Krause - Minkus

STANDARD CATALOG OF U.S. STAMPS

2002 EDITION • LISTINGS 1845 - DATE

Maurice D. Wozniak– Editor

Wayne Youngblood
Publisher, Philatelics Division, Krause Publications

Special Contributors
Mike Bush • Leroy P. Collins III • Francis J. Crown, Jr. • Tony L. Crumbley • James W. Crumpacker
Peter Hoffman • Patricia A. Kaufmann • Joann Lenz • Michael Perry • Peter W.W. Powell • Jerry Palazolo
Francis C. Pogue • Michael Rogers • Richard Spielberg • Vernon Stroupe Jr. • Scott Templin
Marios Theodossiou • Dan Undersander

A fully illustrated collector's catalog for the postage stamps of the United States with stories of the men, women, places and events that have shaped America's history.

Published by

700 E. State Street • Iola, WI 54990-0001
Telephone: 715/445-2214

To place an order or receive our free catalog, call 800-258-0929.
For editorial comment and further information,
use our regular business telephone at (715) 445-2214.

Library of Congress Catalog Number: 98-84632
ISBN: 0-87349-321-4

Printed in the United States of America

Contents

A note from the editor

If you get just half of the enjoyment from using this catalog as I do from bringing it to you, then I think our efforts are worthwhile. Hobbies should be fun, above all, and the venerable and fascinating hobby of stamp collecting provides enjoyment on many levels. This fifth edition of the *Krause-Minkus Standard Catalog of U.S. Stamps* is designed to cater to your search for information and answer your questions.

Foremost, you will find in these pages a complete accounting – in chronological order – of every postage stamp issued by the United States government since the introduction in 1847 of adhesives that signify the payment of a mailing fee. You'll see clear photos of all these stamps and many others, such as provisional stamps issued by postmasters themselves even before the first government issues, and many kinds of revenue stamps issued to raise money, not to pay postage.

Jacques Minkus, when he created this catalog a half-century ago, strove to meet the needs of collectors and offer "more fun and knowledge," in his words. Krause Publications, the world's largest hobby publisher, has revised and expanded Minkus' work.

You'll find the usual philatelic information in this catalog – each stamp numbered, perforation measurements, watermarks, printing methods, colors, and a listing of prices you might encounter in the retail stamp trade. Unique to this catalog are the stories you'll find on every page about each stamp and its subject. How did the $1 stamp known as the "CIA Invert" (No. 730) get its name? Do you know why the U.S. public began using stamps as money? What is unique (so far, at least) about the Padre Felix Varela stamp (CM1954)? Who was Winfield Scott (No. 105)? We hope these vignettes will enhance the hobby for you and maybe influence you to immerse yourself a little deeper into it.

We've tried to offer something new with every edition, and this one is no exception.

You'll find a Booklets section for the first time. The first U.S. booklets, offered for mailers' convenience, were issued in 1900, and only collectors have kept track of the various kinds and their contents.

You'll find Allied Military Government stamps that were printed by the U.S. Bureau of Engraving and Printing for use in four occupied European countries – Italy, France, Germany and Austria – immediately after World War II to help maintain orderly communication. I think the AMG stamps fit well among those other issues that the Minkus catalog has included for many years – the Confederate States of America, Canal Zone, Cuba, Danish West Indies, Guam, Hawaii, Philippines, Puerto Rico and Ryukyu Islands.

Incidentally, you'll find that the section on Confederate Postmasters Provisionals, introduced in the previous edition, has been refined with additional information and several new illustrations, thanks to some cooperative CSA collectors who want others to know what they have learned.

The section on Test Stamps and Test Booklets (or "Dummies"), which debuted last year, also contains additional illustrations and data from collectors who specialize in them. These dummy stamps were produced, typically, to test production or vending equipment or to demonstrate a printer's skill. They were not valid for postage, of course. Most of them were not intended to reach collectors' hands, but this Minkus catalog contains the most comprehensive listing of them you'll find anywhere.

Likewise, the Canal Zone section has been enhanced with the help of members of the Canal Zone Study Group.

In these pages collectors will find tables to aid in the identification of stamps, such as the Washington-Franklin series of 1908-1921 and the modern Transportation and Great Americans series. Decoding the Catalog features give detailed comparisons between stamps that may appear at first to be the same.

The goal from the first has been to produce a catalog that will help you enjoy stamp collecting. I'd like to hear from you if it does, and if you think we can make further improvements I hope you'll write to let us know. Above all, I hope you have fun.

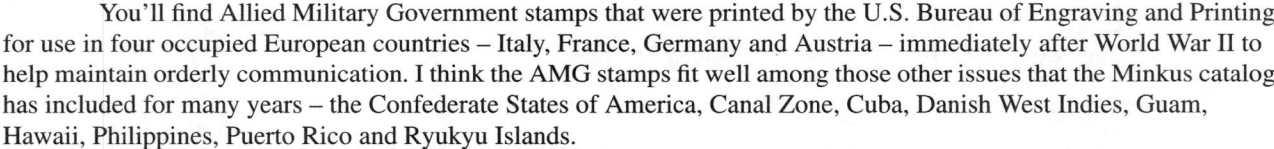

Catalog Introduction

While such factors as age, quantity issued, scarcity and especially demand all have a bearing on the value of a given stamp or cover, the fundamental determinants of value for any given stamp are its grade and its condition. In general, the scarcer and more valuable the basic stamp, the greater the importance of grade or centering in determining its market value.

Grade is a rough measure of the relationship between the printed design of the stamp and its edges or margins, a characteristic that also is often referred to as a stamp's *centering*.

Generally speaking, the more nearly equal in width all margins of a stamp are, and the farther those equal margins are from the printed design, the more desirable the stamp will be to collectors. A stamp with unusually broad margins of identical width on all sides may sell for as much as 100 times the price of an otherwise identical stamp with unbalanced margins and perforations or, in the case of imperforate stamps, a copy with a straightedge cutting the printed design.

Condition refers to the overall appearance and quality of the stamp — the state of its health, so to speak — which can enhance or detract from the desirability (and hence the demand and value) of a stamp.

Stamp Grade

Values shown in this catalog reflect the prices that you may expect to pay for a listed stamp in a grade between **fine** (visibly off-center on two sides, with margins or perforations either just touching or barely clear of the printed design on one side) and **very fine** (barely off-center on one side, with all margins or perforations almost equally distant and well clear of the printed stamp design).

This intermediate grade, which has been the predominant grade in which stamps have been collected for more than a century, is referred to as **fine-to-very fine**, often abbreviated as "**f-vf**." To define the term more explicitly, fine-to-very-fine stamps may be perceptibly off-center to one side, or very slightly off-center on two sides, with the stamp design printed clear of all sides and untouched by any of the margins. (Imperforate stamps graded f-vf will have at least two and usually three margins clear of the printed design.)

Stamps of grades lower than fine-to-very-fine (such as **very good** and **fine**) will usually sell for less than the f-vf copies that are priced here, whereas stamps of grades higher than fine-to-very fine (including **very fine** and the elusive **extremely fine** or **superb**) will sell for more than the stamps that are priced here.

Stamp Condition

Values shown in this catalog reflect the prices that you may expect to pay for a listed stamp in fault-free condition, clear of any detectable defects.

Defects of condition on stamps include (but are not necessarily limited to) tears, scrapes, thins (places where some of the paper is missing from the back of a stamp, often due to inept removal of a hinge), stains, foxing (a yellowish-brown staining) and so-called tropical toning (brown spots on the gum or perforation tips), absence of original gum, the presence of substantial hinge remnants, inclusions (pieces of foreign matter accidentally embedded in the stamp paper during manufacture), heavy, smeared or otherwise disfiguring cancellations or postal markings, pulled, torn or clipped perforations, creases, pinholes, missing corners, and faded, bleached or oxidated pigments and other color changelings (wherein the color of the stamp has changed after it was produced). Extremely defective stamps, with pieces missing, the design unrecognizable due to stains or postmarks and other serious shortcomings, may be virtually uncollectible and unsalable at any price, even if sound, well-centered examples of the same stamp have a high catalog value. The actual, nominal value of stamps in such poor condition has no relationship whatsoever to the values listed in this or any other catalog.

Stamps that have been repaired or altered (with filled thins, regumming, reperforation, repaired tears, bleaching to remove soiling or lighten a cancel, handprinted notes on the back of the stamp) also are generally regarded as defective and valued accordingly. Repaired stamps may be quite presentable and collectible, but they will generally have only a fraction of the value of a comparable, sound example of the same stamp. Knowingly attempting to represent and sell a repaired copy of a damaged stamp as a sound copy in original condition is fraud.

Just as defects and other undesirable traits detract from a stamp's condition, thereby diminishing its value, exceptionally desirable aspects of a stamp's condition can enhance that value, sometimes substantially.

Positive attributes to a stamp's condition can include unusually wide margins on all sides, exceptionally fresh-looking paper and ink color and sharpness of the printing, unusually crisp, sharp and regular perforations (especially on older stamps), the presence of margin selvage (especially with a plate number or other marginal printing of significance) and, on 19th-century stamps, most or all of the original gum.

Minkus Catalog Values

Values in the price columns for early stamps reflect either unused, original-gum fine-very fine stamps (UnFVF) or canceled fine-very fine stamps (UseFVF). For stamps issued since 1940, the price grades reflect mint never-hinged very fine (MNHVF) and canceled very fine (UseVF) stamps. Most unused stamps since 1940 are collected in mint, never-hinged condition, with full, undisturbed and unblemished original gum on the back.

Where a stamp or other catalog-listed item is seldom sold publicly, values appear in italics. Where adequate pricing information for a specific item has proven to be currently unobtainable (as in the case of a recently discovered error or, more prosaically, a common plate block in used condition) in the place of a value a line appears (—).

Every reasonable effort has been made to make the values in this catalog as accurate, realistic and up-to-date as possible. Sources for pricing information may include (but are not necessarily limited to) dealers' published retail price lists and advertisements, auction catalogs with published prices realized, and prices solicited from selected dealers, individuals and collector organizations. This information may have been reviewed for accuracy and consistency by individual specialist-collectors and specialist-dealers.

The minimum stamp value in this catalog (20¢) represents the cost to a retail stamp dealer to maintain in inventory and supply to a collector on demand a single copy of even the most common stamp in fault-free condition and a grade of fine-to-very-fine. The comparable minimum for a first day cover is $1. These figures more accurately reflect a dealer's cost of doing business than the scarcity of a given stamp or FDC.

Values in this catalog do not reflect the generally much lower cost of stamps acquired in mixtures, collections, bulk lots or other large-quantity purchases, nor stamps sold at unusually advantageous prices to attract additional business or offered as approvals, premiums, and so forth. In addition, some stamps can be acquired at lower prices through public auctions and mail-bid sales in which the collector may sometimes secure a lot at an uncontested minimum bid or reserve price.

The publishers of this catalog neither buy nor sell stamps.

Minkus Catalog Listings

Shown here is a typical listing from the catalog, displaying most of the kinds of information that this catalog can provide.

1987. Love Stamp Issue the sixth in the Love Series. *Gravure, perforated 11 1/2 x 11.*

CM1212 *Love*

CM1212		MNHVF	UseVF
22¢	**multicolored,** tagged *(811,560,000)*	.35	.20
	Plate block of 4	2.75	
			1.00

A. Year of Issue

B. Title of Issue, often as assigned by the U.S. Post Office Department or the U.S. Postal Service.

C. Description of Issue, a brief synopsis of the person, place or thing depicted on or commemorated by the issue, with information on any special characteristics or significance and any series of which it is a part.

D. Printing details of the type of printing, printer(s) and gauge of the perforations or rouletting.

E. Minkus Catalog Number appears adjacent to the image of the stamp and also at the beginning of the corresponding price listing for stamps in a grade of fine-to-very-fine. Collectors can use the Minkus catalog numbers to organize their collections, and to identify stamps when buying, selling or exchanging stamps for their collections. Minkus catalog numbers also are used in Minkus stamp albums and supplements.

Each Minkus catalog number refers to a specific stamp. Varieties of that stamp are identified by suffixes appended to the basic catalog number (see item M). Where stamps that are similar in appearance are regarded as distinct issues, collectors are referred to the other issue or issues in a footnote (see item N).

With few exceptions, and unlike other catalogs, Minkus catalog numbers are assigned in strict chronological sequence, and definitive issues (stamps that may go back to press for additional printings at any time to furnish new stocks) are listed separately from commemorative issues (typically printed in a single, much smaller run than their definitive counterparts). Definitive series that extend over many years are identified by series name, but are listed in the order and at the intervals at which they were released by the U.S. Post Office Department or U.S. Postal Service. This avoids the confusing situation of clumps of stamps from an ongoing series being listed at random and arbitrary intervals throughout the catalog, and the necessity of introducing additional subnumbers (e.g., 123B, 123C, 123D) due to a miscalculation of the number of stamps in a given set or series. The stamps are organized into their natural sets in Minkus stamp albums and supplements.

Minkus catalog numbers consist of numerals only for regular definitive issues (e.g., Minkus 123, which refers to the Continental Bank Note Co. 5¢ Prussian blue Zachary Taylor definitive released in 1875). Other types of postage and revenue stamps listed in this catalog are indicated by a prefix. "CM" indicates commemorative stamps (e.g. Minkus CM123, which refers to the 3¢ blue Byrd Antarctic Expedition 11 commemorative of 1933), "A" indicates airmail stamps (e.g. Minkus Al23, which refers to the 45¢ multicolored Hypersonic Airliner stamp in the se-tenant block of four from the Future Mail Transportation issue of 1989), and so on.

F. Description of Image, sometimes but not invariably the same as item B, is intended to represent the design title by which collectors refer to the individual stamp. In practice, many stamps are readily recognized both ways. For example, Minkus CM24 is well-known to stamp collectors both as the $1 denomination from the Trans-Mississippi commemoratives of 1898 (the title of the issue) and as the $1 black Western Cattle in Storm commemorative (the description of the image).

G. Denomination is the numeric value of the stamp (or, in the case of a lettered value issue or an un-valued issue, the equated value at time of issue).

H. Color. When a single color or up to three distinct colors are used they are listed, else the term "multicolor" is used.

I. Tagging. Where relevant, on selected U.S. stamps beginning in the 1960s, the term refers to the presence of a special ink on the face of the stamp visible only under ultraviolet light, used to position the envelope on which the stamp is affixed correctly so that the cancellation will be applied in automated facing-canceling equipment.

J. Quantity Printed is recorded, where available, typically for U.S. commemorative and airmail issues. For U.S. definitives, which may go back to press many times in the course of their working life, accurate figures are rarely available. Quantities include accurate counts and approximate estimates made by the U.S. Post Office Department and Postal Service, counts of quantities shipped but not including stamps returned, unused or destroyed when the issue was taken off sale and, in some cases, accurate counts of copies sold.

K. Catalog Values are expressed in U.S. dollars for unused stamps (UnFVF) and used stamps (UseFVF) in fine-to-very-fine condition for issues prior to 1940, and for mint never-hinged (MNHVF) and used (UseVF) for post 1940 releases. Unused stamps refer to those that have not been canceled with most of their original gum (for 19th century issues) or full original gum, lightly hinged (for early 20th century stamps). Stamps issued without gum are identified in the listings. Used stamps refer to those that have been canceled correctly in the course of performing their intended function.

L. Date of Issue is displayed, in most cases on the same line as that used for the basic first day cover listing.

M. Additional Varieties include (where relevant) plate blocks, se-tenant configurations, paper type, gum type, tagging presence and type, perforation varieties, major errors, plate flaws and varieties.

N. Footnotes convey additional important information about the stamp and related varieties or issues.

Introduction to Stamps

The ability to accurately identify a stamp is indispensible to your full enjoyment of and participation in the stamp hobby. Differences in printing, gum, paper, watermark, ink, perforation, luminescence and design variations that may be slight — but which are readily apparent to the trained eye — can be the key to getting the most out of the time you spend with your collection. They also can be the difference between a common stamp worth a handful of pennies and a rarity valued at thousands of dollars.

There is no substitute for the knowledge that you can gain from the experience of closely examining and working with stamps, not only those in your own collection, but also those that you can read about in philatelic literature and see on display at stamp shows and, if you are fortunate, in the albums of friends at the local stamp club.

The following text is intended to familiarize you with the basic considerations of collecting stamps and the terminology and jargon of the stamp hobby. Inquiries, suggestions and requests for additional clarifications may be addressed to Editor, Krause Minkus Stamp Catalog, Krause Publications, 700 E. State St., Iola WI 54990-0001. (www.krause.com)

Stamp Printing

All stamps may be characterized by the technique or techniques by which they are printed. Although others exist, a few primary printing technologies have been used, alone or in combination, on virtually all United States postal paper: intaglio; lithography; gravure; letterpress; and embossing. (Since 1989, holography also has been used to print the special foil patches that have served as stamp images on several U.S. stamped envelopes and stamps.)

Intaglio (also known as Line-Engraving, Engraving, Etching)

The first step in the intaglio process is creating a **master die**, a small, flat block of soft steel upon which the stamp design is recessed engraved in reverse. The original art intended for use on the stamp is photographically reduced to the appropriate size to serve as a tracing guide for the initial outline of the design on steel.

The highly skilled and detailed work of creating the master die is done by an engraver, who lightly traces the design on the steel, then slowly develops the fully detailed engraving, using gravers, burins and other small chisel-like tools to carve a fine pattern of precisely positioned grooves that collectively form the finished image.

At various points during the engraving process, the engraver hand-inks the dies and makes impressions to check his progress, thereby creating incomplete images of what will become the finished design, known as **progressive die proofs**.

After the engraving is complete, the soft steel of the master die is hardened greatly through various processes so that it will be able to withstand the stress and pressure of the subsequent operations needed to convert it into an intaglio printing plate.

Next, a **transfer roll** is prepared, consisting of a roll of soft steel mounted on a mandrel, which, as the term "transfer roll" implies, is used to transfer the engraved subject from the master die to the intaglio printing plate, a blank roll of soft steel, mounted at the center of a mandrel, which is a metal axle of lesser diameter. The mandrel is placed in a transfer press, in which it rotates freely, and the highly polished soft steel of the transfer roll is brought into contact with the hardened master die in the bed of the press.

The bed of the transfer press is slowly rocked back and forth under increasing pressure, forcing or "rocking in" the soft steel of the transfer roll in every finely engraved line of the hard master die, and eventually transferring the complete engraved image. The resulting design on the transfer roll, now positive in appearance (with its design components as they are intended to appear on the printed stamp), is referred to as a **relief transfer**, because the lines of engraving that were carved into the master die stand out on the completed roll. The soft steel of the transfer roll is hardened, as was the master die before it, after the number of relief transfers that are required have been created.

Because the relief is what is used to create the intaglio printing plate, any imperfections during the creation of the relief transfer may result in flaws that will appear on the finished stamps. A small fleck of foreign material present during the rocking-in process may leave a mark on the relief transfer. Similarly, imperfections in the steel of the transfer roll may cause the loss of part of the design from the master die. These flaws are known as **relief breaks**, which appear as small, uninked areas on the finished stamp. Reliefs also may be deliberately modified to minimize or rectify such flaws, resulting in what is referred to as an **altered relief**, the characteristics of which again will be expressed on the finished stamp.

When the transfer roll has been completed and hardened, it is used to rock in the design to a large plate of polished, soft steel, where it again appears in reversed form as on the original master die. Layout lines or position dots are placed to precisely locate the transfer roll over the plate, and may sometimes later appear on stamps if they are not burnished away during final plate preparation.

It is during this process that double transfers, shifted transfers and dropped transfers occur.

A **shifted transfer** on a plate is one that shows doubling of part of or all the design (typically one edge or corner of the design), usually because the relief transfer shifted slightly while the design was being rocked into the printing plate.

A similar effect also can be achieved on the plate when a defective transfer is incompletely removed, and a second transfer is rocked in over it. Any place where the engraving of the original transfer remains and is not covered by the second transfer is likely to appear on the printed stamp as a **double transfer** (or, in cases where traces of two previous transfers exist, a **triple transfer**). Sometimes the printers need to delete the original transfer from a plate and enter it from scratch again. Should this completed transfer show some traces of the original impression, it is referred to as a **partial double transfer**.

A **dropped transfer** is one that is made normally but is misaligned with respect to the other designs on the plate. A stamp printed from such a dropped transfer will be noticably out of alignment with the stamps around it in the final sheet.

Failure to center the transfer roll correctly on the plate will result in the failure of the relief transfer to completely record all portions of the master die, resulting in the loss of the edge of the engraved design on the finished stamp. This is known as a **short transfer**.

The impressions of the transfer roll on the plate often are referred to as **subjects**, and as many of these subjects are transferred as are required for the final plate (typically 200 or 400 subjects on most plates up to the 1950s and 1960s).

When all the subjects have been put in place, all position dots, layout lines and any minor scratches, burrs or imperfections are removed from the printing surface. With the addition of marginal and other sheet markings including guide lines, arrows and plate numbers, a **plate proof** is printed to confirm that the plate is ready to produce stamps. (**Trial color proofs** may also be printed in a variety of colors other than those eventually selected for the finished stamps, to test the clarity and appearance of the finished print in different hues.) When these impressions are approved, the **printing plate** is machined for fitting onto a press, hardened and sent off to the plate vault, ready to be used.

On the press, the intaglio plate is inked, and its smooth surface is wiped clean, leaving ink only in the lines created by the relief transfer. Paper is then forced under pressure into the engraved recessed lines, the ink of which is transferred to the surface of the stamp paper. When dry, the lines of ink on the intaglio stamp remain slightly raised, giving such stamps their characteristic crisply ridged feel, and slight depressions (known as debossing) on the back of the stamp show where these inked lines appear on the front.

For the first century or so of U.S. intaglio stamp production, prior to the advent of modern, high-speed presses, paper used in intaglio stamp production often was moistened to facilitate the transfer of the ink, known as a **wet printing**. However, this sometimes led to uneven shrinkage by the time the stamps were perforated, resulting in improperly perforated stamps, or misperfs. More modern presses that supplanted early models do not require the use of moistened paper, thus giving rise to stamps that exist in both **wet print** and **dry print** versions.

Until 1915, only **flat press plates** were used to print engraved United States stamps. **Rotary press** printing was introduced in that year and slowly spread to account for an ever larger share of U.S. stamp production. Older **rotary press plates** require additional machining and are curved under pressure to fit the press cylinder. The stretching of the plate during the curving process distorts the subjects on it, with the result that stamps printed from rotary press plates usually are longer or wider than the same stamps printed from flat plate presses. The two basic versions of the Harding Memorial Issue (Minkus CM60 and CM62) provide a good example of this frequently encountered phenomenon. With the exception of the 1919 coil waste issues (Minkus 410-12), all rotary press issues up to 1953 have between one and four **gum breaker ridges** per stamp, impressed on the gum to break its even surface across the back of the stamp during manufacture to inhibit the natural tendency of rotary press-printed stamps to curl.

In the early days of intaglio flat-plate printing, heavily worn plates were sometimes spruced up to give additional service by re-entering their designs, reapplying the transfer roll to the old plate to sharpen worn-down designs. However, if the registration between the transfer roll and the engraving on the worn plate is not exact, or if the original transfer is not completely burnished flat before the design is rocked in again, the result is often a **re-entry**. In a **re-entry**, another kind of **double transfer** can be created, which will appear on stamps printed from such a subject as a design with portions of the previous, worn design still visible.

If the alignment is exact and the placement of the transfer roll is true, a skillful re-entry may be all but undetectable.

Other, slightly less radical techniques of rendering a worn plate fit for continued use usually require that the plate be softened by having its temper drawn (generally by the precise application of heat and cooling) for retooling by hand, Among the techniques involved are **retouching** (the deepening or modification of lines by etching), and **recutting** (the deepening or alteration of lines with an engraving tool). If the resulting inked impression varies slightly from the original, it is referred to as a **re-engraved** stamp.

The intricate line patterns of intaglio printing are an excellent safeguard against would-be counterfeiters, but additional techniques also have been used to make intaglio stamps even more difficult to forge. One of these that was especially popular in the early days of U.S. stamp production was the incorporation of **lathework** and other **engine-turned designs** into the backgrounds and frames of various issues — complicated and precisely repeated designs produced on a mechanical device called an engraving engine. Examples of such patterns can clearly be seen in the frame and spandrels of the 1851 3¢ Washington stamps (Minkus 10-11) and the complex frame of the 1860 24¢ Washington (40).

Bicolored engraved stamps, such as the high values of the 1869 Pictorial issue (92-96), the 1901 PanAmerican commemoratives (CM26-31) and the 24¢ Jenny airmail stamp of 1918 (A3), are created by passing the printing sheet through a flat-bed press two times, once with a plate to print the frame, and a second time, with a second plate inked in a different color, to print the vignette at the center of the design. Performing either of these operations with the sheet incorrectly oriented would result in one part of the stamp being printed upside-down in relation to the rest of the design, creating the category of major error referred to as inverted-center (or inverted-frame) errors, or **inverts**, in common parlance.

Except for such bicolored issues, all other engraved U.S. stamps for more than a century were single-color designs until the advent of the **Giori Press** at the Bureau of Engraving and Printing in 1957. The Giori Press, capable of intaglio printing in two or three colors simultaneously, made its philatelic debut with the 4¢ 48-Star Flag commemorative (CM406) on July 4, 1957, and soon made a distinctive mark on U.S. postage stamps, including the multicolored high values of the Champions of Liberty series, the Conservation series and the American Credo series.

Another innovation in intaglio printing was the **Huck Multicolor Press**, first used in 1969 to print the 6¢ Angel Gabriel stamp from the 1969 Christmas issue (649), starting June 19, 1968, according to BEP data. The Huck Press not only printed in as many as nine colors and applied phosphorescent taggant to stamps, but it also gummed and perforated them all at the same time.

Lithography (also Photolithography, Offset Lithography, Stone Lithography, Dilitho, Planography, Collotype)

To produce a printed design, lithography uses the principle that oil and water do not mix. The design is produced from original artwork and transferred in an oily or greasy ink onto the printing surface, originally a prepared surface of stone (from which lithography takes its name) but now more frequently a metal surface. This greasy design can attract and hold the ink for transfer onto the surface to be printed, while the rest of the plate is moistened with an acidic fluid that repels such ink, corresponding to the uninked portions of the design. To create a plate, special transfer paper is used to make duplicates of the desired design from the original lithographic stone or plate, which are in turn assembled to create the final lithographic printing plate.

In a well-crafted lithographic stamp, the design may have fine and sharply printed lines as in an intaglio stamp, but its design also will have distinct, solidly inked areas that are not to be seen either on intaglio or on gravure issues. Also, unlike either intaglio printing (where lines of ink are raised on the surface of the stamp) or letterpress printing (where the inked areas are impressed into the paper, leaving a debossed surface on the back of the stamp), both sides of a stamp printed by lithography are completely flat.

Offset Lithography, also known as offset printing, refers to a refinement of the basic lithographic technique, whereby a greasy ink impression on a rubber blanket transfers the lithographic image from the printing surface to the paper. The first use of offset lithography on regular United States postage stamps took place with the Washington-Franklin definitives of 1918-20 (Minkus 403-09), when the technique was introduced due to manpower and material restrictions on intaglio printing caused by World War I. Offset lithography and intaglio were used together in printing the 5¢ Homemakers commemorative of 1964 (CM538) and the 1976 Bicentennial souvenir sheets (CM839-42), which showcased the ability of lithography to convey subtle textures, tints and tones.

Because of its greater ease of use and range of applications, offset lithography has largely replaced lithography today, and is now frequently referred to simply as "offset."

Gravure (including such variants as Photogravure, Rotogravure, Heliogravure)

The preparation of stamps for printing by gravure begins with the photographing of the intended design through a fine mesh, referred to as a dot-matrix screen, which renders it onto a metal plate as a pattern of tiny dots. A chemical process etches this fine dot or halftone pattern onto the plate, where it is converted into a multitude of shallow pits or depressions, known as **cells**, which hold the ink during the printing process.

In the gravure printing process, the paper pressed against the gravure plate lifts the ink out of the cells to produce the intended design. Deeper, larger cells produce the more heavily inked and frequently darker portions of the printed design. Shallow, small cells produce more lightly inked and often lightly colored areas on the stamp.

The chief use of gravure is in producing multicolored stamps. Using only the primary colors red, yellow and cyan (blue), along with black, gravure's dot pattern can be combined and recombined to furnish almost any color that might be required. These overlapping patterns of dots, clearly visible under magnification, are the key characteristic by which gravure stamps may be easily identified.

The first gravure U.S. stamps were printed by private firms: the 1967 5¢ Thomas Eakins commemorative (Minkus CM585), printed by Photogravure & Color Co. of Moonachie, N.J.; and the 1968 6¢ Walt Disney issue (CM602), printed by the Achrovure Division of Union-Camp Corp. in Englewood, N.J. In 1970, Guilford Gravure Inc. of Guilford, Conn., produced both the setenant Anti-Pollution issue (CM643-46) and all of the Christmas stamps (655-59) for the Bureau of Engraving and Printing.

The following year, the BEP acquired the multicolor Andreotti Press, and began printing its own gravure stamps, the first of these being the 8¢ Missouri Statehood issue (CM654).

Letterpress (also known as Typography, Surface Printing, Flexography, Dry Offset, High Etch)

Essentially the opposite of intaglio printing, in letterpress printing it is the raised rather than the incised areas of the printing plate that are inked to print the finished design. In fact, the process of creating the printing plate is an inversion of the intaglio process as well, with an additional step in which the design is transferred to another surface before the creation of the transfer roll. This results in the transfer roll's having a recessed rather than a relief design, which means that the final plate will have the areas that are to be inked raised above rather than carved into the surface, similar to a rubber handstamp.

Reproducing a letterpress transfer electromechanically is referred to as **electrotype** or **stereotype** production, and these are then gathered together in the desired configuration to form the plate from which stamps are produced. A plate for letterpress printing, made using the assembled electrotypes, is referred to as an **electroplate**.

The first postage stamps for nationwide use to make use of letterpress printing were the first newspaper and periodical issues of 1865 (Minkus N1-4), which were printed by the National Bank Note Co. in combination with embossing and an engine-turned engraved design to create an almost forgery-proof set. The American Bank Note Co. also combined offset vignettes showing the flags with engraved frames in 1943-44 to produce the Overrun Countries series (CM251-63). More typically (and less dramatically), letterpress was used to create the Molly Pitcher and Hawaii Sesquicentennial overprints of 1928 (CM79-81), the Kansas-Nebraska overprints of 1929 (495-516) and the many different Bureau precancels used over the years.

As with a piece of paper printed using a handstamp or a typewriter, paper printed by letterpress will show a slight depression (debossing) in the printed portion of the printed side of the paper, and a slight elevation (embossing) on the reverse side of the paper. This is characteristic of letterpress.

Embossing (also Colorless Embossing, Blind Embossing, Relief Printing)

Not truly a printing technique (since, technically, ink need not be involved), embossing is, however, an important security technique used on U.S. postal paper (chiefly stamped envelopes). In embossing, a design is carved into a die, which is reproduced to yield a shallow, three-dimensional sculpture from which additional embossing dies are made. A similar back plate, or platen, mirroring the design is created, and the two sides are pressed together to create the embossed image (often with ink on the inside of the die in front, producing the inscribed, denominated printed collar around the embossed portrait or image).

Embossing also has been used on some U.S. stamps, including the first issue newspaper and periodical stamps of 1865.

Holography

The United States produced its first hologram stamps in 2000, 12 years after Austria issued the first one in the world, on Oct. 18, 1988. Brazil followed with a hologram sheetlet of three stamps on Oct. 14, 1989. Fernando Catta-Preta, now president of Trace Holographic Art & Design, Inc., was responsible for the production of both the Brazilian and American hologram stamps.

The United States also has issued four hologram envelopes, three of which used the same hologram scene, a Space Station and Shuttle. The vignette, on foil, was positioned inside the envelope and visible through a die-cut window at the upper right.

The denomination was printed to the left of the window on the envelope, first 25¢ on Dec. 3, 1989 (Minkus EN917), and then 29¢ on Jan. 21, 1992 (Minkus EN925) and 32¢ on Sept. 22, 1995 (Minkus EN945). The other U.S. envelope hologram design was the 25¢ Football Issue (Minkus EN918) of Sept. 9, 1990, which had the same configuration but featured a hologram of a football scene and the National Football League Lombardi Trophy.

Holographic reproduction is technically printing, but ink is not used. Instead, a captured light wave interference pattern that

The first U.S. hologram stamp.

emanated from a three-dimensional object is reproduced on thin foil through microscopic embossing. The resulting ghostly image is visible through reflected ambient light, not an ink laid on paper.

The holographer has three basic starting points — the use of flat images or pictures on different planes, much as a shadowbox; the use of a small three-dimensional model, which might be wafer-thin; and the use of computer-generated images to simulate an actual model.

First, an "H1" image of the model, lit by pure light from a laser, is made in an extremely high-resolution light-sensitive emulsion on a glass plate. A wave of light is essentially flat, but when it reflects off an object, it acquires the shape of that object. When this "deformed" object beam of light crosses an undistorted reference beam at the plate surface, an interference pattern is recorded in the film's emulsion. This pattern is similar to the expanding circular waves you'd see on the smooth surface of a lake if you were to throw two rocks into it. The interference pattern is like a "fingerprint" — an accurate representation of the two beams that created it. When the reference beam is reproduced by shining a light onto it, it "sculpts" this beam and reflects it exactly in the shape (the wavefront) of the other beam, the object beam that illuminated the object.

The H1 image is lined up with the model, and an "H2" image is made of it on another glass plate – a hologram of a hologram. This H2 plate is then silvered and electroplated, producing a thin sheet of nickel with a surface of silver. This coated plate then serves, again in the electroforming part of the process, to generate several copies, or shims as they are known in the industry. These are affixed to the printing cylinders, and embossed with heat and pressure into a polyester film.

Printing of the hologram portions of stamps takes place on a rotary embossing machine whose printing roll is extremely smooth, at the sub-micron level. Heating elements allow the polyester film to deform microscopically and therefore diffract white light into its chromatic components.

Finally, adhesive is applied to the holograms' backs, and they are die cut to shape and applied to the stamp sheet, which has been separately printed through traditional methods.

Under the right light conditions, the viewer sees a true three-dimensional "wavefront" sculpted, as it were, from the very light that illuminates it. Looking at an object and looking at a hologram are essentially the same. In both cases, the same wavefronts reach the viewer's eyes, but in the case of the hologram the object is not physically present.

Stamp Components and Characteristics

If a stamp's image is derived in large measure from its printing (and the techniques used), the rest of the characteristics that define it have to do with the materials used in the stamp's creation — ink, gum, paper and separation technique — and some of the key observable characteristics of these materials, including the watermark, the method of stamp separation and the gauge of its perforations or rouletting, as well as the presence or absence of luminescence.

Examples may be found of otherwise identical stamps that differ in only one or two subtle respects, creating, at the least, two interesting varieties to seek out for your album and, at the most, an opportunity for the observant stamp collector to pick out a gem amid a pile of perfectly common postage. Few of us may ever have such an experience, to be sure, but fortune favors those who have prepared. Contrarily, collectors who are unaware that a rarity exists will never find it.

Ink and Color

Ink is the basic stuff of printing, typically consisting of a finely powdered admixture or suspension of mineral, natural organic or synthetic organic pigment in a liquid solvent or base.

Ink is directly related to color. Many of the inks used in printing 19th-century stamps were mixed by hand to the closely guarded specifications of the private printing firms that did the work, and the color often varied perceptibly from batch to batch. This gave rise to at least some of the many collectible shades and hues found on a number of classic U.S. issues, such as the 24¢ Washington definitives (Minkus 54-56) of 1861-63.

This wealth of color varieties continued briefly even after the Bureau of Engraving and Printing assumed responsibility for printing virtually all U.S. stamps in 1894, best reflected in the many shades of the 2¢ issues of 1894 (170-74) and 1895-98 (189-92). Thereafter, inks became considerably more standardized and the number and variety of color varieties decreased markedly. Still, there are some highly collectible exceptions to this rule, such as the 1922 11¢ Hayes definitive (430).

One consequence of the arrival of single-press-run multicolor printing in the 1950s and 1960s was that minor variations in the individual colors on a stamp became harder to clearly discern, and in time came to be largely ignored, except on monochrome engraved stamps where such varieties remained easy to see. At the same time, however, there slowly developed a considerable increase in the number of color-omitted errors — errors that could never have taken place on monochrome intaglio stamps.

An important transition in inks took place in the 1970s under federal health regulations, when solvent-based inks used at the BEP were screened for potential toxicity and adverse health and environmental effects, and replaced with new, safer water-based inks of similar color. As a result, different shades can be seen on the versions of some values of the Prominent Americans and Americana definitives printed both before and after this period.

In fact, ink is not the only variable that determines the color of a stamp. The quantity of ink, the pressure with which it is applied, the type of paper and its moisture content at the time that the printing takes place and the type of base that carries the pigment in the ink all can affect the apparent color.

Of special concern to collectors are stamps printed in **fugitive ink**, which is soluble and tends to run or dissolve when the stamp is immersed in such otherwise innocuous liquids as water or watermark fluid. Fugitive inks include synthetic organic pigments produced as derivatives of nitrobenzene (aniline inks) and some photogravure stamps as well. Some modern U.S. commemoratives printed in purple can suffer ink damage when immersed in watermark fluid, including the 1963 5¢ Eleanor Roosevelt (CM522), 1964 5¢ Amateur Radio (CM541) and the 1980 15¢ Edith Wharton (CM953).

Stamps that have had their color altered after they were printed, intentionally or accidentally, are referred to as **color changelings**.

Generally such changelings occur as the result of a photochemical reaction (such as prolonged exposure to sunlight or artificial light) or chemical activity (such as the use of a cleaning agent or solvent to remove soiling or lighten a heavy cancel).

One especially notorious kind of accidental color changeling is often seen on 19th-century and early 20th-century yellow, orange and red U.S. stamps in which the oxidation of sulfur compounds in the pigment turns the image a deep brown shade, occasionally approaching black. The immersion of one of these affected stamps in a mild solution of hydrogen peroxide frequently will reverse the effects of such oxidation, though it may not return the stamp precisely to its original color.

While many collectors retain color changelings as curios, they are in fact nothing more than stamps in which the ink has been irreversibly damaged (much as the paper or perforations might be damaged). Color changelings have no place in an authentic collection of the production varieties of U.S. stamps.

Gum

Stamp gum is known in a wide range of textures, shades and degrees of reflectivity. In addition, the gum arabic used on many 19th-century and early 20th century U.S. stamps was applied to the stamps in two formulations — a harder mixture intended to remain dry in storage even during months of relatively high seasonal heat and humidity (summer gum), and a softer gum that was used on stamps produced for use in the drier, cooler months (winter gum). Most stamp gums today use dextrine or polyvinyl alcohol as a base.

Shiny and matte or dull-finish gum varieties are cataloged separately in those instances where both are known to be found on the same U.S. definitive stamps, even though such stamps may not be distinguishable in used condition or used on cover.

The gum on unused stamps encountered by collectors exists in a variety of conditions, which are listed, abbreviated and defined here in decreasing order of desirability:

Mint Never Hinged (MNH) stamps have pristine gum just as originally acquired from the post office, without a blemish, fingerprint or mark of any kind. Mint prices in this catalog for stamps issued since 1940 refer to stamps in this condition.

Lightly Hinged (LH) stamps have 50 percent to 100 percent of their original gum, but show a minor disturbance on the back, such as traces where a stamp hinge was previously located, so-called disturbed gum or a fingerprint. Prices in this catalog for unused stamps issued prior to 1940 are for stamps in this condition. Many earlier 19th-century stamps are less likely to have much of their original gum still intact.

Heavily Hinged (HH) stamps have less than 50 percent of their original gum and/or remnants of older non-peelable paper hinges still affixed to the back of the stamp.

All three of the preceding types of unused stamps are sometimes referred to as **original gum** stamps, their desirability and value increasing according to the the quantity and quality of the gum. However, not all unused stamps have original gum.

No Gum (NG) stamps are stamps from which the original gum has been removed. For purposes of saving the stamp, it may sometimes be advisable to soak off an especially heavy hinge remnant, which may otherwise cause a stamp to warp, buckle or even tear internally. Stamps issued without gum, such as the 1935 Farley issues (CM 142-61) and the Continental Bank Note Co. special printing of the 1875 newspaper and periodical stamps (SPN5-28), are for all practical purposes regarded as mint, never-hinged in that state.

Regummed (R, RG or RE) stamps are stamps from which the original gum has been removed and other gum has been added later. When it is clearly identified as such, there is nothing objectionable about a regummed stamp, and auction catalog realizations often seem to suggest that collectors are willing to pay a bit more for an expertly regummed stamp than for its NG counterpart.

However, it is fraud to knowingly represent and sell regummed stamps as original-gum copies, which is often attempted to obtain the considerably higher price that such OG stamps typically command. Similarly, it is fraudulent to chemically or otherwise remove a light cancellation from a stamp and offer it as unused. Both regumming and removal of cancellations have some skilled practitioners, which is why expertization is recommended for valuable mint stamps.

Paper

Paper, the medium for all printing, consists of dried sheets of processed vegetable fiber laid down on a fine screen from a water suspension. The two basic broad classifications of paper are **laid paper** in which the lines left by the screen during the papermaking process are still visible in transmitted light, and **wove paper**, which has no such visible grain or lines. Papers also may be categorized as thin or thick, soft or hard, and according to their naturally occurring color (as in the listings for some U.S. stamped envelopes).

A very thin, hard translucent paper known as **pelure** also has occasionally been used for U.S. stamps, including the 1847 5¢ and 10¢ St. Louis postmaster provisionals (Minkus PM28-29). **India paper** refers both to a softer, thin translucent paper used for pulling intaglio die and plate proofs and to a tougher, opaque, thin paper, rarely but occasionally used in U.S. stamp printing, including varieties of the 1851 3¢ and 12¢ Washington (10p, 17p).

In addition, **colored paper** has been deliberately selected for use in specific issues, as in the orange paper of the 1956 3¢ Nassau Hall issue (CM395), the light Venetian red paper used for the 1965 5¢ Dante issue (CM549) and the tan paper of the 1976 Telephone Centennial commemorative (CM836).

Ribbed paper, which has actual ridges on the front or back side of the stamp, or both, was used for some of the Continental Bank Note Co. issues of 1873 (119-30). The ribs are parallel and typically run horizontally across the stamp, although vertical ribbed paper is known as well on stamps including the CBNC 15¢ Daniel Webster (128).

Double paper has two-very different meanings. On the previously mentioned 1873 CBNC issues (119-30), it refers to a security paper patented by Charles F. Steel, in which a thin, weak surface paper and a thicker, stronger backing paper were bonded before printing. This produced a two-layer stamp, the printed design of which would be ruined if any attempt were made to clean a cancel after the stamp had been used.

The second meaning of double paper is in reference to the rotary presses that began producing U.S. stamps in 1915. Rotary presses print stamps on a continuous roll of paper, and when one roll of paper ends, the beginning of a new roll is spliced to the end of it so that production will not be interrupted. Stamps printed on the splice, where paper of the old and new rolls overlaps, are typically marked, cut out and discarded when the stamps are separated into sheets and panes. However, stamps printed across the splice do occasionally escape detection and survive to reach collectors, and these are known as **rotary press double paper** varieties.

Paper with silk fibers also was used in printing 1873 CNBC issues (119-30). As the name implies, this is paper with one or several long, colored silk threads embedded in it. In this it differs from some early U.S. revenue stamps printed on so-called "silk paper," in which more numerous short, colored fibers are impressed during the papermaking process. Although it has rarely been used on U.S. stamps, a third silk-related paper is **granite paper** of the sort found on the 1967 5¢ Lions International issue (CM576), in which the grayish paper is shot through with short red and blue silk fibers, mimicking the veins in the rock for which it is named.

In an effort to better control uneven paper shrinkage during stamp manufacturing, in 1909 the Bureau of Engraving and Printing tried using high rag-content paper in place of the wood fiber paper then chiefly used to print stamps. This experimental stock, used for some 1¢ to 15¢ definitives and a small part of the printing of the 1909 2¢ Lincoln Memorial commemorative (CM42), is referred to as **bluish paper**, although many people describe it as actually more gray in color, best seen in comparing the back of the stamp to others of the same period. See the note preceding Minkus 263-72. Unscrupulous fakers have sometimes attempted to simulate these pricey varieties of otherwise relatively inexpensive stamps by tinting them, so competent expertizing is recommended.

A very small number of the definitives of this same period were printed on a grayish, thick, hard stock known as China Clay paper, said to have mineral content of 5 percent to 20 percent rather than the 2 percent that was the standard at the time (although recent research conducted on paper from long-authenticated copies of these stamps failed to confirm the presence of such clay). These **China Clay paper** varieties, which appear even darker than the bluish paper varieties and also are known on the 1¢ to 15¢ definitives, are cataloged here as subvarieties of the 1908-09 definitives (237p-46p).

For information about Hi-Brite paper, fluorescent papers, phosphor-tagged and pre-phosphored papers, and other papers characterized by their response to ultraviolet light, please refer to the luminescence section of this introduction.

Watermarks

A watermark is a pattern laid down on paper during manufacturing. Shallow designs in metal, called bits, are woven into the screen on which the pulp is formed and drained. When the paper is dry and light is transmitted through it, the impression of the designs of these bits shows as a bright pattern in the paper, which is slightly thinner where the bits were positioned.

On most stamps, watermarks may best be seen by immersing them in **watermark fluid**, a nonaqueous fluid that will not moisten the gum on mint stamps. The fluid increases the transparency of the paper, to make watermarks show more clearly as dark patterns when the stamp is placed face-down in the fluid. (Look under Ink for fugitive inks, which notes U.S. stamps printed with inks that are soluble in watermark fluid.)

The widest range of U.S. watermarks on postal paper consists of those on U.S. postal stationery, including 1873-75 postal cards (PC 1-3), Official Mail envelopes of 1991 (PDEN82-83) and a wide range of watermarks on stamped envelopes of 1853-1968 (EN 1-855).

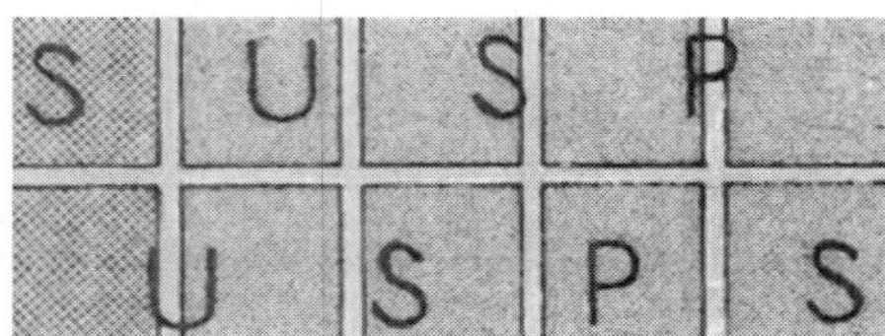

Single line USPS watermark

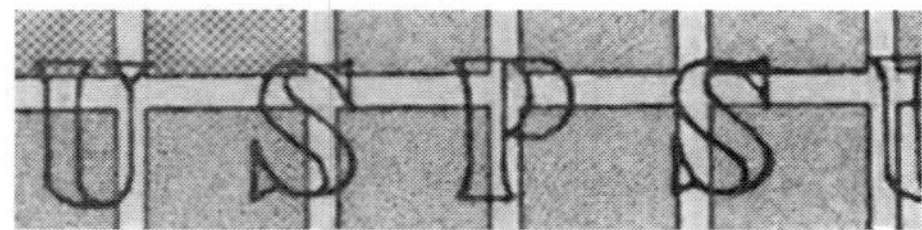

Double line USPS watermark

U.S. postage stamps are known with three watermarks: the double-line watermark "USPS" (for "U.S. Postage Stamp") used on the definitives of 1895-98 (187-210) and the single-line "USPS" watermark used on paper for the 1910-15 Washington-Franklin definitives (273-347); and the double-line watermark "USIR" (for "U.S. Internal Revenue") intended for use on U.S. revenue stamps but used in error for the 1895 6¢ Garfield (198w) and 8¢ Sherman (200w) and a 1951 printing of the $1 Woodrow Wilson stamp from the 1938 Presidential definitive series (553w).

Separation Methods

The makers of the earliest stamps apparently gave little concern to how their users would remove the stamps from the sheets or panes to affix them to mailing pieces. Simply tearing them off or using scissors was time-consuming and messy. The most popular method for separation chosen soon became so universally used that it provided the term for these original stamps – imperforate. After some experimentation, the size and number of holes in lines of perforations were generally standardized for stamp paper to allow the most efficient removal of stamps.

Mostly, perforations consist of round holes punched or ground into the paper, but other methods also have been used, such as hyphen-hole perforations (tiny, rectangular holes) and rouletting (slits, which may be straight or take other shapes). These last two are common on some revenue stamps.

In recent years, the growing popularity of self-adhesive stamps that require no application of moisture to adhere has led to the use of razor-sharp knives that pierce the stamps to allow their removal from a backing paper. This so-called die cutting can consist of straight cuts delineating a traditional rectangular stamp, irregular cuts around an odd-shaped stamp, and (the method preferred by the U.S. Postal Service) cuts that simulate the familiar perforations, usually called a **serpentine die cut**.

The technology of perforation and die cutting could be the subject of a long discourse. For most collectors, however, it is sufficient to know only a few terms and techniques.

Mainly, it is important to know how to gauge the perforations because their size may be the main difference between two catalog listings. A tool called a **perforation gauge** is used to measure the teeth of paper left around a stamp when it is torn along its perforations. If, for example, 10 teeth are found along two centimeters on the side of a stamp, it is said to measure

Horizontal Pair, Imperforate Between

Horizontal Pair, Imperforate Vertically

Horizontal Pair, Imperforate

Vertically Pair, Imperforate Between

Vertical Pair, Imperforate Horizontally

Vertical Pair, Imperforate

"perf 10." In defining a stamp's perforation measurement, the top horizontal side is given first, followed by the right side.

Looking at a single common U.S. stamp design, the Mother's Day issue of 1934, will provide illustration of how stamps that may look the same to the naked eye are actually different. The flat press version of this stamp (CM128) is perforated 11, meaning that its perforations measure 11 all around. However, the perforations on the rotary press version (CM127) measure 11x10 , meaning that it is perf 11 on the top and 10 (or slightly fewer teeth) on the right side. In addition, a third version of the stamp (CM144) is imperforate.

The same perforation measurement applies to other methods of separation, including rouletting and serpentine-shaped die cutting.

Specialists refer to the protruding paper teeth of serpentine due-cut stamps as "peaks" that surround the indented "valleys." In some cases, coil stamps might have a different number of peaks on each side of the stamp. In these cases the number of peaks is used to distinguish the varieties. A stamp with 10 peaks on the left and 11 on the right would be designated as 10x11, for example. The designation does not correlate to the stamp's perforation gauge measurement.

The size of the holes (fine or coarse) and their quality (rough or clean cut) are also used in classifying stamps.

In addition to plate manufacturing errors, which include double impressions in the engraving, and printing errors, which include missing or inverted colors, and folding of the paper in the press, the widest variety of errors occurs in the perforation process. To aid with the explanation of these errors, we have the illustrations on the left and on page XVII. However, none of these errors occur on the stamp illustrated.

Especially in the case where an imperforate version of a same-design stamp has a value considerably more than the perforated version, unscrupulous people may trim the

Left: serpentine die-cut

Right: Straight die-cut

perforations off and purport it to be imperforate. It is always wise to collect imperforate stamps in multiples of at least two and to obtain a certificate of authenticity from a recognized philatelic authority.

Luminescence

Luminescence is the broad general term used to describe all facets of collecting using an ultraviolet light. Luminescence and its characteristics can be used both as an expertizing tool and as a form of collecting specialty. The term breaks down into two main subcategories, fluorescence and phosphorescence.

Fluorescent stamps glow while exposed to UV light, but not after the light source is removed. Phosphorescent stamps glow even after the source of light is removed. This glow can last for only a fraction of a second to close to a minute in some cases. The easiest way to tell the difference, however, is by the type of illumination used.

All luminescent stamps glow under shortwave UV light, but fluorescent stamps also glow under longwave UV light. Phosphorescent stamps do not. Different characteristics of the same stamp can be seen when both light sources are used.

To fully understand luminescence and its significance to stamp collectors it is important to know a bit of background on why stamps glow.

Fluorescence

As previously mentioned, fluorescence simply means that a stamp or piece of postal stationery exhibits some form of glow when illuminated by longwave UV light. Longwave ultraviolet light is the same type of popular black light that is found in poster shops and roller skating rinks. It has no harmful effects to the eyes.

A number of different factors come into play to make a fluorescent stamp glow. Both organic and inorganic substances (either native to the paper or introduced) can react to light, including optical brighteners, ink components, certain pigments and a host of others.

Therefore, as a result of any of these factors, different printings of the same stamp can react differently to UV light, causing collectible varieties to occur. Some of these varieties include the so-called Hi-Brite papers (caused by optical brighteners), fluorescent ink types (caused by ink components) and fluorescent overprintings to aid mail processing. Some of these varieties are intentional, but many are not. They are a result of technological changes in stamp production. Most are highly collectible and some are even rare.

One note of caution, however: Fluorescent varieties on used stamps can be faked, so they are generally bought, sold and traded either as mint examples or on cover. As a result, listings are scarce for fluorescent varieties, and they are valued only as unused examples. Phosphorescent tagging (or the lack thereof) cannot be effectively faked, so listings for these items are more plentiful in both mint and used condition.

As an expertizing tool, the UV light can aid in uncovering many types of fakery, including filled thins, regumming, removed cancellations, altered designs and other repairs. The main principle behind this detection technique is that any paper exhibits some form of fluorescent reaction. None turns completely black under UV light.

Regardless of origin or technological mastery, every batch of paper has different characteristics and a specific weave. Any alteration to this unique pattern (or addition of other fibers) can easily be detected with fluorescent light.

Phosphorescence

Phosphorescent stamps are used by several countries, including the United States and Great Britain. Phosphorescent varieties can be seen only under shortwave UV light. Unlike longwave UV light, shortwave can cause temporary (but painful) eye damage if used improperly. Virtually any pair of prescription glasses provides adequate protection for most collecting activities. Even off-the-shelf reading glasses are usually adequate because they contain UV filters.

Unlike many fluorescent varieties, most stamps with phosphorescent characteristics were intentionally created as such. This is completely true with United States stamps.

After World War II, the U.S. Post Office Departmental faced with a huge challenge. Never before had there been such a high literacy rate among the population, with so much mail traveling through the system. Adding to this burden was the rapidly increasing volume of commercial mail. As a result, mail sorting and processing, which had always been a manual task, could no longer be accomplished in that manner.

By the late 1950s, the USPOD began to seriously explore ideas that had been kicked around since the late 1930s. These ideas ranged from magnetics to color recognition systems.

During the late 1950s, a contract was let to the Pitney-Bowes Corp. (of postage meter fame) to begin experimenting with fluorescence and phosphorescence, and the firm created a number of different stamp and postal stationery essays to test the viability of such systems for automated mail sorting and processing. Fluorescence ultimately was dropped in favor of phosphorescence, and the actual tagging program on live U.S. stamps was piloted by National Cash Register Co. of Dayton, Ohio. Dayton was chosen not only because of the NCR connection, but also because it had a large enough volume of mail to warrant such testing. These tests were to last several years, and the early tagged stamps could be found only in the Dayton area and at the Philatelic Division in Washington, D.C.

A specially tagged label (top) was issued Aug. 1, 1963, for use on airmail letters that did not bear the newly tagged stamp (above).

Although the first tagged stamp was released Aug. 1, 1963, in Dayton, Ohio, it was not the stamp that was being honored! There was no first-day cancel. The cancel simply read "FIRST DAY OF USE LUMINESCENT TAGGING." That stamp, a phosphorescent-coated version of the 8¢ Jet Over Capitol airmail stamp, Minkus A64z, was coated with a calcium silicate suspension that made the stamps glow a bright orange-red.

A special tagged airmail label also was released the same day and was used on many covers. The sole purpose of this early form of U.S. tagging was to separate airmail letters from standard mail. The tests were a success.

Within a few months, the purpose of experimental phosphorescent tagging was expanded to include the automatic facing and canceling of mail. This means the machines were now capable of not only sorting airmail from standard mail, but to line up all envelopes so the stamps were in the same corner and then cancel them! A new form of taggant was introduced for this purpose. It was a suspension of zinc orthosilicate, which glows a bright greenish yellow under shortwave UV light. Thus airmail and standard mail could still be separated (by the color of the taggant) and all letters could be faced and canceled.

Since both types of taggant were mineralogical derivatives, they could not be dissolved to form a solution; they had to be a suspension. A transparent lacquer was chosen as the carrier. Also, as mineralogical derivatives, the two compounds were highly abrasive. This came into play later, with different forms of tagging created to avoid such wear.

This tagged lacquer was applied by a color station on the printing press (sometimes as a separate press run) after all other colors were printed.

On Oct. 26, 1963, the first full printing run of tagged stamps was produced. It was the 5¢ City Mail Delivery commemorative, Minkus CM524. As a result, the first untagged errors also were produced, where no tagging was applied to some stamps. Even though the taggant itself is invisible under standard light, its absence as an untagged error is classified as a form of color-omitted error.

Tagging continued to be an experimental application for several years. Most issues that were released with tagging also exist as issued varieties without tagging, and some of the tagged varieties have become scarce.

By January 1967, stamp production was converted to printing all stamps (except those intended to be precanceled) as phosphorescent tagged issues. By 1969, most post offices had the special facing and canceling equipment designed for use with tagged stamps. By 1973, even the high-value Prominent Americans series stamps had been released as tagged stamps.

There now are numerous types of applications of taggant, each a separate and collectible type, and some stamps exist with more than one type.

The earliest tagged stamps featured overall tagging. This simply means that when a single stamp is viewed under UV light, the entire surface is coated. Several types of this overall tagging were used and are distinguished and collected by specialists.

One major variety of this type of tagging occurs on several issues, most notably the 5¢ National Park Service issue, Minkus CM565z. The basic stamp was untagged, with two types of tagging applied.

The first was the standard form of **overall tagging**, applied to the stamps after printing, but before perforating. The second, and scarcer, type was tagged after perforating (TAP). This allowed tagging to seep through the perforation holes and leave some tagging on the gum side. Also, some markings and tagging flaws can be seen on the face-side of the stamp where perforation hole paper (chad) affected the application. Both types are listed by Minkus and are collected by specialists.

As a direct result of the abrasive nature of taggant on perforating and processing equipment, production shifted to other forms of tagging, the most common being block-over-vignette tagging (**block tagging** for short). This is where most of the surface of a stamp is coated with taggant, but is in the form of a block that does not extend over the perforations. Various sizes of tagging blocks have been used over the years.

Another form of tagging related to block tagging is **cut-to-shape tagging**. This type is one of the more visually stunning of the many that have been tried. With cut-to-shape tagging, the tagging rollers or mats are cut to match a specific area on a stamp design. Recent examples of this form of tagging are the 1999 American Glass or the bugs (CM2072-75), and Insects & Spiders stamps (CM2098), where the taggant covers only the bottles on each stamp.

Some stamps, such as the 1973 Mail Order commemorative, feature a form of **bar tagging** that extends across the center portion of the stamp as a horizontal bar.

The advantages of these two forms of tagging are that a portion of the stamp design is not covered by taggant, which allows cancellation ink to penetrate the surface of the paper. Remember that taggant is suspended in lacquer, which creates an effective barrier between cancel and paper.

A less-frequently used form of tagging involves including the tagging ink in one of the pigmented printing inks. This was most frequently used on U.S. postal cards, but was tried on several stamps as early as 1968, with the release of the 6¢ Leif Erickson issue (CM606).

Although such an inclusion saves a production step and is effective, any pigment affects the visible characteristics of the tagging. Dark colors can so overpower the taggant that it does not give off a strong enough signal to trigger automated equipment.

Beginning with an experimental test stamp in 1987, Minkus 876, the U.S. Postal Service began using paper with the taggant already applied before printing. That stamp, a major variety of the then-current 22¢ Flag over Capitol coil, incorporated a "T" at the bottom of each stamp to designate "Test."

Although that particular form of coated, tagged paper (from England) proved to be too costly to utilize for most issues, the USPS was convinced it wanted to move forward on this form of tagging. Simultaneously, stamp production was reverting from block tagging to overall tagging on many issues, since the abrasive nature of taggant was not as much of a consideration on modern, high-speed equipment. As a result, numerous definitive stamps (particularly the Great Americans series) exist with more than one type of tagging.

By 1989, when the 25¢ Flag over Yosemite definitive, Minkus 891, was released, the USPS was ready to roll out production of stamps printed on phosphored papers. Several different types of these papers exist (both coated and uncoated), and specialists still don't fully agree on correct terminology. But each of these is a collectible type, and at least one stamp (the engraved 25¢ Flag over Mount Rushmore) was printed on both.

At right, misregistered tagging results in two stamps (second row) with no tagging

In some cases, where the stamp design is particularly dark, stamps printed on phosphored papers have been block tagged over the printing as well to ensure a strong enough signal.

All this means there's a whole new world of beautiful collectible stamps available by simply turning on your UV lamp. Just take the time to get to know the stamps and the listings... and keep us posted on your findings. There are more discoveries to be made!

In addition to all the basic types of tagging, there are a number of tagging freaks and errors available.

Besides untagged errors, which exist for most tagged stamps, there also are stamps that were never intended to be tagged but are. This is primarily because they've been accidentally printed on tagged paper. Recently this occurred with the 10¢ Eagle and Shield self-adhesive, (Minkus 1205).

Another form of tagging error (affecting only two stamps so far) is the wrong taggant. The 26¢ Rushmore airmail and 13¢ Letters airmail (booklet) both exist with the zinc-orthosilicate (greenish-yellow) taggant, rather than the calcium silicate (orange-red) taggant intended for them. These stamps, which can't be distinguished under normal light, are truly rare.

The most common form of tagging freak is misregistered tagging, which occurs when the tagging mats are out of alignment with the printing plates. Because these stamps look normal under standard light and give off an adequate tagging signal, they were rarely caught and destroyed by the Bureau of Engraving and Printing. Many of these items are quite visually stunning.

Tagging also can be used as an effective tool for identifying stamps. Different types of stamps printed by different presses are usually easily distinguished by their tagging types. For example, the 14¢ Ice Boat stamp of the Transportation coil series, Minkus 827 and 827A, are easily distinguished without having to pull out a millimeter gauge to measure design width. The original (wider) version printed from the Cottrell presses has overall tagging. The later B-press printings (narrower) has block tagging. There are many other examples as well.

All in all, tagging on U.S. stamps forms a fascinating and colorful collecting specialty that can be as inexpensive or as expensive as you want it to be. There's also the constant thrill of the chase involved because there's always a chance of making a new discovery.

Postmasters' Provisionals

Although the first government-issued adhesive stamps did not appear until 1847, the postmaster at New York City began using his own adhesives in July 1845, immediately after the Congressional act establishing the new postal rates. A number of postmasters in other cities also used either hand-stamps or adhesives of their own design. They are listed here in alphabetical order.

1846. Alexandria, Va. Issue Postmaster Daniel Bryan issued *typeset, imperforate* stamps without gum. Known copies of stamps are cut to shape. The circle of the 5¢ black-on-buff is found with 39 (Type I) or 40 asterisks (Type II).

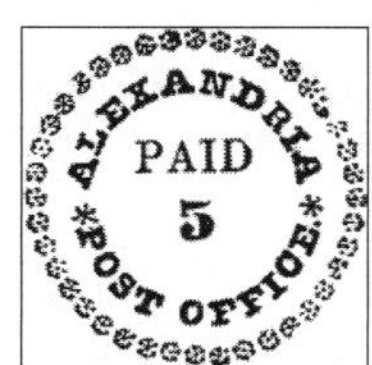

PM1-PM2

		UnFVF	UseFVF
PM1			
5¢	**black,** on buff paper, Type I	78,000.00	—
	v. Type II	—	—

		UnFVF	UseFVF
PM2			
5¢	**black,** on blue paper, Type II	—	—

1846. Annapolis, Md. Issue Postmaster Martin E. Revell issued red stamps printed onto the upper right corner of white envelopes. Envelopes with circular design and figure "2" hand-stamped are known and believed to be locals. Blue circular designs without numeral or "PAID" were used as postmarks.

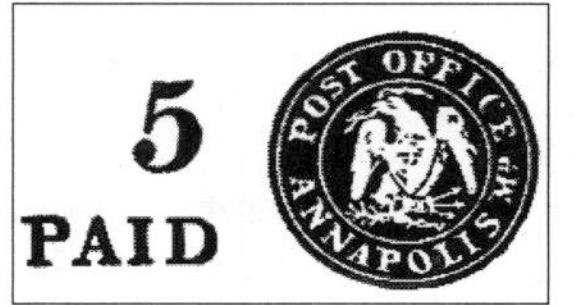

PM3

		UnFVF	UseFVF
PM3			
5¢	**carmine red**		200,000.00

1845. Baltimore, Md. Issue Envelopes in various shades of paper with the signature of the postmaster, James M. Buchanan, printed in black, blue or red. Colors listed below are those of the "PAID" numeral, and oval.

PM4-PM5

		UnFVF	UseFVF
PM4			
5¢	**blue**	—	5,000.00
PM5		UnFVF	UseFVF
5¢	**red**	—	8,500.00
PM6		UnFVF	UseFVF
5¢	**black**	—	18,000.00
PM7		UnFVF	UseFVF
5¢	**blue +5¢ blue**	—	—
PM8		UnFVF	UseFVF
10¢	**red**	—	17,500.00
PM9		UnFVF	UseFVF
10¢	**blue**	—	15,000.00
PM10		UnFVF	UseFVF
10¢	**black**	—	—

1846. Adhesive Stamp Issue Adhesive stamps *printed by intaglio on white or bluish papers, and imperforate.* Eleven varieties of the 5¢ and five varieties of the 10¢ stamps are known.

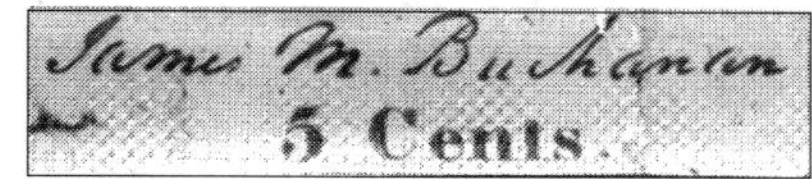

PM11

		UnFVF	UseFVF
PM11			
5¢	**black,** on white paper	—	7,500.00
	p. Bluish paper	25,000.00	7,500.00
PM12		UnFVF	UseFVF
10¢	**black,** on white paper	—	55,000.00
	p. Bluish paper	—	60,000.00

1846. Boscawen, N.H. Issue Postmaster Worcester Webster issued a *typset, imperforate* stamp of which only one copy is known.

PM13

		UnFVF	UseFVF
PM13			
5¢	**dull blue**		—180,000.00

1846. Brattleboro, Vt. Issue Postmaster Frederick N. Palmer issued *intaglio, imperforate* stamps printed from plates of 10 separately engraved subjects. The imprint "Eng'd by Thos. Chubbuck, Bratto," appears below the middle stamp of the bottom row. Eleven varieties are known.

PM14

		UnFVF	UseFVF
PM14			
5¢	**black,** on buff paper	—	6,000.00
	On cover	—	15,000.00

1846. Lockport, N.Y. Issue Postmaster Hezekiah W. Scovell issued adhesive labels with double-lined oval hand-stamped in red, "PAID" in black, and a hand-written "5." One copy and other fragments are known.

PM 15

		UnFVF	UseFVF
PM15			
5¢	**red,** on buff paper, on cover		—150,000.00

1846. Millbury, Mass. Issue Postmaster Asa H. Waters issued imperforate stamps printed singly from a *woodcut on a hand press.*

PM16 *George Washington*

		UnFVF	UseFVF
PM16			
5¢	**black,** on bluish paper	135,000.00	25,000.00
	On cover	—	85,000.00

1846. New Haven, Conn. Issue Postmaster Edward A. Mitchell used a brass hand-stamp to impress envelopes with his provisional stamp as the envelopes were brought to the post office. The postmaster's signature was added to prevent forgery. Reprints are known having been made at various times between 1871 and 1932.

PM17-18

PM17		UnFVF	UseFVF
5¢	**red**	—	75,000.00

PM18		UnFVF	UseFVF
5¢	**blue,** on buff paper	—	75,000.00

1845. New York, N.Y., George Washington Issue Robert H. Morris was the first postmaster to issue adhesive stamps as early as July 15, 1845. They featured George Washington's portrait, adapted from the then-current banknotes. The New York provisionals were also used by postmasters at Albany, Boston, Philadelphia, Washington, and probably other cities with a view of testing the practical usage of adhesive stamps. Reprints in black, blue, green, red, and brown were struck from a new plate.

The original stamps were *printed by intaglio* from plates of 40 by Rawdon, Wright & Hatch. They were *imperforate* and usually initialed "A.C.M." (Alonzo Castle Monson, a clerk in the post office) before sale.

PM19 *George Washington*

PM19		UnFVF	UseFVF
5¢	**black,** on bluish paper	625.00	350.00
	On cover	—	500.00
	Pair	1,600.00	850.00
	a. Signed "R.H.M."	12,500.00	2,500.00
	b. without signature	1,200.00	550.00
	p. blue paper	6,000.00	1,400.00
	p1. gray paper	5,000.00	1,400.00

1846. Providence, R.I. Issue Postmaster Welcome B. Sayles issued *intaglio-printed, imperforate* stamps produced from copper plates containing 12 subjects. The stamps were engraved directly onto the plate.

PM20

PM20		UnFVF	UseFVF
5¢	**black**	200.00	1,250.00

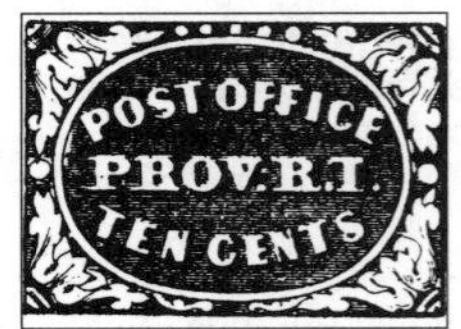

PM21

PM21		UnFVF	UseFVF
10¢	**black**	1,000.00	14,000.00
	Pair, 1 each 5¢ & 10¢	1,400.00	—

Reprints with initials on the back were made in 1898.

1845-46. St. Louis, Mo. Issue Postmaster John M. Wimer issued *imperforate* stamps printed from copper plates of six subjects. Varieties of each stamp are known. *Wove paper.*

PM22-PM29 *Missouri coat of arms*

PM22		UnFVF	UseFVF
5¢	**black,** on greenish paper	5,000.00	2,500.00

PM23		UnFVF	UseFVF
10¢	**black,** on greenish paper	4,500.00	2,500.00

PM24		UnFVF	UseFVF
20¢	**black,** on greenish paper	—	20,000.00

1846. St. Louis, Mo. Issue Previous stamps in new paper color. Varieties exist.

PM25		UnFVF	UseFVF
5¢	**black,** on gray lilac paper	—	4,500.00

PM26		UnFVF	UseFVF
10¢	**black,** on gray lilac paper	4,500.00	2,250.00

PM27		UnFVF	UseFVF
20¢	**black,** on gray lilac paper	—	11,000.00

1847. St. Louis, Mo. Issue Previous stamp designs on pelure paper.

PM28		UnFVF	UseFVF
5¢	**black,** on bluish paper	—	6,500.00

PM29		UnFVF	UseFVF
10¢	**black,** on bluish paper	—	5,500.00

Regular Postal Issues

The First Government stamps were put into use early in July 1847. They superseded Postmasters' Provisionals and other stamps which were thereafter not tolerated by the Postmaster General. The 5¢ stamp paid for carrying an ordinary letter up to 300 miles, and the 10¢ value was used for letters requiring higher postage.

Rawdon, Wright, Hatch & Edson of New York engraved the stamps and printed them in sheets of 200 that were cut into panes of 100 before distribution to the post offices. *The stamps were printed on thin, bluish wove paper. They were unwatermarked and imperforate, intaglio.*

1847. Benjamin Franklin Issue

1 *Benjamin Franklin, first postmaster general, after painting by James B. Longacre*

1		UnFVF	UseFVF
5¢	**red brown**	4,500.00	500.00
	orange brown	4,500.00	600.00
	black brown	4,500.00	525.00
	bright orange brown	5,000.00	600.00
	bright reddish brown	—	—
	brown orange	—	1,100.00
	dark brown	4,500.00	475.00
	dark brown orange	—	—
	dark olive brown	—	—
	gray brown	4,500.00	450.00
	orange	—	—
	reddish brown	—	—
	On cover, numeral *5* cancel	—	600.00
	Mark in "S" at upper right	5,000.00	550.00
	Double impression	—	—
	Double transfer, top frame line	—	550.00
	Double transfer, top and bottom frame lines	—	550.00
	Double transfer, bottom and lower part of left frame line	—	—
	Double transfer, top, bottom, left frame lines	—	1,000.00
	Double transfer. "U," "POST OFFICE," and left numeral	—	—
	Double transfer, top and upper part of side frame lines, "U" "POST OFFICE"	—	—
	FDC *(July 1, 1847)*		

1875. Benjamin Franklin Special Printing Issue Special Printing of the 1847 Regular Issue. New dies were engraved, and the stamps were printed by the Bureau of Engraving and Printing on *gray-blue paper. They are imperforate, without gum and both taller and narrower than the originals. Intaglio.* Reproductions on laid paper are known. Not valid for postage.

1 *Original (1847): The top edge of Franklin's shirt touches the frame on a level with the top of the "F" of "FIVE."*

SP1 *Reproduction (1875): The top of the shirt is on a level with the top of the figure "5."*

SP1		UnFVF	UseFVF
5¢	**red brown** (4,779 copies sold)	800.00	
	brown	800.00	
	dark brown	800.00	

1847. George Washington Issue

2 *George Washington, first president of the United States, after painting by Gilbert Stuart, Boston Museum of Fine Arts*

2		UnFVF	UseFVF
10¢	**black**	17,500.00	1,250.00
	gray black	17,500.00	1,150.00
	greenish black	—	1,150.00
	On cover		1,800.00
	Mark across lips	—	1,800.00
	Mark in necktie	—	1,800.00
	Short transfer at top	18,000.00	1,250.00
	Vertical line through second "F" of "OFFICE"	—	1,400.00
	Double transfer, left and bottom frame line	—	1,800.00
	Double transfer, "POST OFFICE"	—	1,800.00
	Double transfer, "X" at lower right	—	1,800.00
	v. Diagonal bisect on cover		10,000.00
	v1. Horizontal bisect on cover		—
	v2. Vertical bisect on cover		—

Government imitations of the 5¢ (in blue) and 10¢ (in Venetian red) were printed in 1947 and are listed as CM290 in the commemorative stamp section.

Note: The earliest known use of any U.S. stamp is a pen-canceled pair of No. 2 with a New York City postmark of "July 2," 1847, sent to Indianapolis, Ind.

1875. George Washington Special Printing Issue

2 *Original (1847): The left and right vertical outlines of the coat point at the "T" of "TEN" and between the "T" and "S" of "CENTS," respectively.*

SP2 *Reproduction (1875): Above lines point to the right edge of "X" and to the center of the "S" of "CENTS."*

SP2		UnFVF	UseFVF
10¢	**black** (3,883 copies sold)	950.00	
	gray black	950.00	

1851. Benjamin Franklin Issue The 1851-57 Regular Issue consisted of 1¢, 3¢, 5¢, 10¢, and 12¢ denominations, issued to cover the needs of a rapidly expanding postal service.

While the production methods of the day were excellent, they were not of uniform consistency. As a result, more than one type of some of the stamps are recognized by collectors. It will add to your pleasure to determine the correct types of your stamps through the use of illustrations in this catalog.

Toppan, Carpenter, Casilear & Co. printed the stamps on unwatermarked paper. Intaglio, imperforate.

3, 18 *Benjamin Franklin, after bust by Jean Antoine Houdon. For detailed descriptions of Types I-V, see Nos. 3-9 and 18-24.*

DECODING THE CATALOG

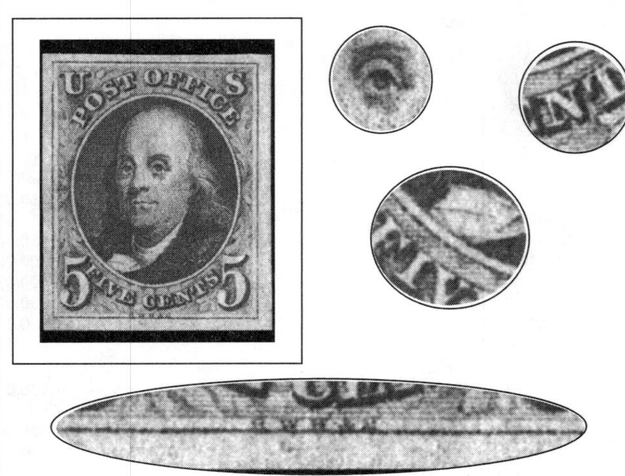

Although the United States had adhesive postages stamps as early as 1842, our first general-issue adhesives — a 5¢ stamp picturing Benjamin Franklin and a 10¢ stamp depicting George Washington —were released July 1, 1847.

The designs, featuring our nation's first postmaster general and first president, were appropriate selections for our first stamps. These issues, Minkus Nos. 1 and 2, were immediately popular. The firm Rawdon, Wright, Hatch and Edson printed them. The 5¢ stamp paid the half-ounce single-letter rate for distances less than 300 miles; the 10¢ paid the same rate for letters traveling more than 300 miles.

Although there is no real problem with identification, our first stamps were reproduced in 1875 as a part of the great centennial celebration for 1876. These new stamps, Minkus SP1 and SP2, are designated as special printings.

The U.S. Post Office Dept. wanted all existing U.S. stamps reprinted for sale to collectors (but not as valid postage), but the original dies for these stamps were no longer available, so the Bureau of Engraving and Printing had to create entirely new dies. The results were predictable, of course: The resulting stamps have numerous differences from the originals.

Most notably, the 1875 versions were printed on an ungummed, slightly bluish paper. Since the 1875 stamps were not valid for postage, most are unused (although some bear cancels). Also, the design size is different. The originals measure 18 millimeters by 23 1/2 mm, while the 1875 versions are taller and shorter (18 1/2 mm by 23 1/2 mm).

Numerous differences are easily spotted in the engravings. These include (on the 5¢) a very differently shaped shirt lace and a more rounded eye on the re-engraved. On the 10¢, there are many mouth and eye differences. The left edge of the coat is straighter on the 1847 version. The initials are more clearly seen on both originals.

3 *Type I is the most complete design of the various types of this stamp. It shows the full scroll work at the top and bottom of the design. The ornaments in the upper right corner are "doubled."*

3		UnFVF	UseFVF
1¢	**blue** Type I	175,000.00	35,000.00
	dark blue	—	—
	pale blue	—	—
	On cover		40,000.00
	Pair, one each Type I and Type II		25,000.00
	FDC *(July 1, 1851)*		

1857. Benjamin Franklin Type Ia Regular Issue

4, 19 *Type Ia has the design complete at the bottom but incomplete at the top.*

4		UnFVF	UseFVF
1¢	**blue** Type Ia	35,000.00	9,500.00
	On cover		11,000.00
	Curl on "C"	37,000.00	10,000.00
	Curl on shoulder	37,000.00	10,500.00
	Earliest documented cover: *April 19, 1857*		

1851. Benjamin Franklin Type Ib Issue

5 *Type Ib has the design at the top complete and the design at the bottom nearly complete. Type Ib is often mistaken for Type I.*

Type Ic has bottom right ornaments incomplete.

5		UnFVF	UseFVF
1¢	**blue** Type Ib	14,000.00	5,500.00
	dark blue	14,000.00	5,000.00
	pale blue	14,000.00	5,000.00
	On cover		6,000.00
	FDC *(July 1, 1851)*		130,000.00
	Type 1c	5,000.00	1,200.00

Catalog prices for the above stamp are for nice examples of the type. Stamps with a slightly less complete design at the bottom are worth about one-fourth of the above prices.

1857. Benjamin Franklin Type II Issue

6, 20 *Type II has the top line always complete, the top ornaments complete or partially cut away. The bottom line is always complete, while the little balls of the bottom scrolls and the bottom of the lower plume ornaments are missing.*

6		UnFVF	UseFVF
1¢	**blue** (Plate 1) Type II	1,100.00	150.00
	dark blue	1,100.00	150.00
	pale blue	1,100.00	150.00
	On cover		190.00
	Double transfer	1,150.00	170.00
	Plate 2 *(Dec. 5, 1855)*	1,100.00	150.00
	Cracked plate	1,300.00	375.00
	Double transfer	1,200.00	200.00
	Triple transfer	1,500.00	375.00
	Plate 3 *(May 6, 1856)*	—	400.00
	Double transfer	—	450.00
	Plate 4 *(April 19, 1857)*	3,400.00	1,100.00
	Curl in hair	—	1,200.00
	FDC *(July 1, 1851)*		17,500.00

1851. Benjamin Franklin Type III Issue

7, 21 *Type III has both the top and bottom lines broken. It should be noted particularly that the side ornaments are complete. If they are not, the stamp has been cut out of a perforated stamp of Type V (No. 24.) The finest examples of No. 7 are found in position 99R2, which is why that item is listed separately.*

7		UnFVF	UseFVF
1¢	**blue** Type III	11,500.00	2,600.00
	On cover		2,800.00
	Position 99R2	15,000.00	4,250.00

1851. Benjamin Franklin Type IIIa Issue 8, 22 Type IIIa has the outer line broken at the top or bottom of the stamp but both lines are not broken on the same stamp.

8		UnFVF	UseFVF
1¢	**blue** (Plate 1E) Type IIIa	4,250.00	975.00
	dark blue	4,250.00	975.00
	pale blue	4,250.00	975.00
	On cover		1,100.00
	Double transfer, 1 inverted (blue)	5,000.00	1,250.00
	Double transfer, 1 inverted (dark blue)	5,000.00	1,250.00
	Double transfer, 1 inverted (pale blue)	5,000.00	1,250.00
	Plate 2	—	—
	Plate 4	—	1,400.00
	FDC *(July 1, 1851)*		

1852. Benjamin Franklin Type IV Issue *Imperforate.*

9, 23 *Type IV, similar to Type II, but with the outer lines recut in several different ways.*

		UnFVF	UseFVF
9			
1¢	**blue** Type IV (recut Type IV) (recut once at top & once at bottom)	600.00	100.00
	On cover		145.00
	Plate block of 8, w/imprint	—	
	Bottom frame line broken	—	250.00
	Cracked plate	800.00	175.00
	Double transfer	725.00	120.00
	Triple transfer, 1 inverted	800.00	175.00
	t. Recut once at top	625.00	120.00
	t1. Recut once at top and twice at bottom	625.00	100.00
	t2. Recut twice at bottom	700.00	130.00
	t3. Recut once at bottom	750.00	155.00
	t4. Recut once at bottom & twice at top	775.00	160.00
	t5. Recut twice at top & twice at bottom	800.00	220.00
	t6. Printed both sides	—	—
	t7. Double impression	—	—
	v. Perforated 12 1/2 (unofficial)	—	3,000.00
	v1. Diagonal bisect on cover		—
	v2. Vertical bisect on cover		—
	Earliest documented cover: *June 18, 1852*		

1851. George Washington Issue *Imperforate.*

10, 11, 25 *George Washington after bust by J.A. Houdon, Mount Vernon, Va. Type I with outer frame lines at top and bottom. For descriptions of Types II and III, see Nos. 26 and 27.*

		UnFVF	UseFVF
10			
3¢	**orange brown** Type I	2,700.00	100.00
	deep orange brown	2,700.00	120.00
	copper brown	2,850.00	150.00
	On cover		—
	Mark on lower right diamond	—	150.00
	Nick on shoulder	—	100.00
	Double transfer	—	120.00
	Triple transfer	—	300.00
	p. Thin, India-like paper	—	450.00
	t. Printed both sides	—	—
	FDC *(July 1, 1851)*		12,000.00

1851. George Washington Issue *Imperforate.*

		UnFVF	UseFVF
11			
3¢	**Venetian red** Type I	220.00	10.00
	claret	270.00	15.00
	bright brown carmine	280.00	18.50
	brown carmine	235.00	10.50
	dark brown carmine	235.00	10.50
	dark violet	235.00	10.50
	dull brown carmine	260.00	12.00
	dull carmine red	275.00	20.00
	dull orange red	220.00	9.00
	dull rose carmine	220.00	9.00
	Plate block of 8	—	
	Mark on lower right diamond	325.00	25.00
	Nick on shoulder	235.00	10.50
	Cracked plate	675.00	95.00
	Worn plate	225.00	10.00
	Double transfer in "CENTS"	350.00	35.00
	Double transfer in "THREE CENTS"	250.00	35.00
	Double transfer in "THREE CENTS" & rosettes double	375.00	45.00
	Triple transfer	350.00	25.00
	t. Double impression	—	5,000.00
	v. Perforated 12 1/2 (unofficial)	—	1,500.00
	Earliest documented cover: *Oct. 4, 1851*		

1856. Thomas Jefferson Issue *Imperforate.*

12, 28-30 *Thomas Jefferson, after painting by Gilbert Stuart. Type I, with full projections at top and bottom as well as the sides. Copies that do not have these complete projections at top and bottom are trimmed from perforated varieties issued at a later date. For a description of Type II see Nos. 31 and 32.*

		UnFVF	UseFVF
12			
5¢	**red brown** Type I	15,500.00	1,000.00
	dark red brown	15,500.00	1,000.00
	Double transfer	—	1,550.00
	Earliest documented cover: *March 24, 1856*		

1855. George Washington Type I Issue

13, 33 *George Washington, after painting by Gilbert Stuart. Type I. For description of Types II-IV, see Nos. 14-16 and 34-37.*

13, 33 *Type I has the "shells" at the lower corners almost complete. The line below "TEN CENTS" is very nearly complete. The outer lines above the middle of the stamp and over the "X" in each upper corner are broken. There are three small circles on each side opposite the words "TEN CENTS."*

		UnFVF	UseFVF
13			
10¢	**green** Type I	13,000.00	700.00
	dark green	13,000.00	700.00
	yellow green	13,000.00	700.00
	On cover		845.00
	Curl in left "X"	13,500.00	860.00
	Double transfer	13,500.00	850.00
	FDC *(May 1855)*		

1855. George Washington Type II Issue *Imperforate.*

14, 34 *Type II has the outer line at the bottom broken in the middle, the "shells" are partially cut away, and the design is complete at the top. There are three small circles on each side.*

		UnFVF	UseFVF
14			
10¢	**green** Type II	1,900.00	200.00

DECODING THE CATALOG

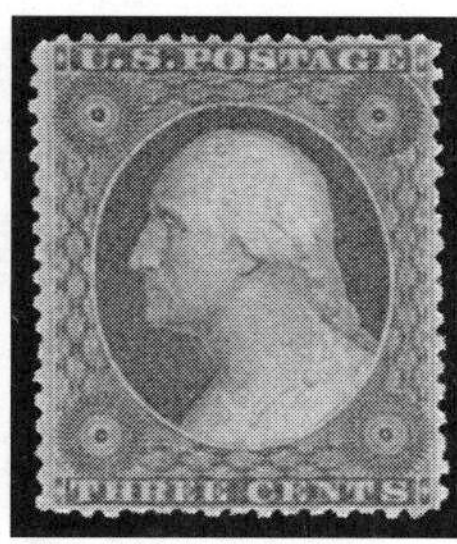

The United States 3¢ 1851 issue has been the single most-studied stamp of the United States and, as a result, there are significant bodies of work to help the collector. The stamp comes in only two formats and three design types. The formats are imperforate and perforated 15 1/2. The imperforate stamps were released in 1851; the perforated ones in 1857. The design types of the 3¢ stamp are all related to the frame lines surrounding the design.

All stamps of the 1851 and 1857 series were demonetized in 1861, after the southern states seceded during the early part of the Civil War.

Type I (left)

Of the three design types found on the 3¢ value, Type I is the only one found both on imperforate and perforated stamps. Since the perforated Type I stamps are worth considerably more than the imperforate ones, there is no incentive to fake imperforates by trimming perforations. The distinguishing feature of Type I is a frame line on all four sides of the design.

There are two main varieties of the Type I imperforate, Minkus 10 and 11. No. 10 is an orange brown stamp, produced from the early 3¢ plates. As a result, the impressions of these stamps are strong and clear, with fine design lines clearly visible.

No. 11 comes in a number of different shades (the most common of these is dull red) from plates used from late 1851 on. Impressions on these stamps range from crisp and clear to blurry and worn.

In 1857, stamps printed from the 1851 plates were perforated, but with what was considered unsatisfactory results. Since the stamp images were laid in on the plates with no idea of later perforating, they appear very close together. As a result, perforating between these stamps was very difficult without cutting into the design.

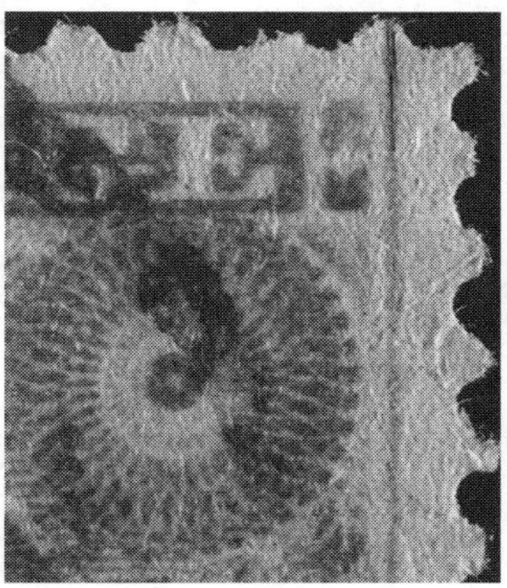

Type II (left)

Type II is found only on perforated stamps.

After some Type I stamps had been perforated, it was decided that the top and bottom frame lines should be removed from future plates to allow for horizontal perforating without cutting the design. The distance between columns of stamps on the plates was considered acceptable with the frame lines, so new plates were prepared using continuous vertical frame lines. This variety, Minkus 26, is the most common type of the 3¢ stamp.

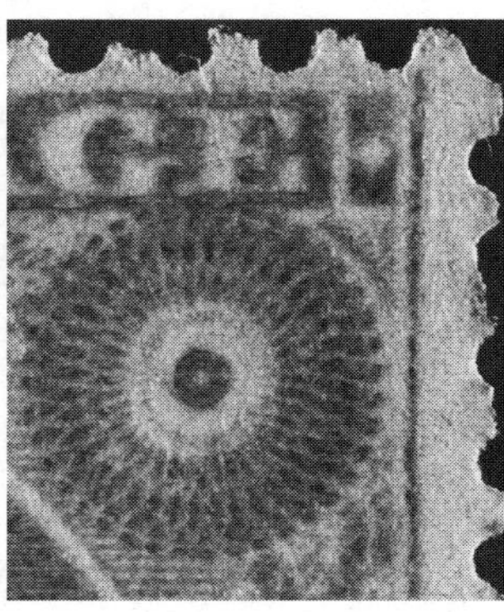

Type III (left)

Type III is a major variety, Minkus 27.

Although similar to Type II, Type III has had a slight design change. The side frame lines extend only to the top and bottom of the stamp design. There are no top or bottom frame lines. Because Type III stamps are considerably more valuable than their Type II counterparts, it is important to be able to tell the type for sure. The most easily mistaken examples are those Type II stamps from the top or bottom of the pane, where the side frame lines stop at the top or bottom of the stamp design. To be sure that your stamp is indeed a Type III example, you should be able to see a frame line break at both the top and the bottom of the stamp design. If one is obscured, then it is best to assume it is a margin copy Type II example.

		UnFVF	UseFVF
	dark green	1,900.00	200.00
	yellow green	1,900.00	200.00
	On cover		260.00
	Curl opposite left "X"	1,950.00	290.00
	Double transfer	1,950.00	270.00
	Earliest documented cover: *May 12, 1855*		

1855. George Washington Type III Issue

15, 35 *Type III has outer lines broken above the top label that contains words "U.S. POSTAGE" and the lines are broken above the "X" numerals. The shells and outer line at the bottom are partially cut away. There are three small circles on each side.*

15		UnFVF	UseFVF
10¢	**green** Type III	1,900.00	200.00
	dark green	1,900.00	200.00
	yellow green	1,900.00	200.00
	On cover		260.00
	Curl on forehead	2,000.00	265.00
	Curl to right of left "X"	2,000.00	265.00
	Double transfer at top and bottom	—	—
	Earliest documented cover: *May 23, 1855*		

1856. George Washington Type IV Issue

16, 36 *Type IV has had the outer lines at the top or bottom of the stamp, or at both places, recut. There are three small circles on each side.*

16		UnFVF	UseFVF
10¢	**green** Type IV (outer line recut at top only)	12,500.00	1,200.00
	dark green	12,500.00	1,200.00
	yellow green	12,500.00	1,200.00
	On cover		1,450.00
	t. Outer line recut at bottom only	12,500.00	1,200.00
	t1. Outer line recut at top and bottom	14,000.00	1,300.00
	Earliest documented cover: *July 10, 1855*		

All four types of the 10¢ stamp occur on the same sheet, so that pairs and blocks showing combination of these types exist.

1851. George Washington Type I Issue

17, 38 *George Washington, Type I, with complete frame lines. For Type II see No. 39.*

17		UnFVF	UseFVF
12¢	**black** Type I	2,600.00	225.00
	deep black	2,600.00	225.00
	gray black	2,600.00	225.00
	On cover		1,250.00
	Double transfer	2,700.00	250.00
	Recut in lower left corner	2,800.00	275.00
	Triple transfer	2,900.00	300.00
	p. Thin, India-like paper	—	550.00
	t. Printed on both sides	—	5,500.00
	y. Diagonal bisect on cover		2,500.00
	On "Via Nicaragua" cover		5,500.00
	y1. Vertical bisect on cover		8,500.00
	y2. Quarter on cover		—
	FDC *(July 1, 1851)*		

1861. Benjamin Franklin Type I Issue

Regular Issue, printed by Toppan, Carpenter & Co., had the same designs and types as the preceding issue, with some further types and values being noted. Three new values, the 24¢, 30¢, and 90¢ stamps, were added to this issue.

This issue marked a great milestone in postal service progress. Due to a pressing need for a faster stamp dispensing method, the stamps were machine perforated and easily and quickly separated, instead of having to be cut apart by scissors. *Intaglio, perforated 15.*

While No. 18 has the complete design like the imperforate stamp No. 3, it does not have the "doubled" ornaments in the upper right corners.

18		UnFVF	UseFVF
1¢	**blue** Type I	725.00	325.00
	On cover		450.00
	Cracked plate	—	500.00
	Double transfer	775.00	400.00
	Earliest documented cover: *Jan. 15, 1861*		

The normal setting of the perforating machine was such that perforations cut the design on almost every stamp. Prices quoted are for such copies. Where the perforations do not cut the design No. 18 stamps command very high premiums.

1857. Benjamin Franklin Type Ia Issue

19		UnFVF	UseFVF
1¢	**blue** Type Ia	12,000.00	3,250.00
	On cover		4,000.00
	Curl on shoulder	12,500.00	3,500.00
	Earliest documented cover: *Nov. 2, 1857*		

1857. Benjamin Franklin Type II Issue

20		UnFVF	UseFVF
1¢	**blue** (Plate 2) Type II	475.00	135.00
	On cover		160.00
	Cracked plate	700.00	325.00
	Double transfer	525.00	150.00
	Plate 4	—	750.00
	Curl in hair	—	650.00
	Double transfer	—	1,000.00
	Plate 11	600.00	175.00
	Double transfer	—	—
	Plate 12	475.00	135.00
	Earliest documented cover: *July 26, 1857*		

1857. Benjamin Franklin Type III Issue

21		UnFVF	UseFVF
1¢	**blue** Type III	5,000.00	1,150.00
	On cover		1,500.00
	Position 99R2	—	7,500.00
	Earliest documented cover: *Nov. 20, 1857*		

The finest examples of No. 21 are found in position 99R2, which is why that item is listed separately.

1857. Benjamin Franklin Type IIIa Issue

22		UnFVF	UseFVF
1¢	**blue** (Plate 4) Type IIIa	800.00	260.00
	On cover		290.00
	Double transfer	850.00	290.00
	v. Horizontal pair, imperforate between	—	4,750.00
	Plate 11	900.00	290.00
	Double transfer	950.00	320.00
	Triple transfer	—	—
	Plate 12	900.00	290.00
	Double transfer	950.00	320.00
	Earliest documented cover: *July 26, 1857*		

1857. Benjamin Franklin Type IV Issue

23		UnFVF	UseFVF
1¢	**blue** Type IV recut top and once at bottom	3,000.00	325.00
	Cracked plate	3,500.00	425.00
	On cover	—	340.00
	Double transfer	3,250.00	350.00

	Triple transfer, 1 inverted	—	—
	t. Recut once at top	—	—
	t1. Recut once at top and twice at bottom	3,250.00	350.00
	t2. Recut twice at bottom	3,500.00	375.00
	t3. Recut once at bottom	3,250.00	360.00
	t4. Recut once at bottom and twice at top	3,250.00	375.00
	t5. Recut twice at top and twice at bottom	3,250.00	410.00
	Earliest documented cover: *July 25, 1857*		

1857. Benjamin Franklin Type V Issue

24 *Type V occurs only on the perforated stamps. The top and bottom lines are broken and the sides of the design have been partially cut away. Trimmed copies of this stamp often are offered as Type III imperforate. They easily can be detected since Type III, and all other types that come imperforate, have the complete design at the sides.*

24		UnFVF	UseFVF
1¢	**blue** Type V	170.00	40.00
	On cover		45.00
	Plate block of 8, w/imprint	3,250.00	
	Curl in hair	220.00	33.00
	Curl on shoulder	—	—
	Curl over "C" of "CENT"	240.00	67.00
	Curl over "E" of "CENT"	270.00	80.00
	Horizontal dash in hair	330.00	80.00
	"Ring" below ear	330.00	80.00
	Double curl in hair	290.00	75.00
	Double transfer, at bottom	295.00	95.00
	Double transfer, at top	230.00	70.00
	Plate 5	495.00	125.00
	Curl in "O" of "ONE"	—	—
	Curl on shoulder	—	—
	p. Laid paper	—	—
	v. Vertical strip of 5, imperforate horizontally	—	—
	Earliest documented cover: *(Nov. 17, 1857)*		

1857. George Washington Type I Issue

25		UnFVF	UseFVF
3¢	**rose** Type I	1,900.00	70.00
	brownish carmine	1,900.00	70.00
	dull red	1,900.00	70.00
	On cover		70.00
	Gash on shoulder	2,000.00	75.00
	Cracked plate	3,200.00	400.00
	Double transfer	2,200.00	100.00
	Double transfer, "GENTS"	—	550.00
	Triple transfer	—	500.00
	Worn plate	2,000.00	75.00
	v. Horizontal pair, imperforate vertically	—	—
	v1. Vertical pair, imperforate horizontally	—	10,000.00
	Earliest documented cover: *Feb. 28, 1857*		

Fakes are known of the horizontal pair, imperforate vertically.

1857. George Washington Type II Issue

26 *Type II has the outer frame removed at the top and bottom of the design. The side frame lines were recut to form continuous lines from the top to the bottom of the plate so they extend beyond the design of the stamp.*

26		UnFVF	UseFVF
3¢	**Venetian red** Type II	75.00	4.50
	bright carmine	—	—
	brown carmine	130.00	14.00
	dull red	75.00	4.50
	dull rose brown	75.00	4.50
	orange brown	—	—
	On cover		6.00
	Cracked plate	725.00	220.00
	Double transfer	100.00	15.00
	Double transfer in rosettes, line through "POSTAGE"	—	350.00
	Left frame line double	100.00	14.00
	Right frame line double	100.00	14.00
	Transfer damage above lower left rosette	75.00	5.50
	Transfer damage, retouched	80.00	7.00
	Transfer damage, retouched w/2 vertical lines	110.00	8.00
	Worn plate	75.00	5.50
	t. Double impression	—	2,500.00
	v. Horizontal pair, imperforate between	—	—
	v1. Horizontal pair, imperforate vertically	4,000.00	
	v2. Vertical pair, imperforate horizontally	—	—
	Earliest documented cover: *Sept. 14, 1857*		

1857. George Washington Type III Issue

27 *Type III has the outer frame lines removed at the top and bottom of the design. The side frame lines extend only to the top and bottom of the stamp design.*

27		UnFVF	UseFVF
3¢	**Venetian red** Type III	200.00	45.00
	brownish carmine	200.00	45.00
	dull red	200.00	45.00
	claret	200.00	45.00
	On cover		75.00
	Damaged transfer, above lower left rosette	220.00	65.00
	Damaged transfer, retouched	200.00	60.00
	Double transfer	300.00	90.00
	Double transfer, bottom part of stamp & rosettes	—	175.00
	Triple transfer	—	300.00
	Worn plate	200.00	45.00
	Earliest documented cover: *July 11, 1857*		

1857. Thomas Jefferson Type I Issue *has full projections at top and bottom.*

28, 28A, 29, 30 *Type I Thomas Jefferson*

28		UnFVF	UseFVF
5¢	**red brown** Type I	3,000.00	260.00
	bright red brown	3,000.00	260.00
	pale red brown	3,000.00	260.00
	Earliest documented cover: *Aug. 23, 1857*		

28A		UnFVF	UseFVF
5¢	**henna brown (Indian red)**	25,000.00	2,500.00
	On cover		3,500.00
	Earliest documented cover: *March 31, 1858*		

1858. Thomas Jefferson Type I Issue

29		UnFVF	UseFVF
5¢	**brick red** Type I	10,000.00	900.00
	On cover	—	1,000.00
	Earliest documented cover: *Oct. 6, 1858*		

1859. Thomas Jefferson Type I Issue

30		UnFVF	UseFVF
5¢	**brown** Type I	1,500.00	250.00
	dark brown	1,500.00	250.00

		UnFVF	UseFVF
	pale brown	1,500.00	250.00
	yellow brown	1,500.00	250.00
	On cover	—	350.00
	Earliest documented cover: *April 4, 1859*		

1860. THOMAS JEFFERSON TYPE II ISSUE 31, 32 *Type II does not have full projections at the top and bottom. These projections have been partially or completely cut away.*

31, 32 *Type III Thomas Jefferson*

31		UnFVF	UseFVF
5¢	**brown** Type II	1,500.00	200.00
	dark brown	1,500.00	200.00
	yellow brown	1,500.00	200.00
	On cover		300.00
	Cracked plate	—	—
	Printed on both sides	3,800.00	4,000.00
	Earliest documented cover: *May 4, 1860*		

1861. THOMAS JEFFERSON TYPE II ISSUE

32		UnFVF	UseFVF
5¢	**orange brown** Type II	1,100.00	800.00
	dark orange brown	1,100.00	800.00
	On cover		2,300.00
	Earliest documented cover: *May 8, 1861*		

1857. GEORGE WASHINGTON TYPE I ISSUE

33		UnFVF	UseFVF
10¢	**green** Type I	8,250.00	500.00
	bluish green	8,250.00	500.00
	dark green	8,250.00	500.00
	yellowish green	8,250.00	500.00
	On cover		825.00
	Curl in left "X"	8,250.00	600.00
	Double transfer	8,250.00	600.00
	Vertical pair, imperforate horizontally		6,600.00
	Earliest documented cover: *Sept. 21, 1857*		

1857. GEORGE WASHINGTON TYPE I ISSUE

34		UnFVF	UseFVF
10¢	**green** Type II	2,500.00	200.00
	bluish green	2,500.00	200.00
	dark green	2,500.00	200.00
	yellowish green	2,500.00	200.00
	On cover		225.00
	Curl opposite left "X"	—	240.00
	Double transfer	2,600.00	210.00
	Earliest documented cover: *July 27, 1857*		

1857. GEORGE WASHINGTON TYPE III ISSUE

35		UnFVF	UseFVF
10¢	**green** Type III	2,600.00	200.00
	bluish green	2,600.00	200.00
	dark green	2,600.00	200.00
	yellowish green	2,600.00	200.00
	On cover		225.00
	Curl in left "X"	—	260.00
	Curl on forehead	—	260.00
	Double transfer	—	—
	Earliest documented cover: *July 25, 1857*		

1857. GEORGE WASHINGTON TYPE IV ISSUE

36		UnFVF	UseFVF
10¢	**green** Type IV, recut at top	17,700.00	1,500.00
	bluish green	17,700.00	1,500.00
	dark green	17,700.00	1,500.00
	yellowish green	17,700.00	1,500.00
	On cover		1,900.00
	t. Recut once at bottom	18,000.00	1,500.00
	t1. Recut at top and bottom	18,500.00	1,600.00
	Earliest documented cover: *July 25, 1857*		

1859. GEORGE WASHINGTON TYPE V ISSUE

37 *Type V had the side ornaments partially cut away. In no case do three small circles remain on each side of the stamp. There usually is one small circle at each side, but some copies show two or three small circles on the right side. The outer lines at the top are complete except over the right "X." Trimmed copies of this stamp are offered as imperforates. If an imperforate does not have three circles at each side it is a trimmed fake.*

37		UnFVF	UseFVF
10¢	**green** Type V	200.00	60.00
	bluish green	200.00	60.00
	dark green	200.00	60.00
	yellowish green	200.00	60.00
	On cover		70.00
	Plate block of 8, /w imprint	—	9,000.00
	Curl in "E" of "CENTS"	250.00	80.00
	Curl in "T" of "CENT"	250.00	80.00
	Curl (small) on forehead	240.00	70.00
	Double transfer at bottom	250.00	80.00
	Cracked plate	—	—
	Earliest documented cover: *April 29, 1859*		

1857. GEORGE WASHINGTON TYPE I ISSUE

38		UnFVF	UseFVF
12¢	**black** Type I	380.00	100.00
	gray black	380.00	100.00
	On cover		485.00
	Double transfer	430.00	110.00
	Triple transfer	525.00	—
	v. Diagonal bisect on cover		17,500.00
	v1. Horizontal pair, imperforate between	—	—
	Earliest documented cover: *July 30, 1857*		

1859. GEORGE WASHINGTON TYPE II ISSUE

39 *Type II has the frame line broken or missing on one or both sides.*

39		UnFVF	UseFVF
12¢	**black** Type II	360.00	115.00
	deep black	360.00	115.00
	On cover		575.00
	Double transfer, frame line at left	390.00	125.00
	Double transfer, frame line at right	390.00	125.00
	Vertical line through rosette	460.00	160.00
	Earliest documented cover: *Dec. 9, 1859*		

1860. GEORGE WASHINGTON ISSUE

40 *George Washington*

40		UnFVF	UseFVF
24¢	**gray lilac**	725.00	210.00
	gray	725.00	210.00
	lilac	725.00	210.00
	On cover		750.00
	Plate block of 12, w/ imprint	32,000.00	

		UnFVF	UseFVF
	v. Imperforate single	1,250.00	
	v1. Pair, imperforate	16,000.00	
	Earliest documented cover: *July 7, 1860*		

1860. Benjamin Franklin Issue

41 *Benjamin Franklin*

41		UnFVF	UseFVF
30¢	**orange**	850.00	300.00
	reddish orange	850.00	300.00
	yellow orange	850.00	300.00
	On cover		1,250.00
	Cracked plate	—	—
	Double transfer	950.00	350.00
	Recut at bottom	1,000.00	450.00
	v. Imperforate single	2,500.00	
	v1. Pair, imperforate	7,500.00	1,250.00
	Earliest documented cover: *Aug. 8, 1860*		

1860. George Washington Issue

42 *Gen. George Washington, after a painting by John Trumbull, Yale University*

42		UnFVF	UseFVF
90¢	**deep blue**	1,300.00	5,500.00
	blue	1,300.00	5,500.00
	On cover		4,500.00
	Double transfer at bottom	1,400.00	—
	Double transfer at top	1,400.00	—
	Short transfer at bottom, left and right	1,350.00	—
	v. Imperforate single	3,000.00	
	v1. Pair, imperforate	—	—
	Earliest documented cover: *Sept. 11, 1860*		

Many fake cancellations exist on this stamp.

1875. Benjamin Franklin Special Printing Issue Special Printing of the 1857-61 Regular Issue. The original dies were intact, but new plates were made of the 1¢, 3¢, 10¢ and 12¢ values. Since these were perforated 12, while the originals were 15, they are quite easy to distinguish from the originals. The issue is very bright in color, *printed on white paper, issued without gum. Printed intaglio by the Continental Bank Note Co.* Not valid for postal use.

SP3		UnFVF	UseFVF
1¢	**brilliant blue** (3,846 copies sold)	500.00	
	Cracked plate	600.00	
	Double transfer	600.00	

1875. George Washington Special Printing Issue

SP4		UnFVF	UseFVF
3¢	**bright vermilion** *(479 copies)*	2,000.00	

1875. Thomas Jefferson Special Printing Issue

SP5		UnFVF	UseFVF
5¢	**bright orange brown** *(878 copies)*	950.00	
	Margin strip of 4, w/plate number	10,000.00	

1875. George Washington Special Printing Issue

SP6		UnFVF	UseFVF
10¢	**bluish green** *(516 copies)*	1,750.00	

1875. George Washington Special Printing Issue

SP7		UnFVF	UseFVF
12¢	**greenish black** *(489 copies)*	2,000.00	

1875. George Washington Special Printing Issue

SP8		UnFVF	UseFVF
24¢	**dark violet black** *(479 copies)*	2,000.00	

1875. Benjamin Franklin Special Printing Issue

SP9		UnFVF	UseFVF
30¢	**yellow orange** *(480 copies)*	2,000.00	

1875. George Washington Special Printing Issue

SP10		UnFVF	UseFVF
90¢	**indigo** *(454 copies)*	3,300.00	

This set is known imperforated.

1861. Benjamin Franklin Issue Upon the outbreak of the War Between the States in 1861, the postal authorities in Washington demonetized all U.S. postage stamps issued up to that time to prevent possible use in the Confederate States and place financial pressure on them. (It is interesting to note that due to the scarcity of metal coins during this period, stamps encased in small containers often were pressed into use as small change.)

The National Bank Note Co. obtained the engraving and printing contract and prepared a set of eight essay designs in the form of finished 1¢, 3¢, 5¢, 10¢, 12¢, 24¢, 30¢ and 90¢ stamps with numerical denominations, and evidently submitted them for approval prior to Aug. 1. At least six of these miscalled "August" designs were not approved. Beginning Aug. 17, postage stamps were issued from new plates of 1¢, 3¢, 5¢, 10¢, 12¢ and 90¢ made from altered designs. The set was completed by regular printings from the 24¢ and 90¢ essay plates after possible alterations on them. A second printing from the 10¢ essay plate was issued and is known used in September 1861.

The second set of designs, regularly issued, are listed here, as well as two denominations, 2¢ and 15¢, added in 1863 and 1866 respectively. The essays as well as the issued stamps are on *unwatermarked paper, intaglio and perforated 12.*

43 *Benjamin Franklin, after bust by Jean Caffert, Pennsylvania Academy of Fine Arts*

Unissued design: There is no dash under the tip of the ornaments at the right of the numeral in the upper left corner.

43 *A dash has been added under the tip of the ornament at the right of the numeral in the upper left corner.*

43		UnFVF	UseFVF
1¢	**blue**	150.00	16.00
	bright blue	150.00	16.00
	pale blue	150.00	16.00
	ultramarine	360.00	45.00
	dark blue	300.00	25.00
	indigo	300.00	25.00

		UnFVF	UseFVF
	On cover	—	21.00
	Plate block of 8, w/imprint	2,450.00	—
	Dot on "U"	160.00	18.00
	Double transfer	—	24.00
	t. Printed on both sides	—	2,500.00
	p. Laid paper	—	—
	v. Vertical pair, imperforate horizontally	—	—
	FDC *(Aug. 17, 1861)*		

1863. Andrew Jackson Issue

44 *Andrew Jackson, after miniature by John Wood Dodge*

44		UnFVF	UseFVF
2¢	**black**	175.00	24.00
	deep black	175.00	24.00
	gray black	175.00	24.00
	On cover		42.00
	Plate block of 8, w/imprint	8,000.00	
	Cracked plate	—	—
	Double transfer	200.00	27.00
	Double transfer of top left corner & "POSTAGE" ("Atherton shift")	6,000.00	—
	Double transfer of right side ("Preston shift")	—	—
	Short transfer	190.00	25.00
	Triple transfer	—	—
	p. Laid paper	—	—
	t. Printed on both sides	—	5,000.00
	y. Diagonal bisect on cover	—	1,250.00
	y1. Horizontal bisect on cover	—	—
	y2. Vertical bisect on cover	—	1,250.00
	Earliest documented cover: *July 6, 1863*		

1861. George Washington Issue

45 *George Washington, after bust by J. A. Houdon*

Unissued Design: The ornaments forming the corners of the design are plain.

45 *A ball has been added to each corner of the design and the ornaments have been enlarged.*

45		UnFVF	UseFVF
3¢	**pink**	4,500.00	450.00
	On cover		500.00
	FDC *(Aug. 17, 1861)*		25,000.00
	a. rose pink	70.00	1.75
	On cover		2.00
	av. Vertical pair, imperforate horizontally	2,500.00	750.00
	b. pigeon blood pink	2,700.00	—
	On cover		4,000.00

It is almost impossible to describe a "pink" in words, but it should be kept in mind that the inking on a "pink" is rather heavy, and the lines of the design do not stand out as sharply as on the other shades. The color, while not as outstanding as a dull pink ribbon, is nevertheless on that order. It is not any of the shades of brown, dull red, rose red, or brown red so often mistaken for the real pink.

1861. George Washington Issue

46		UnFVF	UseFVF
3¢	**brown carmine**	125.00	2.50
	dull brown red	125.00	2.50
	dull red	125.00	2.50
	pale carmine red	125.00	2.50
	dark brown red	225.00	2.50
	On cover		3.50
	Plate block of 8, w/imprint	19,000.00	
	Cracked plate	—	—
	Double impression	150.00	—
	Double transfer	—	—
	p. Laid paper	—	—
	t. Printed on both sides	—	—
	v. Vertical pair, imperforate horizontally	2,500.00	750.00

1861. Thomas Jefferson Issue

47 *Thomas Jefferson. Unissued Design (left): No leaflets project from the corner ornaments. Issued design (right): A leaflet projects from each corner ornament.*

47		UnFVF	UseFVF
5¢	**buff**	9,000.00	425.00
	brown yellow	9,000.00	425.00
	olive yellow	9,000.00	425.00
	On cover		725.00
	Earliest documented cover: *Aug. 18, 1861*		

1862. Thomas Jefferson Issue

48		UnFVF	UseFVF
5¢	**red brown**	2,000.00	225.00
	dark red brown	2,000.00	225.00
	On cover	—	475.00
	Double transfer	2,300.00	250.00
	Earliest documented cover: *Jan. 2, 1862*		

1863. Thomas Jefferson Issue

49		UnFVF	UseFVF
5¢	**brown**	1,000.00	100.00
	dark brown	1,000.00	100.00
	pale brown	1,000.00	100.00
	black brown	1,200.00	140.00
	On cover		150.00
	Double transfer, bottom frame line	1,200.00	125.00
	Double transfer, bottom & top frame lines	1,250.00	140.00
	Double transfer, top frame line	1,200.00	125.00
	p. Laid paper	—	—
	Earliest documented cover: *Feb. 3, 1863*		

1861. George Washington Type I Issue

50, 51 *George Washington*

50 *Type I does not have a heavy curved line cut below the stars, and the ornament directly over the center star at the top has only one outer line. This stamp is found only on thin, semi-transparent paper.*

50		UnFVF	UseFVF
10¢	**green** Type I	4,500.00	550.00
	dark yellow green	4,500.00	550.00
	On cover		900.00
	Double transfer	—	—
	FDC *(Sept. 17, 1861)*		

1861. George Washington Type II Issue

51 *Type II has a heavy curved line cut below the stars. The ornament directly over the center star at the top has a double outer line.*

51		UnFVF	UseFVF
10¢	**green** Type II	325.00	30.00
	dark green	350.00	32.00
	yellow green	325.00	30.00
	blue green	325.00	35.00
	On cover		45.00
	Plate block of 8, w/imprint	5,000.00	
	Double transfer	375.00	40.00
	v. Vertical pair, imperforate horizontally	—	3,500.00

1861. George Washington Issue

52 *George Washington*

Unissued Design. The four corners of the design are rounded.

52 The four corners of the design have had ovals and scrolls added to form "square corners."

52		UnFVF	UseFVF
12¢	**black**	625.00	55.00
	gray black	625.00	55.00
	On cover		85.00
	Double transfer of bottom frame line	650.00	65.00
	Double transfer of top frame line	650.00	65.00
	Double transfer of top & bottom frame lines	675.00	75.00
	FDC *(Aug. 17, 1861)*		

1866. Abraham Lincoln Issue

was released on the anniversary of his assassination at Ford's Theatre.

53 *Abraham Lincoln*

53		UnFVF	UseFVF
15¢	**black**	1,000.00	100.00
	On cover		225.00
	Plate block of 8, w/imprint	—	
	Cracked plate	—	—
	Double transfer	1,200.00	120.00
	Earliest documented cover: *April 14, 1866*		

1861. George Washington Issue

54-56 *George Washington (distinguished primarily by minute color differences)*

54		UnFVF	UseFVF
24¢	**violet**	6,500.00	800.00
	gray violet	1,400.00	500.00

No. 54 is found only on thin, semi-transparent paper, while Nos. 55 and 56 are on a thicker and more opaque paper.

1861. George Washington Issue

55		UnFVF	UseFVF
24¢	**red lilac**	800.00	130.00
	brown lilac	750.00	130.00
	steel blue	5,000.00	400.00
	blackish violet	800.00	80.00
	violet, on thin paper *(Aug. 17, 1861)*	—	—
	grayish lilac, on thin paper	—	—
	On cover		135.00
	Scratch under "A" of "POSTAGE"	—	—
	Earliest documented cover: *Oct. 4, 1861*		

1862. George Washington Issue

56		UnFVF	UseFVF
24¢	**lilac**	400.00	80.00
	gray lilac	400.00	80.00
	gray	400.00	80.00
	dark lilac	40,000.00	1,200.00
	On cover		150.00
	Scratch under "A" of "POSTAGE"	—	—
	p. Printed on both sides	—	3,500.00
	v. Pair, imperforate	—	—
	Earliest documented cover: *Oct. 29, 1862*		

1861. Benjamin Franklin Issue

57 *Benjamin Franklin*

57		UnFVF	UseFVF
30¢	**orange**	650.00	75.00
	deep orange	650.00	75.00
	On cover		350.00
	p. Printed on both sides	—	—
	FDC *(Aug. 17, 1861)*		

1861. George Washington Issue

58 *George Washington*

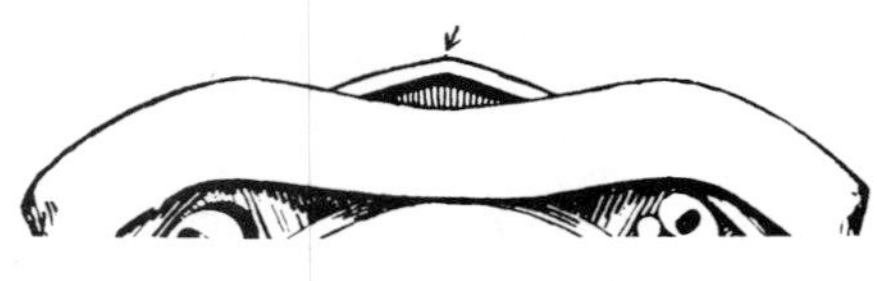

Unissued design. There is no spot of color in the apex of the lower line of the angle at the top of the design. No row of dashes appear between the lines of the angle, and the lines in the leaf at the left of the "U" at the lower left of the design run at an angle.

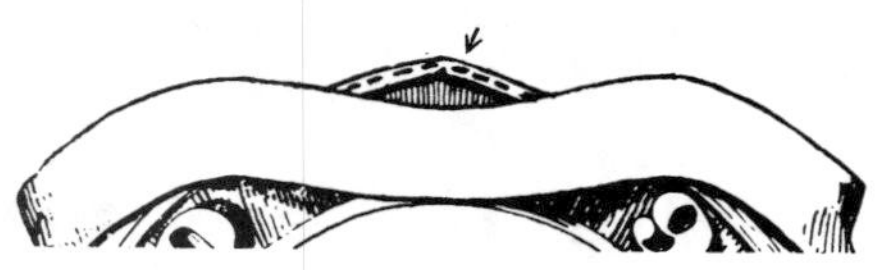

58 *There is a spot of color in the apex of the lower line of the angle at the top of the design. A row of small dashes appear between the lines of the angle, and the lines in the leaf at the lower left corner of the stamp are nearly vertical.*

		UnFVF	UseFVF
58			
90¢	**blue**	1,500.00	250.00
	dark blue	1,650.00	300.00
	pale blue	1,500.00	250.00
	dull blue	1,500.00	250.00
	On cover		13,500.00
	FDC *(Aug. 17, 1861)*		

1875. Benjamin Franklin Special Printing Issue Again the dies were available and new plates were made of the 1¢, 2¢, 10¢ and 12 ¢ values. Printed on hard, extremely white paper, absolutely white gum and without grill. They can be distinguished by their color shades, which are very deep and clear, and the white paper (compared to the slightly yellowish of the originals). *Intagalio by the National Bank Note Co., perforated 12.* Used copies are seldom found.

		UnFVF	UseFVF
SP11			
1¢	**dark ultramarine** *(3,195 copies)*	500.00	800.00

1875. Andrew Jackson Special Printing Issue

		UnFVF	UseFVF
SP12			
2¢	**jet black** *(979 copies)*	2,300.00	4,000.00

1875. George Washington Special Printing Issue

		UnFVF	UseFVF
SP13			
3¢	**brown red** *(465 copies)*	2,500.00	4,300.00

1875. Thomas Jefferson Special Printing Issue

		UnFVF	UseFVF
SP14			
5¢	**light yellow brown** *(672 copies)*	1,850.00	2,300.00

1875. George Washington Special Printing Issue

		UnFVF	UseFVF
SP15			
10¢	**bluish green** *(451 copies)*	2,000.00	3,750.00

1875. George Washington Special Printing Issue

		UnFVF	UseFVF
SP16			
12¢	**deep black** *(389 copies)*	2,800.00	4,500.00

1875. Abraham Lincoln Special Printing Issue

		UnFVF	UseFVF
SP17			
15¢	**deep black** *(397 copies)*	3,250.00	5,500.00

1875. George Washington Special Printing Issue

		UnFVF	UseFVF
SP18			
24¢	**deep brown violet** *(346 copies)*	3,250.00	6,000.00

1875. Benjamin Franklin Special Printing Issue

		UnFVF	UseFVF
SP19			
30¢	**brown orange** *(346 copies)*	3,500.00	6,000.00

1875. George Washington Special Printing Issue

		UnFVF	UseFVF
SP20			
90¢	**dark blue** *(317 copies)*	4,800.00	20,000.00

1867. George Washington w/Grill Issue Stamps of 1861-66, impressed with grills of various sizes. The grills were adopted in order to prevent the removal of cancellation ink for the illegal reuse of stamps. They were impressed into the stamps in the form of small pyramids arranged in parallel rows as noted for each type of grill listed.

Grills with points projecting upward from face of the stamp.

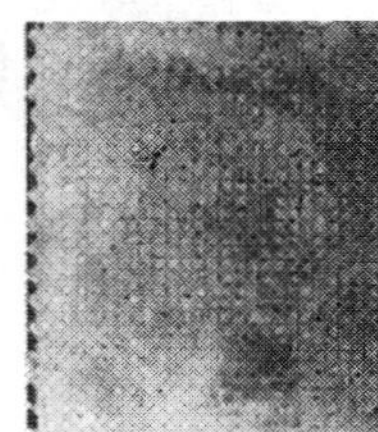

Grill A. *Grill covers the entire stamp and appears as small mounds that have small breaks in their tops. The overall grill was found to weaken the stamps, which tended to tear when being removed from their panes. An essay grill is similar, but paper breaks appear on only a few, if any, of each of the individual mounds that make up the entire grill.*

		UnFVF	UseFVF
59			
3¢	**rose** grill A	2,200.00	2,000.00
	On cover		675.00
	a. Printed on both sides	11,000.00	—
	v. Pair, imperforate	1,750.00	
	Earliest documented cover: *Aug. 13, 1867*		25,000.00

1867. Thomas Jefferson Grill A Issue

		UnFVF	UseFVF
60			
5¢	**brown** grill A	42,000.00	—
	dark brown	—	45,000.00

1867. Benjamin Franklin Grill A Issue

		UnFVF	UseFVF
61			
30¢	**orange** grill A	—	32,500.00

1868. George Washington Grill B Issue Grill B. *This grill, about 18 x 15mm in size, containing 22 x 18 rows of points projecting upward from the face of the stamp, exists on only four copies of the 3¢ rose. The grill points differ from any other issued grill. A variety of Grill C, No. 62, often is mistaken for this item.*

		UnFVF	UseFVF
61A			
3¢	**rose** grill B	—	150,000.00
	Earliest documented cover: *Feb. 1868*		

1867. George Washington Grill C Issue

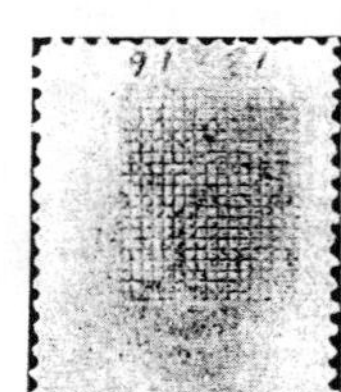

Grill C. *The grill was produced by the same grill roller as Grill A, after the roller had been machined to "erase" portions of the grill so that it now formed groups of grill points on each stamp rather than grilling all over the stamps. This grill is about 13 x 16mm with 16 to 17 by 18 to 21 points projecting upward from the face of the stamp.*

		UnFVF	UseFVF
62			
3¢	**rose** grill C	3,000.00	650.00
	On cover		575.00
	Double grill	4,200.00	1,500.00
	Grill with points down	3,750.00	650.00
	v. Pair, imperforate	1,750.00	
	Earliest documented cover: *Nov. 26, 1867*		

No. 62 shows rows of grill points, not as heavily impressed as the normal grill, forming a grill whose total area is about 18 x 15mm. Caused by a failure to cut deeply enough into the grill roller when it was being machined, which left a few areas on the roller only "partially erased."

1868. Andrew Jackson w/Grill D Issue Grill with points projecting downward. *Grill D. The tips of the grill points form vertical ridg-*

es. This grill is about 12 x 14mm, always has 15 points in each horizontal row, with 17 to 18 points in each vertical row.

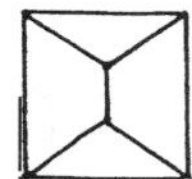

Detail of grill D

63		UnFVF	UseFVF
2¢	**black** grill D	9,500.00	1,500.00
	On cover		1,750.00
	Double transfer	—	—
	Split grill	—	1,600.00
	Earliest documented cover: *Feb. 15, 1868*		

1868. George Washington Grill D Issue

64		UnFVF	UseFVF
3¢	**rose** grill D	3,000.00	2,500.00
	On cover		600.00
	Double grill	—	—
	Split grill	—	525.00
	Earliest documented cover: *Feb. 2, 1868*		

1868. Benjamin Franklin Z Grill Issue only two used copies of No. 65 are known. One is the New York Public Library collection. The other sold at auction in 1998 for the price listed. One reason for the 1¢ Z grill's rarity is that 1¢ stamps were chiefly used on printed circulars and commercial wrappers — the junk mail of the post-Civil War era. Most covers with these stamps were promptly discarded at a time when stamp collecting was just getting under way.

The Z grill itself was not identified as a grill pattern until 1915 — 47 years after the stamp was issued — at which time the first 1¢ Z grill was identified. The second used copy of this rarity was identified the following year.

Grill Z: *When originally discovered by William L. Stevenson, this then unknown grill was given the algebraic "unknown" symbol of "Z" and it has thus remained. It is very easy to distinguish from other pyramid grills as the tip of the pyramids are horizontal ridges, all through the entire area of the grill, while on the D, E and F grills these ridges are vertical. The grill is about 11 x 14mm, with 13 to 14 by 17 to 18 points.*

65

Detail of grill Z

65		UnFVF	UseFVF
1¢	**blue** grill Z		—935,000.00

1868. Andrew Jackson Grill Z Issue

66		UnFVF	UseFVF
2¢	**black** grill Z	3,000.00	400.00
	On cover		550.00
	Double grill	—	—
	Double transfer	3,100.00	450.00
	Earliest documented cover: *March 13, 1868*		

1868. George Washington Grill Z Issue

67		UnFVF	UseFVF
3¢	**rose** grill Z	5,000.00	1,200.00
	On cover		1,600.00
	Double grill	6,000.00	—
	Earliest documented cover: *Feb. 19, 1868*		

1868. George Washington Grill Z Issue

68		UnFVF	UseFVF
10¢	**green** grill Z	47,500.00	—

1868. George Washington Grill Z Issue

69		UnFVF	UseFVF
12¢	**black** grill Z	4,000.00	600.00
	Double transfer of top frame line	—	675.00
	On cover		1,000.00

1868. Abraham Lincoln Grill Z Issue

69A		UnFVF	UseFVF
15¢	**black** grill Z	200,000.00	—

1868. Benjamin Franklin Grill E Issue This grill was created by filing some points from the "D" grill. *It is about 11 x 13mm and has 14 by 15 to 17 points.*

70		UnFVF	UseFVF
1¢	**blue** grill E	1,100.00	275.00
	dull blue	1,000.00	250.00
	On cover		325.00
	Split grill	1,100.00	275.00
	Double grill	—	375.00
	Earliest documented cover: *March 9, 1868*		

1868. Andrew Jackson Grill E Issue

71		UnFVF	UseFVF
2¢	**black** grill E	525.00	75.00
	gray black	525.00	75.00
	intense black	560.00	80.00
	On cover		110.00
	Grill with points up	—	—
	Split grill	575.00	85.00
	Double grill	560.00	80.00
	Double transfer	550.00	80.00
	Triple grill	—	—
	v. Diagonal or Vertical Bisect on cover		2,000.00
	Earliest documented cover: *March 11, 1868*		

1868. George Washington Grill E Issue

72		UnFVF	UseFVF
3¢	**rose** grill E	375.00	10.00
	pale red	375.00	10.00
	pale rose	375.00	10.00
	lake red	475.00	13.00
	On cover		14.00
	Split grill	450.00	12.00
	Double grill	—	—
	Triple grill	—	—
	p. Very thin paper	500.00	12.00
	Earliest documented cover: *May 23, 1868*		

1868. George Washington Grill E Issue

73		UnFVF	UseFVF
10¢	**green** grill E	2,000.00	175.00
	blue green	2,000.00	175.00
	dark green	2,000.00	175.00
	On cover		275.00
	Double transfer	—	225.00
	Split grill	2,100.00	190.00
	Double grill	2,900.00	300.00
	p. Very thin paper	2,100.00	190.00
	Earliest documented cover: *May 6, 1868*		

1868. George Washington Grill E Issue

74		UnFVF	UseFVF
12¢	**black** grill E	2,250.00	210.00
	gray black	2,250.00	210.00
	On cover		340.00
	Double transfer of bottom frame line	2,350.00	225.00
	Double transfer of top frame line	2,350.00	225.00
	Double transfer of top & bottom frame line	2,500.00	260.00
	Split grill	2,400.00	225.00
	Earliest documented cover: *March 3, 1868*		

1868. Abraham Lincoln Grill E Issue

75		UnFVF	UseFVF
15¢	**black** grill E	6,750.00	560.00
	gray black	6,750.00	560.00
	On cover		850.00
	Split grill	—	650.00
	Double grill	—	850.00
	Earliest documented cover: *June 25, 1868*		

1868. Benjamin Franklin Grill F Issue This grill was created by again filing points from the "E" grill. *It is about 9 x 13mm and has 11 to 12 by 15 to 17 points.*

76		UnFVF	UseFVF
1¢	**blue** grill F	500.00	100.00

		UnFVF	UseFVF
	dark blue	500.00	100.00
	pale blue	500.00	100.00
	On cover		130.00
	Split grill	525.00	120.00
	Double grill	—	200.00
	Double transfer	525.00	125.00
	p. Very thin paper	525.00	110.00
	Earliest documented cover: *March 19, 1868*		

1868. Andrew Jackson Grill F Issue

77		UnFVF	UseFVF
2¢	**black** grill F	200.00	35.00
	gray black	200.00	35.00
	On cover		45.00
	Plate block of 8, w/imprint	—	
	Split grill	220.00	40.00
	Double grill	—	125.00
	Double transfer	220.00	40.00
	v. Bisect (any) on cover		1,300.00
	Earliest documented cover: *March 27, 1868*		

1868. George Washington Grill F Issue

78		UnFVF	UseFVF
3¢	**rose** grill F	175.00	3.50
	a. rose red	175.00	3.50
	On cover		3.75
	Plate block of 8, w/imprint	2,500.00	
	Double transfer	200.00	5.50
	Grill with points up	—	—
	Split grill	185.00	4.00
	Quadruple split grill	325.00	85.00
	Double grill	—	—
	Triple grill	—	100.00
	p. Very thin paper	185.00	4.00
	t. Printed on both sides	1,100.00	—
	v. Pair, imperforate	1,000.00	—
	v1. Vertical pair, imperforate horizontally	—	—
	Earliest documented cover: *May 28, 1868*		

1868. Thomas Jefferson Grill F Issue

79		UnFVF	UseFVF
5¢	**brown** grill F	1,500.00	225.00
	black brown	1,600.00	250.00
	On cover		350.00
	Double transfer of top frame line	—	—
	Split grill	1,600.00	250.00
	Double grill	—	—
	p. Very thin paper	1,600.00	250.00
	Earliest documented cover: *Dec. 2, 1868*		

1868. George Washington Grill F Issue

80		UnFVF	UseFVF
10¢	**yellow green** grill F	1,200.00	120.00
	blue green	1,200.00	120.00
	dark green	1,200.00	120.00
	green	1,200.00	120.00
	On cover		145.00
	Double transfer	—	—
	Split grill	1,300.00	125.00
	Quadruple split grill	—	350.00
	Double grill	—	210.00
	p. Very thin paper	1,250.00	130.00
	Earliest documented cover: *Oct. 1, 1868*		

1868. George Washington Grill F Issue

81		UnFVF	UseFVF
12¢	**black** grill F	1,500.00	125.00
	gray black	1,500.00	135.00
	On cover		150.00
	Split grill	1,600.00	145.00
	Double grill	—	270.00
	Double transfer of bottom frame line	1,600.00	135.00
	Double transfer of top frame line	1,600.00	135.00
	Double transfer of top & bottom frame lines	—	165.00
	Triple grill	—	—
	p. Very thin paper	1,550.00	130.00
	Earliest documented cover: *May 27, 1868*		

1868. Abraham Lincoln Grill F Issue

82		UnFVF	UseFVF
15¢	**black** grill F	2,500.00	200.00
	gray black	2,500.00	200.00
	On cover		250.00
	Plate block of 8, w/imprint	25,000.00	
	Double transfer of upper right corner	—	—
	Split grill	2,600.00	250.00
	Quadruple split grill	3,250.00	550.00
	Double grill	—	350.00
	p. Very thin paper	2,500.00	240.00
	Earliest documented cover: *May 4, 1868*		

1869. George Washington Grill F Issue

83		UnFVF	UseFVF
24¢	**gray lilac** grill F	2,100.00	450.00
	gray	2,100.00	450.00
	On cover		900.00
	Plate block of 8, w/imprint	30,000.00	
	Scratch under "A" in "POSTAGE"	—	—
	Split grill	2,200.00	475.00
	Double grill	2,700.00	800.00
	Earliest documented cover: *March 5, 1868*		

1868. Benjamin Franklin Grill F Issue

84		UnFVF	UseFVF
30¢	**orange** grill F	2,750.00	400.00
	deep orange	2,750.00	400.00
	On cover		1,200.00
	Split grill	2,750.00	450.00
	Double grill	3,250.00	750.00
	Double grill, one split	—	—
	Earliest documented cover: *Nov. 21, 1868*		

1869. George Washington Grill F Issue

85		UnFVF	UseFVF
90¢	**blue** grill F	5,000.00	850.00
	dark blue	5,000.00	850.00
	On cover		—
	Split grill	5,250.00	950.00
	Double grill	7,000.00	—
	Earliest documented cover: *May 8, 1869*		

Most of the stamps that bear grills can be found with double grills, triple grills, split grills and quadruple split grills. Double grills are two impressions of the grill on the same stamp, triple grills are three impressions of the grill on the same stamp, split grills are those with about half of a normal grill on each end or on each side of the stamp and quadruple split grills are those that show just a small portion of the grill on each corner of the stamp. The split grill varieties were caused by misplacing the stamps under the grill roller so that the grills were not properly placed on the stamps. Fake grills exist.

1869. National Bank Note Co. Pictorial Series

This series of stamps was printed by the National Bank Note Co. The stamps are square in design. For some reason, now difficult to understand, this series was not popular and was replaced with a new series in about a year. The stamps were grilled with a new size of grill, Grill G, 9 1/2 x 9 1/2mm in size. The stamps were *printed in intaglio on hard wove paper, unwatermarked and were perforated 12.* The series includes the first U.S. bicolored postage stamps. (But see the Documentary R3.)

Three denominations of these stamps are known with inverted centers and are extremely scarce. This was the first time an error of this type was issued and was due to carelessness when printing the bi-colored stamps.

1869. Benjamin Franklin Issue

86 *Benjamin Franklin*

86		UnFVF	UseFVF
1¢	**buff**	275.00	65.00
	brown orange	275.00	65.00
	dark brown orange	275.00	65.00
	On cover		135.00
	Plate block of 10, w/imprint	—	
	Margin block of 4, w/arrow	1,400.00	
	Double transfer	—	—

		UnFVF	UseFVF
	Split grill	300.00	75.00
	Double grill	450.00	150.00
	Double grill, 1 split	—	—
	Grill omitted, original gum	775.00	
	Earliest documented cover: *May 2, 1869*		

1869. Pony Express Issue

87 *Pony Express*

87		UnFVF	UseFVF
2¢	**brown**	225.00	28.00
	dark brown	225.00	28.00
	pale brown	225.00	28.00
	yellow brown	225.00	28.00
	On cover		70.00
	Plate block of 10, w/imprint	—	
	Margin block of 4, w/arrow	975.00	
	Double transfer	—	40.00
	Split grill	250.00	40.00
	Quadruple split grill	—	225.00
	Double grill	—	150.00
	Grill omitted, original gum	600.00	
	p. Printed on both sides	—	—
	v. Bisect (any) on cover		—
	Earliest documented cover: *March 20, 1869*		

1869. Early Locomotive Issue

88 *Early Locomotive*

88		UnFVF	UseFVF
3¢	**ultramarine**	175.00	12.00
	blue	175.00	12.00
	dark blue	175.00	12.00
	dark ultramarine	175.00	12.00
	pale ultramarine	175.00	12.00
	On cover		14.00
	Plate block of 10, w/imprint	7,000.00	
	Margin block of 4, w/arrow	900.00	
	Double transfer	190.00	13.00
	Split grill	185.00	13.00
	Quadruple split grill	400.00	65.00
	Double grill	350.00	45.00
	Triple grill	—	—
	Grill omitted	600.00	—
	t. Double impression	—	—
	Earliest documented cover: *March 27, 1869*		

1869. George Washington Issue

89 *George Washington*

89		UnFVF	UseFVF
6¢	**ultramarine**	950.00	100.00
	pale ultramarine	950.00	100.00
	On cover		300.00
	Margin block of 4, w/arrow	5,000.00	
	Double transfer	—	120.00
	Split grill	1,025.00	120.00
	Quadruple split grill	—	400.00
	Double grill	—	300.00
	v. Vertical bisect on cover		—
	Earliest documented cover: *April 26, 1869*		

1869. Shield and Eagle Issue

90 *Shield and Eagle*

90		UnFVF	UseFVF
10¢	**yellow**	1,000.00	90.00
	yellowish orange	1,000.00	90.00
	On cover		335.00
	Margin block of 4, w/arrow	5,300.00	
	Split grill	1,050.00	110.00
	Double grill	—	275.00
	Earliest documented cover: *April 1, 1869*		

1869. Steamship Adriatic Issue

91 *Steamship Adriatic*

91		UnFVF	UseFVF
12¢	**green**	975.00	100.00
	bluish green	975.00	100.00
	dark green	975.00	100.00
	yellowish green	975.00	100.00
	On cover		375.00
	Margin block of 4, w/arrow	5,000.00	
	Split grill	1,025.00	125.00
	Double grill	—	300.00
	Earliest documented cover: *April 1, 1869*		

1869. Landing of Columbus Type I Issue

92 *Landing of Columbus. Type I has a white area coming to an apex under the "T" of "POSTAGE." It is also known as the "unframed picture."*

92		UnFVF	UseFVF
15¢	**brown & blue** Type I	2,500.00	350.00
	dark brown & blue	2,800.00	350.00
	pale brown & blue	2,800.00	350.00
	On cover		1,000.00
	Split grill	3,000.00	380.00
	Double grill	—	550.00
	Grill omitted	4,000.00	—
	Earliest documented cover: *April 2, 1869*		

1869. Landing of Columbus Type II Issue

93v. *Inverted center*

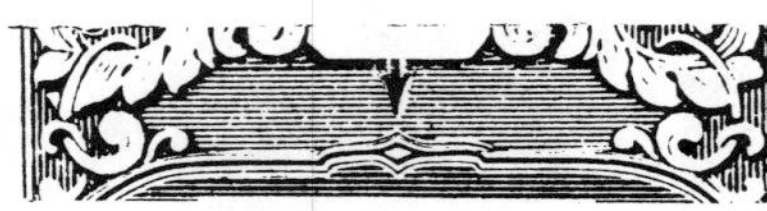

93 *Landing of Columbus. Type II has a diamond ornament under the "T" of "POSTAGE," a line has been drawn around the circumference of the central design so that picture appears to be framed. Some diagonal shading lines have been drawn around the base of the picture.*

93		UnFVF	UseFVF
15¢	**brown & blue** Type II	1,200.00	160.00
	dark brown & blue	1,200.00	160.00
	On cover		800.00
	Plate block of 8, w/imprint	20,000.00	
	Double transfer	—	—
	Split grill	1,300.00	180.00
	Double grill	2,100.00	295.00
	v. Center inverted	—	14,500.00
	v1. Center doubled, 1 inverted	—	—
	v2. Imperforate, horizontally	2,750.00	
	Earliest documented cover: *May 23, 1869*		

1869. Signing of the Declaration of Independence Issue

94 *Declaration of Independence*

94v. *Inverted Center*

94		UnFVF	UseFVF
24¢	**green & violet**	3,100.00	550.00
	bluish green & violet	3,100.00	550.00
	On cover		10,000.00
	Split grill	3,100.00	550.00
	Double grill	—	1,000.00
	Grill omitted	5,600.00	—
	v. Center inverted (83 known)	160,000.00	17,500.00
	On cover		110,000.00
	Earliest documented cover: *April 7, 1869*		

1869. Shield, Eagle and Flags Issue

95 *Shield, Eagle and Flags*

95v Flags Inverted

95		UnFVF	UseFVF
30¢	**blue & carmine**	3,100.00	350.00
	dull blue & dark carmine	3,100.00	350.00
	On cover		16,000.00
	Split grill	3,200.00	300.00
	Double grill	—	650.00
	Grill omitted	4,500.00	—
	Double paper, grill omitted	3,800.00	—
	v. Flags inverted (46 known)	200,000.00	57,000.00
	Earliest documented cover: *May 22, 1869*		

1869. Abraham Lincoln Issue

96 *Abraham Lincoln*

96		UnFVF	UseFVF
90¢	**carmine & black**	6,000.00	1,800.00
	carmine rose & black	6,000.00	1,250.00
	On cover		—
	Split grill	—	—
	Grill omitted	11,000.00	—
	Earliest documented cover: *May 10, 1869*		

1875. Benjamin Franklin Special Printing Pictorial Issue

Again the dies were available, and a new plate was made for the 1¢ and for the frame of the 15¢. The frame is similar to the Type I of the 1869 issue except that it is without the fringe of brown shading lines around the central vignette. *Printed by the National Bank Note Co., without grill, intaglio on hard white paper, with white crackly gum, perforated 12.*

SP21		UnFVF	UseFVF
1¢	**buff** (approx. 2,750 copies sold)	335.00	230.00

1875. Pony Express Special Printing Pictorial Issue

SP22		UnFVF	UseFVF
2¢	**brown** *(4,755 copies)*	385.00	330.00

1875. Early Locomotive Special Printing Pictorial Issue

SP23		UnFVF	UseFVF
3¢	**ultramarine** *(1,406 copies)*	3,000.00	10,000.00

1875. George Washington Special Pictorial Issue

SP24		UnFVF	UseFVF
6¢	**ultramarine** *(2,226 copies)*	900.00	600.00

1875. Shield and Eagle Special Printing Pictorial Issue

SP25		UnFVF	UseFVF
10¢	**yellow** *(1,947 copies)*	1,400.00	1,200.00

1875. Steamship Adriatic Special Printing Pictorial Issue

SP26		UnFVF	UseFVF
12¢	**bright green** *(1,584 copies)*	1,500.00	1,250.00

1875. Landing of Columbus Special Printing Pictorial Issue

SP27		UnFVF	UseFVF
15¢	**brown & blue** Type III *(1,981 copies)*	1,400.00	600.00
	a. Imperforate horizontally (single stamp)	1,650.00	

1875. Declaration of Independence Special Printing Pictorial Issue

SP28		UnFVF	UseFVF
24¢	**deep green & violet** *(2,091 copies)*	1,300.00	600.00

1875. Shield, Eagle and Flags Special Printing Pictorial Issue

SP29		UnFVF	UseFVF
30¢	**bright blue & carmine** *(1,356 copies)*	1,750.00	1,000.00

1875. Abraham Lincoln Special Printing Pictorial Issue

SP30		UnFVF	UseFVF
90¢	**carmine & black** *(1,356 copies)*	3,800.00	4,300.00

1880. Benjamin Franklin Special Printing Pictorial Issue

on soft porous paper, without grill. Perforated 12. Printed by the American Bank Note Co.

SP31		UnFVF	UseFVF
1¢	**buff** without gum *(approx. 2,500 copies)*	210.00	190.00
	Plate block of 10, w/imprint	18,000.00	
	brown orange, without gum (approx 3,000 copies)	180.00	125.00

1870. National Bank Note Co. Portrait Series The short-lived pictorial issue of 1869 was replaced by a series of new portraits, known as the Large Bank Notes. The first issues were produced by the National Bank Note Co. The new stamps were issued both with and without grills, a pattern of indentations in the paper designed to foil reuse of the stamps. The grilled stamps are listed as Nos. 97-107, and the ungrilled stamps are Nos. 108-118. The grills are of two sizes, *Grill H,* about 10 x 12mm with sharp tips on the grill points, and *Grill I,* about 8 1/2 x 10mm having rather blunt tips on the grill points. Grill H was used on all values while Grill I was used only on the 1¢ through 7¢ values. *Intaglio on thin to medium thick white wove paper, unwatermarked and perforated 12.*

1870. Benjamin Franklin Issue

97, 108 *Benjamin Franklin after bust by Rubricht. The pearl at the left of the numeral "1" is clear.*

97		UnFVF	UseFVF
1¢	**ultramarine** grill H	850.00	65.00
	dark ultramarine	850.00	65.00
	dull ultramarine	850.00	65.00
	On cover		90.00
	Double transfer	900.00	70.00
	Split grill	925.00	75.00
	Quadruple split grill	—	225.00
	Double grill	—	130.00
	v. Grill I	—	—
	Earliest documented cover: *April 9, 1870*		

1870. Andrew Jackson Issue

98, 109 *Andrew Jackson after bust by Hiram Powers*

In the notch formed underneath the semi-circular ornament to the left of the "S" of "U.S." the lines forming the notch do not quite join at the apex of the notch. This stamp is always of a red brown shade.

98		UnFVF	UseFVF
2¢	**red brown** grill H	480.00	38.00
	dark red brown	480.00	38.00
	dull red brown	480.00	38.00
	On cover		57.00
	Split grill	525.00	50.00
	Quadruple split grill	1,200.00	125.00
	Double grill	650.00	80.00
	v. Diagonal bisect on cover		—
	v1. Grill I	—	—
	Earliest documented cover: *Sept. 1, 1870*		

1870. George Washington Issue

99, 110 *George Washington. Under the word "THREE," the long tail of the ribbon is lightly shaded along its lower edge.*

99		UnFVF	UseFVF
3¢	**green** grill H	370.00	10.00
	deep green	370.00	10.00
	pale green	370.00	10.00
	yellow green	370.00	10.00
	On cover		15.00
	Plate block of 10, w/imprint	5,500.00	
	Plate block of 12, w/imprint	6,500.00	
	Cracked plate	—	50.00
	Double transfer	—	12.00
	Split grill	400.00	12.00
	Quadruple split grill	—	75.00
	Double grill	550.00	40.00
	v. Grill I	—	—
	v1. Printed on both sides	—	—
	v2. Pair, imperforate	1,250.00	
	Earliest documented cover: *March 25, 1870*		

1870. Abraham Lincoln Issue

100, 111 *Abraham Lincoln after bust by Leonard Volk. The first four vertical lines of the shading in the lower part of the left ribbon, to the left and downward from the "S" of "SIX," are of normal strength.*

100		UnFVF	UseFVF
6¢	**carmine** grill H	2,000.00	300.00
	carmine rose	2,000.00	300.00
	dull carmine	2,000.00	300.00
	On cover		500.00
	Split grill	2,200.00	375.00
	Quadruple split grill	—	570.00
	Double grill	—	500.00
	v. Grill I	—	—
	Earliest documented cover: *Aug. 1870*		

1871. Edwin Stanton Issue

101, 112 *Edwin M. Stanton, Attorney General under Buchanan and Secretary of War under Lincoln and Johnson, actively opposed the latter's Reconstruction policies. An attempt to dismiss him served as the pretext for Johnson's impeachment in 1868. Appointed to the Supreme Court in 1869, Stanton died before he could take office.*

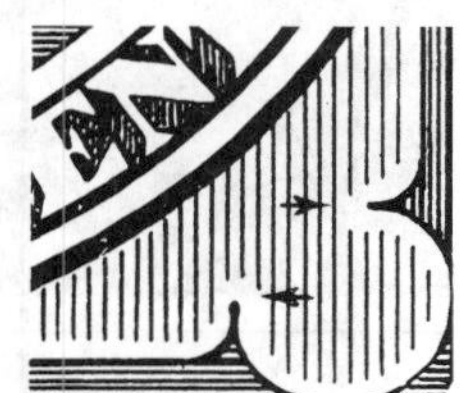

There are no semi-circles around the ends of the lines forming the ball in the lower right corner.

101		UnFVF	UseFVF
7¢	**vermilion** grill H	1,325.00	275.00
	On cover		450.00
	Split grill	1,400.00	300.00
	Quadruple split grill	—	500.00
	Double grill	—	450.00
	v. Grill I	—	—
	Earliest documented cover: *Feb. 12, 1871*		

1871. Thomas Jefferson Issue

102, 113, 138 *Thomas Jefferson after bust by Hiram Powers. The scroll ornament at the right end of the upper label, below the letter "E" of "POSTAGE," is clear.*

DECODING THE CATALOG

Most of the varieties of the United States 3¢ Large Bank Note issue are inexpensive, and all are fairly easy to distinguish, with practice.

As a group, the Large Bank Note issues were in use from 1870-89. The stamps were produced by the National Bank Note Co., the Continental Bank Note Co. and the American Bank Note Co., chronologically in that order. Of these, stamps printed by ABN are on thicker, softer paper than the other two, which are thinner, harder and more translucent. Excluding special printings (which the average collector rarely encounters), the 3¢ divides into six basic different stamps, with three design types.

Type I (left)

The first of these is Type I, produced by NBN, which can be found on Minkus 99 and 110. The biggest distinguishing factor of Type I is the tail of the ribbon in the lower-left area of the stamp, under the word "Three." There is no shading under the ribbon, giving it the appearance of having a white outline. Minkus 99 is grilled; 110 is not. The grills on No. 99 appear very faintly at times. This is normal for these stamps.

Type II (left)

There are two basic stamps of Type II. These are Minkus 122 and 134. These were produced by CBN and ABN, respectively. Type II is characterized by heavy shading under the ribbon ends below "Three." The CBN printing (Minkus 122) is on hard, translucent paper, while the ABN printing (Minkus 134) is on thicker, softer opaque paper.

Type II, re-engraved (left)

The characteristics of Type II, re-engraved, are basically the same as Type II, except that the shading surrounding the vignette oval is about half the previous width, and a horizontal line has been added under the word "Cents."

Two stamps, both printed on ABN soft, opaque paper, exist. The first, Minkus 146, is green. The second, Minkus 135, is vermillion, leaving no confusion as to types.

102		UnFVF	UseFVF
10¢	**brown**	1,800.00	450.00
	dark brown	1,800.00	450.00
	yellow brown	1,800.00	450.00
	On cover		750.00
	Split grill	1,900.00	500.00
	Double grill	—	800.00
	Earliest documented cover: *June 11, 1871*		

1872. Henry Clay Issue

103, 114 *Henry Clay after bust by Joel T. Hart. Clay was the first prominent Speaker of the House and "The Great Pacificator" of the Senate, where he effected compromises between slavery and anti-slavery forces. Twice a candidate for President, in 1824 he threw his electoral votes to John Quincy Adams, defeating Jackson, and served as Adams' Secretary of State.*

The "2" in the figure "12" has balls nearly round in shape at the upper and lower portion of the figure.

103		UnFVF	UseFVF
12¢	**pale violet**	14,000.00	1,750.00
	On cover		4,700.00
	Split grill	—	1,850.00
	Earliest documented cover: *Feb. 9, 1872*		

DECODING THE CATALOG

The United States 6¢ Large Bank Note issue of 1870-89 is one of the easiest to identify of all the Large Bank Note series stamps. It features not only design differences but distinguishable colors as well. All you need is to learn how to decode the catalog listings. All are fairly easy to distinguish once you know what to look for. As is most often the case, the task gets easier with practice.

As a group, the Large Bank Note issues were in use from 1870-89. The stamps were produced by the National Bank Note Co., the Continental Bank Note Co. and the American Bank Note Co., chronologically in that order. Of these, stamps printed by ABN are on thicker, softer paper than the other two, which are thinner, harder and more translucent.

Excluding special printings (which the average collector rarely encounters), the 6¢ divides into five different basic stamps, with three design types.

Type I (left)

The first of these is Type I, produced by NBN, which can be found on Minkus 100 and 111. Both of these stamps are carmine colored (with shades). The biggest distinguishing design factor of Type I is the ribbon end in the lower left (beneath the word "SIX"). Type I examples feature fine, well delineated engraving lines with no shadow in the curl.

Minkus 100 is grilled; 111 is not. The grills on No. 100, as with all in the series, appear very faintly at times. This is normal for these stamps, and all should be expertized due to their value.

Type II (left)

There are two basic stamps of Type II. These are Minkus 124 and 137. These were produced by CBN and ABN, respectively. The basic colors (and respective shades) are dull pink or venetian red, and pink.

Further, the CBN printing (Minkus 124) is on hard, translucent paper, while the ABN printing (Minkus 137) is on thicker, softer opaque paper.

Type II is distinguishable by again looking at the lower-left ribbon curl, which has had shading lines added to the design (the so-called secret mark).

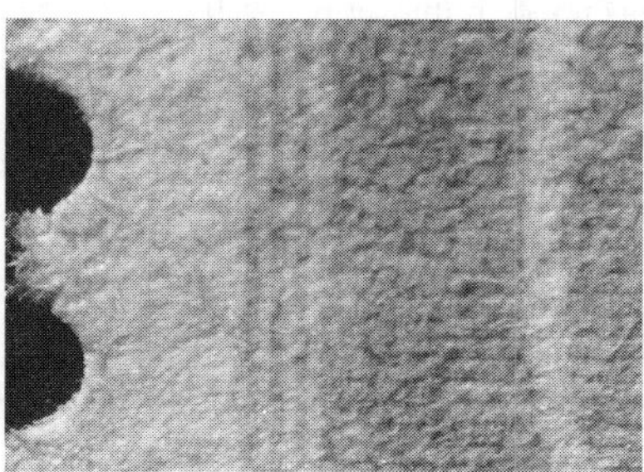

Type II, re-engraved (left)

The general characteristics of Type II, re-engraved, Minkus 147, are the same as the basic Type II, except that identifying it gets even easier. First, the color usually is more of a rose to brown-red color. Again, these shades are unique to these printings.

Unlike either Type I or Type II, the re-engraved version features only three vertical lines to the left of the vignette frame. Previous printings have four (upper right). This is an absolute determiner.

Of all printings, the grilled NBN and re-engraved versions are the most costly and worth looking for.

1870. Daniel Webster Portrait Issue

104, 115 *Daniel Webster after bust by S. V. Clevenger. (For Webster's biography, see CM115). The thin lines shading the triangles, and below the letters "U.S. POSTAGE" are fine but of normal color and strength.*

104 15¢		UnFVF	UseFVF
	orange	2,600.00	750.00
	bright orange	2,600.00	750.00
	dark orange	2,600.00	750.00
	On cover		1,350.00
	Split grill	2,500.00	820.00
	Double grill	—	—
	Earliest documented cover: *Oct. 29, 1870*		

1870. Gen. Winfield Scott Issue

105, 116, 129 *Gen. Winfield Scott after bust by Coffee. A hero of the War of 1812, Scott (1786-1866) is considered the greatest American general between George Washington and Robert E. Lee. (For further biography, see CM173).*

105		UnFVF	UseFVF
24¢	**purple**	—	10,000.00
	dull purple	—	10,000.00
	On cover		—
	Split grill	—	—

1870. Alexander Hamilton Issue

106, 117 *Alexander Hamilton was Washington's aide and secretary during the Revolution and commanded troops at Yorktown. One of the drafters of the Constitution, he advocated an extremely strong central government. As first Secretary of the Treasury, "the Hamiltonian system" established the fiscal policy, strengthened federal government and the public credit, promoted industrialization as opposed to Jefferson's concept of an agricultural economy, and aroused factionalism, which led to the development of political parties in America. Thwarting Aaron Burr's election as President in 1800 and as governor of New York in 1804, he was killed by the latter in a pistol duel.*

Decoding the Catalog

The Large Bank Note issues (1¢-90¢ values) were in use from 1870-89. The stamps were produced by the National Bank Note Co., the Continental Bank Note Co. and the American Bank Note Co., chronologically in that order. Of these, stamps printed by ABN are on thicker, softer paper than the other two, which are thinner, harder and more translucent.

Excluding special printings (which the average collector rarely encounters), the 10¢ issue divides into six basic different stamps, with three design types. The regularly issued stamp types are found here.

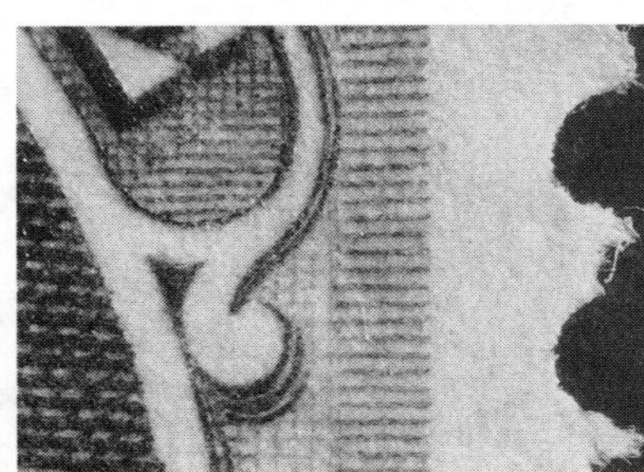

Type I (left)

Design Type I of the 10¢ large Bank Note is easily distinguished. There are three basic stamps. To the left of the portrait oval are five complete vertical lines. This characteristic also is present on Type II. To the upper-right of the portrait (beneath the "E" in "POSTAGE") is a small oval curl. It features strong curled shading lines beneath it and a double diagonal line above it. There are no markings in the curl.

Minkus 102 is printed on white, wove paper and bears a grill. The grill sometimes is quite faint.

Minkus 113 also is on wove paper but has no grill.

Minkus 138 is on softer, thicker paper. It has no grill, and the back, opaque side looks creamy.

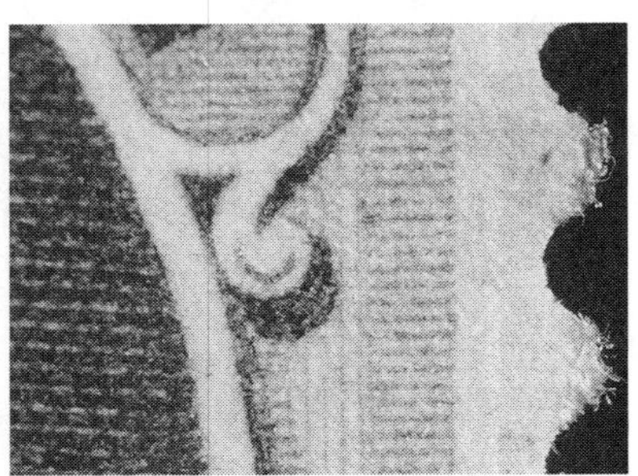

Type II (left)

Type II stamps are quite easily distinguished from Type I. As in Type I, five vertical lines are found to the left of the portrait oval. Unlike Type I, a secret mark has been added to the design. It is a curved line that appears in the curl beneath the "E" of "POSTAGE." In most cases, this is a very pronounced line.

Minkus 126 is on thin, hard translucent paper.

Minkus 139 is printed on thicker, soft opaque paper.

Type III (bottom left)

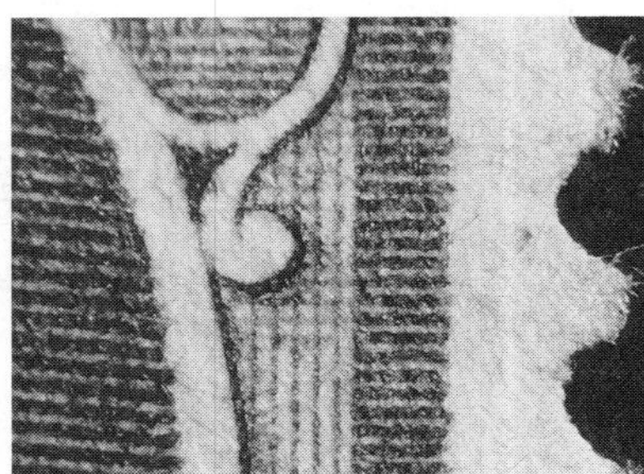

When the American Bank Note Co. produced the reengraved Type III in 1882, it made several changes to the design, including removing the secret mark. As a result of these changes, Type III is the easiest to distinguish at a glance. The entire stamp has a different appearance to it, including a much darker outline and more definition to Jefferson's facial features.

Type III stamps have only four full vertical lines to the left of the portrait oval; the others have five.

Even though the so-called secret mark is no longer present in the upper-right curl, the appearance is quite different. Instead of two curved shading lines there now are cross-hatched straight lines forming the shading. Also, the horizontal shading lines all around the design have been darkened considerably.

There is only one kind of Type III stamp, Minkus 148. However, a black-brown shade of the stamp (recognized as a minor variety) is worth between 5 and 10 times more than the many other shades of the same stamp. It pays to decode the catalog.

106		UnFVF	UseFVF
30¢	**black**	3,750.00	550.00
	deep black	3,750.00	550.00
	On cover		2,100.00
	Double grill		—
	Earliest documented cover: *Aug. 1870*		

1870. Oliver Perry Issue

107 *At the age of 28, Commodore Oliver Hazard Perry (1785-1819) forced a British surrender in the vicious battle of Lake Erie Sept. 10, 1813, and reported, "We have met the enemy, and they are ours." It was the first time in history that an entire British squadron was defeated and every ship captured.*

107		UnFVF	UseFVF
90¢	**carmine**	4,250.00	550.00
	dark carmine	4,250.00	550.00
	On cover		—
	Double grill	—	
	Split grill		1,100.00
	FDC *(April 12, 1870)*		

1870. Benjamin Franklin Issue

108		UnFVF	UseFVF
1¢	**ultramarine**	120.00	5.00
	dark ultramarine	120.00	5.00
	gray blue	120.00	5.00
	pale ultramarine	120.00	5.00
	On cover		—
	Double transfer	—	15.00
	Worn plate	300.00	10.00
	Earliest documented cover: *July 18, 1870*		

1870. Andrew Jackson Issue

109		UnFVF	UseFVF
2¢	**red brown**	90.00	3.50
	dark red brown	90.00	3.50
	orange brown	90.00	3.50
	pale red brown	90.00	3.50
	On cover		7.50
	Bisect (any) on cover		—
	Double transfer	—	8.00
	v. Double impression	—	—
	Earliest documented cover: *June 11, 1870*		

1870. George Washington Issue

110		UnFVF	UseFVF
3¢	**green**	90.00	.50
	dark green	90.00	.50
	pale green	90.00	.50
	yellow green	90.00	.50
	On cover		1.50
	Plate block of 10, w/imprint	1,750.00	
	Double transfer	—	8.00
	Cracked plate	—	4.50
	Worn plate	225.00	1.00
	v. Double impression	—	1,000.00
	v1. Printed both sides	—	1,500.00
	Earliest documented cover: *March 13, 1870*		

1870. Abraham Lincoln Issue

111		UnFVF	UseFVF
6¢	**carmine**	175.00	7.50
	brown carmine	175.00	7.50
	dark carmine	175.00	7.50
	rose	175.00	7.50
	violet carmine	175.00	7.50
	On cover		135.00
	Vertical bisect on cover		—
	Double paper	—	—
	Double transfer	—	—
	v. Double impression	—	1,250.00
	Earliest documented cover: *March 28, 1870*		

1871. Edwin Stanton Issue

112		UnFVF	UseFVF
7¢	**vermilion**	200.00	30.00
	deep vermilion	200.00	30.00
	On cover		140.00
	Cracked plate	—	—
	Double transfer	—	
	Earliest documented cover: *May 11, 1871*		

1870. Thomas Jefferson Issue

113		UnFVF	UseFVF
10¢	**brown**	185.00	9.00
	dark brown	185.00	9.00
	yellow brown	185.00	9.00
	On cover		30.00
	Double transfer	—	60.00
	Earliest documented cover: *May 1870*		

1870. Henry Clay Issue

114		UnFVF	UseFVF
12¢	**pale violet**	400.00	40.00
	dark violet	400.00	40.00
	violet	400.00	40.00
	On cover		350.00
	Earliest documented cover: *July 9, 1870*		

1870. Daniel Webster Issue

115		UnFVF	UseFVF
15¢	**orange**	400.00	50.00
	deep orange	400.00	50.00
	On cover		225.00
	v. Double impression	—	
	Earliest documented cover: *Sept. 24, 1870*		

1870. Gen. Winfield Scott Issue

116		UnFVF	UseFVF
24¢	**purple**	400.00	50.00
	bright purple	400.00	50.00
	dark purple	400.00	50.00
	dull purple	400.00	50.00
	On cover		1,250.00
	Double paper	—	—
	Earliest documented cover: *Nov. 18, 1870*		

1871. Alexander Hamilton Issue

117		UnFVF	UseFVF
30¢	**black**	950.00	75.00
	On cover		675.00
	Earliest documented cover: *Jan. 31, 1871*		

1872. Oliver Perry Issue

118		UnFVF	UseFVF
90¢	**carmine**	950.00	100.00
	dark carmine	950.00	100.00
	On cover		—
	Earliest documented cover: *Sept. 1, 1872*		

1873. Continental Bank Note Co. Portrait Series

The Continental Bank Note Co. was awarded the printing contract for the Large Bank Note Issues for the period of May 1, 1873, through April 30, 1877. This contract later was extended until this company was consolidated with the American Bank Note Co. on Feb. 4, 1879. When Continental took over the printing contract, it took over some of the plates and the dies used by National in the production of the stamps of 1870-71. While the designs of the stamps printed by Continental are similar or identical to those printed by National, the 1¢ through 12¢ easily may be identified because the Continental stamps had so-called "secret marks." The 15¢ can be distinguished by plate wear and some shade variation, and the 30¢ and 90¢ can be distinguished by slight shade differences. The stamps were printed on hard, white wove paper, varying from thin to thick, that generally is difficult or impossible to differentiate from the paper used by National. *The paper is unwatermarked and the stamps are printed by intaglio, perforated 12.*

1873. Benjamin Franklin Issue

119, 132 *Benjamin Franklin. In the pearl at the left of the numeral "1" there is a small dash of color.*

119		UnFVF	UseFVF
1¢	**ultramarine**	70.00	1.25
	blue	70.00	1.25
	dark ultramarine	70.00	1.25
	dull ultramarine	70.00	1.25
	gray blue	70.00	1.25
	On cover		3.25
	Plate block of 12, w/imprint	2,500.00	
	"Cogwheel" punch cut in paper	275.00	
	Cracked plate	—	—
	Double paper	—	
	Double transfer	2.00	5.00
	p. Paper with silk fibers	—	17.50
	p1. Ribbed paper	175.00	3.25
	v. With grill	1,500.00	
	v1. Pair, imperforate	1,150.00	6.00
	Earliest documented cover: *Aug. 22, 1873*		

1873. Andrew Jackson Issue

120, 121, 133 *Andrew Jackson. In the notch formed underneath the semi-circular ornament immediately to the left of the "S" of "U.S." the lines forming the apex of the notch join in a small point of color.*

120		UnFVF	UseFVF
2¢	**brown**	115.00	7.00
	dark brown	115.00	7.00
	dark red brown	115.00	7.00
	yellow brown	115.00	7.00
	On cover		17.50
	Vertical bisect on cover		—
	Cracked plate	—	—
	Double paper	400.00	25.00
	Double transfer	—	17.50
	W/secret mark	325.00	14.00
	p. Ribbed paper	300.00	14.00
	v. Double impression	—	—
	v1. With grill	1,300.00	550.00
	Earliest documented cover: *July 12, 1873*		

1875. Andrew Jackson Issue

121		UnFVF	UseFVF
2¢	**vermilion**	115.00	3.50
	On cover		8.50
	Plate block of 12, w/imprint	—	
	Double paper	—	—
	Double transfer	—	—
	p. Paper with silk fibers	325.00	9.00
	p1. Ribbed paper	—	—
	p2. With grill	350.00	
	v. Pair, imperforate	650.00	
	Earliest documented cover: *July 15, 1875*		

1873. George Washington Issue

122, 134 *George Washington. Under the word "THREE," the long tail of the ribbon is heavily shaded along its lower edge.*

122		UnFVF	UseFVF
3¢	**green**	40.00	.20
	bluish green	40.00	.20
	dark green	40.00	.20
	yellow green	40.00	.20
	dark yellow green	40.00	.20
	olive green	40.00	.20
	On cover		40.00
	Plate block of 10, w/imprint	1,500.00	
	Plate block of 12, w/imprint	2,250.00	
	Plate strip of 5, w/imprint	600.00	
	Plate strip of 6, w/imrpint	675.00	
	"Cogwheel" punch cut in paper	200.00	150.00
	Cracked plate	—	30.00
	Double transfer	—	4.50
	Double paper	150.00	5.00
	Short transfer	—	12.50
	p. Ribbed paper	75.00	1.50
	p1. Paper with silk fibers	—	4.50
	p2. With grill	200.00	
	v. Double impression	—	1,100.00
	v1. Printed on both sides	—	
	v2. Pair, imperforate	850.00	
	v3. Horizontal pair, imperforate between	—	
	v4. Horizontal pair, imperforate vertically	—	
	Earliest documented cover: *July 9, 1873*		

1875. Zachary Taylor Issue

123, 136 *Zachary Taylor. This is a historically interesting stamp for it marked the inauguration of the Universal Postal Union, setting a 5¢ rate for mail abroad and the blue color, which was generally adhered to after 1898. Also unusual in a changing world, the 5¢ rate for a letter to Europe stood for 78 years, until Nov. 1, 1953, when the rate was changed to 8¢.*

123		UnFVF	UseFVF
5¢	**Prussian blue**	145.00	5.50
	bright blue	145.00	5.50
	dark blue	145.00	5.50
	greenish blue	145.00	5.50
	pale blue	145.00	5.50
	On cover		30.00
	Cracked plate	—	390.00
	Double paper	500.00	—
	Double transfer	—	75.00
	p. Paper with silk fibers	—	100.00
	p1. Ribbed paper	—	100.00
	p2. With grill	700.00	
	Earliest documented cover: *July 12, 1875*		

1873. Abraham Lincoln Issue

124, 137 *Abraham Lincoln. The first four vertical lines of the shading in the lower part of the left ribbon, to the left and downward from the "S" in "SIX," have been made heavier.*

124		UnFVF	UseFVF
6¢	**dull Venetian red**	140.00	7.00
	brown rose	140.00	7.00
	rose	140.00	7.00
	On cover		37.50
	Plate block of 12, w/imprint	11,000.00	
	Double paper	—	
	p. Paper with silk fibers	—	32.50
	p1. Ribbed paper	—	14.00
	p2. With grill	1,250.00	
	Earliest documented cover: *July 24, 1873*		

1873. Edwin Stanton Issue

125 *Edwin Stanton. A small semi-circle has been drawn around each end of the two lines that outline the ball in the lower right corner.*

125		UnFVF	UseFVF
7¢	**vermilion**	300.00	30.00
	dark vermilion	300.00	30.00
	On cover		150.00
	Plate block of 12, w/imprint	—	
	Double paper	—	—
	Double transfer of "SEVEN CENTS"	—	175.00
	Double transfer in lower left corner	—	75.00
	p. Paper with silk fibers	—	100.00
	p1. Ribbed paper	—	75.00
	p2. With grill	1,750.00	
	Earliest documented cover: *Oct. 5, 1873*		

1873. Thomas Jefferson Issue

126, 139 *Thomas Jefferson. The scroll ornament at the right end of the upper label, below the letter "E" of "POSTAGE," has a small crescent of color within it.*

126		UnFVF	UseFVF
10¢	**brown**	200.00	8.00
	dark brown	200.00	8.00
	yellow brown	200.00	8.00
	On cover		25.00
	Plate block of 10, w/imprint	8,750.00	
	Plate block of 12, w/imprint	9,250.00	
	Double paper	550.00	
	Double transfer	—	
	p. Paper with silk fibers	—	25.00
	p1. Ribbed paper	—	22.50
	p2. With grill	2,250.00	
	v. Pair, imperforate	—	2,750.00
	v1. Horizontal pair, imperforate between	—	3,500.00
	Earliest documented cover: *Aug. 2, 1873*		

1874. Henry Clay Issue

127 *Henry Clay. The balls of the figure "2" are crescent shaped instead of nearly round.*

127		UnFVF	UseFVF
12¢	**blackish violet**	500.00	40.00
	On cover		300.00
	p. Ribbed paper	—	75.00
	p1. With grill	3,500.00	
	Earliest documented cover: *Jan. 3, 1874*		

1873. Daniel Webster Issue

128, 140 *Daniel Webster. The thin lines shading the triangles and below the letter "U.S. POSTAGE" are worn. These areas show less color and therefore appear more white than the 15¢ National Printing.*

128		UnFVF	UseFVF
15¢	**yellow orange**	475.00	37.50
	dull orange	475.00	37.50
	red orange	475.00	37.50
	On cover		250.00
	Double paper	—	
	p. Paper with silk fibers	1,250.00	80.00
	p1. Paper with vertical ribs	1,100.00	75.00
	p2. With grill	3,500.00	
	Earliest documented cover: *July 22, 1873*		

1874. Gen. Winfield Scott Issue The 24¢ Continental has been the subject of much controversy. It is known that 365,000 copies of this stamp were printed and delivered to the Stamp Agent, but there is no documentation that any of them were issued to post offices. In 1885, 364,950 copies of the 24¢ stamps were destroyed, for they were no longer needed to make up the then-existing postage rates. It is not known whether these were all Continentals. Some experts think that unused examples can be distinguished by their gum, with the Continentals bearing a thinner and lighter-colored gum than the Nationals. Another possible means of identification lies in the paper. The Continental 24¢ was printed from the same plate as the National 24¢, so they are identical in design. The Philatelic Foundation issued a certificate of genuineness to a used 24¢ on vertically ribbed paper; experts believe that only Continental used such paper. The listing below is based on that single item.

129		UnFVF	UseFVF
24¢	**light purple**	—	400,000.00

1874. Alexander Hamilton Issue

130		UnFVF	UseFVF
30¢	**gray black**	600.00	37.50
	greenish black	600.00	37.50
	On cover		625.00
	Double paper	—	85.00
	Double transfer	—	625.00
	p. Paper with silk fibers	—	
	p1. Ribbed paper	1,250.00	75.00
	p2. With grill	3,500.00	
	Earliest documented cover: *Oct. 30, 1874*		

The 30¢ Continental and 30¢ National are identical except in shade.

1874. Oliver Perry Issue

131		UnFVF	UseFVF
90¢	**rose carmine**	1,100.00	105.00
	dull rose carmine	1,100.00	105.00
	On cover		5,500.00

The 90¢ Continental and the 90¢ National are identical except in shade.

1875. Benjamin Franklin Special Printing of the 1873 Pictorial Issue which was still in use. For some reason, these stamps usually were cut apart with scissors so that the perforations generally are mutilated. The special printing can be identified by the color shades and by the very white paper (instead of the yellowish of the original issue). Numbers sold are not known. Some estimate can be made by studying the table that follows SP57. *Printed by the Continental Bank Note Co., intaglio on hard white wove paper, perforated 12, and issued without gum.*

SP32		UnFVF	UseFVF
1¢	**bright ultramarine**	7,250.00	

1875. Andrew Jackson Special Printing Pictorial Issue

SP33		UnFVF	UseFVF
2¢	**blackish brown**	3,000.00	

1875. Andrew Jackson Special Printing Pictorial Issue

SP34		UnFVF	UseFVF
2¢	**carmine vermilion**	20,000.00	

1875. George Washington Special Pictorial Issue

SP35		UnFVF	UseFVF
3¢	**bluish green**	9,250.00	

1875. Zachary Taylor Special Printing Pictorial Issue

SP36		UnFVF	UseFVF
5¢	**bright blue**	27,500.00	

1875. Abraham Lincoln Special Printing Pictorial Issue

SP37		UnFVF	UseFVF
6¢	**pale rose**	8,000.00	

1875. Edwin Stanton Special Printing Pictorial Issue

SP38		UnFVF	UseFVF
7¢	**scarlet vermilion**	1,500.00	

1875. Thomas Jefferson Special Printing Pictorial Issue

SP39		UnFVF	UseFVF
10¢	**yellow brown**	8,000.00	

1875. Henry Clay Special Printing Pictorial Issue

SP40		UnFVF	UseFVF
12¢	**black violet**	2,750.00	

1875. Daniel Webster Special Printing Pictorial Issue

SP41		UnFVF	UseFVF
15¢	**bright orange**	8,000.00	

1875. Winfield Scott Special Printing Pictorial Issue

SP42		UnFVF	UseFVF
24¢	**dull purple**	1,750.00	

1875. Alexander Hamilton Special Printing Pictorial Issue

SP43		UnFVF	UseFVF
30¢	**greenish black**	5,750.00	

1875. Oliver Perry Special Printing Pictorial Issue

SP44		UnFVF	UseFVF
90¢	**violet carmine**	7,500.00	

1879. American Bank Note Co. Portrait Series

The American Bank Note Co. absorbed the Continental Bank Note Co. on Feb. 4, 1879, and continued to print postage, department and newspaper stamps. American used many of the plates bearing the Continental imprints, so the imprint does not always accurately indicate the producing firm. The American Bank Note Co. printed stamps on unwatermarked, soft, porous paper instead of the hard paper used by National and Continental. With the exception of one type of the 10¢, all the stamps from 1¢ through the 12¢ carry the same "secret marks" as the Continentals. With the exception of the color changes on the 3¢, 30¢ and 90¢ that were issued later, these stamps were issued in 1879. *All were printed by intaglio and perforated 12.*

1879. Benjamin Franklin Issue

132		UnFVF	UseFVF
1¢	**dark ultramarine**	75.00	1.00
	blue	75.00	1.00
	gray blue	75.00	1.00
	On cover		2.25
	Plate block of 10, w/imprint	3,000.00	
	Double transfer	—	6.00
	Earliest documented cover: *April 25, 1879*		

1879. Andrew Jackson Issue

133		UnFVF	UseFVF
2¢	**vermilion**	45.00	1.00
	orange vermilion	45.00	1.00
	On cover		2.25
	Plate block of 10, w/imprint	1,250.00	
	Plate block of 12, w/imprint	1,750.00	
	Double transfer	—	
	Double impression	—	400.00
	FDC *(Jan. 17, 1879)*		500.00

1879. George Washington Issue

134		UnFVF	UseFVF
3¢	**green**	35.00	.25
	dark green	35.00	.25
	dull green	35.00	.25
	On cover		.50
	Plate block of 10, w/imprint	800.00	
	Plate block of 12, w/imprint	1,000.00	
	Plate block of 14, w/imprint	1,300.00	
	Double transfer	—	4.00
	Short transfer	—	5.00
	Double impression	—	—
	v. Pair, imperforate	550.00	
	Earliest documented cover: *Aug. 3, 1878*		

1887. George Washington Issue

135		UnFVF	UseFVF
3¢	**vermilion**	45.00	20.00
	On cover		75.00
	Plate block of 10, w/imprint	900.00	
	Plate block of 12, w/imprint	1,100.00	
	Plate strip of 5, w/imprint	350.00	
	Plate strip of 6, w/imprint	400.00	
	Earliest documented cover: *Oct. 18. 1887*		

1879. Zachary Taylor Issue

136		UnFVF	UseFVF
5¢	**blue**	145.00	6.00
	bright blue	145.00	6.00
	dark blue	145.00	6.00
	dull blue	145.00	6.00
	On cover		17.50
	Plate block of 12, w/imprint	7,000.00	
	Earliest documented cover: *May 12, 1879*		

1879. Abraham Lincoln Issue

137		UnFVF	UseFVF
6¢	**dull pink**	257.00	8.50
	brown pink	257.00	8.50
	pink	257.00	8.50
	On cover		32.50
	Earliest documented cover: *July 1, 1879*		

1879. Thomas Jefferson Issue

138		UnFVF	UseFVF
10¢	**brown** like No. 102, but no secret mark	550.00	12.50
	yellow brown	550.00	12.50
	On cover		35.00
	Double transfer	—	30.00
	Earliest documented cover: *Sept. 5, 1879*		

1879. Thomas Jefferson Issue

139		UnFVF	UseFVF
10¢	**brown** like No. 126, with secret mark	425.00	12.50
	black brown	425.00	12.50
	yellow brown	425.00	12.50
	On cover		32.50
	Cracked plate	—	—
	Double transfer	—	35.00
	Pair, 1 each Nos. 138, 139	—	200.00
	v. Vertical pair, imperforate between		—
	Earliest documented cover: *Feb. 21, 1879*		

1879. Daniel Webster Issue

140		UnFVF	UseFVF
15¢	**orange**	300.00	21.00
	red orange	300.00	21.00
	yellow orange	300.00	21.00
	On cover		75.00
	Plate block of 12, w/imprint	5,750.00	
	Earliest documented cover: *Jan. 20, 1879*		

1882. Alexander Hamilton Issue

141		UnFVF	UseFVF
30¢	**black**	300.00	22.50
	greenish black	300.00	22.50
	On cover		375.00
	Plate block of 10, w/imprint	8,500.00	
	Earliest documented cover: *Nov. 13, 1882*		

1888. Alexander Hamilton Issue

142		UnFVF	UseFVF
30¢	**orange brown**	325.00	40.00
	dark orange brown	325.00	40.00
	On cover		1,200.00
	Plate block of 10, w/imprint	6,000.00	
	Plate block of 12, w/imprint	—	
	Plate strip of 5, w/imprint	2,200.00	
	Earliest documented cover: *Sept. 22, 1888*		

1880. Oliver Perry Issue

143		UnFVF	UseFVF
90¢	**carmine**	725.00	95.00
	carmine rose	725.00	95.00
	rose	725.00	95.00
	On cover		4,000.00
	Double paper	—	—
	Earliest documented cover: *June 17, 1880*		

1880. Oliver Perry Issue

144		UnFVF	UseFVF
90¢	**dark red violet**	750.00	85.00
	bright purple	750.00	85.00
	On cover		6,500.00
	Plate block of 10, w/imprint	18,500.00	
	Plate block of 12, w/imprint	—	
	Plate strip of 5, w/imprint	5,000.00	
	v. Pair, imperforate	2,250.00	

1880. Special Printing of the 1879-88 Issue of 1879.

By the American Bank Note Co. Designs on soft porous paper, intaglio, perforated 12.

SP45		UnFVF	UseFVF
1¢	**deep ultramarine**	9,000.00	

		UnFVF	UseFVF
SP46			
2¢	**blackish brown**	5,750.00	
SP47			
2¢	**scarlet vermilion**	13,500.00	
SP48			
3¢	**bluish green**	11,000.00	
SP49			
5¢	**deep blue**	2,000.00	
SP50			
6¢	**pale rose**	9,500.00	
SP51			
7¢	**scarlet vermilion**	3,500.00	
SP52			
10¢	**deep brown**	11,250.00	
SP53			
12¢	**black purple**	3,500.00	
SP54			
15¢	**orange**	7,500.00	
SP55			
24¢	**blackish violet**	8,750.00	
SP56			
30¢	**greenish black**	18,500.00	
SP57			
90¢	**pale carmine**	30,000.00	

The Post Office Department kept no separate records of the sales of the 1875 and 1880 Special Printings but did list the combined sales which we show here. The 1880 printing is the more rare of the two.

1¢	*SP32, SP45*	*388*	*10¢*	*SP39, SP52*	*180*
2¢	*SP33, SP46*	*416*	*12¢*	*SP40, SP53*	*282*
2¢	*SP34, SP47*	*917*	*15¢*	*SP41, SP54*	*169*
3¢	*SP35, SP48*	*267*	*24¢*	*SP42, SP55*	*286*
5¢	*SP36, SP49*	*317*	*30¢*	*SP43, SP56*	*179*
6¢	*SP37, SP50*	*185*	*90¢*	*SP44, SP57*	*170*
7¢	*SP38, SP51*	*473*			

1881-82. Re-Engraved Designs of 1873 Issue for the 1¢, 3¢, 6¢, and 10¢ denominations. They were printed by the American Bank Note Co. by *intaglio on soft porous, unwatermarked paper and were perforated 12.*

132 *1879 Design*

145 *1881 Design, re-engraved: The vertical lines forming the background in the upper part of the stamp have been made much heavier and the background now appears to be almost solid. Lines of shading also have been added to the curving ornaments in the upper corners of the stamps.*

		UnFVF	UseFVF
145			
1¢	**ultramarine**	22.50	.35
	bright ultramarine	22.50	.35
	dull blue	22.50	.35
	gray blue	22.50	.35
	On cover		1.00
	Plate block of 10, w/imprint	900.00	
	Plate block of 12, w/imprint	1,000.00	
	Plate strip of 5, w/imprint	300.00	
	Plate strip of 6, w/imprint	350.00	
	"Cogwheel" punch cut in paper	125.00	
	Double transfer	65.00	3.50

Earliest documented cover: *Dec. 5, 1881*

1881. George Washington Issue

134 *1879 Design*

146 *1881 Design, re-engraved: The shading at the sides of the large central oval is only about half the previous thickness. A short horizontal dash has been added just below the "TS" of "CENTS."*

		UnFVF	UseFVF
146			
3¢	**blue green**	27.50	.20
	green	27.50	.20
	yellow green	27.50	.20
	On cover		.75
	Plate block of 10, w/imprint	1,100.00	
	Plate strip of 5, w/imprint	350.00	
	Cracked plate	—	
	Double transfer	—	7.00
	Punched w/8 small holes in a circle	150.00	
	v1. Plate block of 10, w/imprint	2,000.00	
	v2. Double impression	—	—

Earliest documented cover: *Oct. 24, 1881*

1882. Abraham Lincoln Issue

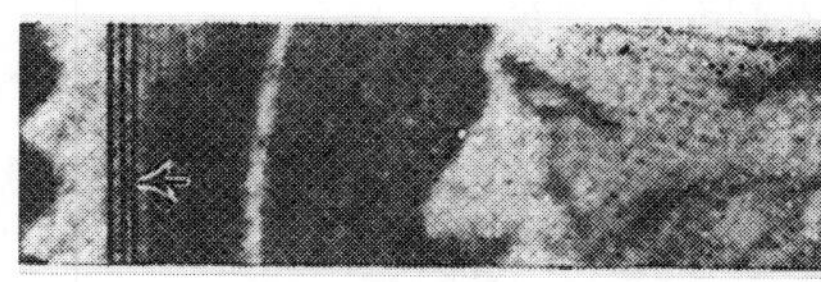

147 *There are only three vertical lines from the outside of the panel to the outside of the stamps. The preceding issue had four lines.*

		UnFVF	UseFVF
147			
6¢	**rose**	150.00	27.50
	dull rose	150.00	27.50
	brown red	125.00	30.00
	On cover		125.00
	Double transfer	450.00	65.00
	Block of 4	1,600.00	

Earliest documented cover: *Sept. 27, 1882*

1882. Thomas Jefferson Issue

148 *There are only four vertical lines between the left side of the oval and the edge of the shield. The preceding issues had five lines. The lines of the background have been made heavier so that these stamps appear much more heavily inked than their predecessors.*

148		UnFVF	UseFVF
10¢	**brown**	50.00	1.50
	olive brown	50.00	1.50
	orange brown	50.00	1.50
	purple brown	50.00	1.50
	yellow brown	50.00	1.50
	black brown	100.00	9.00
	On cover		7.00
	Plate block of 10 w/imprint	1,500.00	
	Plate block of 12, w/imprint	1,800.00	
	Plate strip of 5, w/imprint	650.00	
	Plate strip of 6, w/imprint	750.00	
	v. Double impression	—	
	Earliest documented cover: *May 11, 1882*		

1882-88. American Bank Note Co. Portrait Series

New designs. *Intaglio, unwatermarked soft porous paper, perforated 12.*

1887. Benjamin Franklin Issue

149 *Benjamin Franklin*

149		UnFVF	UseFVF
1¢	**ultramarine**	32.50	.65
	bright ultramarine	32.50	.65
	On cover		1.50
	Plate block of 10, w/imprint	1,000.00	
	Plate block of 12, w/imprint	1,250.00	
	Plate strip of 5, w/imprint	450.00	
	Plate strip of 6, w/imprint	550.00	
	Double transfer	—	
	v. Pair, imperforate	1,000.00	525.00
	Earliest documented cover: *July 28, 1887*		

1883. George Washington Issue

150, 151 *George Washington. This stamp was issued to pay the reduced rate for First Class letters as provided by an Act of Congress approved March 3, 1883, and effective Oct. 1, 1883.*

150		UnFVF	UseFVF
2¢	**red brown**	20.00	.20
	dark red brown	20.00	.20
	orange brown	20.00	.20
	On cover		.50
	Plate block of 10, w/imprint	750.00	
	Plate block of 12, w/imprint	1,000.00	
	Plate strip of 5, w/imprint	225.00	
	Plate strip of 6, w/imprint	375.00	
	Double transfer	40.00	1.25
	v. Pair, imperforate	—	
	v1. Horizontal pair, imperforate between	2,000.00	—
	FDC *(Oct. 1, 1883)*		2,000.00

1887. George Washington Issue

151		UnFVF	UseFVF
2¢	**green**	15.00	.20
	bright green	15.00	.20
	dark green	15.00	.20
	On cover		.75
	Plate block of 10, w/imprint	650.00	
	Plate block of 12, w/imprint	750.00	
	Plate strip of 5, w/imprint	175.00	
	Plate strip of 6, w/imprint	240.00	
	Double transfer	—	2.50
	v. Printed on both sides	—	—
	Pair, imperforate	1,000.00	1,000.00
	Earliest documented cover: *Sept. 21, 1887;* EKU: *Sept. 20, 1887*		

1883. Andrew Jackson Issue

152, 153 *Andrew Jackson. This Denomination was issued to pay the rate on First Class letters of double weight.*

152		UnFVF	UseFVF
4¢	**deep bluish green**	80.00	4.00
	blue green	80.00	4.00
	On cover		32.50
	Plate block of 12, w/imprint	3,500.00	
	Plate block of 6, w/imprint	1,200.00	
	Cracked plate	—	
	Double transfer	—	
	v. Pair, imperforate	—	
	v1. Horizontal pair, imperforate between	—	
	FDC *(Oct. 1, 1883)*		40,000.00

1883. Special Printing Issue of the 2¢ and 4¢ stamps of 1883. *Printed by the American Bank Note Co., intaglio on soft, porous paper, the 2¢ with gum and the 4¢ without gum, both perforated 12.* Quantities are not known.

SP59		UnFVF	UseFVF
2¢	**red brown**	600.00	
	v. Horizontal pair, imperforate between	1,800.00	

1883. Special Printing Issue

SP60		UnFVF	UseFVF
4¢	**blue green**	14,500.00	

1889. Andrew Jackson Issue

153		UnFVF	UseFVF
4¢	**carmine**	75.00	7.50
	dull rose	75.00	7.50
	rose carmine	75.00	7.50
	On cover		50.00
	Plate block of 10, w/imprint	3,000.00	
	Plate block of 12, w/imprint	3,850.00	
	Plate strip of 5, w/imprint	1,000.00	
	Plate strip of 6, w/imprint	1,100.00	
	Double transfer	—	
	Earliest documented cover: *July 11, 1889*		

1882. James Garfield Issue

154 *James Garfield. This design was issued to honor the late President, who was shot on July 2, 1881, after only 200 days in office, by a disgruntled office-seeker, and died Sept. 19 after 11 weeks of botched medical care.*

154		UnFVF	UseFVF
5¢	**olive brown**	80.00	3.00
	brown	80.00	3.00
	gray brown	80.00	3.00
	On cover		20.00
	Plate block of 10 w/imprint	3,000.00	
	Plate block of 12, w/imprint	3,500.00	
	Plate strip of 5, w/imprint	900.00	
	Plate strip of 6, w/imprint	1,100.00	
	FDC *(April 10, 1882)*		

1882. James Garfield Special Printing Issue Special printing of the 5¢ Garfield stamp of 1882 is very difficult to distinguish from the regular printing of the same year. *American Bank Note Co., intaglio on soft, porous paper without gum, perforated 12.*

SP58		UnFVF	UseFVF
5¢	**light brownish gray** *(2,463 sold)*	30,000.00	

1888. James Garfield Issue

155		UnFVF	UseFVF
5¢	**indigo**	75.00	4.00
	dark blue	75.00	4.00
	blue	75.00	4.00
	On cover		20.00
	Plate block of 10, w/imprint	3,000.00	
	Plate block of 12, w/imprint	3,750.00	
	Plate strip of 5, w/imprint	900.00	
	Plate strip of 6, w/imprint	1,100.00	
	v. Pair, imperforate	1,200.00	
	Earliest documented cover: *March 23, 1888*		

1890. American Bank Note Co. Small Size Portrait Series

The American Bank Note Company produced this series in a smaller size than had been used previously. All stamps in this series are *intaglio on unwatermarked soft, porous paper, perforated 12.*

1890. Benjamin Franklin Issue

156 *Benjamin Franklin*

156		UnFVF	UseFVF
1¢	**dull blue**	17.50	.20
	blue	17.50	.20
	dark blue	17.50	.20
	ultramarine	17.50	.20
	On cover		.50
	Plate block of 10, w/imprint	450.00	
	Plate block of 12, w/imprint	600.00	
	Plate block of 14, w/imprint	750.00	
	Plate strip of 5, w/imprint	125.00	
	Plate strip of 6, w/imprint	150.00	
	Plate strip of 7, w/imprint	175.00	
	Double transfer	—	—
	v. Pair, imperforate	150.00	
	FDC *(Feb. 22, 1890)*		

1890. George Washington Issue

157, 158 *George Washington*

158v *Cap on left "2"*

158v2 *Cap on right "2"*

157		UnFVF	UseFVF
2¢	**lake**	125.00	.60
	bright lilac carmine	125.00	.60
	lilac carmine	125.00	.60
	On cover		1.25
	Plate block of 10, w/imprint	2,750.00	
	Plate strip of 5, w/imprint	800.00	
	Double transfer	—	—
	v. Pair, imperforate	100.00	
	FDC *(Feb. 22, 1890)*		17,500.00

158		UnFVF	UseFVF
2¢	**carmine**	14.00	.20
	carmine rose	14.00	.20
	dark carmine	14.00	.20
	On cover		.50
	Plate block of 10, w/imprint	400.00	
	Plate block of 12, w/imprint	500.00	
	Plate block of 14, w/imprint	650.00	
	Plate strip of 5, w/imprint	100.00	
	Plate strip of 6, w/imprint	130.00	
	Plate strip of 7, w/imprint	150.00	
	Double transfer	—	2.50
	v. Cap on left "2"	60.00	1.50
	Plate block of 12, w/imprint	1,250.00	
	v1. Pair, 1 w/cap, 1 without		—
	v2. Cap on both "2's"	150.00	12.50
	v3. Pair, 1 w/cap on 1 "2," 1 w/cap on both "2's"	—	—
	v4. Pair, imperforate	125.00	
	Earliest documented cover: *April 29, 1890*		

1890. Andrew Jackson Issue

159 *Andrew Jackson*

159		UnFVF	UseFVF
3¢	**dark lilac**	47.50	5.00
	bright lilac	47.50	5.00
	lilac	47.50	5.00
	On cover		12.50
	Plate block of 10, w/imprint	1,750.00	
	Plate strip of 5, w/imprint	350.00	
	v. Pair, imperforate	165.00	
	FDC *(Feb. 22, 1890)*		

1890. Abraham Lincoln Issue

160 *Abraham Lincoln*

160		UnFVF	UseFVF
4¢	**dark brown**	47.50	2.00
	black brown	47.50	2.00
	On cover		11.00
	Plate block of 10, w/imprint	1,800.00	
	Plate strip of 5, w/imprint	350.00	
	Double transfer	70.00	
	v. Pair, imperforate	165.00	
	Earliest documented cover: *Oct. 22, 1890*		

1890. Ulysses S. Grant Issue

161 *Ulysses S. Grant*

161		UnFVF	UseFVF
5¢	**chocolate**	47.50	2.00
	yellow brown	47.50	2.00
	On cover		9.00
	Plate block of 10, w/imprint	1,750.00	
	Plate strip of 5, w/imprint	300.00	
	Double transfer	70.00	2.00
	v. Pair, imperforate	165.00	
	Earliest documented cover: *June 14, 1890*		

1890. James Garfield Issue

162 *James Garfield*

162		UnFVF	UseFVF
6¢	**brown red**	50.00	15.00
	dark brown red	50.00	15.00
	On cover		30.00
	Plate block of 10, w/imprint	1,800.00	
	Plate strip of 5, w/imprint	350.00	
	v. Pair, imperforate	175.00	
	FDC *(Feb. 22, 1890)*		

1890. W. T. Sherman Issue

163 *W.T. Sherman, from an 1888 photograph by Napoleon B. Sarony*

163		UnFVF	UseFVF
8¢	**purple brown**	50.00	11.00
	gray lilac	50.00	11.00
	magenta	50.00	11.00
	On cover		25.00
	Plate block of 10, w/imprint	1,650.00	
	Plate strip of 5, w/imprint	300.00	
	v. Pair, imperforate	1,250.00	
	Earliest documented cover: *May 21, 1893*		

1890. Daniel Webster Issue

164 *Daniel Webster*

164		UnFVF	UseFVF
10¢	**deep bluish green**	95.00	2.25
	dark green	95.00	2.25
	green	95.00	2.25
	On cover		7.00
	Plate block of 10, w/imprint	3,000.00	
	Plate strip of 5, w/imprint	800.00	
	Double transfer	—	—
	v. Pair, imperforate	175.00	
	FDC *(Feb. 22, 1890)*		

1890. Henry Clay Issue

165 *Henry Clay*

165		UnFVF	UseFVF
15¢	**indigo**	145.00	16.00
	dark indigo	145.00	16.00
	On cover		55.00
	Plate block of 10, w/imprint	5,500.00	
	Plate strip of 5, w/imprint	750.00	
	Double transfer	—	—
	Triple transfer	—	—
	v. Pair, imperforate	500.00	
	FDC *(Feb. 22, 1890)*		

1890. Thomas Jefferson Issue

166 *Thomas Jefferson*

166		UnFVF	UseFVF
30¢	**black**	225.00	19.00
	gray black	225.00	19.00
	full black	225.00	19.00
	On cover		500.00
	Plate block of 10, w/imprint	1,450.00	
	Plate strip of 5, w/imprint	1,000.00	
	Double transfer	—	—
	v. Pair, imperforate	750.00	
	FDC *(Feb. 22, 1890)*		

1890. Oliver Hazard Perry Issue

167 *Oliver Hazard Perry*

167		UnFVF	UseFVF
90¢	**orange**	325.00	90.00

Decoding the Catalog

Between 1890 and 1898, a sequence of similar series of United States definitive stamps were released. These are known as the Small Bank Notes (1890-93) and the First Bureau Issue (1894-98). These stamps had values ranging between 1¢ and 90¢.

The Small Bank Note stamps, produced by the American Bank Note Co. in 1890-93, are easy to distinguish, since they had no triangles in the upper corners. Beginning in 1894, stamp production was taken over by the Bureau of Engraving and Printing in Washington, D.C. During 1894-98, three basic groups of similar-appearing stamps of this First Bureau Issue were released. These stamps, classed as the 1894, 1895 and 1898 issues, are not difficult to distinguish if you know what you are looking for.

All varieties of the 8¢ value of the series, picturing William Tecumseh Sherman, are perf 12. The first version of the 8¢ Sherman, printed by ABNC in 1893 (Krause-Minkus 163), has no upper corner triangles, making it easy to tell from the Bureau issues that follow. It is known in shades of lilac, gray lilac, magenta and purple brown.

The subsequent Bureau issues were printed in violet brown or purple brown. The first of these was printed on paper without a watermark (Krause-Minkus 179). The perforations for the most part on these stamps are quite crude, making identification fairly simple.

The second 8¢ issue (Minkus 200) was printed on paper bearing a double-line USPS watermark. Any single stamp from this subset should show at least a partial capital "U," "S," "P" or "S" (for "U.S. Postage Stamp"). The watermarked paper was placed into use to help deter the counterfeiting of stamps, which had been a problem.

A small quantity of the 8¢ Shermans was printed on paper intended for use in printing revenue stamps, watermarked "USIR" (for "U.S. Internal Revenue"). This watermark error (Krause-Minkus 200w) is scarce and valuable. A similar error also exists on the 6¢ Garfield definitive of the same series.

Other values from the First Bureau Issue of definitives were reissued in changed colors in 1897-98 to conform to newly introduced Universal Postal Union regulations regarding stamp color, intended to make mail simple to sort and recognize internationally. However, there was no special niche for an 8¢ stamp under the new scheme, so it was not reissued in a new color.

		UnFVF	UseFVF
	red orange	325.00	90.00
	yellow orange	325.00	90.00
	On cover		—
	Plate block of 10, w/imprint	19,500.00	
	Plate strip of 5, w/imprint	2,250.00	
	Short transfer at bottom		
	v. Pair, imperforate	1,000.00	
	FDC *(Feb. 22, 1890)*		

Stamps of all values of the 1890 issue exist imperforate. They are considered finished proofs.

1894. Bureau of Engraving and Printing Portrait Series

Issues from this point through the 1980s, were printed by the Bureau of Engraving and Printing, except where otherwise noted.

The first issue of stamps by the Bureau was very similar in design to the issue of 1890, but triangles were added to the upper corners of the stamps and there were some differences in the denominations issued. The stamps were *printed by intaglio on unwatermarked paper, perforated 12. All of the perforation varieties listed here are believed to have been issued legitimately. Other perforation and imperforate varieties exist on some values, but they were not released through regular postal methods.*

1894. Benjamin Franklin Issue

168, 169, 187, 188 *Benjamin Franklin*

		UnFVF	UseFVF
168			
1¢	**ultramarine**	20.00	3.50
	bright ultramarine	20.00	3.50
	dark ultramarine	20.00	3.50
	On cover		10.00
	Plate block of 6, w/imprint	250.00	
	Plate strip of 3, w/imprint	90.00	
	Double transfer	30.00	4.00
	Earliest documented cover: *Oct. 18, 1894*		

		UnFVF	UseFVF
169			
1¢	**blue**	47.50	2.00
	bright blue	47.50	2.00
	dark blue	47.50	2.00
	On cover		14.00
	Plate block of 6, w/imprint	475.00	
	Plate strip of 3, w/imprint	225.00	
	Double transfer	—	3.00
	Earliest documented cover: *Nov. 11, 1894*		

1894. George Washington Issue

170-174, 189-192 *George Washington*

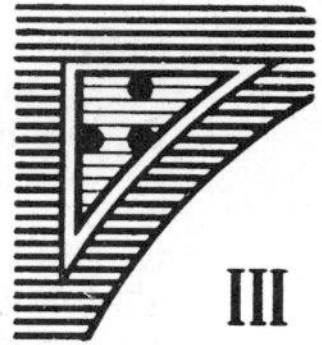

170-172, 189 *Type I. The horizontal lines of background are of same thickness.*

173, 190 *Type II. The horizontal lines are thin within the triangle.*

174, 191, 192 *Type III. The horizontal lines are interrupted by the frame of the triangle and are thin within the triangle.*

Decoding the Catalog

Between 1890-98, two similar United States definitive series of stamps with denominations ranging between 1¢ and 90¢ were released. These are known as the Small Bank Notes and the First Bureau Issue. The Small Bank Note stamps, produced in a smaller size than previously by the American Bank Note Co. in 1890, are easy to distinguish, since they had no triangles in the upper corners.

Beginning in 1894, stamp production was taken over by the Bureau of Engraving and Printing. From 1894-98, three basic groups of similar-appearing stamps of this series were released. These stamps, classed as the 1894, 1895 and 1898 issues, are not difficult to distinguish if you know what you are looking for.

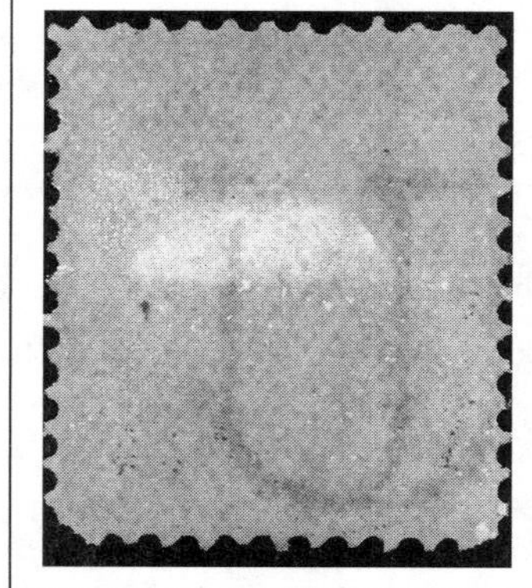

All varieties of the 1¢ value of the series are perforated 12.

The first 1¢ issue (Krause-Minkus 168-169) was printed on unwatermarked paper. The perforations for the most part on these stamps are quite crude, making identification fairly simple. Minkus 168 is ultramarine. Minkus 169 is blue.

The second 1¢ issue (Minkus 187) also is blue but printed on paper bearing a double-line USPS watermark. Any single stamp from this subset should show at least a partial letter U, S or P. The watermarked paper was placed into use to help stem the counterfeiting of stamps, which had been a problem with the 2¢ value.

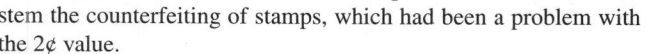

Any single stamp from double-line watermark subset should show at least a partial letter U, S or P, probably not so clear as those shown here.

The third 1¢ issue, (Minkus 188) also was printed on watermarked paper but is easiest to distinguish by its color. It is green and was changed to conform to then-current Universal Postal Union regulations regarding stamp colors.

170		UnFVF	UseFVF
2¢	**pink** triangle I	15.00	3.00
	dull pink	15.00	3.00
	On cover		10.00
	Plate block of 6, w/imprint	175.00	
	Plate strip of 3, w/imprint	75.00	
	Double transfer	—	—
	v. Vertical pair, imperforate horizontally	2,250.00	
	Earliest documented cover: *Oct. 20, 1894*		

171		UnFVF	UseFVF
2¢	**carmine lake** triangle I	95.00	2.00
	dark carmine lake	95.00	2.00
	On cover		7.50
	Plate block of 6, w/imprint	1,000.00	
	Plate strip of 3, w/imprint	400.00	
	Double transfer	—	2.50
	Earliest documented cover: *Oct. 11, 1894*		

172		UnFVF	UseFVF
2¢	**carmine** triangle I	17.50	.35
	dark carmine	17.50	.35
	dull scarlet	17.50	.35
	scarlet	17.50	.35
	On cover		1.50
	Plate block of 6, w/imprint	250.00	
	Plate strip of 3, w/imprint	100.00	
	Double transfer	—	1.25
	v. Vertical pair, imperforate horizontally	1,750.00	
	v1. Horizontal pair, imperforate between	—	
	Earliest documented cover: *Oct. 19, 1894*		

173		UnFVF	UseFVF
2¢	**carmine** triangle II	150.00	3.25
	dark carmine	150.00	3.25
	On cover		10.00
	Plate block of 6, w/imprint	1,900.00	
	Plate strip of 3, w/imprint	700.00	
	Earliest documented cover: *Feb. 18, 1895*		

174		UnFVF	UseFVF
2¢	**carmine** triangle III	85.00	3.50
	dull carmine	85.00	3.50
	On cover		10.00
	Plate block of 6, w/imprint	1,100.00	
	Plate strip of 3, w/imprint	400.00	
	v. Horizontal pair, imperforate between	—	
	v1. Horizontal pair, imperforate vertically	—	
	Earliest documented cover: *Oct. 11, 1894*		

1894. Andrew Jackson Issue

175, 193 *Andrew Jackson*

175		UnFVF	UseFVF
3¢	**dark lilac**	60.00	6.50
	lilac	60.00	6.50
	On cover		20.00
	Plate block of 6, w/imprint	800.00	
	Plate strip of 3, w/imprint	350.00	
	Margin block of 4, w/arrow	375.00	
	v. Pair, imperforate	200.00	
	Earliest documented cover: *Jan. 5, 1895*		

1894. Abraham Lincoln Issue

176, 194, 195 *Abraham Lincoln*

176		UnFVF	UseFVF
4¢	**dark brown**	75.00	3.50
	brown	75.00	3.50
	On cover		15.00
	Plate block of 6, w/imprint	900.00	
	Plate strip of 3, w/imprint	425.00	
	Margin block of 4, w/arrow	500.00	
	v. Pair, imperforate	200.00	
	Earliest documented cover: *Jan. 5, 1895*		

1894. Ulysses S. Grant Issue

177, 196, 197 *Ulysses S. Grant*

177		UnFVF	UseFVF
5¢	**chocolate**	65.00	4.00
	dark chocolate	65.00	4.00
	yellow brown	65.00	4.00
	On cover		15.00
	Plate block of 6, w/imprint	700.00	
	Plate strip of 3, w/imprint	300.00	
	Margin block of 4, w/arrow	325.00	
	Diagonal lines omitted in oval background (worn plate)	80.00	5.00
	Double transfer	85.00	5.00
	v. Pair, imperforate	250.00	
	vl. Vertical pair, imperforate horizontally	1,500.00	
	Earliest documented cover: *Nov. 22, 1894*		

1894. James Garfield Issue

178, 198, 199 *James Garfield*

178		UnFVF	UseFVF
6¢	**red brown**	115.00	17.50
	On cover		37.50
	Plate block of 6, w/imprint	1,800.00	
	Plate strip of 3, w/imprint	525.00	
	Margin block of 4, w/arrow	500.00	
	v. Vertical pair, imperforate horizontally	800.00	
	Earliest documented cover: *Aug. 11, 1894*		

1894. William T. Sherman Issue

179, 200 *W.T. Sherman*

179		UnFVF	UseFVF
8¢	**purple brown**	120.00	12.50
	dark purple brown	120.00	12.50
	On cover		40.50
	Plate block of 6, w/imprint	1,200.00	
	Plate strip of 3, w/imprint	500.00	
	Margin block of 4, w/arrow	525.00	
	Earliest documented cover: *Sept. 15, 1895*		

1894. Daniel Webster Issue

180, 201-203 *Daniel Webster*

180		UnFVF	UseFVF
10¢	**blue green**	150.00	8.50
	dark green	150.00	8.50
	dull green	150.00	8.50
	On cover		30.00
	Plate block of 6, w/imprint	1,800.00	
	Plate strip of 3, w/imprint	700.00	
	Double transfer	200.00	9.00
	v. Pair, imperforate	500.00	
	Earliest documented cover: *Nov. 19, 1894*		

1894. Henry Clay Issue

181, 204, 205 *Henry Clay*

181		UnFVF	UseFVF
15¢	**indigo**	185.00	40.00
	dark blue	185.00	40.00
	On cover		80.00
	Plate block of 6, w/imprint	3,000.00	
	Plate strip of 3, w/imprint	875.00	
	Margin block of 4, w/arrow	900.00	
	Earliest documented cover: *Feb. 20, 1895*		

1894. Thomas Jefferson Issue

182, 206 *Thomas Jefferson*

182		UnFVF	UseFVF
50¢	**orange**	275.00	75.00
	dark orange	275.00	75.00
	On cover		850.00
	Plate block of 6, w/imprint	4,250.00	
	Plate strip of 3, w/imprint	1,300.00	
	Margin block of 4, w/arrow	1,500.00	
	Earliest documented cover: *Jan. 15, 1895*		

1894. Oliver Hazard Perry Issue was the first regular issue dollar-value stamp.

183, 184, 207, 208 *Oliver Hazard Perry*

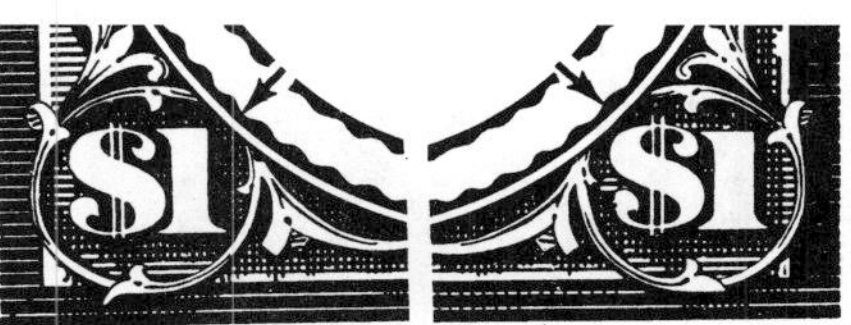

183, 184, 207 *Type I. Circles enclosing "$1" are broken.*

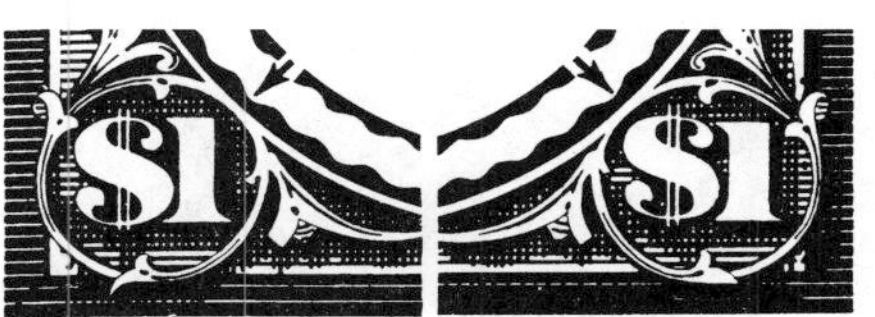

184, 208 *Type II. Circles are complete.*

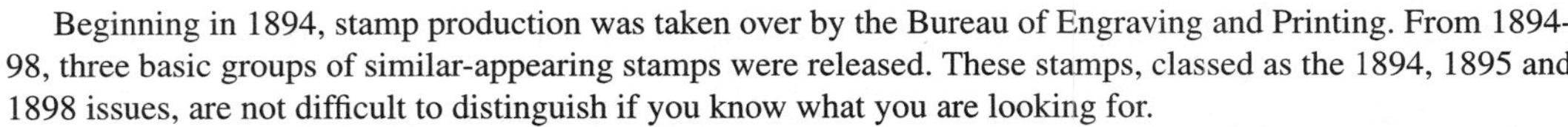

Decoding the Catalog

Between 1890-98, there were two similar United States definitive series of stamps released. These are known as the Small Bank Notes and the First Bureau Issue. These stamps had denominations ranging between 1¢ and 90¢. The Small Bank note stamps, produced by the American Bank Note Co. in 1890, are easy to distinguish, since they had no triangles in the upper-left and upper-right-hand corners.

Beginning in 1894, stamp production was taken over by the Bureau of Engraving and Printing. From 1894-98, three basic groups of similar-appearing stamps were released. These stamps, classed as the 1894, 1895 and 1898 issues, are not difficult to distinguish if you know what you are looking for.

The first 10¢ issue of the series (Minkus 180) was green and printed on unwatermarked paper. The perforations for the most part were quite crude, making identification of these stamps fairly simple. The second 10¢ issue (Minkus 201) also was green, but was printed on paper bearing a double-line USPS watermark. Any single stamp from this subset should show at least a partial letter of U, S, P or S. The watermarked paper was placed into use to help avoid the counterfeiting of stamps, which had been a problem with the 2¢ value. The third 10¢ issue is brown and is broken down into Types I and II. The color was changed from green to conform to Universal Postal Union rules.

Type I

Type I (Minkus 202) is the same as all previous First Bureau 10¢ issues. The tips of the ornamentation surrounding the denomination at both left and right are clear of the white portrait frame line oval.

Type II

Type II, a red-brown stamp, is different. The ornamentation on both the right and left sides intrude into the white portrait frame line oval.

183		UnFVF	UseFVF
$1	**black** Type I	575.00	225.00
	gray black	575.00	225.00
	On cover		1,950.00
	Plate block of 6, w/imprint	12,500.00	
	Plate strip of 3, w/imprint	2,850.00	
	Margin block of 4, w/arrow	3,250.00	
	Earliest documented cover: *Aug. 1895*		

184		UnFVF	UseFVF
$1	**black** Type II	1,500.00	450.00
	gray black	1,500.00	450.00
	On cover		3,400.00
	Plate block of 6, w/imprint (including 2 of No. 183)	22,000.00	
	Plate strip of 3, w/imprint (including 1 of No. 183)	4,800.00	
	Block of 4, 2 each No. 183, 184	6,000.00	
	Pair, 1 each Type I and II	2,850.00	
	Margin block of 4, w/arrow	7,250.00	
	Earliest documented cover: *March 22, 1895*		

1894. James Madison Issue

185, 209 *James Madison*

185		UnFVF	UseFVF
$2	**dark blue**	1,900.00	650.00
	bright blue	1,900.00	650.00
	On cover		3,400.00
	Plate block of 6, w/imprint	28,000.00	
	Plate strip of 3, w/imprint	9,750.00	
	Margin block of 4, w/arrow	10,500.00	
	Earliest documented cover: *July 18, 1895*		

1894. John Marshall Issue

186, 210 *John Marshall, after painting by Henry Inman, the first great Chief Justice of the United States, was appointed to the office by John Adams in 1801. In 34 brilliant and forceful years' service, he firmly established the Constitution as the supreme law of the land, and the Court as its final arbiter. In the case of Marbury vs. Madison in 1803, he created a precedent in setting aside an act of Congress as unconstitutional.*

186		UnFVF	UseFVF
$5	**dark green**	2,900.00	1,250.00
	On cover		—
	Plate strip of 3, w/imprint	18,000.00	
	Margin block of 4, w/arrow	18,000.00	

1895-1898. Bureau of Engraving and Printing Portrait Designs on Watermarked Paper Issue Although in the planning stages for some time, the issuance of U.S. postage stamps on watermarked paper coincided with the discovery of a counterfeit of the 2¢ denomination. It was believed that the new paper would add a measure of protection. The paper is watermarked with the letters "USPS," for "United States Postage Stamp," in double-lined capital letters, each letter 1/2-inch wide and 11/16-inch (16mm) high. The letters are arranged all over the stamp paper, one letter per square inch, so that each pane of 100 stamps has 90 letters. The watermarks appear both horizontally and vertically on the stamps. Seldom does a stamp show a complete letter of the watermark. More commonly, a single stamp will have a portion of one to even four letters.

Denomination portraits remained the same as on the previous series. the color changes of 1898 are integrated with this sequence of stamps. *Intaglio, perforated 12.*

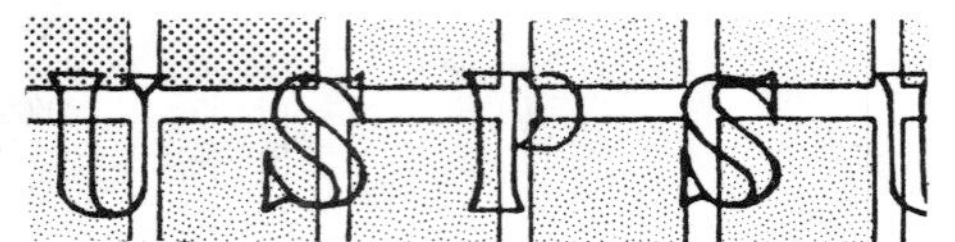

187 *Double-line USPS Watermark (187)*

187		UnFVF	UseFVF
1¢	**deep blue**	5.00	.20
	dark blue	5.00	.20
	indigo	5.00	.20
	pale blue	5.00	.20
	On cover		1.00
	Plate block of 6, w/imprint	150.00	
	Plate strip of 3, w/imprint	20.00	
	Double transfer	—	.75
	Earliest documented cover: *July 7, 1895*		

188		UnFVF	UseFVF
1¢	**deep green**	7.50	.20
	dark green	7.50	.20
	dark yellow green	7.50	.20
	yellow green	7.50	.20
	On cover		.50
	Plate block of 6, w/imprint	150.00	
	Plate strip of 3, w/imprint	32.00	
	Double transfer	10.00	
	v. Pair, imperforate	150.00	
	v1. Horizontal pair, imperforate vertically	—	
	FDC *(Jan. 25, 1898)*		700.00

189		UnFVF	UseFVF
2¢	**carmine** Type I	22.50	.90
	dark carmine	22.50	.90
	dull carmine	22.50	.90
	On cover		2.00
	Plate block of 6, w/imprint	300.00	
	Plate strip of 3, w/imprint	90.00	
	Double transfer	35.00	3.00
	FDC *(July 7, 1895)*		9,500.00

190		UnFVF	UseFVF
2¢	**carmine** Type II	20.00	3.00
	dark carmine	20.00	3.00
	dull carmine	20.00	3.00
	On cover		6.00
	Plate block of 6, w/imprint	300.00	
	Plate strip of 3, w/imprint	90.00	
	Horizontal pair, No. 189, 190	60.00	
	Earliest documented cover: *Oct. 25, 1895*		

191		UnFVF	UseFVF
2¢	**carmine** Type III	4.00	.20
	dark carmine	4.00	.20
	dull carmine	4.00	.20
	On cover		.50
	Plate block of 6, w/imprint	100.00	
	Plate strip of 3, w/imprint	15.00	
	Double transfer	12.50	1.00
	Triple transfer	—	
	Shading omitted in right upper triangle (worn plate)	—	
	v. Pair, imperforate	175.00	
	Earliest documented cover: *July 7, 1895*		

192		UnFVF	UseFVF
2¢	**red** Type III	7.50	.20
	deep red	7.50	.20
	orange red	8.00	.30
	rose carmine	150.00	100.00
	On cover		.50
	Plate block of 6, w/imprint	150.00	
	Plate strip of 3, w/imprint	32.00	
	Double transfer	15.00	
	n. Booklet pane of 6 *(April 18, 1900;* EKU *May 4, 1900)*	325.00	
	Earliest documented cover: *Dec. 19, 1897*		

193		UnFVF	UseFVF
3¢	**dark red violet**	27.50	1.00
	dark purple	27.50	1.00
	dull purple	27.50	1.00
	On cover		5.00
	Plate block of 6, w/imprint	425.00	
	Plate strip of 3, 2/imprint	120.00	
	Margin block of 4, w/arrow	140.00	
	Double transfer	35.00	2.25
	v. Pair, imperforate	200.00	
	Earliest documented cover: *Feb. 18, 1896*		

194		UnFVF	UseFVF
4¢	**dark brown**	27.50	1.50
	black brown	27.50	1.50
	dark yellow brown	27.50	1.50
	On cover		7.50
	Plate block of 6, w/imprint	450.00	
	Plate strip of 3, w/imprint	125.00	
	Margin block of 4, w/arrow	150.00	
	Double transfer	35.00	2.50
	v. Pair, imperforate	200.00	
	Earliest documented cover: *Oct. 12, 1895*		

195		UnFVF	UseFVF
4¢	**chocolate**	22.50	.90
	brownish claret	22.50	.90
	dark orange brown	22.50	.90
	lilac brown	22.50	.90
	orange brown	22.50	.90
	rose brown	22.50	.90
	On cover		8.00
	Plate block of 6, w/imprint	450.00	
	Plate strip of 3, w/imprint	100.00	
	Margin block of 4, w/arrow	120.00	
	Double transfer	.30	1.25
	Extra frame line at top	45.00	3.50
	FDC *(Oct. 7, 1898)*		

196		UnFVF	UseFVF
5¢	**dark orange brown**	27.50	1.65
	brown	27.50	1.65
	dark red brown	27.50	1.65
	reddish brown	27.50	1.65
	On cover		6.00
	Plate block of 6, w/imprint	400.00	
	Plate strip of 3, w/imprint	120.00	
	Diagonal lines omitted in oval background (worn plate)	32.50	2.25
	Double transfer	35.00	3.00
	Margin block of 4, w/arrow	130.00	
	v. Pair, imperforate	200.00	
	Earliest documented cover: *Sept. 14, 1895*		

197		UnFVF	UseFVF
5¢	**dark blue**	25.00	.75
	blue	25.00	.75
	bright blue	25.00	.75
	dull blue	25.00	.75
	On cover		8.00
	Plate block of 6, w/imprint	450.00	
	Plate strip of 3, w/imprint	120.00	
	Diagonal lines omitted in oval background (worn plate)	35.00	.75
	Double transfer	40.00	1.50
	Margin block of 4, w/arrow	140.00	
	FDC *(March 8, 1898)*		

198		UnFVF	UseFVF
6¢	**red brown**	55.00	4.00
	dull brown	55.00	4.00
	On cover		22.50
	Plate block of 6, w/imprint	1,100.00	
	Plate strip of 3, w/imprint	250.00	
	Margin block of 4, w/arrow	395.00	
	p. Thin paper	80.00	4.00
	w. Watermarked "USIR"	2,000.00	325.00
	v. Pair, imperforate	200.00	
	Earliest documented cover: *Sept. 14, 1895*		

199		UnFVF	UseFVF
6¢	**lake**	35.00	2.25
	claret	35.00	2.25
	lilac carmine	35.00	2.25
	purple lake	42.50	3.00
	On cover		14.00
	Plate block of 6, w/imprint	700.00	
	Plate strip of 3, w/imprint	150.00	
	Double transfer	52.50	3.00
	Margin block of 4, w/arrow	150.00	
	v. Pair, imperforate	200.00	
	FDC *(Dec. 31, 1898)*		

200		UnFVF	UseFVF
8¢	**purple brown**	50.00	1.25
	dark lilac brown	50.00	1.25
	lilac brown	40.00	1.25
	On cover		12.00
	Plate block of 6, w/imprint	650.00	
	Plate strip of 3, w/imprint	200.00	
	Double transfer	70.50	2.25
	Margin block of 4, w/arrow	220.00	
	w. Watermarked "USIR"	1,550.00	100.00
	v. Pair, imperforate	300.00	
	Earliest documented cover: *Dec. 24, 1895*		

201, 202 *Type I. Oval below "TEN CENTS" is intact.*

203 *Type II. Oval below "TEN CENTS" is broken by lines.*Un

201		50.00	1.25
10¢	**dark green** Type I		
	green	50.00	1.25
	On cover		12.50
	Plate block of 6, w/imprint	750.00	
	Plate strip of 3, w/imprint	275.00	
	Double transfer	80.00	3.25
	v. Pair, imperforate	225.00	
	Earliest documented cover: *Feb. 16, 1896*		

202		UnFVF	UseFVF
10¢	**brown** Type I	135.00	2.50
	dark brown	135.00	2.50
	On cover		12.50
	Plate block of 6, w/imprint	700.00	
	Plate strip of 3, w/imprint	650.00	
	Double transfer	150.00	4.00
	Pair, 1 each *(202,203)*	13,000.00	
	FDC *(Nov. 11, 1898)*		

203		UnFVF	UseFVF
10¢	**orange brown** Type II	75.00	2.00
	brown	75.00	2.00
	yellow brown	75.00	2.00
	On cover		14.00
	Plate block of 6, w/imprint	950.00	
	Plate strip of 3, w/imprint	400.00	
	Margin block of 4, w/arrow	425.00	
	FDC *(Nov. 11, 1898)*		

204		UnFVF	UseFVF
15¢	**indigo**	150.00	9.00
	blackish blue	150.00	9.00
	On cover		50.00
	Plate block of 6, w/imprint	2,100.00	
	Plate strip of 3, w/imprint	700.00	
	Margin block of 4, w/arrow	725.00	
	v. Pair, imperforate	625.00	
	Earliest documented cover: *Feb. 27, 1897*		

205		UnFVF	UseFVF
15¢	**olive green**	115.00	7.50
	dark olive green	115.00	7.50
	On cover		27.50
	Plate block of 6, w/imprint	1,500.00	
	Plate strip of 3, w/imprint	500.00	
	Margin block of 4, w/arrow	625.00	
	FDC *(Nov. 30, 1898)*		

206		UnFVF	UseFVF
50¢	**orange**	200.00	20.00
	dark red orange	200.00	20.00
	dull red orange	200.00	20.00
	red orange	200.00	20.00
	On cover		325.00
	Plate block of 6, w/imprint	3,750.00	
	Plate strip of 3, w/imprint	850.00	
	Margin block of 4, w/arrow	900.00	
	v. Pair, imperforate	675.00	
	Earliest documented cover: *Feb. 27, 1897*		

207		UnFVF	UseFVF
$1	**black** Type I	450.00	55.00
	greenish black	450.00	55.00
	On cover		2,000.00
	Plate block of 6, w/imprint	3,000.00	

		UnFVF	UseFVF
	Plate strip of 3, w/imprint	2,100.00	
	Margin block of 4, w/arrow	2,200.00	
	Earliest documented cover: *Sept. 5, 1898*		

208		UnFVF	UseFVF
$1	**black** Type II	900.00	125.00
	greenish black	900.00	125.00
	On cover		3,350.00
	Plate block of 6, w/imprint (4 Type II, 2 Type I	19,500.00	
	Plate strip of 3, w/imprint (2 Type II, 1 Type I)	3,750.00	
	Margin block of 4, w/arrow	4,750.00	
	Pair, 1 each Nos. 207, 208	1,950.00	
	v. Pair, imperforate	1,250.00	
	Earliest documented cover: *April 6, 1896*		

209		UnFVF	UseFVF
$2	**dark blue**	775.00	250.00
	bright blue	775.00	250.00
	On cover		3,200.00
	Plate block of 6, w/imprint	14,000.00	
	Plate strip of 3, w/imprint	3,500.00	
	Margin block of 4, w/arrow	4,000.00	
	v. Pair, imperforate	2,250.00	
	Earliest documented cover: *July 16, 1895*		

210		UnFVF	UseFVF
$5	**dark green**	1,600.00	375.00
	On cover		10,000.00
	Plate block of 6, w/imprint	60,000.00	
	Plate strip of 3, w/imprint	7,250.00	
	Margin block of 4, w/arrow	8,500.00	
	v. Pair, imperforate	2,250.00	
	Earliest documented cover: *Nov. 3, 1896*		

1902-03. Regular Issue had only two of its 14 values actually released in 1902, the balance being issued during 1903. All of these stamps were *perforated, with the 1¢, 4¢, and 5¢ being issued imperforate as well,* although the 4¢ imperforate now exists only with the large slots of the Schermack coil cut into the sides. The 1¢ and 5¢ also were issued in coil form. Finally the 1¢ and 2¢ stamps were issued as booklet panes, six stamps to a pane. *Intaglio, double-line watermark USPS, perforated 12.*

211, 225, 228, 230 *Benjamin Franklin*

211		UnFVF	UseFVF
1¢	**deep bluish green**	9.00	.20
	dark green	9.00	.20
	gray green	9.00	.20
	green	9.00	.20
	yellow green	9.00	.20
	On cover		.50
	Plate block of 6, w/imprint	145.00	
	Plate strip of 3, w/imprint	27.50	
	Cracked plate	8.00	.60
	Double transfer	11.00	.75
	Worn plate	8.00	.60
	n. Booklet pane of 6 *(March 6, 1907)*	425.00	
	n1. Pane w/plate number 3472 over left stamp	—	
	v. Arrow block with "color ball"	—	
	EKU *(Feb. 8, 1903)*		

212 *George Washington*

212		UnFVF	UseFVF
2¢	**carmine**	12.00	.20
	bright carmine	12.00	.20
	dark carmine	12.00	.20
	carmine rose	12.00	.20
	On cover		.50
	Plate block of 6, w/imprint	150.00	
	Plate strip of 3, w/imprint	40.00	
	Cracked plate	—	.75
	Double transfer	17.50	.75
	n. Booklet pane of 6 *(Jan. 24, 1903)*	400.00	
	EKU *(Jan. 17, 1903)*		

213 *Andrew Jackson after engraving by A. Sealey*

213		UnFVF	UseFVF
3¢	**dark red violet**	52.50	2.25
	bright violet	52.50	2.25
	violet	52.50	2.25
	Plate block of 6, w/imprint	600.00	
	Plate strip of 3, w/imprint	175.00	
	Cracked plate	—	
	Double transfer	65.00	3.50
	On cover		8.00
	v. Arrow block w/"color ball"	—	
	EKU *(March 21, 1903)*		

214, 226 *U.S. Grant*

214		UnFVF	UseFVF
4¢	**brown**	57.50	1.00
	dark brown	57.50	1.00
	dark yellow brown	57.50	1.00
	orange brown	57.50	1.00
	reddish brown	57.50	1.00
	yellow brown	57.50	1.00
	On cover		10.00
	Plate block of 6, w/imprint	600.00	
	Plate strip of 3, w/imprint	175.00	
	Double transfer	60.00	2.25
	EKU *(March 13, 1903)*		

215, 227, 229 *Abraham Lincoln*

215		UnFVF	UseFVF
5¢	**deep blue**	57.50	1.15
	blue	57.50	1.15
	dark blue	57.50	1.15
	dull blue	57.50	1.15
	On cover		7.00
	Plate block of 6, w/imprint	600.00	
	Plate strip of 3, w/imprint	175.00	
	Cracked plate	55.00	4.00
	Double transfer	65.00	3.00
	EKU *(Feb. 10, 1903)*		

216 *James Garfield*

216		UnFVF	UseFVF
6¢	**brown red**	70.00	2.00
	claret	70.00	2.00
	deep claret	70.00	2.00
	dull brown red	70.00	2.00
	On cover		10.00
	Plate block of 6, w/imprint	700.00	
	Plate strip of 3, w/imprint	200.00	

		UnFVF	UseFVF
	Double transfer	62.50	3.00
	EKU *(May 8, 1903)*		

217 *Martha Washington*

217		UnFVF	UseFVF
8¢	**violet black**	42.50	1.60
	black	42.50	1.60
	blue black	42.50	1.60
	blue lilac	42.50	1.60
	blue violet	42.50	1.60
	On cover		7.50
	Plate block of 6, w/imprint	550.00	
	Plate strip of 3, w/imprint	120.00	
	Double transfer	37.50	2.00
	EKU *(Dec. 27, 1902)*		

218 *Daniel Webster*

218		UnFVF	UseFVF
10¢	**pale red brown**	60.00	1.15
	dark red brown	60.00	1.15
	red brown	60.00	1.15
	On cover		7.00
	Plate block of 6, w/imprint	750.00	
	Plate strip of 3, w/imprint	150.00	
	Double transfer	60.00	8.00
	EKU *(March 12, 1903)*		

219 *Benjamin Harrison died March 13, 1901, and this stamp with his likeness was issued a year later. It was the first U.S. stamp with a 13¢ denomination, the first stamp issued in the 1902 Regular Issue Series. A first-day cover found Nov. 18, 1999, constitutes the first FDC of the 20th century.*

219		UnFVF	UseFVF
13¢	**black brown**	42.50	6.50
	purple black	42.50	6.50
	On cover		32.50
	Plate block of 6, w/imprint	500.00	
	Plate strip of 3, w/imprint	125.00	
	FDC *(Nov. 18, 1902)*		

220 *Henry Clay*

220		UnFVF	UseFVF
15¢	**olive green**	150.00	4.50
	dark olive green	150.00	4.50
	On cover		70.00
	Plate block of 6, w/imprint	1,950.00	
	Plate strip of 3, w/imprint	500.00	
	Double transfer	160.00	8.00
	Margin block of 4, w/arrow	550.00	
	EKU *(Sept. 24, 1903)*		

221 *Thomas Jefferson*

221		UnFVF	UseFVF
50¢	**orange**	425.00	20.00
	deep orange	425.00	20.00
	On cover		600.00
	Plate block of 6, w/imprint	5,250.00	
	Plate strip of 3, w/imprint	1,250.00	
	Margin block of 4, w/arrow	1,500.00	
	EKU *(Feb. 17, 1904)*		

222 *David Farragut (1801-70), known as the Hero of New Orleans and Mobile Boy because of his success in stopping blockade-running in the Civil War. Became the first American Navy admiral in 1866.*

222		UnFVF	UseFVF
$1	**black**	750.00	45.00
	gray black	750.00	45.00
	On cover		1,250.00
	Plate block of 6, w/imprint	10,500.00	
	Plate strip of 3, w/imprint	1,950.00	
	Margin block of 4, w/arrow	2,250.00	
	EKU *(Jan. 23, 1904)*		

223, 365 *James Madison*

223		UnFVF	UseFVF
$2	**dark blue**	1,075.00	140.00
	blue	1,075.00	140.00
	On cover		2,100.00
	Plate block of 6, w/imprint	22,000.00	
	Plate strip of 3, w/imprint	3,200.00	
	Margin block of 4, w/arrow	4,000.00	
	EKU *(Feb. 17, 1904)*		

224, 366 *John Marshall (1755-1835) 4th Chief Justice of the U.S. (1801-35)*

224		UnFVF	UseFVF
$5	**dark green**	2,800.00	525.00
	On cover		4,250.00
	Plate block of 6, w/imprint	42,000.00	
	Plate strip of 3, w/imprint	8,000.00	
	Margin block of 4, w/arrow	10,000.00	
	EKU *(Feb. 17, 1904)*		

1906-08. Regular Issues of 1902-03 *Imperforate.*

225		UnFVF	UseFVF
1¢	**deep bluish green**	20.00	17.50
	dark green	20.00	17.50
	green	20.00	17.50
	On cover		17.50
	Plate block of 6, w/imprint	165.00	
	Margin block of 4, w/arrow	80.00	60.00
	Center line block	120.00	80.00
	Double transfer	30.00	15.00
	EKU *(Feb. 1, 1907)*		

226 *Four Cent, imperforate, with slots at sides. These slots aided in the vending of coil stamps by the machines of the Schermack Co.*

226		UnFVF	UseFVF
4¢	**brown**	30,000.00	25,000.00
	On cover		120,000.00

Washington-Franklin Identifier

PERF.	WMK.	1¢ Text	2c Text	1¢ Numeral	2¢ Numeral	Washington Numeral	Franklin Numeral
12	Double	237, 263	238, 264			239-248, 265-272	313-314
	Single	273	274	297	298	275-282	305-312
Coil 12	Double	254, 258	255, 259			256-257, 260-262	
	Single	285, 287	286, 288			289	
Imperforate	Double	249	250			251-253	
	Single	283	284	299	300, *342*		
	Unwmk.			367, **406**	368, **407-407D**	369-370, **408**	
Coil 8 1/2	Single	290, 292	291, 293	301, 303	302, 304	294-296	
10	Double						331
	Single			315	316	317-321	322-330
	Unwmk.			348, *414*	349	350-355	356-364
Coil 10	Single			333, 335, *340*, *343*	334, 336, *341*, *344*	337-339, *345-347*	
	Unwmk.			371, 374	372, 375	373, 376-378	379
11	Double		399				
	Single				332		
	Unwmk.			380, **403,** *415*, *416*	381, **404-404D,** *417*	382-387, **405-405A**	388-398
12x10, 10x12	Single			315v, 315v1	316v	319v	
12 1/2	Unwmk.			**409**			
11x10, 10x11	Unwmk.			*410, 413*	*411-411A*	*412*	

237 -- Numbers in normal type designate stamps printed by intaglio on a flat-bed press. The design is about 18 1/2-19mm wide and 22mm high

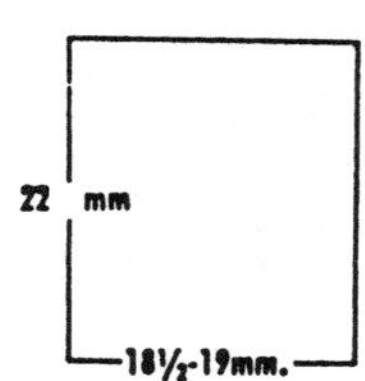

340 -- Numbers in italic designate stamps printed by intaglio on a rotary press.

407 -- Numbers in bold designate stamps printed by offset. These stamps are characterized by the smoothness of the printed surface and by the blurred appearance of the image.

		UnFVF	UseFVF
	Pair	70,000.00	
	Line pair	175,000.00	
	EKU *(May 27, 1908)*		

227		UnFVF	UseFVF
5¢	**blue**	375.00	475.00
	On cover		—
	Plate block of 6, w/imprint	2,800.00	
	Center line block	2,800.00	
	Margin block of 4, w/arrow	1,800.00	
	EKU *(Sept. 15, 1908)*		

Please exercise caution in buying singles of this stamp, particularly used copies. Certification by respected authorities recommended.

1908. Coil Stamp 1902-03 Series Issue were the first coils issued. They have been faked extensively by fraudulently perforating the imperforates in the case of the 1¢ stamps and also by trimming off perforations on both the 1¢ and 5¢ stamps. It is recommended that these stamps be collected in pairs. *Perforated 12 horizontally.*

228		UnFVF	UseFVF
1¢	**blue green** pair	68,500.00	—
	Line pair	110,000.00	
	EKU *(none known)*		

229		UnFVF	UseFVF
5¢	**blue** pair	9,000.00	—
	Line pair	19,500.00	
	EKU *(Sept. 18, 1908)*		

Perforated 12 vertically.

230		UnFVF	UseFVF
1¢	**blue green** pair	6,000.00	—
	Line pair	11,000.00	
	Double transfer	—	
	EKU *(none known)*		

1903. Two-Cent Shield Issue was issued because of public dislike for the 2¢ "Flag" design of the 1902-03 series. The "Shield" stamp comes in a wide range of shades. It was issued perforated, imperforate, in booklet panes, and also in coil form, so that a considerable display can be made of this single denomination. *The stamps were flat-plate printed, double-line watermark USPS, Type I, perforated 12.*

231-236 *George Washington*

Type I: The leaf next to the "2" at left penetrates the border.

Type II: Border to the left of the leaf is formed by a strong line. Lower left inside curve line enlarged.

231		UnFVF	UseFVF
2¢	**carmine** Type I	4.00	.20
	bright carmine	4.00	.20
	red	4.00	.20
	carmine rose	4.50	.20
	scarlet	4.00	.20
	On cover		.50
	Plate block of 6, w/imprint	75.00	
	Plate strip of 3 w/imprint	16.00	
	Double transfer	8.00	1.50
	n. Booklet pane of 6	100.00	
	v. Vertical pair, rouletted between	800.00	
	v1. Vertical pair, imperforate horizontally	2,500.00	
	v2. Vertical pair, imperforate between	1,000.00	
	EKU *(Nov. 19, 1903)*		

232		UnFVF	UseFVF
2¢	**lake** Type II	7.50	.50
	carmine	7.50	.50
	carmine lake	7.50	.50
	scarlet	7.50	.50
	Plate block of 6	150.00	
	n. Booklet pane of 6	150.00	
	EKU *(June 5, 1903)*		

1903. Two-Cent Shield Coil Issue. Imperforate.

233		UnFVF	UseFVF
2¢	**carmine** Type II	20.00	15.00
	carmine rose	20.00	15.00
	scarlet	20.00	15.00
	On cover		15.00
	Plate block of 6, w/imprint	200.00	
	Center line block	140.00	175.00
	Double transfer	22.50	12.50
	Margin block of 4, w/arrow	80.00	85.00
	EKU *(Oct. 26, 1906)*		

234		UnFVF	UseFVF
2¢	**lake** Type II	50.00	40.00
	scarlet	50.00	40.00
	On cover		70.00
	Plate block of 6, w/imprint	700.00	
	Center line block	400.00	
	Margin block of 4, w/arrow	180.00	

1903. Two-Cent Shield Coil Issue. Coil stamp, perforated 12 horizontally.

235		UnFVF	UseFVF
2¢	**carmine** Type I pair	95,000.00	100,000.00
	Line pair	—	
	EKU *(Oct. 2, 1908)*		

Perforated 12 vertically.

236		UnFVF	UseFVF
2¢	**scarlet** Type II pair	7,000.00	4,250.00
	Double transfer	7,750.00	
	Line pair	—	
	EKU *(none known)*		

1908-09 Washington & Franklin Issue consisted of 12 stamps, ranging from 1¢ to $1. The 1¢ stamp has a portrait of Franklin in the central medallion with the words "ONE CENT" at the base of the stamp. The 2¢ stamp, with Washington in the medallion, is inscribed "TWO CENTS." The 3¢ stamp to $1 stamps have Washington in the medallion with numerals of value in each of the lower corners.

As an experiment to counteract the shrinking caused by printing on wet paper, some rows of stamps were separated by 3mm spacing instead of the usual 2mm. Intermediate-size spacings exist and command the lower of the two prices listed for different spacings. *Flat plate printing, watermarked double-line USPS (187), and perforated 12.*

A very few of this series, up through the 15¢ value, were printed on a grayish, hard, thick paper known as *China Clay.* The paper had up to 10 times the mineral content of normal stamp paper of the time.

237 *Benjamin Franklin*

237		UnFVF	UseFVF
1¢	**green**	6.00	.20
	bright green	6.00	.20
	dark green	6.00	.20
	yellow green	6.00	.20
	On cover		.50
	Plate block of 6, w/imprint	45.00	
	Plate block of 6, w/imprint & open star	50.00	
	Plate block of 6, w/small solid star	75.00	
	Block of 4, 2mm spacing	25.00	1.25
	Block of 4, 3mm spacing	27.50	1.50
	Cracked plate	—	
	Double transfer	8.00	.60
	v. Horizontal pair, imperforate between	1,000.00	
	n. Booklet pane of 6 *(Dec. 2, 1908)*	140.00	120.00
	FDC *(Dec. 14, 1908)*		20,000.00
	p. China Clay paper	800.00	

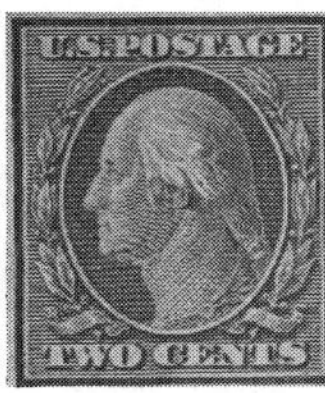

238 *George Washington, value in words.*

238		UnFVF	UseFVF
2¢	**carmine**	6.00	.20
	dark carmine	6.00	.20
	pale carmine	6.00	.20

		UnFVF	UseFVF
	On cover		.50
	Plate block of 6, w/imprint	45.00	
	Plate block of 6, w/imprint & open star	50.00	
	Plate block of 6, w/small solid star	70.00	
	Block of 4, 2mm spacing	22.50	.60
	Block of 4, 3mm spacing	25.00	.75
	Cracked plate	—	
	Double transfer	10.00	
	Double transfer (1¢ design of No. 237)	1,250.00	
	n. Booklet pane of 6 (Nov. 16, 1908)	125.00	110.00
	FDC *(Dec. 1, 1908)*		35,000.00
	p. China Clay paper	1,000.00	

1908. George Washington Type I Issue Details of Type I:

1. The top line of the toga from the front of the neck to the top of the button is very weak, as are the upper parts of the fine lines of shading that join this top line. The top part of the fifth of these shading lines is missing.
2. Two shading lines under the point of the chin are heavy.
3. The line between the lips is thin. This usually is an easy checking point for this type.
4. The lock of hair behind the ear is formed at the bottom by two lines of shading, the lower line being considerably shorter than the upper.
5. The hair lines above and a little to the right of the ear form an "arrowhead."
6. The outline of the inner oval forms a solid line at the bottom.

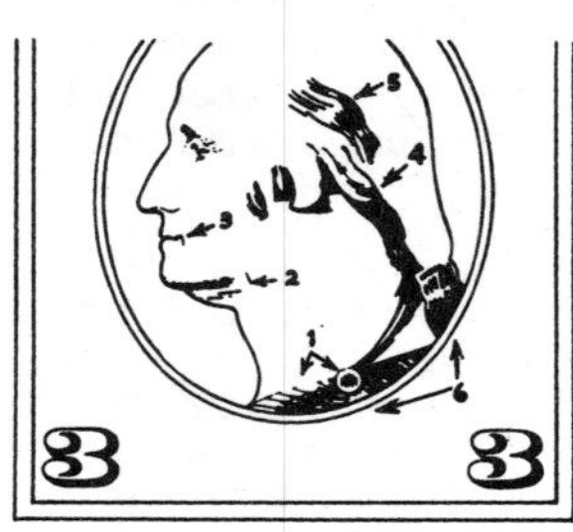

239 George Washington. Type I: All stamps of this design and perforated 12 are Type I. While the description of the type is given here in detail, the areas noted by the small figures "1" and "3" in the drawing will almost always prove sufficient as checking areas.

		UnFVF	UseFVF
239			
3¢	**violet** Type I	27.50	2.50
	dark violet	27.50	2.50
	pale violet	27.50	2.50
	On cover		7.50
	Plate block of 6, w/imprint	200.00	
	Plate block of 6, w/imprint & star	300.00	
	Block of 4, 2mm spacing	110.00	15.00
	Block of 4, 3mm spacing	120.00	17.50
	Double transfer	37.50	4.00
	p. China Clay paper	800.00	
	FDC *(Dec. 26, 1908)*		
240			
4¢	**orange brown**	30.00	1.00
	brown	30.00	1.00
	dark orange brown	30.00	1.00
	dull orange brown	30.00	1.00
	On cover		5.00
	Plate block of 6, w/imprint	300.00	
	Plate block of 6, w/imprint & star	475.00	
	Block of 4, 2mm spacing	140.00	7.50
	Block of 4, 3mm spacing	150.00	9.00
	Double transfer	45.00	
	p. China Clay paper	1,000.00	
	FDC *(Dec. 26, 1908)*		
241			
5¢	**blue**	40.00	2.00
	bright blue	40.00	2.00
	dark blue	40.00	2.00
	On cover		8.00
	Plate block of 6, w/imprint	400.00	
	Plate block of 6, w/imprint & star	600.00	
	Block of 4, 2mm spacing	175.00	12.50
	Block of 4, 3mm spacing	185.00	10.00
	Double transfer	45.00	
	p. China Clay paper	800.00	
	FDC *(Dec. 21, 1908)*		
242			
6¢	**red orange**	47.50	5.00
	dull orange	47.50	5.00
	orange	47.50	5.00
	On cover		17.50
	Plate block of 6, w/imprint	600.00	
	p. China Clay paper	625.00	
	FDC *(Dec. 31, 1908)*		
243			
8¢	**olive green**	37.50	2.50
	dark olive green	37.50	2.50
	On cover		16.00
	Plate block of 6, w/imprint	400.00	
	Double transfer	47.50	
	p. China Clay paper	800.00	
	FDC *(Dec. 18, 1908)*		
244			
10¢	**yellow**	55.00	1.50
	On cover		8.00
	Plate block of 6, w/imprint	650.00	
	Double transfer	—	
	p. China Clay paper	800.00	
	p1. Very thin paper	—	
	FDC *(Jan. 7, 1909)*		
245			
13¢	**blue green**	37.50	20.00
	dark blue green	37.50	20.00
	On cover		90.00
	Plate block of 6, w/imprint	400.00	
	p. China Clay paper	800.00	
	FDC *(Jan. 11, 1909);* EKU *March 5, 1909*		
246			
15¢	**gray blue**	50.00	6.00
	dull gray blue	50.00	6.00
	On cover		110.00
	Plate block of 6, w/imprint	525.00	
	p. China Clay paper	800.00	
	FDC *(Jan. 18, 1909)*		
247			
50¢	**gray lilac**	250.00	17.50
	dull gray lilac	250.00	17.50
	On cover		4,500.00
	Plate block of 6, w/imprint	6,000.00	
	Margin block of 4, w/arrow	1,100.00	
	FDC *(Jan. 13, 1909)*		
248			
$1	**violet brown**	375.00	75.00
	dull violet brown	375.00	75.00
	On cover		5,250.00
	Plate block of 6, w/imprint	11,500.00	
	Margin block of 4, w/arrow	1,900.00	
	Double transfer	—	
	FDC *(Jan. 29, 1909)*		

1908. Washington & Franklin Type I Issue. *Imperforate.*

		UnFVF	UseFVF
249			
1¢	**green**	6.00	4.00
	bright green	6.00	4.00
	dark green	6.00	4.00
	yellow green	6.00	4.00
	On cover		8.00
	Plate block of 6, w/imprint	55.00	
	Plate block of 6, w/imprint & open star	60.00	
	Plate block of 6, w/small solid star	600.00	
	Block of 4, 2mm spacing	25.00	
	Block of 4, 3mm spacing	25.00	
	Center line block	35.00	
	Margin block of 4, 2 or 3mm spacing, w/arrow	30.00	
	Double transfer	—	
	FDC *(Dec. 23, 1908)*		
250			
2¢	**carmine**	7.50	3.00
	dark carmine	7.50	3.00

	pale carmine	7.50	3.00
	On cover		4.50
	Plate block of 6, w/imprint	75.00	
	Plate block of 6, w/imprint & star	80.00	
	Block of 4, 2 or 3mm spacing	30.00	
	Center line block	40.00	
	Double transfer	12.50	3.50
	Double transfer (1¢ design of No. 237)	1,000.00	
	Margin block of 4, 2 or 3mm spacing, w/arrow	35.00	
	FDC *(Dec. 14, 1908)*		

251		UnFVF	UseFVF
3¢	**violet** Type I	17.50	20.00
	On cover		40.00
	Plate block of 6, w/imprint	175.00	
	Center line block	75.00	80.00
	Double transfer	20.00	
	Margin block of 4, w/arrow	60.00	80.00
	FDC *(March 3, 1909)*		

252		UnFVF	UseFVF
4¢	**brown**	27.50	22.50
	orange brown	27.50	22.50
	dark orange brown	27.50	22.50
	dull orange brown	27.50	22.50
	On cover		70.00
	Plate block of 6 w/imprint	200.00	
	Plate block of 6, w/imprint & star	225.00	
	Block of 4, 2 or 3mm spacing	95.00	
	Center line block	125.00	
	Double transfer	40.00	
	Margin block of 4, 2 or 3mm spacing, w/arrow	100.00	
	FDC *(Feb. 25, 1909);* EKU *March 13, 1909*		

253		UnFVF	UseFVF
5¢	**blue**	42.50	30.00
	On cover		90.00
	Plate block of 6, w/imprint	350.00	
	Center line block	220.00	200.00
	Cracked plate	—	
	Margin block of 4, w/arrow	200.00	160.00
	FDC *(Feb. 27, 1909)*		

1908-10. Washington & Franklin Coil Issue *Flat plate printing, double-line USPS watermark, and perforated 12 either on the sides or at the top and bottom of the stamp. Perforated 12 horizontally.*

254		UnFVF	UseFVF
1¢	**green**	22.50	12.50
	dark green	22.50	12.50
	On cover		35.00
	Pair	60.00	65.00
	Line pair	150.00	275.00
	FDC *(Dec. 29, 1908)*		

255		UnFVF	UseFVF
2¢	**carmine**	37.50	8.00
	dark carmine	37.50	8.00
	On cover		25.00
	Pair	65.00	30.00
	Line pair	275.00	135.00
	Double transfer (1¢ design of No. 237)	—	1,350.00
	FDC *(Jan. 2, 1909)*		

256		UnFVF	UseFVF
4¢	**brown**	85.00	70.00
	On cover		150.00
	Pair	225.00	300.00
	Line pair	650.00	550.00
	FDC *(Aug. 15, 1910)*		

257		UnFVF	UseFVF
5¢	**blue**	100.00	85.00
	dark blue	100.00	85.00
	On cover		165.00
	Pair	275.00	300.00
	Line pair	750.00	550.00
	FDC *(Jan. 2, 1909);* EKU *Sept. 21, 1909*		

1908-10. Washington & Franklin Coil Issue *Perforated 12 vertically.*

258		UnFVF	UseFVF
1¢	**green**	50.00	30.00
	On cover		60.00
	Pair, 2mm spacing	135.00	105.00
	Pair, 3mm spacing	120.00	95.00
	Line pair	350.00	200.00
	Double transfer	—	
	FDC *(Jan. 2, 1909)*		

259		UnFVF	UseFVF
2¢	**carmine**	47.50	7.50
	On cover		20.00
	Pair, 2mm spacing	125.00	30.00
	Pair, 3mm spacing	115.00	25.00
	Line pair	350.00	125.00
	FDC *(Jan. 12, 1909)*		

260		UnFVF	UseFVF
4¢	**brown**	115.00	55.00
	On cover		90.00
	Pair, 2mm spacing	325.00	250.00
	Pair, 3mm spacing	340.00	270.00
	Line pair	850.00	400.00
	FDC *(Feb. 23, 1909)*		

261		UnFVF	UseFVF
5¢	**blue**	125.00	75.00
	dark blue	125.00	75.00
	On cover		150.00
	Pair	350.00	325.00
	Line pair	900.00	550.00
	FDC *(Feb. 23, 1909)*		

262		UnFVF	UseFVF
10¢	**yellow**	1,750.00	850.00
	On cover		8,500.00
	Pair	4,200.00	3,800.00
	Line pair	7,500.00	6,850.00
	FDC *(Feb. 23, 1909)*		

1909. Washington & Franklin Issue Stamps of 1908-09 on bluish gray paper. The paper used in this experimental printing was made with a 30% rag stock instead of all wood pulp. Here is a quote from the Report of the Third Assistant Postmaster General for the fiscal year ending June 30, 1909: "The intaglio process by which our postage stamps are printed necessitates a preliminary wetting down of the paper, which is bleached chemical wood stock. This wetting down causes a varying shrinkage, which has resulted in heavy waste from the cutting of the perforations into the stamp design. The Bureau of Engraving and Printing experimented with a paper made of about 30% rag stock, in the hope that it would show less shrinkage, but this paper did not overcome the difficulty as it was found to shrink very unevenly. Some of the stamps printed on this paper, which was of a slightly bluish tinge, were issued to the Postmaster at Washington, D.C., and to others." Actually, the paper is of a color distinctly different from the normal paper, but this shows up better by comparison than it does by the examination of just a single copy of either the normal or the bluish gray paper. We have noted the presence of tiny black specks on much of the blue paper, sometimes only a few to a stamp and best seen with the aid of a magnifying glass. These stamps were *Flat Plate printing, watermarked double-line USPS, and perforated 12.*

263		UnFVF	UseFVF
1¢	**green**	85.00	85.00
	On cover		185.00
	Plate block of 6, w/imprint	900.00	
	Plate block of 6, w/imprint and star	2,500.00	
	Block of 4, 2mm spacing	350.00	375.00
	Block of 4, 3mm spacing	675.00	
	FDC *(Feb. 16, 1909)*		
	Earliest documented cover: *Feb. 22, 1909*		

264		UnFVF	UseFVF
2¢	**carmine**	75.00	70.00
	On cover		150.00
	Plate block of 6, w/imprint	900.00	
	Plate block of 6, w/imprint & star	1,150.00	
	Block of 4, 2mm spacing	340.00	400.00
	Block of 4, 3mm spacing	380.00	
	Double transfer	—	
	FDC *(Feb. 16, 1909)*		
	Earliest documented cover: *Feb. 23, 1909*		

265		UnFVF	UseFVF
3¢	**deep violet** Type I	1,600.00	1,600.00
	On cover		—
	Plate block of 6, w/imprint	15,000.00	
	Earliest documented cover: *Dec. 27, 1910*		

266		UnFVF	UseFVF
4¢	**orange brown**	15,000.00	—

		UnFVF	UseFVF
	Plate block of 6, w/imprint	115,000.00	
	Plate strip of 3, w/imprint	—	
267		**UnFVF**	**UseFVF**
5¢	**blue**	3,500.00	3,750.00
	On cover		5,250.00
	Plate block of 6, w/imprint	30,000.00	
268		**UnFVF**	**UseFVF**
6¢	**red orange**	1,150.00	1,000.00
	On cover		11,000.00
	Plate block of 6, w/imprint	12,500.00	
	Earliest documented cover: *Sept. 14, 1911*		
269		**UnFVF**	**UseFVF**
8¢	**olive green**	16,000.00	—
	Plate block of 6, w/imprint	120,000.00	
	Plate strip of 3 w/imprint	—	
270		**UnFVF**	**UseFVF**
10¢	**yellow**	1,400.00	1,150.00
	On cover		—
	Plate block of 6, w/imprint	15,000.00	
	Earliest documented cover: *Feb. 3, 1910*		
271		**UnFVF**	**UseFVF**
13¢	**blue green**	2,350.00	1,450.00
	On cover		—
	Plate block of 6, w/imprint	17,500.00	
272		**UnFVF**	**UseFVF**
15¢	**pale ultramarine**	1,150.00	1,000.00
	On cover		—
	Plate block of 6, w/imprint	7,500.00	

1910-14. WASHINGTON & FRANKLIN ISSUE This issue was identical with the 1908-09 series in design, but a 7¢ stamp was added while the 50¢ and $1 stamps were discontinued. The stamps were printed on paper with a new watermark, single-line USPS, intended to make the paper stronger and more uniform. For this new watermark, the letters "USPS," for "United States Postage Stamps," are only 5/16 of an inch high, compared with the 9/16-inch height of the double-line watermark previously used on Bureau of Engraving and Printing paper. The letters were arranged in diagonal rows. About 77 letters appear on a pane of 100 stamps, so sometimes stamps will have portions of two or three letters. The letters can be right-side-up or upside-down on sheet stamps; booklet stamps have single-line watermarks sideways. *Flat plate printing. Perforated 12.*

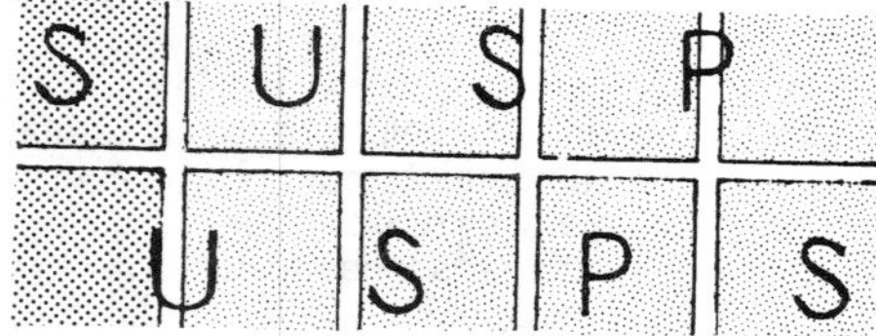

273 *Single-line USPS watermark*

		UnFVF	UseFVF
273		**UnFVF**	**UseFVF**
1¢	**green**	6.00	.20
	dark green	6.00	.20
	pale green	6.00	.20
	yellowish green	6.00	.20
	On cover		.50
	Plate block of 6, w/imprint & "A"	60.00	
	Plate block of 6, w/imprint & star	70.00	
	Block of 4, 2mm spacing	22.50	2.75
	Block of 4, 3mm spacing	22.50	2.75
	Cracked plate	—	
	Double transfer	10.00	
	n. Booklet pane of 6	125.00	100.00
	Earliest documented cover: *Nov. 21, 1911*		
	FDC *(Nov. 23, 1910)*		
274		**UnFVF**	**UseFVF**
2¢	**carmine**	5.75	.20
	dull carmine	5.75	.20
	lake	200.00	—
	On cover		.50
	Plate block of 6, w/imprint & "A"	60.00	
	Plate block of 6, w/imprint & star	65.00	
	Block of 4, 2mm spacing	22.50	1.00
	Block of 4, 3mm spacing	21.00	.80
	Cracked plate	—	
	Double transfer	9.00	—
	Double transfer (1¢ design of No. 273)	—	850.00
	n. Booklet pane of 6	100.00	
	Earliest documented cover: *June 1, 1911*		
	FDC *(Nov. 23, 1910)*		
	FDC booklet *(Nov. 30, 1910)*		

275 *George Washington*

		UnFVF	UseFVF
275		**UnFVF**	**UseFVF**
3¢	**violet** Type I	15.00	1.50
	deep violet	15.00	1.50
	lilac	17.50	1.50
	On cover		7.00
	Plate block of 6	125.00	
	Plate block of 6, w/imprint & star	165.00	
	Block of 4, 2mm spacing	65.00	8.00
	Block of 4, 3mm spacing	67.50	8.00
	FDC *(Jan. 16, 1911)*		
	Earliest documented cover: *June 19, 1911*		

1911. GEORGE WASHINGTON ISSUE

276 *George Washington*

		UnFVF	UseFVF
276		**UnFVF**	**UseFVF**
4¢	**brown**	22.50	.75
	dark brown	22.50	.75
	orange brown	22.50	.75
	On cover		7.00
	Plate block of 6	240.00	
	Plate block of 6, w/imprint & star	200.00	
	Block of 4, 2mm spacing	100.00	
	Block of 4, 3mm spacing	95.00	
	FDC *(Jan. 20, 1911)*		

277

		UnFVF	UseFVF
277		**UnFVF**	**UseFVF**
5¢	**blue**	22.50	.75
	dark blue	22.50	.75
	pale blue	22.50	.75
	On cover		4.50
	Plate block of 6	200.00	
	Plate block of 6 w/imprint	180.00	
	Plate block of 6, w/imprint & "A"	200.00	
	Plate block of 6, w/imprint & star	175.00	
	Block of 4, 2mm spacing	100.00	5.00
	Block of 4, 3mm spacing	95.00	4.50
	Double transfer	—	
	FDC *(Jan. 25, 1911)*		
	Earliest documented cover: *March 28, 1911*		

278

		UnFVF	UseFVF
278		**UnFVF**	**UseFVF**
6¢	**red orange**	30.00	.85
	dull red orange	30.00	.85
	On cover		.40
	Plate block of 6, w/imprint	300.00	

	Plate block of 6, w/imprint & star	275.00	
	Block of 4, 2mm spacing	125.00	8.00
	Block of 4, 3mm spacing	120.00	7.50
	FDC *(Jan. 25, 1911);* EKU: *May 25, 1911*		

279		UnFVF	UseFVF
7¢	**black**	70.00	8.50
	deep black	70.00	8.50
	gray black	70.00	8.50
	On cover		50.00
	Plate block of 6	850.00	
	Earliest documented cover: *May 1, 1914*		

280

280		UnFVF	UseFVF
8¢	**light olive green**	95.00	12.50
	dark olive green	95.00	12.50
	On cover		50.00
	Plate block of 6, w/imprint	900.00	
	Plate block of 6, w/imprint & star	1,100.00	
	Block of 4, 2 or 3mm spacing	400.00	65.00
	FDC *(Feb. 8, 1911)*		

281		UnFVF	UseFVF
10¢	**yellow**	85.00	4.00
	On cover		15.00
	Plate block of 6, w/imprint	900.00	
	Plate block of 6, w/imprint & star	850.00	
	Block of 4, 2 or 3mm spacing	375.00	25.00
	Earliest documented cover: *Feb. 17, 1911*		
	FDC *(Jan. 24, 1911)*		

282		UnFVF	UseFVF
15¢	**pale ultramarine**	225.00	15.00
	On cover		85.00
	Plate block of 6	2,000.00	
	FDC *(March 1, 1911)*		
	Earliest documented cover: *Aug. 31, 1912*		

1910. George Washington Issue *Imperforate.*

283		UnFVF	UseFVF
1¢	**green**	3.00	2.75
	dark green	3.00	2.75
	pale green	3.00	2.75
	yellowish green	3.00	2.75
	On cover		4.00
	Plate block of 6 w/imprint & "A"	40.00	
	Plate block of 6, w/imprint & star	65.00	
	Block of 4, 2 or 3mm spacing	9.50	11.00
	Center line block	20.00	15.00
	Double transfer	6.00	
	Margin block of 4, w/arrow	10.00	11.00
	Earliest documented cover: *March 1, 1911*		
	FDC *(Dec. 1910)*		

284		UnFVF	UseFVF
2¢	**carmine**	5.50	3.00
	On cover		3.00
	Plate block of 6, w/imprint & "A"	115.00	
	Plate block of 6, w/imprint & star	150.00	
	Block of 4, 2 or 3mm spacing	20.00	12.50
	Margin block of 4, w/arrow	25.00	17.50
	Center line block	42.50	40.00
	Cracked plate	—	
	Double transfer	7.50	
	Double transfer (1¢ design of No. 283)	1,200.00	
	Earliest documented cover: *Dec. 15, 1910*		
	FDC *(Dec. 1910)*		

1910. Washington & Franklin Coil Issue *This stamp is relatively common in singles and vertical pairs. Perforated 12 horizontally.*

285		UnFVF	UseFVF
1¢	**green**	22.50	12.50
	dark green	22.50	12.50
	On cover		35.00
	Pair	50.00	35.00
	Line pair	250.00	225.00
	FDC *(Nov. 1, 1910)*		

286		UnFVF	UseFVF
2¢	**carmine**	37.50	17.50
	dark carmine	37.50	17.50
	pale carmine	37.50	17.50
	On cover		40.00
	Pair	135.00	75.00
	Line pair	425.00	
	FDC *(Nov. 1, 1910)*		

1910. Washington & Franklin Coil Issue *Perforated 12 vertically.*

287		UnFVF	UseFVF
1¢	**green**	85.00	37.50
	dark green	85.00	37.50
	On cover		60.00
	Pair, 2mm spacing	200.00	90.00
	Pair, 3mm spacing	220.00	100.00
	Line pair	325.00	260.00
	FDC *(Nov. 1, 1910)*		

288		UnFVF	UseFVF
2¢	**carmine**	575.00	250.00
	dark carmine	575.00	250.00
	pale carmine	575.00	250.00
	On cover		600.00
	Pair, 2 or 3mm spacing	1,950.00	
	Line pair	4,000.00	3,150.00
	FDC *(Nov. 1, 1910)*		

1910. George Washington Orangeburg Coil Issue Known as the "Orangeburg Coil" (because it is only known used from Orangeburg, N.Y.) No. 289 is the rarest of all U.S. coil stamps. One coil of 500 stamps was made, and only about a dozen unused copies are known. The stamps were used by Bell and Co., Inc., manufacturing chemists, of Orangeburg to mail samples of products and used copies bear a wavy-line cancellation used at Orangeburg, N.Y., at the time. *Perforated 12 vertically.*

289

		UnFVF	UseFVF
289			
3¢	**deep violet** Type I	28,500.00	7,000.00
	On cover		15,500.00
	Pair	78,500.00	
	EKU *(March 8, 1911)*		

1910. Washington & Franklin Coil Issue *Perforated 8 1/2 horizontally.*

290		UnFVF	UseFVF
1¢	**green**	4.50	5.00
	dark green	4.50	5.00
	On cover		7.50
	Pair	8.00	16.50
	Line pair	25.00	40.00
	FDC *(Dec. 12, 1910)*		

291		UnFVF	UseFVF
2¢	**carmine**	30.00	12.50
	dark carmine	30.00	12.50
	pale carmine	30.00	12.50
	On cover		20.00
	Pair	75.00	32.50
	Line pair	150.00	125.00
	FDC *(Dec. 23, 1910)*		

1910. Washington & Franklin Coil Issue *Perforated 8 1/2 vertically.*

292		UnFVF	UseFVF
1¢	**green**	20.00	20.00
	dark green	20.00	20.00
	On cover		50.00
	Double transfer	—	—
	Pair	55.00	65.00
	Line pair	115.00	135.00
	FDC *(Dec. 12, 1910)*		

293		UnFVF	UseFVF
2¢	**carmine**	40.00	10.00

		UnFVF	UseFVF
	dark carmine	40.00	10.00
	pale carmine	40.00	10.00
	On cover		20.00
	Pair	85.00	22.50
	Line pair	165.00	80.00
	FDC *(Dec. 16, 1910)*		

		UnFVF	UseFVF
294			
3¢	**violet** Type I	50.00	50.00
	deep violet	50.00	50.00
	red violet	50.00	50.00
	On cover		100.00
	Pair, 2 or 3mm spacing	110.00	125.00
	Line pair	250.00	275.00
	FDC *(Sept. 18, 1911)*		

		UnFVF	UseFVF
295			
4¢	**brown**	50.00	50.00
	dark brown	50.00	50.00
	On cover		100.00
	Pair, 2 or 3mm spacing	110.00	125.00
	Line pair	250.00	250.00
	FDC *(April 15, 1912)*		

		UnFVF	UseFVF
296			
5¢	**blue**	50.00	50.00
	dark blue	50.00	50.00
	On cover		100.00
	Pair	110.00	105.00
	Line pair	250.00	300.00
	FDC *(March 1913)*		

1912. Modified George Washington Issue 1¢ and 2¢ stamps with numerals instead of words for denomination. *Flat Press printing, single-line USPS watermark (wmk 273,) perforated 12.*

297 *George Washington*

		UnFVF	UseFVF
297			
1¢	**green**	5.00	.20
	dark green	5.00	.20
	pale green	5.00	.20
	yellow green	5.00	.20
	On cover		.25
	Plate block of 6	55.00	
	Plate block of 6, w/"A"	60.00	
	Plate block of 6, w/"A" & imprint	65.00	
	Cracked plate	11.00	
	Double transfer	5.00	
	n. Booklet pane of 6 *(Feb. 10, 1912)*	65.00	
	v. Vertical pair, imperforate horizontally	700.00	
	FDC *(Feb. 13, 1912)*		

298 *George Washington*

Input from stamp collectors regarding the content of this catalog and ideas to make it more useful is eagerly sought. Send your comments to :

Minkus Catalog Editor
Krause Publications
700 E State St.
Iola WI 54990

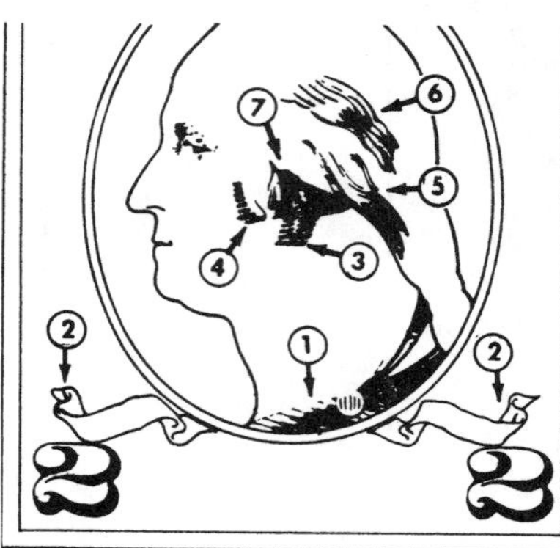

298 *George Washington, Type I. The following detailed description is provided, although any 2¢ that fits Point 1 is a Type I.* 1. The line from the front of the neck to and over the top of the button is very weak. The shading lines that run into this line (top of toga) are thin in the area above the cross hatching lines. 2. One shading line in the first (upper) curve of the ribbon above the left numeral and one line in the second (middle) curve above the right numeral. 3. There is a white dash below the ear. 4. The shading lines of the face terminate in front of the ear and are not joined with each other. 5. The lock of hair behind the ear is formed at the bottom by two lines of shading, the lower one being considerably shorter than the other. 6. The hair lines above the ear and slightly to the right form an arrowhead. 7. The shading lines just to the left of the ear form a fairly solid color.

		UnFVF	UseFVF
298			
2¢	**carmine** Type I	4.50	.20
	dark carmine	4.50	.20
	lilac carmine	4.50	.20
	On cover		.25
	Plate block of 6	70.00	
	Plate block of 6, w/"A"	85.00	
	Double transfer	6.25	
	n. Booklet pane of 6	65.00	
	v. Double impression	—	
	Earliest documented cover: *June 6, 1912*		
	FDC *(Feb. 14, 1912)*		

1912. Modified George Washington Issue *Imperforate.*

		UnFVF	UseFVF
299			
1¢	**green**	1.25	.60
	dark green	1.25	.60
	pale green	1.25	.60
	yellow green	1.25	.60
	On cover		1.00
	Plate block of 6	17.50	
	Plate block of 6, w/"A"	25.00	
	Plate block of 6, w/"A" & imprint	42.50	
	Center line block	8.00	8.00
	Cracked plate	—	
	Double transfer	2.25	.75
	Margin block of 4, w/arrow	4.50	2.75
	FDC *(March 9, 1912)*		

		UnFVF	UseFVF
300			
2¢	**carmine** Type I	1.30	.60
	dark carmine	1.30	.60
	scarlet red	1.30	.60
	On cover		1.00
	Plate block of 6	30.00	
	Plate block of 6, w/"A"	40.00	
	Plate block of 6, w/"A" & imprint	45.00	
	Center line block	9.00	8.00
	Cracked plate	—	
	Margin block of 4, w/arrow	5.50	
	FDC *(Feb. 23, 1912)*		

1912. George Washington Modified Design Coil Issue *Perforated 8 1/2 horizontally.*

		UnFVF	UseFVF
301			
1¢	**green**	5.50	4.50
	dark green	5.50	4.50
	On cover		7.25
	Pair	12.50	8.00
	Line pair	27.50	20.00
	Double transfer	—	
	FDC *(March 18, 1912)*		

		UnFVF	UseFVF
302			
2¢	**carmine** Type I	7.50	4.50

		UnFVF	UseFVF
	dark carmine	7.50	4.50
	On cover		10.00
	Pair	20.00	9.00
	Line pair	35.00	25.00
	Double transfer	10.00	
	FDC *(March 18, 1912)*		

1912. George Washington Modified Design Coil Issue *Perforated 8 1/2 vertically.*

303		UnFVF	UseFVF
1¢	**green**	22.50	6.25
	On cover		12.50
	Pair	45.00	12.50
	Line pair	75.00	40.00
	FDC *(May 18, 1912)*		

304		UnFVF	UseFVF
2¢	**carmine** Type I	35.00	1.25
	dark carmine	35.00	1.25
	On cover		7.00
	Pair	75.00	7.00
	Line pair	150.00	20.00
	Double transfer	35.00	
	FDC *(March 21, 1912)*		

1912-14. Benjamin Franklin Redesigned Issue values from 8¢ through 50¢. *Flat plate printing, single-line USPS watermark (wmk 273,) perforated 12.*

305-314 *Benjamin Franklin*

305		UnFVF	UseFVF
8¢	**pale olive green**	30.00	1.25
	olive green	30.00	1.25
	On cover		12.50
	Plate block of 6, w/imprint & "A"	400.00	
	FDC *(Feb. 14, 1912)*		

306		UnFVF	UseFVF
9¢	**salmon pink**	45.00	12.50
	rose red	45.00	12.50
	On cover		40.00
	Plate block of 6	550.00	
	Earliest documented cover: *May 1, 1914*		
	FDC *(April 1914)*		

307		UnFVF	UseFVF
10¢	**orange yellow**	32.50	.50
	brown yellow	300.00	5.00
	yellow	32.50	.50
	On cover		2.25
	Plate block of 6, w/"A"	370.00	
	Plate block of 6, w/"A" & imprint	420.00	
	Double transfer	—	
	FDC *(Jan. 20, 1912)*		

308		UnFVF	UseFVF
12¢	**chocolate**	40.00	4.25
	deep chocolate	40.00	4.25
	On cover		22.50
	Plate block of 6	450.00	
	Double transfer	47.50	
	Triple transfer	65.00	
	Earliest documented cover: *June 2, 1914*		
	FDC *(April 1914)*		

309		UnFVF	UseFVF
15¢	**gray black**	65.00	4.00
	gray	65.00	4.00
	On cover		15.00
	Plate block of 6	650.00	
	Plate block of 6, w/"A"	625.00	
	Plate block of 6, w/"A" & imprint	600.00	
	Double transfer	—	
	FDC *(Feb. 14, 1912)*		

310		UnFVF	UseFVF
20¢	**gray blue**	150.00	17.50
	ultramarine	150.00	17.50
	On cover		125.00
	Plate block of 6	1,650.00	
	Earliest documented cover: *May 1, 1914*		
	FDC *(April 1914)*		

311		UnFVF	UseFVF
30¢	**orange red**	115.00	17.50
	dark orange red	115.00	17.50
	On cover		225.00
	Plate block of 6	1,250.00	
	Earliest documented cover: *May 1, 1914*		
	FDC *(April 1914)*		

312		UnFVF	UseFVF
50¢	**violet**	350.00	20.00
	pale violet	350.00	20.00
	On cover		1,750.00
	Plate block of 6	8,250.00	
	Earliest documented cover: *May 1, 1914*		
	FDC *(April 1914)*		

1912-14. Benjamin Franklin Redesigned Issue *Double-line USPS watermark (wmk 187.)*

313		UnFVF	UseFVF
50¢	**violet**	225.00	20.00
	On cover		1,750.00
	Plate block of 6, w/"A" & imprint	4,000.00	
	Margin block of 4, w/arrow	950.00	
	FDC *(Feb. 14, 1912)*		

314		UnFVF	UseFVF
$1	**violet brown**	425.00	65.00
	On cover		6,250.00
	Plate block of 6, w/"A" & imprint	9,100.00	
	Double transfer	475.00	
	Margin block of 4, w/arrow	1,950.00	
	FDC *(Feb. 14, 1912)*		

1914-15. Washington & Franklin Issue with *perforation 10. Flat plate printing, single-line USPS watermark (wmk 273.)*

315-321 *George Washington*

315		UnFVF	UseFVF
1¢	**green**	2.75	.20
	bright green	2.75	.20
	dark green	2.75	.20
	yellow green	2.75	.20
	On cover		.25
	Plate block of 6	35.00	
	Plate block of 10, w/"COIL STAMPS"	120.00	
	Cracked plate	—	
	Double transfer	4.00	
	n. Booklet pane of 6	3.75	1.25
	n1v. Booklet pane of 6, ungummed, imperforate	1,000.00	
	v. Perforated 12 x 10	750.00	650.00
	v1. Perforated 10 x 12	—	300.00
	v2. Vertical pair, imperforate horizontally	425.00	—
	v3. Vertical pair, imperforate between	8,000.00	
	Earliest documented cover: *Dec. 20, 1913*		
	FDC *(Sept. 5, 1914)*		

316		UnFVF	UseFVF
2¢	**rose red** Type I	2.25	.20
	dark carmine	2.25	.20
	dark rose	2.25	.20
	scarlet	2.25	.20
	red	2.25	.20
	rose	2.25	.20
	On cover		.25
	Plate block of 6	25.00	
	Plate block of 10, w/"COIL STAMPS"	125.00	
	Cracked plate	8.00	
	Double transfer	—	
	n. Booklet pane of 6	22.50	4.50
	v. Perforated 12 x 10	—	750.00
	Earliest documented cover: *Jan. 6, 1914*		
	FDC *(Sept. 5, 1914)*		

317		UnFVF	UseFVF
3¢	**violet** Type I	12.50	2.00
	bright violet	12.50	2.00
	dark violet	12.50	2.00
	reddish violet	12.50	2.00
	On cover		3.00

	Plate block of 6	160.00	
	FDC *(Sept. 18, 1914)*		

318		UnFVF	UseFVF
4¢	**brown**	30.00	.75
	dark brown	30.00	.75
	orange brown	30.00	.75
	yellow brown	30.00	.75
	On cover		475.00
	Plate block of 6	450.00	
	FDC *(Sept. 7, 1914)*		

319		UnFVF	UseFVF
5¢	**blue**	27.50	.70
	bright blue	27.50	.70
	dark blue	27.50	.70
	indigo blue	27.50	.70
	On cover		2.50
	Plate block of 6	375.00	
	v. Perforated 12 x 10	—	2,000.00
	Earliest documented cover: *April 14, 1915*		
	FDC *(Sept. 14, 1914)*		

320		UnFVF	UseFVF
6¢	**red orange**	45.00	2.00
	dark red orange	45.00	2.00
	pale red orange	45.00	2.00
	On cover		7.50
	Plate block of 6	475.00	
	Plate block of 6, w/imprint & star	375.00	
	Block of 4, 2 or 3mm spacing	170.00	12.50
	FDC *(Sept. 28, 1914)*		

321		UnFVF	UseFVF
7¢	**black**	75.00	5.00
	deep black	75.00	5.00
	gray black	75.00	5.00
	On cover		32.50
	Plate block of 6	800.00	
	FDC *(Sept. 10, 1914)*		

322-331 *Benjamin Franklin*

322		UnFVF	UseFVF
8¢	**yellow olive**	30.00	1.25
	dull yellow olive	30.00	1.25
	On cover		7.00
	Plate block of 6, w/"A"	475.00	
	Plate block of 6, w/"A" & imprint	425.00	
	Double transfer	—	
	v. Double impression	—	
	FDC *(Sept. 26, 1914)*		

323		UnFVF	UseFVF
9¢	**salmon**	35.00	2.00
	dark salmon	35.00	2.00
	On cover		22.50
	Plate block of 6	550.00	
	FDC *(Oct. 6, 1914)*		

324		UnFVF	UseFVF
10¢	**orange yellow**	40.00	.40
	golden yellow	40.00	.40
	yellow	40.00	.40
	On cover		6.50
	Plate block of 6	775.00	
	Plate block of 6, w/"A"	850.00	
	Plate block of 6, w/"A" & imprint	600.00	
	FDC *(Sept. 9, 1914)*		

325		UnFVF	UseFVF
11¢	**deep bluish green**	20.00	9.00
	dark green	20.00	9.00
	green	20.00	9.00
	On cover		22.50
	Plate block of 6	225.00	
	FDC *(Aug. 12, 1915)*		

326		UnFVF	UseFVF
12¢	**maroon**	23.00	4.25
	dark maroon	23.00	4.25
	copper red	25.00	4.50
	On cover		17.50
	Plate block of 6	275.00	
	Double transfer	25.00	
	Triple transfer	30.00	
	FDC *(Sept. 10, 1914)*		

So-called vertical pair, imperforate between, really have at least one perforation hole between the stamps.

327		UnFVF	UseFVF
15¢	**gray black**	110.00	8.50
	gray	110.00	8.50
	On cover		47.50
	Plate block of 6	900.00	
	Plate block of 6, w/"A"	925.00	
	Plate block of 6, w/"A" & imprint	900.00	
	FDC *(Sept. 16, 1914)*		

328		UnFVF	UseFVF
20¢	**pale ultramarine**	175.00	4.50
	ultramarine	175.00	4.50
	On cover		130.00
	Plate block of 6	2,850.00	
	FDC *(Sept. 19, 1914)*		

329		UnFVF	UseFVF
30¢	**orange red**	225.00	20.00
	dark orange red	225.00	20.00
	On cover		225.00
	Plate block of 6	3,250.00	
	FDC *(Sept. 19, 1914)*		

330		UnFVF	UseFVF
50¢	**violet**	600.00	22.50
	On cover		1,500.00
	Plate block of 6	11,500.00	
	FDC *(Dec. 13, 1915)*		

1914-15. Benjamin Franklin Issue This is the only value of the 1914-15 issues, perforated 10, printed on old paper with the double-line USPS watermark (wmk 187).

331		UnFVF	UseFVF
$1	**violet black**	725.00	85.00
	On cover		9,500.00
	Plate block of 6, w/"A" & imprint	10,500.00	
	Margin block of 4, w/arrow	3,000.00	
	Double transfer	750.00	
	FDC *(Feb. 8, 1915)*		

1915. George Washington Issue As an experiment toward finding a more satisfactory perforation, 190,000 Type I 2¢ stamps were perforated 11 and sold through the Washington post offices, mostly to large users who were asked to report concerning the perforations. *Single-line watermark USPS (wmk 273), perforated 11.*

332		UnFVF	UseFVF
2¢	**rose red** Type I	100.00	225.00
	On cover		900.00
	Plate block of 6	950.00	
	Earliest documented cover: *July 19, 1915*		

1914. George Washington Coil Issue *Coil stamps, perforated 10 horizontally.*

333		UnFVF	UseFVF
1¢	**green**	1.25	1.25
	dark green	1.25	1.25
	On cover		2.00
	Pair	2.75	3.50
	Line pair	6.50	6.00
	FDC *(Nov. 14, 1914)*		

334		UnFVF	UseFVF
2¢	**carmine** Type I	8.50	8.00
	dark carmine	8.50	8.00
	On cover		12.50
	Pair	17.50	17.50
	Line pair	45.00	60.00
	FDC *(July 22, 1914)*		

1914. George Washington Coil Issue *Coil stamps, perforated 10 vertically.*

335		UnFVF	UseFVF
1¢	**green**	22.50	7.50
	dark green	22.50	7.50
	On cover		12.50
	Pair	60.00	15.00
	Line pair	125.00	55.00
	FDC *(May 29, 1914)*		

336		UnFVF	UseFVF
2¢	**carmine** Type I	32.50	1.75
	dark carmine	32.50	1.75
	red	32.50	1.75
	On cover		10.00

		UnFVF	UseFVF
	Pair	80.00	5.00
	Line pair	175.00	17.50
	FDC *(April 25, 1914)*		

337		UnFVF	UseFVF
3¢	**violet** Type I	225.00	125.00
	dark violet	225.00	125.00
	On cover		200.00
	Pair	475.00	280.00
	Line pair	900.00	775.00
	FDC *(Dec. 18, 1914)*		

338		UnFVF	UseFVF
4¢	**brown**	120.00	47.50
	On cover		100.00
	Pair	275.00	220.00
	Line pair	600.00	550.00
	FDC *(Oct. 2, 1914)*		

339		UnFVF	UseFVF
5¢	**blue**	47.50	32.50
	On cover		52.50
	Pair	90.00	175.00
	Line pair	200.00	425.00
	FDC *(July 30, 1914)*		

1914-16. Washington & Franklin Rotary Press Coil Issue

The rotary press was first used in production of the following coil stamps. The press plates are curved into a half circle. Two plates are fitted around a cylinder and when the cylinder is rotated it prints on the paper being passed beneath it. An increase in printing speed and efficiency results as the paper is a continuous roll.

When plates are curved to fit the cylinder, there is a slight increase in the size of each stamp design in the direction the plate is curved. Designs on the flat plate presses run about 18 1/2 to 19mm wide by 22mm high. They stretch to 19 1/2 to 22mm wide on the rotary plates that are curved sidewise to the design, and to 22 1/2 to 23mm high when the plates are curved lengthwise to the design. A line of ink is deposited on the paper between stamp designs, where the two plates are joined on the cylinder.

Designs 18 1/2 to 19mm wide by 22 1/2mm high, single-line USPS watermark (wmk 273,) perforated 10 horizontally.

The designs of rotary press stamps are larger in one dimension than those of flat press stamps. The illustrations here shows to the left the rotary press coil No. 340 being taller than the flat press. The other illustration shows the rotary press coil No. 343 being wider than a flat press version No. 335.

340		UnFVF	UseFVF
1¢	**green**	6.50	4.25
	pale green	6.50	4.25
	On cover		8.00
	Pair	15.00	9.00
	Line pair	40.00	27.50
	FDC *(Dec. 12, 1915)*		

341 *Type III. Same as Type II except two lines of shading in the curves of the ribbons.*

341		UnFVF	UseFVF
2¢	**carmine** Type III	10.00	4.25
	carmine rose	10.00	4.25
	red	10.00	4.25
	On cover		9.00
	Pair	25.00	10.00
	Line pair	55.00	22.50
	v. carmine, Type I	2,000.00	325.00
	Earliest documented cover: *Dec. 21, 1915*		

1914. Washington Rotary Press Sidewise Coil Issue *Imperforate, sidewise coil. Design 19 1/2 to 20mm wide by 22mm high.*

342		UnFVF	UseFVF
2¢	**carmine** Type I	375.00	750.00
	On cover		—
	Pair	675.00	2,250.00
	Line pair	1,250.00	8,500.00
	FDC *(June 30, 1914)*		

1914-16. Washington Issue *Perforated 10 vertically. Designs 19 1/2 to 20mm wide by 22mm high.*

343		UnFVF	UseFVF
1¢	**green**	10.00	2.50
	On cover		4.00
	Pair	25.00	2,250.00
	Line pair	65.00	12.50
	Earliest documented cover: *March 22, 1915*		
	FDC *(Nov. 11, 1914)*		

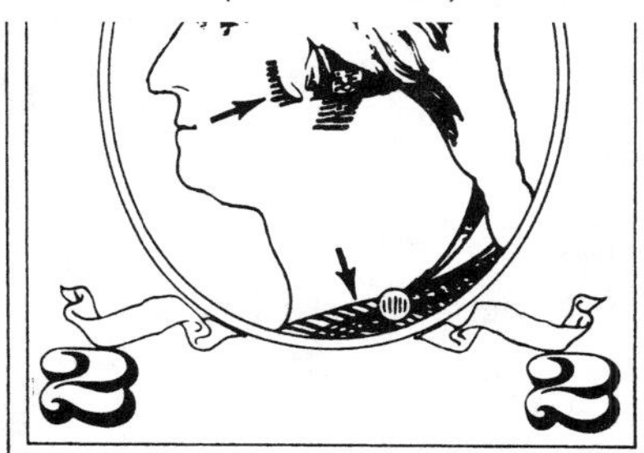

344v *Type II. Shading lines in ribbons same as Type I. The top line of toga rope is heavy, and the rope is heavily shaded. The shading lines on the face, in front of the ear, are joined by a heavy vertical curved line.*

344		UnFVF	UseFVF
2¢	**carmine** Type III	10.00	1.15
	carmine rose	10.00	1.15
	On cover		2.25
	Pair	22.50	2.75
	Line pair	55.00	7.25
	v. carmine, Type II *(June 1915)*	85.00	10.50
	v1. carmine, Type I *(June 30, 1914)*	110.00	4.25
	FDC *(Dec. 1915)*		

345		UnFVF	UseFVF
3¢	**violet** Type I	225.00	115.00
	dark violet	225.00	115.00
	red violet	225.00	115.00
	On cover		180.00
	Pair	550.00	300.00
	Line pair	1,100.00	700.00
	FDC *(Feb. 2, 1916)*		

346		UnFVF	UseFVF
4¢	**yellow brown**	27.50	20.00
	brown	27.50	20.00
	On cover		45.00
	Cracked plate	35.00	
	Pair	60.00	50.00
	Line pair	150.00	100.00
	FDC *(Nov. 5, 1915)*		

347		UnFVF	UseFVF
5¢	**blue**	32.50	17.50
	On cover		42.50
	Pair	75.00	50.00
	Line pair	180.00	100.00
	Double transfer	—	
	FDC *(March 9, 1916)*		

1916-17. Washington & Franklin Issue *Flat plate printing, unwatermarked, perforated 10.*

348		UnFVF	UseFVF
1¢	**green**	6.00	.50
	blue green	6.00	.50
	dark green	6.00	.50
	dull green	6.00	.50

		UnFVF	UseFVF
	On cover		.50
	Plate block of 6	150.00	
	Booklet pane of 6 *(Oct. 15, 1916)*	10.00	
	FDC *(Sept. 27, 1916)*		

349		UnFVF	UseFVF
2¢	**carmine** Type I	4.00	.35
	dark carmine	4.00	.35
	rose red	4.00	.35
	On cover		.50
	Double transfer	6.00	
	Plate block of 6	130.00	
	Booklet pane of 6 *(Oct. 8, 1916)*	85.00	
	FDC *(Sept. 25, 1916)*		

350		UnFVF	UseFVF
3¢	**violet** Type I	65.00	15.00
	dark violet	65.00	15.00
	On cover		40.00
	Plate block of 6	1,400.00	
	Double transfer in "CENTS"	90.00	
	FDC *(Nov. 11, 1916)*		

351		UnFVF	UseFVF
4¢	**yellow brown**	42.50	2.25
	dark brown	42.50	2.25
	On cover		12.50
	Double transfer	—	
	Plate block of 6	675.00	
	FDC *(Oct. 7, 1916)*		

352		UnFVF	UseFVF
5¢	**blue**	65.00	2.25
	dark blue	65.00	2.25
	dull blue	65.00	2.25
	On cover		12.50
	Plate block of 6	900.00	
	FDC *(Oct. 17, 1916)*		

353		UnFVF	UseFVF
5¢	**carmine**	550.00	700.00
	On cover		1,950.00
	Block of 9, one 5¢ error in middle of block of 2¢ stamps	750.00	
	Block of 12, two 5¢ errors (2 middle stamps) w/ten 2¢ stamps	1,500.00	
	Earliest documented cover: *May 25, 1917*		

353 The "Five Cent Red Error" was caused by mistakenly using a 5¢ transfer roll in reentering three positions on plate 7942, a plate of the 2¢ stamps. Of the 400 positions on the plate, 397 copies were 2¢ and three copies were 5¢. The error was not discovered until a considerable number of sheets were in the post offices, and many of them were picked up by collectors. The errors exist perforated 10 (No. 353), perforated 11 (No. 385), and imperforate (No. 370). The shade actually is carmine, but the stamp commonly is called the "Red Error."

354		UnFVF	UseFVF
6¢	**red orange**	80.00	7.50
	orange	80.00	7.50
	On cover		40.00
	Double transfer	—	
	Plate block of 6	1,400.00	
	FDC *(Oct. 10, 1916)*		

355		UnFVF	UseFVF
7¢	**black**	100.00	12.50
	deep black	100.00	12.50
	gray black	100.00	12.50
	On cover		45.00
	Plate block of 6	1,400.00	
	FDC *(Nov. 10, 1916)*		

356		UnFVF	UseFVF
8¢	**yellow olive**	55.00	6.50
	dark yellow olive	55.00	6.50
	On cover		30.00
	Plate block of 6, w/"A"	625.00	
	Plate block of , w/"A" & imprint	575.00	
	FDC *(Nov. 13, 1916)*		

357		UnFVF	UseFVF
9¢	**salmon**	50.00	15.00
	On cover		40.00
	Plate block of 6	775.00	
	FDC *(Nov. 16,1916)*		

358		UnFVF	UseFVF
10¢	**orange yellow**	95.00	1.25
	On cover		8.00
	Plate block of 6	1,400.00	
	FDC *(Oct. 17, 1916)*		

359		UnFVF	UseFVF
11¢	**deep bluish green**	35.00	22.50
	On cover		45.00
	Plate block of 6	375.00	
	FDC *(Nov. 16, 1916)*		

360		UnFVF	UseFVF
12¢	**chocolate**	45.00	5.50
	On cover		22.50
	Plate block of 6	650.00	
	Double transfer	60.00	6.00
	Triple transfer	70.00	9.00
	FDC *(Oct. 10, 1916)*		

361		UnFVF	UseFVF
15¢	**gray black**	165.00	12.50
	gray	165.00	12.50
	On cover		85.00
	Plate block of 6	2,900.00	
	Plate block of 6, w/"A" & imprint	—	
	FDC *(Nov. 16, 1916)*		

362		UnFVF	UseFVF
20¢	**pale blue**	225.00	12.50
	blue	225.00	12.50
	On cover		725.00
	Plate block of 6	3,750.00	
	FDC *(Dec. 5, 1916)*		

362A		UnFVF	UseFVF
30¢	**orange red**	4,500.00	—
	Plate block of 6	—	

362A Two sheets of 100 stamps of the 30¢ denomination were discovered without any trace of watermark, as authenticated by The Philatelic Foundation's expert committee.

363		UnFVF	UseFVF
50¢	**light violet**	950.00	65.00
	On cover		2,250.00
	Plate block of 6	42,500.00	
	FDC *(March 2, 1917)*		

364		UnFVF	UseFVF
$1	**violet black**	625.00	20.00
	On cover		3,000.00
	Block of 6, w/"A" & imprint	14,000.00	
	Margin block of 4, w/arrow	3,250.00	
	Double transfer	850.00	22.50
	FDC *(Dec. 22, 1916)*		

1917. James Madison Issue

365 *James Madison*

365		UnFVF	UseFVF
$2	**dark blue**	325.00	45.00
	On cover		1,750.00
	Plate block of 6	5,000.00	
	Margin block 4, w/arrow	1,450.00	
	Double transfer	—	
	EKU *(April 10, 1917)*		

1917. John Marshall Issue

366 *John Marshall*

		UnFVF	UseFVF
366			
$5	**light green**	250.00	50.00
	On cover	1,750.00	
	Plate block of 6	4,000.00	
	Margin block 4, w/arrow	1,150.00	
	EKU *(April 10, 1917)*		

1916-1917. George Washington Issue *Imperforate.*

		UnFVF	UseFVF
367			
1¢	**green**	1.15	1.00
	bluish green	1.15	1.00
	dark green	1.15	1.00
	On cover		1.50
	Plate block of 6	12.50	
	Center line block	8.50	6.25
	Margin block of 4, w/arrow	4.50	3.25
	Double transfer	2.50	1.25
	FDC *(Dec. 8, 1916)*		

		UnFVF	UseFVF
368			
2¢	**carmine** Type I	1.40	1.30
	carmine rose	1.40	1.30
	dark carmine	1.40	1.30
	dark rose	1.40	1.30
	On cover		2.50
	Plate block of 6	22.50	
	Plate block of 6, from plate No. 7942	175.00	
	Center line block	8.50	7.00
	Cracked plate	—	
	Margin block of 4, w/arrow	6.50	5.75
	FDC *(Dec. 8, 1916)*		

368A	**deep rose,** Type 1a	15,000.00	
2¢	On cover	22,500.00	
	Pair (one example known)	105,000.00	
	EKU *(Feb. 17, 1920)*		

Type Ia is similar to Type I, but lines of the design are stronger. This is particularly noticeable on the toga button, toga rope and rope shading lines, which are heavy. Lines in the ribbons are similar to Type I.

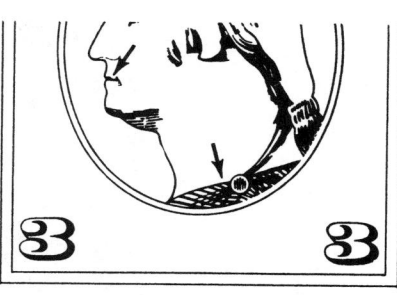

369 *On Type II the top line of the toga rope is heavy and the rope shading lines are also heavy and complete. The line between the lips is heavy.*

		UnFVF	UseFVF
369			
3¢	**violet** Type I	15.00	8.50
	dull violet	15.00	8.50
	On cover		17.50
	Plate block of 6	125.00	
	Center line block	70.00	70.00
	Double transfer	17.50	
	Margin block of 4, w/arrow	60.00	35.00
	Triple transfer	—	
	v. violet, Type II	12.50	5.50
	dark violet	12.50	5.50
	On cover		11.50
	Plate block of 6	100.00	
	Center line block	60.00	60.00
	Margin block of 4, w/arrow	47.50	30.00
	Double transfer	12.50	
	Earliest documented cover: *(April 30, 1918)*		
	FDC *(Oct. 13, 1917)*		

		UnFVF	UseFVF
370			
5¢	**carmine**	12,500.00	
	On cover		—
	Block of 9, one 5¢ error in middle of block of 2¢ stamps	15,000.00	
	Block of 12, two 5¢ errors (two middle stamps) w/ten 2¢ stamps	30,800.00	
	FDC *(March 1917)*		

This stamp commonly is called the "Red Error," but really is carmine. See note with No. 353.

1916-22. Washington Rotary Press Coil Issue *unwatermarked, perforated 10 horizontally. Stamp designs 18 1/2 to 19mm wide by 22 1/2 high.*

		UnFVF	UseFVF
371			
1¢	**green**	.75	.20
	yellowish green	.75	.20
	On cover		.50
	Pair	2.00	.65
	Line pair	4.00	.75
	Cracked plate	—	
	Double transfer	2.25	
	FDC *(Jan. 10, 1918)*		

		UnFVF	UseFVF
372			
2¢	**carmine** Type III	3.00	1.75
	On cover		3.50
	Pair	5.75	4.00
	Line pair	20.00	
	Cracked plate	12.00	7.50
	v. carmine, Type II *(Nov. 15, 1916)*	14.50	4.75
	On cover		10.00
	Pair	32.50	7.50
	Line pair	125.00	
	Cracked plate	—	
	FDC *(1919)*		

		UnFVF	UseFVF
373			
3¢	**violet** Type I	4.50	1.50
	bluish violet	4.50	1.50
	dull violet	4.50	1.50
	On cover		2.50
	Pair	11.00	4.00
	Line pair	27.50	10.00
	FDC *(Oct. 10, 1917)*		

1916-22. Washington Issue *Perforated 10 vertically. Stamp designs 19 1/2 to 20mm wide by 22mm high.*

		UnFVF	UseFVF
374			
1¢	**green**	.60	.20
	yellowish green	.60	.20
	On cover		.50
	Pair	1.25	.65
	Line pair	4.00	1.25
	Cracked plate	7.50	
	Double transfer	—	
	Rosette crack on head	50.00	
	FDC *(Nov. 17, 1916)*		

		UnFVF	UseFVF
375			
2¢	**carmine** Type III	8.50	.20
	carmine rose	8.50	.20
	On cover		.50
	Pair	21.00	.65
	Line pair	50.00	3.50
	Cracked plate	—	
	Double transfer	—	
	v. carmine, Type II *(Nov. 17, 1916)*	1,650.00	800.00
	On cover		850.00
	Pair	4,000.00	17.50
	Line pair	9,000.00	5,000.00
	FDC *(Nov. 17, 1916)*		

		UnFVF	UseFVF
376			
3¢	**violet** Type II	11.50	1.25
	dull violet	11.50	1.25
	gray violet	11.50	1.25
	On cover		1.00
	Pair	24.00	2.25
	Line pair	60.00	2.75
	v1. violet, Type I *(July 23, 1917)*	17.50	3.25
	reddish violet	17.50	3.25
	On cover		7.00
	Pair	35.00	8.00
	Line pair	125.00	45.00
	FDC *(Feb. 4, 1918)*		

		UnFVF	UseFVF
377			
4¢	**yellow brown**	10.50	4.00
	On cover		8.50
	Pair	24.00	10.00
	Line pair	65.00	17.50
	Cracked plate	—	
	FDC *(Oct. 19, 1917)*		

378		UnFVF	UseFVF
5¢	**blue**	3.50	1.25
	On cover		1.75
	Pair	8.00	2.25
	Line pair	25.00	7.00
	FDC *(Jan. 15, 1919)*		

379		UnFVF	UseFVF
10¢	**orange yellow**	19.00	12.50
	On cover		17.50
	Pair	47.50	27.50
	Line pair	125.00	50.00
	FDC *(Jan. 31, 1922)*		5,300.00

1917-19 Washington & Franklin Issue *Flat Press printing, unwatermarked paper, and perforated 11.*

380		UnFVF	UseFVF
1¢	**green**	.55	.20
	dark green	.55	.20
	pale green	.55	.20
	yellowish green	.55	.20
	On cover		.35
	Plate block of 6	17.50	
	Cracked plate	7.50	
	Double transfer	5.50	2.00
	n. Booklet pane of 6	2.75	.35
	n1. Booklet pane of 30	1,100.00	
	v. Double impression	175.00	
	v1. Horizontal pair, imperforate between	200.00	
	v2. Perforated 10 at top	675.00	
	v3. Perforated 10 at bottom	675.00	
	v4. Vertical pair, imperforate between	500.00	
	v5. Vertical pair, imperforate horizontally	150.00	
	Earliest documented cover: *(Sept. 10, 1917)*		
	FDC *(March 23, 1917)*		

381		UnFVF	UseFVF
2¢	**rose red** Type I	.50	.20
	dark rose	.50	.20
	rose carmine	.50	.20
	On cover		.35
	Plate block of 6	18.00	
	Cracked plate	—	
	Double transfer	6.00	
	Retouch in hair	—	
	Double impression	160.00	
	n. Booklet pane of 6 *(March 31, 1917)*	4.50	
	n1. Booklet pane of 30	27,500.00	
	v. Horizontal pair, imperforate vertically	200.00	125.00
	v1. Vertical pair, imperforate between	500.00	250.00
	v2. Vertical pair, imperforate horizontally	150.00	
	a. deep rose, Type Ia	225.00	175.00
	dark rose	225.00	175.00
	On cover		325.00
	Plate block of 6	1,800.00	
	Plate block of 6, two stamps Type I	7,500.00	
	Pair, 1 each Type I & Ia	1,000.00	
	Earliest documented cover: *(Aug. 12, 1917)*		
	FDC *(March 23, 1917)*		

382		UnFVF	UseFVF
3¢	**violet** Type I	12.50	.20
	dark violet	12.50	.20
	dull violet	12.50	.20
	reddish violet	12.50	.20
	On cover		.35
	Plate block of 6	100.00	
	n. Booklet pane of 6 *(Oct. 17, 1917)*	60.00	17.50
	v. Double impression	200.00	
	v1. Vertical pair, imperforate horizontally	400.00	
	FDC *(March 23, 1917)*		

382A		UnFVF	UseFVF
3¢	**violet** Type II	15.00	.40
	dark violet	15.00	.40
	On cover		.65
	Plate block of 6	150.00	
	n. Booklet pane of 6	50.00	
	v. Double impression	200.00	
	v1. Perforated 10 at top	625.00	
	v2. Perforated 10 at bottom	625.00	
	v3. Vertical pair, imperforate horizontally	250.00	150.00
	Earliest documented cover: *(June 18, 1918)*		
	FDC *(Feb. 25, 1918)*		

383		UnFVF	UseFVF
4¢	**yellow brown**	11.50	.30
	brown	11.50	.30
	dark brown	11.50	.30
	orange brown	11.50	.30
	On cover		2.00
	Plate block of 6	140.00	
	Double transfer	15.00	
	v. Double impression	—	
	FDC *(March 23, 1917)*		

384		UnFVF	UseFVF
5¢	**blue**	8.50	.25
	dark blue	8.50	.25
	dull blue	8.50	.25
	On cover		.35
	Plate block of 6	125.00	
	Double transfer	10.50	
	v. Horizontal pair, imperforate between	2,250.00	
	FDC *(March 23, 1917)*		

385		UnFVF	UseFVF
5¢	**carmine**	400.00	500.00
	On cover		1,500.00
	Strip of 3 (Nos. 381-385-381)	500.00	
	Block of 9, one 5¢ error in middle of 2¢ block	600.00	
	Block of 12, two 5¢ errors (2 middle stamps) within ten 2¢ stamps	1,000.00	
	Earliest documented cover: *(March 27, 1917)*		

This stamp commonly is called the "Red Error" but really is carmine. See note with No. 353.

386		UnFVF	UseFVF
6¢	**red orange**	12.50	.40
	orange	12.50	.40
	On cover		2.50
	Plate block of 6	145.00	
	Double transfer	—	
	v. Perforated 10 at bottom	650.00	
	v1. Perforated 10 at top	650.00	
	FDC *(March 23, 1917)*		

387		UnFVF	UseFVF
7¢	**black**	25.00	1.25
	deep black	25.00	1.25
	gray black	25.00	1.25
	On cover		8.00
	Plate block of 6	220.00	
	Double transfer	—	
	FDC *(March 24, 1917)*		

388		UnFVF	UseFVF
8¢	**yellow olive**	12.50	1.00
	dark olive green	12.50	1.00
	olive green	12.50	1.00
	On cover		300.00
	Plate block of 6	125.00	
	Plate block of 6, w/"A"	150.00	
	Plate block of 6, w/"A" & imprint	200.00	
	v. Perforated 10 at bottom		3,250.00
	v1. Perforated 10 at top		3,250.00
	v2. Vertical pair, imperforate between	—	
	FDC *(March 24, 1917)*		

389		UnFVF	UseFVF
9¢	**salmon**	14.00	2.50
	On cover		15.00
	Plate block of 6	125.00	
	Double transfer	20.00	5.00
	v. Perforated 10 at bottom	1,000.00	
	v1. Perforated 10 at top	1,000.00	
	FDC *(March 12,1917)*		

390		UnFVF	UseFVF
10¢	**orange yellow**	17.50	.25
	On cover		2.00
	Plate block of 6	165.00	
	Plate block of 6, w/"A"	300.00	
	FDC *(March 24, 1917)*		

391		UnFVF	UseFVF
11¢	**deep bluish green**	9.00	3.00
	dull green	9.00	3.00
	green	9.00	3.00
	On cover		8.50
	Plate block of 6	115.00	

	Double transfer	12.50	3.25
	v. Perforated 10 at bottom	1,000.00	375.00
	v1. Perforated 10 at top	1,000.00	375.00
	FDC *(May 19, 1917)*		

392		UnFVF	UseFVF
12¢	**brown purple**	9.00	.65
	a. brown carmine	9.00	.65
	On cover		4.00
	Plate block of 6	115.00	
	Double transfer	12.50	
	Triple transfer	20.00	
	v. Perforated 10 at bottom	14.00	6.00
	v1. Perforated 10 at top	14.00	6.00
	FDC *(May 12, 1917)*		

393		UnFVF	UseFVF
13¢	**apple green**	10.50	6.50
	dark apple green	10.50	6.50
	pale apple green	10.50	6.50
	On cover		20.00
	Plate block of 6	125.00	
	FDC *(Jan. 11, 1919)*		

394		UnFVF	UseFVF
15¢	**gray black**	37.50	1.25
	gray	37.50	1.25
	On cover		22.50
	Plate block of 6	450.00	
	Double transfer	—	
	FDC *(May 21, 1917)*		

395		UnFVF	UseFVF
20¢	**pale blue**	47.50	.50
	dark blue	47.50	.50
	gray blue	47.50	.50
	On cover		.75
	Plate block of 6	500.00	
	Double transfer	—	
	v. Double impression	1,250.00	
	v1. Perforated 10 at bottom	1,600.00	
	v2. Perforated 10 at top	1,600.00	
	v3. Vertical pair, imperforate between	425.00	
	FDC *(May 12, 1917)*		

396		UnFVF	UseFVF
30¢	**orange red**	37.50	1.25
	dark orange red	37.50	1.25
	On cover		150.00
	Plate block of 6	500.00	
	Double transfer	—	
	v. Double impression	—	
	v1. Perforated 10 at bottom	1,100.00	
	v2. Perforated 10 at top	1,100.00	
	FDC *(May 12, 1917)*		

397		UnFVF	UseFVF
50¢	**reddish violet**	65.00	.90
	pale violet	65.00	.90
	red violet	65.00	.90
	On cover		400.00
	Plate block of 6	1,650.00	
	Double transfer	100.00	1.50
	v. Perforated 10 at bottom	—	950.00
	v1. Perforated 10 at top	—	950.00
	v2. Vertical pair, imperforate between	1,800.00	1,000.00
	FDC *(May 19, 1917)*		

398		UnFVF	UseFVF
$1	**black purple**	55.00	1.75
	brown purple	55.00	1.75
	blackish brown	1,100.00	750.00
	On cover		550.00
	Plate block of 6, w/"A" & imprint	1,350.00	
	Double transfer	75.00	2.00
	Margin block of 4, w/arrow	250.00	
	FDC *(May 19, 1917)*		

1917. George Washington Issue The 2¢ carmine stamp of 1908-09 issues existed in 1917 in the imperforate form at the New York Post Office. The old stock was returned to the Bureau of Engraving and Printing and was perforated with the then-current perforation. It is identical to No. 238 except for the perforation and is listed here according to the year of its release. *Flat plate printing, double-line USPS watermark (wmk 187), perforated 11.*

399		UnFVF	UseFVF
2¢	**carmine**	275.00	450.00
	On cover		2,000.00
	Plate block of 6, w/imprint	2,250.00	
	Earliest documented cover: *(Oct. 10, 1917)*		

1918-20. Benjamin Franklin Issue New, horizontal designs. *Flat plate printing, unwatermarked, perforated 11.*

400, 401 *Benjamin Franklin*

400		UnFVF	UseFVF
$2	**orange & black**	650.00	225.00
	On cover		1,850.00
	Center line block	3,000.00	
	Margin block of 4, w/arrow	2,800.00	
	Plate block of 8, w/arrow	13,500.00	
	FDC *(Aug. 23, 1918)*		

401		UnFVF	UseFVF
$2	**carmine & black**	190.00	40.00
	lilac carmine & black	190.00	40.00
	Plate block of 8, w/arrow	—	
	Center line block	—	
	Margin block of 4, w/arrow	—	
	On cover		—
	FDC *(Nov. 1, 1920)*		

402 *Benjamin Franklin*

402		UnFVF	UseFVF
$5	**deep green & black**	225.00	35.00
	On cover		1,500.00
	Center line block	1,050.00	
	Margin block of 4, w/arrow	1,000.00	
	Plate block of 8, w/arrow	3,850.00	
	FDC *(Aug. 23, 1918)*		

1918-20. George Washington Issue Offset Printing. This is the first time the Post Office Department did not use engraved plates. It was a direct result of World War I. During this period the Bureau of Engraving and Printing was hard pressed by the demands for stamps and government printing of all types. Printing inks for postage stamps used barites as a base, and as the war went on this basic material grew inferior in quality and contained a gritty substance that wore out the engraved plates more quickly; high quality steel was difficult to obtain, so all conditions combined resulted in the unsatisfactory experiment of offset printing. These stamps can easily be identified by the smoothness of the printed surface when contrast with any of the earlier stamps, all of which were engraved. This can be told apart by actual touch, as the engraved stamps have a "rough" feeling, and the offsets a "soapy" feeling. If you hold an engraved stamp at a flat angle against a light and observe it through a magnifying glass, the actual ridges of the ink may be observed, while on the offsets there is no fine detail, and the stamps have a blurred appearance. The offsets are smaller than the engraved, usually about 1/2mm narrower in width (with the exception of the Type IV 3¢) and from 1/2mm to 1mm less in length. The offsets run from 21 to 21 1/2mm high. Three denominations were made in this style of printing, 1¢, 2¢, and 3¢, each value being *perforated 11* and *imperforate,* and the 1¢ also came *perforated 12 1/2. Unwatermarked, perforated 11.*

Exact dates of issue are not known; dates listed are approximate.

403 *George Washington*

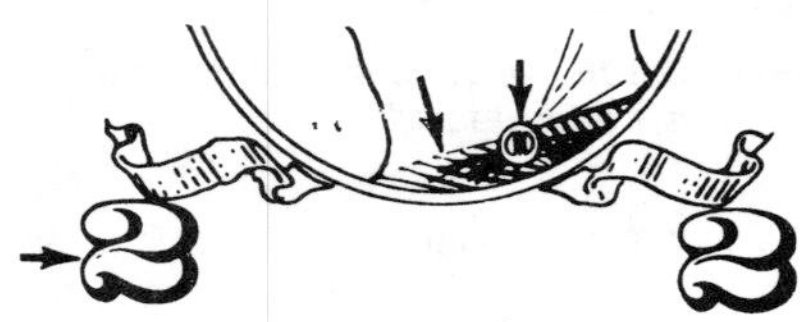

Type IV: *Top line of toga rope is broken. Lines inside toga button read "D (reversed) ID." The line of color in the left "2" is very thin and is usually broken.*

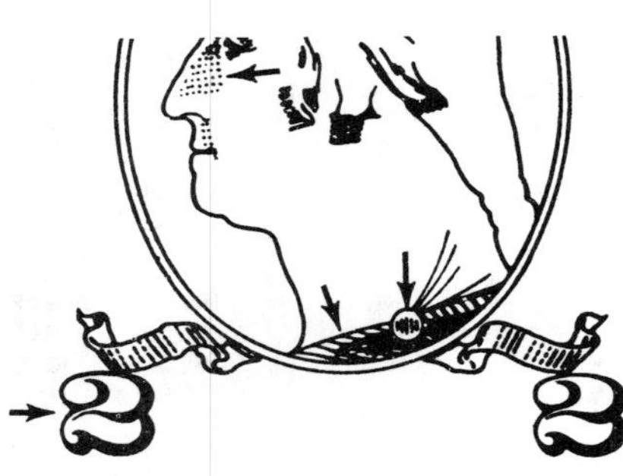

Type V: Top line of the toga is complete. Five vertical shading lines in toga button. Line of color in left "2" is very thin and usually broken. Shading dots on nose from a traingle with six dots in third row from bottom.

Type Va: Same as Type V except on the shading dots on the nose, in which the third row from the bottom has only four dots instead of six.

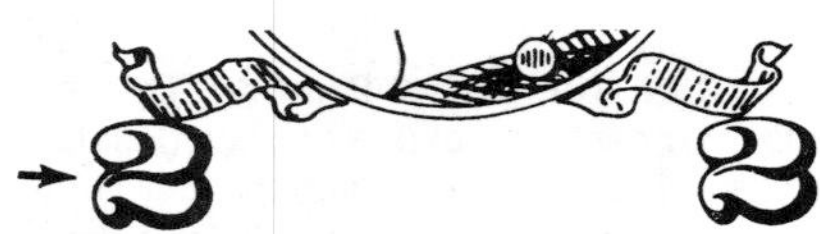

Type VI: Same as Type V but there is a heavy line of color in the left "2."

Type VII: *The line of color in the left "2" is clear and unbroken, heavier than on Type V or Va but not as heavy as on Type VI. An extra vertical row of dots has been added on the lip, making four rows of three dots instead of two dots. Additional dots have been added to the hair on top of the head.*

		UnFVF	UseFVF
403			
1¢	**dull green**	2.00	.75
	a. dark green	2.25	.75
	emerald	2.00	.75
	On cover		1.50
	Plate block of 6	16.50	
	"Flat nose" (nose appears so)	—	
	v. Double impression	25.00	
	v1. Horizontal pair, imperforate between	95.00	
	FDC *(Dec. 24, 1918)*		

404-404D *George Washington. There are five types of the 2¢ offset stamps, each of which appears only on the offset stamps.*

		UnFVF	UseFVF
404			
2¢	**rose red** Type VII	17.50	.35
	On cover		.40
	Plate block of 6	135.00	
	Retouch on cheek	375.00	
	v. Double impression	65.00	
	Earliest documented cover: *(Nov. 10, 1920)*		
404A		**UnFVF**	**UseFVF**
2¢	**rose red** Type V	15.00	1.00
	bright carmine	15.00	1.00
	rose carmine	15.00	1.00
	On cover		2.50
	Plate block of 6	125.00	
	Line through "2" & "EN"	30.00	
	v. Double impression	55.00	8.50
	v1. Horizontal pair, imperforate vertically	—	
	v2. Vertical pair, imperforate horizontally	850.00	
	Earliest documented cover: *(April 20, 1920)*		
404B		**UnFVF**	**UseFVF**
2¢	**rose red** Type Va	8.00	.35
	On cover		65.00
	Plate block of 6	75.00	
	Plate block of 6, w/monogram over number "CRNTS" rather than "CENTS"	90.00	
	Retouch of "P" in "POSTAGE"	50.00	
	Retouch on toga	—	
	v. Double impression	25.00	
	v1. Vertical pair, imperforate between	1,250.00	
	Earliest documented cover: *(July 16, 1920)*		
404C		**UnFVF**	**UseFVF**
2¢	**rose red** Type VI	45.00	1.50
	bright carmine	45.00	1.50
	On cover		3.75
	Plate block of 6	350.00	
	Plate block of 6, w/monogram over number	450.00	
	v. Double impression	150.00	
	v1. Vertical pair, imperforate between	—	
	v2. Vertical pair, imperforate horizontally	—	
	Earliest documented cover: *(July 30, 1920)*		
404D		**UnFVF**	**UseFVF**
2¢	**rose red** Type IV	25.00	4.25
	carmine	25.00	4.25
	On cover		10.00
	Plate block of 6	185.00	
	Misformed "2" at left	35.00	
	Scar on forehead	45.00	
	FDC *(March 15, 1920)*		825.00

1918. George Washington Issue

405 *George Washington. There are two types of the 3¢ offset stamps, each of which appears only on the offset stamps.*

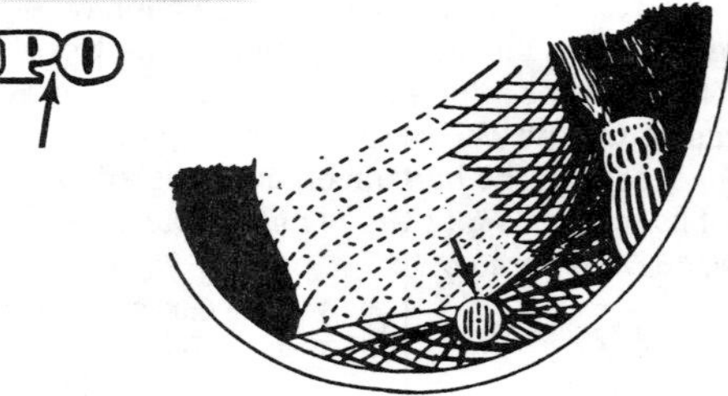

Type III: *Top line of toga is strong but the fifth shading line is missing. The center shading line of the toga button consists of two vertical dashes with a dot between them. The "P" and "O" of "POSTAGE" have a line of color between them.*

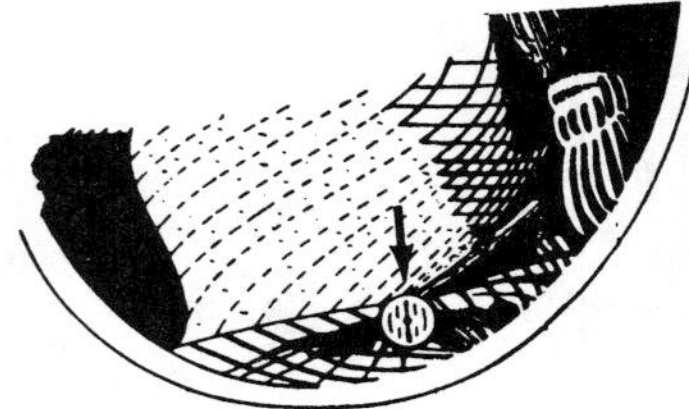

Type IV: *The "P" and "O" of "POSTAGE" are joined with no line of color between them. The center shading line runs right through the dot in the toga button.*

		UnFVF	UseFVF
405			
3¢	**purple** Type III	3.00	.40
	dark purple	3.00	.40
	dull purple	3.00	.40
	On cover		.50
	Plate block of 6	40.00	
	v. Double impression	35.00	
	v1. Printed on both sides	425.00	
	FDC *(March 23, 1918)*		

		UnFVF	UseFVF
405A			
3¢	**purple** Type IV	1.25	.20
	dull purple	1.25	.20
	violet	1.25	.20
	On cover		.25
	Plate block of 6	15.00	
	"Blister" under "U.S."	4.25	
	Retouch under "U.S."	4.25	
	v. Double impression	17.50	6.00
	v1. Printed on both sides	225.00	
	Earliest documented cover: *(June 30, 1918)*		

1919-20. George Washington Issue *Imperforate offset stamps.*

		UnFVF	UseFVF
406			
1¢	**dull green**	10.00	8.50
	green	10.00	8.50
	On cover		15.00
	Plate block of 6	75.00	
	Center line block	55.00	45.00
	Margin block of 4, w/arrow	40.00	36.00
	FDC *(Jan. 21, 1919)*		

		UnFVF	UseFVF
407			
2¢	**rose red** Type IV	35.00	30.00
	On cover		65.00
	Plate block of 6	285.00	
	Center line block	200.00	
	Margin block of 4, w/arrow	175.00	
	Earliest documented cover: *(April 30, 1920)*		

		UnFVF	UseFVF
407A			
2¢	**rose red** Type V	190.00	85.00
	On cover		200.00
	Plate block of 6	1,750.00	
	Center line block	900.00	450.00
	Margin block of 4, w/arrow	800.00	
	Earliest documented cover: *(June 30, 1920)*		

		UnFVF	UseFVF
407B			
2¢	**rose red** Type Va	12.50	8.50
	carmine	12.50	8.50
	On cover		14.00
	Plate block of 6	85.00	
	Plate block of 6, w/monograph over number	200.00	
	Center line block	50.00	60.00
	Margin block of 4, w/arrow	50.00	40.00
	Earliest documented cover: *(July 3, 1920)*		

		UnFVF	UseFVF
407C			
2¢	**rose red** Type VI	35.00	22.50
	On cover		35.00
	Plate block of 6	300.00	
	Center line block	190.00	175.00
	Margin block of 4, w/arrow	165.00	
	Earliest documented cover: *(Sept. 7, 1920)*		

		UnFVF	UseFVF
407D			
2¢	**rose red** Type VII	1,500.00	575.00
	On cover		1,050.00
	Plate block of 6	12,500.00	
	Center line block	7,700.00	
	Margin block of 4, w/arrow	5,500.00	
	Earliest documented cover: *(Nov. 3, 1920)*		

		UnFVF	UseFVF
408			
3¢	**violet** Type IV	8.75	6.00
	On cover		11.00
	Plate block of 6	50.00	
	Center line block	45.00	45.00
	Margin block of 4, w/arrow	40.00	30.00
	v. Double impression	100.00	
	Earliest documented cover: *(Oct. 5, 1918)*		

1919. George Washington Issue The 1¢ offset was issued with a trial perforation 12 1/2 made by the Rossbach perforating machine, a two-way rotary perforator that perforated a single sheet one direction, and then the other. The machine proved unsatisfactory as nearly half of the sheets that were perforated had to be destroyed. Of the 6,641 sheets of 400 images that were perforated by this machine, only 3,466 were good enough to send to the post offices. These were cut into panes of 100 before they were issued. Even the sheets that were released consisted, for the most part, of very badly centered stamps. *Perforated 12 1/2.*

		UnFVF	UseFVF
409			
1¢	**dull green**	14.00	16.50
	On cover		50.00
	Plate block of 6	140.00	
	v. Horizontal pair, imperforate vertically	450.00	
	FDC *(Aug. 15, 1919)*		

The Rotary Press Issues that follow form the final group of issues that bear the Washington design of 1914-15. Here is how rotary press intaglio stamps can be distinguished from stamps of similar designs printed by flat press intaglio or offset:

1. Rotary press stamps are always wider or taller than flat press or offset stamps. This measurement concerns the printed design only.
2. The back of a rotary press stamp is almost always free of color, while flat press stamps often have small bits of color on the back.
3. With the exception of stamps printed from coil waste, the perforated rotary press stamps will show one or more ridges extending across the back of the stamp. These ridges were forced into the paper in an effort to keep the stamps from curling. This easily is apparent on unused stamps, but much more difficult to detect on used stamps. Most flat press stamps do not have these ridges.

1919. George Washington Issue Designs 19 1/2 to 20mm wide by 22mm high. Printed from coil waste sheets, no "breaker bar" ridges on back of stamps, unwatermarked, perforated 11 x 10.

410 *George Washington*

		UnFVF	UseFVF
410			
1¢	**green**	8.00	8.00
	bluish green	8.00	8.00
	yellowish green	8.00	8.00
	On cover		20.00
	Plate block of 4	75.00	
	Plate block of 4, w/star	90.00	
	Plate block of , w/"S 30"	100.00	
	Double transfer	15.00	
	v. Vertical pair, imperforate horizontally		50.00
	v1. Block of 4, imperforate horizontally	100.00	
	v2. Plate block of 6, imperforate horizontally	750.00	
	FDC *(June 14, 1919)*		

Users of this Catalog are invited to write to us if they have information which they feel will supplement or correct any material contained herein. All such communications will be answered.

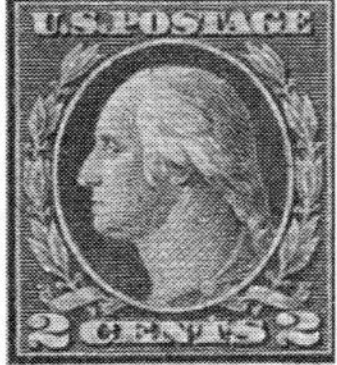

411 *George Washington*

411		UnFVF	UseFVF
2¢	**carmine red** Type II	2,500.00	3,200.00
	Plate block of 4	10,500.00	
	Plate block of 4, w/"S 20"	17,500.00	

411A		UnFVF	UseFVF
2¢	**carmine red** Type III	10.00	9.00
	On cover		22.50
	Plate block of 4	.75	
	Plate block of 4, w/star	125.00	
	Plate block of 4, w/"S 30"	75.00	
	Plate block of 4, w/inverted "S 30"	400.00	
	Double transfer	17.50	
	v. Horizontal pair, imperforate vertically	750.00	
	v1. Vertical pair, imperforate horizontally	50.00	50.00
	v2. Block of 4, imperforate horizontally	100.00	
	FDC *(June 14, 1919)*		

412 *George Washington*

412		UnFVF	UseFVF
3¢	**gray lilac** Type II	32.50	35.00
	On cover		85.00
	Plate block of 4	250.00	
	FDC *(June 14, 1919)*		

1920. George Washington Issue *Rotary press, stamp designs 18 1/2 to 19mm wide by 22 1/2mm high, unwatermarked, perforated 10 x 11, breaker bar ridges on stamps.*

413		UnFVF	UseFVF
1¢	**green**	10.00	1.00
	bluish green	10.00	1.00
	On cover		5.50
	Plate block of 6 (vertical), w/plate number opposite center horizontal row	135.00	
	FDC *(May 26, 1920)*		2,000.00

1921. George Washington Issue *Rotary press, stamp designs 18 1/2 to 19mm wide by 22 1/2mm high, unwatermarked, perforated 10, breaker bar ridges on stamps.*

414		UnFVF	UseFVF
1¢	**green**	.55	.20
	dark green	.55	.20
	On cover		.35
	Plate block of 6 (vertical), number opposite center horizontal row	27.50	
	Plate block of 4	12.50	
	Double transfer	—	
	Triple transfer	—	
	v. Horizontal pair, imperforate between	975.00	
	FDC *(May 26, 1921)*		

1922. George Washington Issue chronologically, the last of the Washington-Franklin stamps, apparently produced to use up waste sheets. *Rotary press, stamp design 19mm wide by 22 1/2mm high, unwatermarked, perforated 11, breaker bar ridges on stamps.*

415		UnFVF	UseFVF
1¢	**green**	15,000.00	3,200.00
	On cover		3,500.00
	Earliest documented cover: *Dec. 21, 1922*		

1921. George Washington Issue *Rotary press, stamp design 19 1/2 to 20mm wide by 22mm high, unwatermarked, perforated 11, no breaker bar ridges.*

416 *George Washington*

416		UnFVF	UseFVF
1¢	**green**	120.00	130.00
	On cover		1,800.00
	Plate block of 4	900.00	
	Plate block of 4, w/star	950.00	
	Plate block of 4, w/"S 30"	850.00	
	Earliest documented cover: *June 25, 1921*		

417 *George Washington*

417		UnFVF	UseFVF
2¢	**carmine** Type III	85.00	115.00
	On cover		700.00
	Plate block of 4	700.00	
	Plate block of 4, w/star	725.00	
	Plate block of 4, w/"S 30"	675.00	
	Recut in hair	120.00	
	v. Perforated 10 on left side	—	
	Earliest documented cover: *May 5, 1921*		

1922-34. Regular Issue Series

Featured famous people and scenes within two similar frames. Some of the denominations were produced, in part, with what are known as "Star Plates." On these particular plates the vertical rows are spaced 3mm apart instead of 2 3/4mm in an effort to improve the perforating. The plates are identified with a large 5-point or 6-point star placed with the plate number. *Flat plate printing, unwatermarked, perforated 11.*

1925. Nathan Hale Issue in the Regular Issue Series of 1922-34 was the first fractional-value postage stamp issued by the United States. Honored Hale, a school teacher and a 21-year-old captain in the Continental Army, who in 1776 volunteered for spy duty behind the British lines on Long Island. Captured by the British on Sept. 21, he was hanged the next morning and his body left hanging for several days. His last words were: "I only regret that I have but one life to lose for my country."

418, 473 *Nathan Hale from a statue by Bela Lyon Pratt, Yale Campus*

418		UnFVF	UseFVF
1/2¢	**olive brown**	.30	.20
	dark olive brown	.25	.20
	dull olive brown	.25	.20
	Plate block of 6	4.50	
	Plate flaw on fraction bar	.75	.20
	FDC *(April 4, 1925)* (Washington, D.C.)		18.00
	FDC (New Haven)		25.00

1923. Benjamin Franklin Issue in the Regular Issue Series of 1922-34.

419, 443, 446, 448, 449A, 450, 461, 469, 474, 495, 506 *Benjamin Franklin*

419		UnFVF	UseFVF
1¢	**green**	1.50	.20
	dark green	1.50	.20

	dull green	1.50	.20
	Plate block of 6	17.50	
	Double transfer	3.50	
	n. Booklet pane of 6	7.00	
	Earliest documented cover: *Jan. 10, 1924*		
	FDC *(Jan. 17, 1923)* FDC (Washington, D.C.)		30.00
	FDC (Philadelphia)		47.50

1925. Warren Harding Issue in the Regular Issue Series of 1922-34. Honored the 29th president, who had died suddenly on a trip to San Francisco, Calif., two years earlier. Harding (1865-1923), an Ohio native, was a newspaper publisher and politician whose administration was rife with corruption.

420, 444, 451, 462, 470, 472, 475, 496, 507 *Warren Harding*

420		UnFVF	UseFVF
1-1/2¢	**yellow brown**	2.50	.25
	brown	2.50	.25
	dull yellow brown	2.50	.25
	Plate block of 6	25.00	
	Double transfer	—	
	FDC *(March 19, 1925)*		30.00

See also CM60-63, a 2¢ black Harding of the same design as 420. Some include it with the 1922-34 Regular Issue Series.

1923. George Washington Type I Issue in the Regular Issue Series of 1922-34.

421, 445, 447, 449, 452, 463, 471, 476, 476A, 497, 508 *George Washington. Type I has thin hair lines at top center of head.*

421		UnFVF	UseFVF
2¢	**carmine** Type I	1.25	.20
	Plate block of 6	17.50	
	Plate block of 6, w/small 5-point star (top only)	450.00	
	Plate block of 6, w/large 5-point star (top only)	550.00	
	Plate block of 6, w/large 5-point star (side only)	60.00	
	Plate block of 6, w/large 6 point star (top only)	700.00	
	Plate block of 6, w/large 6-point star (side only)	850.00	
	Double transfer	2.50	.75
	n. Booklet pane of 6	8.50	1.00
	v. Horizontal pair, imperforate vertically	200.00	
	v1. Vertical pair, imperforate horizontally	500.00	
	v2. Perforated 10 at bottom	3,500.00	
	v3. Perforated 10 at top	3,500.00	
	FDC *(Jan. 15, 1923)*		42.50

1923. Abraham Lincoln Issue in the Regular Issue Series of 1922-34.

422, 453, 464, 477, 498, 509 *Abraham Lincoln*

422		UnFVF	UseFVF
3¢	**reddish violet**	18.00	.65
	bright violet	18.00	.65
	dark violet	18.00	.65
	violet	18.00	.65
	Plate block of 6	125.00	
	FDC *(Feb. 12, 1923)* (Washington, D.C.)		35.00
	FDC (Hodgeville, Ky.)		300.00

1923. Martha Washington Issue in the Regular Issue Series of 1922-34.

423, 454, 465, 478, 499, 510 *Martha Washington*

423		UnFVF	UseFVF
4¢	**yellow brown**	20.00	.20
	brown	20.00	.20
	Plate block of 6	130.00	
	Double transfer	—	
	v. Perforated 10 at bottom	420.00	
	v1. Perforated 10 at top	420.00	
	v2. Horizontal pair, imperforate between	—	
	v3. Vertical pair, imperforate horizontally	—	
	FDC *(Jan. 15, 1923)*		70.00

1922. Theodore Roosevelt Issue in the Regular Issue Series of 1922-34. Honored the 26th president, who took office at the age of 43, upon the assassination of William McKinley. A New York native, Roosevelt (1858-1919), known for his love of nature and conservation, championed the strenuous life in his personal habits and through the force of his personality greatly broadened the use of executive power.

424, 455, 466, 479, 500, 511 *Theodore Roosevelt*

424		UnFVF	UseFVF
5¢	**Prussian blue**	20.00	.20
	Plate block of 6	145.00	
	Double transfer	—	
	v. Horizontal pair, imperforate vertically	1,500.00	
	v1. Pair, imperforate	1,600.00	
	v2. Perforated 10 at bottom	—	450.00
	v3. Perforated 10 at top	—	450.00
	FDC *(Oct. 27, 1922)* (Washington, D.C.)		150.00
	FDC (N.Y.)		200.00
	FDC (Oyster Bay)		1,350.00

1922. James Garfield Issue in the Regular Issue Series of 1922-34.

425, 456, 467, 480, 501, 512 *James Garfield*

425		UnFVF	UseFVF
6¢	**red orange**	35.00	.55
	dull red orange	35.00	.55
	Plate block of 6	300.00	
	Double transfer	50.00	1.75
	Double transfer, recut	50.00	1.75
	FDC *(Nov. 20, 1922)*		250.00

1923. William McKinley Issue in the Regular Issue Series of 1922-34.

426, 457, 481, 502, 513 *William McKinley*

DECODING THE CATALOG

Despite some confusion about the 2¢ value of the 1922 series, it really is not too difficult a stamp to figure out. There are 10 major stamps (and several overprints), but each has its own notable characterisitics.

The 2¢ 1922 issue.

There is only one design type for the flat-plate issues and two types for the rotary press. Beyond that, differentiating the stamps is just a matter of knowing the characteristics of each and their printing types.

During the time the 2¢ value was being produced, the Bureau of Engraving and Printing was switching production from flat-plate presses to rotary presses. Rotary presses, no longer in the experimental stage by then, were far more efficient for rapid stamp production. Flat-plate presses use flat printing plates that leave their inked impressions on single sheets of paper. A rotary press, on the other hand, utitlizes a printing cylinder that prints on a continuous roll of paper.

To create these cylinders, it was necessary to bend two flat printing plates and join them to form a full cylinder. By bending these printing plates, the stamp image became slightly distorted in length or width, depending upon which direction the plate was bent, and the resulting stamp designs were either slightly taller or wider than their flat-plate counterparts.

FLAT-PLATE ISSUES

The 2¢ value was first released on Jan. 15, 1923, as a flat-plate issue with perforations that measure 11 on a standard gauge. This stamp is cataloged as Minkus 421.

One additional flat-plate version of this stamp was released, an imperforate variety, Minkus 445. The basic design dimensions of these stamps are 19 1/4 millimeters by 22 1/4 mm.

Most flat-plate stamps are easy to identify because of light "setoff" on the reverse side; flecks of ink where wet sheets of freshly printed stamps were stacked atop one another, leaving a minor impression.

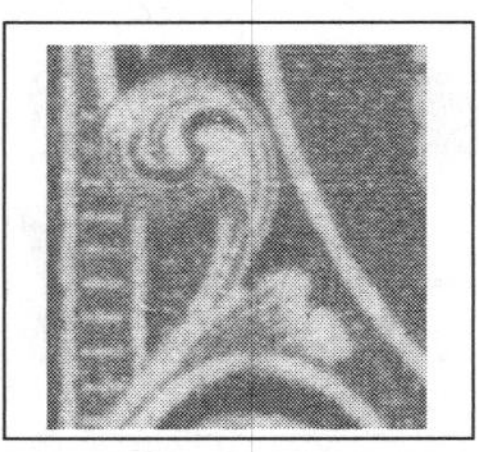

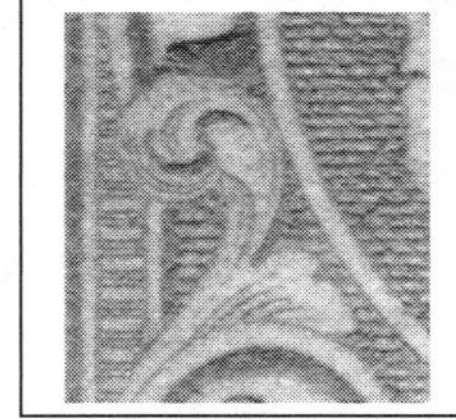

The icanthus scroll area on both sides of the stamp is another simple distinguishable difference between Type I (left) and II (right). Note the heavy line at the top of the scroll and the nicely engraved details in the leaf of Type II.

ROTARY PRESS TYPE I ISSUES

The rotary press stamps give collectors the most trouble. There are six basic types of this stamp but only two different design-size measurements. The remaining differences are determined by format and perforation measurements. This group also contains the scarcest varieties of this stamp.

The design on stamps printed from plates that were curved vertically measures 19 1/4 mm by 22 1/2 mm. This is slightly taller than other 2¢ issues. They are:

• Minkus 452, a sheet stamp with perforations that measure 10 on all four sides.

• Minkus 471, a vertical (or endwise) coil, with perforations that measure 10 at top and bottom. There are straight edges on left and right sides.

• Minkus 476, the most common 2¢ issue. It is a sheet stamp with perforations that measure 10 on all sides.

The design on rotary press-printed stamps printed from plates that were curved horizontally, measures 19 3/4 mm by 22 1/4 mm. This is slightly wider than the other 2¢ issues. They are:

• Minkus 463, the intended stamp from this format. It is a horizontal (or sidewise) coil with perforations that measure 10 on both sides.

• Minkus 447 and Minkus 449, sheet stamps created from coil waste. They are the scarcest of the 2¢ issues and sell for about $100 and $300, respectively, mint or used. In fact, both are worth more used with a demonstrable contemporaneous cancel. Minkus 447 has perforations that measure 11 at top and bottom and 10 on the left and right sides. Minkus 449 has perforations that measure 11 on all four sides.

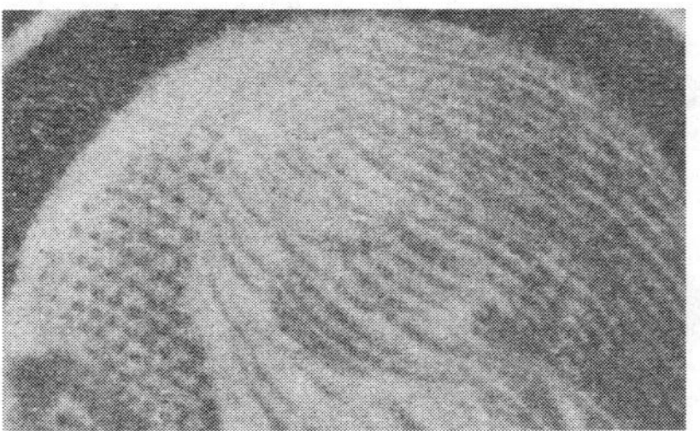

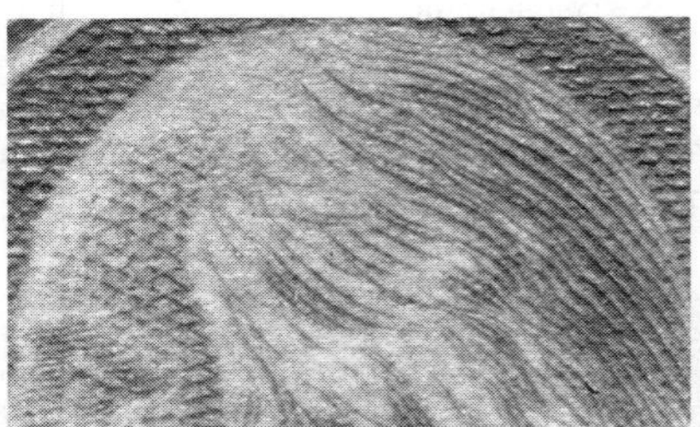

Type I (left) is not as clearly engraved as Type II (right). Type II features greatly strengthened hair lines, eye shadowing and numerous other design differences.

ROTARY PRESS TYPE II ISSUES

The Type II rotary press stamp was created from a new die. Distinguishing the popular and somewhat scarce Type II stamps is very easy, even on a heavily canceled used stamp, because there are several die differences.

Without going into great detail, Die II was created from a transfer of a Die I image. Once the new die was created, there was some touching up done, presumably to strengthen the image. These touch-ups are what create the differences between Types I and II.

The quickest and best way to determine a Type II stamp is by the heavily reinforced lines in the hair. But there are more than 10 other differences to be found. A few are illustrated here.

The Type II stamps are Minkus 463v, a horizontal coil sometimes found in pairs with Minkus 463, a Type I stamp; and 476A, a sheet stamp perforated 11 by 10 1/2.

The corner circles are slightly finer and more distinct on Type II examples (right) than on Type 1 (left).

426		UnFVF	UseFVF
7¢	**black**	9.00	.35
	gray black	9.00	.35
	Plate block of 6	55.00	
	Double transfer	—	
	FDC (May 21, 1923) (Washington, D.C.)		175.00
	FDC (Niles, Ohio)		250.00

1923. ULYSSES S. GRANT ISSUE in the Regular Issue Series of 1922-34.

427, 458, 482, 503, 514 *Ulysses S. Grant*

427		UnFVF	UseFVF
8¢	**yellow olive**	50.00	.85
	dull yellow olive	50.00	.85
	Plate block of 6	550.00	
	Double transfer	—	
	FDC *(May 1, 1923)*		210.00

1923. THOMAS JEFFERSON ISSUE in the Regular Issue Series of 1922-34.

428, 459, 483, 504, 515 *Thomas Jefferson*

428		UnFVF	UseFVF
9¢	**carmine rose**	15.00	.75
	dull carmine rose	15.00	.75
	Plate block of 6	150.00	
	Double transfer	—	
	FDC *(Jan. 15, 1923)*		210.00

1923. JAMES MONROE ISSUE in the Regular Issue Series of 1922-34.

429, 460, 468, 484, 505, 516 *James Monroe*

429		UnFVF	UseFVF
10¢	**orange yellow**	19.00	.25
	dull orange yellow	19.00	.25
	Plate block of 6	150.00	
	v. Pair, imperforate	1,350.00	
	v1. Vertical pair, imperforate horizontally	750.00	
	v2. Perforated 10 at bottom	—	750.00
	v3. Perforated 10 at top	—	750.00
	FDC *(Jan. 15, 1923)*		190.00

1922. RUTHERFORD B. HAYES ISSUE in the Regular Issue Series of 1922-34. Honored the 19th president, who gained office by one electoral vote. Hayes (1822-1893) born in Ohio and wounded in the Civil War, brought honesty and moderate reform to the office after a contentious campaign in 1876, in which he actually lost the popular vote.

430, 485 *Rutherford B. Hayes*

430		UnFVF	UseFVF
11¢	**turquoise blue**	2.50	.30
	dull bluish green	2.50	.30
	dull yellowish green	2.50	.30
	greenish blue	2.50	.30
	Plate block of 6	24.00	
	v. Pair, imperforate	—	
	FDC *(Oct. 4, 1922)* (Washington, D.C.)		650.00
	FDC (Freemont, Ohio)		2,000.00

No. 430 is known in a wide range of color shades between yellow green and light blue.

1923. GROVER CLEVELAND ISSUE in the Regular Issue Series of 1922-34. Honored the 22nd and 24th president, the only president to be married in the White House and the first to have a child born in the White House — popularly known as "Baby Ruth" — and the only president who served two non-consecutive terms. Cleveland (1837-1885) was born and died in New Jersey but achieved political prominence in New York.

431, 486 *Grover Cleveland*

DECODING THE CATALOG

Although it may lack something of the intimidating complexity of the Washington-Franklin series that preceded it, the United States definitive series of 1922-32 nonetheless includes a number of significant catalog-listed varieties of considerable interest to U.S. stamp specialists. The 7¢ McKinley definitive from that series, printed in black as if in belated mourning for the assassinated president, was first issued as a flat-plate-printed stamp on unwatermarked paper on May 1, 1923 (Minkus 426). This first version of the stamp was perforated 11. This perf 11 7¢ stamp is known printed in gray black as well as black, although neither version commands a premium.

A rotary-press-printed version of the 7¢ McKinley, in which the design measures 19 1/4 millimeters by 22 1/2 mm, was issued three years later, on May 29, 1926 (Minkus 457). It is perforated 10.

A third version of the stamp, also printed on the rotary press, was released on July 27, 1927 (Minkus 481). Stamps from this printing, perforated 11 by 10 1/2, are the most common of the three basic versions of the stamp.

Although the design dimensions are identical to those of the earlier rotary press stamp, mint copies of the 1927 stamps have breaker bar ridges in the gum on the back of the stamp, added during production to minimize gum curl.

There are no such breaker bars on the gum of the 1926 rotary press 7¢ McKinleys.

The same is true of the final two collectible versions of this stamp, the Kansas-Nebraska overprints. In 1929, these overprints were added to the 1¢ through 10¢ definitives in an experiment to limit the ability of thieves to sell stamps stolen from post offices by identifying the states in which they were located. (The theory was that the criminals would peddle such large quantities of stamps far from where they had been stolen, but would find no buyers for their purloined postage if it was all overprinted to show its source as a distant state.) Both these overprints were added exclusively to the perf 11 by 10 1/2 McKinleys. Any "Kans." and "Nebr." overprints found on perf 10 or perf 11 7¢ McKinleys are forgeries.

431		UnFVF	UseFVF
12¢	**maroon**	6.25	.20
	deep maroon	6.25	.20
	Plate block of 6	80.00	
	Plate block of 6, w/large 5-point star (side only)	125.00	
	Plate block of 6, w/large 6-point star (side only)	250.00	
	Double transfer	12.50	1.00
	v. Horizontal pair, imperforate vertically	1,000.00	
	v1. Pair, imperforate	—	
	FDC *(March 20, 1923)* (Washington, D.C.)		210.00
	FDC (Boston, Mass.)		210.00
	FDC (Caldwell, N.J.)		240.00

1926. BENJAMIN HARRISON ISSUE in the Regular Issue Series of 1922-34.

432, 487 *Benjamin Harrison*

432		UnFVF	UseFVF
13¢	**green**	10.00	.30
	dull green	10.00	.30
	Plate block of 6	130.00	
	Plate block of 6, w/large 5-point star	1,950.00	
	FDC *(Jan. 11, 1926)* (Washington, D.C.)		25.00
	FDC (Indianapolis, Ind.)		35.00
	FDC (North Bend, Ind.)		175.00

1923. AMERICAN INDIAN ISSUE in the Regular Issue Series of 1922-34.

433, 488 *American Indian from a photograph of Chief Hollow Horn Bear of the Brule Sioux tribe, taken on his visit to Washington, D.C., for the inauguration of Theodore Roosevelt.*

433		UnFVF	UseFVF
14¢	**blue**	4.75	.50
	Plate block of 6	130.00	
	Double transfer	—	
	FDC *(May 1, 1923)* (Washington, D.C.)		450.00
	FDC (Muskogee, Okla.)		1,800.00

1922. STATUE OF LIBERTY ISSUE in the Regular Issue Series of 1922-34.

434, 489 *Statue of Liberty*

434		UnFVF	UseFVF
15¢	**gray black**	25.00	.20
	light gray black	22.50	.20
	Plate block of 6	225.00	
	Plate block of 6, w/large 5-point star (side only)	450.00	
	FDC *(Nov. 11, 1922)*		600.00

1925. WOODROW WILSON ISSUE in the Regular Issue Series of 1922-34. Honored the 28th president, who was a child in Georgia during the Civil War, fought World War I to make the world "Safe for Democracy" and failed to convince Congress of the virtue of a League of Nations. Wilson (1856-1924) was president of Princeton University before launching his political career.

435, 490 *Woodrow Wilson*

435		UnFVF	UseFVF
17¢	**black**	12.00	.20
	gray black	12.00	.20
	Plate block of 6	170.00	
	FDC *(Dec. 28, 1925)* (w/o cachet)		30.00
	FDC (w/cachet)		275.00

1923. GOLDEN GATE ISSUE in the Regular Issue Series of 1922-34 featured the same view as that on the 5¢ value in the Panama-Pacific Exposition commemorative (CM49, CM54) but with different craft on the water.

436, 491 *Golden Gate*

436		UnFVF	UseFVF
20¢	**carmine red**	22.50	.20
	dark carmine red	22.50	.20
	Plate block of 6	220.00	
	Plate block of 6, w/large 5-point star (side only)	425.00	
	v. Horizontal pair, imperforate vertically	2,250.00	
	FDC *(May 1, 1923)* (Washington, D.C.)		550.00
	FDC (San Francisco, Calif.)		3,500.00
	FDC (Oakland, Calif.)		7,250.00

1922. NIAGARA FALLS ISSUE in the Regular Issue Series of 1922-34 featured a view of the American Falls at the popular honeymoon site, over which 20% of the world's freshwater supply is reputed to flow.

437, 492 *Niagara Falls*

437		UnFVF	UseFVF
25¢	**green**	19.00	.50
	yellow green	19.00	.50
	Plate block of 6	175.00	
	Double transfer	—	
	v. Perforated 10 at bottom	—	
	v1. Perforated 10 at top	—	
	v2. Vertical pair, imperforate horizontally	1,000.00	
	FDC *(Nov. 11, 1922)*		700.00

1923. BISON ISSUE was the only one in the Regular Issue Series of 1922-34 without a descriptive ribbon under the vignette.

438, 493 *Bison*

438		UnFVF	UseFVF
30¢	**olive brown**	35.00	.50
	Plate block of 6	220.00	
	Double transfer	50.00	2.00
	FDC *(March 20, 1923)*		900.00

1922. ARLINGTON ISSUE in the Regular Issue Series of 1922-34 featured the amphitheatre at Arlington (Va.) National Cemetery where the unknown soldier of World War I was buried in 1921, in the cenotaph in the foreground.

439, 494 *Arlington*

439		UnFVF	UseFVF
50¢	**gray lilac**	57.00	.20
	dull gray lilac	57.00	.20
	Plate block of 6	625.00	
	FDC *(Nov. 11, 1922)*		1,500.00

1923. Lincoln Memorial Issue in the Regular Issue Series of 1922-34 featured the newly constructed memorial to the slain Civil War president in Washington, D.C.

440 *Lincoln Memorial*

440		UnFVF	UseFVF
$1	**purple brown**	47.00	.50
	purple black	47.00	.50
	Plate block of 6	350.00	
	Double transfer	85.00	1.00
	Margin block of 4, w/arrow	175.00	
	FDC *(Feb. 12, 1923)* (Washington, D.C.)		6,000.00
	FDC (Springfield, Ill.)		6,500.00

1923. U. S. Capitol Issue in the Regular Issue Series of 1922-34 featured the home of the House of Representatives (foreground) and the Senate in Washington, D.C.

441 *U.S. Capitol*

441		UnFVF	UseFVF
$2	**blue**	100.00	6.00
	Plate block of 6	800.00	
	Margin block of 4, w/arrow	400.00	
	FDC *(March 20, 1923)*		17,500.00

1923. Head of Freedom Issue the only bicolor in the Regular Issue Series of 1922-34 featured the head of the statue atop the U.S. Capitol building in Washington, D.C.

442 *Head of Armed Freedom*

442		UnFVF	UseFVF
$5	**carmine & blue**	200.00	13.50
	lilac carmine & dark blue	200.00	13.50
	Plate block of 8, w/arrow & two plate numbers	2,150.00	
	Center line block	850.00	
	Margin block of 4, w/arrow	825.00	
	FDC *(March 20, 1923)*		32,500.00

1923. Issue in the Regular Issue Series of 1922-34. *Imperforate.*

443		UnFVF	UseFVF
1¢	**green**	7.50	3.00
	dark green		3.00
	dull green	7.50	3.00
	Plate block of 6	70.00	
	Center line block	40.00	
	Margin block of 4, w/arrow	35.00	
	FDC *(March 16, 1923)*		

444		UnFVF	UseFVF
1-1/2¢	**yellow brown**	1.50	1.00
	brown	1.50	1.00
	Plate block of 6	17.50	
	Center line block	10.50	
	Margin block of 4, w/arrow	7.00	
	Double transfer	—	
	FDC *(April 4, 1925)*		50.00

No. 444 exists in a rotary press printing, No. 472.

445		UnFVF	UseFVF
2¢	**carmine**	1.50	1.00
	dark carmine	1.50	1.00
	dull carmine	1.50	1.00
	Plate block of 6	25.00	
	Plate block of 6, w/large 5-point star	70.00	
	Center line block	12.50	
	Margin block of 4, w/arrow	7.50	
	FDC *(March 20, 1923)*		

1923-24. Rotary Press Printings in the Regular Issue Series of 1922-34. *From coil waste, no breaker bar ridges on back of stamps, designs 19 1/2 to 20mm wide by 22mm high, unwatermarked, perforated 11 x 10.*

446		UnFVF	UseFVF
1¢	**green**	90.00	90.00
	Plate block of 4, w/star	700.00	
	Earliest documented cover: *March 26, 1924*		

447		UnFVF	UseFVF
2¢	**carmine**	75.00	85.00
	dark carmine	75.00	85.00
	Plate block of 4, w/star	375.00	
	Recut in eye	90.00	125.00
	Earliest documented cover: *Feb. 20, 1923*		

1923-24. Rotary Press Printing Issue in the Regular Issue Series of 1922-34. *Perforated 11.*

448		UnFVF	UseFVF
1¢	**green**	15,000.00	4,000.00
	dark green	15,000.00	4,000.00
	dull green	15,000.00	4,000.00
	Earliest documented cover: *March 25, 1924*		

449		UnFVF	UseFVF
2¢	**carmine**	285.00	300.00
	Plate block of 4, w/star	1,850.00	
	Recut in eye	—	
	Earliest documented cover: *Nov. 17, 1923*		

Nos. 448 and 449 were made from coil waste. Design 18 1/2 to 19mm wide by 22 1/2mm high.

449A		UnFVF	UseFVF
1¢	**green**	—	42,500.00

1923-26. Rotary Press Printing Issue in the Regular Issue Series of 1922-34. *Breaker bar ridges on backs of stamps, designs 18 1/2 to 19mm wide by 22 1/2mm high, unwatermarked, perforated 10.*

450		UnFVF	UseFVF
1¢	**green**	7.50	1.00
	light green	7.50	1.00
	yellow green	7.50	1.00
	Plate block of 4	75.00	
	FDC *(Oct. 17, 1923)*		700.00

451		UnFVF	UseFVF
1-1/2¢	**yellow brown**	3.75	1.00
	dark brown	3.75	1.00
	Plate block of 4	30.00	
	Pair, horizontal or vertical gutter between	150.00	
	FDC *(March 19, 1925)*		45.00

452		UnFVF	UseFVF
2¢	**carmine**	2.00	.35
	Plate block of 4	17.50	
	n. Booklet pane of 6 *(Aug. 27, 1926)*	75.00	
	FDC *(April 1924)*		1,400.00

453		UnFVF	UseFVF
3¢	**reddish violet**	20.00	2.50
	Plate block of 4	170.00	
	FDC *(Aug. 1, 1925)*		60.00

454		UnFVF	UseFVF
4¢	**yellow brown**	14.00	.80
	dark yellow brown	14.00	.80
	Plate block of 4	125.00	
	FDC *(April 4, 1925)*		60.00

455		UnFVF	UseFVF
5¢	**blue**	14.00	.80
	deep blue	14.00	.80
	Plate block of 4	120.00	
	Double transfer	—	
	v. Horizontal pair, imperforate vertically	—	
	FDC *(April 4, 1925)*		65.00

456		UnFVF	UseFVF
6¢	**orange**	6.25	.75
	dull orange	6.25	.75
	Plate block of 4	60.00	
	FDC *(April 4, 1925)*		65.00

457		UnFVF	UseFVF
7¢	**black**	9.00	6.50
	Plate block of 4	65.00	
	FDC *(May 29, 1926)*		70.00

458		UnFVF	UseFVF
8¢	**yellow olive**	20.00	4.00
	pale yellow olive	20.00	4.00
	Plate block of 4	150.00	
	FDC *(May 29, 1926)*		80.00

459		UnFVF	UseFVF
9¢	**red**	4.25	2.50
	Plate block of 4	32.50	
	FDC *(May 29, 1926)*		80.00

460		UnFVF	UseFVF
10¢	**orange yellow**	50.00	.45
	Plate block of 4	325.00	
	FDC *(June 8, 1925)*		100.00

1923-26. Rotary Press Coil Issue in the Regular Issue Series of 1922-34. *Designs 19 1/2 to 20mm wide by 22 1/4mm high, perforated 10 vertically.*

461		UnFVF	UseFVF
1¢	**yellow green**	.35	.20
	green	.35	.20
	Pair	.75	.20
	Line pair	2.00	.25
	Double transfer	2.50	.75
	Gripper cracks	2.50	.75
	FDC *(July 18, 1923)*		550.00

462		UnFVF	UseFVF
1-1/2¢	**yellow brown**	.75	.20
	dark brown	.75	.20
	Pair	2.00	.25
	Line pair	6.00	.50
	FDC *(March 19, 1925)*		55.00

463 *George Washington: Type I (left) and Type II*

463 *Type II. There are three heavy hair lines at the top center of the head.*

463		UnFVF	UseFVF
2¢	**carmine** Type I	.45	.20
	dark carmine	.45	.20
	Pair	.75	.20
	Line pair	2.00	.25
	Line pair, 1 each Type I & Type II	625.00	
	Double transfer	1.75	.50
	Gripper cracks	2.00	1.75
	v. carmine, Type II	115.00	12.50
	dark carmine	115.00	12.50
	Pair	—	
	Line pair	525.00	
	FDC *(Jan. 10, 1923)*		2,000.00

464		UnFVF	UseFVF
3¢	**reddish violet**	5.50	.30
	dark violet	5.50	.30
	Pair	12.50	.50
	Line pair	30.00	1.00
	Cracked plate	—	
	FDC *(May 10, 1924)*		125.00

465		UnFVF	UseFVF
4¢	**yellow brown**	3.75	.50
	brown	3.75	.50
	Pair	9.00	1.00
	Line pair	35.00	2.75

466		UnFVF	UseFVF
5¢	**blue**	1.75	.20
	Pair	3.50	.40
	Line pair	12.50	.60
	FDC *(March 5, 1924)*		100.00

467		UnFVF	UseFVF
6¢	**orange**	9.50	.35
	Pair	22.50	.50
	Line pair	50.00	2.50
	FDC *(Aug. 18, 1932)*		

468		UnFVF	UseFVF
10¢	**orange yellow**	3.50	.20
	Pair	7.50	.25
	Line pair	22.50	1.00
	FDC *(Dec. 1, 1924)*		110.00

1924. Rotary Press Coil Issue in the Regular Issue Series of 1922-34. *Designs 18 1/2 to 19mm wide by 22 1/2mm high, perforated 10 horizontally.*

469		UnFVF	UseFVF
1¢	**yellow green**	.35	.20
	green	.35	.20
	Pair	.75	.25
	Line pair	3.00	.50
	FDC *(July 19, 1924)*		90.00

470		UnFVF	UseFVF
1-1/2¢	**yellow brown**	.35	.20
	brown	.35	.20
	Pair	.75	.25
	Line pair	3.00	.50
	FDC *(May 9, 1925)*		75.00

471		UnFVF	UseFVF
2¢	**carmine**	.35	.20
	Pair	.75	.25
	Line pair	2.00	
	Cracked plate	5.00	2.00
	FDC *(Dec. 31, 1923)*		125.00

1926. Rotary Press Issue in the Regular Issue Series of 1922-34. *Imperforate, design 18 1/2 to 19mm wide by 22 1/2mm high. Most of these stamps show the breaker bars on the back, but there was a printing of this stamp that did not have them. The stamp was issued in sheets of 400, with both vertical and horizontal gutters.*

472		UnFVF	UseFVF
1-1/2¢	**yellow brown**	2.25	2.00
	brown	2.25	2.00
	Plate block of 4	55.00	
	Center block w/crossed gutters & dashes	20.00	22.50
	Block of 4, gutter between	8.50	9.50
	Margin block, w/dash	9.50	13.50
	Without gum breaker ridges	80.00	
	Pair, horizontal or vertical gutter between	200.00	
	FDC *(Aug. 27, 1926)*		50.00

1926-34. Rotary Press Issue in the Regular Issue Series of 1922-34. *Designs 18 1/2 to 19mm wide by 22 1/2mm high, breaker bar ridges on back of stamps, unwatermarked, perforated 11 x 10 1/2.*

473		UnFVF	UseFVF
1/2¢	**olive brown**	.25	.20
	Plate block of 4	1.50	
	Damaged plate	1.35	
	Pair, gutter between	125.00	
	Retouched plate	1.35	
	FDC *(May 25, 1929)*		30.00

474		UnFVF	UseFVF
1¢	**green**	.25	.20
	yellow green	.25	.20
	Plate block of 4	2.00	
	FDC *(June 10, 1927)*		3,500.00
	Cracked plate	—	
	Pair, gutter between	135.00	

	n. Booklet pane of 6 (Nov. 2, 1927)	5.50	
	FDC *(Nov. 2, 1927)* Booklet pane		3,500.00
	v. Horizontal pair, imperforate between	—	
	v1. Vertical pair, imperforate between	2,650.00	—
	Earliest documented cover: *May 24, 1927*		

475		UnFVF	UseFVF
1-1/2¢	**yellow brown**	2.00	.20
	dark brown	2.00	.20
	Plate block of 4	70.00	
	FDC *(May 17, 1927)*		45.00

476		UnFVF	UseFVF
2¢	**carmine red** Type I	.25	.20
	lilac carmine	.25	.20
	Plate (corner) block of 4	2.00	
	Plate block (vertical) of 10, w/number opposite 3rd horizontal row, (experimental electric eye plates)	4.50	
	Margin block of 4, w/electric eye marking	.35	.25
	Pair, gutter between	180.00	
	n. Booklet pane of 6	2.00	
	FDC *(Dec. 10, 1926)*		45.00
	p. Thin (experimental) paper	—	
	v. Horizontal pair, imperforate between	2,250.00	
	v1. Vertical pair, imperforate between	—	
	FDC *(March 28, 1935)* w/electric eye marking		1,300.00

476A		UnFVF	UseFVF
2¢	**carmine red** Type II	300.00	15.00
	Plate block of 4	1,800.00	
	Pair, horizontal or vertical gutter between	1,000.00	
	Earliest documented cover: *(Dec. 19, 1928)*		

477		UnFVF	UseFVF
3¢	**reddish violet**	.55	.20
	Plate block of 4	8.00	
	v. red violet (re-issue) *(Feb. 7, 1934)*	.25	.20
	Plate block of 4	4.75	
	Gripper cracks	3.00	
	FDC *(Feb. 3, 1927)*		47.50

478		UnFVF	UseFVF
4¢	**yellow brown**	2.75	.20
	dark brown	2.75	.20
	Plate block of 4	70.00	
	Pair, gutter between	200.00	
	FDC *(May 17, 1927)*		55.00

479		UnFVF	UseFVF
5¢	**blue**	2.25	.20
	Plate block of 4	15.00	
	Pair, gutter between	275.00	
	Double transfer	—	
	FDC *(March 24, 1927)*		55.00

480		UnFVF	UseFVF
6¢	**orange**	2.25	.20
	dull orange	2.25	.20
	Plate block of 4	15.00	
	Pair, horizontal or vertical gutter between	200.00	
	FDC *(July 27, 1927)*		65.00

481		UnFVF	UseFVF
7¢	**black**	2.25	.20
	Plate block of 4	15.00	
	v. Vertical pair, imperforate between	125.00	75.00
	v1. Block of 4, imperforate between	250.00	
	FDC *(March 24, 1927)*		60.00

482		UnFVF	UseFVF
8¢	**yellow olive**	2.25	.20
	pale yellow olive	2.25	.20
	Plate block of 4	15.00	
	FDC *(June 10, 1927)*		65.00

483		UnFVF	UseFVF
9¢	**red**	2.00	.20
	orange red	2.00	.20
	salmon	2.00	.20
	Plate block of 4	15.00	
	Pair, gutter between	—	
	v. rose *(May 17, 1927)*	2.00	.20
	FDC (1931)		65.00

484		UnFVF	UseFVF
10¢	**orange yellow**	4.00	.20
	Plate block of 4	25.00	
	Double transfer	—	
	FDC *(Feb. 3, 1927)*		90.00

485		UnFVF	UseFVF
11¢	**turquoise green**	2.75	.20
	Plate block of 4	12.50	
	Retouch on forehead	6.50	.75
	FDC *(Sept. 4, 1931)*		125.00

486		UnFVF	UseFVF
12¢	**brown purple**	6.00	.20
	purple brown	6.00	.20
	Plate block of 4	27.50	
	FDC *(Aug. 25, 1931)*	125.00	

487		UnFVF	UseFVF
13¢	**yellow green**	2.25	.20
	blue green	2.25	.20
	pale yellow green	2.25	.20
	Plate block of 4	14.00	
	Pair, gutter between	1.50	
	FDC *(Sept. 4, 1931)*		125.00

488		UnFVF	UseFVF
14¢	**blue**	4.00	.50
	Plate block of 4	20.00	
	FDC *(Sept. 8, 1931)*		125.00

Identifier of the 1922-34 Regular Issues

Frame	Perf. 11	Perf. 11 x 10	Perf. 10	Coil 10	Perf. 11 x 10 1/2 or 10 1/2 x 11	Imperf.
	418-434, 448-449	446-447	450-460	461-471, 520, 522	473-489, 517, 519	443-445 472
	435-442				490-494	

		UnFVF	UseFVF
489			
15¢	**gray black**	8.00	.20
	gray	8.00	.20
	Plate block of 4	35.00	
	FDC *(Aug. 27, 1931)*		140.00

1931. ROTARY PRESS ISSUE in the Regular Issue Series of 1922-34. *The designs of the following stamps are horizontal rather than vertical, so perforation measurements are 10 1/2 x 11.*

		UnFVF	UseFVF
490			
17¢	**black**	5.50	.20
	Plate block of 4	25.00	
	FDC *(July 25, 1931)* (Washington, D.C.)		450.00
	FDC (Brooklyn, N.Y.)		3,000.00
491		**UnFVF**	**UseFVF**
20¢	**carmine rose**	9.50	.20
	Plate block of 4	50.00	
	Double transfer	20.00	
	FDC *(Sept. 8, 1931)*		325.00
492		**UnFVF**	**UseFVF**
25¢	**green**	11.00	.20
	Plate block of 4	50.00	
	FDC *(July 25, 1931)* (Washington, D.C.)		450.00
	FDC (Brooklyn, N.Y.)		2,500.00
493		**UnFVF**	**UseFVF**
30¢	**olive brown**	17.50	.20
	Plate block of 4	85.00	
	Cracked plate	27.50	.75
	Retouch in head	27.50	.75
	FDC *(Sept. 8, 1931)*		325.00
494		**UnFVF**	**UseFVF**
50¢	**lilac**	42.50	.20
	red lilac	42.50	.20
	Plate block of 4	200.00	
	FDC *(Sept. 4, 1931)*		450.00

1929. KANSAS AND NEBRASKA OVERPRINTS ISSUE in the Regular Issue Series of 1922-34 were issued to help prevent loss by post office burglaries. It was thought that stolen stamps in those two states could be traced more easily if they were overprinted. Approximately one year's supply was printed and delivered to the post offices in Kansas and Nebraska for use starting May 1, 1929, but no further printings were made. The overprinting was done on the regular 1¢ to 10¢ stamps of the 1922-34 designs. *Rotary press printing, unwatermarked, perforated 11 x 10 1/2.* All denominations were issued.

"Wide spacing pairs" noted below designate vertical pairs on which the overprints are 32mm apart rather than 22mm.

495 *Kansas overprint* **Kans.**

		UnFVF	UseFVF
495			
1¢	**green**	2.00	1.50
	Plate block of 4	30.00	
	Wide spacing pair	30.00	
	v. Vertical pair, 1 w/out overprint	300.00	
	FDC (Washington, D.C.)		50.00
	FDC (Newton, Kans.)		450.00
496		**UnFVF**	**UseFVF**
1-1/2¢	**yellow brown**	3.00	2.25
	Plate block of 4	40.00	
	Wide spacing pair	60.00	
	v. Vertical pair, 1 w/out overprint	325.00	
	FDC		60.00
497		**UnFVF**	**UseFVF**
2¢	**carmine red**	3.00	1.00
	Plate block of 4	35.00	
	Wide spacing pair	45.00	
	FDC		60.00
498		**UnFVF**	**UseFVF**
3¢	**reddish violet**	15.00	11.00
	Plate block of 4	145.00	
	v. Vertical pair, 1 w/out overprint	400.00	
	FDC		75.00
499		**UnFVF**	**UseFVF**
4¢	**yellow brown**	15.00	8.50
	Plate block of 4	145.00	
	v. Vertical pair, 1 w/out overprint	400.00	
	FDC		100.00
500		**UnFVF**	**UseFVF**
5¢	**blue**	12.50	9.00
	Plate block of 4	120.00	
	FDC		100.00
501		**UnFVF**	**UseFVF**
6¢	**orange**	25.00	15.00
	Plate block of 4	325.00	
	FDC (Washington, D.C.)		125.00
	FDC (Newton, Kans.)		650.00
502		**UnFVF**	**UseFVF**
7¢	**black**	25.00	20.00
	Plate block of 4	375.00	
	v. Vertical pair, 1 w/out overprint	400.00	
	FDC		150.00

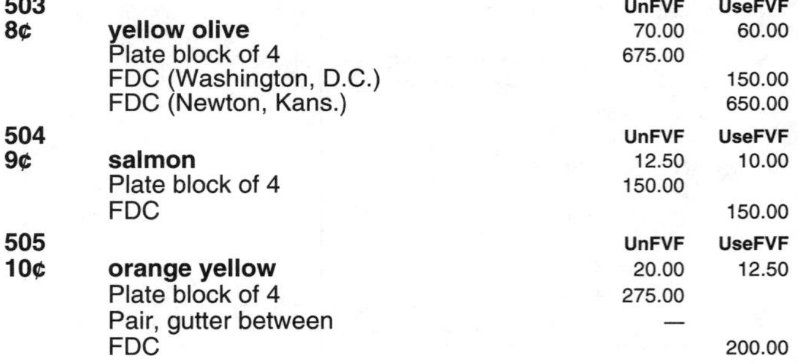

503

		UnFVF	UseFVF
503			
8¢	**yellow olive**	70.00	60.00
	Plate block of 4	675.00	
	FDC (Washington, D.C.)		150.00
	FDC (Newton, Kans.)		650.00
504		**UnFVF**	**UseFVF**
9¢	**salmon**	12.50	10.00
	Plate block of 4	150.00	
	FDC		150.00
505		**UnFVF**	**UseFVF**
10¢	**orange yellow**	20.00	12.50
	Plate block of 4	275.00	
	Pair, gutter between	—	
	FDC		200.00

506 *Nebraska overprint* **Nebr.**

		UnFVF	UseFVF
506			
1¢	**green**	2.25	2.00
	Plate block of 4	30.00	
	v1. Period omitted after "Nebr"	40.00	
	Wide spacing pair	35.00	
	v. Vertical pair, 1 w/out overprint	275.00	
	FDC (Washington, D.C.)		50.00
	FDC (Beatrice, Nebr.)		400.00
507		**UnFVF**	**UseFVF**
1-1/2¢	**yellow brown**	2.25	2.00
	Plate block of 4	40.00	
	Wide spacing pair	35.00	
	FDC (Washington, D.C.)		60.00
	FDC (Hartington, Nebr.)		350.00
508		**UnFVF**	**UseFVF**
2¢	**carmine red**	2.25	1.00
	Plate block of 4	25.00	
	Wide spacing pair	50.00	
	FDC (Washington, D.C.)		60.00
	FDC (Auburn, Beatrice or Hartington, Nebr.)		350.00
509		**UnFVF**	**UseFVF**
3¢	**reddish violet**	11.00	8.00
	Plate block of 4	120.00	
	Wide spacing pair	70.00	
	v. Vertical pair, 1 w/out overprint	400.00	
	FDC (Washington, D.C.)		75.00
	FDC (Beatrice or Hartington, Nebr.)		350.00

510		UnFVF	UseFVF
4¢	**yellow brown**	15.00	10.00
	Plate block of 4	175.00	
	Wide spacing pair	110.00	
	FDC (Washington, D.C.)		100.00
	FDC (Beatrice or Hartington, Nebr.)		350.00

511		UnFVF	UseFVF
5¢	**blue**	12.50	11.50
	Plate block of 4	175.00	
	FDC (Washington, D.C.)		100.00
	FDC (Beatrice or Hartington, Nebr.)		375.00

512		UnFVF	UseFVF
6¢	**orange**	35.00	17.50
	Plate block of 4	350.00	
	FDC		125.00

513		UnFVF	UseFVF
7¢	**black**	18.50	12.50
	Plate block of 4	225.00	
	FDC		150.00

514		UnFVF	UseFVF
8¢	**yellow olive**	25.00	17.50
	Plate block of 4	325.00	
	Wide spacing pair	160.00	
	FDC		150.00

515		UnFVF	UseFVF
9¢	**salmon**	30.00	22.50
	Plate block of 4	350.00	
	Wide spacing pair	140.00	
	v. Vertical pair, 1 w/out overprint	600.00	
	FDC		150.00

516

516		UnFVF	UseFVF
10¢	**orange yellow**	85.00	17.50
	Plate block of 4	775.00	
	FDC		200.00

1930-32. Warren G. Harding New Design Issue in the Regular Issue Series of 1922-34. *Rotary press printing, unwatermarked, perforated 11 x 10 1/2.*

517, 520 *Warren G. Harding*

517		UnFVF	UseFVF
1-1/2¢	**yellow brown**	.25	.20
	dull brown	.25	.20
	Plate block of 4	2.25	
	Pair, horizontal or vertical gutter between	175.00	
	FDC w/o cachet *(Dec. 1, 1930)*		4.50
	FDC w/cachet		45.00

1930-32. George Washington Issue used the design of the 2¢ carmine red stamp issued five months earlier as part of the Washington Bicentennial Issue (CM101) in a new color and denomination.

518, 521, 523 *George Washington*

518		UnFVF	UseFVF
3¢	**reddish violet**	.25	.20
	pale reddish violet	.25	.20
	Plate block of 4	1.25	
	Double transfer	1.00	.25
	Gripper cracks	1.10	.30
	Recut on nose	1.75	.60
	Pair, gutter between	2.00	
	n. Booklet pane of 6 (July 25, 1932)	37.50	
	v. Vertical pair, imperforate between	300.00	
	FDC w/o cachet *(June 16, 1932)*		7.50
	FDC w/cachet		40.00
	FDC Booklet Pane		200.00

1930-32 William H. Taft Issue in the Regular Issue Series of 1922-34 honored the 27th president, who was later appointed Chief Justice of the Supreme Court, a position he embraced more than president. Taft (1857-1930), of Cincinnati, Ohio, had the White House stables converted to a garage for the first presidential automobiles, ordered in 1909.

519, 522 *William H. Taft*

519		UnFVF	UseFVF
4¢	**yellow brown**	.90	.20
	dark brown	.90	.20
	Plate block of 4	11.50	
	Gouge on right "4"	2.00	.60
	Recut on right "4"	2.00	.60
	Pair, gutter between	—	
	FDC w/o cachet *(June 4, 1930)*		6.00
	FDC w/cachet		60.00

1930-32. Warren G. Harding New Design Coil Issue in the Regular Issue Series of 1922-34. *Perforated 10 vertically.*

520 *Line Pair*

520		UnFVF	UseFVF
1-1/2¢	**yellow brown**	1.50	.20
	Pair	3.50	.20
	Line pair	7.50	.50
	FDC w/o cachet *(Dec. 1, 1930)*		5.00
	FDC w/cachet		60.00

1930-32. George Washington Coil Issue *Perforated 10 vertically.*

521		UnFVF	UseFVF
3¢	**reddish violet**	1.75	.20
	pale violet	1.75	.20
	Pair	4.25	.50
	Line pair	5.50	.60
	Gripper cracks	—	
	Recut on nose	—	
	Recut around eyes	—	
	FDC w/o cachet *(June 24, 1932)*		25.00
	FDC w/cachet		95.00

1930-32. William H. Taft Coil Issue in the Regular Issue Series of 1922-34. *Perforated 10 vertically.*

522		UnFVF	UseFVF
4¢	**yellow brown**	2.75	.75
	Pair	6.00	.85
	Line pair	17.50	1.50
	FDC w/o cachet *(Sept. 18, 1930)*		15.00
	FDC w/cachet		50.00

1930-32. George Washington Coil Issue *Perforated 10 horizontally.*

523		UnFVF	UseFVF
3¢	**reddish violet**	1.00	.75
	pale violet	1.00	.75
	Pair	3.00	.80
	Line pair	4.00	1.50
	FDC w/o cachet *(Oct. 12, 1932)*		15.00
	FDC w/cachet		50.00

1938-43. Presidential Series

The first regular issues in almost six years are known as the Presidential Series because all but three of its 32 designs feature the portraits of former presidents of the United States. Sixteen years would pass before the "Prexies" began to be supplemented with another definitive series. *The values from 1/2¢ through 50¢, including coils, are printed by rotary press intaglio and are perforated 11 x 10 1/2. The $1, $2 and $5 values are printed by flat press intaglio, perforated 11.*

1938. Benjamin Franklin Issue in the Presidential Series.

524 *Benjamin Franklin (1706-1790), first Postmaster General appointed by the Continental Congress, began his career as a printer and editor in Philadelphia, where he founded the first circulating library in America, the American Philosophical Society, and the nucleus for the University of Pennsylvania; he invented the Franklin stove, and made important experiments identifying lightning with electricity. He was deputy postmaster at Philadelphia 1737-53 and then (with William Hunter) postmaster general for the colonies until 1774, greatly expanding and improving postal service. An active patriot, both here and in England, for 20 years before the Revolution, he served in the 2nd Continental Congress, was appointed postmaster general, and aided in drafting the Declaration of Independence, of which he was a signer. Sent to France as a diplomat in 1776, he was enormously popular and successful there. With John Jay and John Adams, he negotiated the peace treaty with Great Britain in 1783. An important member of the Constitutional Convention in 1787, he signed the Constitution without entirely approving it. His last public act was in signing a petition to Congress for the abolition of slavery.*

524		UnFVF	UseFVF
1/2¢	**red orange**	.25	.20
	Plate block of 4	.50	
	FDC *(May 19, 1938)*	—	

1938. George Washington Issue in the Presidential Series.

525, 556, 565 *George Washington, unanimously elected first president, mainly supported the federalist and industrialist policies of Alexander Hamilton (see No. 106) against the states' rights and agrarian theories of Thomas Jefferson (see No. 47). He was criticized for "aristocratic tendencies," for the 1794 Jay's Treaty with Great Britain, and for the excise tax that led to the Whiskey Rebellion of 1794; he brought the nation power and prestige, put down severe Indian troubles, and effected treaties opening the Mississippi to navigation.*

525		UnFVF	UseFVF
1¢	**green**	.25	.20
	pale green	.25	.20
	Plate block of 4	.50	
	FDC *(April 25, 1938)*	3.00	
	Pair, gutter between	—	
	n. Booklet pane of 6	2.00	
	FDC Booklet Pane		15.00

Each entry in this catalog has been double-checked for accuracy, but mistakes may crep into any human endeavor, and we ask your assistance in eliminating them. Please call the attention of the editors to any errors in stamp description found in this catalog. Send your comments to:

Minkus Catalog Editor
Krause Publications
700 E. State St.
Iola WI 54990

1938. Martha Washington Issue in the Presidential Series.

526, 557, 566 *Martha Washington, wife of the first president, was known as "the prettiest and richest widow in Virginia" when Washington met her in 1758. Married to him in January 1759, she managed his plantations during the Revolution, visited him at Valley Forge and Newburgh, and was a gracious and popular First Lady.*

526		UnFVF	UseFVF
1-1/2¢	**yellow brown**	.25	.20
	ocher	.25	.20
	Plate block of 4	.50	
	Pair, horizontal or vertical gutter between	175.00	
	v. Horizontal pair, imperforate between	175.00	
	z. Tagged	—	
	FDC *(May 5, 1938)*	—	

No. 526z was produced circa 1955 as a result of experiments conducted by Pitney-Bowes for the Post Office Department. A single copy is known in collectors' hands.

1938. John Adams Issue in the Presidential Series.

527, 558, 567 *John Adams, second president (1797-1801), attacked the Stamp Act in 1765, served in the first and second Continental Congress, nominated George Washington to command the American forces, helped to draft the Declaration of Independence, and (according to Jefferson) was "the pillar of its support on the floor of Congress." He served as commissioner to France 1777-79, went with John Jay and Benjamin Franklin to England to negotiate the peace treaty, and the first American envoy to the Court of St. James. Serving as vice president in both of Washington's terms, he was elected president in 1796. He was opposed by the Jefferson faction for the Alien and Sedition Acts, for which he was directly responsible, and by the Hamilton faction for his concilatory policy toward France, which averted war. Defeated by Jefferson in the election of 1800, he retired to private life in Massachusetts.*

527		UnFVF	UseFVF
2¢	**rose**	.25	.20
	rose pink	.25	.20
	Plate block of 4	.50	
	Plate block of 10 (vertical), with number opposite 3rd horizontal row	7.50	
	Pair, horizontal or vertical gutter between	—	
	Recut at top of head	2.50	1.25
	n. Booklet pane of 6	6.00	
	p. Thin, translucent paper	—	
	FDC *(June 3, 1938)*		3.00
	FDC Booklet Pane		15.00

1938. Thomas Jefferson Issue in the Presidential Series.

528, 559, 568 *Thomas Jefferson, third president (1801-09), was the chief author of the Declaration of Independence and one of its signers. As a wartime legislator and governor in Virginia, he worked to abolish a landed aristocracy, separate church from state, and establish public schools. Returning to Congress in 1783, he headed the committee debating the peace treaty, devised the American monetary system and laid the basis for later organization of western territories. He was minister to France 1785-89, became first secretary of state, and was elected vice president under John Adams. Strongly opposed to Alexander Hamilton, whose policies he felt led toward monarchy, he championed individual liberties, states' rights and an agrarian economy. Tied with Burr for electoral votes in 1800, he was supported by Hamilton and chosen president by the House of Representatives. In his two terms he authorized the Louisiana Purchase (CM32-CM36), warred against the Tripolitan pirates (CM178), dispatched the Lewis and Clark and Pike expeditions, and obtained a Congressional act abolishing the importation of slaves. A distinguished scholar, philosopher and patron of the arts, he founded*

the University of Virginia and greatly influenced the revival of classical architecture in America.

528		UnFVF	UseFVF
3¢	**violet**	.25	.20
	Plate block of 4	.50	
	Plate block of 10 (vertical), with number opposite 3rd horizontal row	.25	
	Pair, horizontal or vertical gutter between	175.00	
	n. Booklet pane of 6	8.50	
	v. Horizontal pair, imperforate between	1,100.00	
	v1. Pair, imperforate	2,750.00	
	FDC *(June 16, 1938)*		3.00
	FDC Booklet Pane		15.00

1938. JAMES MADISON ISSUE in the Presidential Series.

529, 560 *James Madison, fourth president (1809-17), is known as "the father of the Constitution." A Virginian identified with Jefferson's liberal reforms there, he joined with Hamilton in proposing the Constitutional Convention, acted as recorder of the proceedings, took a large part in framing the Constitution, greatly aided its ratification and proposed the first 10 amendments: The Bill of Rights. Criticized as inept in his leadership in the War of 1812, he successfully advocated a protective tariff, a strong military organization and a national system of roads and canals.*

529		UnFVF	UseFVF
4¢	**bright purple**	1.15	.20
	rose lilac	1.15	.20
	Plate block of 4	4.50	
	FDC *(July 1, 1938)*		3.00

1938. WHITE HOUSE ISSUE in the Presidential Series.

530, 561 *The White House*

530		UnFVF	UseFVF
4-1/2¢	**gray**	.25	.20
	dark gray	.25	.20
	Plate block of 4	1.25	
	FDC *(July 11, 1938)*		3.00

1938. JAMES MONROE ISSUE in the Presidential Series.

531, 562 *James Monroe, fifth president (1817-25), fought in the 3rd Virginia Regiment at Harlem Heights, White Plains, Trenton (where he was wounded), Brandywine, Germantown and Monmouth. He studied law under Jefferson, served in the Continental Congress, 1783-86, and fought the Constitution because he believed it made the federal government too powerful. As a senator, he bitterly opposed Washington and Hamilton. As minister to France, he was recalled for over-sympathizing with the French Revolution and failing to follow Washington's instructions. Four times governor of Virginia, he was sent back to France in 1803 to aid in negotiating the Louisiana Purchase (CM34). secretary of state and of war under Madison, he was elected president in 1816, ushering in the "Era of Good Feeling," and re-elected in 1820 with all but one vote, which was given to John Quincy Adams so that only Washington might have the honor of unanimous election. Monroe acquired Florida from Spain, supported the Missouri Compromise, settled the Canadian border and eliminated its forts and proclaimed the Monroe Doctrine prohibiting further European colonization or interference in the Americas.*

531		UnFVF	UseFVF
5¢	**light blue**	.25	.20
	pale blue	.25	.20
	Plate block of 4	1.25	
	Pair, gutter between	—	
	FDC *(July 21, 1938)*		3.00

1938. JOHN QUINCY ADAMS ISSUE in the Presidential Series.

532, 563 *John Quincy Adams, sixth president (1825-29), was the son of John Adams (No. 527). When appointed secretary of state by Monroe, he already had seen diplomatic service in France, the Netherlands, Prussia, Russia and England; spent 5 years in the Senate; taught rhetoric at Harvard; and headed the peace commission that negotiated the Treaty of Ghent in 1814. He obtained the cession of Florida from Spain and shared credit with Monroe in formulating the Monroe Doctrine. Running second to Andrew Jackson in the popular vote in 1824, he was elected president by the House of Representatives through the support of Henry Clay (No. 103). As president, he expanded the executive powers, favored internal improvements and refused to build a personal political machine. Defeated by Jackson in 1828, he was elected to the House of Representatives in 1831 and served there until his death 17 years later.*

532		UnFVF	UseFVF
6¢	**orange**	.35	.20
	Plate block of 4	1.50	
	FDC *(July 28, 1938)*		3.00

1938. ANDREW JACKSON ISSUE in the Presidential Series.

533 *Andrew Jackson, seventh president (1829-37), symbolized the common people's rise in power. A frontiersman, military hero (CM173) and senator from Tennessee, he received the largest popular vote in 1824, but was defeated in the House of Representatives when Henry Clay threw his own electoral votes to John Quincy Adams. Elected by a landslide in 1828, Jackson instituted national political conventions and the "spoils system," expanded the president's power, checked federal spending on internal improvements, paid off the national debt and destroyed the privileged Bank of the United States. Opposed to the states'-rights theories of John Calhoun, he countered South Carolina's refusal to collect protective-tariff duties by sending troops and naval forces to Charleston.*

533		UnFVF	UseFVF
7¢	**sepia**	.45	.20
	lilac brown	.45	.20
	Plate block of 4	2.00	
	FDC *(Aug. 4, 1938)*		3.00

1938. MARTIN VAN BUREN ISSUE in the Presidential Series.

534 *Martin Van Buren, eighth president (1837-41), was a senator, governor of New York and secretary of state and vice president under Jackson, whose policies he attempted to follow as president. He inaugurated the independent treasury, opposed federal spending for internal improvements and advocated tariffs for revenue only. Alienating the North by his appeasement of the British in a Canadian border incident, and the South by his opposition to the annexation of Texas, he was defeated by William Henry Harrison in the 1840 election, failed to win the Democratic nomination in 1844 and was defeated by Zachary Taylor in 1848.*

534		UnFVF	UseFVF
8¢	**olive green**	.45	.20
	light olive green	.45	.20
	olive	.45	.20
	Plate block of 4	2.20	
	FDC *(Aug. 11, 1938)*		3.00

1938. WILLIAM HENRY HARRISON ISSUE in the Presidential Series.

535 *William Henry Harrison, ninth president (1841), fought in the Battle of Fallen Timbers (CM89), served as secretary of the Northwest Territory and as its delegate to Congress, was first governor of the Indiana Territory (CM338), defeated the Indians under Tecumseh at Tippecanoe, defeated the British and Indians in the Battle of the Thames, was a member of both houses of Congress and served briefly as minister to Colombia. After his overwhelming victory in the 1840 election, he died of pneumonia a month after taking office.*

		UnFVF	UseFVF
535			
9¢	**rose pink**	.50	.20
	pink	.50	.20
	Plate block of 4	2.25	
	Pair, gutter between	—	
	FDC *(Aug. 18, 1938)*		3.00

1938. JOHN TYLER ISSUE in the Presidential Series.

536, 564 *John Tyler, 10th president (1841-45), had served as governor of Virginia and as a member of both houses of Congress before his election as vice president in 1840. As president after Harrison's death, he differed with the Whig Party on constitutional principles and lost his party's support. He signed the Pre-emption Act enabling settlers to get government land, reorganized the Navy, annexed Texas and settled the boundary between Maine and Canada. Later, in 1861, he was chairman of the unsuccessful peace conference at Washington and remained loyal to Virginia when it seceded.*

		UnFVF	UseFVF
536			
10¢	**Venetian red**	.45	.20
	dull Venetian red	.45	.20
	Plate block of 4	2.00	
	FDC *(Sept. 2, 1938)*		3.00

1938. JAMES KNOX POLK ISSUE in the Presidential Series.

537 *James Knox Polk, 11th president (1845-49), served as speaker of the House and as governor of Tennessee before his highly successful term as president. He fought the spoils system, settled the Oregon boundary dispute by accepting the 49th parallel and giving Vancouver to the British, reduced the tariff, restored the independent treasury system abolished under Tyler and won a war with Mexico. An expansionist but not an imperialist, he approved the acquisition of Texas, New Mexico and California, but opposed retaining Mexico by force.*

		UnFVF	UseFVF
537			
11¢	**cobalt**	.75	.20
	Plate block of 4	4.25	
	FDC *(Sept. 8, 1938)*		5.00

1938. ZACHARY TAYLOR ISSUE in the Presidential Series.

538 *Zachary Taylor, 12th president (1849-50), came to the White House after a distinguished 40-year Army career in which he gained the nickname "Old Rough and Ready." He fought in the War of 1812, the Black Hawk and Seminole Wars and the Mexican War, which he ended by defeating Santa Anna at Buena Vista in 1847. In his 16 months as president, he resumed the spoils system. A former slave-holder, he worked for California's admission as a free state. He died of typhus in 1850.*

		UnFVF	UseFVF
538			
12¢	**light reddish violet**	1.40	.20
	Plate block of 4	6.00	
	FDC *(Sept. 14, 1938)*		5.00

1938. MILLARD FILLMORE ISSUE in the Presidential Series.

539 *Millard Fillmore, 13th president (1850-53), spent four terms in the House of Representatives before his election as vice president under Taylor. As president he favored the compromise policy in the slavery issue, signed the Fugitive Slave Act, approved the negotiations leading to the opening of Japan (CM363), and maintained neutrality in foreign wars.*

		UnFVF	UseFVF
539			
13¢	**blue green**	2.25	.20
	dark blue green	2.25	.20
	Plate block of 4	9.50	
	FDC *(Sept. 22, 1938)*		5.00

1938. FRANKLIN PIERCE ISSUE in the Presidential Series.

540 *Franklin Pierce, 14th president (1853-57), congressman, senator and brigadier general in the Mexican War, won the Democratic nomination in 1852 on the 49th ballot. As president, he effected the Gadsden Purchase (CM370), sent Matthew Perry to open trade with Japan (CM363), attempted to secure a base in Santo Domingo and annex Cuba, Hawaii and Alaska, and signed the Kansas-Nebraska Bill leaving slavery in those territories to popular vote. Attempting impartiality in domestic policy and imperialism in foreign policy, he generally failed at both and retired to obscurity.*

		UnFVF	UseFVF
540			
14¢	**blue**	1.15	.20
	Plate block of 4	6.00	
	FDC *(Oct. 6, 1938)*		5.00

1938. JAMES BUCHANAN ISSUE in the Presidential Series.

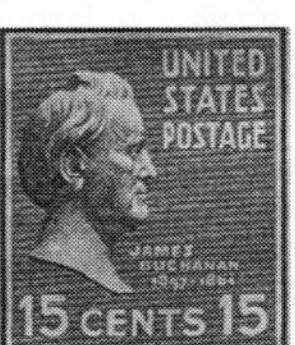

541 *James Buchanan, 15th president (1857-61), had served successively as congressman, minister to Russia, senator, secretary of state under Polk and minister to Great Britain. A conservative and ineffective president, he expressed moral opposition to slavery and secession, but furthered one and condoned the other. His administration saw the growth of the new Republican Party, the Lincoln-Douglas debates and the abolitionist John Brown's raid on the federal armory at Harper's Ferry, Virginia, for which Brown was hanged. Failing to meet the challenge of South Carolina's secession and her firing on Fort Sumter, Buchanan left the office on the brink of the Civil War.*

		UnFVF	UseFVF
541			
15¢	**slate**	.65	.20
	Plate block of 4	3.00	
	FDC *(Oct. 13, 1938)*		5.00

1938. ABRAHAM LINCOLN ISSUE in the Presidential Series.

542 *Abraham Lincoln, 16th president (1861-65), worked as a rail-splitter, surveyor and postmaster of Salem, Ill.; served a term in Congress; and became an outstanding jury lawyer before attaining national prominence through a series of debates with Stephen A. Douglas, against whom he was running for the Senate in 1858. Nominated as the Republican presidential candidate in 1860 because of his conservative views on slavery, his election signaled the secession of seven Southern states. Given almost dictatorial powers in the Civil War, he followed a middle course between the radicals and defeatists, ably commanding the Union war effort and diplomatically handling his cabinet and his generals. Although he had hoped for a gradual, compensated abolition of slavery, in 1863 he issued the Emancipation Proclamation freeing all slaves in rebel territory. The same year marked his Gettysburg Address (CM320). Re-elected in the dark days of 1864, he made his great Second Inaugural Address; "With malice toward none, with charity for all...let us strive on to finish the work we are in; to bind up the nation's wounds...to do all which may achieve a just and lasting peace." His compassionate program for conciliation and reconstruction was never achieved. Ten days later, five days after Lee's surrender at Appomattox, he was assassinated by a Southern fanatic while attending a theater play.*

		UnFVF	UseFVF
542			
16¢	**black**	1.25	.60
	Plate block of 4	6.00	
	FDC *(Oct. 20, 1938)*		6.00

1938. Andrew Johnson Issue in the Presidential Series.

543 *Andrew Johnson, 17th president (1865-69), a self-educated tailor, was a congressman, governor of Tennessee and the only Southern senator to support the Union in the Civil War. His success as military governor of Tennessee led to his election as vice president. As president after Lincoln's death, he attempted to carry out Lincoln's conciliatory policies of Reconstruction, but was thwarted by the radical Republicans in Congress. His removal of War Secretary Edwin M. Stanton (No. 101) for conspiracy led to his impeachment, which fell one vote short of the two-thirds majority needed to remove him from the White House. Elected to the Senate again in 1875, he died the same year.*

		UnFVF	UseFVF
543			
17¢	**rose red**	1.25	.20
	Plate block of 4	6.00	
	FDC *(Oct. 27, 1938)*		6.00

1938. Ulysses S. Grant Issue in the Presidential Series.

544 *Ulysses S. Grant, 18th president (1869-77), led the Union forces to victory in the Civil War (CM174). As president, he authorized harsh Reconstruction policies that kept sectional hatreds alive, and, although he was personally honest, his administration was involved in grave scandals. His achievements included civil service reform and the funding of the national debt. Left penniless by the collapse of a banking house in 1884, he was persuaded by Mark Twain (CM205) to write his "Personal Memoirs," which he finished four days before his death in 1885. They realized almost $450,000.*

		UnFVF	UseFVF
544			
18¢	**brown carmine**	2.25	.25
	rose brown	2.25	.25
	Plate block of 4	10.00	
	FDC *(Nov. 3, 1938)*		6.00

1938. Rutherford B. Hayes Issue in the Presidential Series.

545 *Rutherford B. Hayes, 19th president (1877-81), former congressman and governor of Ohio, ran second to Samuel J. Tilden in the 1876 election, but was chosen president by a partisan electoral commission by a vote of 185-184. His administration returned local government to the South, ending the Reconstruction, and made ineffective attempts at civil service reform.*

		UnFVF	UseFVF
545			
19¢	**light reddish violet**	2.00	.60
	Plate block of 4	9.50	
	FDC *(Nov. 10, 1938)*		6.00

1938. James A. Garfield Issue in the Presidential Series.

546 *James A. Garfield, 20th president (1881), Republican leader of the House, was a senator-elect when chosen president in 1880. Four months after his inauguration, he was fatally shot by a man who had been turned down in a bid to become ambassador to France.*

		UnFVF	UseFVF
546			
20¢	**blue green**	1.25	.20
	bright blue green	1.25	.20
	Plate block of 4	5.00	
	FDC *(Nov. 10, 1938)*		6.00

1938. Chester A. Arthur Issue in the Presidential Series.

547 *Chester A. Arthur, 21st president (1881-85), who succeeded to the office after Garfield's assassination, was an able and honest administrator. He supported civil service reform, arranged a canal treaty (unratified) with Nicaragua, vetoed a Chinese-exclusion bill and began the rebuilding of the Navy.*

		UnFVF	UseFVF
547			
21¢	**slate blue**	2.25	.20
	Plate block of 4	10.00	
	FDC *(Nov. 22, 1938)*		7.00

1938. Grover Cleveland Issue in the Presidential Series.

548 *Grover Cleveland, 22nd and 24th president (1885-89 and 1893-97), reform governor of New York, was an honest and independent president. In his first term he enlarged the civil service, followed a conciliatory policy toward the South, avoided the spoils system, opposed pork-barrel pension bills, and vetoed more than two-thirds of the congressional acts presented to him. Defeated by Benjamin Harrison in 1888, he ran again and was re-elected in 1892. His second term was marked by a severe depression, a fight against inflation, an income tax law (declared unconstitutional), the use of troops to end the mail stoppage in the Pullman strike, and a firm stand against the British use of force in a boundary dispute with Venezuela.*

		UnFVF	UseFVF
548			
22¢	**vermilion**	1.50	.75
	Plate block of 4	12.50	
	FDC *(Nov. 22, 1938)*		7.00

1938. Benjamin Harrison Issue in the Presidential Series.

549 *Benjamin Harrison, 23rd president (1889-93), was a grandson of William Henry Harrison, ninth president. A Union regimental commander in the Civil War and senator for one term, as president he greatly expanded the pension list, signed the McKinley high-tariff bill and the Sherman silver purchase act, followed imperialistic policies in the Pacific, convened the first Pan-American Conference in 1889 and aided the admission to the Union of the Dakotas, Montana and Washington in 1889 and Idaho and Wyoming in 1900.*

		UnFVF	UseFVF
549			
24¢	**gray green**	4.25	.35
	Plate block of 4	20.00	
	FDC *(Dec. 2, 1938)*		8.00

1938. William McKinley Issue in the Presidential Series.

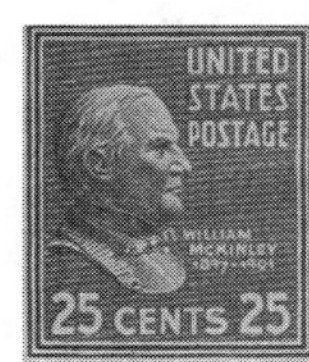

550 *William McKinley, 25th president (1897-1901), former Congressman and governor of Ohio, was elected on a platform of high tariff and maintenance of the gold standard; raised the tariff to the highest level in American history and signed the Gold Standard Act of 1900. After the sinking of the* Maine *at Havana, public opinion forced his intervention in the Cuban rebellion; the resulting Spanish-American War ended in a temporary American protectorate over Cuba, the purchase of the Philippine Islands, the annexation of Puerto Rico and Guam and the establishment of the United States as a world power. His administration also marked the annexation of Hawaii, intervention in China and agitation for a Panama Canal. Re-elected on the "full dinner pail" platform, he was fatally shot by an anarchist the following September while visiting the Pan-American Exposition (CM26-31).*

		UnFVF	UseFVF
550			
25¢	**claret**	1.20	.20

		UnFVF	UseFVF
	rose lilac	1.20	.20
	Plate block of 4	5.00	
	FDC *(Dec. 2, 1938)*		8.00

1938. THEODORE ROOSEVELT ISSUE in the Presidential Series.

551 *Theodore Roosevelt, 26th president (1901-09), achieved early fame as assistant secretary of the Navy under McKinley, as organizer of the Rough Riders (CM315) in the Spanish-American War and as a crusading governor of New York. Given the Republican vice presidential nomination, "to get him out of the way," upon McKinley's death he became, at 43, America's youngest president. He fought government corruption by big business, recognized Panama when it revolted from Colombia, began the construction of the Panama Canal (CM48 and CM198), won the Nobel Peace Prize for his successful mediation of the Russo-Japanese War, organized conservation of national resources and instituted the Pure Food and Drugs Act. Virtually bequeathing the presidency to William Howard Taft, he became dissatisfied with Taft's conservative policies and ran against him in 1912, splitting the Republican ticket so that both lost to Woodrow Wilson. He also was noted as a naturalist, explorer and writer.*

551		UnFVF	UseFVF
30¢	**deep ultramarine**	5.00	.20
	ultramarine	5.00	.20
	blue	15.00	
	deep blue	110.00	
	Plate block of 4	22.50	
	FDC *(Dec. 8, 1938)*		10.00

1938. WILLIAM HOWARD TAFT ISSUE in the Presidential Series.

552 William Howard Taft, 27th president (1909-13), had distinguished careers before and after his presidency. He was a federal judge, solicitor general under Benjamin Harrison, dean of the University of Cincinnati Law School, president of the Philippines Commission, first civil governor of the Philippines, secretary of war and provisional governor of Cuba. His administration dissolved the Standard Oil and American Tobacco Co. trusts, set up the Department of Labor and drafted the 16th and 17th Amendments (authorizing the income tax and the direct election of senators). Defeated in 1912, he became a lecturer and Yale law professor. Appointed chief justice of the United States in 1919, he served until his death in 1930.

552		UnFVF	UseFVF
50¢	**light red violet**	8.50	.20
	Plate block of 4	40.00	
	FDC *(Dec. 8, 1938)*		15.00

Flat plate printing, perforated 11.

1938. WOODROW WILSON ISSUE in the Presidential Series.

553 *Woodrow Wilson, 28th president (1913-21), was president of Princeton University and a reform governor of New Jersey before his election in 1912. His first administration instituted the Federal Reserve Act, Farm Loan Act, Federal Trade Commission, Clayton Anti-Trust Act and Adamson Eight-House Law. (His entire tenure saw three Constitutional Amendments: direct election of Senators, prohibition and women's suffrage). In foreign affairs, in his first term he had difficulties with some Latin American countries, sent the Pershing Expedition into Mexico, established partial protectorates in Santo Domingo, Haiti and Nicaragua, and maintained neutrality in World War I despite foreign pressures and the infringement of American rights. Re-elected with the slogan, "He kept us out of war," within a month of his inauguration he was forced by German sinking of American ships to ask for a declaration of war. An apostle of international cooperation, he went to Paris to negotiate the peace treaty, in which he said the League of Nations was the "most essential part." When the Senate rejected both the treaty and the league, he toured the country for public support, suffered a stroke and became an invalid. He won the Nobel Peace Prize in 1919 and died in 1924.*

553		UnFVF	UseFVF
$1	**dark purple and black**	10.00	.20
	Plate block of 4	45.00	
	Center line block	30.00	
	Margin block of 4, w/arrow	27.50	
	FDC *(Aug. 19, 1938)*		60.00
	w. Watermarked "USIR"	300.00	70.00
	w. Plate block of 4	1,800.00	
	FDC (dry print 1954)		30.00
	v. Vertical pair, imperforate between	2,750.00	
	v1. Vertical pair, imperforate horizontally	1,500.00	
	a. red violet and black *(Aug. 31, 1954)* (dry print)	9.00	.20
	Plate block of 4	40.00	
	av. Vertical pair, imperforate between	7,500.00	
	av1. Vertical pair, imperforate horizontally	1,000.00	

553a is printed on pre-gummed, whiter and thicker paper. It was printed on "dry" print; No. 553 was printed on pre-dampened paper.

1938. WARREN G. HARDING ISSUE in the Presidential Series.

554 *Warren G. Harding, 29th president (1921-23), was an Ohio newspaperman and senator who supported prohibition, anti-strike legislation, women's suffrage and high tariffs; opposed the League of Nations as a threat to national sovereignty. Overwhelmingly elected in 1920 on a "return to normalcy" platform, he worked to repeal excess profits and high income taxes and to revise the tariff. In 1921 he called the Washington Conference to limit naval armaments. Returning from a visit to Alaska in 1923, he died unexpectedly at San Francisco.*

554		UnFVF	UseFVF
$2	**green and black**	27.50	4.75
	yellow green and black	27.50	4.75
	Plate block of 4	135.00	
	Center line block	85.00	35.00
	Margin block of 4, w/arrow	85.00	
	FDC *(Sept. 29, 1938)*		125.00

1938. CALVIN COOLIDGE ISSUE in the Presidential Series.

555 *Calvin Coolidge, 30th president (1923-29), attained prominence in 1919, when, as governor of Massachusetts, he suppressed the Boston police strike on the grounds that "there is no right to strike against the public safety." Elected vice president, he succeeded to the presidency upon Harding's death. In a period of prosperity, his administration was cautious and passive in domestic affairs and isolationist toward Europe. He opposed the League of Nations, approved the World Court, vetoed the Soldiers' Bonus Act, twice vetoed the Farm Relief Bill, refused to intervene in the coal strike of 1927 and reduced the national debt by $2 billion in three years. He declined to run for a third term.*

555		UnFVF	UseFVF
$5	**carmine and black**	115.00	4.50
	red brown and black	3,000.00	1,000.00
	Plate block of 4	500.00	
	Center line block	—	12.50
	Margin block of 4, w/arrow	400.00	
	FDC *(Nov. 17, 1938)*		210.00

1939. PRESIDENTIAL COIL ISSUE in the Presidential Series. Used the same designs as the sheet stamps. *Rotary press, perforated 10 vertically.*

556		UnFVF	UseFVF
1¢	**green**	.25	.20
	light green	.25	.20
	Pair	.50	
	Line pair	1.50	
	FDC *(Jan. 10, 1939)*		5.00

557		UnFVF	UseFVF
1-1/2¢	**yellow brown**	.25	.20
	ocher	.25	.20
	Pair	.50	

			UnFVF	UseFVF
		Line pair	1.50	
		FDC *(Jan. 20, 1939)*		5.00

558			UnFVF	UseFVF
2¢	**rose**		.25	.20
	Pair		.50	
	Line pair		1.50	
	FDC *(Jan. 20, 1939)*			5.00

559		UnFVF	UseFVF
3¢	**violet**	.25	.20
	Pair	.50	
	Line pair	1.50	
	Gripper cracks	—	
	p. Thin, translucent paper	—	
	FDC *(Jan. 20, 1939)*		5.00

560		UnFVF	UseFVF
4¢	**bright purple**	7.50	.75
	Pair	17.50	
	Line pair	32.50	
	FDC *(Jan. 20, 1939)*		5.00

561		UnFVF	UseFVF
4-1/2¢	**gray**	.75	.50
	Pair	1.50	
	Line pair	5.50	
	FDC *(Jan. 20, 1939)*		5.00

562		UnFVF	UseFVF
5¢	**bright blue**	6.00	.50
	Pair	12.50	
	Line pair	27.50	
	FDC *(Jan. 20, 1939)*		5.00

563		UnFVF	UseFVF
6¢	**orange**	1.25	.50
	Pair	2.00	
	Line pair	7.50	
	FDC *(Jan. 20, 1939)*		7.00

564		UnFVF	UseFVF
10¢	**Venetian red**	12.50	1.25
	Pair	22.50	
	Line pair	50.00	
	FDC *(Jan. 20, 1939)*		10.00

1939. PRESIDENTIAL COIL ISSUE in the Presidential Series. *Rotary press, perforated 10 horizontally.*

565		UnFVF	UseFVF
1¢	**green**	.75	.25
	Pair	1.25	
	Line pair	2.25	
	FDC *(Jan. 27, 1939)*		6.00

566		UnFVF	UseFVF
1-1/2¢	**yellow brown**	1.50	.75
	Pair	4.50	
	Line pair	2.75	
	FDC *(Jan. 27, 1939)*		6.00

567		UnFVF	UseFVF
2¢	**rose**	2.50	.75
	Pair	6.00	
	Line pair	4.00	
	FDC *(Jan. 27, 1939)*		6.00

568		UnFVF	UseFVF
3¢	**violet**	2.25	.75
	Pair	6.00	
	Line pair	4.00	
	FDC *(Jan. 28, 1939)*		6.00

1954-73. Liberty Series

The series takes its name from the Statue of Liberty, which was used as the design of the first stamp issued, the 8¢ value, as well as a similar 8¢ value, a 3¢ value and an 11¢ value. The design of the 3¢ and first 8¢ stamp were also used on an imperforate souvenir sheet (CM388) for the Fifth International Philatelic Exhibition. Because of the various printing methods and formats, it is a challenging series for collectors.

1955. BENJAMIN FRANKLIN ISSUE in the Liberty Series. *Rotary press, perforated 11 x 10 1/2.*

569 *Benjamin Franklin*

569		MNHVF	UseVF
1/2¢	**vermilion** wet print	.25	.20
	Plate block of 4	.50	
	FDC *(Oct. 20, 1955)*		1.75
	p. Dry print *(May 1958)*	.25	.20
	Plate block of 4	.50	

1954. GEORGE WASHINGTON ISSUE in the Liberty Series. *Rotary press, perforated 11 x 10 1/2.*

570, 587 *George Washington*

570		MNHVF	UseVF
1¢	**dull green** wet print	.25	.20
	Plate block of 4	.50	
	Pair, gutter between	—	
	FDC *(Aug. 26, 1954)*		1.75
	p. Dry print *(March 1956)*	.25	.20
	Plate block of 4	.50	
	p1. Hi-Brite paper	—	
	Plate block of 4	—	

1956. MOUNT VERNON ISSUE in the Liberty Series. *Rotary press, perforated 10 1/2 x 11.*

571 *Mount Vernon, home of George Washington, on the south bank of the Potomac, 16 miles below Washington, D.C. Land was part of the Royal Grant to Lord Culpepper, who in 1674 granted 5,000 acres to Nicolas Spencer and John Washington, great-grandfather of George. Since 1858 preserved and restored by Mount Vernon Ladies Association.*

571		MNHVF	UseVF
1-1/2¢	**brown carmine** dry print	.25	.20
	Plate block of 4	.50	
	FDC *(Feb. 22, 1956)*		1.75

1954. THOMAS JEFFERSON ISSUE in the Liberty Series. *Rotary press, perforated 11 x 10 1/2.*

572, 588 Thomas Jefferson

572		MNHVF	UseVF
2¢	**rose** dry print	.25	.20
	Plate block of 4	.50	
	Pair, gutter between	—	
	FDC *(Sept. 15, 1954)*		1.75
	p. Silkote paper *(Dec. 1954)*	1,250.00	
	Plate block of 4	—	

Note: *Silkote paper was used for only 50,000 stamps. Silkote varieties need expertization.*

1954. STATUE OF LIBERTY ISSUE in the Liberty Series. *Rotary press, perforated 11 x 10 1/2.*

573, 589 *Statue of Liberty*

573		MNHVF	UseVF
3¢	**violet** wet print	.25	.20
	Plate block of 4	.50	
	Pair, gutter between	150.00	

		MNHVF	UseVF
	n. Booklet pane of 6 *(June 30, 1954)*	4.50	
	nv. Booklet pane of 6, imperforate between vertically	—	
	p. Dry print *(Sept. 1956)*	.25	.20
	Plate block of 4	.50	
	pn. Booklet pane of 6	4.50	
	pz. Tagged, Type II *(July 6, 1966)*	.35	.25
	Plate block of 4	5.00	
	pz1. Tagged, Type III	—	
	Plate block of 4	—	
	p1. Hi-Brite paper	—	
	Plate block of 4	—	
	v. Horizontal pair, imperforate between	2,000.00	
	v1. Pair, imperforate (18 3/4 x 22 1/2mm)	2,250.00	
	FDC *(June 24, 1954)*		1.75
	FDC Booklet Pane		5.00
	FDC Tagged		30.00

Type I tagging: mat tagging. The four separate mats used did not cover the entire sheet of 400 stamps and certain untagged areas help to identify this variety. See expanded definition in the catalog introduction.

Type II tagging: roll tagging. Continuously surfaced rolls replaced the previously used tagging mats. Only the plate number selvage margin is partially tagged, and the plate number blocks have one untagged margin.

Type III tagging: curved metal plate tagging. Sheet margins are almost fully tagged but a "hot line" of intense phosphor-tagging or untagged narrow gap, 1mm or less in width, can appear on stamps from any position in the pane.

1954. ABRAHAM LINCOLN ISSUE. in the Liberty Series. *Rotary press, perforated 11 x 10 1/2.*

574, 590 *Abraham Lincoln*

574		MNHVF	UseVF
4¢	**magenta** wet print	.25	.20
	Plate block of 4	.50	
	Pair, gutter between	—	
	n. Booklet pane of 6 (July 31, 1958)	2.75	
	nv. Booklet pane of 6, imperforate between horizontally	—	
	p. Dry print *(July 1956)*	.25	.20
	Plate block of 4	.50	
	Pair, gutter between	—	
	pn. Booklet pane of 6	2.75	
	pz. Tagged, Type I *(Nov. 2, 1963)*	.50	.45
	Plate block of 4	.50	
	pz1. Tagged, Type II	.50	
	Plate block of 4	.50	
	p1. Hi-Brite paper	—	
	Plate block of 4	—	
	v. Horizontal pair, imperforate between	3,600.00	
	FDC *(Nov. 19, 1954)*		1.75
	FDC Booklet pane		4.00
	FDC tagged		100.00

1954. JAMES MONROE ISSUE in the Liberty Series. *Rotary press, perforated 11 x 10 1/2.*

575 *James Monroe*

575		MNHVF	UseVF
5¢	**blue** dry print	.25	.20
	Plate block of 4	.65	
	Pair, gutter between	—	
	FDC *(Dec. 2, 1954)*		1.75

1955. THEODORE ROOSEVELT ISSUE in the Liberty Series. *Rotary press, perforated 11 x 10 1/2.*

576 *Theodore Roosevelt*

576		MNHVF	UseVF
6¢	**rose red** wet print	.25	.20
	Plate block of 4	1.75	
	p. Dry print *(March 1957)*	.40	.25
	Plate block of 4	1.70	
	v. Block of 4 imperforate (one known)	23,000.00	
	FDC *(Nov. 18, 1955)*		1.75

1956. WOODROW WILSON ISSUE in the Liberty Series. *Rotary press, perforated 11 x 10 1/2.*

577 *Woodrow Wilson*

577		MNHVF	UseVF
7¢	**carmine red** dry print	.25	.20
	Plate block of 4	1.25	
	FDC *(Jan. 10, 1956)*		1.75
	p. Hi-Brite paper	—	
	Plate block of 4	—	

1954. STATUE OF LIBERTY ISSUE in the Liberty Series. *Rotary and flat plate press, perforated 11 (also see 591). The torch extends between "U.S." and "Postage" to the top of the design.*

578, 578A *Statue of Liberty*

578		MNHVF	UseVF
8¢	**deep blue & carmine**	.25	.20
	Plate block of 4, both red & blue numbers	2.00	
	Plate block (corner) of 4, blue number only	—	
	Plate block (corner) of 4, red number only	—	
	v. Double impression, carmine	650.00	
	FDC *(April 9, 1954)*		1.75

Flat plate printing, 22.7mm high. See also 591 for Type II.

1954. STATUE OF LIBERTY ISSUE in the Liberty Series. *Rotary press, perforated 11 x 10 1/2.*

578A		MNHVF	UseVF
8¢	**deep blue and carmine**	.40	.20
	Plate block of 4, both red and blue numbers	3.00	—
	FDC *(April 9, 1954)*		

Rotary press printing, 22.9mm high, slightly taller than No. 578.

1956. THE ALAMO ISSUE in the Liberty Series. *Rotary press, perforated 10 1/2 x 11.*

579 *The Alamo, called the "Cradle of Texas Liberty," founded in 1718 as Mission de San Antonio de Valero, beseiged in 1836 by Gen. Santa Anna and 1,000 Mexicans; the 184 Texan defenders under Col. William Barrett Travis, including Davy Crockett and James Bowie, fought to the last man. Site is now a historic shrine and museum.*

579		MNHVF	UseVF
9¢	**rose lilac** dry print	.25	.20
	Plate block of 4	1.25	
	a. deep rose lilac	—	
	Plate block of 4	—	
	FDC *(June 14, 1956)*		2.00

1956. INDEPENDENCE HALL ISSUE in the Liberty Series. *Rotary press, perforated 10 1/2 x 11.*

580 *Independence Hall, where the Declaration of Independence was adopted and which for many years housed the Liberty Bell.*

580		MNHVF	UseVF
10¢	**brown purple** dry print	.25	.20
	Plate block of 4	1.00	
	a. deep brown purple	—	
	Plate block of 4	—	
	p. Hi-Brite paper	—	
	Plate block of 4	—	
	z. Tagged, Type II *(July 6, 1966)*	2.50	1.50
	Plate block of 4	60.00	
	z1. Tagged, Type III	—	
	Plate block of 4	—	
	FDC *(July 4, 1956)*		2.00
	FDC tagged		30.00

1956. MONTICELLO ISSUE in the Liberty Series. *Rotary press, perforated 10 1/2 x 11.*

581 *Monticello, Thomas Jefferson's estate in Virginia*

581		MNHVF	UseVF
20¢	**bright blue** dry print	.50	.20
	Plate block of 4	1.75	
	a. deep blue	—	
	Plate block of 4	—	
	p. Hi-Brite paper	—	
	Plate block of 4	—	
	FDC *(April 13, 1956)*		2.50

1955. ROBERT E. LEE ISSUE in the Liberty Series. *Rotary press, perforated 11 x 10 1/2.*

582 *Robert E. Lee*

582		MNHVF	UseVF
30¢	**black** wet print	1.50	.25
	Plate block of 4	6.00	
	p. Dry print *(June 1957)*	1.00	.20
	Plate block of 4	5.50	
	FDC *(Sept. 21, 1955)*		2.50

1955. JOHN MARSHALL ISSUE in the Liberty Series. *Rotary press, perforated 11 x 10 1/2.*

583 *John Marshall*

583		MNHVF	UseVF
40¢	**brown carmine** wet print	2.75	.25
	Plate block of 4	13.00	
	p. Dry print *(April 1958)*	2.00	.20
	Plate block of 4	8.00	
	FDC *(Sept. 24, 1955)*		4.00

1955. SUSAN B. ANTHONY ISSUE in the Liberty Series. *Rotary press, perforated 11 x 10 1/2.*

584 *Susan B. Anthony*

584		MNHVF	UseVF
50¢	**red violet** wet print	2.00	.20
	Plate block of 4	13.00	
	Cracked plate (No. 25231, upper left)	—	
	p. Dry print *(April 1958)*	1.50	.20
	Plate block of 4	7.00	
	FDC *(Aug. 25, 1955)*		6.00

1955. PATRICK HENRY ISSUE in the Liberty Series honored the patriot who, in 1775, uttered the famous phrase, "As for me, give me liberty, or give me death." Henry (1736-99) served five one year terms as governor of Virginia and worked hard to secure passage of the Bill of Rights. *Rotary press, perforated 11 x 10 1/2.*

585 *Patrick Henry*

585		MNHVF	UseVF
$1	**dark lilac** wet print	7.00	.20
	Plate block of 4	25.00	
	p. Dry print *(Oct. 1958)*	5.00	.20
	Plate block of 4	22.50	
	FDC *(Oct. 7, 1955)*		10.00

1956. ALEXANDER HAMILTON ISSUE in the Liberty Series. *Flat plate, perforated 11.*

586 *Alexander Hamilton*

586		MNHVF	UseVF
$5	**black** dry print	70.00	6.50
	Plate block of 4	300.00	
	FDC *(March 19, 1956)*		65.00

1954. GEORGE WASHINGTON ISSUE in the Liberty Series. *Horizontal coil, rotary press, perforated 10 vertically.*

587		MNHVF	UseVF
1¢	**dull green** wet print	.45	.25
	Pair	.75	
	Line pair	1.50	
	p. Dry print, large holes *(Aug. 1957)*	.50	.20
	Pair	.35	
	Line pair	.75	
	ps. Dry print, small holes, *(Feb. 1960)*	.50	.20
	Pair	.75	
	Line pair	1.00	
	v. Pair, imperforate	2,250.00	
	FDC *(Oct. 8, 1954)*		1.75

1954. THOMAS JEFFERSON ISSUE in the Liberty Series. *Horizontal coil, rotary press, perforated 10.*

588		MNHVF	UseVF
2¢	**rose** wet print	.25	.20
	Pair	.35	

	Line pair	.75	
	p. Dry print, large holes *(May 1957)*	.25	.20
	Pair	.35	.25
	Line pair	.75	.30
	pss. Dry print, small holes, shiny gum *(Aug. 1961)*	.25	.20
	Pair	.35	.25
	Line pair	1.00	.40
	pssz. Tagged, Type II *(May 6, 1968)*	.25	.20
	Pair	.35	.25
	Line pair	.75	.30
	psszv. Pair, imperforate	600.00	
	Line pair, imperforate	1,200.00	
	psmz. Dry print, small holes, matte gum, tagged	.25	.20
	Pair	.70	
	Line pair	2.00	
	psmv. Pair imperforate, dry print, matte gum, untagged	575.00	
	Line pair, imperforate	—	
	FDC *(Oct. 22, 1954)*		1.75
	FDC tagged		20.00

The imperforate pair, untagged, listed above (588psmv) is known with a Bureau precancel of Riverdale, Md.

1954. STATUE OF LIBERTY ISSUE in the Liberty Series. *Horizontal coil, rotary press, perforated 10.*

589		MNHVF	UseVF
3¢	**purple** wet print, large holes	.25	.20
	Pair	.50	.25
	Line pair	1.00	.45
	p. Dry print, large holes *(May 1957)*	.75	.20
	Pair	1.00	
	Line pair	1.50	
	Gripper cracks	—	
	ps. Dry print, small holes *(July 31, 1958)*	.30	.20
	Pair	.50	.25
	Line pair	.60	.45
	pv. Pair, imperforate, (19 1/2 x 22mm)	1,500.00	850.00
	Line pair, imperforate	—	
	psz. Tagged *Look* Magazine printing *(Oct. 1966)*	6.00	3.00
	Pair	12.00	
	Line pair	150.00	
	psz1. Tagged, Type II philatelic printing *(June 26, 1967)*	2.50	.75
	Pair	5.00	
	Line pair	25.00	
	FDC *(July 20, 1954)*		1.75
	FDC tagged		50.00

No. 589psz1, the so-called "Look Coil," was prepared for Look *magazine in coil rolls of 3,000 subjects. All but 99,000 of this issue were affixed to outgoing mail and return addressed envelopes on an automatic labeling machine at Des Moines, Iowa. The earliest known use was Dec. 29, 1966. The common usage was in combination with a 2¢ Jefferson coil (No. 588). The paper on which the stamps were printed is plain, without fluorescent content, and tagging is uniform and brilliant. A special printing was issued, in coils of 500 subjects, to satisfy collector demands (No. 589psz1). The original printing had a sharper, more well-defined design. The reprint has a more intense shade of purple ink. The philatelic examples were on slightly fluorescent paper, the tagging was less intense and on some coils a tagging plate flaw repeats every 24th stamp, both as a "Hot" line and as an untagged line.*

1958. ABRAHAM LINCOLN ISSUE in the Liberty Series. *Horizontal coil, rotary press, perforated 10.*

590		MNHVF	UseVF
4¢	**bright purple** wet print (Bureau precancel only)	29.00	1.00
	Pair	50.00	2.50
	Line pair	425.00	40.00
	p. Dry print, large holes *(June 1958)*	.75	.20
	Pair	1.00	.25
	Line pair	2.00	.45
	ps. Dry print, small holes *(July 31, 1958)*	.75	.20
	Pair	1.00	.25
	Line pair	2.00	.45
	psv. Pair, imperforate	125.00	75.00
	Line pair, imperforate	250.00	
	p1. Hi-Brite paper	—	
	Pair	—	
	Line pair	—	
	FDC *(July 31, 1958)*	.75	.20

1958. STATUE OF LIBERTY ISSUE in the Liberty Series. *Giori press, perforated 11. The torch and flame do not break through the wording* "U.S. POSTAGE," *the Statue of Liberty is larger than on 578 and the word* "LIBERTY" *is smaller and lower.*

591 *Statue of Liberty*

591		MNHVF	UseVF
8¢	**deep blue & carmine**	.25	.20
	Plate block of 4	1.00	
	FDC *(March 22, 1958)*		1.75

1958. JOHN JAY ISSUE in the Liberty Series. *Rotary press, perforated 11 x 10 1/2.*

592 *John Jay (1745-1829), statesman, first Chief Justice of the Supreme Court (1789-94) and governor of New York (1795-1801). He was a delegate and, in 1778, president of the Continental Congress. Aided Franklin in negotiating peace with Great Britain.*

592		MNHVF	UseVF
15¢	**brown purple** dry print	.75	.20
	Plate block of 4	2.75	
	p1. Hi-Brite paper	—	
	Plate block of 4	—	
	p1z. Tagged, Type II *(July 6, 1966)*	1.25	.50
	Plate block of 4	9.00	
	p1z1. Tagged, Type III	—	
	Plate block of 4	—	
	FDC *(Dec. 12, 1958)*		2.50
	FDC tagged		35.00

1958. PAUL REVERE ISSUE in the Liberty Series. *Rotary press, perforated 11 x 10 1/2.*

593, 614 *Paul Revere (1735-1818), silversmith, copper engraver, and one of three patriots made famous by Longfellow for his ride from Charleston to Lexington, April 18, 1775, to warn of British march. He designed and printed the first issue of continental currency and first official seal for colonies.*

593		MNHVF	UseVF
25¢	**deep blue green**	1.50	.20
	Plate block of 4	5.00	
	p1. Hi-Brite paper	—	
	Plate block of 4	—	
	FDC *(April 18, 1958)*		2.50

1959. BUNKER HILL MONUMENT ISSUE in the Liberty Series. *Rotary press, perforated 11 x 10 1/2.*

594, 598 *Bunker Hill Monument (220 feet high) erected in 1843 on the site (then called Breed's Hill) of the first major battle of the Revolutionary War (June 17, 1775). Gen. Joseph Warren, commander of U.S. forces at this battle, issued the now-famous order, "Don't shoot until you see the whites of their eyes." Outnumbered four-to-one, the colonists lost the battle but inflicted very heavy casualties on the British troops. This moral victory gave the colonists new inspiration. Background of the stamp shows the Pine Tree flag adopted by the Commonwealth of Massachusetts at the beginning of the Revolutionary War.*

594		MNHVF	UseVF
2-1/2¢	**slate blue** dry print	.25	.20
	Plate block of 4	.65	
	FDC *(June 17, 1959)*		1.75

1959. Hermitage Issue in the Liberty Series. *Rotary press, perforated 10 1/2 x 11.*

595, 597 *Hermitage, home of Andrew Jackson*

595		MNHVF	UseVF
4-1/2¢	**blue green** dry print	.25	.20
	Plate block of 4	.75	
	FDC *(March 16, 1959)*		1.75

1959. Benjamin Harrison Issue in the Liberty Series. *Rotary press, perforated 11 x 10 1/2.*

596 *Benjamin Harrison (see No. 549)*

596		MNHVF	UseVF
12¢	**carmine red** dry print	.30	.20
	Plate block of 4	1.50	
	FDC *(June 6, 1959)*		2.00
	Plate block of 4	4.00	
	FDC *(May 6, 1968)*, tagged		12.00
	z. Tagged, Type IIa *(May 6, 1968)*	.35	.20
	FDC tagged		30.00

Type IIa tagging: wide roll tagging. All margins are fully tagged.

1959. Hermitage Coil Issue in the Liberty Series. *Coil, perforated 10 horizontally.*

597		MNHVF	UseVF
4-1/2¢	**blue green** large holes	2.00	1.25
	Pair	3.00	2.50
	Line pair	15.00	5.00
	s. Small holes *(April 1961)*	20.00	2.00
	Pair	30.00	5.00
	Line pair	425.00	60.00
	FDC *(May 1, 1959)*		1.75

1959. Bunker Hill Monument Coil Issue in the Liberty Series. *Rotary press, perforated 10 vertically.*

598		MNHVF	UseVF
2-1/2¢	**slate blue** large holes	.25	.20
	Pair	.50	.40
	Line pair	3.50	1.25
	s. Small holes (Bureau precancel) *(Jan. 1961)*	—	—
	Pair	—	
	Line pair	—	
	FDC *(Sept. 9, 1959)*		2.00

1960. Palace of the Governors in the Liberty Series. *Rotary press, perforated 10 1/2 x 11.*

599, 600 *Palace of the Govenors, Santa Fe, N. Mex., was built in 1610. It is now a historical shrine and memorial to early Spanish life and culture in this country, and reflects the contributions made to the progress and developement of the southwestern United States.*

599		MNHVF	UseVF
1-1/4¢	**turquoise blue**	.25	.20
	Plate block of 4	.50	
	FDC *(June 17, 1960)*		2.00

1960. Palace of the Governors Coil Issue in the Liberty Series. *Rotary press, perforated 10 horizontally.*

600		MNHVF	UseVF
1-1/4¢	**turquoise blue** large holes	15.00	.25
	Pair	25.00	5.00
	Line pair	225.00	50.00
	s. Small holes *(May 1960)*	.20	.20
	Pair	.25	.25
	Line pair	2.25	1.00
	FDC *(June 17, 1960)*		1.75

1961. Statue of Liberty Issue in the Liberty Series. *Giori press, perforated 11.*

601 *Statue of Liberty*

601		MNHVF	UseVF
11¢	**carmine red & blue**	.30	.20
	Plate block of 4	1.25	
	z. Tagged, Type OP *(Jan. 11, 1967)*	2.25	1.75
	Plate block of 4	35.00	
	FDC *(June 15, 1961)*		2.50
	FDC tagged		30.00

Type OP tagging: Used on multicolor stamps previously designated to be printed on Giori presses.

1961. John J. Pershing Issue in the Liberty Series. *Rotary press, perforated 11 x 10 1/2*

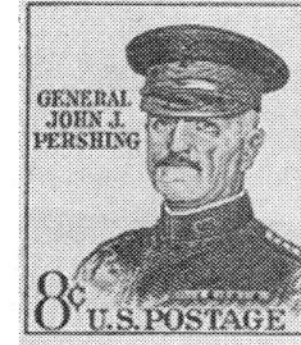

602 *John J. Pershing (1860-1948) commanded the American Expeditionary Forces in Europe during World War I. A leader of vision and courage, Pershing was honored by Congress in 1917 with the title "General of the Armies."*

602		MNHVF	UseVF
8¢	**brown**	.25	.20
	Plate block of 4	1.00	
	FDC *(Nov. 17, 1961)*		2.25

There is disagreement concerning whether No. 602 is actually part of the Liberty Series. Although printed within the same period, it does not match the design characteristics of other stamps in the series.

Christmas Series

1962. Evergreen Wreath and Burning Candles Issue the first Christmas stamp issued by the United States, was intended for use on greeting cards and also to remind the public to shop and mail early. *Giori press, perforated 11.*

603 *Evergreen wreath and burning candles*

603		MNHVF	UseVF
4¢	**green & red**	.25	.20
	Plate block of 4	.75	
	FDC *(Nov. 1, 1962)*		2.00

1962. George Washington Issue *Rotary press, perforated 11 x 10 1/2. Issued to meet increased postal rates, effective Jan. 7, 1963.*

604, 605 *George Washington from bust by Houdon*

604		MNHVF	UseVF
5¢	**gray blue**	.25	.20
	Plate block of 4	.45	

		MNHVF	UseVF
	Pair, gutter between	—	
	v. Horizonal pair, imperforate between	12.50	
	p1. Hi-Brite paper	—	—
	Plate block of 4	—	—
	z. Tagged, Type I *(Oct. 28, 1963)*	—	.20
	Plate block of 4	—	—
	z1. Tagged, Type II *(April 1964)*	—	—
	Plate block of 4	—	—
	z2. Tagged, Type IIa	—	—
	Plate block of 4	—	—
	z3. Tagged, Type III	—	—
	Plate block of 4	—	—
	n1. Booklet pane of 5 with label slogan 1 ("Your Mailman...")	8.00	3.00
	FDC pane *(Nov. 23, 1962)*		3.00
	n2. Booklet pane of 5 with label slogan 2 ("...Use Zone Number...")	20.00	3.50
	n2p. Hi-Brite paper	30.00	—
	n2z. Booklet pane of 5, tagged, with label slogan 2	80.00	7.50
	FDC pane *(Oct. 28, 1963)*	—	—
	n3. Booklet pane of 5 with label slogan 3 ("...Always Use ZIP Code")	4.00	1.50
	n3p. Hi-Brite paper	7.00	10.00
	n3z. Booklet pane of 5, tagged, with label slogan 3	2.50	1.50
	FDC *(Nov. 23, 1962)*	1.75	
	FDC tagged single	25.00	
	FDC tagged booklet pane	100.00	
	FDC tagged booklet pane (Washington, D.C.)	125.00	

1962. GEORGE WASHINGTON COIL ISSUE *Rotary press, perforated 10 vertically.*

605		MNHVF	UseVF
5¢	**gray blue**	.25	.20
	Pair	2.00	
	Line pair	4.00	
	pv. Pair, imperforate	375.00	
	Line pair, imperforate	750.00	
	p1. Hi-Brite paper	—	
	Pair	—	
	Line pair	—	
	z. Tagged, Type I *(Oct. 28, 1963)*	1.25	.30
	Pair	2.50	
	Line pair	5.00	
	z1. Tagged, Type II	—	
	Pair	—	
	Line pair	—	
	FDC *(Nov. 23, 1962)*		1.75
	FDC tagged		30.00

1963. U.S. FLAG AND WHITE HOUSE ISSUE *Giori press, perforated 11.*

606 *U.S. Flag and White House*

606		MNHVF	UseVF
5¢	**blue & red**	.25	.20
	Plate block of 4	.75	
	Pair, gutter between	—	
	z. Tagged, Type OP *(Aug. 25, 1966)*	.25	.20
	Plate block of 4	2.00	
	zv. Horizontal pair, imperforate	1,250.00	
	FDC *(Jan. 9, 1963)*		1.75
	FDC tagged		25.00

1963. ANDREW JACKSON ISSUE *issued to accommodate the 1¢ increase in First Class rates, effective Jan. 7, 1963. Rotary press, perforated 11 x 10 1/2.*

607, 608 *Andrew Jackson*

607		MNHVF	UseVF
1¢	**green**	.25	.20
	Plate block of 4	.75	
	Pair, gutter between	—	
	p1. Hi-Brite paper	—	
	Plate block of 4	—	
	z. Tagged, Type II or III *(July 6, 1966)*	.25	.20
	Plate block of 4	.75	
	FDC *(March 22, 1963)*		1.75
	FDC tagged		25.00

1963. ANDREW JACKSON COIL ISSUE *Rotary press, perforated 10 vertically.*

608		MNHVF	UseVF
1¢	**green**	.25	.20
	Pair	.25	
	Line pair	2.00	
	z. Tagged, Type II *(July 6, 1966)*	.25	.20
	Pair	.25	
	Line pair	.75	
	FDC *(May 31, 1963)*		1.75
	FDC tagged		25.00

1963. CHRISTMAS TREE AND WHITE HOUSE This second Christmas stamp was based on an on-the-spot painting made by artist Lily Spandorf of President Kennedy lighting the National Christmas tree. *Giori press, perforated 11.*

609 *Christmas Tree and White House*

609		MNHVF	UseVF
5¢	**dark blue, indigo & red**	.25	.20
	Plate block of 4	.50	
	Pair, gutter between	—	
	FDC *(Nov. 1, 1963)*		2.00
	z. Tagged, Type OP *(Nov. 2, 1963)*	.65	.50
	Plate block of 4	4.50	
	FDC tagged		60.00

1964. HOLIDAY EVERGREENS ISSUE the third Christmas issue also was a U.S. postal first, featuring four different stamp designs in a regular-size pane of 100 stamps. *Giori press, perforated 11, (carmine, green and black.)*

610 *Holly*

611 *Mistletoe*

612 *Poinsettia*

613 *Conifer sprig*

610		MNHVF	UseVF
5¢	Holly	.25	.20
611		**MNHVF**	**UseVF**
5¢	Mistletoe	.25	.20
612		**MNHVF**	**UseVF**
5¢	Poinsettia	.25	.20
613		**MNHVF**	**UseVF**
5¢	Conifer sprig	.25	.20
	y. Se-tenant block of 4	1.00	1.00
	Plate block of 4	1.25	
	FDC *(Nov. 9, 1964)* any single		2.50
	FDC, Block		4.00
	z. Tagged, Type OP (any single) *Nov. 10, 1964)*	1.75	.50
	zy. Se-tenant block of 4	3.50	
	Plate block of 4	6.00	

		MNHVF	UseVF
	FDC tagged any single		20.00
	FDC tagged block		60.00

1965. Paul Revere Coil Issue in the Liberty Series. *Rotary press, perforated 10 vertically.*

614		MNHVF	UseVF
25¢	**deep blue green** small holes	.45	.25
	Pair	1.00	
	Line pair	2.25	
	v. Pair, imperforate	45.00	
	Line pair, imperforate	90.00	
	zss. Tagged, shiny gum *(April 3, 1973)*	.45	.25
	Pair	1.25	
	Line pair	3.00	
	zsm. Tagged, matte gum *(1980)*	.50	.25
	Pair	1.50	
	Line pair	3.50	
	FDC *(Feb. 25, 1965)*		2.50
	FDC tagge		25.00

1965. Angel Gabriel Issue in the Christmas Series the design is based on a watercolor by Lucille Gloria Chabot. *Giori press printing, perforated 11.*

615 *Angel Gabriel blowing his horn*

615		MNHVF	UseVF
5¢	**red, green & yellow**	.25	.20
	Plate block of 4	.55	
	Pair, gutter between	—	
	FDC *(Nov. 2, 1965)*		1.75
	z. Tagged, Type OP *(Nov. 15, 1965)*	.75	.20
	Plate block of 4	5.50	
	FDC tagged		50.00

1965-78. Prominent Americans Series

The series included a few presidents but generally honored men and women who had gained prominence in many works of life. There was no unifying design theme in the series.

1968. Thomas Jefferson Issue in the Prominent Americans Series, from a portrait by Rembrandt Peale. *Perforated 11 x 10 1/2.*

616, 634 *Thomas Jefferson*

616		MNHVF	UseVF
1¢	**green** tagged Type II or III	.25	.20
	FDC *(Jan. 12, 1968)*		1.75
	Plate block of 4	.25	
	n. Booklet pane of 8	1.00	.25
	FDC *(Jan. 12, 1968)*		2.50
	nm. Booklet pane of 8, matte gum	90.00	1.25
	FDC *(March 1, 1971)*		90.00
	n1. Booklet pane of 4	1.00	
	FDC *(May 10, 1971)*		15.00
	zo. Tagging omitted (error)		
	Plate block of 4	—	
	Plate block of 4, half untagged	—	
	zx. Untagged (Bureau precancel)		.20

1967. Albert Gallatin Issue in the Prominent Americans Series. As treasury secretary under Jefferson, Gallatin (1761-1849) reshaped U.S. financial policy. He was a member of Congress, 1795-1801. *Rotary press, perforated 11 x 10 1/2.*

617 *Albert Gallatin, statesman*

617		MNHVF	UseVF
1-1/4¢	**light green**	.25	.20
	Plate block of 4	7.50	
	FDC *(Jan. 30, 1967)*		1.75

1966. Frank Lloyd Wright Issue in the Prominent Americans Series. Wright (1869-1959) developed a "prairie" style of architecture with horizontal lines and projecting eaves and introduced open planning in houses (see CM1071 and CM1967). New York City's Guggenheim Museum, also on the stamp, was a notable design success. *Rotary press, perforated 11 x 10 1/2.*

618 *Frank Lloyd Wright, architect*

618		MNHVF	UseVF
2¢	**blue** tagged Type II or III	.25	.20
	Plate block of 4	.50	
	Pair, gutter between	—	
	zo. Tagging omitted (error)	—	
	Plate block of 4	—	
	FDC *(June 8, 1966)*		1.75
	n. Booklet pane of 6, shiny gum	1.00	
	FDC booklet pane of 6, shiny gum *(May 7, 1971)*		15.00
	nm. Booklet pane of 6, dull gum	1.00	
	FDC booklet pane of 6, dull gum *(Oct. 31, 1975)*		100.00
	n1. Booklet pane of 5, plus Slogan 4 label ("Mail Early"), shiny gum	1.25	
	FDC booklet pane of 5 *(Jan. 8, 1968)*		4.00
	n2. Booklet pane of 5 plus Slogan 5 label ("Use Zip Code"), shiny gum	1.25	
	FDC booklet pane of 5 *(Jan. 8, 1968)*		4.00
	xz. Untagged (Bureau precancel)	—	
	zxo. Tagged with Bureau precancel (error)	—	

1967. Francis Parkman Issue in the Prominent Americans Series. After travel and study in the American West, Parkman (1823-93) wrote *The Oregon Trail* (see CM1549) and other works. *Rotary press, perforated 10 1/2 x 11.*

619, 693 *Francis Parkman, historian*

619		MNHVF	UseVF
3¢	**purple** tagged Type II	.25	.20
	Plate block of 4	.30	
	zo. Tagging omitted (error)	—	
	Plate block of 4	—	
	zx. Untagged (Bureau precancel)	.50	.20
	FDC *(Sept. 16, 1967)*		1.75

1965. Abraham Lincoln Issue in the Prominent Americans Series, from a photograph by Mathew Brady. *Rotary press, perforated 11 x 10 1/2.*

620, 635 *Abraham Lincoln*

620		MNHVF	UseVF
4¢	**black**	.25	.20
	Plate block of 4	.40	
	Pair, gutter between	—	
	FDC *(Nov. 19, 1965)* (New York, N.Y.)		1.75
	z. Tagged, Type II or III (Dec. 1, 1965)	.25	.20
	Plate block of 4	.55	
	FDC tagged (Dayton, Ohio)		40.00
	FDC tagged (Washington, D.C.		45.00

1965. George Washington Issue in the Prominent Americans Series. The design from a portrait by Rembrandt Peale portrayed the Father of our Country with a creased and pock-marked face and drew strong criticism from the public. The Post Office Department responded by issuing a redesigned stamp (No. 646) with a smoother-appearing face. *Rotary press, perforated 11 x 10 1/2.*

621, 636 *George Washington*

		MNHVF	UseVF
621			
5¢	**deep blue**	.25	.20
	Plate block of 4	.60	
	Pair, gutter between	—	
	FDC *(Feb. 22, 1966)*		1.75
	z. Tagged, Type II or III *(Feb. 23, 1966)*	.25	.20
	Plate block of 4	.60	
	FDC tagged (Dayton, Ohio)		100.00
	FDC tagged (Washington, D.C.)		27.50

1966. Franklin D. Roosevelt Issue in the Prominent Americans Series. This was the first stamp to honor the beloved 32nd president since his memorial series, CM271-274, the first of which was issued June 27, 1945, just two months after his sudden death. *Rotary press, perforated 10 1/2 x 11.*

622 *Franklin D. Roosevelt*

		MNHVF	UseVF
622			
6¢	**black brown**	.25	.20
	Plate block of 4	.65	
	Pair, gutter between		
	FDC *(Jan. 29, 1966)*		2.50
	z. Tagged	.25	.20
	Plate block of 4	1.00	
	FDC *(Dec. 29, 1966)*		20.00
	nz. Booklet pane of 8	1.50	
	FDC Booklet pane of 8 *(Dec. 28, 1967)*		3.00
	n1z. Booklet pane of 5 plus Slogan 4 label ("Mail Early")	1.50	
	FDC Booklet pane of 5 *(Jan. 9, 1968)*		150.00
	n2z. Booklet pane of 5 plus Slogan 5 label ("Use Zip Code")	1.50	
	FDC booklet pane of 5 *(Jan. 9, 1968)*		150.00
	zo. Tagging omitted (error)	—	

1966. Albert Einstein Issue in the Prominent Americans Series. The German-born theoretical physicist (1879-1955) won the Nobel Prize in 1921 and became the living symbol of a scientist to generations of Americans who could not grasp his work (see CM908). *Rotary press, perforated 11 x 10 1/2.*

623 *Albert Einstein, physicist*

		MNHVF	UseVF
623			
8¢	**violet**	.25	.20
	Plate block of 4	1.00	
	FDC *(March 14, 1966)*		2.50
	z. Tagged, Type II or III	.25	.20
	Plate block of 4	1.00	
	FDC tagged *(July 6, 1966)*		40.00

1967. Andrew Jackson Issue in the Prominent Americans Series, honored the seventh president and hero of the war of 1812. *Rotary press, perforated 11 x 10 1/2.*

624 *Andrew Jackson*

		MNHVF	UseVF
624			
10¢	**lavender** tagged Type II or III	.25	.20
	Plate block of 4	1.00	
	FDC *(March 15, 1967)*		1.75
	zo. Tagging omitted (error)	—	
	Plate block of 4	—	
	zx. Untagged (Bureau precancel)	—	.20

1968. Henry Ford Issue in the Prominent Americans Series. The industrialist (1863-1947) grasped the concept of mass production to make him the world's largest maker of inexpensive, standardized cars. *Rotary press, perforated 10 1/2 x 11.*

624A *Henry Ford, auto manufacturer*

		MNHVF	UseVF
624A			
12¢	**black** tagged Type II	.25	.20
	Plate block of 4	1.20	
	FDC *(July 30, 1968)*		2.50
	zo. Tagging omitted (error)	—	
	Plate block of 4	—	
	zx. Untagged (Bureau precancel)	—	.25

1967. John F. Kennedy Issue in the Prominent Americans Series. Kennedy (1917-63), the 34th U.S. president, was the first Catholic and youngest man in the office. He won a Pulitzer Prize in 1956 for *Profiles in Courage.* He was assassinated during a parade in Dallas. *Rotary press, perforated 11 x 10 1/2.*

625 *John F. Kennedy*

		MNHVF	UseVF
625			
13¢	**brown** tagged Type II or III	.25	.20
	Plate block of 4	1.35	
	FDC *(May 29, 1967)*		2.50
	zo. Tagging omitted (error)	—	
	zx. Untagged (Bureau precancel)	—	

1968. Oliver Wendell Holmes Issue in the Prominent Americans Series. As associate justice of the Supreme Court, Holmes (1841-1935) became known as the Great Dissenter who respected human rights and property rights. *Rotary press, perforated 11 x 10 1/2.*

626, 721, 721A *Oliver Wendell Holmes*

		MNHVF	UseVF
626			
15¢	**maroon** design Type I, tagged Type III	.25	.20
	Plate block of 4	1.50	
	FDC *(March 8, 1968)*		1.75
	zx. Untagged (Bureau precancel)		.30

DECODING THE CATALOG

As a result of printing technology advances and the ever-changing needs of the stamp-using public, there frequently are changes made to definitive stamps during their lifetimes that create collectible (and sometimes scarce) varieties. Most of these varieties aren't noticed by the average user, and certainly weren't noted by the United States Post Office Department, but to collectors, each is a different stamp.

Such changes, which affect perforation, printing and design, frequently occurred throughout the 19th and early part of the 20th centuries, and have become less common as stamp designs and series are replaced more frequently.

Type I

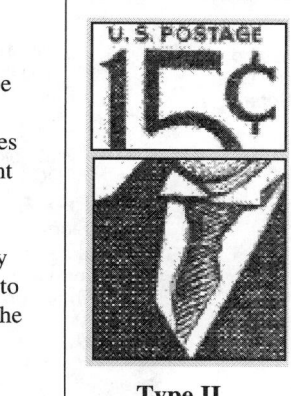

Among the more recent stamps to be affected by design type differences is the 15¢ Oliver Wendell Holmes stamp of the Prominent Americans series. Although none of the varieties is particularly scarce, it is important to know how to decode the catalog and be able to differentiate the three types that collectively make up five different stamps.

First released March 8, 1968, as a sheet stamp, the Holmes issue had a life span of more than 12 years. When the first-class postage rate rose to 15¢ in 1978, it became the workhorse stamp of the U.S. Postal Service. Booklet and coil versions of the stamp were quickly released June 14, 1978, to meet the increased need of the new rate. Later, without notice, re-engraved versions of both the sheet and coil versions were released. These new types had significant differences from the originals, and it did not take collectors long to find them.

Type II

Although several design differences exist among these stamps, it's simplest to focus on the denomination and the necktie areas.

Type I

Type I of the 15¢ Holmes stamp occurs on both sheet and coil versions, Minkus 626 and 721. The top line of the cents sign points to the left of the "E" in "POSTAGE." Also, the tip of Holmes' tie touches the edge of his robe, and there is a consistent cross-hatch pattern throughout the lower part of the tie.

Type II

Like Type I, Type II occurs on both the sheet and coil versions of the stamp, and is quite simple to distinguish. These stamps include Minkus 626A and 721A. On Type II examples, the top line of the cents sign lines up almost squarely with the "E" in "POSTAGE." There is a slight space between the bottom of the tie and the robe, and the crosshatched area on the right side of the tie has an interruption that leaves a small white spot. The engraving on Type II stamps generally looks crisper and cleaner than on Type I.

Type III

Type III

Type III of the Holmes stamp is not only the most easily spotted, but also occurs only on the perf 10 booklet stamps. In this version, Minkus 626B, the entire design has been redrawn and shortened. The top of the cents sign points to the "G" of "POSTAGE," and the length of the tie has been cut nearly in half.

Type I: crosshatching on tie complete and strong; bottom of necktie just touches coat. Type II: crosshatching on tie (lines running upper left to lower right) very faint; necktie does not touch coat. Type III (only known on booklet pane) overall design smaller and "15¢" closer to head.

626A		MNHVF	UseVF
15¢	**maroon** design Type II, tagged	.50	.20
	Plate block of 4	8.50	
	Pair, gutter between	—	
	zo. Tagging omitted (error)	—	
	Plate block of 4	—	

626B		MNHVF	UseVF
15¢	**maroon** design Type III perforated 10	.25	.20
	n. Booklet pane of 8, Type III *(June 14, 1978)*	2.50	1.25
	FDC, single from booklet pane		1.75
	FDC, Booklet pane		3.50
	v. Pair, imperforate between	—	
	nv. Booklet pane of 8, vertically imperforate between	—	

1967. GEORGE C. MARSHALL ISSUE in the Prominent Americans Series. As Army Chief of Staff, Marshall (1880-1959) played a major role in World War II, was secretary of state in 1947-49, and directed the Marshall Plan for European recovery, for which he was given the Nobel Prize in 1953. *Rotary press, perforated 11 x 10 1/2.*

627 *George C. Marshall, diplomat and general*

627		MNHVF	UseVF
20¢	**olive brown**	.35	.20
	Plate block of 4	1.75	
	FDC *(Oct. 24, 1967)*		2.00
	z. Tagged	.40	.20
	Plate block of 4	2.00	
	m. Matte gum	.40	
	FDC tagged, *(April 3, 1973)*		25.00

1967. Frederick Douglass Issue in the Prominent Americans Series paid tribute to a black abolitionist and statesman (1817-1895), son of a slave, who escaped and established the North Star newspaper to fight slavery. *Rotary press, perforated 11 x 10 1/2.*

628 *Frederick Douglass, abolitionist and statesman*

628		MNHVF	UseVF
25¢	**maroon**	.50	.20
	Plate block	1.75	
	FDC *(Feb. 14, 1967)*		3.50
	a. lilac carmine	20.00	
	Plate block of 4	—	
	z. Tagged	.40	.20
	Plate block of 4	2.00	
	FDC tagged *(April 3, 1973)*		25.00
	Matte finish gum	.45	

1968. John Dewey Issue in the Prominent Americans Series honored an educator and philosopher (1859-1952), who argued truth was evolutionary and fought authoritarian methods in education. *Rotary press, perforated 10 1/2 x 11.*

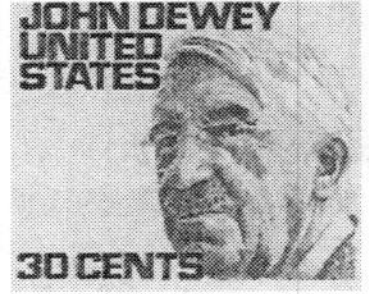

629 *John Dewey, philosopher and educator*

629		MNHVF	UseVF
30¢	**purple**	.55	.25
	Plate block of 4	2.75	
	FDC *(Oct. 21, 1968)*		3.50
	z. Tagged	.45	.25
	Plate block of 4	2.25	
	FDC tagged *(April 3, 1973)*		25.00

1968. Thomas Paine Issue in the Prominent Americans Series honored the American patriot and essayist (1737-1809), who hastened the Declaration of Independence with *Common Sense.* He was prosecuted in England and France for later writings there and alienated many in the United States with his *Letter to Washington* after the war. *Rotary press, perforated 11 x 10 1/2.*

630 *Thomas Paine, essayist*

630		MNHVF	UseVF
40¢	**dark blue**	.75	.25
	Plate block of 4	3.30	
	FDC *(Jan. 29, 1968)*		3.00
	z. Tagged	.75	.25
	Plate block of 4	2.25	
	zm. Matte gum	.75	
	Plate block of 4	3.00	1.00
	FDC tagged *(April 3, 1973)*		25.00

1968. Lucy Stone Issue in the Prominent Americans Series honored the woman suffragist and anti-slavery lecturer (1818-93) who achieved notariety by keeping her own name after marriage. *Rotary press, perforated 11 x 10 1/2.*

631 *Lucy Stone, suffragist and reformer*

631		MNHVF	UseVF
50¢	**maroon**	1.00	.25
	Plate block of 4	4.50	
	FDC *(Aug. 13, 1968)*		4.00
	Pair, gutter between	—	
	z. Tagged	1.00	.25
	Plate block of 4	3.00	
	FDC tagged *(April 3, 1973)*		30.00

1967. Eugene O'Neill Issue in the Prominent Americans Series honored the prolific writer (1888-1953) of plays regarded among the best in American history, including *Mourning Becomes Electra, The Iceman Cometh,* and *Long Day's Journey into Night. Rotary press, perforated 11 x 10 1/2.*

632, 672 *Eugene O'Neill, playwright*

632		MNHVF	UseVF
$1	**dark purple**	2.25	.50
	blackish violet	—	—
	Plate block of 4	10.00	
	FDC *(Oct. 16, 1967)*		7.50
	z. Tagged	1.75	.50
	Plate block of 4	7.00	
	FDC tagged *(April 3, 1973)*		40.00

1966. John Bassett Moore Issue in the Prominent Americans Series. Moore (1860-1947) was an authority on international law and assistant secretary of state in 1898. High values of this series were tagged for use with automated equipment for postmarking large envelopes. *Rotary press, perforated 11 x 10 1/2.*

633 *John Bassett Moore, jurist*

633		MNHVF	UseVF
$5	**dark gray**	10.00	3.00
	Plate block of 4	40.00	
	FDC *(Dec. 3, 1966)*		40.00
	z. Tagged	8.00	3.00
	Plate block of 4	30.00	
	FDC tagged *(April 3, 1973)*		100.00

1968. Thomas Jefferson Coil Issue in the Prominent Americans Series. *Rotary press, perforated 10 vertically.*

634		MNHVF	UseVF
1¢	**green** tagged	.25	.20
	Pair	.25	
	Line pair	.25	
	FDC *(June 12, 1968)*		1.75
	v. Pair, imperforate	30.00	
	Line pair, imperforate	60.00	
	zx. Untagged (Bureau precancel)		.20
	Pair		.25
	Line pair		.60

1966. Abraham Lincoln Coil Issue in the Prominent Americans Series. *Rotary press, perforated 10 vertically.*

635		MNHVF	UseVF
4¢	**black** tagged Type II	.25	.20
	Pair	.25	
	Line pair	.75	
	FDC*(May 28, 1966)*		1.75
	v. Pair, imperforate	850.00	
	Line pair, imperforate	1,500.00	
	v1. Pair, imperforate between	—	
	zo. Tagging omitted (error)	—	
	Pair	—	
	Line pair	—	
	zx. Untagged (Bureau precancel)		1.00

		MNHVF	UseVF
	Pair		10.00
	Line pair		125.00

1966. George Washington Coil Issue in the Prominent Americans Series. *Rotary press, perforated 10 vertically.*

636		MNHVF	UseVF
5¢	**deep blue** tagged Type II	.25	.20
	Pair	.25	
	Line pair	.40	
	FDC *(Sept. 8, 1966)*		1.75
	v. Pair, imperforate	200.00	
	Line pair, imperforate	350.00	
	zo. Tagging omitted (error)	—	
	Pair	—	
	Line pair		
	zx. Untagged (Bureau precancel)		1.00
	Pair		10.00
	Line pair		100.00
	zxv. Pair, imperforate untagged (precanceled)		450.00
	Line pair, imperforate untagged (precanceled)		1,000.00
	m. Matte gum	.25	
	Pair	1.25	
	Line pair	6.00	

1968. Franklin D. Roosevelt Coil Issue in the Prominent Americans Series. *Rotary press, perforated 10 vertically.*

637, 638 *Franklin D. Roosevelt*

637		MNHVF	UseVF
6¢	**black brown** tagged	.25	.20
	Pair	.20	
	Line pair	.55	
	FDC *(Feb. 28, 1968)*		1.75
	v. Pair, imperforate	2,250.00	
	Line pair, imperforate	—	
	zo. Tagging omitted	—	
	Pair	—	
	Line pair	—	
	zx. Untagged (Bureau precancel)	—	
	Pair	17.50	
	Line pair	250.00	

1967. Franklin D. Roosevelt Coil Issue in the Prominent Americans Series. *Rotary press, perforated 10 horizontally.*

638		MNHVF	UseVF
6¢	**black brown** tagged	.25	.20
	Pair	.25	
	Line pair	1.25	
	FDC *(Dec. 28, 1967)*		1.75
	v. Pair, imperforate	70.00	
	Line pair, imperforate	125.00	
	zo. Tagging omitted (error)	—	
	Pair	—	
	Line pair	—	

Nos. 639-643 are not assigned.

1966. Traditional Christmas Issue the fifth in the Christmas Series, featured a design showing a portion of Hans Memling's 15th century painting *Madonna and Child with Angels. Giori press printing and offset, perforated 11.*

644 *Madonna and Child*

644		MNHVF	UseVF
5¢	**multicolored**	.25	.20
	Plate block of 4	.75	
	FDC *(Nov. 1, 1966)*		1.75
	z. Tagged, Type OP	.30	.20
	Plate block of 4	1.75	
	FDC tagged *(Nov. 2, 1966)*		50.00

1967. Traditional Christmas Issue design was the same as the 1966 issue, but printed in much larger size. *Giori press printing and offset, perforated 11.*

645 *Madonna and Child*

645		MNHVF	UseVF
5¢	**multicolored**	.25	.20
	Plate block of 4	.65	
	FDC*(Nov. 6, 1967)*		2.00
	zo. Tagging omitted (error)	—	
	Plate block of 4	—	

1967. George Washington Issue in the Prominent Americans Series was a redesigned version of the original stamp (No. 621) with a so-called "clean shaven" portrait. *Giori press printing and offset, perforated 11.*

646, 747A *Redesigned George Washington*

621 *Original (1965)*

646		MNHVF	UseVF
5¢	**deep blue** tagged, shiny gum	.25	.20
	Plate block of 4	.75	
	FDC *(Nov. 17, 1967)*		1.75
	zo. Tagging omitted shiny gum (error)	—	
	Plate block of 4	—	
	m. Matte gum	.25	.20
	Plate block of 4	1.50	
	mzo. Tagging omitted, matte gum (error)	—	
	Plate block of 4	—	
	zx. Untagged (Bureau precancel)	—	.20

1968. Flag Over White House Issue continued the "Flag Over..." theme begun with the 5¢ stamp, No. 606. *Giori press printing, perforated 11, overall tagging.*

647, 650, 654 *Flag Over White House*

647		MNHVF	UseVF
6¢	**dark blue, green & red** tagged Type OP	.25	.20
	Plate block of 4	.50	
	FDC *(Jan. 24, 1968)*	—	1.75
	v. Vertical pair, imperforate between	500.00	
	v1. Vertical pair, imperforate horizontally	500.00	
	zo. Tagging omitted (error)	—	
	Plate block of 4	—	
	FDC		200.00

1968. Serviceman's Airlift Issue was intended for airlift of parcels to service members overseas in Alaska, Hawaii and Puerto Rico. The design was a late 19th century woodcarving of a flying eagle. *Giori press printing and offset, perforated 11.*

648 *Flying Eagle*

648		MNHVF	UseVF
$1	**multicolored**	3.00	2.00
	Plate block of 4	12.75	
	Pair, gutter between	—	
	FDC *(April 4, 1968)*		7.50

1968. Traditional Christmas Issue featured a design showing a portion of *The Annunciation* by the 15th century Flemish artist Jan van Eyck. This was the first stamp printed on the multicolor *Huck press. Intaglio, perforated 11.*

649 *Angel Gabriel*

649		MNHVF	UseVF
6¢	**multicolored** tagged Type B	.25	.20
	Plate block of 10	2.00	
	v. light yellow omitted	55.00	
	FDC *(Nov. 1, 1968)*		2.00
	v1. Pair, imperforate	250.00	
	zx. Untagged *(Nov. 2, 1968)*	.30	.20
	Plate block of 10	3.00	
	zxv. Pair, imperforate	300.00	

Type B tagging: Billet or bar-like shapes designed to register within the limits of a single stamp. Untagged areas surround the design and were intended to register with the perforations.

1969. Flag Over White House Coil Stamp Issue this was the first multicolored postage stamp produced in coil form. Same design as No. 647. *Coil, Huck press, intaglio, perforated 10 vertically, block tagged.*

650		MNHVF	UseVF
6¢	**dark blue, green & red** tagged	.25	.20
	Pair	.50	.30
	FDC *(May 30, 1969)*		1.75
	v. Pair, imperforate	550.00	
	zo. Tagging omitted (error)	5.00	

1969. Contemporary Christmas Issue in the Christmas Series featured a 19th century painting, *Winter Sunday in Norway, Maine,* by an unknown artist from the collection of the New York State Historical Association, Cooperstown, N.Y. *Intaglio, perforated 11 x 10 1/2.*

651 *Winter Sunday in Norway, Maine*

651		MNHVF	UseVF
6¢	**multicolored** tagged	.25	.20
	Plate block of 10	1.95	
	FDC *(Nov. 3, 1969)*		2.00
	Experimental precancel	.35	.25
	FDC all 4 cities singles		2.75
	Plate block of 10	85.00	
	v. light green omitted	25.00	1.75
	v1. light green, red, and yellow omitted	950.00	
	v2. yellow omitted	2,500.00	
	v3. yellow and red omitted	2,850.00	
	v4. Pair, imperforate	1,100.00	
	zo. Tagging omitted (error)	4.00	
	Plate strip of 10	—	

Experimental precanceled stamps were sold for use by the public, imprinted, "ATLANTA, GA," "BALTIMORE, MD," "MEMPHIS, TN," and "NEW HAVEN, CT."

1970. Dwight D. Eisenhower Issue. in the Prominent Americans Series bore the portrait of the 34th president of the United States (1890-1969). *Rotary press, perforated 11 x 10 1/2.*

652, 653 *Dwight D. Eisenhower*

652		MNHVF	UseVF
6¢	**blue** tagged Type II, shiny gum	.25	.20
	Plate block of 4	1.00	
	FDC *(Aug. 6, 1970)*		1.75
	n. Booklet pane of 8	1.50	
	FDC booklet pane of 8		3.00
	n1. Booklet pane of 5 plus Slogan 4 label ("Mail Early")	1.50	
	FDC booklet pane of 5		75.00
	n2. Booklet pane of 5 plus Slogan 5 label ("Use Zip Code")	1.50	
	FDC booklet pane of 5		75.00
	m. Experimental dull-finish gum	.25	
	Plate block of 4	1.00	
	nm. Booklet pane of 8, dull-finish gum	2.00	
	FDC booklet pane of 8, dull-finish gum		—
	zo. Tagging omitted (error)	—	
	xz. Untagged (Bureau precancel)	—	

1970. Dwight D. Eisenhower Coil Issue in the Prominent Am ericans Series. *Rotary press, perforated 10 vertically.*

653		MNHVF	UseVF
6¢	**blue** tagged, shiny gum	.25	.20
	Pair	.25	
	Line pair	.50	
	FDC *(Aug. 6, 1970)*		
	m. Matte gum	.25	.20
	Pair	.60	
	Line pair	1.50	
	v. Pair, imperforate	1,500.00	
	Line pair, imperforate	—	
	zo. Tagging omitted (error)	8.50	
	zx. Untagged (Bureau Precancel)		.20

1970. Flag Over White House Issue Same design as No. 647 *(Giori press)* and No. 650 *(Huck press). Huck press printings* are 0.05 inches smaller than *Giori printings. Huck press, perforated 11 x 10 1/2.*

654		MNHVF	UseVF
6¢	**dark blue, green & red** tagged Type B	.25	.20
	Margin block of 20	3.25	
	FDC *(Aug. 7, 1970)*		1.75
	v. Horizontal pair, imperforate between	175.00	
	zo. Tagging omitted (error)	3.00	
	Margin block of 20	—	

1970. Contemporary Christmas Issue consisted of four different designs of toys, *printed se-tenant, Gravure at Guilford Gravure, Inc., perforated 11 x 10 1/2.*

655 *Antique toy locomotive*

656 *Toy wheeled horse*

657 *Mechanical tricycle toy*

658 *Doll carriage toy*

655		MNHVF	UseVF
6¢	**multicolored** tagged	.25	.20

656		MNHVF	UseVF
6¢	**multicolored** tagged	.25	.20
	v1. Pair, imperforate (No. 656, 658)	—	

657		MNHVF	UseVF
6¢	**multicolored** tagged	.25	.20

658		MNHVF	UseVF
6¢	**multicolored** tagged	.25	.20
	FDC *(Nov. 5, 1970)* (any single)		2.50
	FDC se-tenant block		6.00
	y. Se-tenant block of 4	1.50	2.50
	Plate block of 8	3.50	
	v. black omitted, any single	2,500.00	
	black omitted, block of 4	—	
	x. Precanceled, any single	.75	.20
	FDC of precanceled single		15.00
	xy. Se-tenant block of 4, precanceled		1.50
	FDC precanceled block of 4		20.00

1970. Traditional Christmas Issue in the Christmas Series. *Gravure at Guilford Gravure, Inc., perforated 10 1/2 x 11.*

659 The Nativity *by Lorenzo Lotto*

659		MNHVF	UseVF
6¢	**multicolored** tagged design Type I	.25	.20
	Plate block of 8	3.50	
	FDC *(Nov. 5, 1970)*		1.75
	v. black omitted	575.00	.20
	x. Precanceled	.25	.20
	Plate block of 8	3.50	
	xv. Precanceled, blue omitted		
	ii. Type II	.25	.20
	Plate block of 8	3.50	
	iix. Type II, precanceled	.25	.20
	Plate block of 8	3.50	
	FDC, Type II		3.00

Type I has a slightly blurry impression and no gum breaker ridges. Type II has a shiny surfaced paper, sharper impression, and both horizontal and vertical gum breaker ridges. Type I precancel is gray black; Type II precancel is intense black.

1971. Ernie Pyle Issue. in the Prominent Americans Series honored the World War II correspondent and newsman who died by enemy gunfire on April 18, 1945. He won the Pulitzer Prize in 1943. *Cottrell press printing, perforated 11 x 10 1/2.*

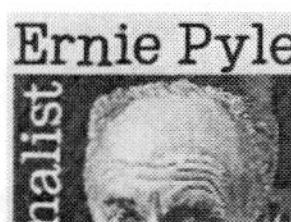

660 *Ernie Pyle*

660		MNHVF	UseVF
16¢	**brown** tagged	.30	.20
	Plate block of 4	1.30	
	FDC *(May 7, 1971)*		2.50
	zo. Tagging omitted (error)	—	
	Plate block of 4	—	
	zx. Untagged (Bureau precancel)	—	.40

1971. Flag Over White House Issue was similar to No. 647, but with the new first-class denomination. *Intaglio, Huck press, perforated 11 x 10 1/2.*

661, 662 *Flag Over White House*

661		MNHVF	UseVF
8¢	**dark blue, red & slate green** tagged Type B	.25	.20
	Margin block of 20	3.75	
	FDC *(May 10, 1971)*		1.75
	v. green omitted	500.00	
	v1. Horizontal pair, imperforate between	55.00	
	v2. Vertical pair, imperforate	55.00	
	Tagging omitted	3.00	

1971. Flag Over White House Coil Issue *Huck press, perforated 10 vertically.*

662		MNHVF	UseVF
8¢	**dark blue, red & slate green** tagged Type B	.20	.20
	Pair	1.75	
	FDC *(May 10, 1971)*		1.75
	v. Pair, imperforate	50.00	
	zo. Tagging omitted (error)	—	
	Pair	—	

1971. Dwight D. Eisenhower Issue in the Prominent Americans Series used the same basic design as Nos. 652 and 653, but with an 8¢ denomination, new colors; and no dot is between "Eisenhower" and "USA" on No. 663. *Giori press printing, perforated 11.*

663 *Dwight D. Eisenhower*

663		MNHVF	UseVF
8¢	**black, blue gray & red** tagged Type OP	.25	.20
	Plate block of 4	.75	
	Pair, gutter between	350.00	
	p. Hi-Brite paper	—	
	Plate block of 4	—	
	zo. Tagging omitted (error)	3.00	
	Plate block of 4	—	
	FDC *(May 10, 1971)*		1.75

1971. Dwight D. Eisenhower Booklet Issue in the Prominent Americans Series had a dot between "Eisenhower" and "USA." *Intaglio, rotary press, perforated 11 x 10 1/2.*

663A *Dwight D. Eisenhower*

663A		MNHVF	UseVF
8¢	**reddish brown** shiny gum Type II, in booklet form only	.25	.20
	FDC single *(May 10, 1971)*		2.00
	n. Booklet pane of 8, shiny gum		2.00
	FDC booklet pane of 8 *(May 10, 1971)*		2.50
	n1. Booklet pane of 7 plus Slogan 4 label ("Mail Early"), dull-finish gum	2.00	
	FDC booklet pane of 7 *(Jan. 28, 1972)*		2.00
	n2. Booklet pane of 7 plus Slogan 5 label ("Use Zip Code"), dull-finish gum	2.00	
	FDC booklet pane of 7 *(Jan. 28, 1972)*		2.00
	n3. Booklet pane of 4 plus two labels (Slogans 5 and 4), dull-finish gum	1.50	
	FDC booklet pane of 4 *(Jan,. 28, 1972)*		2.00

		MNHVF	UseVF
	n4. Booklet pane of 6, shiny gum	1.00	.75
	FDC booklet pane of 6 *(May 10, 1971)*		2.50

All these booklet stamps have 1 or 2 straight edges.

1971. Dwight D. Eisenhower Coil Issue in the Prominent Americans Series. *Coil, intaglio, perforated 10 vertically.*

664		**MNHVF**	**UseVF**
8¢	**reddish brown** tagged	.25	.20
	Pair	.30	
	Line pair	.60	
	v. Pair, imperforate	45.00	
	Line pair, imperforate	75.00	
	v1. Pair, imperforate between	6,250.00	
	zx. Untagged (Bureau precancel)		.25
	FDC *(May 10, 1971)*		1.75

1971. U.S. Postal Service Issue marked the transition from the U.S. Post Office Department to the U.S. Postal Service under the direction of Postmaster General Winton M. Blount. It featured the new logo for the agency, and 16.3 million first-day cancels were applied - nearly double the previous record. *Gravure, perforated 11 x 10 1/2.*

665 *USPS emblem*

665		**MNHVF**	**UseVF**
8¢	**multicolored** tagged	.25	.20
	Plate block of 12	2.00	
	FDC *(July 1, 1971)*		1.75

1971. Contemporary Christmas Issue in the Christmas Series. *Gravure, perforated 10 1/2 x 11.*

666 *A partridge in a pear tree*

666		**MNHVF**	**UseVF**
8¢	**multicolored** tagged	.25	.20
	Plate block of 12	3.00	
	FDC *(Nov. 10, 1971)*		2.00
	zo. Tagging omitted (error)	—	

1971. Traditional Christmas Issue in the Christmas Series. *Gravure, perforated 10 1/2 x 11.*

Christmas

667 Adoration of the Shepherds, *by Giorgione*

667		**MNHVF**	**UseVF**
8¢	**multicolored** tagged	.25	.20
	Plate block of 12	3.00	
	FDC *(Nov. 10, 1971)*		2.00
	v. gold omitted	600.00	

1972. Fiorello H. LaGuardia Issue in the Prominent Americans Series paid tribute to a politician who served his country as a congressman and as mayor of New York City. *Intaglio, perforated 11 x 10 1/2.*

668 *Fiorello H. LaGuardia*

668		**MNHVF**	**UseVF**
14¢	**dark brown** tagged	.25	.20
	Plate block of 4	1.25	
	FDC *(April 24, 1972)*		1.75
	zx. Untagged (Bureau precancel)	—	.25

1972. Benjamin Franklin Issue in the Prominent Americans Series honored the printer, writer, postmaster general and statesman with a stamp intended primarily to pay postage for educational materials. *Intaglio, perforated 10 1/2 x 11.*

669 *Benjamin Franklin*

669		**MNHVF**	**UseVF**
7¢	**light blue** shiny gum, tagged	.25	.20
	Plate block of 4	.75	
	m. Matte gum	.25	
	Plate block of 4	1.35	
	FDC *(Oct. 20, 1972)*		1.75
	zo. Tagging omitted (error)	—	
	Plate block of 4	—	
	zx. Untagged (Bureau precancel)	—	.20

1972. Contemporary Christmas Issue in the Christmas Series. *Photogravure, perforated 10 1/2 x 11.*

670 *Santa Claus*

670		**MNHVF**	**UseVF**
8¢	**multicolored** tagged	.25	.20
	Plate block of 12	3.00	
	FDC *(Nov. 9, 1972)*		1.75

1972. Traditional Christmas Issue *Gravure, perforated 10 1/2 x 11.*

671 *Angels from painting* Mary, Queen of Heaven, *in the National Gallery of Art*

671		**MNHVF**	**UseVF**
8¢	**multicolored** tagged	.25	.20
	Plate block of 12	3.00	
	FDC *(Nov. 9, 1972)*		1.75

		MNHVF	UseVF
	v. black omitted	4,500.00	
	v1. pink omitted	175.00	

1973. Eugene O'Neill Coil Issue see design for No. 632. This was the first dollar-value stamp issued in tagged form. *Intaglio and perforated 10 vertically.*

672		MNHVF	UseVF
$1	**dark purple** tagged, shiny gum	2.00	.75
	Pair	3.50	
	Line pair	5.00	
	FDC *(Jan. 12, 1973)*		5.00
	m. Matte gum	2.00	.75
	Pair	4.00	
	Line pair	10.00	
	v. Pair, imperforate	2,250.00	
	Line pair, imperforate	4,250.00	

1973. Amadeo P. Giannini Issue in the Prominent Americans Series honored the American banker who rose from humble origins to originate consumer bank loans and develop what was the world's largest private bank, the Bank of America. *Intaglio and perforated 11 x 10 1/2.*

673 *Amadeo P. Giannini*

673		MNHVF	UseVF
21¢	**banknote green** tagged	.40	.25
	Plate block of 4	1.60	
	FDC *(June 27, 1973)*		2.25

1973. Traditional Christmas Issue *Gravure, Andreotti press.*

674 Madonna and Child *by Raphael*

674		MNHVF	UseVF
8¢	**multicolored** tagged	.25	.20
	Plate block of 12	3.00	
	Pair, gutter between	—	
	FDC *(Nov. 7, 1973)*		1.75

1973. Contemporary Christmas Issue *Gravure, perforated 10 1/2 x 11.*

675 *Christmas Tree needlepoint by Dolli Tingle*

675		MNHVF	UseVF
8¢	**multicolored** tagged	.25	.20
	Plate block of 12	3.00	
	Vertical pair, gutter between	—	
	FDC *(Nov. 7, 1973)*		1.75
	v. Vertical pair, imperforate between	325.00	

1973. Crossed Flags Issue was made available in anticipation of higher postal rates. Use of the 13-star flag in the design was in tribute to the American Revolution Bicentennial. *Intaglio, Huck press, perforated 11 x 10 1/2.*

676, 677 *50-star and 13-star flags*

676		MNHVF	UseVF
10¢	**red & blue** tagged	.25	.20
	Plate block of 20	4.00	
	FDC *(Dec. 8, 1973)*		1.75
	v. blue omitted	175.00	
	v1. Horizontal pair, imperforate between	60.00	
	v2. Horizontal pair, imperforate vertically	—	
	v3. Vertical pair, imperforate between horizontally	1,150.00	
	v4. Vertical pair, imperforate	950.00	
	zo. Tagging omitted (error)	6.00	

1973. Crossed Flags Coil Issue *Intaglio, Huck press, perforated 10 vertically.*

677		MNHVF	UseVF
10¢	**red & blue** tagged	.40	.25
	Pair	1.00	
	Line pair	1.50	
	FDC *(Dec. 8, 1973)*		1.75
	v. Pair, imperforate	37.50	
	Line pair, imperforate	10.00	
	zo. Tagging omitted (error)	7.50	
	Pair	20.00	

The lines on this issue, which can occur every 4 stamps, are usually incomplete. Full, complete lines sell for a premium.

1973. Jefferson Memorial Issue met the new 10¢ postal rates for first-class mail. *Intaglio, rotary press, perforated 11 x 10 1/2.*

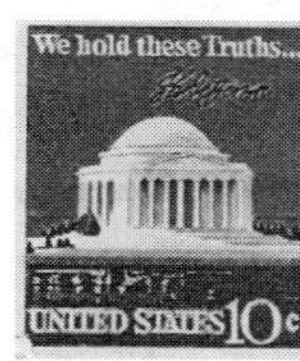

678, 679 *Jefferson Memorial*

678		MNHVF	UseVF
10¢	**blue** tagged, Type II or III	.25	.20
	Plate block of 4	.85	
	FDC *(Dec. 14, 1973)*		1.75
	n. Booklet pane of 5 plus label	1.50	
	FDC *(Dec. 14, 1973)*		2.25
	n1. Booklet pane of 6	5.75	
	FDC *(Aug. 5, 1974)*		5.25
	n2. Booklet pane of 8	1.75	
	FDC *(Dec. 14, 1973)*		2.50
	n2zo. Booklet pane of 8, tagging omitted (error)	—	
	v. Vertical pair, imperforate between	800.00	
	v1. Vertical pair, imperforate horizontally	500.00	
	zo. Tagging omitted (error)	—	
	zx. Untagged (Bureau precancel)		—

1973. Jefferson Memorial Coil Issue *Rotary press, perforated 10 vertically.*

679		MNHVF	UseVF
10¢	**blue** tagged	.25	.20
	Pair	.40	
	Line pair	.75	
	FDC *(Dec. 14, 1973)*		1.75
	v. Pair, imperforate	—	
	Pair, imperforate	40.00	
	Line pair, imperforate	75.00	
	zx. Untagged (Bureau precancel)		.25

1974. ZIP Code Issue another new 10¢ stamp, underlined the importance of moving mail rapidly. *Gravure, perforated 11 x 10 1/2.*

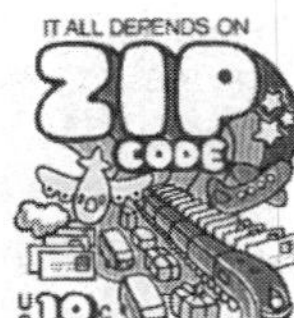

680 *ZIP moves mail rapidly*

680		MNHVF	UseVF
10¢	**multicolored** tagged with small rectangle in center of stamp	.25	.20
	Plate block of 8	1.75	
	Pair, gutter between	—	
	FDC *(Jan. 4, 1974)*		1.75
	v. yellow omitted	50.00	

1974. Elizabeth Blackwell Issue in the Prominent Americans Series honored the first woman medical doctor of modern time. *Intaglio, perforated 11 x 10 1/2.*

681 *Dr. Elizabeth Blackwell*

681		MNHVF	UseVF
18¢	**purple** tagged	.30	.25
	Plate block of 4	1.25	
	FDC *(Jan. 23, 1974)*		2.00

1974. Swinging Bell Coil Issue paid bulk rate. *Intaglio, perforated 10 vertically.*

682 *Swinging bell*

682		MNHVF	UseVF
6.3¢	**brick red** tagged	.25	.20
	Pair	.40	
	Line pair	.75	
	FDC *(Oct. 1, 1974)*		1.75
	v. Pair, imperforate	200.00	
	Line pair, imperforate	600.00	
	zx. Untagged (Bureau precancel)		.20
	Pair		.90
	Line pair		1.50
	zxv. Pair, imperforate		100.00
	Line pair, imperforate		250.00

1974. Contemporary Christmas Issue in the Christmas Series. *Gravure, perforated 11 x 10 1/2.*

683 The Road - Winter, *from Currier and Ives print*

683		MNHVF	UseVF
10¢	**multicolored** tagged	.25	.20
	Plate block of 12	2.25	
	FDC *(Oct. 23, 1974)*		1.75
	v. buff omitted, pane of 50	600.00	

1974. Dove of Peace Issue in the Christmas Series, the first self-adhesive stamp, used glue that was very unstable and has caused most, if not all, stamps to discolor. *Gravure, imperforate, straight die cut, self-adhesive with backing.*

684 *Dove of Peace weather vane atop Mount Vernon*

684		MNHVF	UseVF
10¢	**multicolored** self-adhesive	.25	.20
	Plate block of 20	2.25	
	FDC *(Nov. 15, 1974)*		3.00

Two types of rouletting were used on backing paper.

1974. Traditional Christmas Issue *Gravure, perforated 10 1/2 x 11.*

685 The Perussis Altarpiece, *15th century French artist unknown, Metropolitan Museum of Art, New York City*

685		MNHVF	UseVF
10¢	**multicolored** tagged	.25	.20
	Plate block of 10	2.25	
	FDC *(Oct. 23, 1974)*		1.75

1975. Contemporary Christmas Issue featured stamps that for the first time in U.S. postal history were issued without a printed denomination. The stamps were valid for the first-class rate at the time of issue, 10¢. *Gravure, perforated 11 1/4.*

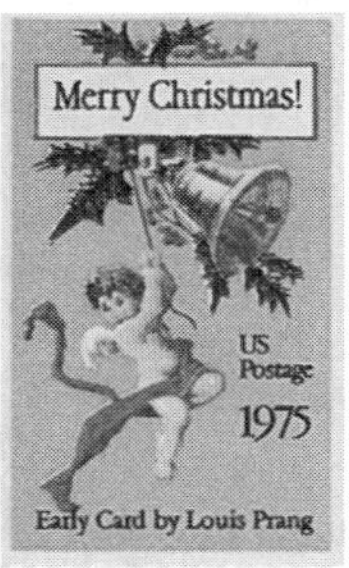

686 *Louis Prang Christmas Card*

686		MNHVF	UseVF
10¢	**multicolored** tagged	.30	.20
	Plate block of 12	3.75	
	FDC *(Oct. 14, 1975)*		1.75
	v. Pair, imperforate	120.00	

1975. Contemporary Christmas Issue *Gravure, perforated 11.*

686A		MNHVF	UseVF
10¢	**multicolored** tagged	.30	.20
	Plate block of 12	5.00	
	FDC *(Oct. 14, 1975)*		1.75

1975. Contemporary Christmas Issue *Gravure, perforated 10 1/2 x 11.*

686B		MNHVF	UseVF
10¢	**multicolored** tagged	.60	.20
	Plate block of 12	15.00	
	FDC *(Oct. 14, 1975)*		1.75

1975. TRADITIONAL CHRISTMAS ISSUE *Gravure, perforated 11.*

687 *Domenico Ghirlandaio* Madonna and Child

687		MNHVF	UseVF
10¢	**multicolored** tagged	.30	.20
	Plate block of 12	3.75	
	Damaged "d" (plate flaw)	5.00	
	FDC *(Oct. 14, 1975)*		1.75
	v. Pair, imperforate	120.00	

1975-81. Americana Series Consisted mainly of symbols of America's principles and goals. When arranged in "blocks" of four by consecutive denomination, phrases on each stamp form a unifying rounded frame.

1975. CAPITOL DOME ISSUE in the Americana Series showed the dome of the U.S. Capitol, home of the Senate and House of Representatives. *Intaglio, rotary press, perforated 11 x 10 1/2.*

688, 697, 702, 702A *Capitol Dome*

688		MNHVF	UseVF
9¢	**green** on gray paper, tagged	.25	.20
	Plate block of 4	.75	
	FDC *(Nov. 24, 1975)*		1.75
	m. Matte gum	1.00	.20
	Plate block of 4	5.25	
	zo. Tagging omitted (error)	—	
	zx. Untagged (Bureau precancel)	—	.20

1975. COLONIAL PRINTING PRESS ISSUE in the Americana Series (see CM199). *Intaglio, perforated 11 x 10 1/2.*

689 *Early printing press*

689		MNHVF	UseVF
11¢	**orange** on gray paper, tagged	.25	.20
	Plate block of 4	1.00	
	Pair, gutter between	—	
	FDC *(Nov. 13, 1975)*		1.75
	zo. Tagging omitted (error)	3.00	

1975. FLAG OVER INDEPENDENCE HALL ISSUE *Huck press, perforated 11 x 10 1/2.*

690, 694, 782 *Flag over Independence Hall*

690		MNHVF	UseVF
13¢	**dark blue & red** tagged	.25	.20
	Plate block of 20	5.50	
	FDC *(Nov. 15, 1975)*		1.75
	v. Horizontal pair, imperforate between	50.00	
	v1. Vertical pair, imperforate	1,000.00	

1975. EAGLE AND SHIELD ISSUE in the Americana Series. *Gravure, perforated 11 1/4.*

691 *Eagle and shield*

691		MNHVF	UseVF
13¢	**multicolored** tagged with eagle-shape untagged area	.25	.20
	Plate block of 12	3.50	
	Pair, gutter between	150.00	
	FDC *(Dec. 1, 1975)*		1.75
	v. yellow omitted	200.00	
	v1. Pair, imperforate	50.00	

691A		MNHVF	UseVF
13¢	**multicolored** perforated 11 (L-perforation)	40.00	15.00
	Plate block of 12	400.00	
	EKU *(March 31, 1976)*		—

1975. OLD NORTH CHURCH ISSUE in the Americana Series pictured the church from whose steeple the patriots were signaled of the advance of the British in the Revolutionary War. *Intaglio, perforated 11 x 10 1/2.*

692 *Old North Church, Boston*

692		MNHVF	UseVF
24¢	**red** on blue paper, tagged	.50	.25
	Plate block of 4	2.00	
	FDC *(Nov. 14, 1975)*		1.75
	zo. Tagging omitted (error)	5.00	
	Plate block of 4	20.00	

1975. FRANCIS PARKMAN COIL ISSUE in the Prominent Americans Series (see No. 619). *Coil, intaglio, perforated 10 horizontally.*

693 *Francis Parkman*

693		MNHVF	UseVF
3¢	**purple** tagged, shiny gum	.25	.20
	Pair	.30	.20
	Line pair	.35	.20
	FDC *(Nov. 4, 1975)*		1.75
	m. Matte gum	.25	
	Pair	.30	
	Line pair	.50	
	v. Pair, imperforate	27.50	
	Line pair, imperforate	45.00	
	zx. Untagged (Bureau precancel)		.25
	Pair		.30
	Line pair		.35
	zxv. Pair, imperforate		6.50
	Line pair, imperforate		20.00

1975. FLAG OVER INDEPENDENCE HALL COIL ISSUE (see 690, 782). *Coil, intaglio, Combination Press, perforated 10 vertically.*

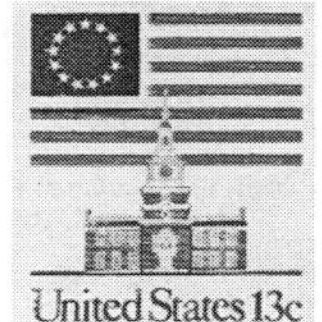

694 *Flag over Independence Hall*

		MNHVF	UseVF
694			
13¢	**dark blue & red** tagged	.25	.20
	Pair	.30	
	Line pair	.45	
	FDC *(Nov. 15, 1975)*		1.75
	v. Pair, imperforate	25.00	
	Line pair, imperforate	50.00	
	zo. Tagging omitted (error)	—	

1975. Liberty Bell Issue in the Americana Series pictured the bell in Independence Hall, Philadelphia, rung in July 1776 to proclaim the signing of the Declaration of Independence. It cracked in 1835. *Booklet panes, intaglio, perforated 11 x 10 1/2, matte gum.*

695, 696 *Liberty Bell*

		MNHVF	UseVF
695			
13¢	**brown** from booklet panes only, tagged	.25	.20
	FDC pane		2.75
	v. Vertical pair, imperforate between	525.00	
	FDC *(Oct. 31, 1975)*		1.75
	n. Booklet pane of 6	2.00	1.00
	FDC pane *(Oct. 31, 1975)*		2.25
	n1. Booklet pane of 7 plus label	1.75	.50
	FDC pane *(Oct. 31, 1975)*		2.50
	n1zo. Booklet pane of 7 plus label, tagging omitted (error)	—	
	n2. Booklet pane of 8	2.00	.75
	FDC pane *(Oct. 31, 1975)*		2.75
	n2zo. Booklet pane of 8, tagging omitted (error)	—	
	n3. Booklet pane of 5 plus label	1.50	.50
	FDC single *(April 2, 1976)*		1.75
	FDC pane *(April 2, 1976)*		2.25

1975. Liberty Bell Coil Issue in the Americana Series. *Coil, intaglio, perforated 10 vertically.*

		MNHVF	UseVF
696			
13¢	**brown** shiny gum, tagged	.25	.20
	Pair	.50	
	Line pair	.80	
	FDC *(Nov. 25, 1975)*		1.75
	m. Matte gum	.30	
	Pair	.60	
	Line pair	2.00	
	v. Pair, imperforate	25.00	
	Line pair, imperforate	60.00	
	v1. Pair, imperforate between	1,400.00	
	zx. Untagged (Bureau precancel)		.50
	Pair		1.00
	Line pair		6.50
	zx1. Untagged (Bureau precancel) matte gum		—
	Pair		—
	Line pair		—
	zo. Tagging omitted (error)		—

1976. Capitol Dome Coil Issue in the Americana Series (see 688). *Coil, perforated 10 vertically.*

697 *Capitol Dome*

		MNHVF	UseVF
697			
9¢	**green** on gray paper, shiny gum, tagged	.25	.20
	Pair	.40	
	Line pair	1.00	
	FDC *(March 5, 1976)*		1.75
	v. Pair, imperforate	160.00	
	v1. Line pair, imperforate	375.00	
	zx. Untagged (Bureau precancel)	—	.35
	Pair		
	Line pair		
	zxv. Pair, imperforate (precanceled Pleasantville, N.Y.)		800.00
	Line pair, imperforate		2,000.00
	zxvm. Untagged (Bureau precancel) matte finish gum		
	Pair		
	Line pair		

1976. American Eagle and Drum Coil Issue in the Americana Series it was the first of several to show musical instruments. *Coil, perforated 10 vertically.*

698 *American eagle on drum*

		MNHVF	UseVF
698			
7.9¢	**red** on canary paper, shiny gum, tagged	.25	.20
	Pair	.50	
	Line pair	.75	
	FDC *(April 23, 1976)*		1.75
	m. Matte gum	.35	
	Pair	.50	
	Line pair	1.50	
	zx. Untagged (Bureau precancel)		.20
	Pair		
	Line pair		
	zxm. Untagged, matte finish gum		
	v. Pair, imperforate	575.00	
	v1. Line pair, imperforate	—	

1976. Contemporary Christmas Issue was based on Nathaniel Currier's *Winter Pastime* lithograph from 1855. Two presses were used in its production — a gravure press and a new multicolor press. The gravure press has all-over tagging, and the lettering at the base is black; the multicolor press printing (70 percent of the issue) has block tagging and grey-black lettering at the base. *Gravure, perforated 11.*

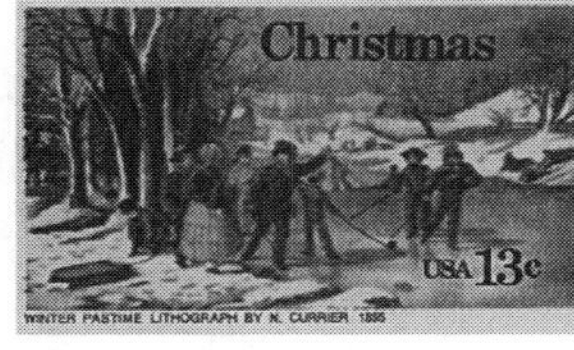

699, 699A *Winter Pastime*

		MNHVF	UseVF
699			
13¢	**multicolored** overall tagged	.40	.25
	Plate block of 10	4.00	
	FDC *(Oct. 27, 1976)*		1.75
	v. Pair, imperforate	100.00	
699A		**MNHVF**	**UseVF**
13¢	**multicolored** block tagged	.40	.25
	Plate block of 20	7.75	
	FDC *(Oct. 27, 1976)*		2.00
	v. Pair, imperforate	120.00	
	v1. Vertical pair, imperforate between	—	
	v2. red omitted	—	
	v3. yellow omitted	—	
	zo. Tagging omitted (error)	12.50	

1976. Traditional Christmas Issue The religious theme featured John Singleton Copley's *Nativity* (1776). *Gravure, perforated 11.*

DECODING THE CATALOG

The 9¢ United States Americana series definitive stamp, originally released Nov. 24, 1975, exists in four basic major types. It is one of the easiest of all U.S. stamps to positively determine all major varieties available. Only one of these four types is significantly valued above the rest. The following information will help you to identify each.

Type I

There are two major Type I Capitol stamps. Both are printed on gray paper and feature a design that measures 18 1/2 by 22 1/2 millimeters. The first, Minkus 688, is a sheet version with perforations measuring 11 by 10 1/2. It was the first type of this stamp. The second variety is Minkus 697, which was released March 5, 1976. It is a coil version (straight edges top and bottom) that has vertical perforations measuring 10.

Type II

The two varieties of the Type II Capitol stamp, released simultaneously on March 11, 1977, were printed on white paper and are told apart by their perforation measurements. Both are from booklets (se-tenant with the 13¢ Flag Over Capitol). There was only one 9¢ stamp in each pane, with a straight edge always at left. The design of the Type II stamps is slightly smaller than that of Type I (17 1/2 by 20 1/2 mm). Minkus 702 has perforations that measure 11 by 10 1/2. Minkus 702A measures 10 on all three sides. The perf 10 variety sells for more than $20 mint, up to 40 times the price of its more common cousin.

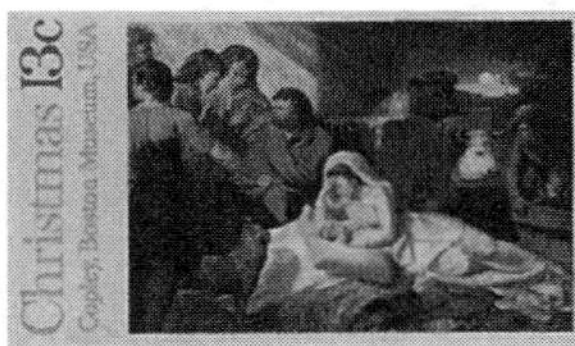

700 *Nativity*

700		MNHVF	UseVF
13¢	**multicolored** tagged	.40	.25
	Plate block of 12	4.75	
	FDC *(Oct. 27, 1976)*		
	v. Pair, imperforate	95.00	

1976. SAXHORNS ISSUE in the Americana Series showed another musical instrument. *Coil, intaglio, perforated 10 vertically.*

701 *Saxhorns*

701		MNHVF	UseVF
7.7¢	**brown** on canary paper, tagged	.25	.20
	Pair	.50	
	Line pair	1.00	
	FDC *(Nov. 20, 1976)*		1.75
	zx. Untagged (Bureau precancel)		.40
	Pair		
	Line pair		
	zxv. Pair, imperforate	1,750.00	
	Line pair, imperforate	4,500.00	

1977. CAPITOL DOME BOOKLET ISSUE in the Americana Series consisted of seven 13¢ stamps and one 9¢ stamp in a single vending machine booklet pane on white paper. *Intaglio, produced with two different perforations.*

702, 703; 702A, 703A *Capitol dome and flag over Capitol*

702		MNHVF	UseVF
9¢	**green** tagged, perforated 11 x 10 1/2	1.00	.20
	FDC *(March 11, 1977)*		10.00

1977. Capitol Dome Booklet Issue in the Americana Series. *Perforated 10.*

702A		MNHVF	UseVF
9¢	**green** tagged	35.00	22.50
	FDC *(March 11, 1977)*		15.00

1977. Flag over Capitol Booklet Issue *Perforated 11 x 10 1/2.*

703		MNHVF	UseVF
13¢	**red & blue** tagged	.25	.20
	FDC *(March 11, 1977)*		2.50
	n. Booklet pane of 8 (7 No. 703 and 1 No. 702)	2.75	
	FDC pane		25.00
	y. Se-tenant pair, No. 702, 703	1.00	1.00

1977. Flag over Capitol Issue in the Americana Series. *Perforated 10.*

703A		MNHVF	UseVF
13¢	**red & blue** tagged	.75	.50
	FDC *(March 11, 1977)*		2.00
	n. Booklet pane of 8 (7 No. 703A and 1 No. 702A)	40.00	25.00
	FDC pane		15.00
	y. Se-tenant pair, No. 702A, 703A	35.00	24.00

1977. Rural Mail Box Issue in the Christmas Series. *Gravure, perforated 11.*

704 *Rural mail box*

704		MNHVF	UseVF
13¢	**multicolored** tagged	.40	.20
	Plate block of 10	4.00	
	FDC *(Oct. 21, 1977)*		1.75
	v. Pair, imperforate	300.00	
	zv. Overall tagging (error)	—	
	Vertical pair, gutter between	—	

1977. Washington Kneeling At Prayer Issue in the Christmas Series was based on a painting by J.C. Leyendecker. *Gravure, Combination Press, perforated 11.*

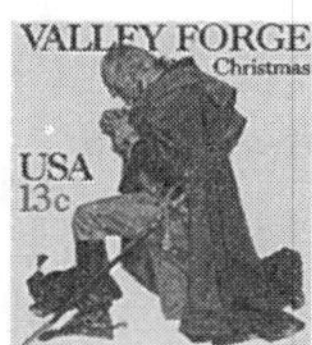

705 *Gen. Washington kneeling at prayer*

705		MNHVF	UseVF
13¢	**multicolored** tagged	.40	.20
	Plate strip of 20	8.00	
	FDC *(Oct. 21, 1977)*		1.75
	v. Pair, imperforate	70.00	
	zv. Overall tagging (error)	—	

The multicolor Combination Press issue (No. 705) has "floating" plate numbers, a set of five numbers sandwiched between two or three blanks, so that on a plate strip of 20 there are five numbers and five blanks, six numbers and four blanks, seven numbers and three blanks or eight numbers and two blanks. There are no ZIP or Mail Early slogans.

Nos. 706-707 are not assigned.

1977. Contemplation of Justice Issue in the Americana Series. *Intaglio, rotary press, perforated 11 x 10 1/2.*

708, 709 *Contemplation of Justice*

708		MNHVF	UseVF
10¢	**purple** on gray paper, shiny gum, tagged	.25	.20
	Plate block of 4	.70	
	FDC *(Nov. 17, 1977)*		1.75
	m. Matte gum	.25	
	Plate block of 4	1.00	
	zo. Tagging omitted (error)	—	
	zx. Untagged (Bureau precancel), shiny gum		—

1977. Contemplation of Justice Coil Issue in the Americana Series. *Coil, intaglio, perforated 10 vertically.*

709		MNHVF	UseVF
10¢	**purple** on gray paper, tagged	.25	.20
	Pair	.40	
	Line pair	1.00	
	FDC *(Nov. 4, 1977)*		1.75
	v. Pair, imperforate	70.00	
	Line pair, imperforate	125.00	
	m. Matte gum	.50	
	Pair	.75	
	Line pair	2.50	
	mv. Pair, imperforate	70.00	
	Line pair, imperforate	120.00	
	zx. Untagged (Bureau precancel), shiny gum		2.00
	Pair		—
	Line pair		—

1977. Quill Pen and Inkwell Issue in the Americana Series highlighted one of four roots of democracy — the ability to write. *Intaglio, rotary press, perforated 11 x 10 1/2.*

710, 742 *Quill pen and inkwell*

710		MNHVF	UseVF
1¢	**blue** on green paper, tagged	.25	.20
	Plate block of 4	.25	
	FDC *(Dec. 8, 1977)*		1.75
	m. Matte gum	.25	.20
	Plate block of 4	.25	
	Horizontal pair, gutter between	—	
	z. Untagged (Bureau precancel)	—	
	zo. Tagging omitted (error)	—	
	p. White paper, dull finish gum	—	
	Plate block of 4	—	

1977. Symbols of Speech Issue in the Americana Series highlighted the freedom to speak out — a root of democracy. *Intaglio, rotary press, perforated 11 x 10 1/2.*

711, 711A *Symbols of speech*

711		MNHVF	UseVF
2¢	**brown** on green paper, shiny gum, tagged	.25	.20
	Plate block of 4	.50	

		MNHVF	UseVF
	FDC *(Dec. 8, 1977)*		
	m. Matte gum	.25	
	Plate block of 4	2.25	
	zo. Tagging omitted (error)	—	
	zx. Untagged (Bureau precancel)		—

1981. Symbols of Speech Issue in the Americana Series.

711A		MNHVF	UseVF
2¢	**brown** on cream paper, matte gum, tagged	.25	.20
	Plate block of 4	.30	
	FDC *(Nov. 7, 1981)*		1.00

1977. Ballot Box Issue in the Americana Series highlighted another root of democracy, the right to vote. *Intaglio, rotary press, perforated 11 x 10 1/2.*

712 *Ballot box*

712		MNHVF	UseVF
3¢	**olive** on green paper, shiny gum, tagged	.25	.20
	Plate block of 4	.30	
	Horizontal pair, gutter between	—	
	FDC *(Dec. 8, 1977)*		1.75
	m. Matte gum	.25	.20
	Plate block of 4	.50	
	zo. Tagging omitted (error)	—	
	zx. Untagged (Bureau precancel)		.20

1977. Reading and Learning Issue in the Americana Series highlighted the importance of reading as a root of democracy. *Intaglio, rotary press, perforated 11 x 10 1/2.*

713 *Reading and learning*

713		MNHVF	UseVF
4¢	**maroon** on cream paper, tagged	.25	.20
	Plate block of 4	.50	
	FDC *(Dec. 8, 1977)*		1.75
	m. Matte gum	.25	
	Plate block of 4	1.25	
	zo. Tagging omitted (error)	—	
	zx. Untagged (Bureau precancel)		1.25

1978. Indian Head Penny Issue For the first time, a U.S. definitive was specially designed in a smaller size so that 150 stamps could be produced in place of the usual 100 stamp pane. *Intaglio, perforated 11.*

714 *Indian Head penny*

714		MNHVF	UseVF
13¢	**brown & blue** on tan paper, tagged	.25	.20
	Plate block of 4	1.75	
	Vertical pair, gutter between	—	
	FDC *(Jan. 11, 1978)*		1.75
	v. Horizontal pair, imperforate vertically	275.00	
	zo. Tagging omitted (error)	—	

1978. Statue of Liberty Issue in the Americana Series featured a stark close-up of the head of the famed symbol of America in New York Harbor. *Intaglio, perforated 11 x 10 1/2.*

715, 716 *Statue of Liberty*

715		MNHVF	UseVF
16¢	**blue** tagged	.30	.20
	Plate block of 4	1.50	
	FDC *(March 31, 1978)*		1.75

1978. Statue of Liberty Coil Issue in the Americana Series. *Coil, intaglio, perforated 10 vertically.*

716		MNHVF	UseVF
16¢	**blue** overall tagged	.35	.20
	Pair	.70	
	Line pair	1.50	
	FDC *(March 31, 1978)*		1.75
	z. Block tagging	.50	.20
	Pair	1.00	.25

716A		MNHVF	UseVF
16¢	**multicolored** block tagged, B Press (design slightly narrower than 716, no joint line)	—	
	Pair	—	

1978. Sandy Hook Lighthouse Issue in the Americana Series showed a lighthouse in New Jersey. *Intaglio, rotary press, perforated 11 x 10 1/2.*

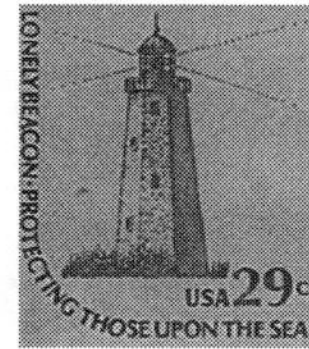

717 *Sandy Hook Lighthouse*

717		MNHVF	UseVF
29¢	**blue** on blue paper, shiny gum, tagged	.50	.65
	Plate block of 4	2.75	
	FDC *(April 14, 1978)*		1.75
	m. Matte gum	2.00	.25
	Plate block of 4	15.25	

1978. "A" Stamp Issue Non-Denominated "A" Stamp Issue marked the new First Class postage rate (15 cents) which went into effect May 29. The stamps were printed in 1975 and 1976 and had been stored for use in this contingency. *Gravure, two perforation sizes.*

718-720 *"A" left of stylized eagle*

718		MNHVF	UseVF
15¢	**orange** perforated 11, tagged	.30	.25
	Plate block of 4	1.50	
	FDC *(May 22, 1978)*		1.75
	v. Pair, imperforate	100.00	
	v1. Vertical pair, imperforate horizontally	750.00	

1978. "A" Stamp Issue

718A		MNHVF	UseVF
15¢	**orange** perforated 11 1/4, tagged	.30	.25
	Plate block of 4	1.50	
	FDC *(May 22, 1978)*		1.75

1978. "A" Booklet Stamp Issue *Booklet stamps, intaglio, perforated 11 x 10 1/2.*

719		MNHVF	UseVF
15¢	**orange** tagged	.25	.20
	FDC *(May 22, 1978)*		1.75
	n. Booklet pane of 8	2.25	.50
	FDC, pane		3.00
	v. Vertical pair, imperforate between	1,750.00	

1978. "A" STAMP COIL ISSUE Coil, intaglio, perforated 10 vertically.

720		MNHVF	UseVF
15¢	**orange** tagged	.25	.15
	Pair	.50	
	Line pair	.75	
	FDC *(May 22, 1978)*		1.75
	v. Pair, imperforate	95.00	
	Line pair, imperforate	195.00	

1978. OLIVER WENDELL HOLMES ISSUE in the Prominent Americans Series used the same design as No. 626 to meet the new postal rate. *Intaglio, coil, perforated 10 vertically.*

721		MNHVF	UseVF
15¢	**maroon,** shiny gum, Type I, tagged	.25	.20
	Pair	.50	
	Line pair	1.25	
	FDC *(June 14, 1978)*		1.75
	m. Matte gum, Type I	.50	
	Pair	1.25	
	Line pair	2.00	
	zx. Untagged (Bureau precancel)		.30
	Pair		
	Line pair		
	v. Pair, imperforate, shiny gum	30.00	
	Line pair, imperforate, shiny gum	75.00	
	mv. Pair, imperforate, matte gum	50.00	
	v1. Pair, imperforate between	225.00	
	Line pair, imperforate between	600.00	

1978. OLIVER WENDELL HOLMES ISSUE in the Prominent Americans Series.

721A		MNHVF	UseVF
15¢	**maroon** Type II matte gum, tagged	.25	.20
	Pair	.50	
	Line pair	2.50	
	mv. Pair, imperforate	90.00	
	Line pair, imperforate	300.00	

For booklet pane issued the same date see No. 626B.

1978. AMERICAN FLAG ISSUE in the Americana Series featured the 15-star Fort McHenry flag, which in 1814 inspired Francis Scott Key to compose *The Star Spangled Banner. Intaglio, Combination Press.*

722, 722A, 723 *American flag*

722		MNHVF	UseVF
15¢	**red, blue & gray** perforated 11, tagged	.30	.20
	Plate block of 20	7.00	
	FDC *(June 30, 1978)*		1.75
	v. gray omitted	600.00	
	v1. Vertical pair, imperforate	25.00	
	zo. Tagging omitted (error)	3.00	

1978. AMERICAN FLAG BOOKLET ISSUE in the Americana Series.

722A		MNHVF	UseVF
15¢	**red, blue & gray** booklet stamp, perforated 11 x 10 1/2, tagged	.35	.20
	FDC *(June 30, 1978)*		1.75
	n. Booklet pane of 8	3.50	2.00
	FDC pane		2.75

1978. AMERICAN FLAG COIL ISSUE in the Americana Series. *Coil, intaglio, perforated 10 vertically.*

723		MNHVF	UseVF
15¢	**red, blue & gray**	.40	.20
	Pair	1.00	
	FDC *(June 30, 1978)*		1.75
	v. Pair, imperforate	25.00	
	v1. Pair, imperforate between	165.00	
	v2. gray omitted	35.00	
	zo. Tagging omitted (error)	5.00	

1978. AMERICAN ROSES BOOKLET ISSUE *Intaglio, perforated 10.*

724 *Two roses: Red Masterpiece (1974 Rose of the Year) and Medallion (winner of two high honors)*

724		MNHVF	UseVF
15¢	**orange, red & green** tagged	.25	.20
	FDC *(July 11, 1978)*		1.75
	n. Booklet pane of 8	2.25	3.00
	FDC, pane		3.75
	nv. Pane of 8, imperforate	—	
	nv1. Pair, imperforate	400.00	
	nzo. Pane of 8, tagging omitted (error)	25.00	

1978. STEINWAY GRAND PIANO COIL ISSUE in the Americana Series of musical instruments. Met the bulk rate. *Intaglio, perforated 10 vertically.*

725 *Steinway grand piano*

725		MNHVF	UseVF
8.4¢	**blue** on canary paper, shiny gum, tagged	.25	.20
	Pair	.40	
	Line pair	3.75	
	FDC *(July 13, 1978)*		1.75
	zx. Untagged (Bureau precancel)	.40	.25
	zxv. Pair, imperforate		15.00
	Line pair, imperforate		25.00
	zxv1. Pair, imperforate between		50.00
	Line pair, imperforate between		135.00
	zxm. Matte gum, untagged (Bureau precancel)	—	
	Pair	—	
	Line pair	—	

1978. BLOCKHOUSE ISSUE in the Americana Series showed the reconstructed blockhouse at Fort Nisqually, Washington. *Intaglio, perforated 11 x 10 1/2.*

726 *Blockhouse*

726		MNHVF	UseVF
28¢	**brown** on blue paper, tagged, shiny gum	.50	.20
	Plate block of 4	2.40	
	FDC *(Aug. 11, 1978)*		1.75
	m. Matte gum	1.25	
	Plate block of 4	10.00	

1978. CONTEMPORARY CHRISTMAS ISSUE in the Christmas Series. *Gravure, perforated 11.*

727 *Child astride a hobby horse, by Dolli Tingle*

727		MNHVF	UseVF
15¢	**multicolored** tagged	.40	.20
	Plate block of 12	5.50	
	Pair, gutter between	—	
	FDC *(Oct, 18, 1978)*		1.75

		MNHVF	UseVF
	v. Pair, imperforate	95.00	
	v1. Vertical pair, imperforate horizontally	2,250.00	

1978. Madonna and Child with Cherubim Issue in the Christmas Series featured a terra cotta sculpture in the National Gallery of Art. *Gravure, perforated 11.*

728 *Madonna and Child with Cherubim, sculpture by Andrea della Robbia*

728		MNHVF	UseVF
15¢	**multicolored** tagged	.40	.20
	Plate block of 12	5.50	
	FDC *(Oct. 18, 1978)*		1.75
	v. Pair, imperforate	90.00	
	v1. Vertical pair, imperforate between	22.50	
	v2. Vertical pair, imperforate horizontally		725.00

1978. Kerosene Table Lamp Issue in the Americana Series was the first of four high-value issues that featured early lamps. *Intaglio and offset, perforated 11.*

729 *Kerosene table lamp*

729		MNHVF	UseVF
$2	**multicolored** tagged	3.50	1.00
	Plate block of 4	14.50	
	FDC *(Nov. 16, 1978)*		7.00

1979. Rush Lamp and Candle Holder Issue in the Americana Series. *Intaglio and offset, perforated 11.*

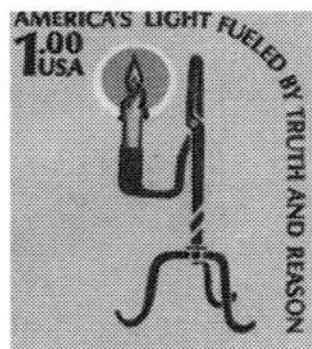

730 *Rush lamp and candle holder*

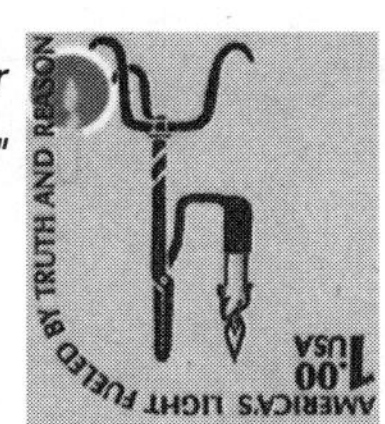

730v *"CIA Invert"*

730		MNHVF	UseVF
$1	**multicolored** tagged	2.00	.25
	Plate block of 4	9.50	
	FDC *(July 2, 1979)*		3.50
	v. brown inverted	15,000.00	
	v1. brown omitted	275.00	
	v2. orange, tan and yellow omitted	350.00	
	zo. Tagging omitted (error)	10.00	

In the spring of 1986, a mail room employee of the United States Central Intelligence Agency, after buying stamps at a post office in the Washington, D.C., suburb of Fairfax, Va., for agency use, discovered he had bought 95 copies of the $1 Rush Lamp and Candle Holder stamp — nearly a full pane of 100 — with an inverted design. He and fellow workers had removed 10 more stamps from the pane to prepare for a mailing before they noticed the disjointed printing.

The Americana Series stamp was printed first in offset for the tan background, the yellow candle and flame and the red halo behind it, and then in intaglio for the engraved candle holder and lettering in dark brown. In this case one sheet of 400 stamps was fed into the intaglio press upside-down so that the two elements did not line up correctly — the brown was inverted.

The finder and some fellow workers each held one copy for themselves, replaced the stamps, and disposed of the remaining error stamps to a dealer. Because of the supersecret nature of the agency's affairs and the fact that the employee used agency money to buy the stamps, controversy erupted over the ownership of the errors. Some employees quit their jobs rather than turn in the stamps they had kept. It has become known as the CIA Invert.

1979. Railroad Conductor's Lantern Issue in the Americana Series. *Intaglio and offset, perforated 11.*

731 *Railroad conductor's lantern*

731		MNHVF	UseVF
$5	**multicolored** tagged	8.50	2.25
	Plate block of 4	33.00	
	FDC *(Aug. 23, 1979)*		13.50

1979. Country Schoolhouse Issue in the Americana Series. *Intaglio, perforated 11 x 10 1/2.*

732 *Country schoolhouse, Morris Township School No. 2, Devils Lake, N.D.*

732		MNHVF	UseVF
30¢	**green** on blue paper, tagged	1.00	.30
	Plate block of 4	2.50	
	FDC *(Aug. 27, 1979)*		1.75
	zo. Tagging omitted (error)	—	

1979. Iron "Betty" Lamp Issue in the Americana Series. *Intaglio and offset, perforated 11.*

733 *Iron "Betty" lamp from the Plymouth Colony*

733		MNHVF	UseVF
50¢	**black, orange & tan** tagged	1.00	.20
	Plate block of 4	3.50	
	FDC *(Sept. 11, 1979)*		2.00
	v. black omitted	300.00	
	v1. Vertical pair, imperforate horizontally	1,750.00	
	zo. Tagging omitted (error)	—	

1979. Santa Claus Christmas Tree Ornament Issue in the Christmas Series. *Gravure, perforated 11.*

734 *Santa Claus Christmas tree ornament*

734		MNHVF	UseVF
15¢	**multicolored** tagged	.40	.20
	Plate block of 12	5.50	
	FDC *(Oct. 18, 1979)*		1.75
	v. green & yellow omitted	575.00	
	v1. green, yellow & tan omitted	650.00	

1979. Traditional Christmas Issue in the Christmas Series. *Black is misaligned on all color-omitted copies. Gravure, perforated 11.*

735 *Madonna and Child from the Gerard David painting* The Rest on the Flight into Egypt. *National Gallery of Art, Washington, D.C.*

735		MNHVF	UseVF
15¢	**multicolored** tagged	.40	.20
	Plate block of 12	5.50	
	FDC *(Oct. 18, 1979)*		1.75
	v. Pair, imperforate	90.00	
	v1. Vertical pair, imperforate between	2,250.00	
	v2. Vertical pair, imperforate horizontally	750.00	

1979. Standard Six-string Guitar Coil Issue in the Americana Series met the non-profit mailing rate. *Intaglio, perforated 10 vertically.*

736 *Standard six-string guitar*

736		MNHVF	UseVF
3.1¢	**brown** on canary paper, tagged	.25	.20
	Pair	.35	
	Line pair	1.50	
	FDC *(Oct. 25, 1979)*		1.75
	v. Pair, imperforate	1,375.00	
	Line pair, imperforate	3,750.00	
	zx. Untagged (Bureau precancel)	4.00	.25
	Pair		—
	Line pair		—

1980. Historic Windmills Issue *Intaglio, perforated 11.*

737 *Robertso Windmill, Williamsburg, Va.;* 738 *Replica of The Old Windmill, Portsmouth, R.I.;* 739 *Cape Cod Windmill, Eastham, Mass.;* 740 *Dutch Mill at Fabyan Park Forest Preserve near Batavia, Ill.;* 741 *A Southwestern Windmill, Texas*

		MNHVF	UseVF
737		MNHVF	UseVF
15¢	Virginia, **brown** on yellow paper, tagged	.30	.20
738		MNHVF	UseVF
15¢	Rhode Island, **brown** on yellow paper, tagged	.30	.20
739		MNHVF	UseVF
15¢	Massachusetts, **brown,** on yellow paper, tagged	.30	.20
740		MNHVF	UseVF
15¢	Illinois, **brown** on yellow paper, tagged	.30	.20
741		MNHVF	UseVF
15¢	Texas, **brown** on yellow paper, tagged	.30	.20
	FDC *(Feb. 7, 1980)* any single		2.00
	y. Se-tenant strip of 5	1.50	1.00
	FDC, strip		6.00
	n. Booklet pane of 10 (2 each Nos. 737-41)	3.50	4.50
	FDC, pane		5.00

1980. Quill Pen and Inkwell Coil Issue in the Americana Series. *Coil, intaglio, perforated 10 vertically.*

742		MNHVF	UseVF
1¢	**blue** on green paper, shiny gum, tagged	.25	.20
	Pair	.25	
	Line pair	.50	
	FDC *(March 6, 1980)*		1.75
	m. Matte gum	.25	
	Pair	.25	
	Line pair	.50	
	mv. Pair, imperforate	175.00	
	Line pair, imperforate	275.00	
	zo. Tagging omitted (error)	—	

1980. Dolley Madison Issue honored the wife (1768-1849) of President James Madison, who influenced Washington, D.C., society and politics with two presidents. The stamp was produced in the mini-stamp format identical in size to the 1978 Indian Head Penny stamp (No. 714). *Intaglio, perforated 11.*

743 *Dolley Madison, pencil sketch from Gilbert Stuart painting*

743		MNHVF	UseVF
15¢	**red brown & sepia** tagged	.40	.20
	Plate block of 4	2.00	
	FDC *(May 20, 1980)*		1.75

1980. Weaver Manufactured Violins Coil Issue in the musical instruments set of the Americana Series met the non-profit organization rate. *Intaglio, perforated 10 vertically.*

744 *Weaver manufactured violins*

744		MNHVF	UseVF
3.5¢	**purple** on yellow paper, tagged	.25	.20
	Pair	.25	
	Line pair	1.00	
	FDC *(June 23, 1980)*		1.75
	v. Pair, imperforate	225.00	
	Line pair, imperforate	400.00	
	zx. Untagged (Bureau precancel)	.25	.20
	Pair	.50	
	Line pair	2.00	

1980. Contemporary Christmas Issue *Gravure, perforated 11.*

745 *Season's Greetings, toys on a window sill*

745		MNHVF	UseVF
15¢	**multicolored** tagged	.50	.20
	Plate block of 20	10.00	
	v. light brown omitted	25.00	
	v1. Pair, imperforate	80.00	
	v2. Vertical pair, imperforate horizontally	—	
	v3. Plate block of 20, imperforate	850.00	
	v4. Horizontal pair, imperforate between	3,400.00	
	zo. Tagging omitted (error)	—	
	FDC *(Oct. 31, 1980)*		1.75

1980. Traditional Christmas Issue *Gravure, perforated 11.*

746 *Vignette of Madonna and Child from the Epiphany Window, Bethlehem Chapel at Washington Cathedral*

746		MNHVF	UseVF
15¢	**multicolored** tagged	.50	.20
	Plate block of 12	5.50	
	Pair, gutter between	—	
	FDC *(Oct. 31, 1980)*		1.75
	v. Pair, imperforate	80.00	
	v1. Plate block of 12, imperforate	650.00	

1980-99. Great Americans Series

The series featured Americans from many walks of life who had distinguished themselves.

1980. Sequoyah Issue the first in the Great Americans Series, honored the unschooled Cherokee Indian scholar (c.1770-1843) who devised a written alphabet for his tribe. *Intaglio, perforated 11 x 10 1/2.*

747 *Sketch from portrait of Sequoyah by Charles Banks Wilson*

747		MNHVF	UseVF
19¢	**brown** overall tagged	.30	.20
	Plate block of 4	2.25	
	FDC *(Dec. 27, 1980)*		1.75

1980. Washington Coil Issue in the Prominent Americans Series. (See No. 646).

747A *"Shaved" Washington coil*

747A		MNHVF	UseVF
5¢	**deep blue** tagged	.25	.20
	Pair	.30	.20
	Line pair	1.25	—
	FDC *(March 31, 1981)*		25.00
	v. Pair, imperforate	1,000.00	

1981. Non-Denominated "B" Stamp Issue marked the change of the First Class domestic postage rate to 18¢ which went into effect March 22, 1981. The design was identical to the "A" stamp except for the background color and the letter. *Gravure, perforated 11 x 10 1/2.*

748-750 *"B" to left of stylized eagle*

748		MNHVF	UseVF
18¢	**purple** tagged	.30	.20
	Plate block of 4	1.40	
	Horizontal pair, gutter between	—	
	FDC *(March 15, 1981)*		2.00

1981. Non-Denominated "B" Booklet Issue *Booklet pane, intaglio, perforated 10.*

749		MNHVF	UseVF
18¢	**purple** tagged	.30	.20
	FDC *(March 15, 1981)*, single		1.75
	n. Booklet pane of 8	3.50	1.50
	FDC pane		4.00

1981. Non-Denominated "B" Coil Issue *Coil, intaglio, perforated 10 vertically.*

750		MNHVF	UseVF
18¢	**purple** tagged	.40	.20
	Pair	.80	
	Line pair	1.65	
	FDC *(March 15, 1981)*		1.75
	v. Pair, imperforate	120.00	
	Line pair, imperforate	200.00	

1981. Freedom of Conscience Issue in the Americana Series highlighted Freedom of Conscience — an American Right with the torch in the upraised hand of the Statue of Liberty. *Intaglio, rotary press, perforated 11 x 10 1/2.*

751, 752 *Torch of the Statue of Liberty*

751		MNHVF	UseVF
12¢	**red brown** on beige paper, tagged	.25	.20
	Plate block of 4	1.15	
	FDC *(April 8, 1981)*		1.75
	zo. Tagging omitted (error)	5.00	

U.S. Postal Service Plate-Numbering Change

In response to collector complaints that its plate-numbering system resulted in many inconvenient and costly blocks of 10, 12 and 20 stamps, the USPS in January 1981 instituted a new plate number arrangement. Under the new system, most sheets were to contain a single plate number consisting of one (for monocolor stamps) to six digits, each digit representing a given printing plate and color. Thus, under this system, most plate blocks returned to blocks of four.

Booklet panes hereafter also contain a plate number in the selvage.

In coils, a plate number was incorporated into some stamps in the roll, at various intervals between stamps, depending on press used.

1981. Freedom of Conscience Coil Issue in the Americana Series. *Coil, intaglio, perforated 10 vertically.*

752		MNHVF	UseVF
12¢	**red brown** on beige paper, tagged	.25	.20
	Pair	.50	.25
	Line pair	1.50	
	FDC *(April 8, 1981)*		1.75
	v. Pair, imperforate	200.00	
	Line pair, imperforate	400.00	
	zx. Untagged (Bureau precancel)		.25
	Pair	—	
	Line pair	—	

1981. America the Beautiful Issue featured an American flag above a landscape and a phrase from the song *America the Beautiful,* written by Katherine Lee Bates (1859-1929) of Falmouth, Mass., in 1893, inspired by the view from Pike's Peak in Colorado. *Intaglio, perforated 11.*

753 *"...for amber waves of grain"*

753		MNHVF	UseVF
18¢	**multicolored** tagged	.30	.20
	Plate block of 20	8.50	
	FDC *(April 24, 1981)*		1.75
	v. Pair, imperforate	100.00	
	v1. Vertical pair, imperforate horizontally	1,000.00	

Great Americans Series Identifier

Entries are in denomination order. All stamps listed provide basic data: denomination, person honored, and catalog number. There is information in the columns for perforation, gum and tagging only when such information better identifies the different varieties of the stamp. This series apparently ended in 1999. If further varieties are found, this listing will be updated and modified in future editions.

Denomination/Name	Cat.	Perf.	Gum	Tagging	Without Tagging
1¢ Dorothea Dix	807	11 1/4 H			
1¢ Dorothea Dix	807A	10 3/4 L		Block (small)	
1¢ Dorothea Dix	807Abz	10 3/4 L		Block (large)	
1¢ Margaret Mitchell	857				Error (857zo)
2¢ Igor Stravinsky	798				Error (798zo)
2¢ Mary Lyon	872				Error (872zo)
2¢ Mary Lyon	872zx				Intentional
3¢ Henry Clay	804				Error (804zo)
3¢ Paul Dudley White, MD	861		Matte		Error (861zo)
3¢ Paul Dudley White, MD	861zxm		Matte		Intentional
3¢ Paul Dudley White, MD	861zxs		Shiny		Intentional
4¢ Carl Schurz	801				Error (801zo)
4¢ Father Flanagan	858				
4¢ Father Flanagan	858zx				Intentional (light gray violet)
4¢ Father Flanagan	858zx1				Intentional (slate violet)
5¢ Pearl Buck	803				
5¢ Hugo L. Black	854				Error (854zo)
5¢ Luis Muñoz Martin	927				Error (927zo)
5¢ Luis Muñoz Martin	927zx				Intentional
6¢ Walter Lippmann	848				
7¢ Abraham Baldwin	819				
8¢ Henry Knox	847				
9¢ Sylvanus Thayer	842				
10¢ Richard Russell	815			Block (small)	
10¢ Richard Russell	815bz			Block (large)	
10¢ Red Cloud	877		Matte	Block (large)	Error (877zo)
10¢ Red Cloud	877pz		Matte	Phosphored paper	
10¢ Red Cloud	877pzs		Shiny	Phosphored paper	
10¢ Red Cloud	877pzs1		Shiny	Carmine, phosphored paper	
11¢ Alden Partridge	823				Error (823zo)
13¢ Crazy Horse	785				Error (785zo)
14¢ Sinclair Lewis	826			Block (small)	
14¢ Sinclair Lewis	826bz			Block (large)	
14¢ Julia Ward Howe	871				
15¢ Buffalo Bill Cody	894			Block (large)	
15¢ Buffalo Bill Cody	894z			Overall	
15¢ Buffalo Bill Cody	894pz			Phosphored paper	Error (894zo)
17¢ Rachel Carson	769				Error (769zo)
17¢ Belva Ann Lockwood	856				Error (856zo)
18¢ George Mason	757				Error (757zo)
19¢ Sequoyah	747				
20¢ Ralph Bunch	784				Error (784zo)
20¢ Thomas H. Gallaudet	802				Error (802zo)
20¢ Harry S. Truman	811	11 L		Block (small)	
20¢ Harry S. Truman	904	11 1/4 H		Block (large)	Error (904zo)*
20¢ Harry S. Truman	904z	11 1/4 H		Overall	Error (904zo)*
20¢ Harry S. Truman	904pz			Phosphored paper	
20¢ Virginia Apgar	1052				
21¢ Chester Carlson	911				Error (911zo)
22¢ John J. Audubon	839	11 L		Block (small)	Error (839zo)
22¢ John J. Audubon	839bz	11 L		Block (large)	Error (83920)
22¢ John J. Audubon	839A	11 1/4 H			
23¢ Mary Cassatt	915			Block (large)	
23¢ Mary Cassatt	915z			Overall	Error (915zo)

Denomination/Name	Cat.	Perf.	Gum	Tagging	Without Tagging
1¢ Dorothea Dix	807	11 1/4 H			
1¢ Dorothea Dix	807A	10 3/4 L		Block (small)	
1¢ Dorothea Dix	807Abz	10 3/4 L		Block (large)	
1¢ Margaret Mitchell	857				Error (857zo)
2¢ Igor Stravinsky	798				Error (798zo)
2¢ Mary Lyon	872				Error (872zo)
2¢ Mary Lyon	872zx				Intentional
3¢ Henry Clay	804				Error (804zo)
3¢ Paul Dudley White, MD	861		Matte		Error (861zo)
3¢ Paul Dudley White, MD	861zxm		Matte		Intentional
3¢ Paul Dudley White, MD	861zxs		Shiny		Intentional
4¢ Carl Schurz	801				Error (801zo)
4¢ Father Flanagan	858				
4¢ Father Flanagan	858zx				Intentional (light gray violet)
4¢ Father Flanagan	858zx1				Intentional (slate violet)
5¢ Pearl Buck	803				
5¢ Hugo L. Black	854				Error (854zo)
5¢ Luis Muñoz Martin	927				Error (927zo)
5¢ Luis Muñoz Martin	927zx				Intentional
6¢ Walter Lippmann	848				
7¢ Abraham Baldwin	819				
8¢ Henry Knox	847				
9¢ Sylvanus Thayer	842				
10¢ Richard Russell	815			Block (small)	
10¢ Richard Russell	815bz			Block (large)	
10¢ Red Cloud	877		Matte	Block (large)	Error (877zo)
10¢ Red Cloud	877pz		Matte	Phosphored paper	
10¢ Red Cloud	877pzs		Shiny	Phosphored paper	
10¢ Red Cloud	877pzs1		Shiny	Carmine, phosphored paper	
11¢ Alden Partridge	823				Error (823zo)
13¢ Crazy Horse	785				Error (785zo)
14¢ Sinclair Lewis	826			Block (small)	
14¢ Sinclair Lewis	826bz			Block (large)	
14¢ Julia Ward Howe	871				
15¢ Buffalo Bill Cody	894			Block (large)	
15¢ Buffalo Bill Cody	894z			Overall	
15¢ Buffalo Bill Cody	894pz			Phosphored paper	Error (894zo)
17¢ Rachel Carson	769				Error (769zo)
17¢ Belva Ann Lockwood	856				Error (856zo)
18¢ George Mason	757				Error (757zo)
19¢ Sequoyah	747				
20¢ Ralph Bunch	784				Error (784zo)
20¢ Thomas H. Gallaudet	802				Error (802zo)
20¢ Harry S. Truman	811	11 L		Block (small)	
20¢ Harry S. Truman	904	11 1/4 H		Block (large)	Error (904zo)*
20¢ Harry S. Truman	904z	11 1/4 H		Overall	Error (904zo)*
20¢ Harry S. Truman	904pz			Phosphored paper	
20¢ Virginia Apgar	1052				
21¢ Chester Carlson	911				Error (911zo)
22¢ John J. Audubon	839	11 L		Block (small)	Error (839zo)
22¢ John J. Audubon	839bz	11 L		Block (large)	Error (83920)
22¢ John J. Audubon	839A	11 1/4 H			
23¢ Mary Cassatt	915			Block (large)	
23¢ Mary Cassatt	915z			Overall	Error (915zo)
23¢ Mary Cassatt	915pzm		Matte	Phosphored paper	
23¢ Mary Cassatt	915z1pzs		Shiny	Phosphored paper	
25¢ Jack London (sheet)	853	11 H			Error (853zo)
25¢ Jack London (booklet)	888	11 L			Error (888zo)
25¢ Jack London (booklet)	889	10 H			Error (889zo)
28¢ Sitting Bull	919				

Denomination/Name	Cat.	Perf.	Gum	Tagging	Without Tagging
29¢ Earl Warren	983				
29¢ Thomas Jefferson	1009				
30¢ Frank C. Laubach	816	11 L	Block (small)		
30¢ Frank C. Laubach	816A	11 1/4 H	Block (large)		
30¢ Frank C. Laubach	816Az	11 1/4 H		Overall	
32¢ Milton S. Hershey	1096				
32¢ Cal Farley	1124				
32¢ Henry R. Luce	1168				
32¢ Lila & DeWitt Wallace	1171				
35¢ Charles R. Drew, MD	770				Error (770zo)
35¢ Dennis Chavez	946				
37¢ Robert Millikan	786				Error (786zo)
39¢ Grenville Clark	825	11 L		Block (small)	
39¢ Grenville Clark	825bz	11 L		Block (large)	
39¢ Grenville Clark	825A	11 1/4 H		Block (large)	
40¢ Lillian M. Gilbreth	813	11 L		Block (small)	
40¢ Lillian M. Gilbreth	813A	11 1/4 H		Block (large)	
40¢ Claire Chennault	932			Overall	
40¢ Claire Chennault	932pzm		Matte	Phosphored paper	
40¢ Claire Chennault	932pzs		Shiny	Phosphored paper	
40¢ Claire Chennault	932pzsg		Low-gloss	Phosphored paper	
45¢ Harvey Cushing, MD	895			Block (large)	Error (895zo)
45¢ Harvey Cushing, MD	895z			Overall	
46¢ Ruth Benedict	1114				
50¢ Chester W. Nimitz	824	11 L	Shiny	Overall	Error (824zo)
50¢ Chester W. Nimitz	824A	11 1/4 H	Matte	Block (large)	Error (824Azo)
50¢ Chester W. Nimitz	824Apz	11 1/4 H	Shiny	Phosphored paper	
50¢ Chester W. Nimitz	824Az1	11 1/4 H	Matte	Overall	
52¢ Hubert H. Humphrey	957		Matte	Phosphored paper	
52¢ Hubert H. Humphrey	957pz		Shiny	Phosphored paper	
55¢ Alice Hamilton, MD	1093				
55¢ Justin S. Morrill	1228				
56¢ John Harvard	860				
65¢ H.H. “Hap” Arnold	916				Error (916zo)
75¢ Wendell Wilkie	981		Matte	Phosphored paper	
75¢ Wendell Wilkie	981pz		Shiny	Phosphored paper	
77¢ Mary Breckinridge	1200				
78¢ Alice Paul	1095				
$1 Bernard Revel	862				
$1 Johns Hopkins	918		Matte	Block (large)	
$1 Johns Hopkins	918z		Matte	Overall	Error (918zo)
$1 Johns Hopkins	918pzm		Matte	Phosphored paper	
$1 Johns Hopkins	918pzs		Shiny	Phosphored paper (Mottled)	
$1 Johns Hopkins	918pzsg		Low-gloss	Phosphored paper (grainy)	
$2 William Jennings Bryan	855				Error (855zo)
$5 Bret Harte	878			Block	Error (878zo)
$5 Bret Harte	878pz			Phosphored paper	

Symbols: (in Perf. column) H = Harrow (perfect corners); L = L perforator

Footnotes

* Impossible to tell if “tagging omitted” version is from block- or overall-tagging version.

1981. America the Beautiful Issue *Coil, intaglio, perforated 10 vertically.*

754 *"...from sea to shining sea"*

754		MNHVF	UseVF
18¢	**multicolored** tagged	.30	.20
	Pair	.60	.20
	v. Pair, imperforate	18.00	
	v1. Pair, imperforate between	—	
	zo. Tagging omitted (error)	—	
	FDC *(April 24, 1981)*		1.75

Listings and prices for plate number coil strips and singles appear at the end of this definitives section of the Krause-Minkus catalog.

1981 America the Beautiful Combination Booklet consisting of two 6¢ and six 18¢ stamps. *Intaglio, perforated 11.*

755 *Circle of Stars*

756 *"...for purple mountain majesties"*

755		MNHVF	UseVF
6¢	**blue** tagged	.55	.25
	FDC *(April 24, 1981)*		2.00
756		**MNHVF**	**UseVF**
18¢	**multicolored** tagged	.30	.20
	FDC *(April 24, 1981)*		1.75
	y. Se-tenant pair, No. 755, 756	.90	
	n. Booklet pane of 8 (2 No. 755, 6 No. 756)	3.00	
	nv. Booklet pane, vertically imperforate between	75.00	
	FDC pane		5.00

1981. George Mason Issue in the Great Americans Series honored an early leader (1725-92) of pre-Revolutionary Virginia patriots, whose draft of a Bill of Rights formed the basis for the first 10 Amendments to the Constitution. *Intaglio, perforated 11 x 10 1/2.*

757 *George Mason*

757		MNHVF	UseVF
18¢	**blue** overall tagged	.30	.20
	Plate block of 4	2.50	
	FDC *(May 7, 1981)*		1.75
	zo. Tagging omitted (error)	4.50	

1981. Wildlife Booklet Issue featured 10 wild animals native to the United States. *Intaglio, perforated 11.*

758 *Bighorn sheep*

759 *Puma*

760 *Harbor seal*

761 *Bison*

762 *Brown bear*

763 *Polar bear*

764 *Elk (Wapiti)*

765 *Moose*

766 *White-tailed deer*

767 *Pronghorn antelope*

758		MNHVF	UseVF
18¢	Bighorn sheep, **brown,** tagged	.50	.20
759		**MNHVF**	**UseVF**
18¢	Puma, **brown,** tagged	.50	.20
760		**MNHVF**	**UseVF**
18¢	Harbor seal, **brown,** tagged	.50	.20
761		**MNHVF**	**UseVF**
18¢	Bison, **brown,** tagged	.50	.20
762		**MNHVF**	**UseVF**
18¢	Brown bear, **brown,** tagged	.50	.20
763		**MNHVF**	**UseVF**
18¢	Polar bear, **brown,** tagged	.50	.20
764		**MNHVF**	**UseVF**
18¢	Elk (Wapiti), **brown,** tagged	.50	.20
765		**MNHVF**	**UseVF**
18¢	Moose, **brown,** tagged	.50	.20
766		**MNHVF**	**UseVF**
18¢	White-tailed deer, **brown,** tagged	.50	.20
767		**MNHVF**	**UseVF**
18¢	Pronghorn antelope, **brown,** tagged	.50	.20
	FDC, any single *(May 14, 1981)*		1.75
	n. Booklet pane of 10 (Nos. 758-67)	8.50	4.00
	nzo. Booklet pane of 10, untagged pane (3 known)	750.00	
	nv. Booklet pane, vertically imperforate between	1,500.00	
	FDC, pane		6.00

1981-95. Transportation Series

featured a wide spectrum of means of moving people or goods. Some — as the initial 18¢ stamp in the series — were famous in history or literature; others had a touch of whimsy.

1981. Surrey Issue in the Transportation Series showed a vehicle with four wheels and two bench seats. *Coil, intaglio, perforated 10 vertically.*

768 *Surrey with the fringe on top*

768		MNHVF	UseVF
18¢	**brown** tagged	.35	.20
	Pair	.60	

		MNHVF	UseVF
	v. Pair, imperforate	125.00	
	FDC *(May 18, 1981)*		2.00

Listings and prices for plate number coil strips and singles appear at the end of this definitives section of the Krause-Minkus catalog.

1981. Rachel Carson Issue in the Great Americans Series honored the scientist and author (1907-1964) of *Silent Spring.* When published, the book touched off an international controversy over pesticides. From March 22, 1981, to April 2, 1988, 17¢ was the additional 1-ounce rate (12-ounce maximum). *Intaglio, perforated 11 x 10 1/2.*

769 *Rachel Carson*

769		MNHVF	UseVF
17¢	**green** overall tagged	.30	.20
	Plate block of 4	1.50	
	FDC *(May 28, 1981)*		1.75
	zo. Tagging omitted (error)	—	

1981. Charles R. Drew Issue in the Great Americans Series honored the scientist and surgeon (1904-1950) who discovered and developed methods to preserve blood plasma in large quantities. He was the first black surgeon selected for membership on the American Board of Surgery. *Intaglio, perforated 11 x 10 1/2.*

770 *Charles R. Drew, MD*

770		MNHVF	UseVF
35¢	**gray** overall tagged	.50	.25
	Plate block of 4	3.50	
	FDC *(June 3, 1981)*		2.50
	zo. Tagging omitted (error)	—	

Note: Plate blocks from plates 3 & 4 carry a premium.

1981. Electric Auto Issue in the Transportation Series showed an electrically powered coupe. From March 22, 1981, to April 2, 1988, 17¢ was the additional-ounce rate (12-ounce maximum). *Coil, intaglio, perforated 10 vertically.*

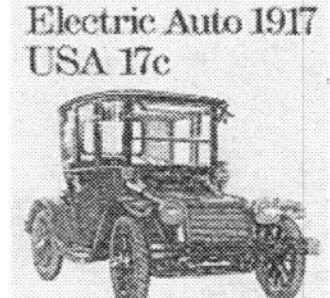

771 *Electric auto, 1917*

771		MNHVF	UseVF
17¢	**blue** tagged	.35	.20
	Pair	.60	
	FDC *(June 25, 1981)*		2.00
	v. Pair, imperforate	—	
	zo. Tagging omitted (error)	—	
	zx1. Untagged (Bureau precancel, Type 1: "PRESORTED" 11 1/2mm)	.35	.35
	zx2. Untagged (Bureau precancel, Type II: "PRESORTED" 12 1/2mm)	.75	.60
	zx3. Untagged (Bureau precancel, Type II: "PRESORTED" 13 1/2mm)	1.00	.50
	zv. Pair, imperforate	650.00	

Listings and prices for plate number coil strips and singles appear at the end of this definitives section of the Krause-Minkus catalog.

1981. Non-Denominated "C" Issue marked the new First Class postage rate of 20¢, which went into effect Nov. 1, 1981. The stamp was intended for domestic use only. Design same as the "A" and "B" issues, except for letter and background color. *Gravure, perforated 11 x 10 1/2, design size 19 x 22mm.*

772-774 *"C" to left of stylized eagle*

772		MNHVF	UseVF
20¢	**brown** tagged	.35	.20
	Plate block of 4	1.50	
	FDC *(Oct. 11, 1981)*		1.75
	zo. Tagging omitted (error)	9.00	

1981. Non-Denominated "C" Booklet Pane Issue *Booklet panes, intaglio, perforated 11 x 10 1/2 design size 15 x 18mm.*

773		MNHVF	UseVF
20¢	**brown** tagged	.50	.20
	FDC *(Oct. 11, 1981)* any single		1.75
	n. Booklet pane of 10	5.00	5.00
	FDC (pane)		5.50

1981. Non-Denominated "C" Coil Issue *Intaglio, perforated 10 vertically, design size 19 x 22mm.*

774		MNHVF	UseVF
20¢	**brown** tagged	.60	.20
	Pair	1.20	
	Line pair	1.50	
	FDC *(Oct. 11, 1981)*	1.75	
	v. Pair, imperforate	2,000.00	
	Line pair, imperforate	—	

1981. Christmas Issue consisted of two stamps. A contemporary design depicting a teddy tear on a sleigh and a traditional design of Madonna and Child by Botticelli. *Gravure, perforated 11.*

775 *Teddy bear on a sleigh*

775		MNHVF	UseVF
20¢	**multicolored** tagged	.50	.20
	Plate block of 4	2.50	
	FDC *(Oct. 28, 1981)*		1.75
	v. Pair, imperforate	250.00	
	v1. Vertical pair, imperforate horizontally	—	

776 Madonna and Child, *detail by Sandro Botticelli, in the collection of The Art Institute of Chicago*

776		MNHVF	UseVF
20¢	**multicolored** tagged	.50	.20
	Plate block of 4	2.50	
	FDC *(Oct. 28, 1981)*		1.75
	v. Pair, imperforate	110.00	
	v1. Vertical pair, imperforate horizontally	1,550.00	

1981. Fire Pumper Issue in the Transportation Series depicted an Amoskeag fire pumper. It carried a steam-producing boiler that operated an engine to pump water from available sources. *Coil, intaglio, perforated 10 vertically.*

777 *Fire pumper, 1860s*

Transportation Series Identifier

As with the Great Americans Identifier, entries here are by denomination, in order of issue of that denomination. All stamps listed provide basic data: denomination, form of transportation depicted, and catalog number. There is information in the gum, tagging and without tagging columns only when such information will assist in properly identifying a stamp.

Denomination/Name	Cat.	Gum	Tagging	Without Tagging
1¢ Omnibus (USA 1)	806			
1¢ Omnibus (1 USA)	867pz		Prephosphored	
1¢ Omnibus	867zxm	Matte		
1¢ Omnibus	867zxs	Shiny		
2¢ Locomotive (USA 2¢)	790			
2¢ Locomotive (2¢ USA)	873			
2¢ Locomotive	873zx			Intentional
3¢ Handcar	800			
3¢ Conestoga Wagon	883			
3¢ Conestoga Wagon	883zxm	Matte		Intentional
3¢ Conestoga Wagon	883zxs	Shiny		Intentional
3.4¢ School Bus	843			
3.4¢ School Bus	843zx			Bureau precancel
4¢ Stagecoach (19 1/2mm long)	791			Error (791zo)
4¢ Stagecoach	791zx			Bureau precancel
4¢ Stagecoach (17mm long)	868	Block		
4¢ Stagecoach	868z	Overall		
4¢ Steam Carriage	943			
4¢ Steam Carriage	943zx			Intentional
4.9¢ Buckboard	846			
4.9¢ Buckboard	846zx			Bureau precancel
5¢ Motorcycle	808			Error (808zo)
5¢ Milk Wagon	879			
5¢ Circus Wagon (05 USA, intaglio)	931			
5¢ Circus Wagon	931z			Intentional
5¢ Circus Wagon (05 USA, gravure)	1007	No		Intentional
5¢ Circus Wagon (USA 5¢)	1077	No		Intentional
5¢ Canoe (brown)	955	No		Bureau service indicator
5¢ Canoe (red)	979	No		Bureau service indicator
5.2¢ Sleigh	799			
5.2¢ Sleigh	799zx			Bureau precancel
5.3¢ Elevator	906			Bureau service indicator
5.5¢ Star Route Truck	865			
5.5¢ Star Route Truck	865zx			Bureau service indicator
5.9¢ Bicycle	787			
5.9¢ Bicycle	787zx			Bureau precancel
6¢ Tricycle	841			
6¢ Tricycle	841zx			Bureau precancel
7.1¢ Tractor	870			
7.1¢ Tractor	870zx			Bureau service indicator ("Nonprofit Org")
7.1¢ Tractor	870zx1			Bureau service indicator ("Nonprofit 5-Digit ZIP+4)
7.4¢ Baby Buggy	814			
7.4¢ Baby Buggy	814zx			Bureau precancel
7.6¢ Carreta	903	No		Bureau service indicator
8.3¢ Ambulance (18 1/2 mm long)	845			
8.3¢ Ambulance	845zx			Bureau precancel
8.3¢ Ambulance (18mm long)	845A	No		Bureau precancel
8.4¢ Wheel Chair	901	No		Bureau service indicator
8.5¢ Tow Truck	869			
8.5¢ Tow Truck	869zx			Bureau service indicator
9.3¢ Mail Wagon	778			
9.3¢ Mail Wagon	778zx			Bureau precancel

Denomination/Name	Cat.	Gum	Tagging	Without Tagging
10¢ Canal Boat	874	Matte	Block	
10¢ Canal Boat	874pz	Shiny	Pre-phosphored	
10¢ Canal Boat	874zm	Matte	Overall	
10¢ Canal Boat	874zs	Shiny	Overall	
10¢ Tractor Trailer	954		No	Bureau service indicator, gray
10¢ Tractor Trailer	1042			Bureau service indicator, black
10.1¢ Oil Wagon	837			
10.1¢ Oil Wagon	837zx			Bureau precancel, black
10.1¢ Oil Wagon	837zx1			Bureau precancel, red
10.9¢ Hansom Cab	788			
10.9¢ Hansom Cab	788zx			Bureau precancel
11¢ Caboose	812			
11¢ Caboose	812zx			Bureau precancel
11¢ Caboose	812zx1			Intentional
11¢ Stutz Bearcat	844			
12¢ Stanley Steamer (18mm long)	831		Block	Error (831zo)
12¢ Stanley Steamer	831p		Hi-Brite Paper	
12¢ Stanley Steamer	831xz		No	Bureau precancel
12¢ Stanley Steamer	831A		No	Bureau precancel
12.5¢ Pushcart	838			
12.5¢ Pushcart	838zx		No	Bureau precancel
13¢ Police Patrol Wagon	914		No	Bureau service indicator
13.2¢ Coal Car	900		No	Bureau service indicator
14¢ Iceboat (17 1/2mm long)	827		Overall	Error (827zo)
14¢ Iceboat (17 1/4mm long)	827A		Block	
15¢ Tugboat	899		Block	Error (899zo)
15¢ Tugboat	899z		Overall	
16.7¢ Popcorn Wagon	898		No	Bureau service indicator
17¢ Electric Auto	771			Error (771zo)
17¢ Electric Auto	771zx1			Bureau precancel 11 1/2mm
17¢ Electric Auto	771zx2			Bureau precancel 12 1/2mm
17¢ Electric Auto	771zx3			Bureau precancel 13 1/2mm
17¢ Dog Sled	859			
17.5¢ Racing Car	880			
17.5¢ Racing Car	880zx			Bureau service indicator
18¢ Surrey	768			
20¢ Fire Pumper	777			
20¢ Cable Car	913		Block	
20¢ Cable Car	913z		Overall	
20¢ Cog Railway	1086			
20.5¢ Fire Engine	907		No	Bureau service indicator
21¢ Railroad Mail Car	902		No	Bureau service indicator
23¢ Lunch Wagon	949	Matte	Overall*	
23¢ Lunch Wagon	949ps	Shiny	Prephosphored*	
24.1¢ Tandem Bicycle	912	No		Bureau service indicator
25¢ Bread Wagon	866			Error (866zo)
32¢ Ferryboat	1085			
$1 Seaplane	928			

Footnotes

* Tagging is solid, smooth-appearing
**Tagging is mottled

777		MNHVF	UseVF
20¢	**red** tagged	.40	.20
	Pair	.80	
	FDC *(Dec. 10, 1981)*		2.00
	v. Pair, imperforate	1,000.00	

Listings and prices for plate number coil strips and singles appear at the end of this definitives section of the Krause-Minkus catalog.

1981. Mail Wagon Issue in the Transportation Series showed a vehicle typical of wagons used in early rural free delivery (RFD) service. Bulk rate. *Coil, printed by intaglio, perforated 10 vertically.*

778 *Mail wagon, 1880s*

778		MNHVF	UseVF
9.3¢	**dark red** tagged	.25	.20
	Pair	.25	
	FDC *(Dec. 15, 1981)*		2.00
	zv. Pair, imperforate	115.00	
	zx. Untagged (Bureau precancel)	.25	.25
	FDC Bureau precancel		300.00

Listings and prices for plate number coil strips and singles appear at the end of this definitives section of the Krause-Minkus catalog.

1981. Flag Over Supreme Court Issue *Intaglio, perforated 11.*

779-781 *Flag over Supreme Court Building; in the foreground is statue* Contemplation of Justice *by noted American James Earle Fraser*

779		MNHVF	UseVF
20¢	**black, dark blue & red** perforated 11, tagged	.35	.20
	Plate block of 20	15.00	
	FDC *(Dec. 17, 1981)*		1.75
	v. Vertical pair, imperforate	35.00	
	v1. Vertical pair, imperforate horizontally	500.00	
	v2. Block of 4, imperforate	75.00	
	v3. black omitted	300.00	
	v4. blue omitted	85.00	
	v5. dark blue omitted	—	

779A		MNHVF	UseVF
20¢	**black, dark blue & red** perforated 11 1/4, tagged	.35	.20
	Plate block of 20	9.00	

1981. Flag Over Supreme Court Coil Issue *Coil, intaglio, perforated 10 vertically.*

780		MNHVF	UseVF
20¢	**black, dark blue & red** tagged	.35	.20
	Pair	.70	
	FDC *(Dec. 17, 1981)*		1.75
	a. slate blue, dark blue and red	—	
	b. black, dark blue and brick red	—	
	v. black omitted	50.00	
	v1. dark blue omitted	1,500.00	
	v2. Pair, imperforate	10.00	
	v3. Pair, imperforate between	1,000.00	
	zx. Untagged (Bureau precancel)	.50	.20
	Pair	1.00	.50
	zo. Tagging omitted (error)	—	

Listings and prices for plate number coil strips and singles appear at the end of this definitives section of the Krause-Minkus catalog.

1981. Flag Over Supreme Court Issue *Intaglio, perforated 11.*

781		MNHVF	UseVF
20¢	**black, dark red & blue** tagged	.35	.20
	FDC *(Dec. 17, 1981)*		1.75
	n. Booklet pane of 6	2.50	3.00
	FDC pane		6.00
	n1. Booklet pane of 10	4.50	4.75
	FDC pane *(June 1, 1982)*		10.00

1981. Flag Over Independence Hall Issue *Intaglio, Combination Press, perforated 11. (See 690, 694.)*

782 *Flag over Independence Hall*

782		MNHVF	UseVF
13¢	**dark blue & red** block tagged	.60	.25
	Plate block of 20	70.00	
	Plate block of 6	17.50	
	v. Vertical pair, imperforate	150.00	
	v1. Horizontal pair, imperforate vertically	—	
	zo. Tagging omitted (error)	3.00	

1982. Bighorn Sheep Issue featured the Bighorn sheep used in the 1981 Wildlife booklet (No. 758). *Booklet pane, intaglio, perforated 11.*

783 *Bighorn sheep*

783		MNHVF	UseVF
20¢	**blue** Type I, overall tagged	.50	.20
	FDC *(Jan. 8, 1982),* 18 3/4mm wide single		1.75
	n. Booklet pane of 10	5.00	5.00
	nv. Booklet pane, imperforate between vertically	110.00	
	zo. Tagging omitted (error)	100.00	
	nzo. Booklet pane of 10, untagged	30.00	

783A		MNHVF	UseVF
20¢	**blue** Type II, block tagged, 18 1/2mm wide	.50	.20
	n. Booklet pane of 10	15.00	.50

Type I: is 18 3/4mm wide, Type II: is 18 1/2mm wide.

1982. Ralph Bunche Issue in the Great Americans Series honored the first black Nobel Peace Prize winner. Bunche, (1904-1971), a United Nations official, was awarded the prize in 1950 for negotiating an armistice between the Palestinian Arabs and the Israelis in 1949. *Intaglio.*

784 *Ralph Bunche*

784		MNHVF	UseVF
20¢	**maroon** overall tagged	.35	.20
	Plate block of 4	2.75	
	FDC *(Jan. 12, 1982)*		2.00
	zo. Tagging omitted (error)	—	

1982. Crazy Horse Issue in the Great Americans Series honored the Oglala Sioux Indian leader (c.1842-77) who, joining Sitting Bull and other Sioux on the Little Big Horn River, was prominent in the defeat of Gen. George A. Custer and the Seventh Cavalry there on June 25, 1876. *Intaglio, perforated 11 x 10 1/2.*

785 *Crazy Horse*

785		MNHVF	UseVF
13¢	**light maroon** overall tagged	.35	.20
	Plate block of 4	1.50	
	FDC *(Jan. 15, 1982)*		1.75
	zo. Tagging omitted (error)	—	

1982. Robert Millikan Issue in the Great Americans Series honored the Nobel Prize-winning physicist, educator, humanitarian, and key figure in the development of the California Institute of Technology (1868-1953). *Intaglio, perforated 11 x 10 1/2.*

786 *Robert Millikan*

786		MNHVF	UseVF
37¢	**blue** overall tagged	.60	.20
	Plate block of 4	3.50	
	FDC *(Jan. 26, 1982)*		1.75
	zo. Tagging omitted (error)	—	

1982. High Wheeler Bicycle Issue in the Transportation Series. Intended for bulk mailings by non-profit organizations. *Coil, intaglio, perforated 10 vertically.*

787 *High Wheeler Bicycle, 1870s*

787		MNHVF	UseVF
5.9¢	**blue** tagged	.25	.20
	Pair	.30	
	FDC *(Feb. 17, 1982)*		2.00
	zx. Untagged (Bureau precancel)		.20
	Pair		
	FDC (Bureau precancel)		200.00
	zv. Pair, imperforate	150.00	
	Line pair, imperforate	—	

1982. Hansom Cab Issue in the Transportation Series pictured a one-horse, two-wheeled vehicle designed by Joseph Hansom. It paid bulk rate. *Coil, intaglio, perforated 10 vertically.*

788 *Hansom cab, 1890s*

788		MNHVF	UseVF
10.9¢	**purple** tagged	.25	.20
	Pair	.50	
	FDC		2.00
	zx. Untagged (Bureau precancel)	.30	.25
	FDC *(March 26, 1982)* (Bureau precancel)		300.00
	zv. Pair, imperforate	160.00	
	Line pair, imperforate	—	

Listings and prices for plate number coil strips and singles appear at the end of this definitives section of the Krause-Minkus catalog.

1982. Consumer Education Issue served to bring attention to consumer education issues by educators, government agencies, consumer organizations, business, labor organizations, and media. *Coil, intaglio, perforated 10 vertically.*

789 *Consumer education, wise shoppers stretch dollars*

789		MNHVF	UseVF
20¢	**blue** tagged	.50	.20
	Pair	.75	
	FDC *(April 27, 1982)*		1.75
	v. Pair, imperforate	95.00	
	Line pair, imperforate	—	
	zo. Tagging omitted (error)	4.00	

Listings and prices for plate number coil strips and singles appear at the end of this definitives section of the Krause-Minkus catalog.

1982. Locomotive Issue in the Transportation Series pictured a steam engine representative of those used in the 1860s and '70s. *Coil, intaglio, perforated 10 vertically.*

790 *Locomotive, 1870s*

790		MNHVF	UseVF
2¢	**black** tagged	.25	.20
	Pair	.30	
	FDC *(May 20, 1982)*		2.00
	v. Pair, imperforate	50.00	
	Line pair, imperforate	—	

(For similar design with "2 USA" see No. 873.)

Listings and prices for plate number coil strips and singles appear at the end of this definitives section of the Krause-Minkus catalog.

1982. Stagecoach Issue in the Transportation Series showed a stagecoach made by Abbott & Downing of Concord, N.H. The precanceled version met the Third Class, non-profit, five-digit-sort bulk rate. "Stagecoach 1890s" measures 19 1/2mm long. *Coil, intaglio, perforated 10 vertically.*

791 *Stagecoach, 1890s*

791		MNHVF	UseVF
4¢	**brown** tagged	.25	.20
	Pair	.30	
	FDC *(Aug. 19, 1982)*		2.00
	v. Pair, imperforate	850.00	
	zo. Tagging omitted (error)	—	
	zx. Untagged (Bureau precancel: "Nonprofit Org")	.25	.20
	zxv. Pair, imperforate, untagged (precanceled)	750.00	

For similar design with "Stagecoach 1890s" measuring 17mm long. see No. 868.

Listings and prices for plate number coil strips and singles appear at the end of this definitives section of the Krause-Minkus catalog.

1982. Christmas Issue consisted of a single traditional design and a block of four contemporary designs. The contemporary design features a block of four children and snow scenes designed by Dolli Tingle. *Gravure, perforated 11.*

792-795

		MNHVF	UseVF
792			
20¢	Sledding, **multicolored,** tagged	.35	.20
793		MNHVF	UseVF
20¢	Building snowman, **multicolored,** tagged	.35	.20
794		MNHVF	UseVF
20¢	Skating, **multicolored,** tagged	.35	.20
795		MNHVF	UseVF
20¢	Decorating tree, **multicolored,** tagged	.35	.20
	FDC *(Oct. 28, 1982)* any single		2.00
	y. Se-tenant block of 4	1.50	
	Plate block of 4	3.50	
	FDC block of 4		4.00
	v. Block of 4, imperforate	3,250.00	
	v1. Block of 4, imperforate horizontally		

1982. Traditional Christmas Issue depicted a Madonna and Child by Giovanni Battista Tiepolo, an 18th century painter. *Gravure, perforated 11.*

796 *Madonna and Child, by Gíovanní Battista Tiepolo, National Gallery of Art*

		MNHVF	UseVF
796			
20¢	**multicolored** tagged	.35	.20
	Plate block of 20	13.75	
	FDC *(Oct. 28, 1982)*		1.75
	v. Horizontal pair, imperforate vertically	—	
	v1. Vertical pair, imperforate horizontally	—	
	v2. Pair, imperforate	—	

1982. Kitten and Puppy Issue was a postcard-rate stamp issued to satisfy demand for those who sent a holiday postcard. *Gravure, perforated 11.*

797 *Kitten and puppy playing in snow*

		MNHVF	UseVF
797			
13¢	**multicolored** tagged	.35	.20
	Plate block of 4	2.00	
	FDC *(Nov. 3, 1982)*		2.00
	v. Pair, imperforate	650.00	

1982. Igor Stravinsky Issue in the Great Americans Series marked the 100th anniversary of the birth of the Russian-born composer (1882-1971) of operas and ballets. He became a U.S. citizen in 1945. *Intaglio.*

798 *Igor Stravinsky*

		MNHVF	UseVF
798			
2¢	**brown** overall tagged	.25	.20
	Plate block of 4	.30	
	Pair, gutter between	7.50	
	FDC *(Nov. 18, 1982)*		1.75
	zo. Tagging omitted (error)	—	

1983. Sleigh Issue in the Transportation Series showed an antique sleigh typical of the 1880s. It was for use by authorized non-profit organizations. *Coil, intaglio, perforated 10 vertically.*

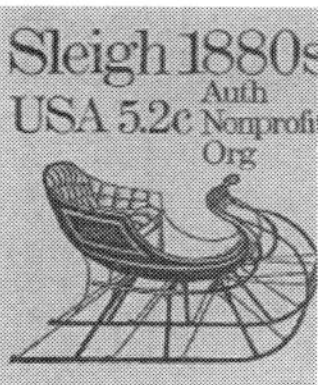

799 *Sleigh, 1880s*

		MNHVF	UseVF
799			
5.2¢	**red** tagged	.25	.20
	Pair	.30	
	FDC *(March 21, 1983)*		2.00
	zx. Untagged (Bureau precancel)	.25	
	FDC (Bureau precancel)		150.00

Listings and prices for plate number coil strips and singles appear at the end of this definitives section of the Krause-Minkus catalog.

1983. Handcar Issue in the Transportation Series showed a manually-operated railroad handcar made in Bucyrus, Ohio. *Coil, intaglio, perforated 10 vertically.*

800 *Handcar, 1880s*

		MNHVF	UseVF
800			
3¢	**green** tagged	.25	.20
	Pair	.30	
	FDC *(March 25, 1983)*		2.00

Listings and prices for plate number coil strips and singles appear at the end of this definitive section of the Krause-Minkus catalog.

1983. Carl Schurz Issue in the Great Americans Series honored the German-born American reformer, public official, and journalist (1829-1906). *Intaglio, perforated 11 x 10 1/2.*

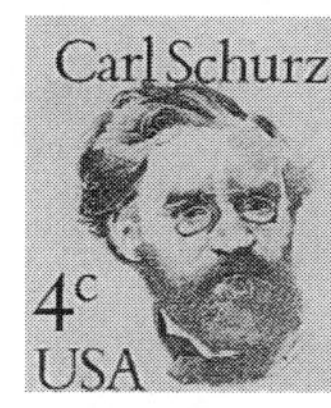

801 *Carl Schurz*

		MNHVF	UseVF
801			
4¢	**purple** overall tagged	.20	.20
	Plate block of 4	.60	
	FDC *(June 3, 1983)*		1.75
	zo. Tagging omitted (error)	4.00	

1983. Thomas H. Gallaudet Issue in the Great Americans Series honored the pioneer educator (1787-1851) who devoted his life to the education of the speaking- and hearing-impaired. *Intaglio, perforated 11 x 10 1/2.*

802 *Thomas H. Gallaudet*

		MNHVF	UseVF
802			
20¢	**green** overall tagged	.40	.20
	Plate block of 4	4.00	
	Plate Nos. 5 & 6 carry a premium	—	
	Plate Nos. 8 & 9 carry a large premium	—	
	FDC *(June 10, 1983)*		2.00
	zo. Tagging omitted (error)	4.00	

1983. Pearl Buck Issue in the Great Americans Series honored the author, humanitarian, and winner of both the Pulitzer and Nobel Prizes (1892-1973). *Intaglio, perforated 11 x 10 1/2.*

803 *Pearl Buck*

803		MNHVF	UseVF
5¢	**red brown** overall tagged	.20	.20
	Plate block of 4	.80	
	FDC *(June 25, 1983)*		1.75

1983. Henry Clay Issue in the Great Americans Series honored the American statesman (1777-1852) known as "The Great Compromiser." *Intaglio, perforated 11 x 10 1/2.*

804 *Henry Clay*

804		MNHVF	UseVF
3¢	**olive** overall tagged	.20	.20
	Plate block of 4	.60	
	zo. Tagging omitted (error)	4.00	
	FDC *(July 13, 1983)*		1.75

1983. Express Mail Issue although not labeled as such nor restricted to that class of mail, was released principally for Express Mail Next Day Service use. *Booklet pane, gravure, perforated 10 vertically.*

805 *Eagle and Moon*

805		MNHVF	UseVF
$9.35	**multicolored** tagged	25.00	20.00
	FDC *(Aug. 12, 1983)*		60.00
	n. Booklet pane of 3	60.00	
	FDC, booklet pane		175.00

1983. Omnibus Issue in the Transportation Series featured a type of transportation popular in the second half of the 19th century. *Coil, intaglio, perforated 10 vertically.*

806 *Omnibus, 1880s*

806		MNHVF	UseVF
1¢	**purple** tagged	.20	.20
	Pair	.20	.20
	FDC *(Aug. 19, 1983)*		2.00
	v. Pair, imperforate	675.00	

For similar design with "1 USA" see No. 867.

Listings and prices for plate number coil strips and singles appear at the end of this definitives section of the Krause-Minkus catalog.

1983. Dorothea Dix Issue in the Great Americans Series honored the 19th century crusader for the poor and mentally impaired (1802-87). *Intaglio, perforated 11 1/4 or 10 3/4.*

807 *Dorothea Dix*

807		MNHVF	UseVF
1¢	**black** tagged (small block) perforated 11 1/4	.20	.20
	Plate block of 20	2.00	
	FDC *(Sept. 23, 1983)*		1.75
	v. Pair, imperforate	450.00	
	v1. Vertical pair, imperforate between	3,000.00	
807A		**MNHVF**	**UseVF**
1¢	**black** tagged (small block) perforated 10 3/4	.20	.20
	Plate block of 20	2.00	
	v. Vertical pair, imperforate horizontally	—	
	bz. Large block tagged (1985)	.20	.20
	Plate block of 20	2.00	

1983. Motorcycle Issue in the Transportation Series was often used as a change-maker in vending machines. The 5¢ denomination met no specific postal value. *Coil, intaglio, perforated 10 vertically.*

808 *Motorcycle, 1913*

808		MNHVF	UseVF
5¢	**dark green** tagged	.25	.20
	Pair	.30	
	FDC *(Oct. 10, 1983)*		2.00
	v. Pair, imperforate	2,750.00	
	zo. Tagging omitted (error)	—	

Listings and prices for plate number coil strips and singles appear at the end of this definitives section of the Krause-Minkus catalog.

1983. Christmas Issue in the Christmas Series consisted of a Santa Claus design and a Madonna and Child by Raphael. *Gravure, perforated 11.*

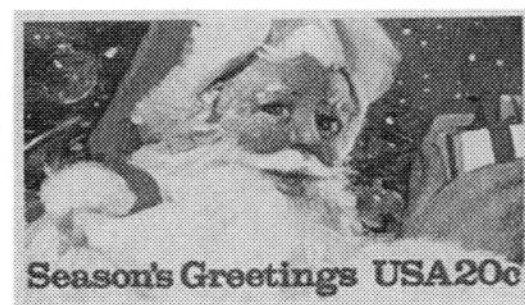

809 *Santa Claus*

809		MNHVF	UseVF
20¢	**multicolored** tagged	.35	.20
	Plate block of 20	12.50	
	FDC *(Oct. 28, 1983)*		2.00
	v. Pair, imperforate	175.00	

810 Madonna and Child, *by Raphael, National Gallery of Art*

810		MNHVF	UseVF
20¢	**multicolored** tagged	.35	.20
	Plate block of 4	2.50	
	FDC *(Oct. 28, 1983)*		1.75

1984. Harry S. Truman Issue in the Great Americans Series honored the 33rd president of the United States, on the centennial of his birth. Truman (1884-1972) came to office upon the death of Franklin D. Roosevelt and made the decision to use the Atomic Bomb to help end World War II. *Intaglio, perforated 11.*

811 *Harry S. Truman*

811		MNHVF	UseVF
20¢	**black** tagged (small block)	.35	.20
	Plate block of 20	12.00	
	FDC *(Jan. 26, 1984)*		2.00

(See also No. 904.)

1984. Railroad Caboose Issue in the Transportation Series. The untagged version was issued to meet the bulk rate. The tagged version met no postal rate; it was issued for collectors. *Coil, intaglio, perforated 10 vertically.*

812 *Railroad caboose, 1890s*

812		MNHVF	UseVF
11¢	**red** tagged	.25	.20
	Pair	.35	
	FDC*(Feb. 3, 1984)*		
	zx. Untagged (Bureau precancel)	.25	.20
	zx1. deep red, untagged (unprecancelled) *(Sept. 25, 1991)*		

Listings and prices for plate number coil strips and singles appear at the end of this definitives section of the Krause-Minkus catalog.

1984. Lillian Gilbreth Issue in the Great Americans Series honored the pioneering American engineer (1878-1972) who searched for efficient working methods in industry and the home. Together with her husband, she laid the foundation for the field of industrial engineering. *Intaglio, perforated 11 or 11 1/4.*

813, 813A *Lillian Gilbreth*

813		MNHVF	UseVF
40¢	**green,** tagged (small block) perforated 11	.60	.20
	Plate block of 20	10.00	
	FDC *(Feb. 24, 1984)*		2.00
813A		**MNHVF**	**UseVF**
40¢	**green** tagged (large block) perforated 11 1/4 (1987)	.60	.20
	Plate block of 4	2.00	

1984. Baby Buggy Issue in the the Transportation Series. The untagged version was issued to meet rate for carrier-route presorted bulk mailings. The tagged stamp was a "collector" issue, meeting no specific postal rate. *Coil, intaglio, perforated 10 vertically.*

814 *Baby buggy, 1880s*

814		MNHVF	UseVF
7.4¢	**brown** tagged	.25	.20
	Pair	.35	
	FDC *(April 7, 1984)*		2.00
	zx. Untagged (Bureau precancel: "Blk. Rt. CAR-RT SORT")	.25	.20
	FDC		300.00

Listings and prices for plate number coil strips and singles appear at the end of this definitives section of the Krause-Minkus catalog.

1984. Richard Russell Issue in the Great Americans Series honored the former U.S. Senator and his 50 years of public service. Two years after becoming, at age 33, the youngest governor in Georgia's history, Russell (1897-1971) was elected to fill the unexpired term of one of the state's U.S. Senators. He was subsequently re-elected six times to the U.S. Senate. *Intaglio, perforated 11.*

815 *Richard Russell*

815		MNHVF	UseVF
10¢	**blue** tagged (small block)	.25	.20
	Plate block of 20	7.00	
	FDC *(May 31, 1984)*		1.75
	bz. Large block tagged	.25	.20
	Plate block of 20	7.00	
	v. Horizontal pair, imperforate between	2,000.00	
	v1. Vertical pair, imperforate between		
	v2. Vertical pair, imperforate horizontally	—	
	v3. Pair, imperforate	1,250.00	

Imperforate printer's waste is known to exist, and in one case was used as postage.

1984. Frank C. Laubach Issue in the Great Americans Series honored the literacy advocate and educator (1884-1970) who developed methods to educate the illiterate and created alphabets and written languages where none previously existed. *Intaglio, perforated 11 or 11 1/4.*

816, 816A *Frank C. Laubach*

816		MNHVF	UseVF
30¢	**green** tagged (small block) perforated 11	.75	.20
	Plate block of 20	18.00	
	FDC *(Sept. 2, 1984)*		1.75
816A		**MNHVF**	**UseVF**
30¢	**green** tagged (large block) perforated 11 1/4	.75	.20
	Plate block of 4	2.25	
	FDC *(June 25, 1988)*		
	z. Overall tagging (1990)	1.00	
	Plate block of 4	4.00	

1984. Christmas Issue in the Christmas Series consisted of a child's drawing of Santa Claus and a Madonna and Child by Lippi. *Gravure, perforated 11.*

817 Santa Claus, *by Danny La Boccetta, winner of a stamp design project*

817		MNHVF	UseVF
20¢	**multicolored** tagged	.25	.20
	Plate block of 4	1.50	
	FDC *(Oct. 30, 1984)*		1.75
	v. Horizontal pair, imperforate vertically	975.00	

818 Madonna and Child, *by Fra Filippo Lippi, National Gallery of Art*

818		MNHVF	UseVF
20¢	**multicolored** tagged	.25	.20
	Plate block of 4	1.50	
			1.75

819 *Abraham Baldwin*

819		MNHVF	UseVF
7¢	**red** tagged (small block)	.25	.20
	Plate block of 20	4.00	
	FDC *(Jan. 25, 1985)*		1.75

1985. Non-Denominated "D" Issue marked the new First Class postage rate of 22¢, which went into effect Feb. 17, 1985. The issue was for domestic use only. Issued in sheet, coil, and booklet form. *Gravure, perforated 11.*

820-822 *"D" and stylized eagle*

820		MNHVF	UseVF
22¢	**green** tagged	.45	.20
	Plate block of 20	25.00	
	FDC *(Feb. 1, 1985)*		1.75
	v. Vertical pair, imperforate	50.00	
	v1. Vertical pair, imperforate horizontally	1,300.00	
	zo. Untagged (error)	—	

1985. Non-Denominated "D" Coil Issue

821		MNHVF	UseVF
22¢	**green** tagged perforated 11	.60	.20
	Pair	1.20	
	FDC *(Feb. 1,1985)*		1.75
	v. Pair, imperforate	45.00	
	vzo. Pair, imperforate, tagging omitted (error)	85.00	

Listing and prices for plate number coil strips and singles appear at the end of this definitives section of the Krause-Minkus catalog.

1985. Non-Denominated "D" Rate Booklet Issue

822		MNHVF	UseVF
22¢	**green** tagged	.40	.20
	FDC *(Feb. 1, 1985)* single		1.75
	n. Booklet pane of 10	8.50	
	nv. Booklet pane of 10, imperforate between horizontally	—	
	FDC (Booklet pane)		7.50

1985. Alden Partridge Issue in the Great Americans Series honored the military educator (1785-1854) on his 200th birthday. After a career at the U.S. Military Academy at West Point, N.Y., Partridge was superintendent there from 1814-17, but refused to step down when Sylvanus Thayer (Minkus No. 842) was named to succeed him. A court martial found Partridge guilty of insubordination, and he resigned from the Army. As a civilian, he founded a school in Vermont that combined academics with military training, and he became known as the Father of the Reserve Officer Training Corps. *Intaglio, perforated 11.*

823 *Alden Partridge*

823		MNHVF	UseVF
11¢	**blue** overall tagged	.25	.20
	Plate block of 4	1.20	
	FDC *(Feb. 12, 1985)*		2.00
	zo. Tagging omitted (error)	.85	

1985. Chester W. Nimitz Issue in the Great Americans Series honored the fleet admiral, whose leadership during World War II brought about key naval victories. Nimitz (1885-1966) was acknowledged as one of the Navy's foremost administrators and strategists. *Gravure, perforated 11 or 11 1/4.*

824, 824A *Chester W. Nimitz*

824		MNHVF	UseVF
50¢	**brown** overall tagged, perforated 11, shiny gum	.90	.20
	Plate block of 4	8.00	
	FDC *(Feb. 22, 1985)*		3.00
	zo. Tagging omitted (error)	7.00	

824A		MNHVF	UseVF
50¢	**brown** tagged (large block) perforated 11 1/4, matte gum	.90	.20
	Plate block of 4	6.50	
	zo. Tagging omitted (error)	7.00	
	z1. Overall tagging	.90	
	Plate block of 4	6.50	
	pz. Prephosphored paper, mottled tagging, shiny gum *(1992)*	.90	
	Plate block of 4	7.00	

1985. Grenville Clark Issue in the Great Americans Series honored a leading advocate (1882-1967) of civil liberties and peace through world federalism. *Intaglio, perforated 11 or 11 1/4.*

825, 825A *Grenville Clark*

		MNHVF	UseVF
825			
39¢	**purple** tagged (small block) perforated 11	.75	.20
	Plate block of 20	24.00	
	FDC *(March 20, 1985)*		2.00
	bz. Large block tagged	.75	.20
	Plate block of 20	24.00	
	v. Vertical pair, imperforate between	2,000.00	
	v1. Vertical pair, imperforate horizontally	575.00	

		MNHVF	UseVF
825A			
39¢	**purple** tagged (large block), perforated 11 1/4	.75	.20
	Plate block of 4	4.00	

1985. Sinclair Lewis Issue in the Great Americans Series honored the novelist and short story writer (1885-1951) on the centennial of his birth. In 1930, Lewis became the first American to win a Nobel Prize for Literature. *Intaglio, perforated 11.*

826 *Sinclair Lewis*

		MNHVF	UseVF
826			
14¢	**gray** tagged (small block)	.25	.20
	Plate block of 20	9.00	
	FDC *(March 21, 1985)*		1.75
	bz. Large block tagged	.25	.20
	Plate block of 20	9.00	
	v. Horizontal pair, imperforate between	10.00	
	v1. Vertical pair, imperforate between	2,000.00	
	v2. Vertical pair, imperforate horizontally	125.00	

1985. Iceboat Issue in the Transportation Series issued to meet the First Class rate for postcards, beginning Feb. 17, 1985. *Coil, intaglio, perforated 10 vertically.*

827, 827A *Iceboat, 1880s*

		MNHVF	UseVF
827			
14¢	**blue** Type I, overall tagged	.25	.20
	Pair	.35	
	FDC *(March 23, 1985)*		1.75
	v. Pair, imperforate	100.00	
	zo. Tagging omitted (error)	—	

		MNHVF	UseVF
827A			
14¢	**blue** Type II, block tagged	.25	.20
	Pair	.35	

Type I is 17 1/2 mm wide with overall tagging. Type II is 17 1/4 mm wide with block tagging.

Listings and prices for plate number coil strips and singles appear at the end of this definitives section of this Krause-Minkus catalog.

1985. Flag over the Capitol Issue consisted of sheet and coil versions, and a booklet stamp the width of two normal definitive stamps. *Coil, intaglio, perforated 11.*

828, 829, 876 *Flag Over the U.S. Capitol*

		MNHVF	UseVF
828			
22¢	**black, blue, & red** tagged	.35	.20
	Plate block of 4	3.00	
	Pair, gutter between	—	
	FDC *(March 29, 1985)*		1.75

1985. Flag Over the U.S. Capitol Coil Issue *Coil, intaglio.*

		MNHVF	UseVF
829			
22¢	**black, blue, & red** tagged	.40	.20
	Pair	1.00	
	FDC *(March 29, 1985)*		1.75
	a. black stars in flag (rather than blue)	1.00	
	b. slate blue, blue, and red	—	
	v. Pair, imperforate	15.00	
	zo. Tagging omitted (error)	3.00	

For similar design with "T" at bottom, see No. 876.

Listings and prices for plate number coil strips and singles appear at the end of this definitives section of the Krause-Minkus catalog.

1985. Flag Over the Capitol Booklet Issue This was the first U.S. booklet pane in the format of a single row of five stamps. *Booklet pane, intaglio, perforated 10 horizontally.*

830 *Flag Over the U.S. Capitol*

		MNHVF	UseVF
830			
22¢	**black, blue, & red** tagged	.40	.20
	FDC *(March 29, 1985)*		1.75
	n. Booklet pane of 5	3.00	2.50
	FDC booklet pane		3.50

Issued for use in vending machines, and was available with one or two panes.

1985. Stanley Steamer Issue in the Transportation Series featured the first successfully operated steam automobile in New England. *Coil, intaglio, perforated 10 vertically.*

831, 831A *Stanley Steamer, 1909*

		MNHVF	UseVF
831			
12¢	**blue** Type I, tagged	.25	.20
	Pair	.30	
	FDC *(April 2, 1985)*		1.75
	p. Hi-Brite paper	—	
	zx. Untagged (Bureau precancel: "PRESORTED FIRST-CLASS")	.25	.20
	Pair	—	
	zo. Tagging omitted (error)	—	

		MNHVF	UseVF
831A			
12¢	**blue** Type II, untagged (Bureau precancel: "PRESORTED FIRST-CLASS")	.25	.20
	Pair	.30	
	FDC *(Sept. 3, 1987)*		60.00

Type I: "Stanley Steamer 1909" is 18mm long;

Type II: "Stanley Steamer 1909" is 17 1/2 mm long.

*Listings and prices for plate number coil strips and singles appear at the end of this definitives section of the Krause-Minkus catalog.*FDC *(Oct. 30, 1984)*

		MNHVF	UseVF
832			
22¢	Frilled dogwinkle, **black & brown** tagged	.35	.20

		MNHVF	UseVF
833			
22¢	Reticulated helmet, **black & multicolored** tagged	.35	.20

		MNHVF	UseVF
834			
22¢	New England neptune, **black & brown,** tagged	.35	.20

		MNHVF	UseVF
835			
22¢	Calico scallop, **black & purple** tagged	.35	.20

836		MNHVF	UseVF
22¢	Lightning whelk, **multicolored,** tagged	.35	.20
	FDC *(April 4, 1985)* any single		2.00
	y. Se-tenant strip of 5	3.00	
	n. Booklet pane of 10 (2 each Nos. 832-36	4.00	
	FDC booklet pane		7.50
	nv. purple omitted, horizontal pair of 835, pane	700.00	
	nv1. Booklet pane of 10, imperforate between vertically	650.00	
	nv2. Booklet pane, imperforate	—	
	zo. Tagging omitted (error)	—	
	nzo. Booklet pane of 10, untagged		

Mis-registered tagging is common on this issue.

1985. OIL WAGON ISSUE in the Transportation Series. The 10.1¢ untagged denomination first was issued to meet the rate for bulk Third Class mail presorted to the 5-digit ZIP code. The tagged stamp was issued for collectors. *Coil, intaglio, perforated 10 vertically.*

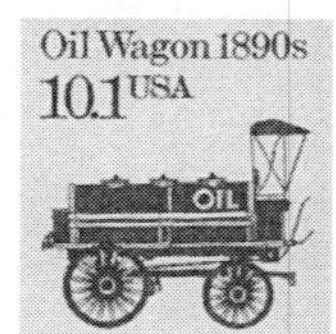

837 *Oil wagon, 1890s*

837		MNHVF	UseVF
10.1¢	**blue** tagged	.25	.20
	Pair	.35	
	FDC *(April 18, 1985)*		1.75
	zx. Untagged (Bureau precancel: in black: "Bulk Rate")	.25	.20
	FDC *(April 18, 1985)*		2.50
	zxv. Pair, imperforate	85.00	
	zx1. Untagged (Bureau precancel: in red: "Bulk Rate/Carrier Route Sort")	.25	.20
	FDC *(June 27, 1988)*		1.75
	zx1v. Pair, imperforate	1.00	

1985. PUSHCART ISSUE in the Transportation Series. The 12.5¢ untagged denomination was issued as the basic rate for bulk Third Class mail. The tagged version originally had no rate use. Covers from a *Reader's Digest* mailing in 1989 used pairs of the 12.5¢ to meet the First Class letter rate.

838 *Pushcart, 1880s*

838		MNHVF	UseVF
12.5¢	**olive** tagged	.25	.20
	Pair	.35	
	FDC *(April 18, 1985)*		1.75
	zx. Untagged (Bureau precancel: "Bulk Rate")	.25	
	zxv. Pair, imperforate	50.00	

Listings and prices for plate number coil strips and singles appear at the end of this definitives section of the Krause-Minkus catalog.

1985. JOHN J. AUDUBON ISSUE in the Great Americans Series celebrated the 200th birthday of the artist-naturalist (1785-1851). *Intaglio, perforated 11 or 11 1/4.*

839, 839A *John J. Audubon*

839		MNHVF	UseVF
22¢	**blue** tagged (small block) perforated 11	.40	.20
	Plate block of 20	16.00	
	FDC *(April 23, 1985)*		2.00
	bz. Large block tagged	.40	.20
	Plate block of 20	16.00	
	v. Horizontal pair, imperforate between	2,750.00	
	v1. Vertical pair, imperforate between	—	
	v2. Vertical pair, imperforate horizontally	2,500.00	
	zo. tagging omitted (error)	4.00	

839A		MNHVF	UseVF
22¢	**blue** tagged (large block) perforated 11 1/4	.40	.20
	Plate block of 4	1.50	

1985. EXPRESS MAIL ISSUE Although valid for use on other classes of mail, was intended for use in four types of Express Mail Service: 1) Same Day Airport Service, 2) Custom Designed Service, 3) Next Day Service, and 4) International Service. *Booklet pane, gravure, perforated 10 vertically.*

840 *Eagle and Moon*

840		MNHVF	UseVF
$10.75	**multicolored** Type I	15.00	9.00
	FDC *(April 29, 1985)*		50.00
	n. Booklet pane of 3	52.00	
	FDC		150.00
	a. Type II *(June 19, 1989)*	17.00	12.00
	FDC		
	an. Booklet pane of 3	52.00	
	FDC		700.00

Type I: overall dull appearance, "$10.75" appears grainy. Type II: more intense colors, "$10.75" smoother, much less grainy.

1985. TRICYCLE ISSUE in the Transportation Series met the basic rate for Third Class bulk mailings by non-profit organizations. The tagged version met no specific domestic postal rate. However, it could be added to a U.S. 15¢ post card when rates to Canada were raised to 21¢ in 1988. *Coil, intaglio, perforated 10 vertically.*

841 *Tricycle, 1880s*

841		MNHVF	UseVF
6¢	**brown** tagged	.25	.20
	Pair	.30	
	FDC *(May 6, 1985)*		1.75
	zx. Untagged (Bureau precancel: "Nonprofit Org.")	.25	.20
	Pair	.30	
	zxv. Pair, imperforate	225.00	

Listings and prices for plate number coil strips and singles appear at the end of this definitives section of the Krause-Minkus catalog.

1985. SYLVANUS THAYER ISSUE in the Great Americans Series honored the former commandant of the U.S. Military Academy at West Point, N.Y. (1785-1872). *Intaglio, perforated 11.*

842 *Sylvanus Thayer*

842		MNHVF	UseVF
9¢	**green** tagged (small block)	.25	.20
	Plate block of 20	4.25	
	FDC *(June 7, 1985)*		2.00

1985. School Bus Issue in the Transportation Series. The untagged version was issued for basic rate for carrier-route presort Third Class bulk mailings by non-profit organizations. The tagged version was issued for collectors. *Coil, intaglio, perforated 10 vertically.*

843 *School bus, 1920s*

843		MNHVF	UseVF
3.4¢	**green** tagged	.20	.20
	Pair	.30	
	FDC *(June 8, 1985)*		1.75
	zx. Untagged (Bureau precancel: "Nonprofit Org. CAR-RT SORT")	.25	.20
	FDC		250.00

Listings and prices for plate number coil strips and singles appear at the end of this definitives section of the Krause-Minkus catalog.

1985. Stutz Bearcat Issue in the Transportation Series showed a 1933 Super Bearcat designed by the H.C.S. Motor Car Co. The 11¢ denomination met no single rate; however, a pair met the first-ounce, First Class letter rate. *Coil, intaglio, perforated 10 vertically.*

844 *Stutz Bearcat, 1933*

844		MNHVF	UseVF
11¢	**green** tagged	.25	.20
	Pair	.30	
	FDC *(June 11, 1985)*		1.75

Listings and prices for plate number coil strips and singles appear at the end of this definitives section of the Krause-Minkus catalog.

1985. Ambulance Issue in the Transportation Series. The untagged 8.3¢ denomination was issued for Third Class mail presorted by carrier route. The tagged version was issued as a "collector" item; it met no postal rate. *Coil, intaglio, perforated 10 vertically.*

845, 845A *Ambulance, 1860s*

845		MNHVF	UseVF
8.3¢	**green** Type I, tagged	.20	.20
	Pair	.30	
	FDC *(June 21, 1985)*		1.75
	zx. Untagged (Bureau precancel: "Blk. Rt. CAR-RT SORT")	.25	.20
	Pair	.30	
	FDC		250.00

845A		MNHVF	UseVF
8.3¢	**green** Type II, untagged (Bureau precancel: "Blk. Rt./CAR-RT/SORT")	.20	.20
	Pair	.30	
	FDC *(Aug. 29, 1986)*		250.00

Type I: "Ambulance 1860s" is 18 1/2mm long. Type II: "Ambulance 1860s" is 18mm long.

1985. Buckboard Issue in the Transportation Series. The 4.9¢ untagged denominat

ion was issued for non-profit Third Class mail presorted to the 5-digit ZIP code. The tagged version met no postal rate and was issued basically for collectors.

846 *Buckboard, 1880s*

846		MNHVF	UseVF
4.9¢	**brown** tagged	.25	.20
	pair	.30	
	FDC *(June 21, 1985)*		1.75
	zx. Untagged (Bureau precancel: "Nonprofit Org.")	.35	.20
	FDC		2.50

Listings and prices for plate number coil strips and singles appear at the end of this definitives section of the Krause-Minkus catalog.

1985. Henry Knox Issue in the Great Americans Series honored the first U.S. Secretary of War (1750-1806) during the 200th anniversary year of his appointment. Fort Knox, in Kentucky, where the bulk of the nation's gold bullion is stored, is named for him. *Intaglio, perforated 11.*

847 *Henry Knox*

847		MNHVF	UseVF
8¢	**olive** overall tagged	.25	.20
	Plate block of 4	.40	
	FDC *(July 25, 1985)*		1.75

1985. Walter Lippmann Issue in the Great Americans Series honored the newsman, political analyst, and author (1889-1974). Among many other awards and prizes, Lippmann earned two Pulitzer Prizes and a Peabody award. *Intaglio, perforated 11.*

848 *Walter Lippmann*

848		MNHVF	UseVF
6¢	**orange** tagged (large block)	.25	.20
	Plate block of 20	2.90	
	FDC *(Sept. 9, 1985)*		1.75

1985. Envelope Stamp Issue prepaid First Class rate for mailers using ZIP + 4. *Coil, gravure, perforated 10 vertically.*

849 *Letters*

849		MNHVF	UseVF
21.1¢	**multicolored** tagged	.35	.20
	Pair	.50	

		MNHVF	UseVF
	FDC *(Oct. 22, 1985)*		1.75
	zx. Untagged, Bureau-printed service indicator: "ZIP+4"	.35	.20
	Pair	.50	

Some precanceled stamps are known with light tagging.

1985. CONTEMPORARY CHRISTMAS ISSUE in the Christmas Series was a painting of poinsettias by James Dean of Annandale, Va. *Gravure, perforated 11.*

850 *Poinsettia plants*

850		MNHVF	UseVF
22¢	**multicolored** tagged	.35	.20
	Plate block of 4	1.40	
	FDC *(Oct. 30, 1985)*		1.75
	v. Pair, imperforate	125.00	

1985. TRADITIONAL CHR ISTMAS ISSUE in the Christmas Series depicted one of four versions of *The Genoa Madonna,* an enameled terra-cotta Madonna and Child by Luca della Robbia. *Gravure, perforated 11.*

851 *Sculpture by Luca della Robbia, Detroit Institute of Arts*

851		MNHVF	UseVF
22¢	**multicolored** tagged	.35	.20
	Plate block of 4	1.50	
	FDC *(Oct. 30, 1985)*		1.75
	v. Pair, imperforate	100.00	

1985. GEORGE WASHINGTON & MONUMENT ISSUE met the basic presort rate for First Class letter mail. *Coil, intaglio, perforated 10 vertically.*

852 *George Washington and the Washington Monument*

852		MNHVF	UseVF
18¢	**multicolored** tagged	.35	.20
	Pair	.70	
	FDC *(Nov. 6, 1985)*		1.75
	v. Pair, imperforate	975.00	
	zx. Untagged (Bureau-printed service indicator: "PRESORTED FIRST-CLASS")	.35	.20
	zo. Tagging omitted (error)	2.00	1.75
	vzo. Pair	4.00	3.50
	zm. Matte gum	.35	
	Pair	.70	
	zxv. Pair, imperforate, precanceled	800.00	

Some precanceled stamps are known with light tagging. Listings and prices for plate number coil strips and singles appear at the end of this definitives section of the Krause-Minkus catalog.

1986. JACK LONDON ISSUE in the Great Americans Series honored the author (1875-1916) of 50 books including *The Call of the Wild, White Fang,* and *The Sea-Wolf. Intaglio, perforated 11.*

853, 888, 889 *Jack London*

853		MNHVF	UseVF
25¢	**blue** tagged (large block) perforated 11	.45	.20
	Plate block of 4	1.50	
	FDC *(Jan. 11, 1986)*		2.00
	zo. Tagging omitted (error)	—	

For booklet panes of 10 and 6, see Nos. 888-889.

1986. HUGO L. BLACK ISSUE in the Great Americans Series honored the Supreme Court justice (1886-1971) on his 100th birthday. *Intaglio, perforated 11.*

854 *Hugo L. Black*

854		MNHVF	UseVF
5¢	**deep olive green** tagged (large block)	.25	.20
	Plate block of 4	.90	
	FDC *(Feb. 27, 1986)*		1.75
	zo. Tagging omitted (error)	—	

1986. WILLIAM JENNINGS BRYAN ISSUE in the Great Americans Series honored the famed orator and legislator (1860-1925). *Intaglio, perforated 11.*

855 *William Jennings Bryan*

855		MNHVF	UseVF
$2	**purple** tagged (large block)	3.25	.75
	Plate block of 4	20.00	
	FDC *(March 19, 1986)*		7.00
	zo. Tagging omitted (error)	10.00	

1986. BELVA ANN LOCKWOOD ISSUE in the Great Americans Series honored the first woman candidate for president and the first woman admitted to practice before the U.S. Supreme Court (1830-1917). *Intaglio, perforated 11.*

856 *Belva Ann Lockwood*

856		MNHVF	UseVF
17¢	**blue green** tagged (large block)	.35	.20
	Plate block of 4	1.75	
	FDC *(June 18, 1986)*		1.75
	zo. Tagging omitted (error)	5.00	

1986. MARGARET MITCHELL ISSUE in the Great Americans Series honored the Pulitzer Prize winning author (1900-49) of *Gone With the Wind. Intaglio, perforated 11.*

857 *Margaret Mitchell*

857		MNHVF	UseVF
1¢	**brown** tagged (large block)	.25	.20
	Plate block of 4	.30	
	FDC *(June 30, 1986)*		2.50
	zo. Tagging omitted (error)	3.00	

1986. FATHER FLANAGAN ISSUE in the Great Americans Series released on the centennial of his birth, honored Rev. Edward Joseph Flanagan (1886-1948), the founder of Boys Town. The center protects and educates abused and underprivileged youth. *Intaglio, perforated 11.*

858 *Father Flanagan*

858		MNHVF	UseVF
4¢	**purple** tagged (large block)	.25	.20
	Plate block of 4	.40	
	FDC *(July 14, 1986)*		1.75
	zx. Untagged, light gray violet (1991)	.25	.20
	Plate block of 4	.40	
	zx1. Untagged, slate violet (1993)	.25	.20
	Plate block of 4	.40	

1986. DOG SLED ISSUE in the Transportation Series. The 17¢ denomination represents the rate for the second ounce of First Class mail. *Coil, intaglio, perforated 10 vertically.*

859 *Dog sled, 1920s*

859		MNHVF	UseVF
17¢	**blue** tagged	.30	.20
	Pair	.50	
	FDC *(Aug. 20, 1986)*		1.75
	v. Pair, imperforate	475.00	

Listings and prices for plate number coil strips and singles appear at the end of this definitives section of the Krause-Minkus catalog.

1986. JOHN HARVARD ISSUE in the Great Americans Series honored the 17th century American colonist and philanthropist (1607-1638), coinciding with the 350th anniversary of Harvard University, the oldest institution of higher learning in the United States. *Intaglio, perforated 11.*

860 *John Harvard*

860		MNHVF	UseVF
56¢	**crimson** tagged (large block)	1.10	.20
	Plate block of 4	5.25	
	FDC *(Sept. 3, 1986)*		2.00

1986. PAUL DUDLEY WHITE ISSUE in the Great Americans Series honored the authority on cardiovascular disease and a pioneer in its diagnosis, treatment, and prevention (1886-1973). *Intaglio, perforated 11.*

861 *Dr. Paul Dudley White*

861		MNHVF	UseVF
3¢	**blue** tagged (large block), matte gum	.25	.20
	Plate block of 4	.35	
	FDC *(Sept. 15, 1986)*		1.75
	zo. Tagging omitted (error) (Plate No. 2 or 3)	—	
	zxm. Untagged (intentional), matte gum (1994)	.25	.20
	Plate block of 4	.35	
	zxs. Untagged (intentional) shiny gum	.25	.20
	Plate block of 4	.35	

1986. BERNARD REVEL ISSUE in the Great Americans Series honored the scholar and educator (1885-1940) in conjunction with the centennial of Yeshiva University, the nation's oldest and largest Jewish institution of higher learning. A six-pointed Star of David is hidden in the engraving for the beard. *Intaglio, perforated 11.*

862 *Dr. Bernard Revel*

862		MNHVF	UseVF
$1	**blue** tagged (large block)	2.00	.25
	Plate block of 4	13.00	
	FDC *(Sept. 23, 1986)*		4.00

1986. CHRISTMAS ISSUE The contemporary stamp featured a winter village scene, which was designed by Dolli Tingle of Westport, Conn. The traditional stamp depicts the oil-on-wood painting *Perugino Madonna,* by Il Perugino. *Gravure, perforated 11.*

863 *Village Scene*

863		MNHVF	UseVF
22¢	**multicolored** tagged	.50	.20
	Plate block of 4	2.75	
	FDC *(Oct. 24, 1986)*		2.00

864 *Perugino Madonna*

864		MNHVF	UseVF
22¢	**multicolored** tagged	.50	.20
	Plate block of 4	2.75	
	FDC *(Oct. 24, 1986)*		2.00

1986. STAR ROUTE TRUCK ISSUE in the Transportation Series showed a truck used to carry mail under contract with the Post Office Dept. The 5.5¢ rate was for nonprofit Third Class mail presorted to the carrier route. The tagged version was a "collector" issue meeting no specific postal rate. *Coil, itaglio, perforated 10 vertically.*

865 *Star Route truck, 1910s*

865		MNHVF	UseVF
5.5¢	**maroon** tagged	.25	.20
	Pair	.35	
	FDC *(Nov. 1, 1986)*		1.75
	zx. Untagged (Bureau-printed service indicator: "Nonprofit Org. CAR-RT SORT")	.25	.20
	FDC		5.00

Listings and prices for plate number coil strips and singles appear at the end of this definitives section of the Krause-Minkus catalog.

1986. Bread Wagon Issue in the Transportation Series. *Coil, intaglio, perforated 10 vertically.*

866 *Bread wagon, 1880s*

866		MNHVF	UseVF
25¢	**orange brown** tagged, plates 2, 3, 4	.40	.20
	brown, plates 1, 5	.40	.20
	Pair	1.00	
	FDC *(Nov. 22, 1986)*		1.75
	v. Pair, imperforate	10.00	
	v1. Pair, imperforate between	500.00	
	zo. Tagging omitted (error)	—	

Listings and prices for plate number coil strips and singles appear at the end of this definitives section of the Krause-Minkus catalog.

1986. Omnibus Issue in the Transportation Series. Type of No. 806, redesigned, ("1 USA" instead of "USA 1"). *Coil, intaglio, perforated 10 vertically.*

867 *Omnibus, 1880s*

867		MNHVF	UseVF
1¢	**violet** tagged	.25	.20
	Pair	.30	
	FDC *(Nov. 26, 1986)*		1.75
	v. Pair, imperforate	2,400.00	
	pz. Prephosphored paper	.25	.20
	Pair	.30	
	zxm. Untagged, matte gum	.25	.20
	Pair	.30	
	zxs. Untagged, shiny gum	.25	.20
	Pair	.30	

(For similar design with "USA 1¢" see No. 806) Listings and prices for plate number coil strips and singles appear at the end of this definitives section of the Krause-Minkus catalog.

1986. Stagecoach Issue in the Transportation Series. Type of No. 791, re-engraved. "Stagecoach 1890s" is 17mm long. *Coil, intaglio, perforated 10 vertically.*

868 *Stagecoach, 1890s*

868		MNHVF	UseVF
4¢	**red brown** block tagged	.25	.20
	Pair	.30	
	FDC *(Aug. 1986)*		1.75
	v. Pair, imperforate	600.00	
	z. Overall tagging *(1990)*	.50	.20
	Pair	.75	

Listings and prices for plate number coil strips and singles appear at the end of this definitives section of the Krause-Minkus catalog.

1987. Tow Truck Issue in the Transportation Series. The 8.5¢ rate was for nonprofit, Third Class mail. *Coil, intaglio, perforated 11 vertically.*

869 *Tow truck, 1920s*

869		MNHVF	UseVF
8.5¢	**dark gray** tagged	.50	.20
	Pair	.50	.20
	FDC *(Jan. 24, 1987)*		1.75
	zx. Untagged (Bureau-printed red service indicator: "Nonprofit Org.")	.25	.20
	Pair	—	
	FDC		5.00

Listings and prices for plate number coil strips and singles appear at the end of this definitives section of the Krause-Minkus catalog.

1987. Tractor Issue in the Transportation Series. The 7.1¢ value was issued for Third Class non-profit mail presorted by ZIP code. *Coil, intaglio, perforated 11.*

870 *Tractor, 1920s*

870		MNHVF	UseVF
7.1¢	**dark red** tagged	.25	.20
	Pair	.50	
	FDC *(Feb. 6, 1987)*		1.75
	zx. Untagged, Bureau-printed service indicator: "Nonprofit Org."	.25	.20
	Pair	.50	
	FDC *(Feb. 6, 1987)*		5.00
	zx1. Untagged (Bureau-printed service indicator: "Nonprofit 5-Digit Zip+4")	.25	.20
	Pair	.50	
	FDC *(May 26, 1989)*		1.75

1987. Julia Ward Howe Issue in the Great Americans Series honored the social reformer and author of *The Battle Hymn of the Republic.* Well-known for her abolitionist sentiment, Howe (1819-1910) also was a champion of the rights of women and the less fortunate. *Intaglio, perforated 11.*

871 *Julia Ward Howe*

871		MNHVF	UseVF
14¢	**red** tagged (large block)	.25	.20
	Plate block of 4	.75	
	FDC *(Feb. 12, 1987)*		1.75

1987. Mary Lyon Issue in the Great Americans Series honored a pioneer of higher education for women. Lyon (1797-1849) organized Wheaton College in 1834 and founded Mount Holyoke College in 1837. *Intaglio, perforated 11.*

872 *Mary Lyon*

872		MNHVF	UseVF
2¢	**blue** tagged (large block)	.25	.20

		MNHVF	UseVF
	Plate block of 4	.30	
	FDC *(Feb. 28, 1987)*		1.75
	zo. Tagging omitted (error) (Plate No. 1)	—	
	zx. Untagged (intentional) (Plate No. 2)	.25	
	Plate block of 4	.30	

1987. Locomotive Issue in the Transportation Series. Type of No. 790, redesigned. *Coil, intaglio, perforated 11.*

873 *Locomotive, 1870s*

873		MNHVF	UseVF
2¢	**black** tagged	.25	.20
	Pair	.30	
	FDC *(March 6, 1987)*		2.00
	zxm. Untagged, matte gum	.25	.20
	zxs. Untagged, shiny gum	.25	

(For similar design with "USA 2¢" see No. 790.) Listings and prices for plate number coil strips and singles appear at the end of this definitives section of the Krause-Minkus catalog.

1987. Canal Boat Issue in the Transportation Series. *Coil, intaglio, perforated 11.*

874 *Canal boat, 1880s*

874		MNHVF	UseVF
10¢	**sky blue** block tagged matte gum	.25	.20
	Pair	.40	.20
	FDC *(April 11, 1987)*		1.75
	v. Pair, imperforate	—	—
	pz. Prephosphored paper, shiny gum	.25	.20
	zm. Overall tagged, matte gum *(1993)*	.25	.20
	zs. Overall tagged, shiny gum *(1994)*	.25	.20

Listings and prices for plate number coil strips and singles appear at the end of this definitives section of the Krause-Minkus catalog.

1987. Flag With Fireworks Issue This stamp replaced the Flag Over Historic Buildings issues. *Gravure, perforated 11.*

875 *Flag with fireworks*

875		MNHVF	UseVF
22¢	**multicolored** tagged	.35	.20
	Plate block of 4	1.75	
	FDC *(May 9, 1987)* single		1.75
	n. Booklet pane of 20	8.50	
	FDC, booklet pane *(Nov. 30, 1987)*		12.00

1987. Flag Over Capitol Coil Issue This stamp was issued to test prephosphored paper, which is tagged before printing. Every stamp has an imprinted "T" in the lower margin. *Coil, intaglio, perforated 10 vertically.*

876		MNHVF	UseVF
22¢	**black, blue, & red** with "T" at bottom	.40	.20
	Pair	.75	
	FDC *(May 23, 1987)*		2.50

Listings and prices for plate number coil strips and singles appear at the end of this definitives section of the Krause-Minkus catalog.

1987. Red Cloud Issue in the Great Americans Series honored the chief (1822-1909) of the Oglala Sioux. *Intaglio, perforated 11.*

877 *Red Cloud*

877		MNHVF	UseVF
10¢	**carmine red** tagged (large block)	.25	.20
	Plate block of 4	.75	
	FDC *(Aug. 15, 1987)*		2.00
	z. Overall tagged (1990)	.25	.20
	Plate block of 4	.75	
	zo. Tagging omitted (error)	—	
	pzm. Phosphored paper, solid tagging, matte gum	.25	.20
	Plate block of 4	.75	
	pzs. Phosphored paper, mottled tagging, shiny gum	.25	.20
	Plate block of 4	.75	
	pzs1. carmine phosphored paper, mottled tagging (1995)	.25	
	Plate block of 4	.75	

1987. Bret Harte Issue in the Great Americans Series honored the author and poet (1836-1902) famous for stories and poems of the American West. *Intaglio, perforated 11.*

878 *Bret Harte*

878		MNHVF	UseVF
$5	**Venetian red** tagged (large block)	8.00	2.00
	Plate block of 4	40.00	
	y. Pane of 20	120.00	
	FDC *(Aug. 25, 1987)*		20.00
	zo. Tagging omitted (error)		
	pz. Phosphored paper, solid tagging *(March 1992)*	8.00	2.00
	Plate block of 4	35.00	
	pzy. Pane of 20	120.00	

1987. Milk Wagon Issue in the Transportation Series met no specific postal rate; it was used as a changemaker in postal vending machines. *Coil, intaglio, perforated 10 vertically.*

879 *Milk wagon, 1900s*

879		MNHVF	UseVF
5¢	**charcoal** tagged	.25	.20
	Pair	.30	
	FDC *(Sept. 25, 1987)*		1.75

Listings and prices for plate number coil strips and singles appear at the end of this definitives section of the Krause-Minkus catalog.

1987. Racing Car Issue in the Transportation Series. The Marmon Wasp, shown here, won the first Indianapolis 500-mile auto race in 1911. Denomination covered the rate for ZIP+4 presorted mail. *Coil, intaglio, perforated 10 vertically.*

880 *Racing car*

880		MNHVF	UseVF
17.5¢	**blue violet** tagged	.30	.20
	Pair	.50	
	FDC *(Sept. 25, 1987)*		1.75
	v. Pair, imperforate	2,250.00	
	zx. Untagged (Bureau-printed red service indicator: "ZIP+4 Pre-sort")	.30	.20
	Pair	.50	

Listings and prices for plate number coil strips and singles appear at the end of this definitives section of the Krause-Minkus catalog.

1987. Christmas Issue The contemporary design consisted of tree ornaments; the traditional design displays a portion of Giovanni Battista Moroni's painting *A Gentleman in Adoration before the Madonna. Gravure, perforated 11.*

881 *Madonna and Child*

881		MNHVF	UseVF
22¢	**multicolored** tagged	.50	.20
	Plate block of 4	2.75	
	FDC *(Oct. 23, 1987)*		2.00

882 *Tree ornament*

882		MNHVF	UseVF
22¢	**multicolored** tagged	.50	.20
	Plate block of 4	2.75	
	Pair, gutter between	—	
	FDC *(Oct. 23, 1987)*		2.00

1988. Conestoga Wagon Coil Issue in the Transportation Series. The wagon was invented by Pennsylvania Dutch to transport produce to markets. *Intaglio, perforated 10 vertically.*

883 *Conestoga wagon, 1800s*

883		MNHVF	UseVF
3¢	**dark lilac purple** tagged	.25	.20
	Pair	.30	
	FDC *(Feb. 29, 1988)*		1.75
	zxm. Untagged, matte gum *(1992)*	.25	.30
	zxs. Untagged, shiny gum *(1995)*	.30	

Listings and prices for plate number coil strips and singles appear at the end of this definitives section of the Krause-Minkus catalog.

1988. Non-Denominated "E" Issue consisted of three versions: sheet, coil, and booklet. The stamps were released to meet the new 25¢ First Class rate. In a departure from previous letter-denominated stamps this showed a picture of the Earth, as in a child's spelling primer. *Gravure, perforated 11.*

884-886 *"E" and Earth*

884		MNHVF	UseVF
28¢	**multicolored** tagged	.50	.20
	Plate block of 4	2.00	
	FDC *(March 22, 1988)*		1.75
	zo. Tagging omitted (error)	—	

1988. Non-Denominated "E" Coil Issue Intaglio, perforated 10 vertically.

885		MNHVF	UseVF
25¢	**multicolored** tagged	.50	.20
	Pair	.75	
	FDC *(March 22, 1988)*		1.75
	v. Pair, imperforate	100.00	

Listings and prices for plate number coil strips and singles appear at the end of this definitives section of the Krause-Minkus catalog.

1988. Non-Denominated "E" Booklet Issue Booklet, perforated 10.

886		MNHVF	UseVF
25¢	**multicolored** tagged	.50	.20
	FDC *(March 22, 1988)*		1.75
	n. Booklet pane of 10	6.50	
	FDC, booklet pane		7.50

1988-99. Flora and Fauna Series

was unannounced as such by the U.S. Postal Service until it consisted of at least 16 stamps over an 11-year period.

1988. Pheasant Booklet Issue designed for sale in vending machines as well as over the counter, this booklet was the first in the Flora and Fauna Series and the first produced for the U.S. Postal Service by the American Bank Note Co. *Gravure, 10 x 11.*

887 *Pheasant*

887		MNHVF	UseVF
25¢	**multicolored** tagged	.50	.20
	FDC *(April 29, 1988)* single		1.75
	n. Booklet pane of 10	6.00	
	a. red removed from background sky	6.00	.50
	an. Booklet pane of 10	75.00	
	nv. Booklet pane of 10, horizontally imperforate between	2,250.00	
	FDC, booklet pane		8.00

Fully imperforate panes were cut from printer's waste.

1988. Jack London Booklet Issue in the Great Americans Series was of the same design as No. 853. *Intaglio, by Bureau of Engraving and Printing, perforated 11 or 10.*

888		MNHVF	UseVF
25¢	**blue** tagged (large block) perforated 11	.45	.20
	FDC single *(May 3, 1988)*		2.00
	n. Booklet pane of 10	4.50	5.00
	FDC booklet pane		8.00
	zo. Tagging omitted (error)	7.00	
	nzo. Booklet pane of 10, tagging omitted		

889		MNHVF	UseVF
25¢	**blue** tagged, (large block) perforated 10	.50	.20
	FDC single *(May 3, 1988)*		1.75
	n. Booklet pane of 6	2.75	
	FDC, booklet pane		4.00
	zo. Tagging omitted (error)	3.00	
	nzo. Booklet pane of 6, tagging omitted	55.00	

1988. Flags with Clouds Issue *Gravure, perforated 11.*

890, 890A *Flag with clouds*

890		MNHVF	UseVF
25¢	**multicolored** tagged	.35	.20
	Plate block of 4	3.25	
	Pair, gutter between	—	
	FDC *(May 6, 1988)*		1.75

1988. Flags With Clouds Booklet Issue Gravure, perforated 11.

890A		MNHVF	UseVF
25¢	**multicolored** tagged	.50	.20
	FDC *(May 6, 1988)* single		1.75
	n. Booklet pane of 6	2.75	3.00
	FDC, booklet pane		4.50

1988. Flag Over Yosemite Issue showed the U.S. flag billowing over Half Dome, Yosemite's most striking example of glacier-carved granite. *Coil, intaglio, perforated 10 vertically.*

891 *Flag over Yosemite*

891		MNHVF	UseVF
25¢	**multicolored** tagged	.40	.20
	Pair	.75	
	FDC *(May 20, 1988)*		1.75
	v. Pair, imperforate	35.00	
	pz. Prephosphored paper	.40	.20
	Pair	.75	
	FDC *(Feb. 14, 1989)*		1.75
	pzv. Pair, imperforate, prephosphored-paper	20.00	
	v1. Pair, imperforate between	450.00	
	a. black trees	150.00	
	zo. Tagging omitted (error)	3.00	

Listings and prices for plate number coil strips and singles appear at the end of this definitives section of the Krause-Minkus catalog.

1988. Owl and Grosbeak Issue in the Flora and Fauna Series depicted two colorful birds in a booklet format. *Gravure, perforated 10.*

892 *Saw-whet owl*

892		MNHVF	UseVF
25¢	**multicolored** tagged	.40	.20
	FDC *(May 28, 1988)*		1.75

893 *Rose-breasted grosbeak*

893		MNHVF	UseVF
25¢	**multicolored** tagged	.40	.20
	y. Se-tenant pair, No. 892-93	1.00	.50
	FDC *(May 28, 1988)*		1.75
	n. Booklet pane of 10 (5 No. 893y)	4.50	6.00
	yzo. Tagging omitted (error), Se-tenant pair	7.50	
	nzo. Booklet pane of 10, tagging omitted	—	

1988. Buffalo Bill Cody Issue in the Great Americans Series honored the military scout, showman, and raconteur (1846-1917) of the Wild West. *Intaglio, perforated 11.*

894 *Buffalo Bill Cody*

894		MNHVF	UseVF
15¢	**maroon** tagged (large block)	.30	.20
	Plate block of 4	3.50	
	FDC *(June 6, 1988)*		2.00
	z. Overall tagged (1990)	.30	.20
	Plate block of 4	2.00	
	pz. Phosphored paper (solid tagging)	.30	.20
	Plate block of 4	2.00	
	zo. Tagging omitted (error)	10.00	

1988. Harvey Cushing Issue in the Great Americans Series honored the "father of neurosurgery" (1869-1939). He is credited with laying the foundation for the field of brain surgery. *Intaglio, perforated 11.*

895 *Harvey Cushing*

895		MNHVF	UseVF
45¢	**blue** tagged (large block)	1.00	.20
	Plate block of 4	4.00	
	FDC *(June 17, 1988)*		2.00
	z. Overall tagged (1990)	1.50	.50
	Plate block of 4	11.00	
	zo. Tagging omitted (error)	7.00	

Nos. 896 and 897 are not assigned.

1988. Popcorn Wagon Issue in the Transportation Series featured the 1902 model of the C. Cretors and Co. No. 1 Wagon. The first completely self-contained model, which could go wherever needed, was introduced in 1893. The value represented the prepaid base bulk mail rate. *Coil, intaglio, perforated 10 vertically.*

898 *Popcorn wagon, 1902*

898		MNHVF	UseVF
16.7¢	**dark rose** (Bureau-printed service indicator "Bulk Rate")	.35	.20
	Pair	.50	
	FDC *(July 7, 1988)*		1.75
	v. Pair, imperforate	175.00	

Listings and prices for plate number coil strips and singles appear at the end of this definitives section of the Krause-Minkus catalog.

1988. Tugboat Issue in the Transportation Series showed a tugboat representative of the type used in the first decade of the 20th century. *Coil, intaglio, perforated 10 vertically.*

899 *Tugboat, 1900s*

899		MNHVF	UseVF
15¢	**purple** block tagged	.30	.20
	Pair	.50	
	FDC *(July 12, 1988)*		1.75
	zo. Tagging omitted (error)		
	z. Overall tagged *(July 1990)*	.30	.20
	zy. Pair, overall tagged	.50	

Listings and prices for plate number coil strips and singles appear at the end of this definitives section of the Krause-Minkus catalog.

1988. Coal Car Issue in the Transportation Series issued to pay a single Third Class bulk mail item presorted to 5-digit ZIP codes. *Coil, intaglio, perforated 10 vertically.*

900 *Coal car, 1870s*

900		MNHVF	UseVF
13.2¢	**dark green** (Bureau-printed red service indicator "Bulk Rate")	.30	.20
	Pair	.50	
	FDC *(July 19, 1988)*		1.75
	v. Pair, imperforate	100.00	

Listings and prices for plate number coil strips and singles appear at the end of this definitives section of the Krause-Minkus catalog.

1988. Wheel Chair Issue in the Transportation Series depicted a 1928 wicker wheelchair produced by the Invacare Corp. of Elyria, Ohio. Issued to pay postage for non-profit bulk rate mail. *Coil, intaglio, perforated 10 vertically.*

901 *Wheel chair, 1920s*

901		MNHVF	UseVF
8.4¢	**dark violet** (Bureau-printed red service indicator: "Non-profit")	.30	.20
	Pair	.50	
	FDC *(Aug. 12, 1988)*		1.75
	v. Pair, imperforate	650.00	

Listings and prices for plate number coil strips and singles appear at the end of this definitives section of the Krause-Minkus catalog.

1988. Railroad Mail Car Issue in the Transportation Series issued to meet the single-piece rate for presorted First Class mail to either the 3 or 5 digit ZIP code. *Coil, intaglio, perforated 10 vertically.*

902 *Railroad mail car, 1920s*

902		MNHVF	UseVF
21¢	**green** (Bureau-printed red service indicator "Presorted 1st Class")	.35	.20
	Pair	.75	
	FDC *(Aug. 16, 1988)*		1.75
	v. Pair, imperforate	65.00	

1988. Carreta Issue in the Transportation Series showed a cart used by settlers in Spanish California. Issued to pay the rate for non-profit bulk mailers. *Coil, gravure, perforated 10 vertically.*

903 *Carreta, 1770s*

903		MNHVF	UseVF
7.6¢	**brown** Bureau-printed red service indicator: "Nonprofit"	.25	.20
	Pair	.30	
	FDC *(Aug. 30, 1988)*		1.75

Listings and prices for plate number coil strips and singles appear at the end of this definitives section of the Krause-Minkus catalog.

1988. Harry S. Truman Issue in the Great Americans Series. A new version. *Perforated 11 1/4.*

904		MNHVF	UseVF
20¢	**black** tagged (large block), matte gum	.35	.20
	Plate block of 4	3.50	
	FDC *(Sept. 1, 1988)*		—
	z. Overall tagged *(1990)*	.35	.20
	Plate block of 4	4.00	
	pz. Phosphored paper, mottled tagging, shiny gum (1993)	.40	.20
	Plate block of 4, shiny gum	2.50	
	zo. Tagging omitted (error)	10.00	

(See also No. 811)

1988. Honeybee Issue in the Flora and Fauna Series. *Coil, intaglio, perforated 11.*

905 *Honeybee*

905		MNHVF	UseVF
25¢	**multicolored** tagged	.40	.20
	Pair	.75	
	FDC *(Sept. 2, 1988)*		1.75
	v. black (intaglio) omitted	65.00	
	v1. black (offset) omitted	550.00	
	v2. yellow (offset) omitted	—	
	v3. Pair, imperforate	55.00	
	v4. Pair, imperforate between	1,000.00	
	zo. Tagging omitted (error)	7.00	

Listings and prices for plate number coil strips and singles appear at the end of this definitives section of the Krause-Minkus catalog.

1988. Elevator Issue in the Transportation Series issued to pay the nonprofit Third Class rate for mail presorted to the carrier route. *Coil, intaglio, perforated 10 vertically.*

906 *Elevator, 1900s*

906		MNHVF	UseVF
5.3¢	**black** (Bureau-printed red service indicator: "Nonprofit/Carrier Route Sort")	.25	.20
	Pair	.30	
	FDC *(Sept. 16, 1988)*		1.75

Listings and prices for plate number coil strips and singles appear at the end of this definitives section of the Krause-Minkus catalog.

1988. Fire Engine Issue in the Transportation Series issued to prepay the First Class mail rate presorted by ZIP+4. *Coil, intaglio, perforated 10 vertically.*

907 *Fire engine, 1900s*

907		MNHVF	UseVF
20.5¢	**red** (Bureau-printed black service indicator: "ZIP+4 Presort")	.35	.20
	Pair	.30	
	FDC *(Sept. 28, 1988)*		2.00

Listings and prices for plate number coil strips and singles appear at the end of this definitives section of the Krause-Minkus catalog.

1988. Eagle and Moon Issue was designed to meet the increased rate for Express Mail. Although intended for that use, it also was valid for postage classes where a high value was needed. *Offset and intaglio, perforated 11.*

908 *Eagle and Moon*

908		MNHVF	UseVF
$8.75	**multicolored** tagged	25.00	8.00
	Plate block of 4	110.00	
	FDC *(Oct. 4, 1988)*		30.00

1988. Christmas Issue The contemporary issue depicted a snowy scene and was released at Berlin, N.H., to honor Irving Berlin and his song *White Christmas. Gravure, perforated 11 1/2.*

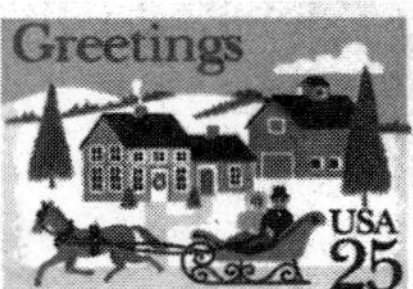

909 *Snowy Village Scene*

909		MNHVF	UseVF
25¢	**multicolored,** tagged	.40	.20
	Plate block of 4	1.50	
	FDC *(Oct. 20, 1988)*		2.00
	Pair, gutter between	—	

1988. Madonna and Child by Botticelli Issue The traditional issue in the Christmas Series, is based on the painting *Madonna and Child* by Italian master Sandro Botticelli. *Intaglio and offset, perforated 11 1/2.*

910 Madonna and Child *by Botticelli*

910		MNHVF	UseVF
25¢	**multicolored** tagged	.40	.20
	Plate block of 4	1.50	
	FDC *(Oct. 20, 1988)*		2.00
	v. gold omitted	30.00	

1988. Chester Carlson Issue in the Great Americans Series honored the man (1906-1968) who invented xerography and began an office copying revolution. *Intaglio, perforated 11.*

911 *Chester Carlson*

911		MNHVF	UseVF
21¢	**blue violet** tagged (large block)	.35	.20
	Plate block of 4	2.25	
	FDC *(Oct. 21, 1988)*		1.75
	zo. Tagging omitted (error)	—	

1988. Tandem Bicycle Issue in the Transportation Series issued to meet the rate for unpresorted ZIP+4 mail, of particular use to mid-size businesses. *Coil, intaglio, perforated 10 vertically.*

912 *Tandem bicycle, 1890s*

912		MNHVF	UseVF
24.1¢	**deep blue violet** (Bureau-printed red service indicator: "ZIP+4")	.40	.20
	Pair	.75	
	FDC *(Oct. 26, 1988)*		1.75

Listings and prices for plate number coil strips and singles appear at the end of this definitives section of the Krause-Minkus catalog.

1988. Cable Car Issue in the Transportation Series featured a conveyance used in many cities in the very late 1900s and still a common sight in San Francisco. Issued to prepay the rate for the second ounce of First Class mail. *Coil, intaglio, perforated 10 vertically.*

913 *Cable car, 1880s*

913		MNHVF	UseVF
20¢	**dark violet,** block tagged	.35	.20
	Pair	.75	
	FDC *(Oct. 28, 1988)*		1.75
	v. Pair, imperforate	75.00	
	z. Overall tagged (1990)	.35	.20
	Pair	.75	

Listings and prices for plate number coil strips and singles appear at the end of this definitives section of the Krause-Minkus catalog.

1988. Police Patrol Wagon Issue in the Transportation Series issued to meet the single-piece rate for presorted First Class mailings of postcards. *Coil, intaglio, perforated 10 vertically.*

914 *Police patrol wagon, 1880s*

914		MNHVF	UseVF
13¢	**black** (Bureau-printed red service indicator: "Presorted First Class")	.30	.20
	Pair	.50	
	FDC *(Oct. 29, 1988)*		1.75

Listings and prices for plate number coil strips and singles appear at the end of this definitives section of the Krause-Minkus catalog.

1988. Mary Cassatt Issue in the Great Americans Series honored the American painter and etcher (1845-1926) who spent most of her life in France. *Intaglio, perforated 11.*

915 *Mary Cassatt*

915		MNHVF	UseVF
23¢	**purple** tagged (large block)	.45	.20
	Plate block of 4	2.25	
	FDC *(Nov. 4, 1988)*		1.75
	z. Overall tagged (1990)	.60	.20
	Plate block of 4	3.00	

		MNHVF	UseVF
	pzm. Phosphored paper (solid tagging) matte gum	.60	.20
	Plate block of 4	3.00	
	pzs. Phosphored paper (mottled tagging) shiny gum	.60	.20
	Plate block of 4	3.25	
	zo. Tagging omitted (error)	7.00	

1988. H.H. "Hap" Arnold Issue in the Great Americans Series honored the "father of the modern air force" (1886-1950). The stamp met the rate for a 3-ounce First Class letter. *Intaglio, perforated 11.*

916 *H.H. "Hap" Arnold*

		MNHVF	UseVF
916			
65¢	**dark blue** tagged (large block)	1.25	.20
	Plate block of 4	5.00	
	FDC *(Nov. 5, 1988)*		2.50
	zo. Tagging omitted (error)	7.50	

No. 917 not assigned.

1989. Johns Hopkins Issue in the Great Americans Series honored the founder of the hospital and university that bears his name. Hopkins (1795-1873) dedicated his fortune to the relief of suffering and advancement of knowledge. *Intaglio, perforated 11.*

918 *Johns Hopkins*

		MNHVF	UseVF
918			
$1	**blackish blue** tagged (large block) matte gum	2.00	.30
	Plate block of 4	7.00	
	y. Pane of 20	35.00	
	FDC *(June 7, 1989)*		5.00
	z. Overall tagged (1990)	1.75	.30
	Plate block of 4	7.00	
	zy. Pane of 20	35.00	
	zo. Tagging omitted (error)	10.00	
	pzm. Phosphored paper (solid tagging) matte gum (1992)	1.75	.30
	Plate block of 4	7.50	
	pzmy. Pane of 20	40.00	
	pzs. Phosphored paper (mottled tagging) shiny gum (1993)	2.00	.30
	Plate block of 4	8.00	
	pzsy. Pane of 20	40.00	
	pzsg. Phosphored paper (grainy tagging) semi-gloss gum	2.00	.30
	Plate block of 4	8.00	
	pzsgy Pane of 20	35.00	

1989. Sitting Bull Issue in the Great Americans Series honored the chief, spiritual and political leader of the Hunkpapa Sioux (c.1831-90). Issued to meet the rate for postcards sent via surface mail from the United States to all foreign destinations other than Canada and Mexico. *Intaglio, perforated 11.*

919 *Sitting Bull*

		MNHVF	UseVF
919			
28¢	**green** tagged (large block)	.50	.20
	Plate block of 4	3.00	
	FDC *(Sept. 14, 1989)*		2.25

1989. Sleigh with Gifts Issue Both the traditional and contemporary stamps were available in both sheet and booklet versions. The two versions of the sleigh contemporary design are noticeably different. The booklet version is printed in five colors, the sheet stamp in four. Sleigh runners of the booklet version are decidedly thicker than on the sheet version. The package to the rear of the sleigh has a bow the same color as the package on the booklet stamp, whereas the bow is of a different color on the sheet version. Finally, the board running under the sleigh is pink on the booklet version and the same color as the sleigh on the sheet version. The two versions of the traditional are identical, other than the booklet stamp having perforations on only two or three sides. *Gravure, perforated 11.*

920, 921 *Sleigh with gifts*

		MNHVF	UseVF
920			
25¢	**multicolored** tagged	.40	.20
	Plate block of 4	1.75	
	FDC *(Oct. 19, 1989)*		1.75
	v. Vertical pair, imperforate horizontally	750.00	

1989. Sleigh with Gifts Booklet Issue in the Christmas Series.

		MNHVF	UseVF
921			
25¢	**multicolored** booklet stamp, tagged	.40	.20
	FDC *(Oct. 19, 1989)* single		1.75
	n. Booklet pane of 10	3.00	
	FDC booklet pane	—	8.00
	nv. Booklet pane of 10, red omitted	7,150.00	
	nv1. Booklet pane of 10, horizontally imperforate between	—	

1989. The Dream of St. Alexandria Issue in the Christmas Series. *Intaglio, perforated 11 1/2.*

922 The Dream of St. Alexandria *by Lucovico Carracci*

		MNHVF	UseVF
922			
25¢	**multicolored** tagged	.40	.20
	Plate block of 4	1.75	
	FDC *(Oct. 19, 1989)* single		1.75
	n. Booklet pane of 10	3.00	
	FDC booklet pane	—	8.00
	nv. Booklet pane of 10, offset red omitted	750.00	
	nv1. Booklet pane of 10, imperforate	—	

No. 923 is not assigned.

1989. Eagle and Shield Self-Adhesive Issue was available in a do-it-yourself booklet format that permitted the purchaser to fold the pane of 18 die-cut stamps into a more convenient pocket-sized package. The stamps also were available in strips of 18 with the stamps spaced apart for use in affixing machines. *Gravure, die cut between.*

924 *Eagle and shield*

		MNHVF	UseVF
924			
25¢	**multicolored** tagged	.40	.20
	n. Booklet pane of 18	12.00	

		MNHVF	UseVF
	FDC *(Nov. 10, 1989)* single		1.75
	v. Vertical pair, no die cutting between	850.00	
	v1. Pair, no die cutting	—	

No. 925 is not assigned.

1990. Beach Umbrella Issue was a vacation-themed stamp meeting the postcard rate. *Booklet stamp, gravure, perforated 11 1/2.*

926 *Beach umbrella*

		MNHVF	UseVF
926			
15¢	**multicolored** booklet stamp, tagged	.30	.20
	n. Booklet pane of 10	4.25	
	FDC *(Feb. 3, 1990)*		1.75
	v. blue omitted	225.00	
	nv. Booklet pane of 10, blue omitted	1,650.00	

1990. Luis Muñoz Marin Issue in the Great Americans Series honored the first popularly elected governor of Puerto Rico (1898-1980). This is a major design change for the Great American series in which a zero precedes denominations of less than 10¢, and information about the subject ("Governor, Puerto Rico") is part of the design. *Intaglio, perforated 11.*

927 *Luis Muñoz Marin*

		MNHVF	UseVF
927			
5¢	**dark rose,** overall tagged	.25	.20
	Plate block of 4	.30	
	FDC *(Feb. 18, 1990)*		1.75
	zo. Tagging omitted (error)	.65	
	Plate block of 4 (Plate No. 1)	2.75	
	zx. Untagged (intentional) (1991)	.25	.20
	Plate block of 4 (Plate No. 2)	.65	

1990. Seaplane Issue in the Transportation Series was the first design in the series to feature aircraft. *Coil, intaglio.*

928 *Seaplane, 1914*

		MNHVF	UseVF
928			
$1	**dark blue & red** overall tagged, matte gum	1.75	.50
	Pair	3.50	1.00
	FDC *(April 20, 1990)*		3.00
	v. Pair, imperforate	2,500.00	—
	pz. Phosphored paper, mottled tagging, shiny gum *(1993)*	1.75	.50
	Pair	3.50	1.00
	pzg. Phosphored paper, grainy tagging, dull gum *(1998)*	1.75	.50
	Pair	3.50	1.00

Listings and prices for plate number coil strips and singles appear at the end of this definitives section of the Krause-Minkus catalog.

1990. Flag Issue for Automatic Teller Machines The USPS tested dispensing of stamps through bank ATM equipment. Available in panes of 12 the same size as a dollar bill and *printed on polyester film by gravure.* This issue was available as a test through 22 machines in the Seattle, Wash., area. *Self-adhesive, straight-line die cut.*

929 *U.S. flag*

		MNHVF	UseVF
929			
25¢	**red & dark blue** tagged	.50	.50
	n. Pane of 12	6.00	
	FDC single *(May 18, 1990)*		1.75

1990. Bobcat Issue in the Flora and Fauna Series was the first high-value stamp. Printed in panes of 20, with four plate numbers, copyright notice and descriptive information on the selvage. *Intaglio and offset, perforated 11.*

930 *Bobcat*

		MNHVF	UseVF
930			
$2	**multicolored** tagged	4.00	1.25
	Plate block of 4	18.00	
	FDC *(June 1, 1990)*		7.00
	v. Intaglio black omitted	350.00	
	zo. Tagging omitted (error)	10.50	7.00

1990. Circus Wagon Issue in the Transportation Series pictured a wagon that could transport live animals from city to city. The wagons could also be loaded on flatbed train cars and were also designed to carry gear or personnel. *Coil, intaglio, Bureau of Engraving and Printing, perforated 10 vertically.*

931 *Circus wagon, 1900s*

		MNHVF	UseVF
931			
5¢	**carmine red** tagged	.25	.20
	Pair	.30	
	FDC *(Aug. 31, 1990)*		1.75
	z. Untagged	.25	.20
	Pair	.30	
	v. Pair, imperforate	875.00	

For stamps of this design inscribed "USA 5¢" see No. 1007 (gravure) or No. 1077 (intaglio).

Listings and prices for plate number coil strips and singles appear at the end of this definitives section of the Krause-Minkus catalog.

1990. Claire Lee Chennault Issue in the Great American Series honored the pioneer air power tactician (1890-1958) who formed and led the Flying Tigers in China in World War II. *Intaglio, perforated 11.*

932 *Claire Lee Chennault*

		MNHVF	UseVF
932			
40¢	**dark blue** overall tagged, matte gum	.75	.20

		MNHVF	UseVF
	Plate block of 4	3.75	
	FDC *(Sept. 6, 1990)*		2.00
	pzm. Phosphored paper (solid tagging) matte gum	.75	
	Plate block of 4	3.75	
	pzs. Phosphored paper (mottled tagging) shiny gum	.75	.20
	Plate block of 4	4.00	
	pzsg. Phosphored paper (grainy tagging) low-gloss gum	.75	
	Plate block of 4	4.00	

1990. Contemporary Christmas Issue featured a cut-paper Christmas tree. There are noticeable design and color differences between the sheet and booklet versions of this stamp. *Gravure, perforated 11 or 11 1/2 x 11.*

933, 934 *Christmas tree*

Perforated 11

		MNHVF	UseVF
933			
25¢	**multicolored** tagged	.40	.20
	Plate block of 4	1.75	
	FDC *(Oct. 18, 1990)*		2.00
	v. Vertical pair, imperforate horizontally	1,100.00	

Perforated 11 1/2 x 11

		MNHVF	UseVF
934			
25¢	**multicolored** booklet stamp, tagged	.40	.20
	FDC *(Oct. 18, 1990)* single		2.00
	n. Booklet pane of 10	5.00	3.50
	FDC booklet pane		6.00

1990. Madonna and Child Issue in the Christmas Series. *Offset and intaglio, perforated 11 1/2.*

935, 936 Madonna and Child *by Antonello da Messina*

		MNHVF	UseVF
935			
25¢	**multicolored** tagged	.40	.20
	Plate block of 4	1.75	
	FDC *(Oct. 18, 1990)*		2.00
936			
25¢	**multicolored** booklet stamp, tagged	.40	.20
	FDC *(Oct. 18, 1990)* single		2.00
	n. Booklet pane of 10	5.00	
	FDC booklet pane		6.50

The booklet version has a much heavier shading in the Madonna's veil where it meets the right frame line.

1991. "F" (Flower) Non-Denominated Issue came in sheet, coil, and two different booklet types with "F" and "Flower" on the face to continue the "alphabet primer" theme. Its face value was 29¢, the new First Class mail rate. *Gravure, perforated 13.*

937-940 *"F" and tulip*

		MNHVF	UseVF
937			
29¢	**multicolored** tagged	.50	.20
	Plate block of 4	2.25	
	FDC *(Jan. 22, 1991)*		1.75
	v. Vertical pair, imperforate	700.00	
	v1. Horizontal pair, imperforate vertically	1,200.00	

1991. "F" (Flower) Non-Denominated Booklet Issue Dark green leaf. *B.E.P., perforated 11 1/4.*

		MNHVF	UseVF
938			
29¢	**multicolored** booklet stamp, tagged	.50	.20
	FDC *(Jan. 22, 1991)*		1.75
	n. Booklet pane of 10	6.00	
	FDC booklet pane		7.50

1991. "F" (Flower) Non-Denominated Booklet Issue Bright green leaf, pale yellow less pronounced, black dies in leaf. *KCS, perforated 11.*

		MNHVF	UseVF
939			
29¢	**multicolored** booklet stamp, printed by KCS Industries, tagged	.50	.20
	FDC *(Jan. 22, 1991)* single		1.75
	n. Booklet pane of 10	25.00	
	FDC, booklet pane	7.50	
	v. Pair, imperforate horizontally	—	

1991. "F" (Flower) Non-Denominated Coil Issue *Coil, perforated 10 vertically.*

		MNHVF	UseVF
940			
29¢	**multicolored** tagged	.60	.20
	Pair	.75	
	FDC *(Jan. 22, 1991)*		1.75
	v. Pair, imperforate	35.00	

1991. Non-Denominated 4¢ Make Up Issue has a value of 4¢, to be used with a 2525¢ stamp to meet the new 29¢ First Class rate. *Offset, perforated 11.*

941 *Text explaining how to use stamp*

		MNHVF	UseVF
941			
4¢	**bister & carmine**	.25	.20
	Plate block of 4	.30	
	FDC *(Jan. 22, 1991)*		1.75
	v. Vertical pair, imperforate horizontally	125.00	

1991. "F" Non-Denominated ATM Flag Issue was identical in design and material to No. 929, with the denomination replaced by an "F" and the inclusion of "For U.S. Addresses Only." *Gravure, straight-line die cut.*

942 *"F" and U.S. flag*

		MNHVF	UseVF
942			
29¢	**black, dark blue & red** tagged	.50	.20
	n. Pane of 12	7.00	
	FDC *(Jan. 22, 1991)* single		1.75
	FDC (pane of 12)		10.00

1991. Steam Carriage Issue in the Transportation Series depicted the "Richard Dudgeon," which is now in the Museum of American History of the Smithsonian Institution. *Coil, intaglio, perforated 10 vertically.*

943 *Steam carriage, 1866*

943		MNHVF	UseVF
4¢	**maroon** tagged	.25	.20
	Pair	.30	
	FDC *(Jan. 25, 1991)*		1.75
	v. Pair, imperforate	625.00	
	zx. Untagged (intentional)	.25	
	Pair	.30	

Listings and prices for plate number coil strips and singles appear at the end of this definitives section of the Krause-Minkus catalog.

1991. Fawn Issue in the Flora and Fauna Series met the rate for postcards. *Gravure, perforated 11.*

944 *Fawn*

944		MNHVF	UseVF
19¢	**multicolored** tagged	.35	.20
	Plate block of 4	1.50	
	FDC *(March 11, 1991)*		1.75
	v. red omitted	850.00	
	zo. Tagging omitted (error)	8.50	

1991. Flag Over Mount Rushmore marked the 50th anniversary of the South Dakota monument that features the carved images of President Washington, Jefferson, T. Roosevelt, and Lincoln. *Coil, intaglio, perforated 10 vertically.*

945, 945A *Flag Over Mount Rushmore; "29" and "USA" outlined in white*

945		MNHVF	UseVF
29¢	**red, blue, & maroon** tagged	.50	.20
	Pair	1.00	.20
	FDC *(March 29, 1991)*		1.75
	v. Pair, imperforate	25.00	
	p. Phosphor-coated "Lenz" paper	5.00	.50

945A		MNHVF	UseVF
29¢	**red, blue & brown** color change "Toledo brown" (error), tagged	5.00	—
	Pair	10.00	
	FDC		1.75

For gravure version of this design, see No. 963.

Listings and prices for plate number coil strips and singles appear at the end of this definitives section of the Krause-Minkus catalog.

1991. Dennis Chavez Issue in the Great Americans Series honored the first U.S. born Hispanic (1888-1962) elected to the U.S. Senate. *Intaglio, by Stamp Venturers, perforated 11.*

946 *Dennis Chavez*

946		MNHVF	UseVF
35¢	**black** phosphored paper, mottled tagging	.75	.20
	Plate block of 4	3.50	
	FDC *(April 3, 1991)*		2.00

1991. Flower Issue is a "denominated" version of the "F" stamp, initially released in sheet and booklet types. *Gravure, perforated 11.*

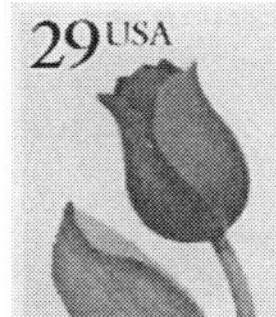

947, 947A, 948, 982 *Tulip*

947		MNHVF	UseVF
29¢	**multicolored** tagged, perforated 11	.40	.20
	Plate block of 4	1.75	
	FDC *(April 5, 1991)*		1.75

1991. Flower Issue *Perforated 13 x 12 3/4.*

947A		MNHVF	UseVF
29¢	**multicolored** *tagged, perforated 12 1/2 x 13*	.40	.20
	Plate block of 4	1.75	

1991. Flower Booklet Issue

948		MNHVF	UseVF
29¢	**multicolored** booklet stamp, tagged, perforated 11	.40	.20
	FDC *(April 5, 1991)* single		1.75
	n. Booklet pane of 10	8.00	
	nv. Pane of 10, vertically imperforate between	1,900.00	
	FDC booklet pane		7.50
	nv1. Pane of 10, imperforate horizontally	2,800.00	
	v. Horizontal pair, imperforate vertically	250.00	
	z. Phosphored paper (1993)	.50	.20
	nz. Booklet pane of 10	25.00	
	m. Low gloss gum (August 1993)	—	
	ng. Booklet pane of 10, low-gloss gum	—	

For coil version of the Flower Issue, see Nos. 966 and 982.

1991. Lunch Wagon Issue in the Transportation Series met the new second-ounce First Class mail rate. *Coil, intaglio, perforated 10 vertically.*

949 *Lunch wagon, 1890s*

949		MNHVF	UseVF
23¢	**blue** tagged, matte gum	.50	.20
	Pair	.75	
	FDC *(April 12, 1991)*		1.75
	ps. Phosphored paper, (mottled tagging), shiny gum (1993)	.50	.20
	Pair	.75	
	pm. Phosphored paper (mottled tagging) matte gum (1993)	.50	.20
	Pair	.75	
	v. Pair, imperforate	150.00	

Listings and prices for plate number coil and singles appear at the end of this definitives section of the Krause-Minkus catalog.

1991. Wood Duck Issue in the Flora and Fauna Series produced by the Bureau of Engraving and Printing with lettering and numbers in black and by KCS Industries with the lettering and numbers in red. *Gravure, perforated 10.*

950, 951 *Wood duck*

950		MNHVF	UseVF
29¢	**multicolored** booklet stamp, black inscription (B.E.P.), tagged	.75	.20
	FDC *(April 12, 1991)*		1.75
	n. Booklet pane of 10	8.00	
	FDC booklet pane	—	9.00
	v. Vertical pair, imperforate horizontally	200.00	
	nv. Pane of 10, horizontally imperforate between	1,000.00	
	z. Phosphored paper	.75	.20
	nz. Pane of 10, phosphored paper	8.00	

1991. Wood Duck Issue in the Flora and Fauna Series. *Perforated 11.*

951		MNHVF	UseVF
29¢	**multicolored** booklet stamp, red inscription (KCS Industries), tagged	1.00	.20
	FDC *(April 12, 1991)*		1.75
	n. Booklet pane of 10	8.75	
	FDC booklet pane		9.00
	v. Vertical pair, imperforate between	—	
	v1. Pair, imperforate	3,960.00	

1991. U.S. Flag with Olympic Rings Issue was a booklet version with a flag motif. *Gravure, perforated 11.*

952 *U.S. Flag With Olympic Rings*

952		MNHVF	UseVF
29¢	**multicolored** booklet stamp, tagged	.75	.20
	FDC *(April 21, 1991)*		1.75
	n. Booklet pane of 10	8.00	
	FDC booklet pane		7.50
	v. Vertical pair, imperforate between	—	
	nv. Pane of 10, horizontally imperforate between	—	

1991. Hot Air Balloon Issue met the postcard rate for First Class mail and was available in booklet form. *Gravure, perforated 10.*

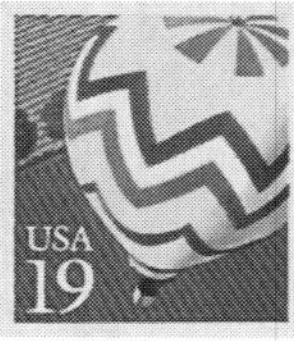

953 *Hot air balloon*

953		MNHVF	UseVF
19¢	**multicolored** booklet stamp, tagged	.30	.20
	FDC *(May 17, 1991)*		1.75
	n. Booklet pane of 10	4.50	
	FDC booklet pane	—	7.50

1991. Tractor Trailer Issue in the Transportation Series was for use by bulk business mailers. Since there was no service endorsement on the stamp, mass mailers were required to endorse each piece of mail franked with this stamp. *Coil, intaglio, B.E.P., perforated 10 vertically.*

954 *Tractor trailer, 1930s*

954		MNHVF	UseVF
10¢	**green** (Bureau-printed gray service indicator: "Additional Presort Postage Paid")	.25	.20
	Pair	.30	
	FDC *(May 25, 1991)*		1.75
	v. Pair, imperforate	150.00	

For version with service indicator in black, see No. 1042.

1991. Canoe Issue in the Transportation Series was for use by nonprofit mailers. *Coil, intaglio, B.E.P., perforated 10 vertically.*

955 *Canoe, 1800s*

955		MNHVF	UseVF
5¢	**brown** (printed gray service indicator: "Additional Nonprofit Postage Paid")	.25	.20
	Pair	.30	
	FDC *(May 25, 1991)*		1.75
	v. Pair, imperforate	325.00	

For gravure version of No. 955 in red, see No. 979.

Listings and prices for plate number coil strips and singles appear at the end of this definitives section of the Krause-Minkus catalog.

1991. Flags on Parade Issue celebrated the 125th anniversary of Memorial Day. *Gravure, perforated 11.*

956 *Flags on parade*

956		MNHVF	UseVF
29¢	**multicolored** tagged	.50	.20
	Plate block of 4	2.00	
	FDC *(May 30, 1991)*		1.75

1991. Hubert H. Humphrey Issue in the Great Americans Series honored the former vice president, Minnesota senator and mayor of Minneapolis (1911-1978). A date error in the selvage inscription, showing the wrong dates of his tenure as vice president, was corrected with a re-release of the stamp in 1993. *Intaglio, perforated 11.*

957 *Hubert H. Humphrey*

957		MNHVF	UseVF
52¢	**purple** phosphored paper (solid tagging) matte gum	1.50	.20
	Plate block of 4	6.00	
	FDC *(June 3, 1991)*		2.00
	pz. Phosphored paper (mottled tagging) shiny gum (1993)	1.00	.20
	Plate block of 4	5.00	

1991. Eagle and Olympic Rings Issue met 8-ounce Express Mail rate. The stamp was valid for other mail as well. *Intaglio and offset, perforated 11.*

958 *Eagle and Olympic rings*

958		MNHVF	UseVF
$9.95	**multicolored** tagged	15.00	7.50
	Plate block of 4	100.00	
	FDC *(June 6, 1991)*		25.00

1991. American Kestrel Issue in the Flora and Fauna Series was the first U.S. stamp issued without a cents sign in the denomination and a "0" preceding the single digit value. *Offset by American Bank Note Co. in shiny-gummed panes of 100, perforated 11.*

959 *American Kestrel*

959		MNHVF	UseVF
1¢	**multicolored**	.25	.20
	Plate block of 4	.30	
	FDC *(June 22, 1991)*		1.75

For versions inscribed "USA 1¢", see No. 1079 (sheet) and No. 1115 (Coil).

1991. Bluebird Issue in the Flora and Fauna Series. *Offset, perforated 11.*

960 *Eastern bluebird*

960		MNHVF	UseVF
3¢	Eastern bluebird	.25	.20
	Plate block of 4	.30	
	FDC *(June 22, 1991)*		1.75

For version inscribed "USA 3¢" see No. 1123.

1991. Cardinal Issue in the Flora and Fauna Series met the post-card rate to Canada and Mexico. *Gravure, perforated 11 1/2 x 11.*

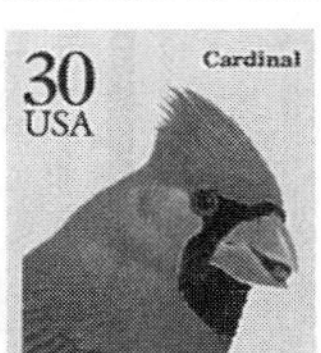

961 *Cardinal*

961		MNHVF	UseVF
30¢	**multicolored** on phosphored paper	.45	.20
	Plate block of 4	2.00	
	FDC *(June 22, 1991)*		1.75
	v. red omitted	850.00	
	zo. Tagging omitted (error)	8.50	

1991. Statue of Liberty Torch Issue was designed for sale through ATM machines. This issue provided 18 stamps on a backing sheet the same size as a dollar bill. Unlike its predecessors (Nos. 929 and 942), this issue was printed on paper. *Gravure, die cut, imperforate.*

962 *Liberty torch*

962		MNHVF	UseVF
29¢	**black, gold & green** tagged, die cut	.60	.30
	FDC *(June 25, 1991)*		1.75
	n. Pane of 18, plain paper back	12.00	
	FDC (pane of 18)		14.00
	nv. Pane of 18, printed backing paper	12.50	
	v. Pair, die cut omitted	3,750.00	

1991. Flag Over Mount Rushmore Coil Issue similar to No. 945. *Coil, gravure, American Bank Note Co., perforated 10 vertically.*

963 *Flag Over Mount Rushmore; "29" and "USA" not outlined in white*

963		MNHVF	UseVF
29¢	**blue, red & brown** tagged	.50	.25
	Pair	1.00	
	FDC *(July 4, 1991)*		1.75

For intaglio version of the same design, see No. 945.

Listings and prices for plate number coil strips and singles appear at the end of this definitives section of the Krause-Minkus catalog.

1991. Eagle and Olympic Rings Issue met the Priority Mail rate for second-day delivery of up to 2 pounds. *Intaglio and offset, perforated 11.*

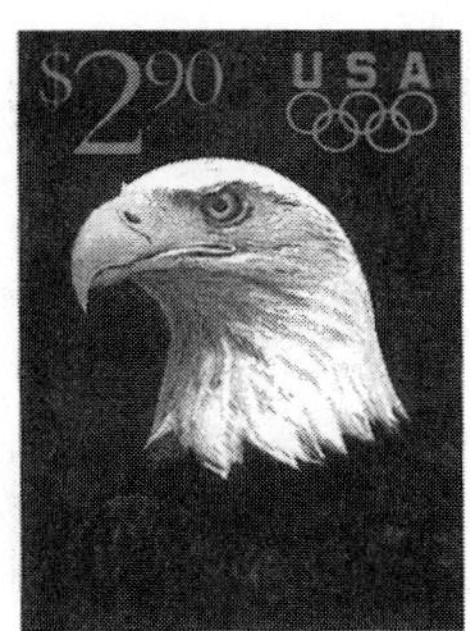

964 *Eagle and Olympic rings*

964		MNHVF	UseVF
$2.90	**multicolored** tagged	5.00	2.75
	Plate block of 4	25.00	
	FDC *(July 7, 1991)*		9.00
	v. Intaglio black omitted	3,500.00	
	v1. Vertical pair, imperforate horizontally	—	

1991. Fishing Boat Coil Issue met the First Class rate for domestic postcards. *Coil, gravure, American Bank Note Co., perforated 10.*

965 *Fishing boat, two rope loops on mooring*

965		MNHVF	UseVF
19¢	**multicolored** Type I, tagged	.40	.20
	Pair	.75	
	FDC *(Aug. 8, 1991)*		1.75
	a. Type II (lighter colors, sharper print) *(1992)*	.40	.20
	Pair	.75	

		MNHVF	UseVF
	zo. Tagging omitted (error, wrong paper used) *(1993)*	1.00	.30
	Pair	2.00	.75

Imperforates in this design came from printer's waste. For version with one loop of rope tying boat to piling, see No. 1044.

1991. Flower Coil Issue "Roulettes," a series of slits, rather than "perforations," or cut holes, facilitate separation. *Coil, gravure, Stamp Venturers, rouletted 10 vertically.*

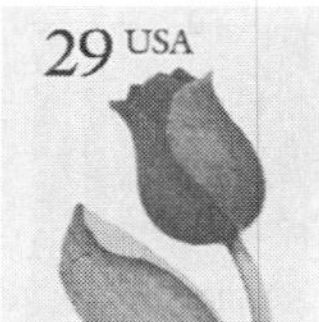

966 *Tulip*

966		MNHVF	UseVF
29¢	**multicolored** tagged	.75	.20
	Pair	1.25	
	FDC *(Aug. 16, 1991)*		1.75

1991. Eagle Over Coastline, Olympic Rings Issue met the rate for international Express Mail pieces weighing up to 8-ounces to 109 countries. *Intaglio and offset, perforated 11.*

967 *Eagle Over Coastline, Olympic rings*

967		MNHVF	UseVF
$14	**multicolored** tagged	30.00	17.50
	Plate block of 4	130.00	
	FDC *(Aug. 31, 1991)*		32.50
	v. Intaglio red omitted (value and rings).	—	

No. 968 is not assigned.

1991. U.S. Flag Issue included a service indicator and met the First Class presort rate. *Coil, gravure, American Bank Note Co., perforated 10 vertically.*

969 *U.S. flag*

969		MNHVF	UseVF
23¢	**red & blue** printed service indicator: "Presorted First Class"	.65	.20
	Pair	1.00	
	FDC *(Sept. 27, 1991)*		1.75

1991. USPS Olympic Sponsor Issue was released to promote the USPS sponsorship of the Olympic Games in Barcelona, Spain. *Gravure, perforated 11.*

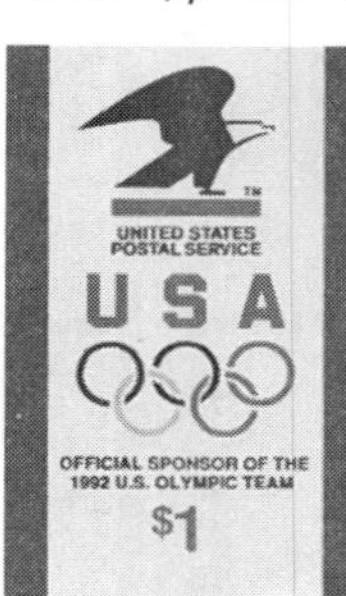

970 *Eagle and Olympic rings*

970		MNHVF	UseVF
$1	**multicolored** tagged	2.75	.75
	Plate block of 4	12.00	
	FDC *(Sept. 20, 1991)*		3.00

1991. Santa Descending a Chimney Issue in the Christmas Series.

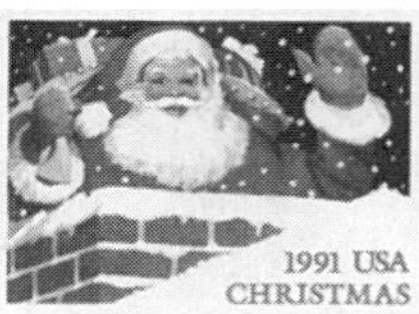

971, 972, 972A *Santa descending a chimney*

971		MNHVF	UseVF
29¢	**multicolored** tagged	.45	.20
	Plate block of 4	2.00	
	FDC *(Oct. 17, 1991)*		1.75
	v. Vertical pair, imperforate horizontally	500.00	
	v1. Horizontal pair, imperforate vertically	325.00	

1991. Santa Booklet Issue Of these six designs, four are totally different and two are modifications of the sheet stamp design. *Perforated 11, gravure.*

972		MNHVF	UseVF
29¢	**multicolored** booklet stamp, Type I, tagged	.45	.20
	FDC *(Oct. 17, 1991)* single		2.00

972A		MNHVF	UseVF
29¢	**multicolored** booklet stamp, Type II, tagged	.45	.20
	FDC single		2.00
	y. Se-tenant pair, Nos. 972, 972A	.90	
	n. Booklet pane, 2 each 4 Nos. 972, 972A	2.00	
	FDC booklet pane	—	4.00
	nv. Booklet pane imperforate	—	

Type I has an extra vertical line of brick in the top row of bricks at left; Type II is missing that vertical line of brick.

973 *Santa checking his list*

973		MNHVF	UseVF
29¢	**multicolored** booklet stamp, tagged	.45	.20
	FDC *(Oct. 17, 1991)* single		2.00
	n. Booklet pane of 4	1.50	
	FDC booklet pane	—	4.00

974 *Santa leaving gifts*

974		MNHVF	UseVF
29¢	**multicolored** booklet stamp, tagged	.45	.20
	FDC single		2.00
	n. Booklet pane of 4	1.50	
	FDC booklet pane	—	4.00
	v. Booklet pane imperforate	—	

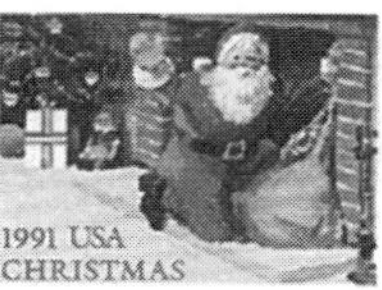

975 *Santa ascending chimney*

975		MNHVF	UseVF
29¢	**multicolored** booklet stamp, tagged	.45	.20
	FDC single		2.00
	n. Booklet pane of 4	1.50	
	FDC booklet pane		4.00
	v. Booklet pane imperforate	—	

976 *Santa departing in sleigh*

976		MNHVF	UseVF
29¢	**multicolored** booklet stamp, tagged	.45	.20
	FDC single		2.00
	n. Booklet pane of 4	1.50	
	FDC booklet pane		4.00
	v. Booklet pane imperforate	—	

1991. TRADITIONAL CHRISTMAS ISSUE Intaglio and offset, perforated 11.

977 *From* Madonna and Child with Donor *by* Antoniazzo Romano

977		MNHVF	UseVF
29¢	**multicolored** tagged	.45	.20
	Plate block of 4	2.00	
	FDC *(Oct. 17, 1991)* single		1.75
	n. Booklet pane of 10	8.00	
	FDC booklet pane		8.00
	v. Booklet single, red & black (intaglio) omitted	3,750.00	

No. 978 is not assigned.

1991. CANOE ISSUE in the Transportation Series. *Coil, gravure, Stamp Venturers, perforated 10 vertically.*

979 *Canoe, 1800s*

979		MNHVF	UseVF
5¢	**red** (printed service indicator: "Additional Nonprofit Postage Paid")	.25	.20
	Pair	.30	
	FDC *(Oct. 22, 1991)*		1.75
	p. Low-gloss gum	.50	—
	Pair	1.00	—

For intaglio version in brown, see No. 955.

Listings and prices for plate number coil strips and singles appear at the end of this definitives section of the Krause-Minkus catalog.

1991. EAGLE AND SHIELD NON-DENOMINATED ISSUE met the needs of permit mailers on presorted bulk mail pieces. The value of the stamp is 10¢, with additional postage paid by mailers at the time of mailing. *Coil, gravure, American Bank Note Co. (plate numbers beginning with "A"), perforated 10 vertically.*

980 *Eagle and shield*

980		MNHVF	UseVF
10¢	**multicolored** (printed service indicator: "Bulk Rate")	.25	.20
	Pair	.30	
	FDC *(Dec. 13, 1991)*		1.75
	v. Pair, imperforate	—	

See Nos. 1011 and 1012 for similar stamps printed by the Bureau of Engraving and Printing and Stamp Venturers.

1992. WENDELL L. WILLKIE ISSUE in the Great Americans Series honored the man (1892-1944) who lost in the 1940 presidential election and then served the Roosevelt administration on a diplomatic mission. *Intaglio, perforated 11.*

981 *Wendell L. Willkie*

981		MNHVF	UseVF
75¢	**maroon** phosphored paper (solid tagging) matte gum	1.25	.50
	Plate block of 4	5.50	
	FDC *(Feb. 16, 1992)*		3.00
	pz. Phosphored paper (mottled tagging) shiny gum	1.25	.50
	Plate block of 4	5.50	

1992. FLOWER PERFORATED COIL ISSUE Gravure, perforated 10 vertically.

982 *Tulip*

982		MNHVF	UseVF
29¢	**multicolored** tagged	.75	.20
	Pair	1.25	
	FDC *(March 3, 1992)*		1.75

Listings and prices for plate number coil strips and singles appear at the end of this definitives section of the Krause-Minkus catalog.

1992. EARL WARREN ISSUE in the Great Americans Series honored the former Chief Justice of the United States. Warren (1891-1974) was the driving force in the landmark case Brown vs. Board of Education that outlawed racial segregation in public schools. *Intaglio, perforated 11.*

983 *Earl Warren*

983		MNHVF	UseVF
29¢	**blue** phosphored paper (mottled tagging)	.50	.20
	Plate block of 4	2.75	
	FDC *(March 9, 1992)*		2.00

1992. FLAG OVER WHITE HOUSE ISSUE honored the 200th anniversary of the home and office of the president of the United States. *Intaglio, perforated 10 vertically.*

984 *U.S. flag, White House*

984		MNHVF	UseVF
29¢	**blue & red** tagged, phosphored paper	.50	.20
	Pair	2.00	

FDC *(April 23, 1992)*
a. indigo & red —
Pair —
v. Pair, imperforate 20.00

1992. USA Issue was for presorted First-Class mailings. The background is a graduated blue; "First-Class" is 9 1/2mm long, and "23" is 6mm long. *Coil, gravure, American Bank Note Co., perforated 10 vertically (plate numbers start with "A").*

985 *"USA"*

985		MNHVF	UseVF
23¢	**multicolored** (printed service indicator: "Presorted First-Class")	.50	.20
	Pair	.75	
	FDC *(July 21, 1992)*		1.75

See Nos. 994 and 1010 for similar stamps printed by the Bureau of Engraving and Printing and by Stamp Venturers.

Listings and prices for plate number coil strips and singles appear at the end of this definitives section of the Krause-Minkus catalog.

1992. ECA GARD Variable Denominated Issue was released as a test of new postage and mail center equipment that weighed items for mailing, determined the postage necessary for the desired level of service, and printed stamps with the appropriate amount of postage. *Coil, intaglio, perforated 10 horizontally.*

986 *Shield & bunting*

986		MNHVF	UseVF
	red & blue variable rate, denomination (.01 to 9.99) printed in black, phosphored paper (solid tagging) matte gum	1.50	.50
	FDC *(Aug. 20, 1992)*		7.50
	pz. embedded taggant, shiny gum	1.50	.50

For narrow, tall format, see No. 1040.

1992. Pledge of Allegiance Issue honored the centennial of the pledge, first recited by school children for the 400th anniversary of Columbus' voyage of discovery. *Gravure, perforated 10.*

987, 1008 *Flag, "I pledge allegiance..."*

987		MNHVF	UseVF
29¢	**multicolored** black inscription, booklet stamp, tagged	.75	.20
	FDC *(Sept. 8, 1992)* single		1.75
	n. Booklet pane of 10	7.50	
	FDC booklet pane		7.00
	a. Perforated 11 x 10 on 2 or 3 sides	1.25	.50
	an. Booklet pane of 10	12.00	
	av. Pair, imperforate	900.00	—

For version with red inscription see No. 1008.

1992. Eagle and Shield Self-Adhesive Issue was produced by three different contractors, each is identifiable through the color of the inscription "(USA 29)": red for Stamp Venturers of Fairfax, Va.; green for Dittler Brothers, Inc., of Oakwood, Ga.; and brown for Bank- note Corporation of America, Inc., of Suffern, N.Y. These stamps were issued in panes of 17 plus a label on flexible backing paper, suitable for folding into a booklet. The stamps also were available in strips of 17 with the stamps spaced apart for use in affixing machines. *Straight-line die cut, gravure.*

988, 990, 992 *Eagle and shield*

988		MNHVF	UseVF
29¢	**multicolored** red inscription, tagged	.45	.30
	FDC *(Sept. 25, 1992)* single		2.00
	n. Pane of 17, plus label	12.00	
	FDC booklet pane		12.00

No. 989 is not assigned.

990		MNHVF	UseVF
29¢	**multicolored** green inscription, tagged	.45	.30
	FDC *(Sept. 25, 1992)* single		2.00
	n. Pane of 17, plus label	15.00	
	FDC booklet pane		12.00

No. 991 is not assigned.

992		MNHVF	UseVF
29¢	**multicolored** brown inscription, tagged	.45	.30
	FDC *(Sept 25, 1992)*		2.00
	n. Pane of 17, plus label	14.50	
	FDC pane of 17		12.00
	v. Pair, imperforate	175.00	
	v1. brown omitted	450.00	

No. 993 is not assigned.

1992. "USA" Issue for presorted First-Class mailings was reformatted in larger coils. The background is solid blue; "First-Class" is 9mm long, and "23" is 6 1/2mm long. *Coil, gravure, Bureau of Printing and Engraving (plate number beginning with a numeral rather than a letter), perforated 10 vertically.*

994, 1010 *"USA"*

994		MNHVF	UseVF
23¢	**multicolored** printed service indicator: "Presorted First-Class," shiny gum	.50	.20
	Pair	.75	
	FDC *(Oct. 9, 1992)*		1.75
	z. Tagged (error)	—	65.00
	m. Matte gum	.50	.20
	Pair	.75	
	v. Pair, imperforate	125.00	
	v1. Imperforate stamp with plate No. 1111	250.00	

See Nos. 985 and 1010 for versions printed by the American Bank Note Co. or by Stamp Venturers.

Listings and prices for plate number coil strips and singles appear at the end of this definitives section of the Krause-Minkus catalog.

1992. Contemporary Christmas Issue consisted of a se-tenant block of four stamps in both sheet and booklet formats with design differences ("Greetings" is 27mm long on the sheet version and 25mm long on the booklet version) and a self-adhesive stamp with essentially the same basic design ("Greetings" is only 21 1/2mm long). Offset, perforated 11 1/2 x 11. Microprinting "Copyright 1992" was used for the first time on a U.S. stamp.

995, 999, 1005, *Locomotive*
996, 1000, *Pony & rider*
997, 1001, *Fire engine*
998, 1002, *Steamship*

		MNHVF	UseVF
995			
29¢	Locomotive **multicolored,** tagged	.45	.20
996			
29¢	Pony & rider **multicolored,** tagged	.45	.20
997			
29¢	Fire engine **multicolored,** tagged	.45	.20
998			
29¢	Steamship **multicolored,** tagged	.45	.20
	FDC *(Oct. 22, 1992)* any single		2.50
	y. Se-tenant block of 4	3.50	
	Plate block of 4	4.50	
	FDC block of 4		4.00

1992. Contemporary Booklet Issue Gravure, Multi-Color Corporation, perforated 11.

		MNHVF	UseVF
999			
29¢	Locomotive **multicolored,** booklet single	.45	.20
1000			
29¢	Pony & rider **multicolored,** booklet single	.45	.20
1001			
29¢	Fire engine **multicolored,** booklet single	.45	.20
1002			
29¢	Steamship **multicolored,** booklet single	.45	.20
	FDC *(Oct. 22, 1992)* any single		2.50
	n. Booklet pane of 4 (Nos. 999-1002)	3.50	
	FDC booklet pane		4.00
	nv. Booklet pane of 4, imperforate	—	
	nv1. Booklet pane of 4, imperforate horizontally	—	

1992. Traditional Christmas Issue in the Christmas Series. *Intaglio and offset, perforated 11 1/2 x 11.*

1003 Madonna and Child *by Bellini*

		MNHVF	UseVF
1003			
29¢	**multicolored** tagged	.45	.20
	Plate block of 4	3.00	
	FDC *(Oct. 22, 1992)* single		1.75
	n. Booklet pane of 10	8.00	
	FDC booklet pane		8.00

No. 1004 is not assigned.

1992. Contemporary Christmas Self-Adhesive ATM Issue featured the toy locomotive design with "Greetings" measuring only 21 1/2mm. *Gravure, die cut, self-adhesive.*

1005 *Toy locomotive*

		MNHVF	UseVF
1005			
29¢	**multicolored** tagged	.75	.20
	FDC *(Oct. 22, 1992)*		1.75
	n. Pane of 18	12.00	
	FDC pane of 18		14.00

1992. Pumpkinseed Sunfish Issue in the Flora and Fauna Series met the second 1/2-ounce rate for international mail and the 1-ounce rate to Mexico. *Intaglio and offset, perforated 11 1/2 x 11.*

1006 *Pumpkinseed sunfish*

		MNHVF	UseVF
1006			
45¢	**multicolored** tagged	1.00	.20
	Plate block of 4	5.50	
	FDC *(Dec. 2, 1992)*		2.00
	v. Intaglio black omitted	600.00	

1992. Circus Wagon Issue in the Transportation Series was a redesigned version of the stamp of 1990 (No. 931). *Coil, gravure, American Bank Note Co., perforated 10 vertically.*

		MNHVF	UseVF
1007			
5¢	**red** untagged	.25	.20
	Pair	.30	
	FDC *(Dec. 8, 1992)*		1.75

For intaglio stamps of this design see No. 931 ("05 USA") and No. 1077 ("USA 5¢").

Listings and prices for plate number coil strips and singles appear at the end of this definitives section of the Krause-Minkus catalog.

1993. Pledge of Allegiance Issue *new version with red, "USA" and denomination, printed by Stamp Venturers. The booklets in which the stamps are found were assembled by KCS, a division of Banta Corp. Gravure, perforated 10.*

		MNHVF	UseVF
1008			
29¢	**multicolored** red inscription, tagged	.75	.20
	FDC *(March 1993)* single		1.75
	n. Booklet pane of 10	7.50	
	FDC booklet pane		7.00
	v. Pair, imperforate	900.00	

For similar stamp with black inscription see No. 987.

1993. Thomas Jefferson Issue in the Great Americans Series honored the third president of the United States (1743-1826) on the 250th anniversary of his birth. *Intaglio, Stamp Venturers, perforated 11 1/2 x 11.*

1009 *Thomas Jefferson*

		MNHVF	UseVF
1009			
29¢	**indigo** phosphored paper (solid tagging)	.50	.30
	Plate block of 4	2.50	
	Plate block of 8, w/position diagram	5.50	
	FDC *(April 13, 1993)*		2.00

1993. USA Issue for presorted First-Class mailings. The background is violet blue; "First-Class" is 8 1/2mm long, and "23" is 6 1/2mm long. *Coil, gravure, Stamp Venturers (plate number beginning with an "S"), perforated 10 vertically.*

		MNHVF	UseVF
1010			
23¢	**multicolored** printed service indicator: "Presorted First-Class"	.75	.20
	Pair	1.00	
	FDC *(May 14, 1993)*		1.75
	v. Pair, imperforate	—	

In this version, "23" is 8 1/2mm long. See No. 985 and No. 994 for versions printed by the American Bank Note Co. and by the Bureau of Engraving and Printing.

1993. Eagle and Shield Non-Denominated Issue met the needs of permit mailers on presorted Bulk Mail pieces. Similar to earlier version, No. 980. Design differences include reversal of "USA" and

"BULK RATE" and colors reversed to "USA" in blue and "BULK RATE" in red. The stamp's face value is 10¢, with additional postage paid by mailers at the time of mailing. *Coil, printed by gravure by the Bureau of Engraving and Printing (plate number beginning with numeral rather than letter) and Stamp Venturers (plate numbers beginning with "S"), perforated 10 vertically. The Stamp Venturers version has the eagle in metallic gold, the B.E.P. version in orange yellow.*

1011, 1012 "USA" before "Bulk Rate"

		MNHVF	UseVF
1011			
(10¢)	**multicolored** (B.E.P.)	.30	.20
	Pair	.60	
	FDC *(May 29, 1993)*		1.75
	v. Pair, imperforate	30.00	
	z. Tagged (error)	2.00	1.50
	v1. Low gloss gum	.20	
	Pair	.40	

		MNHVF	UseVF
1012			
(10¢)	**multicolored** (Stamp Venturers)	.30	.20
	Pair	.40	
	FDC *(May 29, 1993)*		1.75

See No. 980 for similar design printed by the American Bank Note Co.

1993. Futuristic Space Shuttle Issue prepaid the Priority Mail rate. *Offset and intaglio, perforated 11.*

1013 *Futuristic Space Shuttle*

		MNHVF	UseVF
1013			
$2.90	**multicolored**	6.50	2.50
	Plate block of 4	27.50	
	FDC *(June 23, 1993)*		7.50

1993. Red Squirrel Issue in the Flora and Fauna Series. *Self-adhesive First Class letter-rate stamp. Gravure, Dittler Brothers, Inc., die cut.*

1014 *Red squirrel*

		MNHVF	UseVF
1014			
29¢	**multicolored** from booklet or coil, tagged	.50	.20
	FDC *(June 25, 1993)* single		1.75
	n. Pane of 18	12.00	
	FDC pane of 18		14.00

No. 1015 is not assigned.

1993. Rose Issue *self-adhesive stamp* in the Flora and Fauna Series. *Gravure by Stamp Venturers, die cut.*

1016 *Rose*

		MNHVF	UseVF
1016			
29¢	**multicolored** from booklet or coil, tagged	.50	.20
	FDC *(Aug. 19, 1993)* single		1.75
	n. Pane of 18	12.00	
	FDC pane of 18		14.00

No. 1017 is not assigned.

1993. African Violet Booklet Issue in the Flora and Fauna Series. *Gravure by KCS Industries, perforated 10 x 11.*

1018 *African Violet*

		MNHVF	UseVF
1018			
29¢	**multicolored** from booklet, tagged	.75	.20
	FDC *(Oct. 8, 1993)* single		1.75
	n. Booklet pane of 10	8.50	
	FDC booklet pane		8.00

1993. Contemporary Christmas Issue in the Christmas Series consisted of four contemporary designs available in gummed panes (18x25mm, perforated 11 1/2) and booklets (18x21mm, perforated 11x10) and self-adhesive panes. The Snowman design of the Contemporary issues is available self-adhesive both with the other three designs and by itself in panes available through ATM machines. *Printed by gravure by the Bureau of Engraving and Printing (sheets and booklets), and Avery Dennison (self-adhesive); perforated 11.*

1019, 1023, 1029 *Jack-in-the box*

1020, 1024, 1030 *Reindeer*

1021, 1025, 1031 *Snowman*

1022, 1026, 1032 *Toy soldier*

		MNHVF	UseVF
1019			
29¢	Jack-in-the-box, tagged	.50	.20
1020			
29¢	Reindeer, tagged	.50	.20
1021			
29¢	Snowman, tagged	.50	.20
1022			
29¢	Toy soldier, tagged	.50	.20
	FDC *(Oct. 21, 1993) any single*		1.75
	y. Se-tenant block of 4	2.00	.80
	Plate block of 4	3.00	
	FDC block of 4		4.00
1023			
29¢	Jack-in-the-box, tagged	.50	.20
1024			
29¢	Reindeer, tagged	.50	.20
1025			
29¢	Snowman, tagged	.50	.20
1026			
29¢	Toy soldier, tagged	.50	.20
	y. Se-tenant block of 4	2.00	.80
	FDC *(Oct. 21, 1993)*, any single		2.50
	n. Booklet pane of 10 (three each Nos. 1023, 1024; two each Nos. 1025, 1026)	6.50	
	n1. Booklet pane of 10 (two each Nos. 1023, 1024; three each Nos. 1025, 1026)	6.50	
	FDC booklet pane		4.00

1993. Traditional Christmas Issue in the Christmas Series was available in sheet and booklet form. *The booklet version is larger than the sheet version (booklet overall stamp 28.95 x 22.09mm; sheet overall stamp 23.1 x 30.2mm). There are design differences between the two items, also. Perforated 11 (1027) or 11 1/2 x 11 (1028).*

1027, 1028 Madonna and Child in a Landscape, *by Giovanni Battista Cima (1497)* from North Carolina Museum of Art

		MNHVF	UseVF
1027			
29¢	**multicolored** tagged	.50	.20
	Plate block of 4	3.50	
	FDC *(Oct. 21, 1993)*		1.75

		MNHVF	UseVF
1028			
29¢	**multicolored** booklet single, tagged	.50	.20
	FDC *(Oct. 21, 1993)* single		1.75
	n. Booklet pane of 4	4.00	
	FDC booklet pane		4.00
	nv. Booklet pane of 4, imperforate	—	

1993. Contemporary Christmas Self-adhesive Issue Printed by Avery Dennison, die cut.

		MNHVF	UseVF
1029			
29¢	Jack-in-the-box, tagged	.50	.20

		MNHVF	UseVF
1030			
29¢	Reindeer, tagged	.50	.20

		MNHVF	UseVF
1031			
29¢	Snowman, tagged	.50	.20

		MNHVF	UseVF
1032			
29¢	Toy soldier, tagged	.50	.20
	FDC *(Oct. 28, 1993)* any single		2.25
	n. Pane of 12 (3 of each design)	9.50	
	FDC pane of 12		10.00
	y. Se-tenant block of 4	2.00	1.50
	y1. Se-tenant coil strip of 4	2.00	

Nos. 1033-1036 are not assigned.

1993. Snowman ATM Pane Issue Die-cut (self-adhesive.)

1037 *Snowman*

		MNHVF	UseVF
1037			
29¢	**multicolored,** tagged	.75	.25
	FDC *(Oct. 28, 1993)* single		1.75
	n. Pane of 18	12.00	
	FDC pane of 18		14.00

Although the placement is different, the Snowmen depicted on Nos. 1021 and 1031 have three buttons and seven snowflakes beneath the nose. No. 1025 has two buttons and five snowflakes beneath the nose.

1993. Pine Cone Issue *self-adhesive stamp* in the Flora and Fauna Series. *Gravure by the Banknote Corporation of America, die cut.*

1038 *Pine cone*

		MNHVF	UseVF
1038			
29¢	**multicolored** from booklet or coil, tagged	.50	.20
	FDC *(Nov. 5, 1993)* single		1.75
	n. Pane of 18	14.00	
	FDC pane of 18		14.00

1994 4. Eagle Issue Self-adhesive, gravure by National Label Co. for 3M, die cut.

1039 *Eagle*

		MNHVF	UseVF
1039			
29¢	**red, cream & blue** from booklet or coil, tagged	.50	.20
	FDC *(Feb. 4, 1994)* single		1.75
	n. Pane of 18	15.00	
	FDC pane of 18		12.50

1994. Postage and Mail Center (PMC) Issue Similar to No. 986, issued in 1992, this issue is perforated vertically. *Gravure by Guilford Gravure for American Bank Note Co., perforated 10 vertically.*

1040 *Shield & bunting*

		MNHVF	UseVF
1040			
	(variable rate) red and blue, denomination 20¢-$99.99 printed in black, phosphored paper	1.50	.50
	FDC *(Feb. 19, 1994)*		7.50

1994. Surrender of Burgoyne at Saratoga Issue Design of this stamp was taken from an engraving originally prepared to be part of the 1869 definitive series, the first U.S. pictorial postage stamps. John Trumbull's painting *The Surrender of Gen. Burgoyne at Saratoga* is the basis for the stamp design. *Intaglio by Stamp Venturers in panes of 20, perforated 11 1/2.*

1041 *Surrender of Burgoyne at Saratoga*

		MNHVF	UseVF
1041			
$1	**dark blue** tagged	2.00	.75
	Plate block of 4	9.00	
	FDC *(May 5, 1994)*		

1994. Tractor Trailer Issue in the Transportation Series. Reprint of No. 954, showing a 1930s tractor trailer, issued for use by permit mailers. *Coil, gravure, B.E.P., perforated 10 vertically.*

1042 *Tractor trailer*

		MNHVF	UseVF
1042			
10¢	**green** Bureau-printed service indicator (in gray): "Additional Presort Postage Paid"	.25	.20
	Pair	.30	
	FDC *(May 25, 1994)*		1.75
	v. Pair, imperforate	—	

1994. Statue of Liberty Issue Self-adhesive pane. Die cut.

1043 *Statue of Liberty*

		MNHVF	UseVF
1043			
29¢	**multicolored** from booklet or coil, tagged	.50	.20
	FDC *(June 24, 1994)* single		1.75
	n. Pane of 18	12.00	
	FDC pane of 18		12.50

1994. FISHING BOAT ISSUE Originally issued in 1991, (No. 965), this design was reprinted in 1992 in lighter colors (No. 965z1). This 1994 version easily is identifiable by counting the "loops" of rope on the mooring. The original and initial two reprintings had two loops, this version has a single loop. *Coil, gravure by Stamp and Venturers, perforated 10 vertically.*

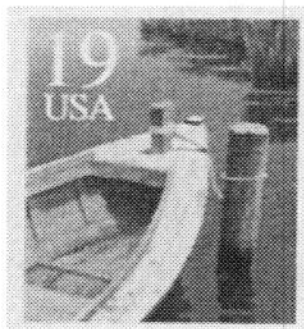
1044 *Boat, single loop on mooring*

		MNHVF	UseVF
1044			
19¢	**multicolored** tagged	.50	.20
	Pair	.60	
	FDC *(June 25, 1994)*		1.75

1994. MOON LANDING ISSUE Celebrated the 25th anniversary of the moon landing with an Express Mail denomination. *Offset and intaglio, perforated 10 1/2 x 11.*

1045 *Moon landing, 25th anniversary*

		MNHVF	UseVF
1045			
$9.95	**multicolored** tagged	25.00	10.00
	Plate block of 4	100.00	
	FDC *(July 20, 1994)*		25.00

1994. WASHINGTON AND JACKSON ISSUE was a design submitted by a firm seeking to win the contract for the 1869 issue. *Intaglio by Stamp Venturers in panes of 20, perforated 11 1/2.*

1046 *Washington and Jackson*

		MNHVF	UseVF
1046			
$5	**dark green** tagged	10.00	3.75
	Plate block of 4	50.00	
	FDC *(Aug. 19, 1994)*		13.50

1994. CONTEMPORARY CHRISTMAS ISSUE consisted of two designs. The Santa Claus stamp was issued only as a self-adhesive. The Holiday Stocking design was issued both in sheet form and in booklets of 20 stamps. *Printed by gravure by Avery Dennison* (Santa self-adhesive), *by Ashton-Potter USA Ltd.* (Holiday Stocking). *Perforated 11* (No. 1047).

1047 *Christmas stocking*

		MNHVF	UseVF
1047			
29¢	**multicolored** from sheet or booklet, tagged	.50	.20
	Plate block of 4	3.50	
	FDC *(Oct. 20, 1994)*		1.75
	v. Pair, imperforate	—	
	n, Booklet pane of 20	8.50	
	FDC booklet pane		15.50
	nv. Booklet pane, imperforate horizontally	—	

1994. TRADITIONAL CHRISTMAS ISSUE *was issued both in sheet and booklet form, with the total size of the booklet version 0.05mm more horizontally and 0.03mm less vertically than the sheet version. Printed by offset and intaglio by the Bureau of Printing and Engraving, perforated 11 (No. 1048), 10 x 11 (No. 1049).*

1048, 1049 Madonna and Child, *by Elisabetta Sirani*

		MNHVF	UseVF
1048			
29¢	**multicolored** shiny gum, tagged	.50	.20
	Plate block of 4	3.50	
	low gloss gum	.50	.20
	Plate block of 4	3.50	
	FDC *(Oct. 20, 1994)*		1.75
1049		**MNHVF**	**UseVF**
29¢	**multicolored** from booklet, tagged	.50	.20
	FDC *(Oct. 20, 1994)* single		1.75
	n. Booklet pane of 10	7.50	
	FDC booklet pane		4.50
	v. Pair, imperforate	—	
	v1. Booklet pane, imperforate	600.00	

1994. CONTEMPORARY SANTA CLAUS BOOKLET ISSUE in the Christmas Series. *Gravure, die cut.*

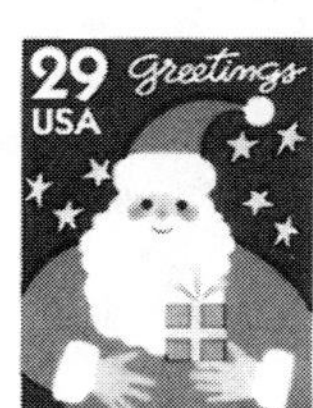
1050 *Santa Claus*

		MNHVF	UseVF
1050			
29¢	**multicolored** from booklet or coil, tagged	.50	.20
	FDC *(Oct. 20, 1994)* single		1.75
	n. Pane of 12	10.50	
	FDC pane of 12		10.00

1994. CARDINAL IN SNOW ATM ISSUE this is a self-adhesive stamp in panes of 18 for automated teller machines (ATM). The stamp released at the same time as the Christmas issues, with the design having a decidely winter holiday motif. *Gravure by Avery Dennison, die cut.*

1051 *Cardinal in snow*

1051		MNHVF	UseVF
29¢	**multicolored** tagged	.50	.20
	FDC *(Oct. 20, 1994)* single		1.75
	n. Pane of 18	14.50	
	FDC pane of 18		

1994. Virginia Apgar Issue in the Great Americans Series honored a medical researcher (1909-1974) whose simple assessment method allows doctors and nurses in the delivery room to make an immediate evaluation of a newborn baby's general condition. This process aids in the identification of those infants who need immediate medical attention. *Intaglio by the Banknote Corporation of America, perforated 11.*

1052 *Virginia Apgar*

1052		MNHVF	UseVF
20¢	**brown** phosphored paper grainy tagging	.50	.20
	a. orange brown	.50	.20
	Plate block of 4	2.50	
	FDC *(Oct. 24, 1994)*		1.75

1994. Postage and Mail Center (PMC) Issue with variable denomination, similar to No. 1040, with different type font. Initial release was in Detroit, Mich.

1053 *Shield and bunting*

1053		MNHVF	UseVF
	(variable rate) red & blue, denomination (.01-9.99) printed in black, phosphored paper (mottled tagging), shiny gum	.75	.50
	FDC *(Nov. 9, 1994)*		7.50
	pz. Phosphored paper (solid tagging), matte gum		

Non-denominated Service-Inscribed Series

1994. Black "G" Sheet Issue the first in the Non-denominated Service-Inscribed Series was the most prolific of the rate-change issues. It pictured "Old Glory" and the letter "G." A total of 16 items were released, including specific items for First Class letter rate, First Class presort, postal card rate, coils and booklets, and two types of self-adhesives. Sheet stamps, overall dimensions 0.84 x 0.99 inches. *Gravure, printed by Bureau of Engraving and Printing, black "G," perforated 11 1/4 x 11.*

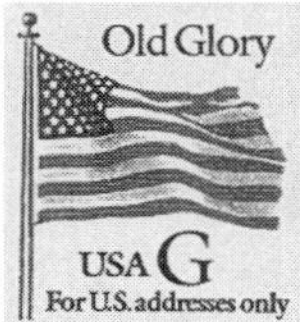

1054 *Old Glory For U.S. addresses only*

1054		MNHVF	UseVF
(32¢)	**red, blue, gray & black** tagged	.50	.20
	Plate block of 4	50.00	
	FDC *(Dec. 13, 1994)*		2.00
	n. Booklet pane of 10	6.00	
	FDC booklet pane		8.50

1994. Red "G" Sheet Issue in the Non-denominated Service-Inscribed Series. *Printed by Stamp Venturers, red "G," perforated 11.*

1055		MNHVF	UseVF
(32¢)	**red, blue, gray & black** tagged	.75	.20
	Plate block of 4	4.00	
	FDC *(Dec. 13, 1994)*		1.90

1994. Black "G" Booklet Issue in the Non-denominated Service-Inscribed Series. *Printed by Bureau of Engraving and printing, black "G," perforated 10.*

1056		MNHVF	UseVF
(32¢)	**red, blue, gray & black** tagged	.50	.20
	FDC single *(Dec. 13, 1994)*		1.90
	n. Booklet pane of 10	6.00	
	FDC booklet pane		8.50

1994. Blue "G" Booklet Issue in the Non-denominated Service-Inscribed Series. *Printed by American Bank Note Co., blue "G," perforated 11.*

1057		MNHVF	UseVF
(32¢)	**red, blue, gray & black** tagged	.50	.20
	FDC single *(Dec. 13, 1994)*		1.90
	n. Booklet pane of 10	9.00	
	FDC booklet pane		8.50
	v. Pair, imperforate	—	
	nv. Booklet pane imperforate	—	

1994. Red "G" Booklet Issue in the Non-denominated Service-Inscribed Series. *Printed by KCS, red "G," perforated 11.*

1058		MNHVF	UseVF
(32¢)	**red, blue, gray & black** tagged	.50	.20
	FDC single *(Dec. 13, 1994)*		1.90
	n. Booklet pane of 10	6.00	
	FDC booklet pane		8.50
	v. Horizontal pair imperforate between	500.00	
	v1. Horizontal pair imperforate between vertically	—	
	nv. Booklet pane of 10, imperforate	—	

1994. Black "G" Coil Issue in the Non-denominated Service-Inscribed Series. *Printed by Bureau of Engraving and Printing, black "G," by gravure, perforated 10.*

1059		MNHVF	UseVF
(32¢)	**red, blue, gray & black** tagged	.50	.20
	Pair	1.00	.30
	FDC *(Dec. 13, 1994)*		1.90
	v. Pair, imperforate	275.00	
	v1. Pair, imperforate between	—	

1994. Blue "G" Coil Issue in the Non-denominated Service-Inscribed Series. *Printed by American Bank Note Co., blue "G," perforated 10 vertically.*

1060		MNHVF	UseVF
(32¢)	**red, blue, gray & black** tagged	.50	.20
	Pair	1.25	.30
	FDC *(Dec. 13, 1994)*		1.90

1994. Red "G" Coil Issue in the Non-denominated Service-Inscribed Series. *Printed by Stamp Venturers, red "G," perforated 10 vertically.*

1061		MNHVF	UseVF
(32¢)	**red, blue, gray & black** tagged	.50	.20
	Pair	1.25	.30
	FDC *(Dec. 13, 1994)*		1.90

1994. Red "G" Coil Issue in the Non-denominated Service-Inscribed Series. *Printed by Stamp Venturers, red "G," rouletted 10 vertically.*

1061A		MNHVF	UseVF
(32¢)	**red, blue, gray & black** tagged	.50	.20
	Pair	1.25	.30
	FDC *(Dec. 13, 1994)*		1.90

1994. "G" Self Adhesive Issue in the Non-denominated Service-Inscribed Series. *Gravure by Avery Dennison, black "G," imperforate and die cut.*

1062 *Old Glory for U.S. addresses only*

1062		MNHVF	UseVF
(32¢)	**red, dark blue, light blue, gray & black,** from booklet or coil, tagged	1.00	.35
	FDC single *(Dec. 13, 1994)*		1.90
	n. Pane of 18	17.50	
	FDC pane of 18		15.00

1994. "G" Self Adhesive ATM Issue in the Non-denominated Service-Inscribed Series. *Dispensed sheetlet, self-adhesive, printed by gravure by Avery Dennison, black "G," imperforate and die cut.*

1063		MNHVF	UseVF
(32¢)	**red, blue & black** tagged	1.00	.35
	FDC single *(Dec. 13, 1994)*		1.90
	n. Pane of 18	17.50	
	FDC pane of 18		15.00

1994. "G" First-Class Presort Rate Issue in the Non-denominated Service-Inscribed Series. *Gravure by Stamp Venturers, black "G," blue background, coil stamp, perforated 10 vertically.*

1064 *Old Glory First-Class Presort*

1064		MNHVF	UseVF
(25¢)	**red, dark blue, gray, black & light blue**	.50	.50
	Pair	1.00	1.00
	FDC *(Dec. 13, 1994)*		1.90

1994. Black "G" Postcard Rate Issue in the Non-denominated Service-Inscribed Series. *Printed by Bureau of Engraving and Printing, black "G", yellow background. Gravure, perforated 11.*

1065 *Old Glory Postcard Rate*

1065		MNHVF	UseVF
(20¢)	**red, blue, gray, yellow & black** tagged	.50	.20
	Plate block of 4	5.00	
	FDC *(Dec. 13, 1994)*		1.90
	v. Pair, imperforate	—	

1994. Red "G" Postcard Rate Issue in the Non-denominated Service-Inscribed Series. *Gravure by Stamp Venturers, red "G," perforated 11.*

1066		MNHVF	UseVF
(20¢)	**red, blue, gray, yellow & black,** tagged	.50	.20
	Plate block of 4	3.00	
	FDC *(Dec. 13, 1994)*		1.95

1994. Non-Denominated "Make-Up " Rate Issue in the Non-denominated Service-Inscribed Series, had a value of 3¢, to be used with a 29¢ stamp to meet the new First Class rate. *Offset, perforated 11, printed by American Bank Note Co., bright blue with thin lettering.*

1067 *Dove*

1067		MNHVF	UseVF
(3¢)	**red, bright blue & tan**	.20	.20
	Plate block of 4	.50	
	FDC *(Dec. 13, 1994)*		1.90
	v. Pair, imperforate	175.00	
	v1. Plate block, imperforate	—	
	v2. Pair, imperforate, bright blue omitted (printer's waste)	—	

1994. Non-Denominated "Make-Up" Rate in the Non-denominated Service-Inscribed Series. *Offset by Stamp Venturers, darker blue with thick lettering, perforated 11.*

1068		MNHVF	UseVF
(3¢)	**red, dark blue & tan**	.20	.20
	Plate block of 4	.50	
	FDC *(Dec. 13, 1994)*		1.90

1995. "G" Nonprofit Presort Coil Issue in the Non-denominated Service-Inscribed Series. *Coil, gravure by American Bank Note Co., black "G," green background, perforated 10 vertically.*

1069 *Old Glory "Nonprofit Presort"*

1069		MNHVF	UseVF
(5¢)	**green & multicolored** untagged	.25	.20
	Pair	.30	.25
	FDC *(Jan. 12, 1995)*		1.90

First-day covers received a Dec. 13, 1994 cancellation although these stamps were not yet available on that date.

1995. Butte and "Nonprofit Organization" Issue in the Non-denominated Service-Inscribed Series. Beginning early in 1995, the USPS introduced several series of coils for use by various mass mailers that showed the service but no denomination. The additional cost of the mail service was prepaid directly by the mailer at the post office where the mailing took place. *Gravure. Printed by J.W. Fergusson & Sons for Stamp Venturers, perforated 10 vertically.*

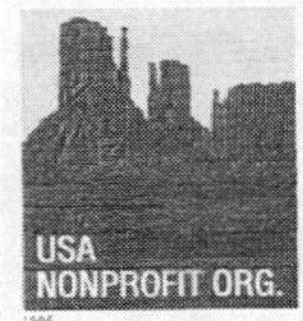

1070, 1130 *Butte and "Nonprofit Org."*

1070		MNHVF	UseVF
(5¢)	**yellow, blue & red** untagged	.25	.20
	Pair	.30	.25
	v. Pair, imperforate	675.00	
	FDC *(March 10, 1995)*		1.90

American Culture Series

1995. Car Hood and "Bulk Rate" Issue in the American Culture Series. *J.W. Fergusson & Sons for Stamp Venturers, perforated 10 vertically.*

1071, 1132 *Car hood and "Bulk Rate"*

1071		MNHVF	UseVF
(10¢)	**black, brown & red brown** untagged	.30	.20
	Pair	.35	.25
	FDC *(March 17, 1995)*		1.90

1995. Tail Fin Presorted First-Class Coil Issue in the American Culture Series. *Printed by B.E.P., perforated 10 vertically.*

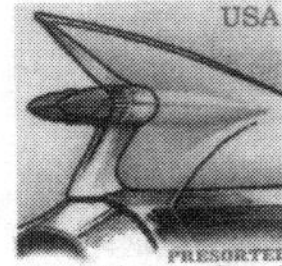

1072 *Tail fin and "Presorted First-Class Card"*

1072		MNHVF	UseVF
(15¢)	**yellow orange & multicolored** untagged	.40	.30
	Pair	.50	.35
	FDC *(March 17, 1995)*		2.25

1995. Tail Fin Presorted First-Class Coil Issue in the American Culture Series. *J.W. Fergusson & Sons for Stamp Venturers, perforated 10 vertically.*

1073, 1133 *Tail fin and "Presorted First-Class Card"*

1073		MNHVF	UseVF
15¢	**buff & multicolored** untagged	.40	.30
	Pair	.50	.35
	FDC *(March 17, 1995)*		2.25

1995. Juke Box Presorted First-Class Coil Issue in the American Culture Series. *Printed by B.E.P., perforated 10 vertically.*

1074-75, 1134, 1153 *Juke Box and "Presorted First-Class"*

1074		MNHVF	UseVF
25¢	**dark red, yellow green & multicolored,** untagged	.65	.40
	Pair	.75	.50
	FDC *(March 17, 1995)*		1.90

1995. Juke Box "Presorted First-Class" Coil Issue in the American Culture Series. *J.W. Fergusson & Sons for Stamp Venturers, perforated 10 vertically.*

1075		MNHVF	UseVF
25¢	**orange red, bright yellow green & multicolored** untagged	.65	.40
	Pair	.75	.50
	FDC *(March 17, 1995)*		1.90

1995. Flag Over Field ATM Issue *Avery Dennison, self-adhesive, die cut.*

1076 *Flag over field*

1076		MNHVF	UseVF
32¢	**multicolored** tagged	1.00	.30
	FDC *(March 17, 1995)*		1.90
	n. Pane of 18	14.50	
	FDC pane of 18		14.50

1995. Circus Wagon Issue in the Transportation Series was a redesigned gravure version of the earlier coil issued in intaglio (No. 931) and gravure (No. 1007). *Coil, intaglio by Stamp Venturers, perforated 9 3/4 vertically.*

1077 *Circus wagon, 1900s*

1077		MNHVF	UseVF
5¢	**red** untagged	.25	.20
	Pair	.30	
	FDC *(March 20, 1995)*		1.90

For intaglio & gravure versions of this design inscribed "05 USA" see Nos. 931 & 1007.

1995. Flag Over Porch Self-Adhesive Booklet Issue *Gravure by Avery Dennison, serpentine die cut 8 3/4.*

1078, 1080, 1081, 1082, 1083 *Flag Over Porch*

1078		MNHVF	UseVF
32¢	**multicolored** from booklet or coil, phosphored paper, large "1995"	.70	.20
	FDC single *(April 19, 1995)*		2.00
	n. Pane of 20 plus label	12.50	
	FDC pane of 20		15.50
	n1. Pane of 15 plus label (various layouts)	9.00	
	n2. Booklet pane of 16 but one stamp removed from upper left or lower right position	—	
	a. Small "1995"	3.00	.20
	an. Pane of 20 plus label	100.00	
	FDC small "1995"		2.00
	FDC pane of 20		45.00

Note: 1078n2 cannot be made from 1078n1 because the label is die cut and, if removed, leaves an impression of the die cutting.

1995. American Kestrel Issue in the Flora and Fauna Series. Redesigned denomination. *Offset by B.E.P., in panes of 100, perforated 11 1/4 X 11.*

1079, 1115 *American Kestrel*

1079		MNHVF	UseVF
1¢	**multicolored** tagged	.25	.20
	m. matte gum	.25	.20
	Plate block of 4	.30	
	FDC *(May 10, 1995)*		1.75

For version inscribed "USA 01" see No. 959. For coil see No. 1115.

1995. Flag Over Porch Issue Gravure by J.W. Fergusson & Sons for Stamp Venturers, blue "1995." Perforated 10 1/4 x 10 1/2.

1080		MNHVF	UseVF
32¢	**multicolored** tagged	.60	.20
	Plate block of 4	2.50	
	FDC *(May 19, 1995)*		2.00
	v. Pair, imperforate (vertical preferred)	75.00	

1995. Flag Over Porch Booklet Issue Perforated 10 3/4 x 9 3/4.

1081		MNHVF	UseVF
32¢	**multicolored** tagged	.80	.20
	FDC *(May 19, 1995)* single		2.00
	n. Booklet pane of 10	6.25	
	FDC booklet pane		8.50
	nv. Booklet pane of 10, imperforate	—	

1995. Flag Over Porch Coil Issue Coil, gravure by B.E.P., perforated 9 3/4 vertically.

1082		MNHVF	UseVF
32¢	**multicolored** tagged, red "1995"	.50	.20
	Pair	1.00	
	FDC *(May 19, 1995)*		2.00
	v. Pair, imperforate	35.00	

1995. Flag Over Porch Coil Issue Coil, gravure by J.W. Fergusson & Sons for Stamp Venturers, perforated 9 3/4 vertically.

1083		MNHVF	UseVF
32¢	**multicolored** tagged, blue "1995"	.75	.20
	Pair	1.00	
	FDC *(May 19,1995)*		2.00

Listings and prices for plate number coil strips and singles appear at the end of this definitives section of the Krause-Minkus catalog.

1995. Pink Rose Issue in the Flora and Fauna Series offered a new color, denomination and die-cut format to simulate perforations in an updated self-adhesive booklet or coil for use in the 32¢ rate period. *Gravure by J.W. Fergusson & Sons for Stamp Venturers, serpentine die cut 11 1/4 x 11 3/4.*

1084 *Pink rose*

1084		MNHVF	UseVF
32¢	**pink, green & black** from booklet or coil, phosphored	.80	.30
	FDC *(June 2, 1995)* single		1.90
	n. Pane of 20 plus label	16.00	
	a. Coil (#S111)	1.00	
	FDC booklet pane		15.50
	n1. Pane of 15 plus label, various layouts (1996)	20.00	
	n2. Pane of 14, no label	22.50	
	n3. Pane of 16, no label	22.50	
	n4. Booklet pane of 16 with one stamp removed, no label, various layouts	22.50	—
	v. Horizontal imperforate between pair (no die cut)	—	
	v1. black omitted	1,000.00	

Note: 1084n4 cannot be made from 1084n3 because the label is die cut and, if removed, leaves an impression of the die cutting.

1995. Ferryboat Issue in the Transportation Series. New York City steam ferryboat. *Coil, intaglio, perforated 9 3/4 vertically.*

Ferryboat 1900s 32USA
1085 *Ferryboat, 1900s*

1085		MNHVF	UseVF
32¢	**deep blue** phosphored paper	.65	.20
	Pair	1.25	
	FDC *(June 2, 1995)*		1.90
	v. Pair, imperforate	—	
	m. Matte gum	60.00	
	a. Bronx (bright) blue	6.00	5.00

1995. Cog Railway Issue in the Transportation Series. The cog railway is used for steep inclines and prevents slippage. *Coil, intaglio, perforated 9 3/4 vertically.*

1086 *Cog Railway 1870s*

1086		MNHVF	UseVF
20¢	**green** phosphored paper	.40	.20
	Pair	.75	
	FDC *(June 9, 1995)*		1.90
	v. Pair, imperforate	.75	

1995. Blue Jay Issue in the Flora and Fauna Series. Produced in booklet form to pay the First Class domestic postcard rate. *Gravure by Stamp Venturers, perforated 11 x 10.*

1087, 1135-36 *Blue jay*

1087		MNHVF	UseVF
20¢	**multicolored** phosphored paper	.45	.20
	FDC *(June 15, 1995)* single		1.90
	n. Booklet pane of 10	4.25	
	FDC booklet pane		8.50

1995. Space Shuttle Challenger Issue prepaid the Priority Mail rate. *Offset and intaglio (panes of 20) by Ashton-Potter (USA) Ltd., perforated 11. (See No. 1119).*

1088 *Space Shuttle Challenger*

1088		MNHVF	UseVF
$3	**multicolored** phosphored paper	6.00	3.00
	Plate block of 4	25.00	
	FDC *(June 22, 1995)*		7.75
	v. Horizontal pair, imperforate between	—	

1995. Peaches and Pear Issue in the Flora and Fauna Series. *Gravure, perforated 11 x 9 3/4.*

1089, 1091, 1091A *Peaches*

1090, 1092, 1092A *Pear*

1089		MNHVF	UseVF
32¢	**multicolored** phosphored paper	.75	.20
	FDC *(July 8, 1995)*		1.90

1090		MNHVF	UseVF
32¢	**multicolored** phosphored paper	.75	.20
	FDC *(July 8, 1995)* single		1.90
	y. Se-tenant pair, No. 1089-90	1.50	1.20
	n. Booklet pane of 10 (5 No. 1090y)	6.25	
	FDC booklet pane		8.50

1995. Peaches and Pear Self-Adhesive Issue (Peaches) in the Flora and Fauna Series. *Gravure by Avery Dennison, self-adhesive, serpentine die cut 8 3/4.*

1091		MNHVF	UseVF
32¢	**multicolored** phosphored paper	.85	.30
	FDC *(July 8, 1995)*		1.90

1995. Peaches and Pear Self-Adhesive Coil Issue (Peaches) in the Flora and Fauna Series. *Gravure by Avery Dennison, serpentine die cut 8 3/4 vertically.*

1091A		MNHVF	UseVF
32¢	**multicolored**	.85	.30
	FDC *(July 8, 1995)*		1.90

1995. Peaches and Pear Self-Adhesive Issue (Pear) in the Flora and Fauna Series. *Gravure by Avery Dennison, self-adhesive, serpentine die cut 8 3/4.*

1092		MNHVF	UseVF
32¢	**multicolored** phosphored paper	.85	.30
	FDC *(July 8, 1995)* single		1.90
	n. Pane of 20 (10 each Nos. 1091-92 plus label)	16.00	
	FDC Pane of 20		15.50

1995. Peaches and Pear Self-Adhesive Coil Issue (Pear) in the Flora and Fauna Series. *Gravure by Avery Dennison, serpentine die cut 8 3/4 vertically.*

1092A		MNHVF	UseVF
32¢	**multicolored**	.85	.30
	FDC *(July 8, 1995)*		1.90
	y. Se-tenant pair (1091A and 1092A)	1.50	
	FDC, pair (1091A and 1092A)		2.50

1995. Alice Hamilton Issue in the Great Americans Series paid tribute to a pioneer in industrial medicine, the first woman on the faculty of Harvard University and a socially committed physician (1869-1970) who played a key role in documenting and taking steps to prevent lead poisoning in the workplace. Issued to pay 2-ounce First Class letter rate. *Intaglio by Banknote Corp. of America, perforated 11 1/4 x 11.*

1093 *Alice Hamilton*

1093		MNHVF	UseVF
55¢	**green** phosphored paper, grainy tagging	1.10	.20
	Plate block of 4	5.50	
	FDC *(July 11, 1995)*		2.25

1995. Space Shuttle Endeavor Issue Prepaid the basic Express Mail rate. *Offset and intaglio (panes of 20) by Ashton-Potter (USA) Ltd., perforated 11.*

1094 *Space Shuttle* Endeavor

1094		MNHVF	UseVF
10.75¢	**multicolored** phosphored paper	21.00	8.00
	Plate block of 4	92.50	
	FDC *(Aug. 4, 1995)*		25.00

1995. Alice Paul Issue in the Great Americans Series recognized a leader in the U.S. movement to extend the right to vote to women (honored about the same time on a commemorative, CM1745) and one of the earliest proponents of the Equal Rights Amendment (1885-1997). Issue to pay 3-ounce First Class letter rate. *Intaglio by Banknote Corporation of America, perforated 11 1/4 x 11.*

1095 *Alice Paul*

1095		MNHVF	UseVF
78¢	**purple** phosphored paper solid tagging	1.75	.25
	Plate block of 4	8.00	
	FDC *(Aug. 18, 1995)*		2.25
	a. Dark violet grainy tagging *(April 1996)*	1.75	—
	Plate block of 4	8.00	

1995. Milton S. Hershey Issue in the Great Americans Series celebrated the chocolate manufacturer and philanthropist (1857-1945) whose orphans' home, established in 1909, has provided a home and education for generations of disadvantaged boys and girls. Issued to pay basic First Class letter rate. *Intaglio by Banknote Corporation of America, perforated 11 1/4 x 11.*

1096 *Milton S. Hershey*

1096		MNHVF	UseVF
32¢	**chocolate brown** phosphored paper solid tagging	.65	.20
	Plate block of 4	3.75	
	FDC *(Sept. 13, 1995)*		1.50

Pioneers of Aviation Series

1995. Eddie Rickenbacker Issue in the Pioneers of Aviation Series honored the racing car driver and automotive and aviation manufacturer (1890-1973) who earned his greatest recognition as a flying ace during World War I, in which he shot down 22 enemy aircraft and four observation balloons. Issued to pay the 1/2-ounce rate for letters to foreign nations other than Canada and Mexico — mail typically carried by air, in keeping with the subject of the stamp, but without the "airmail" designation — no longer needed on such mail, all of which is now typically carried by air. *Gravure by B.E.P., perforated 11 1/4. (See No. 1250).*

1097 *Eddie Rickenbacker*

1097		MNHVF	UseVF
60¢	**multicolored** phosphored paper	.75	.20
	Plate block of 4	6.00	
	FDC *(Sept. 25, 1995)*		1.75

1995. Contemporary Christmas Issue consisted of four Victorian-era designs — two depicting Santa Claus and two portraying children with toys — *produced in sheet, booklet and self-adhesive booklet and coil form. Offset by Sterling Sommer for Ashton-Potter (USA) Ltd., perforated 11 1/2.*

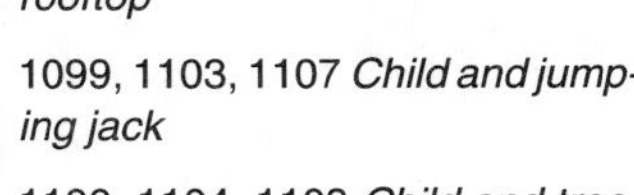

1098, 1102, 1106 *Santa on rooftop*

1099, 1103, 1107 *Child and jumping jack*

1100, 1104, 1108 *Child and tree*

1101, 1105, 1109 *Santa in workshop*

		MNHVF	UseVF
1098			
32¢	Santa on rooftop, phosphored paper	.60	.20
1099			
32¢	Child and jumping jack, phosphored paper	.60	.20
1100			
32¢	Child and tree, phosphored paper	.60	.20
1101			
32¢	Santa in workshop, phosphored paper	.60	.20
	FDC *(Sept. 30, 1995)* any single		2.25
	y. Se-tenant block or strip of 4 Nos. 1098-1101	3.00	
	Plate block of 4	3.50	
	FDC booklet pane		5.00
	n. Booklet pane of 10 (3 of Nos. 1098-99 & 2 of Nos. 1100-01)	6.50	
	n1. Booklet pane of 10 (2 of Nos. 1098-99 & 3 of Nos. 1100-01	6.50	
	v. Block or strip of 4, imperforate	—	

1995. Contemporary Christmas Coil Issue Constituted the first U.S. coil issue with multiple se-tenant designs. *Gravure for Avery Dennison, serpentine die cut 11 1/4 vertically.*

		MNHVF	UseVF
1102			
32¢	Santa on rooftop, phosphored paper	.60	.20
1103			
32¢	Child and Jumping Jack, phosphored paper	.60	.20
1104			
32¢	Child and tree, phosphored paper	.60	.20
1105			
32¢	Santa in workshop, phosphored paper	.60	.20
	FDC *(Sept. 30, 1995) any single*		2.25
	y. Coil strip of 4 (1 each of Nos. 1102-1105)	3.00	
	FDC coil strip of 4		5.00

1995. Contemporary Christmas Booklet Issue Gravure for Avery Dennison, serpentine die cut 11 1/4.

		MNHVF	UseVF
1106			
32¢	**multicolored** phosphored paper	.60	.20
1107			
32¢	**multicolored** phosphored paper	.60	.20
1108			
32¢	**multicolored** phosphored paper	.60	.20
1109			
32¢	**multicolored** phosphored paper	.60	.20
	FDC (Sept. 30, 1995) any single		2.25
	n. Pane of 20 (5 each of 1106-09 plus label	15.00	
	FDC pane of 20		15.50

1995. Midnight Angel Christmas Booklet Issue in the Christmas Series. *Offset by Banknote Corporation of America, serpentine die cut 11 1/2.*

1110, 1110A *Midnight Angel*

		MNHVF	UseVF
1110			
32¢	**multicolored** phosphored paper	.60	.20
	FDC *(Oct. 19, 1995)*		1.90
	n. Pane of 20 plus label	12.00	
	n1. Pane of 15 plus label (various layouts) (1996)	20.00	
	n2. Pane of 16 with one stamp removed, no label, various layouts	22.50	—
	v. Vertical pair, imperforate (no die cutting between)	—	
	FDC Pane of 20		15.50

Note: 1110n2 cannot be made from 1110n1 because the label is die cut and, if removed, leaves an impression of the die cutting.

1995. Midnight Angel Christmas Coil Issue *Offset by Banknote Corporation of America, vertical serpentine die cut.*

		MNHVF	UseVF
1110A			
32¢	**multicolored** phosphored paper	.75	.45
	FDC *(Oct. 19, 1995)*		1.50

Listing and prices for plate number coil strips and singles appear at the end of this definitives section of the Krause-Minkus catalog.

1995. Contemporary Christmas Booklet ATM Issue *Gravure for Avery Dennison, straight-line die cut.*

1111 *Children sledding*

		MNHVF	UseVF
1111			
32¢	**multicolored** phosphored lacquer on surface of stamps	.75	.45
	FDC *(Oct. 19, 1995)*		1.25
	n. Pane of 18	14.00	
	FDC Pane of 18		10.00
	nv. Pane of 18, untagged (error)	—	

1995. Traditional Christmas Issue adapted from an altar panel, *Enthroned Madonna and Child,* by 14th century Florentine artist Giotto di Bodone, was offered in conventional sheet form and booklet form. *Offset and intaglio by B.E.P.*

1112, 1113 Enthroned Madonna and Child *by Giotto*

		MNHVF	UseVF
1112			
32¢	**multicolored** phosphored paper, perforated 11 1/4	.75	.20
	Plate block of 4	3.50	
	FDC *(Oct. 19, 1995)*		1.90
1113			
32¢	**multicolored** phosphored paper, perforated 9 3/4 x 11	.75	.20
	n. Pane of 10, plate number next to LL stamp	6.50	
	FDC *(Oct. 19, 1995)*		1.90
	FDC booklet pane		8.50
	nv. Booklet pane of 10, miscut with a plate number next to UL stamp	25.00	

1995. Ruth Benedict Issue in the Great Americans Series celebrated a social anthropologist (1887-1948) whose 1934 text, *Patterns of Culture,* was influential throughout the world and who fought racism and intolerance through numerous other publications. Issued to pay the 1/2-ounce letter rate to Canada and the ounce letter rate to Mexico. *Intaglio by B.E.P., perforated 11 1/4 x 11.*

1114 *Ruth Benedict*

		MNHVF	UseVF
1114			
46¢	**carmine** phosphored paper (mottled tagging)	1.00	.25
	Plate block of 4	4.75	
	FDC *(Oct. 20, 1995)*		1.60

1996. American Kestrel Coil Issue in the Flora and Fauna Series. *Offset in gummed coils of 500 and 3,000 stamps by B.E.P., perforated 9 3/4 vertically.*

1115 *American Kestrel*

1115		MNHVF	UseVF
1¢	**multicolored** untagged	.25	.20
	Pair	.30	
	FDC *(Jan. 20, 1996)*		1.50

Note: First printed on the B.E.P. "D" Press with the colors of the plate number in the order of BYCM (black, yellow, cyan, magenta), a second version printed on the Optiforma press was printed in BCYM, and first seen in August 1996.

For sheet version see No. 1079. For version inscribed "USA 01" see No. 959.

1996. Flag Over Porch Issue Self-adhesive booklet with stamps showing "1996" in blue. Gravure by Avery Dennison, serpentine die cut 11 1/4.

1116 *Flag Over Porch*

1116		MNHVF	UseVF
32¢	**multicolored** phosphored paper	.75	.30
	n. Pane of 10	8.00	
	FDC *(Jan. 20, 1996)*		2.00
	FDC pane of 10		8.50

1996. Unisys Variable Denomination Issue Vended through postage and mail centers. Coil stamp showing "1996" in red at bottom-left corner of design. *Gravure by B.E.P., perforated 9 3/4.*

1117 *Shield and bunting*

1117		MNHVF	UseVF
32¢	**red & blue** denomination (.20 to $20.00) printed in black, tagged	.95	.50
	FDC *(Jan. 26, 1996)*		1.25

1996. Red-headed Woodpecker Issue in the Flora and Fauna Series. *Offset by B.E.P., perforated 11 1/4 x 11.*

1118 *Red-headed woodpecker*

1118		MNHVF	UseVF
2¢	**multicolored** untagged	.25	.20
	Plate block of 4	.50	
	FDC *(Feb. 2, 1996)*		1.50

1996. Space Shuttle Challenger Issue stamps show "1996" in bottom-left corner. *Offset and intaglio (panes of 20) by Ashton-Potter (USA) Ltd., perforated 11. No first day cancel. (Issued March 1996.) (See No. 1088).*

1119 *Space Shuttle Challenger*

1119		MNHVF	UseVF
$3	**multicolored** phosphored paper	6.00	3.00
	Plate block of 4	25.00	

1996. Jacqueline Cochran Issue in the Pioneers of Aviation Series memoralized the first woman to break the sound barrier, a highly skilled pilot who won the Bendix Transcontinental air race in 1938, and founded the Women's Air Force Service Pilots (WASP) program during World War II (1910-1980). Issued to pay the international postcard rate. *Offset and intaglio by B.E.P., perforated 11 1/4.*

1120 *Jacqueline Cochran*

1120		MNHVF	UseVF
50¢	**multicolored** phosphored paper	1.20	.40
	Plate block of 4	5.00	
	FDC *(March 9, 1996)*		2.00
	v. Intaglio black (inscriptions) omitted	150.00	

1996. Mountain Coil Issue in the Non-denominated Service-Inscribed Series. *Coil stamp with small "1996" in purple in bottom-left corner. Gravure by B.E.P., perforated 9 3/4.*

1121, 1122 *Mountains*

1121		MNHVF	UseVF
5¢	**purple & multicolored** untagged	.25	.20
	FDC *(March 16, 1996)*		1.25
	z. Tagged (error)		

1996. Mountain Coil Issue in the Non-denominated Service-Inscribed Series. Large "1996" in blue in bottom-left corner. *Gravure by J. W. Fergusson & Sons for Stamp Venturers, perforated 9 3/4.*

1122		MNHVF	UseVF
5¢	**blue & multicolored** untagged	.25	.20
	FDC *(March 16, 1996)*		1.25

1996. Eastern Bluebird Issue in the Flora and Fauna Series. Redesigned denomination. *Offset by B.E.P., perforated 11 1/4 x 11.*

1123 *Eastern bluebird*

1123		MNHVF	UseVF
3¢	**multicolored** untagged	.25	.20
	Plate block of 4	.65	
	FDC *(April 3, 1996)*		1.50

For version inscribed "USA03" see No. 960.

1996. Cal Farley Issue in the Great Americans Series recognized the founder (1895-1967) of the Cal Farley's Boys Ranch foster home near Amarillo, Texas. Issued to pay standard First Class letter rate. *Intaglio by Banknote Corporation of America, perforated 11 1/4 x 11.*

1124 *Cal Farley*

1124		MNHVF	UseVF
32¢	**green** phosphored paper (solid tagging)	.65	.20
	Plate block of 4	3.75	
	FDC *(April 26, 1996)*		1.75

1996. Flag Over Porch Booklet Stamp Issue *self-adhesive booklet stamps with small red "1996." Gravure by B.E.P., serpentine die cut 9 3/4 on two or three sides.*

1125 *Flag Over Porch*

1125		MNHVF	UseVF
32¢	**multicolored** phosphored paper	.75	.30
	n. Booklet pane of 10	6.50	
	FDC single *(May 21, 1996)*		2.00
	FDC booklet pane		8.50

1996. Flag Over Porch Coil Stamp Issue *self-adhesive coil stamps with small red "1996." Gravure by B.E.P., serpentine die cut 9 3/4 vertically.*

1126		MNHVF	UseVF
32¢	**multicolored** phosphored paper	1.00	.30
	Pair	2.00	.60
	FDC *(May 21, 1996)*		2.00

1996. Flag Over Porch Coil Stamp Issue *self-adhesive coil stamps with small red "1996." Gravure by B.E.P., serpentine die cut 11 vertically.*

1127		MNHVF	UseVF
32¢	**multicolored** phosphored paper	1.50	.50
	Pair	3.00	1.00
	FDC *(May 21, 1996)*		1.50

1996. Flag Over Porch Coil Stamp Issue *Self-adhesive coil. Serpentine die cut 11 1/2 vertically with large blue "1996."*

1128		MNHVF	UseVF
32¢	**multicolored** phosphored paper	.70	.20
	Pair	1.25	
	FDC *(June 15, 1996)*		2.00

On this issue, stamps are spaced apart on the 10,000 stamp coil roll.

1996. Eagle and Shield Non-Denominated Self-Adhesive Coil Issue *Gravure by J. W. Fergusson & Sons for Stamp Venturers, serpentine die cut 11 1/2 vertically.*

1129 *Eagle and shield*

1129		MNHVF	UseVF
10¢	**multicolored** untagged	.25	.20
	Pair	.50	
	FDC *(May 21, 1996)*		1.50

1996. Butte Coil Issue in the Non-denominated Service-Inscribed Series. *Self-adhesive coils with "1996." Gravure by J. W. Fergusson & Sons for Stamp Venturers, serpentine die cut 11 1/2 vertically.*

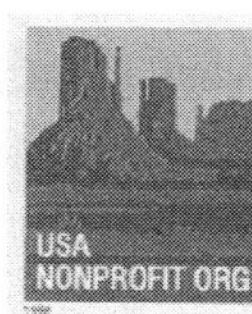

1130 *Butte*

1130		MNHVF	UseVF
5¢	**yellow, blue & red** untagged	.25	.20
	Pair	.50	.25
	FDC *(June 15, 1996)*		1.50

1996. Mountains Coil Issue in the Non-denominated Service-Inscribed Series. *Self-adhesive coils with "1996." Gravure by J. W. Fergusson & Sons for Stamp Venturers, serpentine die cut 11 1/4 vertically.*

1131 *Mountains*

1131		MNHVF	UseVF
5¢	**purple & multicolored** untagged	.25	.20
	Pair	.50	.25
	FDC (June 15, 1996)		1.50

1996. Automobile Coil Issue in the American Culture Series. *Self-adhesive coils with "1996." Gravure by J. W. Fergusson & Sons for Stamp Venturers, serpentine die cut vertically.*

1132 *Auto*

1132		MNHVF	UseVF
10¢	**black, brown & red brown** untagged	.25	.20
	Pair	.50	.25
	FDC		1.50

1996. Auto Tail Fin Coil Issue in the American Culture Series. Self-adhesive coils with "1996." *Gravure by J. W. Fergusson & Sons for Stamp Venturers, serpentine die cut 11 1/2 vertically.*

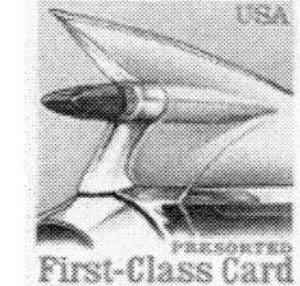

1133 *Auto tail fin*

1133		MNHVF	UseVF
15¢	**buff & multicolored** untagged	.35	.30
	Pair	.70	.60
	FDC *(June 15, 1996)*		1.90

1996. Juke Box Coil Issue in the American Culture Series. *Self-adhesive coils with "1996." Gravure by J. W. Fergusson & Sons for Stamp Venturers, serpentine die cut vertically.*

1134 *Juke box*

1134		MNHVF	UseVF
25¢	**orange red, bright yellow green & multicolored** untagged	.60	.30
	Pair	1.20	.60
	FDC *(June 15, 1996)*		1.90

Listings and prices for plate number coil strips and singles appear at the end of this definitives section of the Krause-Minkus catalog.

1996. Blue Jay Booklet Issue in the Flora and Fauna Series. *Self-adhesive Blue jay booklets and coils with "1996." Gravure by J. W. Fergusson & Sons for Stamp Venturers, serpentine die cut perforations.*

1135, 1136 *Blue jay*

1135		MNHVF	UseVF
20¢	**multicolored** phosphored paper, serpentine die cut 10 1/2 x 10 3/4 on three sides	.45	.25
	n. Pane of 10	4.50	
	FDC *(Aug. 2, 1996)*		1.50
	FDC Pane of 10		8.50

1996. Blue Jay Coil Issue in the Flora and Fauna Series. *Serpentine die cut 11 1/2 vertically.*

1136		MNHVF	UseVF
20¢	**multicolored** phosphored paper	.40	.20
	Pair	.80	.30
	FDC *(Aug. 2, 1996)*		1.50
	v. Coil pair, imperforate	1,000.00	

1996. Contemporary Christmas Issue included se-tenant sheets and self-adhesive booklets of four Christmas Family scenes and a generic Holiday Skater design for sale in ATMs offered in self-adhesive booklets only. Offset by Ashton-Potter (USA) Ltd., perforated 11 1/4.

1137, 1141 *Family at yule hearth*

1138, 1142 *Family trimming tree*

1139, 1143 *Dreaming of Santa*

1140, 1144 *Holiday shopping*

		MNHVF	UseVF
1137		MNHVF	UseVF
32¢	Family at yule hearth, phosphored paper	.60	.20
1138		MNHVF	UseVF
32¢	Family trimming tree, phosphored paper	.60	.20
1139		MNHVF	UseVF
32¢	Dreaming of Santa, phosphored paper	.60	.20
1140		MNHVF	UseVF
32¢	Holiday shopping, phosphored paper	.60	.20
	y. Se-tenant block or strip of 4 Nos. 1137-40	3.00	.50
	FDC *(Oct. 8, 1996)* any single		2.00
	Plate block of 4	3.50	
	FDC block of 4		4.25

1996. Contemporary Self Adhesive Booklet Issue *Offset by Banknote Corporation of America, serpentine die cut 11 3/4 x 11 1/2.*

		MNHVF	UseVF
1141		MNHVF	UseVF
32¢	Family at yule hearth, phosphored paper	.60	.20
1142		MNHVF	UseVF
32¢	Family trimming tree, phosphored paper	.60	.20
1143		MNHVF	UseVF
32¢	Dreaming of Santa, phosphored paper	.60	.20
1144		MNHVF	UseVF
32¢	Holiday shopping, phosphored paper	.60	.20
	n. Pane of 20 (five each of Nos. 1141-44) plus label	15.00	
	FDC *(Oct. 8, 1996)* any single		1.50
	FDC 1141-1144 on one cover		8.00

199106. Holiday Skaters Booklet ATM Issue in the Christmas Series. *Gravure by Avery Dennison, imperforate (die cut).*

1145 *Holiday skaters*

1145		MNHVF	UseVF
32¢	**multicolored,** phosphored lacquer on surface of stamps	.75	.30
	n. Booklet pane of 18	14.00	
	FDC *(Oct. 8, 1996)*		2.00
	FDC Pane of 18		14.75

1996. Traditional Christmas Issue in the Christmas Series. The traditional stamp taken from a detail of *Adoration of the Shepherds* by the 18th century Italian artist Paolo de Matteis, was offered in conventional sheets and self-adhesive booklets, supplemented by new stocks of the Midnight Angel stamps that had proven popular the previous year. *Offset and intaglio by B.E.P.*

1146, 1147 *Madonna and Child* from Virginia Museum of Fine Arts

		MNHVF	UseVF
1146		MNHVF	UseVF
32¢	**multicolored** phosphored paper, perforated 11 1/4	.70	.20
	Plate block of 4	3.50	
	FDC *(Nov. 1, 1996)*		1.80
1147		MNHVF	UseVF
32¢	**multicolored** tagged, serpentine die cut 10	.95	.30
	n. Pane of 20 plus label	15.00	
	FDC *(Nov. 1, 1996)*		2.00
	v. No die cutting (pair)	80.00	

No. 1148 is not assigned.

1996. Yellow Rose Issue in the Flora and Fauna Series got a renewed lease on life in a new color, issued in self-adhesive form convertible booklets of 20 and vending booklets of 15 and 30. *Gravure by J. W. Fergusson & Sons for Stamp Venturers, serpentine die cut die cut 11 1/4 x 11 3/4.*

1149, 1163 *Yellow rose*

1149		MNHVF	UseVF
32¢	**yellow & multicolored** phosphored paper	.75	.25
	n. Pane of 20 plus label	14.00	
	n1. Pane of 15 plus label *(Dec. 1996)*	12.00	
	pn1. Plate number single (bottom left corner of pane)	1.00	
	n2. Pane of 30 *(Dec. 1996)*	17.50	
	pn2. Plate number single (bottom right corner of pane)	1.00	
	FDC *(Oct. 24, 1996)*		2.00

1997. Flag Over Porch Booklet Issue *self-adhesive booklet stamps with red "1997." Gravure by B.E.P., serpentine die cut 9 3/4 on two or three sides.*

1150 *Flag Over Porch*

1150		MNHVF	UseVF
32¢	**multicolored** phosphored paper	.75	.30

		MNHVF	UseVF
	FDC *(Jan. 24, 1997)*		1.90
	n. Booklet pane of 5 plus label	3.50	
	n1. Booklet pane of 10 *(May 21, 1997)*	6.50	

1997. Flag Over Porch Coil Issue *self-adhesive coil stamps with red "1997." Gravure by B.E.P., serpentine die cut 9 3/4 vertically.*

1151		MNHVF	UseVF
32¢	**multicolored** phosphored paper	.75	.30
	FDC *(Jan. 24, 1997)*		1.90

1997. Mountain Coil Issue in the Non-denominated Service-Inscribed Series. *Self-adhesive, 3,000 stamp coil with "1997." Gravure by B.E.P., serpentine die cut 9 3/4 vertically.*

1152 *Mountains*

1152		MNHVF	UseVF
5¢	**purple & multicolored** untagged	.25	.20
	Pair	.50	.25
	FDC *(Jan. 24, 1997)*		1.25

1997. Juke Box Coil Issue in the American Culture Series. *Self-adhesive, 3,000 stamp coils with "1997." Gravure by B.E.P., serpentine die cut 9 3/4 vertically.*

1153 *Juke box*

1153		MNHVF	UseVF
25¢	**multicolored** untagged	.60	.20
	Pair	1.20	.30
	FDC *(Jan. 24, 1997)*		1.25

1997. Statue of Liberty Issue revised denomination version of the 1994 design for use at the 32¢ First Class domestic letter rate. *Self-adhesive vending booklets of 15 and 30 and convertible booklets of 20. Gravure by Avery Dennison, serpentine die cut 11 on two, three or four sides.*

1154 *Statue of Liberty*

1154		MNHVF	UseVF
32¢	**multicolored** phosphored paper	.75	.20
	pn. Plate number single (bottom left corner of pane of 5 or 6)	—	
	n. Booklet pane of 4	2.50	
	n1. Booklet pane of 5 plus label	3.25	
	n2. Booklet pane of 6 with or without plate number	4.00	
	n3. Pane of 20 plus label	13.00	
	FDC *(Feb. 1, 1997)*		1.25
	v. Serpentine die cut 11 1/2 x 11 3/4	40.00	
	n2v. Booklet pane of 6, with or without plate number	—	
	n3v. Pane of 20 plus label	—	

1997. Citron and Insect Issue *self-adhesive convertible-booklet stamps in two distinct sizes and die-cutting gauges, based upon two botanical prints made by Anna Maria Sibylla Merian during her 1699-1701 travels in Surinam. Gravure by Stamp Venturers.*

Design 20 x 27 mm, serpentine die cut 10 3/4 x 10 1/4 on two, three or four sides.

1155 *Citron and insects*

1155		MNHVF	UseVF
32¢	**multicolored** phosphored paper	.75	.20
	FDC *(March 3, 1997)*		2.00
	n. Pane of 20 (10 each Nos. 1155-56 plus label)	12.00	

1997. Flowering Pineapple Issue

1156 *Flowering pineapple*

1156		MNHVF	UseVF
32¢	**multicolored** phosphored paper	.75	.20
	FDC *(March 3, 1997)*		2.00

1997. Citron and Insect Booklet Issue Vending booklet, design 18 1/2 x 24mm, serpentine die cut 11 1/4 x 10 3/4 on two or three sides (Nos. 1157-58).

1157, 1159 Citron and insects

1157		MNHVF	UseVF
32¢	**multicolored** phosphored paper	.75	.20
	FDC *(March 3, 1997)*		2.00

1997. Flowering Pineapple Booklet Issue *design 18 1/2 x 24mm.*

1158, 1160 Flowering pineapple

1158		MNHVF	UseVF
32¢	**multicolored** phosphored paper	.75	.20
	FDC *(March 3, 1997)*		2.00

1997. Citron and Insect Booklet Issue *Design 18 1/2 x 24mm, serpentine die cut 11 1/4 x 11 1/4 x 11 1/4 x 10 3/4 (Nos. 1159-60) on two or three sides.*

1159		MNHVF	UseVF
32¢	**multicolored** phosphored paper	1.25	.50
	FDC *(March 3, 1997)*		2.00
	n. Booklet pane of 5 (one No. 1159 sideways, two each of No. 1157-58)	3.25	

1997. Flowering Pineapple Booklet Issue *design 18 1/2 x 24mm.*

1160		MNHVF	UseVF
32¢	**multicolored** phosphored paper	1.25	.50
	FDC *(March 3, 1997)*		2.00
	n. Booklet pane of 5 (one No. 1160 sideways, two each of No. 1157-58)	3.50	

Nos. 1159-60, which are die cut on all four sides, have a single irregular large serration near the middle of the right side created by die cutting.

1997. Juke Box Issue in the American Culture Series. *Self-adhesive 10,000- and 30,000-stamp experimental linerless (no backing paper) coils, manufactured by 3M Corp. and finished by Stamp Venturers, gravure, imperforate with simulated perforations (black circles) and black bars at top and bottom.*

1161 *Juke box with simulated perforations*

1161		MNHVF	UseVF
25¢	**multicolored** untagged	.60	.20
	Pair	1.20	.40
	FDC *(March 14, 1997)*		1.50

1997. Flag Over Porch Issue *self-adhesive 100-stamp experimental linerless (no backing paper) coils, manufactured by 3M Corp. and finished by Stamp Ventures, gravure, serpentine die cut 10 vertically.*

1162 *Flag Over Porch*

1162		MNHVF	UseVF
32¢	**multicolored** phosphored paper	.60	.20
	Pair	1.25	
	FDC *(March 14, 1997)*		2.00

Listings and prices for plate number coil strips and singles appear at the end of this definitives section of the Krause-Minkus catalog.

1997. Rose Issue in the Flora and Fauna Series. *Self-adhesive coil. Gravure by B.E.P., serpentine die cut 9 3/4 vertically.*

1163 *Yellow rose*

1163		MNHVF	UseVF
32¢	**yellow & multicolored** phosphored paper	.65	.20
	Pair	1.25	.35
	FDC *(Aug. 1, 1997)*		2.00
	v. Coil pair, imperforate	150.00	

1997. Christmas Issue For the first time in several years the Traditional and Contemporary Christmas stamps were issued in moderation — only one design of each, and in a total of four formats. The Traditional design depicts Sano di Pietro's *Madonna and Child with Saints* from the collection of the National Gallery of Art. *Offset by the Bureau of Engraving and Printing, in self-adhesive panes of 20. The Contemporary design depicts American Holly. Offset by Banknote Corporation of America in self-adhesive panes of 20, and self-adhesive booklets of 15 and 30. All with serpentine die-cut perforations on two, three or four sides.*

1164 *Sano di Pietro's* Madonna and Child with Saints

1164		MNHVF	UseVF
32¢	**multicolored** phosphored paper, serpentine die cut 10	.50	.20
	FDC *(Oct. 27, 1997)* single		2.00
	n. Pane of 20 plus label	8.50	

1165 *American holly*

1165		MNHVF	UseVF
32¢	**multicolored** phosphored paper, serpentine die cut 11 1/4 x 11 3/4	.50	.20
	n. Booklet pane of 4	2.50	
	n1. Booklet pane of 5 + label	3.00	
	n2. Booklet pane of 6	3.75	
	n3. Pane of 20 plus label	12.00	
	FDC *(Oct. 30, 1997)*		2.00

1997. Mars Pathfinder Issue this Priority Mail stamp commemorated the Pathfinder's Mission to Mars and the successful landing of July 4, 1997, and the subsequent deployment of the Sojourner rover. The view on the sheetlet is based on one of the first views sent back showing the rover and the Ares Vallis region of Mars. The stamp design incorporates hidden images, repeated "USPS" and "Mars Pathfinder July 4, 1997," visible with a decoder lens. *Gravure, Stamp Venturers perforated 11.*

1166 *Sojourner rover on Mars surface*

1166		MNHVF	UseVF
$3	**multicolored** phosphored paper *(15,000,000 printed)*	4.50	2.50
	FDC *(Dec. 10, 1997)*		4.50

1998. Mars Pathfinder Press Sheet Issue Uncut, but perforated press sheets of 18 subjects of the $3.00 Mars Pathfinder were made available in January 1998. There are vertical perforations between the three columns; thus the single subject measures 152mm wide, rather than the 146mm wide on the single imperforate examples of December 1997.

Varieties exist with perforations on left, right or on both sides. Once the stamp is removed from the pane, it is undistinguishable from No. 1166.

1167		MNHVF	UseVF
$3	**multicolored** phosphored paper (single)	15.00	—
	Uncut press sheet of 18	110.00	

1998. Henry R. Luce Issue in the Great Americans Series honored the magazine editor and publisher, founder of *Time, Fortune, Life,* and *Sports Illustrated.* Luce (1898-1967) also had interests in radio. Design is based on an Alfred Eisenstadt photo. *Intaglio, printed by Banknote Corporation of America, perforated 11.*

1168 *Henry R. Luce*

1168		MNHVF	UseVF
32¢	**lake** phosphored paper (grainy tagging)	.50	.20
	Plate block of 4		
	y. Pane of 20	10.00	
	FDC *(April 3, 1998)*		1.00

1998. Swamp Coil Issue in the Non-denominated Service-Inscribed Series. Nonprofit organization rate. *Printed by Sennett Security Products in 10,000 stamp coils, perforated 10 vertically.*

1169, 1169A *Swamp*

1169		MNHVF	UseVF
5¢	**multicolored** untagged	.25	.20
	Pair	.30	
	FDC *(June 5, 1998)*		1.00

1998. Swamp Self-adhesive Coil Issue in the Non-denominated Service-Inscribed Series. *Self-adhesive coil, untagged, serpentine die cut 9 3/4 vertically.*

1169A		MNHVF	UseVF
5¢	**multicolored** untagged	.20	.20
	Pair	.25	
	FDC *(Dec. 14, 1998)*		1.25

1998. Diner Non-Denominated Coil Issue in the American Culture Series. Presorted First-Class rate. *Printed by Sennett Security Products in 10,000 stamp coils, perforated 10 vertically.*

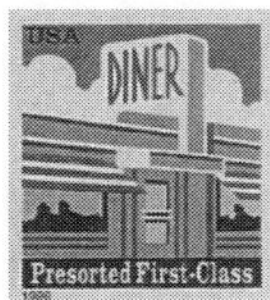

1170, 1177 *Diner*

1170		MNHVF	UseVF
25¢	**multicolored** untagged	.40	.20
	Pair	.80	
	FDC *(June 5, 1998)*		1.00

1998. Lila and De Witt Wallace Issue in the Great Americans Series honored the founders of *Reader's Digest* magazine. Later in life, Lila (1889-1984) and DeWitt (1889-1981) Wallace contributed millions of dollars to charitable causes and set up several charitable foundations. *Printed by Ashton-Potter (USA) Ltd., perforated 11.*

1171 *Lila and DeWitt Wallace*

1171		MNHVF	UseVF
32¢	**blue** phosphored paper (solid tagging)	.50	.20
	Plate block of 4	2.00	
	y. Pane of 20	7.50	
	FDC *(July 16, 1998)*		1.00

1998. Ring-necked Pheasant Coil Issue in the Flora and Fauna Series. *Self-adhesive coil, rolls of 100 stamps. Printed by B.E.P., serpentine die cut 9 3/4 vertically.*

1172, 1173 *Ring-necked pheasant*

1172		MNHVF	UseVF
20¢	**multicolored** phosphored paper	.40	.20
	Pair	.80	
	FDC *(July 30, 1998)*		1.00
	v. Pair, imperforate	—	

1998. Ring-necked Pheasant Booklet Issue in the Flora and Fauna Series. *Self-adhesive convertible booklet, printed by Avery Dennison, serpentine die cut 11 1/4 on two or three sides.*

1173		MNHVF	UseVF
20¢	**multicolored** phosphored paper	.40	.20
	n. Pane of 10	3.50	
	FDC *(July 30, 1998)* single		1.00

1998. Red Fox Issue in the Flora and Fauna Series. A hidden image silhouette of a walking fox is visible with a decoder lens above the rear foot. *Printed by Banknote Corp. of America, serpentine die cut 11 1/2 x 11 1/4.*

1174 *Red Fox*

1174		MNHVF	UseVF
$1	**multicolored** phosphored paper	1.50	.75
	Plate block of 4	10.00	
	y. Pane of 20	25.00	
	FDC *(Aug. 14, 1998)*		2.00

1998. Bicycle Coil Issue non-denominated presorted standard rate with large date. *Printed by Sennett Security Products in coils of 500 and 10,000 stamps with water-activated gum, perforated 10 vertically. (In April 2000 this stamp was issued in coils of 3,000 with no noticeable differences.)*

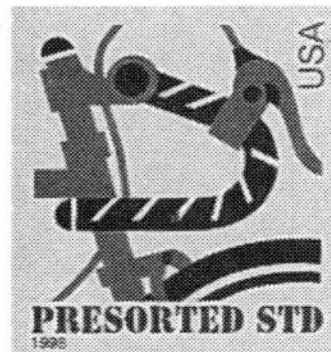

1175 *Bicycle*

1175		MNHVF	UseVF
10¢	**multicolored** untagged	.30	.20
	Pair	.60	
	FDC *(Aug. 14, 1998)*		1.00

1998. Bicycle Coil Issue presorted standard rate with small date. *Printed by Sennett Security Products in coils of 500 and 10,000, and B.E.P. in coils of 3,000 with no distinguishing markings, serpentine die cut 9 3/4.*

1176		MNHVF	UseVF
10¢	**multicolored** untagged	.30	.20
	Pair	.60	
	FDC *(Aug. 14, 1998)*		1.00

1998. Diner Coil Issue *In the American Culture Series self-adhesive 3,000 stamp coil. Printed by B.E.P., serpentine die cut 9 3/4.*

1177		MNHVF	UseVF
25¢	**multicolored** untagged	.30	.20
	Pair	.60	
	FDC *(Sept. 30, 1998)*		1.00

1998. Traditional Christmas Issue a Florentine Terracotta from about 1425 by unknown artisan. It is in the collection of the National Gallery of Art. *Self-adhesive booklet of 20, serpentine die cut 10 on two, three or four sides.*

1178 *Florentine Terracotta*

1178		MNHVF	UseVF
32¢	**multicolored** phosphored paper	.50	.20
	Pane of 20 plus label	7.50	
	FDC *(Oct. 15, 1998)* single		1.00

1998. Contemporary Christmas Issue festive holiday wreaths in a traditional, colonial, chili and tropical design. *Stamp measures 23 x 30mm. Serpentine die cut 11 1/2, on two, three, or four sides. Panes of 20, offset by Banknote Corporation of America.*

1179, 1183, 1187 *Traditional wreath*

1180, 1184, 1188 *Colonial wreath*

1181, 1185, 1189 *Chili wreath*

1182, 1186, 1190 *Tropical wreath*

		MNHVF	UseVF
1179			
32¢	Traditional wreath, phosphored paper	.50	.20
1180			
32¢	Colonial wreath, phosphored paper	.50	.20
1181			
32¢	Chili wreath, phosphored paper	.50	.20
1182			
32¢	Tropical wreath, phosphored paper	.50	.20
	FDC *(Oct. 15, 1998)*, any single		2.00
	FDC 1179-82 on one cover		4.00
	v. Block, red omitted	—	

1998. Contemporary Christmas Booklet Issue had wreathes in traditional, chili, colonial and tropical order and two distinct sizes. *Offset by Bureau of Engraving and Printing (1186n); or Banknote Corporation of America (1190n).*

Convertible booklet, 23 x 30mm, serpentine die cut 11 1/2 on two, three or four sides.

		MNHVF	UseVF
1183			
32¢	Traditional wreath, phosphored paper	.50	.20
1184			
32¢	Colonial wreath, phosphored paper	.50	.20
1185			
32¢	Chili wreath, phosphored paper	.50	.20
1186			
32¢	Tropical wreath, phosphored paper	.50	.20
	FDC *(Oct. 15, 1998)*, any single		1.00
	FDC 1183-86 on one cover		4.00
	n. Pane of 20 (5 each of Nos. 1183-86 plus label)	7.50	

Vending booklet, 21x24mm, serpentine die cut 11 1/4 x 11 1/2.

		MNHVF	UseVF
1187			
32¢	Traditional wreath	.50	.20
1188			
32¢	Colonial wreath	.50	.20
1189			
32¢	Chili wreath	.50	.20
1190			
32¢	Tropical wreath	.50	.20
	FDC *(Oct. 15, 1998)*, any single		1.00
	n. Booklet of 15	6.00	

1998. "H" Make-up Rate, USA White Issue showed a Weather Vane Rooster, a 1¢ stamp to be added to the 32¢ to take the new 33¢ First Class rate of Jan. 10, 1999. The inscription "USA" was in white. Pane of 50. *Printed by Ashton Potter, perforated 11 1/2.*

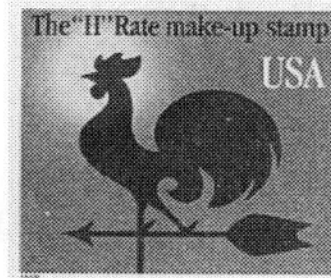

1191 *Rooster, white "USA"*

1191		MNHVF	UseVF
1¢	**multicolored**	.25	.20
	FDC *(Nov. 9, 1998)*		1.00
	Plate block of 4	.30	
	black omitted	—	

1998. "H" Make-Up Rate, USA Light Blue Issue Weather Vane Rooster with inscription "USA" in light blue. *Panes of 50, printed by Banknote Corporation of America, perforated 11 1/2.*

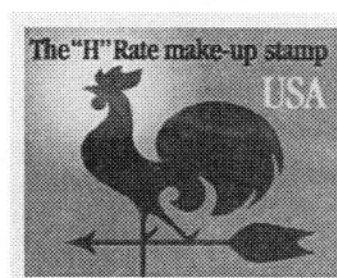

1192 *Rooster, blue "USA"*

1192		MNHVF	UseVF
1¢	**multicolored**	.25	.20
	FDC *(Nov. 9, 1998)*		1.00
	Plate block of 4	.30	

1998. Hat "H" First Class Issue used Uncle Sam's hat to continue the "alphabet primer" stamps. *Gummed pane of 50. Printed by Stamp Venturers, perforated 11.*

1193-1197, 1203 *Hat "H"*

1193		MNHVF	UseVF
33¢	**multicolored** tagged	.50	.20
	Plate block of 4	1.50	

1998. Hat "H" First Class Coil Issue *gummed coil rolls of 100 and 3,000. Printed by B.E.P., perforated 10.*

1194		MNHVF	UseVF
33¢	**multicolored** tagged	.50	.20

1998. Hat "H" First Class Booklet Issue *self-adhesive. Printed by Avery Dennison, serpentine die cut 11.*

1195		MNHVF	UseVF
33¢	**multicolored** tagged	.50	.20
	FDC *(Nov. 9, 1998)*		1.50
	n. Booklet of 10	4.00	1.00
	n1. Booklet of 20	7.00	

1998. Hat "H" First Class Booklet Issue *self-adhesive. Printed by B.E.P., with tiny date, folded booklet, serpentine die cut on two or three sides.*

1196		MNHVF	UseVF
33¢	**multicolored** tagged	.50	.20
	FDC *(Nov. 9, 1998)*		1.00
	n. Booklet of 20	7.00	

1998. Hat "H" First Class Coil Issue *self-adhesive coil roll of 100 or 3,000 stamps. Printed by B.E.P., serpentine die cut 10.*

1197		MNHVF	UseVF
33¢	**multicolored** tagged	.50	.20
	a. Backing paper larger than stamps	.50	
	FDC *(Nov. 9, 1998)*		1.00
	v. Coil pair, imperforate (no die cut)	150.00	
	v1. red omitted (coil pair)	1,500.00	
	v2. black omitted	—	

1998. Uncle Sam Issue Nine months after the first depiction of the venerable symbol of America on a stamp (CM1968i), Uncle Sam got his own definitive. *Panes of 20, serpentine die cut 10 1/2. Printed by Sennett Security Products.*

1198 *Saluting Uncle Sam*

		MNHVF	UseVF
1198			
22¢	**multicolored** tagged	.50	.20
	FDC *(Nov. 9, 1998)*		1.00
	Plate block of 4	1.50	
	y. Pane of 20	7.00	

1998. Uncle Sam Coil Issue self-adhesive, coil rolls of 100. Printed by B.E.P., serpentine die cut 10.

		MNHVF	UseVF
1199			
22¢	**multicolored** tagged	.50	.20
	FDC		1.00

1998. Mary Breckinridge Issue was the first in the Great Americans Series to be issued in a self-adhesive format. Breckinridge (1881-1965) founded the Frontier Nursing Service, which brought healthcare to remote Appalachian homesteads and communities.

Printed by Banknote Corp. of America, serpentine die cut 11 1/2.

1200 *Mary Breckinridge*

		MNHVF	UseVF
1200			
77¢	**blue** phosphored paper solid tagging	1.00	.20
	Plate block of 4	3.50	
	Pane of 20	16.00	

FDC *(Nov. 9, 1998)* 1.25

1998. Shuttle Landing Issue met the Jan.10, 1999, Priority Mail rate. The names of the six space shuttles cover the face of the stamp when viewed through a decoder lens *(Endeavour* is misspelled "Endeavor"). *Self-adhesive, printed by Banknote Corporation of America, serpentine die cut 11 1/2.*

1201 *Shuttle landing*

		MNHVF	UseVF
1201			
$3.20	**multicolored** tagged	4.00	2.75
	FDC *(Nov. 9, 1998)*		4.50
	Plate block of 4	15.00	
	y. Pane of 20	75.00	

1998. Shuttle Piggyback Transport Issue Jan. 10, 1999, Express Mail rate. The Piggyback Shuttle on a converted jumbo jet is how the powerless shuttles are transported from the landing field at Edwards Air Force Base in Cailfornia to the Kennedy Space Center in Florida to prepare for re-use. The names of the six space shuttles cover the face of the stamp when viewed through a decoder lens *(Endeavour* is misspelled "Endeavor"). *Printed by Banknote Corporation of America, serpentine die cut 11 1/2.*

1202 *Shuttle Piggyback transport*

DECODING THE CATALOG

The $3 definitive picturing the Space Shuttle Challenger was issued on June 22, 1995, to pay the then recently increased U.S. Priority Mail rate. Little remarked upon at the time that the stamp was issued was the presence of the year date "1995" below the bottom-left corner under the offset and intaglio printed stamp design. (Below the bottom-right corner is the inscription "Challenger STS-7." The year date was something of an oddity. It wasn't quite small enough to qualify as microprinting as the U.S. Postal Service (which has incorporated most of its microprinting in the printed stamp design) has conventionally used that term. Neither was it big enough to see with the naked eye, as the year dates have been on most U.S. definitives in recent years.

This would have made no difference, except that additional printings of the stamp produced the following March clearly showed a new date — "1996" — indicating that they had been made from new plates.

The "1995" and "1996" versions of the stamp also appear to show slight differences in the offset color of the earth on some copies. However, these may represent mere minor inking varieties.

The "1995" stamp (Minkus 1088) and the "1996" $3 stamp (Minkus 1119) both have the same catalog value at present. In the absence of additional printing information, it may be years before

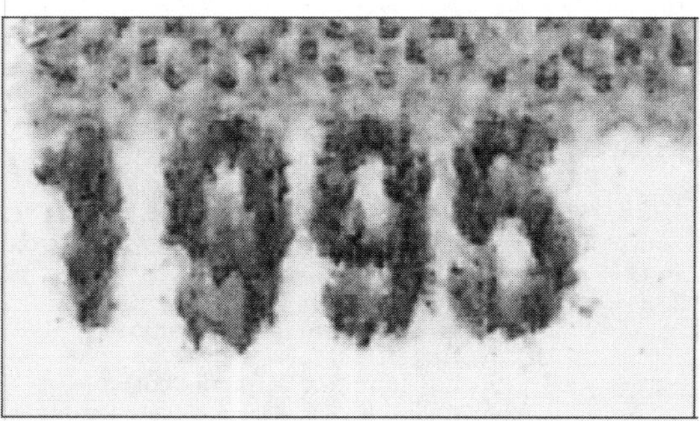

1088

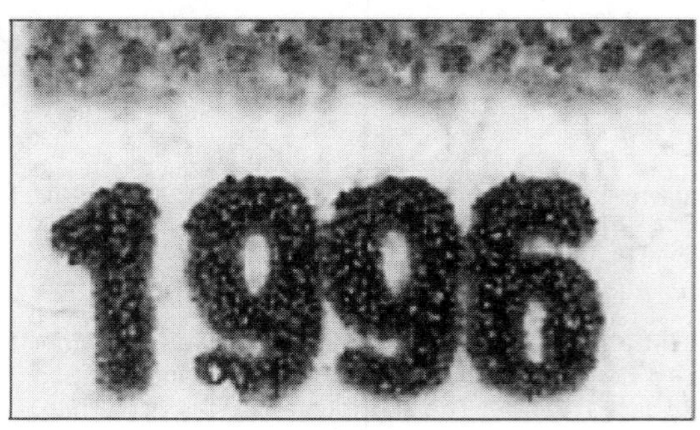

1119

1202		MNHVF	UseVF
$11.75	**multicolored** tagged	14.00	8.00
	FDC *(Nov. 17, 1998)*		16.50
	Plate block of 4	50.00	
	y. Pane of 20	300.00	

1998. Hat "H" First Class ATM Vending Issue *self-adhesive pane of 18 on thin paper, die cut, perforated 8. Gravure by Avery Dennison.n*

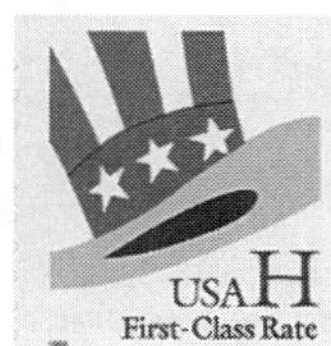

1203 *"H" Hat*

1203		MNHVF	UseVF
33¢	**multicolored**	.50	.20
	FDC *(Nov. 9, 1998)*		1.50
	n. Pane of 18	7.00	

1998. Eagle and Shield Coil Issue in the Non-denominated Service-Inscribed Series featured another redesign of "Bulk Rate" stamps issued in 1991, 1993 and 1996 but with new nomenclature, "USA Presorted Std." *Gravure.*

1204 *Eagle and shield*

1204		MNHVF	UseVF
10¢	**multicolored**	.20	.20
	Pair	.25	
	FDC *(Dec. 14, 1998)*		1.25

See U.S. Nos. 980 ("Bulk Rate USA"), 1011 and 1012 ("USA Bulk Rate") and 1129 ("USA Bulk Rate").

1998. Eagle and Shield Coil Issue in the Non-denominated Service-Inscribed Series. *Self-adhesive coil, serpentine die cut 10.*

1205 *Eagle and shield*

1205		MNHVF	UseVF
10¢	**multicolored**	.20	.20
	Pair	.25	
	FDC *(Dec. 14, 1998)*		1.25

1999. Flag and Skyscrapers Issue Artist Hiro Kimura recalled that, growing up in Japan, he imagined the United States as a land where the American flag flew before skyscrapers that reached to a cloudless sky. Designed by Richard Sheaff. *Glossy gummed panes of 100, gravure by Bureau of Engraving and Printing (200,000,000 printed), perforated 11 1/4.*

1206, 1207, 1208, 1209, 1210, 1211, 1212 *Flag and skyscrapers*

1206		MNHVF	UseVF
33¢	**multicolored,** phosphored paper	.50	.20
	Plate block of four	2.00	
	FDC *(Feb. 25, 1999)*		1.50

1999. Flag and Skyscrapers Coil Issue designed by Richard Sheaff. *Gummed coil rolls of 100, 3,000 and 10,000 gravure by the Bureau of Engraving and Printing (1,200,000,000 printed), perforated 10 vertically.*

1207		MNHVF	UseVF
33¢	**multicolored,** phosphored paper	.50	.20
	Pair	1.00	
	FDC *(Feb. 25, 1999)*		1.50
	v. Large date	.50	.20

1999. Flag and Skyscrapers Coil Issue designed by Richard Sheaff, from art by Hiro Kimura, Brooklyn, N.Y. *Self-adhesive coil rolls of 100, gravure by the Bureau of Engraving and Printing (7,000,000,000 printed), serpentine die cut 9 3/4 vertically, tiny red year date. Corners of stamps are square, backing is same height as stamps.*

1208		MNHVF	UseVF
33¢	**multicolored,** phosphored paper	.50	.20
	Pair	1.00	
	FDC *(Feb. 25, 1999)*		1.50
	v. Large date	.50	.20
	v1. Pair, imperforate	—	

1999. Flag and Skyscrapers Coil Issue designed by Richard Sheaff, from art by Hiro Kimura, Brooklyn, N.Y. Self-adhesive coils of 3,000 and 10,000, *gravure by the Bureau of Engraving and Printing (2,000,000 printed), serpentine die cut 9 3/4 vertically, tiny red year date. Corners of stamps are rounded, backing is higher than stamps.*

1209		MNHVF	UseVF
33¢	**multicolored,** phosphored paper	.50	.20
	Pair	1.00	
	FDC *(Feb. 25, 1999)*		1.50

1999. Flag and Skyscrapers Issue designed by Richard Sheaff, from art by Hiro Kimura, Brooklyn, N.Y. *Self-adhesive booklets of 20, gravure by the Bureau of Engraving and Printing, serpentine die cut 9 3/4, tiny red year date.*

1210		MNHVF	UseVF
33¢	**multicolored,** phosphored paper	.50	.20
	FDC *(Feb. 25, 1999)*		1.50
	n. Booklet pane of 10	8.00	

1999. Flag and Skyscrapers Issue designed by Richard Sheaff, from art by Hiro Kimura, Brooklyn, N.Y. *Printed in self-adhesive convertible booklets of 10 and 20 and vending booklets of 15. Gravure by Avery Dennison, serpentine die cut 11 on two, three or four sides, black year date.*

1211		MNHVF	UseVF
33¢	**multicolored,** phosphored paper	.60	.20
	FDC *(Feb. 25, 1999)*		1.50
	pn. Plate number single (bottom left corner of pane of 5)	.80	.90
	n. Booklet pane of 4	2.50	
	n1. Booklet pane of 5 plus label	3.00	
	n2. Booklet pane of 6	3.75	
	n3. Pane of 10	6.50	
	n4. Pane of 20 plus label	15.00	
	v. Serpentine die cut 11 1/2 x 11 3/4	.60	.20
	nv. Pane of 20 plus label	15.00	

1999. Flag and Skyscrapers Issue designed by Richard Sheaff, from art by Hiro Kimura, Brookly, N.Y. *Gravure in self-adhesive panes of 20, with narrow perforated tips at upper left of all stamps by Avery Dennison (500,000,000 printed), serpentine die cut 11, with red year date.*

1212		MNHVF	UseVF
33¢	**multicolored,** phosphored paper	.60	.20
	Plate block of 4	2.50	
	FDC *(Feb. 25, 1999)*		1.50
	y. Pane of 20	13.00	

1999. Flag in Classroom Issue designed by Richard Sheaff. *Printed in self-adhesive automatic teller machine booklets, serpentine die cut 8.*

1213 *Flag in classroom*

		MNHVF	UseVF
1213			
33¢	**multicolored,** phosphored lacquer on surface	.50	.20
	FDC *(March 13, 1999)*		1.50
	n. Pane of 18	12.00	

1999. Fruit Berries Issue in the Flora and Fauna Series. Designed by Howard Paine, Delaplane, Va., illustrated by Ned Seidler, Hampton Bay, N.Y. Pictured four luscious se-tenant illustrations of edible berries — blueberries, raspberries, strawberries and blackberries. The sequences of the designs are different in each of three formats. *Self-adhesive convertible booklet of 20, gravure by Banknote Corporation of America, (1,200,000,000 printed), serpentine die cut 11 1/4 x 11 3/4 on two, three or four sides.*

1214 *Blueberries*

1215 *Raspberries*

1216 *Strawberries*

1217 *Blackberries*

		MNHVF	UseVF
1214			
33¢	Blueberries, phosphored paper	.50	.20
1215			
33¢	Raspberries, phosphored paper	.50	.20
1216			
33¢	Strawberries, phosphored paper	.50	.20
1217			
33¢	Blackberries, phosphored paper	.50	.20
	y. Se-tenant block of 4 (Nos. 1214-17)	2.00	
	FDC block of 4		5.50
	FDC *(April 10, 1999)* any single		2.00
	n. Pane of 20 plus label	13.00	

1999. Fruit Berries Issue in Flora and Fauna Series. Designed by Howard Paine, Delaplane, Va., illustrated by Ned Seidler, Hampton Bay, N.Y. *Self-adhesive vending booklets of 15, gravure by Banknote Corporation of America, (153,750,000 printed), serpentine die cut 9 1/2 x 10.*

1218 *Blueberries*

1219 *Strawberries*

1220 *Raspberries*

1221 *Blackberries*

		MNHVF	UseVF
1218			
33¢	Blueberries, phosphored paper	.50	.20
1219			
33¢	Strawberries, phosphored paper	.50	.20
1220			
33¢	Raspberries, phosphored paper	.50	.20
1221			
33¢	Blackberries, phosphored paper	.50	.20
	FDC *(April 10, 1999)* any single		2.00
	y. Se-tenant block of 4 (Nos. 1218-21)	2.00	—
	FDC block of 4		5.50
	n. Booklet pane of 4 (Nos. 1218-21)	2.50	—
	n1. Booklet pane of 5 (1 each No. 1218-19, 1221, 2-No. 1220) plus label	3.25	—
	n2. Booklet pane of 6 (2 each Nos. 1218-19, 1 each Nos. 1220-21)	4.00	—

1999. Fruit Berries Coil Issue in Flora and Fauna Series. Designed by Howard Paine, Delaplane, Va., illustrated by Ned Seidler, Hampton Bay, N.Y. *Self-adhesive horizontal coils of 100, gravure by Banknote Corporation of America, (2,000,000,000 printed), serpentine die cut 8 1/2 vertically.*

1222 *Blackberries;* 1223 *Strawberries;* 1224 *Blueberries;* 1225 *Raspberries*

		MNHVF	UseVF
1222			
33¢	Blackberries	.50	.20
1223			
33¢	Strawberries	.50	.20
1224			
33¢	Blueberries	.50	.20
1225			
33¢	Raspberries	.50	.20
	y. Coil strip of 4 (Nos. 1222-25)	2.00	
	FDC *(Feb. 25, 1999)* any single		2.00
	FDC, strip of 4		8.00

Scenic America Series

1999. Niagara Falls Issue first in the Scenic American Landscapes Series, designed by Ethel Kesler, Bethesda, Md., from photo by Kurt Ross, North Tonawanda, N.Y. Paid a new rate for letters under one-half ounce to Canada and featured a view of the mighty falls on the border of the United States and Canada, over which 20% of the world's freshwater supply flows. *Self-adhesive panes of 20, gravure by Avery Dennison, (100,750,000 printed), serpentine die cut 11.*

1226 *Niagara Falls*

		MNHVF	UseVF
1226			
48¢	**multicolored,** phosphored paper	1.00	.20
	Plate block of 4	4.00	
	FDC *(May 12, 1999)*		2.00
	y. Pane of 20	20.00	

Note: With this stamp, the USPS began to add the silhouette of a jetliner next to the denomination on some stamps, indicating they paid an international rate for which air service was used. For many years, virtually all letters and cards have been moved by air. The last U.S. stamp to bear an "Airmail" designation was the William T. Piper Issue of 1993 (A132), and Minkus ceased to classify stamps as airmail after that issue. (See Minkus Nos. 1097, 1120 and 1250.)

1999. Red-headed Woodpecker Issue in the Flora and Fauna Series with "1999" date (see No. 1118). Designed by Michael R. Matherly. *Offset by the Bureau of Engraving and Printing, (100,000,000 printed), in gummed coils of 10,000, perforated 9 3/4 vertically.*

1227 *Red-headed Woodpecker*

1227		MNHVF	UseVF
2¢	**multicolored,** untagged	.25	.20
	Pair	.40	
	FDC *(June 22, 1999)*		1.50

1999. Justin S. Morrill Issue in the Great Americans Series honored a Vermont statesman who served 12 years in the House of Representatives and 32 years in the U.S. Senate. Morrill (1810-1898), who had to leave school at the age of 15, was the chief proponent of the federal college Land Grant Acts of 1862 and 1890, which spawned 105 colleges and universities. Designed by Howard Paine, Delaplane, Va., illustrated by Burt Silverman, New York, N.Y. *Self-adhesive panes of 20, intaglio by the Banknote Corporation of America, (100,000,000 printed), serpentine die cut 11 3/4 x 11 1/2.*

1228 *Justin S. Morrill*

1228		MNHVF	UseVF
55¢	**black,** phosphored paper, (solid tagging)	1.00	.20
	Plate block of four	8.00	
	FDC *(July 17, 1999)*		2.00
	y. Pane of 20	20.00	

1999. American Kestrel Coil Issue in the Flora and Fauna Series bore the same date (1996) as an earlier version (see No. 1115) but in larger type (1.5mm versus 1mm). *Gummed coils, offset by Bureau of Engraving and Printing, perforated 9 3/4 vertically.*

1229 *American Kestrel*

1229		MNHVF	UseVF
1¢	**multicolored,** untagged	.25	.20
	Pair	.50	
	EKU *(July 19, 1999)*		—

1999. Rio Grande Issue in the Scenic American Landscapes Series, designed by Ethel Kessler, Bethesda, Md., from photo by Bruce Dale, Arlington, Va., a view of the river in the southwestern United States from Big Bend Ranch State Park, Texas. The denomination was the rate to mail postcards to Mexico. *Self-adhesive panes of 20, gravure by Avery Dennison, (100,750,000 printed), serpentine die cut 11.*

1230 *Rio Grande*

1230		MNHVF	UseVF
40¢	**multicolored,** phosphored paper	.75	.20
	Plate block of four	3.00	
	FDC *(July 30, 1999)*		2.00
	y. Pane of 20	15.00	

1999. Billy Mitchell Issue designed by Phil Jordan, Falls Church, Va., illustrated by Paul Salmon, Burke, Va. Honored a former Army brigadier general who before World War I and beyond foresaw the potential of military air power and so irritated his superiors with his vitriolic and single-minded pursuit of the revolutionary concept that he was court-marshaled for insubordination and retired from the service in 1926. Mitchell (1879-1936) predicted, years before the occurrence, Japanese aggressiveness in the Pacific and warned of an attack on Pearl Harbor at 7:30 a.m. on a Sunday. *Self-adhesive panes of 20, gravure by Guilford Gravure, (100,750,000 printed), serpentine die cut 9 3/4 x 10.*

1231 *Billy Mitchell*

1231		MNHVF	UseVF
55¢	**multicolored,** phosphored paper	1.00	.40
	Plate block of four	4.00	
	FDC *(July 30, 1999)*		2.25
	y. Pane of 20	15.00	

1999. Coral Pink Rose Issue designed by Derry Noyes, Washington, D.C., illustrated by Ned Seidler, Hampton Beach, N.Y. Provided a popular flower image in convenient *self-adhesive convertible booklets of 20 and vending booklets of 15. Gravure by Armotek Industries for Sennett Security Products, (1,000,000,000 printed), serpentine die cut 11 1/2 on two, three or four sides.*

1232 *Coral Pink Rose*

1232		MNHVF	UseVF
33¢	**multicolored** phosphored paper	.50	.20
	FDC *(Aug. 13, 1999)*		1.50
	n. Booklet pane of 4	2.50	—
	n1. Booklet pane of 5 plus label	3.00	—
	n2. Booklet pane of 6 (plate number on reverse)	3.75	—
	n3. Pane of 20 plus label	12.00	—

1999. Uncle Sam Coil Issue designed by Richard Sheaff, Scottsdale, Ariz., illustrated by David LaFleur, Derby, Kan. A saluting Uncle Sam filled the need for a first-class second-ounce stamp with conventional, water-activated gum (see Nos. 1198-99). *Gummed coil of 3,000 Gravure by Bureau of Engraving and Printing, (150,000,000 printed), perforated 9 3/4 vertically.*

1233 *Saluting Uncle Sam*

1233		MNHVF	UseVF
22¢	**multicolored,** phosphored paper	.50	.20
	Pair	1.00	
	FDC *(Oct. 8, 1999)*		1.50

1999. Madonna And Child Issue designed by Richard Sheaff, Scottsdale, Ariz., from 15th century art by Venetian artist Bartolomeo Vivarini in National Gallery of Art in Washington, D.C. Painted in tempura on a wood panel. It is the second self-adhesive, two-sided convertible booklet from the USPS (the first: Tropical Flowers, CM2056-59, issued May 1, 1999). Booklet of 20, offset by the Banknote Corporation of America, (1,555,560,000 printed) (77,778,000 booklets), serpentine die cut 11 1/4 for two or three sides.

1234 *Madonna and Child*

		MNHVF	UseVF
1234			
33¢	**multicolored,** phosphored paper	.50	.20
	FDC *(Oct. 20, 1999)*		1.50
	n. Pane of 20	10.00	

1999. Greetings Reindeer Issue designed by Tom Nikosey, Bell Canyon, Calif. Featured a leaping stag in antique gold against four different colored backgrounds. *Self-adhesive panes of 20 in four designs, offset by the Banknote Corporation of America, (116,500,000 printed) (5,825,000 panes, 1,456,250 each stamp), serpentine die cut 11 1/4. No stamps have natural straight edges, background color block measures 26 by 19mm, and lower left corner begins between the "1" and first "9" of the "1999" date; on some corners, gold border appears notched.*

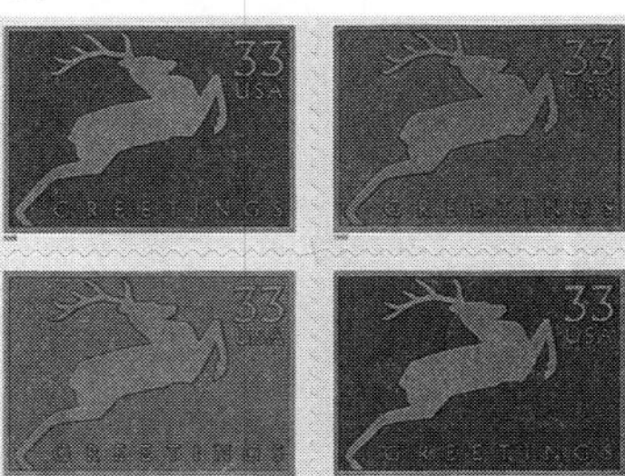
1235-1238 *Leaping reindeer*

		MNHVF	UseVF
1235			
33¢	**red** background, phosphored paper	.50	.20
1236		MNHVF	UseVF
33¢	**blue** background, phosphored paper	.50	.20
1237		MNHVF	UseVF
33¢	**violet** background, phosphored paper	.50	.20
1238		MNHVF	UseVF
33¢	**green** background, phosphored paper	.50	.20
	Plate block of four	2.00	
	y. Block or strip of 4 (Nos. 1235-38)	2.00	
	FDC *(Oct. 20, 1999),* any single		2.00
	FDC, block of 4		8.00
	y1. Pane of 20	10.00	

1999. Greetings Reindeer Booklet Issue designed by Tom Nikosey, Bell Canyon, Calif. *Self-adhesive convertible booklets of 20 in four designs, offset by the Banknote Corporation of America, (1,785,060,000 printed) (89,253,000 booklets), (22,313,250 of each stamp), serpentine die cut 11 1/4 on two or three sides. All but six stamps have at least one natural straight edge, the color block measures 25 1/2 by 18 1/2mm and lower left corner starts between the first and second "9" of the "1999" date, gold border appears thicker than on sheet version.*

1239-1242 *Leaping reindeer*

		MNHVF	UseVF
1239			
33¢	**red** background, phosphored paper	.50	.20
1240		MNHVF	UseVF
33¢	**blue** background, phosphored paper	.50	.20
1241		MNHVF	UseVF
33¢	**violet** background, phosphored paper	.50	.20
1242		MNHVF	UseVF
33¢	**green** background, phosphored paper	.50	.20
	y. Se-tenant block of 4 (Nos. 1239-42)	2.00	—
	FDC *(Oct. 20, 1999),* any single		2.00
	n. Pane of 20	10.00	
	FDC, block of 4		8.00

1999. Greetings Reindeer Vending Booklet Issue designed by Tom Nikosey, Bell Canyon, Calif. *Self-adhesive vending booklets of 15. Offset by Banknote Corporation of America, (118,125,000 printed) (7,875,000 booklets) (1,968,750 of each stamp), serpentine die cut 11 1/2 on two or three sides. All stamps have at least one straight edge, color block measures 20 1/2 by 7 1/2mm, lower left corner of color block begins between the "1" and first "9" of "1999" date.*

1243-1246 *Leaping reindeer*

		MNHVF	UseVF
1243			
33¢	**red** background, phosphored paper	.50	.20
1244		MNHVF	UseVF
33¢	**blue** background, phosphored paper	.50	.20
1245		MNHVF	UseVF
33¢	**violet** background, phosphored paper	.50	.20
1246		MNHVF	UseVF
33¢	**green** background, phosphored paper	.50	.20
	FDC *(Oct. 20, 1999)*		1.50
	n. Booklet pane of 4	2.50	—
	n1. Booklet pane of 5 plus label	3.00	—
	n2. Booklet pane of 6	3.75	—

1999. American Kestrel Issue in the Flora and Fauna Series. *Self-adhesive panes of 50 with "1999" date (see Nos. 1115 and 1229). Offset and intaglio by B.E.P. (1,000,000,000 printed), serpentine die cut 10 1/2.*

1247 *American Kestrel*

		MNHVF	UseVF
1247			
1¢	**multicolored,** untagged	.25	.20
	Plate block of four	.50	
	FDC *(Nov. 19, 1999)*		1.50
	y. Pane of 50	2.00	

1999. Ring-necked Pheasant Booklet Issue in the Flora and Fauna Series. *Self-adhesive vending booklets of 10, serpentine die cut 10 1/2 x 11 (8 upright stamps) or 10 1/2 (2 sideways stamps) (See No. 1173).*

1248 *Ring-necked Pheasant*

DECODING THE CATALOG

The 12 33¢ Reindeer stamps issued for Christmas use in three formats in 1999 have size and design differences that give them all major-variety status. One of the factors that determine a major variety is whether it is easily distinguished on a mint or used single stamp, and these stamps easily pass that test. All production of the Reindeer issue was done by Banknote Corporation of America (BCA) in self-adhesive sheet, convertible booklet and conventional booklet formats. All versions were produced by offset lithography on phosphored paper, using red, blue, green, violet and two shades of gold.

The most notable visual difference between versions is that the stamps produced in the conventional-style booklet are physically smaller than the other two. Die-cut perforations of the larger two types measure 11, while the small stamps measure 11 1/2.

Sheet version

The sheet version of the Reindeer Stamp has been assigned Minkus Nos. 1235 (red), 1236 (blue), 1237 (violet) and 1238 (green). There is no printing on the backside of the liner, and there is selvage surrounding the flat panes of 20. As a result, there are no natural straight edges that occur on these stamps. The simulated die-cut perforations measure 11.

Under long wave ultraviolet light (fluorescent), the gold deer glow slightly. The sheet version is the only one that glows. Another diagnostic is the positioning of the color block near the back hoof, in relation to the date. On sheet-version stamps, the left side of the color block is positioned between the "1" and first "9" in "1999." Both the top antler and rear hoof nearly (and sometimes do) break the color frame. The color block measures about 26 millimeters by 19mm. This makes the overall gold border appear thinner than on the convertible booklet.

When a cut stamp is used as a template, it is easy to see that the color block is larger on stamps from the sheet version. This also makes the gold frame line appear thicker.

Convertible booklet

At first glance, the stamps from the convertible booklet look nearly identical to those from the sheet. But several important distinctions warrant major variety status. The stamps are numbered 1239 (red), 1240 (blue), 1241 (violet) and 1242 (green).

The booklet itself, which contains 20 stamps, has printing on the back of the liner and removable strip down the center, so the pane can be folded. Because the pane is straight cut, there are one or two naturally occurring straight edges on all but six of the stamps. This is the easiest distinguishable feature for most single stamps. The simulated die-cut perforations measure 11.

Under long wave UV light, the reindeer turn almost black, in contrast to the glow found on the sheet version.

The color block positioning near the rear hoof also is significant. The vertical line of the block is positioned between the first and second "9" of "1999." In addition, there is a strong line of color between both the top antler and rear hoof and the frame line.

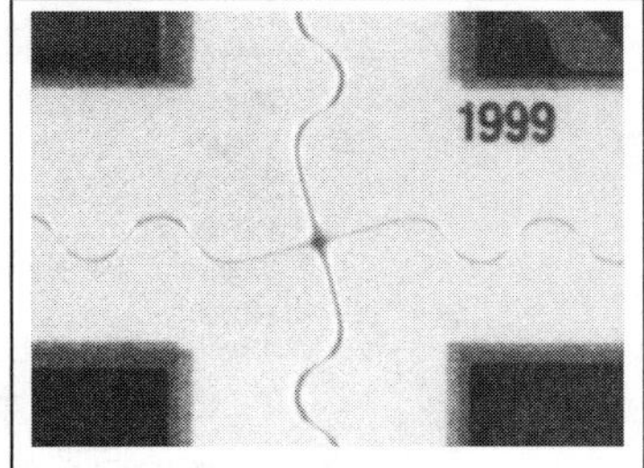

Two colors of gold used in the production of the Reindeer stamp give some stamps the appearance of a doubled frame line.

Both enlargements at top are from the sheet version of the Reindeer stamps. The vertical line of color falls between the "1" and "9," and there is a very thin line of color between the antler, rear hoof and outer frame. The convertible booklet (bottom) features a thicker line of color, and the vertical color line falls between two "9" figures in "1999."

The color block is smaller than on the sheet version. It measures only 25 1/2mm by 18 1/2mm. This difference is easily noted when a cut stamp is used as a template overlay. This size difference also makes the gold border surrounding the design appear much thicker on the convertible booklet than on the sheet version. This is probably the most obvious visible difference between the two.

Conventional booklet

Although there should be no confusion between this version and the other two types, here's a quick run-down of features. The stamps have been numbered 1243 (red), 1244 (blue), 1245 (violet) and 1246 (green). Because the pane of 15 consists of a long strip of two rows, all copies of the stamps have at least one naturally occurring straight edge, and the upper-right stamp has two. The booklet is trifolded and has appropriate printing on the liner's reverse. The simulated die-cut perforations measure 11 1/2, and the stamps are physically smaller than the other versions.

The remaining features of this issue are not diagnostic, due to the diminutive size of the stamps, but are worth noting as they are a bit of a hybrid.

Under long wave UV light, the reindeer turn almost black, much like the convertible booklet. However, the color block and date positioning match the sheet version (between the "1" and "9" of "1999").

There is a strong line of color between both top antler and rear hoof and the gold border. The size of the color block is 20 1/2mm by 17 1/2mm.

Gold features

As a side note, it would seem that gold-omitted errors on this issue would be likely to be easily overlooked. The gold frame, lettering, denomination and deer design were laid down before the color was overprinted. This is why the frame line looks thicker with the smaller color block of the convertible booklet. Why two golds were used remains a mystery. They don't seem to have been printed separately. In fact, the two appear to be printed on top of each other. Because two colors of gold (that are almost indistinguishable) were used for the same design area, even a slight misregistration makes the frame line appear to be doubled.

1248		MNHVF	UseVF
20¢	**multicolored,** phosphored paper, die cut 10 1/2 x 11	.40	.20
	v. sideways stamps, serpentine die cut 10 1/2	.40	.20
	n. Booklet pane of 5 (4 No. 1248, 1 No. 1248v at top)	2.00	
	n1. Booklet pane of 5 (4 No. 1248, 1 No. 1248v at bottom)	2.00	
	EKU *(July 1999)*		

2000. Grand Canyon Issue in the Scenic American Landscapes Series, designed for release in 1999, the stamp included a notation that placed Arizona's scenic natural wonder in Colorado. It was reprinted and released in 2000 and then found to have a reversed image. The rate covered the aerogram rate, the rate for printed matter up to 1 ounce to Mexico and the international 1/2 ounce letter rate to countries other than Canada and Mexico. Designed by Ethel Kessler, Bethesda, Md. *Self-adhesive, offset with microprinting USPS by Banknote Corporation of America, (100,000,000 printed), serpentine die cut 11 1/4 x 11 1/2.*

1249 *Grand Canyon*

1249		MNHVF	UseVF
60¢	**multicolored,** phosphored paper	1.20	.30
	Plate block of 4	5.00	
	FDC *(Jan. 20, 2000)*		1.50
	y. Pane of 20	25.00	

2000. Eddie Rickenbacker Issue in the Pioneers of Aviation series honored the World War I flying ace. Large "1995" date. (See No. 1097 of 1995.) *Gummed pane of 50, gravure by Bureau of Engraving and Printing, perforated 11 1/4.*

1250 *Eddie Rickenbacker*

1250		MNHVF	UseVF
60¢	**multicolored,** phosphored paper	1.00	.30
	Plate block of 4	6.50	
	y. Pane of 50	60.00	
	EKU (Jan., 2000) (printed 10/99)		1.50

2000. Fruit Berries Booklet Issue in the Flora and Fauna Series. Illustrated by Ned Seidler, Hampton Bay, N.Y., and designed by Howard Paine, Delaplane, Va. (See Nos. 1214-17 and 1218-21 of 1999). *In a two-sided convertible booklet format with "2000" date, blueberries, raspberries, strawberries and blackberries. Gravure by Banknote Corporation of America (2,850,000,000 printed). Serpentine die cut 11 1/2 x 11 3/4 on two or three sides.*

1251 *Blueberries;*

1252 *Raspberries;*

1253 *Strawberries;*

1254 *Blackberries*

		MNHVF	UseVF
1251		MNHVF	UseVF
33¢	Blueberries, phosphored paper	.60	.20
1252		MNHVF	UseVF
33¢	Raspberries, phosphored paper	.60	.20
1253		MNHVF	UseVF
33¢	Strawberries, phosphored paper	.60	.20
1254		MNHVF	UseVF
33¢	Blackberries, phosphored paper	.60	.20
	y. Se-tenant block of 4 (Nos. 1251-54)	2.40	—
	FDC *(March 15, 2000),* any single		2.00
	n. Pane of 20	12.00	
	FDC, block of 4		8.00

2000. Coral Pink Rose Booklet Issue designed by Derry Noyes, Washington, D.C., (see No. 1232 of 1999) in a two-sided self-adhesive convertible booklet of 20, *gravure by Sennett Security Products at American Packaging Corp., (350,000,000 printed). Serpentine die cut 10 3/4 x 10 1/2 on two or three sides.*

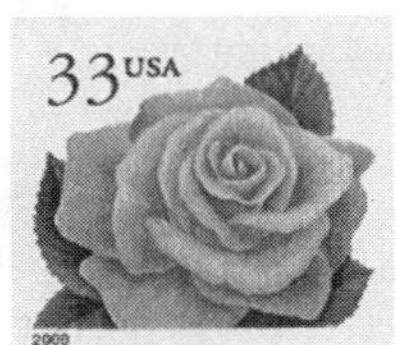

1255 *Coral Pink Rose*

1255		MNHVF	UseVF
33¢	**multicolored,** phosphored paper	.60	.20
	FDC *(April 7, 2000)*		1.50
	n. Booklet pane of 20	12.00	

2000. Fruit Berries Vertical Coil Issue was a linerless coil version of the design introduced in 1999 as part of the Flora and Fauna Series. Designed by Howard Paine, Delaplane, Va. Serpentine die cut 8 1/2 horizontally. (See Nos. 1222-25). *Self-adhesive coils of 100, gravure by Guilford Gravure. (330,000,000 printed).*

1256 *Raspberries;*

1257 *Blueberries;*

1258 *Strawberries;*

1259 *Blackberries*

		MNHVF	UseVF
1256		MNHVF	UseVF
33¢	Raspberries, phosphored paper	.60	.20
1257		MNHVF	UseVF
33¢	Blueberries, phosphored paper	.60	.20
1258		MNHVF	UseVF
33¢	Strawberries, phosphored paper	.60	.20
1259		MNHVF	UseVF
33¢	Blackberries, phosphored paper	.60	.20
	y. Strip of 4	2.40	
	FDC *(June 16, 2000),* any single		2.00
	FDC strip of 4		8.00

Distinguished Americans Series

2000. Joseph W. Stillwell Issue the first in the Distinguished Americans Series, honored Gen. "Vinegar Joe" Stillwell (1883-1946), who spent most of World War II in Asia. He was chief of staff for

DECODING THE CATALOG

A 60¢ stamp picturing World War I flying ace and commercial aviation mogul Eddie Rickenbacker (Minkus No. 1097) was issued on Sept. 25, 1995. The Bureau of Engraving and Printing produced the stamps with the copyright date "1995" printed in the bottom-left corner of the design.

After four years of service, the stamp was scheduled for replacement in summer 1999 by a 60¢ self-adhesive Grand Canyon definitive (No. 1249), release of which was postponed by an erroneous inscription that would have placed the canyon in Colorado, not Arizona. In the meantime, the Postal Service ordered an additional printing of the 60¢ Rickenbacker (No. 1250). These stamps, also printed by the BEP, were sent to post offices without public notice, and their presence was not detected until 2000.

The difference in the size of the copyright date on each stamp — 1.2 millimeters on the original, 1.8mm on the new version — means the stamps were printed from new plates, making them identifiably different and justifying separate major catalog listings.

The original stamps were printed on LP-748V paper, which does not fluoresce under ultraviolet light, whereas the later Rickenbakers were printed on LP-840 Universal paper, which has a "high bright" appearance, shining brilliantly under UV light.

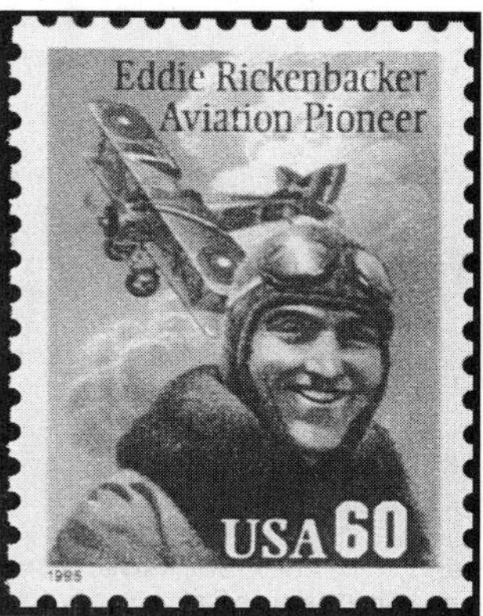

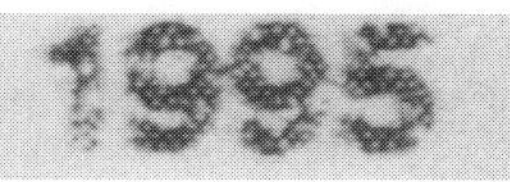

1097 1250

A reported modest "color variation" may be the result of this difference in papers, rather than any difference in the ink or printing. Examples of the new stamp may have a flatter, less crisp and colorful appearance than the originals.

Chiang Kaishek and commander of U.S. forces in China-Burma-India 1942-44. Designed by Mark Summers, Waterdown, Ontario, Canada. *Offset and intaglio by Banknote Corporation of America (100,000,000 printed, perforated 11.*

1260 *Joseph W. Stillwell*

		MNHVF	UseVF
1260			
10¢	**multicolored**	.20	.20
	Plate block of 4	.80	
	FDC *(Aug. 24, 2000)*		1.25

2000. Claude Pepper Issue in the Distinguished Americans Series. Pepper (1900-1989) served in both the House of Representatives and the Senate and became known for advocating programs for the elderly. When he died at age 88 he was the oldest member of Congress. Designed by Richard Sheaff, Scottsdale, Ariz., illustration by Mark Summers, Waterdown, Ontario, Canada. *Offset and intaglio in gummed panes of 20, by Banknote Corporation of America (56,000,000 printed), perforated 11.*

1261 *Claude Pepper*

		MNHVF	UseVF
1261			
33¢	**multicolored**	.50	.20
	Plate block of 4	2.00	
	FDC *(Sept. 7, 2000)*		1.50

2000. The New York Public Library Lion Issue featured a stylized image of one of the trademark stone lions, sculpted by Edward Clark Potter, that flank the 5th Ave. entrance to the New York Public Library, the largest in the United States. After the original design was revealed, the library insisted that its name be included on the stamp. Designed by Carl Herrman, Carlsbad, Calif., from the illustration by Nancy Stahl, New York, N.Y. *Issued in nonphosphored, self-adhesive coils of 10,000, printed by American Packaging Corp., Columbus, Wis., for Sennett Security Products (100,000,000 printed), die cut 11 1/2.*

1262 *New York Public Library Lion*

		MNHVF	UseVF
1262			
(10¢)	**multicolored**	.20	.20
	Plate No. strip of 5	1.00	
	FDC *(Nov. 9, 2000)*		1.50

2000. Blue Kestrel Issue in the Flora and Fauna Series had the identification "American Kestrel" in blue. It was issued without notice. *Self-adhesive panes of 50, offset by Banknote Corporation of America.*

1263 *Blue Kestrel*

		MNHVF	UseVF
1263			
1¢	**multicolored**	.20	.20
	Plate block of 4	.80	
	EKU *(Oct. 2000)*		—

2000. Farm Flag Issue featured an American flag against a farm field, with a tiny "USPS" over the doors on the shed in the background. Designed by Richard Sheaff, based on illustration by Hiro Kimura, Brooklyn, N.Y. No. 1264 *offset by Ashton Potter (USA) Ltd., with mi-*

croprinting "USPS" on shed, gummed panes of 20, perforated 11 1/2 (25,000,000 printed). No. 1265 *self-adhesive panes of 20, offset by Ashton Potter (USA) Ltd. with microprinting "USPS" on shed, die cut 11.*

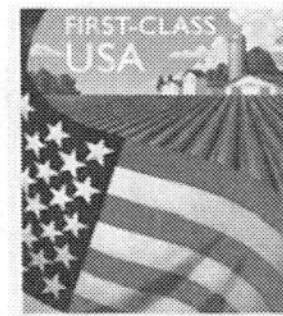

1264, 1265 *Farm flag*

		MNHVF	UseVF
1264			
(34¢)	**multicolored**	.50	.20
	Plate block of 4	2.00	
	FDC *(Dec. 15, 2000)*		1.50
1265		MNHVF	UseVF
(34¢)	**multicolored**	.50	.20
	Plate block of 4	2.00	
	FDC *(Dec. 15, 2000)*		1.50

2000. Farm Flag Booklet Issue had no tiny inscription over the doors on the shed in the background. *Booklet panes of 18, gravure by Avery Dennison, die cut 8.*

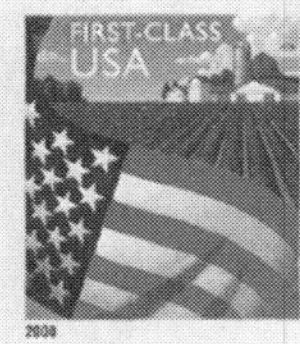

1266 *Farm flag*

		MNHVF	UseVF
1266			
(34¢)	**multicolored**	.50	.20
	Plate block of 4	2.00	
	FDC *(Dec. 15, 2000)*		1.50
	n. Pane of 18	9.00	

2000. Statue of Liberty Issue featured a view of the icon of freedom in a vertical-format, water-activated-gum coil. Designed by Derry Noyes, from photo by Paul Hardy, New York, N.Y. No. 1267, *gummed, vertical coil of 3,000, gravure by Bureau of Engraving and Printing, perforated 10 (200,000,000 printed).* No. 1268, *self-adhesive, vertical coils of 100, gravure by Bureau of Engraving and Printing, perforated 10 (1,000,000,000 printed).*

1267, 1268 *Statue of Liberty*

		MNHVF	UseVF
1267			
(34¢)	**multicolored**	.50	.20
	FDC *(Dec. 15, 2000)*		1.50
	n. Plate No. strip of 5	2.50	
1268		MNHVF	UseVF
(34¢)	**multicolored**	.50	.20
	FDC *(Dec. 15, 2000)*		1.50
	n. Plate No. strip of 5	2.50	

2000. Statue of Liberty Booklet Issue featured a view of the icon of freedom in horizontal-format, self-adhesive booklets. Die cuts on four sides of some convertible booklet stamps and a plate number on one of the vending booklet stamps help to distinguish them. *Booklets of 20, gravure by Avery Dennison (1,500,000,000 convertible booklets and 200,000,000 vending booklets), perforated 10 1/2.*

1269 *Statue of Liberty*

		MNHVF	UseVF
1269			
(34¢)	**multicolored**	.50	.20
	FDC *(Dec. 15, 2000)*		1.50
	n. Pane of 20 (convertible booklet)	10.00	
	n1. Pane of 20 (vending booklet)	10.00	

2000. Flowers Coil Issue featured close-up photos of four flowers — freesia (green backgound), Asian hybrid lily (red), cymbidium orchid (tan), and longiforum lily (purple). Designed by Derry Noyes from photos by Robert Peak, Winter Park, Fla. *Self-adhesive coil of 100, gravure by Banknote Corporation of America, die cut 8 1/2, (500,000,000 printed).*

1270-1273 *Flowers*

		MNHVF	UseVF
1270			
(34¢)	**multicolored**	.50	.20
1271		MNHVF	UseVF
(34¢)	**multicolored**	.50	.20
1272		MNHVF	UseVF
(34¢)	**multicolored**	.50	.20
1273		MNHVF	UseVF
(34¢)	**multicolored**	.50	.20
	FDC *(Dec. 15, 2000)*		1.50
	y. Strip of 4 (4 designs)	2.00	
	y1. Plate No. strip of 5	2.50	
	y2. Plate No. strip of 9	4.50	

2000. Flowers Booklet Issue featured close-up photos of four flowers — longiflorum lily (purple background), cymbidium orchid (tan), freesia (green), and Asian hybrid lily (red). *Self-adhesive vending booklet of 20 and convertible (two-sided) booklet of 20, gravure by Sennett Security Products (200,000,000 vending, 1,500,000,000 convertible), die cut 10 1/4 x 10 3/4; some convertible booklets die cut 11 1/2 x 11 3/4 on 12-stamp side or 8-stamp side.*

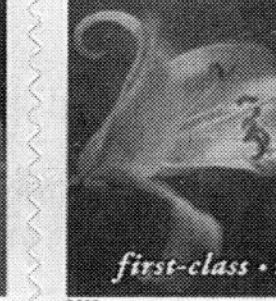

1274-1277, 1278-1281 *Flowers*

		MNHVF	UseVF
1274			
(34¢)	Longiflorum lily, **purple** background, 10 1/4 x 10 3/4	.50	.20
1275		MNHVF	UseVF
(34¢)	Cymbidium orchid, **tan,** 10 1/4 x 10 3/4	.50	.20
1276		MNHVF	UseVF
(34¢)	Freesia, **green,** 10 1/4 x 10 3/4	.50	.20
1277		MNHVF	UseVF
(34¢)	Asian hybrid lily, **red,** 10 1/4 x 10 3/4	.50	.20
	FDC *(Dec. 15, 2000)*		1.50
	n. Vending Booklet of 20	10.00	
	n1. Convertible Booklet of 20	10.00	
1278		MNHVF	UseVF
(34¢)	Longiflorum lily, **purple** background, 11 1/2 x 11 3/4	.50	.20
1279		MNHVF	UseVF
(34¢)	Cymbidium orchid, **tan,** 11 1/2 x 11 3/4	.50	.20
1280		MNHVF	UseVF
(34¢)	Freesia, **green,** 11 1/2 x 11 3/4)	.50	.20

1281		MNHVF	UseVF
(34¢)	Asian hybrid lily, **red,** 11 1/2 x 11 3/4)	.50	.20
	FDC *(Dec. 15, 2000)*		1.50
	n. Double-sided Convertible Booklet, 8-stamp side 11 1/2 x 11 3/4		
	n1. Double-sided Convertible Booklet, 12-stamp side 11 1/2 x 11 3/4		

2001. Statue of Liberty Coil Issue A denominated version of the self-adhesive coil stamp released in December 2000 for a mail rate increase. Designed by Derry Noyes, Washington, D.C., based on photo by Paul Hardy, New York, N.Y. *Gummed, vertically formatted, rolls of 3,000 and 10,000 with rounded corners and backing paper higher than the stamp, gravure by Bureau of Engraving and Printing on phosphored paper, serpentine die cut 9 3/4 vertically, tagged.*

1282 *Statue of Liberty*

1282		MNHVF	UseVF
34¢	**multicolored**	.65	.20
	Pair	1.30	
	FDC *(Jan. 7, 2001)*		1.50

2001. Capitol Dome Issue Featured a night-time photo of the Capital Dome taken by Robert Llewellyn, Earlysville, Va. The stamp paid the newly established Priority Mail rate. *Self-adhesive, panes of 20, offset with hidden image of a line, "Priority Mail," gravure by Banknote Corporation of America (800,000,000) printed on phosphored paper, serpentine die cut 11 1/4x11 1/2.*

1283 *Capitol Dome*

1283		MNHVF	UseVF
$3.50	**multicolored**	7.00	3.00
	FDC *(Jan. 29, 2001)*		7.00

2001. Washington Monument Issue Featured a photo of the Washington Monument by Patricia Fisher, Washington, D.C., with other distinctive Washington, D.C. landmarks in the background. Designed by Derry Noyes, Washington, D.C. The stamp paid the newly established Express Mail rate up to one pound. *Self-adhesive, panes of 20, offset with hidden image of a line,* "Express Mail," *gravure by Banknote Corporation of America (35,000,000) printed on phosphored paper, serpentine die cut 11 1/4x11 1/2.*

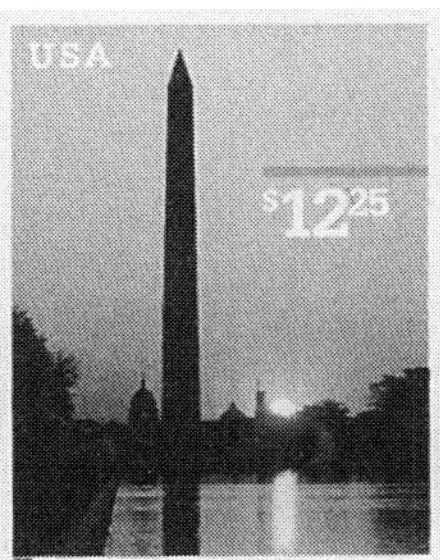

1284 *Washington Monument*

1284		MNHVF	UseVF
$12.25	**multicolored**	24.50	10.00
	FDC *(Jan. 29, 2001)*		24.00

2001. Farm Flag Issue a denominated version of the rate-change stamp issued late in 2000. *Gummed pane of 100, offset by Ashton-Potter (USA) Ltd., perforated 11 1/4.*

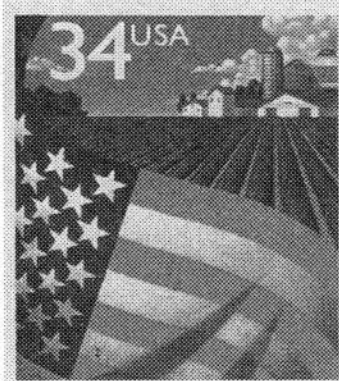

1285 *Farm flag*

1285		MNHVF	UseVF
34¢	**multicolored**	.65	.20
	Plate block of 4	2.60	
	y. Pane of 100	65.00	
	FDC *(Feb. 7, 2001)*		1.50

2001. Flowers Coil Issue in the Flora and Fauna Series, denominated versions of the rate-change stamps issued late in 2000- freesia (green background, Asian hybrid lily (red), cymbidium orchid (tan), and longiforum lily (purple). *Offset by Guilford Gravure for Banknote Corporation of America, serpentine die cut 8 1/2 vertically.*

1286-1289 *Flowers*

1286		MNHVF	UseVF
34¢	**multicolored**	.65	.20
1287		MNHVF	UseVF
34¢	**multicolored**	.65	.20
1288		MNHVF	UseVF
34¢	**multicolored**	.65	.20
1289		MNHVF	UseVF
34¢	**multicolored**	.65	.20
	y. Plate strip of 5	3.25	
	y1. Plate strip of 9	6.00	
	FDC *(Feb. 7, 2001)*		1.50

2001. Flowers Booklet Issue in the Flora and Fauna Series denominated versions of the rate-change stamps issued late in 2000 longiflorum lily (purple background), cymbidium orchid (tan), freesia (green), and Asian hybrid lily (red). *Gravure by Guilford Gravure for Banknote Corporation of America, serpentine die cut 10 1/4x10 3/4 on 2 or 3 sides.*

1290-1293 *Flowers*

1290		MNHVF	UseVF
34¢	Longiflorum lily, **purple** background	.65	.20
1291		MNHVF	UseVF
34¢	Cymbidium orchid, **tan**	.65	.20
1292		MNHVF	UseVF
34¢	Freesia, **green**	.65	.20
1293		MNHVF	UseVF
34¢	Asian hybrid lily, **red**	.65	.20
	n. Vending booklet pane of 20	13.00	
	n1. Convertible booklet of 20	13.00	
	FDC *(Feb. 7, 2001)*		1.50

2001. Statue of Liberty Coil Issue A water-activated-gum version of the coil stamp released in January 2001. *Gummed, vertically formatted, gravure by Bureau of Engraving and Printing on phosphored paper, perforated 9 3/4 vertically, tagged.*

1294 *Statue of Liberty*

1294		MNHVF	UseVF
34¢	**multicolored**	.65	.20
	Pair	1.30	
	y. Plate number strip of 5	3.50	
	FDC *(Feb. 7, 2001)*		1.50

2001. Statue of Liberty Coil Issue A second self-adhesive version of the coil stamp released in January 2001. *Vertically formatted, gravure by Bureau of Engraving and Printing on phosphored paper, with square corners and backing paper the same height as the stamp, serpentine die cut 9 3/4 vertically, tagged.*

1295 *Statue of Liberty*

1295		MNHVF	UseVF
34¢	**multicolored**	.65	.20
	Pair	1.30	
	y. Plate number strip of 5	3.50	
	FDC *(Feb. 7, 2001)*		1.50

2001. Statue of Liberty Booklet Issue a self-adhesive booklet version of the coil stamp released in January 2000. *Gravure, serpentine die cut 11 on 2, 3 or 4 sides.*

1296 *Statue of Liberty*

1296		MNHVF	UseVF
34¢	**multicolored**	.65	.20
	FDC *(Feb. 7, 2001)*		1.50
	n. Convertible booklet pane of 10	6.50	
	n1. Convertible booklet pane of 20	13.00	
	n2. Vending booklet of 20	13.00	

2001. Hattie Caraway Issue third in the Distinguished Americans Series, honored the first woman elected to the U.S. Senate. In November 1931, Caraway (1878-1950) was appointed to the Senate after the death of her husband, Sen. Thaddeus Caraway (D-Ark.), and on Jan. 12, 1932, she won a special election to the post and was re-elected in 1938. She left the Senate in 1945. *Designed by Richard Sheaff, offset and intaglio by Banknote Corporation of America, serpentine die cut 11.*

1297 *Hattie Caraway*

1297		MNHVF	UseVF
76¢	**multicolored**	1.50	.20
	Plate block of 4	6.00	
	FDC *(Feb. 21, 2001)*		1.75

2001. George Washington Booklet Issue featured a bust of the nation's first president by French sculptor Jean Antoine Houdon. The bust, housed at Mount Vernon, was also used as the basis for CM99 and (facing left) for the Washington-Franklin series. The stamp was issued on the 269th anniversary of Washington's birth. *Self-adhesive pane of 10 designed by Richard Sheaff, offset by Ashton-Potter (USA) Ltd., serpentine die cut 11 1/4x11 on 3 sides.*

1298 *George Washington*

1298		MNHVF	UseVF
20¢	**dark carmine**	.40	.20
	y. Pane of 10	4.00	
	FDC *(Feb. 22, 2001)*		1.50

2001. George Washington Booklet Issue Designed by Richard Sheaff. *Self-adhesive pane of 10, serpentine die cut 10 1/2x11 on 3 sides.*

1299		MNHVF	UseVF
20¢	**multicolored**	.40	.20
	y. Pane of 10	4.00	
	FDC *(Feb. 22, 2001)*		1.50
	y1. Pane of 10, 5 of No. 1298 at left, 5 of No. 1299 at right	—	

2001. Bison Issue glorified the majestic symbol of the American Wild West. *Self-adhesive pane of 20 designed by Carl Herrman from an illustration by Tom Nikosey, Bell Canyon, Calif., gravure by Avery Dennison (200 million stamps), serpentine die cut 11.*

1300, 1301 *Bison*

1300		MNHVF	UseVF
21¢	**multicolored**	.40	.20
	Plate block of 4	1.60	
	FDC *(Feb. 22, 2001)*		1.50

2001. Bison Coil Issue *Self-adhesive coil of 100 designed by Carl Herrman, gravure by Avery Dennison (600 million stamps), serpentine die cut 8 1/2 vertically.*

1301		MNHVF	UseVF
21¢	**multicolored**	.40	.20
	Pair	.80	
	Plate number strip of 5	2.25	
	FDC *(Feb. 22, 2001)*		1.50

2001. Art Deco Eagle Issue bronze-look illustration based on a 1930s lobby mailbox design. *Self-adhesive pane of 20, designed by Carl Herrman from an illustration by Nancy Stahl, New York, N.Y., gravure by American Packaging Corp. for Senett Security Printers (100 million stamps), serpentine die cut 10 3/4.*

1302 *Eagle*

1302		MNHVF	UseVF
55¢	**multicolored**	1.00	.20
	Plate block of 4	4.00	
	FDC *(Feb. 22, 2001)*		1.50

2001. Apple and Orange Issue in the Flora and Fauna Series showed the two fruits as a se-tenant pair. The stamps were designed at the same time as the 1995 Peaches and Pear Issue (Nos. 1089-90). *Self-adhesive convertible booklet of 20, designed by Ned Seidler, offset by Banknote Corporation of America, serpentine die cut 11 1/4 on 2, 3 or 4 sides.*

1303, 1308 *Apple*

1304, 1309 *Orange*

		MNHVF	UseVF
1303			
34¢	**multicolored** (Apple)	.65	.20
	FDC *(March 6, 2001)*		1.50
1304		MNHVF	UseVF
34¢	**multicolored** (Orange)	.65	.20
	FDC *(March 6, 2001),* either single		1.50
	y. Se-tenant pair, Nos. 1303-04	1.30	
	n. Booklet pane of 20 (10 each, 1303-04)	13.00	
	FDC *(March 6, 2001),* pair		2.50

2001. Nine-Mile Prairie Issue seventh in the Scenic American Landscapes Series featured a native prairie near Lincoln, Neb. While its design included the silhouette of an airliner adjacent to the denomination, representing the postcard rate to foreign destinations outside Canada and Mexico, it was not classified by the USPS as an airmail stamp. *Self-adhesive pane of 20, designed by Ethel Kessler, offset by Ashton-Potter (USA) Ltd., die cut 11 1/4x11 1/2, tagged.*

1305 *Nine-Mile Prairie*

		MNHVF	UseVF
1305			
70¢	**multicolored**	1.40	.30
	Plate block of 4	5.70	
	FDC *(March 6, 2001)*		1.60

2001. Farm Flag Issue a denominated version of the "first class" stamps issued earlier to meet the requirments of a rate change in early 2001. *Self-adhesive pane of 20, designed by Richard Sheaff, offset by Ashton-Potter (USA) Ltd., serpentine die cut 11 1/4.*

1306 *Farm flag*

		MNHVF	UseVF
1306			
34¢	**multicolored**	.65	.20
	Plate block of 4	2.60	
	FDC *(March 6, 2001)*		1.50

2001. Mount McKinley Issue eighth in the Scenic American Series featured the highest mountain in North America (20,320 feet), which is part of Alaska's Denali National Park and Preserve. *Self-adhesive pane of 20, designed by Ethel Kessler from a photo by John Eastcott and Yva Momatiuk, gravure by Avery Dennison (85,000,000), serpentine die cut 11.*

1307 *Mount McKinley*

		MNHVF	UseVF
1307			
80¢	**multicolored**	1.50	.35
	Plate block of 4	6.00	
	FDC *(April 17, 2001)*		2.00

2001. Apple and Orange Issue in the Flora and Fauna Series showed the two fruits as a se-tenant pair in a self-adhesive vending booklet of 20 (see 1303-04). The USPS did not announce the issue date, probably April 2001. *Designed by Ned Seidler, offset by Banknote Corporation of America, serpentine die cut 11 1/2x10 3/4.*

		1MNHVF	UseVF
1308			
34¢	**multicolored** (Apple)	.65	.20
1309		MNHVF	UseVF
34¢	**multicolored** (Orange)	.65	.20
	y. Se-tenant pair, Nos. 1308-09	1.30	
	4-stamp pane, Apple upper left	2.60	
	6-stamp pane, Apple upper left	3.90	
	6-stamp pane, Orange upper left	3.90	
	4-stamp pane, Apple upper left, plate No. B1111 on Orange at lower left	2.60	
	n. Booklet of 20 (10 each, 1308-09)	13.00	

2001. Acadia National Park Issue ninth in the Scenic American Landscapes Series, highlighted the park in Maine, the first national park established east of the Mississippi River. *Self-adhesive pane of 20, designed by Ethel Kessler from a photo by Carr Clifton, Taylorsville, Calif., offset with microprinting "USPS" by Banknote Corporation of America (100,000,000) serpentine die cut 11 1/4x11 1/2.*

1310 *Acadia National Park*

		MNHVF	UseVF
1310			
60¢	**multicolored**	1.20	.30
	Plate block of 4	4.80	
	FDC *(May 30, 2001)*		2.00

Plate Number Coil Strips

	Strip of 5	Strip of 3	Single Used
806			
1¢ Omnibus, (USA 1¢)			
Pl# 1, 2, 3, 4, 5, 6	.70	.60	.25
867			
1¢ Omnibus, (1¢ USA), block tagged			
Pl# 1, 2	.50	.45	.25
867pz			
1¢ Omnibus, (1¢ USA), phosphored paper			
Pl# 3	10.00	10.00	10.00
867zxm			
1¢ Omnibus, (1¢ USA), untagged, matte gum			
Pl# 2, 3	.60	.55	.40
867zxm			
1¢ Omnibus, (1¢ USA), untagged, low-gloss gum			
Pl# 3	.80	.75	.65
867zxs			
1¢ Omnibus, (1¢ USA), shiny gum, untagged			
Pl# 3	.90	.80	.80
1115			
1¢ Kestrel, (small date)			
Pl# 1111 (varieties)	1.00	.75	.30
1229			
1¢ Kestrel, (large date)			
Pl# 1111, 2222	.85	.50	.55
790			
2¢ Locomotive, (USA 2¢)			
Pl# 2, 3, 4, 6, 8, 10	.60	.45	.30
873			
2¢ Locomotive, (2¢ USA), tagged			
Pl# 1	.80	.40	.35
873zx			
2¢ Locomotive, untagged			
Pl# 2 (matte gum)	.70	.60	.50
Pl# 2 (shiny gum)	1.20	1.10	.65
1227			
2¢ Red-headed Woodpecker			
Pl# 11111, 22222	.80	.60	.60
800			
3¢ Handcar			
Pl# 1, 2, 3, 4	.70	.65	.50
883			
3¢ Conestoga Wagon, tagged			
Pl# 1	.80	.70	.40
883zxm			
3¢ Conestoga Wagon, untagged, matte gum			
Pl# 2, 3	1.25	1.00	.90

	Strip of 5	Strip of 3	Single Used
883zxs			
3¢ Conestoga Wagon, untagged, shiny gum			
Pl# 3	1.25	1.00	.85
Pl# 6	2.25	1.60	1.00
883zxs			
3¢ Conestoga Wagon, untagged, low gloss gum			
Pl# 5	1.25	1.00	.85
843			
3.4¢ School Bus			
Pl# 1, 2	.90	.80	.75
843zx			
3.4¢ School Bus, Nonprofit Org., untagged			
Pl# 1, 2	4.25	4.25	3.50
791			
4¢ Stagecoach, title 19 1/5mm long			
Pl# 1, 2, 3, 4	1.00	.85	.60
Pl# 5, 6	2.00	2.00	2.00
791zx			
4¢ Stagecoach, Nonprofit Org., untagged			
Pl# 3, 4, 5, 6	5.00	5.00	4.25
868			
4¢ Stagecoach, title 17mm long, block tagged			
Pl# 1	1.20	1.00	.75
868z			
4¢ Stagecoach, overall tagging			
Pl# 1	11.00	10.50	5.00
943			
4¢ Steam Carriage, overall tagged			
Pl# 1	1.00	1.00	.85
943zx			
4¢ Steam Carriage, untagged			
Pl# 1	1.00	1.00	.50
846			
4.9¢ Buckboard			
Pl# 3, 4	1.00	.90	.75
846zx			
4.9¢ Buckboard, Nonprofit Org., untagged			
Pl# 1, 2, 3, 4, 5, 6	1.50	1.40	1.00
808			
5¢ Motorcycle			
Pl# 1, 2, 3, 4	.90	.80	.75
808zo			
5¢ Motorcycle (untagged error)			
Pl# 1, 2	250.00		

	Strip of 5	Strip of 3	Single Used
879			
5¢ Milk Wagon			
Pl# 1	.90	.75	.50
931			
5¢ Circus Wagon, Intaglio, Tagged			
Pl# 1	1.20	1.00	.85
931z			
5¢ Circus Wagon, untagged			
Pl# 1 (matte gum)	1.20	1.00	1.00
Pl# 2 (low gloss gum)	1.40	1.30	1.20
955			
5¢ Canoe, Brown, Intaglio			
Pl# 1, 2, 3	1.40	1.30	1.00
979			
5¢ Canoe, Red, Gravure			
Pl# S11	1.25	1.25	1.00
Pl# S11, low gloss gum	10.00	9.75	-
1007			
5¢ Circus Wagon, Gravure			
Pl# Al, A2	1.50	1.45	1.00
Pl# A3, luminescent ink	2.00	2.00	2.00
1069			
(5¢) "G" Non Profit			
Pl# A11111, A21111	1.85	1.70	1.35
1070			
(5¢) Butte Non Profit			
Pl# S111, S222, S333	1.40	1.40	1.00
1077			
5¢ Circus Wagon ("¢" sign)			
Pl# S1, S2	1.45	1.35	1.25
1121			
(5¢) Mountain, BEP			
Pl# 11111	1.50	1.50	1.00
1121z			
(5¢) Mountain, BEP			
Tagged error #11111	84.00	80.00	70.00
1122			
(5¢) Mountain, SVS			
Pl# S111	1.75	1.50	1.00
1130			
(5¢) Butte Non Profit S/A			
Pl# S111	1.40	1.40	1.10
1169			
(5¢) Swamp			
Pl# S111	1.40	1.40	1.00
799			
5.2¢ Sleigh			
Pl# 1, 2	8.00	5.50	5.00
Pl# 3	220.00	170.00	150.00
Pl# 5	170.00	145.00	140.00
799zx			
5.2¢ Sleigh, untagged, precancel			
Pl# 1, 2, 3, 5	10.00	9.50	3.00
Pl# 4, 6	12.50	12.00	10.00
906			
5.3¢ Elevator			
Pl# 1	1.25	1.00	.80
865			
5.5¢ Star Route Truck			
Pl# 1	1.50	1.50	1.25
865zx			
5.5¢ Star Route Truck, Nonprofit Org., untagged			
Pl# 1	1.75	1.65	1.00
Pl# 2	2.25	2.25	1.75
787			
5.9¢ Bicycle			
Pl# 3, 4	12.25	7.00	5.75
787zx			
5.9¢ Bicycle, precancel, untagged			
Pl# 3, 4	30.00	24.00	5.50
Pl# 5, 6	95.00	85.00	80.00
841			
6¢ Tricycle			
Pl# 1	1.50	1.40	1.00
841zx			
6¢ Tricycle, Nonprofit Org., untagged			
Pl# 1	1.70	1.50	1.00
Pl# 2	7.00	6.75	2.75
870			
7.1¢ Tractor			
Pl# 1	2.20	2.00	1.50
870zx			
7.1¢ Tractor, Nonprofit Org., untagged			
Pl# 1	2.90	3.00	1.75
870zx1			
7.1¢ Tractor, Zip + 4, untagged			
Pl# 1	1.50	1.50	1.50
814			
7.4¢ Baby Buggy			
Pl# 2	8.20	8.00	6.00
814zx			
7.4¢ Baby Buggy, Blk. Rt. Car. Rt. Sort, untagged			
Pl# 2	5.00	5.00	4.00
903			
7.6¢ Carreta			
Pl# 1, 2	2.20	2.00	1.50
Pl# 3	6.00	5.50	4.00

	Strip of 5	Strip of 3	Single Used
845			
8.3¢ Ambulance, title 18 1/2mm long			
Pl# 1, 2	1.45	1.40	1.00
845zx			
8.3¢ Ambulance, Blk. Rt., untagged			
Pl# 1, 2	1.50	1.45	1.25
Pl# 3, 4	4.50	4.50	3.50
845A			
8.3¢ Ambulance, Blk. Rt. title 18mm long, untagged			
Pl# 1	4.75	4.50	3.00
Pl# 2	5.75	5.50	4.50
901			
8.4¢ Wheel Chair			
Pl# 1, 2	2.00	1.75	1.00
Pl# 3	12.50	12.00	5.50
869			
8.5¢ Tow Truck			
Pl# 1	2.90	2.50	2.25
869zx			
8.5¢ Tow Truck, Nonprofit Org., untagged			
Pl# 1	2.40	2.25	2.00
Pl# 2	12.00	11.50	8.00
778			
9.3¢ Mail Wagon			
Pl# 1, 2	12.00	7.00	7.00
Pl# 3, 4	31.00	20.00	17.50
Pl# 5, 6	275.00	250.00	200.00
778zx			
9.3¢ Mail Wagon, Bulk Rate, untagged			
Pl# 1	11.50	8.00	7.50
Pl# 2	10.00	9.50	10.00
Pl# 3	25.50	21.00	12.00
Pl# 4	18.00	16.00	10.00
Pl# 5, 6	2.80	2.75	1.75
Pl# 8	245.00	240.00	225.00
874			
10¢ Canal Boat, block tagged			
Pl# 1	2.25	2.00	1.00
874pz			
10¢ Canal Boat, phosphored paper, also shiny gum			
Pl# 1, 2	3.25	3.00	2.50
Pl# 3, 4	3.65	3.65	2.00
Pl# 5 (low gloss gum)	3.65	—	—
874zm			
10¢ Canal Boat, overall tagged, matte gum			
Pl# 1	3.70	3.60	3.25
874zs			
10¢ Canal Boat, overall tagging, shiny gum			
Pl# 4	3.70	3.60	2.75

	Strip of 5	Strip of 3	Single Used
954			
10¢ Tractor Trailer, Intaglio			
Pl# 1	2.00	2.00	1.50
980			
(10¢) Eagle & Shield			
A11111, A11112, A21112, A22112, A22113, A43324, A43324, A43326, A43334, A53335, A43335,	2.40	2.30	2.00
A12213	17.00	17.00	17.00
A21113, A33335, A43426, A54444, A54445, A33333	2.70	2.70	2.70
A34424, A34426	4.00	3.50	3.00
A32333	275.00	265.00	265.00
A33334	85.00	84.00	78.00
A77777, A88888, A88889, A89999, A99998, A99999	2.80	2.75	2.25
A1010101010, A1011101011, A1011101012, A1110101010, A1110111010, A1111101010, A1111111010, A1411101010, A1411101011, A1412111110, A1412111111	3.00	2.80	2.00
A1011101010	5.00	4.75	3.50
A1211101010	4.80	4.75	4.50
A1110101011	11.70	11.50	7.00
1011			
(10¢) Eagle & Shield, BEP, shiny gum			
Pl# 11111, 22221, 22222	3.00	2.80	1.75
(10¢) Eagle & Shield, low gloss			
Pl# 11111, 22222, 33333, 44444	2.95	2.90	1.75
1011z			
(10¢) Eagle & Shield, tagged			
Pl# 11111, 22221	12.50	12.00	12.00
Pl# 22222	290.00	—	285.00
1012			
(10¢) Eagle & Shield, SVS			
Pl# S11111, S22222	3.00	2.50	2.00
Pl# S22222 (shiny gum)	3.20	2.90	1.75
1042			
10¢ Tractor Trailer, Gravure			
Pl# 11, 22	2.10	2.00	1.80
1071			
(10¢) Automobile Hood, Bulk rate			
Pl# S111, S222, S333	2.50	2.00	1.75
1175			
(10¢) Bicycle			
Pl# S111	2.50	2.50	1.75
1204			
(10¢) Eagle & Shield			
Pl# 11111, 22222	2.50	2.50	1.75

	Strip of 5	Strip of 3	Single Used
837			
10.1¢ Oil Wagon			
Pl# 1	2.50	2.40	2.00
837zx			
10.1¢ Oil Wagon, Black precancel, untagged			
Pl# 1, 2	2.50	2.40	1.50
837zx1			
10.1¢ Oil Wagon, Red precancel, untagged			
Pl# 2, 3	2.25	2.00	2.00
788			
10.9¢ Hansom Cab			
Pl# 1, 2	29.00	15.00	12.00
788zx			
10.9¢ Hansom Cab, Precancel, untagged			
Pl# 1, 2	29.00	20.00	8.75
Pl# 3, 4	335.00	300.00	75.00
812			
11¢ Caboose			
Pl# 1	3.80	3.60	3.00
812zx			
11¢ Caboose, untagged, precanceled			
Pl# 1	3.20	3.10	2.75
812zx1			
11¢ Caboose, untagged, unprecanceled			
Pl# 2	2.75	2.30	2.00
844			
11¢ Stutz Bearcat			
Pl# 1, 2, 3, 4	1.40	1.35	1.00
831			
12¢ Stanley Steamer, title 18mm long			
Pl# 1, 2	2.20	2.00	1.50
831zx			
12¢ Stanley Steamer, precancel, untagged			
Pl# 1, 2	2.40	2.10	1.75
831A			
12¢ Stanley Steamer, title 17 1/2mm long, precancel, untagged			
Pl# 1	20.00	18.00	17.00
838			
12.5¢ Pushcart			
Pl# 1	3.00	2.50	2.25
Pl# 2	4.60	4.50	3.00
838zx			
12.5¢ Pushcart, precancel, untagged			
Pl# 1	3.00	2.70	1.75
Pl# 2	3.60	3.30	3.00
914			
13¢ Patrol Wagon			
Pl# 1	3.25	3.00	2.00
900			
13.2¢ Coal Car			
Pl# 1, 2	2.70	2.60	1.50

	Strip of 5	Strip of 3	Single Used
827			
14¢ Iceboat, overall tagged			
Pl# 1, 2, 3, 4	2.25	2.00	1.50
827A			
14¢ Iceboat, block tagged			
Pl# 2	3.25	3.10	2.50
899			
15¢ Tugboat, block tagged			
Pl# 1	2.00	1.80	1.50
Pl# 2	2.50	2.25	1.50
899z			
15¢ Tugboat, overall tagged			
Pl# 2	3.50	3.00	2.75
899z1			
15¢ Tugboat - untagged			
Pl# 2	170.00	—	—
1072			
(15¢) Tail Fin			
Pl# 11111	2.90	2.75	2.00
1073			
(15¢) Tail Fin			
Pl# S11111	2.80	2.65	1.75
898			
16.7¢ Popcorn Wagon			
Pl# 1	2.80	2.50	1.75
Pl# 2	3.75	3.60	2.75
771			
17¢ Electric Car			
Pl# 1, 2, 3, 4, 5	2.20	2.00	1.50
Pl# 6	14.00	13.50	12.00
Pl# 7	5.30	5.00	4.50
771zx1			
17¢ Electric Car, precancel 11 1/2mm long			
Pl# 3, 4, 5	3.80	3.60	3.00
Pl# 6, 7	11.50	11.00	10.00
771zx2			
17¢ Electric Car, precancel 12 1/2mm long			
Pl# 3	25.00	23.50	21.00
Pl# 4	23.00	22.50	21.00
Pl# 5, 6	28.00	27.50	28.00
771zx2 / 771zx1			
17¢ Electric Car, combination strips			
Pl# 5	69.00	—	—
Pl# 6	75.00	—	—
771zx3			
17¢ Electric Car, precancel 13 1/2mm long			
Pl# 1, 2, 3, 4	9.40	9.00	7.50
Pl# 5	32.00	32.00	32.00
Pl# 7	27.00	25.00	25.00
859			
17¢ Dog Sled			
Pl# 2	3.10	2.90	1.50

	Strip of 5	Strip of 3	Single Used
880			
17.5¢ Racing Car			
Pl# 1	3.00	2.90	2.50
880zx			
17.5¢ Racing Car, Zip+4 Presort, untagged			
Pl# 1	3.50	2.90	2.75
754			
18¢ Flag			
Pl# 1	360.00	98.00	2.50
Pl# 2	45.00	16.00	1.00
Pl# 3	850.00	235.00	10.00
Pl# 4	7.00	6.00	1.00
Pl# 5	5.75	4.50	3.50
Pl# 6	—	2,050.00	625.00
Pl# 7	30.00	27.75	25.00
768			
18¢ Surrey			
Pl# 1	90.00	65.00	9.50
Pl# 2, 5, 6, 8, 13, 14, 17, 18	3.50	3.50	3.75
Pl# 3, 4	67.00	62.00	9.25
Pl# 7	32.00	32.00	9.50
Pl# 9, 10, 11, 12	12.80	11.50	4.00
Pl# 15, 16	21.00	19.00	18.00
852			
18¢ George Washington & Monument			
Pl# 1112	3.50	3.50	2.00
Pl# 3333	4.10	3.90	3.25
852zo			
18¢ Washington & Monument, untagged error			
Pl# 3333	—	—	—
852zx			
18¢ Washintgon & Monument, precancel, low gloss gum, untagged			
Pl# 11121	6.00	5.50	5.00
Pl# 33333	2.80	2.80	2.00
852zm			
18¢ George Washington & Monument, precancel, matte gum, untagged			
Pl# 33333	4.00	3.85	1.75
Pl# 43444	6.50	6.25	5.50
Tagged error (light)			
Pl# 33333	50.00	—	35.00
Tagged error (heavy)			
Pl#33333	148.00	—	125.00
965			
19¢ Fishing Boat, Type I			
Pl# A1111, A1212, A2424	3.20	3.00	2.25
Pl# A1112	6.00	5.50	5.00
965a			
19¢ Fishing Boat, Type II, Gravure			
Pl# A5555, A5556, A6667, A7667, A7679, A7766, A7779	3.80	3.50	2.50
965zo			
19¢ Fishing Boat, Type II, untagged error			
Pl# A5555	7.75	7.50	5.00
1044			
19¢ Fishing Boat, Type III SVS			
Pl# S11	7.25	4.50	3.00
777			
20¢ Fire Pumper			
Pl# 1	140.00	30.00	1.00
Pl# 2	755.00	165.00	7.50
Pl# 3, 4, 13, 15, 16	4.30	3.80	3.65
Pl# 5, 9, 10	2.70	2.00	.75
Pl# 6	37.50	33.00	1.20
Pl# 7, 8	175.00	85.00	1.00
Pl# 11	75.00	29.00	1.00
Pl# 12, 14	8.50	7.00	6.25
780			
20¢ Flag Over Supreme Court			
Pl# 1	75.00	5.00	.75
Pl# 2, 11, 12	8.00	7.50	1.00
Pl# 3, 5, 9, 10, 13, 14	4.20	3.30	1.00
Pl# 4	615.00	35.00	1.00
Pl# 6	145.00	90.00	2.50
Pl# 8	12.50	3.50	.75
780zx			
20¢ Flag Over Supreme Court precancel			
Pl# 14	60.00	60.00	50.00
789			
20¢ Consumer Education			
Pl# 1, 2	157.00	25.00	1.50
Pl# 3, 4	100.00	25.00	1.50
913			
20¢ Cable Car, block tagged			
Pl# 1, 2	3.30	3.20	1.50
913z			
20¢ Cable Car, overall tagged			
Pl# 2	6.00	5.25	5.00
1086			
20¢ Cog Railway			
Pl# 1, 2	4.10	3.80	2.25
907			
20.5¢ Fire Engine			
Pl# 1	4.75	3.75	3.25
902			
21¢ Railroad Mail Car			
Pl# 1, 2	3.50	3.40	2.50
849			
21.1¢ Envelopes			
Pl# 111111	3.20	2.80	2.50
Pl# 111121	4.75	4.25	3.65

	Strip of 5	Strip of 3	Single Used
849zx			
21.1¢ Envelopes, ZIP+4			
Pl# 111111	3.20	2.80	2.50
Pl# 111121	4.75	4.25	3.75
821			
(22¢) "D" Series, Eagle			
Pl# 1, 2	6.25	5.00	4.50
Untagged error Pl# 1	—	—	—
829			
22¢ Flag Over Capitol			
Pl# 1, 7	11.75	10.00	8.50
Pl# 2, 8, 10, 12, 15, 19, 22	3.20	3.00	.55
Pl# 3	49.00	10.50	.50
Pl# 4, 5, 11	5.90	5.00	.55
Pl# 6	6.50	6.50	6.50
Pl# 16, 17, 18, 20, 21	6.00	5.00	2.25
Pl# 13	11.75	10.50	9.00
Pl# 14	28.00	24.00	20.00
876			
22¢ Flag Over Capitol Test Coil			
Pl# T1	3.20	3.00	3.00
1233			
22¢ Uncle Sam			
Pl# 1111	3.50	3.25	2.50
949			
23¢ Lunch Wagon, tagged, matte gum			
Pl# 2, 3	3.75	3.00	2.00
Pl# 4	5.20	5.00	2.75
Pl # 5	12.00	10.00	5.50
949pm			
23¢ Lunch Wagon, phosphored, matte gum			
Pl# 3	4.40	3.45	2.75
949zs			
23¢ Lunch Wagon, phosphored, shiny gum			
Pl# 3	4.40	3.45	2.75
Pl# 4	5.10	5.00	2.75
Pl# 5	12.00	10.00	5.50
969			
23¢ Flag, Presorted First-Class			
Pl# A111, A212, A222 (Thick)	3.40	3.00	2.00
Pl# A112, A122, A222 (Thin), A333	3.90	3.30	2.25
985			
23¢ USA, Presorted First-Class, ABNCo.			
Pl# A1111, A2222, A2232, A3333, A4364, A4443, A4444, A4453	3.90	3.40	2.25
994			
23¢ USA, Presorted First-Class, BEP, shiny gum			
Pl# 1111	5.00	4.00	3.00
994z			
23¢ USA, Presorted First-Class			
Tagged (error)			
Pl# 1111	125.00	—	65.00

	Strip of 5	Strip of 3	Single Used
994m			
23¢ USA, Presorted First-Class, BEP, matte gum			
Pl# 1111	4.00	3.50	2.25
1010			
23¢ USA, Presorted First-Class, SVS			
Pl# S111	4.40	3.75	2.50
912			
24.1¢ Tandem Bicycle			
Pl# 1	3.90	3.00	2.50
866			
25¢ Bread Wagon			
Pl# 1, 5	3.60	3.30	2.50
Pl# 2, 3, 4	3.55	3.25	.65
885			
(25¢) "E" Series, Earth			
Pl# 1111, 1222	2.85	2.50	.65
Pl# 1211	4.15	3.80	1.25
Pl# 2222	4.50	4.50	3.50
891			
25¢ Flag Over Yosemite, block tagged			
Pl# 1, 7	6.35	5.65	2.50
Pl# 2, 3, 4, 5, 8	3.00	3.50	.75
Pl# 9	9.35	8.50	2.00
891pz			
25¢ Flag Over Yosemite, phosphored tagged			
Pl# 1	38.00	36.00	30.00
Pl# 2, 3, 7, 8, 9, 10, 11, 13, 14	3.50	3.00	.75
Pl# 5, 15	6.35	5.50	2.00
Pl# 6	12.00	10.50	5.00
905			
25¢ Honeybee			
Pl# 1, 2	3.80	3.00	.65
1064			
(25¢) "G" Series, Old Glory			
Pl# S11111	4.55	3.95	2.50
1074			
(25¢) Juke Box, BEP			
Pl# 111111, 212222, 222222, 332222	4.35	4.00	2.50
1075			
(25¢) Juke Box, SVS			
Pl# S11111, S22222	3.70	3.50	2.25
1170			
(25¢) Diner			
Pl# S11111	3.90	3.60	2.00
940			
(29¢) "F" Series, Tulip flower			
Pl# 1111, 1222, 2222	3.60	3.25	.75
Pl# 1211	18.50	18.00	14.00
Pl# 2211	4.85	4.25	3.00

	Strip of 5	Strip of 3	Single Used
945			
29¢ Flag Over Mt. Rushmore, Intaglio			
Pl# 1, 2, 3, 4, 5, 6, 7	4.20	3.85	.60
Pl# 8	6.00	5.35	2.00
Pl# 9	9.00	9.50	2.00
945p			
29¢ Flag Over Mt. Rushmore ("Lenz")			
Pl# 2	550.00	300.00	150.00
Pl# 6	150.00	100.00	125.00
945A			
29¢ Flag Over Mt. Rushmore ("Toledo Brown")			
Pl# 1	3750.00	2000.00	150.00
Pl# 7	160.00	150.00	150.00
963			
29¢ Flag Over Mt. Rushmore, Gravure			
Pl# A11111, A22211	4.00	3.85	2.50
966			
29¢ Tulip Flower, rouletted			
Pl# S1111, S2222	4.50	4.00	.75
982			
29¢ Tulip Flower, perforated			
Pl# S2222	4.50	4.00	2.50
984			
29¢ Flag Over White House			
Pl# 1, 2, 3, 4, 6, 7, 8	4.50	4.30	.75
Pl# 5	4.50	4.30	2.25
Pl# 9, 10, 11, 12, 13, 14, 15, 16, 18	5.50	5.20	1.00
1059			
(32¢) Black "G" Series, Old Glory			
Pl# 1111, 2222	9.45	6.50	3.50
1060			
(32¢) Blue "G" Series, Old Glory			
Pl# A1111, A1112, A1212, A1211, A1311, A1314, A1324, A2211, A2212, A2213, A2214, A3113, A3314, A3323, A3324, A3433, A3435, A3436, A4426, A4427, A5327, A5417, A5427,	4.50	4.30	3.25
Pl# A1113, A1211, A2313	5.60	4.50	4.00
Pl# A1417, A1433, A3114	8.50	8.00	5.00
Pl# A2223, A3315	8.40	4.30	4.50
Pl# A3423, A5437	8.00	7.00	4.00
Pl# A1222, A3426	6.50	6.00	4.50
Pl# A4435	220.00	210.00	210.00
1061			
(32¢) Red "G" Series, Old Glory			
Pl# S1111	4.75	4.65	1.00
1061A			
(32¢) "G" Series, Old Glory, rouletted			
Pl# S1111, S2222	5.40	5.25	1.00
1082			
32¢ Flag Over Porch, BEP, shiny gum			
Pl# 11111, 22222	5.25	5.00	.65
Pl# 22221	5.25	5.00	3.00

	Strip of 5	Strip of 3	Single Used
32¢ Flag Over Porch, low-gloss gum			
Pl# 11111, 22222, 33333, 44444	5.75	4.75	.65
Pl# 45444, 66646, 77767	5.75	4.50	.95
Pl# 34333, 78767, 91161	5.75	4.50	2.00
Pl# 99969	5.75	4.85	3.00
Pl# 22322	12.00	9.00	4.50
Pl# 66666	12.00	10.00	8.75
1083			
32¢ Flag Over Porch, SVS			
Pl# S11111	5.75	4.75	2.50
1085			
32¢ Ferry Boat, shiny gum			
Pl# 2, 3, 4	5.50	5.00	2.30
Pl# 5	10.00	9.50	2.75
1085a			
32¢ Ferry Boat, low gloss gum (Bronx Blue)			
Pl# 5	100.00	95.00	94.00
1085m			
32¢ Ferry Boat, low gloss gum			
Pl# 3, 5	6.25	5.75	2.50
Pl# 4	14.50	13.00	2.50
1194			
33¢ H (Hat), includes low gloss			
Pl# 1111, 3333, 3433, 3444	5.00	4.50	2.50
Pl# 3344	7.20	7.00	10.75
1207			
33¢ Flag and Skyscrapers			
Pl# 1111, 2222, 3333	5.00	4.50	2.50
928			
$1 Seaplane, all gum varieties			
Pl# 1, 3	8.50	7.50	3.00
OF130			
20¢ Official			
Pl# 1	56.00	16.00	15.00
OF132			
(22¢) "D" Official			
Pl# 1	65.00	36.00	32.00

Variable-Denomination Coils

	Strip of 5	Strip of 3	Single Used
986			
Shield, horizontal, matte gum			
Pl# 1	9.00	8.00	6.75
986pz			
Shield, horizontal, shiny gum			
Pl# 1	9.00	8.00	6.75

	Strip of 5	Strip of 3	Single Used
1040			
Shield, vertical design			
Pl# A11	7.50	6.00	5.50
1053			
Shield, horizontal, shiny gum			
Pl# 1	14.00	12.00	7.00
1053pz			
Shield, horizontal, matte gum			
Pl# 1	15.00	13.00	7.50
1117			
Shield, vertical design			
Pl# 11	7.50	6.00	6.00

Self-Adhesive Plate Number Coil Strips

	Strip of 5	Strip of 3	Single Used
1130			
(5¢) Butte			
Pl# S111	1.45	1.40	1.10
1131			
(5¢) Mountain (1996)			
Pl# V222222, V333323, V333333, V333342	1.80	1.60	1.25
Pl# V333343	2.15	2.15	2.15
1152			
(5¢) Mountain (1997)			
Pl# 1111	1.50	1.50	1.25
1169A			
(5¢) Swamp			
Pl# 1111, 2222, 3333	1.45	1.40	1.00
1129			
(10¢) Eagle & Shield (1996)			
Pl# S11111	2.85	2.50	2.00
1205			
(10¢) Eagle & Shield (1998)			
Pl# 11111, 22222	2.80	2.50	1.75
Pl# 11111 (tagged, error)	10.50	9.90	9.50
1132			
(10¢) Automobile			
Pl# S111	2.50	2.00	1.75

	Strip of 5	Strip of 3	Single Used
1176			
(10¢) Bicycle			
Pl# 111, 221, 222, 333, 344, 444, 555, 666, 777, 888, 999	2.65	2.50	1.80
1133			
(15¢) Auto Tail Fin			
Pl# S11111	2.85	2.65	1.75
1136			
20¢ Blue Jay			
Pl# S1111	3.10	3.00	2.00
1172			
20¢ Ring-necked Pheasant			
Pl# 1111, 2222	3.25	3.15	2.25
1199			
22¢ Uncle Sam			
Pl# 1111	3.50	3.25	2.50
1134			
(25¢) Juke Box (1996)			
Pl# S11111, S22222	3.85	3.55	2.00
1153			
(25¢) Juke Box (1997)			
Pl# 111111, 22222	3.95	3.60	2.00
1161			
(25¢) Juke Box, Linerless			
Pl# M11111	4.75	4.00	2.50
1177			
(25¢) Diner			
Pl# 11111, 22211, 22222, 33333, 4444	4.00	3.65	2.00
1029-32			
29¢ Contemporary Christmas			
Pl# V1111111 (Strip of 8, $7.00)	5.50		3.50
1038			
29¢ Pine Cone			
Pl# B1	6.85	5.90	3.75
1039			
29¢ Eagle			
Pl# 111	6.00	4.00	1.00
CM1616			
29¢ Love & Sunrise			
Pl# B1	6.80	5.90	3.75
1043			
29¢ Statue of Liberty			
Pl# D1111	6.80	5.90	4.00
1050			
29¢ Santa Claus			
Pl# V1111	6.80	5.90	3.75

	Strip of 5	Strip of 3	Single Used
1062			
(32¢) "G" Series			
Pl# V11111	5.35	5.00	3.25
1078			
32¢ Flag Over Porch, die cut 8-3/4, stamps separate			
Pl# V11111	8.00	6.75	2.00
1084			
32¢ Pink Rose			
Pl# S111	5.70	5.00	3.00
1091A-1092A			
32¢ Peaches/Pear			
Pl# V11111	5.60	5.00	3.50
1102-1105			
32¢ Santa & Children			
Pl# V1111 (Strip of 8, $6.50)	4.75		3.50
1110A			
32¢ Midnight Angel			
Pl# B1111	5.60	5.00	3.00
1126			
32¢ Flag Over Porch, die cut 9 3/4			
Pl# 11111, 22222, 23222, 33333, 44444, 45444, 55555, 66666, 78777, 88888, 89878, 99999, 11111A, 13231A, 13311A, 22222A, 33333A, 44444A, 55555A, 66666A, 77777A, 78777A, 88888A	5.25	4.85	1.25
Pl# 66666	—	—	—
Pl# 78777	—	—	—
Pl# 87888, 89888	27.50	20.00	4.75
Pl# 87898	12.00	10.00	3.75
Pl# 88898	300.00	245.00	—
Pl# 89898	12.00	10.00	2.50
Pl# 89899	425.00	350.00	—
Pl# 97898	8.00	6.00	4.25
Pl# 99899	27.50	20.00	
Pl# 13211A	27.50	12.00	1.25
1127			
32¢ Flag Over Porch, die cut 11			
Pl# 55555, 66666	8.00	6.75	2.00
1128			
32¢ Flag Over Porch, die cut 11 1/2			
Pl# S11111	5.00	4.50	2.75

	Strip of 5	Strip of 3	Single Used
1151			
32¢ Flag Over Porch (1997)			
Pl# 11111			
1162			
32¢ Flag Over Porch, Linerless			
Pl# M11111	6.00	5.25	3.00
1163			
32¢ Yellow Rose			
Pl# 1111, 1112, 1122, 2222, 2223, 2233, 2333, 3344, 3444, 4455, 5455, 5555, 5556, 5566, 5666, 6666, 6677, 6777, 7777, 8888	5.50	5.00	2.50
1197			
(33¢) "H" Hat			
Pl# 1111, 1131, 2222, 3333	5.20	4.50	2.00
Pl# 1111 (gap between stamps)	5.00	4.50	3.50
1208			
33¢ Flag and Skyscrapers			
Pl# 1111, 2222, 3333, 3433, 4443, 4444, 5555, 6666, 7777, 8888, 9999 "A" Nos.	5.00	4.50	2.00
1209			
33¢ Flag and Skyscrapers (gap between stamps)			
Pl# 1111, 2222	5.00	4.50	3.00
1222-25			
33¢ Fruit Berries (vertical die cut)			
Pl# B1111, B1112, B2211, B2221, B2222 (Strip of 9, $7.50)	5.00		2.50
1256-59			
33¢ Fruit Berries (horizontal, die cut, linerless)			
Pl# G1111 (Strip of 9, $7.50)	5.00	4.50	2.50

Self-Adhesive Panes and Convertible Booklets

	Full Pane
1135n	
20¢ Blue Jay (10)	
Pl# S1111, S2222	4.50
1173	
20¢ Pheasant (10)	
Pl# V1111, V2222, V2232, V2333, V2342, V2343, V3232, V3233, V3243, V3333	3.50
924n	
25¢ Eagle & Shield (18)	
Pl# A1111	12.00

	Full Pane
929	
25¢ Flag, Plastic (12)	
No Plate Number	6.00
942	
(29¢) "F" Flag (12)	
No Plate Number	7.00
962n	
29¢ Statue of Liberty Torch (18)	
No Plate Number	12.00
962nv	
29¢ Statue of Liberty Torch, revised back	
No Plate Number	12.50
988n	
29¢ Eagle, Red text (17)	
Pl# S1111	12.00
990n	
29¢ Eagle, Green text (17)	
Pl# D11111, D21221, D22322, D32322, D32332, D54573, D65784	15.00
Pl# D54561, D54563	16.00
Pl# D32342, D42342, D43352, D43452, D43453, D54571, D54673, D61384,	20.00
992n	
29¢ Eagle, Brown text (17)	
Pl# B1111-1, B1111-2, B3434-1, B4344-1, B4444-1, B4444-3	14.50
Pl# B2222-1, B2222-2, B3333-1, B3333-3, B3434-3	18.00
Pl# 4344-3	225.00
1005n	
29¢ Toy Train ATM (18)	
PL# V11111	12.00
1014n	
29¢ Red Squirrel (18)	
Pl# D11111, D22211, D23133	12.00
Pl# D22221, D22222	20.00
1016n	
29¢ Red Rose (18)	
Pl# S111	12.00
1032n	
29¢ Christmas (12)	
Pl# V111-1111, V222-1222, V222-2112, V222-2122, V222-2221, V222-2222, V333-3333	10.00
1037n	
29¢ Snowman (18)	
Pl# V1111	12.00
Pl# V2222	20.00
1038n	
29¢ Pine Cone (18)	
Pl# B1	18.00
Pl# B3, B4, B6, B7, B9, B10, B11, B13, B14, B16	14.00
Pl# B2, B5, B8, B12, B15	15.00

	Full Pane
1039n	
29¢ Eagle (18)	
Pl# M111, M112	15.00
1043n	
29¢ Statue of Liberty (18)	
Pl# D1111, D1212	12.00
CM1616n	
29¢ Love & Sunrise (18)	
Pl# B111-1, B111-2, B111-3, B111-4, B222-4, B222-5, B222-6, B333-9, B333-10, B333-11, B333-12, B333-17, B344-12, B344-13,B444-7, B444-8, B444-9, B444-10, B444-13, B444-14, B444-15, B444-17, B444-18, B444-19, B555-20, B555-21	15.00
Pl# B111-5	50.00
Pl# B121-5, B221-5	16.00
Pl# B333-5, B333-7, B333-8	25.00
Pl# B333-14	90.00
Pl# B334-11	750.00
Pl# B344-11	75.00
Pl# B434-10	120.00
Pl# B444-16	16.00
1050n	
29¢ Santa Claus (12)	
Pl# V1111	10.50
1051n	
29¢ Cardinal in Snow (18)	
Pl# V1111, V2222	14.50
1062n	
(32¢) "G" (18)	
Pl# V11111, V22222	17.50
1063n	
(32¢) "G" ATM (18)	
No Plate Number	17.50
1076n	
32¢ Flag Over Field (18)	
Pl# V1111, V1311, V1433, V2111, V2222, V2322	14.50
1078n	
32¢ Flag Over Porch, (large 1995) **(20)**	
Pl# V12211, V12212, V12312, V12321, V12322, V12331, V13322, V13831, V13834, V13836, V22211, V23322, V23422, V23432, V34743, V34745, V36743, V42556, V45554, V56663, V56665, V56763, V65976, V78989	17.50
(The Following Demand a Premium)	
Pl# V23522, V57663	

	Full Pane
1078an	
32¢ Flag Over Porch, (small 1995) **(20)**	
Pl# V11111	38.00
1084n	
32¢ Pink Rose (20)	
Pl# S111, S112, S333, S444	16.00
1084n1	
32¢ Pink Rose, Die-Cut "Time to Reorder"	
Pl# S444, S555	11.00
1092n	
32¢ Peach & Pear (20)	
Pl# V11111, V11122, V11131, V11132, V12131, V12132, V12211, V12221, V12232, V22212, V22221, V22222, V33142, V33143, V33243, V33323, V33333, V33343, V33353, V33363, V33453, V44424, V44434, V44454	16.00
Pl# V45434, V45464, V54365, V54565, V55365, V55565	20.00
Pl# V11232	250.00
CM1695n	
(32¢) Love & Cherub (20)	
Pl# B1111-1, B2222-1, B2222-2, B3333-2	16.00
1109n	
32¢ Santa & Children (20)	
Pl# V1111, V1211, V3233, V3333, V4444	15.00
Pl# V1212	—
1110n	
32¢ Midnight Angel (20)	
Pl# B1111, B2222, B3333	15.00
1111n	
32¢ Children Sledding (18)	
Pl# V1111	14.00
1116n	
32¢ Flag Over Porch, die cut 11-1/4 **(10)**	
Pl# V11111, V12111, V23222, V31121, V32111, V32121, V44322, V44333, V44444, V55555, V66666, V66886, V67886, V68886, V68896, V76989, V77666, V77668, V77766, V77776, V78698, V78886 V78896, V78898, V78989, V89999	8.00
Pl# 78986	17.50
CM1798n	
32¢ Love Cherub (20)	
Pl# B1111-1, B1111-2, B2222-1, B2222-2	16.50
1144n	
32¢ Family Scenes (20)	
Pl# B1111, B2222, B3333	15.00

	Full Pane
1145n	
32¢ Skaters (18)	
Pl# V1111, V2111	14.00
CM1830n	
32¢ Tennessee (20)	
Pl# S11111	16.00
CM1848n	
32¢ Iowa (20)	
Pl# B1111	16.00
1147n	
32¢ Madonna (20)	
Pl# 1111-1, 1211-1, 2212-1, 2222-1, 2323-1, 3333-1, 3334-1, 4444-1, 5556-2, 5656-2, 6666-2, 6766-1, 7887-1, 7887-2, 7888-2, 7988-2	15.00
Pl# 5544-1	75.00
Pl# 5555-1, 5556-1, 6656-2	30.00
Pl# 3323-1, 6666-1	25.00
1149n	
32¢ Yellow Rose (20)	
Pl# S1111, S2222	14.00
1154n3	
32¢ Liberty & Torch (die cut 11) (20)	
Pl# V1111, V1211,V1311, V2122, V2222, V2311, V2331, V3233, V3333, V3513,V4532	13.00
1154n3v	
32¢ Liberty & Torch, (die cut 11-1/2 x 11-3/4) **(20)**	
Pl# V1111, V1211, V2122, V2222	40.00
1155n	
32¢ Botanical Prints (20)	
Pl# S11111, S22222	13.00
Pl# S33333	12.00
1159n (5)	3.50
1160n (5)	3.75
CM1884n	
32¢ Love & Swans (20)	
Pl# B1111, B2222, B3333, B4444, B5555, B6666, B7777	13.00
CM1892	
32¢ Bugs Bunny (10)	
No Plate Number	7.50
CM1893	
32¢ Bugs Bunny, imperforate stamp on right panel **(10)**	
No Plate Number	200.00
1164n	
32¢ Madonna and Child (20)	
Pl# 1111, 2222, 3333	8.50
1165n3	
32¢ American Holly (20)	
Pl# B1111, B2222, B3333	8.50
CM1891	
32¢ Sylvester and Tweety (10)	
No Plate Number	5.00

CM1892
32¢ Sylvester and Tweety, imperforate stamp on right panel **(10)**
No Plate Number 5.00

1178n
32¢ Madonna (20)
Pl# 11111, 22222, 33333 7.50

1186n
32¢ Wreath (20)
Pl# B111111, B222222, B333333, B444444, B555555 7.50

1195n
33¢ "H" Hat (10)
Pl# V1111, V1211, V2211, V2222 4.00

1195n1
33¢ "H" Hat (20)
Pl# V1111, V1112, V1113, V1122, V1213, V1222, V2113, V2122, V2213, V2222, V2223 7.00

1203n
33¢ "H" Hat ATM **(18)**
Pl# V1111 7.00

CM2040n
33¢ Victorian Love (20)
Pl# V1111, V1112, V1117, V1118, V1211, V1212, V1213, V1233, V1313, V1314, V1333, V1334, V1335, V2123, V2221, V2222, V2223, V2324, V2424, V2425, V2426, V3123, V3124, V3125, V3133, V3134, V3323, V3327, V3333, V3334, V3336, V4529, V4549, V5650 7.50

1211n3
33¢ Flag and Skyscrapers (10)
Pl# V1111, V1112, V1113, V2222, V2322, V2324, V3434, V3545 6.00

1211n4
33¢ Flag and Skyscrapers, diecut 11 **(20)**
Pl# V1111, V1211, V2122, V2222, V2223, V3333, V4444, V8789 13.00

1211nv
33¢ Flag and Skyscrapers, diecut 11-1/2 x 11-3/4 **(20)**
Pl# V1111, V1131, V2222, V2223, V2227, V2243, V2323, V2423, V2443, V3333, V4444, V5428, V5445, V5546, V5576, V5578, V6423, V6456, V6546, V6556, V6575, V6576, V7567, V7663, V7667, V7676, V8789 13.00

Full Pane

1213n
33¢ Flag In Classroom ATM (18)
Pl# V1111 12.00

1217n
33¢ Fruit Berries (20)
Pl# B1111, B1112, B2211, B2222, B3331, B3332, B3333, B4444, B5555 13.00

CM2053
33¢ Daffy Duck (10)
No plate number 7.50

CM2053
33¢ Daffy Duck, imperforate stamp on right pane **(10)**
No plate number 7.50

CM2059n
33¢ Tropical Flowers (20)
Pl# S11111, S22222, S22244, S22344, S22444, S22452, S22462, S23222, S24222, S24224, S24242, S24244, S24422, S24442, S24444, S26462, S32323, S32333, S32444, S33333, S44444, S45552, S46654, S55452, S55552, S56462, S62544, S62562, S64452, S64544, S65552, S66462, S66544, S66552, S66562, S66652 13.00

1232n3
33¢ Coral Rose, 1-sided **(20)**
Pl# S111, S222 13.00

1255n
33¢ Coral Rose, 2-sided **(20)**
Pl# S111 12.00

CM1706n
55¢ Love Cherub (20)
Pl# B1111-1, B2222-1 22.50

CM1885n
55¢ Love & Swans (20)
Pl# B1111, B2222, B3333, B4444 22.50

U. S. Government Commemorative Issues

1893. Columbian Issues released in connection with the World's Columbian Exposition held in Chicago, Ill., commemorated the 400th anniversary of the first voyage to America by Christopher Columbus. They are considered to be the first true commemoratives. All the stamps except the 8¢ were issued Jan. 2. The 8¢ value, not originally planned with the others, appeared on March 3, 1893, to meet a new registry note.

Christoforo Colombo was born in Genoa, Italy, ca. 1451. He went to sea at an early age and settled in Portugal. His wife was Felipa Perestrello, daughter of a distinguished navigator who left many charts that Columbus studied with care. He conceived the idea of reaching Asia by sailing due west and vainly sought support in Portugal, Spain, Italy and England for such an expedition.

In 1491, Columbus (CM15, CM16) was on his way to France when he paused to stay with old friends at the monastery of La Rabida (CM10) in Spain. Juan Perez, former confessor to Queen Isabella, obtained for him an audience with the queen, who listened to his theories (CM5) and brought him before King Ferdinand.

Columbus was turned down by the sovereigns, whose treasury had been depleted by war with the Moors. Setting out overland for France, he had gone only six miles when a royal courier overtook him (CM11) to summon him back to court. Isabella (CM15) had decided to raise the needed money, tradition says, by pledging her jewels (CM12). An agreement was signed giving Columbus three caravels: the *Santa Maria* (CM3), a 100-ton ship with a crew of 52; the 50-ton *Pinta;* and the 40-ton *Niña*. The latter two each had a crew of 18. The little fleet sailed from Palos on Aug. 2, 1492, (CM4).

After rebellious outbursts among the crews, on the night of Oct. 11, 1492, Columbus thought he saw a light. The next morning Rodrigo de Triana sighted land (CM1): Guanahani, now believed to be Watling's Island in the Bahamas. Naming the place San Salvador (Holy Savior), Columbus kissed the soil and gave thanks to God (CM2).

Excited by the native tales of gold, the fleet sailed south, finding Cuba on Oct. 28 and Hispaniola on Dec. 6. Leaving a colony of 40 men to build a fort at Hispaniola, where the *Santa Maria* had run aground, Columbus returned to Spain. At court, in Barcelona, he was given a great welcome (CM6), reported his discoveries (CM9) and displayed the natives he brought back with him (CM8).

Columbus sailed again Sept. 25, 1493, with 3 galleons, 14 caravels, and 1,500 men. He reached Dominica, Guadaloupe, and Puerto Rico, found his Haitian colony destroyed by natives, and returned to Spain in March with 225 men and 30 natives.

Charged by enemies in court with mistreating the natives, he successfully defended himself, but his third voyage was delayed until May 1498. Given six vessels, he sent three to Hispaniola and took the others south to explore.

Returning to Hispaniola, he was put in chains (CM13) by Francisco de Bobadilla, sent from Spain to investigate new rumors of mistreatment of natives. Stripped of his honors and returned to Spain, he was released by the queen (CM7). Telling of the discoveries of his third expedition (CM14), he obtained four vessels and set out again in May 1502, discovering Honduras and Panama. The queen's death after his return in 1504 marked the end of his fortunes. He died at Valladolid in 1504, convinced that he had discovered the coast of Asia.

Intaglio by the American Bank Note Company, the last U.S. stamps of the 19th century produced by a private printer, unwatermarked paper, perforated 12.

CM1 *Columbus in Sight of Land, from a painting by William H. Powell*

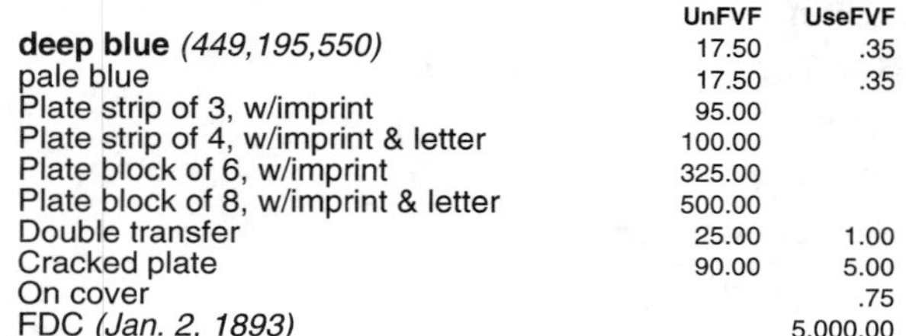

CM1		UnFVF	UseFVF
1¢	**deep blue** *(449,195,550)*	17.50	.35
	pale blue	17.50	.35
	Plate strip of 3, w/imprint	95.00	
	Plate strip of 4, w/imprint & letter	100.00	
	Plate block of 6, w/imprint	325.00	
	Plate block of 8, w/imprint & letter	500.00	
	Double transfer	25.00	1.00
	Cracked plate	90.00	5.00
	On cover		.75
	FDC *(Jan. 2, 1893)*		5,000.00

CM2 *Columbus Landing on Guanahani, from a painting by Vanderlyn in the Rotunda of the Capitol in Washington, D.C.*

CM2		UnFVF	UseFVF
2¢	**dull purple** *(1,464,588,750)*	17.50	.20
	brown violet	20.00	.20
	gray violet	20.00	.20
	Plate strip of 3, w/imprint	75.00	
	Plate strip of 4, w/imprint & letter	125.00	
	Plate block of 6, w/imprint	225.00	
	Plate block of 8, w/imprint & letter	450.00	
	Double transfer	25.00	.30
	Triple transfer	75.00	
	Quadruple transfer	90.00	
	v1. Broken frame line	25.00	.20
	Recut frame lines	25.00	.20
	Cracked plate	90.00	
	On cover		.50
	FDC *(Jan. 2, 1893);* EKU *Jan. 1, 1893*		3,750.00

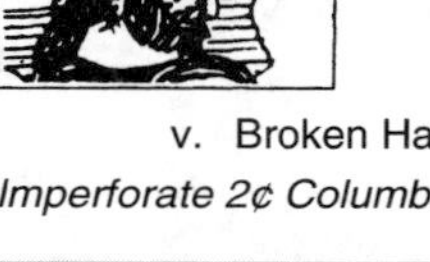

CM2v The Broken Hat variety is found in the hat of the knight to the left of Columbus

	UnFVF	UseFVF
v. Broken Hat variety	65.00	.50

Imperforate 2¢ Columbians are from printer's waste.

CM3 *Columbus' flagship,* Santa Maria, *from a Spanish engraving*

CM3		UnFVF	UseFVF
3¢	**deep bluish green** *(11,501,250)*	40.00	11.00
	dull green	40.00	11.00
	Plate strip of 3, w/imprint	200.00	
	Plate strip of 4, w/imprint & letter	275.00	
	Plate block of 6, w/imprint	650.00	
	Plate block of 8, w/imprint & letter	1,200.00	
	Double transfer	75.00	
	On cover		35.00
	FDC *(Jan. 2, 1893)*		10,000.00

CM4 Santa Maria, Pinta *and* Niña, *from a Spanish engraving*

CM4		UnFVF	UseFVF
4¢	**gray blue** *(19,181,550)*	60.00	5.50
	dull ultramarine	60.00	
	Plate strip of 3, w/imprint	275.00	
	Plate strip of 4, w/imprint & letter	3.50	
	Plate block of 6, w/imprint	1,100.00	
	Plate block of 8, w/imprint & letter	2,000.00	
	Double transfer	125.00	25.00

DECODING THE CATALOG

Although the 2¢ Columbian issue of 1893 is not particularly complicated, there are three main types that every collector should know, as they are widely collected minor varieties listed in most catalogs. These are the normal, Broken Hat and broken frame line varieties. There are many types of the latter two varieties, but most of them are visually similar.

"Broken Hat" Variety

Broken frame line (lower right) variety

Recutting

The 2¢ Columbian (Minkus CM2) is part of what is generally considered to be the first United States commemorative set. The set was produced by the American Bank Note Co. and marked the last stamps of the 19th century produced by a private printer.

A group of 15 stamps, with denominations ranging from 1¢ to $5, was placed on sale Jan. 2, 1893. The 8¢ value, not originally planned as part of the set, was released March 3, 1893, to meet the new registry rate. Of all stamps produced until that time, the 2¢ Columbian had the largest printing. A total of about 1.5 billion stamps were produced, leading to a wealth of varieties for the specialized collector.

The first variety of the 2¢ Columbian is the so-called normal type, which is the most common form of this stamp. This simply means there are no noticeable major varieties.

The second is the famous "Broken Hat" variety, shown in the illustration at left. Note the notched hat on the third figure to the left of Columbus. This variety, one of the best known in all U.S. collecting, has frequently been erroneously referred to as a plate variety. It is not. The Broken Hat variety was caused by a flaw on one or more of the transfer rolls used to create the printing plate.

The third variety, also caused by a relief break on a transfer roll, is known as the broken frame line variety. An example of that stamp is shown at left center. When the image on the transfer roll (a relief) is rocked into the printing plate (a depressed image), bits of the metal can beak off the roll, leaving no impression on the steel of the printing plate. The resulting unprinted area is called a relief break. It will appear on every stamp produced from any image on the printing plate created from that transfer roll.

This is different from plate varieties in that several stamps from a pane may exhibit the same transfer roll variety, whereas only a single stamp will show a plate variety. For example, a plate crack must always appear on the same stamp from the same position of the same plate. A relief break may affect several positions on several different printing plates until the use of a particular transfer roll is discontinued.

In the case of the Broken Hat and broken frame line varieties, there are different stages and different breaks, all of which are classified the same but have slightly different appearances.

Although of less consequence to the average collector, the illustration on the canceled stamp at lower left illustrates yet another type of variety that frequently occurs on stamps with long printing histories: recut designs. Recutting is usually done to solidify fading details and to gain extra life from a worn-out printing plate.

If you take a look at the figures in the enlargements, you'll note that the men each look different from one stamp to another. This is because portions of the design and shading have been recut (more than likely directly on the printing plate), resulting in altered appearances. These, too, are collectible.

		UnFVF	UseFVF
	On cover		
	FDC *(Jan. 2, 1893)*		10,500.00
	v. blue (error)		
	Plate strip of 4, w/imprint & letter		

CM5 *Columbus Soliciting Aid of Isabella, from a painting by Brozik in the Metropolitan Museum of Art, New York*

CM5		UnFVF	UseFVF
5¢	**brown** *(35,248,250)*	65.00	6.00
	pale brown	65.00	6.00
	yellow brown	65.00	6.00
	Plate strip of 3, w/imprint	300.00	
	Plate strip of 4, w/imprint & letter	450.00	
	Plate block of 6, w/imprint	1,400.00	
	Plate block of 8, w/imprint & letter	2,400.00	
	Double transfer	125.00	25.00
	On cover		25.00
	FDC *(Jan. 2, 1893)*		17,500.00

CM6 *Columbus Welcomed at Barcelona, from a panel by Randolph Rogers in the bronze doors of the Capitol, Washington, D.C.*

CM6		UnFVF	UseFVF
6¢	**dark lilac** *(4,707,550)*	60.00	17.50
	dull purple	60.00	17.50
	Plate strip of 3, w/imprint	275.00	
	Plate strip of 4, w/imprint & letter	360.00	
	Plate block of 6, w/imprint	1,250.00	
	Plate block of 8, w/imprint & letter	2,250.00	
	Double transfer	125.00	
	On cover		3,500.00
	FDC *(Jan. 2, 1893)*		22,500.00
	a. red violet	—	

CM7 *Columbus Restored to Favor, from a painting by Francesco Jover*

CM7		UnFVF	UseFVF
8¢	**brown purple** *(10,656,550)*	50.00	7.00
	pale brown purple	50.00	7.00
	Plate strip of 3, w/imprint	225.00	
	Plate strip of 4, w/imprint & letter	300.00	
	Plate block of 6, w/imprint	750.00	
	Plate block of 8, w/imprint & letter	1,150.00	
	Double transfer	75.00	
	On cover		25.00
	Earliest known use: *March 3, 1893*		

CM8 *Columbus Presenting Natives, from a painting by Luigi Gregori at the University of Notre Dame, South Bend, Ind.*

CM8		UnFVF	UseFVF
10¢	**black brown** *(16,516,950)*	95.00	5.50
	a. dark brown	95.00	5.50
	gray black	95.00	5.50
	Plate strip of 3, w/imprint	475.00	
	Plate strip of 4, w/imprint & letter	650.00	
	Plate block of 6, w/imprint	2,800.00	
	Plate block of 8, w/imprint & letter	4,250.00	
	Double transfer	175.00	12.00

		UnFVF	UseFVF
	Triple transfer	—	
	On cover		35.00
	FDC *(Jan. 2, 1893)*		

CM9 *Columbus Announcing His Discovery, from a painting by R. Baloca in Madrid, Spain*

CM9		UnFVF	UseFVF
15¢	**deep bluish green** *(1,576,950)*	175.00	50.00
	a. dull green	175.00	50.00
	Plate strip of 3, w/imprint	900.00	
	Plate strip of 4, w/imprint & letter	1,200.00	
	Plate block of 6, w/imprint	4,800.00	
	Plate block of 8, w/imprint & letter	7,500.00	
	Double transfer	—	
	On cover		250.00
	Earliest known use: *Jan. 26, 1893*		

CM10 *Columbus at La Rabida, from a painting by R. Maso*

CM10		UnFVF	UseFVF
30¢	**orange brown** *(617,250)*	225.00	65.00
	bright orange brown	225.00	65.00
	Plate strip of 3, w/imprint	1,250.00	
	Plate strip of 4, w/imprint & letter	1,600.00	
	Plate block of 6, w/imprint	7,500.00	
	Plate block of 8, w/imprint & letter	11,500.00	
	On cover		400.00
	Earliest known use: *Feb. 8, 1893*		

CM11 *Recall of Columbus, from a painting by Augustus G. Heaton in the Capitol, Washington, D.C.*

CM11		UnFVF	UseFVF
50¢	**slate black** *(243,750)*	350.00	125.00
	dull slate black	350.00	125.00
	Plate strip of 3, w/imprint	1,750.00	
	Plate strip of 4, w/imprint & letter	2,500.00	
	Plate block of 6, w/imprint	12,000.00	
	Plate block of 8, w/imprint & letter	17,500.00	
	Double transfer	—	
	Triple transfer	—	
	On cover		650.00
	Earliest known use: *Feb. 8, 1893*		

CM12 *Isabella pledging her jewels, from a painting by Muñoz Degrain in the Hall of Legislature in Madrid, Spain*

CM12		UnFVF	UseFVF
$1	**Venetian red** *(55,050)*	1,000.00	450.00
	pale Venetian red	1,000.00	450.00
	Plate strip of 3, w/imprint	5,250.00	
	Plate strip of 4, w/imprint & letter	7,250.00	
	Plate block of 6, w/imprint	35,000.00	
	Plate block of 8, w/imprint & letter	55,000.00	
	Double transfer	—	
	On cover		2,850.00
	Earliest known use: *Jan. 21, 1893*		

CM13 *Columbus In Chains, from a painting by K. Leutze, Germantown, Pa. It was the first dollar-value U.S. stamp.*

CM13		UnFVF	UseFVF
$2	**brown red** *(45,550)*	1,100.00	400.00
	dark brown red	1,100.00	400.00
	Plate strip of 3, w/imprint	1,650.00	
	Plate strip of 4, w/imprint & letter	8,000.00	
	Plate block of 6, w/imprint	45,000.00	
	Plate block of 8, w/imprint & letter	2,500.00	
	On cover		
	FDC *(Jan. 2, 1893)*		65,000.00

CM14 *Columbus Describing His Third Voyage, from a painting by Francesco Jover*

CM14		UnFVF	UseFVF
$3	**bronze green** *(27,650)*	1,700.00	725.00
	pale bronze green	1,700.00	725.00
	Plate strip of 3, w/imprint	8,500.00	
	Plate strip of 4, w/imprint & letter	14,000.00	
	Plate block of 6, w/imprint	65,000.00	
	Plate block of 8, w/imprint & letter	85,000.00	
	On cover		4,000.00
	a. olive green	2,300.00	850.00
	Earliest known use: *April 4, 1893*		

CM15 *Queen Isabella and Columbus, Isabella from a painting in Madrid, Columbus by Lotto*

CM15		UnFVF	UseFVF
$4	**deep rose** *(26,350)*	2,250.00	1,000.00
	pale analine rose	2,250.00	1,000.00
	Plate strip of 3, w/imprint	12,500.00	
	Plate strip of 4, w/imprint & letter	—	
	Plate block of 6, w/imprint	—	
	Plate block of 8, w/imprint & letter	—	
	On cover		4,000.00
	a. rose carmine	3,000.00	1,250.00
	Earliest known use: *Jan. 6, 1893*		

CM16 *Profile of Columbus, from the sculpture of the commemorative half dollar*

CM16		UnFVF	UseFVF
$5	**black** *(27,350)*	2,750.00	1,600.00
	gray black	2,750.00	1,600.00
	Plate strip of 3, w/imprint	14,000.00	
	Plate strip of 4, w/imprint & letter	20,000.00	
	Plate block of 6, w/imprint	—	
	Plate block of 8, w/imprint & letter	—	
	On cover		5,000.00
	Earliest known use: *Jan. 6, 1893*		

For stamps of these designs, but with "1992" instead of "1893" in the top-right corner see Nos. CM1456-61.

1898. Trans-Mississippi Issue was released for the Trans-Mississippi Exposition held at Omaha, Neb., commemorating the settling of the Middle West.

All denominations issued June 17. *Printed in Intaglio, Bureau of Engraving and Printing, Washington, D.C., on paper with double-line "USPS" watermark.*

CM17 *Marquette Exploring the Mississippi, from a painting by Lamprecht. (The scene is actually on the Wisconsin River.) Jacques Marquette (CM17), a French Jesuit, founded a mission and in 1673 explored the Mississippi with Louis Jolliet.*

CM17		UnFVF	UseFVF
1¢	**green** *(70,993,400)*	22.50	4.75
	dark yellow green	22.50	4.75
	yellow green	22.50	4.75
	Plate pair, w/imprint	75.00	
	Plate strip of 3, w/imprint	95.00	
	Plate block of 4, w/imprint	200.00	
	Plate block of 6, w/imprint	300.00	
	Margin block of 4, w/arrow	95.00	
	Double transfer	40.00	7.50
	On cover		10.00
	FDC *(June 17, 1898)*		12,500.00

CM18 *Farming in the West, from a photograph, was the first U.S. stamp to portray people still alive: Evan Nybakken (foreground, partially obscured by his arm) and Arthur John De Lance (facing front with wide-brimmed hat and holding dog).*

CM18		UnFVF	UseFVF
2¢	**brown red** *(159,720,800)*	19.00	1.25
	pale brown red	19.00	1.25
	Plate pair, w/imprint	55.00	
	Plate strip of 3, w/imprint	85.00	
	Plate block of 4, w/imprint	175.00	
	Plate block of 6, w/imprint	240.00	
	Margin block of 4, w/arrow	85.00	
	Double transfer	35.00	2.50
	Worn plate	25.00	2.00
	On cover		2.50
	FDC *(June 17, 1898)*		11,500.00
	Earliest known use: *June 16, 1898*		

CM19 *Indian Hunting Buffalo, from an engraving in Schoolcraft's* History of the Indian Tribes

CM19		UnFVF	UseFVF
4¢	**orange red** *(94,924,500)*	100.00	17.50
	orange	100.00	17.50
	Plate pair, w/imprint	250.00	20.00
	Plate strip of 3, w/imprint	450.00	20.00
	Plate block of 4, w/imprint	750.00	
	Plate block of 6, w/imprint	1,250.00	
	Margin block of 4, w/arrow	500.00	
	On cover		75.00
	FDC *(June 17, 1898)*		20,000.00

CM20 *Fremont on Rocky Mountains, from old wood engraving. John Charles Fremont (CM20) mapped the Oregon Trail in 1842 and later surveyed railway routes in the Southwest.*

CM20		UnFVF	UseFVF
5¢	**deep blue** *(7,694,180)*	100.00	17.50
	bright blue	100.00	17.50

		UnFVF	UseFVF
	dull blue	100.00	17.50
	Plate pair, w/imprint	150.00	17.50
	Plate strip of 3, w/imprint	250.00	
	Plate block of 4, w/imprint	700.00	
	Plate block of 6, w/imprint	1,250.00	
	Margin block of 4, w/arrow	450.00	
	On cover		75.00
	FDC *(June 17, 1898)*		20,000.00

CM21 *Troops Guarding Train, from a drawing by Frederic Remington*

CM21		UnFVF	UseFVF
8¢	**chocolate** *(2,927,200)*	135.00	32.50
	violet brown	135.00	32.50
	Plate pair, w/imprint	350.00	
	Plate strip of 3, w/imprint	500.00	
	Plate block of 4, w/imprint	1,750.00	
	Plate block of 6, w/imprint	2,500.00	
	Margin block of 4, w/arrow	650.00	
	On cover		150.00
	FDC *(June 17, 1898)*		25,000.00
	v. Horizontal pair, imperforate vertically between	17,500.00	
	v1. Plate block of 4, w/imprint	75,000.00	

CM22 *Hardships of Emigration, from a painting by A. G. Heaton*

CM22		UnFVF	UseFVF
10¢	**violet black** *(4,629,760)*	135.00	17.50
	gray violet	135.00	17.50
	Plate pair, w/imprint	250.00	
	Plate strip of 3, w/imprint	525.00	
	Plate block of 4, w/imprint	1,750.00	
	Plate block of 6, w/imprint	2,750.00	
	Margin block of 4, w/arrow	750.00	
	On cover		100.00
	FDC *(June 17, 1898)*		30,000.00

CM23 *Western Mining Prospector, from a drawing by Frederic Remington*

CM23		UnFVF	UseFVF
50¢	**bronze green** *(530,400)*	450.00	130.00
	dark bronze green	450.00	130.00
	Plate pair, with imprint	150.00	
	Plate strip of 3, w/imprint	2,000.00	
	Plate block of 4, w/imprint	10,250.00	
	Plate block of 6, w/imprint	16,000.00	
	Margin block of 4, w/arrow	2,250.00	
	On cover		1,500.00
	FDC *(June 17, 1898)*		35,000.00

CM24 *Western Cattle in a Storm, based on a painting,* The Vanguard, by *John A. MacWhirter of cattle in the Scottish highlands during a snowstorm*

CM24		UnFVF	UseFVF
$1	**black** *(56,900)*	950.00	400.00
	Plate pair, w/imprint	2,750.00	
	Plate strip of 3, w/imprint	5,500.00	
	Plate block of 4, w/imprint	30,000.00	
	Plate block of 6, w/imprint	42,500.00	
	Margin block of 4, w/arrow	5,500.00	
	On cover		4,500.00
	FDC *(June 17, 1898)*		20,000.00

CM25 *Mississippi River Bridge at St. Louis, Mo., from a photograph*

CM25		UnFVF	UseFVF
$2	**red brown** *(56,200)*	2,700.00	700.00
	dark red brown	2,700.00	700.00
	Plate pair, w/imprint	4,750.00	
	Plate strip of 3, w/imprint	7,500.00	
	Plate block of 4, w/imprint	65,000.00	
	Plate block of 6, w/imprint	100,000.00	
	Margin block of 4, w/arrow	10,500.00	
	On cover		60,000.00
	FDC *(June 17, 1898);* EKU *(June 24, 1898)*		—

For bicolor versions of the Trans-Mississippi Issue, see Nos. CM1985 and CM1986.

1901. Pan-American Issue commemorated the Pan-American Exposition at Buffalo, N.Y., promoting friendly relations among the countries of the New World. The stamps illustrating engineering achievements of the age were printed in two colors, and the first three denominations are known with inverted centers (actually, inverted frames, because the black vignettes were printed first). The stamps were on sale only during the exposition, from May 1 to Oct. 31. *Intaglio, perforated 12.*

CM26 *Navigation on the Great Lakes* (S.S. City of Alpena)

CM26v

CM26		UnFVF	UseFVF
1¢	**emerald & black** *(91,401,500)*	15.00	2.75
	dark blue green & black	15.00	2.75
	Plate strip of 3, w/imprint	100.00	
	Plate block of 4, w/imprint & arrow	—	
	Plate strip of 5 (2 numbers), w/imprint	175.00	
	Plate block of 6, w/imprint	275.00	
	Plate block of 10 (2 numbers), w/imprint	—	
	Margin block of 4, w/imprint and arrow	125.00	
	Double transfer	22.50	2.75
	On cover		8.00
	FDC *(May 1, 1901)*		5,000.00
	v. Center inverted *(1,000 reported)*	12,500.00	6,000.00
	v1. Center inverted plate strip of 3, w/imprint	45,000.00	
	v2. Center inverted single on cover		18,500.00

CM27 *Fast rail transportation (Empire State Express)*

CM27v

CM27		UnFVF	UseFVF
2¢	**rose red & black** *(209,759,700)*	15.00	1.00
	carmine & gray black	15.00	1.00
	Plate strip of 3, w/imprint	85.00	
	Plate block of 4, w/imprint & arrow	—	
	Plate strip of 5 (2 numbers), w/imprint	200.00	
	Plate block of 6, w/imprint	275.00	
	Plate block of 10 (2 numbers), w/imprint	—	
	Margin block of 4, w/imprint & arrow	100.00	
	Double transfer	30.00	4.00
	On cover		2.00
	FDC *(May 1, 1901)*		2,750.00
	v. Center inverted *(158 known)*	—	
	v1. Center inverted block of 4	—	

CM28 *Columbia Electric Vehicle Co. automobile, world's first depiction of an auto on stamp*

CM28v

CM28		UnFVF	UseFVF
4¢	**orange brown & black** *(5,737,100)*	70.00	12.50
	red brown & black	70.00	12.50
	Plate strip of 3, w/imprint	350.00	
	Plate block of 4, w/imprint & arrow	—	
	Plate strip of 5 (2 numbers), w/imprint	600.00	
	Plate block of 6, w/imprint	2,500.00	
	Plate block of 10 (2 numbers), w/imprint	4,500.00	
	Margin block of 4, w/imprint & arrow	350.00	
	On cover		50.00
	FDC *(May 1, 1901)*		8,500.00
	v. Center inverted *(206 known)*	25,000.00	
	v1. Center inverted plate strip of 4, w/imprint	135,000.00	
	v2. Center inverted, overprinted "Specimen"	—	

CM29 *Bridge at Niagara Falls*

CM29		UnFVF	UseFVF
5¢	**gray blue & black** *(7,201,300)*	75.00	12.50
	dark gray blue & black	75.00	12.50
	Plate strip of 3, w/imprint	400.00	
	Plate block of 4, w/imprint & arrow	—	
	Plate strip of 5 (2 numbers), w/imprint	725.00	
	Plate block of 6, w/imprint	3,000.00	
	Plate block of 10 (2 numbers), w/imprint & arrow	5,250.00	
	Margin block of 4, w/imprint & arrow	425.00	
	On cover		55.00
	FDC *(May 1, 1901)*		16,000.00

CM30 *Canal Locks, Sault Ste. Marie*

CM30		UnFVF	UseFVF
8¢	**chocolate & black** *(4,921,700)*	100.00	45.00
	purple brown & black	100.00	45.00
	Plate strip of 3, w/imprint	500.00	
	Plate block of 4, w/imprint & arrow	—	
	Plate strip of 5 (2 numbers), w/imprint	900.00	
	Plate block of 6, w/imprint	4,500.00	
	Plate block of 10 (2 numbers), w/imprint	8,000.00	
	Margin block of 4, w/imprint & arrow	500.00	
	On cover		125.00
	FDC *(May 1, 1901)*		—

CM31 *Fast Ocean Navigation* (S.S. St. Paul)

CM31		UnFVF	UseFVF
10¢	**yellow brown & black** *(5,043,700)*	140.00	22.50
	dark yellow brown & black	140.00	22.50
	Plate strip of 3, w/imprint	750.00	
	Plate block of 4, w/imprint & arrow	—	
	Plate strip of 5 (2 numbers), w/imprint	1,400.00	
	Plate block of 6, w/imprint	7,000.00	
	Plate block of 10 (2 numbers), w/imprint	12,500.00	
	Margin block of 4, w/imprint & arrow	800.00	
	On cover		150.00
	FDC *(May 1, 1901)*		—

1904. Louisiana Purchase Exposition Issue prepared for the World's Fair at St. Louis, Mo., commemorating the 1803 acquisition of the Louisiana Territory from France. All values were placed on sale April 30, the opening day of the fair.

Robert Livingston (CM32) was appointed minister to France in 1801. In 1803 President Jefferson (CM33) instructed him to negotiate with Napoleon for the purchase of New Orleans and the mouth of the Mississippi. James Monroe (CM34), former minister to France, was sent to aid in the negotiations. Francois de Barbe-Marbois, Napoleon's finance minister, astounded them by offering to sell the entire Louisiana Territory, an offer which they accepted without delay or authority. The price was $11,250,000; claims and interest accruals raised it to $27,000,000, about 4¢ an acre. The territory (CM36) eventually became 10 entire states and parts of three others. President McKinley (CM35) signed the Act of Congress approving the 1904 World's Fair but never lived to see it. In September 1901 he was assassinated while attending the Pan-American Exposition. *Intaglio, perforated 12.*

CM32 *Robert Livingston, from a painting by Gilbert Stuart*

CM32		UnFVF	UseFVF
1¢	**green** *(79,779,200)*	20.00	3.50
	dark green	20.00	3.50
	Plate pair, w/imprint	65.00	
	Plate strip of 3, w/imprint	100.00	
	Plate block of 4, w/imprint	160.00	
	Plate block of 6, w/imprint	175.00	
	Margin block of 4, w/arrow	75.00	
	Diagonal line through left "1"	50.00	10.00
	Double transfer	—	
	On cover		75.00
	FDC *(April 30, 1904)*		6,500.00

CM33 *Thomas Jefferson, from a painting attributed to Gilbert Stuart*

CM33		UnFVF	UseFVF
2¢	**carmine** *(192,732,400)*	19.00	1.25
	bright carmine	19.00	1.25
	Plate pair, w/imprint	75.00	
	Plate strip of 3, w/imprint	125.00	
	Plate block of 4, w/imprint	160.00	
	Plate block of 6, w/imprint	175.00	
	Margin block of 4, w/arrow	100.00	
	On cover		6.00
	FDC *(April 30, 1904)*		5,000.00
	v. Vertical pair, imperforate horizontally	—	

CM34 *James Monroe, from a painting by Vanderlyn in New York City Hall*

CM34		UnFVF	UseFVF
3¢	**dark red violet** *(4,542,600)*	60.00	25.00
	Plate pair, w/imprint	150.00	
	Plate strip of 3, w/imprint	275.00	
	Plate block of 4, w/imprint	550.00	
	Plate block of 6, w/imprint	800.00	
	Margin block of 4, w/arrow	325.00	
	Double transfer	—	
	On cover		75.00
	FDC *(April 30, 1904)*		18,000.00

CM35 *William McKinley*

CM35		UnFVF	UseFVF
5¢	**indigo** *(6,926,700)*	75.00	17.50
	Plate pair, w/imprint	200.00	
	Plate strip of 3, w/imprint	325.00	
	Plate block of 4, w/imprint	625.00	
	Plate block of 6, w/imprint	900.00	
	Margin block of 4, w/arrow	350.00	
	On cover		75.00
	FDC *(April 30, 1904)*		26,000.00

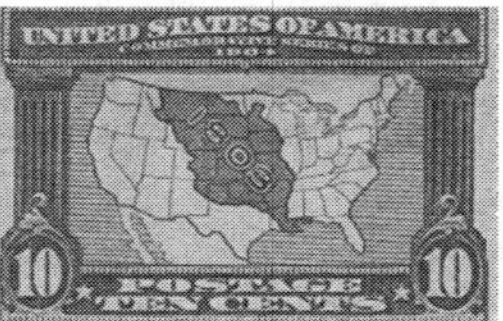

CM36 *Map of Louisiana Purchase*

CM36		UnFVF	UseFVF
10¢	**red brown** *(4,011,200)*	125.00	25.00
	dark red brown	125.00	25.00
	Plate pair, w/imprint	325.00	
	Plate strip of 3, w/imprint	500.00	
	Plate block of 4, w/imprint	1,250.00	
	Plate block of 6, w/imprint	1,750.00	
	Margin block of 4, w/arrow	575.00	
	On cover		125.00
	FDC *(April 30, 1904)*		27,500.00

1907. Jamestown Issue was created for the Jamestown Exposition at Hampton Roads, Va., commemorating the 300th anniversary of the oldest permanent English settlement in America. In 1607, on their way to reattempt a settlement at Roanoke Island, three London Company ships with 105 men were blown off course and discovered the entrance to Chesapeake Bay. Sailing 50 miles up a river they named the James (for King James I), they began a settlement called Jamestown (CM38). Constant Indian trouble brought out the leadership qualities of Capt. John Smith (CM37). Captured while foraging and condemned to death by the Indian Chief Powhatan, Smith is said by legend to have been saved by the chief's beautiful daughter Pocahontas (CM39). Married to a settler named John Rolfe, she was received with royal honors in England, where she died in 1617. The 1¢ and 2¢ stamps were placed on sale April 25, 1907. The 5¢ value was first sold May 3, 1907. *Intaglio, perforated 12.*

CM37 *Captain John Smith, from a painting in the State Library, Virginia*

CM37		UnFVF	UseFVF
1¢	**deep bluish green** *(77,728,794)*	17.50	3.00
	dark green	17.50	3.00
	Plate strip of 3, w/imprint	65.00	
	Plate block of 6, w/imprint	275.00	
	Margin block of 4, w/arrow	75.00	
	Double transfer	25.00	8.00
	On cover		12.50
	FDC *(April 6, 1907)*		12,000.00

CM38 *Founding of Jamestown, from a lost painting*

CM38		UnFVF	UseFVF
2¢	**rose red** *(149,497,994)*	22.50	2.75
	bright rose red	22.50	2.75
	Plate strip of 3, w/imprint	75.00	
	Plate block of 6, w/imprint	375.00	
	Margin block of 4, w/arrow	90.00	
	Double transfer		6.00
	On cover		7.50
	FDC *(April 6, 1907)*		12,000.00

CM39 *Pocahontas, from a painting in Norfolk, England*

CM39		UnFVF	UseFVF
5¢	**indigo** *(7,980,594)*	85.00	22.50
	blue	85.00	22.50
	Plate strip of 3, w/imprint	300.00	
	Plate block of 6, w/imprint	2,100.00	
	Margin block of 4, w/arrow	350.00	
	Double transfer	125.00	45.00
	On cover		75.00
	Earliest known use: *May 9, 1907*		

1909. Lincoln Memorial Centennial Issue commemorated the 100th anniversary of the birth of Abraham Lincoln. It was designed, using the existing Washington-Franklin series frame, and produced within 31 days. As an experiment to counteract the shrinking caused by printing on wet paper, some rows of stamps were separated by 3mm spacing instead of the usual 2mm. Some of the perforated stamps were printed on a 35-percent-rag stock known as "bluish paper," which is actually grayish in appearance. *Intaglio, perforated 12 and imperforate.*

CM40-42 *Abraham Lincoln, from The Head of State statue by Augustus Saint Gaudens, Grant Park, Chicago*

Perforated 12.

CM40		UnFVF	UseFVF
2¢	**carmine** *(148,387,191)*	5.00	1.75
	bright carmine	5.00	1.75
	Block of 4 (2mm spacing)	25.00	17.50
	Block of 4 (3mm spacing)	25.00	17.50
	Plate block of 6, w/imprint	125.00	
	Double transfer	12.50	5.00
	On cover		9.00
	FDC *(Feb. 12, 1909)*		500.00

Imperforate.

CM41		UnFVF	UseFVF
2¢	**carmine** *(1,273,900)*	22.50	1,750.00
	Block of 4 (2mm spacing)	100.00	
	Block of 4 (3mm spacing)	100.00	
	Plate block of 6, w/imprint	225.00	
	Center line block	200.00	
	Margin block of 4, w/arrow	100.00	
	Double transfer	60.00	30.00
	On cover		50.00
	FDC *(Feb. 12, 1909)*		17,000.00

Bluish gray paper, perforated 12 (Feb. 1909).

CM42		UnFVF	UseFVF
2¢	**carmine** *(637,000)*	175.00	195.00
	Block of 4 (2mm spacing)	900.00	750.00
	Block of 4 (3mm spacing)	900.00	750.00
	Plate block of 6, w/imprint	3,000.00	
	On cover		450.00
	Earliest known use: *March 27, 1909*		

1909. Alaska-Yukon Issue released in connection with a Seattle, Wash., exposition commemorating the development of the Alaska-Yukon-Pacific Territory. William H. Seward, Secretary of State under Lincoln and Johnson, negotiated the purchase of Alaska from Russia, begun in 1859 but postponed by the Civil War. The treaty of March 30,

1867, set the purchase price at $7,200,000. The formal transfer was made Oct. 18 at Sitka. *Intaglio, perforated 12 and imperforate.*

CM43, 44 *William Seward, from a drawing by Marcus W. Baldwin*

Perforated 12.

CM43		UnFVF	UseFVF
2¢	**carmine** *(152,887,311)*	7.00	1.50
	bright carmine	7.00	1.50
	Plate block of 6, w/imprint	250.00	
	Double transfer	1,750.00	6.00
	On cover		7.50
	FDC *(June 1, 1909)*		4,500.00

Imperforate.

CM44		UnFVF	UseFVF
2¢	**carmine** *(525,400)*	30.00	22.50
	Plate block of 6, w/imprint	275.00	
	Center line block	175.00	150.00
	Margin block of 4, w/arrow	150.00	120.00
	Double transfer	55.00	35.00
	On cover		45.00
	Earliest known use: *June 9, 1909*		

1909. HUDSON-FULTON ISSUE commemorated historic voyages 200 years apart up the Hudson River to Albany, N.Y. Henry Hudson, an English navigator commanding the Dutch East India Company ship, *Half Moon,* explored the river when he sailed into New York Bay Sept. 3, 1609. Robert Fulton, aided by Robert Livingston (CM32), constructed the first practical steamship, named *Clermont* after Livingston's home, and steamed to Albany and back Aug. 17-22, 1807. *Intaglio, perforated 12 and imperforate.*

CM45 Half Moon *and* S.S. Clermont

Perforated 12.

CM45		UnFVF	UseFVF
2¢	**carmine** *(72,634,631)*	10.00	3.50
	Plate block of 6, w/imprint	350.00	
	Double transfer	25.00	7.50
	On cover		800.00
	FDC *(Sept. 25, 1909);* EKU *Sept. 23, 1909*		—

Imperforate.

CM46		UnFVF	UseFVF
2¢	**carmine** *(216,480)*	35.00	22.50
	Plate block of 6, w/imprint	350.00	
	Center line block	275.00	140.00
	Margin block of 4, w/arrow	175.00	120.00
	Double transfer	55.00	35.00
	On cover		45.00
	FDC *(Sept. 25, 1909)*		7,500.00

1913-15. PANAMA-PACIFIC ISSUE commemorated Balboa's sighting of the Pacific Ocean in 1513; the opening of the Panama Canal in 1914; and the Panama-Pacific Exposition at San Francisco, Calif., in 1915.

Vasco Nuñez de Balboa (CM47), Spanish governor of Darien (Panama), marched across the isthmus and from the peak of Mount Darien sighted the waters of "the South Sea" on Sept. 25, 1513. Ferdinand Magellan named it the Pacific Ocean in 1520. A canal connecting the Atlantic and Pacific oceans (CM48) was built by the United States during 1904-14 at a cost of $336,650,000. San Francisco Bay (CM99) is said to have been sighted by Francis Drake in 1579, but the city's site was discovered (CM50), in 1770 by Don Gaspar de Portola, Spanish governor of the Californias, who, with the Franciscan missionary Junipero Serra (A116), led a 1,000-mile march establishing settlements from Lower California to Monterey. *Stamps issued on paper with single-line "USPS" watermark. Intaglio, perforated 12 (1913) and perforated 10 (1914-15). (Quantities shown include both perforation types).*

CM47, 52 *Vasco Nuñez de Balboa*

CM47		UnFVF	UseFVF
1¢	**green** *(334,796,926)*	15.50	1.25
	yellow green	15.50	1.25
	Plate block of 6	160.00	
	Double transfer	25.00	5.00
	On cover		7.50
	FDC *(Jan. 1, 1913)*		5,000.00

CM48, CM53 *Panama Canal, from a model of the Pedro Miguel Locks*

CM48		UnFVF	UseFVF
2¢	**rose red** *(503,713,086)*	20.00	.50
	deep carmine	20.00	.50
	brown lake	—	
	Plate block of 6	250.00	
	Double transfer	45.00	5.00
	On cover		4.00
	FDC *(Jan. 18, 1913)*		2,000.00
	a. carmine lake	575.00	
	Earliest known use: *Jan. 17, 1913*		

CM49, CM54 *The Golden Gate, from a photograph*

CM49		UnFVF	UseFVF
5¢	**blue** *(29,088,726)*	75.00	9.00
	dark blue	75.00	9.00
	Plate block of 6	2,000.00	
	On cover		45.00
	FDC *(Jan. 1, 1913)*		22,000.00

CM50-51, CM55 *Dicovery of San Francisco Bay, from a painting by Charles F. Matthews, San Francisco Art Museum*

CM50		UnFVF	UseFVF
10¢	**orange yellow** *(16,968,365)*	125.00	20.00
	Plate block of 6	2,500.00	
	On cover		100.00
	FDC *(Jan. 1, 1913)*		17,500.00

CM51		UnFVF	UseFVF
10¢	**orange** *(16,968,365)* (Aug. 1913)	200.00	15.00
	Plate block of 6	10,250.00	
	On cover		125.00

1914-15. PANAMA-PACIFIC ISSUE *Perforated 10.*

CM52		UnFVF	UseFVF
1¢	**green**	22.00	5.25
	dark green	22.00	5.25
	Plate block of 6	330.00	
	On cover		30.00
	Earliest known use: *Dec. 21, 1914*		

CM53		UnFVF	UseFVF
2¢	**rose red**	70.00	1.50

		UnFVF	UseFVF
	dark carmine	70.00	1.50
	red	70.00	1.50
	Plate block of 6	1,700.00	
	On cover		12.50
	Earliest known use: *Jan. 13, 1915*		

CM54		UnFVF	UseFVF
5¢	**blue**	160.00	14.50
	dark blue	160.00	14.50
	Plate block of 6	4,250.00	
	On cover		75.00
	Earliest known use: *Feb. 6, 1915*		

CM55		UnFVF	UseFVF
10¢	**orange**	900.00	60.00
	Plate block of 6	13,000.00	
	On cover		225.00
	Earliest known use: *Aug. 27, 1915*		

1919. Victory Issue commemorated the winning of World War I by the Allies. The design shows a female allegory of "Victory" and the U.S. flag flanked by the flags of Great Britain, Belgium, Italy and France. *Intaglio, perforated 11.*

CM56 *"Victory" and Flags*

CM56		UnFVF	UseFVF
3¢	**dark lilac** *(99,585,200)*	7.50	3.00
	Plate block of 6	75.00	
	FDC *(March 3, 1919)*		200.00
	a. dark red lilac	600.00	150.00
	a1. Plate block of 6	—	
	b. pale red lilac	13.50	3.50
	b1. Plate block of 6	—	
	c. bright red lilac	40.00	15.00
	c1. Plate block of 6	—	

1920. Pilgrim Tercentenary Issue marked the 300th anniversary of the landing of the Pilgrims at Plymouth, Mass. (CM58), in December 1620. Of the *Mayflower's* (CM57) 102 passengers, 41 Pilgrim "fathers" en route signed a compact (CM59) in which they pledged to

Decoding the Catalog

The Panama-Pacific stamps of 1913-15 are notable among early United States commemorative issues by virtue of their extraoridinary longevity, which gave rise to collectible perforation and color varieties. At first, most U.S. commemoratives were issued at and used for the duration of various expositions. When the show ended, the stamps were taken off sale, and unsold remainders were soon destrayed. The idea of releasing stamps prior to an event for advance publicity and promotion came to fruition with the Panama-Pacific commemoratives.

The issue ostensibly celebrated three events — the 400th anniversary of Balboa's sighting of the Pacific Ocean in 1513, the opening of the Panama Canal in 1914 and the Panama-Pacific Exposition in 1915. However, the impetus behind the stamps and the exposition was the surprisingly rapid recovery of San Francisco from the devastating earthquake and fire of April 18, 1906. Unlike the first U.S. commemoratives, which had been widely opposed by collectors, the Panama-Pacific issue actually had some respected philatelic publications calling for the stamps, in addition to local civic boosters.

Panama-Pacific Exposition

1913 — Perforated 12

Minkus	Value & Shade	Unused	Used
CM47	1¢ green	15.50	1.25
	yellow green	15.50	1.25
CM48	2¢ carmine	20.00	.50
	deep carmine	20.00	.50
	carmine lake	575.00	—
CM49	5¢ blue	75.00	9.00
	dark blue	75.00	9.00
CM50	10¢ orange yellow	125.00	20.00
CM51	10¢ orange	200.00	15.00

1914-15 — Perforated 10

Minkus	Value & Shade	Unused	Used
CM52	1¢ green	22.00	5.25
	dark green	22.00	5.25
CM53	2¢ carmine	70.00	1.50
	dark carmine	70.00	1.50
	red	70.00	1.50
CM54	5¢ blue	160.00	14.50
	dark blue	160.00	14.50
CM55	10¢ orange	900.00	60.00

The first of the stamps, perforated 12, were issued Jan. 1, 1913 — more than two years before the exhibition, which ran from Feb. 20 to Dec. 4, 1915. The final stamps were shipped in mid-January 1916 — an unprecendented run.

In the middle of that run, the Bureau of Engraving and Printing changed perforations to 10 gauge in late 1914 to increase the strength of the sheets, and as the perf 12 stock became low additional quantities were given gauge 10 perforations. "This later group was current for only about a year, and as the majority of collectors paid little or no attention to the change of perforation it is very much scarcer than the early perf 12," Max Johl noted in *U.S. Postage Stamps of the 20th Century."*

The reprinting of the 10¢ stamp in a darker orange perf 12 version in August 1913 was no accident. It was done at the behest of the Post Office Department in response to complaints that the original orange yellow was too light a shade. The perf 10 orange, Johl wrote, "was current for less than six months and was almost entirely overlooked by both collectors and dealers," accounting for its higher value today.

Johl rated the perf 12 2¢ carmine lake as extremely scarce. "Only 40 copies from one pane of 70 of this shade were said to have been found... although it hardly seems possible that only one sheet could have been printed in this darker color," he wrote.

adhere to the principles of self-government in the colony. *Intaglio, perforated 11.*

CM57 *The Mayflower, from a watercolor by Harrison Eastman, Smithsonian Institution, Washington, D.C.*

CM57		UnFVF	UseFVF
1¢	**green** *(137,978,207)*	3.50	2.50
	dark green	3.50	2.00
	Plate block of 6	35.00	
	Double transfer	—	
	On cover		8.00
	FDC *(Dec. 21, 1920)*		1,600.00

CM58 *Landing of the Pilgrims, from an 1846 engraving by Burt based on a sketch by White*

CM58		UnFVF	UseFVF
2¢	**rose red** *(196,037,327)*	5.25	1.75
	carmine	5.25	1.75
	rose	5.25	1.75
	Plate block of 6	50.00	
	On cover		5.00
	FDC *(Dec. 20, 1920)*		1,500.00

CM59 *Signing of the Compact, from a painting by Edwin White*

CM59		UnFVF	UseFVF
5¢	**deep blue** *(11,321,607)*	35.00	12.50
	dark blue	35.00	12.50
	Plate block of 6	375.00	
	On cover		30.00
	FDC *(Dec. 21, 1920)*		3,000.00

1923. Harding Memorial Issue honored President Warren G. Harding, who died Aug. 2, 1923, in San Francisco, Calif. An Ohio newspaper editor elected to the U.S. Senate in 1914, he won the presidency in 1920 on a platform pledging a "return to normalcy." First President to visit Alaska, he died on the way home. An immediate scramble to release a memorial stamp ensued. Unlike today, there was no one-year waiting period for a president. By Sept. 1, 1923, less than one month after Harding's death, a stamp had been designed, engraved, printed, distributed and issued, a remarkable feat. However, this led to several varieties of the stamp, due primarily to changing printing technology. Four varieties of the stamp exist: two printed by flat plate *(perforated 11 and imperforate)* and two produced by rotary press *(perforated 10 and the rare perforated 11). No. CM63 is known only in used condition, and only 43 examples are recorded. Intaglio.*

The printed design of the flat plate printing measures 19 x 21 7/8mm. Small specks of black color usually are seen on the backs of these stamps, a characteristic of almost all flat-press-printed stamps. The color is a true black.

The printed design of the rotary press printings measures 19 x 22 1/2mm. Color specks are almost always absent from the backs of these stamps. The color is a grayish black.

Some consider these commemorative mourning stamps to be part of the 1922-34 Regular Issue Series. In fact, a similar design with 1 1/2¢ value (No. 420) is part of that series.

CM60-63 *Warren G. Harding*

Flat plate printing, perforated 11.

CM60		UnFVF	UseFVF
2¢	**black** *(1,459,487,085)*	.60	.20
	grayish black	.60	.20
	Plate block of 6	27.50	
	Double transfer	3.00	.75
	On cover		1.00
	FDC *(Sept. 1, 1923)*		40.00
	v. Horizontal pair, imperforate vertically	1,500.00	

Flat plate printing, imperforate.

CM61		UnFVF	UseFVF
2¢	**black** *(770,000)*	6.50	4.50
	Plate block of 6	90.00	
	Block of 4, w/arrow	50.00	
	Center line block of 4	75.00	
	On cover		12.50
	FDC *(Nov. 15, 1923)*		125.00

Rotary press printing, perforated 10.

CM62		UnFVF	UseFVF
2¢	**gray black** *(99,950,300)*	15.00	1.75
	black	15.00	1.75
	Plate block of 4	275.00	
	Pair, gutter between	400.00	
	On cover		6.00
	FDC *(Sept. 12, 1923)*		175.00

Rotary press printing, perforated 11.

CM63		UnFVF	UseFVF
2¢	**gray black**		30,000.00

1924. Huguenot-Walloon Issue commemorated the 300th anniversary of the Walloon settlement of New York, and the restoration of a monument to earlier Huguenot settlements in the South.

During the religious wars of the 16th century, thousands of French and Belgian Protestants, known as Huguenots, settled in Holland, where they were called Walloons (foreigners). Although Dutch traders had visited Manhattan since 1613, the first Dutch immigrants were 30 Walloon families sent by the Dutch West India Company in 1624. Under Peter Minuit they bought Manhattan from the Indians and tried founding settlements all the way from the Delaware River to Fort Orange, now Albany (CM65). In 1562, French Huguenots unsuccessfully had tried a settlement at Port Royal, S.C. In 1564 a colony was established at Fort Caroline (now Mayport) on the St. Johns River in Florida, and had a stone column erected bearing the French coat of arms. The colony was massacred in 1565 by the Spanish under Pedro Menendez de Aviles. This column was replaced and dedicated May 2, 1924. *Intaglio, perforated 11.*

CM64 *The* New Netherland

CM64		UnFVF	UseFVF
1¢	**green** *(51,378,023)*	2.75	2.75
	dark green	2.75	2.75
	Plate block of 6	30.00	
	Double transfer	10.00	6.50
	On cover		7.00
	FDC *(May 1, 1924)*		40.00

CM65 *Landing of Walloons at Fort Orange, from* History of New York *by Martha Lamb*

CM65		UnFVF	UseFVF
2¢	**carmine red** *(77,753,423)*	5.00	2.00
	Plate block of 6	55.00	
	Double transfer	15.00	4.25
	On cover		5.00
	FDC *(May 1, 1924)*		60.00

CM66 *Monument of Huguenots at Mayport, Fla.*

CM66		UnFVF	UseFVF
5¢	**Prussian blue** *(5,659,023)*	27.50	14.00
	dark blue	27.50	14.00
	Plate block of 6	250.00	
	On cover (UPU rate)		30.00
	FDC *(May 1, 1924)*		85.00
	v. Broken circle below right numeral "5"	65.00	22.50

1925. Lexington-Concord Issue commemorated the 150th anniversary of the first armed conflicts of the American Revolution, which took place on April 19, 1775.

When Gen. Thomas Gage, colonial governor of Massachusetts, sent 800 troops to Lexington and Concord to destroy military supplies stored there by the colonists, Paul Revere made his famous ride on horseback to warn the colonists. Calling themselves the Minute Men (ready to fight on a minute's notice) (CM69), the colonists gathered on the Green at Lexington with the watchword, "If they mean to have a war, let it begin here" (CM68). Eight of the 70 Minute Men were killed; the rest fell back, and the British went to Concord. In fighting on the North Bridge there, and continuing all the way back to the protection of naval guns at Charlestown Harbor, the British suffered 273 casualties; the colonists 93. Chosen to head a Continental Army, George Washington took command at Cambridge in July (CM67). *Intaglio, perforated 11.*

CM67 *Washington at Cambridge, from an engraving in the Cambridge Public Library*

CM67		UnFVF	UseFVF
1¢	**green** *(15,615,000)*	2.75	2.50
	dark green	2.75	2.50
	Plate block of 6	40.00	
	On cover		5.00
	FDC *(April 4, 1925)*		30.00

CM68 Battle of Lexington, *painting by Henry Sandham, Town Hall, Lexington, Mass.*

CM68		UnFVF	UseFVF
2¢	**carmine red** *(26,596,600)*	5.00	3.50
	Plate block of 6	65.00	
	On cover		7.50
	FDC *(April 4, 1925)*		35.00

CM69 *The Minute Man, from a statue by Daniel Chester French in Concord; poetry by Ralph Waldo Emerson*

CM69		UnFVF	UseFVF
5¢	**Prussian blue** *(5,348,800)*	25.00	14.00
	Plate block of 6	225.00	
	On cover (UPU rate)		22.50
	FDC *(April 4, 1925)*		85.00
	v. Line over head	65.00	25.00

1925. Norse-American Issue commemorated the 100th anniversary of the first Norwegian immigrants' arrival on the *Restaurationen* on Oct. 9, 1825. Sagas tell of Norse exploration of the North American coast ca. 1000 A.D. *Intaglio, perforated 11.*

CM70 *Sloop* Restaurationen, *adapted from a drawing of a sister ship*

CM70		UnFVF	UseFVF
2¢	**carmine & black** *(9,104,983)*	4.00	3.00
	dark carmine and black	4.00	3.00
	Plate block of 8 w/2 numbers & arrow	200.00	
	Plate block of 8, w/carmine number (only) & arrow	3,250.00	
	Center line block of 4	27.50	
	Margin block of 4, w/arrow	35.00	
	On cover		8.00
	FDC *(May 18, 1925)*		20.00

CM71 *Viking ship built in Norway, by popular subscription, as a gift to the people of the United States*

CM71		UnFVF	UseFVF
5¢	**indigo & black** *(1,900,983)*	15.00	12.50
	Plate block of 8, w/2 numbers & arrow	575.00	
	Center line block of 4	90.00	
	Margin block of 4, w/arrow	85.00	
	On cover (UPU rate)		22.50
	FDC *(May 18, 1925)*		30.00
	FDC CM70 & 71 on 1 cover		50.00

1926. Sesquicentennial Issue in connection with the exposition at Philadelphia, Pa., commemorated the 150th anniversary of the Declaration of Independence. *Intaglio, perforated 11.*

CM72 *The Liberty Bell, designed from the entrance to the exposition*

CM72		UnFVF	UseFVF
2¢	**carmine red** *(307,731,900)*	2.50	.50
	Plate block of 6	35.00	
	Double transfer	—	
	FDC *(May 10, 1926)*		10.00

1926. Ericsson Memorial Issue honored John Ericsson, the Swedish-born engineer who built the ironclad *USS Monitor,* which engaged the Confederate ironclad *Virginia* (formerly *USS Merrimac)* off Hampton Roads, Va., in 1862. Ericsson's inventions included a screw propeller that revolutionized shipbuilding. The stamp shows a statue of him unveiled in Washington by the Crown Prince of Sweden. *Intaglio, perforated 11.*

Users of this Catalog are invited to write us if they have information which they feel will supplement or correct any material contained herein. All such communications will be answered.

CM73 *Statue of John Ericsson, sculpted by James Earl Fraser, Washington, D.C.*

CM73		UnFVF	UseFVF
5¢	**slate violet** *(20,280,500)*	6.00	2.50
	Plate block of 6	75.00	
	FDC *(May 29, 1929)*		25.00

1926. White Plains Issue commemorated the 150th anniversary of the Battle of White Plains, N.Y., Oct. 28, 1776. The British, attempting to outflank Washington's forces in upper Manhattan, caused him to withdraw his main force northward. In a sharp battle at White Plains, the British captured a key hill, but Washington escaped while they were awaiting reinforcements. *Intaglio, perforated 11.*

CM74 *Alexander Hamilton's battery, from a painting by E. L. Ward*

CM74		UnFVF	UseFVF
2¢	**carmine red** *(40,639,485)*	2.00	1.50
	Plate block of 6	40.00	
	FDC *(Oct. 18, 1926)*		8.00
	v. Vertical pair, imperforated between	2,500.00	

1926. White Plains Philatelic Exhibition Issue Sheets of 25 stamps with marginal inscription noting the International Philatelic Exhibition, Oct. 16-23, 1926, in New York, N.Y. Sheet size 161 x 149mm.

CM75 *White Plains souvenir sheet of 25*

CM75		UnFVF	UseFVF
2¢	**carmine red** *(107,398)*	400.00	425.00
	v. Dot over first "S" of "States" on stamp in position 9 of lower left pane of plate 18774 or position 11 of the lower left pane of plate 18773.	425.00	450.00
	FDC Full sheet *(Oct. 18, 1926)*		1,700.00

1927. Vermont Sesquicentennial Issue commemorated the 150th anniversary of the Battle of Bennington and the independence of the State of Vermont. In 1777, badly needing supplies at Saratoga, N.Y., British Gen. John Burgoyne sent a force to capture American military stores at Bennington, Vt. In a battle Aug. 16 with 2,600 militiamen (the "Green Mountain Boys") under Gen. John Stark, almost the entire British force was killed or captured. *Intaglio, perforated 11.*

CM76 *Green Mountain Boy*

CM76		UnFVF	UseFVF
2¢	**carmine red** *(39,974,900)*	1.25	1.00
	Plate block of 6	40.00	
	FDC *(Aug. 3, 1927)*		6.00

1927. Burgoyne Campaign Issue commemorated the Battle of Bennington, Oriskany, Fort Stanwix and Saratoga. On Oct. 17, 1777, surrounded by a force three times his own, British Gen. John Burgoyne surrendered to the Americans at Saratoga. His 5,700 men went back to England, pledged not to fight again in the war. *Intaglio, perforated 11.*

CM77 *Surrender of Gen. John Burgoyne, from a painting by John Trumbull in the Capitol Rotunda, Washington, D.C.*

CM77		UnFVF	UseFVF
2¢	**carmine red** *(25,628,450)*	3.50	2.25
	Plate block of 6	40.00	
	FDC *(Aug. 3, 1927)*		11.00

1928. Valley Forge Issue recalled the 150th anniversary of Washington's winter encampment at Valley Forge, about 20 miles northwest of Philadelphia, Pa. Beaten at Brandywine and Germantown, desperately short of food, clothing and supplies, the American troops at Valley Forge showed courage in the darkest period of American history. *Intaglio, perforated 11.*

CM78 *General Washington at Prayer, from an engraving by John C. McRae*

CM78		UnFVF	UseFVF
2¢	**carmine red** *(101,330,328)*	1.00	.50
	Plate block of 6	25.00	
	FDC *(May 26, 1928)*		5.00

1928. Hawaiian Sesquicentennial Issue marked the 150th anniversary of the arrival in the Hawaiian Islands of English navigator Capt. James Cook. These makeshift commemoratives, made by overprinting ordinary definitive stamps (Nos. 476 and 479), disappointed collectors who expected something more elaborate. The overprints available only in the Territory of Hawaii and at the Philatelic Sales Agency in Washington, D.C., caused confusion when some postal clerks would not honor them because they thought they were precancels. *Intaglio, perforated 11 x 10 1/2.*

CM79 2¢ overprint

CM80 5¢ overprint

HAWAII
1778 - 1928

CM79		UnFVF	UseFVF
2¢	**carmine** *(5,519,897)*	4.50	4.50
	Plate block of 4	100.00	
	Vertical pair with wide spacing (28mm rather than 18mm)	100.00	
	FDC *(Aug. 13, 1928)*		15.00

CM80		UnFVF	UseFVF
5¢	**blue** *(1,459,897)*	12.50	12.50
	Plate block of 4	200.00	
	FDC *(Aug. 13, 1928)*		20.00
	FDC CM79 & 80 on 1 cover		40.00

1928. Molly Pitcher Issue another two-line overprint of No. 476, commemorated the 150th anniversary of the Battle of Monmouth, N.J., June 28, 1778, and honored Mary Ludwig Hays McCauly, whose husband was a cannoneer in the battle. Called "Molly Pitcher" because she carried water to the tired and wounded soldiers, she also took her husband's place when he was wounded, and manned his cannon throughout the rest of the battle. (See also the 1978 10¢ postal card, No. PC73.) *Intaglio, perforated 11.*

CM81 *2¢ Molly Pitcher overprint*

CM81		UnFVF	UseFVF
2¢	**carmine** *(9,779,896)*	1.00	1.25
	Plate block of 4	25.00	
	Vertical pair with wide spacing (28mm rather than 18mm)	27.50	
	FDC *(Oct. 20, 1928)*		12.50

1928. Aeronautics Conference Issue in connection with the International Civil Aeronautics Conference held Dec. 12-14 in Washington, D.C., commemorated the 25th anniversary of the first airplane flight (Dec. 17, 1903) by the Wright brothers at Kitty Hawk, N.C. The plane (CM80), in England for 20 years, was returned to the United States in 1948 and is now on view at the Smithsonian Institution in Washington, D.C. *Intaglio, perforated 11.*

CM82 *Wright airplane*

CM82		UnFVF	UseFVF
2¢	**carmine red** *(51,342,273)*	1.25	1.00
	Plate block of 6	12.50	
	FDC *(Dec. 12, 1928)*		6.00

CM83 *Globe and airplane*

CM83		UnFVF	UseFVF
5¢	**Prussian blue** *(10,319,700)*	5.00	3.00
	Plate block of 6	55.00	
	"Prairie dog" plate flaw (position 50 of bottom-lower left pane of plate 19658)	30.00	
	FDC *(Dec. 12, 1928)*		10.00

1929. George Rogers Clark Issue commemorated the 150th anniversary of Clark's recapture of Fort Sackville (now Vincennes, Ind.), from a force of British, Loyalists and Indians commanded by Col. Henry Hamilton. From winter quarters at Kaskaskia, Clark sent 40 men by boat, led another 130 across the flooded plains, tricked Hamilton's Indians into deserting, took the fort on Feb. 25, and secured the Northwest for the colonists. *Intaglio, perforated 11.*

CM84 *Surrender of Fort Sackville, from a painting by Frederick C. Yohn*

CM84		UnFVF	UseFVF
2¢	**carmine & black** *(16,684,674)*	.60	.50
	Plate block of 6, w/two numbers & "TOP"	12.50	
	Plate block of 10, w/red number only	—	
	Margin block of 4, w/arrow	3.50	
	Double transfer	5.50	3.00
	FDC *(Feb. 25, 1929)*		5.00

1929. Edison Commemorative Issue celebrated the 50th anniversary of the invention of the incandescent electric lamp by Thomas Alva Edison (CM287). *Issued in both flat and rotary press intaglio printings and as a rotary press coil stamp. The rotary press sheet version is taller than the other two, and the coil version is wider, due to the stretching of the plates as they were curved to fit the continuous rotary press. Huge quantities of the rotary press stamps were used (and subsequently destroyed) on business mailings, leaving relatively few for the philatelic trade.*

CM85-87 *Edison's first electric lamp*

Flat press, perforated 11.

CM85		UnFVF	UseFVF
2¢	**carmine red** *(31,679,200)*	.75	.75
	Plate block of 6	30.00	
	FDC *(June 5, 1929)*		40.00

Rotary press, perforated 11 x 10 1/2.

CM86		UnFVF	UseFVF
2¢	**carmine red** *(210,119,474)*	.75	.25
	Plate block of 4	35.00	
	FDC *(June 11, 1929)*		375.00

Rotary press coil, perforated 10 vertically.

CM87		UnFVF	UseFVF
2¢	**carmine red** *(133,530,000)*	12.50	1.50
	Pair	22.50	7.00
	Joint line pair	60.00	40.00
	FDC *(June 11, 1929)*		375.00

1929. Sullivan Expedition Issue noted the 150th anniversary of the campaign by Gens. John Sullivan and James Clinton against the Loyalists and Iroquois Indians ravaging Pennsylvania and New York frontier settlements. They defeated the Iroquois at Newtown (now Elmira), N.Y., Aug. 29, 1779. *Intaglio, perforated 11.*

CM88 *Maj. Gen. John Sullivan*

CM88		UnFVF	UseFVF
2¢	**carmine red** *(51,451,880)*	.75	.75
	Plate block of 6	25.00	
	FDC *(June 17, 1929)* w/o cachet		4.00
	FDC w/cachet		27.50

1929. Battle of Fallen Timbers Issue commemorated Gen. Anthony Wayne's defeat of Chief Little Turtle, Aug. 1794, near what is now Toledo, Ohio. His victory led to the settlement of Ohio. *Intaglio, perforated 11.*

CM89 *Gen. Wayne Memorial, monument by Bruce W. Laville at Fallen Timbers Park, Ohio*

CM89		UnFVF	UseFVF
2¢	**carmine red** *(29,338,274)*	.75	.75
	Plate block of 6	25.00	
	FDC *(Sept. 14, 1929)* w/o cachet		3.50
	FDC w/cachet		35.00

1929. Ohio River Canalization Issue saluted the Army Engineers' completion of America's most extensive canal system. Its 46 locks and dams provided a dependable 9-foot channel between Pittsburgh, Pa., and Cairo, Ill., a distance of 981 miles. *Intaglio, perforated 11.*

CM90 *Monongahela River lock*

CM90		UnFVF	UseFVF
2¢	**carmine red** *(32,680,900)*	.50	.75
	Plate block of 6	17.50	35.00
	FDC *(Oct. 19, 1929)* w/o cachet		3.50
	FDC w/cachet		30.00

1930. Massachusett's Bay Colony Issue commemorated the 300th anniversary of the arrival of the Puritans under Gov. John Winthrop. When the charter given to the Massachusetts Bay Company neglected to specify where its annual meetings were to be held, the company took advantage of the oversight by moving itself to New England as a self-governing commonwealth, the first in the New World. *Intaglio, perforated 11.*

CM91 *Seal of the Massachusetts Bay Colony*

CM91		UnFVF	UseFVF
2¢	**carmine red** *(74,000,774)*	.75	.45
	Plate block of 6	25.00	
	FDC *(April 8, 1930)* w/o cachet		3.50
	FDC w/cachet		35.00

1930. Carolina-Charleston Issue commemorated the 260th anniversary of the Province of Carolina and 250th anniversary of the City of Charleston. In 1670, Gov. William Sayle and 150 colonists landed at Albemarle Point on the Ashley River, founding a settlement called Charles Town. In 1680 they moved into a walled city they had built at Oyster Point, present site of Charleston. This was the first permanent settlement in the Carolinas. *Intaglio, perforated 11.*

CM92 *Colonial governor and Indian*

CM92		UnFVF	UseFVF
2¢	**carmine red** *(25,215,574)*	1.25	1.00
	Plate block of 6	40.00	
	FDC *(April 10, 1930)* w/cachet		35.00
	FDC w/o cachet		3.50

1930. Braddock's Field Issue commemorated the 175th anniversary of the Battle of the Wilderness in the French and Indian War. Advancing on Fort Duquesne (now Pittsburgh), Gen. Braddock's forces were defeated, and Braddock was killed. Lt. Col. George Washington, 23, commanding Braddock's colonials, led the remnant troops in a safe retreat. *Intaglio, perforated 11.*

CM93 *Col. George Washington, monument by Frank Vittor, at Braddock's Field, Pa.*

CM93		UnFVF	UseFVF
2¢	**carmine red** *(25,609,470)*	1.00	1.00
	Plate block of 6	30.00	
	FDC *(July 9, 1930)* w/cachet		30.00
	FDC w/o cachet		4.00

1930. Von Steuben Issue commemorated the 200th birthday of Baron Friedrich Wilhelm von Steuben, a Prussian officer who joined Washington at Valley Forge to serve as inspector general. Von Steuben reorganized and trained the army, lifted its morale, and fought at Monmouth and Yorktown. Naturalized in 1783, he was given 16,000 acres of land by New York State and an annual pension by Congress. *Intaglio, perforated 11.*

CM94 *Gen. von Steuben, from a memorial tablet by Karl Dautert, Magdeburg, Germany*

CM94		UnFVF	UseFVF
2¢	**carmine red** *(66,487,000)*	.50	.50
	Plate block of 6	20.00	
	FDC *(Sept. 17, 1930)* w/cachet		30.00
	FDC w/o cachet		4.00
	v1. Pair, imperforate	3,000.00	
	v2. Plate block of 6, imperforate	12,000.00	

1931. Pulaski Issue tardily commemorated the 150th anniversary of the Oct. 11, 1779, death of Count Casimir Pulaski, Polish patriot and hero of the American Revolution. Known as the Father of the U.S. Cavalry, he was mortally wounded leading a cavalry charge against the British at Savannah, Ga. *Intaglio, perforated 11.*

CM95 *Gen. Casimir Pulaski, from an etching by H. B. Hall*

CM95		UnFVF	UseFVF
2¢	**carmine red** *(96,559,400)*	.25	.20
	dark carmine red	.25	.20
	Plate block of 6	12.50	
	FDC *(Jan. 16, 1931)* w/cachet		30.00
	FDC w/o cachet		4.00

1931. Red Cross Issue commemorated the 50th anniversary of the founding of the American Red Cross Society at Dansville, N.Y. Clara Barton (see CM309, CM1723) was its first president. The design of the stamp is adapted from the popular poster, *The Greatest Mother,* by Laurence Wilbur. *Intaglio, perforated 11.*

CM96 *Red Cross nurse and globe*

CM96		UnFVF	UseFVF
2¢	**black & scarlet** *(99,074,600)*	.25	.20
	Plate block of 4	2.00	

	UnFVF	UseFVF
Margin block of 4, w/arrow	1.00	
Double transfer	1.25	
FDC *(May 21, 1931)* w/cachet		30.00
FDC w/o cachet		3.00
v. Red (cross) omitted	40,000.00	

1931. Yorktown Issue commemorated the 150th anniversary of Lord Cornwallis' surrender at Yorktown, the last important battle of the Revolutionary War. When Lafayette's small force in Virginia was joined in June 1781 by Wayne and von Steuben, Cornwallis moved to Yorktown to maintain sea communication with Clinton's forces in New York. The sudden arrival of De Grasse's French fleet with 3,000 troops hemmed Cornwallis in completely. Washington, who had been preparing an attack on New York, suddenly marched his troops and the French forces of Rochambeau to Virginia, where, with almost 17,000 men, he began the siege of Yorktown. Cornwallis' attempt to escape across the York River by night was thwarted by a storm. On Oct. 19 he surrendered almost 8,000 British and Hessian troops.

Flat press, two plate layouts used. Most panes have a straight edge along one side, but about 10% of printing was from plates that permitted perforation all around, and thus these sheets have no straight edges. Perforated 11.

CM97 *Rochambeau, Washington, De Grasse, from paintings by J. D. Court and J. Trumbull (see CM105) and an engraving*

CM97

2¢		UnFVF	UseFVF
	carmine red & black *(25,006,400)*	.35	.20
	Plate block of 4, 2 numbers	3.50	
	Plate block of 4, 2 numbers & arrow	3.50	
	Plate block of 6, 2 numbers, "TOP" & arrow	4.50	
	Plate block of 8, 2 numbers & "TOP"	6.00	
	Center line block of 4	2.75	
	Margin block of 4, w/arrow	2.75	
	Double transfer	4.50	
	a. dark lake & black	375.00	
	a1. Plate block of 4, 2 numbers	2,000.00	
	b. lake & black	4.50	
	v. Horizontal pair, imperforated vertically	4,500.00	
	FDC *(Oct. 19, 1931)*		45.00

1932. Washington Bicentennial Issue commemorated the 200th birthday of George Washington, Feb. 22, 1932, in Westmoreland County, Va. *Intaglio, perforated 11 x 10 1/2.*

CM98 *Washington at 45, after miniature by Charles W. Peale, Metropolitan Museum of Art, New York, N.Y.*

CM98

1/2¢		UnFVF	UseFVF
	olive brown *(87,969,700)*	.25	.20
	Plate Block of 4	3.75	
	Broken circle (position 8 of top-right pane of plate No. 20560)	.60	
	FDC *(Jan. 1, 1932)*		17.50

CM99 *Washington at 53, from bust by Jean A. Houdon, Mount Vernon, Va.*

CM99

1¢		UnFVF	UseFVF
	yellow green *(1,265,555,100)*	.25	.20
	Plate block of 4	3.75	
	Gripper cracks (top left & top-right panes of plate No. 20742)	2.50	
	FDC *(Jan. 1, 1932)*		17.50

CM100 *Washington at 40, after painting by Peale, Washington & Lee University, Lexington, Va.*

CM100

1-1/2¢		UnFVF	UseFVF
	yellow brown *(304,926,800)*	.50	.20
	Plate block of 4	19.00	
	FDC *(Jan. 1, 1932)*		17.50

CM101 *Washington at 64, after painting by Gilbert Stuart, Boston Museum, Boston, Mass.*

CM101

2¢		UnFVF	UseFVF
	carmine red *(4,222,198,300)*	.25	.20
	Plate block of 4	2.00	
	Pair, gutter between	—	
	Gripper cracks	1.75	
	FDC *(Jan. 1, 1932)*		17.50

CM102 *Washington at 46, painted by Peale at Valley Forge, West Chester (Pa.) State University*

CM102

3¢		UnFVF	UseFVF
	slate purple *(456,198,500)*	.50	.20
	Plate block of 4	15.00	
	Broken top frame line (position 8 of bottom-left pane of plate No. 20847)	3.75	
	Double transfer	1.60	
	FDC *(Jan. 1, 1932)*		17.50

CM103 *Washington at 49, after painting by Polk, Rhinebeck, N.Y.*

CM103

4¢		UnFVF	UseFVF
	yellow brown *(151,201,300)*	.40	.20
	Plate block of 4	7.50	
	Broken bottom frame line (position 100 of bottom-right pane of plate No. 20568)	1.50	
	Retouch in eyes (position 89 of bottom-right pane of plate No. 20568)	2.00	
	Double transfer	1.50	
	FDC *(Jan. 1, 1932)*		17.50

CM104 *Washington at 63, after painting by Peale, New York Historical Society, N.Y.C.*

CM104

5¢		UnFVF	UseFVF
	Prussian blue *(170,656,100)*	1.75	.20
	Plate block of 4	19.00	
	Cracked plate (position 80 of top-right pane of plate No. 20637)	5.00	
	FDC *(Jan. 1, 1932)*		17.50

CM105 *Washington at 60, after a painting by John Trumbull, Yale University, New Haven, Conn.*

CM105		UnFVF	UseFVF
6¢	**orange** *(111,739,400)*	3.50	.20
	Plate block of 4	65.00	
	FDC *(Jan. 1, 1932)*		17.50

CM106 *Washington at 48, after painting by Trumbull, Metropolitan Museum of Art, New York, N.Y.*

CM106		UnFVF	UseFVF
7¢	**black** *(83,257,400)*	.40	.20
	Plate block of 4	7.00	
	Double transfer	—	
	FDC *(Jan. 1, 1932)*		20.00

CM107 *Washington at 66, after drawing by Charles Saint Memin, Brooklyn, N.Y.*

CM107		UnFVF	UseFVF
8¢	**bister** *(96,506,100)*	3.00	.75
	Plate block of 4	65.00	
	FDC *(Jan. 1, 1932)*		20.00

CM108 *Washington at 62, after drawing by W. Williams, Alexandria, Va.*

CM108		UnFVF	UseFVF
9¢	**salmom** *(75,706,200)*	2.50	.20
	orange red	2.50	.20
	Plate block of 4	40.00	
	FDC *(Jan. 1, 1932)*		20.00

CM109 *Washington at 63, after portrait by Gilbert Stuart, Metropolitan Museum of Art, New York, N.Y.*

CM109		UnFVF	UseFVF
10¢	**orange yellow** *(147,216,000)*	12.50	.20
	Plate block of 4	125.00	
	FDC *(Jan. 1, 1932)*		20.00

1932. Olympic Winter Games Issue anticipated the Third Winter games, Feb. 4-13 at Lake Placid, N.Y. *Intaglio, perforated 11.*

CM110 *Ski jumper*

CM110		UnFVF	UseFVF
2¢	**carmine red** *(51,102,800)*	.40	.25
	dark carmine red	.40	.25
	Plate block of 6	12.50	
	Cracked plate	5.00	
	Recut (position 61 of top-right pane of plate No. 20823)	3.00	
	"Snowball" (position 64 of top-right pane of plate No. 20815)	25.00	
	FDC *(Jan. 25, 1932)*		25.00

1932. Arbor Day Issue hailed the 60th anniversary of Arbor Day, observed in many individual states for the planting of trees. First celebrated in Nebraska, it was originated by Julius Sterling Morton, agriculturist, newspaper editor, secretary of the Nebraska Territory, and national secretary of agriculture from 1893 to 1897. *Intaglio, perforated 11 x 10 1/2.*

CM111 *Children planting tree*

CM111		UnFVF	UseFVF
2¢	**carmine red** *(100,869,300)*	.25	.20
	Plate block of 4	7.00	
	FDC *(April 22, 1932)*		15.00

1932. Olympic Summer Games Issue anticipated the 10th modern Olympic Games, held July 30-Aug. 14 in Los Angeles, Calif. The ancient games began in 776 B.C. and were banned in 394 A.D. Through the efforts of Pierre de Coubertin, French educator and sportsman, they were revived in 1896 in Greece. *Intaglio, perforated 11 x 10 1/2.*

CM112 *Modern athlete preparing to run*

CM112		UnFVF	UseFVF
3¢	**reddish violet** *(168,885,300)*	1.50	.20
	dark reddish violet	1.50	.20
	Plate block of 4	15.00	
	Gripper cracks	4.00	
	FDC *(June 15, 1932)*		25.00

CM113 *Discus Thrower, by Myron, 5 B.C.*

CM113		UnFVF	UseFVF
5¢	**blue** *(52,376,100)*	2.25	.30
	dark blue	2.25	.30
	Plate block of 4	27.50	
	Gripper cracks	4.00	
	FDC *(June 15, 1932)*		25.00

1932. William Penn Issue commemorated the 250th anniversary of the arrival of William Penn (1644-1718) to found a colony. A Quaker at 18, Penn was imprisoned three times for religious nonconformity before he was 26. Inheriting a £16,000 claim against King Charles II, he asked for a grant of land in America and was given Pennsylvania in 1681. Landing Oct. 24, 1682, at New Castle, Del., he organized the colony on a liberal basis guaranteeing freedom of conscience, made fair treaties with the Indians, laid out the city of Philadelphia and established the first successful postal system in America. *Intaglio, perforated 11.*

CM114 *Young William Penn, from a painting, Pennsylvania Historical Society, Philadelphia, Pa.*

CM114		UnFVF	UseFVF
3¢	**reddish violet** *(49,949,000)*	.35	.25
	Plate block of 6	12.50	
	Vertical pair, imperforate horizontally	—	
	FDC *(Oct. 24, 1932)*		17.50

1933. Daniel Webster Issue commemorated the 150th anniversary of the birth of Daniel Webster and the 80th anniversary of his death. Famed orator, constitutional lawyer and statesman, Webster was elected four times to the Senate and twice appointed secretary of state. In 1840 he submitted a Senate resolution advocating reduced postal rates and the use of postage stamps in America. *Intaglio, perforated 11.*

CM115 *Daniel Webster, from a bust by Daniel Chester French, Franklin, N.H.*

CM115		UnFVF	UseFVF
3¢	**reddish violet** *(49,538,500)*	.35	.40
	light violet	.35	.40
	Plate block of 6	20.00	
	FDC *(Oct. 24, 1932)*		17.50

1933. Oglethorpe Issue commemorated the 200th anniversary of the founding of Georgia and the city of Savannah, and honored Gen. James Edward Oglethorpe. A philanthropist concerned with religious tolerance and the relief of debtors, Oglethorpe obtained a royal charter and led 120 immigrants in settling the colony. He successfully repulsed Spanish attacks and attempted a siege of St. Augustine, Fla. *Intaglio, perforated 11.*

CM116 *Gen. James Edward Oglethorpe, from a painting at Oglethorpe University, Atlanta, Ga.*

CM116		UnFVF	UseFVF
3¢	**reddish violet** *(61,719,200)*	.35	.25
	Plate block of 6	14.00	
	FDC *(Feb. 12, 1933)*		17.50

1933. Newburgh Issue commemorated the 150th anniversary of the Proclamation of Peace issued by Gen. George Washington from his headquarters at Newburgh, ending the Revolutionary War. *Perforated 10 1/2 x 11.*

CM117, CM142 *Washington's headquarters at Newburgh, N.Y., from an engraving by James Smille*

CM117		UnFVF	UseFVF
3¢	**reddish violet** *(73,382,400)*	.25	.20
	Plate block of 4	6.00	
	Block of 4, horizontal gutter between	—	
	Block of 4, vertical gutter between	—	
	Center block, w/crossed gutters	—	
	FDC *(April 19, 1933)*		17.50

For ungummed stamps (Farley Issue), see CM142.

Although not regularly issued that way, CM117 was also available in full sheets of 400 subjects.

1933. Century of Progress Issue commemorated the World's Fair held in Chicago, Ill., to honor the 100th anniversary of its incorporation as a city. *Intaglio, perforated 10 1/2 x 11.*

CM118, CM156 *Fort Dearborn blockhouse, from a painting by Dwight Benton*

CM118		UnFVF	UseFVF
1¢	**yellow green** *(348,266,800)*	.25	.20
	Plate block of 4	3.00	
	Block of 4, horizontal gutter between	—	
	Block of 4, vertical gutter between	—	
	Center block, w/crossed gutters	—	
	Gripper cracks	—	
	FDC *(May 25, 1933)*		17.50

CM119, CM157 *Federal building at fair*

CM119		UnFVF	UseFVF
3¢	**reddish violet** *(480,239,300)*	.25	.20
	Plate block of 4	3.00	
	Block of 4, horizontal gutter between	—	
	Block of 4, vertical gutter between	—	
	Center block, w/crossed gutters	—	
	FDC *(May 25, 1933)*		17.50

Although not regularly issued that way, CM118 and CM119 were also available in full sheets of 400 subjects.

1933. Century of Progress Souvenir Sheets were issued in honor of the American Philatelic Society convention held in Chicago in August. *Each sheet measures 134 x 120mm, contains 25 ungummed, imperforate stamps and is inscribed in the margin:* "PRINTED BY THE TREASURY DEPARTMENT, BUREAU OF ENGRAVING AND PRINTING / UNDER AUTHORITY OF JAMES A. FARLEY, POSTMASTER GENERAL AT A CENTURY OF PROGRESS / IN COMPLIMENT TO THE AMERICAN PHILATELIC SOCIETY FOR ITS CONVENTION AND EXHIBITION / CHICAGO, ILLINOIS, AUGUST 1933." *Intaglio, imperforate.*

CM120, CM156 *Sheet of 25*

CM120		UnFVF	UseFVF
1¢	**yellow green** *(456,704)*	35.00	32.50
	FDC *(Aug. 25, 1933)*		200.00
	a. Single stamp	.75	.20
	FDC (single stamp)		15.00

CM121, CM157 *Sheet of 25*

CM121

		UnFVF	UseFVF
3¢	**reddish violet** *(441,172)*	30.00	27.50
	FDC *(Aug. 25, 1933)*		200.00
	a. Single stamp	.75	.50
	FDC (single stamp)		15.00

For ungummed stamps (Farley issue) see CM156 & CM157.

1933. NRA Issue publicized the National Recovery Administration, one of the first acts of the New Deal aimed at recovery from the Depression of the 1930s. The NRA was declared unconstitutional in 1935. In the original drawing for this stamp, the second figure was said by some to resemble President Franklin D. Roosevelt. A mustache was added since postal custom is against depicting a living person on a stamp. *Intaglio, perforated 10 1/2 x 11.*

CM122 *Workers Marching Forward, from a poster drawn by Rudolph L. Bortel*

CM122

		UnFVF	UseFVF
3¢	**reddish violet** *(1,978,707,300)*	.25	.20
	Plate block of 4	2.00	
	Gripper cracks	—	
	Recut at right (position 47 of top-right pane of plate No. 21151)	—	
	FDC *(Aug. 15, 1933)*		17.50

1933. Byrd Antarctic Issue publicized the second expedition of Rear Adm. Richard E. Byrd to the South Pole. Flight routes used by Byrd, as well as proposed new routes, are indicated on the stamp. Letters mailed with this 3¢ stamp from the camp at Little America, Antarctica, were subject to an additional service charge of 50¢ each. *Intaglio, perforated 11.*

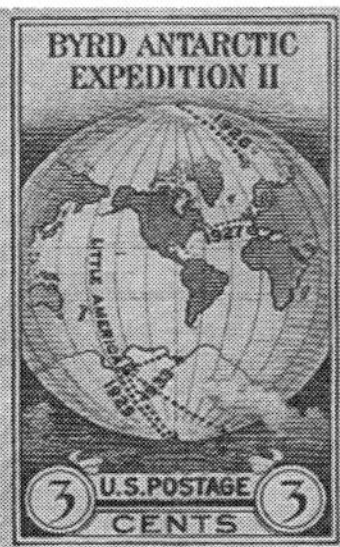

CM123, CM143, CM158 *Globe with Antarctic routes*

CM123

		UnFVF	UseFVF
3¢	**blue** *(5,735,944)*	.75	.60
	Plate block of 6	17.50	
	Double transfer	—	
	FDC *(Oct. 9, 1933)*		25.00

For ungummed stamps (Farley issue), see CM143.

1933. Kosciuszko Issue commemorated Polish patriot Tadeusz Kosciuszko and the 150th anniversary of his naturalization as an American citizen. Gen. Kosciuszko fought throughout the Revolutionary War, served as aide to Washington, and laid out the fortifications of West Point. Afterward he led a rebellion that briefly liberated his native Poland from Russia. *Intaglio, perforated 11.*

CM124 *Gen. Tadeusz Kosciuszko, from a statue by Anton Popiel, Lafayette Park, Washington, D.C.*

CM124

		UnFVF	UseFVF
5¢	**blue** *(45,137,700)*	.75	.35
	Plate block of 6	35.00	
	Cracked plate	—	
	FDC *(Oct. 13, 1933)*		17.50
	v. Horizontal pair, imperforate vertically	2,250.00	

1934. Byrd Souvenir Sheet honored the National Stamp Exhibition held in New York. *It measured 87 x 93mm, contained six imperforate stamps without gum. The margins of the sheets inscribed:* "PRINTED BY THE TREASURY DEPARTMENT, BUREAU OF ENGRAVING AND PRINTING / UNDER AUTHORITY OF JAMES A. FARLEY, POSTMASTER GENERAL / IN COMPLIMENT TO THE NATIONAL STAMP EXHIBITION OF 1934 / NEW YORK, N.Y. FEBRUARY 10-18, 1934." *Intaglio, imperforated.*

CM125, CM158 *Globe with Antarctic routes, souvenir sheet of 6*

CM125

		UnFVF	UseFVF
3¢	**blue** *(811,404)*	17.50	16.50
	FDC *(Feb. 10, 1934)*		75.00
	a. Single stamp	3.00	2.75
	FDC (single stamp)		15.00

For ungummed stamps (Farley issue), see CM158.

1934. Maryland Tercentenary Issue marked the 300th anniversary of the settlement of Maryland by about 200 colonists under a charter held by Cecilius Calvert, second Lord Baltimore, a Catholic. He made the colony a haven of religious tolerance. The *Ark* and the *Dove* were sailing vessels used in the voyage to America. *Intaglio, perforated 11.*

CM126 *The* Ark *and the* Dove, *from a drawing by Edwin Tunis*

CM126

		UnFVF	UseFVF
3¢	**carmine red** *(46,258,300)*	.25	.20
	Plate block of 6	10.00	
	Double transfer (position 1 of top-left pane of plate No. 21190)	—	
	FDC *(March 23, 1934)*		15.00
	v. Horizontal pair, imperforated horizontally	6,500.00	

1934. Mother's Day Issue commemorated the 20th anniversary of Woodrow Wilson's proclamation of the second Sunday in May as Mother's Day. The design shows an adaptation of the painting popularly known as "Whistler's Mother," a world symbol of motherhood, although the painter, James Abbott McNeill Whistler (1834-1903), called the picture simply *Arrangement in Grey and Black: The Painter's Mother (1871). Stamp issued in both rotary and flat-press printings. Intaglio.*

CM127-128, CM144 *Whistler's Mother, from a painting by James McNeill Whistler, the first painting by an American in the Louvre Museum, Paris, France*

Rotary press, perforated 11 x 10 1/2.

CM127		UnFVF	UseFVF
3¢	**reddish violet** *(193,239,100)*	.25	.20
	Plate block of 4	1.25	
	FDC *(May 2, 1934)*		15.00

Flat press, perforated 11.

CM128		UnFVF	UseFVF
3¢	**reddish violet** *(15,432,200)*	.25	.20
	Plate block of 6	5.00	
	FDC *(May 2, 1934)*		1.00

For ungummed stamps (Farley issue), see CM144.

1934. Wisconsin Tercentenary Issue memorialized the 300th anniversary of the arrival of the French explorer Jean Nicolet onto the shores of Green Bay on Lake Michigan. The first white man to reach that region, he appears in oriental garb as he thought he was landing in China. *Intaglio.*

CM129, CM145 *Nicolet's Landing on Green Bay, from a painting by Edward W. Deming, Wisconsin Historical Society*

CM129		UnFVF	UseFVF
3¢	**reddish violet** *(64,525,400)*	.25	.20
	violet	.25	.20
	Plate block of 6	4.00	
	FDC *(July 7, 1934)*		15.00
	v. Horizontal pair, imperforate vertically	325.00	
	v1. Vertical pair, imperforate horizontally	275.00	

For ungummed stamps (Farley issue), see CM145.

1934. National Parks Issue commemorated National Parks Year and publicized the great American park system. *Intaglio.*

CM130, CM146, CM159 *El Capitan, Yosemite (California)*

CM130		UnFVF	UseFVF
1¢	**green** *(84,896,350)*	.25	.20
	light green	.25	.20
	Plate block of 6	1.50	
	Recut	—	
	FDC *(July 16, 1934)*		10.00
	v. Vertical pair, imperforate horizontally (with gum)	550.00	

CM131, CM147 *Grand Canyon (Arizona)*

CM131		UnFVF	UseFVF
2¢	**red** *(74,400,200)*	.25	.20
	Plate block of 6	1.75	
	Double transfer	—	
	FDC *(July 24, 1934)*		10.00
	v. Horizontal pair, imperforate vertically (with gum)	300.00	
	v1. Vertical pair, imperforate horizontally (with gum)	400.00	

CM132, CM148, CM160 *Mt. Rainier and Mirror Lake (Washington)*

CM132		UnFVF	UseFVF
3¢	**reddish violet** *(95,089,000)*	.25	.20
	Plate block of 6	2.00	
	Recut	—	
	FDC *(Aug. 3, 1934)*		10.00
	v. Vertical pair, imperforate horizontally (with gum)	450.00	

CM133, CM149 *The Cliff Palace, Mesa Verde (Colorado)*

CM133		UnFVF	UseFVF
4¢	**yellow brown** *(19,178,650)*	.50	.35
	light brown	8.00	
	Plate block of 6	—	
	FDC *(Sept. 25, 1934)*		10.00
	v. Vertical pair, imperforate horizontally (with gum)	650.00	

CM134, CM150 *Old Faithful, Yellowstone (Wyoming)*

CM134		UnFVF	UseFVF
5¢	**light blue** *(30,980,100)*	1.00	.75
	blue	1.00	.75
	Plate block of 6	10.00	
	FDC *(July 30, 1934)*		10.00
	v. Horizontal pair, imperforate vertically (with gum)	475.00	

CM135, CM151 *Crater Lake (Oregon)*

CM135		UnFVF	UseFVF
6¢	**blue** *(16,923,350)*	1.25	1.00
	Plate block of 6	20.00	
	FDC *(Sept. 5, 1934)*		22.50

CM136, CM152 *Great Head, Bar Harbor, Acadia (Maine)*

CM136		UnFVF	UseFVF
7¢	**black** *(15,988,250)*	1.00	.75
	Plate block of 6	12.50	
	Double transfer	—	
	FDC *(Oct. 2, 1934)*		10.00
	v. Horizontal pair, imperforate vertically (with gum)	550.00	

CM137, CM153 *Great White Throne, Zion (Utah)*

CM137		UnFVF	UseFVF
8¢	**gray green** *(15,288,700)*	2.00	1.75
	Plate block of 6	20.00	
	FDC *(Sept. 18, 1934)*		10.00

CM138, CM154 *Mt. Rockwell and Two Medicine Lake, Glacier (Montana)*

CM138		UnFVF	UseFVF
9¢	**orange red** *(17,472,600)*	2.00	.75
	orange	2.00	.75
	Plate block of 6	20.00	
	FDC *(Aug. 17, 1934)*		10.00

CM139, CM155 *Great Smokey Mountains (North Carolina)*

CM139		UnFVF	UseFVF
10¢	**gray black** *(18,874,300)*	3.25	1.25
	gray	3.25	1.25
	Plate block of 6	30.00	
	FDC *(Oct. 8, 1934)*		10.00

For ungummed stamps, (Farley issue), see CM146-CM155.

1934. Trans-Mississippi Philatelic Exposition Issue was released in honor of the Philatelic Exposition and Convention held at Omaha, Nebr. *The sheet measured 94 x 99mm, contained six imperforate, gummed 1¢ National Parks stamps, and was inscribed in the margin:* "PRINTED BY THE TREASURY DEPARTMENT, BUREAU OF ENGRAVING AND PRINTING / UNDER AUTHORITY OF JAMES A. FARLEY, POSTMASTER GENERAL / IN COMPLIMENT TO THE TRANS-MISSISSIPPI PHILATELIC EXPOSITION AND CONVENTION / OMAHA, NEBRASKA, OCTOBER 1934."

CM140, CM159 *El Capitan, Yosemite (California)*

CM140		UnFVF	UseFVF
1¢	**green,** sheet of 6 *(793,551)*	14.00	12.50
	FDC *(Oct. 10, 1934)*		75.00
	a. Single stamp	2.00	1.75
	FDC, single stamp		20.00

For ungummed stamps, (Farley issue), see CM159.

1934. American Philatelic Society Issue honored the American Philatelic Society convention and exhibition held at Atlantic City, N.J. *The sheet measured 97 x 99mm, contained six imperforate, gummed 3¢ National Parks stamps, and was inscribed in the margin:* "PRINTED BY THE TREASURY DEPARTMENT, BUREAU OF ENGRAVING AND PRINTING / UNDER AUTHORITY OF JAMES A. FARLEY, POSTMASTER GENERAL / IN COMPLIMENT TO THE AMERICAN PHILATELIC SOCIETY FOR ITS CONVENTION AND EXHIBITION / ATLANTIC CITY, NEW JERSEY, AUGUST 1934."

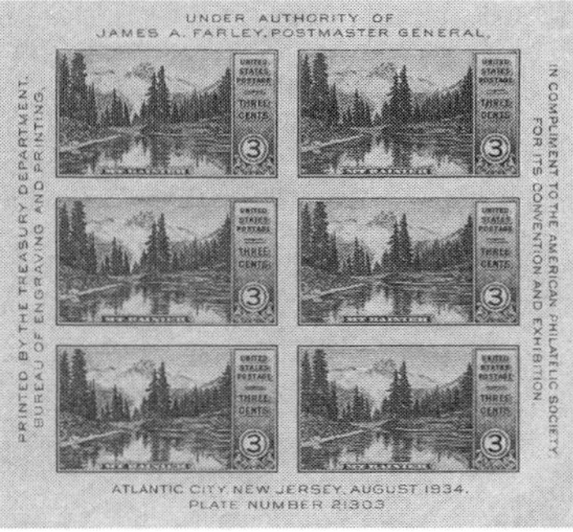

CM141, CM160 *Mt. Rainier and Mirror Lake (Washington)*

CM141		UnFVF	UseFVF
3¢	**reddish violet,** sheet of 6 *(511,391)*	40.00	30.00
	FDC *(Aug. 28, 1934)*		75.00
	a. Single stamp	4.50	4.00
	FDC, single stamp		20.00

For ungummed stamps (Farley issue), see CM160.

The Farley Series (CM142-CM161) is a collective term commonly applied to 20 stamps issued to the public as a direct result of protests by collectors against the practice of presenting to a few favored collectors full sheets of stamps in forms not available to the general public. Original "Farley Sheets" — signed by government officials, including Franklin D. Roosevelt, president; Harold L. Ickes, secretary of the interior; and James A. Farley, postmaster general — were given as philatelic favors to political friends.

The full sheets of the Farley Series contained four or more post office panes separated by spaces (called gutters) or by guidelines and arrows (to guide the cutting machine). Blocks showing two crossed gutters or crossed lines are called "cross gutter" and "center line" blocks, respectively.

All of the Farley stamps were issued ungummed. In 1940 the Post Office Department gummed full sheets of CM144-61 sent in by collectors for that purpose. With the exception of CM142-43, all Farley stamps were imperforate.

The Farley Series sheets were first placed on sale March 15, 1935, at the Philatelic Agency in Washington, D.C., and were sold through June 15, 1935.

1935. NEWBURGH FARLEY ISSUE was printed in sheets of 400 stamps: 4 panes of 100 stamps, separated by gutters. Newburgh Farley stamps differ slightly in color from the original Newburgh issue (CM117); there seems to be a tinge of blue in the violet. They usually are not well-centered and the perforations are ragged. *Intaglio, ungummed and perforated 10 1/2 x 11.*

CM142		UnFVF	UseFVF
3¢	**reddish violet** *(3,274,556)*	.25	.20
	Plate block of 4	16.50	
	Plate block of 4, w/arrow at top or bottom	15.00	
	Plate block of 4, w/arrow at side	8.50	
	Pair w/vertical gutter	7.50	
	Pair w/horizontal gutter	4.00	
	Center line block	50.00	
	FDC *(March 15, 1935)*		35.00

1935. BYRD FARLEY ISSUE was printed in sheets of 200, so that arrows and guidelines, along which the sheets normally were cut into panes of 50 before being sent to the post office, are complete. The stamps were issued *without gum and perforated 11.* Since it is virtually impossible to distinguish between a used copy of this and the original Byrd stamp (CM123), they must be considered interchangeable in used condition.

CM143		UnFVF	UseFVF
3¢	**blue** *(2,040,760)*	.50	.45
	Plate block of 6	17.50	
	Pair, w/vertical line	2.00	
	Pair, w/horizontal line	40.00	
	Block of 4, w/arrow at top or bottom	85.00	
	Block of 4, w/arrow at side	4.00	
	Center line block	90.00	
	FDC *(March 15, 1935)*		35.00

1935. MOTHER'S DAY FARLEY ISSUE was printed on a flate-plate press in sheets of 200 with arrows and guidelines, identical in design to CM127, but issued *without gum* and *imperforate.*

CM144		UnFVF	UseFVF
3¢	**reddish violet** *(2,389,288)*	.60	.60
	Plate block of 6	18.50	
	Block of 4, w/arrow at top or bottom	—	
	Block of 4, w/arrow at side	4.50	
	Pair, w/vertical line	1.75	
	Pair, w/horizontal line	2.25	
	Center line block	10.00	
	FDC *(March 15, 1935)*		35.00

1935. WISCONSIN FARLEY ISSUE was printed in sheets of 200 with arrows and guidelines, identical in design to CM129, but issued *without gum* and *imperforate.*

CM145		UnFVF	UseFVF
3¢	**reddish violet** *(2,294,948)*	.60	.60
	Plate block of 6	18.50	
	Block of 4, w/arrow at top or bottom	3.50	
	Block of 4, w/arrow at side	4.50	
	Pair, w/vertical line	1.75	
	Pair, w/horizontal line	2.25	
	Center line block	10.00	
	FDC *(March 15, 1935)*		35.00

1935. NATIONAL PARKS FARLEY ISSUE were printed in sheets of 200 with arrows and guidelines. The designs are identical to CM130-39, but the Farley versions were issued *without gum* and *imperforate.*

CM146		UnFVF	UseFVF
1¢	**green** *(3,217,636)*	.25	.20
	Plate block of 6	6.50	
	Block of 4, w/arrow at top or bottom	1.25	
	Block of 4, w/arrow at sides	1.00	
	Pair, w/vertical line	.60	
	Pair, w/horizontal line	.45	
	Center line block	4.50	
	FDC *(March 15, 1935)*		30.00

CM147		UnFVF	UseFVF
2¢	**red** *(2,746,640)*	.25	.20
	Plate block of 6	7.50	
	Block of 4, w/arrow at top or bottom	1.50	
	Block of 4, w/arrow at sides	1.50	
	Pair, w/vertical line	.60	
	Pair, w/horizontal line	.65	
	Center line block	5.00	
	Double transfer	—	
	FDC *March 15, 1935)*		30.00

CM148		UnFVF	UseFVF
3¢	**reddish violet** *(2,168,088)*	.50	.45
	Plate block of 6	17.50	
	Block of 4, w/arrow at top or bottom	3.00	
	Block of 4, w/arrow at sides	3.75	
	Pair, w/vertical line	1.25	
	Pair, w/horizontal line	1.75	
	Center line block	12.50	
	FDC *(March 15, 1935)*		30.00

CM149		UnFVF	UseFVF
4¢	**yellow brown** *(1,822,684)*	1.25	1.25
	Plate block of 6	22.50	
	Block of 4, w/arrow at top or bottom	5.50	
	Block of 4, w/arrow at sides	6.50	
	Pair, w/vertical line	2.50	
	Pair, w/horizontal line	3.00	
	Center line block	12.50	
	FDC *(March 15, 1935)*		30.00

CM150		UnFVF	UseFVF
5¢	**light blue** *(1,724,576)*	1.75	1.75
	Plate block of 6	27.50	
	Block of 4, w/arrow at top or bottom	12.00	
	Block of 4, w/arrow at sides	10.00	
	Pair, w/vertical line	5.25	
	Pair, w/horizontal line	4.25	
	Center line block	20.00	
	Double transfer	—	
	FDC *(March 15, 1935)*		30.00

CM151		UnFVF	UseFVF
6¢	**blue** *(1,647,696)*	2.25	2.25
	Plate block of 6	40.00	
	Block of 4, w/arrow at top or bottom	12.50	
	Block of 4, w/arrow at sides	15.00	
	Pair, w/vertical line	6.00	
	Pair, w/horizontal line	6.75	
	Center line block	22.50	
	FDC *(March 15, 1935)*		30.00

CM152		UnFVF	UseFVF
7¢	**black** *(1,682,948)*	2.00	1.75
	Plate block of 6	37.50	
	Block of 4, w/arrow at top or bottom	10.00	
	Block of 4, w/arrow at sides	12.00	
	Pair, w/vertical line	4.50	
	Pair, w/horizontal line	5.00	
	Center line block	2.00	
	Double transfer	—	
	FDC *(March 15, 1935)*		30.00

CM153		UnFVF	UseFVF
8¢	**gray green** *(1,638,644)*	2.00	2.00
	Plate block of 6	45.00	
	Block of 4, w/arrow at top or bottom	14.00	
	Block of 4, w/arrow at sides	12.50	
	Pair, w/vertical line	6.50	
	Pair, w/horizontal line	5.00	
	Center line block	22.50	
	FDC *(March 15, 1935)*		30.00

CM154		UnFVF	UseFVF
9¢	**orange red** *(1,625,224)*	2.00	2.00
	Plate block of 6	47.50	
	Block of 4, w/arrow at top or bottom	12.50	
	Block of 4, w/arrow at sides	14.00	
	Pair, w/vertical line	12.50	
	Pair, w/horizontal line	10.00	
	Center line block	35.00	
	FDC *(March 15, 1935)*		30.00

CM155		UnFVF	UseFVF
10¢	**gray black** *(1,644,900)*	4.00	3.50
	Plate block of 6	55.00	
	Block of 4, w/arrow at top or bottom	25.00	
	Block of 4, w/arrow at sides	22.50	
	Pair, w/vertical line	12.50	
	Pair, w/horizontal line	10.00	
	Center line block	35.00	
	FDC *(March 15, 1935)*		30.00

1935. Century of Progress Souvenir Sheet, Farley Issue contained nine souvenir sheets of 25 stamps each, separated by gutters, issued *without gum* and *imperforate.* Identification of single stamps is possible only with stamps that come from the outside rows of the miniature sheets, in which the margins are wider than those from the regular sheets. CM120-21.

CM156		UnFVF	UseFVF
1¢	**yellow green** *(2,467,800)*	22.50	22.50
	Horizontal gutter block	—	
	Vertical gutter block	—	
	Cross-gutter block	12.50	
	a. Single stamp	.75	.30
	FDC *(March 15, 1935)*		40.00

CM157		UnFVF	UseFVF
3¢	**reddish violet** *(2,147,856)*	20.00	20.00
	Horizontal gutter block	—	
	Vertical gutter block	—	
	Cross-gutter block	12.50	
	a. Single stamp	.75	.30
	FDC *(March 15, 1935)*		40.00

1935. Byrd Souvenir Sheet, Farley Issue contained 25 souvenir sheets of six stamps each, separated by gutters, issued *without gum* and *imperforate.* Identification of single stamps is possible only if their margins are wider than those from the regular sheet, CM125.

CM158		UnFVF	UseFVF
3¢	**blue** *(1,603,200)*	17.50	12.50
	Horizontal gutter block	—	
	Vertical gutter block	—	
	Cross-gutter block	17.50	
	a. Single stamp	2.75	2.25
	FDC *(March 15, 1935)*		40.00

1935. National Parks Souvenir Sheets, Farley Issue contained 20 souvenir sheets of six stamps each, separated by gutters, issued *without gum* and *imperforate.* Identification of single stamps is possible only if their margins are wider than those from the regular sheets CM140-41.

CM159		UnFVF	UseFVF
1¢	**green** *(1,679,760)*	10.00	9.00
	Horizontal gutter block	—	
	Vertical gutter block	—	
	Cross-gutter block	12.50	
	a. Single stamp	1.75	1.75
	FDC *(March 15, 1935)*		40.00

CM160		UnFVF	UseFVF
3¢	**reddish violet** *(1,295,520)*	25.00	20.00
	Horizontal gutter block	—	
	Vertical gutter block	—	
	Cross-gutter block	25.00	
	a. Single stamp	3.00	2.75
	FDC *(March 15, 1935)*		40.00

1935. Airmail Special Delivery Farley Issue was printed in sheets of 200 stamps with arrows and guidelines. It is listed in this section of the catalog because it always has been considered an integral part of the Farley Series. *Intaglio, without gum, imperforate.*

CM161		UnFVF	UseFVF
16¢	**blue** *(1,370,560)*	2.75	2.50
	Plate block of 6	70.00	
	Block of 4, w/arrow at top or bottom	13.50	
	Block of 4, w/arrow at sides	17.00	
	Horizontal gutter block	—	
	Vertical gutter block	—	
	Center line block	77.50	
	FDC *(March 15, 1935)*		40.00

1935. Connecticut Tercentenary Issue commemorated the 300th anniversary of the settlement of Connecticut by dissatisfied members of the Massachusetts Bay Colony. The tree depicted is the oak in which the Colonial charter was hidden when it was demanded by the British in 1687. *Intaglio, perforated 11 x 10 1/2.*

CM162 *The Charter Oak, from a painting by Charles D. Brownell, (1822-1909), State Library, Hartford, Conn.*

CM162		UnFVF	UseFVF
3¢	**purple** *(70,726,800)*	.25	.20
	rose violet	.25	.20
	Plate block of 4	2.00	
	Defect in ¢ sign (position 4 of top-right pane of plate No. 21395)	—	
	FDC *(April 26, 1935)*		10.00

For imperforates, see No. CM168.

1935. California-Pacific Issue commemorated the California-Pacific Exposition at San Diego, Calif. *Intaglio, perforated 11 x 10 1/2.*

CM163 *View of the San Diego Exposition, from a sketch by Larrinague*

CM163		UnFVF	UseFVF
3¢	**dark lilac** *(100,839,600)*	.25	.20
	Plate block of 4	1.50	
	Pair, gutter between	—	
	FDC *(May 29, 1935)*		12.50

For imperforates, see No. CM168.

1935. Boulder Dam Issue commemorated the dedication of the largest dam on the Colorado River. Built to supply power, water and flood control, its name was changed in 1933 to Boulder Dam, which appears on the stamp. Its original name, Hoover Dam, was restored in 1947. *Intaglio, perforated 11.*

CM164 *Boulder (Hoover) Dam*

CM164		UnFVF	UseFVF
3¢	**dark lilac** *(73,610,650)*	.25	.20
	purple	.25	.20
	Plate block of 6	2.25	
	FDC *(Sept. 30, 1935)*		15.00

1935. Michigan Centennial Issue commemorated the 100th anniversary of the admission of Michigan as the 26th state. *Intaglio, perforated 11 x 10 1/2.*

CM165 *Michigan state seal*

CM165		UnFVF	UseFVF
3¢	**dark lilac** *(75,823,900)*	.25	.20
	Plate block of 4	1.50	
	FDC *(Nov. 1, 1935)*		12.50

For imperforates, see No. CM168.

1936. Texas Centennial Issue commemorated the 100th anniversary of Texas independence, established after the Texans under Gen. Sam Houston defeated the Mexicans at the Battle of San Jacinto. The first Texas colony was founded by Stephen P. Austin under a Mexican charter in 1821. *Intaglio, perforated 11 x 10 1/2.*

CM166 *Sam Houston, Stephen F. Austin and The Alamo, from artwork by S. Salamo, T. A. Butler and F. Pauling*

CM166		UnFVF	UseFVF
3¢	**dark lilac** *(124,324,500)*	.25	.20
	Plate block of 4	1.50	
	FDC *(March 2, 1936)*		15.00

For imperforates, see No. CM168.

1936. Rhode Island Tercentenary Issue honored the 300th anniversary of the founding of Rhode Island as a haven of tolerance by Roger Williams. This was the only New England colony to tolerate a permanent Jewish community in the 17th century. *Intaglio, perforated 10 1/2 x 11.*

CM167 *Roger Williams, a statue by Franklin Simmons in Williams Park, Providence, R.I.*

CM167		UnFVF	UseFVF
3¢	**dull purple** *(67,127,650)*	.25	.20
	rose violet	.25	.20
	Plate block of 4	1.50	
	Pair, gutter between	—	
	FDC *(May 4, 1936)*		10.00

1936. TIPEX Souvenir Sheet was issued in complement to the Third International Philatelic Exhibition held in New York City. *The sheet measures 98 x 66mm and contains one each of the Connecticut, California-Pacific, Michigan and Texas stamps. Intaglio, imperforate. The sheet is inscribed in the margins:* "PRINTED BY THE TREASURY DEPARTMENT, BUREAU OF ENGRAVING AND PRINTING / UNDER AUTHORITY OF JAMES A. FARLEY, POSTMASTER GENERAL / IN COMPLIMENT TO THE THIRD INTERNATIONAL PHILATELIC EXHIBITION OF 1936 / NEW YORK, N.Y., MAY 9-17, 1936."

CM168 *TIPEX souvenir sheet of 4*

CM168		UnFVF	UseFVF
4x3c	**reddish purple** *(2,809,039)*	2.75	2.50
	FDC *(May 9, 1936)*		17.50
	a. Connecticut single from souvenir sheet	.75	.60
	b. California single from souvenir sheet	.75	.60
	c. Michigan single from souvenir sheet	.75	.60
	d. Texas single from souvenir sheet	.75	.60

1936. Arkansas Centennial Issue commemorated the 100th anniversary of the admission of Arkansas into the Union as the 25th state. *Intaglio, perforated 11 x 10 1/2.*

CM169 *Old State House in Little Rock, Ark.*

CM169		UnFVF	UseFVF
3¢	**dark lilac** *(72,992,650)*	.25	.20
	Plate block of 4	1.50	
	FDC *(June 15, 1936)*		10.00

1936. Oregon Territory Centennial Issue commemorated the 100th anniversary of the opening of the Oregon Territory, comprising the present states of Oregon, Washington, Idaho and parts of Montana and Wyoming. *Intaglio, perforated 11 x 10 1/2.*

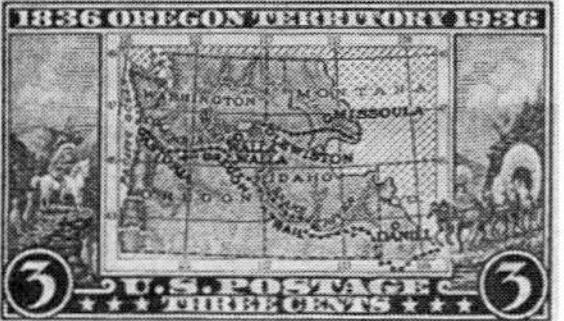

CM170 *Map of Oregon Territory*

CM170		UnFVF	UseFVF
3¢	**dark lilac** *(74,407,450)*	.25	.20
	Plate block of 4	1.25	
	Double transfer	—	
	FDC *(July 14, 1936)*		1.50

1936. Susan B. Anthony Issue in an election year, honored the 16th anniversary of the ratification of the 19th Amendment, which granted suffrage to women. Anthony (1820-1906) was a pioneer in temperance and social reform, and in part through her leadership and effort, women in the United States won the right to vote. Beginning with this issue, plate numbers were placed 4mm from the frame line of the nearest stamp. Previously, they were separated by less than 2mm. *Intaglio, perforated 11 x 10 1/2.*

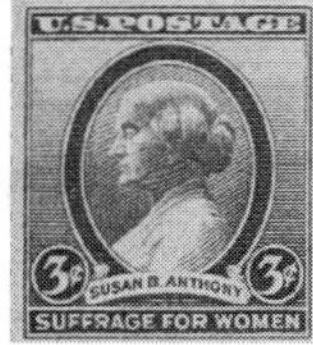

CM171 *Susan B. Anthony*

CM171		UnFVF	UseFVF
3¢	**reddish purple** *(269,522,200)*	.25	.20
	Plate block of 4	1.25	
	FDC *(Aug. 20, 1936)*		10.00

1936-37. Army Issue honored the U.S. Army and paid tribute to its early leaders and heroes. *Intaglio, perforated 11 x 10 1/2.*

CM172 *George Washington commanded the Continental Army throughout the Revolutionary War. (See CM98-CM109) Mount Vernon was his home in Virginia. Nathanael Greene led the patriot forces in the Southern theater. Both portraits are from Trumbull paintings.*

CM172		UnFVF	UseFVF
1¢	**green** *(105,196,150)*	.25	.20
	Plate block of 4	1.00	
	FDC *(Dec. 15, 1936)*		7.50

CM173 *Andrew Jackson (from a statue by Belle Scholtz in the U.S. Hall of Fame) defeated the Creek Indians at Horseshoe Bend in 1814, and the British at New Orleans in 1815. The Hermitage was his Tennessee home. Winfield Scott (from a statue by Launt Thomas in the U.S. Soldiers' Home at Washington) fought gallantly at Chippewa and Lundy's Lane in the War of 1812 and led the U.S. Army in the Mexican War.*

CM173		UnFVF	UseFVF
2¢	**rose red** *(93,848,500)*	.25	.20
	Plate block of 4	1.00	
	FDC *(Jan. 15, 1937)*		10.00

CM174 *William Tecumseh Sherman has been called "the first modern general." His march from Atlanta to the sea in the Civil War aimed at weakening his adversaries by the destruction of supplies rather than lives. Ulysses S. Grant split the Confederacy in two by capturing Vicksburg in 1863. After his successful Tennessee campaigns, he was given command under Lincoln of all Union forces and fought a war of attrition that brought the war to an end in 1865. Philip H. Sheridan, a cavalry commander, distinguished himself at Chickamauga and Chattanooga, and commanded the army that laid waste to the Shenandoah Valley.*

CM174		UnFVF	UseFVF
3¢	**dull purple** *(87,741,150)*	.25	.20
	Plate block of 4	1.50	
	FDC *(Feb. 18, 1937)*		7.50

CM175 *Robert E. Lee, to whom Lincoln offered command of the Union field forces in 1861, resigned his commission instead to command the forces of Virginia. After his defeat at Gettysburg, July 1863, he fought bravely and brilliantly against hopeless odds, surrendering to Grant in 1865. Stratford Hall was his birthplace. Thomas J. Jackson, greatest of Lee's generals, won his nickname "Stonewall" by holding off strong Union assaults at the first Battle of Bull Run. After forcing back the Union troops at Chancellorsville, he was mistakenly shot by one of his own pickets.*

CM175		UnFVF	UseFVF
4¢	**slate** *(35,794,150)*	.50	.20
	Plate block of 4	10.00	
	FDC *(March 23, 1937)*		7.50

CM176 *The U.S. Military Academy at West Point, N.Y., was established in 1802. Upon completion of a four-year course, cadets are eligible for commission as second lieutenants in the Army. Its graduates include all five generals pictured on CM174 and CM175. Among its civilian alumni were James Abbott McNeill Whistler (CM227) and Edgar Allan Poe (CM328).*

CM176		UnFVF	UseFVF
5¢	**gray blue** *(36,839,250)*	.75	.20
	Plate block of 4	12.50	
	FDC *(May 26, 1937)*		7.50

1936-37. Navy Issue honored the U.S. Navy and paid tribute to early naval leaders and heroes. *Intaglio, perforated 11 x 10 1/2.*

CM177 *John Paul Jones (from a painting by Peale) destroyed British ships, preyed upon the British coast and captured the man-of-war* Serapis *in a battle in which his own flagship* Bonhomme Richard *(shown) was sunk. John Barry (from a painting by Stuart) commanded the* Lexington *when he captured the first ship ever taken by a commanding officer of the U.S. Navy.*

CM177		UnFVF	UseFVF
1¢	**green** *(104,773,450)*	.25	.20
	Plate block of 4	1.00	
	FDC *(Dec. 15, 1936)*		7.50

CM178 *Stephen Decatur (from a painting by Alonzo Chappel), fighting the Tripolitan pirates, effected the daring recapture of the frigate* Philadelphia. *He commanded the ship* United States *in the War of 1812. The stamp shows a contemporary warship under full sail. Thomas Macdonough (from a painting by Carl Becker), commanded the American fleet on Lake Champlain, where his brilliant victory over the British in 1814 saved New York and Vermont from invasion. The* Saratoga *was his flagship.*

CM178		UnFVF	UseFVF
2¢	**rose red** *(92,054,550)*	.25	.20
	Plate block of 4	1.00	
	FDC *(Jan. 15, 1937)*		7.50

CM179 *David Farragut (from a photograph by Brady), in 1862 destroyed the Confederate fleet at New Orleans. His foster brother David Dixon Porter aided him there and at Vicksburg; later, as superintendent of the U.S. Naval Academy, Porter greatly improved its organization and curriculum. The stamp mentions ships commanded and depicts a warship of the period.*

CM179		UnFVF	UseFVF
3¢	**dull purple** *(93,291,650)*	.25	.20
	Plate block of 4	1.50	
	FDC *(Feb. 18, 1937)*		7.50

CM180 *William T. Sampson commanded the North Atlantic Squadron that destroyed the Spanish fleet at Santiago, Cuba, in 1898, sharing the victory with Winfield S. Schley, his second in command. Schley earlier had led the expedition that rescued the Artic explorer Adolphus Greely in 1884. George Dewey, commanding the Asiatic Squadron, destroyed the Spanish fleet in the Philippines in 1898.*

CM180		UnFVF	UseFVF
4¢	**slate** *(34,521,950)*	.50	.20
	Plate block of 4	10.00	
	FDC *(March 23, 1937)*		7.50

CM181 *The U.S. Naval Academy at Annapolis, Maryland, was established in 1805. Upon completion of a four-year course, midshipmen are eligible for commissions as ensigns in the Navy. Its graduates include all three admirals pictured on CM180. The stamp pictures the academy's seal and cadets of early days and the 1930s.*

CM181		UnFVF	UseFVF
5¢	**gray blue** *(36,819,050)*	.75	.20
	Plate block of 4	12.50	
	Pair, gutter between	—	
	FDC *(May 26, 1937)*		7.50

1937. Northwest Ordinance Issue of 1787 marked the 150th anniversary of the adoption of the Northwest Ordinance by the Congress of the Confederation. The confederation's greatest achievement, it provided for the governing of the Northwest Territory, dividing it into five parts that are now Ohio, Indiana, Illinois, Wisconsin and Michigan. The Rev. Manasseh Cutler, a distinguished botanist, aided in drafting the ordinance and organizing the colonization. Rufus Putnam led the first settlers (see CM192), who founded Marietta, Ohio. *Intaglio, perforated 11 x 10 1/2.*

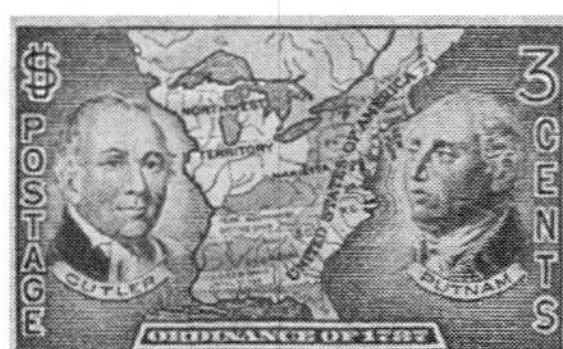

CM182 *Manasseh Cutler (from an engraving by J. C. Buttre), Rufus Putnam (from a Trumbull miniature), map of the Northwest Territory*

CM182		UnFVF	UseFVF
3¢	**dull purple** *(84,825,250)*	.25	.20
	Plate block of 4	8.50	
	FDC *(July 13, 1937)*		10.00

1937. Virginia Dare Issue commemorated the 350th birthday of Virginia Dare, first child of English parentage born in America, at Roanoke Island off the North Carolina coast. Her grandfather, John White, leader of the expedition for Sir Walter Raleigh, returned to England for supplies a week after her birth in 1579. The Spanish War delayed his return until 1591, by which time the entire colony had mysteriously vanished. The stamps were printed 48 to the pane. *Flat plate printing, intaglio, perforated 11.*

CM183 *Virginia Dare and parents, from a drawing by William A. Roache*

CM183		UnFVF	UseFVF
5¢	**light slate blue** *(25,040,400)*	.25	.20
	Plate block of 6	8.50	
	FDC *(Aug. 18, 1937)*		10.00

Users of this Catalog are invited to write to us if they have information which they feel will supplement or correct any material contained herein. All such communications will be answered.

1937. Society of Philatelic Americans Souvenir Sheet was issued for the 43rd annual convention of the S.P.A. at Asheville, N.C. It consisted of a single stamp, the 10¢ Great Smokey Mountains National Park design (CM139), *printed in blue green on a sheet measuring 67 x 78mm. Intaglio, imperforate. The margin is inscribed:* "PRINTED BY THE TREASURY DEPARTMENT, BUREAU OF ENGRAVING AND PRINTING / UNDER THE AUTHORITY OF JAMES A. FARLEY, POSTMASTER GENERAL / IN COMPLIMENT TO THE 43RD ANNUAL CONVENTION OF THE SOCIETY OF PHILATELIC AMERICANS / ASHEVILLE, N.C., AUGUST 26-28, 1937."

CM184 *Society of Philatelic Americans souvenir sheet*

CM184		UnFVF	UseFVF
10¢	**blue green** *(5,277,445)*	.75	.65
	FDC *(Aug. 26, 1937)*		10.00

1937. Constitution Sesquicentennial Issue marked the 150th anniversary of the signing of the U.S. Constitution. The Articles of Confederation having proved ineffectual, a convention was called in Philadelphia to revise and strengthen them. The convention, presided over by Washington, sat for four months in closed sessions, scrapping the Articles altogether and vigorously debating a new constitution point by point. On Sept. 17, 1787, a final draft was signed by 39 of the 42 delegates present and sent to Congress for submission to the states. *Intaglio, perforated 11 x 10 1/2.*

CM185 *Adoption of the Constitution, from a painting by J. B. Sterns*

CM185		UnFVF	UseFVF
3¢	**bright purple** *(99,882,300)*	.25	.20
	Plate block of 4	1.75	
	FDC *(Sept. 17, 1937)*		7.50

1937. Hawaii Territory Issue honored Hawaii, which voluntarily joined the United States in 1898. King Kamehameha the Great (1737-1819) united the Hawaiian Islands under one rule and allowed the first foreign traders to settle there. *Intaglio, perforated 10 1/2 x 11.*

CM186 *Kamehameha I, from a statue by T. R. Gould, Iolani Castle, Honolulu*

CM186		UnFVF	UseFVF
3¢	**violet** *(78,454,450)*	.25	.20
	Plate block of 4	1.50	
	FDC *(Oct. 18, 1937)*		20.00

1937. Alaska Territory Issue honored Alaska, purchased from Russia in 1867 (see CM43). Mount McKinley, pictured on the stamp, is the highest North American peak. *Intaglio, perforated 10 1/2 x 11.*

CM187 *Mount McKinley*

CM187		UnFVF	UseFVF
3¢	**violet** *(77,004,200)*	.25	.20
	Plate block of 4	1.50	
	Pair, gutter between	—	
	FDC *(Nov. 12, 1937)*		15.00

1937. Puerto Rico Territory Issue honored Puerto Rico, ceded to the United States by Spain after the Spanish-American War of 1898. The stamp shows the old Governor's Palace in San Juan, known as La Fortaleza. *Intaglio, perforated 10 1/2 x 11.*

CM188 *La Fortaleza Palace*

CM188		UnFVF	UseFVF
3¢	**light reddish violet** *(81,292,450)*	.25	.20
	Plate block of 4	1.50	
	FDC *(Nov. 25, 1937)*		15.00

1937. Virgin Islands Issue honored the Virgin Islands Territory, purchased from Denmark in 1917 to serve as a naval base for the defense of the Panama Canal. *Intaglio, perforated 10 1/2 x 11.*

CM189 *Harbor at Charlotte Amalie, St. Thomas, Virgin Islands*

CM189		UnFVF	UseFVF
3¢	**lilac** *(76, 474,550)*	.25	.20
	Plate block of 4	.50	
	Pair, gutter between	—	
	FDC *(Dec. 15, 1937)*		15.00

1938. Constitution Ratification Issue commemorated the 150th anniversary of the ratification of the Constitution of the United States. The endorsement of nine states was needed to make the Constitution effective. Maryland was the first state to ratify it. New Hampshire became the ninth (June 21, 1788). *Intaglio, perforated 11 x 10 1/2.*

CM190 *Colonial Court House, Williamsburg, Va.*

CM190		UnFVF	UseFVF
3¢	**violet** *(73,043,650)*	.50	.20
	Plate block of 4	4.50	
	FDC *(June 21, 1938)*		10.00

1938. Swedes and Finns Issue commemorated the 300th anniversary of the settlement by Swedish and Finnish colonists of Fort Christina (now Wilmington, Del.). They were led by Peter Minuit, who was a leader in the earlier settlement of New York (see CM64). The stamps were printed 48 to the sheet. *Intaglio, perforated 11.*

CM191 *Landing of the Swedes and Finns, from a painting by Stanley M. Arthurs, Wilmington, Del.*

CM191		UnFVF	UseFVF
3¢	**carmine purple** *(58,564,368)*	.25	.20
	Plate block of 6	3.25	
	FDC *(June 27, 1938)*		10.00

1938. Northwest Territory Issue commemorated the 150th anniversary of the settlement of the Northwest Territory after the Northwest Ordinance of 1787 (see CM182). *Intaglio, perforated 11 x 10 1/2.*

CM192 *Colonization of the West, from a statue by Gutzon Borglum, Marietta, Ohio*

CM192		UnFVF	UseFVF
3¢	**light reddish violet** *(65,939,500)*	.25	.20
	violet	.25	.20
	Plate block of 4	10.00	
	FDC *(July 15, 1938)*		10.00

1938. Iowa Territory Issue commemorated the 100th anniversary of the establishment of the Iowa Territory, July 3, 1838. The stamp was placed on sale in Des Moines at the opening of the Iowa State Fair. The building pictured was the old Iowa capitol in Iowa City. *Intaglio, perforated 11 x 10 1/2.*

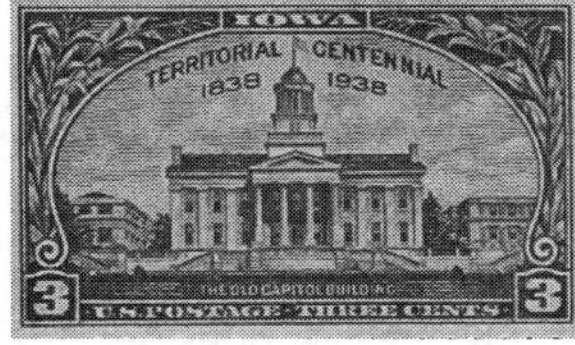

CM193 *Old Capitol Building, Iowa City, Iowa*

CM193		UnFVF	UseFVF
3¢	**violet** *(47,064,300)*	.25	.20
	Plate block of 4	7.50	
	Pair, gutter between	—	
	FDC *(Aug. 24, 1938)*		10.00

1939. Golden Gate Exposition Issue commemorated the international fair held in San Francisco, Calif. The exposition's Tower of the Sun is shown. *Intaglio, perforated 10 1/2 x 11.*

CM194 *Tower of the Sun*

CM194		UnFVF	UseFVF
3¢	**light reddish violet** *(114,439,600)*	.25	.20
	Plate block of 4	1.75	
	FDC *(Feb. 18, 1939)*		10.00

1939. New York World's Fair Issue commemorated the enormous fair and exhibition, "The World of Tomorrow," held in New York City during 1939-40. The futuristic Trylon and Perisphere served as a focal point for the fair. *Intaglio, perforated 10 1/2 x 11.*

CM195 *Trylon and Perisphere*

CM195		UnFVF	UseFVF
3¢	**bluish violet** *(101,699,550)*	.25	.20
	Plate block of 4	2.25	
	FDC *(April 1, 1939)*		12.00

1939. Washington Inauguration Issue commemorated the 150th anniversary of George Washington's inauguration as first President of the United States. The oath of office was administered on the balcony of Federal Hall, at the corner of Wall and Broad Streets in New York City, by Robert Livingston, chancellor of New York State. *Intaglio, perforated 11.*

CM196 *Washington Taking the Oath of Office, from an engraving by Alonzo Chappel*

CM196		UnFVF	UseFVF
3¢	**bright purple** *(73,764,550)*	.25	.20
	Plate block of 6	5.50	
	FDC *(April 30, 1939)*		9.00

1939. Baseball Centennial Issue commemorated the 100th anniversary of this popular American sport. According to a story now generally held to be spurious, while attending school at Cooperstown, N.Y., in 1839, Abner Doubleday laid out the base and player pattern still used today. The National Baseball Hall of Fame and Museum at Cooperstown was selected as the first-day site. *Intaglio, perforated 11 x 10 1/2.*

CM197 *Sandlot baseball game*

CM197		UnFVF	UseFVF
3¢	**violet** *(81,269,600)*	2.25	.20
	Plate block of 4	11.00	
	FDC *(June 12, 1939)*		40.00

1939. Panama Canal Issue commemorated the 25th anniversary of the opening of the Panama Canal (see CM48). Authorized by President Theodore Roosevelt, who arranged the requisite treaty with Panama in 1904, it was built under the direction of Col. George W. Goethals. *Intaglio, perforated 11.*

CM198 *Theodore Roosevelt, George W. Goethals and a ship in the Gaillard Cut of the Panama Canal*

CM198		UnFVF	UseFVF
3¢	**deep reddish purple** *(67,813,350)*	.50	.20
	Plate block of 6	4.00	
	FDC *(Aug. 15, 1939)*		10.00

1939. Printing Tercentenary Issue recalled the 300th anniversary of printing in Colonial America. The press shown was brought to the colonies by the Rev. Joseph Glover, who died en route. Stephen Daye set up the press at Cambridge, Mass. Its first publication, in March 1639, was a single sheet, "Oath of a Free-man." In 1640 it printed *The Bay Psalm Book,* the first American book in English. The press is now in the Harvard University Museum. *Intaglio, perforated 10 1/2 x 11.*

CM199 *Stephen Daye press*

CM199		UnFVF	UseFVF
3¢	**violet** *(71,394,750)*	.25	.20
	Plate block of 4	1.50	
	FDC *(Sept. 25, 1939)*		8.00

1940. Four States Issue commemorated the 50th anniversary of the states of North Dakota, South Dakota, Montana and Washington. The stamp had three different first-day dates (Nov. 2 for the Dakotas, Nov. 8 for Montana and Nov. 11 for Washington) before being placed on general sale Nov. 13. *Intaglio, perforated 11 x 10 1/2.*

CM200 *Map of North Dakota, South Dakota, Montana and Washington*

CM200		UnFVF	UseFVF
3¢	**reddish purple** *(66,835,000)*	.25	.20
	Plate block of 4	1.50	
	FDC *(Nov. 2, 1939)*		7.50

1940. Famous Americans Series issued over a nine-month period, paid tribute to America's men and women who had distinguished themselves and their country in their creative dedication to the betterment of all mankind. They were grouped by the following topics: authors, poets, educators, scientists, musicians, artists, and inventors. Honorees were chosen mainly through a poll conducted by the National Federation of Stamp Clubs. *Intaglio, perforated 10 1/2 x 11.*

CM201 *Washington Irving (1783-1859), America's first internationally accepted man of letters, is best remembered for his stories such as* The Legend of Sleepy Hollow *(see CM754) and* Rip Van Winkle.

CM201		MNHVF	UseVF
1¢	**emerald** *(56,348,320)*	.25	.20
	Plate block of 4	1.25	
	FDC *(Jan. 29, 1940)*		4.00

CM202 *James Fenimore Cooper (1789-1851) lives on through his adventure stories, notably* The Leather-Stocking Tales, *five novels about a pioneer scout named Natty Bumppo.*

CM202		MNHVF	UseVF
2¢	**carmine** *(53,177,110)*	.25	.20
	Plate block of 4	1.25	
	FDC *(Jan. 29, 1940)*		4.00

CM203 *Ralph Waldo Emerson (1803-82), New England philosopher, is known for the practical idealism of his essays and for poems such as "The Concord Hymn."*

CM203		MNHVF	UseVF
3¢	**bright purple** *(53,260,270)*	.25	.20
	Plate block of 4	1.25	
	FDC *(Feb. 5, 1940)*		4.00

CM204 *Louisa May Alcott (1832-88), teacher, social reformer and Civil War nurse, wrote the spectacularly popular novel* Little Women *and many others.*

CM204		MNHVF	UseVF
5¢	**gray blue** *(22,104,950)*	.40	.25
	Plate block of 4	12.00	
	FDC *(Feb. 5, 1940)*		5.00

CM205 *Samuel Langhorne Clemens (1835-1910), is known to the world as Mark Twain. His best-known character is Tom Sawyer, his greatest work* Adventures of Huckleberry Finn, *published in 1884.*

CM205		MNHVF	UseVF
10¢	**sepia** *(13,201,270)*	2.25	1.75
	Plate block of 4	45.00	
	FDC *(Feb. 13, 1940)*		10.00

CM206 *Henry Wadsworth Longfellow (1807-1882), Harvard professor and America's best-loved poet, wrote "The Song of Hiawatha," "Evangeline" and "The Village Blacksmith."*

CM206		MNHVF	UseVF
1¢	**emerald** *(51,603,580)*	.25	.20
	Plate block of 4	2.00	
	FDC *(Feb. 16, 1940)*		4.00

CM207 *John Greenleaf Whittier (1807-92), poet and abolitionist, is best remembered for his "Snow-Bound," "The Barefoot Boy," "Maude Muller" and "Barbara Frietchie."*

CM207		MNHVF	UseVF
2¢	**carmine** *(52,100,510)*	.25	.20
	Plate block of 4	2.00	
	FDC *(Feb. 16, 1940)*		4.00

CM208 *James Russell Lowell (1819-91), also was a diplomat, teacher and satirist. His best-known works are "The Biglow Papers" and "The Vision of Sir Launfal."*

CM208		MNHVF	UseVF
3¢	**bright purple** *(51,666,580)*	.25	.20
	Plate block of 4	2.75	
	FDC *(Feb. 20, 1940)*		4.00

CM209 *Walt Whitman (1819-92), poet of democracy and the individual, pioneered the free-verse form with a collection of poems called* Leaves of Grass, *first published in 1855.*

CM209		MNHVF	UseVF
5¢	**gray blue** *(22,207,780)*	.45	.25
	Plate block of 4	12.00	
	FDC *(Feb. 20, 1940)*		5.00

CM210 *James Whitcomb Riley (1849-1916) wrote kindly, cheerful poems in Indiana dialect. His best-known works are "Little Orphant Annie" and "The Raggedy Man."*

CM210		MNHVF	UseVF
10¢	**sepia** *(11,835,530)*	2.25	1.75
	Plate block of 4	50.00	
	FDC *(Feb. 24, 1940)*		10.00

CM211 *Horace Mann (1796-1859) founded the nation's first normal school and revolutionized the organization and teaching of the American public school system.*

CM211		MNHVF	UseVF
1¢	**emerald** *(52,471,160)*	.25	.20
	Plate block of 4	2.75	
	FDC *(March 14, 1940)*		4.00

CM212 *Mark Hopkins (1802-87), for 36 years president of Williams College in Massachusetts, did much to raise American educational standards.*

CM212		MNHVF	UseVF
2¢	**carmine** *(52,366,440)*	.25	.20
	Plate block of 4	1.25	
	FDC *(March 14, 1940)*		4.00

CM213 *Charles W. Eliot (1834-1926), president of Harvard, 1869-1909, made the school America's leading university and edited the* Harvard Classics, *commonly known as "Dr. Eliot's Five-Foot Shelf of Books."*

CM213		MNHVF	UseVF
3¢	**bright purple** *(51,636,270)*	.25	.20
	Plate block of 4	2.75	
	FDC *(March 28, 1940)*		4.00

Please do not send us stamps to be authenticated. This type of service requires elaborate equipment and facilities not regularly available to us.

CM214 *Frances E. Willard (1839-98), dean of women at Northwestern University, was a pioneer worker for the improvement of education for women.*

CM214		MNHVF	UseVF
5¢	**gray blue** *(20,729,030)*	.40	.30
	Plate block of 4	12.00	
	FDC *(March 28, 1940)*		5.00

CM215 *Booker T. Washington (1856-1910), born a slave, was America's leading Black educator. In 1881 he founded Tuskegee Normal and Industrial Institute.*

CM215		MNHVF	UseVF
10¢	**sepia** *(14,125,580)*	2.50	1.75
	Plate block of 4	42.50	
	FDC *(April 7, 1940)*		10.00

CM216 *John James Audubon (1785-1851), ornithologist, painted birds from life. His* Birds of America, *published 1827-38, has been called "the most magnificent monument yet raised by art to science."*

CM216		MNHVF	UseVF
1¢	**emerald** *(59,409,000)*	.25	.20
	Plate block of 4	1.25	
	FDC *(April 8, 1940)*		4.00

CM217 *Dr. Crawford W. Long (1815-78), a Georgia physician, is believed to have been the first surgeon to use ether as an anaesthetic in 1842.*

CM217		MNHVF	UseVF
2¢	**carmine** *(57,888,600)*	.25	.20
	Plate block of 4	1.25	
	FDC *(April 8, 1940)*		4.00

CM218 *Luther Burbank (1849-1926), horticulturist, developed the Burbank potato and many new and better varieties of fruits, flowers and vegetables.*

CM218		MNHVF	UseVF
3¢	**bright purple** *(58,273,180)*	.25	.20
	Plate block of 4	1.25	
	FDC *(April 17, 1940)*		4.00

CM219 *Dr. Walter Reed (1851-1902), led the experiments in Cuba establishing that yellow fever is transmitted by a variety of mosquito, a discovery that made possible the virtual elimination of that disease.*

CM219		MNHVF	UseVF
5¢	**gray blue** *(23,779,000)*	.50	.20
	Plate block of 4	7.75	
	FDC *(April 17, 1940)*		5.00

CM220 *Jane Addams (1860-1935), noted humanitarian, in 1889 founded Hull House, a social settlement to improve community life in the slums of Chicago. It was the first institution of its kind in the United States.*

CM220		MNHVF	UseVF
10¢	**sepia** *(15,112,580)*	1.50	1.50
	Plate block of 4	32.50	
	FDC *(April 26, 1940)*		6.00

CM221 *Stephen Collins Foster (1826-64), most popular of all American composers, wrote such songs as "O Susanna," "Swanee River," "Camptown Races," and "Jeannie with the Light Brown Hair."*

CM221		MNHVF	UseVF
1¢	**emerald** *(57,322,790)*	.25	.20
	Plate block of 4	1.25	
	FDC *(May 3, 1940)*		4.00

CM222 *John Philip Sousa (1854-1932), a bandmaster and composer, was known as the March King. His most popular march is "The Stars and Stripes Forever." (See CM1941.)*

CM222		MNHVF	UseVF
2¢	**carmine** *(58,281,580)*	.25	.20
	Plate block of 4	1.25	
	FDC *(May 3, 1940)*		4.00

CM223 *Victor Herbert (1859-1924), Irish-born cellist and conductor, wrote many operettas, including* Babes in Toyland, The Red Mill *and* Naughty Marietta. *His best-known song is "Ah, Sweet Mystery of Life."*

CM223		MNHVF	UseVF
3¢	**bright purple** *(56,398,790)*	.25	.20
	Plate block of 4	1.25	
	FDC *(May 13, 1940)*		4.00

CM224 *Edward A. MacDowell (1861-1908), composed piano and orchestral works and songs. He is best known for his "Woodland Sketches" and "To a Wild Rose."*

CM224		MNHVF	UseVF
5¢	**gray blue** *(21,147,000)*	.75	.30
	Plate block of 4	12.50	
	FDC *(May 13, 1940)*		5.00

CM225 *Ethelbert Nevin (1862-1901), composed 70 songs, including "Narcissus," The Rosary" and "Mighty Lak a Rose."*

CM225		**MNHVF**	**UseVF**
10¢	**sepia** *(13,328,000)*	5.00	2.00
	Plate block of 4	50.00	
	FDC *(June 10, 1940)*		6.00

226 *Gilbert Charles Stuart (1755-1828), was one of the first eminent American painters. His portraits of contemporaries, especially George Washington, have been used on many U.S. stamps.*

CM226		**MNHVF**	**UseVF**
1¢	**emerald** *(54,389,510)*	.25	.20
	Plate block of 4	1.00	
	FDC *(Sept. 5, 1940)*		4.00

CM227 *James Abbott McNeill Whistler (1834-1903), a brilliant American painter and etcher, made his success in Europe. His portrait of his mother (see CM127) is his best-known work.*

CM227		**MNHVF**	**UseVF**
2¢	**carmine** *(53,636,580)*	.25	.20
	Plate block of 4	1.00	
	FDC *(Sept. 5, 1940)*		4.00

CM228 *Augustus Saint-Gaudens (1848-1907), great Irish-born sculptor, is best known for his equestrian statue of Sherman in New York City and his statue of Lincoln.*

CM228		**MNHVF**	**UseVF**
3¢	**bright purple** *(55,313,230)*	.25	.20
	Plate block of 4	1.25	
	FDC *(Sept. 16, 1940)*		4.00

CM229 *Daniel Chester French (1850-1931), New Hampshire sculptor, created* The Minute Man *(CM69) on Lexington Green and the seated Abraham Lincoln in the Lincoln Memorial at Washington, D.C.*

CM229		**MNHVF**	**UseVF**
5¢	**gray blue** *(21,720,580)*	.75	.30
	Plate block of 4	11.00	
	FDC *(Sept. 16, 1940)*		5.00

CM230 *Frederic Remington (1861-1909), was a painter, illustrator and sculptor, known for his depiction of lively action in Western scenes. His artwork is seen on CM21, CM23, CM496 and CM993.*

CM230		**MNHVF**	**UseVF**
10¢	**sepia** *(13,600,580)*	2.00	1.75
	Plate block of 4	35.00	
	FDC *(Sept. 30, 1940)*		6.00

CM231 *Eli Whitney (1765-1825), revolutionized the cotton industry in 1793 by inventing the cotton gin, a machine that separated cotton seed from the fiber 50 times faster than it could be done by hand.*

CM231		**MNHVF**	**UseVF**
1¢	**emerald** *(47,599,580)*	.25	.20
	Plate block of 4	2.00	
	FDC *(Oct. 7, 1940)*		4.00

CM232 *Samuel F. B. Morse (1791-1872), a portrait painter, invented the electric telegraph (CM266) and the telegraphic alphabet known as Morse Code.*

CM232		**MNHVF**	**UseVF**
2¢	**carmine** *(53,766,510)*	.25	.20
	Plate block of 4	1.25	
	FDC *(Oct. 7, 1940)*		4.00

CM233 *Cyrus Hall McCormick (1809-84), in 1831 invented a reaping machine with all key features of the harvesting machines of today. It increased American farm output and settlement of the West.*

CM233		**MNHVF**	**UseVF**
3¢	**bright purple** *(54,193,580)*	.25	.20
	Plate block of 4	2.00	
	FDC *(Oct. 14, 1940)*		4.00

CM234 *Elias Howe (1819-67), invented the sewing machine in 1846, which revolutionized clothesmaking, lowered costs, increased quality and eventually brought many women into American industry.*

CM234		**MNHVF**	**UseVF**
5¢	**gray blue** *(20,264,580)*	1.25	.50
	Plate block of 4	17.50	
	FDC *(Oct. 14, 1940)*		7.50

CM235 *Alexander Graham Bell (1847-1922), whose interest in acoustics stemmed from his work in teaching the deaf, invented the telphone in 1876.*

CM235		**MNHVF**	**UseVF**
10¢	**sepia** *(13,726,580)*	15.00	3.25
	Plate block of 4	70.00	
	FDC *(Oct. 28, 1940)*		7.50

1940. Pony Express Issue marked the 80th anniversary of the Central Overland California and Pike's Peak Express Company, the "Pony Express" that carried letters at $5 an ounce from St. Joseph, Mo., to Sacramento, Calif. Using 80 young riders, 420 horses and 190 relay stations, it made the 1,900-mile trip in 10 days (winter) or eight days (summer). *Intaglio, perforated 11 x 10 1/2.*

CM236 *Pony Express rider*

CM236		MNHVF	UseVF
3¢	**chestnut** *(46,497,400)*	.35	.20
	Plate block of 4	3.50	
	FDC *(April 3, 1940)*		7.50

1940. Pan-American Union Issue commemorated the 50th anniversary of the founding of the International Bureau of American Republics, now known as the Pan-American Union. It was created by the various republics of North, Central and South America for the development of trade relations and peace. *Intaglio, perforated 10 1/2 x 11.*

CM237 *Three Graces, from Botticelli's painting,* Spring

CM237		MNHVF	UseVF
3¢	**lilac** *(47,700,000)*	.30	.20
	Plate block of 4	4.25	
	FDC *(April 14, 1940)*		5.00

1940. Idaho Statehood Issue commemorated the 50th anniversary of Idaho's admission as the 43rd state. The region, crossed by Lewis and Clark in 1806, was a part of the Oregon Territory (CM170) in 1848-63, before becoming Idaho Territory. *Intaglio, perforated 11 x 10 1/2.*

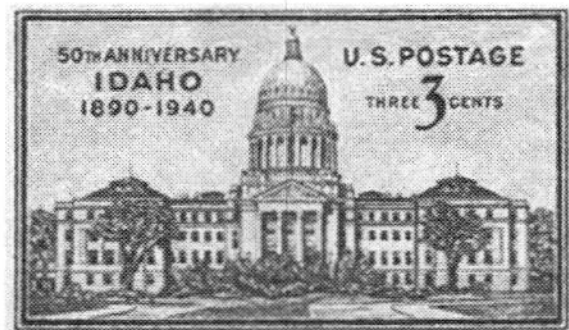

CM238 *State Capitol at Boise*

CM238		MNHVF	UseVF
3¢	**light reddish violet** *(50,618,150)*	.25	.20
	Plate block of 4	2.50	
	FDC *(July 3, 1940)*		5.00

1940. Wyoming Statehood Issue commemorated the 50th anniversary of Wyoming's admission as the 44th state. The state seal's central figure, a female on a pedestal under the banner "Equal Rights," is a reminder that in Wyoming Territory women were given the right to vote in 1869. *Intaglio, perforated 10 1/2 x 11.*

CM239 *Wyoming state seal*

CM239		MNHVF	UseVF
3¢	**purple brown** *(50,034,400)*	.25	.20
	Plate block of 4	2.25	
	FDC *(July 10, 1940)*		5.00

1940. Coronado Expedition Issue observed the 400th anniversary of the expedition by Francisco Vasquez de Coronado, seeking the fabled Seven Cities of Cibola. Coronado's men discovered the Grand Canyon, explored what is now southern California and the Rio Grande, captured Zuni Indian settlements in New Mexico, and crossed the Arkansas River into Kansas. *Intaglio, perforated 11 x 10 1/2.*

CM240 Coronado and his captains, *painting by Gerald Cassidy*

CM240		MNHVF	UseVF
3¢	**reddish lilac** *(60,943,700)*	.25	.20
	Plate block of 4	1.75	
	FDC *(Sept. 7, 1940)*		5.00

1940. National Defense Issue focused attention upon the necessity for building an adequate national defense. Original sketches by President Roosevelt were the basis for the final designs. *Intaglio, perforated 11 x 10 1/2.*

CM241 *The Statue of Liberty, rising 305 feet above the waters of New York harbor, is the work of Alsatian sculptor Frederic Auguste Bartholdi (CM1163), who conceived the idea on a visit to the United States. A centennial gift from the people of France, it was up to America to supply the funds to build the pedestal, which was completed 10 years later in 1886, after the efforts of Pulitzer and his New York* World *newspaper. Its full name is "Liberty Enlightening the World;" and it has become a universal symbol of the freedom and security of democracy in America.*

CM241		MNHVF	UseVF
1¢	**emerald** *(6,081,409,300)*	.25	.20
	Plate block of 4	.50	
	Cracked plate	—	
	Gripper cracks	—	
	Pair, gutter between	—	
	FDC *(Oct. 16, 1940)*		5.00
	v. Horizontal pair, imperforate between	35.00	
	v1. Vertical pair, imperforate between	500.00	

CM242 *90mm anti-aircraft gun*

CM242		MNHVF	UseVF
2¢	**rose** *(5,211,708,200)*	.25	.20
	Plate block of 4	.50	
	Pair, gutter between	—	
	FDC *(Oct. 16, 1940)*		5.00
	v. Horizontal pair, imperforate between	40.00	

CM243 *Torch symbolizing enlightenment*

CM243		MNHVF	UseVF
3¢	**light reddish violet** *(8,384,867,600)*	.25	.20
	Plate block of 4	.75	
	Pair, gutter between	—	
	FDC *(Oct. 16, 1940)*		5.00
	v. Horizontal pair, imperforate between	25.00	

1940. Thirteenth Amendment Issue commemorated the abolition of slavery in the United States. President Lincoln's Emancipation Proclamation of 1863 freed only the slaves in states that had seceded from the Union, leaving the status of nearly a million others in northern and border states unchanged. The Thirteenth Amendment, proclaimed in force Dec. 18, 1865, abolished all involuntary servitude except as a punishment for crime. *Intaglio, perforated 10 1/2 x 11.*

CM244 *Emancipation Monument of President Lincoln and Archer Alexander, an escaped slave who won freedom in Missouri, by Thomas Ball (1819-1911) in Lincoln Park, Washington, D.C.*

CM244		MNHVF	UseVF
3¢	**violet** *(44,389,550)*	.35	.20
	Plate block of 4	3.75	
	FDC *(Oct. 20, 1940)*		7.50

1941. Vermont Statehood Issue commemorated the 150th anniversary of Vermont's admission into the Union as the 14th state. *Intaglio, perforated 11 x 10 1/2.*

CM245 *State Capitol at Montpelier, Vt.*

CM245		MNHVF	UseVF
3¢	**violet** *(54,574,550)*	.25	.20
	Plate block of 4	2.00	
	FDC *(March 4, 1941)*		7.50

1942. Kentucky Statehood Issue commemorated the 150th anniversary of its admission as the 15th state. Kentucky was explored in 1767 by Daniel Boone who in 1775 led a party of settlers through the Cumberland Gap and over the Wilderness Road to erect a fort at what later became Boonesborough. *Intaglio, perforated 11 x 10 1/2.*

CM246 *Daniel Boone and Frontiersmen, mural by Gilbert White, State Capitol, Frankfort, Ky.*

CM246		MNHVF	UseVF
3¢	**reddish violet** *(63,558,400)*	.25	.20
	Plate block of 4	1.25	
	FDC *(June 1, 1942)*		5.00

1942. Win the War Issue following Pearl Harbor, replaced the 3¢ National Defense stamp (CM243) and symbolized the nation's war effort and its goal of victory. *Intaglio, perforated 11 x 10 1/2.*

CM247 *Victory Eagle*

CM247		MNHVF	UseVF
3¢	**violet** *(20,642,793,300)*	.25	.20
	light violet	.25	.20
	Plate block of 4	.75	
	Pair, gutter between	—	
	FDC *(July 4, 1942)*		5.00
	a. purple	—	

1942. Chinese Commemorative Issue honored five years of Chinese resistance to Japanese aggression. Chinese characters below the portrait of Sun Yat-sen, founder of the Republic, are Abraham Lincoln's words: "of the people, by the people, for the people." *Intaglio, perforated 11 x 10 1/2.*

CM248 *Abraham Lincoln, map of China, Sun Yat-sen*

CM248		MNHVF	UseVF
5¢	**Prussian blue** *(21,272,800)*	.60	.30
	Plate block of 4	12.00	
	FDC *(July 7, 1942)*		10.00

1943. Allied Nations Issue commemorated the strength and unity with which nations of the free world were fighting to establish peace and freedom. *Intaglio, perforated 11 x 10 1/2.*

CM249 *Nations United for Victory*

CM249		MNHVF	UseVF
2¢	**carmine** *(1,671,564,200)*	.25	.20
	Plate block of 4	.50	
	Pair, gutter between	—	
	FDC *(Jan. 14, 1943)*		5.00

1943. Four Freedoms Issue symbolized principles enunciated by President Roosevelt in the 1941 State of the Union message to Congress: freedom of speech and expression, freedom of worship, freedom from want and freedom from fear. *Intaglio, perforated 11 x 10 1/2.*

CM250 *Liberty bearing the torch of freedom and enlightenment*

CM250		MNHVF	UseVF
1¢	**emerald** *(1,227,334,200)*	.25	.20
	Plate block of 4	.60	
	FDC *(Feb. 12, 1943)*		5.00

1943-44. Overrun Countries Issue recognized the countries occupied by the Axis powers, which implied the free world's determination to liberate them.

For the first time since 1893, the Bureau of Engraving and Printing contracted with a private firm, the American Bank Note Co., so that the stamps could be printed in color. The frames of all values were engraved slate violet. The vignettes were printed by offset in two or three colors of the flags. *Letterpress and offset, perforated 12.*

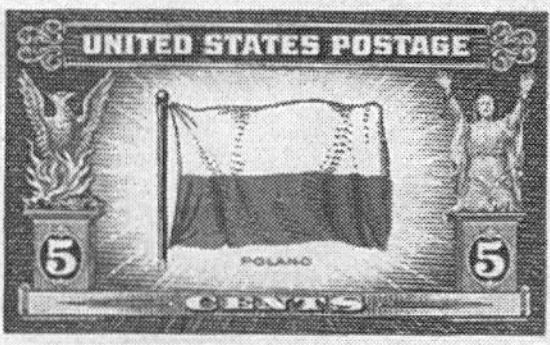

CM251 *Flag of Poland*

CM251		MNHVF	UseVF
5¢	**slate violet, scarlet & black** *(19,999,646)*	.25	.20
	"Poland" block of 4	7.25	
	"Poland" block of 6, w/guide markings	—	
	FDC *(June 22, 1943)*		5.00

CM252 *Flag of Czechoslovakia*

CM252		MNHVF	UseVF
5¢	**slate violet, blue, scarlet & black** *(19,999,646)*	.25	.20
	"Czechoslovakia" block of 4	4.00	
	"Czechoslovakia" block of 6 w/guide markings	—	
	v. "Czechoslovakia" Doubled inscription	—	
	FDC *(July 12, 1943)*		5.00

CM253 *Flag of Norway*

CM253		MNHVF	UseVF
5¢	**slate violet, rose red, ultramarine & black** *(19,999,616)*	.25	.20
	"Norway" block of 4	1.75	
	"Norway" block of 6, w/guide markings	—	
	FDC *(July 27, 1943)*		5.00

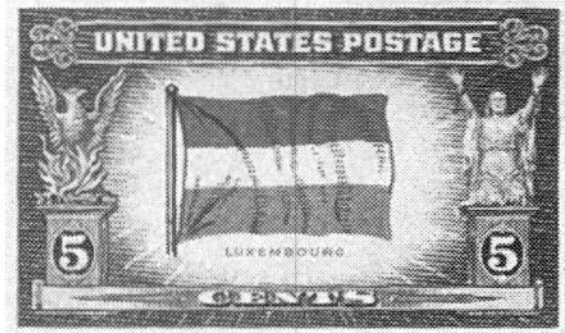

CM254 *Flag of Luxembourg*

CM254		MNHVF	UseVF
5¢	**slate violet, rose red, light blue & black** *(19,999,646)*	.25	.20
	"Luxembourg" block of 4	1.75	
	"Luxembourg" block of 6, w/guide markings	—	
	FDC *(Aug. 10, 1943)*		5.00

CM255 *Flag of Netherlands*

CM255		MNHVF	UseVF
5¢	**slate violet, scarlet, blue & black** *(19,999,646)*	.25	.20
	"Netherlands" block of 4	1.75	
	"Netherlands" block of 6, w/guide markings	—	
	FDC *(Aug. 24, 1943)*		5.00

CM256 *Flag of Belgium*

CM256		MNHVF	UseVF
5¢	**slate violet, scarlet, greenish yellow & black** *(19,999,646)*	.25	.20
	"Belgium" block of 4	1.75	
	"Belgium" block of 6, w/guide markings	—	
	FDC *(Sept. 14, 1943)*		5.00

CM257 *Flag of France*

CM257		MNHVF	UseVF
5¢	**slate violet, blue, red & black** *(19,999,648)*	.25	.20
	"France" block of 4	1.75	
	"France" block of 6, w/guide markings	—	
	FDC *(Sept. 28, 1943)*		5.00

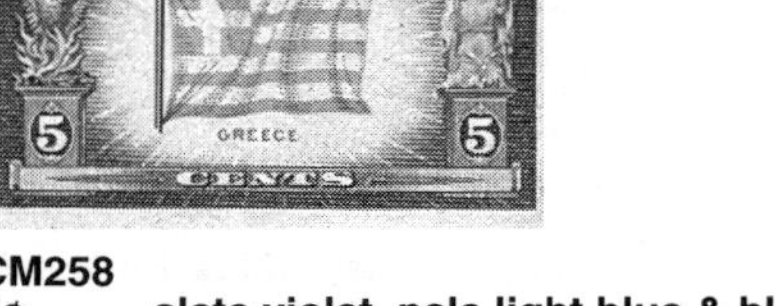

CM258 *Flag of Greece*

CM258		MNHVF	UseVF
5¢	**slate violet, pale light blue & black** *(14,999,646)*	.50	.20
	"Greece" block of 4	15.00	
	"Greece" block of 6, w/guide markings	—	
	FDC *(Oct. 12, 1943)*		5.00

CM259 *Flag of Yugoslavia*

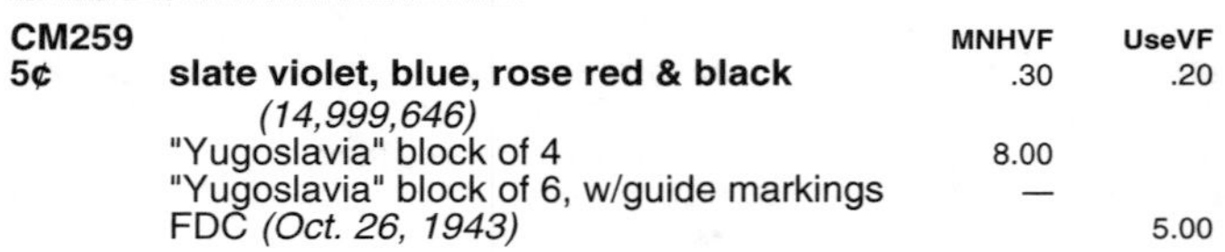

CM259		MNHVF	UseVF
5¢	**slate violet, blue, rose red & black** *(14,999,646)*	.30	.20
	"Yugoslavia" block of 4	8.00	
	"Yugoslavia" block of 6, w/guide markings	—	
	FDC *(Oct. 26, 1943)*		5.00

CM260 *Flag of Albania*

CM260		MNHVF	UseVF
5¢	**slate violet, red & black** *(14,999,646)*	.30	.20
	"Albania" block of 4	8.00	
	"Albania" block of 6, w/guide markings	—	
	FDC *(Nov. 9, 1943)*		5.00

CM261 *Flag of Austria*

CM261		MNHVF	UseVF
5¢	**slate violet, red & black** *(14,999,646)*	.30	.20
	"Austria" block of 4	5.25	
	"Austria" block of 6, w/guide markings	—	
	v. Doubled inscription "Austria"	—	
	FDC *(Nov. 23, 1943)*		5.00

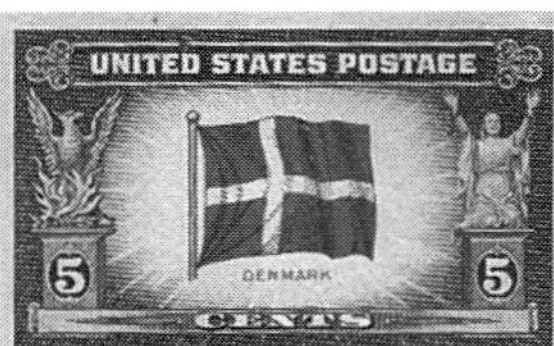

CM262 *Flag of Denmark*

CM262		MNHVF	UseVF
5¢	**slate violet, scarlet & black** *(14,999,646)*	.30	.20
	"Denmark" block of 4	6.25	
	"Denmark" block of 6, w/guide markings	—	
	FDC *(Dec. 7, 1943)*		5.00

CM263 *Flag of Korea*

CM263		MNHVF	UseVF
5¢	**slate violet, scarlet, bright blue & gray** *(14,999,646)*	.30	.20
	"Korea" block of 4	5.25	
	"Korea" block of 6, w/guide markings	—	
	v. "KORPA" plate flaw	27.50	
	FDC *(Nov. 2, 1944)*		5.00

1944. Transcontinental Railroad Issue marked the 75th anniversary of the completion of the first transcontinental railroad. A golden spike driven at Promontory Point, near Ogden, Utah, on May 10, 1869, marked the meeting of the Union Pacific tracks from the west with the Central Pacific from the east. *Intaglio, perforated 11 x 10 1/2.*

CM264 *Golden Spike Ceremony, mural by John McQuarrie, Union Pacific Station, Salt Lake City, Utah*

CM264		MNHVF	UseVF
3¢	**violet** *(61,303,000)*	.30	.20
	Plate block of 4	1.75	
	FDC *(May 10, 1944)*		7.50

1944. Steamship Issue commemorated the 125th anniversary of the first steamship crossing of the Atlantic. The first-day date was National Maritime Day. The ship *Savannah,* sailing with an auxiliary steam engine, crossed from Savannah, Ga., to Liverpool, England, in 19 days. *Intaglio, perforated 11 x 10 1/2.*

CM265 *S.S.* Savannah, *from ship model, Marine Museum, Newport News, Va.*

CM265		MNHVF	UseVF
3¢	**violet** *(61,001,450)*	.25	.20
	Plate block of 4	1.50	
	FDC *(May 22, 1944)*		7.50

1944. Telegraph Centennial Issue commemorated the 100th anniversary of the first message sent by telegraph. The inventor, Samuel F. B. Morse (CM232), sent the historic words, "What hath God wrought!" from Washington, D.C., to Baltimore, Md., where they were received by his associate, Alfred Vail. *Intaglio, perforated 11 x 10 1/2.*

CM266 *Telegraph wires and posts*

CM266		MNHVF	UseVF
3¢	**bright purple** *(60,605,000)*	.25	.20
	Plate block of 4	1.00	
	FDC *(May 24, 1944)*		7.50

1944. Corregidor Issue paid tribute to the gallant resistance of Gen. Jonathan M. Wainwright's American and Philippine troops besieged there by the Japanese in 1942. After the fall of Bataan, the surviving forces withdrew to Corregidor in Manila Bay and withstood the invaders for almost a month before surrendering May 6, 1942. *Intaglio, perforated 11 x 10 1/2.*

CM267 *Corregidor Island*

CM267		MNHVF	UseVF
3¢	**violet** *(50,129,350)*	.25	.20
	Plate block of 4	1.25	
	FDC *(Sept. 27, 1944)*		7.50

1944. Motion Picture Issue commemorated the 50th anniversary of motion pictures and paid tribute to the cinema industry's contributions to the war effort. *Intaglio, perforated 11 x 10 1/2.*

CM268 *Motion pictures for the troops*

CM268		MNHVF	UseVF
3¢	**violet** *(53,479,400)*	.25	.20
	Plate block of 4	1.00	
	FDC *(Oct. 31, 1944)*		7.50

1945. Florida Centennial Issue marked the 100th anniversary of Florida's admission as the 27th state. Explored by Juan Ponce de Leon in 1513, Florida was not settled by Europeans until 1565 when Pedro Menendez de Aviles set up a colony at St. Augustine, now the oldest city in the United States. West Florida was seized by the United States in 1813; East Florida was ceded by Spain in 1819. *Intaglio, perforated 11 x 10 1/2.*

CM269 *Gates of St. Augustine, state seal and state capitol*

CM269		MNHVF	UseVF
3¢	**bright purple** *(61,617,350)*	.25	.20
	Plate block of 4	.75	
	FDC *(March 3, 1945)*		7.50

1945. United Nations Conference Issue honored the conference in San Francisco at which the delegates of 50 nations met to draft the Charter of the United Nations Organization. President Roosevelt, who had invited them there, died 13 days before the conference. His words "Toward United Nations, April 25, 1945," were inscribed on the stamp as a memorial to him. *Intaglio, perforated 11 x 10 1/2.*

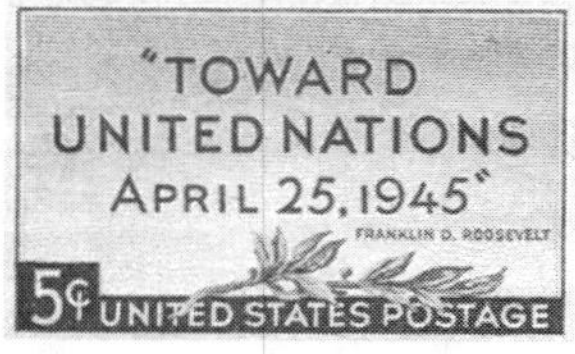

CM270 *"Toward United Nations, April 25, 1945"*

CM270		MNHVF	UseVF
5¢	**ultramarine** *(75,500,000)*	.25	.20
	Plate block of 4	.75	
	FDC *(April 25, 1945)*		8.00

1945-46. ROOSEVELT SERIES paid tribute to President Franklin Delano Roosevelt (1882-1945), who died April 12, 1945. The only American president for whom the "no third term" tradition was set aside, he was elected to the presidency four times. First taking office in a time of grave economic depression, he began the vast economic and social program known as the New Deal. He gave substantial support to Great Britain after the fall of France in 1940, wrote (with British Prime Minister Winston S. Churchill) the Atlantic Charter in 1941, defined the Four Freedoms (CM250), helped lead the fight to victory in World War II and called the conference to organize the United Nations. Thirteen days before it opened, he died of a cerebral hemorrhage at the "Summer White House" in Warm Springs, Ga. (CM272), where he had set up a foundation for children who had, like himself, been stricken by infantile paralysis. He was buried in the garden of his home at Hyde Park, N.Y. (CM271).

An ardent stamp collector for 56 years, Roosevelt added greatly to the popularity of the hobby and suggested the designs of a number of postage stamps issued during his presidency. "I owe my life to my hobbies," he said, "especially stamp collecting." Many countries have honored him on their postage stamps. *Intaglio, perforated 11 x 10 1/2.*

CM271 *Roosevelt and Hyde Park*

CM271		MNHVF	UseVF
1¢	**blue green** *(128,140,000)*	.25	.20
	Plate block of 4	.50	
	FDC *(July 26, 1945)*		4.00
	p. printed on thin, translucent paper	—	

CM272 *Roosevelt and "Little White House" at Warm Springs, Ga.*

CM272		MNHVF	UseVF
2¢	**carmine red** *(67,255,000)*	.25	.20
	Plate block of 4	.50	
	FDC *(Aug. 24, 1945)*		4.00

CM273 *Roosevelt and the White House*

CM273		MNHVF	UseVF
3¢	**lilac** *(138,870,000)*	.25	.20
	Plate block of 4	.50	
	FDC *(June 27, 1945)*		4.00

CM274 *Roosevelt, Globe and Four Freedoms*

CM274		MNHVF	UseVF
5¢	**light blue** *(76,455,400)*	.25	.20
	Plate block of 4	.75	
	FDC *(Jan. 30, 1946)*		3.00

1945-46. Armed Forces Series of five stamps paid tribute to the nation's fighting forces and Merchant Marine for their valiant efforts toward victory in World War II.

1945. MARINE COMMEMORATIVE honored the U.S. Marine Corps. The design is taken from the famous photograph by Joseph Rosenthal of the Associated Press, showing the Marines raising the American Flag on Mount Suribachi on the Japanese island of Iwo Jima. The color was intended to match that of the Marine uniform. *Intaglio, perforated 10 1/2 x 11.*

CM275 *U.S. Marines raising the flag on Mount Suribachi, Iwo Jima*

CM275		MNHVF	UseVF
3¢	**dark yellow green** *(137,321,000)*	.25	.20
	Plate block of 4	.75	
	FDC *(July 11, 1945)*		7.50

1945. ARMY COMMEMORATIVE honored the U.S. Army, particularly the infantry, in World War II. The design was devised from a group of photographs of the 28th Division marching through Paris. The color was selected to match the olive-drab uniform of the Army. *Intaglio, perforated 11 x 10 1/2.*

CM276 *U.S. infantry, bombers and L'Arc de Triomphe, Paris, France*

CM276		MNHVF	UseVF
3¢	**brown olive** *(128,357,750)*	.25	.20
	Plate block of 4	.65	
	FDC *(Sept. 28, 1945)*		7.50

1945. NAVY COMMEMORATIVE honored the U.S. Navy in World War II. The design reproduces an official Navy photograph made at the Corpus Christi Naval Air Station. It may be the first U.S. stamp to show people smiling. *Intaglio, perforated 11 x 10 1/2.*

CM277 *U.S. Navy sailors*

CM277		MNHVF	UseVF
3¢	**blue** *(138,863,000)*	.25	.20
	Plate block of 4	.65	
	FDC *(Oct. 27, 1945)*		7.50

1945. Coast Guard Commemorative honored the U.S. Coast Guard service in World War II. The nation's oldest uniformed service, the Coast Guard participated in every major invasion of the war. *Intaglio, perforated 11 x 10 1/2.*

CM278 *Coast Guard landing craft and supply ship*

CM278		MNHVF	UseVF
3¢	**blue green** *(111,616,700)*	.25	.20
	Plate block of 4	.65	
	FDC *(Nov. 10, 1945)*		7.50

1946. Merchant Marine Commemorative honored the achievements of the U.S. Merchant Marine in World War II. Photographs of two Liberty Ships, the *James Madison* and the *John W. Troy,* were used in the composite design. *Intaglio, perforated 11 x 10 1/2.*

CM279 *Liberty ship and goods*

CM279		MNHVF	UseVF
3¢	**blue green** *(135,927,000)*	.25	.20
	Plate block of 4	.65	
	FDC *(Feb. 26, 1946)*		7.50

1945. Alfred E. Smith Issue honored the colorful and popular American who rose from humble beginnings to serve four terms as governor of New York. Known as "The Happy Warrior," he was the Democratic candidate for president in 1928, but was defeated by Herbert Hoover. He died in 1944. *Intaglio, perforated 11 x 10 1/2.*

CM280 *Alfred E. Smith*

CM280		MNHVF	UseVF
3¢	**dark lilac** *(308,587,700)*	.25	.20
	Plate block of 4.	.55	
	Pair, gutter between	—	
	FDC *(Nov. 26, 1945)*		5.00

1945. Texas Statehood Issue commemorated the 100th anniversary of Texas as the 28th state. A former Mexican state whose American settlers revolted in 1836 and set up a republic (CM166), Texas was granted Congressional authority to divide its vast territory into as many as five states of "convenient size" and "sufficient population" without further permission of Congress. *Intaglio, perforated 11 x 10 1/2.*

CM281 *U.S. and Texas flags and the "Lone Star"*

CM281		MNHVF	UseVF
3¢	**Prussian blue** *(170,640,000)*	.25	.20
	Plate block of 4	.55	
	FDC *(Dec. 29, 1945)*		5.00

1946. Honorable Discharge Stamp honored the members of the armed forces who were returning to civilian life after having served their country in World War II. *Intaglio, perforated 10 X 11 1/2.*

CM282 *Honorable discharge emblem*

CM282		MNHVF	UseVF
3¢	**violet** *(269,339,100)*	.25	.20
	Plate block of 4	.55	
	FDC *(May 9, 1946)*		5.00

1946. Tennessee Statehood Issue commemorated the 150th anniversary of Tennessee as the 16th state. First settled in 1757 as part of North Carolina, it was ceded in 1784 to the federal government, which gave it neither administration nor protection. Settlers under John Sevier set up the independent State of Franklin in 1785-88, and he later served as first governor of Tennessee. *Intaglio, perforated 11 x 10 1/2.*

CM283 *Capitol at Nashville, Andrew Jackson and John Sevier*

CM283		MNHVF	UseVF
3¢	**violet** *(132,274,500)*	.25	.20
	Plate block of 4	.55	
	FDC *(June 1, 1946)*		3.00

1946. Iowa Statehood Issue commemorated the 100th anniversary of Iowa's admission as the 29th state. *Intaglio, perforated 11 x 10 1/2.*

CM284 *Iowa map and flag*

CM284		MNHVF	UseVF
3¢	**Prussian blue** *(132,430,000)*	.25	.20
	Plate block of 4	.55	
	FDC *(Aug. 3, 1946)*		3.00

1946. Smithsonian Institution Issue commemorated the 100th anniversary of its establishment at Washington, D.C. James Smithson, an English chemist, willed more than £100,000 as a gift to the United States for "an establishment for the increase and diffusion of knowledge among men." Today it includes a great library and several museums, including the National Postal Museum (CM1589-92). *Intaglio, perforated 11 x 10 1/2.*

CM285 *Smithsonian Institution*

CM285		MNHVF	UseVF
3¢	**brown purple** *(139,209,500)*	.25	.20
	Plate block of 4	.55	
	FDC *(Aug. 10, 1946)*		3.00

1946. Kearny Expedition Issue commemorated the 100th anniversary of the march of Gen. Stephen W. Kearny's Army of the West from Fort Leavenworth, Kans., to New Mexico. Kearny's unopposed entry into Santa Fe on Aug. 18, 1846, ended the Mexican War and established New Mexico as a part of the United States. *Intaglio, perforated 11 x 10 1/2.*

CM286 *Capture of Santa Fe, from a painting by Kenneth M. Chapman*

CM286		MNHVF	UseVF
3¢	**brown purple** *(114,684,450)*	.25	.20
	Plate block of 4	.55	
	FDC *(Oct. 16, 1946)*		3.00
	Plate block of 4 FDC *(Feb. 1947)*	3.00	
		.55	
		.55	
			3.00
			3.00

1947. Thomas A. Edison Issue commemorated the 100th anniversary of the birth of America's greatest practical scientist. Thomas Alva Edison's more than 1,200 inventions include the incandescent electric bulb (CM85), the automatic telegraph repeater, teleprinter, mimeograph, phonograph, microphone, Ediphone, storage battery, electric dynamo, electric automobile, electric locomotive, carbon telephone transmitter, many motion picture developments, and telegraphic communication with moving trains. *Intaglio, perforated 10 1/2 x 11.*

CM287 *Thomas A. Edison*

CM287		MNHVF	UseVF
3¢	**bright purple** *(156,540,510)*	.25	.20
	Plate block of 4	.55	
	FDC *(Feb. 11, 1947)*		3.00

1947. Joseph Pulitzer Issue commemorated the 100th anniversary of the birth of Joseph Pulitzer, the Hungarian-born journalist who published the *St. Louis Post-Dispatch* and the *New York World.* It was a drive by Pulitzer's *World* that raised the funds to build the base for the Statue of Liberty. He founded and endowed the Columbia School of Journalism, which awards annual Pulitzer Prizes in journalism and letters. *Intaglio, perforated 11 x 10 1/2.*

CM288 *Joseph Pulitzer and the Statue of Liberty*

CM288		MNHVF	UseVF
3¢	**dark lilac** *(120,452,600)*	.25	.20
	Plate block of 4	.55	
	FDC *(April 10, 1947)*		3.00

1947. Postage Stamp Centenary Issue marked the 100th anniversary of the first regular issue U.S. postage stamps. *Intaglio, perforated 11 x 10 1/2.*

CM289 *Washington and Franklin and new methods of carrying the mail*

CM289		MNHVF	UseVF
3¢	**blue** *(127,104,300)*	.25	.20
	Plate block of 4	.55	
	FDC *(May 17, 1947)*		3.00
		.55	

1947. CIPEX Souvenir Sheet featured reproductions of the two stamps of the 1847 issue produced for the Centenary International Philatelic Exhibition. Stamps cut out of the sheet are valid for postage and sometimes are mistaken for the 1847 originals by those who have not checked the colors. The reproduced 5¢ Franklin is light blue instead of the original red brown and the 10¢ Washington reproduction is Venetian red instead of black. The sheet is inscribed in the margin:

"PRINTED BY THE TREASURY DEPARTMENT, BUREAU OF ENGRAVING AND PRINTING / UNDER AUTHORITY OF ROBERT E. HANNEGAN, POSTMASTER GENERAL / IN COMPLIMENT TO THE CENTENARY INTERNATIONAL PHILATELIC EXHIBITION / NEW YORK, N.Y., MAY 17-25, 1947." *Intaglio (flat plate), imperforate.*

CM290 *CIPEX Souvenir Sheet*

CM290		MNHVF	UseVF
15¢	**Complete sheet of 2 stamps** *(10,299,600)*	.75	.65
	a. 5¢ light blue, from sheet	.30	.25
	b. 10¢ Venetian red, from sheet	.45	.25
	FDC *(May 19, 1947)*		4.00

1947. The Doctors Issue paid tribute to the physicians of America. *Intaglio, perforated 11 x 10 1/2.*

CM291 *The Doctor, from a painting by Sir Luke Fildes*

CM291		MNHVF	UseVF
3¢	**brown purple** *(132,902,000)*	.25	.20
	Plate block of 4	.75	
	FDC *(June 9, 1947)*		7.00

1947. Utah Issue commemorated the 100th anniversary of the settlement of Utah by the Mormons under Brigham Young. Driven out of the Midwest by religious persecution, members of the Church of Jesus Christ of Latter-Day Saints made a mass migration to the valley of the Great Salt Lake and founded a territory called Deseret, which in 1850 became the Utah Territory. *Intaglio, perforated 11 x 10 1/2*

CM292 *Pioneers entering the Valley of Great Salt Lake, Utah*

CM292		MNHVF	UseVF
3¢	**violet** *(131,968,000)*	.25	.20
	Plate block of 4	.75	
	FDC *(July 24, 1947)*		3.00

1947. U.S. Frigate Constitution Issue commemorated the 150th anniversary of the launching of the great fighting ship *Constitu-*

tion. Ordered dismantled in 1830, she was saved by public sentiment aroused by Oliver Wendell Holmes' poem, "Old Ironsides." *Intaglio, perforated 11 x 10 1/2.*

CM293 *Drawing of the U.S. Frigate* Constitution

CM293		MNHVF	UseVF
3¢	**blue green** *(131,488,000)*	.25	.20
	Plate block of 4	.55	
	FDC *(Oct. 21, 1947)*		3.50

1947. Everglades National Park Issue commemorated the dedication of the park on Dec 6. The park contains more than a million acres of subtropical land in southern Florida, with extensive watercourses and profuse bird life. *Intaglio, perforated 11 x 10 1/2.*

CM294 *Great white heron and map of Florida*

CM294		MNHVF	UseVF
3¢	**emerald** *(122,362,000)*	.25	.20
	Plate block of 4	.75	
	FDC *(Dec. 5, 1947)*		3.00

1948. George Washington Carver Issue memorialized the fifth anniversary of the death of the agricultural chemist. Born into slavery, and illiterate until he was almost 20, Dr. Carver (1864-1943) spent 47 years as director of agricultural research at Tuskegee Institute, discovered hundreds of industrial uses for the peanut, sweet potato and soybean, aided Southern agriculture, and developed a new cotton strain known as Carver's Hybrid. *Intaglio, perforated 10 1/2 x 11.*

CM295 *George Washington Carver*

CM295		MNHVF	UseVF
3¢	**bright purple** *(121,548,000)*	.25	.20
	Plate block of 4	.55	
	FDC *(Jan. 5, 1948)*		4.00

1948. California Gold Centennial Issue celebrated the 100th anniversary of the discovery of gold by James W. Marshall at Sutter's Mill in California. News of the discovery brought 100,000 gold-seeking "Forty-Niners" to the state from all parts of the world. *Intaglio, perforated 11 x 10 1/2.*

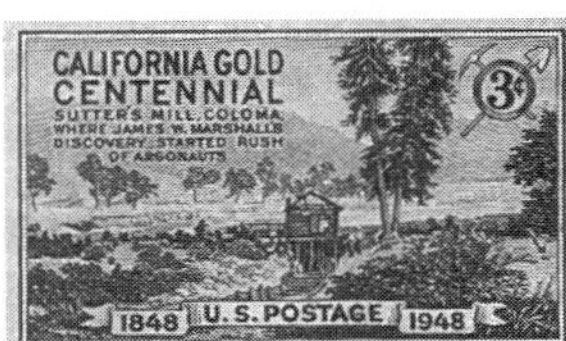

CM296 *Sutter's Mill, California*

CM296		MNHVF	UseVF
3¢	**violet** *(131,109,500)*	.25	.20
	Plate block of 4	.55	
	FDC *(Jan. 24, 1948)*		2.00

1948. Mississippi Territory Issue commemorated the 150th anniversary of the establishment of the Mississippi Territory, comprising the present states of Mississippi and Alabama. Winthrop Sargent was its first governor. *Intaglio, perforated 11 x 10 1/2*

CM297 *Map and original seal of the territory and Sargent*

CM297		MNHVF	UseVF
3¢	**brown purple** *(122,650,500)*	.25	.20
	Plate block of 4	.55	
	FDC *(April 7, 1948)*		2.00

1948. Four Chaplains Issue honored the heroic chaplains — George L. Fox, Clark V. Poling, John P. Washington and Alexander D. Goode — who sacrificed themselves for their comrades when the S.S. *Dorchester* sank on Feb. 3, 1943. Two ministers, a priest, and a rabbi, they gave up their life preservers so that others might live. *Intaglio, perforated 11 x 10 1/2.*

CM298 *Four chaplains and the sinking S.S.* Dorchester

CM298		MNHVF	UseVF
3¢	**black** *(121,953,500)*	.25	.20
	Plate block of 4	.55	
	FDC *(May 28, 1948)*		2.00

1948. Wisconsin Centennial Issue commemorated the 100th anniversary of Wisconsin's admission as the 30th state. First explored by Jean Nicolet in 1634, it was surrendered by France to the British in 1760 and ceded by the British to the United States in 1783. It was part of the Northwest, Indiana, Illinois, and Michigan Territories before becoming the Wisconsin Territory in 1836. *Intaglio, perforated 11 x 10 1/2.*

CM299 *Scroll with map of Wisconsin and State Capitol at Madison*

CM299		MNHVF	UseVF
3¢	**violet** *(115,250,000)*	.25	.20
	Plate block of 4	.75	
	FDC *(May 29, 1948)*		2.00

1948. Swedish Pioneers Issue hailed the 100th anniversary of the arrival of Swedish pioneers in the Midwest. The 12 stars on the stamp represent the 12 states in which the immigrants settled. *Intaglio, perforated 11 x 10 1/2.*

CM300 *Swedish pioneer and covered wagon*

CM300		MNHVF	UseVF
5¢	**blue** *(64,198,500)*	.25	.20
	Plate block of 4	.75	
	FDC *(June 4, 1948)*		2.00

1948. The Progress of Women Issue observed the 100th anniversary of the first women's rights convention, held at Seneca Falls, N.Y., July 19-20, 1848. The convention, called by pioneer feminists Elizabeth Stanton and Lucretia Mott, began the women's suffrage movement to which both devoted the rest of their lives. Carrie Chapman Catt led the suffrage campaign to its final victory in 1920, when the 19th Amendment gave women the vote. *Intaglio, perforated 11 x 10 1/2.*

CM301 *Elizabeth Stanton, Carrie Chapman Catt, and Lucretia Mott*

CM301		MNHVF	UseVF
3¢	**violet** *(117,642,500)*	.25	.20
	Plate block of 4	.55	
	FDC *(July 19, 1948)*		2.00

1948. William Allen White Issue honored the distinguished editor of the *Emporia Gazette,* from 1896, when his editorial "What's the Matter with Kansas?" attracted nationwide attention, until his death in 1944. White was known for his intellectual greatness and honesty, and he made the *Gazette* one of the most notable newspapers in American history. *Intaglio, perforated 10 1/2 x 11*

CM302 *William Allen White*

CM302		MNHVF	UseVF
3¢	**bright purple** *(77,649,000)*	.25	.20
	Plate block of 4	.55	
	FDC *(July 31, 1948)*		2.00

1948. United States - Canada Friendship Issue commemorated a century of friendship between the United States and Canada. The 3,000-mile frontier between the two countries is the longest undefended border in the world. *Intaglio, perforated 11 x 10 1/2.*

CM303 *The Niagara Gorge railway suspension bridge joining the United States and Canada*

CM303		MNHVF	UseVF
3¢	**blue** *(113,474,500)*	.25	.20
	Plate block 4	.55	
	FDC *(Aug. 2, 1948)*		2.00

1948. Francis Scott Key Issue honored the author of our national anthem, "The Star Spangled Banner." Negotiating the exchange of an American held by the British fleet off Baltimore, Key was detained aboard a warship while the British bombarded Fort McHenry on Sept. 13, 1814. After the fort endured a 25-hour bombardment of more than 1,500 shells, Key was thrilled to see the American flag still flying over the parapet. The verses were written there on the back of an envelope, published as "The Defense of Fort McHenry," and set to an old English tune, "To Anacreon in Heaven." The song was made the U.S. national anthem March 3, 1931. *Intaglio, perforated 11 x 10 1/2.*

CM304 *Francis Scott Key and American flags*

CM304		MNHVF	UseVF
3¢	**carmine** *(120,868,500)*	.25	.20
	Plate block of 4	.55	
	FDC *(Aug. 9, 1948)*		2.00

1948. American Youth Issue paid tribute to the young people of America and was a part of the celebration of Youth Month. *Intaglio, perforated 11 x 10 1/2.*

CM305 *Girl and boy*

CM305		MNHVF	UseVF
3¢	**blue** *(77,800,500)*	.25	.20
	Plate block of 4	.55	
	FDC *(Aug. 11, 1948)*		2.00

1948. Oregon Territory Issue commemorated the 100th anniversary of the signing of the Oregon Bill by President James Polk. The bill, passed after seven months' wrangling between slavery and anti-slavery elements in Congress, established a non-slaveholding Oregon Territory. Jason Lee, a Methodist minister, had petitioned Congress for territorial status as early as 1836. Dr. John McLoughlin, who founded Fort Vancouver in 1824 and for 22 years served as administrator for the Hudson's Bay Company, is known as the "Father of Oregon." *Intaglio, perforated 11 x 10 1/2.*

CM306 *John McLoughlin, Jason Lee, and wagon on Oregon Trail*

CM306		MNHVF	UseVF
3¢	**Venetian red** *(52,214,000)*	.25	.20
	Plate block of 4	.55	
	FDC *(Aug. 14, 1948)*		2.00

1948. Harlan Fiske Stone Issue honored the great American jurist, appointed to the U.S. Supreme Court by President Calvin Coolidge in 1925. Stone was named 12th chief justice of the United States by President Franklin D. Roosevelt in 1941, and served until his death in 1946. *Intaglio, perforated 10 1/2 x 11.*

CM307 *Harlan Fiske Stone*

CM307		MNHVF	UseVF
3¢	**bright purple** *(53,958,100)*	.25	.20
	Plate block of 4	.75	
	FDC *(Aug. 25, 1948)*		2.00

1948. Palomar Mountain Observatory Issue commemorated the dedication of the world's largest telescope on Palomar Mountain, 66 miles north of San Diego, Calif. The 200-inch reflecting telescope, named in honor of the astronomer George Ellery Hale, penetrates a billion light years into the sky. *Intaglio, perforated 10 1/2 x 11.*

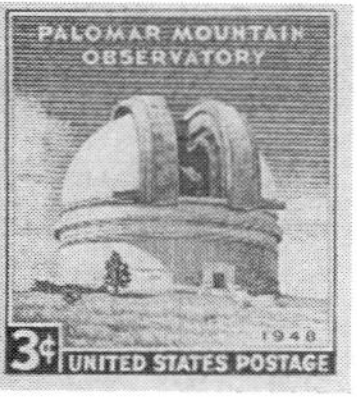

CM308 *Palomar Mountain Observatory*

CM308		MNHVF	UseVF
3¢	**blue** *(61,120,010)*	.25	.20
	Plate block of 4	1.00	
	FDC *(Aug. 30, 1948)*		2.00
	v. Vertical pair, imperforate between	450.00	

1948. Clara Barton Issue honored the founder of the American Red Cross (CM96, CM358). A humanitarian, Barton organized supply and nursing services for Union casualties in the Civil War (CM1723), successfully campaigned for an American society of the International Red Cross, and served as its first president, 1882-1904. *Intaglio, perforated 11 x 10 1/2.*

CM309 *Clara Barton and Red Cross*

CM309		MNHVF	UseVF
3¢	**carmine** *(57,823,000)*	.25	.20
	Plate block of 4	.60	
	FDC *(Sept. 7, 1948)*		2.00

1948. Poultry Industry Centennial Issue marked the 100th anniversary of the establishment of the American poultry industry. *Intaglio, perforated 11 x 10 1/2.*

CM310 *Light Brahma rooster*

CM310		MNHVF	UseVF
3¢	**sepia** *(52,975,000)*	.25	.20
	Plate block of 4	.60	
	FDC *(Sept. 9, 1948)*		2.00

1948. Gold Star Mothers Issue honored mothers of those members of the armed forces who lost their lives in both World Wars. *Intaglio, perforated 10 1/2 X 11.*

CM311 *Gold star and palm branch*

CM311		MNHVF	UseVF
3¢	**yellow** *(77,149,000)*	.25	.20
	Plate block of 4	.60	
	FDC *(Sept. 21, 1948)*		2.00

1948. Fort Kearny Issue commemorated the 100th anniversary of the establishment of Fort Kearny, Neb., an important frontier post in protecting settlers. *Intaglio, perforated 11 x 10 1/2.*

CM312 *Fort Kearny and pioneers*

CM312		MNHVF	UseVF
3¢	**violet** *(58,332,000)*	.25	.20
	Plate block of 4	.60	
	FDC *(Sept. 22, 1948)*		2.00

1948. Volunteer Fireman Issue commemorated the 300th anniversary of the organization of America's first volunteer fire department in New Amsterdam (now New York City) by Peter Stuyvesant, director-general of the Dutch colony of New Netherland. *Intaglio, perforated 11 x 10 1/2.*

CM313 *Peter Stuyvesant and fire engines*

CM313		MNHVF	UseVF
3¢	**rose carmine** *(56,228,000)*	.25	.20
	Plate block of 4	.60	
	FDC *(Oct. 4, 1948)*		2.00

1948. Indian Centennial Issue commemorated the arrival of the five civilized Indian tribes in the Indian Territory, which later became the State of Oklahoma. The Cherokee, Choctaw, Chickasaw, Muskogee (Creek), and Seminole tribes were called "civilized" because of their willingness to adopt the ways of white culture. *Intaglio, perforated 11 x 10 1/2.*

CM314 *Map of Oklahoma and the seals of the five civilized tribes*

CM314		MNHVF	UseVF
3¢	**brown** *(57,832,000)*	.25	.20
	Plate block of 4	.60	
	FDC *(Oct. 15, 1948)*		2.00

1948. Rough Riders Issue marked the 50th anniversary of the First U.S. Volunteer Calvalry Regiment, composed of cowboys and adventurous young Easterners, and known as the Rough Riders. Commanded by Col. Leonard Wood and Lt. Col. Theodore Roosevelt, they fought a spectacular dismounted action in the Battle of San Juan Hill, Cuba (July 1, 1898), seizing the heights and exposing Santiago and the Spanish fleet to artillery bombardment. Capt. William "Bucky" O'Neill, killed in the battle, was one of 1,572 American casualties. *Intaglio, perforated 11 x 10 1/2.*

CM315 *Capt. William O'Neill on horse, from statue by Solon H. Borglum, Prescott, Ariz.*

CM315		MNHVF	UseVF
3¢	**brown purple** *(53,875,000)*	.25	.20
	Plate block of 4	.60	
	FDC *(Oct. 27, 1948)*		2.00

1948. Juliette Low Issue honored the Girl Scouts of America and the memory of founder Juliette Gordon Low, who organized its first troop in Savannah, Ga., in 1912. *Intaglio, perforated 11 x 10 1/2.*

CM316 *Juliette Gordon Low and Girl Scout emblem*

CM316		MNHVF	UseVF
3¢	**blue green** *(63,834,000)*	.25	.20
	Plate block of 4	.60	
	FDC *(Oct. 9, 1948)*		1.00

1948. Will Rogers Issue memorialized America's beloved cowboy philosopher and humorist. A part-Indian native of Oklahoma, Rogers began as a vaudeville entertainer, delivering humorous monologues while doing lasso tricks. As a lecturer, movie actor and newspaper columnist, he was known for his shrewd but kindly commentary on current events. He died in an airplane crash at Point Barrow, Alaska, in 1935 with his friend Wiley Post (A96-97), holder of the 'round-the-world flight record. (See also CM929). *Intaglio, perforated 10 1/2 x 11.*

CM317 *Will Rogers*

CM317		MNHVF	UseVF
3¢	**bright purple** *(67,162,200)*	.25	.20
	Plate block of 4	.60	
	FDC *(Nov. 4, 1948)*		1.00

1948. Fort Bliss Centennial Issue commemorated the 100th anniversary of Fort Bliss, Texas, largest cavalry post in America and later a center for guided-missile training. *Intaglio, perforated 10 1/2 x 11.*

CM318 *Fort Bliss and rocket launch*

CM318		MNHVF	UseVF
3¢	**chestnut** *(64,561,000)*	.35	.20
	Plate block of 4	1.50	
	FDC*(Nov. 5, 1948)*		1.00

1948. Moina Michael Issue honored the originator of the Memorial Poppy. John McCrae's poem, "In Flanders Fields," spoke of wild poppies growing in the cemeteries of the dead of World War I. By an annual Memorial Day sale of poppies made by disabled veterans, Moina Michael used this symbol of the dead to assist the living. *Intaglio, perforated 11 x 10 1/2.*

CM319 *Moina Michael and poppies*

CM319		MNHVF	UseVF
3¢	**rose carmine** *(64,079,500)*	.25	.20
	Plate block of 4	.55	
	FDC *(Nov. 9, 1948)*		1.00

1948. Gettysburg Address Issue commemorated the 85th anniversary of the brief speech with which Abraham Lincoln dedicated the military cemetery at Gettysburg, Pa., (CM174), Nov. 19, 1863. The 11 sentences, which Lincoln said "the world will little note nor long remember," have since been recognized as one of the noblest and most eloquent orations in the English language. *Intaglio, perforated 11 x 10 1/2.*

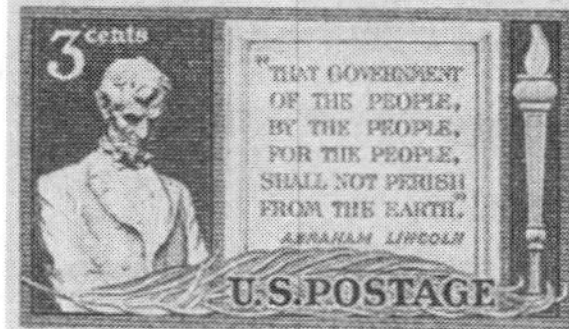

CM320 *Abraham Lincoln, from the statue by Daniel Chester French, State Capitol, Lincoln, Neb.*

CM320		MNHVF	UseVF
3¢	**light blue** *(63,388,000)*	.25	.20
	Plate block of 4	.55	
	FDC *(Nov. 19, 1948)*		1.00

1948. American Turners Issue recalled the centennial of the formation in Cincinnati of an association of gymnasts and athletes, known as the American Turners Society, which comes from the German *"turnverein,"* meaning an exercise club. The organizer was Friedrich Hecker, a German refugee. *Intaglio, perforated 10 1/2 x 11.*

CM321 *American Turners emblem*

CM321		MNHVF	UseVF
3¢	**carmine** *(62,285,000)*	.25	.20
	Plate block of 4	.80	
	FDC *(Nov. 20, 1948)*		1.00

1948. Joel Chandler Harris Issue commemorated the 100th anniversary of the birth of the Georgia journalist and author of *Uncle Remus* and *Br'er Rabbit.* His stories, written for children, also are treasured by adults for their insights into human nature. The richness of their background and humor rank them among the greatest works in the school of folk literature. *Intaglio, perforated 10 1/2 x 11.*

CM322 *Joel Chandler Harris*

CM322		MNHVF	UseVF
3¢	**bright purple** *(57,492,610)*	.25	.20
	Plate block of 4	.60	
	FDC *(Dec. 9, 1948)*		1.00

1949. Minnesota Territory Issue commemorated the 100th anniversary of the Minnesota Territory, with Alexander Ramsey as its first governor. It encompassed part of the Northwest Territory and part of the Louisiana Purchase. *Intaglio, perforated 11 x 10 1/2.*

CM323 *Pioneer and ox cart*

CM323		MNHVF	UseVF
3¢	**blue green** *(99,190,000)*	.25	.20
	Plate block of 4	.55	
	FDC *(March 3, 1949)*		1.00

1949. Washington and Lee University Issue commemorated the 200th anniversary of the founding of Augusta Academy at Lexington, Va. In 1776, as a patriotic gesture, it was renamed Liberty Hall Academy. In 1798, endowed with $50,000 by George Washington, it became Washington Academy. It was renamed Washington and Lee University in 1871 after the death of its president, Gen. Robert E. Lee (CM175). *Intaglio, perforated 11 x 10 1/2.*

CM324 *George Washington, University, and Robert E. Lee*

CM324

		MNHVF	UseVF
3¢	**bright blue** *(104,790,000)*	.25	.20
	Plate block of 4	.55	
	FDC *(April 12, 1949)*		1.00

1949. Puerto Rico Election Issue celebrated Puerto Rico's first gubernatorial election, Nov. 2, 1948. Acquired from Spain in 1898, the island was an unorganized territory until 1917, when its residents were made U.S. citizens. A bill signed by President Harry Truman in 1947 gave it the right to choose its own chief executive by popular vote. Luis Muñoz Marin (927), its first elected governor, was sworn into office Jan. 2, 1949. *Intaglio, perforated 11 x 10 1/2.*

CM325 *Puerto Rican farmer with cog wheel and ballot box*

CM325

		MNHVF	UseVF
3¢	**dull green** *(108,805,000)*	.25	.20
	Plate block of 4	.55	
	FDC *(April 27, 1949)*		1.00

1949. Annapolis Tercentenary Issue marked the 300th anniversary of the founding of Annapolis by the colonists of Lord Baltimore's Maryland Plantation (CM126). Named for Queen Anne of England, it is the site of the U.S. Naval Academy (CM181). *Intaglio, perforated 11 x 10 1/2.*

CM326 *Map of 1718 and seal of Lord Baltimore*

CM326

		MNHVF	UseVF
3¢	**turquoise green** *(107,340,000)*	.25	.20
	Plate block of 4	.55	
	FDC *(May 23, 1949)*		1.00

1949. GAR Issue commemorated the 83rd and final encampment, Aug. 28 at Indianapolis, Ind., of the Civil War Union-veterans' organization known as the Grand Army of the Republic. Founded in 1866 by Benjamin Frankin Stevenson, its members had included five presidents of the United States. *Intaglio, perforated 11 x 10 1/2.*

CM327 *Union soldier and GAR veteran*

CM327

		MNHVF	UseVF
3¢	**carmine** *(117,020,000)*	.25	.20
	Plate block of 4	.55	
	FDC *(Aug. 19, 1949)*		1.00

1949. Edgar Allan Poe Issue commemorated the 100th anniversary of the death of a world-renowned American writer. Born 1809 in Richmond, he was expelled from the University of Virginia for bad debts and from the U.S. Military Academy for disobedience and neglect of duty, and went on to a brilliant but erratic career. Now recognized as one of the world's great lyric poets, he also was one of the originators of the modern detective story. *Intaglio, perforated 10 1/2 x 11.*

CM328 *Edgar Allan Poe*

CM328

		MNHVF	UseVF
3¢	**bright purple** *(122,633,000)*	.25	.20
	Plate block of 4	.65	
	Top inner frame line missing (position 42 of bottom-left pane of plate 24143)	—	
	FDC *(Oct. 7, 1949)*		1.00

1950. American Bankers Association Issue commemorated the 75th anniversary of its founding at Saratoga Springs, N.Y. The group made valuable contributions to the growth and development of American industry and life. *Intaglio, perforated 11 x 10 1/2.*

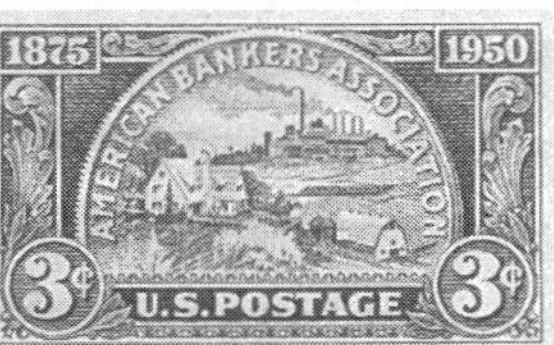

CM329 *Areas of banking service*

CM329

		MNHVF	UseVF
3¢	**green** *(130,960,000)*	.25	.20
	Plate block of 4	.55	
	FDC *(Jan. 3, 1950)*		1.00

1950. Samuel Gompers Issue commemorated the 100th anniversary of the birth of the British-born labor leader who helped to found the American Federation of Labor and served as its president from 1886 until his death in 1924. Acknowledged leader of the American labor movement, Gompers concentrated on the betterment of wages, hours and working conditions. *Intaglio, perforated 10 1/2 x 11.*

CM330 *Samuel Gompers*

CM330

		MNHVF	UseVF
3¢	**bright purple** *(128,478,000)*	.25	.20
	Plate block of 4	.55	
	FDC *(Jan. 27, 1950)*		1.00

1950. National Capital Sesquicentennial Issue celebrated 150 years of the U.S. Capitol in Washington, D.C. *Intaglio, perforated 10 1/2 x 11 (CM331) and 11 x 10 1/2 (CM332-34).*

CM331 *The statue of* Armed Freedom *by Thomas Crawford tops the Capitol dome (see No. 442)*

CM331

		MNHVF	UseVF
3¢	**light blue** *(132,090,000)*	.25	.20
	Plate block of 4	.60	
	FDC *(April 20, 1950)*		1.00

Read the introduction to this catalog carefully. It contains much valuable information for all stamp collectors, and makes the catalog easier to use.

CM332 *The Executive Mansion, which Congress in 1902 officially designated The White House, was designed in 1792 by James Hoban (CM994-95), who is believed to have patterned it after the Duke of Leinster's palace in Dublin. Its sandstone walls were painted white after the British burned it in 1814. It was enlarged by William Howard Taft and by both Roosevelts. In 1951-52, in bad disrepair, it was completely reconstructed within its original walls during the presidency of Harry Truman.*

CM332		MNHVF	UseVF
3¢	**dull green** *(130,050,000)*	.25	.20
	Plate block of 4	.65	
	FDC *(June 12, 1950)*		1.00

CM333 *The Supreme Court building is the home of the chief judicial offices in the United States.*

CM333		MNHVF	UseVF
3¢	**bluish violet** *(131,350,000)*	.25	.20
	Plate block of 4	.60	
	FDC *(Aug. 2, 1950*		1.00

CM334 *The U.S. Capitol is the seat of the Congress. Designed by William Thornton, it was built during 1793-1800, restored in 1814-17 after being burned by British troops in the War of 1812, and greatly enlarged in 1861-65, when the central dome was added.*

CM334		MNHVF	UseVF
3¢	**bright purple** *(129,980,000)*	.25	.20
	Plate block of 4	.80	1.00
	Gouge marks at "GT" and "ITA"	1.00	.50
	FDC *(Nov. 22, 1950)*		1.00

1950. Railroad Engineers Issue paid tribute to American railway and pictured the fabled hero, "Casey" Jones. Born John Luther Jones in 1864, he acquired the nickname "Casey" for having lived at one time in Cayce, Ky. A railroader from boyhood, he spent the last 10 years of his life as an engineer with the Illinois Central Railroad. The "big eight-wheeler" in which he won his fame was a part of the Cannonball Express between Chicago and New Orleans, and Jones' run was between Canton, Miss., and Memphis, Tenn. He was killed April 30, 1900, when his train crashed into the rear of a freight train near Vaughn, Miss. The ballad about the wreck is known throughout America. *Intaglio, perforated 11 x 10 1/2.*

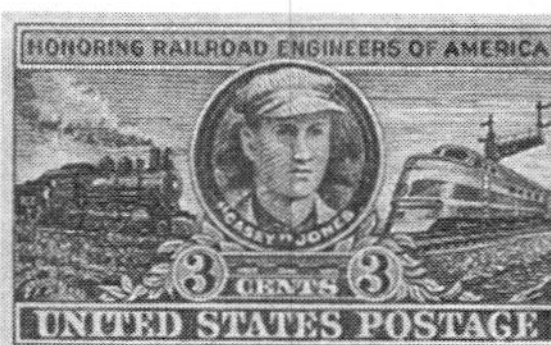

CM335 *"Casey" Jones, steam and diesel locomotives*

CM335		MNHVF	UseVF
3¢	**brown purple** *(122,315,000)*	.25	.20
	Plate block of 4	.60	
	FDC *(April 29, 1950)*		1.00

1950. Kansas City Centennial Issue commemorated the 100th anniversary of the incorporation of Kansas City, Mo. The "Gateway to the West" was first settled by a French fur trapper named Louis Barthelot. *Intaglio, perforated 11 x 10 1/2.*

CM336 *Kansas City in 1950 and Westport Landing in 1850*

CM336		MNHVF	UseVF
3¢	**violet** *(122,170,000)*	.25	.20
	Plate block of 4	.55	
	FDC *(June 3, 1950)*		1.00

1950. Boy Scout Issue honored the 40th anniversary of the Boy Scouts of America, and the second National Jamboree at Valley Forge, Pa. The organization (CM454, CM1173) was incorporated Feb. 8, 1910, formed by uniting Ernest Thompson Seton's *Woodcraft Indians* with Daniel Beard's *Sons of Daniel Boone,* with ideas from the English program of Robert Baden-Powell. *Intaglio, perforated 11 x 10 1/2.*

CM337 *Scouts, Statue of Liberty, and Scout badge*

CM337		MNHVF	UseVF
3¢	**sepia** *(131,635,000)*	.25	.20
	Plate block of 4	.60	
	FDC *(June 30, 1950)*		1.00

1950. Indiana Territory Sesquicentennial Issue marked the 150th anniversary of the Indiana Territory. William Henry Harrison, later a military hero and ninth president, was the territory's first governor. *Intaglio, perforated 11 x 10 1/2.*

CM338 *Gov. William Henry Harrison and first capitol at Vincennes*

CM338		MNHVF	UseVF
3¢	**light blue** *(121,860,000)*	.25	.20
	Plate block of 4	.55	
	FDC *(July 4, 1950)*		1.00

1950. California Statehood Centennial Issue commemorated the 100th anniversary of California's admission as the 31st state. First settled by the Spaniards under Gaspar de Portola, the territory was ceded to the United States by Mexico in 1848. Its development was greatly accelerated by the discovery of gold that year at Sutter's Mill (CM296). *Intaglio, perforated 11 x 10 1/2.*

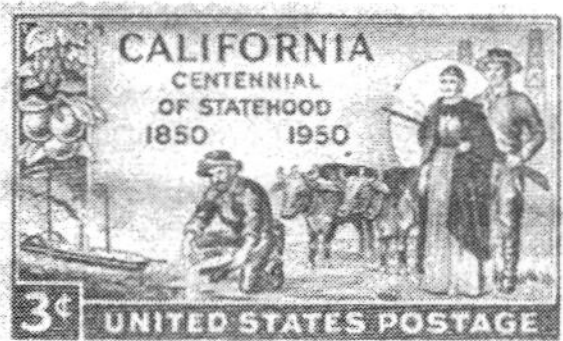

CM339 *Gold miner, pioneers and S.S.* Oregon

CM339		MNHVF	UseVF
3¢	**yellow** *(121,120,000)*	.25	.20
	Plate block of 4	.55	
	FDC *(Sept. 9, 1950)*		1.00

1951. Confederate Veterans Issue commemorated the final reunion, May 30 at Norfolk, Va., of the United Confederate Veterans, organized in New Orleans in 1889. *Intaglio, perforated 11 x 10 1/2.*

CM340 *Confederate soldier and veteran*

CM340		MNHVF	UseVF
3¢	**gray** *(119,120,000)*	.25	.20
	Plate block of 4	.60	
	FDC *(May 30, 1951)*		1.00

1951. Nevada Centennial Issue commemorated the first settlement of Nevada in 1851. The discovery of the Comstock Lode in 1856 led to rapid development of the territory; by 1863 it had 40,000 inhabitants and was producing as much as $30,000,000 worth of silver a year. Nevada was admitted to statehood in 1864. *Intaglio, perforated 11 x 10 1/2.*

CM341 *Carson Valley homestead*

CM341		MNHVF	UseVF
3¢	**light olive green** *(112,125,000)*	.25	.20
	Plate block of 4	.55	
	FDC *(July 14, 1951)*		1.00

1952. Detroit Issue noted the 250th anniversary of the landing of Antoine de la Mothe Cadillac, at what is now Detroit, with a charter from King Louis XIV of France. Established by Cadillac as a military post to protect his fur trade, Detroit became the automotive capital of the world. *Intaglio, perforated 11 x 10 1/2.*

CM342 *Landing of Cadillac at Detroit, modern skyline*

CM342		MNHVF	UseVF
3¢	**light blue** *(114,140,000)*	.25	.20
	Plate block of 4	.55	
	FDC *(July 24, 1951)*		1.00

1951. Colorado Statehood Issue commemorated the 75th anniversary of Colorado's admission as the 38th state. Formed of lands that were once part of the Louisiana Purchase and of the Texas and Mexican cessions, it became a territory in 1861. *Intaglio, perforated 11 x 10 1/2.*

CM343 *Capitol at Denver, Mount of the Holy Cross, bronco buster*

CM343		MNHVF	UseVF
3¢	**violet blue** *(114,490,000)*	.25	.20
	Plate block of 4	.55	
	FDC *(Aug. 1, 1951)*		1.00

1951. American Chemical Society Issue marked the 75th anniversary of the American Chemical Society. *Intaglio, perforated 11 x 10 1/2.*

CM344 *ACS Emblem, industrial chemical equipment*

CM344		MNHVF	UseVF
3¢	**brown purple** *(117,200,000)*	.25	.20
	Plate block of 4	.55	
	FDC *(Sept. 4, 1951)*		1.00

1951. Battle of Brooklyn Issue commemorated the 175th anniversary of the Battle of Long Island, Aug. 27, 1776. British and Hessian troops, under Clinton, Howe, Percy, Cornwallis and DeHesiter, attacked the American fortifications at what is now Prospect Park in Brooklyn, overpowered the desperate Americans and captured their commander, Gen. John Sullivan (CM88). General Washington arrived late in the day with additional troops, saw the futility of making a stand, and withdrew the remaining American forces in a skillful night retreat. *Intaglio, perforated 11 x 10 1/2.*

CM345 *Gen. George Washington evacuating the army*

CM345		MNHVF	UseVF
3¢	**violet** *(16,130,000)*	.25	.20
	Plate block of 4	.60	
	FDC *(Dec. 10, 1951)*		1.00

1952. Betsy Ross Issue celebrated the 200th birthday of Betsy Ross, the Philadelphia upholsterer whom the Continental Congress engaged in 1777 to make the first American flag. The legend that she designed the original Stars and Stripes generally is disputed, and the credit given to Francis Hopkinson, one of the signers of the Declaration of Independence. *Intaglio, perforated 11 x 10 1/2.*

CM346 Birth of Our Nation's Flag, *from a painting by C.H. Weisgerber*

CM346		MNHVF	UseVF
3¢	**carmine red** *(116,175,000)*	.25	.20
	Plate block of 4	.55	
	FDC *(Jan. 2, 1952)*		1.00

1952. 4-H Club Issue honored the farm youth organization whose emblem — the letter H on each leaf of a four-leaf-clover — signifies the 4-H pledge: "I pledge My Head to clear thinking; My Heart to great Loyalty; My Hands to larger service; My Health to better living, for my club, my community, and my country." *Intaglio, perforated 11 x 10 1/2.*

CM347 *American farm, 4-H emblem and members*

CM347		MNHVF	UseVF
3¢	**blue green** *(115,945,000)*	.25	.20
	Plate block of 4	.55	
	FDC *(Jan. 15, 1952)*		1.00

1952. American Railroads Issue commemorated the 125th anniversary of the chartering of the B & O Railroad by the Maryland Legislature. The first passenger railroad in the United States, it was begun on July 4, 1828, with Charles Carroll of Carrollton, the last living signer of the Declaration of Independence, in attendance. The first 14-mile section opened to horse-drawn traffic May 24, 1830. *Intaglio, perforated 11 x 10 1/2.*

CM348 *Charter, horse-drawn car, Tom Thumb and modern diesel*

CM348		MNHVF	UseVF
3¢	**light blue** *(112,540,000)*	.25	.20
	Plate block of 4	.55	
	FDC *(Feb. 28, 1952)*		1.00

1952. AAA ISSUE commemorated the 50th anniversary of the American Automobile Association, (the Triple-A) and honored its contribution to motoring safety and convenience. *Intaglio, perforated 11 x 10 1/2.*

CM349 *Children and crossing guard, automobiles of 1902 and 1952*

CM349		MNHVF	UseVF
3¢	**blue** *(117,415,000)*	.25	.20
	Plate block of 4	.55	
	FDC *(March 4, 1952)*		1.00

1952. NATO ISSUE commemorated the third anniversary of the signing of the North Atlantic Treaty Organization, in which the United States, Canada and 10 Western European nations pledged that an armed attack against any of them would be considered an attack against all. *Intaglio, perforated 11 x 10 1/2.*

CM350 *The torch of liberty, globe*

CM350		MNHVF	UseVF
3¢	**violet** *(2,899,580,000)*	.25	.20
	Plate block of 4	.55	
	FDC *(April 4, 1952)*		1.00
	v. thin, translucent paper		—

1952. GRAND COULEE DAM ISSUE commemorated 50 years of federal cooperation in developing western rivers, and paid tribute to the world's largest concrete dam, the Grand Coulee, built and operated by the Bureau of Reclamation on Washington's Columbia River. *Intaglio, perforated 11 x 10 1/2.*

CM351 *Grand Coulee Dam spillway*

CM351		MNHVF	UseVF
3¢	**blue green** *(114,540,000)*	.25	.20
	Plate block of 4	.55	
	FDC *(May 15, 1952)*		1.00

1952. LAFAYETTE ISSUE commemorated the 175th anniversary of the arrival in America of Marquis de Lafayette (CM409, CM866) to fight for American freedom. Commissioned a major general at 20 by the Continental Congress, he fought valiantly at Brandywine and Monmouth and in the Virginia campaign ending in the British surrender at Yorktown (CM97). After the war he was a significant figure in the French Revolution. He returned briefly to the United States in 1784 and again for a triumphant tour in 1824. *Intaglio, perforated 11 x 10 1/2.*

CM352 *Lafayette, flags of the United States and France*

CM352		MNHVF	UseVF
3¢	**bright blue** *(113,135,000)*	.25	.20
	Plate block of 4	.55	
	FDC *(June 13, 1952)*		1.00

1952. MOUNT RUSHMORE MEMORIAL ISSUE marked the 25th anniversary of the dedication of the monument in the Black Hills of South Dakota. The first such memorial authorized by the government, it was financed by South Dakota. The sculptor Gutzon Borglum designed and carved the enormous heads of Washington, Jefferson, Lincoln and Roosevelt from the solid rock of the mountain. *Intaglio, perforated 11 x 10 1/2.*

CM353 *Mount Rushmore*

CM353		MNHVF	UseVF
3¢	**blue green** *(116,255,000)*	.25	.20
	Plate block of 4	.55	
	FDC *(Aug. 11, 1952)*		1.00

1952. ENGINEERING CENTENNIAL ISSUE commemorated the 100th anniversary of the American Society of Civil Engineers. The George Washington Bridge in New York City, shown on the stamp, was chosen as a symbol of the great engineering projects for which society members are responsible. *Intaglio, perforated 11 x 10 1/2.*

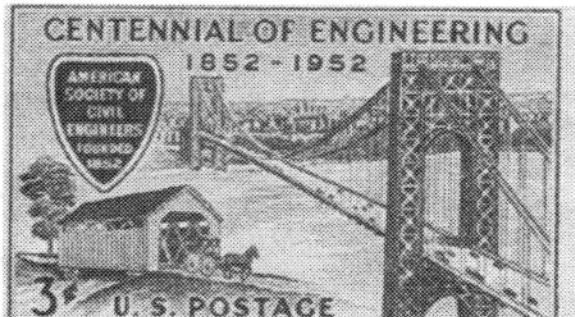

CM354 *The George Washington Bridge and an old covered bridge*

CM354		MNHVF	UseVF
3¢	**ultramarine** *(113,860,000)*	.25	.20
	Plate block of 4	.55	
	FDC *(Sept. 6, 1952)*		1.00

1952. SERVICE WOMEN ISSUE honored women in the U.S. armed services. More than 40,000 women served in World War II and contributed immeasurably to Allied victory. *Intaglio, perforated 11 x 10 1/2.*

CM355 *Marine Corps., Army, Navy and Air Force service women*

CM355		MNHVF	UseVF
3¢	**blue** *(124,260,000)*	.25	.20
	Plate block of 4	.55	
	FDC *(Sept. 11, 1952)*		1.00

1952. Gutenberg Bible Issue commemorated the 500th anniversary of the first European book published from movable type, attributed to Johann Gutenberg of Mainz, Germany. Movable type replaced the tedious and costly process of hand copying. It made books available to many people, thus spreading knowledge on an unprecedented scale. *Intaglio, perforated 11 x 10 1/2.*

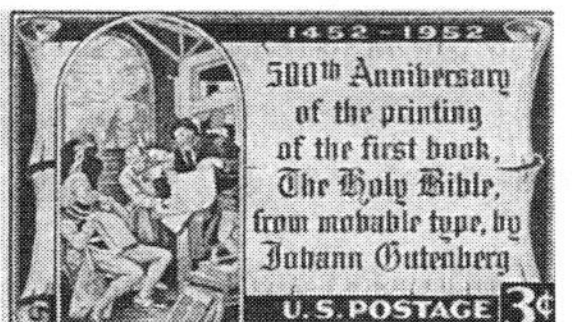

CM356 *Gutenberg showing a proof to the elector of Mainz, from a mural by Edward Laning in the New York Public Library*

CM356		MNHVF	UseVF
3¢	**violet** *(115,735,000)*	.25	.20
	Plate block of 4	.55	
	FDC *(Sept. 30, 1952)*		1.00

1952. Newspaperboys of America Issue recognized America's newsboys and the value of their early business training. It also complemented the meeting of the International Circulation Managers Association, at Philadelphia, Pa., in October. *Intaglio, perforated 11 x 10 1/2.*

CM357 *Paperboy, torch of "free enterprise" and neighborhood*

CM357		MNHVF	UseVF
3¢	**violet** *(115,430,000)*	.25	.20
	Plate block of 4	.55	
	FDC *(Oct. 4, 1952)*		1.00

1952. International Red Cross Issue honored the humanitarian society founded by Jean Henri Dunant and others in 1864. Its headquarters in Geneva, Switzerland, provides an exchange for all the Red Cross societies of the world. Maintaining strict neutrality, the organization extends relief to civilian victims of war, furnishes aid to war prisoners and monitors their treatment by their captors. (See also CM96, CM525 and CM969). *Intaglio and letterpress, perforated 11 x 10 1/2.*

CM358 *Red Cross enlightening the world*

CM358		MNHVF	UseVF
3¢	**ultramarine & scarlet** *(136,220,000)*	.25	.20
	Plate block of 4	.55	
	FDC *(Nov. 21, 1952)*		1.00

1953. National Guard Issue honored the oldest military organization in the United States, a service older than the nation itself. The Guard, under state control except in war, has served with distinction in every national conflict. In peacetime, it aids in disasters such as floods, forest fires and hurricanes. *Intaglio, perforated 11 x 10 1/2.*

CM359 *National Guard in war and peace*

CM359		MNHVF	UseVF
3¢	**light blue** *(114,894,600)*	.25	.20
	Plate block of 4	.55	
	FDC *(Feb. 23, 1953)*		1.00

1953. Ohio Sesquicentennial Issue commemorated the 150th anniversary of Ohio as the 17th state. A part of the Northwest Territory, Ohio became a state March 1, 1803, with Chillicothe as its capital. Columbus has been the capital since 1817. Ohio has given the nation eight presidents, and its history is reflected in many U.S. stamps. *Intaglio, perforated 11 x 10 1/2.*

CM360 *Ohio map and seal*

CM360		MNHVF	UseVF
3¢	**sepia** *(117,706,000)*	.25	.20
	Plate block of 4	.55	
	FDC *(March 2, 1953)*		1.00

1953. Washington Territory Issue commemorated the 100th anniversary of the Washington Territory. Visited by the Lewis and Clark Expedition in 1803, it was settled in 1811. *Intaglio, perforated 11 x 10 1/2.*

CM361 *Centennial crest, pioneer and vista*

CM361		MNHVF	UseVF
3¢	**blue green** *(114,190,000)*	.25	.20
	Plate block of 4	.55	
	FDC *(March 2, 1953)*		1.00

1953. Louisiana Purchase Issue commemorated the 150th anniversary of the Louisiana Purchase from France. (See CM32-CM36.) *Intaglio, perforated 11 x 10 1/2.*

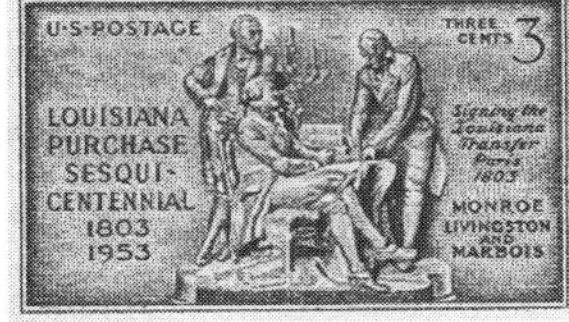

CM362 *Monroe, Livingston and de Barbe-Marbois signing transfer, from the sculpture by Karl Bitter in the Jefferson Memorial, St. Louis, Mo.*

CM362		MNHVF	UseVF
3¢	**brown purple** *(113,990,000)*	.25	.20
	Plate block of 4	.55	
	FDC *(April 30, 1953)*		1.00

1953. Opening of Japan Issue commemorated the centennial of negotiations between Commodore Matthew C. Perry and representatives of the emperor of Japan, leading to the Treaty of Kanagawa in 1854. Japan, isolated since the early 17th century, agreed to open two ports to U.S. trade and make provision for shipwrecked American seamen. In 1858 Japan opened additional ports, granted residence rights to Americans, and exchanged diplomatic representatives. *Intaglio, perforated 11 x 10 1/2.*

CM363 *Commodore Perry and vessels in Tokyo Bay*

CM363		MNHVF	UseVF
5¢	**blue green** *(89,289,600)*	.25	.20
	Plate block of 4	.75	
	FDC *(July 14, 1953)*		1.00

1953. American Bar Association Issue honored the organization's 75th anniversary and its efforts in securing uniform state laws, promoting sound legislation and advancing the administration of justice. *Intaglio, perforated 11 x 10 1/2.*

CM364 *Wisdom, Justice, Divine Inspiration and Truth, frieze on a wall of the Supreme Court*

CM364		MNHVF	UseVF
3¢	**light reddish violet** *(114,865,000)*	.25	.20
	Plate block of 4	.75	
	FDC *(Aug. 24, 1953)*		1.00

1953. Sagamore Hill Issue commemorated its dedication as a national shrine, June 14. Sagamore Hill was the Oyster Bay, N.Y., home of Theodore Roosevelt, and it was there that Roosevelt died on Jan. 6, 1919. *Intaglio, perforated 11 x 10 1/2.*

CM365 *Sagamore Hill, home of Theodore Roosevelt*

CM365		MNHVF	UseVF
3¢	**green** *(115,780,000)*	.25	.20
	Plate block of 4	.55	
	FDC *(Sept. 14, 1953)*		1.00

1953. Future Farmers of America Issue honored the 25th anniversary of the founding of the Future Farmers of America under the auspices of the U.S. Office of Education. *Intaglio, perforated 11 x 10 1/2.*

CM366 *Future farmer and farmland*

CM366		MNHVF	UseVF
3¢	**bright blue** *(115,224,600)*	.25	.20
	Plate block of 4	.55	
	FDC *(Oct. 13, 1953)*		1.00

1953. Trucking Industry Issue marked the 50th anniversary of the American Trucking Association and its convention in Los Angeles. *Intaglio, perforated 11 x 10 1/2.*

CM367 *Truck, farm and city*

CM367		MNHVF	UseVF
3¢	**violet** *(123,709,600)*	.25	.20
	Plate block of 4	.55	
	FDC *(Oct. 27, 1953)*		1.00

1953. General Patton Issue honored Gen. George S. Patton, Jr., (1885-1945) and the armored forces of the U.S. Army. Patton was a hero of the Battle of the Bulge in World War II. *Intaglio, perforated 11 x 10 1/2.*

CM368 *Gen. Patton and Patton tanks in action*

CM368		MNHVF	UseVF
3¢	**bluish violet** *(114,789,600)*	.25	.20
	Plate block of 4	.65	
	FDC *(Nov. 11, 1953)*		1.00

1953. New York City Tercentenary Issue commemorated the 300th anniversary of the incorporation of New Amsterdam as a city. Feb. 2, 1653. *Intaglio, perforated 11 x 10 1/2.*

CM369 *Dutch ship and New Amsterdam, modern New York City skyline*

CM369		MNHVF	UseVF
3¢	**bright purple** *(115,759,600)*	.25	.20
	Plate block of 4	.55	
	FDC *(Nov. 20, 1953)*		1.00

1953. Gadsden Purchase Issue commemorated the 100th anniversary of the purchase of territory from Mexico to add territory to the states of Arizona and New Mexico and settle a dispute dating from the Guadelupe-Hildalgo Treaty of 1848. *Intaglio, perforated 11 x 10 1/2.*

CM370 *Gadsen Purchase map and pioneers*

CM370		MNHVF	UseVF
3¢	**Venetian red** *(115,759,600)*	.25	.20
	Plate block of 4	.55	
	FDC *(Dec. 30, 1953)*		1.00

1953. Columbia University Issue commemorated the 200th anniversary of King's College, which closed during the Revolution to reopen as Columbia College. It now includes many colleges such as Teacher's College, Barnard College, and schools of medicine, pharmacy, engineering, law, architecture, and journalism among others. Located in New York City, it is one of the oldest and largest U.S. universities. *Intaglio, perforated 11 x 10 1/2.*

CM371 *Low Memorial Library*

CM371		MNHVF	UseVF
3¢	**cobalt blue** *(118,540,000)*	.25	.20
	Plate block of 4	.55	
	FDC *(Jan. 4, 1954)*		1.00

1954. Nebraska Territorial Centennial Issue honored the centennial of the Nebraska Territory, under the Kansas-Nebraska Bill. *Intaglio, perforated 11 x 10 1/2.*

CM372 *Mitchell Pass, Scotts Bluff and* The Sower, *from a statue by Lee Lawrie from a painting by Millet*

CM372		MNHVF	UseVF
3¢	**violet** *(115,810,000)*	.25	.20
	Plate block of 4	.55	
	FDC *(May 7, 1954)*		1.00

1954. Kansas Territorial Centennial Issue commemorated the centennial of the Kansas Territory from unorganized Indian reservations. The Kansas-Nebraska bill repealed the 1820 Missouri Compromise that had drawn a line, north of which slavery could not exist. The politicians intended Kansas to be a slave state and Nebraska free, by "popular sovereignty." The rivalry for settling the status of these two new territories was one of the direct causes of the War Between the States. *Intaglio, perforated 11 x 10 1/2.*

CM373 *Wagon train and wheat field*

CM373		MNHVF	UseVF
3¢	**salmon** *(113,603,700)*	.25	.20
	Plate block of 4	.55	
	FDC *(May 31, 1954)*		1.00

1954. George Eastman Issue commemorated the 100th birthday of George Eastman at Waterville, N.Y. At an early age he went to Rochester where he gained fame as an inventor and philanthropist. His inventions made photography possible for virtually everyone, and his invention of transparent film created motion pictures. He gave $100 million to educational and musical institutions and dental clinics around the world. He was a proponent of the Community Chest, and profit sharing with employees. *Intaglio, perforated 10 1/2 x 11.*

CM374 *George Eastman*

CM374		MNHVF	UseVF
3¢	**brown purple** *(121,100,000)*	.25	.20
	Plate block of 4	.55	
	FDC *(July 12, 1954)*		1.00

1954. Lewis and Clark Expedition Issue commemorated the exploration by Meriwether Lewis and William Clark (brother of George Rogers Clark) at the request of President Jefferson to secure more information about the country west of the Mississippi. The party of 30 made its way overland to Oregon and the Pacific Ocean, leaving St. Louis in May 1804, and returning in 1806 after having been given up as lost. They owed much of the success of the venture to Sacagawea (Birdwoman), a Shoshone Indian woman who acted as their guide (CM1690). *Intaglio, perforated 11 x 10 1/2.*

CM375 *Lewis and Clark, from a statue by Charles Keck at Charlottesville, Va., and Sacagawea from a statue by Leonard Crunekle at Bismark, N.D.*

CM375		MNHVF	UseVF
3¢	**brown** *(116,078,150)*	.25	.20
	Plate block of 4	.55	
	FDC *(July 28, 1954)*		1.00

1955. Pennsylvania Academy of Fine Arts Issue honored the 150th anniversary of that institution. The design of the stamp is a reproduction of the painting *Peale in his Museum,* a self-portrait of Charles Willson Peale (1741-1827), now in the collection of the Pennsylvania Academy, of which Peale was one of the founders. *Intaglio, perforated 10 1/2 X 11.*

CM376 *Charles Willson Peale in his museum*

CM376		MNHVF	UseVF
3¢	**brown purple** *(116,139,800)*	.25	.20
	Plate block of 4	.55	
	FDC *(Jan. 15, 1955)*		1.00

1955. First Land-Grant College Issue commemorated the centennial of the establishment of Michigan State University and Pennsylvania State University. Land grants, originally intended for settlers and homesteaders, were extended in 1854 to various groups for services for the national welfare. *Intaglio, perforated 11 x 10 1/2.*

CM377 *Open book and symbols of agriculture, mining, chemistry, engineering*

CM377		MNHVF	UseVF
3¢	**emerald green** *(120,484,800)*	.25	.20
	Plate block of 4	.55	
	FDC *(Feb. 12, 1955)*		1.00

1955. Rotary International Issue marked the 50th anniversary of the organization founded Feb. 23, 1905, by Chicago lawyer Paul P. Harris. Rotary became national in 1910, international in 1912. It is an organization of business and professional men founded to further the ideal of service to others in all relationships. *Intaglio, perforated 11 x 10 1/2.*

CM378 *Rotary insignia, globe and torch*

CM378		MNHVF	UseVF
8¢	**deep blue** *(53,854,750)*	.25	.20
	Plate block of 4	1.95	
	FDC *(Feb. 23, 1955)*		1.00

1955. The Armed Forces Reserve Issue honored the Reserves of all the U.S. armed forces. *Intaglio, perforated 11 x 10 1/2.*

CM379 *Marines, Coast Guard, Army, Navy and Air Force Reservists*

CM379		MNHVF	UseVF
3¢	**bright purple** *(176,075,000)*	.25	.20
	Plate block of 4	.55	
	FDC *(May 21, 1955)*		1.00

1955. Old Man of the Mountains Issue commemorated the sesquicentennial of the discovery of New Hampshire's famous landmark of that name (see also CM1312). Also called "The Great Stone Face," it was immortalized in prose by Hawthorne. *Intaglio, perforated 10 1/2 X 11.*

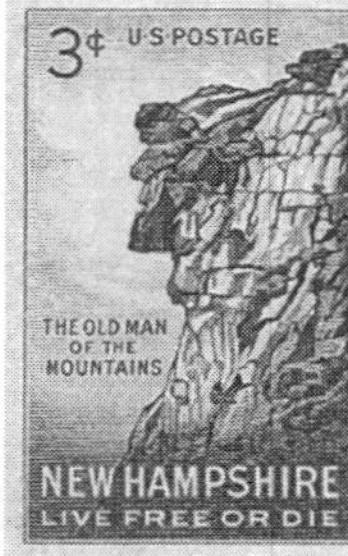

CM380 *Old Man of the Mountains as seen from Franconia, N.H.*

CM380		MNHVF	UseVF
3¢	**blue green** *(125,944,400)*	.25	.20
	Plate block of 4	.55	
	FDC *(June 21, 1955)*		1.00

1955. Soo Locks Centennial Issue was released in conjuction with the opening of the Soo Locks Exposition at Sault Ste. Marie, Mich., celebrating a century of Great Lakes transportation. *Intaglio, perforated 11 x 10 1/2.*

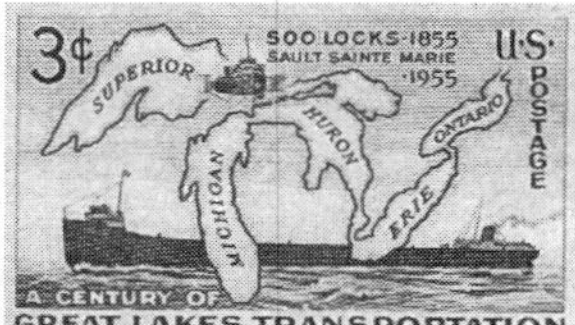

CM381 *Map of the Great Lakes and freighter*

CM381		MNHVF	UseVF
3¢	**blue** *(122,284,600)*	.25	.20
	Plate block of 4	.55	
	FDC *(June 28, 1955)*		1.00

1955. Atoms for Peace Issue symbolized the intention of the United States to put atomic energy to peaceful uses. The stamp features the words "To find the way by which the inventiveness of man shall be consecrated to his life" from President Eisenhower's speech before the U.N. General Assembly on Dec. 8, 1953. *Intaglio, perforated 11 x 10 1/2.*

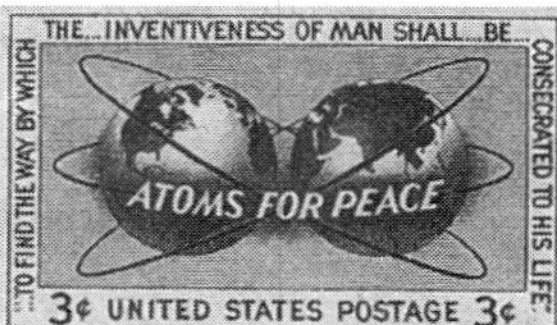

CM382 *Atomic emblem and hemispheres*

CM382		MNHVF	UseVF
3¢	**deep blue** *(133,638,850)*	.25	.20
	Plate block of 4	.55	
	FDC *(July 28, 1955)*		1.00

1955. Fort Ticonderoga Bicentennial Issue marked the building of the fort in 1755 by the French, who named it Fort Carillon. During the French & Indian War it was unsuccessfully attacked by Abercrombie in 1758, but a year later was captured by Lord Amherst. Ethan Allen and his Green Mountain Boys (see CM76) took the fort at the outbreak of the Revolution (1775). *Intaglio, perforated 11 x 10 1/2.*

CM383 *Plan of Fort Ticonderoga, officer and cannon*

CM383		MNHVF	UseVF
3¢	**dark red brown** *(118,664,600)*	.25	.20
	Plate block of 4	.55	
	FDC *(Sept. 18, 1955)*		1.00

1955. Andrew Mellon Issue commemorated the 100th anniversary of the birth of Mellon (1855-1937), Secretary of the Treasury under Harding, Coolidge and Hoover. He negotiated the payments of war debts owed to the United States, and reduced internal debt and income taxes. He later served as ambassador to England. He donated a gallery and his very valuable art collection to the United States. *Intaglio, perforated 10 1/2 x 11.*

CM384 *Andrew W. Mellon, portrait by O. Birely*

CM384		MNHVF	UseVF
3¢	**carmine red** *(112,434,000)*	.25	.20
	Plate block of 4	.55	
	FDC *(Dec. 20, 1955)*		1.00

1956. Franklin 250th Anniversary Issue commemorated the birth of the great inventor, writer and public official Benjamin Franklin (see 524). *Intaglio, perforated 10 1/2 X 11.*

CM385 Franklin Taking Electricity from the Sky, *Benjamin West painting*

CM385		MNHVF	UseVF
3¢	**carmine** *(129,384,550)*	.25	.20
	Plate block of 4	.55	
	FDC *(Jan. 17, 1956)*		1.00

1956. Booker T. Washington Issue commemorated the 100th anniversary of the great educator's birth (CM215). *Intaglio, perforated 11 x 10 1/2.*

CM386 *Log cabin*

CM386		MNHVF	UseVF
3¢	**deep blue** *(121,184,600)*	.25	.20
	Plate block of 4	.55	
	FDC *(April 5, 1956)*		1.00

1956. FIPEX Issue celebrated the fifth International Philatelic Exhibition (April 28 to May 6, 1956). Stamp, photography and auto exhibitions, held simultaneously, opened the New York Coliseum at Columbus Circle, New York City. *Intaglio, perforated 11 x 10 1/2.*

CM387 *New York Coliseum and Columbus Monument*

CM387		MNHVF	UseVF
3¢	**violet** *(119,784,200)*	.25	.20
	Plate block of 4	.55	
	FDC *(April 28, 1956)*		1.00

1956. Fifth International Philatelic Exhibition (FIPEX) Souvenir Sheet pictured two oversize versions of stamps from the Liberty Definitive Series (see 573, 578). *Measure 108 x 73mm, flat plate printing, intaglio, imperforate.*

CM388 *FIPEX souvenir sheet*

CM388		MNHVF	UseVF
11¢	**Complete sheet of 2 stamps** *(9,802,025)*	2.50	2.00
	a. 3¢ dark violet, from sheet		.80
	b. 8¢ deep blue and rose, from sheet		1.00
	FDC *(April 28, 1956)*		2.50

Wildlife Conservation Series

Wildlife Conservation Series highlighted the importance of protecting wildlife.

1956. Wild Turkey Issue in the Wildlife Conservation Series called attention to this aspect of America's heritage. The turkey had once been proposed as the national bird. *Intaglio, perforated 11 x 10 1/2.*

CM389 *Wild turkey*

CM389		MNHVF	UseVF
3¢	**brown purple** *(123,159,400)*	.25	.20
	Plate block of 4	.55	
	FDC *(May 5, 1956)*		1.00

1956. Pronghorn Antelope Issue in the Wildlife Conservation Series showed a buck and two does. This species had dwindled to only 17,000, but multiplied rapidly under protection and now is widely hunted. *Intaglio, perforated 11 x 10 1/2.*

CM390 *Pronghorn antelope*

CM390		MNHVF	UseVF
3¢	**sepia** *(123,138,800)*	.25	.20
	Plate block of 4	.55	
	FDC *(June 22, 1956)*		1.00

1956. King Salmon Issue in the Wildlife Conservation Series showed salmon migrating to spawning ground. Construction of fish ladders and elevators, and elimination of log jams and high waterfalls aid salmon migration and reproduction. *Intaglio, perforated 11 x 10 1/2.*

CM391 *King salmon*

CM391		MNHVF	UseVF
3¢	**blue green** *(109,275,000)*	.25	.20
	Plate block of 4	.55	
	FDC *(Nov. 9, 1956)*		1.00

1956. Pure Food and Drug Laws Issue commemorated the 50th anniversary of their passage. Harvey W. Wiley (1844-1930) was a chemist and teacher who single-handedly devoted himself to the cause of pure food. While chief of the Bureau of Chemistry in the U.S. Department of Agriculture he secured passage of the 1906 laws, which required government inspection and accurate labeling of foods and drugs. Wiley was the author of hundreds of scientific papers and pamphlets. *Intaglio, perforated 10 1/2 x 11.*

CM392 *Harvey W. Wiley*

CM392		MNHVF	UseVF
3¢	**blue green** *(112,932,200)*	.25	.20
	Plate block of 4	.55	
	FDC *(June 27, 1956)*		1.00

1956. Wheatland Issue honored President James Buchanan and his Pennsylvania home, Wheatland. *Intaglio, perforated 11 x 10 1/2.*

CM393 *Wheatland, Lancaster, Pa.*

CM393		MNHVF	UseVF
3¢	**black brown** *(125,475,000)*	.25	.20
	Plate block of 4	.55	
	FDC *(Aug. 5, 1956)*		1.00

1956. Labor Day Issue celebrated the national holiday honoring workers. The movement for a Labor Holiday was begun by the Knights of Labor, who paraded on the first Monday of September in 1882-84. The holiday first was recognized by Oregon (1887) then by New York, New Jersey and Colorado, and by the U.S. Congress in 1894. *Intaglio, perforated 10 1/2 x 11.*

CM394 Labor is Life *mural by L. Winter in AFL-CIO headquarters building, Washington, D.C.*

CM394		MNHVF	UseVF
3¢	**deep blue** *(117,855,000)*	.25	.20
	Plate block of 4	.55	
	FDC *(Sept. 3, 1956)*		1.00

1956. Nassau Hall Issue commemorated the 200th anniversary of the oldest building at Princeton University. Named for William of Nassau (later King William III of England), it was at its completion the largest academic building in the American colonies. In 1783, in Nassau Hall, Congress formally thanked George Washington for his leadership in the Revolutionary War. *Intaglio, perforated 11 x 10 1/2.*

CM395 *Nassau Hall, from the Henry Dawkins engraving of 1764. The first U.S. Postage stamp on colored paper featured Princeton's school colors - orange and black.*

CM395		MNHVF	UseVF
3¢	**black on orange** *(122,100,00)*	.25	.20
	Plate block of 4	.55	
	FDC *(Sept. 22, 1956)*		1.00

1956. Devils Tower Issue commemorated the 50th anniversary of the establishment of the 1,200-acre area as the first U.S. national monument. The natural 600-foot rock formation is the eroded core of a long-extinct volcano. *Intaglio, perforated 10 1/2 x 11.*

CM396 *Devils Tower National Monument, Wyoming*

CM396		MNHVF	UseVF
3¢	**lilac** *(118,180,000)*	.25	.20
	Plate block of 4	.55	
	Pair, gutter between		
	FDC *(Sept. 24, 1956)*		1.00

1956. Children's Issue featured the theme "Friendship — The Key to World Peace," and promoted friendship among children throughout the world. The stamp design, by Ronald Dias, a 1956 high school graduate, was selected in a nationwide competition. *Intaglio, perforated 11 x 10 1/2.*

CM397 *Children of the world and key of friendship*

CM397		MNHVF	UseVF
3¢	**blue** *(100,975,000)*	.25	.20
	Plate block of 4	.55	
	FDC *(Dec. 15, 1956)*		1.00

1957. Alexander Hamilton Bicentennial Issue commemorated the 200th anniversary of the birth of this great patriot, the first secretary of the treasury and one of the signers of the Constitution. *Intaglio, perforated 11 x 10 1/2.*

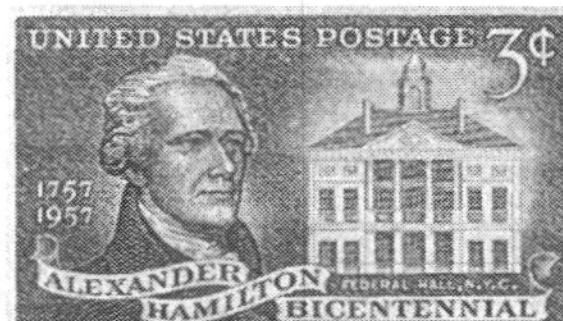

CM398 *Alexander Hamilton and Federal Hall, New York, N.Y.*

CM398		MNHVF	UseVF
3¢	**rose red** *(115,299,450)*	.25	.20
	Plate block of 4	.55	
	FDC *(Jan. 11, 1957)*		1.00

1957. Anti-Polio Issue was a tribute to those who helped fight this dread disease, from children who contributed pennies to scientists who devoted their lives to the battle against a terrifying affliction. It marked 20th anniversary of the National Foundation for Infantile Paralysis and the March of Dimes. *Intaglio, perforated 10 1/2 x 11.*

CM399 *Boy, Girl and allegorical figure with shield Caduceus*

CM399		MNHVF	UseVF
3¢	**bright purple** *(186,949,250)*	.25	.20
	Plate block of 4	.55	
	FDC *(Jan. 15, 1957)*		1.00

1957. Coast and Geodetic Survey Issue commemorated the 150th anniversary of this government service, devoted to charting and surveying America's coasts and harbors and land masses. *Intaglio, perforated 11 x 10 1/2.*

CM400 *Coast and Geodetic Survey flag and ships*

CM400		MNHVF	UseVF
3¢	**deep blue** *(115,235,000)*	.25	.20
	Plate block of 4	.55	
	FDC *(Feb. 11, 1957)*		1.00

1957. Architects of America Issue honored the centennial of the founding of the American Institute of Architects, and its members who create buildings, structures and communities of lasting beauty and usefulness. *Intaglio, perforated 11 x 10 1/2.*

CM401 *Corinthian capitol and modern pillar*

CM401		MNHVF	UseVF
3¢	**rose lilac** *(106,647,500)*	.25	.20
	Plate block of 4	.55	
	FDC *(Feb. 23, 1957)*		1.00

1957. Steel Industry in America Issue marked the centennial of this great industry, which has contributed to social progress, economic welfare and comforts in daily life. *Intaglio, perforated 10 1/2 x 11.*

CM402 *Eagle and pouring ladle*

CM402		MNHVF	UseVF
3¢	**bright blue** *(112,010,000)*	.25	.20
	Plate block of 4	.55	
	FDC *(May 22, 1957)*		1.00

1957. International Naval Review Issue commemorated the Jamestown Festival and the naval review. Its theme was "Freedom of the Seas," and it was the largest representation of nations in an event of this type. *Intaglio, perforated 11 x 10 1/2.*

CM403 *Aircraft carrier and Jamestown festival emblem*

CM403		MNHVF	UseVF
3¢	**blue green** *(118,399,600)*	.25	.20
	Plate block of 4	.55	
	FDC *(June 10, 1957)*		1.00

1957. Oklahoma Statehood Issue celebrated the 50th anniversary of statehood, growth and progress of a land that was once the Indian Territory. *Intaglio, perforated 11 x 10 1/2.*

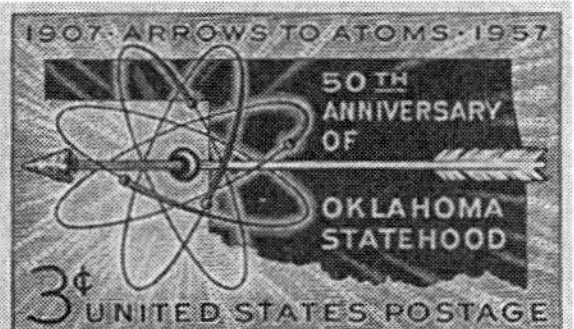

CM404 *Arrow, atom and Oklahoma map*

CM404		MNHVF	UseVF
3¢	**bright blue** *(102,209,500)*	.25	.20
	Plate block of 4	.55	
	FDC *(June 14, 1957)*		1.00

1957. Teachers of America Issue honored the National Education Association and the teaching profession that has contributed to the development of America through its school systems. *Intaglio, perforated 11 x 10 1/2.*

CM405 *Teacher, students and globe*

CM405		MNHVF	UseVF
3¢	**brown purple** *(103,045,000)*	.25	.20
	Plate block of 4	.55	1.00
	FDC *(July 1, 1957)*		1.00

1957. American Flag Issue saluted "Old Glory," symbol of freedom throughout the world. *Intaglio (Giori Press), perforated 11.*

CM406 *48-star American flag*

CM406		MNHVF	UseVF
4¢	**deep blue & carmine** *(84,054,400)*	.25	.20
	Plate block of 4	.55	
	FDC *(July 4, 1957)*		1.00

1957. Virginia of Sagadahock Issue commemorated the 350th anniversary of shipbuilding in the United States, and featured the first American built ship to participate in world commerce. *Intaglio, perforated 10 1/2 x 11.*

CM407 Virginia of Sagadahock *and state seal of Maine*

CM407		MNHVF	UseVF
3¢	**violet** *(126,266,000)*	.25	.20
	Plate block of 4	.55	
	FDC *(Aug. 15, 1957)*		1.00

Champions of Liberty Series was a five-year-long series honoring Champions of Liberty and freedom fighters of other nations.

1957. Ramon Magsaysay Issue honored a man of humble birth, who became president of the Philippines. (See also CM419-20, CM423-24, CM434-35, CM445-46, CM456-57, CM474-75, CM477-78 and CM483-84.) *Intaglio (Giori Press), perforated 11.*

CM408 *Ramon Magsaysay*

CM408		MNHVF	UseVF
8¢	**scarlet, deep ultramarine & ocher** *(39,489,600)*	.25	.20
	Plate block of 4, 2 numbers	.75	
	v. Plate block of 4, deep ultramarine, number omitted	—	
	FDC *(Aug. 31, 1957)*		1.00

1957. Lafayette Issue commemorated the 200th birthday of the French officer who came to America in 1777 and helped the fight for independence. *Intaglio, perforated 10 1/2 x 11.*

CM409 *Lafayette, flintlock rifle and sword*

CM409		MNHVF	UseVF
3¢	**brown purple** *(122,990,000)*	.25	.20
	Plate block of 4	.55	
	FDC *(Sept. 6, 1957)*		1.00

Users of this catalog are invited to write to us if they have information they feel will supplement or correct any material contained herein. All such communications will be answered.

1957. Whooping Crane Issue in the Wildlife Conservation Series brought to the attention of the American public the need to protect and preserve wildlife resources (see CM389-CM391). The whooping crane at the time was almost extinct. *Intaglio (Giori Press), perforated 11.*

CM410 *Whooping cranes*

CM410		MNHVF	UseVF
3¢	**gray blue, yellow & blue green** *(174,372,800)*	.25	.20
	Plate block of 4	.55	
	FDC *(Nov. 22, 1957)*		1.00

1957. Flushing Remonstrance Issue recalled a 1657 demonstration for religious freedom and liberty by the citizens of Flushing, N.Y. *Intaglio, perforated 10 1/2 x 11.*

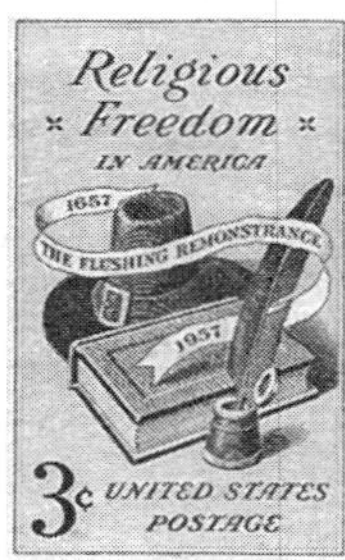

CM411 *Bible, hat, pen and inkwell*

CM411		MNHVF	UseVF
3¢	**brown black** *(114,365,000)*	.25	.20
	Plate block of 4	.55	
	FDC *(Dec. 27, 1957)*		1.00

1958. Garden and Horticultural Issue marked the 100th birthday of Liberty Hyde Bailey, famous botanist, author, and teacher whose horticultural achievements contributed to American prosperity. *Intaglio, perforated 10 1/2 x 11.*

CM412 *Allegory of the Good Earth with Horn of Plenty*

CM412		MNHVF	UseVF
3¢	**dull green** *(122,765,200)*	.25	.20
	Plate block of 4	.55	
	FDC *(March 15, 1958)*		1.00

1958. Brussels Universal and International Exhibition Issue paid tribute to the World's Fair and U.S. participation in it. *Intaglio, perforated 11 x 10 1/2.*

CM413 *U.S. fair pavilion*

CM413		MNHVF	UseVF
3¢	**brown purple** *(113,660,200)*	.25	.20
	Plate block of 4	.55	
	FDC *(April 17, 1958)*		1.00

1958. James Monroe Issue commemorated the 200th birthday of the fifth president of the United States. *Intaglio, perforated 11 x 10 1/2.*

CM414 *James Monroe, from a portrait by Gilbert Stuart*

CM414		MNHVF	UseVF
3¢	**violet** *(120,196,580)*	.25	.20
	Plate block of 4	.55	
	FDC *(April 28, 1958)*		1.00

1958. Minnesota Statehood Centennial Issue commemorated the 100th anniversary of Minnesota's admission as the 32nd state. *Intaglio, perforated 11 x 10 1/2.*

CM415 *Minnesota lake scene*

CM415		MNHVF	UseVF
3¢	**emerald green** *(120,805,200)*	.25	.20
	Plate block of 4	.55	
	FDC *(May 11, 1958)*		1.00

1958. International Geophysical Year Issue paid tribute to geophysicists in more than 60 countries who pool their knowledge for mankind's welfare in exploring outer space and the oceans and Earth. *Intaglio (Giori Press), perforated 11.*

CM416 *Detail from Michelangelo's* The Creation of Adam *and solar surface*

CM416		MNHVF	UseVF
3¢	**black & red** *(125,815,200)*	.25	.20
	Plate block of 4	.55	
	FDC *(May 31, 1958)*		1.00

1958. Gunston Hall Bicentennial Issue honored the completion of the home of George Mason, Revolutionary patriot and friend of George Washington. The house, about 15 miles south of Alexandria, Va., was opened to the public in 1952. *Intaglio, perforated 11 x 10 1/2.*

CM417 *Gunston Hall*

CM417		MNHVF	UseVF
3¢	**dull green** *(108,415,200)*	.25	.20
	Plate block of 4	.55	
	FDC *(June 12, 1958)*		1.00

1958. Mackinac Straits Bridge Issue marked the formal opening and dedication of the suspension span that connects St. Ignace and Mackinaw City, in Michigan's Upper and Lower Peninsulas. *Intaglio, perforated 10 1/2 x 11.*

CM418 *Ore boat under Mackinac Bridge*

CM418		MNHVF	UseVF
3¢	**turquoise blue** *(107,195,200)*	.25	.20
	Plate block of 4	.55	
	FDC *(June 25, 1958)*		1.00

1958. Simon Bolívar Issue The first two-stamp installment in the Champions of Liberty Series honored the South American freedom fighter known as "The Liberator" who dedicated his life to bringing happiness, social security and political stability to his countrymen. *Intaglio, perforated 10 1/2 x 11.*

CM419-20 *Simon Bolívar, from portrait by Acevedo Bernal*

CM419		MNHVF	UseVF
4¢	**olive buff** *(115,745,280)*	.25	.20
	Plate block of 4	.60	
	FDC *(July 24, 1958)*		1.00

1958. Simon Bolívar Issue *Intaglio (Giori Press), perforated 11*

CM420		MNHVF	UseVF
8¢	**scarlet, deep ultramarine & deep ocher** *(39,743,640)*	.25	.20
	Plate block of 4, 2 numbers	1.30	
	v. Plate block of 4, ocher number only	—	
	FDC *(July 25, 1958)*		1.00

1958. Atlantic Cable Centennial Issue commemorated the linking by cable of the eastern and western hemispheres in 1858. The first formal messages were exchanged by President Buchanan and Queen Victoria. *Intaglio, perforated 11 x 10 1/2.*

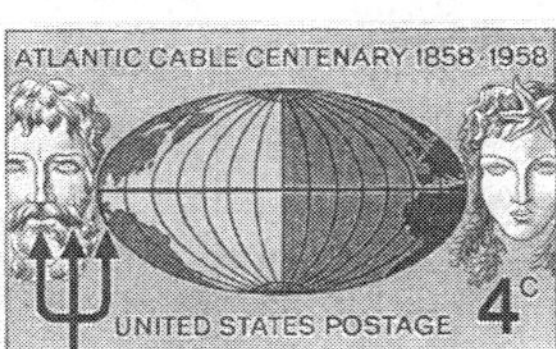

CM421 *Globe, Neptune and mermaid*

CM421		MNHVF	UseVF
4¢	**red violet** *(114,570,200)*	.25	.20
	Plate block of 4	.60	
	FDC *(Aug. 15, 1958)*		1.00

1958. Lincoln Douglas Debate Issue the first of four stamps issued to note the 150th anniversary of Lincoln's birth, marked the 100th anniversary of the Lincoln-Douglas debates held as part of the 1859 campaign for U.S. Senator. Although Douglas was re-elected, Lincoln gained national prominence and two years later was elected to the presidency. *Intaglio, perforated 11 x 10 1/2.*

CM422 *Lincoln and Douglas debating*

CM422		MNHVF	UseVF
4¢	**brown** *(114,860,200)*	.25	.20
	Plate block of 4	.85	
	FDC *(Aug. 27, 1958)*		1.00

1958. Lajos Kossuth Issue the third honoree in the Champions of Liberty Series, honored the famous Hungarian patriot who fought to liberate Hungary from Austrian control. He lived in exile until his death in 1894, never giving up hope that some day his beloved country would be free. *Intaglio, perforated 10 1/2 x 11.*

CM423-24 *Lajos Kossuth, from a photo taken in the United States in 1852*

CM423		MNHVF	UseVF
4¢	**dull green** *(120,561,280)*	.25	.20
	Plate block of 4	.60	
	FDC *(Sept. 19, 1958)*		1.00

1958. Lajos Kossuth Issue *Intaglio (Giori Press), perforated 11.*

CM424		MNHVF	UseVF
8¢	**scarlet, deep ultramarine & deep ochre** *(44,064,576)*	.25	.20
	Plate block of 4	1.30	
	FDC *(Sept. 19, 1958)*		1.00

1958. Journalism and Freedom of the Press Issue marked the 50th anniversary of the establishment of the world's first school of journalism at the University of Missouri. *Intaglio, perforated 10 1/2 x 11.*

CM425 *Symbols of a free press*

CM425		MNHVF	UseVF
4¢	**gray black** *(118,390,200)*	.25	.20
	Plate block of 4	.60	
	FDC *(Sept. 22, 1958)*		1.00

1958. Overland Mail Centennial Issue honored the pioneer mail service established in 1858. "The Great Overland Mail Route" started its run from Memphis and St. Louis and went to San Francisco. It was important in the settlement of the Southwest. *Intaglio, perforated 11 x 10 1/2.*

CM426 *Overland mail coach and map of route*

CM426		MNHVF	UseVF
4¢	**orange red** *(125,770,200)*	.25	.20
	Plate block of 4	.60	
	FDC *(Oct. 10, 1958)*		1.00

1958. Noah Webster Bicentennial Issue commemorated the 200th birthday of the noted lexicographer. He fought for American independence in the Revolutionary War, and his *Elementary Spelling Book* sold a million copies. *Intaglio, perforated 10 1/2 x 11.*

CM427 *Noah Webster, from a painting by James Herring*

CM427		MNHVF	UseVF
4¢	**magenta** *(114,114,280)*	.25	.20
	Plate block of 4	.60	
	FDC *(Oct. 16, 1958)*		1.00

1958. Forest Conservation Issue honored the 100th birthday of Theodore Roosevelt, one of the first leaders in the movement to preserve the nation's natural resources. *Intaglio (Giori Press), perforated 11.*

CM428 *Forest and deer*

CM428		MNHVF	UseVF
4¢	**deep green, yellow & brown** *(156,600,200)*	.25	.20
	Plate block of 4	.60	
	FDC *(Oct. 27, 1958)*		1.00

1958. Fort Duquesne Bicentennial Issue commemorated the 200th anniversary of the historic site that was so important in the conflict between England and France for control of North America. *Intaglio, perforated 11 x 10 1/2.*

CM429 *Composite drawing showing Gen. Forbes, Col. Washington, and Col. Henry Bouquet*

CM429		MNHVF	UseVF
4¢	**light blue** *(124,200,200)*	.25	.20
	Plate block of 4	.60	
	FDC *(Nov. 25, 1958)*		1.00

1959. Lincoln Sesquicentennial Issue *Intaglio, perforated 10 1/2 x 11.*

CM430 Beardless Lincoln, *painting by George P.A. Healy*

CM430		MNHVF	UseVF
1¢	**deep green** *(120,400,200)*	.25	.20
	Plate block of 4	.45	
	FDC *(Feb. 12, 1959)*		1.00

1959. Head of Lincoln Issue *Intaglio, perforated 11 x 10 1/2.*

CM431 Head of Lincoln, *sculpture by Gutzon Borglum*

CM431		MNHVF	UseVF
3¢	**deep plum** *(91,160,200)*	.25	.20
	Plate block of 4	.60	
	FDC *(Feb. 27, 1959)*		1.00

1959. Lincoln Statue Issue *Intaglio, perforated 11 x 10 1/2.*

CM432 Lincoln statue, *by Daniel Chester French, taken from a line and pastel drawing by Fritz Busse*

CM432		MNHVF	UseVF
4¢	**blue** *(126,500,000)*	.25	.20
	Plate block of 4	1.25	
	FDC *(May 30, 1959)*		1.00

1959. Oregon Statehood Issue commemorated the 100th anniversary of Oregon's admission as a state. *Intaglio, perforated 11 x 10 1/2.*

CM433 *Mount Hood and covered wagon*

CM433		MNHVF	UseVF
4¢	**blue green** *(120,740,200)*	.25	.20
	Plate block of 4	.60	
	FDC *(Feb. 14, 1959)*		1.00

1959. José de San Martin Issue the fourth of the Champions of Liberty Series paid tribute to the "hero of the Andes," a great general who fought for freedom in his native Argentina and other South American nations. *Intaglio, perforated 10 1/2 x 11.*

CM434-35 *Portrait of José de San Martin, from a print provided by the Library of Congress*

CM434		MNHVF	UseVF
4¢	**blue** *(113,623,280)*	.25	.20
	Plate block of 4	.60	
	FDC *(Feb. 25,1959)*		1.00
	v. Horizontal pair, imperforate between	1,250.00	

CM435		MNHVF	UseVF
8¢	**carmine, blue & ocher** *(45,569,088)*	.25	.20
	Plate block of 4	1.25	
	FDC *(Feb. 25, 1959)*		1.00

1959. NATO Issue honored the 10th anniversary of the North Atlantic Treaty Organization, binding 15 nations "to safeguard the freedom, common heritage and civilization of their people, founded on the principles of democracy, individual liberty and the rule of law." *Intaglio, perforated 10 1/2 x 11.*

CM436 *NATO emblem*

CM436		MNHVF	UseVF
4¢	**blue** *(122,493,280)*	.25	.20
	Plate block of 4	.60	
	FDC *(April 1, 1959)*		1.00

1959. Arctic Explorations Issue marked the conquest of the north polar regions and commemorated the 50th anniversary of Adm. Peary's expedition. The nuclear-powered submarine, USS *Nautilus,* joined the anniversary celebration, making the first underwater crossing of the North Pole. *Intaglio, perforated 11 x 10 1/2.*

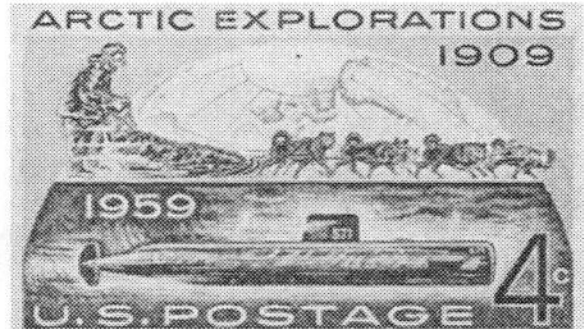

CM437 *Dog team and USS* Nautilus

CM437		MNHVF	UseVF
4¢	**turquoise blue** *(131,260,200)*	.25	.20
	Plate block of 4	.60	
	FDC *(April 6, 1959)*		1.00

1959. Peace through Trade Issue was released in association with the 17th Congress of the International Chamber of Commerce, held in Washington, D.C., April 19-25. *Intaglio, perforated 11 x 10 1/2.*

CM438 *Globe and laurel spray*

CM438		MNHVF	UseVF
8¢	**brown purple** *(47,125,200)*	.25	.20
	Plate block of 4	.60	
	FDC *(April 20, 1959)*		1.00

1959. Silver Centennial Issue commemorated the 100th anniversary of the discovery of the Comstock Lode, which produced about $300,000,000 worth of silver in its first 20 years. *Intaglio, perforated 11 x 10 1/2.*

CM439 *Henry Comstock and miners*

CM439		MNHVF	UseVF
4¢	**black** *(123,105,000)*	.25	.20
	Plate block of 4	.60	
	FDC *(June 8, 1959)*		1.00

1959. St. Lawrence Seaway Issue commemorated the opening of a link joining the United States and Canada in friendship and commerce, and providing a source of electric energy for both countries. Canada issued a commemorative stamp on the same day (Canada 480). Artists of both nations contributed to the design of both stamps, which are identical in design except for captions and denominations. *Intaglio (Giori Press), perforated 11 .*

CM440 *Linked eagle and maple leaf over Great Lakes*

CM440		MNHVF	UseVF
4¢	**blue & red** *(126,105,050)*	.25	.20
	Plate block of 4	.60	
	Pair, gutter between	—	
	FDC *(June 26, 1959)*		1.00

1959. 49-Star Flag Issue commemorated the admission of Alaska as the 49th state. *Intaglio (Giori Press), perforated 11.*

CM441 *49-star American flag*

CM441		MNHVF	UseVF
4¢	**deep blue & carmine** *(209,170,000)*	.25	.20
	Plate block of 4	.60	
	FDC *(July 4, 1959)*		1.00

1959. Soil Conservation Issue was a tribute to the effort to prevent erosion and conserve soil, vital to successful farming and ranching. *Intaglio (Giori Press), perforated 11.*

CM442 *Soil conservation methods*

CM442		MNHVF	UseVF
4¢	**blue green & yellow orange** *(120,835,000)*	.25	.20
	Plate block of 4	.60	
	FDC *(Aug. 26, 1959)*		1.00
	v. orange brown omitted	5,280.00	

1959. Petroleum Industry Centennial Issue marked the 100th anniversary of the completion of the first oil well at Titusville, Pa., by Edwin L. Drake. *Intaglio, perforated 10 1/2 x 11.*

CM443 *Oil derrick*

CM443		MNHVF	UseVF
4¢	**brown** *(115,715,000)*	.25	.20
	Plate block of 4	.60	
	FDC *(Aug. 27, 1959)*		1.00

1959. Dental Health Issue honored the centennial of the American Dental Association. *Intaglio, perforated 11 x 10 1/2.*

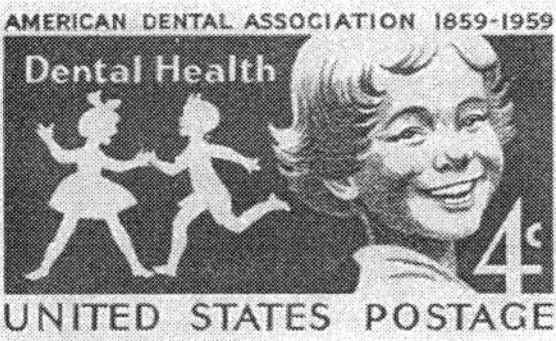

CM444 *Children playing and smiling girl with feather-cut hair style*

CM444		MNHVF	UseVF
4¢	**dark green** *(118,445,000)*	.25	.20
	Plate block of 4	.90	
	FDC *(Sept. 14, 1959)*		1.00

1959. Ernst Reuter Issue fifth in the Champions of Liberty Series, honored Ernst Reuter (1889-1953). He was persecuted and imprisoned by the Nazis, went into exile and after World War II returned to help rebuild his country. He was elected mayor of Berlin in 1947, holding that office until his death. *Intaglio, perforated 10 1/2 x 11.*

CM445-46 *Ernst Reuter*

CM445		MNHVF	UseVF
4¢	**black** *(111,685,000)*	.25	.20
	Plate block of 4	.60	
	FDC *(Sept. 29, 1959)*		1.00

1959. Ernst Reuter Issue *Intaglio (Giori Press), perforated 11.*

CM446		MNHVF	UseVF
8¢	**carmine, blue & ocher** *(43,099,200)*	.25	.20
	Plate block of 4	1.25	
	FDC *(Sept. 29, 1959)*		1.00

1959. Ephraim McDowell Issue paid tribute to an American who performed the first successful abdominal operation of its kind in the world at Danville, Ky., in 1809. *Intaglio, perforated 10 1/2 x 11.*

CM447 *Ephraim McDowell*

CM447		MNHVF	UseVF
4¢	**brown purple** *(115,444,000)*	.25	.20
	Plate block of 4	.65	
	FDC *(Dec. 3, 1959)*		1.00
	v. Vertical pair, imperforate between	500.00	
	v1. Vertical pair, imperforate horizontally	300.00	

1960. George Washington Issue *Intaglio (Giori Press), perforated 11.*

CM448 *"Observe good faith and justice toward all nations," George Washington*

CM448		MNHVF	UseVF
4¢	**deep blue & carmine** *(126,470,000)*	.25	.20
	Plate block of 4	.65	
	FDC *(Jan. 20, 1960)*		1.00

1960. Benjamin Franklin Issue Intaglio (Giori Press), perforated 11.

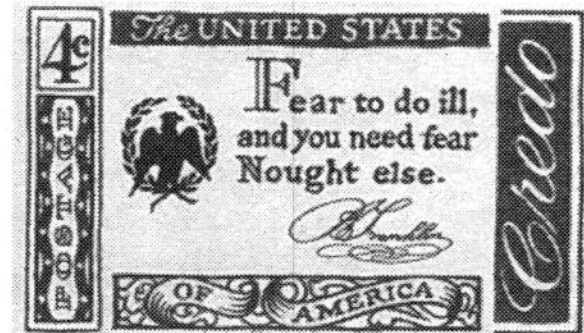

CM449 *"Fear to do ill, and you need fear nought else," Benjamin Franklin*

CM449		MNHVF	UseVF
4¢	**brown bister & emerald** *(124,460,000)*	.25	.20
	Plate block of 4	.65	
	FDC *(March 31, 1960)*		1.00

1960. Thomas Jefferson Issue Intaglio (Giori Press), perforated 11.

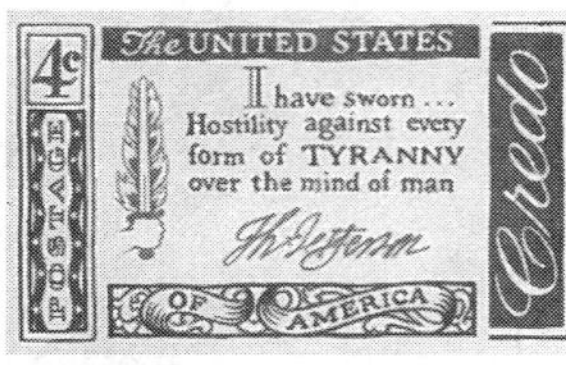

CM450 *"I have sworn hostility against every form of tyranny over the mind of man," Thomas Jefferson*

CM450		MNHVF	UseVF
4¢	**gray & scarlet** *(115,445,000)*	.25	.20
	Plate block of 4	.65	
	FDC *(May 18, 1960)*		1.00

1960. Francis Scott Key *Intaglio (Giori Press), perforated 11.*

CM451 *"And this be our motto, in God is our Trust," Francis Scott Key*

CM451		MNHVF	UseVF
4¢	**carmine red & deep blue** *(122,060,000)*	.25	.20
	Plate block of 4	.65	
	FDC *(Sept. 14, 1960)*		1.00

1960. Abraham Lincoln Issue Intaglio (Giori Press), perforated 11.

CM452 *"Those who deny freedom to others deserve it not for themselves," Abraham Lincoln*

CM452		MNHVF	UseVF
4¢	**bright purple & green** *(120,540,000)*	.25	.20
	Plate block of 4	.90	
	FDC *(Nov. 19, 1960)*		1.00

1960. Patrick Henry Issue *Intaglio (Giori Press), perforated 11.*

CM453 *"Give me liberty or give me death," Patrick Henry*

CM453		MNHVF	UseVF
4¢	**green & brown** *(113,075,000)*	.25	.20
	Plate block of 4	.90	
	Pair, gutter between	—	
	FDC *(Jan. 11, 1961)*		1.00

1960. Boy Scout Issue commemorated the 50th anniversary of the Boy Scout movement in America. Norman Rockwell designed the stamp. *Intaglio (Giori Press), perforated 11.*

CM454 *Boy Scout giving the Scout sign*

CM454

		MNHVF	UseVF
4¢	**red, deep blue & deep ocher** *(139,325,000)*	.25	.20
	Plate block of 4	.90	
	FDC *(Feb. 8, 1960)*		1.00

1960. Winter Olympic Games Issue marked the eighth Winter Games at Squaw Valley, Calif. It was the second time this important athletic contest was held in the United States (see CM110). *Intaglio, perforated 10 1/2 x 11.*

CM455 *Olympic emblem and snowflake*

CM455

		MNHVF	UseVF
4¢	**turquoise blue** *(124,445,000)*	.25	.20
	Plate block of 4	.60	
	FDC *(Feb. 18, 1960)*		1.00
		.60	
			1.00

1960. Tomas G. Masaryk Issue sixth in the Champions of Liberty Series, honored the first president of Czechoslovakia, who rose from humble origin to lead the movement for an independent nation. The two stamps were issued on the 41st anniversary of the republic. *Intaglio, perforated 10 1/2 x 11.*

CM456-57 *Tomas G. Masaryk*

CM456

		MNHVF	UseVF
4¢	**blue** *(113,792,000)*	.25	.20
	Plate block of 4	.60	
	v. Vertical pair, imperforate between	3,250.00	
	FDC *(March 7, 1960)*		1.00

CM457

		MNHVF	UseVF
8¢	**carmine, deep blue & ocher** *(44,215,200)*	.25	.20
	Plate block of 4	1.10	
	v. Horizontal pair, imperforate between	—	
	FDC *(March 7, 1960)*		1.00

1960. World Refugee Year Issue focused attention on the world's homeless and destitute and the importance of universal participation in aiding them. *Intaglio, perforated 11 x 10 1/2.*

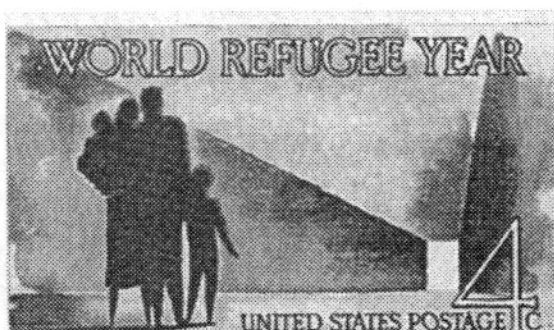

CM458 *Family facing doorway to a new life*

CM458

		MNHVF	UseVF
4¢	**gray black** *(113,195,000)*	.25	.20
	Plate block of 4	.60	
	FDC *(April 7, 1960)*		1.00

1960. Water Conservation Issue in conjunction with the Seventh National Watershed Congress, emphasized the importance of conserving this precious natural resource. *Intaglio (Giori Press), perforated 11.*

CM459 *Watershed and dependent farm and factories*

CM459

		MNHVF	UseVF
4¢	**blue, green & orange brown** *(120,570,000)*	.25	.20
	Plate block of 4	.60	
	FDC *(April 18, 1960)*		1.00

1960. SEATO Issue commemorated the South East Asia Treaty Organization Conference (May 31-June 3) and the organization's efforts on behalf of peace and freedom. This defensive alliance of nations includes Australia, France, New Zealand, Pakistan, Philippines, Thailand, United Kingdom and the United States. *Intaglio, perforated 10 1/2 x 11.*

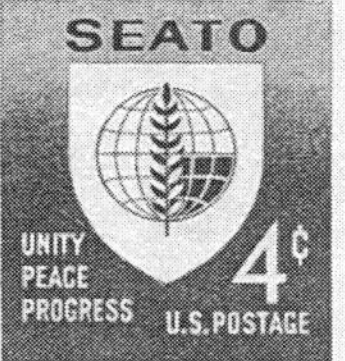

CM460 *SEATO emblem*

CM460

		MNHVF	UseVF
4¢	**blue** *(115,353,000)*	.25	.20
	Plate block of 4	.60	
	FDC *(May 31, 1960)*		1.00
	v. Vertical pair, imperforate between	150.00	

1960. American Women Issue emphasized the important contributions American women have made to social, spiritual, economic and political progress. *Intaglio, perforated 11 x 10 1/2.*

CM461 *Mother, daughter, and open book*

CM461

		MNHVF	UseVF
4¢	**violet** *(111,080,000)*	.25	.20
	Plate block of 4	.60	
	FDC *(June 2, 1960)*		1.00

1960. 50-Star Flag Issue commemorated the admission of Hawaii as the 50th state. *Intaglio (Giori Press), perforated 11.*

CM462 *50-star American flag*

CM462

		MNHVF	UseVF
4¢	**deep blue & scarlet** *(153,025,000)*	.25	.20
	Plate block of 4	.60	
	FDC *(July 4, 1960)*		1.00

1960. Pony Express Centenary Issue commemorated the contribution to progress by this pioneer transportation service, which provided a faster mail service vitally needed at the time. A stamped envelope (EN844) also was issued in conjunction with this event (see also CM236). *Intaglio, perforated 11 x 10 1/2.*

CM463 *Pony Express rider and map of route*

CM463		MNHVF	UseVF
4¢	**sepia** *(119,665,000)*	.25	.20
	Plate block of 4	.70	
	FDC *(July 19, 1960)*		1.00

1960. Employ the Handicapped Issue focused on the need to promote employment of physically handicapped people who could be trained for gainful activity in American industry. *Intaglio, perforated 10 1/2 x 11.*

CM464 *Drill press operator in wheelchair*

CM464		MNHVF	UseVF
4¢	**blue** *(117,855,000)*	.25	.20
	Plate block of 4	.60	
	FDC *(Aug. 28, 1960)*		1.00

1960. Fifth World Forestry Congress Issue paid tribute to the 2,000 foresters from more than 60 nations who gathered to explore the many uses of forest land. The congress was sponsored by the Food and Agriculture Organization of the United Nations. *Intaglio, perforated 10 1/2 X 11.*

CM465 *Seal of World Forestry Congress*

CM465		MNHVF	UseVF
4¢	**blue green** *(118,185,000)*	.25	.20
	Plate block of 4	.60	
	FDC *(Aug. 29, 1960)*		1.00

1960. Mexican Independence Issue marked the 150th anniversary of the Republic of Mexico. Mexico issued a stamp on the same day (Mexico 1373), different only in captions and denomination. *Intaglio (Giori Press), perforated 11.*

CM466 *Freedom Bell of the National Palace, Mexico City*

CM466		MNHVF	UseVF
4¢	**deep green & carmine red** *(112,260,000)*	.25	.20
	Plate block of 4	.60	
	FDC *(Sept. 16, 1960)*		1.00

1960. United States of America-Japan Centennial Issue commemorated the 100th anniversary of the first treaty between the two countries to promote good will and understanding. *Intaglio (Giori Press), perforated 11.*

CM467 *Washington Monument and cherry blossoms*

CM467		MNHVF	UseVF
4¢	**light blue & carmine** *(125,010,000)*	.25	.20
	Plate block of 4	.65	
	FDC *(Sept. 28, 1960)*		1.00

1960. Ignace Jan Paderewski Issue seventh in the Champions of Liberty Series, honored the world-famous statesman, pianist and Polish patriot. *Intaglio, perforated 10 1/2 x 11.*

CM468-69 *Ignace Jan Paderewski*

CM468		MNHVF	UseVF
4¢	**blue** *(119,798,000)*	.25	.20
	Plate block of 4	.60	
	FDC *(Oct. 8, 1960)*		1.00
CM469		**MNHVF**	**UseVF**
8¢	**red, blue & ocher** *(42,696,000)*	.25	.20
	Plate block of 4	1.10	
	FDC *(Oct. 8, 1960)*		1.00

1960. Robert A. Taft Issue honored the memory of an American (1889-1953) who served his country as a senator from 1939 until his death on July 31, 1953. A native of Ohio, he distinguished himself as Senate majority leader. *Intaglio, perforated 10 1/2 x 11.*

CM470 *Robert A. Taft*

CM470		MNHVF	UseVF
4¢	**violet** *(115,171,000)*	.25	.20
	Plate block of 4	.60	
	FDC *(Oct. 10, 1960)*		1.00

1960. Wheels of Freedom Issue was issued as a tribute to the automotive industry. It was released in conjunction with the National Automobile Show in Detroit. *Intaglio, perforated 11 x 10 1/2.*

CM471 *Hemispheres and steering wheel, symbol of automobile industry*

CM471		MNHVF	UseVF
4¢	**blue** *(109,695,000)*	.25	.20
	Plate block of 4	.60	
	FDC *(Oct. 15, 1960)*		1.00

1960. Boys' Club of America Issue commemorated the 100th anniversary of the movement that provided excellent recreational facilities for the underprivileged. *Intaglio (Giori Press), perforated 11.*

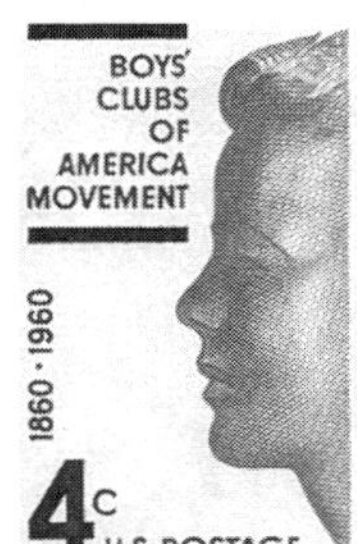

CM472 *American youth*

CM472		MNHVF	UseVF
4¢	**deep blue, black & red** *(123,690,000)*	.25	.20
	Plate block of 4	.60	
	FDC *(Oct. 18, 1960)*		1.00

1960. First Automated Post Office Issue commemorated the establishment of the first fully automated post office at Providence, R.I. Considered a milestone in postal progress, the specially created machinery was expected to speed mail delivery. *Intaglio (Giori Press), perforated 11.*

CM473 *Automated post office*

CM473		MNHVF	UseVF
4¢	**deep blue & scarlet** *(127,970,000)*	.25	.20
	Plate block of 4	.60	
	FDC *(Oct. 20, 1960)*		1.00

1960. Baron Karl Gustaf Emil Mannerheim Issue the eighth of the Champions of Liberty Series, honored the great Finnish soldier, statesman and leader for his heroic devotion to his country, in peace and war. Born in Askainen, June 4, 1867, he rose to the rank of marshal and led Finnish forces three times in his country's struggle for independence. He served twice as Finland's chief of state. *Intaglio, perforated 10 1/2 x 11.*

CM474-75 *Karl Gustaf Emil Mannerheim*

CM474		MNHVF	UseVF
4¢	**blue** *(124,796,000)*	.25	.20
	Plate block of 4	.60	
	FDC *(Oct. 26, 1960)*		1.00
CM475		**MNHVF**	**UseVF**
8¢	**red, blue & ocher** *(42,076,800)*	.25	.20
	Plate block of 4	1.10	
	FDC *(Oct. 26,1960)*		1.00

1960. Campfire Girls Issue commemorated the Golden Jubilee Convention celebration of the organization that was created in 1910 for girls 7 to 18 years of age. *Intaglio (Giori Press), perforated 11.*

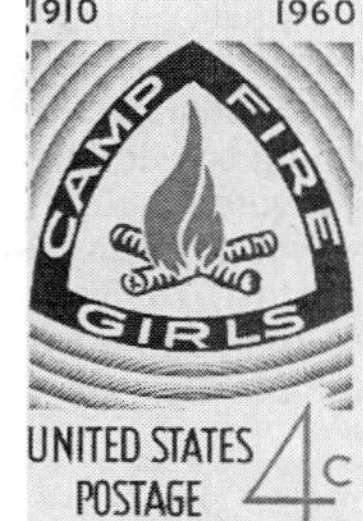

CM476 *Campfire Girls insignia*

CM476		MNHVF	UseVF
4¢	**blue & red** *(116,215,000)*	.25	.20
	Plate block of 4	.60	
	FDC *(Nov. 1, 1960)*		1.00

1960. Giuseppe Garibaldi Issue the ninth of the Champions of Liberty Series, commemorated Italy's great patriot and fighter for freedom. A born leader, Garibaldi helped unify Italy and fought for the cause of liberty in South America and Europe. *Intaglio, perforated 10 1/2 x 11.*

CM477-78 *Giuseppe Garibaldi*

CM477		MNHVF	UseVF
4¢	**green** *(126,252,000)*	.25	.20
	Plate block of 4	.60	
	FDC *(Nov. 2, 1960)*		1.00
CM478		**MNHVF**	**UseVF**
8¢	**red, blue & ocher** *(42,746,400)*	.25	.20
	Plate block of 4	1.10	
	FDC *(Nov. 2, 1960)*		1.00

1960. Walter F. George Issue honored the distinguished public servant (1878-1957) who served as a senator from Georgia and as special assistant for President Eisenhower to NATO in 1957. *Intaglio, perforated 10 1/2 x 11.*

CM479 *Walter F. George*

CM479		MNHVF	UseVF
4¢	**violet** *(124,117,000)*	.25	.20
	Plate block of 4	.60	
	FDC *(Nov. 5, 1960)*		1.00

1960. John Foster Dulles Issue paid tribute to an American (1888-1959) who died while serving as secretary of state. His long, distinguished career included service as secretary to the Hague Peace Conference in 1907 and as U.S. senator from New York. *Intaglio, perforated 10 1/2 x 11.*

CM480 *John Foster Dulles*

CM480		MNHVF	UseVF
4¢	**violet** *(177,187,000)*	.20	.20
	Plate block of 4	.60	
	FDC *(Dec. 6, 1960)*		1.00

1960. Andrew Carnegie Issue honored the industrialist on his 125th birthday and the 50th anniversary of the establishment of the Carnegie Endowment for International Peace. Born in Scotland, Carnegie (1835-1919), came to the United States as a young boy and became one of the great leaders of world industry. He devoted a good portion of his life and wealth to the cause of social and educational advancements and the promotion of international peace. In 1910, in an effort to abolish the horrors of war, he founded the Carnegie Endowment for International Peace with a gift of $10 million. *Intaglio, perforated 10 1/2 x 11.*

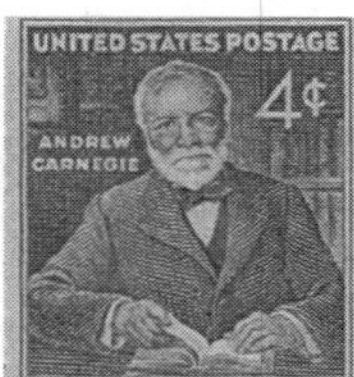

CM481 *Andrew Carnegie*

CM481		MNHVF	UseVF
4¢	**claret** *(119,840,000)*	.20	.20
	Plate block of 4	.60	
	FDC *(Nov. 25, 1960)*		1.00

1960. Echo I Satellite Issue commemorated the world's first communications satellite launched by NASA into orbit on Aug. 12, 1960. *Intaglio, perforated 11 x 10 1/2.*

CM482 *Echo I satellite in orbit*

CM482		MNHVF	UseVF
4¢	**violet** *(125,290,000)*	.25	.20
	Plate block of 4	1.00	
	FDC *(Dec. 15, 1960)*		1.00

1961. Mahatma Gandhi Issue the 10th and final Champions of Liberty Series, honored the Indian who led his country to freedom. A physically frail man, he endured many hardships that inspired his countrymen to work non-violently for independence, equality and social justice. *Intaglio, perforated 10 1/2 x 11.*

CM483-84 *Mahatma Gandhi*

CM483		MNHVF	UseVF
4¢	**red orange** *(112,966,000)*	.20	.20
	Plate block of 4	.60	
	FDC *(Jan. 26, 1961)*		1.00

CM484		MNHVF	UseVF
8¢	**red, blue & ocher** *(41,644,200)*	.25	.20
	Plate block of 4	1.20	
	FDC *(Jan. 26.1961)*		1.00

1961. Range Conservation Issue was released in conjunction with the annual meeting of the American Society of Range Management, devoted to conservation, forestry, livestock and land management. *Intaglio (Giori Press), perforated 11.*

CM485 *Trail boss and cattle grazing*

CM485		MNHVF	UseVF
4¢	**blue, orange & indigo** *(110,850,000)*	.20	.20
	Plate block of 4	.60	
	FDC *(Feb. 2, 1961)*		1.00

1961. Horace Greeley Issue honored the publisher and editor (1811-1872) who advised the youth of America, "Go West, young man, go West." He established the *New York Tribune* in 1841. *Intaglio, perforated 10 1/2 x 11.*

CM486 *Horace Greeley*

CM486		MNHVF	UseVF
4¢	**violet** *(98,616,000)*	.20	.20
	Plate block of 4	.60	
	FDC *(Feb. 3, 1961)*		1.00

1961-65. Civil War Centennial Series

1961-65. Civil War Centennial Series saluted the 10th anniversary of the bloodiest conflict in the nation's history with one centennial stamp for each of the war's five years.

1961. Fort Sumter Issue in the Civil War Centennial Series marked the anniversary of the assault and capture of the Charleston fort. This attack committed the Confederate states to war. *Intaglio, perforated 10 1/2 x 11.*

CM487 *Coastal gun at Fort Sumter*

CM487		MNHVF	UseVF
4¢	**green** *(101,125,000)*	.25	.20
	Plate block of 4	1.65	
	FDC *(April 12, 1961)*		1.00

1962. Battle of Shiloh Issue in the Civil War Centennial Series commemorated the valiant stand of Confederate troops under Gen. Albert S. Johnston and Union soldiers under Gen. Ulysses S. Grant in the fields of Tennessee. (See also CM1725). *Intaglio, perforated 11 x 10 1/2.*

CM488 *Infantryman in action*

CM488		MNHVF	UseVF
4¢	**black on pink** *(124,865,000)*	.25	.20
	Plate block of 4	1.10	
	FDC *(April 7, 1962)*		1.00

1963. Battle of Gettysburg Issue in the Civil War Centennial Series honored the heroes of one of the most important battles of the Civil War, which was fought July 1-3, 1863, in eastern Pennsylvania. (See CM1740). *Intaglio (Giori Press), perforated 11.*

CM489 *Union and Confederate soldiers fighting*

CM489		MNHVF	UseVF
5¢	**gray & blue** *(79,905,000)*	.25	.20

	Plate block of 4	1.75	
	FDC *(July 1, 1963)*		1.00

1964. Battle of the Wilderness Issue in the Civil War Centennial Series saluted the fierce battle between the armies of Grant and Lee that took place in densely wooded terrain near Fredericksburg, Va. *Intaglio (Giori Press), perforated 11.*

CM490 *Artillery in action*

CM490		MNHVF	UseVF
5¢	**brown, purple & black** *(125,410,000)*	.25	.20
	Plate block of 4	1.50	
	FDC *(May 5, 1964)*		1.00

1965. Appomattox Issue in the Civil War Centennial Series celebrated the end of the War between the States. At Appomattox Court House, Va., on Sunday, April 9, 1865, the Confederate Army under the command of Gen. Robert E. Lee surrendered to Gen. Ulysses S. Grant and the Union forces. *Intaglio (Giori Press), perforated 11.*

CM491 *Civil War soldier and rifles*

CM491		MNHVF	UseVF
5¢	**blue & black** *(112,845,000)*	.25	.20
	Plate block of 4	3.75	
	FDC *(April 9, 1965)*		1.00
	v. Horizontal pair, imperforate vertically	—	

1961. Kansas Statehood Centennial Issue marked 100 years of statehood for Kansas, admitted in 1861 as the 34th state. *Intaglio (Giori Press), perforated 11.*

CM492 *Sunflower, pioneers and fort*

CM492		MNHVF	UseVF
4¢	**brown, lake & green** on yellow paper *(106,210,000)*	.20	.20
	Plate block of 4	.60	
	FDC *(May 10, 1961)*		1.00

1961. George William Norris Issue honored the Nebraska senator on his 100th birthday. Among his many achievements was a key role in the creation of the Tennessee Valley Authority. *Intaglio, perforated 11 x 10 1/2.*

CM493 *George W. Norris and Norris Dam*

CM493		MNHVF	UseVF
4¢	**blue green** *(110,810,000)*	.20	.20
	Plate block of 4	.60	
	FDC *(July 11, 1961)*		1.00

1961. Naval Aviation Issue saluted the golden jubilee of the Navy's participation and development in aviation. *Intaglio, perforated 11 x 10 1/2.*

CM494 *Naval air wings and first naval airplane (1911 Curtis A-1)*

CM494		MNHVF	UseVF
4¢	**blue** *(116,995,000)*	.20	.20
	Plate block of 4	.65	
	Pair, gutter between	—	
	FDC *(Aug. 20, 1961)*		1.00

1961. Workman's Compensation Issue marked the 50th anniversary of the first U.S. legislation to compensate workers injured on the job. The Wisconsin law of 1911 set a pattern that was followed by nine other states that year. *Intaglio, perforated 10 1/2 x 11.*

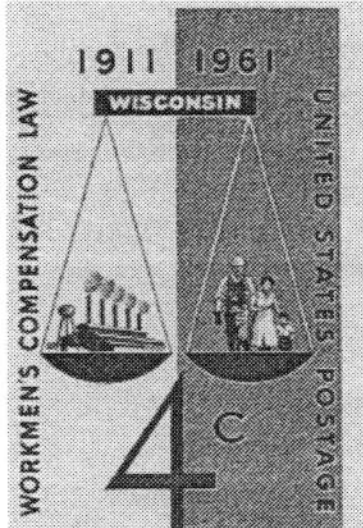

CM495 *Factory and family in scales of justice*

CM495		MNHVF	UseVF
4¢	**ultramarine** on bluish paper *(121,015,000)*	.20	.20
	Plate block of 4	.60	
	v. Plate block of 4, plate number inverted	.60	
	FDC *(Sept. 4, 1961)*		1.00

Fine Arts Series

1961. Frederic Remington Issue first stamp in a Fine Arts Series, honored the 100th birthday of this American artist of the West (CM230) who won fame for his paintings and sculptures of North American Indians, U.S. soldiers and cowboys on the western plains. (See also CM993). *Intaglio (Giori Press), perforated 11.*

CM496 *Detail from* The Smoke Signal *by Remington (left side of painting)*

CM496		MNHVF	UseVF
4¢	**blue, red & yellow** *(111,600,000)*	.20	.20
	Plate block of 4	.65	
	FDC *(Oct. 4, 1961)*		1.00

1961. 50th Anniversary of the Republic of China Issue honored Sun Yat-sen (1866-1925), the founder of the republic who fought against dynastic rule for the freedom of China. (See also CM248). *Intaglio, perforated 10 1/2 x 11.*

CM497 *Sun Yat-Sen*

CM497		MNHVF	UseVF
4¢	**blue** *(110,620,000)*	.20	.20
	Plate block of 4	.85	
	FDC *(Oct. 10, 1961)*		1.00

1961. Naismith-Basketball Issue commemorated the 100th birthday of Dr. James A. Naismith (1861-1939), Canadian-born inventor of basketball. An athletic instructor at the YMCA, Naismith saw the need for a fast-moving, exciting indoor sport that could be played in the winter. In 1891 he founded the game, which today draws millions of participants and spectators. *Intaglio, perforated 10 1/2 x 11.*

CM498 *Basketball, hand and net*

CM498		MNHVF	UseVF
4¢	**brown** *(109,110,000)*	.25	.20
	Plate block of 4	1.00	
	FDC *(Nov. 6, 1961)*		1.00

1961. Nursing Issue noted the 100th anniversary of the nursing profession in the United States. An urgent need for skilled nurses was created by the Civil War. The training programs then established laid the foundations for the profession, which thousands of Americans enter each year. *Intaglio, (Giori Press), perforated 11.*

CM499 *Nurse lighting candle*

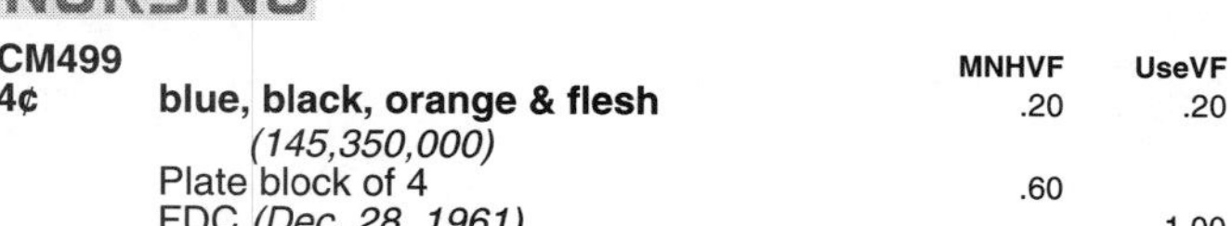

CM499		MNHVF	UseVF
4¢	**blue, black, orange & flesh** *(145,350,000)*	.20	.20
	Plate block of 4	.60	
	FDC *(Dec. 28, 1961)*		1.00

1962. New Mexico Statehood Issue commemorated the 50th anniversary of its admission as the 47th state (see CM286). *Intaglio (Giori Press), perforated 11.*

CM500 *Shiprock Mesa*

CM500		MNHVF	UseVF
4¢	**light blue, bister & brown purple** *(112,870,000)*	.20	.20
	Plate block of 4	.60	
	FDC *(Jan. 6, 1962)*		1.00

1962. Arizona Statehood Issue marked the 50th anniversary of the admission of the 48th state. *Intaglio (Giori Press), perforated 11.*

CM501 *Giant Saguaro cactus in bloom at night*

CM501		MNHVF	UseVF
4¢	**scarlet, deep blue & green** *(121,820,000)*	.20	.20
	Plate block of 4	.60	
	FDC *(Feb. 14, 1962)*		1.00

1962. Project Mercury Issue paid tribute to the successful three-orbit flight of Lt. Col. John H. Glenn, Jr. The stamp was released at the moment the flight was completed — the first time the United States honored a historic event with an unannounced, simultaneous commemorative. Glenn, the first American astronaut to orbit the earth, traveled at 17,500 miles per hour in his Mercury capsule, *Friendship 7. Intaglio (Giori Press), perforated 11.*

CM502 *Mercury capsule circling Earth*

CM502		MNHVF	UseVF
4¢	**deep blue & yellow** *(289,240,000)*	.20	.20
	Plate block of 4	.80	
	FDC *(Feb. 20, 1962)*		1.00

1962. Malaria Eradication Issue pledged U.S. support to the World Health Organization in its campaign to eliminate malaria, a disease that claims countless lives each year. *Intaglio (Giori Press), perforated 11.*

CM503 *United States seal and WHO emblem*

CM503		MNHVF	UseVF
4¢	**blue & bister** *(120,155,000)*	.20	.20
	Plate block of 4	.60	
	FDC *(March 30, 1962)*		1.00

Read the introduction to this catalog carefully. It contains much valuable information for all stamp collectors and makes the catalog easier to use.

1962. Charles Evans Hughes Issue honored the 100th birthday of a statesman-jurist (1862-1948) who served as governor of New York, secretary of state under President Harding and chief justice of the U.S. Supreme Court (1930-41). *Intaglio, perforated 10 1/2 x 11.*

CM504 *Charles Evans Hughes*

CM504		**MNHVF**	**UseVF**
4¢	**black** on yellow paper *(124,595,000)*	.20	.20
	Plate block of 4	.60	
	FDC *(April 11, 1962)*		1.00

1962. Seattle World's Fair Issue marked the International Exposition held in Seattle, Wash., April 21-Oct. 21, 1962. This was America's first space-age world's fair, with the 550-foot-high Space Needle as its most distinctive structure and symbol. *Intaglio (Giori Press), perforated 11.*

CM505 *Space Needle and monorail*

CM505		**MNHVF**	**UseVF**
4¢	**red & deep blue** *(147,310,000)*	.20	.20
	Plate block of 4	.60	
	FDC *(April 25, 1962)*		1.00

1962. Louisiana Statehood Commemorative Issue marked the 150th anniversary of the admission of Louisiana as the 18th state. *Intaglio (Giori Press), perforated 11.*

CM506 *Mississippi riverboat*

CM506		**MNHVF**	**UseVF**
4¢	**gray green, blue & vermilion** *(118,690,000)*	.20	.20
	Plate block of 4	.60	
	FDC *(April 30, 1962)*		1.00

1962. Homestead Act Issue commemorated the 100th anniversary of the act signed by Abraham Lincoln that opened the Great Plains to settlers. A homesteader could acquire 160 acres by living and working on the land for five years. *Intaglio, perforated 11 1/4 x 10 1/2.*

CM507 *Sod hut and homesteaders*

CM507		**MNHVF**	**UseVF**
4¢	**slate blue** *(122,730,000)*	.20	.20
	Plate block of 4	.60	
	FDC *(May 20, 1962)*		1.00

1962. Girl Scouts of America Issue commemorated the 50th anniversary of the movement, which has grown into an organization of millions. (See CM316). *Intaglio, perforated 11 1/4 X 10 1/2.*

CM508 *Girl Scout, American flag*

CM508		**MNHVF**	**UseVF**
4¢	**red** *(126,515,000)*	.20	.20
	Plate block of 4	.60	
	Pair, gutter between	—	
	FDC *(July 24, 1962)*		1.00

1962. Brien McMahon Issue honored the Connecticut senator who saw the vast potential of the atom for medical, industrial and scientific purposes. McMahon (1903-1952) formed the Atomic Energy Commission. (See CM382). *Intaglio, perforated 11 1/4 X 10 1/2.*

CM509 *James O'Brien McMahon and atomic symbol*

CM509		**MNHVF**	**UseVF**
4¢	**violet** *(130,960,000)*	.20	.20
	Plate block of 4	.60	
	FDC *(July 28, 1962)*		1.00

1962. National Apprenticeship Issue marked the 25th anniversary of the program, under which the U.S. Department of Labor, unions and management join in sponsoring apprenticeship training. *Intaglio, perforated 11 1/4 X 10 1/2.*

CM510 *Young hand receiving micrometer*

CM510		**MNHVF**	**UseVF**
4¢	**black,** on buff *(120,055,000)*	.20	.20
	Plate block of 4	.60	
	FDC *(Aug. 31, 1962)*		1.00

1962. Sam Rayburn Issue honored the Texan who served as a Congressman from 1913 until 1961. Rayburn (1882-1961) was Speaker of the House of Representatives for 17 years, longer than any other. *Intaglio (Giori Press), perforated 11.*

CM511 *Sam Rayburn and Capitol dome*

CM511		**MNHVF**	**UseVF**
4¢	**brown & blue** *(120,715,000)*	.20	.20
	Plate block of 4	.60	
	FDC *(Sept. 16, 1962)*		1.00

1962. Dag Hammarskjöld Issue honored the secretary-general of the United Nations who lost his life while on a peace mission in Africa. *Intaglio (Giori Press), perforated 11.*

CM512-13 *Dag Hammarskjöld and U.N. building*

CM512		MNHVF	UseVF
4¢	**black, brown & yellow** *(121,440,000)*	.20	.20
	Plate block of 4	.60	
	FDC *(Oct. 23, 1962)*		1.00

1962. Dag Hammarskjöld Special Issue Shortly after the commemorative was released, a yellow inverted error was discovered by collectors in New Jersey and Ohio. The Post Office Department deliberately reprinted this error — the first U.S. invert error since the 24¢ Jenny airmail of 1918. Only the yellow is inverted and there are three distinct varieties as noted below. *Intaglio (Giori Press), perforated 11.*

CM513 *Inverted yellow*

CM513		MNHVF	UseVF
4¢	**black, brown & yellow** *(40,270,000)*	.55	.25
	Type I, the non-yellow strip at left is 3.5mm wide	.55	.25
	Type II, the non-yellow strip at left is 11.5mm wide	.55	.25
	Type III, the non-yellow strip at left is 9.75mm wide	.55	.25

1962. Higher Education Issue commemorated the centennial of the law creating land-grant colleges and universities and pointed out the role higher education has played in the development of the United States (see also CM377). *Intaglio (Giori Press), perforated 11.*

CM514 *Lamp of learning and U.S. map*

CM514		MNHVF	UseVF
4¢	**blue, green & black** *(120,035,000)*	.20	.20
	Plate block of 4	.65	
	FDC *(Nov. 14, 1962)*		1.00

1962. Winslow Homer Issue honored the American artist who painted *Breezing Up,* on display in the National Gallery of Art in Washington, D.C. This is the second issue in the Fine Arts Series. *Intaglio (Giori Press), perforated 11.*

CM515 Breezing Up *by Winslow Homer*

CM515		MNHVF	UseVF
4¢	**multicolored** *(117,870,000)*	.20	.20
	Plate block of 4	.65	
	v. Horizontal pair, imperforate between	6,750.00	
	FDC *(Dec. 15, 1962)*		1.00

1963. Carolina Charter Issue commemorated the 300th anniversary of the granting of the charter by Charles II to eight supporters who helped him regain the English throne. The land grant covered 1.5 million square miles. *Intaglio (Giori Press), perforated 11.*

CM516 *Charter and quill pen*

CM516		MNHVF	UseVF
5¢	**dark carmine & brown** *(129,445,000)*	.20	.20
	Plate block of 4	.65	
	FDC *(April 6, 1963)*		1.00

1963. Food for Peace Issue paid tribute to the World Food Congress and joined nearly 150 other nations and territories in publicizing the international Freedom from Hunger campaign on stamps. *Intaglio (Giori Press), perforated 11.*

CM517 *Stalk of wheat*

CM517		MNHVF	UseVF
5¢	**green, yellow & red** *(135,620,000)*	.20	.20
	Plate block of 4	.65	
	FDC *(June 4, 1963)*		1.00

1963. West Virginia Statehood Issue commemorated the 100th anniversary of the admission of the Mountain State to the union as the 35th state. *Intaglio (Giori Press), perforated 11.*

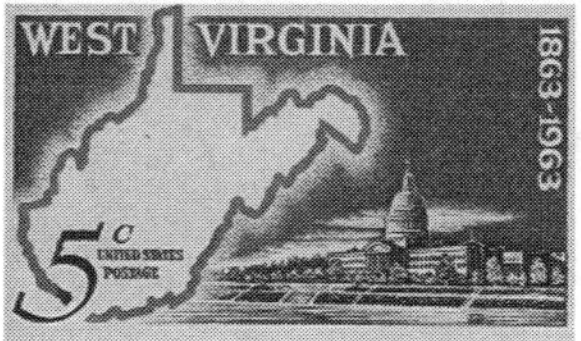

CM518 *Map and state capitol of West Virginia*

CM518		MNHVF	UseVF
5¢	**green, red & black** *(137,540,000)*	.20	.20
	Plate block of 4	.65	
	FDC *(June 20, 1963)*		1.00

1963. Emancipation Proclamation Issue commemorated the centennial of President Lincoln's action to abolish slavery in the United States. *Intaglio (Giori Press), perforated 11.*

CM519 *Broken chain*

CM519		MNHVF	UseVF
5¢	**bright blue, scarlet & indigo** *(132,435,000)*	.20	.20
	Plate block of 4	.85	
	FDC *(Aug. 16, 1963)*		1.00

1963. Alliance for Progress Issue marked the second anniversary of an inter-American program for peaceful coexistence and economic improvement. Other members of the Organization of American States to issue stamps honoring the event include Argentina, Bolivia, Costa Rica, Uruguay and Canal Zone. *Intaglio (Giori Press), perforated 11.*

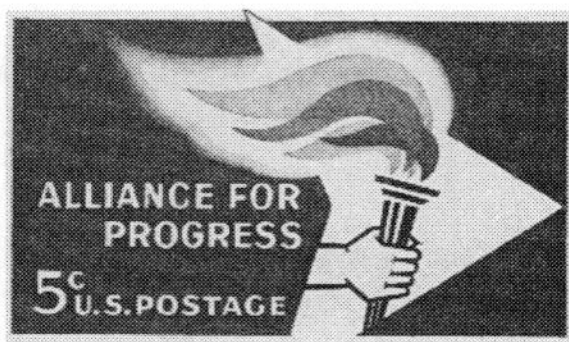

CM520 *Torch of progress*

CM520		MNHVF	UseVF
5¢	**bright blue & green** *(135,520,000)*	.20	.20
	Plate block of 4	.65	
	FDC *(Aug. 17, 1963)*		1.00

1963. Cordell Hull Issue paid tribute to the secretary of state during the administration of Franklin Roosevelt, from 1933 until 1944. Hull (1871-1955) was awarded the Nobel Peace Prize in 1945. *Intaglio, perforated 10 1/2 X 11.*

CM521 *Cordell Hull*

CM521		MNHVF	UseVF
5¢	**blue green** *(131,420,000)*	.20	.20
	Plate block of 4	.65	
	FDC *(Oct. 5, 1963)*		1.00

1963. Eleanor Roosevelt Issue honored Franklin D. Roosevelt's widow (1884-1962), a champion of liberty and a formidable fighter for human rights. The likeness on the stamp was taken from a photograph she liked best. *Intaglio, perforated 11 X 10 1/2.*

CM522 *Eleanor Roosevelt*

CM522		MNHVF	UseVF
5¢	**purple** *(133,170,000)*	.20	.20
	Plate block of 4	.65	
	FDC *(Oct. 11, 1963)*		1.00

1963. National Academy of Science Issue saluted this organization on its 100th anniversary. Abraham Lincoln signed into law the legislation that created the academy, which was originally composed of 50 American scientists. *Intaglio (Giori Press), perforated 11.*

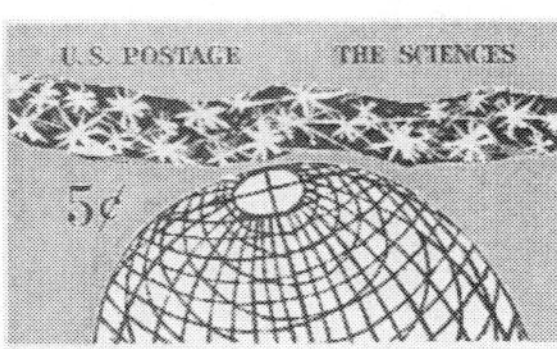

CM523 *Astral belt over globe*

CM523		MNHVF	UseVF
5¢	**turquoise, blue & black** *(139,195,000)*	.20	.20
	Plate block of 4	.65	
	FDC *(Oct. 14, 1963)*		1.00

1963. City Mail Delivery Issue marked the centennial of the service begun at the suggestion of Postmaster General Montgomery Blair, who convinced Congress to pass a law providing for the free delivery of city mail. Designed by Norman Rockwell, this commemorative is considered the first expression of humor on a U.S. stamp. It was also the first U.S. commemorative issue tagged with an invisible compound of zinc-orthosilicate that glows green under ultraviolet light in automated mail handling equipment. *Intaglio (Giori Press), perforated 11.*

CM524 *Postman flanked by boy and dog*

CM524		MNHVF	UseVF
5¢	**red, gray & blue,** tagged *(128,450,000)*	.20	.20
	Plate block of 4	.65	
	FDC *(Oct. 26, 1963)*		1.00
	zo. Tagging omitted	15.00	

1963. International Red Cross Issue marked the centennial of the organization and saluted the Red Cross for its participation in the Cuban prisoner exchange program. *Intaglio (Giori Press), perforated 11.*

CM525 *Cuban refugees on S.S.* Morning Light

CM525		MNHVF	UseVF
5¢	**deep gray & red** *(116,665,000)*	.20	.20
	Plate block of 4	.65	
	FDC *(Oct. 29, 1963)*		1.00

1963. John James Audubon Issue honored the great American artist and ornithologist who died in 1851. This is the third in the Fine Arts Series and is the second time Audubon has been honored with a stamp (see CM216 and A71). *Intaglio (Giori Press), perforated 11.*

CM526 *Audubon's Columbia jays*

CM526		MNHVF	UseVF
5¢	**multicolored** *(175,175,000)*	.20	.20
	Plate block of 4	.80	
	FDC *(Dec. 7, 1963)*		1.00

1964. Sam Houston Issue saluted the first president of the Republic of Texas, commander of the army that defeated Santa Ana in 1836 and thus gained independence for the Lone Star state. This was the first use of the Mr. ZIP marginal inscription. (See also CM166 and CM168.) *Intaglio, perforated 10 1/2 X 11.*

CM527 *Sam Houston*

CM527		MNHVF	UseVF
5¢	**black** *(125,995,000)*	.20	.20

		MNHVF	UseVF
	Plate block of 4	.85	
	FDC *(Jan. 10, 1964)*		1.00

1964. CHARLES M. RUSSELL ISSUE noted the 100th anniversary of the artist's birth with the fourth stamp in the Fine Arts Series. Famous for his Western themes, Russell's art has themes of gunmen, longhorn steers, broncos and dancehall girls. *Intaglio (Giori Press), perforated 11.*

CM528 *Russell's* Jerked Down

CM528		MNHVF	UseVF
5¢	**multicolored** *(128,025,000)*	.20	.20
	Plate block of 4	.85	
	FDC *(March 19, 1964)*		1.00

1964. NEW YORK WORLD'S FAIR ISSUE commemorated the opening of the international exposition dedicated to "Peace Through Understanding." Approximately 175 separate pavilions and other structures presented the achievements of more than 509 nations, states and major industries. *Intaglio, perforated 11 x 10 1/2.*

CM529 *Unisphere and World's Fair mall*

CM529		MNHVF	UseVF
5¢	**green** *(145,700,000)*	.20	.20
	Plate block of 4	.85	
	FDC *(April 22, 1964)*		1.00

1964. JOHN MUIR ISSUE honored the naturalist and conservationist (1838-1914) whose efforts helped save California's priceless forests. *Intaglio (Giori Press), perforated 11.*

CM530 *John Muir and redwoods*

CM530		MNHVF	UseVF
5¢	**brown, green, brownish gray & olive green** *(120,310,000)*	.20	.20
	Plate block of 4	.85	
	FDC *(April 29, 1964)*		1.00

1964. JOHN F. KENNEDY MEMORIAL ISSUE paid tribute to the 35th president of the United States, assassinated in Dallas, Texas, Nov. 22, 1963. Many nations mourned his passing and issued stamps in his memory. Although Boston was the official first-day city, the stamp was released nationwide that same day. *Intaglio, perforated 11 x 10 1/2.*

CM531 *John F. Kennedy and eternal flame*

CM531		MNHVF	UseVF
5¢	**gray blue** *(500,000,000)*	.20	.20
	Plate block of 4	1.85	
	FDC *(May 29, 1964)*		1.00

1964. NEW JERSEY TERCENTENARY ISSUE marked the 300th anniversary of the colonization of the Garden State by the British. The stamp was first issued in Elizabeth, the state's first capital and oldest city. *Intaglio, perforated 10 1/2 X 11.*

CM532 *Philip Carteret at Elizabethtown*

CM532		MNHVF	UseVF
5¢	**ultramarine** *(123,845,000)*	.20	.20
	Plate block of 4	.65	
	FDC *(June 15, 1964)*		1.00

1964. NEVADA STATEHOOD ISSUE commemorated the centenary of the entry of Nevada as the 36th state. *Intaglio (Giori Press), perforated 11.*

CM533 *Virginia City and map of Nevada*

CM533		MNHVF	UseVF
5¢	**multicolored** *(122,825,000)*	.20	.20
	Plate block of 4	.65	
	FDC *(July 22, 1964)*		1.00

1964. REGISTER AND VOTE ISSUE encouraged Americans to take part in the forthcoming election and was endorsed by both the Democratic and Republican parties. *Intaglio (Giori Press), perforated 11.*

CM534 *U.S. flag*

CM534		MNHVF	UseVF
5¢	**blue & red** *(325,000,000)*	.20	.20
	Plate block of 4	.65	
	FDC *(Aug. 1, 1964)*		1.00

1964. WILLIAM SHAKESPEARE ISSUE commemorated the 400th birthday of the Bard of Avon. His contribution to the world included such masterpieces as *Romeo & Juliet, Hamlet, Othello, Macbeth* and *King Lear. Intaglio, perforated 10 1/2 X 11.*

CM535 *William Shakespeare*

CM535		MNHVF	UseVF
5¢	**brown** on tan paper *(123,245,000)*	.20	.20
	Plate block of 4	.65	
	FDC *(Aug. 14, 1964)*		1.00

1964. Doctors Mayo Issue honored the birth of William J. Mayo and his brother Charles H. Mayo and the 50th anniversary of the founding of the world-famous Mayo Clinic in Rochester, Minn. *Intaglio, perforated 10 1/2 X 11.*

CM536 *Statue of the Mayo brothers*

CM536		MNHVF	UseVF
5¢	**green** *(123,355,000)*	.20	.20
	Plate block of 4	1.50	
	FDC *(Sept. 11, 1964)*		1.00

1964. American Music Issue commemorated the 50th anniversary of the American Society of Composers, Authors and Publishers. *Intaglio (Giori Press), perforated 11.*

CM537 *Lute and horn, music score, oak and laurel*

CM537		MNHVF	UseVF
5¢	**red, gray & blue** on granite paper *(126,370,000)*	.20	.20
	Plate block of 4	.85	
	v. blue omitted	1,000.00	
	FDC *(Oct. 15, 1964)*		1.00

1964. Homemakers Issue commemorated the 50th anniversary of the Smith-Lever Act that improved home life in America. It was issued in conjunction with the annual meeting of the National Extension Homemakers Council. This was the first time the Bureau of Engraving and Printing combined offset and intaglio printing on a stamp, a method used by the American Bank Note Company to print the Overrun Countries stamps (CM251-63). *Intaglio (Giori Press) and offset, perforated 11.*

CM538 *Needlepoint sampler of American farm scene*

CM538		MNHVF	UseVF
5¢	**multicolored** on buff *(121,250,000)*	.20	.20
	Plate block of 4	.85	
	FDC *(Oct. 26, 1964)*		1.00

We regret that we cannot pass upon the authenticity of any stamp. Should you have stamps for which you desire authenticiation, we suggest that you contact a recognized expertizing service. Expertizing committees offer opinions only, not guarantees. Opinions may vary among services, and over the years an opinion may change.

1964. Verrazano-Narrows Bridge Issue marked the dedication of what was the longest single suspension bridge in the world. Named for the Florentine explorer who discovered New York Bay in 1524, the span links Staten Island and Brooklyn, N.Y. *Intaglio, perforated 10 1/2 X 11.*

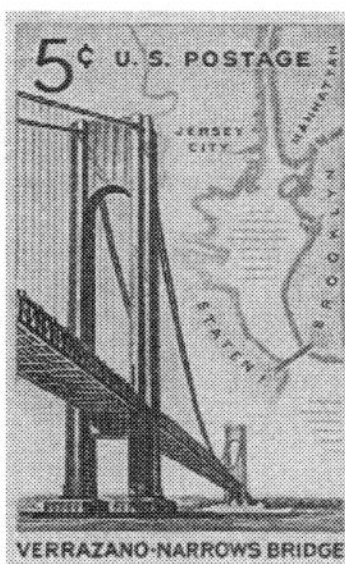

CM539 *Verrazano-Narrows Bridge and map*

CM539		MNHVF	UseVF
5¢	**green** *(125,005,000)*	.20	.20
	Plate block of 4	.65	
	FDC *(Nov. 21, 1964)*		1.00

1964. Abstract Art Issue is the fifth in the Fine Arts Series commemoratives. It is based on a lithograph by the late Stuart Davis. *Intaglio (Giori Press), perforated 11.*

CM540 Melange of Squiggles *by Stuart Davis*

CM540		MNHVF	UseVF
5¢	**blue, black & red** *(125,800,000)*	.20	.20
	Plate block of 4	.65	
	FDC *(Dec. 2, 1964)*		1.00

1964. Amateur Radio Operators Issue paid tribute to the nation's 250,000 "hams" and their long record of service to the country in emergencies and marked the 50th anniversary of the American Radio Relay League. *Intaglio, perforated 10 1/2 X 11.*

CM541 *Radio dial and wave*

CM541		MNHVF	UseVF
5¢	**purple** *(122,230,000)*	.20	.20
	Plate block of 4	.90	
	FDC *(Dec. 15, 1964)*		1.00

1965. Battle of New Orleans Issue saluted 150 years of peace between England and the United States and the sesquicentennial of the famous battle between American forces under Gen. Andrew Jackson and the British troops led by Sir Edward Packenham. *Intaglio (Giori Press), perforated 11.*

CM542 *Gen. Andrew Jackson leading troops in battle and sesquicentennial medal*

CM542		MNHVF	UseVF
5¢	**carmine, blue & slate** *(115,695,000)*	.20	.20
	Plate block of 4	.65	
	FDC *(Jan. 8, 1964)*		1.00

1965. Sokol Centennial - Physical Fitness Issue paid tribute to the program initiated by President Kennedy and the 100th anniversary of the Sokol educational and physical fitness organization. *Intaglio (Giori Press), perforated 11.*

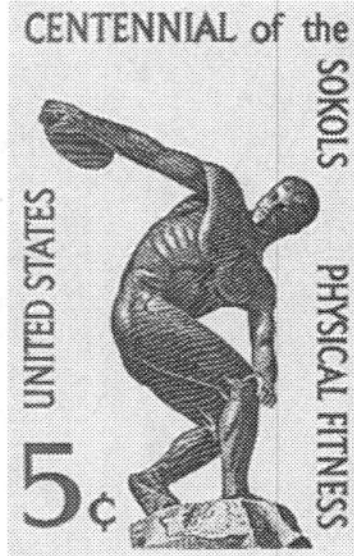

CM543 *Discus thrower*

CM543		MNHVF	UseVF
5¢	**lake & deep slate** *(115,095,000)*	.20	.20
	Plate block of 4	.65	
	FDC *(Feb. 15, 1965)*		1.00

1965. Crusade Against Cancer Issue publicized the importance of medical checkups and prompt treatment and saluted the efforts of those dedicated to eradicating cancer. *Intaglio (Giori Press), perforated 11.*

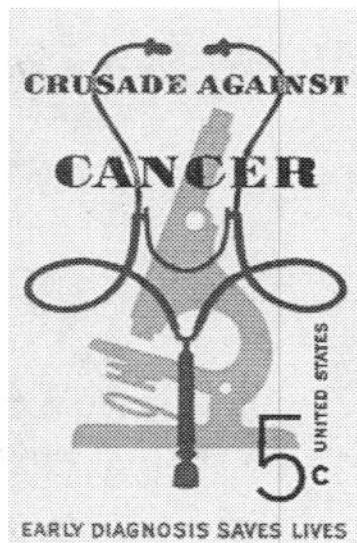

CM544 *Stethoscope and microscope*

CM544		MNHVF	UseVF
5¢	**reddish violet, black & red** *(116,560,000)*	.20	.20
	Plate block of 4	.65	
	FDC *(April 1, 1965)*		1.00

1965. Winston Churchill Memorial Issue honored the World War II British leader (1874-1965) who was an honorary American citizen. *Intaglio, perforated 10 1/2 X 11.*

CM545 *Winston Churchill*

CM545		MNHVF	UseVF
5¢	**black** *(125,180,000)*	.20	.20
	Plate block of 4	.65	
	FDC *(May 13, 1965)*		1.00

1965. Magna Carta Issue commemorated the 750th anniversary of the document signed by King John that became the first detailed statement of English feudal law esteemed by many as a cornerstone of later British and American law. *Intaglio (Giori Press), perforated 11.*

CM546 Triumph of the People Over the King, *symbolic design by Brook Temple*

CM546		MNHVF	UseVF
5¢	**black, yellow & reddish-violet** *(120,135,000)*	.20	.20
	Plate block of 4 (2 numbers)	.65	
	v. Plate block of 4, black plate number omitted	—	
	FDC *(June 15, 1965)*		1.00

1965. UN International Cooperation Year Issue commemorated the 20th anniversary of the United Nations. The United States and other U.N. member nations issued stamps dedicated to the theme, and the United Nations issued a set of two stamps and a souvenir sheet on the same day as this U.S. stamp. *Intaglio (Giori Press), perforated 11.*

CM547 *International Cooperation Year emblem*

CM547		MNHVF	UseVF
5¢	**turquoise blue & slate** *(115,405,000)*	.20	.20
	Plate block of 4	.65	
	FDC *(June 26, 1965)*		1.00

1965. Salvation Army Issue marked the 100th anniversary of this non-sectarian international organization. Founded in London by William Booth in 1865, the Salvation Army was established in the United States in 1880. *Intaglio (Giori Press), perforated 11.*

CM548 *Salvation Army*

CM548		MNHVF	UseVF
5¢	**red, black & deep blue** *(115,855,000)*	.20	.20
	Plate block of 4	.65	
	FDC *(July 2, 1965)*		1.00

1965. Dante Alighieri Issue marked the 700th birthday of Italy's poet who wrote *The Divine Comedy. Intaglio, perforated 10 1/2 X 11.*

CM549 *Dante Alighieri, adapted from a 16th-century painting*

CM549		MNHVF	UseVF
5¢	**carmine red** on light venetian red paper *(115,340,000)*	.20	.20
	Plate block of 4	.65	
	FDC *(July 17, 1965)*		1.00

1965. Herbert Hoover Issue paid tribute to the 31st president of the United States (1874-1964) who died Oct. 20, 1964. He was a talented mining engineer and served the country in many capacities, including secretary of commerce under Harding. *Intaglio, perforated 10 1/2 X 11.*

CM550 *Herbert Hoover*

CM550		MNHVF	UseVF
5¢	**red** *(114,840,000)*	.20	.20
	Plate block of 4	.65
	FDC *(Aug. 10, 1965)*		1.00

1965. Robert Fulton Issue commemorated the 200th birthday of the inventor (1765-1815) who built the first successful steamship, *The Clermont,* in 1807. *Intaglio (Giori Press), perforated 11.*

CM551 *Robert Fulton* and The Clermont

CM551		MNHVF	UseVF
5¢	**blue & black** *(116,140,000)*	.20	.20
	Plate block of 4	.65
	FDC *(Aug. 19, 1965)*		1.00

1965. European Settlement Issue commemorated the 400th anniversary of the establishment by Spanish colonists of a permanent settlement in Florida in September 1565. Spain released a joint issue marking this event (Spain 1715). *Intaglio (Giori Press), perforated 11.*

CM552 *Spanish explorer and ships*

CM552		MNHVF	UseVF
5¢	**yellow, red & black** *(116,900,000)*	.20	.20
	Plate block of 4	.65
	v. yellow omitted	400.00
	FDC *(Aug. 28, 1965)*		1.00

1965. Traffic Safety Issue called attention to the urgent need to reduce automotive accidents. *Intaglio (Giori Press), perforated 11.*

CM553 *Traffic signal*

CM553		MNHVF	UseVF
5¢	**green, black & red** *(114,085,000)*	.20	.20
	Plate block of 4	.65
	FDC *(Sept. 3, 1965)*		1.00

1965. John Singleton Copley Issue the sixth stamp in the Fine Arts Series, featured a portrait of the artist's daughter, part of a family group painted in 1776 by Copley. The original hangs in the National Gallery of Art, Washington, D.C. *Intaglio (Giori Press), perforated 11.*

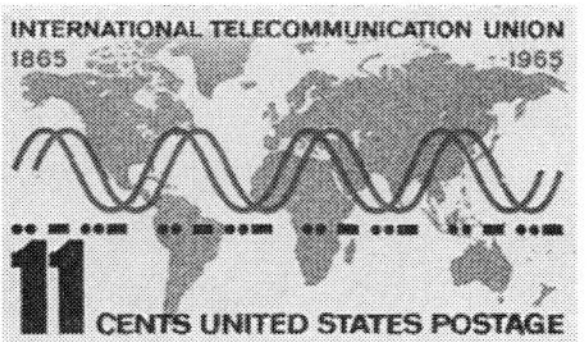

CM554 *Elizabeth Clarke Copley*

CM554		MNHVF	UseVF
5¢	**black & tones of brown & olive** *(114,880,000)*	.20	.20
	Plate block of 4	.65
	FDC *(Sept. 17, 1965)*		1.00

1965. International Telecommunication Union Issue commemorated the 100th anniversary of this international organization created in 1865 to develop electronic communication among nations. *Intaglio (Giori Press), perforated 11.*

CM555 *World map and radio wave*

CM555		MNHVF	UseVF
11¢	**yellow, red & black** *(26,995,000)*	.20	.20
	Plate block of 4	5.50
	FDC *(Oct. 6, 1965)*		1.00

1965. Adlai Stevenson Issue paid tribute to the late U.S. ambassador to the United Nations, governor of Illinois, and presidential candidate (1900-1965). *Intaglio (Giori Press) and offset, perforated 11.*

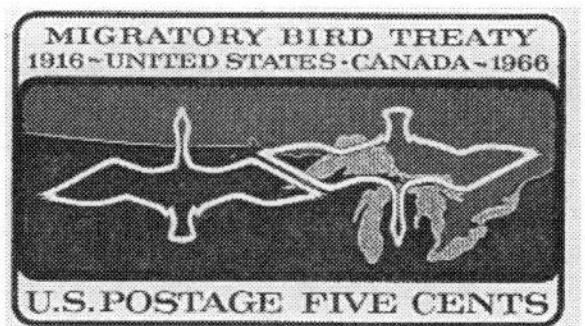

CM556 *Adlai Stevenson, U.N. wreath and U.S. colors*

CM556		MNHVF	UseVF
5¢	**light blue gray, black, red & blue** *(128,495,000)*	.20	.20
	Plate block of 4	.65
	FDC *(Oct. 23, 1965)*		1.00

1966. Migratory Bird Treaty Issue marked the 50th anniversary of cooperation between the United States and Canada in protecting birds. *Intaglio (Giori Press), perforated 11.*

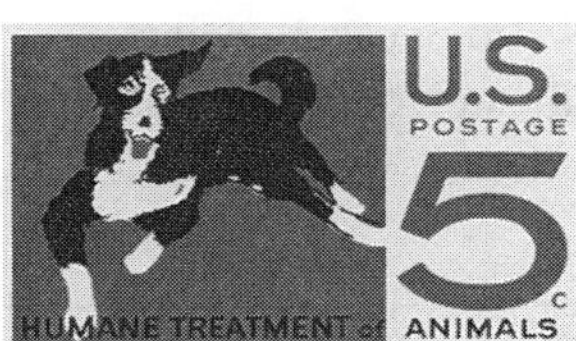

CM557 *Birds over the Great Lakes*

CM557		MNHVF	UseVF
5¢	**red, blue & light blue** *(116,835,000)*	.25	.20
	Plate block of 4	.65
	FDC *(March 16, 1966)*		1.00

1966. Humane Treatment of Animals Issue paid tribute to The American Society for the Prevention of Cruelty to Animals, founded in 1866 by Henry Bergh. *Intaglio (Giori Press) and offset, perforated 11.*

CM558 *"Babe" the dog*

CM558		MNHVF	UseVF
5¢	**reddish brown & black** *(117,470,000)*	.25	.20
	Plate block of 4	.65
	FDC *(April 9, 1966)*		1.00

1966. Indiana Statehood Issue marked the 150th anniversary of Indiana's admission to the union as the 19th state. The event was officially celebrated at Corydon, the first capital of Indiana. *Intaglio (Giori Press), perforated 11.*

CM559 *Map of Indiana and old capitol*

CM559		MNHVF	UseVF
5¢	**blue, yellow & brown** *(123,770,000)*	.25	.20
	Plate block of 4	.65	
	FDC *(April 16, 1966)*		1.00

1966. American Circus Issue saluted the Big Top and those who bring fun and thrills to audiences throughout the nation. *Intaglio (Giori Press), perforated 11.*

CM560 *Circus clown*

CM560		MNHVF	UseVF
5¢	**red, blue, pink & black** *(131,270,000)*	.25	.20
	Plate block of 4	.90	
	FDC *(May 2, 1966)*		1.00

1966. Sixth International Philatelic Exhibition Issue commemorated the show, held in Washington, D.C., May 21-30. This commemorative stamp and souvenir sheet (and a related airmail postal card, PCA5) were issued to mark the event. *Intaglio (Giori Press) and offset, perforated 11.*

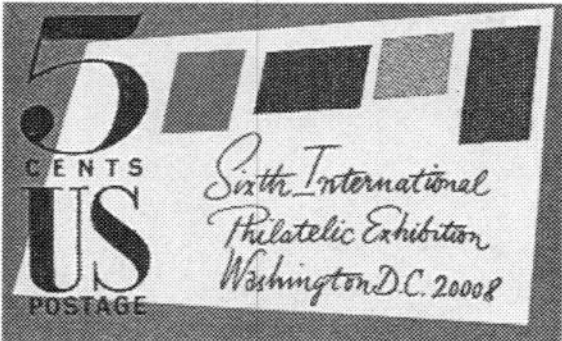

CM561 *Envelope with stamps*

CM561		MNHVF	UseVF
5¢	**multicolored** *(122,285,000)*	.25	.20
	Plate block of 4	.65	
	FDC *(May 21, 1966)*		1.00

Users of this catalog are invited to write to us if they have information they feel will supplement or correct any material contained herein. All such communications will be answered.

1966. SIPEX Souvenir Sheet dedicated to stamp collectors also features the words "Discover America," the theme of President Johnson's program to stimulate travel and tourism in the United States. *Intaglio (Giori Press) and offset, imperforate.*

CM562 *Envelope and Capitol scene*

CM562		MNHVF	UseVF
5¢	**multicolored** *(14,680,000)*	.30	.25
	FDC *(May 23, 1966)*		1.00

1966. Bill of Rights Issue commemorated the 175th anniversary of the first 10 amendments to the U.S. Constitution. The stamp was designed by Herbert L. Block, renowned editorial cartoonist. *Intaglio (Giori Press), perforated 11.*

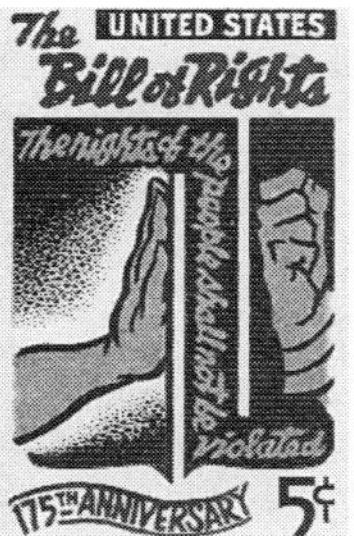

CM563 *"Freedom Conquers Tyranny"*

CM563		MNHVF	UseVF
5¢	**red & blue** *(114,160,000)*	.25	.20
	Plate block of 4	.65	
	FDC *(July 1, 1966)*		1.00

1966. Polish Millennium Issue commemorated the 1,000th anniversary of Poland and paid tribute to the longstanding friendship between Americans and the Polish people. *Intaglio, perforated 10 1/2 x 11.*

CM564 *Polish eagle*

CM564		MNHVF	UseVF
5¢	**red** *(126,475,000)*	.25	.20
	Plate block of 4	.65	
	FDC *(July 30, 1966)*		1.00

1966. National Park Service Issue paid tribute to the 50th anniversary of the National Park Service. Although the national park system dates back to 1872, it was first established as a bureau under the Department of Interior Aug. 25, 1916. *Intaglio (Giori Press) and offset, perforated 11.*

CM565 *National Park Service emblem*

CM565		MNHVF	UseVF
5¢	**multicolored** *(119,535,000)*	.25	.20
	Plate block of 4	.80	
	FDC *(Aug. 25, 1966)*		1.00
	z. Tagged	.30	.25

		MNHVF	UseVF
	Plate block of 4, tagged	2.00	
	FDC, tagged *(Aug. 26, 1966)*	—	30.00
	zl. Tagged after perforating	.30	
	Plate block of 4, with untagged left margin	2.00	
	FDC (Washington, D.C.) *(Aug. 26, 1966)*		—
	z2. Tagging inverted		
	Plate block of 4	—	
	z3. Error (untagged), side-margin strip of 20 with plate and ZIP, with tagged and untagged errors on same piece	1.40	

Stamps tagged after perforation can be distinguished by a grid of tagging which connects the perforation holes on the gummed side of unused stamps and perforation-sized disc-like blemishes in the tagging on the face of the stamps. Untagged gripper margins, about 3/8-inch in width, were intended to appear in left sheet margins, but some sheets were put through the offset tagging press with the underlying design inverted, resulting in errors with tagging absent in the opposite margins.

Values shown for the untagged errors are for strips of at least five stamps with both tagged and untagged specimens on a single piece.

For more information on tagging, see the introduction.

1966. Marine Corps Reserve Issue celebrated the 50th anniversary of the military organization. *Intaglio (Giori Press) and offset, perforated 11.*

CM566 *U.S. Marines 1775-1966*

CM566		MNHVF	UseVF
5¢	**black, olive, red & blue** *(125,110,000)*	.25	.20
	Plate block of 4	.65	
	FDC *(Aug. 29, 1966)*		1.00
	z. Tagged	.30	.25
	Plate block of 4, tagged	2.00	
	FDC, tagged *(Aug. 29, 1966)*		30.00
	z1. Error (untagged), strip of 5 showing both tagged and untagged on same piece.	—	
	v. black and olive omitted	15,400.00	

1966. General Federation of Women's Clubs Issue commemorated 75 years of service ranging from aiding school dropouts to aiding international understanding, and the millions of women who are members of the clubs and associate organizations. *Intaglio (Giori Press), perforated 11.*

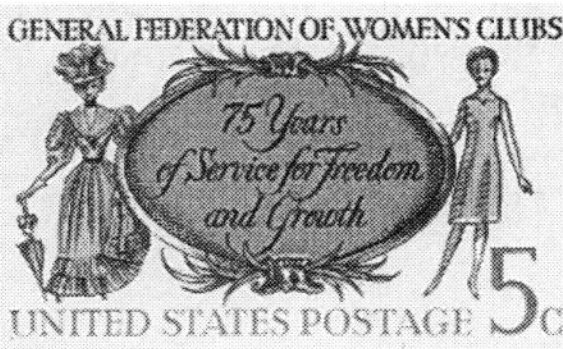

CM567 *Women of 1890s and 1960s*

CM567		MNHVF	UseVF
5¢	**pink, blue & black** *(114,853,000)*	.25	.20
	Plate block of 4	.65	
	FDC *(Sept. 12, 1966)*		30.00
	z. Tagged	.30	.25
	Plate block of 4	2.00	
	FDC *(Sept. 13, 1966)*		30.00

American Folklore Series

1966. Johnny Appleseed Issue the inaugural stamp in the American Folklore Series, honored John Chapman, eccentric nurseryman who devoted his life to planting apple trees in Pennsylvania, Ohio and Indiana. It is reputed that he covered over 100,000 square miles before his death in 1845. *Intaglio (Giori Press), perforated 11.*

CM568 *Johnny Appleseed and apple*

CM568		MNHVF	UseVF
5¢	**black, red & green** *(124,290,000)*	.25	.20
	Plate block of 4	.65	
	FDC *(Sept. 24, 1966)*		1.00
	z. Tagged	.30	.25
	Plate block of 4	2.00	
	FDC *(Sept. 26, 1966)*		1.00

1966. Beautification of America Issue publicized the campaign to restore and enhance the beauty of the country. *Intaglio (Giori Press), perforated 11.*

CM569 *Jefferson Memorial and cherry blossoms*

CM569		MNHVF	UseVF
5¢	**black, green & pink** *(128,460,000)*	.25	.20
	Plate block of 4	.65	
	FDC *(Oct. 5, 1966)*		1.00
	z. Tagged	.30	.25
	Plate block of 4	2.00	
	FDC *(Oct. 5, 1966)*		30.00
	z1. Tagged after perforating	.30	
	Plate block of 4, untagged right margin	2.00	
	z2. Tagged after perforating (error), untagged *left* margin	1.75	
	Plate block of 4	2.00	

1966. Great River Road Issue publicized the longest parkway in the world, stretching from Kenora, Canada, southward to New Orleans, a distance of 5,600 miles. *Intaglio (Giori Press) and offset, perforated 11.*

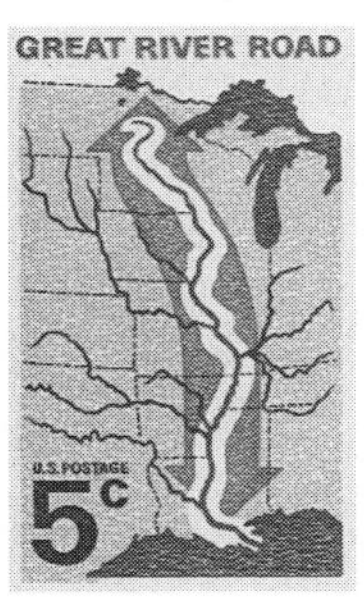

CM570 *Map of Mississippi River and road*

CM570		MNHVF	UseVF
5¢	**salmon, blue, olive yellow & yellow green** *(127,585,000)*	.25	.20
	Plate block of 4	.65	
	FDC *(Oct. 21, 1966)*		1.00
	z. Tagged	.30	.25
	Plate block of 4	2.00	
	FDC *(Oct. 22, 1966)* tagged		30.00

1966. U.S. Savings Bond Issue saluted 25 years of bond sales and carried the message, "We Appreciate Our Servicemen." *Intaglio (Giori Press) and offset, perforated 11.*

CM571 *Statue of Liberty and U.S. flag*

CM571		**MNHVF**	**UseVF**
5¢	**red, blue & black** *(115,875,000)*	.25	.20
	Plate block of 4	.75	
	FDC *(Oct. 26, 1966)*		1.00
	v. red, black and dark blue omitted	5,000.00	
	v1. dark blue omitted	8,000.00	
	z. Tagged	.30	.25
	Plate block of 4	2.00	
	FDC *(Oct. 27, 1966)* tagged		30.00

1966. Mary Cassatt Issue the seventh in the Fine Arts Series, paid tribute to the American painter whom many critics regard as the greatest female artist. Cassatt (1844-1926) was the only American, besides Whistler, to have her work hang in the Louvre. (See No. 915.) *Intaglio (Giori Press), perforated 11.*

CM572 The Boating Party

CM572		**MNHVF**	**UseVF**
5¢	**multicolored** *(114,015,000)*	.25	.20
	Plate block of 4	.75	
	FDC *(Nov. 17, 1966)*		1.00
	z. Tagged	.30	.25
	Plate block of 4	—	
	FDC *(Nov. 17, 1966)* tagged		30.00

1967. National Grange Issue commemorated the 100th anniversary of the farmers' organization founded by Oliver H. Kelley to help farmers develop economically and culturally. Its sphere of activities has broadened to include scholarships and aid to underdeveloped nations. *Intaglio (Giori Press), perforated 11.*

CM573 *Grange poster of 1870*

CM573		**MNHVF**	**UseVF**
5¢	**brownish orange, green, orange & black** *(121,105,000)*	.25	.20
	Plate block of 4	.65	
	FDC *(April 17, 1967)*		1.00
	zo. Tagging omitted	3.50	

1967. Canada Centennial Issue commemorated the anniversary of Canada's Confederation. The stamp was first sold at the U.S. pavilion at Expo '67 in Montreal. *Intaglio (Giori Press), perforated 11.*

CM574 *Abstract Canadian landscape*

CM574		**MNHVF**	**UseVF**
5¢	**blue, green, dark blue & olive green,** tagged *(132,045,000)*	.25	.20
	Plate block of 4	.65	
	FDC *(May 26, 1967)*		1.00
	zo. Tagging omitted	4.50	

1967. Erie Canal Sesquicentennial Issue celebrated the engineering feat that linked Lake Erie with New York City. This 363-mile man-made waterway contributed to the economic development of the young nation. *Intaglio (Giori Press) and offset, perforate 11.*

CM575 *Canal boat*

CM575		**MNHVF**	**UseVF**
5¢	**dark blue, light blue, black red,** tagged *(118,780,000)*	.25	.20
	Plate block of 4	.65	
	FDC *(July 4, 1967)*		1.00
	zo. Tagging omitted	10.00	

1967. Lions International Issue saluted the world's largest volunteer service organization on its 50th anniversary. The theme of the stamp, "Search for Peace," was that of an essay contest sponsored by the Lions. *Intaglio (Giori Press), perforated 11.*

CM576 *Dove of peace and olive branch*

CM576		**MNHVF**	**UseVF**
5¢	**red, blue & black** on granite paper, tagged *(121,985,000)*	.25	.20
	Plate block of 4	.80	
	FDC *(July 5, 1967)*		1.00
	zo. Tagging omitted	4.00	

1967. Henry David Thoreau Issue honored the 19th-century essayist (1817-62) on the 150th anniversary of his birth. His writings reflect his love of nature and his belief in the dignity of all mankind. *Intaglio (Giori Press) and offset, perforated 11.*

CM577 *Henry David Thoreau*

CM577		**MNHVF**	**UseVF**
5¢	**red, black & green** tagged *(111,850,000)*	.25	.20
	Plate block of 4	.65	
	FDC *(July 12, 1967)*		1.00
	zo. Tagging omitted	—	

1967. Nebraska Statehood Issue marked the centennial of the state's entry into the union as the 37th state. *Intaglio (Giori Press), perforated 11.*

CM578 *Cattle and corn*

CM578		MNHVF	UseVF
5¢	**yellow, green & brown** tagged *(117,225,000)*	.25	.20
	Plate block of 4	.65	
	FDC *(July 29, 1967)*		1.00
	zo. Tagging omitted	5.00	

1967. Voice of America Issue paid tribute to the radio branch of the U.S. Information Agency on its 25th anniversary. *Intaglio (Giori Press), perforated 11.*

CM579 *Radio tower transmitting*

CM579		MNHVF	UseVF
5¢	**red, blue & black** tagged *(111,515,000)*	.25	.20
	Plate block of 4	.65	
	FDC *(Aug. 1, 1967)*		1.00
	zo. Tagging omitted	5.00	

1967. Davy Crockett Issue the second stamp in the American Folklore Series, honored the Tennessee backwoodsman who gained fame as a trapper, hunter, soldier and public official and died at the Alamo. *Intaglio (Giori Press), perforated 11.*

CM580 *Davy Crockett*

CM580		MNHVF	UseVF
5¢	**green, black & yellow** tagged *(114,270,000)*	.25	.20
	Plate block of 4	.85	
	FDC *(Aug. 17, 1967)*		1.00
	v. green omitted	—	
	v1. green and black omitted	—	
	v2. green and yellow omitted	—	
	v3. Vertical pair, imperforate between	6,000.00	
	zo. Tagging omitted	4.50	

1967. Space Twins Issue saluted America's achievements in space. For the first time, the United States printed two se-tenant stamps that blend into one complete design. *Intaglio (Giori Press) and offset, perforated 11.*

CM581-82 *Spacewalking astronaut and Gemini capsule*

CM581		MNHVF	UseVF
5¢	**dark blue, black & red** tagged *(120,865,000)*	1.00	.35

CM582		MNHVF	UseVF
5¢	**dark blue, red & blue, green** tagged	1.00	.35
	y. Se-tenant pair, CM581-82	2.00	1.50
	Plate block of 4	4.50	
	FDC, single *(Sept. 29, 1967)*		5.00
	FDC, pair		10.00
	zo. Tagging omitted, any single	5.00	
	zoy. Tagging omitted, pair	10.00	

1967. Urban Planning Issue publicized the need to improve and develop American cities. *Intaglio (Giori Press), perforated 11.*

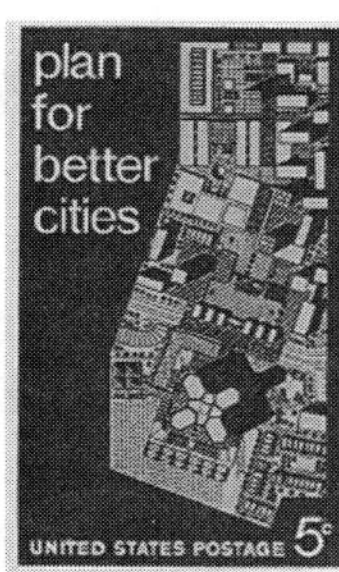

CM583 *Overhead view of model city*

CM583		MNHVF	UseVF
5¢	**dark blue, light blue & black** tagged *(110,675,000)*	.25	.20
	Plate block of 4	.65	
	FDC *(Oct. 2, 1967)*		1.00
	zo. Tagging omitted	—	

1967. Finland Independence Issue honored the 50th anniversary of Finnish sovereignty. *Intaglio (Giori Press), perforated 11.*

CM584 *Finnish coat of arms*

CM584		MNHVF	UseVF
5¢	**blue** tagged *(110,670,000)*	.25	.20
	Plate block of 4	.65	
	FDC *(Oct. 6, 1967)*		1.00
	zo. Tagging omitted	—	

1967. Thomas Eakins Issue the eighth stamp in the Fine Arts Series, honored an American artist who gained fame for his paintings of athletic events, portraits and early American life. A professor of anatomy at the Pennsylvania Academy of Fine Arts, Eakins' thorough knowledge of this subject is reflected in his works. The first U.S. postage stamp using the *gravure* method. The issue was printed by the Photogravure and Color Co., Moonachie, N.J. *Perforated 12.*

CM585 The Biglin Brothers Racing

CM585		MNHVF	UseVF
5¢	**gold & multicolored** tagged *(113,825,000)*	.25	.20
	Plate block of 4	.65	
	FDC *(Nov. 2, 1967)*		1.00
	zo. Tagging omitted	6.00	

1967. Mississippi Statehood Issue honored the 150th anniversary of the Magnolia State's entry into the union as the 20th state. *Intaglio (Giori Press), perforated 11.*

CM586 *Magnolia blossom*

CM586		MNHVF	UseVF
5¢	**green blue, blue green & brown** tagged *(113,330,000)*	.25	.20
	Plate block of 4	.75	
	FDC *(Dec. 11, 1967)*		1.00
	zo. Tagging omitted	5.00	

1968. Illinois Statehood Issue marked the 150th anniversary of the state's entry into the union as the 21st state. *Intaglio (Giori Press), perforated 11.*

CM587 *Illinois farm scene*

CM587		MNHVF	UseVF
6¢	**multicolored** tagged *(141,350,000)*	.25	.20
	Plate block of 4	.85	
	FDC *(Feb. 12, 1968)*		1.00
	zo. Tagging omitted	—	

1968. Hemisfair '68 Issue celebrated the international exposition that opened in San Antonio, Texas, April 6. The theme was "The Confluence of Civilizations in the Americas," and the stamp also commemorated the 250th anniversary of San Antonio. *Intaglio (Giori Press) and offset, perforated 11.*

CM588 *North and South America with lines converging on San Antonio*

CM588		MNHVF	UseVF
6¢	**blue, pink, & white** tagged *(117,470,600)*	.25	.20
	Plate block of 4	.85	
	FDC *(March 30, 1968)*		1.00
	v. white omitted	1,400.00	

1968. Support Our Youth Issue honored the Benevolent and Protective Order of Elks' centennial year and the expansion of its youth service program. *Intaglio (Giori Press), perforated 11.*

CM589 *Young Americans*

CM589		MNHVF	UseVF
6¢	**red & blue** tagged *(147,120,000)*	.25	.20
	Plate block of 4	.85	
	FDC *(May 1, 1968)*		1.00
	zo. Tagging omitted	5.00	

1968. Law and Order Issue publicized the work of the law enforcement officer as a protector and friend of the people. *Intaglio (Giori Press), perforated 11.*

CM590 *Policeman and young friend*

CM590		MNHVF	UseVF
6¢	**red, blue & black** tagged *(130,125,000)*	.25	.20
	Plate block of 4	.85	
	FDC *(May 17, 1968)*		1.00
	zo. Tagging omitted	—	

1968. Register and Vote Issue supported the efforts of the American Heritage Foundation and others in making the public aware of its civic obligation to vote. *Intaglio (Giori Press) and offset, perforated 11.*

CM591 *Eagle weathervane*

CM591		MNHVF	UseVF
6¢	**gold and black** tagged *(158,070,000)*	.25	.20
	Plate block of 4	.85	
	FDC *(June 27, 1968)*		1.00
	zo. Tagging omitted	—	

1968. Historic Flags Issue saluted 10 banners from America's struggle for independence. Nine of the flags were selected because of their important roles in the Revolutionary War period. One flag, the one flown at Fort McHenry, inspired Francis Scott Key to write the "Star Spangled Banner" during the War of 1812. *Intaglio (Giori Press) and offset, perforated 11.*

CM592 *Fort Moultrie flag (1776)*

CM592		MNHVF	UseVF
6¢	**blue** tagged *(228,040,000)*	.40	.30

CM593 *Fort McHenry flag (1795-1818)*

CM593		MNHVF	UseVF
6¢	**red & blue** tagged	.40	.30

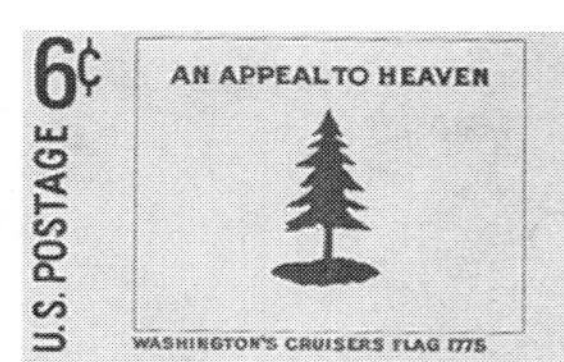

CM594 *Washington's Cruisers flag (1775)*

CM594		MNHVF	UseVF
6¢	**green & blue** tagged	.40	.30

CM595 *Bennington flag (1777)*

CM595		MNHVF	UseVF
6¢	**red & blue** tagged	.40	.30

CM596 *Rhode Island flag (1775)*

CM596		MNHVF	UseVF
6¢	**gold & blue** tagged	.40	.30

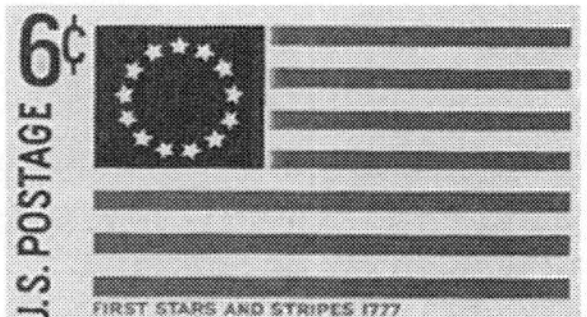

CM597 *First Stars and Stripes (1777)*

CM597		MNHVF	UseVF
6¢	**red & blue** tagged	.40	.30

CM598 *Bunker Hill flag (1775)*

CM598		MNHVF	UseVF
6¢	**red, green & blue** tagged	.40	.30

CM599 *Grand Union flag (1776)*

CM599		MNHVF	UseVF
6¢	**red & blue** tagged	.40	.30

CM600 *Philadelphia Light Horse flag (1775)*

CM600		MNHVF	UseVF
6¢	**multicolored** tagged	.40	.30

CM601 *First Navy Jack (1775)*

CM601		MNHVF	UseVF
6¢	**red, gold & blue** tagged	.40	.30
	Plate block of 20	7.50	
	y. Se-tenant strip of 10 (CM592-601)	3.50	4.00
	FDC, *(July 4, 1968),* any single		2.00
	FDC, strip of 10		8.50
	zo. Tagging omitted, any single	—	
	zoy. Tagging omitted se-tenant strip of 10	—	

Because the plate number is attached to a vertical column of 10 different stamps, plate block of 20 is listed.

1968. Walt Disney Issue hailed the creative genius who brought a new dimension to entertainment with his animated cartoons, full-length films and theme parks. The creator of Mickey Mouse, Donald Duck and other lovable characters built a multi-million dollar entertainment empire. *Gravure by Achrovure Division of Union-Camp Corp., Englewood, N.J., perforated 12.*

CM602 *Walt Disney and cartoon children*

CM602		MNHVF	UseVF
6¢	**multicolored** tagged *(153,015,000)*	.25	.20
	Plate block of 4	2.10	
	FDC *(Sept. 11, 1968)*		1.00
	v. Horizontal pair, imperforate between	5,000.00	
	v1. Pair, imperforate	675.00	
	v2. Vertical pair, imperforate horizontally	650.00	
	v3. black omitted	2,000.00	
	v4. blue omitted	2,150.00	
	v5. yellow omitted	600.00	
	zo. Tagging omitted	7.50	

1968. Father Jacques Marquette Issue honored the French explorer-missionary (CM17) who in 1668 established what is considered the oldest permanent settlement in Michigan. *Intaglio (Giori Press) and offset, perforated 11.*

CM603 *Jacques Marquette and Louis Joliet in canoe*

CM603		MNHVF	UseVF
6¢	**black, green & brown** tagged *(132,560,000)*	.25	.20
	Plate block of 4	.85	
	FDC *(Sept. 20, 1968)*		1.00
	zo. Tagging omitted	6.00	

1968. Daniel Boone Issue the third commemorative in the American Folklore Series, recalled the frontiersman whose exploits inspired historians and fiction writers to record the remarkable achievements of this heroic hunter, trapper, soldier and public servant. *Intaglio (Giori Press) and offset, perforated 11.*

CM604 *Pipe tomahawk, powder horn, rifle, and knife*

CM604		MNHVF	UseVF
6¢	**red brown, brown, yellow & black** tagged *(130,385,000)*	.25	.20
	Plate block of 4	.85	
	FDC *(Sept. 26, 1968)*		1.00
	zo. Tagging omitted	—	

1968. Arkansas River Navigation Issue paid tribute to this important waterway and the economic potential of the $1.2 billion project. *Intaglio (Giori Press) and offset, perforated 11.*

CM605 *Ship's wheel and transmission tower*

CM605		MNHVF	UseVF
6¢	**blue, black & dark blue** tagged *(132,265,000)*	.25	.20
	Plate block of 4	.85	
	FDC *(Oct. 1, 1968)*		1.00
	zo. Tagging omitted	—	

1968. Leif Erikson Issue honored the 11th century Norseman, whose navigational skills and daring brought him to the Americas 500 years before Christopher Columbus. *Intaglio (Giori Press) and offset, perforated 11.*

CM606 *Statue of Leif Erikson by A. Stirling Calder*

CM606		MNHVF	UseVF
6¢	**brown** *(128,710,000)*	.25	.20
	Plate block of 4	.85	
	FDC *(Oct. 9, 1968)*		1.00

1968. Cherokee Strip Issue marked the 75th anniversary of the historic land run by more than 100,000 would-be homesteaders into northern Oklahoma, competing for the 40,000 available homesites. *Rotary press printing, perforated 11.*

CM607 *Racing for homesteads*

CM607		MNHVF	UseVF
6¢	**brown** tagged *(124,775,000)*	.25	.20
	Plate block of 4	.85	
	FDC *(Oct. 15 1968)*		1.00
	zo. Tagging omitted	5.00	

1968. John Trumbull Issue the ninth stamp in the Fine Arts Series, honored an artist noted for his paintings of Revolutionary War scenes. The design came from an original painting at Yale University, New Haven, Conn. *Intaglio (Giori Press) and offset, perforated 11.*

CM608 *Lt. Thomas Grosvenor and Peter Salem, detail from* The Battle of Bunker's Hill

CM608		MNHVF	UseVF
6¢	**multicolored** tagged *(128,295,000)*	.25	.20
	Plate block of 4	.90	
	FDC *(Oct. 18, 1968)*		1.00
	zo. Tagging omitted	20.00	
	Pane, black (engraved) omitted	21,000.00	

1968. Waterfowl Conservation Issue pointed out the need for protecting waterfowl and their habitats. *Intaglio (Giori Press) and offset, perforated 11.*

CM609 *Wood ducks in flight*

CM609		MNHVF	UseVF
6¢	**multicolored** *(142,245,000)*	.25	.20
	Plate block of 4	1.10	
	FDC *(Oct. 24, 1968)*		1.00
	v. dark blue and red omitted	800.00	
	v1. Vertical pair, imperforate between	525.00	

1968. Chief Joseph Issue was released in conjunction with the dedication of the National Portrait Gallery in Washington, D.C. A portrait of the stamp subject, Chief Joseph, hangs in the gallery, which is part of the Smithsonian Institution. *Intaglio and offset, perforated 11.*

CM610 Chief Joseph, *painting by Cyrenius Hall*

CM610		MNHVF	UseVF
6¢	**multicolored** tagged *(125,100,000)*	.25	.20
	Plate block of 4	1.10	
	FDC *(Nov. 4, 1968)*		1.00
	zo. Tagging omitted	—	

1969. Beautification of America Issue encouraged the participation of all Americans in a nationwide natural beauty campaign. Four se-tenant stamp designs appear in the same pane of 50 stamps. *Intaglio (Giori Press), perforated 11.*

CM611 *Azaleas, Tulips and Capitol building*

CM612 *Daffodils, Washington Monument and Potomac River*

CM613 *Highway, poppies and lupines*

CM614 *Flowering crabapples on tree-lined street*

CM611		MNHVF	UseVF
6¢	**multicolored** tagged *(102,570,000)*	.30	.25

CM612		MNHVF	UseVF
6¢	**multicolored** tagged	.30	.25

CM613		MNHVF	UseVF
6¢	**multicolored** tagged	.30	.25

CM614		MNHVF	UseVF
6¢	**multicolored** tagged	.30	.25
	Plate block of 4	2.50	
	y. Se-tenant block of 4	2.00	
	FDC *(Jan. 16, 1969),* any single		2.00
	FDC block of 4		5.00
	zo. Tagging omitted, any single		
	zoy. Tagging omitted, se-tenant block of 4	—	

1969. American Legion Issue saluted the 50th anniversary of the veterans' organization incorporated by an act of Congress and signed by Woodrow Wilson on Sept. 16, 1919. *Intaglio (Giori Press) and offset, perforated 11.*

CM615 *Eagle with olive branch, from the Great Seal of the United States*

CM615		MNHVF	UseVF
6¢	**red, black & blue** tagged *(148,770,000)*	.25	.20
	Plate block of 4	.85	
	FDC *(March 15, 1969)*		1.00
	zo. Tagging Omitted	5.00	

1969. Grandma Moses Issue honored the grand old lady of American painting, who took up art at the age of 76 and continued until her death at 101. *Intaglio (Giori Press) and offset, perforated 11.*

CM616 July 4th, *detail from a Grandma Moses painting*

CM616		MNHVF	UseVF
6¢	**multicolored** tagged *(139,475,000)*	.25	.20
	Plate block of 4	.85	
	FDC *(May 1, 1969)*		1.00
	v. black and Prussian blue omitted	750.00	
	v1. Horizontal pair, imperforate between	225.00	
	zo. Tagging omitted	—	

1969. Apollo 8 Issue commemorated a vital space mission, in which the lunar surface was televised to Earth, prior to the moon landing. *Intaglio (Giori Press), perforated 11.*

CM617 *Earth rising over lunar surface*

CM617		MNHVF	UseVF
6¢	**gray, deep blue & blue** tagged *(187,165,000)*	.25	.20
	Plate block of 4	1.30	
	FDC *(May 5, 1969)*		1.00
	zo. Tagging omitted	—	

Note: Imperforate varieties, from printer's waste, exist.

1969. W.C. Handy Issue honored the memory of the great African-American composer and jazz musician who composed such immortal hits as "The St. Louis Blues," "The Memphis Blues" and "The Beale Street Blues." *Intaglio (Giori Press) and offset, perforated 11.*

CM618 *W.C. Handy and horn*

CM618		MNHVF	UseVF
6¢	**multicolored** tagged *(125,555,000)*	.25	.20
	Plate block of 4	1.30	
	FDC *(May 17, 1969)*		1.00
	zo. Tagging omitted	6.00	

1969. Settlement of California Issue commemorated the 200th anniversary of European settlement in the state. On July 16, 1769, a Spanish expedition led by Capt. Gasper de Portola entered San Diego, which became the first European settlement in California. *Intaglio (Giori Press) and offset, perforated 11.*

CM619 *Mission bells at Carmel, Calif.*

CM619		MNHVF	UseVF
6¢	**multicolored** tagged *(144,425,000)*	.25	.20
	Plate block of 4	.85	
	FDC *(July 16, 1969)*		1.00
	zo. Tagging omitted	5.50	

1969. John Wesley Powell Issue honored the eminent geologist who in 1869 explored the Colorado River. *Intaglio (Giori Press) and offset, perforated 11.*

CM620 *Maj. Powell leading Colorado River expedition*

CM620		MNHVF	UseVF
6¢	**multicolored** tagged *(133,100,000)*	.25	.20
	Plate block of 4	.85	
	FDC *(Aug. 1, 1969)*		1.00
	zo. Tagging omitted	4.50	

1969. Alabama Statehood Issue marked the 150th anniversary of the entry of Alabama into the union as the 22nd state. *Intaglio (Giori Press) and offset, perforated 11.*

CM621 *Camelia and yellow-shafted flicker*

CM621		MNHVF	UseVF
6¢	**multicolored** tagged *(136,900,000)*	.25	.20
	Plate block of 4	.85	
	FDC *(Aug. 2, 1969)*		1.00
	zo. Tagging omitted	—	

1969. 11TH INTERNATIONAL BOTANICAL CONGRESS ISSUE saluted the first international meeting of botanists held in the United States. Four se-tenant stamp designs appear in the same pane of 50 stamps; each design represents a region of the country. *Intaglio (Giori Press) and offset, perforated 11.*

CM622 *Douglas fir*
CM623 *Lady's-slipper*
CM624 *Ocotillo*
CM625 *Franklinia*

CM622		MNHVF	UseVF
6¢	**multicolored** tagged *(158,695,000)*	.30	.25
CM623		**MNHVF**	**UseVF**
6¢	**multicolored** tagged	.30	.25
CM624		**MNHVF**	**UseVF**
6¢	**multicolored** tagged	.30	.25
CM625		**MNHVF**	**UseVF**
6¢	**multicolored** tagged	.30	.25
	Plate block of 4	2.75	
	y. Se-tenant block of 4	2.25	2.50
	FDC *(Aug. 23, 1969),* any single		2.00
	FDC, block of 4		6.00

1969. DARTMOUTH COLLEGE CASE ISSUE commemorated the 150th anniversary of the legal decision that protected college charters and reasserted the sanctity of contracts. Daniel Webster won the case before the U.S. Supreme Court. *Intaglio, perforated 10 1/2 X 11.*

CM626 *Daniel Webster and Dartmouth Hall*

CM626		MNHVF	UseVF
6¢	**green** tagged *(124,075,000)*	.25	.20
	Plate block of 4	.95	
	FDC *(Sept. 22, 1969)*		1.00

1969. PROFESSIONAL BASEBALL ISSUE marked the 100th anniversary of the use of salaried players on a baseball team. The Red Stockings of Cincinnati, Ohio, in 1869 became the first club to pay its team members. *Intaglio (Giori Press) and offset, perforated 11.*

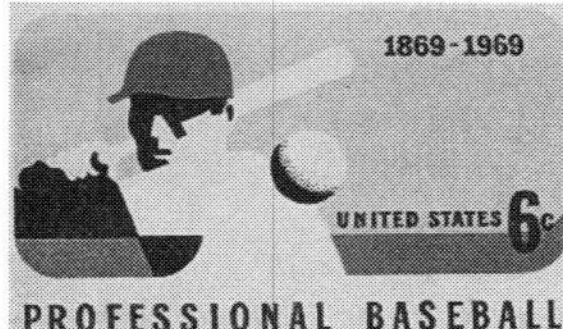

CM627 *Player at bat*

CM627		MNHVF	UseVF
6¢	**yellow, red, black & green** tagged *(129,925,000)*	1.25	.20
	Plate block of 4	4.95	
	FDC *(Sept. 24, 1969)*		1.00
	v. black omitted	950.00	

1969. INTERCOLLEGIATE FOOTBALL ISSUE celebrated the 100th anniversary of the popular college sport that started Nov. 6, 1869, when Rutgers defeated Princeton. *Intaglio and offset, perforated 11.*

CM628 *Coach and football player*

CM628		MNHVF	UseVF
6¢	**red & green** tagged *(129,860,000)*	.45	.20
	Plate block of 4	2.00	
	FDC *(Sept. 26, 1969)*		1.00
	zo. Tagging omitted	—	

The intaglio portion of CM628 was printed on a rotary press normally used for currency.

1969. DWIGHT D. EISENHOWER ISSUE paid tribute to the 34th president of the United States. Eisenhower (1890-1969) was a West Point graduate who went on to become a five-star general and the Supreme Allied Commander in Europe during World War II. *Intaglio (Giori Press), perforated 11.*

CM629 *Dwight D. Eisenhower and flag*

CM629		MNHVF	UseVF
6¢	**blue, black & reddish purple** tagged *(138,976,000)*	.25	.20
	Plate block of 4	.85	
	FDC *(Oct. 14, 1969)*		1.00
	zo. Tagging omitted	—	

1969. HOPE FOR THE CRIPPLED ISSUE encouraged aid in research and therapy for the handicapped. *Intaglio (Giori Press) and offset, perforated 11.*

CM630 *Child rising from wheelchair*

CM630		MNHVF	UseVF
6¢	**multicolored** tagged *(124,565,000)*	.25	.20
	Plate block of 4	.85	
	FDC *(Nov. 20, 1969)*		1.00
	zo. Tagging omitted	—	

1969. WILLIAM M. HARNETT ISSUE honored an artist (1848-92) noted for his realistic work. *Intaglio (Giori Press) and offset, perforated 11.*

CM631 *Still life* Old Models

CM631		MNHVF	UseVF
6¢	**multicolored** tagged *(124,729,000)*	.25	.20
	Plate block of 4	.85	
	FDC *(Dec. 3, 1969)*		1.00

1970. Natural History Issue commemorated the centenary of the American Museum of Natural History in New York City. Four se-tenant stamp designs appear in the same 32-image pane. *Intaglio (Giori Press) and offset, perforated 11.*

HAIDA CEREMONIAL CANOE

CM632 *American Bald Eagle, detail from a display in The American Museum of Natural History*
CM633 *Herd of African Elephants, a display in Carl Akeley Memorial Hall*
CM634 *Northwest Coast Canoe (Haida Indians), the figures in the canoe represent a Tlingit chief and his party on their way to a marriage ceremony*
CM635 *Jurassic Dinosaurs, from a mural at Yale University's Peabody Museum of Natural History*

CM632		MNHVF	UseVF
6¢	**multicolored** tagged *(201,794,600)*	.25	.20
CM633		**MNHVF**	**UseVF**
6¢	**multicolored** tagged	.25	.20
CM634		**MNHVF**	**UseVF**
6¢	**multicolored** tagged	.25	.20
CM635		**MNHVF**	**UseVF**
6¢	**multicolored** tagged	.25	.20
	Plate block of 4	1.00	
	y. Se-tenant block of 4 (CM632-35)		
	FDC *(May 6, 1970)*, any single		2.00
	FDC block of 4		4.00
	zo. Tagging omitted, any single	—	
	zoy. Tagging omitted, block of 4	—	

1970. Maine Statehood Issue honored the 150th anniversary of its entry into the union as the 23rd state. *Intaglio (Giori Press) and offset, perforated 11.*

CM636 The Lighthouse at Two Lights, *Edward Hopper oil painting in New York's Metropolitan Museum of Art*

CM636		MNHVF	UseVF
6¢	**multicolored** tagged *(171,850,000)*	.25	.20
	Plate block of 4	1.00	
	FDC *(July 9, 1970)*		1.75
	zo. Tagging omitted	—	

1970. Wildlife Conservation Issue reminded Americans of the continuing need to protect wildlife. Issued in Custer, S.Dak., near Custer State Park, home to the largest bison herd in the country. *Intaglio, perforated 11 x 10 1/2.*

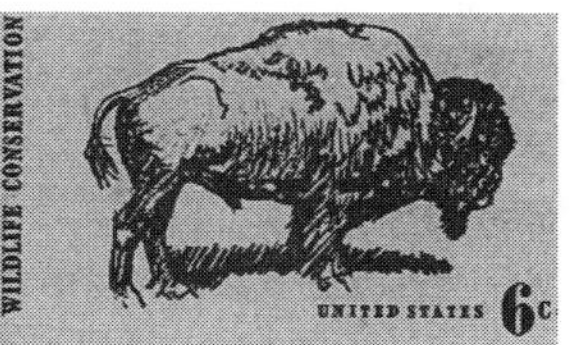

CM637 *American bison*

CM637		MNHVF	UseVF
6¢	**black** on tan *(142,205,000)*	.25	.20
	Plate block of 4	1.00	
	FDC *(July 20, 1970)*		1.75

American Poets Series

1970. Edgar Lee Masters Issue first in an American Poets Series, paid tribute to the author of *Spoon River Anthology.* Its ruthless exposure of small-town mores won instant acclaim as well as outraged criticism. *Intaglio (Giori Press) and offset, perforated 11.*

CM638 *Edgar Lee Masters*

CM638		MNHVF	UseVF
6¢	**black** tagged *(137,660,000)*	.25	.20
	Plate block of 4	.85	
	FDC *(Aug. 22, 1970)*		1.75
	zo. Tagging omitted	—	

1970. The 50th Anniversary of Woman Suffrage Issue celebrated the ratification of the 19th Amendment, which gave women the right to vote. *Intaglio (Giori Press), perforated 11.*

CM639 *Suffragettes of 1920 and modern voter*

CM639		MNHVF	UseVF
6¢	**blue** tagged *(135,125,000)*	.25	.20
	Plate block of 4	.85	
	FDC *(Aug. 25, 1970)*		1.75

1970. South Carolina Issue marked the 300th anniversary of the state's first permanent European settlement, established by the English at Charles Town (now Charleston). *Intaglio (Giori Press) and offset, perforated 11.*

CM640 *Aspects of South Carolina*

CM640		MNHVF	UseVF
6¢	**brown, black & red** tagged *(135,895,000)*	.25	.20
	Plate block of 4	.85	
	FDC *(Sept. 12, 1970)*		1.75

1970. Stone Mountain Issue commemorated the carving in a huge granite outcropping in Georgia of the mounted figures of Robert E. Lee, Jefferson Davis and Stonewall Jackson. *Intaglio (Giori Press), perforated 11.*

CM641 *Stone Mountain memorial*

CM641		MNHVF	UseVF
6¢	**gray black** tagged *(132,675,000)*	.25	.20
	Plate block of 4	1.10	
	FDC *(Sept. 19, 1970)*		1.75

1970. Fort Snelling Sesquicentennial Issue highlighted the importance of this outpost in settling the Northwestern United States. The fort was named after Col. Joshiah Snelling. *Intaglio (Giori Press) and offset, perforated 11.*

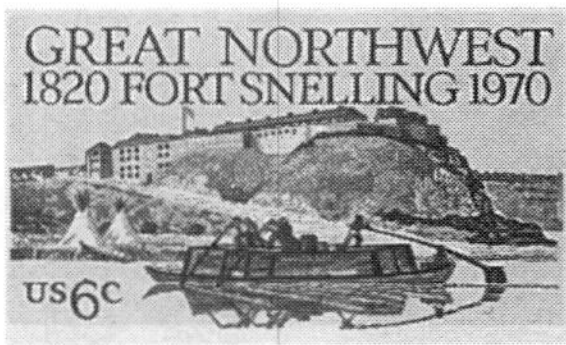

CM642 *Fort Snelling and surrounding area*

CM642		MNHVF	UseVF
6¢	**multicolored** tagged *(134,795,000)*	.25	.20
	Plate block of 4	.85	
	FDC *(Oct. 17, 1970)*		1.00
	zo. Tagging omitted	—	

1970. Anti-Pollution Issue emphasized the importance of world ecology. Four se-tenant designs appear in the pane. *Printed in gravure by the Bureau of Engraving and Printing at Guilford Gravure, Inc., perforated 11 x 10 1/2.*

CM643 *Save Our Soil*

CM644 *Save Our Cities*

CM645 *Save Our Water*

CM646 *Save Our Air*

CM643		MNHVF	UseVF
6¢	**multicolored** tagged *(161,600,000)*	.25	.20
CM644		**MNHVF**	**UseVF**
6¢	**multicolored** tagged	.25	.20
CM645		**MNHVF**	**UseVF**
6¢	**multicolored** tagged	.25	.20
CM646		**MNHVF**	**UseVF**
6¢	**multicolored** tagged	.25	.20
	Plate block of 4	3.50	
	y. Se-tenant block of 4	—	
	FDC *(Oct. 28, 1970)*, any single		2.00
	FDC, block of 4		5.00

1970. United Nations Issue marked the 25th anniversary of the international organization, chartered in San Francisco on June 26, 1945. *Intaglio (Giori Press) and offset, perforated 11.*

UNITED STATES POSTAGE 6 CENTS
UN
United Nations 25th Anniversary

CM647 *United Nations initials, logo*

CM647		MNHVF	UseVF
6¢	**black, red & blue** tagged *(127,610,000)*	.25	.20
	Plate block of 4	.85	
	Pair, gutter between	—	
	FDC *(Nov. 20, 1970)*		1.75
	zo. Tagging omitted	—	

1970. Landing of the Pilgrims Issue commemorated the 350th anniversary of the arrival of the *Mayflower* and the landing of the Pilgrims at Plymouth, Mass. *Intaglio (Giori Press) and offset, perforated 11.*

CM648 Mayflower *and Pilgrims*

CM648		MNHVF	UseVF
6¢	**multicolored** tagged *(129,785,000)*	.25	.20
	Plate block of 4	.85	
	FDC *(Nov. 21, 1970)*		1.75
	v. orange and yellow omitted	950.00	

1970. U.S. Servicemen Issue paid tribute to the Disabled American Veterans, prisoners of war and those missing and killed in action. Two se-tenant stamp designs alternate in the pane. *Intaglio (Giori Press) and offset, perforated 11.*

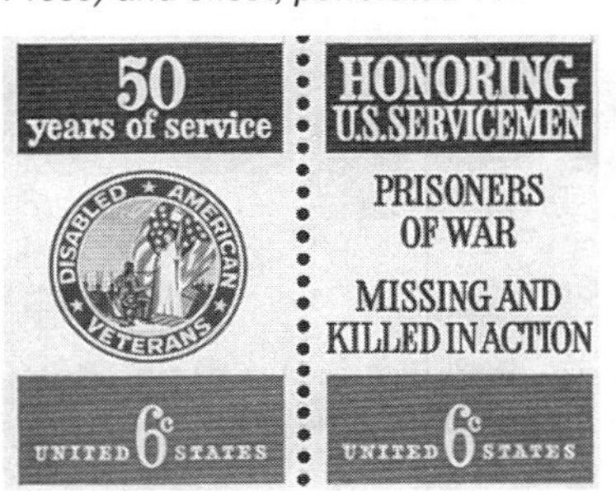

CM649 *Crest of Disabled American Veterans*

CM650 *Prisoners of war, missing and killed in action*

CM649		MNHVF	UseVF
6¢	**multicolored** tagged *(134,380,000)*	.25	.20
CM650		**MNHVF**	**UseVF**
6¢	**dark blue, black & red** tagged	.25	.20
	Plate block of 4	1.30	
	y. Se-tenant pair	.50	
	FDC *(Nov. 24, 1970)*, either single		1.75
	FDC, pair		2.00
	zo. Tagging omitted, single	—	
	zoy. Tagging omitted, se-tenant Pair	—	

1971. American Wool Issue commemorated the 450th anniversary of the introduction of sheep in America. *Intaglio (Giori Press) and offset, perforated 11.*

CM651 *Ewe and lamb*

CM651		MNHVF	UseVF
6¢	**multicolored** tagged *(135,305,000)*	.25	.20
	Plate block of 4	.85	
	FDC *(Jan. 19, 1971)*		1.75
	zo. Tagging omitted	5.00	

1971. Douglas MacArthur Issue honored the five-star Army general (1880-1964) who commanded the Pacific theater Allied forces in World War II, headed occupation forces in Japan and was U.N. commander in the Korean War. *Intaglio (Giori Press), perforated 11.*

CM652 *Douglas MacArthur*

CM652		MNHVF	UseVF
6¢	**red, blue & black** tagged *(134,840,000)*	.25	.20
	Plate block of 4	.85	
	FDC *(Jan. 26, 1971)*		2.00
	zo. Tagging omitted	—	

1971. Blood Donors Issue pointed out the need for more Americans to increase their participation. *Intaglio (Giori Press) and offset, perforated 11.*

CM653 *Giving Blood Saves Lives*

CM653		MNHVF	UseVF
6¢	**red & blue** tagged *(130,975,000)*	.25	.20
	Plate block of 4	.85	
	FDC *(March 12, 1971)*		1.75
	zo. Tagging omitted	5.00	

1971. Missouri Statehood Issue honored the 150th anniversary of entry into the union of the "Show Me" state, the 24th state. *Gravure (Andreotti Press), perforated 11 x 10 1/2.*

CM654 Independence and the Opening of the West, *detail of a mural by Thomas Hart Benton*

CM654		MNHVF	UseVF
8¢	**multicolored** tagged *(161,235,000)*	.25	.20
	Plate block of 12	3.25	
	FDC *(May 8, 1971)*		1.75
	zo. Tagging omitted	—	

1971. Wildlife Conservation Issue stressed the importance of preserving nature's creatures from extinction. Four different representatives of wildlife are featured in the pane of 32 stamps. *Intaglio (Giori Press) and offset, perforated 11.*

CM655 *Polar bear*

CM656 *Condor*

CM657 *Alligator*

CM658 *Trout*

CM655		MNHVF	UseVF
8¢	**multicolored** tagged *(175,680,000)*	.25	.20

CM656		MNHVF	UseVF
8¢	**multicolored** tagged	.25	.20

CM657		MNHVF	UseVF
8¢	**multicolored** tagged	.25	.20

CM658		MNHVF	UseVF
8¢	**multicolored** tagged	.25	.20
	Plate block of 4	1.20	
	y. Se-tenant block of 4	.75	
	FDC *(June 12, 1971)* any single		2.00
	FDC, block of 4		4.00
	v. red omitted, block of 4	9,500.00	
	v1. light green and dark green omitted, block of 4	4,500.00	
	zo. Tagging omitted, any single	—	
	zoy. Tagging omitted, se-tenant block of 4	—	

1971. Antarctic Treaty Issue marked the 10th anniversary of the treaty that pledged 12 nations to scientific cooperation and peaceful use of Antarctica: Argentina, Australia, Belgium, Chile, France, Japan, New Zealand, Norway, South Africa, Soviet Union, United Kingdom and United States. *Intaglio (Giori Press), perforated 11.*

CM659 *Antarctic Treaty emblem*

CM659		MNHVF	UseVF
8¢	**red & dark blue** tagged *(138,700,000)*	.25	.20
	Plate block of 4	1.00	
	FDC *(June 23, 1971)*		1.75
	zo. Tagging omitted	5.00	

American Revolution Bicentennial Series

1971. American Revolution Bicentennial Issue commemorated the struggle that led to the birth of the United States, and was the first in a series of stamps to pay tribute to the men, women, places and events of the Revolutionary War. *Intaglio (Giori Press) and offset, perforated 11.*

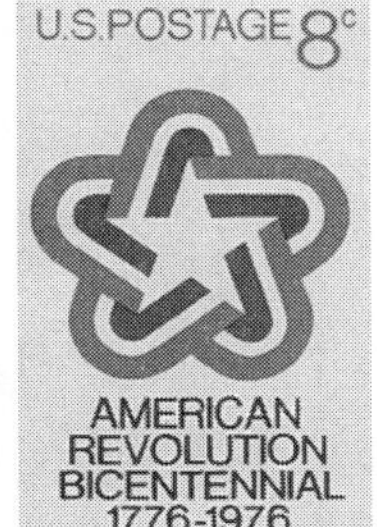

CM660 *American Revolution Bicentennial symbol*

CM660		MNHVF	UseVF
8¢	**gray, red, blue & black** tagged *(138,165,000)*	.25	.20
	Plate block of 4	1.10	
	FDC *(July 4, 1971)*		1.75
	v. gray (top legend) omitted	1,250.00	
	v1. black and gray omitted	700.00	

1971. Space Achievements Decade Issue marked 10 years of extraordinary accomplishments in space with a se-tenant pair. *Intaglio (Giori Press) and offset, perforated 11.*

CM661 *Landing craft on Moon's surface;* CM662 *Astronauts in Lunar Rover*

		MNHVF	UseVF
CM661			
8¢	**multicolored** tagged *(176,295,000)*	.25	.20
	v. blue and red omitted	600.00	

		MNHVF	UseVF
CM662			
8¢	**multicolored** tagged	.25	.20
	y. Se-tenant pair, CM661-62	.50	
	Plate block of 4	1.15	
	FDC *(Aug. 2, 1971)*, either single		1.75
	v. blue and red omitted	600.00	
	y1. Se-tenant pair, blue and red omitted	1,500.00	
	zo. Tagging omitted, any single	6.00	
	zoy.Se-tenant pair, tagging omitted	22.50	
	FDC, pair		2.50

1971. John Sloan Issue honored the artist on the centennial of his birth at Lock Haven, Pa. Part of Fine Arts Series. *Intaglio (Giori Press) and offset, perforated 11.*

CM663 The Wake of the Ferry, *Phillips Gallery, Washington, D.C.*

		MNHVF	UseVF
CM663			
8¢	**multicolored** tagged *(152,125,000)*	.25	.20
	Plate block of 4	1.00	
	FDC *(Aug. 2, 1971)*		1.75
	zo. Tagging omitted	—	

1971. Emily Dickinson Issue in the American Poets Series honored the reclusive poet (1830-86), who was born in Amherst, Mass. Only after she died were her works widely published and acclaimed. *Intaglio (Giori Press) and offset, perforated 11.*

CM664 *Emily Dickinson*

		MNHVF	UseVF
CM664			
8¢	**multicolored** tagged *(142,845,000)*	.25	.20
	Plate block of 4	1.00	
	FDC *(Aug. 28, 1971)*		1.75
	v. black and olive omitted	850.00	
	v1. pale rose omitted	7,500.00	
	zo. Tagging omitted	—	

1971. San Juan Issue marked the 450th anniversary of the founding of the Puerto Rican city. *Intaglio (Giori Press) and offset, perforated 11.*

CM665 *Battlement at El Morro Castle*

		MNHVF	UseVF
CM665			
8¢	**multicolored** tagged *(148,755,000)*	.25	.20
	Plate block of 4	1.00	
	FDC *(Sept. 12, 1971)*		1.75
	zo. Tagging omitted	6.00	

1971. Prevent Drug Abuse Issue publicized drug addiction as a national menace of concern to every American. *Gravure (Andreotti Press), perforated 10 1/2 x 11.*

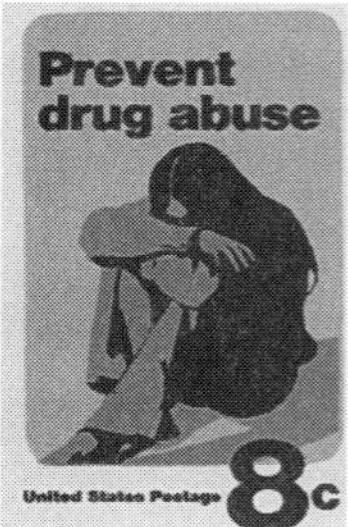

CM666 *Drug addict*

		MNHVF	UseVF
CM666			
8¢	**blue, deep blue & black** tagged *(139,080,000)*	.25	.20
	Plate block of 6	1.50	
	FDC *(Oct. 4, 1971)*		1.75
	zo. Tagging omitted	—	

1971. CARE Issue honored the 25th anniversary of the American-Canadian Cooperative for American Relief Everywhere. *Intaglio (Giori Press), perforated 11.*

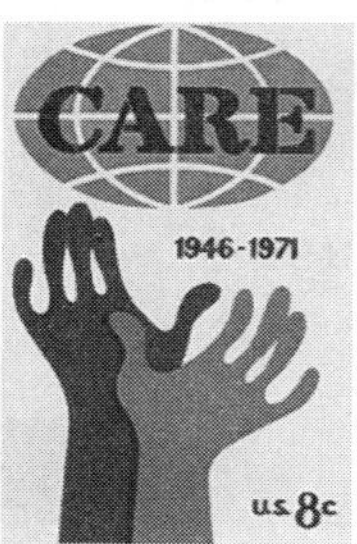

CM667 *Hands and CARE emblem*

		MNHVF	UseVF
CM667			
8¢	**black, blue, violet & red lilac** tagged *(130,755,000)*	.25	.20
	Plate block of 8	1.95	
	FDC *(Oct. 27, 1971)*		1.75
	a. black omitted		4,750.00
	zo. Tagging omitted	4.00	

1971. Historic Preservation Issue paid tribute to important artifacts of America's past. *Intaglio (Giori Press) and offset, perforated.*

CM668 *Decatur House, Washington, D.C.*

CM669 *Whaling Ship* Charles W. Morgan, *Mystic, Conn.*

CM670 *Cable Car, San Francisco, Calif.*

CM671 *San Xavier del Bac Mission, Tucson, Ariz.*

		MNHVF	UseVF
CM668			
8¢	**brown & dark beige** on buff, tagged *(170,208,000)*	.25	.20

		MNHVF	UseVF
CM669			
8¢	**brown & dark beige** on buff, tagged	.25	.20

		MNHVF	UseVF
CM670			
8¢	**brown & dark beige** on buff, tagged	.25	.20

		MNHVF	UseVF
CM671			
8¢	**brown & dark beige** on buff, tagged	.25	.20
	Plate block of 4	1.20	
	y. Se-tenant block of 4 (CM668-71)	.75	
	FDC *(Oct. 29, 1971)* any single		2.00
	FDC, block of 4		4.00
	v. brown omitted (any single)	—	
	v1. dark beige omitted (any single)	—	

	vy. brown omitted, se-tenant block of 4	2,600.00	
	vly. dark beige omitted, se-tenant block of 4	—	
	zo. Tagging omitted, any single	—	
	zoy. Tagging omitted, se-tenant block of 4	50.00	

1972. American Poets Issue in the American Poets Series honored a man, who had a brief but distinguished career as a lawyer, teacher, musician and poet. Born in Macon, Ga., he died in 1881 at the age of 39. *Intaglio (Giori Press), perforated 11.*

CM672 *Sidney Lanier*

CM672		MNHVF	UseVF
8¢	**black, reddish brown & blue** tagged *(137,355,000)*	.25	.20
	Plate block of 4	1.00	
	FDC *(Feb. 3, 1972)*		1.75
	zo. Tagging omitted	12.50	

1972. Peace Corps Issue paid tribute to a government organization created to aid developing countries. *Gravure (Andreotti Press), perforated 10 1/2 x 11.*

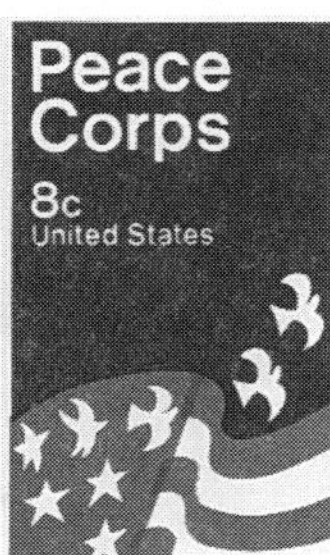

CM673 *Flag and Doves, from poster by David Battle*

CM673		MNHVF	UseVF
8¢	**dark blue, light blue & red** tagged *(150,400,000)*	.25	.20
	Plate block of 6	1.60	
	FDC *(Feb. 11, 1972)*		1.75
	zo. Tagging omitted	4.00	

National Parks Centennial Series

released over a five-month period consisted of eight stamps (one is an airmail stamp, A82).

1972. Yellowstone Park Issue marked the centennial of the establishment of the first national park in the world, located in Western Wyoming. *Intaglio (Giori Press) and offset, perforated 11.*

CM674 *Old Faithful, Yellowstone Park*

CM674		MNHVF	UseVF
8¢	**multicolored** tagged *(164,096,000)*	.25	.20
	Plate block of 4	1.00	
	FDC *(March 1, 1972)*		1.75
	zo. Tagging omitted	14.00	

1972. Cape Hatteras Issue in the National Parks Centennial Series called attention to the National Seashore, established in 1937, which includes perhaps the most photographed lighthouse in the world. *Intaglio (Giori Press) and offset, perforated 11.*

CM675-78 *Cape Hatteras National Seashore* scenes: *squall, lighthouse, laughing gulls, and beach grass*

CM675		MNHVF	UseVF
2¢	**multicolored** tagged *(172,730,000)*	.25	.20
CM676		**MNHVF**	**UseVF**
2¢	**multicolored** tagged	.25	.20
CM677		**MNHVF**	**UseVF**
2¢	**multicolored** tagged	.25	.20
CM678		**MNHVF**	**UseVF**
2¢	**multicolored** tagged	.25	.20
	Plate block of 4	.60	
	y. Se-tenant block of 4 (CM675-78)		
	FDC *(April 5, 1972)*, block of 4		1.75
	v. black omitted (any single)	—	
	vy. black omitted, se-tenant block of 4	2,750.00	
	zo. Tagging omitted, any single	—	
	zoy. Tagging omitted, se-tenant block of 4	—	

1972. Wolf Trap Farm Issue in the National Parks Centennial Series called attention to the national park for performing arts, established in 1966. *Intaglio (Giori Press) and offset, perforated 11.*

CM679 *Theater at Wolf Trap Farm, Va., at night*

CM679		MNHVF	UseVF
6¢	**multicolored** tagged *(104,090,000)*	.25	.20
	Plate block of 4	.85	
	FDC *(June 26, 1972)*		1.75
	zo. Tagging omitted	6.00	

1972. Mount McKinley Issue in the National Parks Centennial Series celebrated the park including the highest peak (20,270 feet) in North America. *Intaglio (Giori Press) and offset, perforated 11.*

CM680 *Mount McKinley, Alaska*

CM680		MNHVF	UseVF
15¢	**multicolored** tagged *(53,920,000)*	.25	.20
	Plate block of 4	1.90	
	FDC *(July 28, 1972)*		1.75
	zo. Tagging omitted	19.00	

1972. Family Planning Issue reminded people of the need for planning to have a better America and a better world. *Intaglio (Giori Press), perforated 11.*

Family Planning CM681 *Planned family*

CM681		MNHVF	UseVF
8¢	**multicolored** tagged *(153,025,000)*	.25	.20
	Plate block of 4	1.10	
	FDC *(March 18, 1972)*		1.75
	v. dark brown omitted	9,350.00	
	v1. dark brown and olive omitted	—	
	v2. yellow omitted	1,650.00	
	zo. Tagging omitted	—	

1972. Colonial Craftsmen Issue commemorated the contributions of Colonial artisans to the early development of America. *Intaglio, perforated 11 x 10 1/2.*

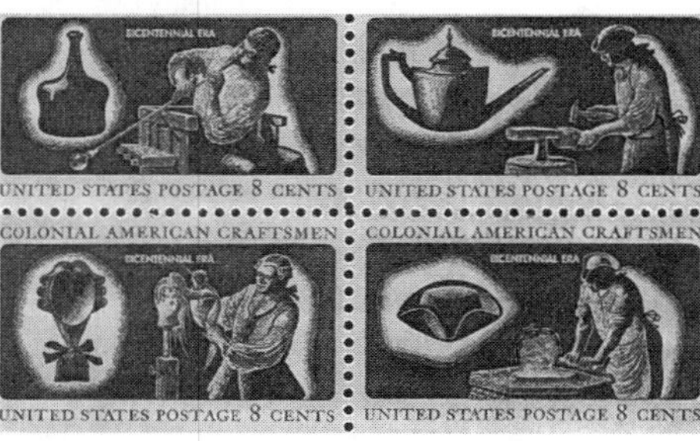

CM682 *Glassmaker*

CM683 *Silversmith*

CM684 *Wigmaker*

CM685 *Hatter*

CM682		MNHVF	UseVF
8¢	**deep brown** on buff paper, tagged *(201,890,000)*	.25	.20
CM683		MNHVF	UseVF
8¢	**deep brown** on buff paper, tagged	.25	.20
CM684		MNHVF	UseVF
8¢	**deep brown** on buff paper, tagged	.25	.20
CM685		MNHVF	UseVF
8¢	**deep brown** on buff paper, tagged	.25	.20
	Plate block of 4	1.25	
	y. Se-tenant block of 4, (CM682-85)	.75	
	FDC *(July 4, 1972),* any single		2.00
	FDC, block of 4		4.00
	zo. Tagging omitted, any single	—	
	zoy. Tagging omitted, se-tenant block of 4	—	

Olympic Games Series

1972. Olympic Games Issue saluted international athletic meets in Sapporo, Japan (Winter Games) and Munich, Germany (Summer Games) (See also A837). *Gravure (Andreotti Press), perforated 11 x 10 1/2. (See A83).*

CM686 *Cycling*

CM686		MNHVF	UseVF
6¢	**multicolored** tagged *(67,335,000)*	.25	.20
	Plate block of 10	2.10	
	v. Plate flaw, broken red ring (position 43 of top-left pane of plate No. 33313)	10.00	
	FDC *(Aug. 17, 1972)*		1.75

CM687 *Bobsled racing*

CM687		MNHVF	UseVF
8¢	**multicolored** tagged *(96,240,000)*	.25	.20
	Plate block of 10	2.75	
	FDC *(Aug. 17, 1972)*		1.75
	zo. Tagging omitted	5.00	

CM688 *Foot racing*

CM688		MNHVF	UseVF
15¢	**multicolored** tagged *(46,340,000)*	.25	.20
	Plate block of 10	5.25	
	FDC *(Aug. 17, 1972)*		1.75

1972. Parent Teacher Association Issue saluted the 75th anniversary of an organization dedicated to improving educational methods furthering development of young minds. *Gravure (Andreotti Press), perforated 11 x 10 1/2.*

CM689 *Blackboard, symbol of education*

CM689		MNHVF	UseVF
8¢	**yellow & black** tagged *(180,155,000)*	.25	.20
	Plate block of 4	1.00	
	Plate block, yellow inverted	—	
	FDC *(Sept. 15, 1972)*		1.75
	zo. Tagging omitted	—	

1972. Wildlife Conservation Issue showcased the importance and beauty of nature's creatures. *Intaglio (Giori Press) and offset, perforated 11.*

CM690 *Fur seal*

CM691 *Cardinal*

CM692 *Brown pelican*

CM693 *Bighorn sheep*

CM690		MNHVF	UseVF
8¢	**multicolored** tagged *(198,364,800)*	.25	.20
CM691		MNHVF	UseVF
8¢	**multicolored** tagged	.25	.20
CM692		MNHVF	UseVF
8¢	**multicolored** tagged	.25	.20
CM693		MNHVF	UseVF
8¢	**multicolored** tagged	.25	.20
	Plate block of 4	1.10	
	y. Se-tenant block of 4 (CM690-93)		
	FDC *(Sept. 20, 1972),* any single		2.00
	FDC, block of 4		4.00
	v. brown omitted	—	
	vy. Se-tenant block of 4 brown omitted	4,500.00	
	v1. green and blue omitted	—	

v1y. Se-tenant block of 4, green and blue omitted	4,500.00	
v2. red and brown omitted	—	
Se-tenant block of 4, red and brown omitted	4,500.00	

1972. Mail Order Centennial Issue marked the 100th anniversary of the introduction of merchandising by mail. *Gravure (Andreotti Press), perforated 11 x 10 1/2.*

CM694 *Rural Post Office store*

CM694		MNHVF	UseVF
8¢	**multicolored** tagged *(185,490,000)*	.25	.20
	Plate block of 12	3.00	
	FDC *(Sept. 27, 1972)*		1.75

Tagging on this issue typically consists of a vertical bar, 10mm wide.

1972. Osteopathic Medicine Issue marked the 75th anniversary of the American Osteopathic Association established by Dr. Andrew Still. *Gravure (Andreotti Press), perforated 10 1/2 x 11.*

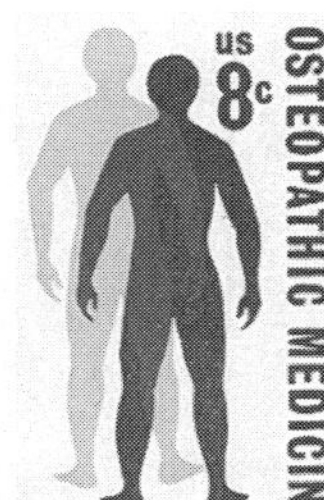

CM695 *Osteopathic medicine*

CM695		MNHVF	UseVF
8¢	**multicolored** tagged *(162,335,000)*	.25	.20
	Plate block of 6	1.60	
	FDC *(Oct, 9, 1972)*		2.50

1972. Tom Sawyer Issue the fourth stamp in the American Folklore Series, recalled the exciting, carefree adventures of the fictional mischievous boy created by Mark Twain (see CM205). *Intaglio (Giori Press) and offset, perforated 11.*

CM696 *Tom Sawyer, painted by Norman Rockwell*

CM696		MNHVF	UseVF
8¢	**multicolored** tagged *(162,789,950)*	.25	.20
	Plate block of 4	1.10	
	FDC *(Oct. 13, 1972)*		2.50
	v. black and red omitted	2,250.00	
	v1. yellow and tan omitted	2,100.00	
	v2. Horizontal pair, imperforate between	5,500.00	
	zo. Tagging omitted	15.00	

1972. Pharmacy Issue saluted the nation's druggists and their contribution to keeping Americans healthy. *Intaglio (Giori Press) and offset, perforated 11.*

CM697 *Bowl of Hygeia, mortar and pestle*

CM697		MNHVF	UseVF
8¢	**multicolored** tagged *(165,895,000)*	.25	.20
	Plate block of 4	1.75	
	FDC *(Nov. 10, 1972)*		10.00
	v. blue omitted	2,000.00	
	v1. blue and orange omitted	875.00	
	v2. orange omitted	2,000.00	
	zo. Tagging omitted	—	

1972. Stamp Collecting Issue paid tribute to the nation's stamp collectors and the hobby of philately. *Intaglio (Giori Press) and offset, perforated 11.*

CM698 *First U.S. stamp under magnifying glass*

CM698		MNHVF	UseVF
8¢	**multicolored** tagged *(166,508,000)*	.25	.20
	Plate block of 4	1.00	
	FDC *(Nov. 17, 1972)*		2.00
	v. black omitted	900.00	
	zo. Tagging omitted	—	

Love Series

1973. Love Issue the first in a series issued for use on birthdays, anniversaries and other occasions, featured a classic design by Robert Indiana. *Photogravure (Andreotti), perforated 11 x 10 1/2.*

CM699 *Love sculpture by Robert Indiana*

CM699		MNHVF	UseVF
8¢	**red, green, violet & blue** tagged *(330,055,000)*	.25	.20
	Plate block of 6	1.50	
	FDC *(Jan. 26, 1973)*		2.25

1973. Rise of the Spirit of Independence Issue highlighted the role of communications in spurring the American revolution. *Intaglio (Giori Press) and offset, perforated 11.*

CM700 *Pamphlets printed by press*

CM700		MNHVF	UseVF
8¢	**blue, greenish black & red** tagged *(166,005,000)*	.25	.20
	Plate block of 4	1.00	
	FDC *(Feb. 16, 1973)*		1.75
	zo. Tagging omitted	12.50	

CM701 *Posting a broadside*

CM701		MNHVF	UseVF
8¢	**black, orange & ultramarine** tagged *(163,050,000)*	.25	.20
	Plate block of 4	1.00	
	FDC *(April 13, 1973)*		1.75
	Pair, gutter between	—	
	zo. Tagging omitted	—	

CM702 *Colonial post rider*

CM702		MNHVF	UseVF
8¢	**blue, black, red & green** tagged *(159,005,000)*	.25	.20
	Plate block of 4	1.00	
	FDC *(June 22, 1973)*		1.75
	zo. Tagging omitted	—	

CM703 *Drummer summoning minutemen*

CM703		MNHVF	UseVF
8¢	**blue, black, yellow & red** tagged *(147,295,000)*	.25	.20
	Plate block of 4	1.00	
	FDC *(Sept. 28, 1973)*		1.75
	zo. Tagging omitted	—	

1973. George Gershwin Issue honored the American composer who created music for more than 400 songs, including "Rhapsody in Blue" and *Porgy and Bess* (CM1586), a folk opera. *Gravure (Andreotti Press), perforated 11.*

CM704 *George Gershwin and* Porgy and Bess *montage*

CM704		MNHVF	UseVF
8¢	**multicolored** *(139,152,000)*	.25	.20
	Plate block of 12	3.25	
	FDC *(Feb. 28, 1973)*		1.75
	v. Vertical pair, imperforate horizontally	225.00	

1973. Nicolaus Copernicus Issue paid tribute to the father of modern astronomy on the 500th anniversary of his birth. *Intaglio (Giori Press) and offset, perforated 11.*

CM705 *Nicolaus Copernicus*

CM705		MNHVF	UseVF
8¢	**black & yellow** tagged *(159,475,000)*	.25	.20
	Plate block of 4	1.10	
	FDC *(April 23, 1973)*		2.00
	v. Engraved black omitted	1,300.00	
	v1. yellow omitted	1,000.00	
	zo. Tagging omitted	15.00	

The yellow may be removed chemically. Competent expertization is recommended of CM705v1.

1973. Postal Service Employee Issue saluted the 700,000 employees of the U.S. Postal Service. Ten different stamps in a pane of 50 depict some of the services performed by postal employees, with text describing those activities printed on the reverse side of the stamp, under the gum, a U.S. stamp first. *Gravure (Andreotti Press), perforated 10 1/2 x 11.*

CM706-CM715 *Postal people performing services*

		MNHVF	UseVF
CM706			
8¢	**multicolored** tagged *(486,020,000)*	.25	.20
CM707			
8¢	**multicolored** tagged	.25	.20
CM708			
8¢	**multicolored** tagged	.25	.20
CM709			
8¢	**multicolored** tagged	.25	.20
CM710			
8¢	**multicolored** tagged	.25	.20
CM711			
8¢	**multicolored** tagged	.25	.20
CM712			
8¢	**multicolored** tagged	.25	.20
CM713			
8¢	**multicolored** tagged	.25	.20
CM714			
8¢	**multicolored** tagged	.25	.20
CM715			
8¢	**multicolored** tagged	.25	.20
	Plate block of 20	5.50	
	y. Se-tenant strip of 10, (CM706-15)	4.00	
	FDC *(April 30, 1973)*, any single		2.00
	FDC, strip of 10		20.00
	zo. Tagging omitted, any single	—	
	zoy. Tagging omitted, se-tenant strip of 10	—	

Tagging consists of a 1/2 inch high horizontal band.

1973. Harry S. Truman Issue honored the 33rd president of the United States, who died Dec. 26, 1972. *Intaglio (Giori Press), perforated 11.*

CM716 *Harry S. Truman, from a photograph by Leo Stern*

CM716		MNHVF	UseVF
8¢	**red, black & blue** tagged *(157,052,800)*	.25	.25
	Plate block of 4	1.10	
	FDC *(May 8, 1973)*		2.00
	zo. Tagging omitted	5.00	

1973. Boston Tea Party Issue used four different se-tenant designs to form a single scene depicting this historical event that preceded the War of Independence. *Intaglio (Giori Press) and offset, perforated 11.*

CM717-20 *Boston Tea Party*

CM717		MNHVF	UseVF
8¢	**multicolored** tagged *(196,275,000)*	.25	.20
CM718		**MNHVF**	**UseVF**
8¢	**multicolored** tagged	.25	.20
CM719		**MNHVF**	**UseVF**
8¢	**multicolored** tagged	.25	.20
CM720		**MNHVF**	**UseVF**
8¢	**multicolored** tagged	.25	.20
	Plate block of 4	1.15	
	y. Se-tenant block of 4, (CM717-20)	.75	
	FDC *(July 4, 1973),* any single		2.00
	FDC, block of 4		8.00
	vy. Se-tenant block of 4, intaglio black omitted	1,500.00	
	vy1. Se-tenant block of 4, intaglio black omitted	500.00	
	zo. Tagging omitted, any single	—	
	zoy. Se-tenant block of 4, tagging omitted	—	

1973. Progress in Electronics Issue commemorated advances and developments in electronic communications. (See also A84). *Intaglio (Giori Press) and offset, perforated 11.*

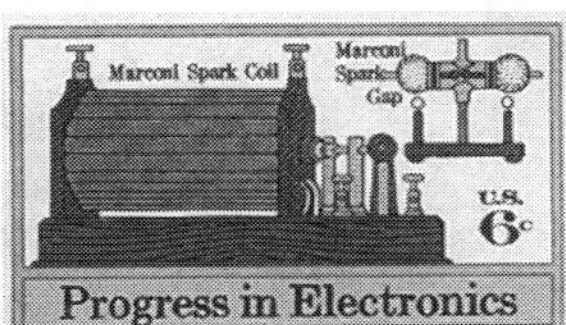

CM721 *Marconi spark coil and gap*

CM721		MNHVF	UseVF
6¢	**multicolored** tagged *(53,005,000)*	.25	.20
	Plate block of 4	.85	
	FDC *(July 10, 1973)*		1.75
	zo. Tagging omitted	—	

CM722 *Transistors and electronic circuit*

CM722		MNHVF	UseVF
8¢	**multicolored** tagged *(159,775,000)*	.25	.20
	Plate block of 4	1.00	
	FDC *(July 10, 1973)*		1.75
	a. black (inscription) omitted	650.00	
	b. lilac and tan (background) omitted	1,300.00	
	zo. Tagging omitted	—	

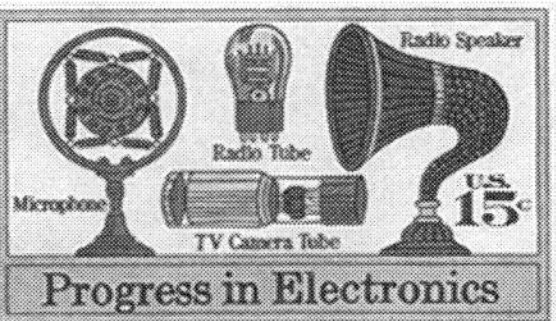

CM723 *Radio and television components*

CM723		MNHVF	UseVF
15¢	**multicolored** tagged *(39,005,000)*	.25	.20
	Plate block of 4	1.85	
	FDC *(July 10, 1973)*		1.75
	v. black omitted	1,500.00	

1973. Robinson Jeffers Issue paid tribute to the poet whose works were mainly allegories influenced by his love of the classical Greek and Roman tragedies. *Gravure (Andreotti Press), perforated*

CM724 *Robinson Jeffers and children with burro*

CM724		MNHVF	UseVF
8¢	**multicolored** tagged *(128,048,000)*	.25	.20
	Plate block of 12	3.00	
	FDC *(Aug. 13, 1973)*		1.75
	v. Vertical pair, imperforate horizontally	250.00	

1973. Lyndon B. Johnson Issue honored the 36th president of the United States, who died Jan. 22, 1973. *Gravure (Andreotti Press), perforated 11.*

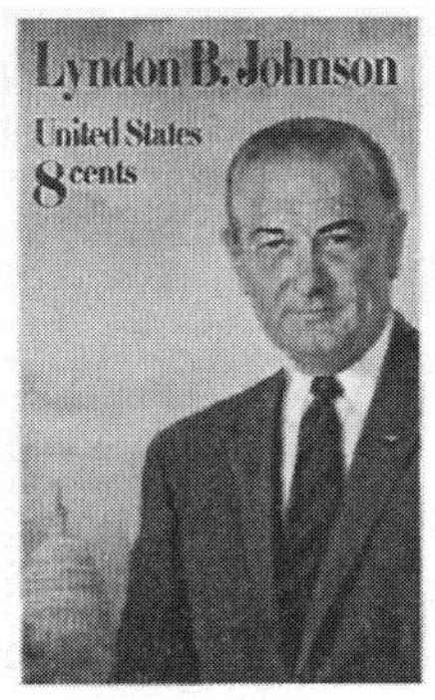

CM725 *Lyndon B. Johnson*

CM725		MNHVF	UseVF
8¢	**multicolored** *(152,624,000)*	.25	.20
	Plate block of 12	3.50	
	FDC *(Aug. 27, 1973)*		1.75
	v. Horizontal pair, imperforate vertically	350.00	

1973. Henry O. Tanner Issue saluted the artist who studied art under Thomas Eakins. Many of his works were based on Biblical themes. *Gravure (Andreotti Press), perforated 11.*

CM726 *Henry O. Tanner, palette and rainbow*

CM726

		MNHVF	UseVF
8¢	**multicolored** tagged *(146,008,000)*	.25	.20
	Plate block of 12	3.00	
	FDC *(Sept. 10, 1973)*		2.50

1973. Willa Cather Issue saluted a novelist who won a 1922 Pulitzer Prize. *Gravure (Andreotti Press), perforated 11.*

CM727 *Willa Cather, pioneers and covered wagon*

CM727

		MNHVF	UseVF
8¢	**multicolored** tagged *(139,608,000)*	.25	.20
	Plate block of 12	3.00	
	FDC *(Sept. 20, 1973)*		1.75
	v. Vertical pair, imperforate horizontally	275.00	

Rural America Series

1973. Angus Cattle Issue first of a series of three stamps honoring rural America, saluted the 100th anniversary of the introduction of Aberdeen Angus cattle into the United States (See also CM751-752). *Intaglio (Giori Press) and offset, perforated 11.*

CM728 *Angus cattle and longhorn cattle on prairie*

CM728

		MNHVF	UseVF
8¢	**multicolored** tagged *(145,430,000)*	.25	.20
	Plate block of 4	1.00	
	FDC *(Oct. 5, 1973)*		1.75
	v. green and red brown omitted	975.00	
	v1. Vertical pair, imperforate between	4,500.00	
	zo. Tagging omitted	14.00	

1974. Veterans of Foreign Wars Issue saluted the men and women in America's military service since the Revolutionary War. *Intaglio (Giori Press), perforated 11.*

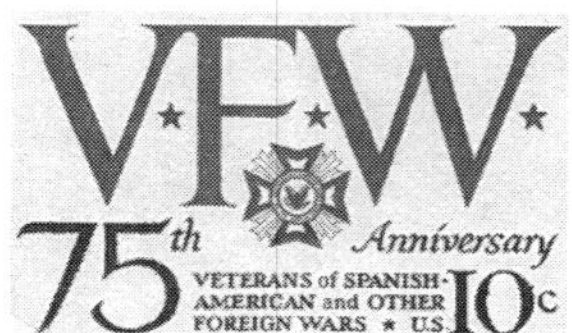

CM729 *VFW emblem*

CM729

		MNHVF	UseVF
10¢	**red & blue** tagged *(145,430,000)*	.25	.20
	Plate block of 4	1.30	
	FDC *(March 11, 1974)*		1.75
	zo. Tagging omitted	5.00	

1974. Robert Frost Issue in the American Poets Series honored the New England poet (1873-1963) and four-time winner of the Pulitzer Prize. *Intaglio, perforated 10 1/2 x 11.*

CM730 *Robert Frost*

CM730

		MNHVF	UseVF
10¢	**black** tagged *(145,235,000)*	.25	.20
	Plate block of 4	1.30	
	FDC *(March 26, 1974)*		1.75

1974. Expo 74 World's Fair Issue featured the theme "Preserve the Environment," magically rendered by Peter Max in his images Cosmic Jumper and Smiling Sage. *Gravure (Andreotti Press), perforated 11.*

CM731 *Expo 74*

CM731

		MNHVF	UseVF
10¢	**multicolored** tagged *(135,052,000)*	.25	.20
	Plate block of 12	4.25	
	FDC *(April 18, 1974)*		1.75

1974. Horse Racing Issue commemorated the 100th running of the Kentucky Derby. *Gravure (Andreotti Press), perforated 11 x 10 1/2.*

CM732 *Horses at the turn*

CM732

		MNHVF	UseVF
10¢	**multicolored** tagged *(156,750,000)*	.25	.20
	Plate block of 12	3.75	
	FDC *(May 4, 1974)*		3.00
	v. blue "Horse Racing" omitted	900.00	
	b. red "U.S. Postage 10 cents" omitted	—	
	zo. Tagging omitted	15.00	

Beware of stamps with minute traces of red being offered as CM732b. They are printing freaks, and do not have comparable value to a full color-omitted error.

1974. Skylab Project Issue paid tribute to the Skylab I program, devoted to experimentation in space.

CM733 *Skylab*

CM733

		MNHVF	UseVF
10¢	**multicolored** tagged *(164,670,000)*	.25	.20
	Plate block of 4	1.30	
	FDC *(May 14, 1974)*		2.00
	v. Vertical pair, imperforate between	—	
	zo. Tagging omitted	7.50	

1974. Universal Postal Union Issue marked the centenary of the international organization that helped standardize mail rates and expedite mail delivery worldwide. *Gravure (Andreotti Press), perforated 11.*

CM734 Lady Writing a Letter *by Terboch* CM735 Still Life *by Chardin* CM736 Mrs. John Douglas *by Gainsborough* CM737 Don Antonio Noriega *by Goya* CM738 Portrait of Michelangelo *by Raphael* CM739 5 Feminine Virtues *by Hokusai* CM740 Old Scraps (Old Letter Rack) *by Peto* CM741 The Lovely Reader *by Liotard*

		MNHVF	UseVF
CM734			
10¢	**multicolored** tagged *(190,154,680)*	.25	.20
CM735		MNHVF	UseVF
10¢	**multicolored** tagged	.25	.20
CM736		MNHVF	UseVF
10¢	**multicolored** tagged	.25	.20
CM737		MNHVF	UseVF
10¢	**multicolored** tagged	.25	.20
CM738		MNHVF	UseVF
10¢	**multicolored** tagged	.25	.20
CM739		MNHVF	UseVF
10¢	**multicolored** tagged	.25	.20
CM740		MNHVF	UseVF
10¢	**multicolored** tagged	.25	.20
CM741		MNHVF	UseVF
10¢	**multicolored** tagged	.25	.20
	Plate block of 10	3.50	
	y. Se-tenant block or strip of 8, CM734-41	2.00	
	FDC *(June 6, 1974)*		2.50
	FDC, block or strip of 8		5.00
	v. Se-tenant block or strip of 8 imperforate vertically	7,500.00	

1974. Mineral Heritage Issue focused attention on the significant contributions minerals have made to making the United States a leader among nations. *Intaglio (Giori Press) and offset, perforated 11.*

CM742 *Amethyst*

CM743 *Petrified wood*

CM744 *Rhodochrosite*

CM745 *Tourmaline*

		MNHVF	UseVF
CM742			
10¢	**multicolored** tagged *(167,212,800)*	.25	.20
	v. light blue and yellow omitted	—	
CM743		MNHVF	UseVF
10¢	**multicolored** tagged	.25	.20
	v. light blue and yellow omitted	—	
CM744		MNHVF	UseVF
10¢	**multicolored** tagged	.25	.20
	v. light blue omitted	—	
	v1. black and red omitted	—	
CM745		MNHVF	UseVF
10¢	**multicolored** tagged	.25	.20
	v. light blue omitted	—	
	v1. black and purple omitted	—	
	Plate block of 4	1.00	
	y. Se-tenant block or strip of 4	—	
	FDC *(June 13, 1974)*		2.00
	FDC, block of 4		4.00
	vy. Se-tenant block or strip of 4, light blue & yellow omitted		
	zo. Tagging omitted, any single	—	
	zoy. Se-tenant block or strip of 4, tagging omitted	58.00	

1974. Settlement of Kentucky Issue saluted the 200th anniversary of the founding of Fort Harrod, the first British settlement west of the Allegheny Mountains. *Intaglio (Giori Press) and offset, perforated 11.*

CM746 *Settlers at Fort Harrod*

		MNHVF	UseVF
CM746			
10¢	**multicolored** tagged *(156,265,000)*	.25	.20
	Plate block of 4	1.30	
	FDC *(June 15, 1974)*		1.75
	v. Offset dull black omitted	800.00	
	v1. green & black (intaglio & offset) & blue omitted	4,250.00	
	v2. green intaglio & offset black omitted	—	
	v3. intaglio green omitted	—	
	zo. Tagging omitted	10.00	

1974. First Continental Congress Issue commemorated the 200th anniversary of the assemblage that paved the way for the creation of the United States. *Intaglio (Giori Press), perforated 11.*

CM747 *Carpenters' Hall*

CM748 *Independence Hall*

CM749 *Quote from 1st Continental Congress*

CM750 *Quote from Declaration of Independence*

		MNHVF	UseVF
CM747			
10¢	**dark blue & red** tagged *(195,585,000)*	.25	.20
CM748		MNHVF	UseVF
10¢	**red & dark blue** tagged	.25	.20
CM749		MNHVF	UseVF
10¢	**gray, dark blue & red** tagged	.25	.20

CM750		MNHVF	UseVF
10¢	**gray, dark blue & red** tagged	.25	.20
	Plate block of 4	1.40	
	y. Se-tenant block of 4, CM747-50	.75	
	FDC *(July 4, 1974),* any single		2.00
	FDC, block of 4		4.00
	zo. Tagging omitted, any single	—	
	zoy. Se-tenant block of 4, tagging omitted	50.00	

1974. Chautauqua Tent Issue the second stamp in the Rural America Series, commemorated the 100th anniversary of the founding of the Chautauqua (N.Y.) Institution, which developed into a teachers' training center for Sunday school and, later, public school. *Intaglio (Giori Press) and offset, perforated 11.*

CM751 *Chautauqua tent*

CM751		MNHVF	UseVF
10¢	**multicolored** tagged *(151,335,000)*	.25	.20
	Plate block of 4	1.30	
	FDC *(Aug. 6, 1974)*		1.75
	v. Black omitted	—	—

1974. Winter Wheat and Train Issue the third and final stamp in the Rural America Series marked the 100th anniversary of hard winter wheat. *Intaglio (Giori Press) and offset, perforated 11.*

CM752 *Winter wheat and train*

CM752		MNHVF	UseVF
10¢	**multicolored** tagged *(141,085,000)*	.25	.20
	Plate block of 4	1.30	
	FDC *(Aug. 16, 1974)*		1.75
	v. black and intaglio blue omitted	875.00	
	zo. Tagging omitted	15.00	

1974. Energy Conservation Issue focused attention upon the national fuel shortage and the need to save energy. *Intaglio (Giori Press) and offset, perforated 11.*

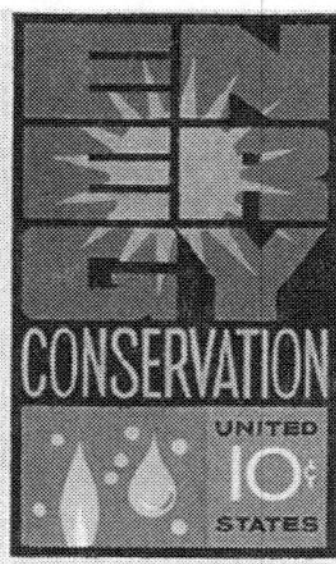

CM753 *Energy conservation*

CM753		MNHVF	UseVF
10¢	**multicolored** tagged *(148,850,000)*	.25	.20
	Plate block of 4	1.30	
	FDC *(Sept. 23, 1974)*		1.75
	v. blue and orange omitted	950.00	
	v1. green omitted	875.00	
	v2. orange and green omitted	800.00	
	zo. Tagging omitted	5.00	

1974. Legend of Sleepy Hollow Issue the fifth in the American Folklore Series, commemorated Washington Irving's *Legend of Sleepy Hollow. Intaglio (Giori Press) and offset, perforated 11.*

CM754 *Headless Horseman pursuing Ichabod Crane*

CM754		MNHVF	UseVF
10¢	**dark blue, black, orange, & yellow** tagged *(157,270,000)*	.25	.20
	Plate block of 4	1.30	
	FDC *(Oct. 10, 1974)*		2.00

1974. Help for Retarded Children Issue encouraged efforts to help mentally retarded persons. *Intaglio (Giori Press), perforated 11.*

CM755 *Retarded girl and helping hand*

CM755		MNHVF	UseVF
10¢	**light & dark brown** tagged *(150,245,000)*	.25	.20
	Plate block of 4	1.30	
	FDC *(Oct. 12, 1974)*		1.75
	zo. Tagging omitted	6.00	

American Arts Series

1975. Benjamin West Issue part of a brief American Arts Series, commemorated Benjamin West, the first American-born painter to gain an international reputation working abroad. *Gravure (Andreotti Press), perforated 10 1/2 x 11.*

CM756 Self Portrait, *Benjamin West*

CM756		MNHVF	UseVF
10¢	**multicolored** tagged *(156,995,000)*	.25	.20
	Plate block of 10	3.25	
	FDC *(Feb. 10, 1975)*		1.75

1975. Pioneer Space Issue saluted the unmanned Pioneer space mission, which probed the planet Jupiter in 1973-74. *Intaglio (Giori Press) and offset, perforated 11.*

CM757 Pioneer 10 *and Jupiter*

CM757		MNHVF	UseVF
10¢	**dark blue, yellow & red** tagged *(173,685,000)*	.25	.20
	Plate block of 4	1.30	
	FDC *(Feb. 28, 1975)*		1.75
	v. intaglio blue omitted	950.00	

v1. red and yellow omitted 1,350.00
zo. Tagging omitted 7.50

Imperforate varieties came from printer's waste.

1975. Collective Bargaining Issue commemorated the 40th anniversary of collective bargaining law in the Wagner Act, which stabilized labor-management relations in the United States. *Gravure (Andreotti Press), perforated 11.*

CM758 *Collective bargaining*

CM758		MNHVF	UseVF
10¢	**multicolored** tagged *(153,355,000)*	.25	.20
	Plate block of 8	2.50	
	FDC *(March 13, 1975)*		1.75
	v. Pair, imperforate	350.00	

Imperforate varieties came from printer's waste.

1975. Contributors to the Cause Issue honored four heroes of the American Revolution. Emerald green inscriptions on the back of the stamp telling the story of each individual are printed under the gum. *Gravure (Andreotti Press), perforated 11 x 10 1/2.)*

CM759 *Sybil Ludington, youthful heroine*

CM759		MNHVF	UseVF
10¢	**multicolored** tagged *(63,205,000)*	.25	.20
	Plate block of 10	2.50	
	FDC *(March 25, 1975)*		1.75
	v. Inscription on back omitted	250.00	

CM760 *Salem Poor, gallant soldier*

CM760		MNHVF	UseVF
10¢	**multicolored** tagged *(157,865,000)*	.25	.20
	Plate block of 10	3.25	
	FDC *(March 25, 1975)*		2.50
	v. Inscription on back omitted	250.00	

CM761 *Haym Solomon, financial hero*

CM761		MNHVF	UseVF
10¢	**multicolored** tagged *(166,810,000)*	.25	.20
	Plate block of 10	3.25	
	FDC *(March 25, 1975)*		1.75
	v. Inscription on back omitted	250.00	
	v1. red omitted	275.00	

CM762 *Peter Francisco, fighter extraordinary*

CM762		MNHVF	UseVF
18¢	**multicolored** tagged *(44,825,000)*	.25	.20
	Plate block of 10	6.25	
	FDC *(March 25, 1975)*		1.75

1975. Mariner Space Issue honored the *Mariner 10* unmanned space mission to Venus and Mercury. *Intaglio (Giori Press) and offset, perforated 11.*

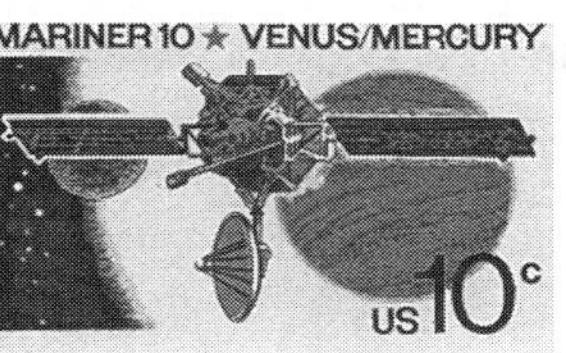

CM763 Mariner 10, *Venus and Mercury*

CM763		MNHVF	UseVF
10¢	**black, red, ultramarine & bister** tagged *(158,600,000)*	.25	.20
	Plate block of 4	1.30	
	FDC *(April 4, 1975)*		1.75
	v. red omitted	575.00	
	v1. ultramarine and bister omitted	1,750.00	
	zo. Tagging omitted	7.50	

1975. Lexington and Concord Issue commemorated these 1775 battles, the first of the Revolutionary War. *Gravure (Andreotti Press), perforated 11.*

CM764 *Lexington and Concord, based on painting* Birth of Liberty *by Henry Sandham*

CM764		MNHVF	UseVF
10¢	**multicolored** tagged *(114,028,000)*	.25	.20
	Plate block of 12	3.75	
	FDC *(April 19, 1975)*		1.75
	v. Vertical pair, imperforate horizontally	425.00	

1975. Paul Laurence Dunbar Issue in the American Arts Series honored the African-American poet. *Gravure (Andreotti Press), perforated 11.*

CM765 *Paul Lawrence Dunbar*

CM765		MNHVF	UseVF
10¢	**multicolored** tagged *(146,365,000)*	.25	.20
	Plate block of 10	3.25	
	FDC *(May 1, 1975)*		2.50
	v. Pair, imperforate	1,300.00	

1975. D.W. Griffith Issue of the American Arts Series commemorated motion picture pioneer D.W. Griffith. *Intaglio (Giori Press) and offset, perforated 11.*

CM766 *D.W. Griffith, motion picture camera*

CM766		MNHVF	UseVF
10¢	**multicolored** tagged *(148,805,000)*	.25	.20
	Plate block of 4	1.30	
	FDC *(May 27, 1975)*		1.75
	v. intaglio dark brown omitted	650.00	

1975. Bunker Hill Issue commemorated the 200th anniversary of the Battle of Bunker Hill. *Gravure (Andreotti Press), perforated 11.*

CM767 *Detail from the painting* The Battle of Bunker Hill *by John Trumbull*

CM767		MNHVF	UseVF
10¢	**multicolored** tagged *(139,928,000)*	.25	.20
	Plate block of 12	3.75	
	FDC *(June 17, 1975)*		1.75

1975. Military Services Bicentennial Issue honored the 200th anniversary year of the U.S. military services. Designs depict uniforms worn by the Continental Army, Navy, Marines and Militia during the Revolutionary War. *Gravure (Andreotti Press), perforated 11.*

CM768 *Soldier*

CM769 *Sailor*

CM770 *Marine*

CM771 *Militiaman*

CM768		MNHVF	UseVF
10¢	**multicolored** tagged *(179,855,000)*	.25	.20
CM769		**MNHVF**	**UseVF**
10¢	**multicolored** tagged	.25	.20
CM770		**MNHVF**	**UseVF**
10¢	**multicolored** tagged	.25	.20
CM771		**MNHVF**	**UseVF**
10¢	**multicolored** tagged	.25	.20
	Plate block of 12	4.25	
	y. Se-tenant block of 4, CM768-71	.75	
	FDC *(July 4, 1975)*, any single		2.00
	FDC, block of 4		4.00

1975. Apollo Soyuz Issue honored the first combined space mission between the United States and Soviet Union. The se-tenant designs used by both nations are identical except for language and denomination (Russia Nos. 4472-4473). *Gravure (Andreotti Press), perforated 11.*

CM772 *Spacecraft in docked position*

CM772		MNHVF	UseVF
10¢	**multicolored** tagged *(161,863,200)*	.25	.20

CM773 *Spacecraft prior to docking*

CM773		MNHVF	UseVF
10¢	**multicolored** tagged	.25	.20
	Plate block of 12	4.00	
	y. Se-tenant pair, CM772-73	.45	
	Pair, gutter between	—	
	FDC *(July 15, 1975)*, either single		2.00
	FDC, pair		3.00
	v. Vertical pair, imperforate horizontally	2,500.00	
	zo. Tagging omitted, either single	—	
	zoy. Se-tenant pair, tagging omitted	25.00	

1975. World Peace Through Law Issue was a prelude to the Seventh World Law Conference of the World Peace Through Law Center and commemorated man's effort toward the universal goal of a peaceful world order with justice. *Intaglio (Giori Press), perforated 11.*

CM774 *Olive branch, globe, gavel and law book*

CM774		MNHVF	UseVF
10¢	**green, gray blue & brown** tagged *(146,615,000)*	.25	.20
	Plate block of 4	1.35	
	FDC *(Sept. 29, 1975)*		2.00
	v. Horizontal pair, imperforate vertically (only 1 plate block)	14,000.00	
	zo. Tagging omitted	6.00	

1975. International Women's Year Issue celebrated the significance of women. *Gravure (Andreotti Press), perforated 11 x 10 1/2.*

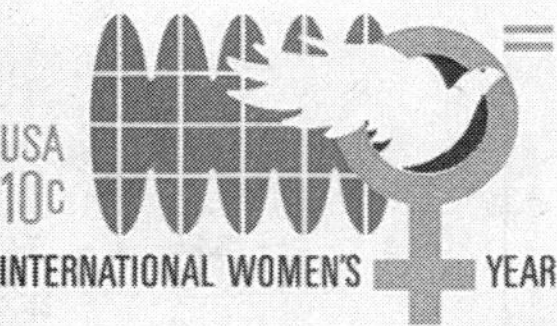

CM775 *Stylized dove, globe and gender sign*

CM775		MNHVF	UseVF
10¢	**blue, orange & dark blue** tagged *(145,640,000)*	.25	.20
	Plate block of 6	1.90	
	FDC *(Aug. 26, 1975)*		1.75

1975. U.S. Postal Service Bicentennial Issue commemorated the 200th anniversary of Postal Service in the United States. *Gravure (Andreotti Press), perforated 11 x 10 1/2.*

CM776 *Stagecoach and modern trailer truck*

CM777 *Early and modern locomotives*

CM778 *Early mail plane and jumbo jet*

CM779 *Satellite for Mailgram transmissions*

CM776 MNHVF UseVF
10¢ **multicolored** tagged *(168,655,000)* .25 .20

CM777 MNHVF UseVF
10¢ **multicolored** tagged .25 .20

CM778 MNHVF UseVF
10¢ **multicolored** tagged .25 .20

CM779 MNHVF UseVF
10¢ **multicolored** tagged .25 .20

	MNHVF	UseVF
Plate block of 12	4.25	
y. Se-tenant block of 4 CM776-79	1.25	
FDC *(Sept. 3, 1975)*, any single		2.00
FDC, block of 4		8.00
vy. Se-tenant block of 4, red "10¢" omitted	7,500.00	

1975. Banking and Commerce Issue focused on the importance of these commercial activities in the nation's development. *Intaglio (Giori Press) and offset, perforated 11.*

CM780 *Coins and currency motif;* CM781 *Coins and currency motif*

CM780 MNHVF UseVF
10¢ **multicolored** tagged *(146,196,000)* .25 .20

CM781 MNHVF UseVF
10¢ **multicolored** tagged .25 .20

	MNHVF	UseVF
Plate block of 4	1.50	
y. Se-tenant pair, CM780-81	.75	.50
FDC *(Oct. 6, 1975)*, either single		1.00
FDC, pair		2.00
vy. Se-tenant pair, brown and blue (offset) omitted	2,500.00	
vly. Se-tenant pair, brown, blue and yellow (offset) omitted	2,750.00	

1976. Spirit of 76 Issue reproduced a classic image of the American Revolution. *Gravure (Andreotti Press), perforated 11.*

CM782-84 Revolutionary War Fife and Drum Trio, *painting by Archibald M. Willard*

CM782 MNHVF UseVF
13¢ **multicolored** tagged *(219,455,000)* .25 .20

CM783 MNHVF UseVF
13¢ **multicolored** tagged .25 .20

CM784 MNHVF UseVF
13¢ **multicolored** tagged .25 .20

	MNHVF	UseVF
Plate block of 12	5.00	
y. Se-tenant strip of 3, CM782-84	.75	1.00
FDC *(Jan. 1, 1976)*, any single		1.75
FDC, strip of 3		5.75
v. Vertical pair, CM784, imperforate	900.00	
v1. Se-tenant strip of 3, imperforate	1,300.00	

1976. INTERPHIL Issue commemorated the Seventh International Philatelic Exhibition. May 29-June 6, 1976, in Philadelphia, Pa. *Intaglio (Giori Press) and offset, perforated 11.*

CM785 *Interphil 76*

CM785 MNHVF UseVF
13¢ **blue, red & ultramarine** tagged *(157,825,000)* .25 .20

	MNHVF	UseVF
Plate block of 4	1.60	
FDC *(Jan. 17, 1976)*		1.75

1976. 50-State Flag Issue included in one sheet the flag of every state, arranged in order of its admission to the union. (The Tennessee flag is shown on CM801 upside-down, altering subtly but discernably the orientation of the three stars.) *Gravure (Andreotti Press), perforated 11, all stamps multicolored.*

CM786-CM835 *State Flags*

CM786 MNHVF UseVF
13¢ **Delaware,** tagged *(436,005,000)* .55 .40

CM787 MNHVF UseVF
13¢ **Pennsylvania,** tagged .55 .40

		MNHVF	UseVF
CM788		MNHVF	UseVF
13¢	**New Jersey,** tagged	.55	.40
CM789		MNHVF	UseVF
13¢	**Georgia,** tagged	.55	.40
CM790		MNHVF	UseVF
13¢	**Connecticut,** tagged	.55	.40
CM791		MNHVF	UseVF
13¢	**Massachusetts,** tagged	.55	.40
CM792		MNHVF	UseVF
13¢	**Maryland,** tagged	.55	.40
CM793		MNHVF	UseVF
13¢	**South Carolina,** tagged	.55	.40
CM794		MNHVF	UseVF
13¢	**New Hampshire,** tagged	.55	.40
CM795		MNHVF	UseVF
13¢	**Virginia,** tagged	.55	.40
CM796		MNHVF	UseVF
13¢	**New York,** tagged	.55	.40
CM797		MNHVF	UseVF
13¢	**North Carolina,** tagged	.55	.40
CM798		MNHVF	UseVF
13¢	**Rhode Island,** tagged	.55	.40
CM799		MNHVF	UseVF
13¢	**Vermont,** tagged	.55	.40
CM800		MNHVF	UseVF
13¢	**Kentucky,** tagged	.55	.40
CM801		MNHVF	UseVF
13¢	**Tennessee,** tagged	.55	.40
CM802		MNHVF	UseVF
13¢	**Ohio,** tagged	.55	.40
CM803		MNHVF	UseVF
13¢	**Louisiana,** tagged	.55	.40
CM804		MNHVF	UseVF
13¢	**Indiana,** tagged	.55	.40
CM805		MNHVF	UseVF
13¢	**Mississippi,** tagged	.55	.40
CM806		MNHVF	UseVF
13¢	**Illinois,** tagged	.55	.40
CM807		MNHVF	UseVF
13¢	**Alabama,** tagged	.55	.40
CM808		MNHVF	UseVF
13¢	**Maine,** tagged	.55	.40
CM809		MNHVF	UseVF
13¢	**Missouri,** tagged	.55	.40
CM810		MNHVF	UseVF
13¢	**Arkansas,** tagged	.55	.40
CM811		MNHVF	UseVF
13¢	**Michigan,** tagged	.55	.40
CM812		MNHVF	UseVF
13¢	**Florida,** tagged	.55	.40
CM813		MNHVF	UseVF
13¢	**Texas,** tagged	.55	.40
CM814		MNHVF	UseVF
13¢	**Iowa,** tagged	.55	.40
CM815		MNHVF	UseVF
13¢	**Wisconsin,** tagged	.55	.40
CM816		MNHVF	UseVF
13¢	**California,** tagged	.55	.40
CM817		MNHVF	UseVF
13¢	**Minnesota,** tagged	.55	.40
CM818		MNHVF	UseVF
13¢	**Oregon,** tagged	.55	.40
CM819		MNHVF	UseVF
13¢	**Kansas,** tagged	.55	.40
CM820		MNHVF	UseVF
13¢	**West Virginia,** tagged	.55	.40
CM821		MNHVF	UseVF
13¢	**Nevada,** tagged	.55	.40
CM822		MNHVF	UseVF
13¢	**Nebraska,** tagged	.55	.40
CM823		MNHVF	UseVF
13¢	**Colorado,** tagged	.55	.40
CM824		MNHVF	UseVF
13¢	**North Dakota,** tagged	.55	.40
CM825		MNHVF	UseVF
13¢	**South Dakota,** tagged	.55	.40
CM826		MNHVF	UseVF
13¢	**Montana,** tagged	.55	.40
CM827		MNHVF	UseVF
13¢	**Washington,** tagged	.55	.40
CM828		MNHVF	UseVF
13¢	**Idaho,** tagged	.55	.40
CM829		MNHVF	UseVF
13¢	**Wyoming,** tagged	.55	.40
CM830		MNHVF	UseVF
13¢	**Utah,** tagged	.55	.40
CM831		MNHVF	UseVF
13¢	**Oklahoma,** tagged	.55	.40
CM832		MNHVF	UseVF
13¢	**New Mexico,** tagged	.55	.40
CM833		MNHVF	UseVF
13¢	**Arizona,** tagged	.55	.40
CM834		MNHVF	UseVF
13¢	**Alaska,** tagged	.55	.40
CM835		MNHVF	UseVF
13¢	**Hawaii,** tagged	.55	.40
	FDC, *(Feb. 23 1976),* any single		3.00
	y. Pane of 50	13.00	
	FDC, pane of 50		150.00

1976. Telephone Centennial Issue honored the 100th anniversary of the first telephone call by Alexander Graham Bell (CM235). *Intaglio (Giori Press), perforated 11.*

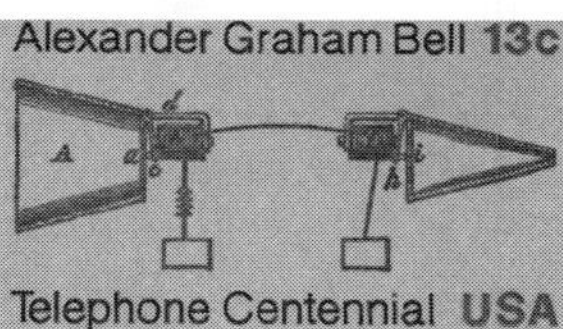

CM836 *Patent application of Bell's 1876 telephone*

CM836		MNHVF	UseVF
13¢	**black, purple & red,** on tan paper, tagged *(159,915,000)*	.25	.20
	Plate block of 4	1.60	
	FDC *(March 10, 1976)*		1.75

1976. Commercial Aviation Issue saluted the 50th anniversary of the first contract airmail flights. The stamp depicts a Ford-Pullman monoplane and a Laird Swallow biplane. *Gravure (Andreotti Press), perforated 11.*

CM837 *Early contract airmail planes*

CM837		MNHVF	UseVF
13¢	**multicolored** tagged *(156,960,000)*	.25	.20
	Plate block of 10	4.70	
	FDC *(March 19, 1976)*		2.00

1976. Chemistry Issue paid tribute to that science and saluted the 100th anniversary of the American Chemical Society. *Gravure (Andreotti Press), perforated 11.*

CM838 *Laboratory flasks, computer tape*

CM838		MNHVF	UseVF
13¢	**multicolored** tagged *(158,470,000)*	.25	.20
	Plate block of 12	4.70	
	Pair, gutter between		
	FDC *(April 6, 1976)*		1.75

1976. Bicentennial Souvenir Sheets issued to coincide with the Seventh International Philatelic Exhibition, held in Philadelphia, Pa., May 29-June 6. Each contained five stamps of the same denomination. *Lithographed, perforated 11.*

CM839 Surrender of Cornwallis at Yorktown *by John Trumbull (five 13¢ stamps)*

CM839		MNHVF	UseVF
65¢	**multicolored** tagged *(1,990,500)*	4.75	4.50
	a. 13c 2 British officers	.95	.90
	b. 13c Gen. Benjamin Lincoln	.95	.90
	c. 13c Gen. George Washington	.95	.90
	d. 13c John Trumbull, Col. Cobb, von Steuben, Lafayette & Thomas Nelson	.95	.90
	e. Alexander Hamilton, John Laurens & Walter Stewart	.95	.90
	FDC *(May 29, 1976),* sheetlet		10.00
	v. "USA/13c" omitted on CM839b, CM839c & CM839d, imperforate	500.00	
	v1. "USA/13c" omitted on CM839b, CM839c & CM839d	900.00	
	v2. "USA/13c" omitted on CM839a & CM839e	500.00	
	v3. "USA/13c" omitted on CM839c & CM838d	500.00	
	v4. "USA/13c" omitted on CM839e	600.00	
	v5. "USA/13c" double on CM839b	—	
	v6. Tagging and "USA/13c" omitted imperforate	—	
	zo. Tagging omitted	—	
	zov. Tagging omitted, imperforate	2,250.00	

CM840 Declaration of Independence, *by John Trumball*

CM840		MNHVF	UseVF
90¢	**multicolored** tagged *(1,983,000)*	6.00	5.75
	a. 18c John Adams, Roger Sherman & Robert Livingston	1.35	1.30
	b. 18c Jefferson and Franklin	1.35	1.30
	c. 18c Thomas Nelson, Jr., Francis Lewis, John Witherspoon & Samuel Huntington	1.35	1.30
	d. 18c John Hancock and Charles Thompson	1.35	1.30
	e. 18c George Read, John Dickenson & Edward Rutledge	1.35	1.30
	FDC *(May 29, 1976),* sheetlet		10.00
	v. black omitted in design	1,250.00	
	v1. Design and marginal inscriptions omitted	—	
	v2. "USA/18c" and tagging omitted, imperforate	—	
	v3. "USA/18c" omitted on CM840a & CM840c	600.00	
	v4. "USA/18c" omitted on CM840b, CM840d & CM840e	500.00	
	v5. "USA/18c" omitted on CM840d	550.00	
	v6. "USA/18c" omitted on CM840b & CM840e	550.00	
	zo. Tagging omitted	—	

CM841 Washington Crossing the Delaware, *by Emmanuel Leutze/Eastman Johnson (five 24¢ stamps)*

CM841		MNHVF	UseVF
$1.20	**multicolored** tagged *(1,953,000)*	8.25	8.00
	a. 24c Boatsman	1.80	1.70
	b. 24c Gen. George Washington	1.80	1.70
	c. 24c Flag bearer	1.80	1.70
	d. 24c Men in boat	1.80	1.70
	e. 24c Men on shore	1.80	1.70
	FDC *(May 29, 1976),* sheetlet		10.00
	v. Design & marginal inscription omitted	3,250.00	
	v1. "USA/24c" omitted, imperforate	—	
	v2. "USA/24c" omitted on CM841a, CM841b & CM841C	600.00	
	v3. "USA/24c" omitted on CM841d & CM841e	550.00	
	v4. "USA/24c" of CM841d & CM841e inverted	500.00	
	zo. Tagging omitted	—	
	zov. Tagging omitted, imperforate	2,500.00	

CM842 Washington Reviewing His Ragged Army at Valley Forge, *by William T. Trego*

CM842		MNHVF	UseVF
$1.55	**multicolored** tagged *(1,903,000)*	10.75	10.50
	a. 31c 2 officers	2.25	2.15
	b. 31c Gen. George Washington	2.25	2.15
	c. 31c Officer on black horse	2.25	2.15
	d. 31c Officer and white horse	2.25	2.15
	e. 31c 3 foot soldiers	2.25	2.15
	FDC *(May 29, 1976),* sheetlet		10.00
	v. black omitted in design	—	
	v1. "USA/31c" omitted, imperforate	2,500.00	
	v2. "USA/31c" omitted on CM842a, CM842b & CM842e	—	
	v3. "USA/31c" and tagging omitted on CM842a, CM842b & CM842c, imperforate	—	
	v4. "USA/31c" omitted on CM842a & CM842c	550.00	
	v5. "USA/31c" and tagging omitted on CM842a & CM842c, imperforate	—	
	v6. "USA/31c"omitted on CM842b, CM842d & CM842e	—	
	v7. "USA/31c" and tagging omitted on CM842b, CM842d & CM842e, imperforate	2,500.00	
	v8. "USA/31c" omitted on CM842b & CM842d	—	
	v9. "USA/31c" omitted on CM842d & CM842e	1,250.00	
	v10. "USA/31c" omitted on CM842e	550.00	
	zo. Tagging omitted, imperforate	2,250.00	

1976. Benjamin Franklin Issue honored America's first postmaster general, appointed by the Continental Congress. *Intaglio (Giori Press) and offset, perforated 11.*

CM843 *Benjamin Franklin and map of North America*

CM843		MNHVF	UseVF
13¢	**multicolored** tagged *(164,890,000)*	.25	.20
	Plate block of 4	1.60	
	FDC *(June 1, 1976)*		1.75
	v. light blue omitted	275.00	
	zo. Tagging omitted	4.00	

1976. Declaration of Independence Issue celebrated the anniversary of the approval of the document on July 4, 1776, by the members of the Continental Congress. *Gravure (Andreotti Press), perforated 11.*

CM844-47 The Declaration of Independence, *painting by John Trumbull*

CM844		MNHVF	UseVF
13¢	**multicolored** tagged *(208,035,000)*	.25	.20

CM845		MNHVF	UseVF
13¢	**multicolored** tagged	.25	.20

CM846		MNHVF	UseVF
13¢	**multicolored** tagged	.25	.20

CM847		MNHVF	UseVF
13¢	**multicolored** tagged	.25	.20
	Plate block of 16	11.00	
	y. Se-tenant strip of 4, CM844-47	1.00	1.00
	FDC *(July 4, 1976)* any single		2.00
	FDC, strip of 4		8.00

1976. Olympic Games Issue saluted the 1976 Winter Games in Innsbruck, Austria, and the Summer Games in Montreal, Canada. *Gravure (Andreotti Press), perforated 11.*

CM848 *Diving*

CM849 *Skiing*

CM850 *Running*

CM851 *Skating*

CM848		MNHVF	UseVF
13¢	**multicolored** tagged *(185,715,000)*	.25	.20

CM849		MNHVF	UseVF
13¢	**multicolored** tagged	.25	.20

CM850		MNHVF	UseVF
13¢	**multicolored** tagged	.25	.20

CM851		MNHVF	UseVF
13¢	**multicolored** tagged	.25	.20
	Plate block of 12	6.50	
	y. Se-tenant block of 4	1.25	1.50
	FDC *(July 16, 1976),* any single		2.00
	FDC, block of 4		4.00
	v. Se-tenant block of 4, imperforate	750.00	
	vl. Pair (either), imperforate	275.00	

1976. Clara Maass Issue honored the 100th birthday of the nurse who gave her life during yellow fever research. *Gravure (Andreotti Press), perforated 11.*

CM852 *Nurse Clara Maass and hospital pin*

CM852		MNHVF	UseVF
13¢	**multicolored** tagged *(130,592,000)*	.25	.20
	Plate block of 12	5.75	
	FDC *(Aug. 18, 1976)*		2.00
	v. Horizontal pair, imperforate vertically	500.00	

1976. Adolph S. Ochs Issue commemorated the 125th anniversary of *The New York Times.* Ochs was the publisher of the *Times* from 1896 until his death in 1935. *Intaglio (Giori Press), perforated 11.*

CM853 *Adolph S. Ochs from portrait by S.J. Woolf*

CM853		MNHVF	UseVF
13¢	**gray & black** tagged *(158,332,800)*	.25	.20
	Plate block of 4	1.60	
	FDC *(Sept. 18, 1976)*		1.75

1977. Washington at Princeton Issue commemorated the American victory at Princeton, N.J., over the British led by Lord Cornwallis. *Gravure (Andreotti Press), perforated 11.*

CM854 George Washington *painting by Charles Willson Peale*

CM854		MNHVF	UseVF
13¢	**multicolored** tagged *(150,328,000)*	.25	.20
	Plate block of 10	3.95	

FDC *(Jan. 3, 1977)* 1.75
v. Horizontal pair, imperforate vertically 550.00

1977. Sound Recording Issue paid tribute to a century of progress in the field of sound recording. *Intaglio (Giori Press) and offset, perforated 11.*

CM855 *Early sound recorder*

CM855		MNHVF	UseVF
13¢	**multicolored** tagged *(176,830,000)*	.25	.20
	Plate block of 4	1.60	
	FDC *(March 23, 1977)*		2.00

American Folk Art Series

1977. Pueblo Indian Art Issue first installment in the all se-tenant American Folk Art Series showcased the artistic achievements of the Pueblo Indians in the craft of pottery. *Gravure (Andreotti Press), perforated 11.*

CM856 *Zia Pueblo*

CM857 *San Ildefonso Pueblo*

CM858 *Hopi Pueblo*

CM859 *Acoma Pueblo*

CM856		MNHVF	UseVF
13¢	**multicolored** tagged *(195,976,000)*	.25	.20
CM857		MNHVF	UseVF
13¢	**multicolored** tagged	.25	.20
CM858		MNHVF	UseVF
13¢	**multicolored** tagged	.25	.20
CM859		MNHVF	UseVF
13¢	**multicolored** tagged	.25	.20
	Plate block of 10	4.50	
	y. Se-tenant block or strip of 4	.75	
	FDC *(April 13, 1977)*, any single		2.00
	FDC, block of 4		4.00
	v. Se-tenant block or strip of 4, imperforate vertically	2,500.00	

1977. 50th Anniversary of Transatlantic Flight Issue commemorated the epic solo flight of Charles A. Lindbergh across the Atlantic Ocean (see A10). *Gravure (Andreotti Press), perforated 11.*

CM860 The Spirit of St. Louis *over the Atlantic Ocean*

CM860		MNHVF	UseVF
13¢	**multicolored** tagged *(208,820,000)*	.25	.20
	Plate block of 12	4.75	
	FDC *(May 20, 1977)*		2.50
	v. Pair, imperforate	1,250.00	

Privately applied overprints on this stamp have no official status.

1977. Colorado Statehood Issue celebrated the centennial of Colorado's entry into the union as the 38th state. *Gravure (Andreotti Press), perforated 11.*

CM861 *Columbine and mountain peak*

CM861		MNHVF	UseVF
13¢	**multicolored** tagged *(190,005,000)*	.25	.20
	Plate block of 12	4.75	
	FDC *(May 21, 1977)*		1.75
	v. Horizontal pair, imperforate between	900.00	
	v1. Horizontal pair, imperforate vertically	900.00	
	v2. Perforated 11 1/4	.35	

1977. Butterfly Issue commemoratives displayed representatives of different regions of the United States. *Gravure (Andreotti Press), perforated 11.*

CM862 *Swallowtail*

CM863 *Checkerspot*

CM864 *Dogface*

CM865 *Orange-Tip*

CM862		MNHVF	UseVF
13¢	**multicolored** tagged *(219,830,000)*	.25	.20
CM863		MNHVF	UseVF
13¢	**multicolored** tagged	.25	.20
CM864		MNHVF	UseVF
13¢	**multicolored** tagged	.25	.20
CM865		MNHVF	UseVF
13¢	**multicolored** tagged	.25	.20
	Plate block of 12	5.50	
	y. Se-tenant block of 4, CM1712-1715	1.00	.80
	FDC *(June 6, 1977)*, any single		2.00
	FDC, block of 4		4.00
	v. Se-tenant block of 4, imperforate horizontally	13,000.00	

1977. Lafayette Issue marked the 200th anniversary of Marquis de Lafayette's landing on the coast of South Carolina, north of Charleston. *Intaglio (Giori Press), perforated 11.*

CM866 *Marquis de Lafayette*

CM866		MNHVF	UseVF
13¢	**blue, black & red** *(159,852,000)*	.25	.20
	Plate block of 4	1.60	
	FDC *(June 13, 1977)*		1.75

1977. Skilled Hands of Independence Issue saluted representatives of four American industries — blacksmiths, wheelwrights, leatherworkers and seamstresses — who contributed to winning the Revolutionary War. *Gravure (Andreotti Press), perforated 11.*

CM867 *Seamstress*

CM868 *Blacksmith*

CM869 *Wheelwright*

CM870 *Leatherworker*

		MNHVF	UseVF
CM867			
13¢	**multicolored** tagged *(188,310,000)*	.25	.20
CM868			
13¢	**multicolored** tagged	.25	.20
CM869			
13¢	**multicolored** tagged	.25	.20
CM870			
13¢	**multicolored**	.25	.20
	Plate block of 12	5.50	
	y. Se-tenant block of 4, CM1717-1720	1.00	.80
	FDC *(July 4, 1977)*		2.00
	FDC, block of 4		4.00

1977. Peace Bridge Issue marked the 50th anniversary of the Peace Bridge between Buffalo (Fort Porter), N.Y., and Fort Erie, Ontario, Canada. *Intaglio, perforated 11 x 10 1/2.*

CM871 *Dove over peace bridge*

		MNHVF	UseVF
CM871			
13¢	**blue** tagged *(163,625,000)*	.25	.20
	Plate block of 4	1.60	
	FDC *(Aug. 4, 1977)*		1.75

1977. Herkimer at Oriskany Issue honored Gen. Nicholas Herkimer's contribution to the American War for Independence and the 200th anniversary of the Battle of Oriskany. *Gravure (Andreotti Press), perforated 11.*

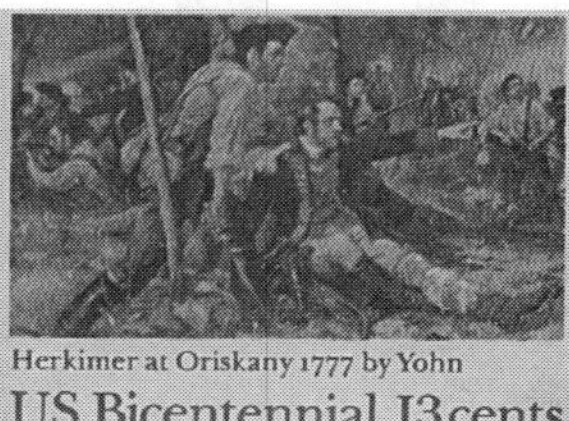

CM872 *Wounded Gen. Herkimer at Battle of Oriskany*

		MNHVF	UseVF
CM872			
13¢	**multicolored** tagged *(156,296,000)*	.25	.20
	Plate block of 10	3.95	
	FDC *(Aug. 6, 1977)*		1.75

1977. Alta California Issue commemorated the bicentennial of the first Spanish civil settlement in Alta (northern) California. *Intaglio (Giori Press) and offset, perforated 11.*

CM873 *Spanish colonial farms*

		MNHVF	UseVF
CM873			
13¢	**multicolored** tagged *(154,495,000)*	.25	.20
	Plate block of 4	1.60	
	FDC *(Sept. 9, 1977)*		1.75

1977. Articles of Confederation Issue marked the 200th anniversary of the drafting of the Articles of Confederation in 1777. *Intaglio (Giori Press), perforated 11.*

CM874 *Drafting the Articles of Confederation*

		MNHVF	UseVF
CM874			
13¢	**red & dark brown** on cream paper, tagged *(168,050,000)*	.25	.20
	Plate block of 4	1.60	
	FDC *(Sept. 30, 1977)*		1.75
	zo. Tagging omitted	10.00	

1977. Talking Pictures Issue marked 50 years since the introduction of sound in films. *The Jazz Singer,* starring Al Jolson, is accepted as the first feature-length talking picture. *Intaglio (Giori Press) and offset, perforated 11.*

CM875 *Early projector and phonograph*

		MNHVF	UseVF
CM875			
13¢	**multicolored** tagged *(156,810,000)*	.25	.20
	Plate block of 4	1.60	
	FDC *(Oct. 6, 1977)*		2.25

1977. Surrender at Saratoga marked the surrender of British Gen. John Burgoyne to Gen. Horatio Gates in 1777 (See CM77). *Gravure (Andreotti Press), perforated 11.*

CM876 Surrender of Burgoyne, *painted by John Trumbull*

		MNHVF	UseVF
CM876			
13¢	**multicolored** *(153,736,000)*	.25	.20
	Plate block of 10	4.00	
	FDC *(Oct. 7, 1977)*		1.75

1977. Energy Issue stressed the importance of conserving energy and developing new sources. *Gravure (Andreotti Press), perforated 11.*

CM876A *"Conservation"*

CM876B *"Development"*

CM876A		MNHVF	UseVF
13¢	**multicolored** tagged	.25	.20
	Plate block of 12	5.00	
	FDC *(Oct. 20, 1977)*, either single		1.50
	y. Se-tenant pair CM876A & CM876B	.50	.40
	FDC se-tenant pair		3.00

CM876B		MNHVF	UseVF
13¢	**multicolored** tagged	.25	.20
	FDC *(Oct. 20, 1977)*		1.50

1978. Carl Sandburg Issue honored "The Poet of the People" on the 100th anniversary of his birth. He won the Pulitzer Prize three times for his works. *Intaglio (Giori Press), perforated 11.*

CM877 *Carl Sandburg*

CM877		MNHVF	UseVF
13¢	**brown & black** tagged *(156,560,000)*	.25	.20
	Plate block of 4	1.60	
	FDC *(Jan. 6, 1978)*		1.75
	v. brown omitted		

1978. Captain Cook Issue featuring two stamps oriented differently in the same sheet, marked the 200th anniversary of the explorer's arrival in Hawaii and Alaska. *Intaglio (Giori Press), perforated 11.*

CM878 *Capt. James Cook*

CM879 *Cook's ships* Resolution *and* Discovery

CM878		MNHVF	UseVF
13¢	**blue** tagged *(202,155,000)*	.25	.20
	FDC *(Jan. 20, 1978)*		1.75

CM879		MNHVF	UseVF
13¢	**green** tagged	.25	.20
	Plate block of 4, CM878 & CM879	1.60	
	Plate block of 20, 10 each CM878-79	5.25	
	y. Se-tenant pair CM878-79	.50	
	FDC *(Jan. 20, 1978)*, either single		1.75
	FDC, Se-tenant pair		2.00
	v. Se-tenant pair, imperforate between	4,250.00	
	v1. Vertical pair (CM879), imperforate horizontally	—	

Please do not send us stamps to be authenticated. This type of service requires elaborate equipment and facilities not regularly available to us.

Black Heritage Series

1978. Harriet Tubman Issue first stamp in the long-running Black Heritage Series, honored the woman known as the "Moses of her people" (c1820-1913). Born into slavery, she is credited with helping more than 300 slaves to escape via the "Underground Railway." (See also CM1731) *Gravure (Andreotti Press), perforated 10 1/2 x 11.*

CM880 *Harriet Tubman*

CM880		MNHVF	UseVF
13¢	**multicolored** tagged *(156,525,000)*	.25	.20
	Plate block of 12	6.50	
	FDC *(Feb. 1, 1978)*		2.50

1978. American Quilts Issue the second se-tenant set in the American Folk Art Series, showed four different basket design quilt patterns. *Gravure (Andreotti Press), perforated 11.*

CM881-884
Basket design by Christopher Pullman after 1875 quilt made in New York City

CM881		MNHVF	UseVF
13¢	**multicolored** tagged *(165,182,000)*	.25	.20

CM882		MNHVF	UseVF
13¢	**multicolored** tagged	.25	.20

CM883		MNHVF	UseVF
13¢	**multicolored** tagged	.25	.20

CM884		MNHVF	UseVF
13¢	**multicolored** tagged	.25	.20
	Plate block of 12	5.50	
	y. Se-tenant block of 4, CM881-84	1.00	.95
	FDC *(May 8, 1978)*, any single		2.00
	FDC, block of 4		4.00

1978. American Dance Issue celebrated various styles of popular dancing. *Gravure (Andreotti Press), perforated 11.*

CM885 *Ballet*

CM886 *Theater*

CM887 *Folk*

CM888 *Modern*

CM885		MNHVF	UseVF
13¢	**multicolored** tagged *(157,598,400)*	.25	.20

CM886		MNHVF	UseVF
13¢	**multicolored** tagged	.25	.20

CM887		MNHVF	UseVF
13¢	**multicolored** tagged	.25	.20

CM888		MNHVF	UseVF
13¢	**multicolored** tagged	.25	.20

		MNHVF	UseVF
	Plate block of 12	5.50	
	y. Se-tenant block of 4, CM885-88	1.50	.95
	FDC *(April 26, 1978)*, any single		2.00
	FDC, block of 4		4.00

1978. French Alliance Issue marked the 200th anniversary of the signing of the French Alliance in 1778. *Intaglio (Giori Press) and offset, perforated 11.*

CM889 *King Louis XVI and Benjamin Franklin. Porcelain statuette by Charles Gabriel Sauvage*

CM889		MNHVF	UseVF
13¢	**blue, black, & red** tagged *(102,856,000)*	.25	.20
	Plate block of 4	1.60	
	FDC *(May 4, 1978)*		1.75

1978. George Papanicolaou Issue commemorated the noted cancer researcher for his development of an early cancer detection procedure, the use of which has saved the lives of thousands of women. *Intaglio, perforated 10 1/2 x 11.*

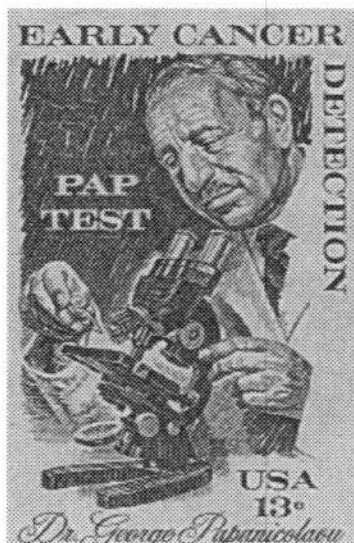

CM890 *Dr. Papanicolaou and microsope*

CM890		MNHVF	UseVF
13¢	**brown** tagged *(152,270,000)*	.25	.20
	Plate block of 4	2.10	
	FDC *(May 13, 1978)*		1.75

Performing Artists Series

1978. Jimmie Rodgers Issue the first stamp in the Performing Artists Series, commemorated the country and western singer known as the "Singing Brakeman" and the "Father of Country Music." Rodgers was the first person inducted into the Country Music Hall of Fame in 1967. *Gravure (Andreotti Press), perforated 11.*

CM891 *Jimmie Rodgers*

CM891		MNHVF	UseVF
13¢	**multicolored** tagged *(94,600,000)*	.25	.20
	Plate block of 12	5.00	
	FDC *(May 24, 1978)*		1.75

1978. Canadian International Philatelic Exhibition Souvenir Sheet commemorated the 1978 CAPEX stamp show in Toronto, Canada. The souvenir sheet contains eight perforated stamps depicting animals and birds indigenous to the United States and Canada. *Intaglio (Giori Press) and offset, perforated 11.*

CM892 *CAPEX souvenir sheet*

CM892		MNHVF	UseVF
$1.04	**multicolored** *(10,400,000)*	2.75	2.00
	Souvenir sheet w/ plate number attached	3.25	2.25
	a. 13¢ Cardinal, tagged	.25	.20
	b. 13¢ Mallard, tagged	.25	.20
	c. 13¢ Canada Goose, tagged	.25	.20
	d. 13¢ Blue Jay, tagged	.25	.20
	e. 13¢ Moose, tagged	.25	.20
	f. 13¢ Chipmunk, tagged	.25	.20
	g. 13¢ Red Fox, tagged	.25	.20
	h. 13¢ Raccoon, tagged	.25	.20
	y. Se-tenant block of 8 CM892 a-h	3.00	
	FDC *(June 6, 1978)* souvenir sheet		3.50
	FDC, any single		2.00
	v. Yellow, green, red, brown, blue & offset black omitted	7,000.00	
	v1. Strip of 4 (a-d), imperforate vertically	7,500.00	
	v2. Strip of 4 (e-h), imperforate vertically	6,500.00	

1978. Photography Issue celebrated the colorful, popular art form. *Gravure (Andreotti Press), perforated 11.*

CM893 *Camera, filters and photo equipment*

CM893		MNHVF	UseVF
15¢	**multicolored** tagged *(161,228,000)*	.30	.20
	Plate block of 12	5.75	
	FDC *(June 26, 1978)*		1.75

1978. George M. Cohan Issue the second stamp in the Performing Artists Series, marked the 100th birthday of George M. Cohan, a patriotic and world-renowned actor, popular song writer, playwright and producer. *Gravure (Andreotti Press), perforated 11.*

CM894 *George M. Cohan*

CM894		MNHVF	UseVF
15¢	**multicolored** tagged *(151,570,000)*	.30	.20
	Plate block of 12	5.75	
	FDC *(July 3, 1978)*		1.75

1978. Viking Missions Issue commemorated the historic Viking space voyages; issued on the second anniversary of the landing of Viking 1 on Mars. *Intaglio (Giori Press) and offset, perforated 11.*

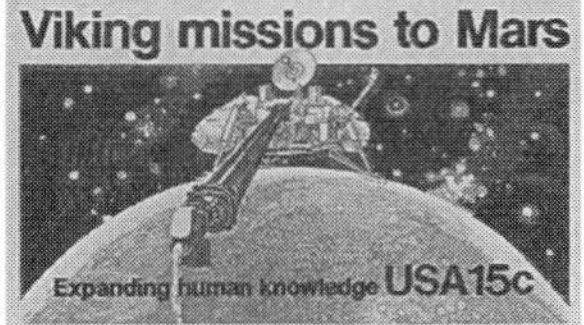

CM895 *Viking I lander and Mars*

CM895		MNHVF	UseVF
15¢	**multicolored** tagged *(158,880,000)*	.30	.20
	Plate block of 4	2.25	
	FDC *(July 20, 1978)*		1.75

1978. Wildlife Conservation Issue featured four species of owls native to the United States. *Intaglio (Giori Press) and offset, perforated 11.*

CM896 *Great Gray Owl*

CM897 *Saw Whet Owl*

CM898 *Barred Owl*

CM899 *Great Horned Owl*

CM896		MNHVF	UseVF
15¢	**Great Gray Owl,** tagged *(186,550,000)*	.30	.20
CM897		MNHVF	UseVF
15¢	**Saw Whet Owl,** tagged	.30	.20
CM898		MNHVF	UseVF
15¢	**Barred Owl,** tagged	.30	.20
CM899		MNHVF	UseVF
15¢	**Great Horned Owl,** tagged	.30	.20
	Plate block of 4	2.00	
	y. Se-tenant block of 4 CM896-99	1.50	1.00
	FDC *(Aug. 26, 1978),* any single		2.00
	FDC, block of 4		4.00

1978. American Trees Issue highlighted four different trees native to the United States and reflected a variety in both appearance and geographic location. *Gravure, perforated 11.*

CM900 *Giant Sequoia*

CM901 *Eastern White Pine*

CM902 *White Oak*

CM903 *Gray Birch*

CM900		MNHVF	UseVF
15¢	**Giant Sequoia,** tagged *(168,136,000)*	.30	.20
CM901		MNHVF	UseVF
15¢	**Eastern White Pine,** tagged	.30	.20
CM902		MNHVF	UseVF
15¢	**White Oak,** tagged	.30	.20
CM903		MNHVF	UseVF
15¢	**Gray Birch,** tagged	.30	.20
	Plate block of 12	6.00	
	y. Se-tenant block of 4, CM900-03	1.25	1.00
	FDC *(Oct. 9, 1978)*		2.00
	FDC, block of 4		4.00
	vy. Se-tenant block of 4, imperforate horizontally	12,250.00	

1979. Robert F. Kennedy Issue honored the assassinated U.S. senator and presidential hopeful. *Intaglio, perforated 11.*

CM904 *Robert F. Kennedy*

CM904		MNHVF	UseVF
15¢	**blue** tagged *(159,297,000)*	.30	.20
	Plate block of 4	1.80	
	FDC *(Jan. 12, 1979)*		2.00
	zo. Tagging omitted	—	

1979. Martin Luther King Jr. Issue in the Black Heritage Series, honored the civil rights leader and his role in the struggle for racial equality. *Gravure (Andreotti Press), perforated 11.*

CM905 *Martin Luther King Jr.*

CM905		MNHVF	UseVF
15¢	**multicolored** tagged *(166,435,000)*	.30	.20
	Plate block of 12	6.25	
	FDC *(Jan. 13, 1979)*		2.50
	v. Imperforate pair	1,750.00	

1979. International Year of the Child Issue acknowledged the declaration by the U.N. General Assembly of 1979 as a year of concern for the condition and well-being of the children of the world. *Intaglio, perforated 11.*

CM906 *Portraits of four children*

CM906		MNHVF	UseVF
15¢	**light & dark brown** tagged *(162,535,000)*	.30	.20
	Plate block of 4	1.80	
	FDC *(Feb. 15, 1979)*		1.75

Literary Arts Series

1979. John Steinbeck Issue the first release in the Literary Arts Series, honored the prolific novelist (1902-68) of *The Grapes of Wrath* and *Travels With Charley* who won the Pulitzer Prize in 1940 and the Nobel Prize for Literature in 1962. *Intaglio, perforated 10 1/2 x 11.*

CM907 *John Steinbeck, from photograph by Philippe Halsman*

CM907		MNHVF	UseVF
15¢	**dark blue** tagged *(155,000,000)*	.30	.20
	Plate block of 4	1.80	
	FDC *(Feb. 27, 1979)*		1.75

1979. Albert Einstein Issue honored the physicist, philosopher and humanitarian best known as the creator of the special and general theories of relativity. *Intaglio, perforated 10 1/2 x 11.*

CM908 *Albert Einstein, from photograph by Hermann Landshoff*

CM908		MNHVF	UseVF
15¢	**brown** tagged *(157,310,000)*	.30	.20
	Plate block of 4	1.80	
	Gutter pair, vertical	—	
	FDC *(March 4, 1979)*		1.75

1979. Pennsylvania Toleware Issue the third se-tenant installment in the American Folk Art Series, depicted four examples of Pennsylvania Toleware, work known for its colorful design motifs. *Gravure (Andreotti Press), perforated 11, multicolored.*

CM909 *Coffee pot with straight spout*

CM910 *Tea caddy*

CM911 *Sugar bowl with lid*

CM912 *Coffee pot with gooseneck spout*

CM909		MNHVF	UseVF
15¢	**Coffee pot with straight spout** *(174,096,000)*	.30	.20

CM910		MNHVF	UseVF
15¢	**Tea caddy**	.30	.20

CM911		MNHVF	UseVF
15¢	**Sugar bowl with lid**	.30	.20

CM912		MNHVF	UseVF
15¢	**Coffee pot with gooseneck spout**	.30	.20
	Plate block of 12	5.00	
	y. Se-tenant block of 4, CM909-12	1.50	1.00
	FDC *(April 19, 1979)*		2.00
	FDC, block of 4		4.00
	vy. Se-tenant block of 4, imperforate horizontally	4,250.00	

1979. American Architecture Issue the first of four se-tenant quartets on this subject designed by Walter D. Richards, commemorated successful early American architecture of enduring beauty, strength and usefulness. *Intaglio (Giori Press), perforated 11, multicolored.*

CM913 *Virginia Rotunda, designed by Thomas Jefferson*

CM914 *Baltimore Cathedral, designed by Benjamin Latrobe*

CM915 *Boston State House, designed by Charles Bulfinch*

CM916 *Philadelphia Exchange, designed by William Strickland*

CM913		MNHVF	UseVF
15¢	**University of Virginia Rotunda,** tagged *(164,793,000)*	.30	.20

CM914		MNHVF	UseVF
15¢	**Baltimore Cathedral,** tagged	.30	.20

CM915		MNHVF	UseVF
15¢	**Boston State House,** tagged	.30	.20

CM916		MNHVF	UseVF
15¢	**Philadelphia Exchange,** tagged	.30	.20
	Plate block of 4	2.50	
	y. Se-tenant block of 4 CM913-16	1.50	1.00
	FDC *(June 4, 1979)*, any single		2.00
	FDC, block of 4		4.00

1979. Endangered Flora Issue portrayed four of the more than 1,700 plant species in the United States seriously threatened with extinction. *Gravure (Andreotti Press), perforated 11, multicolored.*

CM917 *Persistent Trillium*

CM918 *Hawaiian Wild Broadbean*

CM919 *Contra Costa Wallflower*

CM920 *Antioch Dunes Evening Primrose*

CM917		MNHVF	UseVF
15¢	**Persistent Trillium,** tagged *(163,055,000)*	.30	.20

CM918		MNHVF	UseVF
15¢	**Hawaiian Wild Broadbean,** tagged	.30	.20

CM919		MNHVF	UseVF
15¢	**Contra Costa Wallflower,** tagged	.30	.20

CM920		MNHVF	UseVF
15¢	**Antioch Dunes Evening Primrose,** tagged	.30	.20
	Plate block of 12	6.50	
	FDC *(June 7, 1979)*		2.00
	FDC, block of 4		4.00
	Horizontal gutter block of 4	—	
	y. Se-tenant block of 4 CM917-20	2.00	1.00
	vy. Imperforate se-tenant block of 4	600.00	

1979. Seeing Eye Dog Issue commemorated the 50th anniversary of the first guide dog program in the United States, founded by Dorothy Harrison. *Gravure (Combination Press), perforated 11.*

CM921 *German shepherd leading man*

CM921		MNHVF	UseVF
15¢	**multicolored** tagged *(161,860,000)*	.30	.20
	Plate block of 20	9.00	
	FDC *(June 15, 1979)*		1.75
	v. Imperforate pair	425.00	
	zo. Tagging omitted	6.00	

1979. Special Olympics Issue honored the international program of sports training, physical fitness and athletic competition for mentally and physically retarded children and adults. *Gravure (Andreotti Press), perforated 11.*

CM922 *Child with Special Olympics Medal*

CM922		MNHVF	UseVF
15¢	**multicolored** tagged *(165,775,000)*	.30	.20
	Plate block of 10	4.50	
	FDC *(Aug. 9, 1979)*		1.75

1979. Summer Games Issue Gravure, perforated 11, multicolored.

CM923 *Decathlete throwing javelin*

CM923		MNHVF	UseVF
10¢	**multicolored** tagged *(67,195,000)*	.25	.25
	Plate block of 12	4.50	
	FDC *(Sept. 5, 1979)*		1.75

1979. John Paul Jones Issue honored the naval hero (1747-92), of the American Revolution on the 200th anniversary of his victory over the British in the 1779 battle between *Bonhomme Richard* and *HMS Serapis.* This stamp was the first to be printed privately under terms of a contract awarded by the U.S. Postal Service in 1978. *Gravure by J.W. Fergusson and Sons, Richmond, Va., with perforating, cutting and final processing by Americn Bank Note Co., New York, N.Y. perforated 11 x 12.*

CM924, 924A, 924B *John Paul Jones, based on portrait by Charles Willson Peale*

CM924		MNHVF	UseVF
15¢	**multicolored** tagged *(160,000,000, all perforation types)*	.30	.20
	Plate block of 10	4.50	
	FDC *(Sept. 23, 1979)*		2.00
	v. Vertical pair, imperforate horizontally	65.00	

Imperforate errors are from printer's waste.

CM924A		MNHVF	UseVF
15¢	**multicolored** tagged, perforated 11	.75	.25

DECODING THE CATALOG

In the cases of the 15¢ United States John Paul Jones issue of 1979 it really pays to be able to decode the catalog. This single stamp exists in three major types, with values that range from 20¢ to more than $2,000.

The John Paul Jones issue was the first modern-day stamp-printing job to be let out to a contractor. The American Bank Note Co. held the contract, with the stamps being produced on a four-color gravure press owned by J.W. Fergusson and Sons of Richmond, Va. The processing, which included perforating and trimming, was completed byABNC in New York City. There are no significant printing differences on the Jones stamp that created major collectible types, but processing was quite another matter.

When the stamps were first processed on a line perforator, perforations on all four sides gauged 12. These stamps are cataloged as Minkus CM924B.

Shortly after production began, the perforation wheels that perforated the stamps horizontally were replaced with perf 11 wheels. The resulting stamps measured perf 11 by 12. The stamps created by this processing switch are Minkus CM924.

Some time later, the vertical perforations were changed as well, making the remainder of the stamps measure perf 11. These stamps are Minkus CM924A.

Ironically, the rarest of the three stamp types is not a variety, but the originally intended version. Both inexpensive types are varieties. The catalog lists the inexpensive variety as the primary issue, partly so collectors won't feel compelled to purchase the rare type simply because it is the major listing. Both the perf 11 and perf 11 by 12 stamps are fairly common. However, only a few mint panes and a handful of used singles of the perf 12 type were located.

Today, the perf 12 Jones stamp is worth more than $2,000 mint and $1,000 used. The perf 11 version has a slight premium value over face, and the hybrid perforation type is a common commemorative.

		MNHVF	UseVF
	Plate block of 10	8.50	
	FDC *(Sept. 23, 1979)*		2.00
	v. Vertical pair, imperforate horizontally	140.00	
CM924B		**MNHVF**	**UseVF**
15¢	**multicolored** tagged, perforated 12	2,800.00	1,000.00
	v. Vertical pair, imperforate horizontally	175.00	

1979. Summer Games Issue *Gravure, perforated 11, multicolored.*

CM925 *Women runners*

CM926 *Women swimmers*

CM927 *Pair of rowers*

CM928 *Horse and rider*

		MNHVF	UseVF
CM925		**MNHVF**	**UseVF**
15¢	**Women runners,** tagged *(186,905,000)*	.25	.20
CM926		**MNHVF**	**UseVF**
15¢	**Women swimmers,** tagged	.25	.20
CM927		**MNHVF**	**UseVF**
15¢	**Pair of rowers,** tagged	.25	.20
CM928		**MNHVF**	**UseVF**
15¢	**Horse & Rider,** tagged	.25	.20
	Plate block of 12	6.50	
	y. Se-tenant block of 4 CM925-28	1.50	1.10
	FDC *(Sept. 28, 1979),* any single		2.00
	FDC, block of 4		4.00
	vy. Se-tenant block of 4, imperforate	1,500.00	
	v1. Vertical pair, imperforate (either)	650.00	

1979. Will Rogers Issue in the Performing Arts Series, honored the American humorist on the 100th anniversary of his birth. (See also CM317.) *Gravure (Andreotti Press), perforated 11.*

CM929 *Will Rogers*

		MNHVF	UseVF
CM929		**MNHVF**	**UseVF**
15¢	**multicolored** tagged *(161,290,000)*	.30	.20
	Plate block of 12	6.00	
	FDC *(Nov. 4, 1979)*		1.75
	v. Imperforate pair	200.00	

1979. Vietnam Veterans Issue paid tribute to the veterans of the war in Southeast Asia. *Gravure (Andreotti Press), perforated 11.*

CM930 *Vietnam Service ribbon*

		MNHVF	UseVF
CM930		**MNHVF**	**UseVF**
15¢	**multicolored** tagged *(172,740,000)*	.30	.20
	Plate block of 10	5.95	
	FDC *(Nov. 11, 1979)*		2.50

1980. W.C. Fields Issue in the Performing Arts Series honored the juggler, actor and comedian on the 100th anniversary of his birth. *Gravure, perforated 11.*

CM931 *W.C. Fields*

		MNHVF	UseVF
CM931		**MNHVF**	**UseVF**
15¢	**multicolored** tagged *(168,995,000)*	.30	.20
	Plate block of 12	6.00	
	FDC *(Jan. 29, 1980)*		2.50
	v. Pair, imperforate	—	

1980. Winter Games Issue included four commemoratives for events from the Winter Games, and honored the 13th Winter Games at Lake Placid, N.Y. *Gravure, perforated 11 x 10 1/2, multicolored.*

CM932, CM935A *Speed skater*

CM933, CM935B *Ski jumper*

CM934, CM935C *Downhill skier*

CM935, CM935D *Hockey goaltender*

		MNHVF	UseVF
CM932		**MNHVF**	**UseVF**
15¢	**Speed skater,** tagged *(208,295,000) (both perforation types)*	.30	.20
CM933		**MNHVF**	**UseVF**
15¢	**Ski jumper,** tagged	.30	.20
CM934		**MNHVF**	**UseVF**
15¢	**Downhill skier,** tagged	.30	.20
CM935		**MNHVF**	**UseVF**
15¢	**Hockey goaltender,** tagged	.30	.20
	Plate block of 12	6.50	
	y. Se-tenant block of 4 CM932-35	1.50	1.10
	FDC *(Feb. 1, 1980),* any single		2.00
	FDC, block of 4		4.00
CM935A		**MNHVF**	**UseVF**
15¢	**Speed Skater,** perforated 11, tagged	.80	.75
CM935B		**MNHVF**	**UseVF**
15¢	**Ski jumper,** perforated 11, tagged	.80	.75
CM935C		**MNHVF**	**UseVF**
15¢	**Downhill skier,** perforated 11, tagged	.80	.75
CM935D		**MNHVF**	**UseVF**
15¢	**Hockey goaltender,** perforated 11, tagged	.80	.75
	Plate block of 12	14.00	
	y. Se-tenant block of 4 CM935A- 935D	4.00	4.00

1980. Benjamin Banneker Issue in the Black Heritage Series honored a pioneer American scientist and mathematician. Born free in 1731, he became both a noted astronomer and surveyor. *Gravure by J.W. Fergusson and Sons for American Bank Note Co., perforated 11.*

CM936 *Benjamin Banneker*

CM936		MNHVF	UseVF
15¢	**multicolored** tagged *(160,000,000)*	.30	.20
	Plate block of 12	5.50	
	FDC *(Feb. 15, 1980)*		2.50
	v. Horizontal pair, imperforate vertically	750.00	
	v1. Imperforate pair	50.00	

Imperforates with misregistered colors are from printers' waste, have been fraudulently perforated to simulate CM936v. Genuine examples of this error have colors correctly registered. Expert certification recommended.

1980. National Letter Writing Issue focused attention on the importance of letter writing. Three sets of vertical pairs. *Gravure, perforated 11, multicolored.*

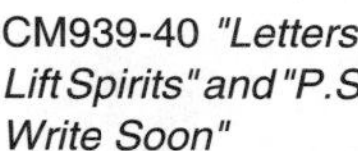
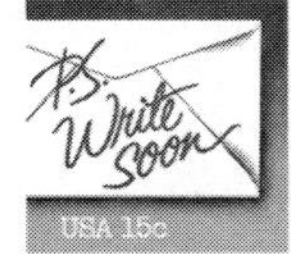

CM937-38 *"Letters Preserve Memories" and "P.S. Write Soon"*

CM939-40 *"Letters Lift Spirits" and "P.S. Write Soon"*

CM41-42 *"Letters Shape Opinions" and "P.S. Write Soon"*

CM937		MNHVF	UseVF
15¢	**"Letters Preserve Memories"** *(232,134,000)*	.30	.20
CM938		**MNHVF**	**UseVF**
15¢	**"Write Soon," (purple),** tagged	.30	.20
CM939		**MNHVF**	**UseVF**
15¢	**"Letters Lift Spirits,"** tagged	.30	.20
CM940		**MNHVF**	**UseVF**
15¢	**"Write Soon", (green),** tagged	.30	.20
CM941		**MNHVF**	**UseVF**
15¢	**"Letters Shape Opinions,"** tagged	.30	.20
CM942		**MNHVF**	**UseVF**
15¢	**"Write Soon," (red),** tagged	.30	.20
	Plate block of 36	19.50	
	y. Se-tenant vertical strip of 6 CM937-42	2.00	
	FDC *(Feb. 25, 1980),* any single		1.75
	FDC, strip of 6		4.00

1980. Frances Perkins Issue honored the first woman to serve as a member of a U.S. presidential cabinet. Perkins (1882-1965), a social reformer, was Franklin Roosevelt's Secretary of Labor. *Intaglio, perforated 10 1/2 x 11.*

CM943 *Frances Perkins*

CM943		MNHVF	UseVF
15¢	**blue** tagged *(163,510,000)*	.30	.20
	Plate block of 4	1.95	
	FDC *(April 10, 1980)*		1.75

1980. Emily Bissell Issue celebrated the crusader against tuberculosis who introduced Christmas seals to the United States. *Intaglio, perforated 11.*

CM944 *Emily Bissell*

CM944		MNHVF	UseVF
15¢	**black & red** tagged *(95,695,000)*	.30	.20
	Plate block of 4	1.80	
	FDC *(May 31, 1980)*		1.75
	v. Vertical pair, imperforate horizontally	375.00	

1980. Helen Keller and Anne Sullivan Issue commemorated blind, deaf author and lecturer Helen Keller (1880-1968) and her teacher, Anne Sullivan, her constant companion for almost 50 years. *Offset and intaglio, perforated 11.*

CM945 *Helen Keller and Anne Sullivan*

CM945		MNHVF	UseVF
15¢	**multicolored** tagged *(153,975,000)*	.30	.20
	Plate block of 4	1.80	
	FDC *(June 27, 1980)*		2.00

1980. Veterans Administration Issue marked the 50th anniversary of the Veterans Administration. *Gravure by J.W. Fergusson and Sons for American Bank Note Co., perforated 11.*

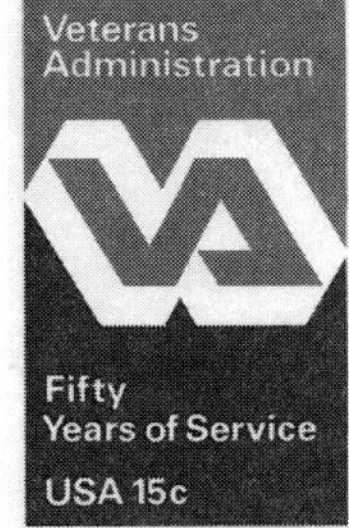

CM946 *Veterans Administration emblem*

CM946		MNHVF	UseVF
15¢	**red & dark blue** tagged *(160,000,000)*	.30	.20
	Plate block of 4	1.80	
	FDC *(July 21, 1980)*		2.00
	v. Horizontal pair, imperforate vertically	475.00	

1980. Bernardo de Galvez Issue honored the governor of Spanish Louisiana during the American Revolution, a major contributor to the winning of the war. *Intaglio and offset, perforated 11.*

CM947 *Bernardo de Galvez from statue in Spanish Plaza, Mobile, Ala.*

CM947		MNHVF	UseVF
15¢	**multicolored** tagged *(103,850,000)*	.30	.20
	Plate block of 4	1.80	
	FDC *(July 23, 1980)*		1.75
	v. blue, brown, red & yellow omitted	1,350.00	
	v1. red, brown & blue omitted	750.00	

1980. Coral Reefs Issue showcased corals found in the waters of the United States, its territories and possessions. *Gravure, perforated 11, multicolored.*

CM948 *Brain Coral, U.S. Virgin Islands*

CM949 *Elkhorn Coral, Florida*

CM950 *Chalice Coral, American Samoa*

CM951 *Finger Coral, Hawaii*

CM948		MNHVF	UseVF
15¢	**Brain Coral,** tagged *(204,715,000)*	.30	.20
CM949		**MNHVF**	**UseVF**
15¢	**Elkhorn Coral,** tagged	.30	.20
CM950		**MNHVF**	**UseVF**
15¢	**Chalice Coral,** tagged	.30	.20
CM951		**MNHVF**	**UseVF**
15¢	**Finger Coral,** tagged	.30	.20
	Plate block of 12	6.00	
	y. Se-tenant block of 4 CM948-51	1.50	
	FDC *(Aug. 26, 1980),* any single		2.00
	FDC, block of 4		4.00
	v. Se-tenant block of 4, imperforate	1,200.00	
	v1. Se-tenant block of 4, imperforate between vertically	3,750.00	
	v2. Se-tenant block of 4, imperforate vertically	3,000.00	

1980. Organized Labor Issue honored the American labor movement, an integral part of the history of democracy and freedom in the United States. *Gravure, perforated 11.*

CM952 *Bald eagle*

CM952		MNHVF	UseVF
15¢	**multicolored** tagged *(166,545,000)*	.30	.20
	Plate block of 12	5.50	
	FDC *(Sept. 1, 1980)*		1.75
	v. Imperforate pair	375.00	

1980. Edith Wharton Issue 2nd in the Literary Arts Series honored the Pulitzer Prize-winning author (1862-1937) of *The Age of Innocence* and other novels, as well as short stories and poetry. *Intaglio, perforated 10 1/2 x 11.*

CM953 *Edith Wharton*

CM953		MNHVF	UseVF
15¢	**purple** tagged *(163,310,000)*	.30	.20
	Plate block of 4	2.00	
	FDC *(Sept. 5, 1980)*		1.75

1980. Education in America Issue commemorated American education and called attention to the newly established U.S. Education Department. *Gravure by J.W. Fergusson and Sons for the American Bank Note Co., perforated 11.*

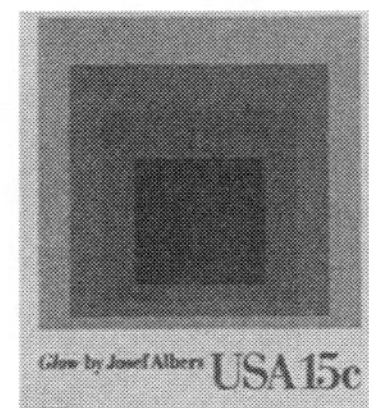

CM954 Homage to the Square: Glow, *acrylic printing by Josef Albers*

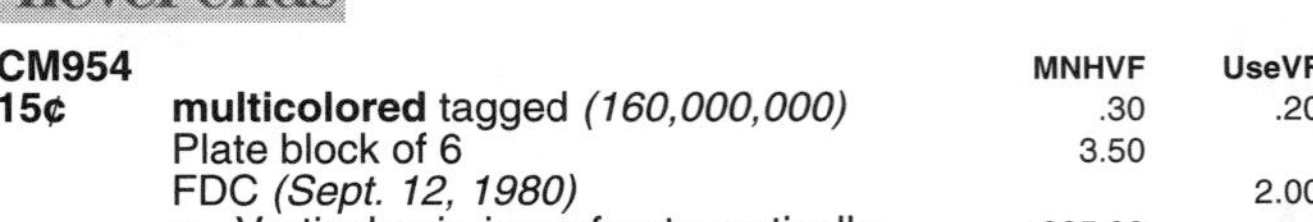

CM954		MNHVF	UseVF
15¢	**multicolored** tagged *(160,000,000)*	.30	.20
	Plate block of 6	3.50	
	FDC *(Sept. 12, 1980)*		2.00
	v. Vertical pair, imperforate vertically	225.00	

1980. Pacific Northwest Masks Issue the fourth set in the American Folk Art Series, featured four carved masks representing the craftsmanship of tribes in the Pacific Northwest coastal region. *Gravure, perforated 11.*

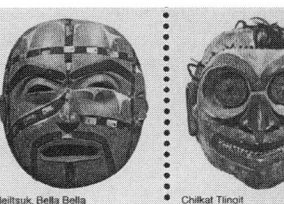

CM955 *Heiltsuk Bella Bella mask*

CM956 *Chilkat Tlingit mask*

CM957 *Tlingit mask*

CM958 *Bella Coola mask*

CM955		MNHVF	UseVF
15¢	**Heiltsuk Bella Bella mask,** tagged *(152,404,000)*	.30	.20
CM956		**MNHVF**	**UseVF**
15¢	**Chikat Tlingit mask,** tagged	.30	.20
CM957		**MNHVF**	**UseVF**
15¢	**Tlingit mask,** tagged	.30	.20
CM958		**MNHVF**	**UseVF**
15¢	**Bella Coola mask,** tagged	.30	.20
	Plate block of 10	7.00	
	y. Se-tenant block of 4 CM955-58	2.25	1.50
	FDC *(Sept. 24, 1980),* any single		2.00
	FDC, block of 4		4.00

1980. American Architecture Issue second of four se-tenant quartets, represented 19th-century architecture of enduring beauty, strength and usefulness. *Intaglio (Giori Press), perforated 11.*

CM959 *Smithsonian I nstitution in Washington, D.C., designed by James Renwick*

CM960 *Trinity Church in Boston, designed by Henry Hobson Richardson*

CM961 *Pennsylvania Academy of the Fine Arts in Philadelphia, designed by Frank Furness*

CM962 *Lyndhurst at Tarrytown, New York, designed by Alexander Jackson Davis*

		MNHVF	UseVF
CM959			
15¢	**Smithsonian Institution,** tagged *(152,720,000)*	.30	.20
CM960			
15¢	**Trinity Church,** tagged	.30	.20
CM961			
15¢	**Pennsylvania Academy of the Fine Arts,** tagged	.30	.20
CM962			
15¢	**Lyndhurst,** tagged	.30	.20
	Plate block of 4	2.50	
	y. Se-tenant block of 4 CM959-62	2.25	1.50
	FDC *(Oct. 9, 1980)*		2.00
	FDC, block of 4		4.00

1981. Everett Dirksen Issue commemorated a public servant (1896-1969) first elected from Illinois to the U.S. House of Representatives in 1932, then in 1950 to the U.S. Senate, where he served until his death. Dirksen was noted for his oratory and attention to legislative detail. *Intaglio, perforated 11.*

CM963 *Everett Dirksen*

		MNHVF	UseVF
CM963			
15¢	**gray** tagged *(160,155,000)*	.30	.20
	Plate block of 4	2.50	
	FDC *(Jan. 4, 1981)*		1.75

1981. Whitney Moore Young Issue part of the Black Heritage Series, honored the civil rights leader who was executive director of the National Urban League at his death. Young was an author, former dean of the Atlanta School of Social Work and a recipient of the Medal of Freedom. *Gravure, perforated 11.*

CM964 *Whitney M. Young*

		MNHVF	UseVF
CM964			
15¢	**multicolored** tagged *(159,505,000)*	.30	.20
	Plate block of 4	1.80	
	FDC *(Jan. 30, 1981)*		2.50

1981. Flower Issue featured the designs of four flowers cultivated in the United States, reproduced from original paintings by Lowell Nesbitt in se-tenant form. *Gravure, perforated 11, multicolored.*

CM965 *Rose*

CM966 *Camellia*

CM967 *Dahlia*

CM968 *Lily*

		MNHVF	UseVF
CM965			
18¢	**Rose,** tagged *(210,633,000)*	.30	.20
CM966			
18¢	**Camellia,** tagged	.30	.20
CM967			
18¢	**Dahlia,** tagged	.30	.20
CM968			
18¢	**Lily,** tagged	.30	.20
	Plate block of 4	2.60	
	y. Se-tenant block of 4 CM965-68	2.00	1.50
	FDC *(April 23, 1981)*		2.00
	FDC, block of 4		4.00

1981. American Red Cross Issue marked the centennial of the organization and honored the thousands of Red Cross volunteers who have given freely of their time to help people throughout the country. *Gravure, perforated 10 1/2 x 11.*

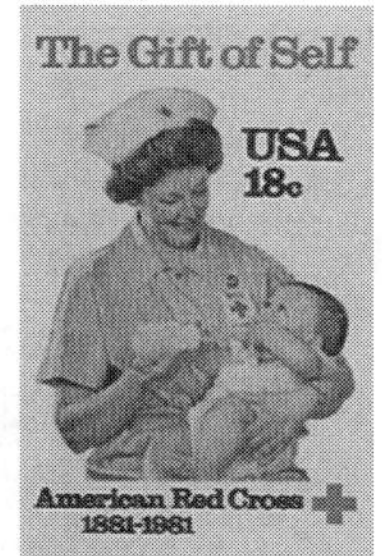

CM969 *Nurse and baby*

		MNHVF	UseVF
CM969			
18¢	**multicolored** tagged *(165,175,000)*	.30	.20
	Plate block of 4	2.80	
	FDC *(May 1, 1981)*		2.00

1981. Savings and Loan Issue marked the sesquicentennial of the first savings and loan organization in the United States and emphasized the importance of thrift and home ownership. *Gravure, perforated 11.*

CM970 *Savings and loan building coin bank*

		MNHVF	UseVF
CM970			
18¢	**multicolored** tagged *(107,240,000)*	.30	.20

		MNHVF	UseVF
	Plate block of 4	2.50	
	FDC *(May 8, 1981)*		1.75

1981. SPACE ACHIEVEMENT ISSUE saluted the U.S. accomplishments and technology in space research. *Gravure, perforated 11, multicolored.*

CM971 *Astronaut on Moon;* CM972 *Pioneer II and Saturn;* CM973 *Skylab and Sun;* CM974 *Hubble Space Telescope;* CM975 *Space Shuttle In orbit;* CM976 *Space Shuttle with arm deployed;* CM977 *Space Shuttle at launch;* CM978 *Space Shuttle prior to landing*

		MNHVF	UseVF
CM971			
18¢	**Astronaut on Moon,** tagged *(337,819,000)*	.30	.20
CM972			
18¢	**Pioneer II & Saturn,** tagged	.30	.20
CM973			
18¢	**Skylab & Sun,** tagged	.30	.20
CM974			
18¢	**Hubble Space Telescope,** tagged	.30	.20
CM975			
18¢	**Space Shuttle in orbit,** tagged	.30	.20
CM976			
18¢	**Space Shuttle with arm deployed,** tagged	.30	.20
CM977			
18¢	**Space Shuttle at launch,** tagged	.30	.20
CM978			
18¢	**Space Shuttle at landing,** tagged	.30	.20
	Plate block of 8	6.00	
	y. Se-tenant block of 8 CM971-78	5.00	4.00
	FDC *(May 5, 1981)*		2.00
	FDC, block of 8		6.00
	v. Se-tenant block of 8, imperforate	9,500.00	

1981. PROFESSIONAL MANAGEMENT ISSUE marked the 100th anniversary of professional management education in the United States, and honored Joseph Wharton, founder of the Wharton School of Business. *Gravure, perforated 11.*

CM979 *Joseph Wharton*

		MNHVF	UseVF
CM979			
18¢	**blue & black** tagged *(99,420,000)*	.30	.20
	Plate block of 4	2.40	
	FDC *(June 18, 1981)*		1.75

1981. SAVE WILDLIFE HABITATS ISSUE focused on the necessity for the preservation of the natural environment of our native birds and mammals. *Gravure, perforated 11, multicolored.*

CM980 *Blue heron*

CM981 *Badger*

CM982 *Grizzly bear*

CM983 *Ruffed grouse*

		MNHVF	UseVF
CM980			
18¢	**Blue heron,** tagged *(178,930,000)*	.30	.20
CM981			
18¢	**Badger,** tagged	.30	.20
CM982			
18¢	**Grizzly bear,** tagged	.30	.20
CM983			
18¢	**Ruffed grouse,** tagged	.30	.20
	Plate block of 4	2.50	
	y. Se-tenant block of 4 CM980-83	2.25	1.50
	FDC *(June 26, 1981)*		2.00
	FDC, block of 4		4.00

1981. DISABLED PERSONS ISSUE hailed the U.N.'s International Year of Disabled Persons, and the worldwide effort to promote education, prevention of impairments and rehabilitation. *Gravure, perforated 11.*

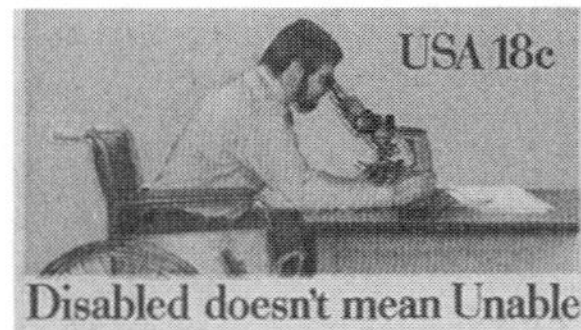

CM984 *Disabled man using microscope*

		MNHVF	UseVF
CM984			
18¢	**multicolored** tagged *(100,265,000)*	.30	.20
	Plate block of 4	2.40	
	FDC *(June 29, 1981)*		1.75
	v. Vertical pair, imperforate horizontally	2,750.00	

1981. EDNA ST. VINCENT MILLAY ISSUE 3rd in the Literary Arts Series honored the poet and author who received, among other awards, the Pulitzer Prize for Poetry in 1923. *Offset and intaglio, perforated 11.*

CM985 *Edna St. Vincent Millay, from miniature painting by Glenora Case Richards*

		MNHVF	UseVF
CM985			
18¢	**multicolored** tagged *(99,615,000)*	.30	.25
	Plate block of 4	2.40	
	FDC *(July 10, 1981)*		1.75
	v. Intaglio block (inscriptions) omitted	525.00	

1981. BEAT ALCOHOLISM ISSUE conveyed the message that alcoholism is a treatable disease. *Intaglio, perforated 11.*

CM986 *Alcoholism - You Can Beat It !*

CM986		MNHVF	UseVF
18¢	**blue & black** tagged *(97,535,000)*	.65	.20
	Plate block of 20	40.00	
	FDC *(Aug. 19, 1981)*		3.00
	v. Pair, imperforate	425.00	
	v1. Vertical pair, imperforate horizontally	1,850.00	

1981. American Architecture Issue the third of four issues on this subject featured examples of successful work by late 19th and early 20th century American architects. *Intaglio, perforated 11, multicolored.*

CM987 *New York University Library, designed by Stanford White;* CM988 *Biltmore House, Asheville, N.C., designed by Richard Morris Hunt;* CM989 *Palace of Arts, San Francisco, Calif., designed by Bernard Maybeck;* CM990 *National Farmers Bank Building, Owatonna, Minn., designed by Louis Sullivan*

CM987		MNHVF	UseVF
18¢	**N.Y. University Library,** tagged *(167,308,000)*	.30	.20
CM988		MNHVF	UseVF
18¢	**Biltmore House,** tagged	.30	.20
CM989		MNHVF	UseVF
18¢	**Palace of Arts,** tagged	.30	.20
CM990		MNHVF	UseVF
18¢	**National Farmers Bank Building,** tagged	.30	.20
	Plate block of 4	3.00	
	y. Se-tenant block of 4 CM987-90	2.75	
	FDC *(Aug. 28, 1981),* any single		2.00
	FDC, block of 4		4.00

American Sports Series

1981. Bobby Jones Issue inaugurated the American Sports Series honoring famous American athletes. In 1930 Bobby Jones became the only golfer in history to win the Grand Slam of Golf. *Intaglio, perforated 10 1/2 x 11.*

CM991 *Bobby Jones*

CM991		MNHVF	UseVF
18¢	**green** tagged *(99,170,000)*	.30	.20
	Plate block of 4	7.75	
	FDC *(Sept. 22, 1981)*		12.00

1981. (Mildred) Babe Zaharias Issue also part of the American Sports Series, honored one of the greatest athletes of the first half of the 20th century, who broke four track records in the 1932 Olympics and then won virtually every women's golf title, both as an amateur and as a professional. *Intaglio, perforated 10 1/2 x 11.*

CM992 *Mildred "Babe" Didrickson Zaharias*

CM992		MNHVF	UseVF
18¢	**light violet** tagged *(101,625,000)*	.30	.20
	Plate block of 4	4.00	
	FDC *(Sept. 22, 1981)*		8.00

1981. Frederic Remington Issue honored the American painter, illustrator and sculptor. *Offset and intaglio, perforated 11.*

CM993 *Frederic Remington's* Coming Through the Rye *Sculpture*

CM993		MNHVF	UseVF
18¢	**multicolored** tagged *(101,155,000)*	.30	.20
	Plate block of 4	2.40	
	FDC *(Oct. 9, 1981)*		1.75
	v. Brown omitted	550.00	
	v1. Vertical pair, imperforate between	250.00	

1981. James Hoban Issue honored the Irish-American architect of the White House. The Irish Postal Administration and the U.S. Postal Service jointly issued stamps identical in design except for country designation and denomination (Ireland 528). The issue was released by the USPS in two denominations: the lower to accommodate the then current first-class letter rate; and the higher to accommodate the rate that went into effect a little more than two weeks following the release of the stamps. *Gravure, perforated 11.*

CM994 *James Hoban and White House*

CM994		MNHVF	UseVF
18¢	**multicolored** tagged *(101,200,000)*	.30	.20
	Plate block of 4	2.40	
	FDC *(Oct. 13, 1981)*		1.75

CM995 *James Hoban and White House*

CM995		MNHVF	UseVF
20¢	**multicolored** tagged *(167,360,000)*	.30	.20
	Plate block of 4	2.50	
	FDC *(Oct. 13, 1981)*		1.75

1981. Battle of Yorktown and the Virginia Capes Issue commemorated the bicentennial of the two battles with *se-tenent stamps.* The Battle of the Virginia Capes of Sept. 6, 1781, prevented the British fleet from aiding British troops, a critical turning point in the Revolutionary War. The Battle of Yorktown, Oct. 16-19, ending with the surrender of the British, marked the end of the war. *Intaglio and offset, perforated 11.*

CM996 *Map of Yorktown Capes;* CM997 *Map of Virginia Capes*

CM996		**MNHVF**	**UseVF**
18¢	**multicolored** tagged *(162,420,000)*	.30	.20
	v. intaglio back (inscriptions) omitted	175.00	
	zo. Tagging omitted	—	

CM997		**MNHVF**	**UseVF**
18¢	**multicolored** tagged	.30	.20
	Plate block of 4	3.00	
	y. Se-tenant pair CM996-97	.60	.60
	FDC *(Oct. 16, 1981),* either single		1.50
	FDC, pair		2.00
	v. Intaglio black (inscriptions) omitted	175.00	
	vy. Se-tenant pair, intaglio black, (inscriptions) omitted	425.00	
	zo. Tagging omitted	—	
	zoy. Se-tenant pair, tagging omitted	—	

1981. John Hanson Issue commemorated the American Revolutionary leader elected first president of the Continental Congress Nov. 5, 1781. Elected "President of the United States in Congress Assembled," and therefore considered by some the first president of the United States, Hanson (1715-83) was a congressional presiding officer and had none of the powers of the president under the Constitution. *Gravure, perforated 11.*

CM998 *John Hanson*

CM998		**MNHVF**	**UseVF**
20¢	**multicolored** tagged *(167,130,000)*	.30	.20
	Plate block of 4	2.50	
	FDC *(Nov. 5, 1981)*		1.75

1981. Desert Plants Issue depicted four plants that grow in the arid American West. Three are in the cactus family, and the agave is a succulent plant of the amaryllis family. *Intaglio, perforated 11, multicolored.*

CM999 *Barrel cactus* CM1000 *Agave* CM1001 *Beavertail cactus* CM1002 *Saguaro*

CM999		**MNHVF**	**UseVF**
20¢	**Barrel cactus,** tagged *(191,560,000)*	.35	.20

CM1000		**MNHVF**	**UseVF**
20¢	**Agave,** tagged	.35	.20

CM1001		**MNHVF**	**UseVF**
20¢	**Beavertail cactus,** tagged	.35	.20

CM1002		**MNHVF**	**UseVF**
20¢	**Saguaro,** tagged	.35	.20
	Plate block of 4	3.25	
	FDC *(Dec. 11, 1981),* any single		2.00
	FDC, block of 4		4.00
	v. Vertical pair (CM1002), imperforate	6,500.00	
	y. Se-tenant block of 4 C999-1002	2.00	
	vy. Se-tenant block of 4, intaglio brown omitted	8,000.00	

1982. Franklin D. Roosevelt Issue commemorated the 100th birthday of the 32nd president of the United States. The only president to be elected four times, Roosevelt was inaugurated in 1933 and served as president through the New Deal era and World War II until his death in April 1945. *Intaglio, perforated 11.*

CM1003 *Franklin D. Roosevelt*

CM1003		**MNHVF**	**UseVF**
20¢	**blue** tagged *(163,939,200)*	.35	.20
	Plate block of 4	2.50	
	FDC *(Jan. 3, 1982)*		1.75

1982. Love Issue celebrated special occasions, such as birthdays, anniversaries, weddings and other special sentiments. Flowers form the letters "L": miniature poppy; "O": painted daisies and miniature pansies; "V": cornflower; "E": coralbells. *Gravure, perforated 11.*

CM1004-04A

CM1004		**MNHVF**	**UseVF**
20¢	**multicolored** tagged	.35	.20
	Plate block of 4	3.25	

CM1004A		**MNHVF**	**UseVF**
20¢	**multicolored** tagged, perforated 11 x 10 1/2	1.00	.25
	Plate block of 4	5.50	
	FDC *(Feb. 1, 1982)*		1.75
	v. Blue omitted	225.00	
	v1. Pair, imperforate	275.00	

1982. George Washington Issue commemorated the 250th anniversary of his birth. *Gravure, perforated 11.*

CM1005 *George Washington*

CM1005		**MNHVF**	**UseVF**
20¢	**multicolored** tagged *(180,700,000)*	.35	.20
	Plate block of 4	2.75	
	FDC *(Feb. 22, 1982)*		2.00

1982. State Birds and Flowers commemorated the official birds and flowers of all 50 states. Arranged in alphabetical order in the pane, from top-left to bottom right, these stamps were designed by the father-and-son team of Arthur and Alan Singer. Arthur, the father, created the bird designs, and Alan contributed the flower designs. *Gravure, perforated 10 1/2 x 11 and 11 ("v" numbers).*

		MNHVF	UseVF
CM1006			
20¢	**Alabama, multicolored,** tagged *(666,950,000)*	1.00	.50
	v. Perforated 11	1.00	.50
CM1007		**MNHVF**	**UseVF**
20¢	**Alaska, multicolored,** tagged	1.00	.50
	v. Perforated 11	1.00	.50
CM1008		**MNHVF**	**UseVF**
20¢	**Arizona, multicolored,** tagged	1.00	.50
	v. Perforated 11	1.00	.50
CM1009		**MNHVF**	**UseVF**
20¢	**Arkansas, multicolored,** tagged	1.00	.50
	v. Perforated 11	1.00	.50
CM1010		**MNHVF**	**UseVF**
20¢	**California, multicolored,** tagged	1.00	.50
	v. Perforated 11	1.00	.50
CM1011		**MNHVF**	**UseVF**
20¢	**Colorado, multicolored,** tagged	1.00	.50
	v. Perforated 11	1.00	.50
CM1012		**MNHVF**	**UseVF**
20¢	**Connecticut, multicolored,** tagged	1.00	.50
	v. Perforated 11	1.00	.50
CM1013		**MNHVF**	**UseVF**
20¢	**Delaware, multicolored,** tagged	1.00	.50
	v. Perforated 11	1.00	.50
CM1014		**MNHVF**	**UseVF**
20¢	**Florida, multicolored,** tagged	1.00	.50
	v. Perforated 11	1.00	.50
CM1015		**MNHVF**	**UseVF**
20¢	**Georgia, multicolored,** tagged	1.00	.50
	v. Perforated 11	1.00	.50
CM1016		**MNHVF**	**UseVF**
20¢	**Hawaii, multicolored,** tagged	1.00	.50
	v. Perforated 11	1.00	.50
CM1017		**MNHVF**	**UseVF**
20¢	**Idaho, multicolored,** tagged	1.00	.50
	v. Perforated 11	1.00	.50
CM1018		**MNHVF**	**UseVF**
20¢	**Illinois, multicolored,** tagged	1.00	.50
	v. Perforated 11	1.00	.50
CM1019		**MNHVF**	**UseVF**
20¢	**Indiana, multicolored,** tagged	1.00	.50
	v. Perforated 11	1.00	.50
CM1020		**MNHVF**	**UseVF**
20¢	**Iowa, multicolored,** tagged	1.00	.50
	v. Perforated 11	1.00	.50
CM1021		**MNHVF**	**UseVF**
20¢	**Kansas, multicolored,** tagged	1.00	.50
	v. Perforated 11	1.00	.50
CM1022		**MNHVF**	**UseVF**
20¢	**Kentucky, multicolored,** tagged	1.00	.50
	v. Perforated 11	1.00	.50
CM1023		**MNHVF**	**UseVF**
20¢	**Louisiana, multicolored,** tagged	1.00	.50
	v. Perforated 11	1.00	.50

CM1006-55 *State Birds and Flowers*

CM1024

		MNHVF	UseVF
20¢	**Maine, multicolored,** tagged	1.00	.50
	v. Perforated 11	1.00	.50

CM1025

		MNHVF	UseVF
20¢	**Maryland, multicolored,** tagged	1.00	.50
	v. Perforated 11	1.00	.50

CM1026

		MNHVF	UseVF
20¢	**Massachusetts, multicolored,** tagged	1.00	.50
	v. Perforated 11	1.00	.50

CM1027

		MNHVF	UseVF
20¢	**Michigan, multicolored,** tagged	1.00	.50
	v. Perforated 11	1.00	.50

CM1028

		MNHVF	UseVF
20¢	**Minnesota, multicolored,** tagged	1.00	.50
	v. Perforated 11	1.00	.50

CM1029

		MNHVF	UseVF
20¢	**Mississippi, multicolored,** tagged	1.00	.50
	v. Perforated 11	1.00	.50

CM1030

		MNHVF	UseVF
20¢	**Missouri, multicolored,** tagged	1.00	.50
	v. Perforated 11	1.00	.50

CM1031

		MNHVF	UseVF
20¢	**Montana, multicolored,** tagged	1.00	.50
	v. Perforated 11	1.00	.50

CM1032

		MNHVF	UseVF
20¢	**Nebraska, multicolored,** tagged	1.00	.50
	v. Perforated 11	1.00	.50

CM1033

		MNHVF	UseVF
20¢	**Nevada, multicolored,** tagged	1.00	.50
	v. Perforated 11	1.00	.50

CM1034

		MNHVF	UseVF
20¢	**New Hampshire, multicolored,** tagged	1.00	.50
	v. Perforated 11	1.00	.50

CM1035

		MNHVF	UseVF
20¢	**New Jersey, multicolored,** tagged	1.00	.50
	v. Perforated 11	1.00	.50

CM1036

		MNHVF	UseVF
20¢	**New Mexico, multicolored,** tagged	1.00	.50
	v. Perforated 11	1.00	.50

CM1037

		MNHVF	UseVF
20¢	**New York, multicolored,** tagged	1.00	.50
	v. Perforated 11	1.00	.50

CM1038

		MNHVF	UseVF
20¢	**North Carolina, multicolored,** tagged	1.00	.50
	v. Perforated 11	1.00	.50

CM1039

		MNHVF	UseVF
20¢	**North Dakota, multicolored,** tagged	1.00	.50
	v. Perforated 11	1.00	.50

CM1040

		MNHVF	UseVF
20¢	**Ohio, multicolored,** tagged	1.00	.50
	v. Perforated 11	1.00	.50

CM1041

		MNHVF	UseVF
20¢	**Oklahoma, multicolored,** tagged	1.00	.50
	v. Perforated 11	1.00	.50

CM1042

		MNHVF	UseVF
20¢	**Oregon, multicolored,** tagged	1.00	.50
	v. Perforated 11	1.00	.50

CM1043

		MNHVF	UseVF
20¢	**Pennsylvania, multicolored,** tagged	1.00	.50
	v. Perforated 11	1.00	.50

CM1044

		MNHVF	UseVF
20¢	**Rhode Island, multicolored,** tagged	1.00	.50
	v. Perforated 11	1.00	.50

CM1045

		MNHVF	UseVF
20¢	**South Carolina, multicolored,** tagged	1.00	.50
	v. Perforated 11	1.00	.50

CM1046

		MNHVF	UseVF
20¢	**South Dakota, multicolored,** tagged	1.00	.50
	v. Perforated 11	1.00	.50

CM1047

		MNHVF	UseVF
20¢	**Tennessee, multicolored,** tagged	1.00	.50
	v. Perforated 11	1.00	.50

CM1048

		MNHVF	UseVF
20¢	**Texas multicolored,** tagged	1.00	.50
	v. Perforated 11	1.00	.50

CM1049

		MNHVF	UseVF
20¢	**Utah, multicolored,** tagged	1.00	.50
	v. Perforated 11	1.00	.50

CM1050

		MNHVF	UseVF
20¢	**Vermont, multicolored,** tagged	1.00	.50
	v. Perforated 11	1.00	.50

CM1051

		MNHVF	UseVF
20¢	**Virginia, multicolored,** tagged	1.00	.50
	v. Perforated 11	1.00	.50

CM1052

		MNHVF	UseVF
20¢	**Washington, multicolored,** tagged	1.00	.50
	v. Perforated 11	1.00	.50

CM1053

		MNHVF	UseVF
20¢	**West Virginia, multicolored,** tagged	1.00	.50
	v. Perforated 11	1.00	.50

CM1054

		MNHVF	UseVF
20¢	**Wisconsin, multicolored,** tagged	1.00	.50
	v. Perforated 11	1.00	.50

CM1055

		MNHVF	UseVF
20¢	**Wyoming, multicolored,** tagged	1.00	.50
	v. Perforated 11	1.00	.50
	y. Se-tenant pane of 50	45.00	
	y1. Se-tenant pane of 50, perforated 11	47.50	
	FDC *(April 14, 1982),* any single		1.50
	FDC, pane of 50		45.00
	vy1. Pane of 50, imperforate	23,000.00	

Because most plate block collectors consider that a plate block contains at least one copy of each stamp in the issue, a plate block of the State Birds and Flowers Issue is considered to be a full pane of 50 stamps.

1982. Netherlands Issue marked the 200th anniversary of Netherlands' diplomatic recognition of the United States. The Netherlands released two stamps at the same time as this one (Netherlands 1365-66). *Gravure, perforated 11.*

CM1056 *200th anniversary of Netherlands diplomatic recognition of the United States*

CM1056

		MNHVF	UseVF
20¢	**orange, red, blue & dark gray** tagged *(109,245,000)*	.35	.20
	Plate block of 6	13.95	
	FDC *(April 20, 1982)*		1.75
	v. Pair, imperforate	300.00	

1982. Library of Congress Issue saluted the library for the services and information it provides to Congress and many other organizations and researchers who use it every year. *Intaglio, perforated 11.*

CM1057 *Library of Congress*

CM1057

		MNHVF	UseVF
20¢	**black & red** tagged *(112,535,000)*	.35	.20
	Plate block of 4	2.50	
	FDC *(April 21, 1982)*		1.75

1982. Knoxville World's Fair Issue commemorated the Knoxville, Tenn., World's Fair, the theme of which was energy. Four stamps depict solar, synthetic, nuclear and fossil fuel energy sources. *Gravure, perforated 11, multicolored.*

CM1058 *Solar energy;* CM1059 *Synthetic fuels;* CM1060 *Breeder reactor;* CM1061 *Fossil fuels*

		MNHVF	UseVF
CM1058			
20¢	**Solar energy,** tagged *(124,640,000)*	.35	.20
CM1059		MNHVF	UseVF
20¢	**Synthetic fuels,** tagged	.35	.20
CM1060		MNHVF	UseVF
20¢	**Breeder reactor,** tagged	.35	.20
CM1061		MNHVF	UseVF
20¢	**Fossil fuels,** tagged	.35	.20
	Plate block of 4	3.25	
	y. Se-tenant block of 4 CM1058-61	2.00	1.50
	FDC *(April 29, 1982),* Block of 4		1.75
	FDC, block of 4		4.00

1982. Horatio Alger Issue honored the 150th birthday of Alger, a best-selling author of books for boys, with more than 100 of his works published during his lifetime. Alger's *Phil the Fiddler, or The Story of a Young Street Musician* is credited with bringing public and legislative attention to forced child labor. The stamp is generally not considered to be part of the Literary Arts Series, although no stamp in that series was issued in 1982. *Intaglio, perforated 11.*

CM1062 *Horatio Alger, frontispiece from Ragged Dick series by Alger*

		MNHVF	UseVF
CM1062			
20¢	**red & black** on tan paper tagged *(107,605,000)*	.35	.20
	Plate block of 4	2.50	
	FDC *(April 30, 1982)*		1.75
	v. Red and black omitted	—	

1982. Aging Together Issue heightened awareness that older persons enrich society with their wealth of experience and creative energy. *Intaglio, perforated 11.*

CM1063 *Aging together*

		MNHVF	UseVF
CM1063			
20¢	**brown** tagged *(173,160,000)*	.35	.20
	Plate block of 4	2.50	
	FDC *(May 21, 1982)*		1.75

1982. Barrymore Family Issue in the Performing Arts Series honored the distinguished American theatrical family, featuring likenesses of Lionel, Ethel, and John Barrymore. *Gravure, perforated 11.*

CM1064 *Lionel, Ethel, and John Barrymore*

		MNHVF	UseVF
CM1064			
20¢	**multicolored** tagged *(107,285,000)*	.35	.20
	Plate block of 4	2.50	
	FDC *(June 8, 1982)*		1.75

1982. Mary Walker Issue commemorated the Civil War surgeon who gave care and treatment to the sick and the wounded. *Gravure, perforated 11.*

CM1065 *Dr. Mary Walker*

		MNHVF	UseVF
CM1065			
20¢	**multicolored** tagged *(109,040,000)*	.35	.20
	Plate block of 4	3.00	
	FDC *(June 10, 1982)*		1.75

1982. International Peace Garden Issue recognized the 50th anniversary of the garden shared by Dunseith, N.Dak., and Boissevain, Manitoba. It remains a symbol of more than 150 years of peace and friendship between the United States and Canada. *Offset and intaglio, perforated 11.*

CM1066 *Maple leaf and rose*

		MNHVF	UseVF
CM1066			
20¢	**multicolored** tagged *(183,270,000)*	.35	.20
	Plate block of 4	2.50	
	FDC *(June 30, 1982)*		1.75
	v. Black & intaglio green omitted	275.00	

1982. America's Libraries Issue honored the contribution of libraries to the growth and development of the United States. *Intaglio, perforated 11*

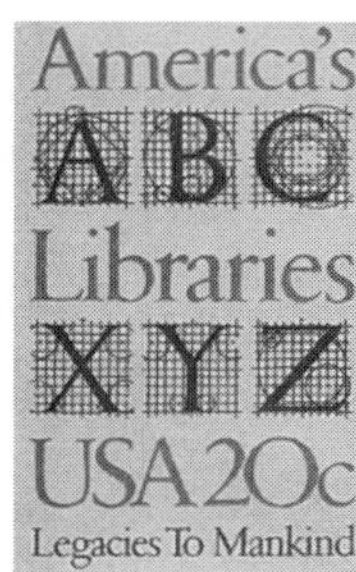

CM1067 *America's Libraries*

		MNHVF	UseVF
CM1067			
20¢	**red & black** tagged *(169,495,000)*	.35	.20
	Plate block of 4	2.50	

	FDC *(July 13, 1982)*		1.75
	v. Vertical pair, imperforate horizontally	325.00	
	zo. Tagging omitted	6.00	

1982. Jackie Robinson Issue honored the athlete who broke major league baseball's racial barrier. Hired in football after starring at UCLA to play for the Brooklyn Dodgers' top farm team and then for the Dodgers in 1947, he withstood racial hostility to become one of the most exciting baseball players of his era. Black Heritage Series. *Gravure, perforated 10 1/2 x 11.*

CM1068 *Jackie Robinson*

CM1068		MNHVF	UseVF
20¢	**multicolored** tagged *(164,235,000)*	2.50	.20
	Plate block of 4	11.00	
	FDC *(Aug. 2, 1982)*		7.00

1982. Touro Synagogue Issue honored the oldest existing synagogue in the United States. Designated a National Historical Site in 1946, the synagogue was built in 1763 principally by Sephardic Jews from Spain and Portugal who fled the Inquisition and found religious freedom in the Rhode Island colony. *Gravure and intaglio, perforated 11.*

CM1069 *Touro Synagogue*

CM1069		MNHVF	UseVF
20¢	**multicolored** tagged *(110,130,000)*	.35	.20
	Plate block of 20	13.75	
	FDC *(Aug. 22, 1982)*		2.00
	v. Pair, imperforate	2,750.00	

1982. Wolf Trap Farm Issue saluted the Wolf Trap Farm Park for the Performing Arts, a theater in wooded surroundings in Virginia. (See also CM679.) *Gravure, perforated 11.*

CM1070 *Wolf Trap Farm Park*

CM1070		MNHVF	UseVF
20¢	**multicolored** tagged *(110,995,000)*	.35	.20
	Plate block of 4	2.50	
	FDC *(Sept. 1, 1982)*		1.75

1982. American Architecture Issue the fourth and final installment in the series, which honored key structures and architects of the 20th century. *Intaglio, perforated 11.*

CM1071 *Fallingwater, Mill Run, Pa., designed by Frank Lloyd Wright*

CM1072 *Illinois Institute of Technology, Chicago, Ill., designed by Ludwig Mies van der Rohe*

CM1073 *Gropius House, Lincoln, Mass., designed by Walter Gropius in collaboration with Marcel Breuer*

CM1074 *Dulles International Airport, Washington, D.C. designed by Eero Saarinen*

CM1071		MNHVF	UseVF
20¢	**Falling Water,** tagged *(165,340,000)*	.35	.20
CM1072		**MNHVF**	**UseVF**
20¢	**Illinois Intitute of Technology,** tagged	.35	.20
CM1073		**MNHVF**	**UseVF**
20¢	**Gropius House,** tagged	.35	.20
CM1074		**MNHVF**	**UseVF**
20¢	**Washington International Airport,** tagged	.35	.20
	Plate block of 4	4.25	
	y. Se-tenant block of 4 CM1071-74	2.00	
	FDC *(Sept. 30, 1982),* any single		2.00
	FDC, block of 4		4.00

1982. Francis of Assisi Issue honored the 800th birthday of the man (1182-1226) whose compassion earned him reverence transcending religious bounds. He formed the Franciscan Order, the members of which still minister to the sick and needy. *Gravure by J.W. Fergusson and Sons for American Bank Note Co., perforated 11.*

CM1075 *Francis of Assisi*

CM1075		MNHVF	UseVF
20¢	**multicolored** tagged *(174,180,000)*	.35	.20
	Plate block of 4	2.75	
	FDC *(Oct. 7, 1982)*		1.75

1982. Ponce de Leon Issue honored the Spaniard (1527-1591) who explored Puerto Rico in 1508-09 and Florida in 1513. *Gravure (Combination Press), perforated 11.*

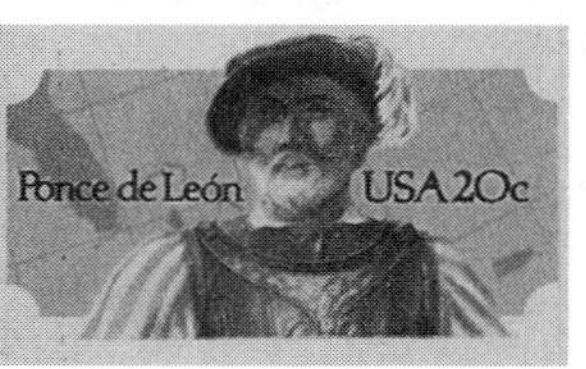

CM1076 *Ponce de Leon*

CM1076		MNHVF	UseVF
20¢	**multicolored** tagged *(110,261,000)*	.35	.20
	Plate block of 6	16.00	
	FDC *(Oct. 12, 1982)*		1.75
	v. Pair, imperforate	500.00	
	v1. Vertical pair, imperforate between	—	

1983. Science and Industry Issue saluted their contributions to the growth and development of the United States. *Offset and intaglio, perforated 11.*

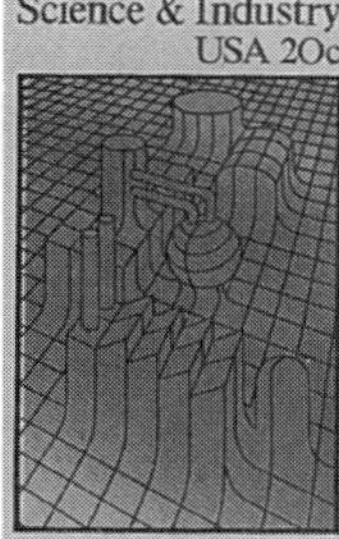

CM1077 *Science and Industry*

CM1077		MNHVF	UseVF
20¢	**multicolored** tagged *(118,555,000)*	.35	.20
	Plate block of 4	2.50	
	FDC *(Jan. 19, 1983)*		1.75
	a. Intaglio black omitted	1,400.00	

1983. SWEDEN ISSUE marked the 200th anniversary of the signing of the Treaty of Amity and Commerce between Sweden and the United States. A stamp of similar design was issued simultaneously by Sweden (Sweden 1247). *Intaglio, perforated 11.*

CM1078 *Benjamin Franklin and Treaty Seal*

CM1078		MNHVF	UseVF
20¢	**multicolored** tagged *(118,225,000)*	.30	.20
	Plate block of 4	2.50	
	FDC *(March 24, 1983)*		1.75

1983. BALLOONING ISSUE honored the sport of hot air ballooning. Balloons were successfully flown in June 1783 by two brothers, Joseph and Jacques Montgolfier, in France. Used for surveillance and scientific research over the years, they are today enjoyed by thousands of recreational enthusiasts. *Gravure, perforated 11.*

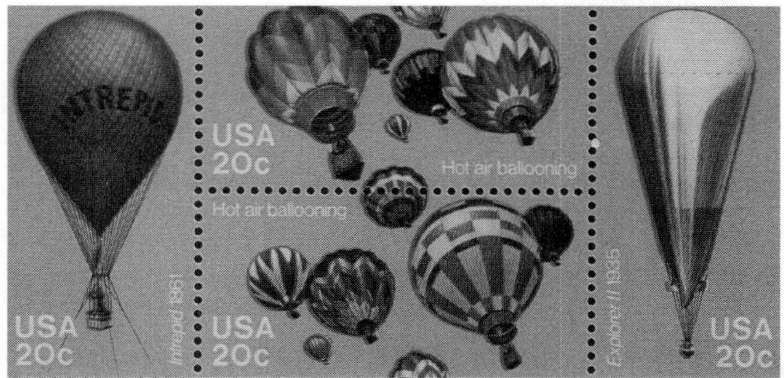

CM1079 Intrepid, *1861;* CM1080 and CM1081 *Hot air ballooning;* CM1082 Explorer II, *1935*

CM1079		MNHVF	UseVF
20¢	***Intrepid,*** tagged *(226,128,000)*	.35	.20
CM1080		MNHVF	UseVF
20¢	**Hot air ballooning,** tagged	.35	.20
CM1081		MNHVF	UseVF
20¢	**Hot air ballooning,** tagged	.35	.20
CM1082		MNHVF	UseVF
20¢	***Explorer II,*** tagged	.35	.20
	Plate block of 4	3.00	
	y. Se-tenant block of 4 CM1079-82	2.00	
	FDC *(March 31, 1983),* any single		2.00
	FDC, block of 4		4.00
	vy. Se-tenant block of 4, imperforate	5,500.00	

1983. CIVILIAN CONSERVATION CORPS ISSUE honored the 50th anniversary of the Great Depression programs, which recruited thousands of unemployed young men to develop and conserve the nation's natural resources. *Gravure, perforated 11.*

CM1083 *Civilian Conservation Corps*

CM1083		MNHVF	UseVF
20¢	**multicolored** tagged *(114,290,000)*	.35	.20
	Plate block of 4	2.50	
	FDC *(April 5, 1983)*		1.75
	v. Pair, imperforate	2,750.00	

1983. JOSEPH PRIESTLY ISSUE commemorated the clergyman and chemist (1733-1804) who discovered oxygen. *Gravure, perforated 11.*

CM1084 *Joseph Priestly*

CM1084		MNHVF	UseVF
20¢	**multicolored** tagged *(165,000,000)*	.35	.20
	Plate block of 4	3.00	
	FDC *(April 13, 1983)*		1.75

1983. VOLUNTEER ISSUE recognized the contribution volunteers have made to the development of the United States. *Intaglio, perforated 11.*

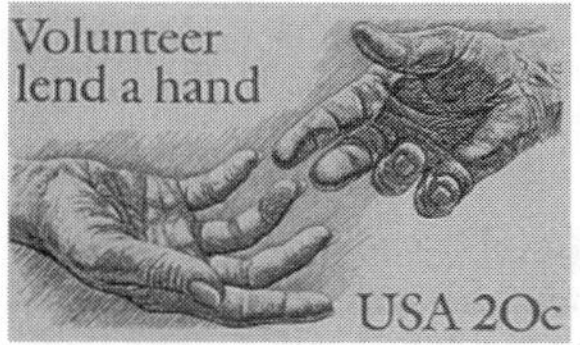

CM1085 *Helping hands*

CM1085		MNHVF	UseVF
20¢	**red & black** tagged *(120,430,000)*	.35	.20
	Plate block of 20	13.95	
	FDC *(April 20, 1983)*		1.75
	v. Pair, imperforate	800.00	

1983. GERMAN CONCORD ISSUE honored the 300th anniversary of the arrival of the first 13 families of German immigrants to the United States in the ship *Concord.* A stamp of similar design was issued May 5, six days after the U.S. issue, by West Germany (2363). *Intaglio, perforated 11.*

CM1086 Concord, *1683, German immigration tricentennial*

CM1086		MNHVF	UseVF
20¢	**brown** tagged *(117,025,000)*	.35	.20
	Plate block of 4	2.50	
	FDC *(April 29, 1983)*		1.75

1983. PHYSICAL FITNESS ISSUE saluted physical fitness activities for maintaining good physical health. *Gravure (Combination Press), perforated 11.*

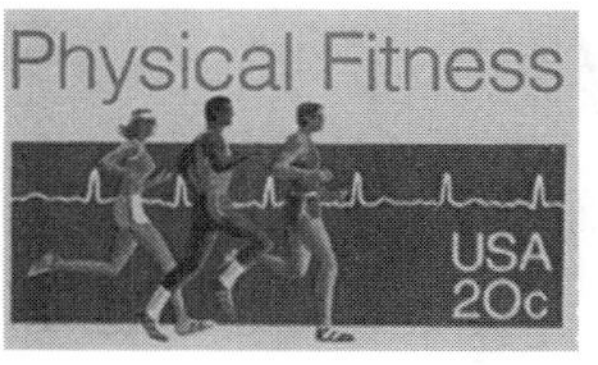

CM1087 *Physical fitness*

CM1087		MNHVF	UseVF
20¢	**multicolored** tagged *(111,775,000)*	.35	.20
	Plate block of 20	13.95	
	FDC *(May 14, 1983)*		2.00

1983. Brooklyn Bridge Issue honored the 100th anniversary of the completion of the bridge, created by 19th-century civil engineer John A. Roebling and his son Washington. It opened on May 24, 1883. *Intaglio, perforated 11.*

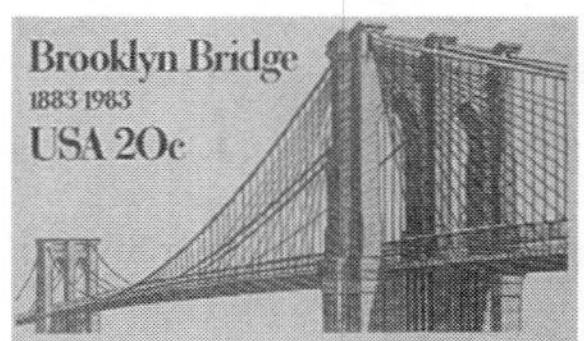

CM1088 *Brooklyn Bridge*

CM1088		MNHVF	UseVF
20¢	**blue** tagged *(181,700,000)*	.35	.20
	"Short bridge"	.50	.30
	Plate block of 4	2.50	
	FDC *(May 17, 1983)*		2.00
	zo. Tagging omitted		

1983. Tennessee Valley Authority Issue marked the 50th anniversary of its establishment, providing flood control through a system of dams and locks, developing the natural resources of the area and creating industry. *Gravure and intaglio (Combination Press), perforated 11.*

CM1089 *Norris Hydroelectric Dam*

CM1089		MNHVF	UseVF
20¢	**multicolored** tagged *(114,250,000)*	.35	.20
	Plate block of 20	13.95	
	FDC *(May 18, 1983)*		1.75

1983. Medal of Honor Issue saluted the United States' highest military award and all those who have been awarded the medal. It is awarded for "courage above and beyond the call of duty." *Offset and intaglio, perforated 11.*

CM1090 *Medal of Honor*

CM1090		MNHVF	UseVF
20¢	**multicolored** tagged *(108,820,000)*	.35	.20
	Plate block of 4	3.00	
	FDC *(June 7, 1983)*		6.00
	v. Red omitted	325.00	

1983. Scott Joplin Issue honored the ragtime composer (1868-1917) who successfully combined the charm of late Victorian music and the lively qualities of pioneer American folk song and dance. Black Heritage Series. *Gravure, perforated 11.*

CM1091 *Scott Joplin*

CM1091		MNHVF	UseVF
20¢	**multicolored** tagged *(115,200,000)*	.35	.20
	Plate block of 4	3.00	
	FDC *(June 9, 1983)*		2.50
	v. Pair, imperforate	550.00	

1983. Babe Ruth Issue the third issue in the American Sports Series, commemorated the great baseball player and Hall of Fame member George Herman Ruth (1895-1948). *Intaglio, perforated 10 1/2 x 11.*

CM1092 *George Herman "Babe" Ruth*

CM1092		MNHVF	UseVF
20¢	**blue** tagged *(184,950,000)*	.35	.20
	Plate block of 4	9.75	
	FDC *(July 6, 1983)*		6.00

1983. Nathaniel Hawthorne Issue 4th in the Literary Arts Series honored the American author of the novel, *The House of Seven Gables.* A master at writing tales, Hawthorne (1804-1864) was one of the first American writers who built his stories around the New England of his forefathers. *Gravure, perforated 11.*

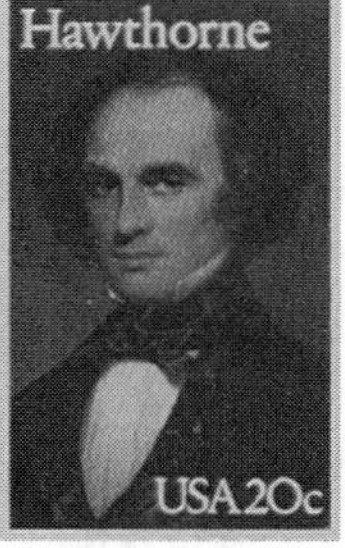

CM1093 *Nathaniel Hawthorne*

CM1093		MNHVF	UseVF
20¢	**multicolored** tagged *(110,925,000)*	.35	.20
	Plate block of 4	2.50	
	FDC *(July 8, 1983)*		1.75

1983. 1984 Olympic Issue was the first of an array of postal paper designed by Robert Peak, commemorating the Summer Games in Los Angeles and the Winter Games in Sarajevo, Yugoslavia. (see also CM1111-14, CM1126-29, A101-12, ALS19, PC96 and PC98.) *Gravure, perforated 11, multicolored.*

CM1094 *Discus;* CM1095 *High jump;* CM1096 *Archery;* CM1097 *Boxing*

		MNHVF	UseVF
CM1094			
13¢	**Discus,** tagged *(395,424,000)*	.25	.20
CM1095			
13¢	**High jump,** tagged	.25	.20
CM1096			
13¢	**Archery,** tagged	.25	.20
CM1097			
13¢	**Boxing,** tagged	.25	.20
	Plate block of 4	3.75	
	y. Se-tenant block of 4 CM1094-97	2.00	
	FDC *(July 28, 1983),* any single		2.00
	FDC, block of 4		4.00

1983. Treaty of Paris Issue marked the 200th anniversary of the Treaty of Paris, which officially ended the American Revolution and was signed by John Adams, Benjamin Franklin, and John Jay. The treaty established the boundaries of the new nation at the Great Lakes, the Mississippi River and the northern border of Florida. *Gravure, perforated 11.*

CM1098 *Treaty of Paris*

		MNHVF	UseVF
CM1098			
20¢	**multicolored** tagged *(104,340,000)*	.35	.20
	Plate block of 4	2.75	
	FDC *(Sept. 2, 1983)*		1.75

1983. Civil Service Issue marked 100 years of federal civil service. *Gravure and intaglio, perforated 11.*

CM1099 *Civil Service*

		MNHVF	UseVF
CM1099			
20¢	**beige, blue & red** tagged *(114,725,000)*	.35	.20
	Plate block of 20	13.95	
	FDC *(Sept. 9, 1983)*		1.75

1983. Metropolitan Opera Issue celebrated the centennial of the Metropolitan Opera in New York, combining features from the original Metropolitan Opera (the proscenium arch above the stage) and the new building at Lincoln Center (the five-arched entrance). *Offset and intaglio, perforated 11.*

CM1100 *Metropolitan Opera*

		MNHVF	UseVF
CM1100			
20¢	**dark carmine & yellow orange** tagged *(112,525,000)*	.35	.20
	Plate block of 4	2.75	
	FDC *(Sept. 14, 1983)*		1.75
	zo. Tagging omitted	7.00	

1983. American Inventors Issue honored Charles Steinmetz, Edwin Armstrong, Nikola Tesla, and Philo T. Farnsworth. Steinmetz pioneered research on alternating current and high-voltage power. Armstrong's crowning achievement is wide-band frequency modulation, now used in FM radio. Tesla, creator of more than 700 inventions, is best known for the induction motor. Farnsworth, with more than 300 inventions in television and related fields, is most famous for the first all-electronic television transmission in 1927. *Offset and intaglio, perforated 11, multicolored.*

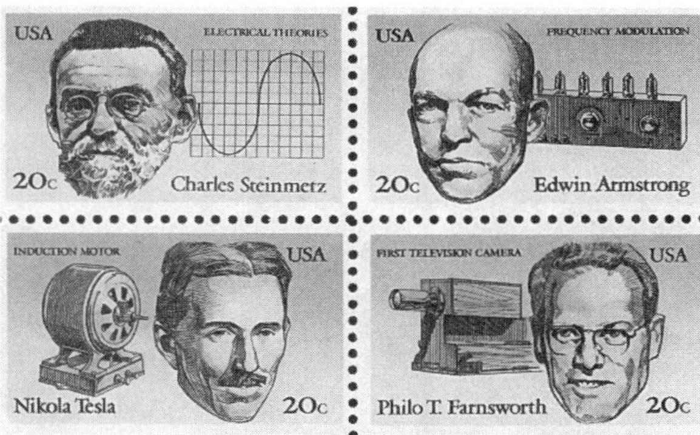

CM1101 *Charles Steinmetz* CM1102 *Edwin Armstrong* CM1103 *Nikola Tesla* CM1104 *Philo T. Farnsworth*

		MNHVF	UseVF
CM1101			
20¢	**Charles Steinmetz,** tagged *(193,055,000)*	.35	.20
CM1102			
20¢	**Edwin Armstrong,** tagged	.35	.20
CM1103			
20¢	**Nikola Tesla,** tagged	.35	.20
CM1104			
20¢	**Philo T. Farnsworth,** tagged	.35	.20
	Plate block of 4	4.25	
	y. Se-tenant block of 4 CM1101-04	2.00	
	FDC *(Sept. 21, 1983),* any single		2.00
	FDC, block of 4		4.00
	vy. Block of 4, black (engraved) omitted	425.00	
	vy1.black (engraved) omitted, any single	100.00	

1983. Streetcar Issue paid tribute to the evolution of importance of the streetcar in the United States. *Offset and intaglio, perforated 11.*

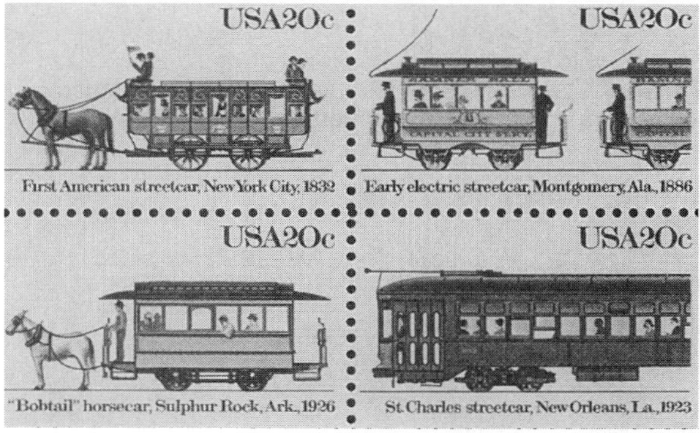

CM1105 *1st American streetcar New York City, 1832;* CM1106 *Early electric streetcar, Montgomery, Ala., 1886;* CM1107 *"Bobtail" horse car, Sulphur Rock, Ark., 1926;* CM1108 *St. Charles streetcar, New Orleans, La., 1923*

		MNHVF	UseVF
CM1105			
20¢	**NYC's First Horsecar,** tagged	.35	.20
CM1106			
20¢	**Montgomery electric,** tagged	.35	.20
CM1107			
20¢	**"Bobtail" Horse Car,** tagged	.35	.20
CM1108			
20¢	**St. Charles Streetcar,** tagged	.35	.20
	Plate block of 4	4.25	
	y. Se-tenant block of 4 CM1105-08	2.00	

		MNHVF	UseVF
	FDC *(Oct. 8, 1983)*, any single		2.00
	FDC, block of 4		4.00
	vy. Block of 4 black (engraved) omitted	425.00	
	vy1. black (engraved) omitted, any single	75.00	

1983. MARTIN LUTHER ISSUE commemorated the 500th birthday of religious reformer Martin Luther (1483-1546). *Gravure (American Bank Note Co.), perforated 11.)*

CM1109 *Martin Luther*

CM1109		MNHVF	UseVF
20¢	**multicolored** tagged *(165,000,000)*	.35	.20
	Plate block of 4	2.50	
	FDC *(Nov. 10, 1983)*		1.75

1984. ALASKA STATEHOOD ISSUE honored the 25th anniversary of the 49th state. *Gravure by J.W. Fergusson and Sons for the American Bank Note Co., perforated 11.*

CM1110 *Alaska statehood*

CM1110		MNHVF	UseVF
20¢	**multicolored** tagged *(120,000,000)*	.35	.20
	Plate block of 4	2.50	
	FDC *(Jan. 3, 1984)*		1.75

1984. WINTER OLYMPICS ISSUE featured events of the games in Sarajevo, Yugoslavia. Designed by Robert Peak. *Gravure, perforated 10 1/2 x 11.*

CM1111 *Ice dancing*

CM1112 *Alpine sking*

CM1113 *Cross-country skiing*

CM1114 *Ice hockey*

CM1111		MNHVF	UseVF
20¢	**Ice dancing,** tagged *(319,675,000)*	.35	.20

CM1112		MNHVF	UseVF
20¢	**Alpine skiing,** tagged	.35	.20

CM1113		MNHVF	UseVF
20¢	**Cross-country skiing,** tagged	.35	.20

CM1114		MNHVF	UseVF
20¢	**Ice hockey,** tagged	.35	.20
	Plate block of 4	4.25	
	y. Se-tenant block of 4 CM1111-14	2.00	
	FDC *(Jan. 6, 1984)*		2.00
	FDC, block of 4		4.00

1984. FEDERAL DEPOSIT INSURANCE CORPORATION ISSUE honored the 50th anniversary of the institution, which gives bank depositors limited protection in the event of bank insolvency. *Gravure, perforated 11.*

CM1115 *Federal Deposit Insurance Corporation*

CM1115		MNHVF	UseVF
20¢	**multicolored** tagged *(103,975,000)*	.35	.20
	Plate block of 4	2.50	
	FDC *(Jan. 12, 1984)*		1.75

1984. LOVE ISSUE for use on Valentine's Day as well as other special occasions. From a design by Bradbury Thompson. *Gravure and intaglio (Combination Press), perforated 11.*

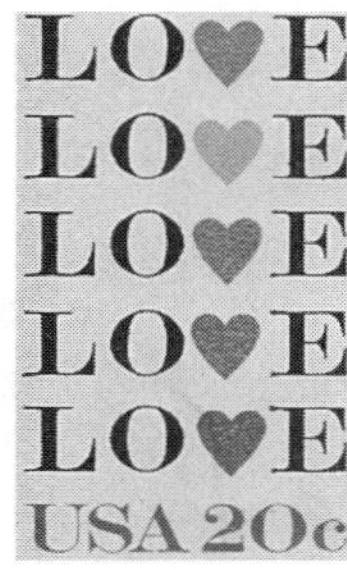

CM1116 *Love*

CM1116		MNHVF	UseVF
20¢	**multicolored** tagged *(554,675,000)*	.35	.20
	Plate block of 20	14.50	
	FDC *(Jan. 31, 1984)*		1.75
	v. Horizontal pair, imperforate vertically	175.00	
	zo. Tagging omitted	5.00	

1984. CARTER G. WOODSON ISSUE part of the Black Heritage Series, honored the African-American historian, teacher and administrator, as well as editor of the *Journal of Negro History. Gravure by American Bank Note Co., perforated 11.*

CM1117 *Carter G. Woodson*

CM1117		MNHVF	UseVF
20¢	**multicolored** tagged *(120,000,000)*	.35	.20

		MNHVF	UseVF
	Plate block of 4	2.75	
	FDC *(Feb. 1, 1984)*		2.50
	v. Horizontal pair, imperforate vertically	1,750.00	

1984. Soil and Water Conservation Issue recognized the 50th anniversary of government efforts to abate soil erosion and conserve water resources. *Gravure, perforated 11.*

CM1118 *Soil and water conservation*

CM1118		MNHVF	UseVF
20¢	**multicolored** tagged *(106,975,000)*	.35	.20
	Plate block of 4	2.50	
	FDC *(Feb. 6, 1984)*		1.75

1984. Credit Union Act of 1934 Issue honored the 50th anniversary of the act that enabled credit unions to be organized everywhere in the United States under charters from the federal government. *Gravure, perforated 11.*

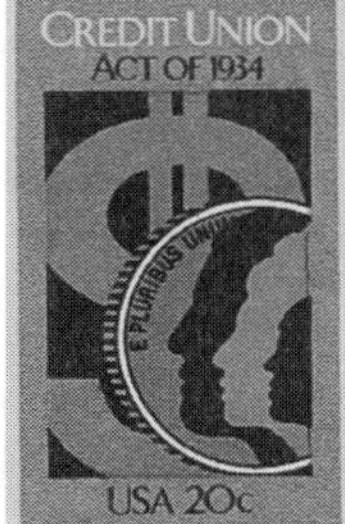

CM1119 *Credit Union Act of 1934*

CM1119		MNHVF	UseVF
20¢	**multicolored** tagged *(107,325,000)*	.35	.20
	Plate block of 4	2.50	
	FDC *(Feb. 10, 1984)*		1.75

1984. Orchids Issue featured four different native American orchids: the Wild Pink orchid of Florida; Yellow Lady's Slipper of the Midwest; Spreading Pogonia of the Northeast; and the Pacific Calypso found along the Pacific Coast. *Gravure, perforated 11.*

CM1120 *Wild Pink*

CM1121 *Yellow Lady's-Slipper*

CM1122 *Spreading Pogonia*

CM1123 Pacific Calypso

CM1120		MNHVF	UseVF
20¢	**Wild Pink Orchid,** tagged *(306,912,000)*	.35	.20
CM1121		**MNHVF**	**UseVF**
20¢	**Yellow Lady's-Slipper,** tagged	.35	.20
CM1122		**MNHVF**	**UseVF**
20¢	**Spreading Pogonia,** tagged	.35	.20
CM1123		**MNHVF**	**UseVF**
20¢	**Pacific Calypso Orchid,** tagged	.35	.20
	Plate block of 4	3.50	
	y. Se-tenant block of 4 CM1120-23	2.00	
	FDC *(March 6, 1984),* any single		2.00
	FDC, block of 4		4.00

1984. Hawaii Statehood Issue honored the 25th anniversary of Hawaii statehood. Hawaii was admitted as the 50th state Aug. 21, 1959. *Gravure by American Bank Note Co., perforated 11.*

CM1124 *Hawaii statehood*

CM1124		MNHVF	UseVF
20¢	**multicolored** tagged *(120,000,000)*	.35	.20
	Plate block of 4	2.75	
	FDC *(March 12, 1984)*		2.00

1984. National Archives Issue marked the 50th anniversary of the National Archives in Washington, D.C., which preserves the Declaration of Independence, the Constitution of the United States, the Bill of Rights and other treasures of America's past such as photographs, maps, and sound recordings of film. *Gravure, perforated 11.*

CM1125 *National Archives*

CM1125		MNHVF	UseVF
20¢	**multicolored** tagged *(108,000,000)*	.35	.20
	Plate block of 4	2.75	
	FDC *(April 16, 1984)*		1.75

1984. Summer Olympics Issue featured events at the Los Angeles Summer Games. *Gravure, perforated 11.*

CM1126 *Men's diving*

CM1127 *Women's long jump*

CM1128 *Wrestling*

CM1129 *Women's kayacking*

CM1126		MNHVF	UseVF
20¢	**Men's diving,** tagged *(313,350,000)*	.35	.20
CM1127		**MNHVF**	**UseVF**
20¢	**Women's long jump,** tagged	.35	.20

CM1128		MNHVF	UseVF
20¢	**Wrestling,** tagged	.35	.20
CM1129		MNHVF	UseVF
20¢	**Women's kayacking,** tagged	.35	.20
	Plate block of 4	5.50	
	v. Block of 4, imperforate vertically	—	
	Pair (Wrestling and Kayacking) imperforate vertically	—	
	y. Se-tenant block of 4 CM1126-29	2.00	
	FDC *(May 4, 1984)*		2.00
	FDC, block of 4		4.00

1984. Louisiana World Exposition Issue honored the exposition that celebrated fresh water, spotlighting rivers and ports of the world through displays and exhibitions. *Gravure, perforated 11.*

CM1130 *Louisiana World Exposition*

CM1130		MNHVF	UseVF
20¢	**multicolored** tagged *(130,320,000)*	.35	.20
	Plate block of 4	2.75	
	FDC *(May 11, 1984)*		1.75

1984. Health Research Issue hailed the professionals who have worked to prevent disease and prolong life. *Gravure by American Bank Note Co., perforated 11.*

CM1131 *Health Research*

CM1131		MNHVF	UseVF
20¢	**multicolored** tagged *(120,000,000)*	.35	.20
	Plate block of 4	3.00	
	FDC *(May 17, 1984)*		1.75

1984. Douglas Fairbanks Issue recalled the actor as part of the Performing Arts Series. Together with Charlie Chaplin, D.W. Griffith and Mary Pickford, in 1919 Fairbanks (1883-1939) formed United Artists Corp. *Gravure and intaglio (Combination Press), perforated 11.*

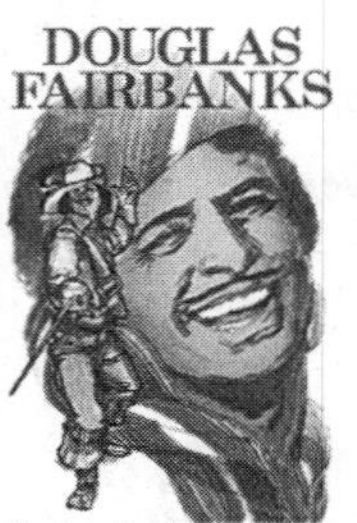

CM1132 *Douglas Fairbanks*

CM1132		MNHVF	UseVF
20¢	**multicolored** tagged *(117,050,000)*	.35	.20
	Plate, block of 20	17.50	
	FDC *(May 23, 1984)*		1.75
	v. Horizontal pair, imperforate vertically (one copy known)	—	
	zo. Tagging omitted	7.50	

1984. Jim Thorpe Issue saluted the American athlete whose feats in track, baseball and football are legendary. In 1912, at the Summer Olympics in Stockholm, Thorpe (1888-1953) became the first athlete to win both the pentathlon and the decathlon. Later, he was stripped of his medals when it was learned that he had briefly played semi-professional baseball in 1910. In 1938, the International Olympic Committee returned replicas of Thorpe's 1912 medals to his family, restoring his place in Olympic history. Part of the American Sports Series. *Intaglio, perforated 11.*

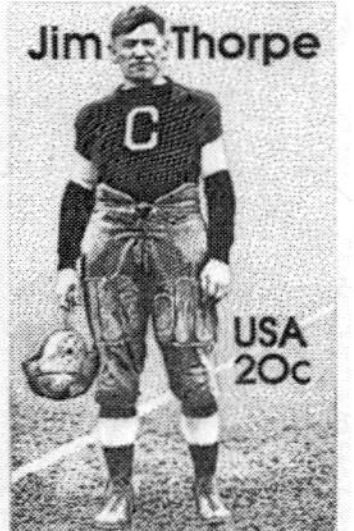

CM1133 *Jim Thorpe*

CM1133		MNHVF	UseVF
20¢	**dark brown** tagged *(115,725,000)*	.75	.20
	Plate block of 4	3.00	
	FDC *(May 24, 1984)*		5.00

1984. John McCormack Issue in the Performing Arts Series honored the 100th birthday of the Irish-American singer and world-famous tenor (1884-1945) who sang with the outstanding opera companies in North America and performed Irish folk songs and ballads in major cities of the world. This stamp was released jointly with an Irish stamp (Ireland 622). *Gravure, perforated 11.*

CM1134 *John McCormack*

CM1134		MNHVF	UseVF
20¢	**multicolored** tagged *(116,600,000)*	.35	.20
	Plate block of 4	2.50	
	FDC *(June 6, 1984)*		1.75

1984. St. Lawrence Seaway Issue commemorated the 25th anniversary of the opening of the seaway, which stretches from the Atlantic Ocean to Duluth, Minn. This was a joint issue with Canada (Canada 1085). *Gravure by American Bank Note Co., perforated 11.*

CM1135 *St. Lawrence Seaway*

CM1135		MNHVF	UseVF
20¢	**multicolored** tagged *(120,000,000)*	.35	.20
	Plate block of 4	2.50	
	FDC *(June 26, 1984)*		1.75

1984. Wetlands Preservation Issue marked the 50th anniversary of the Migratory Bird Hunting and Conservation Stamp Act, enacted in 1934 as a result of a proposal by conservationist Jay Norwood ("Ding") Darling for a federal revenue stamp required to be purchased by waterfowl hunters. Funds from the sale of these stamps go to buy and lease waterfowl habitats. The stamp design is the same Darling art as that on the first Duck stamp, RH1. *Intaglio, perforated 11.*

CM1136 Mallards Dropping In, *by Jay Norwood Darling*

CM1136		MNHVF	UseVF
20¢	**blue** tagged *(123,575,000)*	.35	.20
	Plate block of 4	4.50	
	FDC *(July 2, 1984)*		1.75
	v. Horizontal pair, imperforate vertically	375.00	

1984. Roanoke Voyages Issue commemorated the 400th anniversary of the establishment of an English colony in the New World. An expedition landed in 1584 on what is now the coast of North Carolina and took possession of the new land in the name of Queen Elizabeth. Two groups landed in 1585 and 1587. In 1590, the crew of a ship carrying supplies to the colony landed and could find no evidence of the colonists, whose fate remains a mystery. *Gravure by American Bank Note Co., perforated 11.*

CM1137 *Roanoke Voyages*

CM1137		MNHVF	UseVF
20¢	**multicolored** tagged *(120,000,000)*	.35	.20
	Plate block of 4	2.80	
	Gutter Pair	—	
	FDC *(July 13, 1984)*		1.75

1984. Herman Melville Issue 5th in the Literary Arts Series honored the 19th century American author (1819-91) of *Moby Dick. Intaglio, perforated 11.*

CM1138 *Herman Melville*

CM1138		MNHVF	UseVF
20¢	**blue green** tagged *(117,125,000)*	.35	.20
	Plate block of 4	2.50	
	FDC *(Aug. 1, 1984)*		1.75

1984. Horace Moses Issue saluted the man who created Junior Achievement because of his interest in career-oriented educational opportunities for city youth. *Intaglio (Combination Press), perforated 11.*

CM1139 *Horace Moses*

CM1139		MNHVF	UseVF
20¢	**orange & dark brown** tagged *(117,225,000)*	.35	.20
	Plate block of 20	17.00	
	FDC *(Aug. 6, 1984)*		1.75

1984. Smokey Bear Issue celebrated the symbol for forest fire prevention used by the Forest Service of the U.S. Department of Agriculture. *Combination of offset and intaglio, perforated 11.*

CM1140 *Smokey and bear cub*

CM1140		MNHVF	UseVF
20¢	**multicolored** tagged *(95,525,000)*	.35	.20
	Plate block of 4	3.00	
	FDC *(Aug. 13, 1984)*		2.00
	v. Horizontal pair, imperforate between	275.00	
	v1. Horizontal pair, imperforate vertically	1,750.00	
	v2. Vertical pair, imperforate between	225.00	
	v3. Block of 4, imperforate between horizontally & vertically	6,000.00	

1984. Roberto Clemente Issue in the American Sports Series commemorated the 18-year Pittsburgh Pirates veteran inducted into the Baseball Hall of Fame in 1973, the year following his untimely death while on a volunteer humanitarian mission. The Puerto Rican flag in the background symbolizes the place of his birth. *Gravure, perforated 11.*

CM1141 *Roberto Clemente*

CM1141		MNHVF	UseVF
20¢	**multicolored** tagged *(119,125,000)*	2.75	.20
	Plate block of 4	12.75	
	FDC *(Aug. 17, 1984)*		10.00
	v. Horizontal pair, imperforate vertically	2,000.00	

1984. American Dogs Issue depicted eight pedigreed dogs that represent the types most often bred in the United States. The stamps were issued in conjunction with the American Kennel Club's centennial. *Gravure, perforated 11.*

CM1142 *Beagle, Boston Terrier;* CM1143 *Chesapeake Bay Retriever, Cocker Spaniel;* CM1144 *Alaskan Malamute, Collie;* CM1145 *Black and Tan Coonhound, American Foxhound*

		MNHVF	UseVF
CM1142			
20¢	**Beagle & Terrier,** tagged *(216,260,000)*	.35	.20
CM1143			
20¢	**Retriever & Cocker Spaniel,** tagged	.35	.20
CM1144			
20¢	**Malamute & Collie,** tagged	.35	.20
CM1145			
20¢	**Coonhound & Foxhound,** tagged	.35	.20
	Plate block of 4	4.25	
	y. Se-tenant block of 4 CM1142-45	2.00	
	FDC *(Sept. 7, 1984),* any single		2.00
	FDC, block of 4		4.00

1984. Crime Prevention Issue depicted McGruff, the Crime Dog, popularized to boost public confidence and encourage participation in citizen crime-prevention activities. *Gravure by American Bank Note Co., perforated 11.*

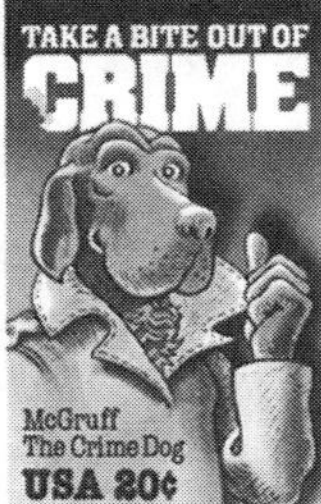

CM1146 *McGruff, the Crime Dog*

		MNHVF	UseVF
CM1146			
20¢	**multicolored** tagged *(120,000,000)*	.35	.20
	Plate block of 4	2.50	
	FDC *(Sept. 26, 1984)*		2.00

1984. Family Unity Issue was designed by high school student Molly LaRue. *Gravure and intaglio (Combination Press), perforated 11.*

CM1147 *Stick-figure family*

		MNHVF	UseVF
CM1147			
20¢	**multicolored** tagged *(117,625,000)*	.35	.20
	Plate block of 20	17.75	
	FDC *(Oct. 1, 1984)*		1.75
	v. Horizontal pair, imperforate vertically	525.00	
	v1. Vertical pair, imperforate between	—	
	zo. Tagging omitted	4.00	

1984. Eleanor Roosevelt Issue honored the woman who distinguished herself both as the first lady and as a humanitarian who fought for human rights as a delegate to the United Nations. *Intaglio, perforated 11.*

CM1148 *Eleanor Roosevelt*

		MNHVF	UseVF
CM1148			
20¢	**blue** tagged *(112,896,000)*	.35	.20
	Plate block of 4	2.50	
	FDC *(Oct. 11, 1984)*		1.75

1984. Nation of Readers Issue recognized the importance of reading in American society, including the traditions of public education and the public library. *Intaglio, perforated 11.*

CM1149 *Abraham Lincoln and son Tad, from a daguerreotype by Matthew Brady*

		MNHVF	UseVF
CM1149			
20¢	**brown & dark red** tagged, *(116,500,000)*	.35	.20
	Plate block of 4	2.95	
	FDC *(Oct. 16, 1984)*		1.75

1984. Hispanic Americans Issue honored Hispanic Americans and their contribution to national defense. Many have received the nation's highest honors and awards for gallantry in the armed services. *Gravure, perforated 11.*

CM1150 *Hispanic Americans*

		MNHVF	UseVF
CM1150			
20¢	**multicolored** tagged *(108,140,000)*	.35	.20
	Plate block of 4	2.50	
	FDC *(Oct. 31, 1984)*		1.75
	v. Vertical pair, imperforate horizontally	1,850.00	

1984. Vietnam Veterans Memorial Issue commemorated the second anniversary of the dedication of the Vietnam Veterans Memorial. The Washington, D.C., memorial contains the names of 58,196 Americans killed or missing in action during the war. *Intaglio, perforated 11.*

CM1151 *Vietnam Veterans Memorial*

		MNHVF	UseVF
CM1151			
20¢	**multicolored** tagged *(105,300,000)*	.35	.20
	Plate block of 4	4.25	
	FDC *(Nov. 10, 1984)*		1.75
	zo. Tagging omitted		

1985. Jerome Kern Issue in the Performing Arts Series celebrated the 100th birthday of the composer who wrote more than 108 complete theatrical scores and 1,000 songs and earned two Academy Awards. He perhaps is best known for *Show Boat.* The stamp was the first with the 22¢ First Class denomination. *Gravure by American Bank Note Co., perforated 11.*

CM1152 *Jerome Kern*

		MNHVF	UseVF
CM1152			
22¢	**multicolored** tagged *(124,500,000)*	.35	.20
	Plate block of 4	3.00	

		MNHVF	UseVF
	FDC *(Jan. 23, 1985)*		1.75
	zo. Tagging omitted	7.00	

1985. Mary McLeod Bethune Issue in the Black Heritage Series commemorated the noted educator and social activist (1875-1955). She founded the school that became Bethune-Cookman College in Daytona, Fla., and advised president Franklin Roosevelt on minority affairs. *Gravure by American Bank Note Co., perforated 11.*

CM1153 *Mary McLeod Bethune*

CM1153		MNHVF	UseVF
22¢	**multicolored** tagged *(120,000,000)*	.35	.20
	Plate block of 4	3.25	
	FDC *(March 5, 1985)*		2.50

1985. Duck Decoys Issue in the American Folk Art Series had designs based on actual decoys: a broadbill decoy carved by Ben Holmes of Stratford, Conn., 1890; a mallard decoy by Percy Grant of Osbornville, N.J., 1900; a canvasback by Bob McGraw of Havre de Grace, Md., 1929; and a redhead by Keyes Chadwick of Martha's Vineyard, Mass., 1925. *Gravure by American Bank Note Co., perforated 11.*

CM1154 *Broadbill decoy;* CM1155 *Mallard decoy;* CM1156 *Canvasback decoy;* CM1157 *Redhead decoy*

CM1154		MNHVF	UseVF
22¢	**Broadbill decoy,** tagged *(300,000,000)*	.40	.20
CM1155		**MNHVF**	**UseVF**
22¢	**Mallard decoy,** tagged	.40	.20
CM1156		**MNHVF**	**UseVF**
22¢	**Canvasback decoy,** tagged	.40	.20
CM1157		**MNHVF**	**UseVF**
22¢	**Redhead decoy,** tagged	.40	.20
	Plate block of 4	12.00	
	y. Se-tenant block of 4 CM1154-57	2.00	1.50
	FDC *(March 22, 1985)*		2.00
	FDC, block of 4		4.00

1985. Special Olympics Issue saluted the largest program of sports training and athletic competition for mentally and physically impaired people in the world. With assistance of 550,000 volunteers worldwide, more than 1 million children and adults participate. *Gravure, perforated 11.*

CM1158 *Winter Special Olympics*

CM1158		MNHVF	UseVF
22¢	**multicolored** tagged *(120,580,000)*	.35	.20
	Plate block of 4	2.95	
	FDC *(March 25, 1985)*		1.75
	v. Vertical pair, imperforate horizontally	575.00	

1985. Love Issue was the fourth issue for use on special occasions throughout the year. Color lines by Corita Kent. *Gravure, perforated 11.*

CM1159 *Love*

CM1159		MNHVF	UseVF
22¢	**multicolored** tagged *(729,700,000)*	.35	.20
	Plate block of 4	3.25	
	FDC *(April 17, 1985)*		1.75
	v. Pair, imperforate	1,500.00	

1985. Rural Electrification Administration Issue marked the 50th anniversary of the organization, which has served as a lending agency as well as developing programs for rural electrification. *Gravure and intaglio (Combination Press), perforated 11.*

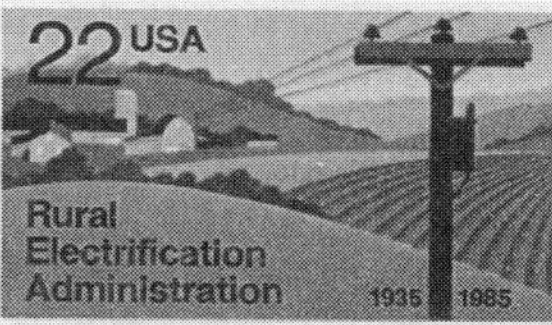

CM1160 *Rural Electrification Administration*

CM1160		MNHVF	UseVF
22¢	**multicolored** tagged *(124,750,000)*	.35	.20
	Plate block of 20	32.50	
	FDC *(May 11, 1985)*		1.75
	v. Vertical pair, imperforate between	—	

1985. Ameripex 86 Issue honored the 1986 international stamp show hosted by the United States in suburban Chicago, Ill. The stamp depicted is the 1¢ National Bank Note of 1870 (No. 97). *Offset and intaglio, perforated 11.*

CM1161 *Ameripex 86*

CM1161		MNHVF	UseVF
22¢	**multicolored** tagged *(203,496,000)*	.35	.20
	Plate block of 4	2.75	
	FDC *(May 25, 1985)*		1.75
	v. red omitted	2,250.00	
	v1. red and black omitted	1,250.00	
	v2. black, blue, and red omitted	200.00	

1985. Abigail Adams Issue honored the wife of John Adams, second president of the United States. She acted as adviser to her husband, maintained the family estate, raised four children (son John Quincy Adams became the sixth president of the United States), and distinguished herself as one of the leading women writers of her era (1744-1818). *Gravure, perforated 11.*

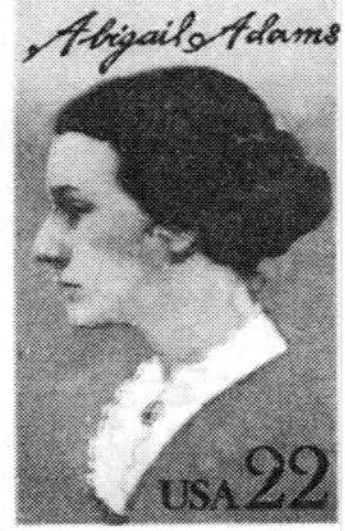

CM1162 *Abigail Adams*

CM1162		MNHVF	UseVF
22¢	**multicolored** tagged *(126,325,000)*	.35	.20
	Plate block of 4	2.75	
	FDC *(June 14, 1985)*		1.75
	v. Pair, imperforate	250.00	

Examples exist with minute traces of the intaglio black remaining, which are worth far less than a complete color-omitted error. Competent expertizing is required.

1985. Frederic Auguste Bartholdi Issue saluted the sculptor of the Statue of Liberty. *Offset and intaglio, perforated 11.*

CM1163 *F.A. Bartholdi and Statue of Liberty*

CM1163		MNHVF	UseVF
22¢	**multicolored** tagged *(130,000,000)*	.35	.20
	Plate block of 4	2.75	
	FDC *(July 18, 1985)*		1.75
	v. Intaglio black omitted	—	

1985. Korean War Veterans Issue honored Americans who served during the Korean War of 1950-53, the first conflict in which U.S. troops fought under the flag of the United Nations. *Intaglio, perforated 11.*

CM1164 *Troops marching, from a photograph by David Duncan*

CM1164		MNHVF	UseVF
22¢	**gray green & rose red** tagged *(119,975,000)*	.35	.20
	Plate block of 4	3.50	
	FDC*(July 26, 1985)*		2.00

1985. Social Security Act Issue marked the 50th anniversary of the Social Security Act, which, along with later amendments, brought workers essential protection. These include old age, survivor, disability and health insurance; compensation for unemployment; public assistance; and health and welfare services. *Gravure by American Bank Note Co., perforated 11.*

CM1165 *Social Security Act*

CM1165		MNHVF	UseVF
22¢	**dark blue & light blue** tagged *(120,000,000)*	.35	.20
	Plate block of 4	3.50	
	FDC *(Aug. 14, 1985)*		1.75

1985. World War I Veterans Issue honored American sacrifice in "the War to End all Wars" based on a drawing, *The Battle of the Marne* by Capt. Harvey Dunn, one of eight official artists for the American Expeditionary Force. *Intaglio, perforated 11.*

CM1166 The Battle of the Marne

CM1166		MNHVF	UseVF
22¢	**green & red** tagged *(119,975,000)*	.35	.20
	Plate block of 4	3.50	
	FDC *(Aug. 26, 1985)*		2.00

1985. American Horses Issue featured four breeds of horses representing the many types of horses, mules and donkeys in North America. *Gravure, perforated 11.*

CM1167 *Quarter horse;* CM1168 *Morgan;* CM1169 *Saddlebred;* CM1170 *Appaloosa*

CM1167		MNHVF	UseVF
22¢	**Quarter horse,** tagged *(147,940,000)*	2.75	.20
CM1168		MNHVF	UseVF
22¢	**Morgan,** tagged	2.75	.20
CM1169		MNHVF	UseVF
22¢	**Saddlebred,** tagged	2.75	.20
CM1170		MNHVF	UseVF
22¢	**Appaloosa,** tagged	2.75	.20
	Plate block of 4	15.00	
	y. Se-tenant block of 4 CM1167-70	13.00	6.50
	FDC *(Sept. 25, 1985),* any single		2.00
	FDC, block of 4		4.00

1985. Public Education Issue recognized the importance of public education in the development of America. *Gravure by American Bank Note Co., perforated 11.*

CM1171 *Pen and inkwell, glasses, penmanship drill*

CM1171		MNHVF	UseVF
22¢	**multicolored** tagged *(120,000,000)*	.35	.20
	Plate block of 4	6.50	
	FDC *(Oct. 1, 1985)*		2.00

1985. International Youth Year Issue honored youth groups with outdoor scenes and representative individuals from each group. *Gravure by American Bank Note Co., perforated 11.*

CM1172 *YMCA youth camping;* CM1173 *Boy Scouts;* CM1174 *Big Brothers/Big Sisters;* CM1175 *Camp Fire*

		MNHVF	UseVF
CM1172			
22¢	**YMCA youth camping,** tagged *(130,000,000)*	1.00	.20
CM1173			
22¢	**Boy Scouts,** tagged	1.00	.20
CM1174			
22¢	**Big Brothers/Sisters,** tagged	1.00	.20
CM1175			
22¢	**Camp Fire,** tagged	1.00	.20
	Plate block of 4	8.00	
	y. Se-tenant block of 4 CM1172-75	3.50	3.00
	FDC *(Oct. 7, 1985)*		2.00
	FDC, block of 4		4.00

1985. Help End Hunger Issue focused on the plight of millions suffering from hunger worldwide. *Gravure by American Bank Note Co., perforated 11.*

CM1176 *Help end hunger*

		MNHVF	UseVF
CM1176			
22¢	**multicolored** tagged *(129,000,000)*	.35	.20
	Plate block of 4	3.00	
	FDC *(Oct. 15, 1985)*		1.75

1986. Arkansas Statehood Issue marked the 150th anniversary of Arkansas' entry into the Union as the 25th state. *Gravure by American Bank Note Co., perforated 11.*

CM1177 *Old State House, Little Rock, Ark.*

		MNHVF	UseVF
CM1177			
22¢	**multicolored** tagged	.35	.20
	Plate block of 4	3.00	
	FDC *(Jan. 3, 1986)*		1.75
	v. Vertical pair, imperforate horizontally	—	

1986. Stamp Collecting Booklet Issue celebrated philately. This first booklet of commemorative stamps was issued by the U.S. Postal Service on the same day as a booklet about stamp collecting was issued by the postal administration of Sweden (Sweden 1368). The U.S. also paid tribute to the centennial of the Smithsonian Institution's first acceptance of philatelic items and to the centennial year of the American Philatelic Society. The cover of the U.S. stamp collecting booklet was an acceptable admission ticket to the international stamp show, Ameripex '86. *Offset and intaglio, perforated 10 vertically on 1 or 2 sides.*

CM1178 *Handstamp, magnifying glass, 1883 stamps;* CM1179 *Boy with his stamp collection;* CM1180 *2 Swedish stamps and U.S. CM191;* CM1181 *First-day cover of 1986 Presidents souvenir sheet*

		MNHVF	UseVF
CM1178			
22¢	**Covers & handstamp,** tagged *(67,996,800)*	.40	.20
CM1179			
22¢	**Youth w/albums,** tagged	.40	.20
CM1180			
22¢	**Magnifier & stamp,** tagged	.40	.20
CM1181			
22¢	**AMERIPEX '86 souvenir sheet,** tagged	.40	.20
	FDC *(Jan. 23, 1986)*, any single		2.00
	n. Booklet pane of 4 CM1178-1181	2.00	
	FDC, pane of 4		5.00
	nv. Booklet pane with black omitted CM1178 & CM1181	45.00	150.00
	nv1. Booklet pane with blue omitted CM1178-CM1180	2,500.00	
	nv2. Booklet pane with light brown omitted	—	

1986. Love Stamp Issue was the fifth U.S. Love stamp. *Gravure, perforated 11.*

CM1182 *Puppy*

		MNHVF	UseVF
CM1182			
22¢	**multicolored** tagged *(947,450,000)*	.35	.20
	Plate block of 4	3.50	
	FDC *(Jan. 30, 1986)*		1.75
	zo. Tagging omitted		

1986. Sojourner Truth Issue in the Black Heritage Series honored the woman who, after acquiring her freedom, took a new name and dedicated her life to the enfranchisement and education of freed slaves and to the cause of human rights (1797-1853). *Gravure by American Bank Note Co., perforated 11.*

CM1183 *Sojourner Truth*

		MNHVF	UseVF
CM1183			
22¢	**multicolored** tagged *(130,000,000)*	.35	.20
	Plate block of 4	3.50	
	FDC *(Feb. 4, 1986)*		2.50

1986. Republic of Texas Issue commemorated the 150th anniversary of Texan independence from Mexico. *Gravure by American Bank Note Co., perforated 11.*

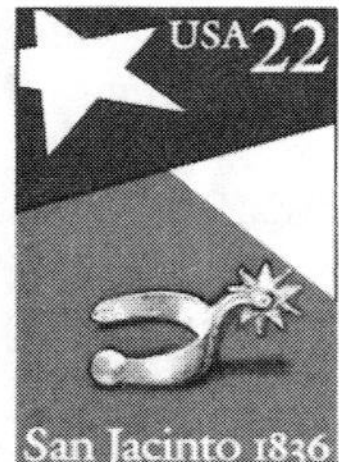

CM1184 *Spur on Texas state flag*

CM1184		MNHVF	UseVF
22¢	**dark blue, dark red & dark gray** tagged *(136,500,000)*	.35	.20
	Plate block of 4	3.50	
	FDC *(March 2, 1986)*		2.00
	v. dark red omitted	2,550.00	
	v1. Horizontal pair, imperforate vertically	1,100.00	

1986. Fish Booklet Issue featured five fish common to the U.S. waters. *Gravure, perforated 10 horizontally on 1 or 2 sides.*

CM1185 *Muskellunge*

CM1186 *Atlantic cod*

CM1187 *Largemouth bass*

CM1188 *Bluefin tuna*

CM1189 *Catfish*

CM1185		MNHVF	UseVF
22¢	**Muskellunge,** tagged *(219,990,000)*	1.75	.20
CM1186		**MNHVF**	**UseVF**
22¢	**Atlantic cod,** tagged	1.75	.20
CM1187		**MNHVF**	**UseVF**
22¢	**Largemouth bass,** tagged	1.75	.20
CM1188		**MNHVF**	**UseVF**
22¢	**Bluefin tuna,** tagged	1.75	.20
CM1189		**MNHVF**	**UseVF**
22¢	**Catfish,** tagged	1.75	.20
	FDC *(March 21, 1986),* any single		2.00
	n. Booklet pane of 5 CM1185-89	8.50	
	FDC, pane of 5		6.00

1986. Public Hospitals Issue honored U.S. public hospitals that trace their history back to Philadelphia General Hospital, which opened about 1731 (closed in 1977). *Gravure by American Bank Note Co., perforated 11.*

CM1190 *Public hospitals*

CM1190		MNHVF	UseVF
22¢	**multicolored** tagged *(130,000,000)*	.35	.20
	Plate block of 4	3.25	
	FDC *(April 11, 1986)*		1.75
	v. Horizontal pair, imperforate vertically	1,250.00	
	v1. Vertical pair, imperforate horizontally	375.00	

1986. Duke Ellington Issue in the Performing Arts Series paid homage to the renowned jazz composer on the 75th anniversary of his birth. Edward Kennedy Ellington (1899-1974) was a creative master of jazz composition, songwriting, film scoring, ballet and sacred music alike. *Gravure by American Bank Note Co., perforated 11.*

CM1191 *Duke Ellington*

CM1191		MNHVF	UseVF
22¢	**multicolored** tagged *(130,000,000)*	.35	.20
	Plate block of 4	3.00	
	FDC *(April 29, 1986)*		2.75
	v. Vertical pair, imperforate horizontally	900.00	375.00

1986. Presidents Souvenir Sheets honored U.S. presidents on four souvenir sheets of nine stamps (one for each president and one featuring the White House). The sheets were issued in conjunction with Ameripex '86, in Chicago. *Intaglio, perforated 11.*

CM1192
Presidents I

CM1192		MNHVF	UseVF
$1.98	**Souvenir sheet of 9** *(5,825,050)*	5.25	4.50
	a. 22¢ George Washington, tagged		
	b. 22¢ John Adams, tagged	.50	.40
	c. 22¢ Thomas Jefferson, tagged		
	d. 22¢ James Madison, tagged	.50	.40
	e. 22¢ James Monroe, tagged	.50	.40
	f. 22¢ John Quincy Adams, tagged		
	g. 22¢ Andrew Jackson, tagged	.50	.40
	h. 22¢ Martin Van Buren, tagged		
	i. 22¢ William Henry Harrison, tagged	.50	.40
	FDC *(May 22, 1986),* any single		1.75
	FDC, souvenir sheet		8.00
	v. black (inscription) omitted	2,000.00	—
	v1. Intaglio blue omitted	3,500.00	
	v2. Pane of 9, imperforate	10,500.00	

CM1193
Presidents II

CM1193		MNHVF	UseVF
$1.98	**Souvenir sheet of 9** *(5,825,050)*	5.25	4.50
	a. 22¢ John Tyler, tagged	.50	.40
	b. 22¢ James K. Polk, tagged	.50	.40
	c. 22¢ Zachary Taylor, tagged	.50	.40
	d. 22¢ Millard Fillmore, tagged	.50	.40
	e. 22¢ Franklin Pierce, tagged	.50	.40
	f. 22¢ James Buchanan, tagged	.50	.40
	g. 22¢ Abraham Lincoln, tagged	.50	.40
	h. 22¢ Andrew Johnson, tagged	.50	.40
	i. 22¢ Ulysses S. Grant, tagged	.50	.40
	FDC *(May 22, 1986),* any single		1.75
	FDC, souvenir sheet		8.00
	v. black (inscription) omitted	3,000.00	

We regret that we cannot pass upon the authenticity of any stamp. Should you have stamps for which you desire authentication, we suggest that you contact a recognized expertizing service. Expertizing committees offer opinions only, not guarantees. Opinions may vary among services, and over the years an opinion may change.

CM1194
Presidents III

CM1194		MNHVF	UseVF
$1.98	**Souvenir sheet of 9** *(5,825,050)*	5.25	4.50
	a. 22¢ Rutherford B. Hayes, tagged	.50	.40
	b. 22¢ James A. Garfield, tagged	.50	.40
	c. 22¢ Chester A. Arthur, tagged	.50	.40
	d. 22¢ Grover Cleveland, tagged	.50	.40
	e. 22¢ Benjamin Harrison, tagged	.50	.40
	f. 22¢ William McKinley, tagged	.50	.40
	g. 22¢ Theodore Roosevelt, tagged	.50	.40
	h. 22¢ William H. Taft, tagged	.50	.40
	i. 22¢ Woodrow Wilson, tagged	.50	.40
	FDC *(May 22, 1986),* any single		1.75
	FDC, souvenir sheet		8.00
	v. black (inscription) omitted	—	
	v1. Intaglio brown omitted	2,750.00	

CM1195
Presidents IV

CM1195		MNHVF	UseVF
$1.98	**Souvenir sheet of 9** *(5,825,050)*	5.25	4.50
	a. 22¢ Warren G. Harding, tagged	.50	.40
	b. 22¢ Calvin Coolidge, tagged	.50	.40
	c. 22¢ Herbert C. Hoover, tagged	.50	.40
	d. 22¢ Franklin D. Roosevelt, tagged	.50	.40
	e. 22¢ White House, tagged	.50	.40
	f. 22¢ Harry S. Truman, tagged	.50	.40
	g. 22¢ Dwight D. Eisenhower, tagged	.50	.40
	h. 22¢ John F. Kennedy, tagged	.50	.40
	i. 22¢ Lyndon B. Johnson, tagged	.50	.40
	FDC *(May 22, 1986),* any single		2.75
	FDC, souvenir sheet		8.00
	v. Intaglio blue black inscription omitted on 6 stamps at left (a-b, d-e, g-h)	2,250.00	
	zo. Tagging omitted on 3 stamps at right (c,f,i)	—	

1986. Arctic Explorers Issue honored five pioneers of popular exploration who accomplished a variety of geographical, anthropological, mapping, and other scientific work. *Gravure, perforated 11.*

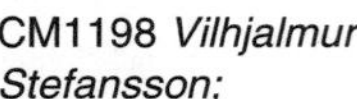

CM1196 *Elisha Kent Kane;*

CM1197 *Adolphus W. Greely;*

CM1198 *Vilhjalmur Stefansson;*

CM1199 *Robert E. Peary and Matthew Henson*

CM1196		MNHVF	UseVF
22¢	**E.K. Kane,** *(130,000,000)*	1.10	.20
CM1197		**MNHVF**	**UseVF**
22¢	**A.W. Greely**	1.10	.20
CM1198		**MNHVF**	**UseVF**
22¢	**V. Stefansson**	1.10	.20
CM1199		**MNHVF**	**UseVF**
22¢	**R.E. Peary & M. Henson**	1.10	.20
	Plate block of 4	8.00	
	y. Se-tenant block of 4 CM1196-99	5.50	3.75
	FDC *(May 28, 1986),* any single		2.00
	FDC, block of 4		5.00
	vy. Se-tenant block of 4, engraved black omitted	11,550.00	
	vy1. Se-tenant block of 4, engraved black omitted from CM1196-97 only	—	

1986. Statue of Liberty Issue commemorated the 100th anniversary of this sculpture, a gift to the United States from the people of France as a demonstration of their empathy with the nation's founding principles. France simultaneously released a 2.20-franc stamp (France 2764) with matching design. *Intaglio, perforated 11.*

CM1200 *Statue of Liberty*

CM1200		MNHVF	UseVF
22¢	**red & blue** *(220,725,000)*	.35	.20
	Plate block of 4	4.00	
	FDC *(July 4, 1986)*		2.00

1986. Navajo Art Issue depicted four Navajo blankets. This sixth issue in the Folk Art Series celebrated native American handicrafts. *Offset and intaglio, perforated 11.*

CM1201, CM1202, CM1203, CM1204 *Navajo blankets*

CM1201		MNHVF	UseVF
22¢	**multicolored** *(240,525,000)*	.40	.20
CM1202		**MNHVF**	**UseVF**
22¢	**multicolored**	.40	.20
CM1203		**MNHVF**	**UseVF**
22¢	**multicolored**	.40	.20
CM1204		**MNHVF**	**UseVF**
22¢	**multicolored**	.40	.20
	Plate block of 4	6.00	
	y. Se-tenant block of 4 CM1201-04	3.00	1.50
	FDC *(Sept. 4, 1986),* any single		2.00
	FDC, block of 4		4.00
	vy. Se-tenant block of 4 (engraved) black omitted	375.00	

1986. T.S. Eliot Issue 6th in the Literary Arts Series commemorated Thomas Stearns Eliot (1888-1965), prominent poet ("The Love Song of J. Albert Prufrock"), critic, editor, and dramatist, awarded the Nobel Prize for Literature. *Gravure, perforated 11.*

CM1205 *T.S. Eliot*

CM1205		MNHVF	UseVF
22¢	**copper red** *(131,700,000)*	.35	.20
	Plate block of 4	2.75	
	FDC *(Sept. 26, 1986)*		1.75

Each entry in this catalog has been double-checked for accuracy, but mistakes may creep into any human endeavor, and we ask your assistance in eliminating them. Please call the attention of the editors to any errors in stamp description found in this catalog. Send your comments to:
Minkus Catalog Editor
Krause Publications
700 E. State St.
Iola WI 54990

1986. Woodcarved Figurines Issue was the seventh in the American Folk Art Series. Since Colonial times, woodcarved figurines frequently served as advertisements by merchants, displayed outside their shop doors. *Gravure by American Bank Note Co., perforated 11.*

CM1206 *Highlander figure*

CM1207 *Ship figurehead*

CM1208 *Nautical figure*

CM1209 *Cigar store figure*

CM1206		MNHVF	UseVF
22¢	**Highlander figure,** tagged *(240,000,000)*	.40	.20

CM1207		MNHVF	UseVF
22¢	**Ship figurehead,** tagged	.40	.20

CM1208		MNHVF	UseVF
22¢	**Nautical figure,** tagged	.40	.20

CM1209		MNHVF	UseVF
22¢	**Cigar Store figure,** tagged	.40	.20
	Plate block of 4	4.50	
	y. Se-tenant block of 4 CM1206-09	3.25	1.50
	FDC *(Oct. 1, 1986),* any single		2.00
	FDC, block of 4		4.00
	vy. Block of 4, imperforate vertically	1,450.00	
	vy1. Pair, any, imperforate vertically	300.00	

1987. Michigan Statehood Issue honored the 150th anniversary of Michigan's admission as the 26th state of the Union. *Gravure, perforated 11.*

CM1210 *White pine*

CM1210		MNHVF	UseVF
22¢	**multicolored** tagged *(167,430,000)*	.35	.20
	Plate block of 4	2.75	
	Pair, gutter between		
	FDC *(Jan. 26, 1987)*		1.75

1987. Pan-American Games Issue commemorated the international sports competition held every four years since 1957. *Gravure, perforated 11.*

CM1211 *Runners*

CM1211		MNHVF	UseVF
22¢	**multicolored** tagged *(166,555,000)*	.35	.20
	Plate block of 4	2.75	
	FDC *(Jan. 29, 1987)*		1.75
	v. metallic silver omitted	1,600.00	

1987. Love Stamp Issue the sixth in the Love Series. *Gravure, perforated 11 1/2 x 11.*

CM1212 *Love*

CM1212		MNHVF	UseVF
22¢	**multicolored** tagged *(811,560,000)*	.35	.20
	Plate block of 4	2.75	
	FDC *(Jan. 30, 1987)*		1.75

1987. Jean-Baptiste du Sable Issue in the Black Heritage Series honored the founder of Chicago in the year of that city's sesquicentennial. Du Sable played an active role in the frontier settlement on the Chicago River as a general merchant, fur trader, farmer and Indian overseer. *Gravure, perforated 11.*

CM1213 *Jean-Baptiste du Sable*

CM1213		MNHVF	UseVF
22¢	**multicolored** tagged *(142,905,000)*	.35	.20
	Plate block of 4	3.25	
	FDC *(Feb. 20, 1987)*		2.50

1987. Enrico Caruso Issue in the Performing Arts Series honored one of the most popular opera tenors (1873-1921) of all time and the world's highest paid performer in his day. *Gravure by American Bank Note Co., perforated 11.*

CM1214 *Enrico Caruso*

CM1214		MNHVF	UseVF
22¢	**multicolored** tagged *(130,000,000)*	.35	.20
	Plate block of 4	2.75	
	FDC *(Feb. 27, 1987)*		1.75
	v. Intaglio black omitted	5,000.00	

1987. Girl Scouts Issue marked the 75th anniversary of the Girl Scouts. Juliette Low (CM316) formed the first Girl Scout troop in the United States, patterned after the English Girl Guides. *Intaglio (Giori Press), perforated 11.*

CM1215 *Girl Scout badges*

CM1215		MNHVF	UseVF
22¢	**multicolored** tagged *(149,980,000)*	.35	.20
	Plate block of 4	3.25	
	FDC *(March 12, 1987)*		3.00
	v. black, yellow, magenta, cyan & green omitted	2,750.00	
	v1. Intaglio black & red omitted	—	

1987. Special Occasions Issue consisted of eight designs (CM1216 and CM1221 each are repeated once and CM1216 has two different perforation configurations) in a booklet pane of 10. The stamps were intended for use on greeting cards and other special personal mail. *Gravure, perforated 10 on 1, 2 or 3 sides.*

CM1216 *Congratulations!*
CM1217 *Get Well!*
CM1218 *Thank You!*
CM1219 *Love You, Dad!*
CM1220 *Best Wishes!*
CM1221 *Happy Birthday!*
CM1222 *Love You, Mother!*
CM1223 *Keep in Touch!*

		MNHVF	UseVF
CM1216			
22¢	**Congratulations,** tagged *(610,425,000)*	1.75	.40
CM1217			
22¢	**Get Well,** tagged	1.75	.40
CM1218			
22¢	**Thank You,** tagged	1.75	.40
CM1219			
22¢	**Love You, Dad,** tagged	1.75	.40
CM1220			
22¢	**Best Wishes,** tagged	1.75	.40
CM1221			
22¢	**Happy Birthday,** tagged	1.75	.40
CM1222			
22¢	**Love You, Mother,** tagged	1.75	.40
CM1223			
22¢	**Keep in Touch,** tagged	1.75	.40
	FDC *(April 20, 1987) any single*		1.00
	n. Booklet pane of 10, (2 each CM1216, CM1221 and 1 each CM1217-20, CM1222-23)	16.00	12.00
	FDC, pane of 10		7.00

Nos. CM1224 and CM1225 are not assigned.

1987. United Way Issue celebrated the community-based charity's 100th anniversary. *Offset and intaglio, perforated 11.*

CM1226 *Faces in profile*

CM1226		MNHVF	UseVF
22¢	**multicolored** tagged *(156,995,000)*	.35	.20
	Plate block of 4	2.75	
	FDC *(April 28, 1987)*		1.75

1987. American Wildlife Issue 50 different stamps se-tenant in one pane released during Capex 87 in Toronto, Canada. Stamps feature animals indigenous to North America and Hawaii. *Gravure, perforated 11.*

		MNHVF	UseVF
CM1227			
22¢	**Barn Swallow,** tagged	1.50	.55
CM1228			
22¢	**Monarch Butterfly,** tagged	1.50	.55
CM1229			
22¢	**Bighorn Sheep,** tagged	1.50	.55
CM1230			
22¢	**Broad-tailed Hummingbird,** tagged	1.50	.55
CM1231			
22¢	**Cottontail,** tagged	1.50	.55
CM1232			
22¢	**Osprey,** tagged	1.50	.55
CM1233			
22¢	**Mountain Lion,** tagged	1.50	.55
CM1234			
22¢	**Luna Moth,** tagged	1.50	.55
CM1235			
22¢	**Mule Deer,** tagged	1.50	.55
CM1236			
22¢	**Gray Squirrel,** tagged	1.50	.55
CM1237			
22¢	**Armadillo,** tagged	1.50	.55
CM1238			
22¢	**Eastern Chipmunk,** tagged	1.50	.55
CM1239			
22¢	**Moose,** tagged	1.50	.55
CM1240			
22¢	**Black Bear,** tagged	1.50	.55
CM1241			
22¢	**Tiger Swallowtail,**	1.50	.55
CM1242			
22¢	**Bobwhite,** tagged	1.50	.55
CM1243			
22¢	**Ringtail,** tagged	1.50	.55
CM1244			
22¢	**Red-winged Blackbird,** tagged	1.50	.55
CM1245			
22¢	**American Lobster,** tagged	1.50	.55
CM1246			
22¢	**Black-tailed Jack Rabbit, Rabbit,** tagged	1.50	.55
CM1247			
22¢	**Scarlet Tanager,** tagged	1.50	.55
CM1248			
22¢	**Woodchuck,** tagged	1.50	.55
CM1249			
22¢	**Roseate Spoonbill,** tagged	1.50	.55
CM1250			
22¢	**Bald Eagle,** tagged	1.50	.55
CM1251			
22¢	**Alaskan Brown Bear,** tagged	1.50	.55

		MNHVF	UseVF
CM1252			
22¢	**Iiwi,** tagged	1.50	.55
CM1253			
22¢	**Badger,** tagged	1.50	.55
CM1254			
22¢	**Pronghorn,** tagged	1.50	.55
CM1255			
22¢	**River Otter,** tagged	1.50	.55
CM1256			
22¢	**Ladybug,** tagged	1.50	.55
CM1257			
22¢	**Beaver,** tagged	1.50	.55
CM1258			
22¢	**White-tailed Deer,** tagged	1.50	.55
CM1259			
22¢	**Blue Jay,** tagged	1.50	.55
CM1260			
22¢	**Pika,** tagged	1.50	.55
CM1261			
22¢	**Bison,** tagged	1.50	.55
CM1262			
22¢	**Snowy Egret,** tagged	1.50	.55
CM1263			
22¢	**Gray Wolf,** tagged	1.50	.55
CM1264			
22¢	**Mountain Goat,** tagged	1.50	.55
CM1265			
22¢	**Deer Mouse,** tagged	1.50	.55
CM1266			
22¢	**Black-tailed Prairie Dog,** tagged	1.50	.55
CM1267			
22¢	**Box Turtle,** tagged	1.50	.55
CM1268			
22¢	**Wolverine,** tagged	1.50	.55
CM1269			
22¢	**American Elk,** tagged	1.50	.55
CM1270			
22¢	**California Sea Lion,** tagged	1.50	.55
CM1271			
22¢	**Mockingbird,** tagged	1.50	.55
CM1272			
22¢	**Raccoon,** tagged	1.50	.55
CM1273			
22¢	**Bobcat,** tagged	1.50	.55
CM1274			
22¢	**Black-footed Ferret,** tagged	1.50	.55
CM1275			
22¢	**Canada Goose,** tagged	1.50	.55
CM1276			
22¢	**Red Fox,** tagged	1.50	.55
	y. Pane of 50	65.00	20.00
	FDC *(June 13, 1987)*, any single		1.50
	FDC, pane of 50		30.00
	v. red omitted, any single	—	

Constitution Ratification Bicentennial Series

1987. Delaware Statehood Issue was the first stamp in a series commemorating the bicentennial of the Constitution. Delaware was the first state to vote for ratification. *Offset and intaglio by B.E.P., perforated 11.*

CM1277 *Delaware State seal*

CM1227-1276 *Examples of American Wildlife*

CM1277		MNHVF	UseVF
22¢	**multicolored** tagged *(166,725,000)*	.35	.20
	Plate block of 4	3.00	
	FDC *(July 4, 1987)*		2.00

1987. Friendship with Morocco Issue marked the bicentennial of diplomatic relations between the United States and Morocco. Morocco issued a stamp at the same time (Morocco 1281). *Intaglio (Giori Press), perforated 11.*

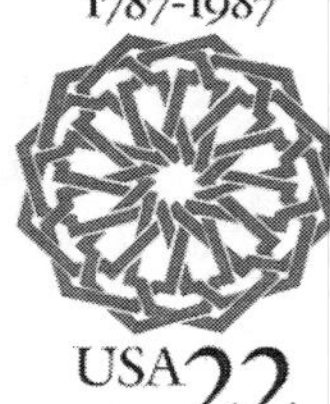

CM1278 *Arabesque from door of Dar Batha Palace, Fez, Morocco*

CM1278		MNHVF	UseVF
22¢	**red & black** tagged *(157,475,000)*	.35	.20
	Plate block of 4	2.75	
	FDC *(July 17, 1987)*		1.75
	v. Intaglio black omitted	350.00	

1987. William Faulkner Issue 7th in the Literary Arts Series honored the novelist and poet (1897-1962) who won the Nobel Prize in 1955. He was noted for his writings about life in the South. *Intaglio, perforated 11.*

CM1279 *William Faulkner*

CM1279		MNHVF	UseVF
22¢	**green** tagged *(156,225,000)*	.35	.20
	Plate block of 4	2.75	
	FDC *(Aug. 3, 1987)*		1.75
	v. Single, imperforate		

Note: Imperforate singles are untagged and from printer's waste.

1987. Lacemaking Issue in the American Folk Art Series featured four different designs of delicate needlework. *Offset and intaglio, perforated 11. Intaglio white ink was printed on top of offset blue to achieve the lace effect.*

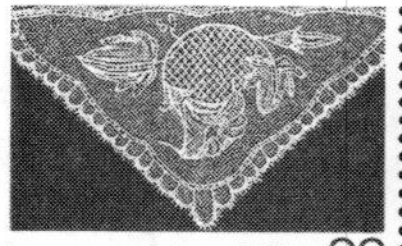

CM1280 *Squash blossoms*

CM1281 *Floral design*

CM1282 *Floral lace*

CM1283 *Dogwood blossoms*

CM1280		MNHVF	UseVF
22¢	**Squash blossoms,** tagged *(163,980,000)*	.40	.20

CM1281		MNHVF	UseVF
22¢	**Floral design,** tagged	.40	.20

CM1282		MNHVF	UseVF
22¢	**Floral lace design,** tagged	.40	.20

CM1283		MNHVF	UseVF
22¢	**Dogwood blossoms,** tagged	.40	.20
	Plate block of 4	5.00	
	y. Se-tenant block of 4 CM1280-83	2.50	1.50
	FDC *(Aug. 14, 1987),* any single		2.00
	FDC, block of 4		4.00
	vy. Se-tenant block of 4, white omitted	900.00	
	vy1. White omitted, any single	165.00	

1987. Pennsylvania Statehood Issue second in the Constitution Ratification Bicentennial Series. The Keystone State ratified the U.S. Constitution on Dec. 12, 1787. *Gravure by American Bank Note Co., perforated 11.*

CM1284 *Independence Hall, Philadelphia*

CM1284		MNHVF	UseVF
22¢	**multicolored** tagged *(186,575,000)*	.35	.20
	Plate block of 4	3.95	
	FDC *(Aug. 26, 1987)*		2.00

1987. Constitution Bicentennial Issue released in booklet format, commemorated the 200th anniversary of the drafting of the U.S. Constitution with excerpts from the preamble. *Gravure, perforated 10 horizontally on 1 or 2 sides.*

CM1285 *The Bicentennial...*

CM1286 *We the people...*

CM1287 *Establish justice...*

CM1288 *And secure... liberty...*

CM1289 *Do ordain...*

CM1285		MNHVF	UseVF
22¢	**The Bicentennial...,** tagged *(584,340,000)*	.75	.25

CM1286		MNHVF	UseVF
22¢	**We the people...,** tagged	.75	.25

CM1287		MNHVF	UseVF
22¢	**Establish justice...,** tagged	.75	.25

CM1288		MNHVF	UseVF
22¢	**And secure... liberty...,** tagged	.75	.25

CM1289		MNHVF	UseVF
22¢	**Do ordain...,** tagged	.75	.25
	FDC *(Aug. 28, 1987),* any single		2.00
	n. Booklet pane of 5 (CM1285-89)	4.25	3.50
	FDC, pane of 5		5.00
	v. greenish gray (background) omitted	—	

1987. New Jersey Statehood Issue third in the Constitution Ratification Bicentennial Series. New Jersey ratified the document Dec. 18, 1787. *Gravure by American Bank Note Co., perforated 11.*

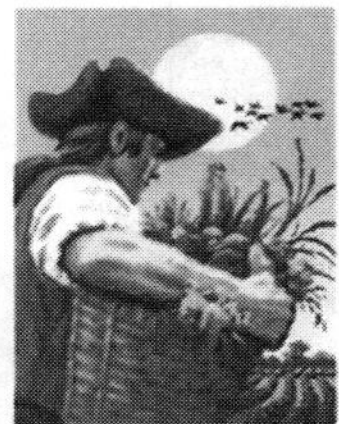

CM1290 *Farmer carrying produce*

CM1290		MNHVF	UseVF
22¢	**multicolored** tagged *(184,325,000)*	.35	.20
	Plate block of 4	3.50	
	FDC *(Sept. 11, 1987)*		2.00
	v. Intaglio black omitted	6,500.00	

1987. Constitution Bicentennial Issue honored the 200th anniversary of the signing of the document. *Offset and intaglio, perforated 11.*

CM1291 *Constitution and feather pen*

CM1291		MNHVF	UseVF
22¢	**multicolored** tagged *(168,995,000)*	.35	.20
	Plate block of 4	3.25	
	FDC *(Sept. 17, 1987)*		2.00

1987. Certified Public Accountants Issue honored the centennial of the accounting profession in the United States. *Intaglio, perforated 11.*

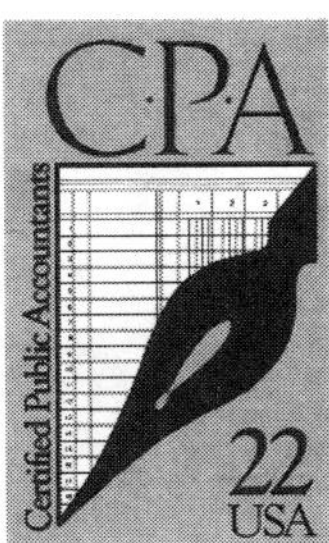

CM1292 *Spreadsheet and pen*

CM1292		MNHVF	UseVF
22¢	**multicolored** tagged *(163,120,000)*	.35	.20
	Plate block of 4		
	FDC *(Sept. 21, 1987)*		12.00
	v. Intaglio black omitted	900.00	

Please do not send us stamps to be authenticated. This type of service requires elaborate equipment and facilities not regularly available to us.

1987. Steam Locomotive Issue a five-stamp booklet, paid tribute to the steam locomotives that drove the railroad revolution in America. *Offset and intaglio, perforated 10, horizontally.*

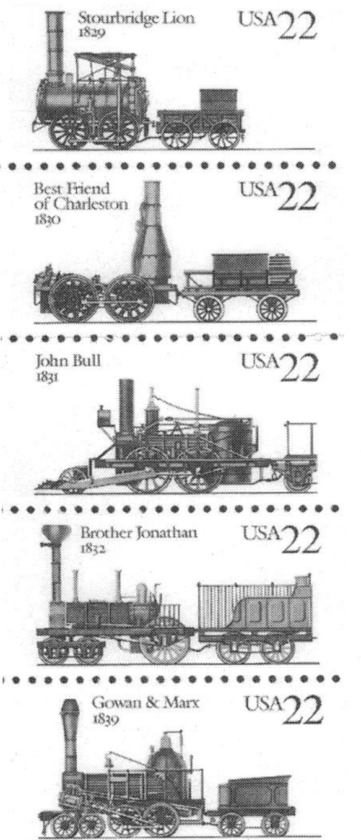

CM1293 Stourbridge Lion

CM1294 Best Friend of Charleston

CM1295 John Bull

CM1296 Brother Jonathan

CM1297 Gowan & Marx

		MNHVF	UseVF
CM1293		MNHVF	UseVF
22¢	***Stourbridge Lion,*** tagged	.75	.25
CM1294		MNHVF	UseVF
22¢	***Best Friend of Charleston,*** tagged	.75	.25
CM1295		MNHVF	UseVF
22¢	***John Bull,*** tagged	.75	.25
CM1296		MNHVF	UseVF
22¢	***Brother Jonathan,*** tagged	.75	.25
	v. red omitted	1,100.00	
CM1297		MNHVF	UseVF
22¢	***Gowan & Marx,*** tagged	.75	.25
	v. blue omitted	—	
	FDC *(Oct. 1, 1993),* any single		2.00
	n. Booklet pane of 5, (CM1293-97)	3.75	2.50
	FDC, pane of 5		4.00
	nv. Booklet pane of 5, black omitted	—	
	nzo.Booklet pane of 5, untagged	—	

1988. Georgia Statehood Issue fourth in the Constitution Ratification Bicentennial Series. Georgia ratified the Constitution Jan. 2, 1788. *Gravure, perforated 11.*

CM1298 *Live oak and Atlanta skyline*

CM1298		MNHVF	UseVF
22¢	**multicolored** tagged *(165,845,000)*	.35	.20
	Plate block of 4	3.50	
	FDC *(Jan. 6, 1988)*		2.00

1988. Connecticut Statehood Issue fifth in the Constitution Ratification Bicentennial Series. Connecticut ratified the Constitution Jan. 9, 1788. *Offset and intaglio, perforated 11.*

CM1299 *Harbor scene*

CM1299		MNHVF	UseVF
22¢	**multicolored** tagged *(155,170,000)*	.35	.20
	Plate block of 4	3.50	
	FDC *(Jan. 9, 1988)*		2.00

1988. Winter Olympics Issue honored the 1988 Winter Games at Calgary, Alberta, Canada. *Gravure by American Bank Note Co., perforated 11.*

CM1300 *Alpine skier*

CM1300		MNHVF	UseVF
22¢	**multicolored** tagged *(158,870,000)*	.35	.20
	Plate block of 4	3.25	
	FDC *(Jan. 10, 1988)*		1.75

1988. Australia Bicentennial Issue marked the 200th anniversary of the first European settlement in Australia. The stamp was issued at the same time as one by Australia (Australia 1175). *Gravure, perforated 11.*

CM1301 *Cartoon of Australian koala and American bald eagle*

CM1301		MNHVF	UseVF
22¢	**multicolored** tagged *(145,560,000)*	.35	.20
	Plate block of 4	2.75	
	FDC *(Jan. 26, 1988)*		1.75

1988. James Weldon Johnson Issue in the Black Heritage Series honored the educator, diplomat, lawyer, author and lyricist (1871-1938). *Gravure by American Bank Note Co., perforated 11.*

CM1302 *James Weldon Johnson*

CM1302		MNHVF	UseVF
22¢	**multicolored** tagged *(97,300,000)*	.35	.20
	Plate block of 4	3.00	
	FDC *(Feb. 2, 1988)*		2.50

1988. Cats Issue depicted eight popular feline breeds. *Gravure by American Bank Note Co., perforated 11.*

CM1303 *Siamese, Exotic Shorthair;* CM1304 *Abyssinian, Himalayan;* CM1305 *Maine Coon Cat, Burmese;* CM1306 *American Shorthair, Persian*

CM1303		MNHVF	UseVF
22¢	**Siamese, Exotic Shorthair,** tagged *(158,556,000)*	1.00	.20
CM1304		**MNHVF**	**UseVF**
22¢	**Abyssinian, Himalayan,** tagged	1.00	.20
CM1305		**MNHVF**	**UseVF**
22¢	**Maine Coon Cat, Burmese,** tagged	1.00	.20
CM1306		**MNHVF**	**UseVF**
22¢	**American Shorthair, Persian,** tagged	1.00	.20
	Plate block of 4	5.75	
	y. Se-tenant block of 4 CM1303-06	4.50	2.50
	FDC *(Feb. 5, 1988), any single*		3.00
	FDC, block of 4		8.00

1988. Massachusetts Statehood Issue sixth in the Constitution Ratification Bicentennial Series. Massachusetts' own constitution was a model for the federal document, which it ratified Feb. 6, 1788. *Intaglio, perforated 11.*

CM1307 *Old Statehouse*

CM1307		MNHVF	UseVF
22¢	**dark blue & dark red** tagged *(102,100,000)*	.35	.20
	Plate block of 4	3.50	
	FDC *(Feb. 6, 1988)*		2.00

1988. Maryland Statehood Issue seventh in the Constitution Ratification Bicentennial Series. Maryland ratified the document April 28, 1788. *Offset and intaglio, perforated 11.*

CM1308 *Skipjack sailboat and Annapolis*

CM1308		MNHVF	UseVF
22¢	**multicolored** tagged *(103,325,000)*	.35	.20
	Plate block of 4	3.50	
	FDC *(Feb. 15, 1988)*		2.00

1988. Knute Rockne Issue in the American Sports Series honored the famed player and Notre Dame University football coach (1888-1931) credited with helping to develop the forward pass with quarterback Gus Dorais. *Offset and intaglio, perforated 11.*

CM1309 *Knute Rockne*

CM1309		MNHVF	UseVF
22¢	**multicolored** tagged *(97,300,000)*	.35	.20
	Plate block of 4	3.95	
	FDC *(March 9, 1988)*		4.00

1988. South Carolina Statehood Issue eighth in the Constitution Ratification Bicentennial Series. South Carolina ratified the Constitution May 23, 1788. This was the first commemorative stamp paying the 25¢ First Class rate. *Gravure by American Bank Note Co., perforated 11.*

CM1310 *Palmetto trees*

CM1310		MNHVF	UseVF
25¢	**multicolored** tagged *(162,045,000)*	.40	.20
	Plate block of 4	3.95	
	FDC *(May 23, 1988)*		2.00
	v. Horizontal strip of 3, vertically imperforate between	10,450.00	

1988. Francis Ouimet Issue in the American Sports Series honored the 75th anniversary of his victory at the U.S. Open Golf Championship, which made him the first amateur to win the event. *Gravure by American Bank Note Co., perforated 11.*

CM1311 *Francis Ouimet*

CM1311		MNHVF	UseVF
25¢	**multicolored** tagged *(153,045,000)*	.40	.20
	Plate block of 4	5.75	
	FDC *(June 13, 1988)*		7.50

1988. New Hampshire Statehood Issue ninth in the Constitution Ratification Bicentennial Series (see also CM380). New Hampshire ratified the Constitution June 21, 1788. *Gravure by American Bank Note Co., perforated 11.*

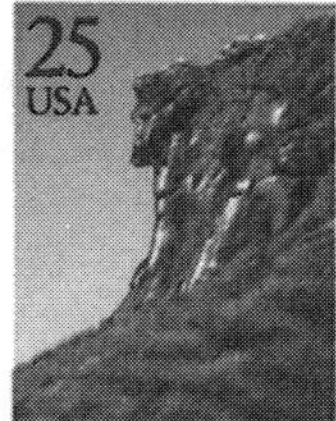

CM1312 *Old Man of the Mountains*

CM1312		MNHVF	UseVF
25¢	**multicolored** tagged *(153,295,000)*	.40	.20
	Plate block of 4	3.95	
	FDC *(June 21, 1988)*		2.00

1988. Virginia Statehood Issue 10th in the Constitution Ratification Bicentennial Series. Virginia ratified the document June 25, 1788. *Offset and intaglio, perforated 11.*

CM1313 *Old Capitol Building, Williamsburg*

CM1313		MNHVF	UseVF
25¢	**multicolored** tagged *(153,295,000)*	.40	.20
	Plate block of 4	3.95	
	FDC *(June 25, 1988)*		2.00

1988. Love Issue seventh in the series begun in 1982, featured a rose and was released in Pasadena, Calif., home of the Rose Bowl. *Gravure, perforated 11.*

CM1314 *Rose*

CM1314		MNHVF	UseVF
25¢	**multicolored** tagged *(841,240,000)*	.40	.20
	Plate block of 4	3.25	
	FDC *(July 4, 1988)*		1.75
	v. Pair, imperforate	2,750.00	

1988. New York Statehood Issue 11th in the Constitution Ratification Bicentennial Series. New York ratified the Constitution July 26, 1788. *Offset and intaglio, perforated 11.*

CM1315 *Federal Hall, Wall Street and Trinity Church steeple*

CM1315		MNHVF	UseVF
25¢	**multicolored** tagged *(183,290,000)*	.40	.20
	Plate block of 4	3.25	
	FDC *(July 26, 1988)*		2.00

1988. LOVE ISSUE the second of the year, this one in a 45¢ denomination, was released to cover the postal rate for 2 ounces of First Class mail (such as a standard wedding invitation and R.S.V.P. envelope). *Gravure, perforated 11.*

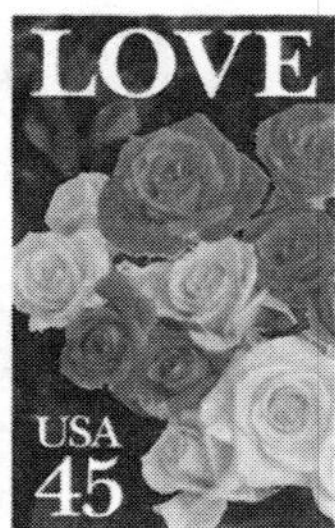

CM1316 *Roses*

CM1316		MNHVF	UseVF
45¢	**multicolored** tagged *(169,765,000)*	1.35	.20
	Plate block of 4	5.75	
	FDC *(Aug. 8, 1988)*		2.00

1988. SUMMER OLYMPIC GAMES ISSUE honored the 14th Summer Games in Seoul, Korea. *Gravure, perforated 11.*

CM1317 *Gymnast on rings*

CM1317		MNHVF	UseVF
25¢	**multicolored** tagged *(157,215,000)*	.40	.20
	Plate block of 4	3.50	
	FDC *(Aug. 19, 1988)*		1.75

1988. CLASSIC CARS ISSUE featured five antique automobiles in se-tenant booklet pane. *Offset and intaglio, perforated 10 horizontally.*

CM1318 *Locomobile, 1928*

CM1319 *Pierce-Arrow, 1929*

CM1320 *Cord, 1931*

CM1321 *Packard, 1932*

CM1322 *Duesenberg, 1935*

CM1318		MNHVF	UseVF
25¢	**Locomobile,** tagged *(635,238,000)*	2.00	.50
CM1319		MNHVF	UseVF
25¢	**Pierce-Arrow,** tagged	2.00	.50
CM1320		MNHVF	UseVF
25¢	**Cord,** tagged	2.00	.50
CM1321		MNHVF	UseVF
25¢	**Packard,** tagged	2.00	.50
CM1322		MNHVF	UseVF
25¢	**Duesenberg,** tagged	2.00	.50
	FDC *(Aug. 25, 1988), any single*		2.00
	n. Booklet pane of 5, (CM1318-22)	10.00	
	FDC, booklet pane		4.00

1988. ANTARCTIC EXPLORERS ISSUE saluted four men who first explored the vast ice-capped continent of Antarctica. *Gravure by American Bank Note Co., perforated 11.*

CM1323 *Nathaniel Palmer*

CM1324 *Lt. Charles Wilkes*

CM1325 *Richard E. Byrd*

CM1326 *Lincoln Ellsworth*

CM1323		MNHVF	UseVF
25¢	**Nathaniel Palmer,** tagged *(162,142,500)*	1.00	.20
CM1324		MNHVF	UseVF
25¢	**Lt. Charles Wilkes,** tagged	1.00	.20
CM1325		MNHVF	UseVF
25¢	**Richard E. Byrd,** tagged	1.00	.20
CM1326		MNHVF	UseVF
25¢	**Lincoln Ellsworth,** tagged	1.00	.20
	Plate block of 4	8.00	
	y. Se-tenant block of 4 CM1323-26	4.75	3.00
	FDC *(Sept. 14, 1988),* any single		2.00
	FDC, block of 4		4.00
	v. Block of 4, intaglio black omitted	1,500.00	
	v1. Block of 4, imperforate horizontally	3,000.00	

1988. CAROUSEL ANIMAL ISSUE in the American Folk Art Series presented examples of a popular art form. *Offset and intaglio, perforated 11.*

CM1327 *Deer*

CM1328 *Horse*

CM1329 *Camel*

CM1330 *Goat*

CM1327		MNHVF	UseVF
25¢	**Deer,** tagged *(305,015,000)*	1.00	.20
CM1328		MNHVF	UseVF
25¢	**Horse,** tagged	1.00	.20
CM1329		MNHVF	UseVF
25¢	**Camel,** tagged	1.00	.20
CM1330		MNHVF	UseVF
25¢	**Goat,** tagged	1.00	.20
	Plate block of 4	6.00	
	y. Se-tenant block of 4 CM1327-30	4.75	2.00
	FDC *(Oct. 1, 1988),* any single		2.00
	FDC, block of 4		6.00

1988. Special Occasions Issue had four different designs. Each booklet pane contains six stamps, three each of two designs. The two different panes bring the total to 12 stamps (three of each design). *Gravure by American Bank Note Co., perforated 11 on 2 or 3 sides.*

CM1331 *Happy Birthday*

CM1331		MNHVF	UseVF
25¢	**multicolored** tagged *(480,000,000)*	1.00	.20

CM1332 *Best Wishes*

CM1332		MNHVF	UseVF
25¢	**multicolored** tagged	1.00	.20
	n. Booklet pane of 6 (3 each CM1331-32) with gutter between	5.00	4.00
	FDC, *(Oct. 22, 1988),* either single		1.25
	FDC, booklet pane		5.00

CM1333 *Thinking of You*

CM1333		MNHVF	UseVF
25¢	**multicolored** tagged	1.00	.20

CM1334 *Love You*

CM1334		MNHVF	UseVF
25¢	**multicolored** tagged	1.00	.20
	n. Booklet pane of 6 (3 each CM1333-34 with gutter between)	5.00	4.00
	nv. Booklet pane, imperforate	—	
	FDC *(Oct. 22, 1988),* any single		1.25
	FDC, booklet pane		5.00

1989. Montana Statehood Issue commemorated the state's centennial with a design by Western artist Charles Russell (see also CM528). Montana became the 41st state Nov. 8, 1889. *Offset and intaglio, perforated 11.*

CM1335 *C.M. Russell and Friends*

CM1335		MNHVF	UseVF
25¢	**multicolored** tagged	.40	.20
	Plate block of 4	4.00	
	v. Pair, imperforate	—	
	FDC *(Jan. 15, 1989)*		2.00

1989. A. Philip Randolph Issue in the Black Heritage Series honored a prominent, respected and indefatigable voice (1889-1979) for the rights of minority labor. *Gravure, perforated 11.*

CM1336 *Asa Philip Randolph*

CM1336		MNHVF	UseVF
25¢	**multicolored** tagged *(151,675,000)*	.40	.20
	Plate block of 4	3.75	
	FDC *(Feb. 3, 1989)*		2.50

1989. North Dakota Statehood Issue marked the centennial of the 39th state to enter the Union — Nov. 2, 1889. *Gravure by American Bank Note Co., perforated 11.*

CM1337 *Grain elevator*

CM1337		MNHVF	UseVF
25¢	**multicolored** tagged *(163,000,000)*	.40	.20
	Plate block of 4	3.50	
	FDC *(Feb. 21, 1989)*		1.75

1989. Washington Statehood Issue marked the centennial of the 42nd state to enter the Union — Nov. 11, 1889. *Gravure by American Bank Note Co., perforated 11.*

CM1338 *Mount Rainier*

CM1338		MNHVF	UseVF
25¢	**multicolored** tagged *(264,625,000)*	.40	.20
	Plate block of 4	2.00	
	FDC *(Feb. 22, 1989)*		1.75

Users of this catalog are invited to write to us if they have inforamtion they feel will supplement or correct any material contained herein. All such communications will be answered.

1989. Steamboats Issue a setenant five-stamp booklet issue depicted five of America's earliest and most innovative crafts. *Offset and intaglio, perforated 11 on 1 or 2 sides.*

CM1339 Experiment

CM1340 Phoenix

CM1341 New Orleans

CM1342 Washington

CM1343 Walk in the Water

		MNHVF	UseVF
CM1339			
25¢	***Experiment,*** tagged *(204,984,000)*	.75	.20
CM1340			
25¢	***Phoenix,*** tagged	.75	.20
CM1341			
25¢	***New Orleans,*** tagged	.75	.20
CM1342			
25¢	***Washington,*** tagged	.75	.20
CM1343			
25¢	***Walk in the Water,*** tagged	.75	.20
	FDC *(March 3, 1989),* any single		2.00
	n. Booklet pane of 5 (CM1339-43)	3.60	1.00
	FDC, booklet pane		4.00

1989. World Stamp Expo 89 Issue honored the first-ever international stamp show to be sponsored by the U.S. Postal Service. The stamp depicted is the 90¢ Lincoln from the 1869 Pictorial Series (No. 96). *Offset and intaglio, perforated 11.*

CM1344 *World Stamp Expo 89*

		MNHVF	UseVF
CM1344			
25¢	**red, gray & black** *(103,835,000)*	.40	.20
	Plate block of 4	3.00	
	FDC *(March 16, 1989)*		1.75

1989. Arturo Toscanini Issue in the Performing Arts Series saluted an Italian (1867-1957) who many consider the greatest orchestra conductor of all time. *Gravure by American Bank Note Co., perforated 11.*

CM1345 *Arturo Toscanini*

		MNHVF	UseVF
CM1345			
25¢	**multicolored** tagged *(152,250,000)*	.40	.20
	Plate block of 4	3.50	
	FDC *(March 25, 1989)*		1.75

Branches of Government Series

1989. House of Representatives Issue was the first of four stamps honoring the three branches of government set by the U.S. Constitution. *Offset and intaglio, perforated 11.*

CM1346 *Marble clock by Carlo Franzoni*

		MNHVF	UseVF
CM1346			
25¢	**multicolored** tagged *(138,760,000)*	.40	.20
	Plate block of 4	3.75	
	FDC *(April 4, 1989)*		2.00

1989. Senate Issue honored the bicentennial of the U.S. Senate; the second in a series to honor branches of government established by the U.S. Constitution. *Offset and intaglio, perforated 11.*

CM1347 *Old Senate Chamber eagle and shield*

		MNHVF	UseVF
CM1347			
25¢	**multicolored** tagged *(137,985,000)*	.40	.20
	Plate block of 4	3.75	
	FDC *(April 6, 1989)*		2.00

1989. Executive Branch Issue honored George Washington as the first person to head this government branch established by the Constitution. *Offset and intaglio, perforated 11.*

CM1348 *George Washington*

CM1348		MNHVF	UseVF
25¢	**multicolored** tagged *(138,580,000)*	.40	.20
	Plate block of 4	4.25	
	FDC *(April 16, 1989)*		2.00

1989. South Dakota Statehood Issue honored the centennial of the 40th state, which entered the Union — Nov. 2, 1889. *Gravure by American Bank Note Co., perforated 11.*

CM1349 *Pasque flower, pioneer woman and sod house*

CM1349		MNHVF	UseVF
25¢	**multicolored** tagged *(164,680,000)*	.40	.20
	Plate block of 4	3.00	
	FDC *(May 3, 1989)*		1.75

1989. Lou Gehrig Issue in the American Sports Series recognized one of baseball's immortals (1903-1941), the "Iron Horse" of the New York Yankees. *Gravure by American Bank Note Co., perforated 11.*

CM1350 *Lou Gehrig*

CM1350		MNHVF	UseVF
25¢	**multicolored** tagged *(138,760,000)*	1.10	.20
	Plate block of 4	5.25	
	FDC *(June 10, 1989)*		5.50

1989. Ernest Hemingway Issue 8th in the Literary Arts Series honored the Nobel Prize-winning author (1899-1961) of *The Sun Also Rises* and *For Whom the Bell Tolls. Gravure by American Bank Note Co., perforated 11.*

CM1351 *Ernest Hemingway*

CM1351		MNHVF	UseVF
25¢	**multicolored** tagged *(191,755,000)*	.40	.20
	Plate block of 4	3.00	
	Pair, imperforate horizontally	—	
	FDC *(July 17, 1989)*		1.75
	v. Vertical pair, imperforate horizontally	—	

1989. Moon Landing Anniversary Issue commemorated the 20th anniversary of man's first steps on the Moon. The stamp was the first to meet the basic Priority Mail rate. *Offset and intaglio, perforated 11.*

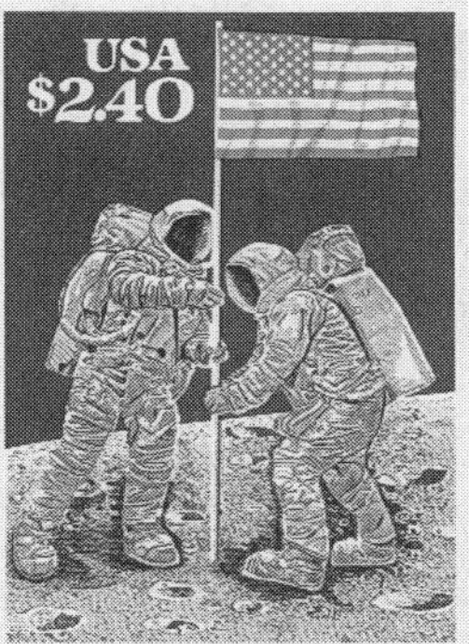

CM1352 *Astronauts and flag on Moon*

CM1352		MNHVF	UseVF
$2.40	**multicolored** tagged	6.00	2.25
	Plate block of 4	28.50	
	FDC *(July 20, 1989)*		7.00
	v. Intaglio black omitted	2,750.00	
	v1. Offset black omitted	4,500.00	
	v2. Pair, imperforate	850.00	

1989. North Carolina Statehood Issue the 12th in the Constitution Ratification Bicentennial Series. North Carolina ratified the Constitution Nov. 21, 1789. *Gravure by American Bank Note Co., perforated 11.*

CM1353 *Dogwood*

CM1353		MNHVF	UseVF
25¢	**multicolored** tagged *(179,800,000)*	.40	.20
	Plate block of 4	3.95	
	FDC *(Aug. 22, 1989)*		2.00

1989. Letter Carriers Issue paid tribute to those who carry America's mail to 100 million delivery points. *Gravure by American Bank Note Co., perforated 11.*

CM1354 *Letter carrier caricatures*

CM1354		MNHVF	UseVF
25¢	**multicolored** tagged *(188,400,000)*	.40	.20
	Plate block of 4	3.95	
	FDC *(Aug. 30, 1989)*		2.00

1989. Bill of Rights Issue commemorated the freedoms guaranteed in the first 10 Amendments to the Constitution. *Offset and intaglio, perforated 11.*

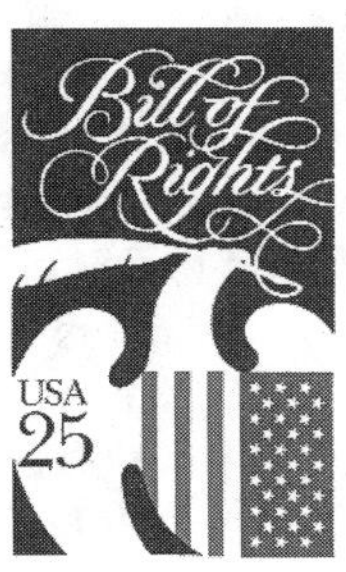

CM1355 *Eagle, Stars and Stripes*

CM1355		MNHVF	UseVF
25¢	**multicolored** tagged *(191,860,000)*	.40	.20
	Plate block of 4	5.50	
	FDC *(Sept. 25, 1989)*		1.75
	v. Intaglio black omitted	350.00	

1989. Dinosaurs Issue celebrated the great prehistoric beasts, kicked off Stamp Collecting Month and served as a promotional tie-in with the videocassette release of the movie *The Land Before Time. Intaglio (Giori Press), perforated 11.*

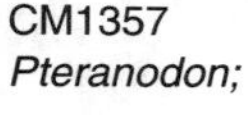

CM1356 *Tyrannosaurus;*
CM1357 *Pteranodon;*
CM1358 *Stegosaurus;*
CM1359 *Apatosaurus ("Brontosaurus")*

CM1356		MNHVF	UseVF
25¢	**Tyrannosaurus,** tagged	1.25	.20
CM1357		MNHVF	UseVF
25¢	**Pteranodon,** tagged	1.25	.20
CM1358		MNHVF	UseVF
25¢	**Stegosaurus,** tagged	1.25	.20
CM1359		MNHVF	UseVF
25¢	**Apatosaurus,** tagged	1.25	.20
	Plate block of 4	5.75	
	y. Se-tenant block of 4 CM1356-59	4.50	2.50
	FDC *(Oct. 1, 1989),* any single		2.00
	FDC, block of 4		5.00
	vy. Block of 4, intaglio black omitted	1,600.00	
	vy1. Any single, intaglio black omitted	175.00	

1989. America Issue honored the customs, images and traditions of native Americans prior to Columbus. Part of a 1989-91 Columbian Series by members of the Postal Union of the Americas and Spain (PUAS). *Gravure by American Bank Note Co., perforated 11.*

CM1360 *Southwest carved figure*

CM1360		MNHVF	UseVF
25¢	**multicolored** tagged *(137,410,000)*	.40	.20
	Plate block of 4	3.00	
	FDC *(Oct. 12, 1989)*		1.75

1989. World Stamp Expo 89 Souvenir Sheet featured a reproduction of the 90¢ stamp from the 1869 Pictorials (No. 96) and three trial color proofs on a single imperforate sheet. *Offset and intaglio, perforated 11.*

WORLD STAMP EXPO'89
The classic 1869 U.S. Abraham Lincoln stamp is reborn in these four larger versions commemorating World Stamp Expo'89, held in Washington, D.C. during the 20th Universal Postal Congress of the UPU. These stamps show the issued colors and three of the trial proof color combinations.

CM1361 *World Stamp Expo 89 souvenir sheet*

CM1361		MNHVF	UseVF
$3.60	**Souvenir sheet of 4** *(2,017,225)*	20.00	13.50
	a. 90¢ like No. 96, carmine frame, black vignette	2.50	2.00
	b. 90¢ blue frame, brown vignette	2.50	2.00
	c. 90¢ green frame, blue vignette	2.50	2.00
	d. 90¢ scarlet frame, blue vignette	2.50	2.00
	FDC *(Nov. 17, 1989)*		14.50

1989. Classic Mail Transportation Issue depicted vehicles that delivered mail in the 19th and the early 20th century. Issued in conjunction with the 20th UPU Congress. *Offset and intaglio, perforated 11.*

CM1362, 1366a *Stagecoach*
CM1363, 1366b *Steamboat*
CM1364, 1366c *Biplane*
CM1365, 1366d *Early automobile*

CM1362		MNHVF	UseVF
25¢	**Stagecoach,** tagged *(163,824,000)*	.75	.20
CM1363		MNHVF	UseVF
25¢	**Steamboat,** tagged	.75	.20
CM1364		MNHVF	UseVF
25¢	**Biplane,** tagged	.75	.20
CM1365		MNHVF	UseVF
25¢	**Early automobile,** tagged	.75	.20
	Plate block of 4	6.00	
	y. Se-tenant block of 4 CM1362-65	3.00	2.00
	FDC *(Nov. 19, 1989),* any single		2.00
	FDC, block of 4		4.00
	vy. Block of 4, intaglio dark blue omitted	1,250.00	
	vy1. Any single, intaglio blue omitted	200.00	

1989. Classic Mail Transportation Souvenir Sheet Issue

Each entry in this catalog has been double-checked for accuracy, but mistakes may creep into any human endeavor, and we ask your assistance in eliminating them. Please call the attention of the editors to any errors in stamp description found in this catalog. Send your comments to:
Minkus Catalog Editor
Krause Publications
700 E. State St.
Iola WI 54990

20th Universal Postal Congress
A review of historical methods of delivering the mail in the United States is the theme of these four stamps issued in commemoration of the convening of the 20th Universal Postal Congress in Washington, D.C. from November 13 through December 14, 1989. The United States, as host nation to the Congress for the first time in ninety-two years, welcomed more than 1,000 delegates from most of the member nations of the Universal Postal Union to the major international event.

USA
25

USA
25

USA
25

USA
25

CM1366 *Classic Mail Transportation Souvenir Sheet*

CM1366		MNHVF	UseVF
$1	**multicolored Souvenir sheet,** tagged	5.00	4.00
	a. 25¢ like CM1362	1.25	.75
	b. 25¢ like CM1363	1.25	.75
	c. 25¢ like CM1364	1.25	.75
	d. 25¢ like CM1365	1.25	.75
	FDC *(Nov. 28, 1989)*		4.50
	v. Souvenir sheet, dark blue & gray omitted	5,500.00	

1990. Idaho Statehood Issue honored its centennial as the 43rd state to join the Union — July 3, 1890. *Gravure, American Bank Note Co., perforated 11.*

IDAHO
Mountain Bluebird
USA 25 1890

CM1367 *Mountain bluebird and Sawtooth Mountains*

CM1367		MNHVF	UseVF
25¢	**multicolored** tagged	.40	.20
	Plate block of 4	3.00	
	FDC *(Jan. 6, 1990)*		2.00

1990. Love Issue was the first in the series to include a booklet version of the winning Pennsylvania Dutch-inspired design, which came from a design project for Yale University graduate students. *Gravure, U.S. Banknote Corp. (sheet) and B.E.P. (booklet).*

L O V E
USA
25

CM1368-69 *Lovebirds*

CM1368		MNHVF	UseVF
25¢	**multicolored** tagged perforated 12 1/2 x 13	.40	.20
	Plate block of 4	3.00	
	FDC *(Jan. 18, 1990)*		2.00
	v. Pair, imperforate	800.00	

CM1369		MNHVF	UseVF
25¢	**multicolored** tagged perforated 11 1/2 on 2 or 3 sides	.40	.20
	FDC *(Jan. 18, 1990)*		1.75
	v. Single, pink omitted	200.00	
	n. Booklet pane of 10	5.00	3.50
	FDC, pane of 10		8.00
	nv. Pane of 10, pink omitted	1,900.00	

1990. Ida B. Wells Issue in the Black Heritage Series honored the civil rights activist (1862-1930) who was born a slave and spent her life educating others about the horrors of discrimination and lynching. *Gravure, American Bank Note Co., perforated 11.*

Ida B. Wells
25
Black Heritage USA

CM1370 *Ida B. Wells*

CM1370		MNHVF	UseVF
25¢	**multicolored** tagged	.40	.20
	Plate block of 4	3.75	
	FDC *(Feb. 1, 1990)*		2.50

1990. Supreme Court Issue the fourth and final stamp in the series honoring the three branches of the federal government established by the U.S. Constitution, honored the 200th anniversary of the judicial branch. *Offset and intaglio, perforated 11.*

BICENTENNIAL
U.S. SUPREME COURT
USA
25
Chief Justice John Marshall

CM1371 *Bust of John Marshall, fourth chief justice of the Supreme Court*

CM1371		MNHVF	UseVF
25¢	**multicolored** tagged	.40	.20
	Plate block of 4	4.00	
	FDC *(Feb. 2, 1990)*		2.00

1990. Wyoming Statehood Issue commemorated the centennial of the state's entry July 10, 1890, as the 44th state in the Union. *Offset and intaglio, perforated 11.*

1890
USA
Wyoming 25

CM1372 High Mountain Meadows *by Conrad Schwiering*

CM1372		MNHVF	UseVF
25¢	**multicolored** tagged	.40	.20
	Plate block of 4	3.85	
	FDC *(Feb. 23, 1990)*		1.75
	v. Intaglio black omitted	2,500.00	

1990. Classic Films Issue showcased four works of Hollywood's Golden Era on the 50th anniversary of their nomination for the Academy Award. *Gravure, American Bank Note Co., perforated 11.*

The WIZARD OF Oz
USA
25

USA
25
GONE WITH THE WIND

USA
25
BEAU GESTE
STAGECOACH
USA
25

CM1373 *Judy Garland and Toto,* The Wizard of Oz

CM1374 *Clark Gable and Vivien Leigh,* Gone with the Wind

CM1375 *Gary Cooper,* Beau Geste

CM1376 *John Wayne,* Stagecoach

		MNHVF	UseVF
CM1373			
25¢	***Wizard of Oz,*** tagged	2.00	.20
CM1374			
25¢	***Gone with The Wind,*** tagged	2.00	.20
CM1375			
25¢	***Beau Geste,*** tagged	2.00	.20
CM1376			
25¢	***Stagecoach,*** tagged	2.00	.20
	Plate block of 4	10.00	
	y. Se-tenant block of 4 CM1373-76	9.00	
	FDC *(March 23, 1990),* any single		3.00
	FDC, block of 4		7.50

1990. MARIANNE MOORE ISSUE 9th in the Literary Arts Series paid tribute to the Pulitzer Prize-winning poet (1887-1972). *Gravure, American Bank Note Co., perforated 11.*

CM1377 *Marianne Moore*

		MNHVF	UseVF
CM1377			
25¢	**multicolored** tagged	.40	.20
	Plate block of 4	3.00	
	FDC *(April 18, 1990)*		2.00

1990. AMERICAN LIGHTHOUSES ISSUE a se-tenant booklet issue of five designs, portrayed oceanside lighthouses. *Offset and intaglio, perforated 10, vertically on 1 or 2 sides.*

CM1378 *Admiralty Head, Wash.;* CM1379 *Cape Hatteras, N.C.;* CM1380 *West Quoddy Head, Maine;* CM1381 *American Shoals, Fla.;* CM1382 *Sandy Hook, N.J.*

		MNHVF	UseVF
CM1378			
25¢	**Admiralty Head,** tagged	.40	.20
	v. white "25 / USA" omitted	15.00	
CM1379			
25¢	**Cape Hatteras,** tagged	.40	.20
	v. white "25 / USA" omitted	15.00	
CM1380			
25¢	**West Quoddy Head,** tagged	.40	.20
	v. white "25 / USA" omitted	15.00	
CM1381			
25¢	**American Shoals,** tagged	.40	.20
	v. white "25 / USA" omitted	15.00	
CM1382			
25¢	**Sandy Hook,** tagged	.40	.20
	FDC *(April 26, 1990),* any single		2.00
	v. white "25 / USA" omitted	15.00	
	n. Booklet pane of 5 (CM1378-82)	4.00	
	FDC, booklet pane		4.00
	nv. Booklet pane of 5, white omitted	75.00	

1990. RHODE ISLAND STATEHOOD ISSUE the 13th and final stamp in the Constitution Ratification Bicentennial Series. Rhode Island ratified the Constitution May 29, 1790. *Offset and intaglio, perforated 11.*

CM1383 *Slater Mill, R.I.*

		MNHVF	UseVF
CM1383			
25¢	**multicolored** tagged	.40	.20
	Plate block of 4	3.95	
	FDC *(May 29, 1990)*		2.00

1990. OLYMPIC ATHLETES ISSUE honored five of the greatest U.S. Olympic athletes of the first half of the 20th century. *Gravure, American Bank Note Co., perforated 11.*

CM1384 *Jesse Owens;* CM1385 *Ray Ewry;* CM1386 *Hazel Wightman;* CM1387 *Eddie Eagan;* CM1388 *Helene Madison*

		MNHVF	UseVF
CM1384			
25¢	**Jesse Owens,** tagged	.40	.20
CM1385			
25¢	**Ray Ewry,** tagged	.40	.20
CM1386			
25¢	**Hazel Wightman,** tagged	.40	.20
CM1387			
25¢	**Eddie Eagan,** tagged	.40	.20
CM1388			
25¢	**Helene Madison,** tagged	.40	.20
	Plate block of 10	8.00	
	y. Se-tenant strip of 5 CM1384-88	3.00	
	FDC *(July 6, 1990),* any single		2.50
	FDC, strip of 5		5.00

1990. AMERICAN INDIAN HEADDRESSES ISSUE featured five different native headdresses or war bonnets. Folk Art series. *Offset and intaglio, perforated 11 on 2 or 3 sides.*

CM1389 *Assiniboine;* CM1390 *Cheyenne;* CM1391 *Commanche;* CM1392 *Flathead;* CM1393 *Shoshone*

		MNHVF	UseVF
CM1389			
25¢	**Assiniboine,** tagged	.40	.20
CM1390			
25¢	**Cheyenne,** tagged	.40	.20
CM1391			
25¢	**Commanche,** tagged	.40	.20
CM1392			
25¢	**Flathead,** tagged	.40	.20
CM1393			
25¢	**Shoshone,** tagged	.40	.20
	FDC *(Aug. 17, 1990)* any single		2.00
	v. Any single, intaglio black omitted	300.00	
	y. Se-tenant strip of 5 CM1389-93	8.50	7.50
	vy. Strip of 5, intaglio black omitted	1,500.00	
	n. Booklet of 10 (2 each CM1389-93)	5.00	
	nv. Booklet of 10, intaglio black omitted	3,500.00	
	FDC, booklet pane		8.00

1990. MICRONESIA AND MARSHALL ISLANDS ISSUE commemorated the relationship between the United States and the Federated States of Micronesia and the Republic of the Marshall Islands. This was a joint issue among the three postal administrations (Micronesia 188-190, Marshall Islands 300). *Offset and intaglio, perforated 11.*

CM1394 *Micronesia flag*

CM1395 *Marshall Islands flag*

CM1394		MNHVF	UseVF
25¢	**Micronesia,** tagged	.40	.20
	v. Intaglio black omitted	1,000.00	

CM1395		MNHVF	UseVF
25¢	**Marshall Islands,** tagged	.40	.20
	Plate block of 4	3.85	
	Intaglio, black omitted	1,000.00	
	FDC *(Sept. 28, 1990),* either single		2.00
	FDC, pair		3.00
	y. Se-tenant pair CM1394-95	1.00	1.00
	vy. Se-tenant pair, intaglio black omitted	4,250.00	

1990. Sea Mammals Issue a joint release by the United States and the Soviet Union (Russia 6228-6231), focused on the beauty and significance of marine mammals. *Offset and intaglio, perforated 11.*

CM1396 *Killer whales*

CM1397 *Northern sea lions*

CM1398 *Sea otter*

CM1399 *Dolphin*

CM1396		MNHVF	UseVF
25¢	**Killer Whale,** tagged *(278,264,000)*	.75	.20

CM1397		MNHVF	UseVF
25¢	**Northern Sea Lion,** tagged	.75	.20

CM1398		MNHVF	UseVF
25¢	**Sea Otter,** tagged	.75	.20

CM1399		MNHVF	UseVF
25¢	**Dolphin,** tagged	.75	.20
	Plate block of 4	3.95	
	FDC *(Oct. 3, 1990),* any single		2.00
	FDC, block of 4		5.00
	zo. Tagging omitted, any single		
	y. Se-tenant block of 4 CM1396-99	3.00	2.00
	vy. Block of 4, intaglio black omitted	1,900.00	
	vy1. Any single, intaglio black omitted	250.00	
	zoy. Block of 4, tagging omitted		

1990. America Issue honored natural wonders of the Americas as part of the joint release by the 24 participating postal administrations of the Postal Union of the Americas and Spain (PUAS). (See also A127.) *Gravure, American Bank Note Co., perforated 11.*

CM1400 *Grand Canyon*

CM1400		MNHVF	UseVF
25¢	**multicolored** tagged *(143,995,000)*	.40	.20
	Plate block of 4	3.00	
	FDC *(Oct. 12, 1990)*		2.00

1990. Dwight D. Eisenhower Issue paid tribute on the centennial of his birth, to the 34th president. Eisenhower (1890-1969) also was the supreme commander of Allied Forces in Europe during World War II. *Gravure by American Bank Note Co., perforated 11.*

CM1401 *Dwight D. Eisenhower*

CM1401		MNHVF	UseVF
25¢	**multicolored** tagged *(142,692,000)*	.45	.20
	Plate block of 4	5.00	
	FDC *(Oct. 13, 1990)*		2.00
	v. Pair, imperforate	2,300.00	

1991. Switzerland 700th Anniversary Issue honored the small country founded in 1291. Switzerland issued a matching stamp at the same time (Switzerland 1579). *Gravure by American Bank Note Co., perforated 11.*

CM1402 *U.S. Capitol, Swiss Federal Palace*

CM1402		MNHVF	UseVF
50¢	**multicolored** tagged *(103,648,000)*	.75	.35
	Plate block of 4	6.50	
	FDC *(Feb. 22, 1991)*		2.00

1991. Vermont Statehood Issue marked the bicentennial of the Green Mountain State, which remained an independent republic until admitted to the Union as the 14th state, March 4, 1791. *Gravure by American Bank Note Co., perforated 11.*

CM1403 *Vermont farmland*

CM1403		MNHVF	UseVF
29¢	**multicolored** tagged *(179,990,000)*	.45	.20
	Plate block of 4	3.50	
	FDC *(March 1, 1991)*		2.25

1991. U.S. Savings Bond Issue honored the 50th anniversary of the E-Series Savings Bond. *Gravure, perforated 11.*

CM1404 *Bald Eagle*

CM1404		MNHVF	UseVF
29¢	**multicolored** tagged *(150,560,000)*	.45	.20
	Plate block of 4	3.95	
	FDC *(April 30, 1991)*		1.75

1991. Love Issue part of the Love Series. *Gravure (29¢ sheet by U.S. Banknote Co., 29¢ booklet by BEP, 52¢ sheet by American Bank Note Co.)*

CM1405-06 *Heart-shaped Earth*

CM1405		MNHVF	UseVF
29¢	**multicolored** tagged, perforated 12 1/2 x 13	.45	.20
	Plate block of 4	3.75	
	FDC *(May 9, 1991)*		1.75
	v. Pair, imperforate	2,500.00	

CM1405A		MNHVF	UseVF
29¢	**multicolored** tagged, perforated 11	.45	.20
	Plate block of 4	5.00	

CM1406		MNHVF	UseVF
29¢	**multicolored** tagged, perforated 11 on 2 or 3 sides	.45	.20
	FDC *(May 9, 1991)*		1.75
	n. Booklet pane of 10	7.50	
	FDC, booklet pane		7.50

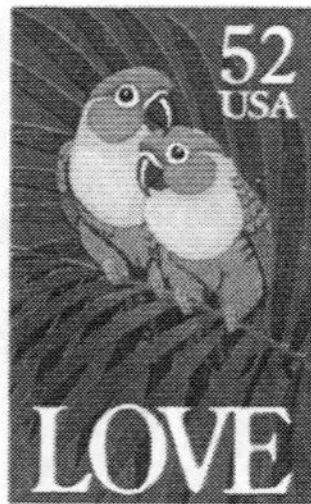

CM1407 *Fischer's Lovebirds*

CM1407		MNHVF	UseVF
52¢	**multicolored** tagged, perforated 11	.75	.35
	Plate block of 4	5.75	
	FDC *(May 9, 1991)*		2.00

1991. William Saroyan Issue 10th in the Literary Arts Series honored the Armenian-American novelist, playwright and short story writer (1908-81). He won a Pulitzer Prize in 1940 for his play, *The Time of Your Life.* This was a joint issue with Russia (Russia 6300). *Gravure, J.W. Fergusson Co. for the American Bank Note Co., perforated 11.*

CM1408 *William Saroyan*

CM1408		MNHVF	UseVF
29¢	**multicolored** tagged *(161,498,000)*	.45	.20
	Plate block of 4	3.50	
	FDC *(May 22, 1991)*		2.25

Users of this catalog are invited to write to us if they have information they feel will supplement or correct any material contained herein. All such communications will be answered.

1991. Fishing Flies Issue showed classic and carefully crafted lures in a five stamp se-tenant booklet format. *Gravure by American Bank Note Co., perforated 11 horizontally on 1 or 2 sides.*

CM1409 *Royal Wulff*

CM1410 *Jock Scott*

CM1411 *Apte Tarpon Fly*

CM1412 *Lefty's Deceiver*

CM1413 *Muddler Minnow*

CM1409		MNHVF	UseVF
29¢	**Royal Wulff,** tagged *(744,918,000)*	.45	.20
	v. black omitted	—	

CM1410		MNHVF	UseVF
29¢	**Jack Scott,** tagged	.45	.20
	v. black omitted	—	

CM1411		MNHVF	UseVF
29¢	**Apte Tarpon,** tagged	.45	.20
	v. black omitted	—	

CM1412		MNHVF	UseVF
29¢	**Lefty's Deceiver,** tagged	.45	.20

CM1413		MNHVF	UseVF
29¢	**Muddler Minnow,** tagged	.45	.20
	FDC *(May 31, 1991)* any single		2.00
	n. Booklet pane of 5 (CM1409-13)	5.50	3.25
	FDC, booklet pane		5.00
	nv. Booklet pane, black omitted from CM1409-11		—

1991. Cole Porter Issue in the Performing Arts Series, honored the 20th-century composer (1891-1964) of light, cheery songs and plays, including *Anything Goes. Gravure by American Bank Note Co., perforated 11.*

CM1414 *Cole Porter*

CM1414		MNHVF	UseVF
29¢	**multicolored** tagged *(149,848,000)*	.45	.20
	Plate block of 4	3.75	
	FDC *(June 8, 1991)*		1.75
	v. Vertical pair, imperforate between	600.00	

1991. Desert Shield-Desert Storm Issue paid tribute to those who served in the Gulf War. *Gravure (sheet version by J.W. Fergusson & Sons for Stamp Ventures, perforated 11.*

CM1415-16 *Southwest Asia Service Medal*

CM1415		MNHVF	UseVF
29¢	**multicolored** tagged *(200,003,000)*	.45	.20
	Plate block of 4	3.50	
	FDC *(July 2, 1991)*		2.00
	v. Vertical pair, imperforate horizontally	2,000.00	

1991. Desert Shield-Desert Storm Booklet Issue by the Multi-color Corp. for the American Bank Note Co., perforated 11 vertically on 1 or 2 sides.

CM1416		MNHVF	UseVF
29¢	**multicolored** tagged *(200,000,000)*	.45	.20
	FDC *(July 2, 1991)*		2.00
	n. Booklet pane of 5	2.00	
	FDC, booklet pane		4.50

1991. Olympic Track and Field Issue promoted the USPS' sponsorship of the 1992 Winter and Summer Olympics. *Gravure by American Bank Note Co., perforated 11.*

CM1417 *Pole vault;* CM1418 *Discus;* CM1419 *Women's sprint;* CM1420 *Javelin;* CM1421 *Women's hurdles*

CM1417		MNHVF	UseVF
29¢	**Pole vault,** tagged *(170,025,000)*	.45	.20
CM1418		MNHVF	UseVF
29¢	**Discus,** tagged	.45	.20
CM1419		MNHVF	UseVF
29¢	**Women's sprint,** tagged	.45	.20
CM1420		MNHVF	UseVF
29¢	**Javelin,** tagged	.45	.20
CM1421		MNHVF	UseVF
29¢	**Women's hurdles,** tagged	.45	.20
	Plate block of 10	9.75	
	y. Se-tenant strip of 5, CM1417-21	2.25	
	FDC *(July 12, 1991)* any single		1.00
	FDC, strip of 5		4.50

1991. Numismatics Issue saluted the hobby of coin and currency collecting. *Offset and intaglio, perforated 11.*

CM1422 *Coins and banknotes*

CM1422		MNHVF	UseVF
29¢	**multicolored** tagged *(150,310,000)*	.45	.20
	Plate block of 4	4.50	
	FDC *(Aug. 13, 1991)*		1.00

1991. Basketball Centennial Issue commemorated the 100th anniversary of one of the world's most popular sports. Many basketball fans pointed out the design looks like an illegal "goaltending" block. (See CM498.) *Gravure, perforated 11.*

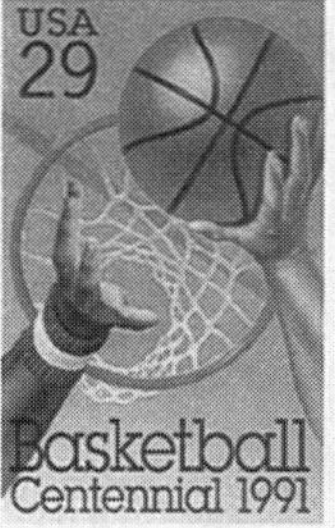

CM1423 *Hands above basketball hoop*

CM1423		MNHVF	UseVF
29¢	**multicolored** tagged *(149,810,000)*	.45	.20
	Plate block of 4	4.50	
	FDC *(Aug. 28, 1991)*		3.00

1991. American Comedians Issue showcased comedians and comedy teams of the first half of the 20th century. The stamps were the first designed by the famed caricaturist Al Hirschfeld. *Offset and intaglio, perforated 11 on 2 or 3 sides.*

CM1424 *Stan Laurel, Oliver Hardy;* CM1425 *Edgar Bergen, Charlie McCarthy;* CM1426 *Jack Benny;* CM1427 *Fanny Brice;* CM1428 *Bud Abbott, Lou Costello*

CM1424		MNHVF	UseVF
29¢	**Laurel & Hardy,** tagged *(699,978,000)*	.45	.20
CM1425		MNHVF	UseVF
29¢	**Bergen & McCarthy,** tagged	.45	.20
CM1426		MNHVF	UseVF
29¢	**Jack Benny,** tagged	.45	.20
CM1427		MNHVF	UseVF
29¢	**Fanny Brice,** tagged	.45	.20
CM1428		MNHVF	UseVF
29¢	**Abbott & Costello,** tagged	.45	.20
	y. Se-tenant strip of 5 CM1424-28	3.00	
	FDC *(Aug. 28, 1991),* any single		2.00
	a. Intaglio purple & red omitted, any single	—	
	n. Booklet pane of 10 (2 each CM1424-28)	6.00	
	nv. Booklet pane, intaglio purple & red omitted	850.00	
	FDC, strip of 5		4.50
	nv1. Booklet pane, intaglio red omitted		
	nv2. Booklet pane, intaglio purple omitted	—	

World War II Commemorative Series

1991. 1941: A World At War Issue was the first in an annual World War II Commemorative Series issued through 1995 to trace the history of World War II. *Offset and intaglio, perforated 11.*

CM1429		MNHVF	UseVF
$2.90	**Commemorative pane of 10**	9.00	5.00
	a. 29¢ Military Vehicles, tagged	.80	.45
	b. 29¢ Draft Recruits, tagged	.80	.45
	c. 29¢ Dockside View, tagged	.80	.45
	d. 29¢ Roosevelt and Churchill, tagged	.80	.45
	e. 29¢ Tank, tagged	.80	.45
	f. 29¢ Sinking of *Reuben James,* tagged	.80	.45
	g. 29¢ Gas Mask and Helmet, tagged	.80	.45
	h. 29¢ Liberty Ship, tagged	.80	.45
	i. 29¢ Pearl Harbor, tagged	.80	.45
	j. 29¢ Congress Declares War, tagged	.80	.45
	FDC *(Sept. 3, 1991)* any single		3.00
	FDC Complete pane of 10		12.00
	v. black omitted, complete sheet of 20	12,650.00	

1991. District of Columbia Bicentennial Issue marked the 200th anniversary of the federal district selected by George Washington as a site for the permanent capital. *Offset and intaglio, perforated 11.*

CM1430 *Early view up Pennsylvania Avenue*

CM1430		MNHVF	UseVF
29¢	**multicolored** tagged *(699,978,000)*	.45	.20
	Plate block of 4	3.50	
	FDC *(Sept. 7, 1991)*		1.75
	v. Intaglio black omitted	100.00	
	Plate block of 4, intaglio black omitted	650.00	

1991. Jan E. Matzeliger Issue in the Black Heritage Series honored the man (1852-89) who patented a machine for shaping shoes, which revolutionized shoe manufacturing in the United States and cut the price in half. *Gravure, J.W. Fergusson & Sons for the American Bank Note Co., perforated 11.*

CM1431 *Jan E. Matzeliger*

CM1431		MNHVF	UseVF
29¢	**multicolored** tagged *(148,973,000)*	.45	.20
	Plate block of 4	4.25	
	FDC *(Sept. 15, 1991)*		2.50
	v. Horizontal pair, imperforate vertically	1,500.00	
	v1. Vertical pair, imperforate horizontally	1,500.00	
	v2. Pair, imperforate	1,250.00	

1991. Space Exploration Issue a se-tenant 10-stamp booklet pane featured unmanned spacecraft launched to the Earth's Moon and each of the nine planets that orbit the sun, with the exception of Pluto, which is depicted as well. *Gravure, perforated 11 on two or three sides.*

CM1432 *Mercury, Mariner 10;* CM1433 *Venus, Mariner 2;* CM1434 *Earth, Landsat;* CM1435 *Moon, Lunar Orbiter;* CM1436 *Mars, Viking Orbiter;* CM1437 *Jupiter, Pioneer II;* CM1438 *Saturn, Voyager 2;* CM1439 *Uranus, Voyager 2;* CM1440 *Neptune, Voyager 2;* CM1441 *Pluto*

CM1432		MNHVF	UseVF
29¢	**Mercury,** tagged *(333,948,000)*	.45	.20
CM1433		MNHVF	UseVF
29¢	**Venus,** tagged	.45	.20
CM1434		MNHVF	UseVF
29¢	**Earth,** tagged	.45	.20
CM1435		MNHVF	UseVF
29¢	**Moon,** tagged	.45	.20
CM1436		MNHVF	UseVF
29¢	**Mars,** tagged	.45	.20
CM1437		MNHVF	UseVF
29¢	**Jupiter,** tagged	.45	.20
CM1438		MNHVF	UseVF
29¢	**Saturn,** tagged	.45	.20
CM1439		MNHVF	UseVF
29¢	**Uranus,** tagged	.45	.20
CM1440		MNHVF	UseVF
29¢	**Neptune,** tagged	.45	.20
CM1441		MNHVF	UseVF
29¢	**Pluto,** tagged	.45	.20
	FDC *(Oct. 1, 1991),* any single		2.00
	n. Booklet pane of 10 (CM1432-41)	8.75	
	FDC, booklet pane		8.00

1992. Winter Olympics Issue honored five of the sporting events of the games held in Albertville, France. *Gravure, J.W. Fergusson for Stamp Venturers, perforated 11.*

CM1442 *Ice hockey*

CM1429 *1941: A World at War*

CM1442		MNHVF	UseVF
29¢	**multicolored** tagged	.45	.20

CM1443 *Figure skating*

CM1443		MNHVF	UseVF
29¢	**multicolored** tagged	.45	.20

CM1444 *Speed skating*

CM1444		MNHVF	UseVF
29¢	**multicolored** tagged	.45	.20

CM1445 *Skiing*

CM1445		MNHVF	UseVF
29¢	**multicolored** tagged	.45	.20

CM1446 *Bobsledding*

CM1446		MNHVF	UseVF
29¢	**multicolored** tagged	.45	.20
	Plate block of 10	9.75	
	y. Se-tenant strip of 5 (CM1442-46)	3.00	
	FDC *(Jan. 11, 1992)* any single		2.00
	FDC, strip of 5		5.00

1992. World Columbian Stamp Expo '92 Issue promoted the international stamp show in Chicago. The stamp shows a detail from the 1869 15¢ Pictorial (No. 92). *Offset and intaglio, perforated 11.*

CM1447 *World Columbian Stamp Expo*

CM1447		MNHVF	UseVF
29¢	**multicolored** tagged	.45	.20
	Plate block of 4	3.50	
	FDC *(Jan. 24, 1992)*		1.75
	zo. Tagging omitted	—	

1992. W.E.B. Du Bois Issue in the Black Heritage Series honored the noted writer, historian, critic, scholar and educator (1868-1963). The Niagara Movement he founded in 1905 evolved into the NAACP. *Offset and intaglio, perforated 11.*

CM1448 *W.E.B. Du Bois*

CM1448		MNHVF	UseVF
29¢	**multicolored** tagged	.45	.20
	Plate block of 4	3.75	
	FDC *(Jan. 31, 1992)*		2.50

1992. Love Issue part of the Love Series. *Gravure, U.S. Bank Note Co., perforated 11.*

CM1449 *Heart in an envelope*

CM1449		MNHVF	UseVF
29¢	**multicolored** tagged	.45	.20
	Plate block of 4	3.50	
	FDC *(Feb. 6, 1992)*		1.75
	v. Horizontal pair, imperforate between	800.00	

CM1432 *Mercury, Mariner 10* CM1433 *Venus, Mariner 2* CM1434 *Earth, Landsat* CM1435 *Moon, Lunar Orbiter* CM1436 *Mars, Viking Orbiter* CM1437 *Jupiter, Pioneer II* CM1438 *Saturn, Voyager 2* CM1439 *Uranus, Voyager 2* CM1440 *Neptune, Voyager 2* CM1441 *Pluto*

1992. Olympic Baseball Issue commemorated the acceptance of baseball as an official Olympic sport. *Gravure, perforated 11.*

CM1450 *Player sliding into home*

CM1450		MNHVF	UseVF
29¢	**multicolored** tagged	1.00	.20
	Plate block of 4	4.75	
	FDC *(April 3, 1992)*		3.50

1992. Voyage of Columbus Issue a joint issue with Italy (Italy 2416-2419), honored the explorer's historic first voyage to the New World with four related se-tenant designs. *Offset and intaglio, perforated 11.*

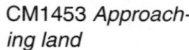

CM1451 *Seeking Queen Isabella's Support*

CM1452 *Crossing the Atlantic*

CM1453 *Approaching land*

CM1454 *Coming ashore*

CM1451		MNHVF	UseVF
29¢	**Seeking Support,** tagged	1.00	.20
CM1452		**MNHVF**	**UseVF**
29¢	**Atlantic Crossing,** tagged	1.00	.20
CM1453		**MNHVF**	**UseVF**
29¢	**Approaching Land,** tagged	1.00	.20
CM1454		**MNHVF**	**UseVF**
29¢	**Coming Ashore,** tagged	1.00	.20
	Plate block of 4	4.75	
	y. Se-tenant block of 4 (CM1451-54)	4.00	3.00
	FDC *(April. 24, 1992)* any single		2.00
	FDC, se-tenant block of 4		4.00

1992. New York Stock Exchange Issue commemorated the bicentennial of the exchange, originally formed by 24 brokers and dealers who met regularly under a tree. *Offset and intaglio by Jeffries Bank Note Co. for the American Bank Note Co., perforated 11.*

CM1455 *Stock certificate*

CM1455		MNHVF	UseVF
29¢	**multicolored** tagged	.45	.20
	Plate block of 4	3.50	
	FDC *(May 17, 1992)*		3.00

1992. Columbian Souvenir Sheets were a joint issue with Italy, Portugal and Spain at the World Columbian Expo '92 (Italy 2423-28, Portugal 2102-07, Spain 3177-82). Stamps depicted on the sheets are close in appearance to the original Columbian commemoratives of 1893 (CM1-16), but are inscribed "1992" at upper right. *Offset and intaglio by American Bank Note Co., perforated 10 1/2, block tagging on stamps over 10¢ value.*

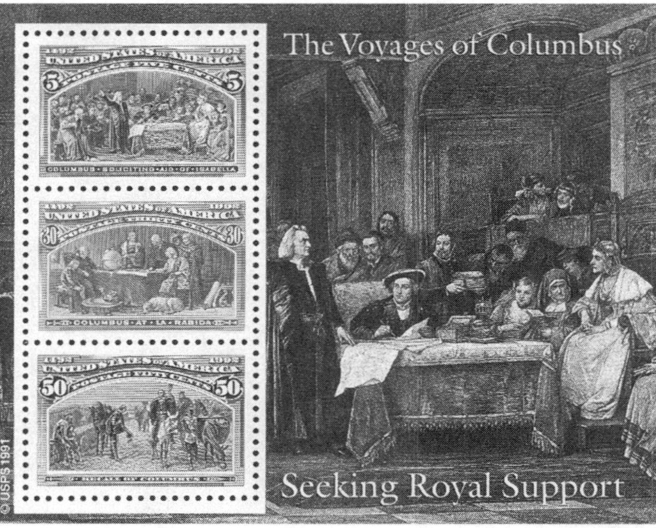

CM1456 *Seeking royal support*

CM1456		MNHVF	UseVF
85¢	**Sheet of three**	3.00	
	a. 5¢ brown like CM5		.75
	b. 30¢ orange brown like CM10		1.00
	c. 50¢ slate black like CM11		1.00
	FDC *(May 22, 1992),* souvenir sheet		4.00
	v. Souvenir sheet, imperforate	—	

Note: Imperforate Columbian souvenir sheets are very probably the result of printer's waste.

CM1457 *First sighting of land*

CM1457		MNHVF	UseVF
$1.05	**Sheet of three**	2.50	
	a. 1¢ deep blue like CM1		.50
	b. 4¢ gray blue like CM4		.75
	c. $1 Venetian red like CM12		2.50
	FDC *(May 22, 1992)*		4.00
	v. Souvenir sheet, imperforate	—	

Read the introduction to this catalog carefully. It contains much valuable information for all stamp collectors and makes the catalog easier to use.

CM1458 *Reporting discoveries*

		MNHVF	UseVF
CM1458			
$2.25	**Sheet of three**	5.00	
	a. 10¢ black brown like CM8		.75
	b. 15¢ deep bluish green like CM9		.75
	c. $2 brown red like CM13		4.50
	FDC *(May 22, 1992)*		9.00
	v. Souvenir sheet, imperforate	—	

CM1459 *Royal favor restored*

		MNHVF	UseVF
CM1459			
$3.14	**Sheet of three**	8.50	
	a. 6¢ dark lilac like CM6		1.00
	b. 8¢ brown purple like CM7		1.00
	c. $3 bronze green like CM14		5.50
	FDC *(May 22, 1992)*		10.00
	v. Souvenir sheet, imperforate	—	

CM1460 *Claiming a new world*

		MNHVF	UseVF
CM1460			
$4.05	**Sheet of three**	9.00	
	a. 2¢ dull purple like CM2		.75
	b. 3¢ dark bluish green like CM3		.75
	c. $4 deep rose like CM15		7.00
	FDC *(May 22, 1992)*		15.00
	v. Souvenir sheet, imperforate	—	

CM1461 *Christopher Columbus*

		MNHVF	UseVF
CM1461			
$5	**Sheet of one, black** like CM15	12.00	8.50
	FDC *(May 22, 1992)*		20.00
	Full set of 6 s/s	40.00	37.50
	v. Souvenir sheet, imperforate	—	

1992. Space Achievements Issue a joint issue with Russia (Russia 6376-79), honored a broad spectrum of space exploration by the two countries. *Gravure, perforated 11.*

We regret that we cannot pass upon the authenticity of any stamp. Should you have stamps for which you desire authentication, we suggest that you contact a recognized expertizing service. Expertizing committees offer opinions only, not guarantees. Opinions may vary among services, and over the years an opinion may change.

CM1462 *Space Shuttle;*

CM1463 *Astronaut, Space Shuttle, space station;*

CM1464 *Lunar Lander, Apollo and Vostok spacecraft, Sputnik;*

CM1465 *Soyuz, Mercury and Gemini spacecraft*

		MNHVF	UseVF
CM1462			
29¢	**Space Shuttle,** tagged	1.00	.20
CM1463			
29¢	**Space station,** tagged	1.00	.20
CM1464			
29¢	**Apollo & Vostok craft,** tagged	1.00	.20
CM1465			
29¢	**Soyuz, Mercury & Gemini craft,** tagged	1.00	.20
	Plate block of 4	4.50	
	y. Se-tenant block of 4, (CM1462-65)	4.00	2.50
	FDC *(May 29, 1992)* any single		2.00
	FDC, block of 4		4.00

1992. Alaska Highway Issue marked the 50th anniversary of the completion of the 1,500-mile route connecting Army installations in Alaska and the United States during World War II. *Offset and intaglio, perforated 11.*

CM1466 *Alaska Highway*

		MNHVF	UseVF
CM1466			
29¢	**multicolored** tagged	.45	.20
	Plate block of 4	3.50	
	FDC *(May 30, 1992)*		1.75
	v. Intaglio black omitted	900.00	

1992. Kentucky Statehood Issue celebrated the bicentennial of the entry of the Bluegrass State as the 15th state in the Union. *Gravure, J.W. Fergusson & Sons for Stamp Venturers, perforated 11.*

CM1467 *My Old Kentucky Home State Park*

		MNHVF	UseVF
CM1467			
29¢	**multicolored** tagged	.45	.20
	Plate block of 4	3.50	
	FDC *(June 1, 1992)*		1.75

1992. Summer Olympic Games Issue presented five events contested in the quadrennial games held in Barcelona, Spain. *Gravure, J.W. Fergusson & Sons for Stamp Venturers.*

		MNHVF	UseVF
CM1468			
29¢	**Soccer,** tagged	.45	.20
CM1469			
29¢	**Gymnastics,** tagged	.45	.20
CM1470			
29¢	**Vollyball,** tagged	.45	.20
CM1471			
29¢	**Boxing,** tagged	.45	.20
CM1472			
29¢	**Swimming,** tagged	.45	.20
	Plate block of 10	10.00	
	y. Se-tenant strip of 5 (CM1468-72)	8.00	
	FDC *(June 11, 1992)* any single		2.00
	FDC, strip of 5		5.00

1992. Hummingbirds Issue a popular booklet release, featured five varieties of these colorful birds. *Gravure, Multi-Color Corp. for the American Bank Note Co., perforated 11 on 1 or 2 sides.*

CM1473 *Ruby-throated hummingbird;* CM1474 *Broad-billed hummingbird;* CM1475 *Costa's hummingbird;* CM1476 *Rufous hummingbird;* CM1477 *Calliope hummingbird*

		MNHVF	UseVF
CM1473			
29¢	**Ruby-throated,** tagged	.45	.20
CM1474			
29¢	**Broad-billed,** tagged	.45	.20
CM1475			
29¢	**Costa's,** tagged	.45	.20
CM1476			
29¢	**Rufous,** tagged	.45	.20
CM1477			
29¢	**Calliope,** tagged	.45	.20
	FDC *(June 15,1992)* any single		2.00
	n. Booklet pane of 5 (CM1473-77)	4.50	
	FDC, booklet pane		5.00
	nv. Booklet pane, imperforate	—	

1992. Wildflowers Issue showcased 50 colorful, blooming native plants. While no specific states are attached to each flower, one or more of the flowers are found in each of the states. *Offset, Ashton-Potter America, Inc., perforated 11.*

Two simultaneous printings were produced, one with four panes (plate number positions) per sheet and the other with six panes (plate number positons) per sheet. Stamps from the four-pane press were assigned odd plate numbers and stamps from the six-pane press were assigned even plate numbers. Further, an illustration is found in the selvage of each pane depicting an uncut sheet and the location of the specific pane in hand. Screening of the "29" inscription apparently was a test leading toward microprinting, which began in 1992 (see Nos. 995-998).

		MNHVF	UseVF
CM1478			
29¢	**Indian Paintbrush,** tagged	.95	.60
CM1479			
29¢	**Fragrant Water Lily,** tagged	.95	.60
CM1480			
29¢	**Meadow Beauty,** tagged	.95	.60
CM1481			
29¢	**Jack-in-the-Pulpit,** tagged	.95	.60
CM1482			
29¢	**California Poppy,** tagged	.95	.60

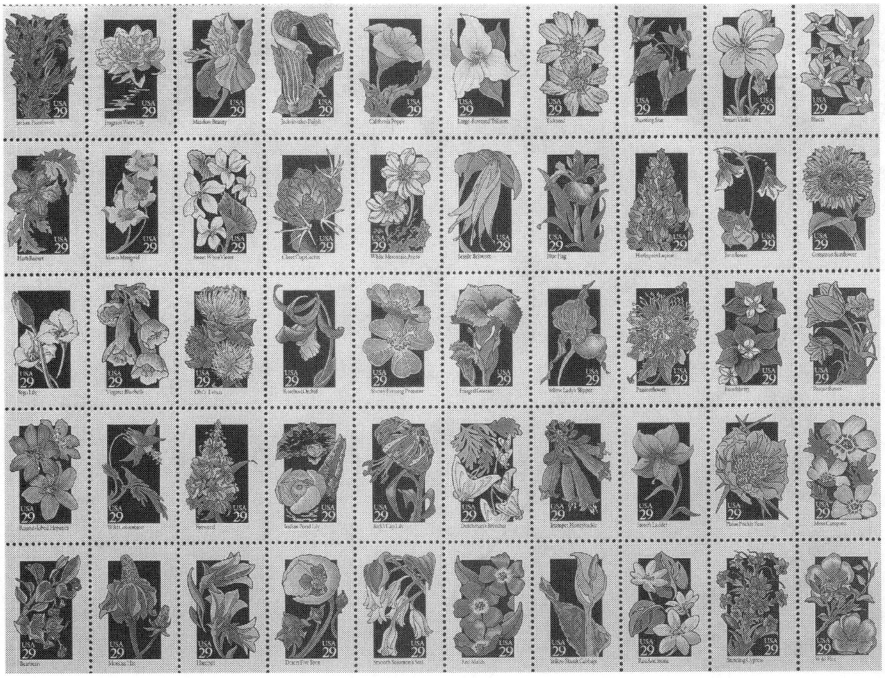

CM1478-1527 *Wildflowers from around the nation*

Number	Value	Description	MNHVF	UseVF
CM1483	**29¢**	**Large-Flowered Trillium,** tagged	.95	.60
CM1484	**29¢**	**Tickseed,** tagged	.95	.60
CM1485	**29¢**	**Shooting Star,** tagged	.95	.60
CM1486	**29¢**	**Stream Violet,** tagged	.95	.60
CM1487	**29¢**	**Bluets,** tagged	.95	.60
CM1488	**29¢**	**Herb Robert,** tagged	.95	.60
CM1489	**29¢**	**Marsh Marigold,** tagged	.95	.60
CM1490	**29¢**	**Sweet White Violet,** tagged	.95	.60
CM1491	**29¢**	**Claret Cup Cactus,** tagged	.95	.60
CM1492	**29¢**	**White Mountain Avens,** tagged	.95	.60
CM1493	**29¢**	**Sessile Bellwort,** tagged	.95	.60
CM1494	**29¢**	**Blue Flag,** tagged	.95	.60
CM1495	**29¢**	**Harlequin Lupine,** tagged	.95	.60
CM1496	**29¢**	**Twinflower,** tagged	.95	.60
CM1497	**29¢**	**Common Sunflower,** tagged	.95	.60
CM1498	**29¢**	**Sego Lily,** tagged	.95	.60
CM1499	**29¢**	**Virginia Bluebells,** tagged	.95	.60
CM1500	**29¢**	**Ohi'a Lehua,** tagged	.95	.60
CM1501	**29¢**	**Rosebud Orchid,** tagged	.95	.60
CM1502	**29¢**	**Showy Evening Primrose,** tagged	.95	.60
CM1503	**29¢**	**Fringed Gentian,** tagged	.95	.60
CM1504	**29¢**	**Yellow Lady's Slipper,** tagged	.95	.60
CM1505	**29¢**	**Passionflower,** tagged	.95	.60
CM1506	**29¢**	**Bunchberry,** tagged	.95	.60
CM1507	**29¢**	**Pasqueflower,** tagged	.95	.60
CM1508	**29¢**	**Round-Lobed Hepatica,** tagged	.95	.60
CM1509	**29¢**	**Wild Columbine,** tagged	.95	.60
CM1510	**29¢**	**Fireweed,** tagged	.95	.60
CM1511	**29¢**	**Indian Pond Lily,** tagged	.95	.60
CM1512	**29¢**	**Turk's Cap Lily,** tagged	.95	.60
CM1513	**29¢**	**Dutchman's Breeches,** tagged	.95	.60
CM1514	**29¢**	**Trumpet Honeysuckle,** tagged	.95	.60
CM1515	**29¢**	**Jacob's Ladder,** tagged	.95	.60
CM1516	**29¢**	**Plains Prickly Pear,** tagged	.95	.60
CM1517	**29¢**	**Moss Campion,** tagged	.95	.60
CM1518	**29¢**	**Bearberry,** tagged	.95	.60
CM1519	**29¢**	**Mexican Hat,** tagged	.95	.60
CM1520	**29¢**	**Harebell,** tagged	.95	.60
CM1521	**29¢**	**Desert Five Spot,** tagged	.95	.60
CM1522	**29¢**	**Smooth Solomon's Seal,** tagged	.95	.60
CM1523	**29¢**	**Red Maids,** tagged	.95	.60
CM1524	**29¢**	**Yellow Skunk Cabbage,** tagged	.95	.60
CM1525	**29¢**	**Rue Anemone,** tagged	.95	.60
CM1526	**29¢**	**Standing Cypress,** tagged	.95	.60

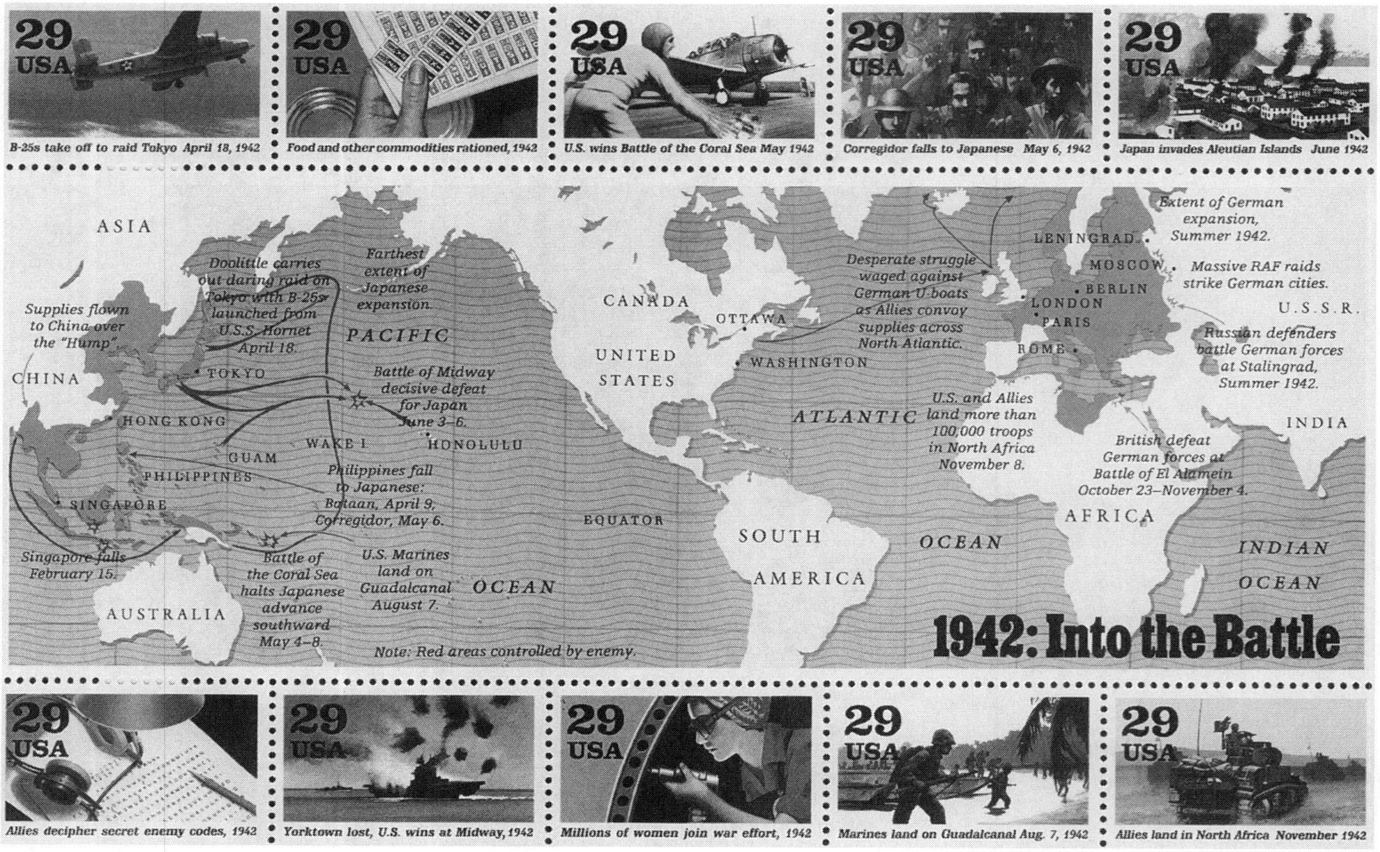

CM1528 *1942: Into the Battle.*

CM1527		MNHVF	UseVF
29¢	**Wild Flax,** tagged	.95	.60
	y. Pane of 50 (CM1478-1527)	42.50	
	FDC *(July 24, 1992)* any single		1.75
	FDC, pane of 50		50.00

1992. 1942: INTO THE BATTLE ISSUE of the World War II Commemorative Series included a map and stamps showing events of the war in 1942. *Offset and intaglio, perforated 11.*

CM1528		MNHVF	UseVF
$2.90	**Commemorative pane of 10**	9.00	5.00
	a. 29¢ B-25 Raid on Tokyo, tagged	.75	.45
	b. 29¢ Ration Stamps, tagged	.75	.45
	c. 29¢ Carrier Crewman & fighter tagged	.75	.45
	d. 29¢ Prisoners of War, tagged	.75	.45
	e. 29¢ Attack on Aleutian Islands, tagged	.75	.45
	f. 29¢ Coded Message, tagged	.75	.45
	g. 29¢ *USS Yorktown,* tagged	.75	.45
	h. 29¢ Woman Defense Worker, tagged	.75	.45
	i. 29¢ Marines at Guadalcanal, tagged	.75	.45
	j. 29¢ Tank in Desert, tagged	.75	.45
	FDC *(Aug. 17, 1992)* any single		2.00
	FDC, complete pane of 10		10.00
	v. Red omitted	6,000.00	

1992. DOROTHY PARKER ISSUE 11th in the Literary Arts Series honored the writer, poet and critic (1893-1967) noted for her wit. *Gravure by J.W. Fergusson & Sons for Stamp Venturers, perforated 11.*

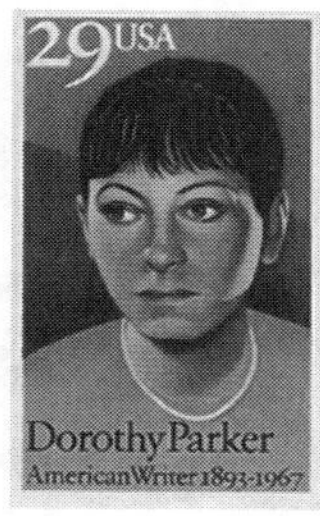

CM1529 *Dorothy Parker*

CM1529		MNHVF	UseVF
29¢	**multicolored** tagged	.45	.20
	Plate block of 4	3.50	
	FDC *(Aug. 22, 1992)*		1.75

1992. THEODORE VON KÁRMÁN ISSUE paid tribute to the aerospace scientist credited with establishing the center for rocket research that now is the Jet Propulsion Laboratory at the California Institute of Technology. *Gravure, J.W. Fergusson & Sons for Stamp Venturers, perforated 11.*

CM1530 *Theodore von Kármán*

CM1530		MNHVF	UseVF
29¢	**multicolored** tagged	.45	.20
	Plate block of 4	3.50	
	FDC *(Aug. 31, 1992)*		1.75

1992. MINERALS ISSUE featured specimens from the Smithsonian Institution's National Museum of Natural History collection. *Offset and intaglio, perforated 11.*

CM1531 *Azurite*

CM1532 *Copper*

CM1533 *Variscite*

CM1534 *Wulfenite*

		MNHVF	UseVF
CM1531			
29¢	**Azurite,** tagged	.45	.20
CM1532		MNHVF	UseVF
29¢	**Copper,** tagged	.45	.20
CM1533		MNHVF	UseVF
29¢	**Variscite,** tagged	.45	.20
CM1534		MNHVF	UseVF
29¢	**Wulfenite,** tagged	.45	.20
	Plate block of 4	4.50	
	y. Se-tenant block or strip of 4, (CM1531-34)	3.00	
	FDC *(Sept. 17, 1992),* any single		2.00
	FDC, block or strip of 4		4.00
	v. silver omitted	—	

1992. Juan Rodríguez Cabrillo Issue recalled the Spanish explorer who named San Miguel Harbor, later the site of San Diego, Calif. *Printed by The Press and J.W. Fergusson & Sons for Stamp Venturers, perforated 11.*

CM1535 *Juan Rodríguez Cabrillo*

		MNHVF	UseVF
CM1535			
29¢	**multicolored** tagged	.45	.20
	Plate block of 4	3.50	
	FDC *(Sept. 28, 1992)*		1.75

Each entry in this catalog has been double-checked for accuracy, but mistakes may creep into any human endeavor, and we ask your assistance in eliminating them. Please call the attention of the editors to any errors in stamp description found in this catalog. Send your comments to:

Minkus Catalog Editor
Krause Publications
700 E. State St.
Iola WI 54990

1992. Wild Animals Issue depicted five popular animals in U.S. zoos. *Gravure, J.W. Fergusson & Sons for Stamp Venturers, perforated 11 horizontally on 1 or 2 sides.*

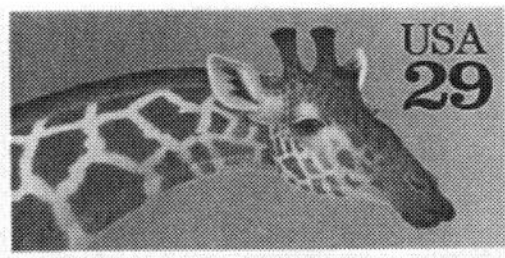

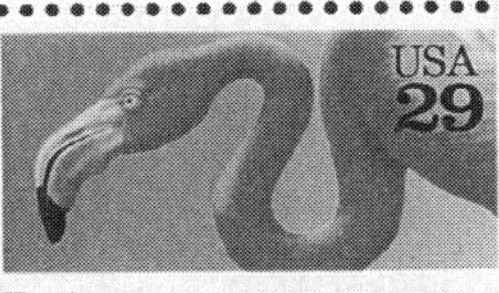

CM1536 *Giraffe*

CM1537 *Giant Panda*

CM1538 *Flamingo*

CM1539 *King Penguins*

CM1540 *White Bengal Tiger*

		MNHVF	UseVF
CM1536			
29¢	**Giraffe,** tagged	.45	.20
CM1537		MNHVF	UseVF
29¢	**Giant Panda,** tagged	.45	.20
CM1538		MNHVF	UseVF
29¢	**Flamingo,** tagged	.45	.20
CM1539		MNHVF	UseVF
29¢	**King Penquins,** tagged	.45	.20
CM1540		MNHVF	UseVF
29¢	**White Bengal Tiger,** tagged	.45	.20
	FDC *(Oct. 1, 1992)* any single		2.00
	n. Booklet pane of 5 (CM1536-40)	2.25	
	FDC Booklet pane of 5		5.00
	nv. Pane of 5, imperforate (6 reported)	3,500.00	

Lunar New Year Series

1992. New Year Issue was the first U.S. stamp in the Lunar New Year Series to honor the Asian lunar holiday. *Offset and intaglio, American Bank Note Co., perforated 11.*

CM1541 *Rooster and Chinese characters*

		MNHVF	UseVF
CM1541			
29¢	**multicolored** tagged	.45	.20
	Plate block of 4	3.95	
	FDC *(Dec. 30, 1992)*		3.00
	y. Pane of 20	12.00	

American Music Series

1993. Elvis Presley Issue of 500 million stamps represented a massive press run for a single commemorative, reflecting the interest in the rock 'n roll entertainer. The public in a write-in poll voted for the design of this stamp over a second design showing an older-looking portrait of the pop icon. This stamp is also the first in a lengthy and eclectic American Music Series. *Gravure, perforated 11.*

CM1542 *Elvis Presley*

CM1542		MNHVF	UseVF
29¢	**multicolored** tagged	.45	.20
	Plate block of 4	3.50	
	FDC *(Jan. 8, 1993)*		2.00

1993. Space Fantasy Issue was reminiscent of the 1930s vision of space travel made popular in movie and comic-book adventure. *Gravure, perforated 11 vertically on 1 or 2 sides.*

CM1543; CM1544; CM1545; CM1546; CM1547

CM1543		MNHVF	UseVF
29¢	**Saturn Rings,** tagged	.45	.20
CM1544		MNHVF	UseVF
29¢	**Two oval crafts,** tagged	.45	.20
CM1545		MNHVF	UseVF
29¢	**Spacemen & Jet Pack,** tagged	.45	.20
CM1546		MNHVF	UseVF
29¢	**Craft & lights,** tagged	.45	.20
CM1547		MNHVF	UseVF
29¢	**Three craft,** tagged	.45	.20
	FDC *(Jan. 25, 1993),* any single		2.00
	n. Booklet pane of 5 (CM1541-45)	3.50	
	FDC, booklet pane		5.00

1993. Percy Lavon Julian Issue in the Black Heritage Series honored the research chemist (1898-1975) who synthesized cortisone for treatment of arthritis. *Offset and intaglio, perforated 11.*

CM1548 *Percy Lavon Julian*

CM1548		MNHVF	UseVF
29¢	**multicolored** tagged	.45	.20
	Plate block of 4	3.50	
	FDC *(Jan. 29, 1993)*		2.50

1993. Oregon Trail Issue recalled the 2,000-mile stretch from Independence, Mo., to Oregon City, Ore., that was a popular route used by settlers traveling west. *Offset and intaglio, perforated 11.*

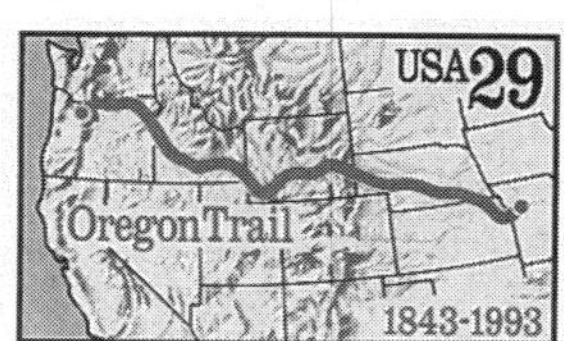

CM1549 *The Oregon Trail*

CM1549		MNHVF	UseVF
29¢	**multicolored** tagged	.45	.20
	Plate block of 4	3.50	
	FDC *(Feb. 12, 1993)*		1.75
	zo. Tagging omitted	—	

The official first day city was Salem, Ore., but the stamp was available Feb. 12 at 36 cities along the Trail.

1993. World University Games Issue celebrated the first time this biennial competition was held in the United States. *Gravure, perforated 11.*

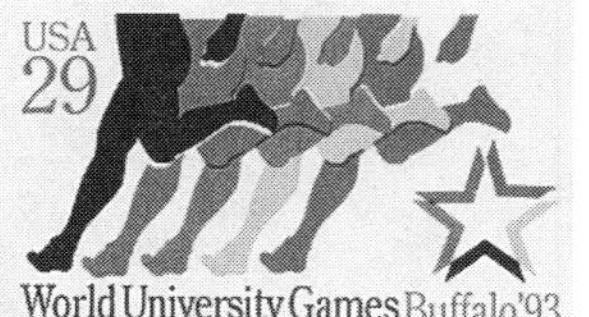

CM1550 *World University Games*

CM1550		MNHVF	UseVF
29¢	**multicolored** tagged	.45	.20
	Plate block of 4	4.00	
	FDC *(Feb. 25, 1993)*		2.00

1993. Grace Kelly Issue memoralized the American actress who became Princess of Monaco (1928-1982). Monaco and the United States jointly issued similar stamps (Monaco 2127). *Intaglio, Stamp Venturers, perforated 11.*

CM1551 *Grace Kelly*

CM1551		MNHVF	UseVF
29¢	**blue** tagged	.45	.20
	Plate block of 4	3.50	
	FDC *(March 24, 1993)*		2.50

1993. Oklahoma! Issue paid tribute to the landmark American musical. The stamp was available for sale in every post office in the state on its first day, rather than at a single outlet. American Music Series. *Gravure, perforated 10.*

CM1552 *Oklahoma*

CM1552		MNHVF	UseVF
29¢	**multicolored** tagged	.45	.20
	Plate block of 4	3.50	
	FDC *(March 30, 1993)*		1.75

1993. Circus Issue honored the 200th anniversary of the first circus performance in America. *Offset, Ashton-Potter America, perforated 11.*

CM1553 *Trapeze Artist*

CM1554 *Elephant*

CM1555 *Clown*

CM1556 *Ringmaster*

		MNHVF	UseVF
CM1553			
29¢	**Trapeze Artist,** tagged	.45	.20
CM1554		MNHVF	UseVF
29¢	**Elephant,** tagged	.45	.20
CM1555		MNHVF	UseVF
29¢	**Clown,** tagged	.45	.20
CM1556		MNHVF	UseVF
29¢	**Ringmaster,** tagged	.45	.20
	Plate block of 6	6.75	
	Plate block of 4	4.00	
	y. Se-tenant block of 4 (CM1553-56)	3.00	
	FDC *(April 6, 1993),* any single		2.50
	FDC, block of 4		4.00

1993. Cherokee Strip Land Run Centennial Issue commemorated the events of Sept. 16, 1893, when more than 100,000 pioneers raced to stake out land claims in the 8 million acre parcel of land known as the "Cherokee Strip." *Offset and intaglio, by American Bank Note Co., perforated 11.*

CM1557 *Pioneers on wagon and horseback racing*

		MNHVF	UseVF
CM1557			
29¢	**multicolored** tagged	.45	.20
	Plate block of 4	3.50	
	FDC *(April 17, 1993)*		1.75
	y. Pane of 20	10.00	

1993. Dean Acheson Issue honored the former U.S. Secretary of State (1893-1971). *Intaglio, Stamp Venturers, perforated 11.*

CM1558 *Dean Acheson*

		MNHVF	UseVF
CM1558			
29¢	**green** tagged	.45	.20
	Plate block of 4	3.50	
	FDC *(April 21, 1993)*		1.75

1993. Sporting Horses Issue commemorated four equestrian events. *Offset and intaglio, Stamp Venturers, perforated 11 x 11 1/2.*

CM1559 *Steeplechase*

CM1560 *Throughbred racing*

CM1561 *Harness racing*

CM1562 *Polo*

		MNHVF	UseVF
CM1559			
29¢	**Steeplechase,** tagged	.45	.20
CM1560		MNHVF	UseVF
29¢	**Thoroughbred racing,** tagged	.45	.20
CM1561		MNHVF	UseVF
29¢	**Harness racing,** tagged	.45	.20
CM1562		MNHVF	UseVF
29¢	**Polo,** tagged	.45	.20
	Plate block of 4	4.25	
	FDC *(May 1, 1993),* any single		2.00
	FDC, block of 4		4.00
	y. Se-tenant block of 4 (CM1559-62)	1.80	
	v. Any single, intaglio, black omitted	375.00	
	vy. Block of 4, intaglio black omitted	1,650.00	

Garden Flowers Series

1993. Garden Flowers Issue the first in a Garden Flowers Series of four that showed popular spring blooms in a booklet format. *Offset and intaglio, perforated 11 vertically on 1 or 2 sides.*

CM1563 *Hyacinth;* CM1564 *Daffodil;* CM1565 *Tulip;* CM1566 *Iris;* CM1567 *Lilac*

		MNHVF	UseVF
CM1563			
29¢	**Hyacinth,** tagged	.45	.20
CM1564		MNHVF	UseVF
29¢	**Daffodil,** tagged	.45	.20
CM1565		MNHVF	UseVF
29¢	**Tulip,** tagged	.45	.20
CM1566		MNHVF	UseVF
29¢	**Iris,** tagged	.45	.20
CM1567		MNHVF	UseVF
29¢	**Lilac,** tagged	.45	.20
	FDC *(May 15, 1993),* any single		2.00
	n. Booklet pane of 5 (CM1563-67)	5.50	
	FDC, booklet pane		5.00
	nv. Booklet pane, imperforate	2,000.00	
	nv1. Booklet pane, intaglio black omitted	275.00	

1993. 1943: Turning The Tide Issue in the World War II Commemorative Series included a map and stamps showing events of the war in 1943. *Offset and intaglio, perforated 11.*

		MNHVF	UseVF
CM1568			
$2.90	**Commemorative pane of 10**	8.75	7.00
	a. Allied Escort ships, tagged	.75	.45
	b. Military Medics, tagged	.75	.45
	c. Sicily Attacked, tagged	.75	.45

Allied forces battle German U-boats, 1943

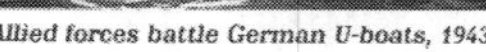

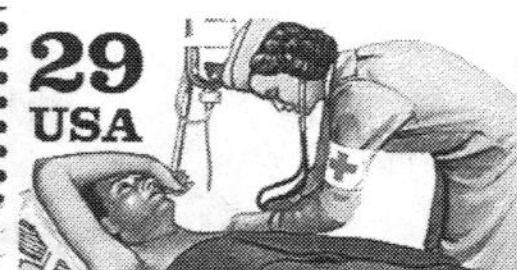
Military medics treat the wounded, 1943

Sicily attacked by Allied forces, July 1943

B-24s hit Ploesti refineries, August 1943

V-mail delivers letters from home, 1943

Italy invaded by Allies, September 1943

Bonds and stamps help war effort, 1943

"Willie and Joe" keep spirits high, 1943

Gold Stars mark World War II losses, 1943

Marines assault Tarawa, November 1943

CM1568 *1943: Turning the Tide*

d. B-24's Hit Ploesti, tagged	.75	.45
e. V-mail Delivers Letters, tagged	.75	.45
f. Italy Invaded (PT boat), tagged	.75	.45
g. War Bonds & Stamps, tagged	.75	.45
h. "Willie and Joe," tagged	.75	.45
i. Gold Stars, tagged	.75	.45
j. Marines Assault Tarawa, tagged	.75	.45
FDC *(May 31, 1993)* any single		2.00
FDC, complete pane of 10		10.00

1993. Hank Williams Issue in the American Music Series honored the country singer and composer credited with integrating country music and rock 'n roll. *Gravure, Stamp Venturers, perforated 11.*

CM1569 *Hank Williams*

CM1569		MNHVF	UseVF
29¢	**multicolored** tagged	.45	.20
	Plate block of 4	3.50	
	FDC *(June 9, 1993)*		1.75
	v. Perforated 11 1/4 x 11 1/2	20.00	15.00
	Plate block of 4	125.00	

1993. Rock 'n Roll - Rhythm & Blues Issue honored seven stars in a continuation of the American Music Series, including a second Elvis Presley stamp that spells out his last name. Additional personalities featured in this issue are Buddy Holly, Ritchie Valens, Bill Haley, Dinah Washington, Otis Redding, and Clyde McPhatter. The stamps were released in a pane of 35 stamps and a booklet of 20 stamps. The booklet consists of two panes of eight (with six of seven honorees appearing once and Elvis Presley appearing twice), and one pane of four (the bottom four stamps of the pane of eight).

Although the stamp designs are similar, the stamps in the booklet panes are printed in magenta, cyan, yellow, and black, while the commemorative sheet is printed in those four colors plus additional blue and red inks. The sheet stamps are 31.5mm high, and booklet stamps are 31.1mm high. *Gravure, Stamp Ventures, perforated 10 on 4 sides.*

Input from stamp collectors regarding the content of this catalog and ideas to make it more useful is eagerly sought. Send your comments to:

Minkus Catalog Editor
Krause Publications
700 E. State St.
Iola WI 54990

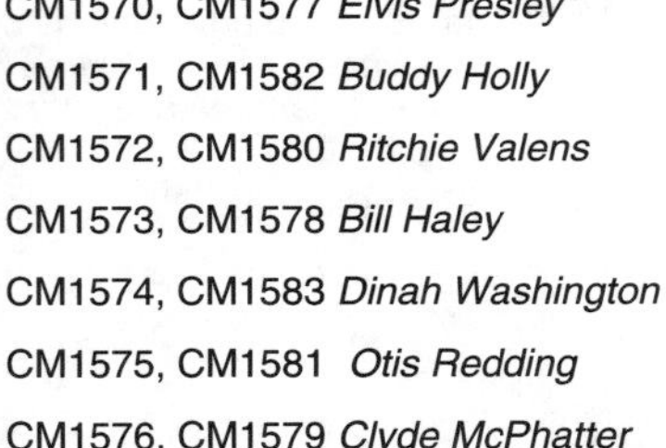
CM1570, CM1577 *Elvis Presley*

CM1571, CM1582 *Buddy Holly*

CM1572, CM1580 *Ritchie Valens*

CM1573, CM1578 *Bill Haley*

CM1574, CM1583 *Dinah Washington*

CM1575, CM1581 *Otis Redding*

CM1576, CM1579 *Clyde McPhatter*

CM1570		MNHVF	UseVF
29¢	**Elvis Presley,** tagged	.45	.20
CM1571		MNHVF	UseVF
29¢	**Buddy Holly,** tagged	.45	.20
CM1572		MNHVF	UseVF
29¢	**Richie Valens,** tagged	.45	.20
CM1573		MNHVF	UseVF
29¢	**Bill Haley,** tagged	.45	.20
CM1574		MNHVF	UseVF
29¢	**Dinah Washington,** tagged	.45	.20
CM1575		MNHVF	UseVF
29¢	**Otis Redding,** tagged	.45	.20
CM1576		MNHVF	UseVF
29¢	**Clyde McPhatter,** tagged	.45	.20
	Commemorative sheet of 35 (includes 4 plate nos.)		
	y. Se-tenant vertical strip of 7 (CM1570-76)	3.00	—
	y1. Pane of 35	15.00	—
	FDC *(June 16, 1993)* any single		2.50
	FDC, strip of 7		8.00

Gravure, Multi-Color Corp. Perforated 11 on one or two sides.

CM1577		MNHVF	UseVF
29¢	**multicolored** tagged	.45	.20
CM1578		MNHVF	UseVF
29¢	**multicolored** tagged	.45	.20
CM1579		MNHVF	UseVF
29¢	**multicolored** tagged	.45	.20
CM1580		MNHVF	UseVF
29¢	**multicolored** tagged	.45	.20
CM1581		MNHVF	UseVF
29¢	**multicolored** tagged	.45	.20
CM1582		MNHVF	UseVF
29¢	**multicolored** tagged	.45	.20
CM1583		MNHVF	UseVF
29¢	**multicolored** tagged	.45	.20
	FDC *(June 16, 1993)* any single		2.50
	n. Booklet pane of 8 (2 of CM1577, 1 each CM-1578-83)	4.50	2.25
	FDC, booklet pane of 8		8.00
	nl. Booklet pane of 4 (CM1577 & CM1581-83)	2.50	
	FDC, booklet pane of 4		4.50

The vertically oriented pane of eight consists of the following stamps, from top to bottom: CM1577, CM1578, CM1579, CM1580, CM1581, CM1582, CM1583, CM1577. The vertically oriented pane of four consists of the following stamps, from top to bottom: CM1581, CM1582, CM1583, CM1584. A complete booklet consists of two panes of eight and one pane of four. CM1583n1 without tab is indistinguishable from a strip of the bottom four stamps of CM1583n.

1993. Joe Louis Issue honored the heavyweight boxing champion known as the "Brown Bomber" (1914-1981) and was issued on the 55th anniversary of his knockout win over Max Schmeling. *Offset and intaglio, perforated 11.*

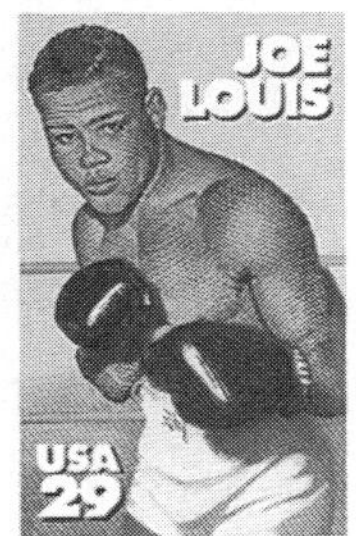

CM1584 *Joe Louis*

CM1584		MNHVF	UseVF
29¢	**multicolored** tagged	.45	.20
	Plate block of 4	4.75	
	FDC *(June 22, 1993)*		3.00

1993. Broadway Musicals Issue in the American Music Series honored four of the most celebrated musicals in American theater. *Gravure, Multi-Color Corp. for the American Bank Note Co., perforated 11 horizontallyon 1 or 2 sides.*

CM1585 Show Boat

CM1586 Porgy & Bess

CM1587 Oklahoma!

CM1588 My Fair Lady

		MNHVF	UseVF
CM1585			
29¢	***Show Boat,*** tagged	.45	.20
CM1586			
29¢	***Porgy & Bess,*** tagged	.45	.20
CM1587			
29¢	***Oklahoma!,*** tagged	.45	.20
CM1588			
29¢	***My Fair Lady,*** tagged	.45	.20
	FDC *(July 14, 1993)* any single		2.50
	n. Booklet pane of 4 (CM1585-88)	4.95	
	FDC, booklet pane of 4		5.00

1993. National Postal Museum Issue marked the opening of the Washington, D.C., facility, part of the Smithsonian Institution. *Offset and intaglio, American Bank Note Co., perforated 11.*

CM1589 *Benjamin Franklin, Liberty Hall, printing press*

CM1590 *Civil War soldier writing letter, stagecoach*

CM1591 *Mail plane, Charles Lindbergh, railway mail car and mail truck*

CM1592 *Miner's letter, stamps, barcode and date stamp*

		MNHVF	UseVF
CM1589			
29¢	**Benjamin Franklin,** tagged	.45	.20
CM1590			
29¢	**Civil War soldier writing letter**	.45	.20
CM1591			
29¢	**Charles Lindbergh,** tagged	.45	.20
CM1592			
29¢	**Letters & date stamp,** tagged	.45	.20
	Plate block of 4	4.25	
	y. Se-tenant block or strip of 4 (CM1589-92)	1.80	.80
	y1. Pane of 20	9.00	
	FDC *(July 30, 1993)* any single		2.50
	FDC, block of 4		4.00
	v. Block of 4, imperforate	3,500.00	

1993. Recognizing Deafness/American Sign Language Issue showed nonverbal communication used with the hearing impaired. Both stamps show the sign for "I love you." *Gravure, Stamp Venturers, perforated 11 1/2.*

CM1593-CM1594 *"I Love You"*

		MNHVF	UseVF
CM1593			
29¢	**Mother and child,** tagged	.45	.20
CM1594			
29¢	**Sign "I love you"**	.45	.20
	y. Se-tenant pair (CM1593-94)	.90	.40
	Plate block of 4	3.95	
	FDC *(Sept. 20, 1993),* either single		2.00
	FDC, pair		2.25
	y1. Pane of 20	9.00	

1993. Country Music Issue in the American Music Series included an earlier design that featured Hank Williams (CM1569). Added were The Carter Family, Patsy Cline and Bob Wills. The stamps were available as a 20-stamp pane with a large title across the top, or a booklet with each stamp appearing once on each of the five panes. Although the designs and sizes are identical, the sheet stamps used burgundy and blue in addition to yellow, magenta, cyan, and black, while the booklet stamps were produced using pink and line black in addition to the four process colors. *Gravure, Stamp Venturers, perforated 10 on 4 sides (sheet stamps) or on 1 or 2 sides (booklet stamps).*

CM1595, CM1599 *Hank Williams*

CM1596, CM1600 *The Carter Family*

CM1597, CM1601 *Patsy Cline*

CM1598, CM1602 *Bob Wills*

		MNHVF	UseVF
CM1595			
29¢	**Hank Williams,** tagged	.45	.20
CM1596			
29¢	**The Carter Family,** tagged	.45	.20
CM1597			
29¢	**Patsy Cline,** tagged	.45	.20
CM1598			
29¢	**Bob Wills,** tagged	.45	.20
	Plate block of 4	3.95	
	y. Se-tenant block or strip of 4 (CM1595-98)	2.50	
	y1. Pane of 20	9.00	
	FDC *(Sept. 25, 1993),* any single		2.00
	FDC, block or strip of 4		5.00

Gravure by American Bank Note Co., perforated 11 on 1 or 2 sides, from booklet panes.

		MNHVF	UseVF
CM1599			
29¢	**Hank Williams,** tagged	.45	.20
CM1600			
29¢	**The Carter Family,** tagged	.45	.20
CM1601			
29¢	**Patsy Cline,** tagged	.45	.20
CM1602			
29¢	**Bob Wills,** tagged	.45	.20
	FDC *(Sept. 25, 1993) any single*		1.75
	n. Booklet pane of 4, (CM1599-1602)	3.50	
	FDC, booklet pane		5.00
	nv. Booklet pane, imperforate	—	

1993. Youth Classics Issue was a se-tenant block showing four of the best-loved and popular stories for young readers. Louisa May Alcott's *Little Women* was published in two volumes in 1868-69. Kate Douglas Smith Wiggin's *Rebecca of Sunnybrook Farm,* the story of a fatherless little girl who goes to live with her maiden aunts, was a best-seller in 1903. Laura Ingalls Wilder drew upon her own childhood and travels on the frontier as inspiration for her books, including *Little House on the Prairie,* published in 1935. *The Adventures of Huckleberry Finn* also is a peek into the childhood of its author, Samuel Clemens (Mark Twain). *Offset and Intaglio on phosphored paper by American Bank Note Co., perforated.*

CM1603
Rebecca of Sunny brook Farm

CM1604
Little House on the Prairie

CM1605
The Adventures of Huckleberry Finn

CM1606
Little Women

		MNHVF	UseVF
CM1603			
29¢	***Rebecca,*** block tagged	.45	.20
CM1604			
29¢	***Little House***	.60	.20
CM1605			
29¢	***Huck Finn***	.60	.20
CM1606			
29¢	***Little Women,*** block tagged	.45	.20
	Plate block of 4	4.50	
	y. Se-tenant block or strip of 4 (CM1603-06)	3.50	
	FDC *(Oct. 23, 1993)* any single		2.00
	FDC, block of 4		4.00
	v. Block of 4, imperforate	3,000.00	

1993. Commonwealth of the Northern Mariana Islands Issue saluted a group of 16 islands in the western Pacific Ocean administered by the United States following World War II as part of the U.N. Trust Territories of the Pacific Islands. In 1978, following a referendum, the archipelago became a self-governing entity in union with the United States. Mail to and from the Mariana Islands is sent at domestic U.S. postage rates from a U.S. post office. *Offset and intaglio, perforated 11.*

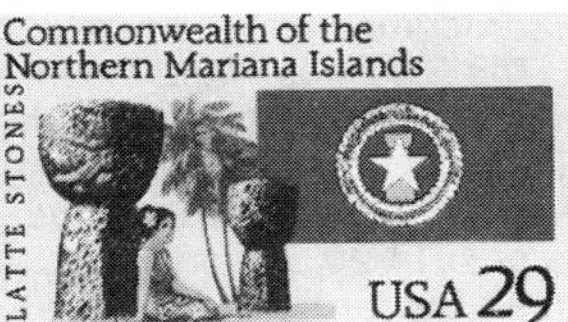

CM1607 *Flag and limestone pillars*

		MNHVF	UseVF
CM1607			
29¢	**multicolored** tagged	.45	.20
	Plate block of 4	3.50	
	FDC *(Nov. 4, 1993)*		1.75
	y. Pane of 20	9.00	

1993. Columbus Landing in Puerto Rico Issue marked the 500th anniversary of the arrival of Columbus. *Gravure, perforated 11.*

CM1608 *Caravels in Boqueron Bay*

		MNHVF	UseVF
CM1608			
29¢	**multicolored** tagged	.45	.20
	Plate block of 4	3.50	
	FDC *(Nov. 19, 1993)*		1.75

1993. AIDS Awareness Issue symbolized compassion and awareness for those afflicted by this disease. The stamps were sold nationwide on their first day of issue and were available in sheet form or in 10-stamp booklets. *Gravure, perforated 11.*

CM1609 *Symbolic ribbon*

		MNHVF	UseVF
CM1609			
29¢	**red & black** tagged, perforated 11 1/4	.45	.20
	Plate block of 4	2.50	
	FDC (Dec. 1, 1993)		1.75
CM1609A			
29¢	**red & black** tagged, perforated 11 vertically on 1 or 2 sides	.75	.25
	FDC *(Dec. 1 1993)*		1.75
	FDC, booklet pane		5.00
	n. Booklet pane of 5	2.50	

1994. Winter Olympics Issue honored the 1994 Winter Games. *Offset, Ashton-Potter, perforated 11.*

CM1610 *Downhill skiing;* CM1611 *Luge;* CM1612 *Figure skating;* CM1613 *Cross-country skiing;* CM1614 *Hockey*

		MNHVF	UseVF
CM1610			
29¢	**Downhill skiing,** tagged	.45	.20
CM1611			
29¢	**Luge,** tagged	.45	.20
CM1612			
29¢	**Figure skating,** tagged	.45	.20
CM1613			
29¢	**Cross-country skiing,** tagged	.45	.20
CM1614			
29¢	**Hockey,** tagged	.45	.20
	Plate block of 10	7.50	
	y. Se-tenant strip of 5 (CM-1610-14)	3.00	
	FDC *(Jan. 6, 1994)* any single		2.00
	FDC, strip of 5		5.00

1994. Edward R. Murrow Issue honored the broadcast journalist (1908-65) who joined CBS in 1935 and directed its European bureau through World War II. In 1945 he was made CBS vice president in charge of news, education and discussion programs. *Intaglio, perforated 11.*

CM1615 *Edward R. Murrow*

		MNHVF	UseVF
CM1615			
29¢	**brown** tagged	.45	.20
	Plate block of 4	3.50	
	FDC *(Jan. 21, 1994)*		1.75

1994. Love Issue in the popular Love Series was a self-adhesive stamp, one of four 1994 stamps with this theme. (See CM1619-20, CM1642). *Offset and intaglio, straight line die cut).*

CM1616 *Love — Heart*

CM1616		MNHVF	UseVF
29¢	**multicolored** tagged	.45	.20
	FDC *(Jan. 27, 1994)*		1.75
	n. Pane of 18	15.00	
	Plate No. strip of 3	3.50	—
	Plate No. strip of 5	4.00	—

1994. Dr. Allison Davis Issue in the Black Heritage Series honored the influential social anthropologist and educator (1902-83) who challenged the cultural bias of standardized intelligence tests and helped end racial segregation. *Intaglio by Stamp Venturers, perforated 11.*

CM1617 *Dr. William Allison Davis*

CM1617		MNHVF	UseVF
29¢	**red brown & brown** tagged	.45	.20
	Plate block of 4	4.00	
	FDC *(Feb. 1, 1994)*		2.75

1994. New Year Issue second in the Lunar New Year Series featured the royal dog of China, a Pekinese, and marked the Year of the Dog. *Gravure, perforated 11.*

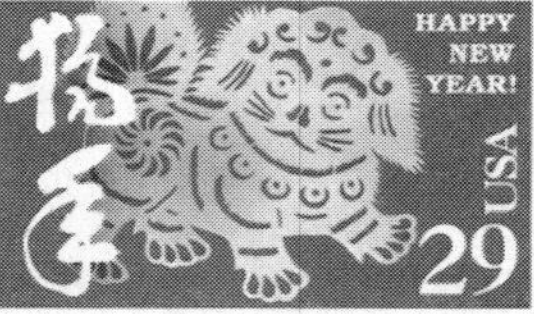

CM1618 *Lunar New Year*

CM1618		MNHVF	UseVF
29¢	**multicolored** tagged	.45	.20
	Plate block of 4	3.75	
	FDC *(Feb. 5, 1994)*		2.50

1994. Love Issues in the Love Series were two lick-and-stick stamps released on Valentine's Day, complementing the earlier self-adhesive issue, CM1616. (See also CM1642.) *Gravure and intaglio, perforated 10 3/4 by 11 on 2 or 3 sides.*

CM1619 *Love — Dove and roses*

CM1619		MNHVF	UseVF
29¢	**multicolored** tagged	.45	.20
	FDC *(Feb. 14, 1994)*		1.75
	n. Booklet pane of 10	6.00	
	FDC, booklet pane		7.00
	v. Pair, imperforate	—	
	v1. Horizontal pair, imperforate between	—	
	nv. Booklet pane of 10, imperforate	—	

CM1620 *Love — Doves and roses*

CM1620		MNHVF	UseVF
52¢	**multicolored** tagged	1.50	.35
	Plate block of 4	7.00	
	FDC *(Feb. 14, 1994)*		2.00

1994. Buffalo Soldiers Issue honored the U.S. Army's regiments, predominantly black cavalry and infantry, that played a major role in the settlement of the American West. Black troops of the Buffalo Soldier regiments were the first authorized to serve in the Army during peacetime. *Offset and intaglio, perforated 11 1/2 x 11.*

CM1621 *Buffalo Soldiers*

CM1621		MNHVF	UseVF
29¢	**multicolored** tagged	.45	.20
	Plate block of 4	1.25	
	FDC *(April 22, 1994)*		2.50

1994. Silent Screen Stars Issue featured 10 early film stars, drawn by Al Hirschfeld. Rudolph Valentino is one of the world's best-known film stars remembered for *The Four Horsemen of the Apocalypse, The Sheik,* and *Blood and Sand.* Film star Clara Bow first arrived in Hollywood as the result of a high school beauty contest. Charlie Chaplin's *"Little Tramp"* character became famous worldwide. Lon Chaney used his incredible make-up and characterization in *The Hunchback of Notre Dame, Phantom of the Opera* and *The Unholy Three.* John Gilbert began with a stage career that led to romantic roles in such films as *The Merry Widow, The Big Parade* and *Flesh and the Devil.* Zasu Pitts began as an extra, moving to both comedy and dramatic roles. Comedian Harold Lloyd made more than 500 movies, beginning in 1914. Mack Sennett's Keystone Cops kept audiences laughing through many short films of 1914-20. Theda Bara's work in *The Vampire* led to the term "vamp." Buster Keaton is known for slapstick comedy and his deadpan stare. *Offset and intaglio, perforated 11.*

CM1622 *Rudolph Valentino;* CM1623 *Clara Bow;* CM1624 *Charlie Chaplin;* CM1625 *Lon Chaney;* CM1626 *John Gilbert;* CM1627 *Zasu Pitts;* CM1628 *Harold Lloyd;* CM1629 *Keystone Cops;* CM1630 *Theda Bara;* CM1631 *Buster Keaton*

CM1622 MNHVF UseVF
29¢ **Rudolph Valentino,** tagged .45 .20

CM1623 MNHVF UseVF
29¢ **Clara Bow,** tagged .45 .20

CM1624 MNHVF UseVF
29¢ **Charlie Chaplin,** tagged .45 .20

CM1625 MNHVF UseVF
29¢ **Lon Chaney,** tagged .45 .20

CM1626 MNHVF UseVF
29¢ **John Gilbert,** tagged .45 .20

CM1627 MNHVF UseVF
29¢ **Zasu Pitts,** tagged .45 .20

CM1628 MNHVF UseVF
29¢ **Harold Lloyd,** tagged .45 .20

CM1629 MNHVF UseVF
29¢ **Keystone Cops,** tagged .45 .20

CM1630 MNHVF UseVF
29¢ **Theda Bara,** tagged .45 .20

CM1631 MNHVF UseVF
29¢ **Buster Keaton,** tagged .45 .20
Plate block of 10 9.00
y. Se-tenant block of 10 (CM1622-31) 8.00
vy. Block of 10, offset black omitted —
vy1. Block of 10, offset black & intaglio red & purple omitted —
FDC *(April 27, 1994)*, any single 2.00
FDC, block of 10 8.00

1994. Garden Flowers Issue the second in a Garden Flowers Series of five-stamp booklets showing bright and popular flowers that bloom in summer. *Offset and intaglio, perforated 11.*

CM1632 *Lily;* CM1633 *Zinnia;* CM1634 *Gladiola;* CM1635 *Marigold;* CM1636 *Rose*

CM1632 MNHVF UseVF
29¢ **multicolored** tagged .45 .20

CM1633 MNHVF UseVF
29¢ **multicolored** tagged .45 .20

CM1634 MNHVF UseVF
29¢ **multicolored** tagged .45 .20

CM1635 MNHVF UseVF
29¢ **multicolored** tagged .45 .20

CM1636 MNHVF UseVF
29¢ **multicolored** tagged .45 .20
FDC *(April 28, 1994)*, any single 2.00
n. Booklet pane of 5 (CM1632-36) 4.50
FDC, booklet pane of 5 5.00
nv. Pane of 5, intaglio black omitted 375.00
nv1. Pane of 5, imperforate 2,250.00

1994. World Cup Soccer Championship Issue of three stamps and a souvenir sheet noted the first time the United States hosted the final rounds of soccer's quadrennial World Cup. Stamps issued in panes of 20 were printed on phosphor-coated paper; those within the souvenir sheet are block tagged. The 50¢ stamp in the souvenir sheet (CM1640c) has part of the yellow map from the sheet in the lower-right corner of its design. *Gravure, perforated 11.*

CM1637 MNHVF UseVF
29¢ **multicolored** phosphored paper .75 .20
Plate block of 4 4.00
FDC *(May 26, 1994)* 1.75

CM1638 MNHVF UseVF
40¢ **multicolored** phosphored paper 1.00 .35
Plate block of 4 5.50
FDC *(May 26, 1994)* 2.00

CM1639 MNHVF UseVF
50¢ **multicolored** phosphored paper 1.50 .50
Plate block of 4 6.50
FDC *(May 26, 1994)* 2.00

CM1640 MNHVF UseVF
$1.19 **Souvenir Sheet** 3.75 3.00
a. **29¢** like CM1637, block tagged .75
b. **40¢** like CM1638, block tagged 1.00
c. **50¢** like CM1639, block tagged 1.25

1994. 1944: Road to Victory Issue in the World War II Commemorative Series included a map and stamps showing events of the war in 1944. *Offset and intaglio, perforated 11.*

CM1641 MNHVF UseVF
$2.90 **Commemorative pane of 10,** tagged 8.75 7.00
a. **29¢** Forces Retake New Guinea .75 .70
b. **29¢** P-51s escort B-17s .75 .70
c. **29¢** Allies Free Normandy .75 .70
d. **29¢** Airborne Units .75 .70
e. **29¢** Submarines .75 .70
f. **29¢** Allies Free Rome, Paris .75 .70
g. **29¢** U.S. Troops Clear Saipan .75 .70
h. **29¢** Red Ball Express .75 .70
i. **29¢** Battle of Leyte Gulf .75 .70
j. **29¢** Bastogne and The Bulge .75 .70

CM1640 *World Cup Souvenir Sheet*

CM1641 *1944: Road to Victory*

FDC *(June 6, 1994)* any single	2.00
FDC complete pane of 10	10.00

1994. Love Issue in the Love Series was a slightly longer sheet version of the 29¢ booklet stamp (CM1619) released on Valentine's Day. *Offset and intaglio, perforated 11.*

CM1642 *Love*

CM1642

		MNHVF	UseVF
29¢	**multicolored** tagged	.50	.20
	Plate block of 4	3.50	
	FDC *(June 11, 1994)*		1.75

1994. Norman Rockwell Issue honored the artist best known as a chronicler of 20th century America for more than 4,000 works, including 321 original *Saturday Evening Post* covers between 1916 and 1963. The commemoration consisted of a single stamp and a commemorative sheet of four stamps depicting Franklin D. Roosevelt's Four Freedoms. *Offset and intaglio, perforated 11.*

CM1643 *Norman Rockwell*

CM1643

		MNHVF	UseVF
29¢	**multicolored** tagged	.50	.20
	Plate block of 4	3.50	
	FDC *(July 1, 1994)*		1.75

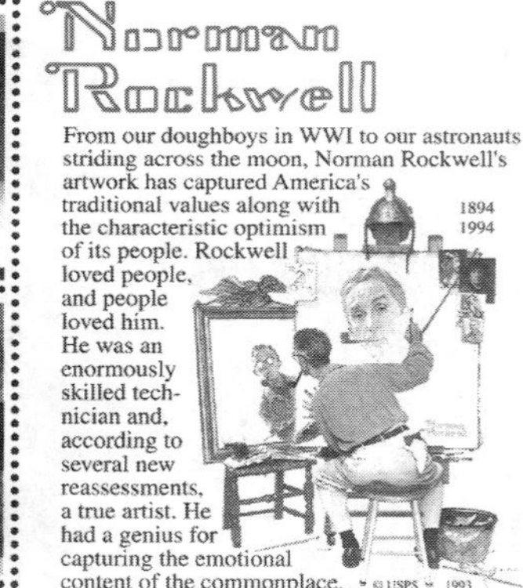

CM1644a *Freedom from Want;* CM1644b *Freedom from Fear;* CM1644c *Freedom of Speech;* CM1644d *Freedom of Worship*

CM1644

		MNHVF	UseVF
$2	**multicolored** tagged	6.00	5.00
	a. 50¢ Freedom from Want	1.00	1.00
	b. 50¢ Freedom from Fear	1.00	1.00
	c. 50¢ Freedom of Speech	1.00	1.00
	d. 50¢ Freedom of Worship	1.00	1.00
	FDC *(July 1, 1994)*, any single		2.00
	FDC, souvenir sheet		5.75

1994. Moon Landing Anniversary Issue released in special 12-stamp sheetlets, celebrated the 25th anniversary of man's first landing on the Moon. (See also No. 1045). *Gravure, by Stamp Venturers, perforated 11.*

CM1645 *Moon Landing, 25th anniversary*

CM1645		MNHVF	UseVF
29¢	**multicolored** tagged	.50	.25
	FDC *(July 20, 1994)*		1.75
	n. Sheetlet of 12	9.00	7.50
	FDC, sheetlet		10.75

1994. Locomotives Issue a five-stamp booklet, depicted historically significant locomotives. (See also CM1293-97.) *Gravure, by J.W. Ferguson & Sons for Stamp Venturers, perforated 11 horizontally.*

CM1646 *Hudson's General*

CM1647 *McQueen's Jupiter*

CM1648 *Eddy's No. 242*

CM1649 *Ely's No. 10*

CM1650 *Buchannan's No. 999*

CM1646		MNHVF	UseVF
29¢	**Hudson's General,** tagged	.75	.50
CM1647		MNHVF	UseVF
29¢	**McQueen's Jupiter,** tagged	.75	.50
CM1648		MNHVF	UseVF
29¢	**Eddy's No. 242,** tagged	.75	.50
CM1649		MNHVF	UseVF
29¢	**Ely's No. 10,** tagged	.75	.50
CM1650		MNHVF	UseVF
29¢	**Buchannan's No. 999,** tagged	.75	.50
	FDC *(July 29, 1994),* any single		2.00
	n. Booklet pane of 5 (CM1646-50)	4.50	
	FDC, booklet pane of 5		5.00
	nv. Pane of 5, imperforate		—

1994. George Meany Issue honored one of the most influential labor leaders in American history (1894-1980), president of the American Federation of Labor (AFL) from 1952-55 and first president of the AFL and Congress of Industrial Organizations (CIO) from 1955 until his retirement in 1979. *Intaglio, perforated 11.*

CM1651 *George Meany*

CM1651		MNHVF	UseVF
29¢	**blue** tagged	.50	.20
	Plate block of 4	3.50	
	FDC *(Aug. 16, 1994)*		1.75

1994. Popular Singers Issue in the American Music Series honored five showstoppers of this century. *Gravure by J.W. Fergusson & Sons for Stamp Venturers, perforated 11.*

CM1652 *Al Jolson*

CM1653 *Bing Crosby*

CM1654 *Ethel Waters*

CM1655 *Nat "King" Cole*

CM1656 *Ethel Merman*

CM1652		MNHVF	UseVF
29¢	**Al Jolson,** tagged	.75	.50
CM1653		MNHVF	UseVF
29¢	**Bing Crosby,** tagged	.75	.50
CM1654		MNHVF	UseVF
29¢	**Ethel Waters,** tagged	.75	.50
CM1655		MNHVF	UseVF
29¢	**Nat "King" Cole,** tagged	.47	.50
CM1656		MNHVF	UseVF
29¢	**Ethel Merman,** tagged	.75	.50

		MNHVF	UseVF
	Plate block of 6 (vertical)	6.00	
	Plate block of 12 (horizontal)	11.00	
	FDC *(Sept. 1, 1994)* any single		2.00
	a. Pane of 20	17.50	
	FDC, strip of 5		6.00

1994. James Thurber Issue 12th in the Literary Arts Series hailed the author, humorist, playwright and cartoonist (1894-1961) whose 31 books gave humorous views of life in America. *Offset and intaglio, perforated 11.*

CM1657 *James Thurber*

CM1657		MNHVF	UseVF
29¢	**multicolored** tagged	.50	.20
	Plate block of 4	3.50	
	FDC *(Sept. 10. 1994)*		1.75

1994. Blues and Jazz Singers Issue in the American Music Series honored seminal artists in these distinctive American musical genres. *Offset by Manhardt-Alexander for Ashton-Potter (USA) Ltd., perforated 11 x 10 3/4.*

CM1658 *Bessie Smith*

CM1659 *Muddy Waters*

CM1660 *Billie Holiday*

CM1661 *Robert Johnson*

CM1662 *Jimmy Rushing*

CM1663 *"Ma" Rainy*

CM1664 *Mildred Bailey*

CM1665 *Howlin' Wolf*

		MNHVF	UseVF
CM1658			
29¢	**Bessie Smith,** tagged	.50	.25
CM1659		MNHVF	UseVF
29¢	**Muddy Waters,** tagged	.50	.25
CM1660		MNHVF	UseVF
29¢	**Billie Holiday,** tagged	.50	.25
CM1661		MNHVF	UseVF
29¢	**Robert Johnson,** tagged	.50	.25
CM1662		MNHVF	UseVF
29¢	**Jimmy Rushing,** tagged	.50	.25
CM1663		MNHVF	UseVF
29¢	**"Ma" Rainy,** tagged	.50	.25
CM1664		MNHVF	UseVF
29¢	**Mildred Bailey,** tagged	.50	.25
CM1665		MNHVF	UseVF
29¢	**Howlin' Wolf,** tagged	.50	.25
	Plate block of 10	9.00	
	y. Se-tenant block of 9, plus 1 extra stamp, (CM-1658-65)	8.50	
	FDC *(Sept. 17, 1994)* any single		2.00
	a. Pane of 35	27.50	
	FDC, strip of 8		10.00

1994. Wonders of the Seas Issue used four se-tenant stamps to form a single underwater fantasy scene. *Offset by Barton Press for the Banknote Corp., of America, perforated 11.*

CM1666 *Porcupine fish*

CM1667 *Dolphin*

CM1668 *Nautilus and ship's sheel*

CM1669 *Fish and coral*

		MNHVF	UseVF
CM1666			
29¢	**Porcupine fish,** tagged	.75	.25
CM1667		MNHVF	UseVF
29¢	**Dolphin,** tagged	.75	.25
CM1668		MNHVF	UseVF
29¢	**Nautilus & ship's wheel,** tagged	.75	.25
CM1669		MNHVF	UseVF
29¢	**Fish & coral,** tagged	.75	.25
	Plate block of 4	4.00	
	y. Se-tenant block of 4 (CM1666-69)	3.00	
	FDC *(Oct. 3, 1994),* any single		2.00
	vy. Block of 4, imperforate	2,500.00	
	FDC, block of 4		4.00

1994. Cranes Issue depicted two of the world's rarest birds, the North American Whooping Crane and the Chinese Black-necked Crane. A joint issue of the United States and the People's Republic of China, (CNP3784-3785), the issues of the two countries show the same designs, with the Chinese issue as two separate stamps and the U.S. issue as a se-tenant pair. *Offset and intaglio by Barton Press for the Banknote Corp. of America, perforated 11.*

CM1670 *Black-necked Crane*

CM1671 *Whooping Crane*

		MNHVF	UseVF
CM1670			
29¢	**Black-necked crane,** tagged	.45	.20
CM1671		MNHVF	UseVF
29¢	**Whooping crane,** tagged	.45	.20
	Plate block of 4	1.25	
	y. Se-tenant pair (CM1670-71)		
	FDC *(Oct. 9, 1994)* either single		2.00
	v. Se-tenant pair, black and red omitted	4,000.00	
	FDC, pair		2.25

Classic Collections Series

1993-1994. Legends of the West Issue late in 1993, the Postal Service printed more than 5 million Legends of the West panes and forwarded them to postal distribution centers and post offices throughout the country, even though the stamps were not scheduled to be issued until 1994. These stamps were to be the first in a new series formatted by USPS as *"Classic Collections"*— special panes of 20 different first-class letter rate stamps with explanatory text on the back of each and a banner across the top of the pane describing its collective subject — in this case, legendary personalities and themes from the early days of the Western frontier.

At least 183 of these panes inadvertently were sold at four post offices long before the planned first day of issue, beginning with a full pane that was purchased and used to frank a parcel mailed in Bend, Ore., Dec. 14, 1993. The other three post offices at which the stamps were sold early were McLean, Va., High Point, N.C., and Princeton, N.J.

About the same time, the USPS learned that one stamp in the original pane, purported to have depicted black cowboy and rodeo showman Bill Pickett, was actually a portrait of his brother, Ben. Bill Pickett's descendants demanded that the Postal Service withdraw and destroy panes with the incorrect portrait and print new ones with an accurate portrait of Bill Pickett, and the USPS agreed to do so.

However, the early release and use of the panes from the original printing containing the stamp with the incorrect portrait made that impossible.

After a great deal of public and private debate as to the best solution (including two lawsuits), the Postal Service decided to print a second Legends of the West pane as promised with a revised, accurate portrait of Bill Pickett, but also to offer 150,000 original Legends of the West panes with the Ben Pickett portrait to collectors in a special lottery. The remainder of the original Legends of the West — about 5 million panes — would then be destroyed.

The USPS stuck to this plan despite considerable criticism from stamp collectors, even when it was revealed that, in the revised pane, 16 of the 20 stamps in the pane were different from those in the original pane. (The red framelines around the stamps portraying people in the original pane are about half the thickness of those in the revised pane.) *Gravure by J.W. Fergusson & Sons for Stamp Ventures, perforated 11.*

CM1671A *Legends of the West commemorative pane (original version)*
CM1671Ag *Bill (Ben) Pickett (incorrect portrait in original pane)*

		MNHVF	UseVF
CM1671A			
$5.80	**Legends of the West commemorative pane,** tagged, *(earliest known use Dec. 14, 1993)*	195.00	

1994. Revised Legends of the West Issue with a stamp showing an accurate portrait of Bill Pickett and thicker red framelines around his portrait and the portraits on the other 15 stamps in the pane that depict individuals. Because the overwhelming majority of the 150,000 original Legends of the West commemorative panes that were sold to collectors by lottery were retained as panes by collectors, it has been listed as a single number (CM1671), with the individual stamps as minor varieties of that number. Because the revised panes were sold at face value, and stamps from them were used relatively more extensively on mail, stamps from the revised pane are listed and numbered individually. *Gravure by J.W. Fergusson & Sons for Stamp Ventures, perforated 11.*

CM1691y *Legends of the West commemorative pane (revised version)*
CM1678 *Bill Pickett (correct portrait in revised pane)*

		MNHVF	UseVF
CM1672			
29¢	**Home on the Range,** tagged	.45	.20
CM1673			
29¢	**Buffalo Bill,** tagged	.45	.20
CM1674			
29¢	**Jim Bridger,** tagged	.45	.20
CM1675			
29¢	**Annie Oakley,** tagged	.45	.20
CM1676			
29¢	**Native American Culture,** tagged	.45	.20
CM1677			
29¢	**Chief Joseph,** tagged	.45	.20
CM1678			
29¢	**Bill Pickett,** tagged	.45	.20
CM1679			
29¢	**Bat Masterson,** tagged	.45	.20
CM1680			
29¢	**John Fremont,** tagged	.45	.20
CM1681			
29¢	**Wyatt Earp,** tagged	.45	.20
CM1682			
29¢	**Nellie Cashman,** tagged	.45	.20
CM1683			
29¢	**Charles Goodnight,** tagged	.45	.20
CM1684			
29¢	**Geronimo,** tagged	.45	.20

		MNHVF	UseVF
CM1685		MNHVF	UseVF
29¢	**Kit Carson,** tagged	.45	.20
CM1686		MNHVF	UseVF
29¢	**Wild Bill Hickok,** tagged	.45	.20
CM1687		MNHVF	UseVF
29¢	**Western Wildlife,** tagged	.45	.20
CM1688		MNHVF	UseVF
29¢	**Jim Beckwourth,** tagged	.45	.20
CM1689		MNHVF	UseVF
29¢	**Bill Tilghman,** tagged	.45	.20
CM1690		MNHVF	UseVF
29¢	**Sacagawea,** tagged	.45	.20
CM1691		MNHVF	UseVF
29¢	**Overland Mail,** tagged	.45	.20
	FDC *(Oct. 18, 1994),* any single		2.00
	y. Se-tenant pane of 20	16.00	14.00
	Six pane press sheet	125.00	
	FDC, pane of 20		25.00

Because this issue also was made available to collectors in full six-pane printing sheets, gutter pairs and blocks and cross-gutter multiples also exist.

1994. Bureau of Engraving and Printing Centennial Souvenir Issue marked the 100th anniversary of the national security printer with a souvenir sheet containing four $2 James Madison definitives of a design first used almost a century before (No. 185, 1894), when the B.E.P. began printing U.S. stamps. *Offset and intaglio, perforated 11.*

CM1692 *B.E.P. centennial souvenir sheet*

CM1692		MNHVF	UseVF
$8	**multicolored** tagged *(Nov. 3, 1994)*	20.00	14.50
	a. single stamp	5.00	3.50
	Major double transfer on right $2 stamp in sheet of 4	—	
	Major double transfer, single $2 stamp	—	
	Minor double transfer on $2 stamp in sheet of 4	—	
	Minor double transfer, single $2 stamp	—	
	FDC *(Nov. 3, 1994),* any single		7.00
	FDC souvenir sheet of 4		24.00

Listings for minor double transfers refer to any of approximately 10 different ones that are known.

1994. New Year Issue in Lunar New Year Series for the Year of the Boar was the third installment. This stamp was released only two days before the first-class letter rate increased from 29¢ to 32¢. *Gravure by Stamp Venturers, perforated 11.*

CM1693 *Lunar New Year, Boar*

CM1693		MNHVF	UseVF
29¢	**multicolored** tagged	.50	.20
	Plate block of 4	3.50	
	FDC *(Dec. 30, 1994)*		2.50

1995. Love Cherub Issue in the Love Series featured non-denominated conventional and self-adhesive stamps depicting a cherub from the 16th-century *Sistine Madonna* by Raphael. *Offset and intaglio (B.E.P.), perforated 11 1/2.*

CM1694 *Love Cherub, tall design*

CM1694		MNHVF	UseVF
32¢	**multicolored** phosphored paper	.50	.20
	Plate block of 4	1.25	
	FDC *(Feb. 1, 1995)*		1.90

Self-adhesive booklet, offset and intaglio by Banknote Corp. of America, imperforate (die cut).

CM1695 *Love Cherub, short design*

CM1695		MNHVF	UseVF
32¢	**multicolored** phosphored paper	.50	.20
	FDC *(Feb. 1, 1995)*		1.90
	n. Pane of 20, plus label	16.00	
	vn. Pane of 20, intaglio red (inscriptions) omitted	1,000.00	

1995. Florida Sesquicentennial Issue marked the 150th anniversary of Florida statehood. It was the 27th state in the Union. *Offset by Sterling Sommer for Ashton-Potter (USA) Ltd., perforated 11.*

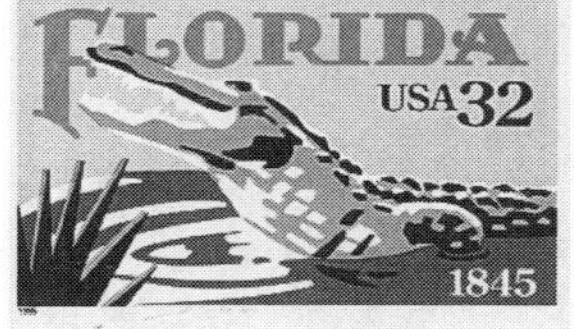

CM1696 *Florida statehood sesquicentennial*

CM1696		MNHVF	UseVF
32¢	**multicolored** phosphored paper	.50	.20
	Plate block of 4	3.50	
	FDC *(March 3, 1995)*		1.90

1995. Earth Day Issue showcased the four winning designs created by children in a nationwide contest to produce stamps for the 25th anniversary of Earth Day. The winning quartet was issued in a pane of 16 (four se-tenant blocks of four) with a "Kids Care!" banner across selvage at the top of the pane and the details of the contest in the selvage at the foot of the pane. *Offset by Sterling Sommer for Ashton-Potter (USA) Ltd., perforated 11.*

CM1697 *Clean Earth*

CM1698 *Solar Power*

CM1699 *Tree Planting*

CM1700 *Clean Beaches*

		MNHVF	UseVF
CM1697		MNHVF	UseVF
32¢	**Clean Earth,** phosphored paper	.50	.20
CM1698		MNHVF	UseVF
32¢	**Solar Power,** phosphored paper	.50	.20

CM1699		MNHVF	UseVF
32¢	**Tree Planting,** phosphored paper	.50	.20

CM1700		MNHVF	UseVF
32¢	**Clean Beaches,** phosphored paper	.50	.20
	Plate block of 4	3.50	
	y. Se-tenant block of 4	2.00	
	FDC *(April 20, 1995),* any single		2.00
	a. Pane of 16	13.50	
	FDC, block of 4		4.35

1995. Richard M. Nixon Issue marked the death on April 22, 1994, of the 37th president of the United States, Richard Milhous Nixon (1913-1994). He ended the divisive Vietnam war and improved relations with the USSR and China, but he resigned from office over a burglary of Democratic offices in Washington, D.C. *Offset and intaglio by Barton Press and Banknote Corp. of America, perforated 11.*

CM1701 *Richard M. Nixon*

CM1701		MNHVF	UseVF
32¢	**multicolored** phosphored paper	.50	.20
	Plate block of 4	3.50	
	FDC *(April 26, 1995)*		1.90
	v. Intaglio red ("Richard Nixon") omitted	1,500.00	

1995. Bessie Coleman Issue commemorated the first African-American woman aviator, who traveled to France to learn the language in order to earn her pilot's license there in 1921 after American flying schools had refused to admit her. She died in a fall from a plane (1896-1926). *Intaglio by B.E.P., perforated 11.*

CM1702 *Bessie Coleman*

CM1702		MNHVF	UseVF
32¢	**red & black** phosphored paper	.50	.20
	Plate block of 4	3.50	
	FDC *(April 27, 1995)*		3.00

1995. Love Cherub Issue in the Love Series added stamps with a 32¢ face value in matching designs to follow the non-denominated versions issued in February (CM1695-96), along with 55¢ stamps showing the cherub on the right in the same Raphael painting, paying the rate for letters under 2 ounces (such as most wedding invitations with response cards and envelopes enclosed). *Offset and intaglio, by B.E.P. Perforated 11 1/4.*

CM1703 *Love Cherub*

CM1703		MNHVF	UseVF
32¢	**multicolored** phosphored paper	.50	.20
	Plate block of 4	2.50	
	FDC *(May 12, 1995)*		1.90

1995. Love Cherub Booklet Issue in the Love Series *perforated 9 3/4 x 11 on 2 or 3 sides.*

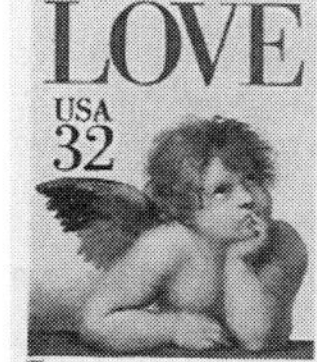

CM1704 *Love Cherub*

CM1704		MNHVF	UseVF
32¢	**multicolored** phosphored paper	.50	.20
	FDC *(May 12, 1995)*		1.90
	n. Booklet pane of 10	5.50	
	FDC, booklet pane		8.50

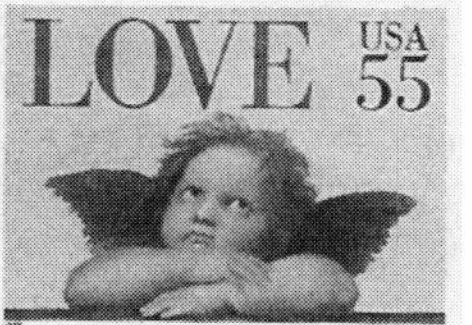

CM1705 *Love Cherub*

CM1705		MNHVF	UseVF
55¢	**multicolored** phosphored paper	1.00	.35
	Plate block of 4	5.00	
	FDC *(May 12, 1995)*		2.25

1995. Love Cherub Self-Adhesive Booklet Issue in the Love Series *printed in offset and intaglio by Banknote Corp. of America, imperforate (die cut).*

CM1706 *Love Cherub*

CM1706		MNHVF	UseVF
55¢	**multicolored** phosphored paper	1.00	.35
	FDC *(May 12, 1995)*		2.25
	n. Pane of 20, plus label	22.50	

1995. Recreational Sports Issue depicted popular American pastimes in five se-tenant designs. *Offset by Barton Press for Banknote Corp. of America, perforated 11 x 11 1/4.*

CM1707 *Bowling*

CM1708 *Tennis*

CM1709 *Golf*

CM1710 *Volleyball*

CM1711 *Baseball*

CM1707		MNHVF	UseVF
32¢	**Bowling,** phosphored paper	.50	.20

CM1708		MNHVF	UseVF
32¢	**Tennis,** phosphored paper	.50	.20

CM1709		MNHVF	UseVF
32¢	**Golf,** phosphored paper	.50	.20

CM1710		MNHVF	UseVF
32¢	**Volleyball,** phosphored paper	.50	.20

CM1711		MNHVF	UseVF
32¢	**Baseball,** phosphored paper	.50	.20
	Plate block of 10	8.50	
	y. Se-tenant vertical strip of 5 (CM1708-12)	3.00	
	FDC *(May 20, 1995),* any single		2.00
	a. Sheetlet of 20	16.00	
	vy. Strip of 5, imperforate	2,750.00	
	vyl. Vertical strip of 5, yellow omitted	2,500.00	
	vy2. Vertical strip of 5, yellow, cyan & magenta omitted	2,500.00	
	FDC, strip of 5		5.50

1995. POW & MIA ISSUE saluted personnel in the U.S. armed forces who were prisoners of war or who were unaccounted for after the end of hostilities. *Offset by Sterling Sommer for Ashton-Potter (USA) Ltd., perforated 11.*

CM1712 *POW & MIA*

CM1712		MNHVF	UseVF
32¢	**multicolored** phosphored paper	.50	.20
	Plate block of 4	3.50	
	FDC *(May 29, 1995)*		1.90
	y. Sheetlet of 20	14.50	

Legends of Hollywood Series

1995. MARILYN MONROE ISSUE first installment in the USPS Legends of Hollywood Series, with a pane of 20 (each stamp having its corner perforations in the shape of a star), bearing the likeness and facsimile autograph of Marilyn Monroe (1926-1962), with the large all-around selvage in the commemorative pane of 20 showing an enlargement of a portrait of the movie star near the height of her powers. *Gravure by J.W. Fergusson & Sons for Stamp Venturers, perforated 11.*

CM1713 *Marilyn Monroe*

CM1713		MNHVF	UseVF
32¢	**multicolored** block tagged	.75	.20
	Plate block of 4	3.50	
	FDC *(June 1, 1995)*		4.00
	a. Pane of 20	14.50	
	v. Pair, imperforate	625.00	
	Six-pane press sheets	125.00	

Because this issue also was made available to collectors in full six-pane printing sheets, gutter pairs and blocks and cross-gutter multiples also exist.

1995. TEXAS SESQUICENTENNIAL ISSUE marked the 150th anniversary of Texas statehood. Texas was the 28th state in the Union. *Offset by Sterling Sommer for Ashton-Potter (USA) Ltd., perforated 11.*

CM1714 *Texas statehood sesquicentennial*

CM1714		MNHVF	UseVF
32¢	**multicolored** phosphored paper	.50	.20
	Plate block of 4	3.50	
	FDC *(June 16, 1995)*		1.90

1995. LIGHTHOUSES ISSUE used the same format and design as the 1990 Lighthouses issue (CM1378-82) to create a booklet showcasing lighthouses of the Great Lakes. *Gravure by J.W. Ferguson & Sons for Stamp Venturers, perforated 11 vertically on one or two sides.*

CM1715 *Split Rock;* CM1716 *St. Joseph;* CM1717 *Spectacle Reef;* CM1718 *Marblehead;* CM1719 *Thirty Mile Point*

CM1715		MNHVF	UseVF
32¢	**Split Rock,** phosphored paper	.50	.20

CM1716		MNHVF	UseVF
32¢	**St. Joseph,** phosphored paper	.50	.20

CM1717		MNHVF	UseVF
32¢	**Spectacle Reef,** phosphored paper	.50	.20

CM1718		MNHVF	UseVF
32¢	**Marblehead,** phosphored paper	.50	.20

CM1719		MNHVF	UseVF
32¢	**Thirty Mile Point,** phosphored paper	.50	.20
	FDC *(June 17, 1995),* any single		2.00
	n. Booklet pane of 5 (CM1715-19)	4.00	3.50
	FDC, booklet pane		5.50

1995. UNITED NATIONS ISSUE marked the 50th anniversary of that organization. *Intaglio by Banknote Co. of America, perforated 11 1/4 x 11.*

CM1720 *United Nations*

CM1720		MNHVF	UseVF
32¢	**blue** phosphored paper	.50	.20
	Plate block of 4	3.00	
	FDC *(June 26, 1995)*		1.90

1995. CIVIL WAR ISSUE was the second release in the USPS Classic Collections Series to showcase 20 stamps on a single theme in a pane with a colorful banner across the top selvage identifying the subject — in this case, the Civil War. As on the 1994 Legends of the West pane that introduced the concept, the four corner stamps detail events (battles, in this instance) while the other 16 stamps are painstakingly researched portraits of individuals who played a significant role in the era, and text printed on the back of the stamps provides information on the subject of each. *Gravure by J.W. Fergusson & Sons for Stamp Venturers, perforated 10 1/4 x 10. Multicolored, block tagged (June 29, 1995).*

CM1721 *Monitor* and *Virginia;* CM1722 *Robert E. Lee;* CM1723 *Clara Barton;* CM1724 *Ulysses S. Grant;* CM1725 *Battle of Shiloh;* CM1726 *Jefferson Davis;* CM1727 *David Farragut;* CM1728 *Frederick Douglass;* CM1729 *Raphael Semmes;* CM1730 *Abraham Lincoln;* CM1731 *Harriet Tubman;* CM1732 *Stand Watie;* CM1733 *Joseph E. Johnston; CM1734 Winfield Hancock;* CM1735 *Mary Chesnut;* CM1736 *Battle of Chancellorsville;* CM1737 *William T. Sherman;* CM1738 *Phoebe Pember;* CM1739 *Stonewall Jackson;* CM1740 *Battle of Gettysburg*

		MNHVF	UseVF
CM1721			
32¢	***Monitor and Virginia***	.75	.50
CM1722			
32¢	**Robert E. Lee**	.75	.50
CM1723			
32¢	**Clara Barton**	.75	.50
CM1724			
32¢	**Ulysses S. Grant**	.75	.50
CM1725			
32¢	**Battle of Shiloh**	.75	.50
CM1726			
32¢	**Jefferson Davis**	.75	.50
CM1727			
32¢	**David Farragut**	.75	.50
CM1728			
32¢	**Frederick Douglass**	.75	.50
CM1729			
32¢	**Raphael Semmes**	.75	.50
CM1730			
32¢	**Abraham Lincoln**	.75	.50
CM1731			
32¢	**Harriet Tubman**	.75	.50
CM1732			
32¢	**Stand Watie**	.75	.50
CM1733			
32¢	**Joseph E. Johnston**	.75	.50
CM1734			
32¢	**Winfield Hancock**	.75	.50
CM1735			
32¢	**Mary Chesnut**	.75	.50
CM1736			
32¢	**Battle of Chancellorsville**	.75	.50
CM1737			
32¢	**William T. Sherman**	.75	.50
CM1738			
32¢	**Phoebe Pember**	.75	.50
CM1739			
32¢	**"Stonewall" Jackson**	.75	.50
CM1740			
32¢	**Battle of Gettysburg**	.75	.50
	y. Pane of 20 (CM1721-40)	16.00	14.00
	FDC, any single		2.00
	FDC, pane of 20		20.00
	vy. Pane of 20, imperforate	2,000.00	
	v1y. Pane with CM1721-25 imperforated, (CM1726-30) part perforated	—	
	v2y. Pane with CM1731-35 imperforated, (CM1736-40) part perforated	—	
	v3. Block of 9 (CM1726-28, CM1731-33, CM1736-38), imperforate vertically	—	
	Six pane press sheet	150.00	

Because this issue also was made available to collectors in full six-pane printing sheets, gutter pairs and blocks and cross-gutter multiples also exist.

1995. Carousel Horses Issue used the same design and much the same format as the the popular 1988 Carousel Animals issue (CM1327-30) in portraying four stalwart steeds from the classic American carnival ride. *Offset by Sterling Sommer for Ashton-Potter (USA) Ltd., perforated 11.*

CM1741 *Golden horse*

CM1742 *Black horse*

CM1743 *Armored horse*

CM1744 *Brown horse*

		MNHVF	UseVF
CM1741			
32¢	**Golden horse,** phosphored paper	.50	.20
CM1742			
32¢	**Black horse,** phosphored paper	.50	.20
CM1743			
32¢	**Armored horse,** phosphored paper	.50	.20
CM1744			
32¢	**Brown horse,** phosphored paper	.50	.20
	Plate block of 4	3.75	
	y. Se-tenant block of 4	2.00	
	FDC *(July 21, 1995)* any single		2.00
	FDC, block of 4		4.35

1995. Woman Suffrage Issue memorialized the 75th anniversary of the Aug. 18, 1920, ratification of the 19th Amendment to the Constitution: "The right of citizens of the United States to vote will not be denied or abridged by the United States or by any state on account of sex." *Offset and intaglio by Ashton-Potter (USA) Ltd., perforated 11.*

CM1745 *U.S. Constitution's 19th Amendment*

CM1745		MNHVF	UseVF
32¢	**multicolored,** phosphored paper	.50	.20
	Plate block of 4	3.50	
	FDC *(Aug. 26, 1995)*		1.90
	v. Pair, imperforate	1,500.00	
	v1. Intaglio black omitted	450.00	

1995. Louis Armstrong Issue honored the New Orleans-born trumpet player, composer, improviser and unofficial U.S. goodwill ambassador (1900-1971) who made giant contributions to jazz. *Offset by Sterling Sommer for Ashton-Potter (USA) Ltd., perforated 11.*

CM1746 *Louis Armstrong*

CM1746		MNHVF	UseVF
32¢	**multicolored,** phosphored paper	.50	.20
	Plate block of 4	3.50	
	FDC *(Sept. 1, 1995)*		2.75

For a similar design with "32" in black, see CM1749.

1995. 1945: Victory at Last Issue the final installment in the five-year, 50-stamp World War II Commemorative Series, featured a map and stamps covering events of the war in 1945. *Offset and intaglio by B.E.P., perforated 11.*

CM1747		MNHVF	UseVF
$3.20	**Commemorative pane of 10,** overall tagged	9.00	8.00
	a. **32¢** Flag raised on Iwo Jima	.80	.75
	b. **32¢** Manila freed	.80	.75
	c. **32¢** Okinawa	.80	.75
	d. **32¢** U.S. & Soviets at Elbe	.80	.75
	e. **32¢** Liberated Camps	.80	.75
	f. **32¢** Germany surrenders	.80	.75
	g. **32¢** Displaced persons	.80	.75
	h. **32¢** Japan surrenders	.80	.75
	i. **32¢** News of victory	.80	.75
	j. **32¢** Hometowns honor veterans	.80	.75
	FDC, any single		2.50
	FDC, pane of 10		10.00

We regret that we cannot pass upon the authenticity of any stamp. Should you have stamps for which you desire authentication, we suggest that you contact a recognized expertizing service. Those listed here are considered competent general authorities. Expertizing committees offer opinions only, not guarantees. Opinions may vary among services, and over the years an opinion may change.

American Philatelic Expertizing Service (APEX)
P.O. Box 8000
State College, PA 16803-8000

Philatelic Foundation
501 Fifth Ave., Room 1901
New York, NY 10017

Professional Stamp Experts (PSE), Inc.
P.O. Box 43-0055
Miami, FL 33243-0055

1995. Jazz Musicians Issue in the American Music Series a se-tenant pane of 20 stamps depicting 10 jazz greats included a second version of the Louis Armstrong commemorative (CM1746) released Sept. 1. *Offset by Sterling Sommer for Ashton-Potter (USA) Ltd., perforated 11.*

CM1748 *Coleman Hawkins*

CM1749 *Louis Armstrong*

CM1750 *James P. Johnson*

CM1751 *"Jelly Roll" Morton*

CM1752 *Charlie Parker*

CM1753 *Eubie Blake*

CM1754 *Charles Mingus*

CM1755 *Thelonious Monk*

CM1756 *John Coltrane*

CM1757 *Erroll Garner*

		MNHVF	UseVF
CM1748			
32¢	**Coleman Hawkins,** phosphored paper	.50	.20
CM1749		MNHVF	UseVF
32¢	**Louis Armstrong,** phosphored paper	.50	.20
CM1750		MNHVF	UseVF
32¢	**James P. Johnson,** phosphored paper	.50	.20
CM1751		MNHVF	UseVF
32¢	**"Jelly Roll" Morton,** phosphored paper	.50	.20
CM1752		MNHVF	UseVF
32¢	**Charles Parker,** phosphored paper	.50	.20
CM1753		MNHVF	UseVF
32¢	**Eubie Blake,** phosphored paper	.50	.20
CM1754		MNHVF	UseVF
32¢	**Charlie Mingus,** phosphored paper	.50	.20
CM1755		MNHVF	UseVF
32¢	**Thelonious Monk,** phosphored paper	.50	.20
CM1756		MNHVF	UseVF
32¢	**John Coltrane,** phosphored paper	.50	.20
CM1757		MNHVF	UseVF
32¢	**Erroll Garner,** phosphored paper	.50	.20
	Plate block of 10	8.50	
	FDC *(Sept. 16, 1995)* any single		2.00
	y. Se-tenant vertical block of 10 (CM1748-57)	9.50	
	a. Pane of 20	25.00	
	va. Pane of 20, dark blue omitted	—	
	FDC, block of 10		10.00

1995. Garden Flowers Issue the third in a Garden Flowers Series of colorful and popular se-tenant five-stamp booklets, depicted late summer and early autumn blooms. *Offset and intaglio by B.E.P., perforated 11 vertically on one or two sides.*

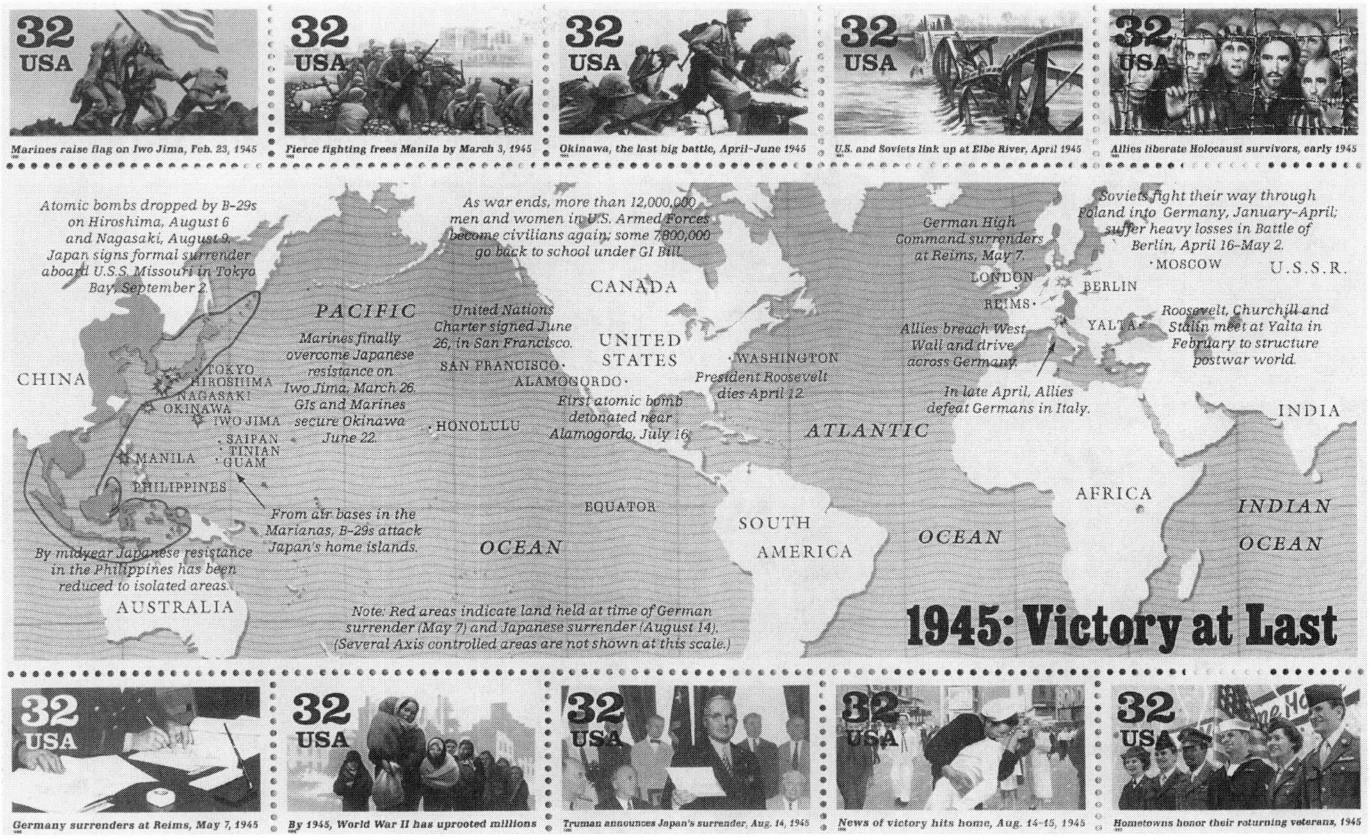

CM1747 *1945: Victory at Last*

CM1758 *Aster;* CM1759 *Chrysanthemum;* CM1760 *Dahlia;* CM1761 *Hydrangea;* CM1762 *Rudbeckia*

		MNHVF	UseVF
CM1758		**MNHVF**	**UseVF**
32¢	**Aster,** overall tagged	.50	.20
CM1759		**MNHVF**	**UseVF**
32¢	**Chrysanthemum,** overall tagged	.50	.20
CM1760		**MNHVF**	**UseVF**
32¢	**Dahlia,** overall tagged	.50	.20
CM1761		**MNHVF**	**UseVF**
32¢	**Hydrangea,** overall tagged	.50	.20
CM1762		**MNHVF**	**UseVF**
32¢	**Rudbeckia,** overall tagged	.50	.20
	FDC *(Sept. 19, 1995)* any single		2.00
	n. Booklet pane of 5 (CM1758-62)	4.00	
	FDC, booklet pane		5.50
	nv. Pane of 5, imperforate	—	

1995. Republic of Palau Issue celebrated the first anniversary of independence for this former U.S. trust territory of the western Pacific Ocean, which released a joint issue almost identical in design (Palau No. 815) on Oct. 1. This stamp also is complementary in design to those of earlier U.S. issues honoring each of the other three territories previously administered by the United States: Marshall Islands (CM1394); Micronesia (CM1395); and the Northern Mariana Islands (CM1607). *Offset by Sterling Sommer for Ashton-Potter (USA) Ltd., perforated 11.*

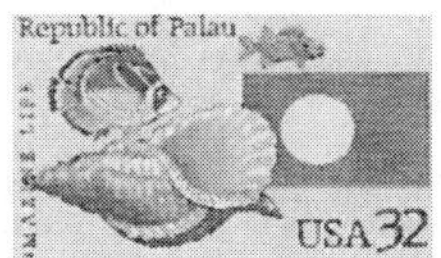

CM1763 *Republic of Palau*

		MNHVF	UseVF
CM1763		**MNHVF**	**UseVF**
32¢	**multicolored** phosphored paper	.50	.20
	Plate block of 4	3.50	
	FDC *(Sept. 29, 1995)*		1.90

1995. Comic Strip Classics Issue was the third USPS Classic Collection Series of 20 stamps on a single theme in a se-tenent pane with a header across the top and explanatory text on the back of each stamp. This issue, on the subject of influential U.S. comic strips, was issued to mark the 100th anniversary of *The Yellow Kid*, which appeared in the *New York World* in May 1895 and is recognized as one of the first modern comic strip characters. *Gravure by J.W. Fergusson & Sons for Stamp Venturers, perforated 10 1/4 x 10. Multicolored, block tagged (Oct. 1, 1995).*

		MNHVF	UseVF
CM1764		**MNHVF**	**UseVF**
32¢	**The Yellow Kid**	.75	.50
CM1765		**MNHVF**	**UseVF**
32¢	**Katzenjammer Kids**	.75	.50
CM1766		**MNHVF**	**UseVF**
32¢	**Little Nemo in Slumberland**	.75	.50
CM1767		**MNHVF**	**UseVF**
32¢	**Bringing Up Father**	.75	.50
CM1768		**MNHVF**	**UseVF**
32¢	**Krazy Kat**	.75	.50
CM1769		**MNHVF**	**UseVF**
32¢	**Rube Goldberg's Inventions**	.75	.50

CM1764 *The Yellow Kid*
CM1765 *Katzenjammer Kids*
CM1766 *Little Nemo in Slumb erland*
CM1767 *Bringing Up Father*
CM1768 *Krazy Kat*
CM1769 *Rube Goldberg's Inventions*
CM1770 *Toonerville Folks*
CM1771 *Gasoline Alley*
CM1772 *Barney Google*
CM1773 *Little Orphan Annie*
CM1774 *Popeye*
CM1775 *Blondie*
CM1776 *Dick Tracy*
CM1777 *Alley Oop*
CM1778 *Nancy*
CM1779 *Flash Gordon*
CM1780 *Li'l Abner*
CM1781 *Terry and the Pirates*
CM1782 *Prince Valiant*
CM1783 *Brenda Starr, Reporter*

		MNHVF	UseVF
CM1770			
32¢	**Toonerville Folks**	.75	.50
CM1771		**MNHVF**	**UseVF**
32¢	**Gasoline Alley**	.75	.50
CM1772		**MNHVF**	**UseVF**
32¢	**Barney Google**	.75	.50
CM1773		**MNHVF**	**UseVF**
32¢	**Little Orphan Annie**	.75	.50
CM1774		**MNHVF**	**UseVF**
32¢	**Popeye**	.75	.50
CM1775		**MNHVF**	**UseVF**
32¢	**Blondie**	.75	.50
CM1776		**MNHVF**	**UseVF**
32¢	**Dick Tracy**	.75	.50
CM1777		**MNHVF**	**UseVF**
32¢	**Alley Oop**	.75	.50
CM1778		**MNHVF**	**UseVF**
32¢	**Nancy**	.75	.50
CM1779		**MNHVF**	**UseVF**
32¢	**Flash Gordon**	.75	.50
CM1780		**MNHVF**	**UseVF**
32¢	**Li'l Abner**	.75	.50
CM1781		**MNHVF**	**UseVF**
32¢	**Terry & the Pirates**	.75	.50
CM1782		**MNHVF**	**UseVF**
32¢	**Prince Valiant**	.75	.50
CM1783		**MNHVF**	**UseVF**
32¢	**Brenda Starr**	.75	.50
	FDC, any single	—	2.50
	y. Se-tenant pane of 20 (CM1764-83)	15.00	14.00
	FDC, pane of 20		25.00
	v. Pane of 20, imperforate	3,000.00	
	v1. Pane with CM1764-71 imperforate, CM1772-75 part perforated	—	
	Six pane press sheets	125.00	

Because this issue also was made available to collectors in full six-pane printing sheets, gutter pairs and blocks and cross-gutter multiples also exist.

1995. U.S. Naval Academy Issue marked the 150th anniversary of the Annapolis, Md., institution with a stamp showing the racing sloop *Swift* crewed by academy midshipmen. *Offset by Sterling Sommer for Ashton-Potter (USA) Ltd., perforated 11.*

CM1784 *U.S. Naval Academy sesquicentennial*

		MNHVF	UseVF
CM1784			
32¢	**multicolored** phosphored paper	.50	.20
	Plate block of 4	3.50	
	FDC *(Oct. 10, 1995)*		1.90

1995. Tennessee Williams Issue 13th in the Literary Arts Series memorialized the Mississippi-born playwright and author. Williams (1911-1983), among the most influential U.S. dramatists of the 20th century, wrote such powerful works as *The Glass Menagerie, Suddenly Last Summer* and *A Streetcar Named Desire. Offset by Sterling Sommer for Ashton-Potter (USA) Ltd., perforated 11.*

CM1785 *Tennessee Williams*

		MNHVF	UseVF
CM1785			
32¢	**multicolored** phosphored paper	.50	.20
	Plate block of 4	3.50	
	FDC *(Oct. 13, 1995)*		1.90

1995. James K. Polk Issue with its frame design adapted from the 1932 1/2¢ Washington Bicentennial stamp (CM98), commemorated the 200th birthday of the 11th president of the United States. *Intaglio by Banknote Corp. of America, perforated 11 1/4 x 11.*

CM1786 *James K. Polk*

CM1786		MNHVF	UseVF
32¢	**reddish brown** phosphored paper	.50	.20
	Plate block of 4	3.50	
	FDC *(Nov. 2, 1995)*		1.90

1995. Antique Automobiles Issue depicted in a se-tenant pane of 25 stamps five of the earliest types of automobiles made in the United States at the turn of the century. *Gravure by J.W. Fergusson & Sons for Stamp Venturers, perforated 10 x 11.*

CM1787 *Duryea*

CM1788 *Haynes*

CM1789 *Columbia*

CM1790 *Winton*

CM1791 *White*

CM1787		MNHVF	UseVF
32¢	**Duryea,** phosphored paper	.75	.50
CM1788		MNHVF	UseVF
32¢	**Haynes,** phosphored paper	.75	.50
CM1789		MNHVF	UseVF
32¢	**Columbia,** phosphored paper	.75	.50
CM1790		MNHVF	UseVF
32¢	**Winton,** phosphored paper	.75	.50
CM1791		MNHVF	UseVF
32¢	**White,** phosphored paper	.75	.50
	Plate block of 10	9.00	
	y. Se-tenant strip of 5 (CM1787-91)	4.00	
	FDC *(Nov. 3, 1995)* any single		1.70
	FDC, strip of 5		3.75

1996. Utah Centennial Issue marked the 100th anniversary of Utah statehood with a colorful rendering of a natural rock formation from the state's Arches National Park. Utah was the 45th state in the Union. *Offset by Sterling Sommer for Ashton-Potter (USA) Ltd., perforated 11.*

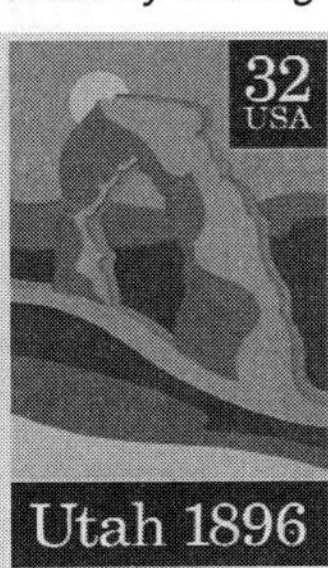

CM1792 *Utah state centennial*

CM1792		MNHVF	UseVF
32¢	**multicolored** tagged *(120,000,000)*	.50	.20
	Plate block of 4	3.50	
	FDC *(Jan. 4, 1996)*		1.90

1996. Garden Flowers Issue was the fourth in a Garden Flower Series of colorful five-stamp pane booklets, this one depicting blooms that appear at various locations in the United States during the winter months. *Offset and intaglio by B.E.P., perforated 11 vertically on one or two sides.*

CM1793 *Crocus;* CM1794 *Winter Aconite;* CM1795 *Pansy;* CM1796 *Snowdrop;* CM1797 *Anemone*

CM1793		MNHVF	UseVF
32¢	**Crocus,** phosphored paper *(160,000,000)*	.50	.20
CM1794		MNHVF	UseVF
32¢	**Winter Aconite,** phosphored paper	.50	.20
CM1795		MNHVF	UseVF
32¢	**Pansy,** phosphored paper	.50	.20
CM1796		MNHVF	UseVF
32¢	**Snowdrop,** phosphored paper	.50	.20
CM1797		MNHVF	UseVF
32¢	**Anemone,** phosphored paper	.50	.20
	FDC *(Jan. 19, 1996)* any single		2.00
	n. Booklet pane of 5 (CM1793-97)	3.50	
	FDC, booklet pane		5.50
	nv. Pane of 5, imperforate	—	

1996. Love Cherub Issue in the Love Series is slightly reformatted self-adhesive version of the 32¢ Cherub design (CM1703-04) in booklet form with "32" and "USA" side-by-side. *Offset and intaglio by Banknote Corp. of America, serpentine die cut 11 1/4.*

CM1798 *Love*

CM1798		MNHVF	UseVF
32¢	**multicolored** tagged *(2,550,000,000)*	.50	.20
	FDC *(Jan. 20, 1996)*		1.90
	n. Pane of 20 plus label	16.50	
	FDC, pane of 20		15.50
	n1. Pane of 15 plus label, various layouts	10.00	
	v. red omitted	—	

1996. Ernest E. Just Issue in the Black Heritage Series honored marine biologist, scientist and professor Ernest Everett Just (1883-1941) whose research on abnormal cell development contributed to understanding leukemia, sickle-cell anemia and cancer. *Offset by Banknote Corp. of America, perforated 11.*

CM1799 *Ernest E. Just*

CM1799		MNHVF	UseVF
32¢	**black & gray** tagged *(92,100,000)*	.50	.20

		MNHVF	UseVF
	Plate block of 4	3.50	
	FDC *(Feb. 1, 1996)*		2.75

1996. Smithsonian Institution Sesquicentennial Issue marked the 150th anniversary of the national museum, begun in 1829 with a $508,318 bequest from a British chemist named Smithson, "to found at Washington...an establishment for the increase & diffusion of knowledge among men." (See also CM285 and CM959). *Offset by Sterling Sommer for Ashton-Potter (USA) Ltd., perforated 11.*

CM1800 *Smithsonian Institution sesquicentennial*

CM1800		MNHVF	UseVF
32¢	**multicolored** tagged *(115,600,000)*	.50	.20
	Plate block of 4	3.50	
	FDC *(Feb. 7, 1996)*		1.90

1996. New Years Issue in the Lunar New Year Series for the Year of the Rat was the fourth in the on-going series celebrating the lunar holiday. *Gravure by Stamp Venturers, perforated 11 1/4.*

CM1801 *Year of the Rat*

CM1801		MNHVF	UseVF
32¢	**multicolored** tagged *(93,150,000)*	.50	.20
	Plate block of 4	3.50	
	FDC *(Feb. 8, 1996)*		2.00
	v. Single, imperforate	—	
	v1. Pair, imperforate	—	
	v2. Plate block, imperforate	—	

1996. Pioneers of Communications Issue saluted a quartet of 19th-century innovators in photographic and print technology. Eadweard Muybridge (1830-1904) pioneered the conversion of photographs to moving images. Ottmar Mergenthaler (1854-99) invented the Linotype, which vastly reduced the cost of printing newspapers and boosted circulation. Chief among the many inventions of Frederic E. Ives (1856-1937) was the half-tone printing process, which enabled newspapers to reproduce photographs. William Kennedy Laurie Dickson (1860-1935), an Edison employee, devised the Kinetoscope, in which precise synchronization gives motion pictures the illusion of movement. *Offset by Ashton-Potter (USA) Ltd., perforated 11.*

CM1802 *Eadweard Muybridge*

CM1803 *Ottmar Mergenthaler*

CM1804 *Frederic E. Ives*

CM1805 *William Dickson*

CM1802		MNHVF	UseVF
32¢	**Eadweard Muybridge,** phosphored paper *(23,292,500)*	.50	.20

CM1803		MNHVF	UseVF
32¢	**Ottmar Mergenthaler,** phosphored paper	.50	.20

CM1804		MNHVF	UseVF
32¢	**Frederic E. Ives,** phosphored paper	.50	.20

CM1805		MNHVF	UseVF
32¢	**William Dickson,** phosphored paper	.50	.20
	Plate block of 4	3.50	
	y. Se-tenant block or strip of CM1802-05	3.00	2.50
	FDC *(Feb. 22, 1996)*		1.75
	FDC, block of 4		3.50

1996. Fulbright Scholarships Issue marked the 50th anniversary of the annual awards, named for Arkansas Senator and long-time Foreign Relations Committee Chairman J. William Fulbright (1905-1995), sponsor of the 1946 act that created the program. To date, about a quarter million Fulbright scholars either have traveled from the United States to study abroad or have come from abroad to study in the United States. *Offset and intaglio by B.E.P., perforated 11.*

CM1806 *Fulbright scholarships*

CM1806		MNHVF	UseVF
32¢	**multicolored** tagged *(111,000,000)*	.50	.20
	Plate block of 4	3.50	
	FDC *(Feb. 28, 1996)*		1.90

1996. Marathon Issue saluted the 100th running of the annual 26.2-mile Boston Marathon. *Offset by Banknote Corp. of America, perforated 11.*

CM1807 *Marathon*

CM1807		MNHVF	UseVF
32¢	**multicolored** tagged *(209,450,000)*	.50	.20
	Plate block of 4	3.50	
	FDC *(April 11, 1996)*		1.00

1996. Atlanta 1996 Centennial Olympic Games Issue was the fourth USPS Classic Collections Series of 20 stamps on a single theme in a se-tenant pane with a header across the top and descriptive text on the back of each stamp. This issue celebrated the 100th anniversary of the first modern Olympiad. *Gravure by J.W. Fergusson & Sons for Stamp Venturers, perforated 10 1/4 x 10. Multicolored, block tagged (May 2, 1996)*

CM1808		MNHVF	UseVF
32¢	**Javelin**	.75	.50
CM1809		MNHVF	UseVF
32¢	**Whitewater canoeing**	.75	.50
CM1810		MNHVF	UseVF
32¢	**Women's running**	.75	.50
CM1811		MNHVF	UseVF
32¢	**Women's platform diving**	.75	.50
CM1812		MNHVF	UseVF
32¢	**Men's cycling**	.75	.50
CM1813		MNHVF	UseVF
32¢	**Freestyle wrestling**	.75	.50
CM1814		MNHVF	UseVF
32¢	**Women's gymnastics**	.75	.50
CM1815		MNHVF	UseVF
32¢	**Women's sailboarding**	.75	.50

CM1808 *Javelin*
CM1809 *Whitewater canoeing*
CM1810 *Women's running*
CM1811 *Women's platform diving*
CM1812 *Men's cycling*
CM1813 *Freestyle wrestling*
CM1814 *Women's gymnastics*
CM1815 *Women's sailboarding*
CM1816 *Men's shot Put*
CM1817 *Women's soccer*
CM1818 *Beach volleyball*
CM1819 *Men's rowing*
CM1820 *Men's sprinting* event
CM1821 *Women's swimming*
CM1822 *Women's softball*
CM1823 *Men's hurdles*
CM1824 *Men's swimming (backstroke)*
CM1825 *Men's gymnastics (pommel horse)*
CM1826 *Equestrian events*
CM1827 *Men's basketball*

		MNHVF	UseVF
CM1816			
32¢	**Men's shot put**	.75	.50
CM1817		MNHVF	UseVF
32¢	**Women's soccer**	.75	.50
CM1818		MNHVF	UseVF
32¢	**Beach volleyball**	.75	.50
CM1819		MNHVF	UseVF
32¢	**Men's rowing**	.75	.50
CM1820		MNHVF	UseVF
32¢	**Men's sprinting events**	.75	.50
CM1821		MNHVF	UseVF
32¢	**Women's swimming**	.75	.50
CM1822		MNHVF	UseVF
32¢	**Women's softball**	.75	.50
CM1823		MNHVF	UseVF
32¢	**Men's hurdles**	.75	.50
CM1824		MNHVF	UseVF
32¢	**Men's swimming (backstroke)**	.75	.50
CM1825		MNHVF	UseVF
32¢	**Men's gymnastics (pommel Horse)**	.75	.50
CM1826		MNHVF	UseVF
32¢	**Equestrian events**	.75	.50
CM1827		MNHVF	UseVF
32¢	**Men's basketball**	.75	.50
	FDC *(May 2, 1996)* any single		1.00
	y. Pane of CM1808-27	14.00	
	vy. Pane of 20, imperforate	—	
	vy1. Partially perforated pane of 20	—	
	Six pane press sheet	150.00	

Because this issue also was made available to collectors in full six-pane printing sheets, gutter pairs and blocks and cross-gutter multiples also exist.

1996. Georgia O'Keeffe Issue commemorated the artist whose distinctive, vibrant presentation of images from nature in abstract, creative settings marked her as a true American original. One of 200 early flower paintings created by O'Keeffe (1887-1986) was reproduced in a 15-stamp commemorative pane with selvage picturing the painter and a quotation by her. *Gravure by J.W. Fergusson & Sons for Stamp Venturers, perforated 11 1/2.*

CM1828 *Georgia O'Keeffe's* Red Poppy, 1927

		MNHVF	UseVF
CM1828			
32¢	**multicolored** tagged *(156,300,000)*	.50	.20
	Plate block of 4	3.50	
	y. Pane of 15	16.00	
	FDC *(May 23, 1996)*		1.00
	v. Pair, imperforate	200.00	

1996. Tennessee Bicentennial Issue marked the 200th anniversary of Tennessee's entering the Union as the 16th state. It was the first conventional commemorative issued simultaneously both in lick-and-stick panes and self-adhesive booklets sold only in Tennessee. *Gravure by J.W. Fergusson & Sons for Stamp Venturers, perforated 11.*

CM1829-30 *Tennessee statehood*

CM1829		MNHVF	UseVF
32¢	**multicolored** tagged *(100,000,000)*	.50	.20
	Plate block of 4	3.25	
	FDC *(May 31, 1996)*		1.00

1996. Tennessee Bicentennial Booklet Issue *Serpentine die cut 10 x 10 3/4.*

CM1830		MNHVF	UseVF
32¢	**multicolored** tagged *(60,120,000)*	.75	.20
	FDC *(May 31, 1996)*		1.00
	n. Pane of 20	16.00	
	v. Horizontal pair, imperforate (no die cutting) between	—	

1996. American Indian Dances Issue pictured an important component of native American culture and ritual in a 20-stamp commemorative pane. *Gravure by Ashton-Potter (USA) Ltd., perforated 11.*

CM1831 *Fancy Dance;* CM1832 *Butterfly Dance;* CM1833 *Traditional Dance;* CM1834 *Raven Dance;* CM1835 *Hoop Dance*

CM1831		MNHVF	UseVF
32¢	**Fancy Dance,** tagged *(27,850,000)*	.75	.50
CM1832		MNHVF	UseVF
32¢	**Butterfly Dance,** tagged	.75	.50
CM1833		MNHVF	UseVF
32¢	**Traditional Dance,** tagged	.75	.50
CM1834		MNHVF	UseVF
32¢	**Raven Dance,** tagged	.75	.50
CM1835		MNHVF	UseVF
32¢	**Hoop Dance,** tagged	.75	.50
	Plate block of 10	8.00	
	y. Se-tenant strip of CM1831-53	3.50	
	FDC *(June 7, 1996)* any single		1.00
	Pane of 20	14.50	

1996. Prehistoric Animals Issue featured dramatic portraits of four important North American animals of the Cenozoic Era (or Age of Mammals), comprising the last 65 million years. *Offset by Ashton-Potter (USA) Ltd., perforated 11.*

CM1836 *Eohippus*

CM1837 Woolly Mammoth

CM1838 *Mastodon*

CM1839 *Saber-tooth Cat*

CM1836		MNHVF	UseVF
32¢	**Eohippus,** tagged *(22,218,000)*	.75	.50
CM1837		MNHVF	UseVF
32¢	**Woolly Mammoth,** tagged	.75	.50
CM1838		MNHVF	UseVF
32¢	**Mastodon,** tagged	.75	.50
CM1839		MNHVF	UseVF
32¢	**Saber-tooth Cat,** tagged	.75	.50
	Plate block of 4	3.50	
	y. Se-tenant block or strip of CM1836-39	3.00	
	FDC *(June 8, 1996)* any single		1.00

1996. Breast Cancer Awareness Issue took note of a serious health risk to American women to raise awareness and encourage early detection. Special postmarks, clinics and screening in conjunction with this stamp across the nation increased public attention, and helped spark Congress to request a breast cancer semipostal stamp (CMSP1) in 1998. *Offset by Ashton-Potter (USA) Ltd., perforated 11.*

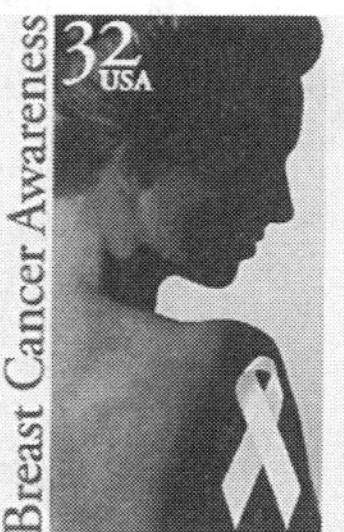

CM1840 *Breast Cancer Awareness*

CM1840		MNHVF	UseVF
32¢	**multicolored** tagged *(95,600,000)*	.50	.20
	Plate block of 4	3.25	
	FDC *(June 15, 1996)*		1.00

1996. James Dean Issue the second in the Legends of Hollywood Series again consisted of a 20-stamp commemorative pane with star-shaped corner perforations and a large area of selvage displaying an enlargement of the actor. Dean (1931-55) had enormous impact in three films — *East of Eden, Rebel Without a Cause* and *Giant* — before his death in a car crash at the age of 24. *Gravure by J.W. Fergusson & Sons for Stamp Venturers, perforated 11.*

CM1841 *James Dean*

CM1841		MNHVF	UseVF
32¢	**multicolored** tagged *(300,000,000)*	.50	.20
	Plate block of 4	3.25	
	FDC *(June 24, 1996)*		1.00
	a. Pane of 20	14.50	
	Six pane press sheet		
	v. Pair, imperforate	—	495.00

v1. Pane, imperforate —
v2. Partially perforate pane —

Because this issue also was made available to collectors in full six-pane printing sheets, gutter pairs and blocks and cross-gutter multiples also exist.

1996. Folk Heroes Issue featured bold portraits of larger-than-life characters made famous in popular American fiction: Mighty Casey, whose turn at the bat in Ernest L. Thayer's 1888 poem tragically came to naught; legendary lumberjack Paul Bunyan, who transformed America together with Babe, his giant blue ox; John Henry, the "steel drivin' man" who beat a steam drill in carving out a West Virginia railway tunnel, but perished in the attempt; and the cyclone-taming Texas cowboy Pecos Bill, who wears a rattlesnake for a scarf on the stamp. *Offset by Ashton-Potter (USA) Ltd., perforated 11.*

CM1842 *Mighty Casey*

CM1843 *Paul Bunyan*

CM1844 *John Henry*

CM1845 *Pecos Bill*

		MNHVF	UseVF
CM1842			
32¢	**Mighty Casey,** tagged *(23,681,250)*	.50	.20
CM1843		MNHVF	UseVF
32¢	**Paul Bunyan,** tagged	.50	.20
CM1844		MNHVF	UseVF
32¢	**John Henry,** tagged	.50	.20
CM1845		MNHVF	UseVF
32¢	**Pecos Bill,** tagged	.50	.20
	Plate block of 4	3.50	
	y. Se-tenant block or strip of CM1842-45	3.00	
	FDC *(July 11, 1996)* any single		1.00

1996. Olympic Games Centennial Issue was another single-design 20-stamp commemorative pane to mark the 100th anniversary of the first modern Olympiad in 1896 in Athens, Greece. Left margin selvage showed an enlargement of *Discobolus,* after the original bronze created by the Greek sculptor Myron in the 5th century B.C. *Offset and intaglio by Ashton-Potter (USA) Ltd., perforated 11.*

CM1846 *Discus Thrower, centennial Olympics*

		MNHVF	UseVF
CM1846			
32¢	**brown** tagged *(133,613,000)*	.50	.20
	Plate block of 4	3.00	
	FDC *(July 19, 1996)*		1.00
	y. Pane of 20	14.00	

1996. Iowa Sesquicentennial Issue marked the 150th anniversary of Iowa's entering the Union as the 29th state. The conventional commemorative was available throughout the country, whereas the self-adhesive booklet version of the stamp was sold only in Iowa and at philatelic centers out of state. *Perforated 11, Offset by Ashton-Potter (USA) Ltd.*

CM1847, CM1848 *Iowa sesquicentennial*

		MNHVF	UseVF
CM1847			
32¢	**multicolored** tagged *(103,400,000)*	.50	.20
	Plate block of 4	3.00	
	FDC *(Aug. 1, 1996)*		1.00

1996. Iowa Sesquicentennial Self Adhesive Issue *Serpentine die cut 10 x 10 3/4.*

		MNHVF	UseVF
CM1848			
32¢	**multicolored** tagged *(60,000,000)*	.75	.30
	FDC *(Aug. 1, 1996)*		1.00
	n. Pane of 20	16.00	

1996. Rural Free Delivery Centennial Issue saluted a century of the service that brought mail for the first time directly to the homes of America's farmers and other rural residents. *Offset and intaglio by B.E.P., perforated 11.*

CM1849 *Rural Free Delivery*

		MNHVF	UseVF
CM1849			
32¢	**multicolored** tagged *(134,000,000)*	.50	.20
	Plate block of 4	3.00	
	FDC *(Aug. 7, 1996)*		1.00

1996. Riverboats Issue is a se-tenant presentation of five self-adhesive stamps saluting historic 19th-century steamboats that carried passengers and important cargo on the inland waterways of America. *Gravure by Avery Dennison Security Printing Division, serpentine die cut 11.*

CM1850 Robt. E. Lee

CM1851 Sylvan Dell

CM1852 Far West

CM1853 Rebecca Everingham

CM1854 Bailey Gatzert

		MNHVF	UseVF
CM1850			
32¢	***Robt. E. Lee,*** tagged *(32,000,000)*	.75	.50
CM1851		MNHVF	UseVF
32¢	***Sylvan Dell,*** tagged	.75	.50
CM1852		MNHVF	UseVF
32¢	***Far West,*** tagged	.75	.50
CM1853		MNHVF	UseVF
32¢	***Rebecca Everingham,*** tagged	.75	.50
CM1854		MNHVF	UseVF
32¢	***Bailey Gatzert,*** tagged	.75	.50
	Plate block of 10	8.00	
	y. Se-tenant vertical strip of CM1850-54	3.50	
	v. Die Cut through backing full pane	35.00	
	FDC *(Aug. 22, 1996)* any single		1.00

1996. Big Band Leaders Issue honored outstanding orchestra leaders of the Big Band era who popularized the swing music that had its heyday in the 1930s and '40s. Count Basie (1904-84), a brilliant composer whose bands for almost 50 years featured many of the nation's finest jazz soloists, is best remembered for tunes including "One O'Clock Jump," "Swingin' the Blues" and "Jumpin' at the Woodside." The Dorsey Brothers, clarinetist Jimmy (1904-57) and trombonist Tommy (1905-56), headed dance bands separately and together, notable for melodies such as "Tangerine" and "I'm Sentimental Over You." Glenn Miller (1904-44), a gifted trombonist and arranger, presided over one of the most successful Swing era orchestras, the distinctive sound of which is recognizable in classics such as "In the Mood," "Kalamazoo," and "Sunrise Serenade." Benny Goodman (1909-86), known as the "King of Swing," was a clarinet prodigy and a perfectionist as band leader, with "King Porter Stomp," "Don't Be That Way" and "Sing, Sing, Sing" among his hits. *Offset by Ashton-Potter (USA) Ltd., perforated 11.*

CM1855 *Count Basie;* CM1856 *Tommy & Jimmy Dorsey;* CM1857 *Glen Miller;* CM1858 *Benny Goodman*

		MNHVF	UseVF
CM1855			
32¢	**Count Basie,** tagged *(23,025,000)*	.50	.20
CM1856		MNHVF	UseVF
32¢	**Tommy & Jimmy Dorsey,** tagged	.50	.20
CM1857		MNHVF	UseVF
32¢	**Glenn Miller,** tagged	.50	.20
CM1858		MNHVF	UseVF
32¢	**Benny Goodman,** tagged	.50	.20
	Plate block of 4	3.50	
	y. Se-tenant block or strip of CM1855-58	3.00	
	FDC *(Sept. 11, 1996)* any single		1.00
	n. Pane of 20	14.00	

1996. Songwriters Issue honored four of the finest songwriters of the 20th century. Harold Arlen (1905-86) is best known for his scores for two Judy Garland films, *The Wizard of Oz* (co-written with Yip Harburg) and *A Star is Born* (co-written with Ira Gershwin), and tunes written for Harlem's renowned Cotton Club including "Stormy Weather." Songwriter, singer and Capitol Records founder Johnny Mercer (1909-76) penned the lyrics to more than 1,000 songs, from "I'm an Old Cowhand" to "Moon River." The nation's finest female songwriter, Dorothy Fields (1905-74) credits include "Sunny Side of the Street," "The Way You Look Tonight," and "A Fine Romance." Hoagy Carmichael (1899-1981) may be most closely associated with "Stardust" but authored many other great songs as well, including "Heart and Soul" and "Georgia on My Mind." *Offset by Ashton-Potter (USA) Ltd., perforated 11.*

CM1859 *Harold Arlen;* CM1860 *Johnny Mercer;* CM1861 *Dorothy Fields;* CM1862 *Hoagy Carmichael*

		MNHVF	UseVF
CM1859			
32¢	**Harold Arlen,** tagged *(23,025,000)*	.50	.20
CM1860		MNHVF	UseVF
32¢	**Johnny Mercer,** tagged	.50	.20
CM1861		MNHVF	UseVF
32¢	**Dorothy Fields,** tagged	.50	.20
CM1862		MNHVF	UseVF
32¢	**Hoagy Carmichael,** tagged	.50	.20
	Plate block of 4	3.50	
	y. Se-tenant block or strip of CM1859-62	3.00	
	FDC *(Sept. 11, 1996)* any single		1.00
	n. Pane of 20	14.00	

1996. F. Scott Fitzgerald Issue 14th in the Literary Arts Series celebrated the 100th birthday of the novelist (1896-1940) who immortalized the Jazz Age of the 1920s in such works as *The Beautiful and the Damned, The Great Gatsby* and *Tender is the Night.* The stamp prepays the 23¢ fee for each additional ounce over the basic 32¢ first-class letter rate. *Gravure by B.E.P., perforated 11.*

CM1863 *F. Scott Fitzgerald*

		MNHVF	UseVF
CM1863			
23¢	**multicolored** tagged *(300,000,000)*	.50	.20
	Plate block of 4	2.75	
	FDC *(Sept. 27, 1996)*		1.00

1996. Endangered Species Issue was a 15-stamp se-tenant commemorative pane with a banner and marginal text, each stamp featuring an indigenous American animal currently threatened with extinction. Although not a joint issue technically speaking, a pane of 24 stamps depicting native endangered species was issued simultaneously by Mexico. *Offset (14,910,000 panes) by Sterling Sommer for Ashton-Potter (USA) Ltd., perforated 11. Multicolored, block tagged (Oct 2, 1996).*

		MNHVF	UseVF
CM1864			
32¢	**Black-footed ferret**	.50	.20
CM1865		MNHVF	UseVF
32¢	**Thick-billed parrot**	.50	.20

Endangered Species
National Stamp Collecting Month 1996 highlights these 15 species to promote awareness of endangered wildlife. Each generation must work to protect the delicate balance of nature, so that future generations may share a sound and healthy planet.
© USPS 1995
.32 x 15 = $4.80

CM1864 *Black-footed ferret*

CM 1865 *Thick-billed parrot*

CM1866 *Hawaiian Monk seal*

CM1867 *American crocodile*

CM1868 *Ocelot*

CM1869 *Schaus swallowtail butterfly*

CM1870 *Wyoming toad*

CM1871 *Brown pelican*

CM1872 *California condor*

CM1873 *Gila trout*

CM1874 *San Francisco garter snake*

CM1875 *Woodland caribou*

CM1876 *Florida panther*

CM1877 *Piping plover*

CM1878 *Florida manatee*

		MNHVF	UseVF
CM1866			
32¢	**Hawaiian Monk seal**	.50	.20
CM1867			
32¢	**American crocodile**	.50	.20
CM1868			
32¢	**Ocelot**	.50	.20
CM1869			
32¢	**Schaus swallowtail butterfly**	.50	.20
CM1870			
32¢	**Wyoming toad**	.50	.20
CM1871			
32¢	**Brown pelican**	.50	.20
CM1872			
32¢	**California condor**	.50	.20
CM1873			
32¢	**Gila trout**	.50	.20
CM1874			
32¢	**San Francisco garter snake**	.50	.20
CM1875			
32¢	**Woodland caribou**	.50	.20
CM1876			
32¢	**Florida panther**	.50	.20
CM1877			
32¢	**Piping plover**	.50	.20
CM1878			
32¢	**Florida manatee**	.50	.20
	FDC *(Oct. 2, 1996)* any single		1.00
	y. Se-tenant pane of CM1864-78	11.00	

1996. Computer Technology Issue marked the 50th anniversary of the Electronic Numerical Integrator and Calculator (ENIAC), regarded widely as the first general-purpose electronic digital computer, forerunner to the millions in use today. *Offset and intaglio, by Ashton-Potter (USA) Ltd., perforated 11.*

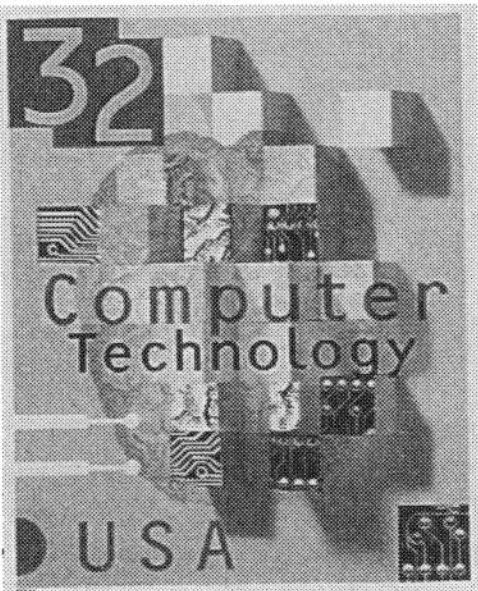

CM1879 *Computer Technology*

		MNHVF	UseVF
CM1879			
32¢	**multicolored** tagged *(93,612,000)*	.50	.20
	Plate block of 4	3.00	
	FDC *(Oct. 8, 1996)*		1.00

Holiday Celebration Series

1996. Hanukkah Issue first in a Holiday Celebration Series, honored the Jewish Festival of Lights and shared its design with a joint issue from Israel (Israel No. 1360). The self-adhesive stamp shows a stylized menorah and the colorful candles with which Jews mark the eight-day observance. Due to its popularity, it was reprinted in 1997 with no major differences. *Gravure by Avery Dennison Security Printing Division, serpentine die cut 11.*

CM1880 *Hanukkah*

CM1880		MNHVF	UseVF
32¢	**multicolored** tagged *(103,520,000)*	.75	.20
	Plate block of 4	3.00	
	FDC *(Oct. 22, 1996)*		1.00
	n. Booklet pane of 20	12.50	

1996. Cycling Souvenir Sheet was issued to sell at international cycling meets in which the USPS Pro Cycling Team competed, to defray the team's cost. *Gravure by J.W. Fergusson & Sons for Stamp Venturers, perforated 11.*

CM1881 *Cycling souvenir sheet*

CM1881		MNHVF	UseVF
50¢	**multicolored** tagged *(20,000,000)*	2.50	1.00
	a. **50¢** multicolored & orange	1.50	1.00
	b. **50¢** multicolored & blue green	1.50	1.00
	FDC *(Nov. 1, 1996)*		1.00

1997. New Years Issue for the Year of the Ox in the Lunar New Year Series was the fifth in celebrating the Chinese holiday. *Gravure by Stamp Venturers, perforated 11 1/4.*

CM1882 *Year of the Ox*

CM1882		MNHVF	UseVF
32¢	**multicolored** tagged *(160,000,000)*	.50	.20
	Plate block of 4	3.00	
	FDC *(Jan. 5, 1996)*		1.00

1997. Benjamin O. Davis Issue in the Black Heritage Series saluted with a self-adhesive stamp the nation's first black brigadier general, a soldier who began as a private and rose through the ranks in a 50-year career to become both a force for and a symbol of integration in America's military. *Offset by Banknote Corp. of America, serpentine die cut 11 1/2.*

CM1883 *Benjamin O. Davis, Sr.*

CM1883		MNHVF	UseVF
32¢	**gray, green & black** phosphored paper *(112,000,000)*	.50	.20
	Plate block of 4	3.00	
	FDC *(Jan. 28, 1997)*		1.00

1997. Love Issue in the Love Series used bilaterally symmetrical profiles of two elegant swans outlining a heart in two self-adhesive booklets paying the 32¢ standard First Class 1-ounce letter rate and the 55¢ rate for 2-ounce letters (useful for wedding invitations containing reply cards and envelopes), respectively. *Serpentine die cut 11 3/4 x 11 1/2 on two, three, or four sides. Offset by Banknote Corp. of America.*

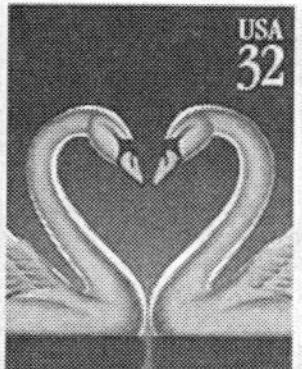

CM1884 *32¢ Love swans*

CM1884		MNHVF	UseVF
32¢	**multicolored** tagged	.50	.20
	FDC *(Feb. 7, 1997)*		1.00
	n. Pane of 20 plus label	13.00	
	v. Pair, imperforate (no die cutting)	275.00	
	vn. Pane of 20, imperforate (no die cutting)	—	

1997. Love Issue *Serpentine die cut 11 1/2 x 11 3/4 on two, three, or four sides.*

CM1885 *55¢ Love swans*

CM1885		MNHVF	UseVF
55¢	**multicolored** tagged	1.00	.30
	FDC *(Feb. 7, 1997)*		1.00
	n. Pane of 20 plus label	22.50	

1997. Helping Children Learn Issue a self-adhesive stamp called attention to the developmental importance and simple pleasure of reading as an activity for adults to share with children. The issue coincided with the centennial of the PTA, the nation's oldest and largest volunteer association working for children. *Gravure by Avery Dennison Security Printing Division, serpentine die cut 11 1/2 x 11 3/4.*

CM1886 *Helping Children Learn*

CM1886		MNHVF	UseVF
32¢	**multicolored** tagged	.50	.20
	Plate block of 4	3.00	
	FDC *(Feb. 18, 1997)*		1.00

1997. Pacific 97 Issue the first triangular stamps in U.S. philatelic history, used two early means of moving the mail — the stagecoach and the clipper ship — to promote the Pacific 97 International Philatelic Exhibition May 29 to June 8 in San Francisco, Calif. *Intaglio by Banknote Corp. of America, perforated 11 1/4.*

CM1887 *Stagecoach*

CM1887		MNHVF	UseVF
32¢	**red** phosphored paper *(65,000,000)*	.50	.20

CM1888 *Clipper ship*

CM1888		MNHVF	UseVF
32¢	**blue** phosphored paper	.50	.20
	Plate block of 4	3.00	
	y. Se-tenant pair (CM1887-88)	1.25	
	FDC *(March 13, 1997)*		2.00
	Six pane press sheets	150.00	

Because this issue also was made available in full 96-subject printing sheets of six 16-stamp panes, gutter pairs and blocks and cross-gutter multiples also exist.

1997. Thornton Wilder Issue 15th in the Literary Arts Series celebrated the 100th birthday of the three-time Pulitzer Prize-winning author (1897-1975) of the novel *The Bridge of San Luis Rey* and the plays *Our Town* (symbolically depicted on the stamp) and *The Skin of Our Teeth. Offset by Ashton-Potter (USA) Ltd., perforated 11.*

CM1889 *Thornton Wilder*

CM1889		MNHVF	UseVF
32¢	**multicolored** tagged *(97,500,000)*	.50	.20
	Plate block of 4	3.00	
	FDC *(April 17, 1997)*		1.00

1997. Raoul Wallenberg Issue commemorated the Swedish diplomat who in 1944 risked his own life to save over 20,000 Hungarian Jews from Nazi genocide by issuing them falsified Swedish passes. In 1945, Wallenberg was taken prisoner by the Soviets, who only in 1957 announced that he had died a decade earlier, of a purported heart attack, while in Moscow's Lubyanka Prison. *Offset by Sterling Sommer for Ashton-Potter (USA) Ltd., perforated 11.*

CM1890 *Wallenberg and refugees*

CM1890		MNHVF	UseVF
32¢	**multicolored** tagged *(96,000,000)*	.50	.20
	Plate block of 4	3.00	
	FDC *(April 24, 1997)*		1.00

1997. The World of Dinosaurs Issue a 15-stamp pane showcased two panoramic dioramas by James Gurney of life in the age of the giant reptiles: a scene in Colorado 150 million years ago in the top panel; and a 75-million-year-old scene from Montana in the bottom panel of the pane. The pane portrays many species never before shown on stamps. *Offset by Sterling Sommer for Ashton-Potter (USA) Ltd., perforated 11.*

CM1891		MNHVF	UseVF
$4.80	**Sheet of 15,** tagged *(14,600,000)*	15.00	9.50
	a. **32¢** Ceratosaurus	.75	.50
	b. **32¢** Camptosaurus	.75	.50
	c. **32¢** Camarasaurus	.75	.50
	d. **32¢** Brachiosaurus	.75	.50
	e. **32¢** Goniopholis	.75	.50
	f. **32¢** Stegosaurus	.75	.50
	g. **32¢** Allosaurus	.75	.50
	h. **32¢** Opisthias	.75	.50
	i. **32¢** Edmontonia	.75	.50
	j. **32¢** Einiosaurus	.75	.50
	k. **32¢** Daspletosaurus	.75	.50
	l. **32¢** Palaeosaniwa	.75	.50
	m. **32¢** Corythosaurus	.75	.50
	n. **32¢** Ornithomimus	.75	.50
	o. **32¢** Parasaurolophus	.75	.50
	FDC *(May 1, 1997)* any single		2.00
	FDC pane of 15		12.50
	v. All colors omitted, untagged	—	
	v1. Perforations inverted	—	
	v2. Perforate CM1891 a-g, Imperforate CM1891 h-o	—	
	v3. Imperforate CM1891 a-g, perforated CM1891 h-o	6,875.00	

Warner Bros. Cartoon Characters Series

1997. Bugs Bunny Issue first in the Warner Bros. Cartoon Characters Series, showcased in two types of self-adhesive 10-stamp panes (rouletted vertically through the middle) the wisecracking "Oscar-winning rabbit" with the Brooklyn accent who has been a fixture on American movie and television screens for more than half a century. *Gravure by Avery Dennison Security Printing Division.*

CM1892 *Bugs Bunny*

CM1892		MNHVF	UseVF
$3.20	**Pane of 10,** tagged	7.50	
	n. Right half of pane (single die cut CM1892a superimposed on enlarged image in right selvage)	1.00	
	n1. Left half of pane (block of 9 CM1892a)	5.00	
	a. 32¢ single	.75	.25
	FDC *(May 22, 1997)*		1.00

Serpentine die cut 11 through stamps and backing.

CM1893		MNHVF	UseVF
$3.20	**Pane of 10,** tagged	200.00	
	n. Right half of pane (single imperforate CM1893a on enlarged image in right selvage)	150.00	
	n1. Left half of pane (block of 9 CM1893a)	5.00	
	a. 32¢ single	.75	.25

THE WORLD OF DINOSAURS

CM1891 *The World of Dinosaurs*

This issue also was made available in top and bottom half printing sheets of six 10-stamp panes each. A single plate number, trimmed away on individual panes, appears adjacent to the bottom-left pane in the bottom half of the printing sheet only. Value of plate number half is $225.

A gummed, non-denominated, untagged item similar to CM1893n on the same backing paper as the normal stamps lacks Bugs' "autograph" and single stamp, the latter of which is replaced by "32 USA" as on the issued stamp. Though printed for the USPS, this item was an advertising piece and was not postally valid.

1997. Pacific 97 U.S. Stamp Sesquicentennial Issue marked the 150th anniversary of the first regular-issue U.S. postage stamps (Minkus 1-2, depicted in the selvage of the souvenir sheets) and hailed the opening of the Pacific 1997 International Philatelic Exhibition in San Francisco, Calif. The souvenir sheets were sold only during the 11 days of the show. *Offset and intaglio by B.E.P., perforated 10 1/2.*

CM1894 *Benjamin Franklin souvenir sheet*

CM1894		MNHVF	UseVF
$6	**Pane of 12,** tagged	11.50	9.00
	a. 50¢ single	1.00	.50
	FDC *(May 29, 1997)*		1.00

1997. Pacific 97 U.S. Stamp Sesquicentennial Issue marked the 150th anniversary of the first regular-issue U.S. postage stamps (Minkus 1-2, depicted in the selvage of the souvenir sheets) and hailed the opening of the Pacific 1997 International Philatelic Exhibition in San Francisco, Calif. The souvenir sheets were sold only during the 11 days of the show. *Offset and intaglio by B.E.P., perforated 10 1/2.*

CM1895 *George Washington souvenir sheet*

CM1895		MNHVF	UseVF
$7.20	**Pane of 12,** tagged	12.50	10.00
	a. 60¢ single	1.25	.75
	FDC *(May 29, 1997)*		1.00
	Six subject press sheets (3 each of CM1894 & CM1895)	150.00	

Because this issue also was made available to collectors in full six-pane printing sheets, gutter pairs and blocks and cross-gutter multiples also exist.

1997. Marshall Plan 50th Anniversary Issue saluted the post-World War II European Recovery Program unveiled in 1947 by Gen. George C. Marshall (1880-1959). The U.S.-backed, multi-billion-dollar plan to help a devastated Western Europe regain its economic health and halt the expansion of Soviet influence earned Marshall the Nobel Peace Prize. *Offset and Intaglio by Stevens Security Press for Ashton-Potter (USA) Ltd., perforated 11.*

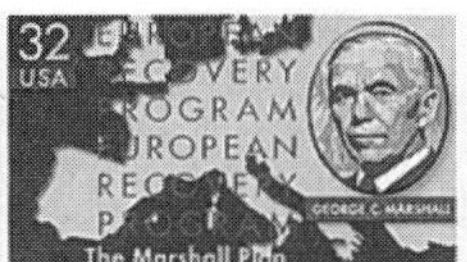

CM1896 *The Marshall Plan*

CM1896		MNHVF	UseVF
32¢	**multicolored** tagged *(45,250,000)*	.50	.20
	Plate block of 4	3.50	
	FDC *(June 4, 1997)*		1.00

1997. Classic American Aircraft Issue was the fifth USPS issue of 20 se-tenant single-theme stamps in a pane with a header across the top and descriptive text on the back of each stamp. This issue showcased 20 U.S. aircraft of the first half-century of powered flight. *Gravure (8,050,000 panes) by Stamp Venturers, perforated 10. Multicolored, block tagged.*

CM1897 *North American P-51 Mustang fighter;* CM1898 *Wright Model B Flyer;* CM1899 *Piper J-3 Cub;* CM1900 *Lockheed Vega;* CM1901 Northrop Alpha; CM1902 *Martin B-10 bomber;* CM1903 Chance Vought Corsair F4U fighter; CM1904 *Boeing B-47 Stratojet bomber;* CM1905 *Gee Bee Super-Sportster;* CM1906 *Beech Model C17L Staggerwing;* CM1907 *Boeing B-17 Flying Fortress bomber;* CM1908 *Stearman PT-13 training aircraft;* CM1909 *Lockheed Constellation;* CM1910 *Lockheed P-38 Lightning fighter;* CM1911 *Boeing P-26 Peashooter fighter;* CM1912 *Ford Tri-Motor;* CM1913 *Douglas DC-3 passenger plane;* CM1914 *Boeing 314 Clipper flying boat;* CM1915 *Curtiss JN-4 Jenny training aircraft;* CM1916 *Grumman F4F Wildcat fighter*

CM1897		MNHVF	UseVF
32¢	**North American P-51 Mustang fighter**	.75	.50
CM1898		MNHVF	UseVF
32¢	**Wright Model B Flyer**	.75	.50
CM1899		MNHVF	UseVF
32¢	**Piper J-3 Cub**	.75	.50
CM1900		MNHVF	UseVF
32¢	**Lockheed Vega**	.75	.50
CM1901		MNHVF	UseVF
32¢	***Northrop Alpha***	.75	.50
CM1902		MNHVF	UseVF
32¢	**Martin B-10 bomber**	.75	.50
CM1903		MNHVF	UseVF
32¢	**Chance Vought Corsair F4U fighter**	.75	.50
CM1904		MNHVF	UseVF
32¢	**Boeing B-47 Stratojet bomber**	.75	.50
CM1905		MNHVF	UseVF
32¢	**Gee Bee Super-Sportster**	.75	.50
CM1906		MNHVF	UseVF
32¢	**Beech Model C17L Staggerwing**	.75	.50
CM1907		MNHVF	UseVF
32¢	**Boeing B-17 Flying Fortress bomber**	.75	.50
CM1908		MNHVF	UseVF
32¢	**Stearman PT-13 training aircraft**	.75	.50
CM1909		MNHVF	UseVF
32¢	**Lockheed Constellation**	.75	.50
CM1910		MNHVF	UseVF
32¢	**Lockheed P-38 Lightning fighter**	.75	.50
CM1911		MNHVF	UseVF
32¢	**Boeing P-26 Peashooter fighter**	.75	.50
CM1912		MNHVF	UseVF
32¢	**Ford Tri-Motor**	.75	.50
CM1913		MNHVF	UseVF
32¢	**Douglas DC-3 passenger plane**	.75	.50
CM1914		MNHVF	UseVF
32¢	**Boeing 314 Clipper flying boat**	.75	.50
CM1915		MNHVF	UseVF
32¢	**Curtiss JN-4 Jenny training aircraft**	.75	.50
CM1916		MNHVF	UseVF
32¢	**Grumman F4F Wildcat fighter**	.75	.50
	FDC *(July 19, 1997)*		1.00
	y. Se-tenant pane of CM1897-1906	15.00	
	FDC		10.00
	Six pane press sheets	150.00	

Because this issue also was made available to collectors in full six-pane printing sheets, gutter pairs and blocks and cross-gutter multiples also exist.

1997. Legendary Football Coaches Issue recalled four of the greatest who ever coached the game in a se-tenant issue released at Canton, Ohio, home of the professional Football Hall of Fame. Slightly revised designs of all four stamps were issued in August in the states where the coaches became famous (CM1937-40). *Offset by Sterling Sommer for Ashton-Potter (USA) Ltd., perforated 11.*

CM1917 *Paul "Bear" Bryant;* CM1918 *Glenn "Pop" Warner;* CM1919 *Vince Lombardi;* CM1920 *George Halas*

CM1917		MNHVF	UseVF
32¢	**Paul "Bear" Bryant,** tagged *(22,500,000)*	.50	.20
CM1918		MNHVF	UseVF
32¢	**Glen "Pop" Warner,** tagged	.50	.20
CM1919		MNHVF	UseVF
32¢	**Vince Lombardi,** tagged	.50	.20

CM1920		MNHVF	UseVF
32¢	**George Halas,** tagged	.50	.20
	Plate block of 4	3.50	
	y. Se-tenant block or strip of CM1917-20	2.00	
	FDC *(July 25, 1997)*		2.00

1997. Classic American Dolls Issue depicted these beloved toys of childhood (and, increasingly, collectibles for adults) dating from as far back as the 1850s up to the 1960s in a commemorative 15-stamp pane with a banner and descriptions in the margins. *Offset (7,000,000 panes) by Sterling Sommer for Ashton-Potter (USA) Ltd., perforated 11. Multicolored, tagged (July 28, 1997)*

CLASSIC
American Dolls
The above names include doll makers, designers, trade names and common names.

CM1921 *"Alabama Baby" and Martha Chase Doll;* CM1922 *Rutta Sisters "The Columbian Doll";* CM1923 *Johnny Gruelle's "Raggedy Ann";* CM1924 *Martha Chase Cloth Doll;* CM1925 *Effanbee Doll Co. "American Child";* CM1926 *Ideal Novelty & Toy Co. "Baby Coos";* CM1927 *Plains Indian Doll 1920s;* CM1928 *Izannah Walker Oil-Painted Cloth Doll;* CM1929 *All-Cloth "Babyland Rag" Doll;* CM1930 *Rose O'Neill "Scootles" Doll;* CM1931 *Ludwig Greiner First U.S. Patent Doll;* CM1932 *"Betsy McCall" American Character Doll;* CM1933 *Percy Crosby's "Skippy";* CM1934 *Alexander Doll Co. "Maggie Mix-up";* CM1935 *Schoenut "All Word Perfection Art Dolls";*

CM1921		MNHVF	UseVF
32¢	**"Alabama Baby" and Martha Chase Doll**	.75	.50
CM1922		MNHVF	UseVF
32¢	**Rutta Sisters "The Columbian Doll"**	.75	.50
CM1923		MNHVF	UseVF
32¢	**Johnny Gruelle's "Raggedy Ann"**	.75	.50
CM1924		MNHVF	UseVF
32¢	**Martha Chase Cloth Doll**	.75	.50
CM1925		MNHVF	UseVF
32¢	**Effanbee Doll Co. "American Child"**	.75	.50
CM1926		MNHVF	UseVF
32¢	**Ideal Novelty & Toy Co. "Baby Coos"**	.75	.50
CM1927		MNHVF	UseVF
32¢	**Plains Indian Doll 1920s**	.75	.50
CM1928		MNHVF	UseVF
32¢	**Izannah Walker Oil-Painted Cloth Doll**	.75	.50
CM1929		MNHVF	UseVF
32¢	**All-Cloth "Babyland Rag" Doll**	.75	.50
CM1930		MNHVF	UseVF
32¢	**Rose O'Neill "Scootles" Doll**	.75	.50
CM1931		MNHVF	UseVF
32¢	**Ludwig Greiner First U.S. Patent Doll**	.75	.50
CM1932		MNHVF	UseVF
32¢	**"Betsy McCall" American Character Doll**	.75	.50
CM1933		MNHVF	UseVF
32¢	**Percy Crosby's "Skippy"**	.75	.50
CM1934		MNHVF	UseVF
32¢	**Alexander Doll Co. "Maggie Mix-up"**	.75	.50
CM1935		MNHVF	UseVF
32¢	**Schoenut "All Word Perfection Art Dolls"**	.75	.50
	FDC *(July 28, 1997)* any single		1.00
	y. Se-tenant pane of CM1921-35	12.50	
	y. FDC, pane of 15		10.00

1997. Humphrey Bogart Issue third in the Legends of Hollywood Series, was a 20-stamp commemorative pane with a large area of selvage displaying a portrait of the actor on the stamp. Bogart was one of the giants of American film in the 1930s and '40s in such movies as *Casablanca, The Maltese Falcon* and *To Have and Have Not.* Bogart was nominated for an Academy Award for *Treasure of the Sierra Madre* and *The Caine Mutiny,* and finally won an Oscar for *The African Queen. Gravure by Stamp Venturers, perforated 11.*

CM1936 *Humphrey Bogart*

CM1936		MNHVF	UseVF
32¢	**multicolored** tagged *(195,000,000)*	.50	.20
	FDC *(July 31, 1997)*		1.00
	Plate block of 4	3.50	
	y. Pane of 20	8.00	
	Six subject press sheet	125.00	

Because this issue also was made available to collectors in full six-pane printing sheets, gutter pairs and blocks and cross-gutter multiples also exist.

1997. Vince Lombardi Issue recalled the legendary coach of the Green Bay Packers, a member of the Pro Football Hall of Fame, with a stamp issued in Green Bay, Wis., similar to CM1917 but with a red bar over Lombardi's name. *Printed by Sterling Sommer for Ashton-Potter (USA) Ltd., perforated 11.*

CM1937 *Vince Lombardi*

CM1937		MNHVF	UseVF
32¢	**multicolored** tagged *(20,000,000)*	.50	.20
	FDC *(Aug. 5, 1997)*		1.00
	Plate block of 4	3.50	
	y. Pane of 20	10.00	

1997. Paul "Bear" Bryant Issue honored the fabled coach of the University of Alabama — "the Crimson Tide" — with a stamp issued in Tuscaloosa, Ala., similar to CM1918 but with a red bar over Bryant's name. *Printed by Sterling Sommer for Ashton-Potter (USA) Ltd., perforated 11.*

CM1938 *Paul "Bear" Bryant*

CM1938		MNHVF	UseVF
32¢	**multicolored** tagged *(20,000,000)*	.50	.20
	FDC *(Aug. 7, 1997)*		1.00
	Plate block of 4	3.50	
	y. Pane of 20	10.50	

1997. Glen "Pop" Warner Issue commemorated the outstanding LaSalle University coach who gave his name to the nationwide Pop Warner Youth Football League with a stamp issued in Philadelphia, Pa., similar to CM1919 but with a red bar over Warner's name. *Printed by Sterling Sommer for Ashton-Potter (USA) Ltd., perforated 11.*

CM1939 *Glen "Pop" Warner*

CM1939		MNHVF	UseVF
32¢	**multicolored** tagged *(10,000,000)*	.50	.20
	FDC *(Aug. 8, 1997)*		1.00
	Plate block of 4	3.50	
	y. Pane of 20	10.00	

1997. George Halas Issue recalled the longtime coach of the Chicago Bears, a member of the Pro Football Hall of Fame, with a stamp issued in Chicago, Ill., similar to CM1920 but with a red bar over Halas' name. *Printed by Sterling Sommer for Ashton-Potter (USA) Ltd., perforated 11.*

CM1940 *George Halas*

CM1940		MNHVF	UseVF
32¢	**multicolored** tagged *(10,000,000)*	.50	.20
	FDC *(Aug. 16, 1997)*		1.00
	Plate block of 4	3.50	
	y. Pane of 20	10.00	

1997. "The Stars And Stripes Forever" Issue saluted the centennial of the premiere of "The Stars and Stripes Forever!" arguably the best-loved and most frequently played composition of John Philip Sousa (CM222), the celebrated "March King." *Gravure by B.E.P., perforated 11 1/2.*

CM1941 *"The Stars and Stripes Forever!"*

CM1941		MNHVF	UseVF
32¢	**multicolored** tagged *(323,000,000)*	.50	.20
	Plate block of 4	3.50	
	FDC *(Aug. 21, 1997)*		1.00

1997. Opera Singers Issue in the American Music Series was a se-tenant quartet of renowned vocalists in costumes from their greatest roles, celebrating the 400th anniversary of their art, which originated in 16th-century Florence, Italy. Lily Pons (1898-1976), a diminutive coloratura, made her debut at New York's Metropolitan Opera in 1931 as the heroine of *Lucia di Lammermoor.* Tenor Richard Tucker (1913-75), depicted in foreground of his stamp as the Duke in Verdi's *Rigoletto,* enjoyed a 30-year career at the Met and was regarded as the nation's foremost opera performer of the postwar era. Baritone Lawrence Tibbett (1896-1960), celebrated as the first American male to achieve operatic stardom in his own right, is portrayed as the Toreador in *Carmen,* one of many roles in which he excelled. A 21-year-old soprano, Rosa Ponselle (1897-1981), held her own opposite Caruso at the Met's premiere of Verdi's *La Forza del Destino,* much to the delight of critics and audiences as well, and is pictured in her costume from *Norma. Offset by Ashton-Potter (USA) Ltd., perforated 11.*

CM1942 *Lily Pons;* CM1943 *Richard Tucker;* CM1944 *Lawrence Tibbett;* CM1945 *Rosa Ponselle*

CM1942		MNHVF	UseVF
32¢	**Lily Pons,** tagged *(21,500,000)*	.50	.20
CM1943		MNHVF	UseVF
32¢	**Richard Tucker,** tagged	.50	.20
CM1944		MNHVF	UseVF
32¢	**Lawrence Tibbett,** tagged	.50	.20
CM1945		MNHVF	UseVF
32¢	**Rosa Ponselle,** tagged	.50	.20
	Plate block of 4	3.50	
	FDC *(Sept. 10, 1997)* any single		1.00
	y. Se-tenant block or strip of CM1942-45	3.50	
	FDC		3.00
	Pane of 20	8.00	

1997. Classical Composers and Conductors Issue in the American Music Series celebrated four composers and four conductors in a se-tenant 20-stamp pane. Leopold Stokowski began conducting the Cincinnati Symphony at the age of 27, and in 1912 moved to Philadelphia where he was to wield the baton for more than 25 years, making that city's symphony orchestra one of the finest in the world. Arthur Fiedler, who began as a viola player in the Boston Symphony, gained world fame and brought classical music to vast new audiences as conductor of the Boston Pops Orchestra. George Szell fashioned the Cleveland Orchestra into one of the finest in the nation. Eugene Ormandy was musical director of the Philadelphia Symphony for over 35 years, and in 1948 conducted the first symphony concert on American television. Composer Samuel Barber won the Pulitzer Prize for his operas *Vanessa* and his *Piano Concerto.* Composer, pianist and arranger Ferde Grofe brilliantly scored Gershwin's *Rhapsody In Blue* for the symphony in 1924, and merged jazz and simple ballads with equal creativity in his own compositions. Charles Ives was an innovative composer who used daring techniques to mold hymns and folk tunes into unusual symphonies. Louis Moreau Gottschalk gained international celebrity as a dazzling pianist whose compositions were built on the Creole rhythms of his native New Orleans. *Offset by Sterling Sommer for Ashton-Potter (USA) Ltd., perforated 11.*

CM1946 *Leopold Stokowski;* CM1947 *Arthur Fiedler;* CM1948 *George Szell;* CM1949 *Eugene Ormandy;* CM1950 *Samuel Barber;* CM1951 *Ferde Grofe;* CM1952 *Charles Ives;* CM1953 *Louis Moreau Gottschalk*

		MNHVF	UseVF
CM1946			
32¢	**Leopold Stokowski,** tagged *(4,300,000)* *20-stamp panes*	.50	.20
CM1947		MNHVF	UseVF
32¢	**Arthur Fiedler,** tagged	.50	.20
CM1948		MNHVF	UseVF
32¢	**George Szell,** tagged	.50	.20
CM1949		MNHVF	UseVF
32¢	**Eugene Ormandy,** tagged	.50	.20
CM1950		MNHVF	UseVF
32¢	**Samuel Barber,** tagged	.50	.20
CM1951		MNHVF	UseVF
32¢	**Ferde Grofe,** tagged	.50	.20
CM1952		MNHVF	UseVF
32¢	**Charles Ives,** tagged	.50	.20
CM1953		MNHVF	UseVF
32¢	**Louis Moreau Gottschalk,** tagged	.50	.20
	Plate block of 10	5.00	
	FDC *(Sept. 12, 1997)* any single		1.00
	y. Se-tenant block of CM1946-53	4.00	
	FDC		3.50
	y1. Pane of 20	8.00	

1997. Padre Felix Varela Issue memorialized the priest, educator and social reformer whose humanitarian works for more than 30 years earned him high esteem. Varela (1788-1853) was educated in Cuba but is best known for his work in New York City, beginning in the 1820s, when he concentrated on helping the poor, organized the New York Catholic Temperance Association, founded nurseries and orphanages and risked infection during an 1832 cholera epidemic. He also founded the first Hispanic newspaper in the United States, which chronicled social injustice, urged religious and ethnic tolerence and promoted the importance of education. The stamp is notable for its use of the microprinted letters "USPS" to form Varela's portrait. *Offset by Sterling Sommer for Ashton-Potter (USA) Ltd., perforated 11 3/4.*

CM1954 *Padre Felix Varela*

		MNHVF	UseVF
CM1954			
32¢	**purple** tagged *(25,250,000)*	.50	.20
	FDC *(Sept. 15, 1997)*		1.00
	Plate block of 4	3.50	
	y. Pane of 20	7.50	

1997. U.S. Department of the Air Force Issue marked the 50th anniversary of the youngest branch of the U.S. armed forces as a separate military department. The stamp shows the Thunderbirds USAF demonstration team flying its custom-painted F-18 jet fighters in close "Diamond-Four" formation. This also was the first U.S. issue to include hidden images in the background of the stamp, designs visible only with a special USPS "Stamp Decoder." *Offset by Sterling Sommer for Ashton-Potter (USA) Ltd., perforated 11.*

CM1955 *U.S. Department of the Air Force*

		MNHVF	UseVF
CM1955			
32¢	**multicolored** tagged *(45,250,000)*	.50	.20
	FDC *(Sept. 18, 1997)*		1.00
	Plate block of 4	3.50	
	y. Pane of 20	7.50	

1997. Classic Movie Monsters Issue a 20-stamp pane with a banner across the top released for National Stamp Collecting Month saluted monsters from Universal Studios films of the 1920s, '30s, and '40s and the actors who brought them to life. The stamps included hidden images to be viewed with the USPS decoder. *Gravure by Stamp Venturers, perforated 10.*

CM1956 *Lon Chaney,* as The Phantom of the Opera; CM1957 *Bela Lugosi,* as Dracula; CM1958 *Boris Karloff,* in Frankenstein; CM1959 *Boris Karloff,* as The Mummy; CM1960 *Lon Chaney Jr.,* as The Wolf Man

		MNHVF	UseVF
CM1956			
32¢	**Lon Chaney, as Phantom of the Opera,** *(29,000,000)*	.50	.20
CM1957		MNHVF	UseVF
32¢	**Bela Lugosi, as Dracula,** tagged	.50	.20
CM1958		MNHVF	UseVF
32¢	**Boris Karloff, in Frankenstein,** tagged	.50	.20
CM1959		MNHVF	UseVF
32¢	**Boris Karloff, as The Mummy,** tagged	.50	.20
CM1960		MNHVF	UseVF
32¢	**Lon Chaney Jr., as The Wolf Man,** tagged	.50	.20
	Plate block of 10	5.00	
	FDC *(Sept. 30, 1997)* any single		1.00
	y. Se-tenant strip of CM1956-60	4.00	
	FDC		4.00
	y1. Pane of 20	8.00	
	Press sheets of 9 panes	150.00	

Because this issue also was made available to collectors in full nine-pane printing sheets, gutter pairs and blocks and cross-gutter multiples also exist.

1997. First Supersonic Flight Issue a self-adhesive stamp hailed the 50th anniversary of the historic 1947 flight at Edwards Air Force Base in which a Bell X-1 rocket aircraft piloted by Chuck Yeager became the first to break the sound barrier and travel faster than Mach 1. *Offset by Banknote Corp. of America, serpentine roulette 11 1/2.*

CM1961 *First supersonic flight*

		MNHVF	UseVF
CM1961			
32¢	**multicolored** tagged *(173,000,000)*	.50	.20
	FDC *(Oct. 14, 1997)*		1.00
	Plate block of 4	3.50	
	y. Pane of 20	7.50	

1997. Women in Military Service Issue saluted the nearly 2 million women who have served in the U.S. armed forces in conjunction with the Oct. 18 dedication of the Women in Military Service for America Memorial in Arlington National Cemetery near Washington, D.C. (See also CM355). *Offset by Banknote Corp. of America, perforated 11.*

CM1962 *Women in military service*

CM1962		MNHVF	UseVF
32¢	**multicolored** tagged *(37,000,000)*	.50	.20
	FDC *(Oct. 18, 1997)*		1.00
	Plate block of 4	3.50	
	y. Pane of 20	7.50	

1997. Kwanzaa Issue a colorful self-adhesive design and the second annual installment in the Postal Service's Holiday Celebration Series, honored the non-sectarian African-American festival of family, community and culture that takes its name from the Swahili phrase meaning "first fruits." Available in panes of 50 or booklets of 15. *Gravure by Avery Dennison Security Printing Division, serpentine die cut 11.*

CM1963 *Kwanzaa*

CM1963		MNHVF	UseVF
32¢	**multicolored** tagged *(133,000,000)*	.50	.20
	FDC *(Oct. 22, 1997)*		1.00
	Plate block of 4	3.50	
	n. Booklet of 15	6.00	
	Six subject press sheet	150.00	

Because this issue also was made available to collectors in full six-pane printing sheets, gutter pairs and blocks and cross-gutter multiples also exist.

1998. Year of The Tiger New Year Issue the sixth in the Lunar New Year Series. *Gravure by Stamp Venturers, perforated 11.*

CM1964 *Year of The Tiger*

CM1964		MNHVF	UseVF
32¢	**multicolored** tagged	.50	.20
	FDC *(Jan. 5, 1998)*		1.50
	Plate block of 4	2.00	
	y. Pane of 20	7.50	

1998. Winter Sports Issue celebrated alpine skiing. The USPS circumvented the licensing fee to the International Olympic Committee for use of the five-ring trademark, and still was able to honor the games held in Nagano, Japan; thus this is a substitute Winter Olympics stamp. *Banknote Corporation of America, perforated 11.*

CM1965 *Winter sports - alpine skier*

CM1965		MNHVF	UseVF
32¢	**multicolored** tagged	.50	.20
	FDC *(Jan. 22, 1998)*		1.50
	Plate block of 4	2.00	1.50
	y. Pane of 20	7.50	

1998. Madam C.J. Walker Issue in the Black Heritage Series saluted, with a self-adhesive stamp, the successful cosmetic and hair-care products businesswoman of the early 20th century. She earned praise as a philanthropist championing such causes as the NAACP and Tuskegee Institute. The portrait photo is from the Scurlock Studio. *Offset, Banknote Corporation of America. Serpentine die cut.*

CM1966 *Madam C.J. Walker*

CM1966		MNHVF	UseVF
32¢	**multicolored** tagged	.50	.20
	Plate block of 4	2.00	
	y. Pane of 20	7.50	
	FDC *(Jan. 28, 1998)*		1.50

Celebrate the Century Series

1998. Celebrate the Century 1900s Issue was the first of a series of distinctive commemorative panes of 15 stamps that highlighted notable events, personalities and things of each decade of the 20th century. Historical text is printed on the back of each stamp. *Offset, with one intaglio stamp in the pane, printed by Ashton-Potter USA, perforated 11 3/4.*

CM1967 *Celebrate the Century 1900s*

CM1967		MNHVF	UseVF
$4.80	**Pane of 15,** tagged	12.50	9.50
	a. Model T Ford	.50	.50

b. President Theodore Roosevelt	.50	.50
c. The Great Train Robbery	.50	.50
d. Crayola Crayons	.50	.50
e. 1904 St. Louis World's Fair	.50	.50
f. 1906 Pure Food and Drugs Act	.50	.50
g. Kitty Hawk (1903)	.50	.50
h. Ash Can Painters	.50	.50
i. Immigrants Arrive	.50	.50
j. John Muir Preservationist	.50	.50
k. "Teddy" Bear Created	.50	.50
l. W.E.B. DuBois, Social Activist	.50	.50
m. Gibson Girl (intaglio)	.50	.50
n. First World Series	.50	.50
o. Robie House, Chicago	.50	.50
FDC *(Feb. 3, 1998)* any single		2.00
Pane of 15, red engraved omitted (one known)	—	

1998. Celebrate the Century 1910s Issue was the second pane of 15 stamps in the series. *Offset, with one intaglio stamp in the pane, by Ashton-Potter USA, perforated 11 3/4.*

CM1968 *Celebrate the Century 1910s*

CM1968		MNHVF	UseVF
$4.80	**Pane of 15,** tagged	12.50	9.50
	a. Charlie Chaplin	.50	.50
	b. Federal Reserve (intaglio)	.50	.50
	c. George Washington Carver	.50	.50
	d. Armory Show	.50	.50
	e. Transcontinental phone line	.50	.50
	f. Panama Canal	.50	.50
	g. Jim Thorpe	.50	.50
	h. Grand Canyon	.50	.50
	i. World War I	.50	.50
	j. Scouting	.50	.50
	k. Woodrow Wilson	.50	.50
	l. Crossword puzzle	.50	.50
	m. Jack Dempsey	.50	.50
	n. Construction toys	.50	.50
	o. Child labor	.50	.50
	v. Pane of 15, 5 stamps imperforate (one known)	—	
	FDC *(Feb. 3, 1998)* any single		2.00

1998. Spanish American War Issue marked the centennial of this very short hostility, which began after the sinking of the battleship *Maine* in Havana harbor. *Printed by B.E.P., perforated 11 1/4.*

CM1969 *Battleship* Maine

CM1969		MNHVF	UseVF
32¢	**red & black** tagged	.50	.20
	Plate block of 4	2.00	
	y. Pane of 20	7.50	
	FDC *(Feb. 15, 1998)*		1.50

1998. Flowering Trees Issue highlighted in self-adhesive form these native North American trees. *Offset, serpentine die cut 11 1/4, printed by Banknote Corporation of America.*

CM1970-1974 *Flowering trees*

		MNHVF	UseVF
CM1970			
32¢	**Southern Magnolia,** tagged	.50	.20
CM1971			
32¢	**Blue Paloverde,** tagged	.50	.20
CM1972			
32¢	**Yellow Poplar,** tagged	.50	.20
CM1973			
32¢	**Prairie Crab Apple,** tagged	.50	.20
CM1974			
32¢	**Pacific Dogwood,** tagged	.50	.20
	FDC, *(March 19, 1998)* any single		1.50
	a. Strip of 5 (CM1970-74)	3.00	
	y. Pane of 20	7.50	
	Plate block of 10	5.50	

1998. Alexander Calder Issue honored the abstract sculptor on the centennial of his birth. His dramatic mobiles and stabiles helped popularize the art form. *Gravure, Stamp Venturers, perforated 10 1/4.*

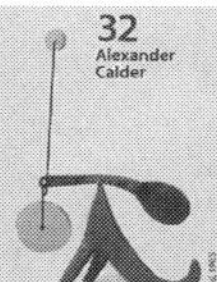
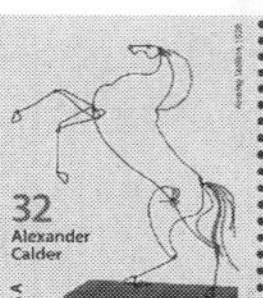

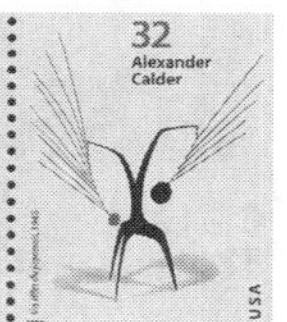

CM1975-1979 *Calder sculptures*

		MNHVF	UseVF
CM1975			
32¢	**Black Cascade, 13 verticals,** tagged	.50	.20
CM1976			
32¢	**Untitled,** tagged	.50	.20
CM1977			
32¢	**Rearing Stallion,** tagged	.50	.20
CM1978			
32¢	**Portrait of a young man,** tagged	.50	.20
CM1979			
32¢	**Un Effet du Japonais,** tagged	.50	.20
	FDC *(March 25, 1998)* any single		1.50
	Plate block of 10	4.50	
	a. Strip of 5 (CM1975-79)	2.00	
	y. Pane of 20	7.50	

1998. Cinco de Mayo Issue honored the festival of Mexican Heritage commemorating the Mexican victory over French invaders at the Battle of Puebla in 1862. The stamp, a joint issue with Mexico, (Mexico 2946), featured a couple dancing in traditional costumes. A 33¢ version (CM2055), with the same design was released in 1999. *Self-adhesive, Gravure, Stamp Venturers, serpentine die cut 11 3/4 x 11.*

CM1980 *Cinco de Mayo festival*

CM1980		MNHVF	UseVF
32¢	**multicolored**	.50	.20
	FDC *(April 16, 1998)*		1.50
	Plate block of 4	2.00	
	y. Pane of 20	7.50	

1998. Sylvester and Tweety Issue second in the Warner Bros. Cartoon Characters Series, pictured the two cartoon antagonists. *Self-adhesive, Gravure, printed by Avery Dennison, serpentine die cut 11 1/4 x 11.*

CM1981 *Sylvester and Tweety*

CM1981		MNHVF	UseVF
$3.20	**Pane of 10,** tagged	5.00	
	n. Right half of pane (single die cut CM1981a superimposed on enlarged image in right selvege)	1.00	
	n1. Left half of pane (block of 9 CM1981a)	5.00	
	a. 32¢ single	.50	.25
	6 pane top press sheet	175.00	
	6 pane bottom press sheet	225.00	
	FDC *(April 27, 1998)* single		1.50

1998. Sylvester and Tweety Issue *self-adhesive — Gravure, printed by Avery Dennison, 9 stamps serpentine die cut, and one imperforate on right panel.*

CM1982		MNHVF	UseVF
$3.20	**Pane of 10,** tagged	5.00	
	n. Right half of pane (single imperforate CM1982a) enlarged image in right selvege	1.00	
	n1. Left half of pane (block of 9 CM1982a)	5.00	
	a. 32¢ single	.50	

This issue also was made available in top and bottom half printing sheets of six 10-stamp panes each. Vertical rouletting between the two panes is missing on these half sheets. A plate number, trimmed away or individual panes, appears adjacent to the bottom-left pane in the bottom half of the printing sheet only.

1998. Breast Cancer Research Semipostal Issue the first official money-raising U.S. stamp, raised $7.8 million in one year of sales. The undenominated First Class stamp sold for 40¢, with the amount over standard postage (8¢ before the rate increase in 1999, then 7¢ and 6¢ after the rate increase to 34¢ in 2001) earmarked for cancer research. By August 2001, sales had generated $21.5 million for research. *Self-adhesive, printed by Avery Dennison, serpentine, die cut.*

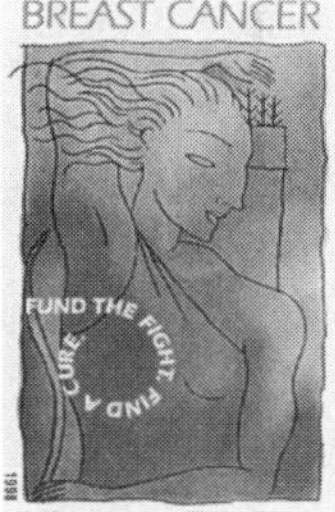

CMSP1 *Breast cancer self-examination*

CMSP1		MNHVF	UseVF
40¢	**multicolored**	.75	.20
	Plate block of 4	3.00	
	FDC *(July 29, 1998)*		1.25

1998. Celebrate the Century, 1920s Issue was the third in the series honoring each decade of the 20th Century. *Offset, with one intaglio stamp in the pane, printed by Ashton-Potter USA, perforated 11 3/4.*

CM1983 *Celebrate the Century 1920s*

CM1983		MNHVF	UseVF
$4.80	**Sheetlet of 15,** tagged	15.00	9.50
	a. Babe Ruth	.75	.50
	b. The Gatsby Style	.75	.50
	c. Prohibition Enforced	.75	.50
	d. Electric toy trains	.75	.50
	e. 19th Amendment	.75	.50
	f. Emily Post's Etiquette	.75	.50
	g. Margaret Mead, Anthropologist	.75	.50
	h. Flappers do the Charleston	.75	.50
	i. Radio Entertains America	.75	.50
	j. Art Deco style	.75	.50
	k. Jazz flourishes	.75	.50

l.	Four Horsemen of Notre Dame	.75	.50
m.	Lindbergh Flies Atlantic (intaglio)	.75	.50
n.	American Realism	.75	.50
o.	Stock Market Crash of 1929	.75	.50
	FDC *(May 28, 1998)* any single		2.00

1998. Wisconsin Statehood Sesquicentennial Issue honored the 1848 entry of Wisconsin as the 40th state in the Union. Sale of the stamp was restricted. It contains a hidden image of a badger, the state animal, in the sky, visible only with a USPS Decoder. *Self-adhesive, printed by American Packaging Corp. for Sennett Security Products, serpentine die cut 11.*

CM1984 *Door County farm scene*

CM1984		MNHVF	UseVF
32¢	**multicolored**	.50	.20
	Plate block of 4	1.50	
	Pane of 20	7.50	
	FDC *(May 29, 1998)*		1.50

1998. Trans-Mississippi Color Issue highlighted nine views of westward expansion. Orginally issued in single colors for the 1898 Trans-Mississippi Exposition held in Omaha, Neb. *Gravure, printed by Banknote Corp. of America, perforated 12 1/4 x 12 1/2.*

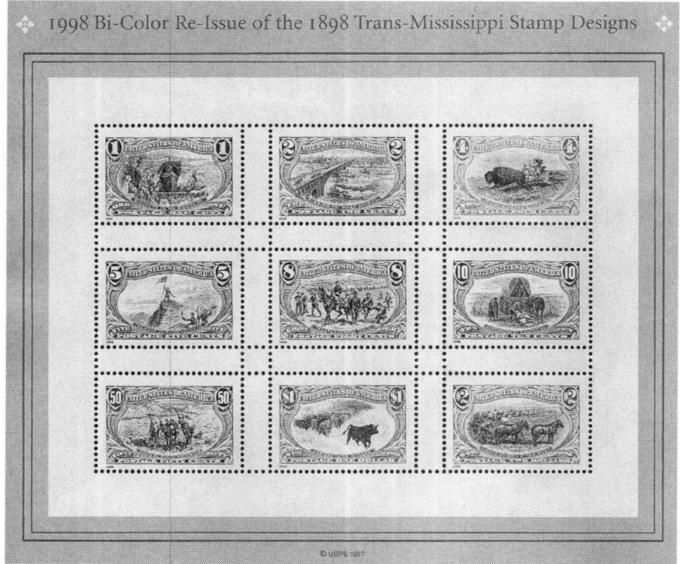

CM1985 *1898 Trans-Mississippi*

CM1985		MNHVF	UseVF
$3.80	**Pane of 9**	7.50	3.50
	a. **1¢** dark green & black	.25	.20
	b. **2¢** copper red & black	.25	.20
	c. **4¢** orange & black	.25	.20
	d. **5¢** dark blue & black	.25	.20
	e. **8¢** dark lilac & black	.25	.20
	f. **10¢** purple & black	.50	.50
	g. **50¢** olive & black	1.50	.50
	h. **$1.00** red & black	2.00	.50
	i. **$2.00** brown & black	3.00	1.00
	FDC *(June 18, 1998)*, pane of 9		10.75
	Uncut press sheet of 3-9 design CM1985a-i	50.00	

1998. Trans-Mississippi Color Issue highlighted nine views of westward expansion. Orginally issued in single colors for the 1898 Trans-Mississippi Exposition held in Omaha, Neb. *Gravure, printed by Banknote Corp. of America, perforated 12 1/4 x 12 1/2.*

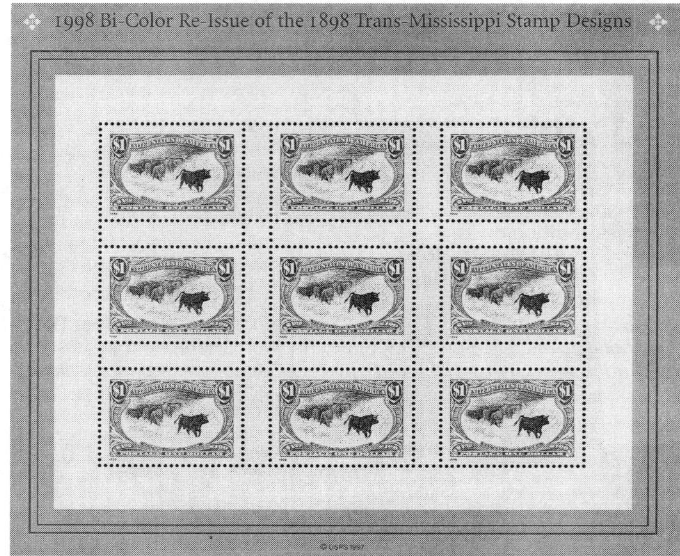

CM1985 *1898 Trans-Mississippi*

CM1986		MNHVF	UseVF
$9	**Pane,** 9 examples of CM1985h	15.00	
	FDC *(June 18, 1998)*, pane of 9		15.00
	Uncut press sheet of 3-9 cattle CM1986	50.00	

1998. Berlin Airlift Issue commemorated the 50th anniversary of the U.S. Air Force operation to assist the citizens of war-ravaged Berlin from a land and water blockade set up by the Soviets. The flights of C-47s and C-54s lasted from June 26, 1948, through Sept. 30, 1949. *Offset by Banknote Corporation of America, perforated 11.*

CM1987 *Berliners watching arriving C-54*

CM1987		MNHVF	UseVF
32¢	**multicolored**	.50	.20
	Plate block of 4	1.50	
	y. Pane of 20	7.50	
	FDC *(June 26, 1998)*		2.00

1998. Folk Musicians Issue in the American Music Series honored four performers whose songs reflected the soul of America. Woodrow "Woody" Guthrie (1912-1967), maybe the most famous folk singer of all time, wrote 1,000 songs, including "This Land Is Your Land" and "So Long, It's Been Good To Know You." Sonny Terry (1911-1986), a blind harmonica player, also produced an array of sounds on the harp. "Leadbelly" Ledbetter (1888-1949), master of the 12-string guitar, drew upon the breadth of southern black music and wrote the popular sentimental hit, "Goodnight Irene." Josh White (1908-1969) played guitar for President Franklin Roosevelt at the White House. A favorite song was "Careless Love." Gravure, American Packaging Corp. for Sennett Security Products, perforated 10 1/4.

CM1988 *Woody Guthrie;* CM1989 *Sonny Terry;* CM1990 *Huddie "Leadbelly" Ledbetter;* CM1991 *Josh White*

CM1988		MNHVF	UseVF
32¢	**Woody Guthrie,** tagged	.50	.20
CM1989		MNHVF	UseVF
32¢	**Sonny Terry,** tagged	.50	.20
CM1990		MNHVF	UseVF
32¢	**Huddie "Leadbelly" Ledbetter**	.50	.20
CM1991		MNHVF	UseVF
32¢	**Josh White**	.50	.20
	FDC *(June 26, 1998)* any single		2.00
	Plate block of 4	1.50	
	y. Pane of 20	7.50	
	FDC, block or strip of 4		4.25

1998. Spanish Settlement of the Southwest Issue noted the 400th anniversary of the oldest European road in the southwestern U.S., "El Camino Real de Tierra Adentro" (the royal road to the interior land), and the founding of the settlement of San Gabriel in what is now New Mexico. The mission replica in Española, N. Mex., is depicted. *Offset by Banknote Corporation of America, perforated 11 1/4.*

CM1992 *Mission de San Miguel de San Gabriel*

CM1992		MNHVF	UseVF
32¢	**multicolored**	.50	.20
	FDC *(July 11, 1998)*		2.00
	Plate block of 4	1.50	
	y. Pane of 20	7.50	

1998. Gospel Singers Issue in the American Music Series. Mahalia Jackson's magnificent voice and fervent faith made her gospel music's first superstar. Clara Ward was the leader of the most successful female gospel group of the 1950s. Roberta Martin founded the Roberta Martin Singers. Sister Rosetta Tharpe was the first gospel singer to record with a major record company. *Gravure. American Packaging Corp. for Sennett Security Products.*

CM1993 *Mahalia Jackson;* CM1994 *Roberta Martin;* CM1995 *Clara Ward;* CM1996 *Sister Rosetta Tharpe*

CM1993		MNHVF	UseVF
32¢	**Mahalia Jackson**	.50	2.00
CM1994		MNHVF	UseVF
32¢	**Roberta Martin**	.50	.20
CM1995		MNHVF	UseVF
32¢	**Clara Ward**	.50	.20
CM1996		MNHVF	UseVF
32¢	**Sister Rosetta Tharpe**	.50	.20
	FDC *(July 15, 1998)* any single		2.00
	Plate block of 4	1.50	
	y. Pane of 20	7.50	
	FDC, strip or block of 4		5.00

1998. Stephen Vincent Benét Issue 16th in the Literary Arts Series honored the poet (1898-1943) on his birth centennial. Pulitzer Prize winning author of *John Brown's Body* and *The Devil and Daniel Webster.* Benét's portrait is set against part of Augustus St. Gauden's Shaw Memorial on Boston Common. *Offset by Sterling Sommer for Ashton-Potter, with microprinting "John Brown's Body" on rifle barrel under "B." Perforated 11.*

CM1997 *Stephen Vincent Benét*

CM1997		MNHVF	UseVF
32¢	**multicolored**	.50	.20
	FDC *(July 22, 1998)*		2.00
	Plate block of 4	1.50	
	Pane of 10	7.50	

1998. Tropical Birds Issue featured two birds of Puerto Rico, and one each from the the rain forest of Maui and the island of Samoa. *Offset, Banknote Corporation of America, perforated 11.*

CM1998-2001 *Tropical Birds*

CM1998		MNHVF	UseVF
32¢	**Antillean Euphonia**	.50	.20
CM1999		MNHVF	UseVF
32¢	**Green-throated Carib**	.50	.20
CM2000		MNHVF	UseVF
32¢	**Crested Honeycreeper**	.50	.20
CM2001		MNHVF	UseVF
32¢	**Cardinal Honeyeater**	.50	.20
	FDC *(July 29, 1998)* any single		2.00
	Plate block of 4	2.00	
	y. Pane of 20	7.50	
	FDC, strip or block of 4		5.50

1998. Alfred Hitchcock Issue in the Legends of Hollywood Series honored the British born director (1899-1980) who became an American citizen. He was a master of dramatic suspense. The caricature sketch at upper left on the stamp is die cut, not printed. *Printed by Sennett Security Products, perforated 11 1/4.*

CM2002 *Alfred Hitchcock*

CM2002		MNHVF	UseVF
32¢	**black & gray**	.75	.20
	FDC *(Aug. 3, 1998)*		2.00
	Plate block of 4	2.00	
	y. Pane of 20	8.50	

1998. Organ & Tissue Donation Issue called attention to a life-saving medical practice. *Self-adhesive. Printed by Avery Dennison. Serpentine die cut.*

CM2003 *Organ & Tissue Donation*

CM2003		MNHVF	UseVF
32¢	**multicolored**	.50	.20
	FDC *(Aug. 5, 1998)*		1.00

1998. Bright Eyes Pet Issue aimed at children, showed bug-eyed examples of popular pets. *Self-adhesive die cut, printed by Banknote Corporation of America.*

CM2004 *Dog*

CM2005 *Goldfish*

CM2006 *Cat*

CM2007 *Parakeet*

CM2008 *Hamster*

		MNHVF	UseVF
CM2004			
32¢	**Dog,** tagged	.50	.20
CM2005			
32¢	**Goldfish,** tagged	.50	.20
CM2006			
32¢	**Cat,** tagged	.50	.20
CM2007			
32¢	**Parakeet,** tagged	.50	.20
CM2008			
32¢	**Hamster,** tagged	.50	.20
	FDC (Aug. 20, 1998), any single		1.90
	y. Pane of 20	7.50	
	FDC, strip of 5		5.50

1998. Klondike Gold Rush Issue dramatically portrayed the gold-seekers who crossed Alaska to the Klondike gold fields a century earlier. *Printed by Ashton-Potter, perforated 11.*

CM2009 *Klondike Gold Rush*

		MNHVF	UseVF
CM2009			
32¢	**multicolored** tagged	.50	.20
	y. Pane of 20	7.50	
	FDC *(August 21, 1998)*		1.90

Each entry in this catalog has been double-checked for accuracy, but mistakes may creep into any human endeavor, and we ask your assistance in eliminating them. Please call the attention of the editors to any errors in stamp description found in this catalog. Send your comments to:

Minkus Catalog Editor
Krause Publications
700 E. State St.
Iola WI 54990

1998. American Art Issue featured works of four centuries of American Artists. *Sennett Security Products, perforated 10 1/2 x 10.*

CM2010-2029

		MNHVF	UseVF
CM2010			
32¢	**John Foster**	.50	.20
CM2011			
32¢	**The Freake Limner**	.50	.20
CM2012			
32¢	**Ammi Phillips**	.50	.20
CM2013			
32¢	**Rembrandt Peale**	.50	.20
CM2014			
32¢	**John J. Audubon**	.50	.20
CM2015			
32¢	**George Caleb Bingham**	.50	.20
CM2016			
32¢	**Asher B. Durand**	.50	.20
CM2017			
32¢	**Joshua Johnson**	.50	.20
CM2018			
32¢	**William M. Harnett**	.50	.20
CM2019			
32¢	**Winslow Homer**	.50	.20
CM2020			
32¢	**George Catlin**	.50	.20
CM2021			
32¢	**Thomas Moran**	.50	.20
CM2022			
32¢	**Albert Bierstadt**	.50	.20
CM2023			
32¢	**Frederic Edwin Church**	.50	.20
CM2024			
32¢	**Mary Cassatt**	.50	.20
CM2025			
32¢	**Edward Hopper**	.50	.20
CM2026			
32¢	**Grant Wood**	.50	.20
CM2027			
32¢	**Charles Sheeler**	.50	.20
CM2028			
32¢	**Franny Kline**	.50	.20
CM2029			
32¢	**Mark Rothko**	.50	.20

		MNHVF	UseVF
	FDC *(Aug. 27, 1998)* any single		1.00
	y. Pane of 20	8.50	

1998. Celebrate the Century, 1930s Issue was the fourth in the series honoring each decade of the 20th century. *Printed by Ashton-Potter. Offset, with one intaglio stamp per pane, perforated 11 3/4.*

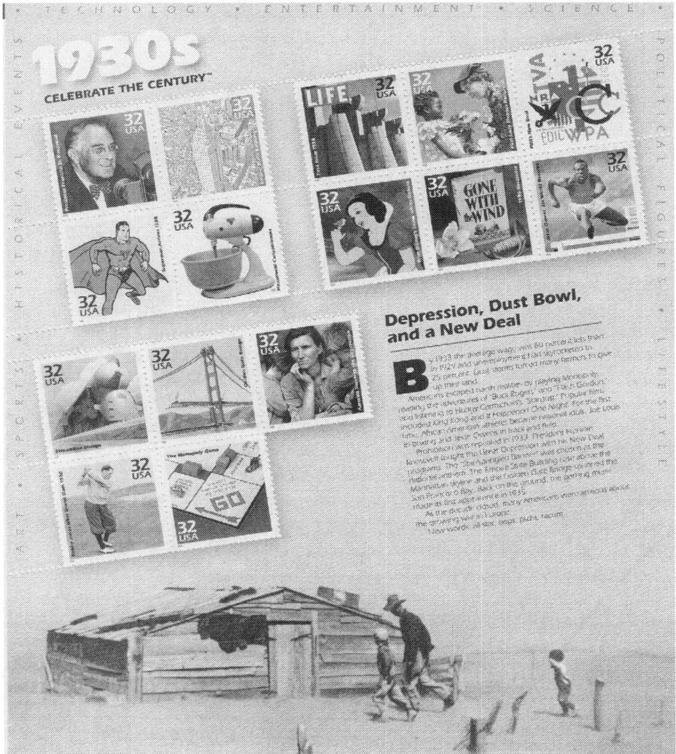

CM2030 *Celebrate the Century 1930s*

CM2030		MNHVF	UseVF
$4.80	**Sheetlet of 15,** tagged	10.00	7.50
	a. Franklin D. Roosevelt	.75	.50
	b. Empire State Building (intaglio)	.75	.50
	c. Life Magazine	.75	.50
	d. Eleanor Roosevelt	.75	.50
	e. FDR's New Deal Programs	.75	.50
	f. Superman Arrives	.75	.50
	g. Household Conveniences	.75	.50
	h. Disney's Snow White	.75	.50
	i. Gone with the Wind	.75	.50
	j. Jesse Owens	.75	.50
	k. Streamline Design	.75	.50
	l. Golden Gate Bridge	.75	.50
	m. America Survives the Depression	.75	.50
	n. Bobby Jones	.75	.50
	o. Monopoly Game	.75	.50
	FDC (any single)		1.50
	Sheet of 4 panes	4.00	
	FDC		7.50

1998. Ballet Issue Ballerina performing the step "en pointe" in an "attitude derriere" pose honored the art form. *Printed by Ashton-Potter, perforated 11.*

CM2031 *Ballet*

CM2031		MNHVF	UseVF
32¢	**multicolored**	.50	.20
	FDC *(Sept. 16, 1998)*		2.00
	y. Pane of 20	12.80	

1998. Space Discovery Issue a panoramic scene by artist Attila Hejja depicted exotic spacecraft, a city on an alien planet and colonists. There are views of space ships as hidden indicia visible only with the USPS optical Decoder. *Gravure by American Packaging Corp., for Sennett Security Products, block tagged.*

CM2032-2036

		MNHVF	UseVF
CM2032			
32¢	**Land craft**	.50	.20
CM2033			
32¢	**Space ship**	.50	.20
CM2034			
32¢	**Figure**	.50	.20
CM2035			
32¢	**Jagged hills**	.50	.20
CM2036			
32¢	**Moon**	.50	.20
	Plate Block of 10 (2 each CM2032-2036)	4.50	
	y. Se-tenant strip of 5 (CM2032-2036)	2.00	
	FDC *(Oct. 1 1998),* any single		1.50
	y1. Pane of 20	7.50	
	FDC, strip of 5		2.00

1998. Giving & Sharing Issue paid tribute to philanthropy. The bee and flower is a metaphor for the symbolic relationship between the "giver" and the "receiver." *Gravure by Avery Dennison, serpentine die cut, phosphored paper, self-adhesive.*

CM2037 *Giving & Sharing*

CM2037		MNHVF	UseVF
32¢	**multicolored**	.50	.20
	Plate block of 4	2.00	
	FDC *(Oct. 7, 1998)*		2.00
	y. Pane of 20	7.50	

1999. Year of the Hare Issue was the seventh in the Lunar New Year Series designed by Clarence Lee, Honolulu, Hawaii, and executed in paper-cut style. *Gravure by American Packaging Corp. for Sennett Security Products, (51,000,000 printed), gummed, die cut 11, tagged.*

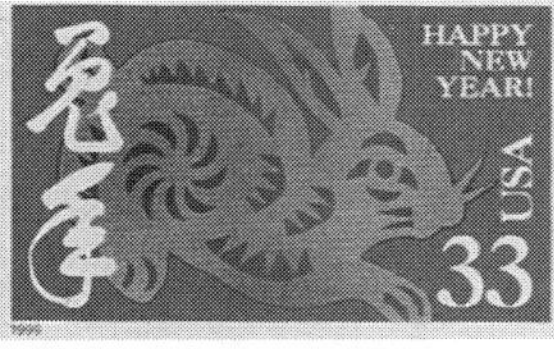

CM2038 *Year of the Hare*

CM2038		MNHVF	UseVF
33¢	**multicolored** tagged	.50	.20
	Plate block of 4	2.50	
	FDC *(Jan. 5, 1999)*		2.25
	y. Pane of 20	7.50	

1999. Malcolm X Issue 22nd stamp in the Black Heritage Series, saluted the founder (born Malcolm Little) of the Organization of Afro-American Unity (1963). Once a fiery spokesman for the black separatism teachings of the Nation of Islam, Malcolm X (1925-1965) broke away from the organization and promoted a more neutral solution to racial inequality. He was shot to death during a speech Feb. 21, 1965. The black-and-white stamp image is from an Associated Press news photo. Designed by Richard Sheaff, Scottsdale, Ariz. *Self-adhesive,* *serpentine die cut 11 1/2. Offset by Banknote Corporation of America, (100,000,000 printed).*

CM2039 *Malcolm X*

CM2039		MNHVF	UseVF
33¢	**multicolored**	.50	.20
	Plate block of 4	2.00	
	FDC *(Jan. 20, 1999)*		2.50
	y. Pane of 20	7.50	

1999. Victorian Hearts Issue in the Love Series initiated in 1973 constituted the first die-cut-to-shape United States postage stamps. Designed by Richard Sheaff, Scottsdale, Ariz., computer design by John Grossman and Holly Sudduth of Point Richmond, Calif. The word "love" was not included in the design for only the second time in the series (see CM1884 and CM1885). The paper-lace-and-flowers motif was reminiscent of the late 1880s. *Self-adhesive, die-cut convertible booklets (33¢) and panes (55¢) of 20. Gravure by Avery Dennison, (1,500,000,000 printed).*

CM2040 *Victorian hearts*

CM2040		MNHVF	UseVF
33¢	**multicolored**	.50	.20
	FDC *(Jan. 28, 1999)*		1.90
	n. Pane of 20 (convertible booklet)	12.00	

1999. Victorian Hearts Issue in the Love Series. Designed by Richard Sheaff, Scottsdale, Ariz., computer design by John Grossman and Holly Sudduth of Point Richmond, Calif. *Self-adhesive die cut to shape. Offset by Banknote Corporation of America, (300,000,000 printed).*

CM2041 *Victorian hearts*

CM2041		MNHVF	UseVF
55¢	**multicolored**	.85	.25
	Plate block of 4	3.20	
	FDC *(Jan. 28, 1999)*		2.25
	y. Pane of 20	13.20	

1999. Hospice Care Issue was intended to raise awareness of the concept of a team oriented medical care program to treat and comfort terminally ill patients in a home-like setting. Designed by Phil Jordan, Falls Church, Va. *Self-adhesive serpentine die cut 11 1/2. Offset by Banknote Corporation of America (100,000,000 printed).*

CM2042 *Hospice care*

CM2042		MNHVF	UseVF
33¢	**multicolored** phosphored paper	.50	.20
	Plate block of 4	2.00	
	FDC *(Feb. 9, 1999)*		2.25
	y. Pane of 20	7.50	

1999. Celebrate the Century 1940s Issue in the Celebrate the Century Series was the fifth in the series highlighting each decade of the 20th century. Designed by Carl Herrman, Laguna Nigel, Calif., illustrated by Howard Koslow, Toms River, N.J., engraver Ron Becker (Internatinal Style of Architecture design). *Gummed pane of 15. Offset, with one intaglio stamp in the pane; by Ashton-Potter USA, (188,000,000 or 12,533,333 panes printed). Perforated 11 3/4, tagged.*

CM2043 *Celebrate the Century 1940s*

CM2043		MNHVF	UseVF
$4.95	**Commemorative pane of 15, multicolored** tagged	10.00	7.50
	FDC *(Feb. 18, 1999)*	15.50	
	a. World War II	.75	.50
	b. Antibiotics Save Lives	.75	.50
	c. Jackie Robinson	.75	.50
	d. President Harry S. Truman	.75	.50
	e. Women Support War Effort	.75	.50
	f. TV Entertains America	.75	.50
	g. Jitterbug Sweeps Nation	.75	.50
	h. Abstract Expressionism	.75	.50
	i. GI Bill 1944	.75	.50
	j. The Big Band Sound	.75	.50

k. International Style of Architecture (intaglio)	.75	.50
l. Postwar Baby Boom	.75	.50
m. Slinky Craze Begins 1945	.75	.50
n. Broadway Hit 1947	.75	.50
o. Orson Welles' *Citizen Kane*	.75	.50
FDC *(Feb. 18, 1999)*		7.50
FDC, any single		1.90
Sheet of 4 panes	40.00	

1999. Irish Immigration Issue acknowledged the second-largest ancestral group in the United States on the 150th anniversary of the potato famine, which drove many Irish to America for survival. It was a joint issue with an Irish Emigration stamp from Ireland. Designed by Howard Paine, Delaplane, Va., from illustration by Dennis Lyall of Bridgeport, Conn. *Gummed pane of 20. Offset by Ashton-Potter USA, (40,400,000 printed). Perforated 11, tagged.*

CM2044 *Irish immigration*

CM2044		MNHVF	UseVF
33¢	**multicolored**	.50	.20
	Plate block of 4	2.00	
	FDC *(Feb. 26, 1999)*		1.90
	y. Pane of 20	7.50	

1999. Alfred Lunt and Lynn Fontanne Issue in the Performing Arts Series honored one of the greatest husband-and-wife acting teams ever to take the stage. Lunt (1892-1977) and Fontanne (1887-1983) met and first acted together in 1919, married in 1922, and never appeared separately on stage after 1928. They last appeared in the Broadway play, *The Visit,* in 1958. The illustration was based on a 1931 publicity photo for a film that was never made, *Lullaby.* The first-day ceremony took place at the Lunt-Fontanne Theatre in New York City. Designed by Carl Herrman, Laguna Nigel, Calif., from illustration by Drew Struzan, Pasadena, Calif. *Offset by Sterling Sommer for Ashton-Potter USA, (42,500,000 printed). Perforated 11, tagged.*

CM2045 *Alfred Lunt and Lynn Fontanne*

CM2045		MNHVF	UseVF
33¢	**multicolored**	.50	.20
	Plate block of 4	2.00	
	FDC *(March 2, 1999)*		1.90
	y. Pane of 20	7.50	

1999. Arctic Animals Issue pictured five animals adapted to thrive in the extreme cold of the Arctic. The stamps are based on close-up photographs. Designed by Derry Noyes, Washington, D.C., photos by Art Wolfe (Artic Hare), Joe McDonald (Timber Wolf), Zig Leszczynski (Snowy Owl), Gary Schultz (Artic Fox), Jeff Foott (Polar Bear), and Johnny Johnson (Polar Bear family in header). *Offset by Banknote Corporation of America, (73,155,000 or 4,877,000 panes printed), block tagged, perforated 11.*

CM2046 *Arctic Hare;* CM2047 *Arctic Fox;* CM2048 *Snowy Owl;* CM2049 *Polar Bear;* CM2050 *Gray Wolf*

CM2046		MNHVF	UseVF
33¢	**Arctic Hare, multicolored**	.60	.20

CM2047		MNHVF	UseVF
33¢	**Arctic Fox, multicolored**	.60	.20

CM2048		MNHVF	UseVF
33¢	**Snowy Owl, multicolored**	.60	.20

CM2049		MNHVF	UseVF
33¢	**Polar Bear, multicolored**	.60	.20

CM2050		MNHVF	UseVF
33¢	**Gray Wolf, multicolored**	.60	.20
	Plate block of 10	6.00	
	FDC *(March 12, 1999)*		1.50
	y. Pane of 15	10.00	
	y1. Se-tenant strip of CM2046-2050	3.30	
	FDC, pane		4.00

Nature of America Series

1999. Sonoran Desert Issue the first of a planned educational Nature of America Series, pictured a Southwestern desert scene teeming with wildlife. On the back of the pane, the USPS identified 25 species, including those not on the stamps die-cut into the scene, ranging from an elf owl in a cactus cavity, three collared peccary and a tarantula, but not including a trail of ants near the bottom of the pane. Designed by Ethel Kessler, Bethesda, Md., illustrated by John Dawson, Hilo, Hawaii. *Self-adhesive commemorative pane of 10 offset by Banknote Corporation of America, (10,000,000 panes printed). Serpentine die cut 11, tagged.*

CM2051a *Saguaro cactus;* CM2051b *White-winged dove, prickly pear;* CM2051c *Desert mule deer;* CM2051d *Gila woodpecker;* CM2051e *Cactus wren, brittlebush, teddy bear cholla;* CM2051f *Desert tortoise;* CM2051g *Gambel quail;* CM2051h *Desert cottontail, hedgehog cactus;* CM2051i Gila monster; CM2051j Western diamondback rattlesnake, cactus mouse

CM2051		MNHVF	UseVF
$3.30	**multicolored Sheetlet of 10,** blocked tagged	7.50	3.00
	a. Saguaro cactus	.75	.50
	b. White-winged dove, prickly pear	.75	.50
	c. Desert mule deer	.75	.50
	d. Gila woodpecker	.75	.50
	e. Cactus wren, brittlebush, teddy bear cholla	.75	.50
	f. Desert tortoise	.75	.50
	g. Gambel quail	.75	.50
	h. Desert cottontail, hedgehog cactus	.75	.50
	i. Gila monster	.75	.50
	j. Western diamondback rattlesnake, cactus mouse	.75	.50
	any single	.70	.25
	FDC, pane of 10 *(April 6, 1999)*		10.00
	FDC, any single		1.00

1999. Daffy Duck Issue the third in the Warner Bros. Cartoon Characters Series, featured the underachieving Looney Tunes duck famous for his lisping, "That's despicable." Designed by Ed Wleczyk,

Los Angeles, Calif. *Self-adhesive, gravure by Avery Dennison, (427,000,000 stamps printed), (42,700,000 panes). Serpentine die cut 11 on all stamps, "Double prong" tooth at upper right corner of each stamp, tagged.*

CM2052 *Daffy Duck*

CM2052		MNHVF	UseVF
$3.30	**Pane of 10,** tagged	7.50	
	n. Right half of pane (single die cut CM2052a superimposed on enlarged image)	1.00	
	n1. Left half of pane (block of 9 CM2052a)	5.00	
	a. 33¢ single	.75	.25
	FDC *(April 16, 1999)*		2.50

This issue also was made available in top- and bottom-half printing sheets of six 10-stamp panes each. Vertical rouletting between the two panes is missing on these half sheets. A single plate number, trimmed away on individual panes, appears adjacent to the bottom-left pane in the bottom half of the printing sheet only.

1999. Daffy Duck Issue in the Warner Bros. Cartoon Characters Series. Designed by Ed Wleczyk, Los Angeles, Calif. *Self-adhesive, gravure by Avery Dennison, (50,000 panes), nine stamps serpentine die cut 11 through stamps and backing on left pane, one stamp imperforate on right pane. The two sides are separated by a vertical line of tiny perforations.*

CM2053 *Daffy Duck*

CM2053		MNHVF	UseVF
$3.30	**Pane of 10,** tagged	7.50	
	n. Right half of pane (single imperforate CM2053a superimposed on enlarged image)	1.00	1.00
	n1. Left half of pane (block of 9 CM2053a)	6.00	
	a. 33¢ single	.75	.25

1999. Ayn Rand Issue 17th in the Literary Arts Series honored the writer (and stamp collector) whose philosophy of individual freedom and effort shaped her novels such as *Atlas Shrugged* and *The Fountainhead.* Born Alissa Rosenbaum in Russia, she came to the United States at the age of 21, became a U.S. citizen, changed her name (Ayn rhymes with fine; Rand she found on her Remington-Rand typewriter), and moved to Hollywood, where she continued writing and worked in movies. Designed by Phil Jordan, Falls Church, Va., illustrated by Nicholas Gaetano, Fletcher, N.C. *Offset by Sterling Sommer for Ashton Potter USA, (42,500,000 printed). Perforated 11, tagged.*

CM2054 *Ayn Rand*

CM2054		MNHVF	UseVF
33¢	**multicolored**	.50	.20
	Plate block of 4	2.00	
	FDC *(April 22, 1999)*		1.90
	y. Pane of 20	7.50	

1999. Cinco de Mayo Issue part of the Holiday Celebration Series. Was printed with "33" denomination and 1999 date (see CM1980). *Gravure by Banknote Corporation of America, (105,000,000 printed), die cut 11 1/2, tagged.*

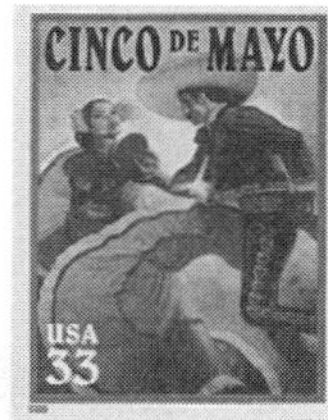

CM2055 *Cinco de Mayo*

CM2055		MNHVF	UseVF
33¢	**multicolored**	.50	.20
	FDC *(April 27, 1999)*		1.90
	y. Pane of 20	7.50	

1999. Tropical Flowers Issue continued the USPS fascination with floral issues and included several innovations. It was the first self-adhesive convertible booklet with stamps on both sides of the pane, the first U.S. stamps printed with a 550-line screen rather than the more common 300-line screen to give the illustrations more sharpness, the first with a completely recyclable adhesive, and the first on paper stock with 20% post-consumer waste. The flowers, arranged as in a bouquet, are the bird of paradise, whose showy flowers resemble the heads of birds; the royal poinciana, a 50-foot tree with fiery blooms in the rainy season; the gloriosa lily, a climbing plant whose flowers are four inches across; and the Chinese hibiscus whose vibrant flowers last only a day each but are replaced quickly for a long-lasting bloom. Designed by Carl Herrman, Laguna Niguel, Calif., illustrations by Steve Buchanan, Winstead, Conn. *Gravure at American Packaging Corp. for Sennett Security Products on phosphored paper (1,500,000,000 stamps), (75,000,000 booklets), serpentine die cut 11.*

CM2056 *Bird of paradise*

CM2057 *Royal poinciana*

CM2058 *Gloriosa lily*

CM2059 *Chinese hibiscus*

		MNHVF	UseVF
CM2056			
33¢	**Bird of paradise, multicolored**	.50	.20
CM2057		MNHVF	UseVF
33¢	**Royal poinciana, multicolored**	.50	.20
CM2058		MNHVF	UseVF
33¢	**Gloriosa lily, multicolored**	.50	.20
CM2059		MNHVF	UseVF
33¢	**Chinese hibiscus, multicolored**	.50	.20
	FDC *(May 1, 1999)*		1.50
	n. Pane of 20	13.00	
	FDC (one of each stamp)		3.00
	FDC (single stamp)		1.50

1999. John & William Bartram Issue brought to attention John Bartram (1699-1777), who established in Philadelphia the oldest existing botanical garden in America. He and his son, William Bartram (1739-1823) introduced 200 native American plants there. The stamp shows a detail of a handcolored engraving by William Bartram. *Offset with microprinting "Botanists" by Banknote Corporation of America, (145,375,000 printed), self-adhesive, phosphored paper, serpentine die cut, perforated 11 1/2.*

CM2060 *Botanical engraving*

		MNHVF	UseVF
CM2060			
33¢	**multicolored**	.60	.20
	Plate block of 4	2.00	
	y. Pane of 20	13.00	
	y1. block of 4	—	
	FDC *(May 18, 1999)*		1.90

We regret that we cannot pass upon the authenticity of any stamp. Should you have stamps for which you desire authentication, we suggest that you contact a recognized expertizing service. Expertizing committees offer opinions only, not guarantees. Opinions may vary among services, and over the years an opinion may change.

1999. Celebrate the Century 1950s Issue in the Celebrate the Century Series was the sixth in the series highlighting each decade of the 20th century. Designed by Howard Paine, Delaplane, Va., with illustrations by Dean Ellis, Amagansett, N.Y. *Gummed pane of 15, offset, with one intaglio stamp in each pane, by Ashton-Potter USA, (188,000,000 printed), (12,533,333 panes). Perforated 11 1/2.*

CM2061 *Celebrate the Century 1950s*

		MNHVF	UseVF
CM2061			
$4.95	**Commemorative page of 15, multicolored** tagged	10.00	7.50
	FDC *(May 26, 1999)*		1.50
	a. Polio Vaccine Developed (intaglio)	.65	.30
	b. Teen Fashions	.65	.30
	c. The "Shot Heard 'Round the World"	.65	.30
	d. U.S. Launches Satellites	.65	.30
	e. The Korean War	.65	.30
	f. Desegregating Public Schools	.65	.30
	g. Tail Fins and Chrome	.65	.30
	h. Dr. Seuss' *The Cat in the Hat*	.65	.30
	i. Drive-in Movies	.65	.30
	j. World Series Rivals	.65	.30
	k. Rockey Marciano, Undefeated	.65	.30
	l. *I Love Lucy*	.65	.30
	m. Rock 'n' Roll	.65	.30
	n. Stock Car Racing	.65	.30
	o. Movies Go 3-D	.65	.30
	Sheet of 4 panes	40.00	

1999. Prostate Cancer Awareness Issue focused attention on the second leading cause of cancer death (after lung cancer) in men and the second most common cancer (after skin cancer) in men. Designed by Michael Cronan, San Francisco, Calif. *Gravure by Avery Dennison, (78,100,000 printed), phosphored paper, self-adhesive, serpentine die cut, perforated 11.*

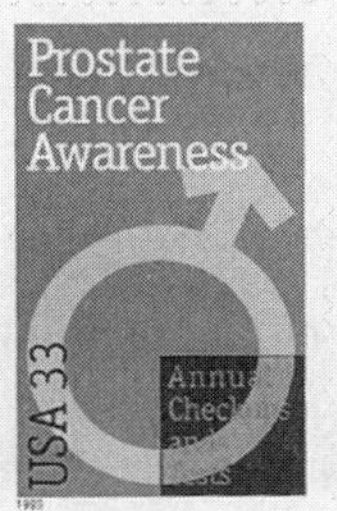

CM2062 *Prostate Cancer Awareness*

		MNHVF	UseVF
CM2062			
33¢	**multicolored**	.50	.20

	Plate block of 4	2.60	
	FDC *(May 28, 1999)*		1.90
	y. Pane of 20	7.50	

1999. California Gold Rush Issue honored the thousands of hopeful "Forty-Niners" who rushed to California after gold was discovered at Sutter's Mill in January 1848. Designed by Howard Paine, Delaplane, Va., illustrated by John Berkey, Excelsior, Minn. *Offset by Ashton-Potter USA Ltd., (89,270,000 printed). In gummed panes of 20, perforated 11.*

CM2063 *Gold miners*

CM2063		MNHVF	UseVF
33¢	**multicolored**	.50	.20
	Plate block of 4	2.00	
	FDC *(June 18, 1999)*		1.90
	y. Pane of 20	7.50	

1999. Aquarium Fish Issue displayed on a strip of four multicolored stamps in an illustrated sheetlet a fish tank scene with corals, sea anemones, fish and other species found at reefs in different parts of the world. Designed by Richard Sheaff, Scottsdale, Ariz., illustrations by Teresa Fasolino, New York, N.Y. *Offset by Banknote Corporation of America, (152,375,000 printed), block tagged (7,618,500 panes), serpentine die cut 11 1/2.*

CM2064-2067 *Aquarium Fish*

		MNHVF	UseVF
CM2064		MNHVF	UseVF
33¢	**Black-and-white fish**	.50	.20
CM2065		MNHVF	UseVF
33¢	**Thermometer**	.50	.20
CM2066		MNHVF	UseVF
33¢	**Blue-and-yellow fish**	.50	.20
CM2067		MNHVF	UseVF
33¢	**red-and-white fish**	.50	.20
	Plate block of 8	4.00	
	FDC *(June 24, 1999)*		1.50
	y. Pane of 20	10.00	

This issue was also made available in press sheets.

1999. Xtreme Sports Issue designed by Carl Herrman, Laguna Nigel, Calif., from photos by J. Grant Brittain (Skateboarding), Keith Mulligan (BMX Biking), Scott Spiker (Snowboarding) and Mike Powell (Inline Skating). Captured, in four multicolored stamps on an illustrated sheetlet, the speed and action of participants in four high-excitement and daring pastimes — skateboarding, BMX biking, snowboarding and in-line skating. Slang words detectable only with a special USPS decoder appear on the stamps — "Gnarly," "Rad," "Stoked," and "Phat," respectively. *Gravure by Avery Dennison on phosphored paper (7,598,750 panes), serpentine die cut 11.*

CM2068 *Skateboarding*

CM2069 *BMX biking*

CM2070 *Snowboarding*

CM2071 *In-line skating*

		MNHVF	UseVF
CM2068		MNHVF	UseVF
33¢	**Skateboarding**	.50	.20
CM2069		MNHVF	UseVF
33¢	**BMX biking**	.50	.20
CM2070		MNHVF	UseVF
33¢	**Snowboarding**	.50	.20
CM2071		MNHVF	UseVF
33¢	**In-line skating**	.50	.20
	Plate block of 4	2.00	
	FDC *(June 25, 1999)*		1.50
	y. Pane of 20	10.00	

1999. American Glass Issue designed by Richard Sheaff, Scottsdale, Ariz. from photos by Robert Schlowsky, Weston, Mass. (Mold-Blown and Pressed Glass) and Nicholas Williams, Corning, N.Y. (Art Glass and Freeblown Glass). Showcased on an illustrated sheetlet American glassmaking designs and techniques from 18th to 20th century. Presented are examples of freeblown, mold-blown, pressed and art glass. They were the first U.S. stamps to feature digital photography. Tagging was in selective-cut blocks only on the glass items in the stamps. *Offset by Ashton Potter USA (116,083,500 printed), (7,738,900 panes), perforated 11.*

CM2072 *Freeblown glass*

CM2073 *Mold-blown glass*

CM2074 *Pressed glass*

CM2075 *Art glass*

		MNHVF	UseVF
CM2072		MNHVF	UseVF
33¢	**Freeblown glass**	.50	.20
CM2073		MNHVF	UseVF
33¢	**Mold-blown glass**	.50	.20

CM2074		MNHVF	UseVF
33¢	**Pressed glass**	.50	.20

CM2075		MNHVF	UseVF
33¢	**Art glass**	.50	.20
	FDC *(June 29, 1999)*		1.50
	y. Pane of 15	8.50	

1999. James Cagney Issue in the Legends of Hollywood Series. Designed by Howard Paine, Delaplane, Va., illustrated by Thomas Blackshear, Colorado Springs, Colo. Honored the star of stage and screen (1899-1986) who was equally proficient playing a song-and-dance man or a tough guy. He appeared in 65 films, won his only Oscar playing George M. Cohan in *Yankee Doodle Dandy* (portrayed in the selvage illustration), and turned out numerous seminal performances of bad men, including *The Public Enemy* and *White Heat. Gravure by American Packaging Corp. for Sennett Security Products, (75,500,000 printed), (3,775,000 panes), block tagged.*

2076 *James Cagney*

CM2076		MNHVF	UseVF
33¢	**multicolored**	.50	.20
	Plate block of 4	2.00	
	FDC *(July 22, 1999)*		1.90
	y. Gummed pane of 20	7.50	

1999. Honoring Those Who Served Issue paid tribute to the millions of military veterans, firefighters and law enforcement officers who have risked or given their lives to protect the welfare of their fellow Americans. Designed by Richard Sheaf, Scottsdale, Ariz., and Uldis Purins, Newton, Mass. *Gravure by Avery Dennison on phosphored paper, (101,800,000 printed), serpentine die cut 11.*

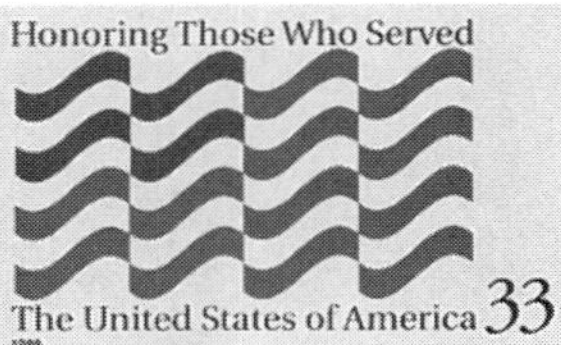

CM2077

CM2077		MNHVF	UseVF
33¢	**multicolored**	.50	.20
	Plate block of 4	2.00	
	FDC *(Aug. 16, 1999)*		1.90
	y. Self-adhesive pane of 20	10.00	

1999. Universal Postal Union Issue Commemorated 125 years of the world governing body for postal matters. Designed by Gerald Gallo, Bethesda, Md. The stamp was issued in Beijing, China. *Offset by Ashton Potter USA, (43,150,000 printed).*

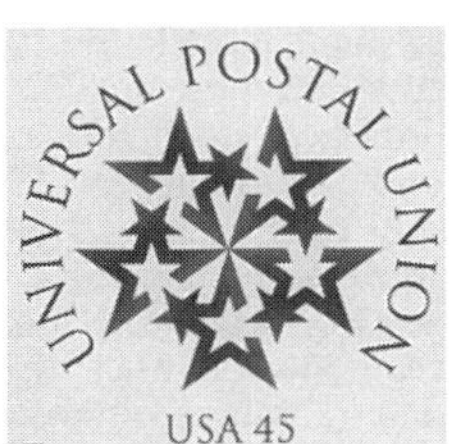

CM2078

CM2078		MNHVF	UseVF
45¢	**multicolored**	.90	.40
	Plate block of 4	3.60	
	FDC *(Aug. 25, 1999)*		2.50
	y. Pane of 20	18.00	

1999. All Aboard! Issue pictured watercolor illustrations of five legendary passenger trains of the 1930s and 1940s. Designed by Howard Paine, Delaplane, Va., illustrated by Ted Rose, Santa Fe, N.M. The Daylight, called "the Most Beautiful Train in the World," connected Los Angeles and San Francisco along Pacific Ocean beaches. The Congressional, which ran between New York City and Washington, D.C., boasted, "Every Mile Electrified," thanks to Public Works Administration help. The 20th Century Limited offered 16 hour travel between Chicago and New York. The Hiawatha traveled over 100 mph on its twice-daily run connecting Chicago, Milwaukee and Minneapolis-St. Paul. The Super Chief, which ran between Chicago and Los Angeles, became known as "the Train of the Stars" because it was the preferred mode of transportation for Hollywood's elite. *Gummed pane of 20, offset by Ashton Potter USA (120,000,000 printed).*

CM2079 *Daylight;*

CM2080 *Congressional;*

CM2081 *20th Century Limited;*

CM2082 *Hiawatha;*

CM2083 *Super Chief*

CM2079		MNHVF	UseVF
33¢	**multicolored**	.50	.20

CM2080		MNHVF	UseVF
33¢	**multicolored**	.50	.20

CM2081		MNHVF	UseVF
33¢	**multicolored**	.50	.20

CM2082		MNHVF	UseVF
33¢	**multicolored**	.50	.20

CM2083		MNHVF	UseVF
33¢	**multicolored**	.50	.20
	Plate block of 10	6.50	
	FDC *(Aug. 26, 1999)*		1.90
	y. Pane of 20	7.50	
	FDC, strip of 5		5.50

1999. Frederic Law Olmsted Issue called attention to the ideals and artistry of one of America's most prolific park designers, who was a founder of American landscape architecture. Among many other projects Olmsted designed New York's Central Park and the Capitol grounds in Washington, D.C. Designed by Ethel Kessler, Bethesda, Md. *Offset by Ashton Potter USA Ltd., (42,500,000 printed) on phosphored paper.*

CM2084 *Frederic Law Olmsted*

CM2084		MNHVF	UseVF
33¢	**multicolored**	.50	.20
	Plate block of 4	2.00	
	FDC *(Sept. 12, 1999)*		1.90
	y. Pane of 20	7.50	

1999. Hollywood Composers Issue in the Legends of American Music Series. Featured six distinguished composers of music for films. Max Steiner, a pioneer of Hollywood composing provided music for more than 200 films, including *Gone With the Wind,* and won three Academy Awards. Dimitri Tiomkin, a concert pianist, won Oscars for his music for *High Noon, The High and the Mighty* and *The Old Man and the Sea.* Alfred Newman pioneered a method of synchronizing film music that is still in use and won Oscars for films that included *Alexander's Ragtime Band, The Song of Bernadette, Love Is a Many Splendored Thing, The King and I,* and *Camelot.* Bernard Herrmann worked with Alfred Hitchcock on films such as *Vertigo* and *Psycho.* Franz Waxman was a cabaret pianist in Berlin before moving to Hollywood, where he composed music for more than 200 films and won Academy Awards for *Sunset Boulevard* and *A Place in the Sun.* Erich Wolfgang Korngold, a child prodigy in Vienna, won Oscars for *Anthony Adverse* and *The Adventures of Robin Hood.* Designed by Howard Paine, Delaplane, Va., illustrated by Drew Struzan, Pasadena, Calif. *Offset by Sterling Sommer for Ashton Potter USA Ltd., (42,500,000 printed), (2,125,000 gummed panes), block tagged.*

CM2085 *Max Steiner;* CM2086 *Dimitri Tiomkin;* CM2087 *Bernard Herrmann;* CM2088 *Franz Waxman;* CM2089 *Alfred Newman;* CM2090 *Erich Wolfgang Korngold*

CM2085		MNHVF	UseVF
33¢	**multicolored**	.50	.20
CM2086		MNHVF	UseVF
33¢	**multicolored**	.50	.20
CM2087		MNHVF	UseVF
33¢	**multicolored**	.50	.20
CM2088		MNHVF	UseVF
33¢	**multicolored**	.50	.20
CM2089		MNHVF	UseVF
33¢	**multicolored**	.50	.20
CM2090		MNHVF	UseVF
33¢	**multicolored**		
	Plate block of 6	4.00	
	FDC, block of 6 *(Sept. 16, 1999)*		4.00
	y. Pane of 20	10.00	

1999. Celebrate the Century 1960s Issue in the Celebrate the Century series. Was the seventh in the series highlighting each decade of the 20th century. Designed by Carl Herrman, Laguna Nigel, Calif., illustrated by Keith Birdsong, Muskogee, Okla. *Offset with one stamp intaglio by Ashton Potter USA Ltd., (120,000,000 printed), (8,000,000 panes), perforated 11 3/4.*

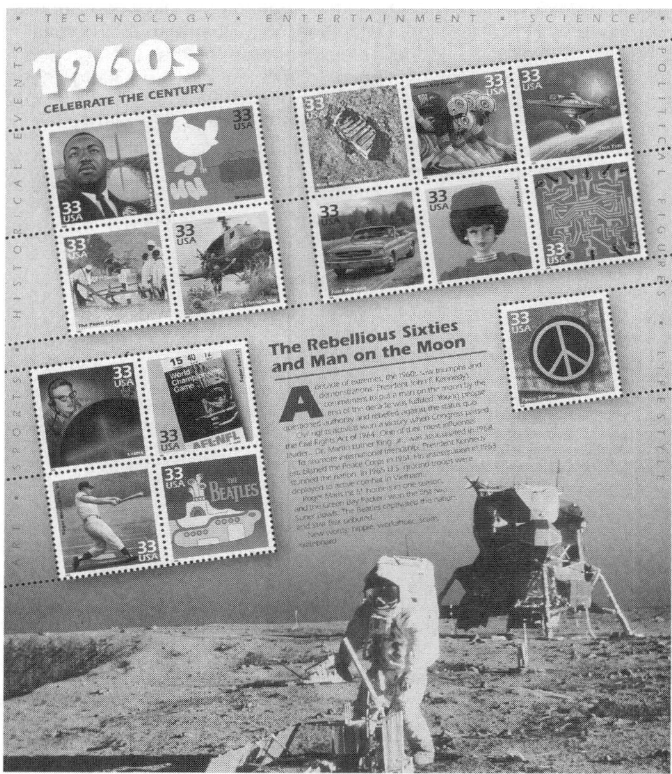

CM2091a-2091o *Celebrate the Century 1960s*

CM2091		MNHVF	UseVF
$4.95	**Commemorative pane of 15, multicolored,** tagged	10.00	7.50
	FDC *(Sept. 17, 1999)*		1.50
	a. Martin Luther King Jr.	.50	.25
	b. Woodstock	.50	.25
	c. Man Walks on Moon (intaglio)	.50	.25
	d. Green Bay Packers	.50	.25
	e. Star Trek	.50	.25
	f. Peace Corps	.50	.25
	g. Vietnam War	.50	.25
	h. Ford Mustang	.50	.25
	i. Barbie Doll	.50	.25
	j. Integrated circuit	.50	.25
	k. Lasers	.50	.25
	l. Super Bowl I	.50	.25
	m. Peace symbol	.50	.25
	n. Roger Maris, "61 in '61"	.50	.25
	o. The Beatles' "Yellow Submarine"	.50	.25

1999. Broadway Songwriters Issue Final installment in the Legends of American Music series. Honored, on six stamps, nine world-renowned songwriters whose works on Broadway delighted music lovers for decades. Brothers Ira (lyrics) and George (music) Gershwin worked together from the early 1920s to 1937 for shows including *Of Thee I Sing* (1931), the first musical to win a Pulitzer Prize. Alan Jay Lerner and Frederick Loewe collaborated from 1942 until the 1970s on musicals including *Brigadoon, Paint Your Wagon, My Fair Lady,* and *Camelot.* Lorenz Hart is best known for memorable turns of phrase in such musicals as *Pal Joey* and *Babes in Arms.* Richard Rogers and Oscar Hammerstein II were noted for innovative integration of music and plot in musicals such as *Oklahoma!, Carousel, South Pacific, The King and I* and *The Sound of Music.* Besides his signature *Music Man,* Meredith Willson wrote *The Unsinkable Molly*

Brown and *Here's Love*. Frank Loesser wrote *Guys and Dolls, The Most Happy Fella* and *How To Succeed in Business Without Really Trying.* Designed by Howard Paine, Delaplane, Va., illustrated by Drew Struzan, Pasadena, Calif. *Offset by Sterling Sommer for Ashton Potter USA Ltd., (42,500,000 printed), (2,125,000 panes), block tagged, perforated 11.*

CM2092 *Ira & George Gershwan;*

CM2093 *Alan Jay Lerner & Frederick Loewe;*

CM2094 *Lorenz Hart;*

CM2095 *Richard Rogers & Oscar Hammerstein II;*

CM2096 *Meredith Willson;*

CM2097 *Frank Loesser*

		MNHVF	UseVF
CM2092			
33¢	**multicolored**	.50	.20
CM2093		MNHVF	UseVF
33¢	**multicolored**	.50	.20
CM2094		MNHVF	UseVF
33¢	**multicolored**	.50	.20
CM2095		MNHVF	UseVF
33¢	**multicolored**	.50	.20
CM2096		MNHVF	UseVF
33¢	**multicolored**	.50	.20
CM2097		MNHVF	UseVF
33¢	**multicolored**	.50	.20
	Plate block of 6	2.00	
	FDC *(Sept. 21, 1999)*		1.50
	y. Pane of 20	10.00	

1999. Insects and Spiders Issue in the Classic Collection series. Presented 20 lifelike crawly creatures aimed at appealing to children's curiosity. Designed by Carl Herrman, Laguna Nigel, Calif., illustrated by Steven Buchanan, Winsted, Conn., from specimens at the Connecticut Agriculture Experiment Station, New Haven, Conn. *Phosphor tagging on stamps took the shape of the bugs. Printing on the back of each stamp included its Latin name and a description. Offset by Ashton Potter USA, (84,700,000 printed), (4,235,000 panes).*

CM2098 *Insects and Spiders*

		MNHVF	UseVF
CM2098			
33¢	**Pane of 20, multicolored**	10.00	.50
	FDC *(Oct. 1, 1999)*		1.50
	a. Black widow spider	.50	.20
	b. Elderberry longhorn beetle	.50	.20
	c. Lady beetle	.50	.20
	d. Yellow garden spider	.50	.20
	e. Dogbane beetle	.50	.20
	f. Flower fly	.50	.20
	g. Assassin bug	.50	.20
	h. Ebony jewelring damselfly	.50	.20
	i. Velvet ant	.50	.20
	j. Monarch caterpillar	.50	.20
	k. Monarch butterfly	.50	.20
	l. Eastern Hercules beetle	.50	.20
	m. Bombardier beetle	.50	.20
	n. Dung beetle	.50	.20
	o. Spotted water beetle	.50	.20
	p. True katydid	.50	.20
	q. Spinybacked spider	.50	.20
	r. Periodical cicada	.50	.20
	s. Scorpionfly	.50	.20
	t. Jumping spider	.50	.20

1999. Hanukkah Issue in the Holiday Celebrations series. A redenominated version of a stamp that kicked off the series in 1996, it features a Jewish menorah for the Festival of Lights. Designed by Hannah Smotrich. *Printed by Avery Dennison, (65,000,000 printed), serpentine die cut 11.*

CM2099 *Festival of Lights*

		MNHVF	UseVF
CM2099			
33¢	**multicolored**	.50	.20
	Plate block of 4	2.00	
	FDC *(Oct. 8, 1999)*		1.50
	y. Pane of 20	7.50	

1999. North Atlantic Treaty Organization Issue Featured the Dove of Peace to celebrate 50 years of the European defense organization. Its release date was delayed while NATO bombed Serbia during the Kosovo crisis. Designed by Michael Cronan, San Francisco, Calif. *Gummed panes of 20, gravure by Ashton Potter USA, (44,600,000 printed) on phosphored paper, perforated 11.*

CM2100 *Dove of Peace*

		MNHVF	UseVF
CM2100			
33¢	**multicolored**	.50	.20
	Plate block of 4	2.00	
	FDC *(Oct. 13, 1999)*		1.50
	y. Pane of 20	7.50	

1999. Kwanzaa Issue in the Holiday Celebrations series. A redenominated version of a stamp issued in 1997, it pictures a couple in colorful African garb and the seven symbols of the relatively new year-end celebration. Designed by Synthia St. James. *Self-adhesive pane of 20, gravure by Avery Dennison, (95,000,000 printed) on phosphored paper, serpentine die cut 10 1/2.*

CM2101 *African couple*

		MNHVF	UseVF
CM2101			
33¢	**multicolored**	.50	.20
	Plate block of 4	2.00	
	FDC *(Oct. 29, 1999)*		1.50
	y. Pane of 20	7.50	

1999. Celebrate the Century 1970s Issue in the Celebrate the Century series was the eighth in a series highlighting each decade of the 20th century. Designed by Howard Paine, Delaplane, Va., illustrations by Kazuhiko Sano, Mill Valley, Calif. *Offset (with one stamp* *intaglio) by Ashton Potter USA, (90,000,000 printed), (6,000,000 panes), perforated 11 3/4.*

CM2102a-2102o *Celebrate the Century 1970s*

CM2102		MNHVF	UseVF
$4.95	**Sheetlet of 15,** tagged	10.00	7.00
	FDC *(Nov. 18, 1999)*		12.50
	a. Earth Day Celebrated	.50	.25
	b. TV Series ("All in the Family")	.50	.25
	c. "Sesame Street"	.50	.25
	d. Disco Music	.50	.25
	e. (Pittsburgh) Steelers Win Four Super Bowls	.50	.25
	f. U.S. Celebrates 200th Birthday	.50	.25
	g. Secretariat Wins Triple Crown	.50	.25
	h. VCRs Transform Entertainment (intaglio)	.50	.25
	i. "Pioneer 10"	.50	.25
	j. Women's Rights Movement	.50	.25
	k. 1970s Fashion	.50	.25
	l. "Monday Night Football"	.50	.25
	m. America Smiles	.50	.25
	n. Jumbo Jets	.50	.25
	o. Medical Imaging	.50	.25

1999. YEAR 2000 ISSUE Used a traditional, festive "New Year's Baby" illustration by J.C. Leyendecker (1874-1951) that originally appeared on the cover of the Jan. 2, 1937, issue of the *Saturday Evening Post.* The "1999" date is included at lower right in the vignette. Designed by Carl Herrman, Carlsbad, Calif. *Self-adhesive panes of 20, offset by Banknote Corporation of America, (120,000,000 printed) on phosphor-tagged paper, serpentine die cut 11.*

CM2103 *"New Year's Baby"*

CM2103		MNHVF	UseVF
33¢	**multicolored**	.50	.20
	Plate block of 4	2.00	
	FDC *(Dec. 27, 1999)*		1.50
	y. Pane of 20	7.50	

2000. YEAR OF THE DRAGON ISSUE in the Lunar New Year series. Was the eighth in a series featuring the creatures of the Chinese zodiac designed in paper cut fashion and calligraphy by artist Clarence Lee, Hololulu, Hawaii. *Gummed panes of 20, offset by Ashton Potter, (56,000,000 printed), on phosphored paper, perforated 11 1/4, (56,000,000 printed).*

CM2104 *Dragon*

CM2104		MNHVF	UseVF
33¢	**multicolored**	.50	.20
	Plate block of 4	2.00	
	FDC *(Jan. 6, 2000)*		1.25
	y. Pane of 20	10.00	

2000. CELEBRATE THE CENTURY 1980S ISSUE was the ninth in the Celebrate the Century series highlighting each decade of the 20th century. Designed by Carl Herrman, Carlsbad, Calif. *Gummed panes of 15, offset by Ashton Potter USA, (90,000,000 printed), perforated 11 1/2.*

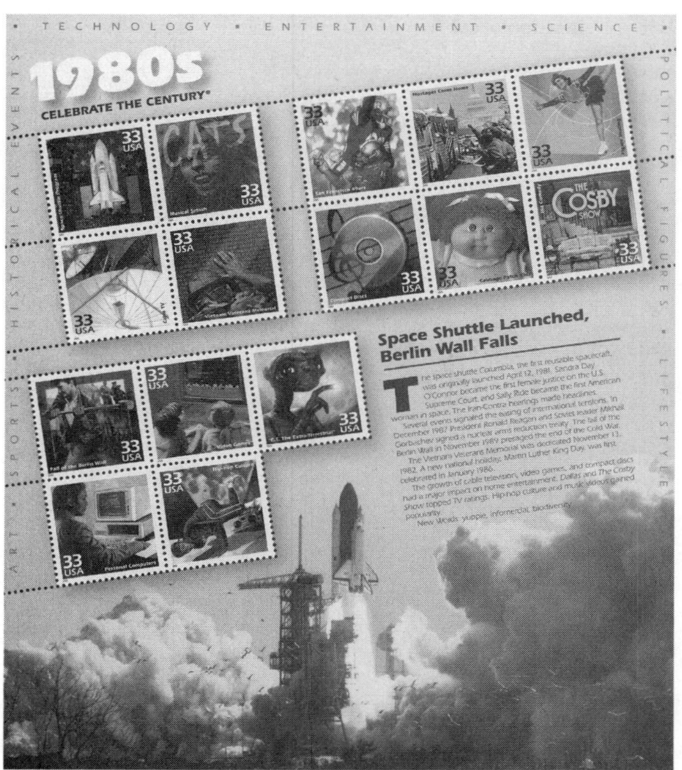

CM2105a-2105o *Celebrate the Century 1980s*

CM2105		MNHVF	UseVF
33¢	**Commemorative pane of 15, multicolored,** tagged	10.00	7.00
	FDC *(Jan. 12, 2000)*		12.50
	a. Space Shuttle Program	.50	.25
	b. *Cats* Broadway Show	.50	.25
	c. San Francisco 49ers	.50	.25
	d. American Hostages Freed	.50	.25
	e. Figure Skating	.50	.25
	f. Cable TV	.50	.25
	g. Vietnam Veterans Memorial	.50	.25
	h. Compact Discs	.50	.25
	i. Cabbage Patch Kids	.50	.25
	j. *The Cosby Show*	.50	.25

		MNHVF	UseVF
k.	Fall of the Berlin Wall	.50	.25
l.	Video Games	.50	.25
m.	*ET The Extra-Terrestrial* Movie	.50	.25
n.	Personal Computers	.50	.25
o.	Hip-Hop Culture	.50	.25
	FDC (any single)		1.50
	Sheet of 4 panes	—	

2000. Patricia Roberts Harris Issue in the Black Heritage Series. The daughter of a Pullman dining car waiter, Patricia Roberts Harris (1924-1985) graduated first in her law school class and became known as "a woman of firsts." She was the first African-American woman ambassador (to Luxembourg, under President Lyndon Johnson), the first black to hold a U.S. cabinet position (secretary of Housing and Urban Development under President Carter), the first to hold two cabinet posts (adding secretary of Health, Education and Welfare — then HHS), the first black woman on a major company's corporate board of directors, and the first black woman to serve as dean of the Howard University School of Law. This is the 23rd stamp in the series. Designed by Howard Paine. *Self-adhesive panes of 20, offset by Ashton Potter USA Ltd., (150,000,000 printed) on phosphored paper, perforated 11 1/2 x 11 1/4.*

CM2106 *Patricia Roberts Harris*

CM2106		MNHVF	UseVF
33¢	**multicolored**	.50	.20
	Plate block of 4	2.00	
	FDC *(Jan. 27, 2000)*		1.25
	y. Pane of 20	10.00	

2000. U.S. Navy Submarines Issue was issued at Groton, Conn., which in World War I was named the first U.S. submarine base and in 1954 became the launch site of the USS *Nautilus,* the first nuclear-powered sub and the only other one to be pictured on a U.S. stamp (CM437). Images depict the USS *Holland* (60¢), S Class submarine (22¢), *Gato*-class submarine ($3.20), *Los Angeles* class attack submarine (33¢), *Trident* class intercontinental ballistic missile submarine (55¢). Designed by Carl Herrman, Carlsbad, Calif. *Prestige booklet panes of 5, offset by Banknote Corporation of America, (1,500,000 booklets printed), (15,000,000 stamps printed).*

CM2107 *USS* Holland; CM2108 *S Class submarine;* CM2109 Gato-*class submarine;* CM2110 Los Angeles *class attack submarine;* CM2111 Trident-*class ICBM submarine*

		MNHVF	UseVF
CM2107			
60¢	**USS *Holland***	1.20	1.00
CM2108			
22¢	**S Class submarine**	.40	.30
CM2109			
$3.20	***Gato*-class submarine**	6.00	2.50
CM2110			
33¢	***Los Angeles*-class attack submarine**	.60	.30
CM2111			
55¢	**Trident-*class ICBM submarine***	1.00	1.00
	Pane of 5	10.00	7.00
	FDC *(March 27, 2000),* booklet pane		10.50
	n. Booklet pane of 5 plus descriptive text	10.00	

Note: CM2111 was issued with two different descriptive texts.

2000. Los Angeles Class Submarine Issue Designed by Carl Herrman, Carlsbad, Calif. *Gummed panes of 20, offset by Banknote Corporation of America, (65,150,000 printed) with microprinting USPS at base of sail.*

CM2112 Los Angeles *class submarine*

CM2112		MNHVF	UseVF
33¢	**multicolored**	.50	.20
	Plate block of 4	2.00	
	FDC *(March 27, 2000)*		1.50
	y. Pane of 20	10.00	

2000. Pacific Coast Rain Forest Issue second in the Nature in America series, featured 10 plants and animals in an overall scene. Designed by John D. Dawson of Hilo, Hawaii (art director Ethel Kessler of Bethesda, Md.) *Self-adhesive panes of 10, offset by Banknote Corporation of America with (100,000,000 printed), microprinting USPS.*

CM2113a *Roosevelt elk;* CM2113b *Harlequin duck;* CM2113c *Snail-eating ground beetle;* CM2113d *American dipper;* CM2113e *Winter wren;* CM2113f *Douglas squirrel;* CM2113g *Pacific giant salamander;* CM2113h *Western tiger swallowtail;* CM2113i *Banana slug;* CM2113j *Cutthroat trout*

CM2113		MNHVF	UseVF
33¢	**multicolored,** pane of 10	7.50	—
	a. Roosevelt elk	.50	.20
	b. Harlequin duck	.50	.20
	c. Snail-eating ground beetle	.50	.20
	d. American dipper	.50	.20
	e. Winter wren	.50	.20
	f. Douglas squirrel	.50	.20
	g. Pacific giant salamander	.50	.20
	h. Western tiger swallowtail	.50	.20
	i. Banana slug	.50	.20
	j. Cutthroat trout	.50	.20
	FDC *(March 29, 2000)*		1.50

2000. Louise Nevelson Issue honored a pioneering sculptor who arranged carved, recycled, and painted wooden objects in boxes and stacked to create sculptural walls. Nevelson (1899-1988) was born in Kiev and came to the United States with her family in 1905. She lived and worked in New York City for most of her life. The pane selvage includes a portrait of the artist. Designed by Ethel Kessler, Bethesda, Md. *Gummed pane of 20, offset by Ashton Potter USA Ltd., (55,000,000 printed).*

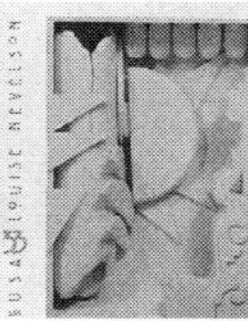

CM2114 Silent Music I; CM2115 Royal Tide I; CM2116 Black Chord; CM2117 Night-Sphere-Light; CM2118 Wedding Chapel I

CM2114		MNHVF	UseVF
33¢	**multicolored**	.50	.20
CM2115		MNHVF	UseVF
33¢	**multicolored**	.50	.20
CM2116		MNHVF	UseVF
33¢	**multicolored**	.50	.20
CM2117		MNHVF	UseVF
33¢	**multicolored**	.50	.20
CM2118		MNHVF	UseVF
33¢	**multicolored**	.50	.20
	Plate block of 10	5.00	
	FDC *(April 6, 2000)*		5.00
	y. Pane of 20	10.00	
	y1. Strip of 5	2.50	1.00

2000. Edwin Powell Hubble Issue honored an American astronomer who vastly expanded mankind's concept of the universe. The five designs feature remarkable images of distant celestial features captured by the orbiting Hubble Space Telescope named after him. The selvage depicts Hubble (1889-1953) at the 48-inch Schmidt Telescope at Palomar Observatory. Designed by Phil Jordan, Falls Church, Va. *Gummed panes of 20, gravure by Sennett Security Products, (105,350,000 printed).*

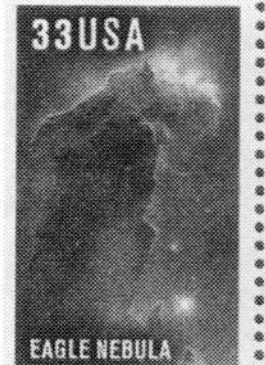

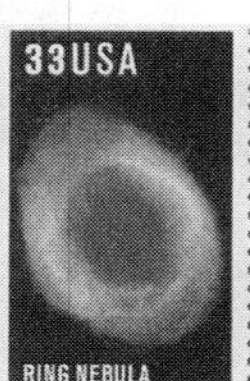

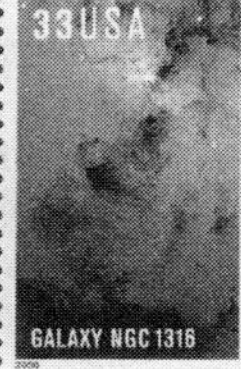

CM2119-23

CM2119		MNHVF	UseVF
33¢	**Eagle Nebula**	.50	.20
CM2120		MNHVF	UseVF
33¢	**Ring Nebula**	.50	.20
CM2121		MNHVF	UseVF
33¢	**Lagoon Nebula**	.50	.20
CM2122		MNHVF	UseVF
33¢	**Egg Nebula**	.50	.20
CM2123		MNHVF	UseVF
33¢	**Galaxy NGC 1316**	.50	.20
	Plate block of 10	5.00	
	FDC *(April 10, 2000)*		5.00
	y. Pane of 20	10.00	
	y1. Strip of 5	2.50	1.00

2000. American Samoa Issue marked the 100th anniversary of the union between the U.S. and the South Pacific Ocean territory. The stamp features an 'alia, the traditional double canoe of the Samoans, sailing near Sunuitao Peak on the island of Ofu. The territory consists of five volcanic islands and two coral atolls. Designed by Howard Paine, Delaplane, Va. *Gummed panes of 20, offset by Ashton Potter USA Ltd., (16,000,000 printed) with microprinting Samoa.*

CM2124 *American Samoa canoe*

CM2124		MNHVF	UseVF
33¢	**multicolored**	.50	.20
	Plate block of 4	2.00	
	FDC *(April 17, 2000)*		1.50
	y. Pane of 20	10.00	

2000. Library of Congress Issue Designed by Ethel Kessler, from a photo by Michael Freeman, London, England. *Gummed panes of 20, offset with microprinting USPS by Ashton Potter USA Ltd., (55,000,000 printed).*

CM2125 *Library of Congress*

CM2125		MNHVF	UseVF
33¢	**multicolored**	.50	.20
	Plate block of 4	2.00	
	FDC *(April 24, 2000)*		1.50
	y. Pane of 20	10.00	

2000. Celebrate the Century 1990-1999 Issue the 10th and last in the Celebrate the Century Series highlighting each decade of the 20th century. Designed by Howard Paine, Delaplane, Va. *Gummed panes of 15, offset by Ashton Potter USA Ltd., (82,500,000 printed), (5,500,000 panes).*

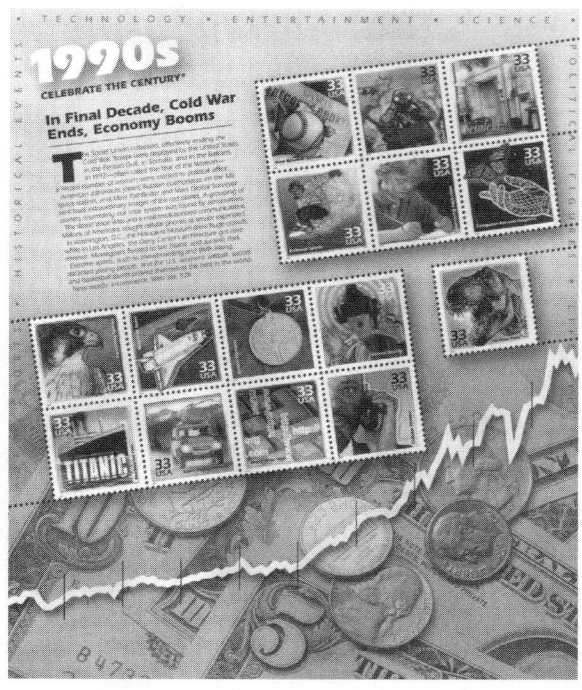

CM2126a-2126o *Celebrate the Century 1990s*

CM2126

		MNHVF	UseVF
33¢	**Commemorative pane of 15, multicolored,** tagged	10.00	7.00
	FDC *(May 2, 2000)*	—	
	a. New Baseball Records	.50	.20
	b. Gulf War	.50	.20
	c. Sitcom Sensation *(Seinfeld)*	.50	.20
	d. Extreme Sports	.50	.20
	e. Improving Education	.50	.20
	f. Computer Art and Graphics	.50	.20
	g. Recovering Species	.50	.20
	h. Return to Space	.50	.20
	i. Special Olympics	.50	.20
	j. Virtual Reality	.50	.20
	k. *Jurassic Park*	.50	.20
	l. Blockbuster Film *(Titanic)*	.50	.20
	m. Sport Utility Vehicles	.50	.20
	n. World Wide Web	.50	.20
	o. Cellular Phones	.50	.20
	FDC *(May 2, 2000)*		—
	FDC (any single)	—	
	Sheet of 4 panes	10.00	

2000. Wile E. Coyote & Road Runner Issue the fourth in the Warner Bros. Cartoon Characters Series, featured the nonchalant Road-runner and his conniving but perennially thwarted nemisis, Wile E. Coy-ote. Designed and illustrated by Ed Wleczyk, Los Angeles, Calif. *Offset with microprinting by Banknote Corporation of America. 300,000,000 printed, (30,000,000 panes).*

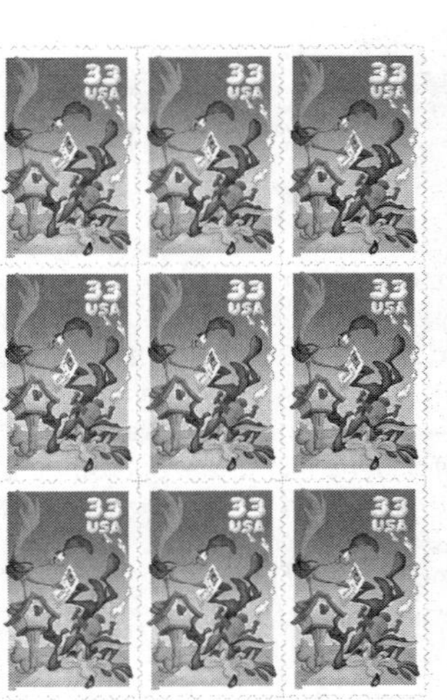

CM2127-CM2128 *Wile E. Coyote & Road Runner*

CM2127

		MNHVF	UseVF
33¢	**multicolored**	7.50	
	Pane of 10, tagged (30,000,000 panes)	7.50	
	n. Right half of pane (single die cut CM2127a superimposed on enlarged image)	1.00	1.00
	n1. Left half of pane (block of 9 CM2127a)	6.00	
	a. 33¢ single	.75	.20
	FDC *(April 26, 2000)* (Pane of 10)		10.00
	FDC (single)		2.00

CM2128 *Wile E. Coyote & Road Runner*

CM2128

		MNHVF	UseVF
33¢	**multicolored**	7.50	
	Pane of 10, tagged	7.50	
	n. Right half of pane (single imperforate CM2128a superimposed on enlarged image)	1.00	
	n1. Left of pane (block of 9 CM2128a)	6.00	
	a. 33¢ single	.75	.20
	FDC *(April 26, 2000)* (Pane of 10, 1 imperforate)		15.00
	FDC (Pane of 1 imperforate)		12.00

2000. Distinguished Soldiers Issue saluted four American war heroes. John L. Hines (1868-1968) took part in the Battle of San Juan Hill in the Spanish-American War, was ajutant to Gen. John J. Pershing in the Mexican Expedition, and was promoted from major to major general during World War I and succeeded Pershing as Army Chief of Staff in 1924. Omar Bradley (1893-1981) commanded the American ground forces in the invasion of Normandy during World War II, the largest American field command in history. He headed the Veterans Administration after the war and became the first chairman of the Joint Chiefs of Staff in 1949. Alvin C. York (1887-1964) won the Medal of Honor for his exploits in a battle at the Argonne Forest during World War I. He was credited with killing 25 Germans, capturing 132 and silencing 35 machine guns. It was "the greatest thing accomplished by any private soldier of all the armies of Europe," according to Allied Commander Marshall Ferdinand Foch. Audie L. Murphy (1924-1971) won the Medal of Honor for his actions during a German attack in World War II. Ordering the men to retreat, he remained to man a machine gun and break up the attack, killing 240 of the enemy. He wrote a book about his war experiences and played himself in a motion picture based upon it. Designed by Phil Jordan, Falls Church, Va. *Offset by Sterling Sommer. 55,000,000 printed, (2,750,000 panes).*

CM2129 *John L. Hines;* CM2130 *Omar Bradley;* CM2131 *Alvin C. York;* CM2132 *Audie L. Murphy*

CM2129

		MNHVF	UseVF
33¢	**multicolored**	.50	.20

CM2130

		MNHVF	UseVF
33¢	**multicolored**	.50	.20

CM2131

		MNHVF	UseVF
33¢	**multicolored**	.50	.20

CM2132

		MNHVF	UseVF
33¢	**multicolored**	.50	.20
	Plate block of 4	2.00	
	FDC *(May 3, 2000),* single		1.50
	y1. Block of 4	2.00	.80
	FDC (block)		6.00
	y. Pane of 20	10.00	

2000. Summer Sports Issue portrayed through a blurred photograph the speed of a track event. Designed by Richard Sheaff, Scottsdale, Ariz., from a photograph by David Madison, Portola Valley, Calif. *Offset, with microprinting "USPS" under the runner's numeral 4, by Ashton-Potter, USA. Perforated 11. 90,600,000 printed.*

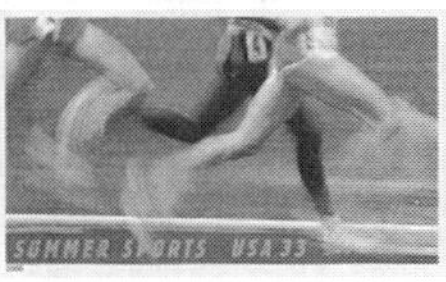

CM2133 *Runners*

CM2133		MNHVF	UseVF
33¢	**multicolored**	.50	.20
	Plate block of 4	2.00	
	FDC *(May 5, 2000)*		1.50

2000. Adoption Issue intended to raise awareness that more than 100,000 children are available for adoption in the United States each year. Designed by Greg Berger, Bethesda, Md. *Offset with microprinting "USPS" at corner of house, by Banknote Corporation of America. Die cut perforation 11. 200,000,000 printed.*

CM2134 *Adoption awareness*

CM2134		MNHVF	UseVF
33¢	**multicolored**	.50	.20
	Plate block of 4	2.00	
	FDC *(May 10, 2000)*		1.50
	y. Pane of 20	10.00	

2000. Youth Team Sports Issue captured typical moments of kids playing four popular team sports. Photos were by William Sallaz, basketball; Mike Powell, football; Zoran Milich, soccer; and Bob Wickley, baseball. Designed by Derry Noyes, Washington, D.C. *Offset by Sterling Sommer. Perforated 10 3/4. 88,000,000 printed.*

CM2135 *Basketball;* CM2136 *Football;* CM2137 *Soccer;* CM2138 *Baseball*

CM2135		MNHVF	UseVF
33¢	**multicolored**	.50	.20
CM2136		MNHVF	UseVF
33¢	**multicolored**	.50	.20
CM2137		MNHVF	UseVF
33¢	**multicolored**	.50	.20
CM2138		MNHVF	UseVF
33¢	**multicolored**	.50	.20
	Plate block of 4	2.00	
	FDC *(May 27, 2000)*, single		1.50
	FDC (block)		6.00
	y. Pane of 20	10.00	
	y1. Strip of 4	2.00	.80

> Input from stamp collectors regarding the content of this catalog and ideas to make it more useful is eagerly sought. Send your comments to:
>
> Minkus Catalog Editor
> Krause Publications
> 700 E. State St.
> Iola WI 54990

2000. Stars and Stripes Issue in the Classic Collection Series tracked the 225-year evolution of the American flag, with text on the backs of the stamps written by Dr. Whitney Smith of the Flag Research Center. Designed by Richard Sheaff, Scottsdale, Ariz. *Offset by Sennett Security Products. Perforated 10 1/2. 80,000,000 printed.*

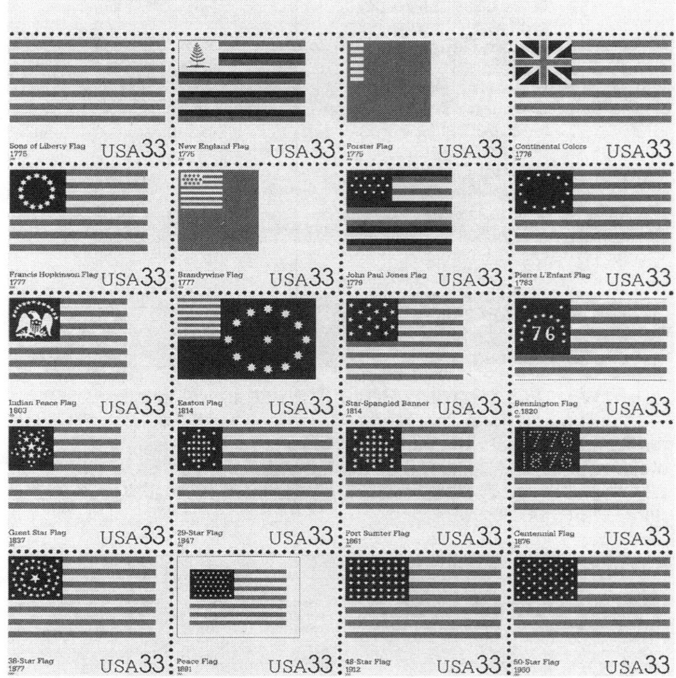

CM2139 *Sons of Liberty Flag, 1775, represented the unity of the 13 colonies, probably inspired the stripes in Old Glory;* CM2140 *New England Flag, 1775, featured a pine tree and red, white and blue stripes;* CM2141 *Forster Flag, 1775, captured from the British, the altered red and white canton represented the colonies;* CM2142 *Continental Colors, 1776, carried the British Union Jack as a canton and 13 stripes;* CM2143 *Francis Hopkinson Flag, 1777, constituted the first "Stars and Stripes;"* CM2144 *Brandywine Flag, 1777, may have been a militia color carried at the Battle of Brandywine;* CM2145 *John Paul Jones Flag, 1779, was hoisted in victory when* Bonhomme Richard *captured* HMS Serapis; CM2146 *Pierre L'Enfant Flag, 1783, was sketched by the man who drew up the original plans for the layout of Washington, D.C.;* CM2147 *Indian Peace Flag, 1803, displayed the U.S. coat of arms and was presented to friendly Indian nations by the government;* CM2148 *Easton Flag, 1814, presented to volunteers from Easton, Pa., in the War of 1812, reversed the official placement of the stars and stripes;* CM2149 *Star-Spangled Banner, 1814, featured the "broad stripes and bright stars" that inspired Francis Scott Key to write the poem that became our national anthem;* CM2150 *Bennington Flag, c.1820, has an uncertain origin;* CM2151 *Great Star Flag, 1837, contained its stars in a star pattern;* CM2152 *29-Star Flag, 1847, featured a diamond pattern of stars in the canton, with stars for four more states added in the corners;* CM2153 *Fort Sumter Flag, 1861, was flying over the fort at Charleston, S.C., when the first shots of the Civil War were fired;* CM2154 *Centennial Flag, 1876, was unofficial but reflected the patriotism of the people who made it;* CM2155 *38-Star Flag, 1877, features another imaginative star design; rows did not become standard until 1912;* CM2156 *Peace Flag, 1891, carried the Stars and Stripes within a field of white;* CM2157 *48-Star Flag, 1912, was official for 47 years, the longest period for any fixed star pattern;* CM2158 *50-Star Flag, 1960, represents the current configuration*

CM2139		MNHVF	UseVF
33¢	**multicolored**	.50	.20
CM2140		MNHVF	UseVF
33¢	**multicolored**	.50	.20
CM2141		MNHVF	UseVF
33¢	**multicolored**	.50	.20
CM2142		MNHVF	UseVF
33¢	**multicolored**	.50	.20

CM2143 MNHVF UseVF
33¢ multicolored .50 .20
CM2144 MNHVF UseVF
33¢ multicolored .50 .20
CM2145 MNHVF UseVF
33¢ multicolored .50 .20
CM2146 MNHVF UseVF
33¢ multicolored .50 .20
CM2147 MNHVF UseVF
33¢ multicolored .50 .20
CM2148 MNHVF UseVF
33¢ multicolored .50 .20
CM2149 MNHVF UseVF
33¢ multicolored .50 .20
CM2150 MNHVF UseVF
33¢ multicolored .50 .20
CM2151 MNHVF UseVF
33¢ multicolored .50 .20
CM2152 MNHVF UseVF
33¢ multicolored .50 .20
CM2153 MNHVF UseVF
33¢ multicolored .50 .20
CM2154 MNHVF UseVF
33¢ multicolored .50 .20
CM2155 MNHVF UseVF
33¢ multicolored .50 .20
CM2156 MNHVF UseVF
33¢ multicolored .50 .20
CM2157 MNHVF UseVF
33¢ multicolored .50 .20
CM2158 MNHVF UseVF
33¢ multicolored .50 .20
FDC *(June 14, 2000)*, single 1.50
FDC, pane 20.00
y. Pane of 20 10.00

2000. Legends of Baseball Issue in the Classic Collections Series honored 20 players chosen as Major League Baseball's All-Century Team. Designed by Phil Jordan, Falls Church, Va., with illustrations by Joseph Saffold, Savannah, Ga. *Offset by Ashton-Potter, USA. Die cut perforation 11. 225,000,000 printed.*

CM2159 *Jackie Robinson;* CM2160 *Eddie Collins;* CM2161 *Christy Mathewson;* CM2162 *Ty Cobb;* CM2163 *George Sisler;* CM2164 *Rogers Hornsby;* CM2165 *Mickey Cochrane;* CM2166 *Babe Ruth;* CM2167 *Walter Johnson;* CM2168 *Roberto Clemente;* CM2169 *Lefty Grove;* CM2170 *Tris Speaker;* CM2171 *Cy Young;* CM2172 *Jimmie Foxx;* CM2173 *Pie Traynor;* CM2174 *Satchel Paige;* CM2175 *Honus Wagner;* CM2176 *Josh Gibson;* CM2177 *Dizzy Dean;* CM2178 *Lou Gehrig*

CM2159 MNHVF UseVF
33¢ multicolored .50 .20
CM2160 MNHVF UseVF
33¢ multicolored .50 .20
CM2161 MNHVF UseVF
33¢ multicolored .50 .20
CM2162 MNHVF UseVF
33¢ multicolored .50 .20
CM2163 MNHVF UseVF
33¢ multicolored .50 .20
CM2164 MNHVF UseVF
33¢ multicolored .50 .20
CM2165 MNHVF UseVF
33¢ multicolored .50 .20
CM2166 MNHVF UseVF
33¢ multicolored .50 .20
CM2167 MNHVF UseVF
33¢ multicolored .50 .20
CM2168 MNHVF UseVF
33¢ multicolored .50 .20
CM2169 MNHVF UseVF
33¢ multicolored .50 .20
CM2170 MNHVF UseVF
33¢ multicolored .50 .20
CM2171 MNHVF UseVF
33¢ multicolored .50 .20
CM2172 MNHVF UseVF
33¢ multicolored .50 .20
CM2173 MNHVF UseVF
33¢ multicolored .50 .20
CM2174 MNHVF UseVF
33¢ multicolored .50 .20
CM2175 MNHVF UseVF
33¢ multicolored .50 .20
CM2176 MNHVF UseVF
33¢ multicolored .50 .20
CM2177 MNHVF UseVF
33¢ multicolored .50 .20
CM2178 MNHVF UseVF
33¢ multicolored .50 .20
FDC *(July 6, 2000)*, single 1.50
FDC, pane 20.00
y. Pane of 20 10.00

2000. Space Achievement and Exploration Issue was the first holographic stamp and first circular stamp issued by the United States. The Express Mail rate hologram, on a souvenir sheet for World Stamp Expo 2000 (which had a Space theme), showed the western hemisphere of the Earth from space. (For previous hologram envelopes, see Minkus Nos. EN917, EN918, EN925 and EN945.) Designed by Richard Sheaff, Scottsdale, Ariz. *Gravure and Hologram by Sennett Security Products. Perforated 10 1/2. 1,695,000 printed.*

CM2179 *Earth from space*

CM2179 MNHVF UseVF
$11.75 multicolored 22.00 10.00
FDC *(July 7, 2000)* 25.00
y. Sheetlet 22.00 11.00

Note: The foil hologram is affixed with water-soluble adhesive and may release from the stamp while soaking.

2000. Landing on the Moon Issue was a second Express Mail rate hologram stamp issued on an illustrated sheetlet of one during World Stamp Expo 2000. It depicted the Lunar Landar blasting off from the Moon, formed with computer images and a model of the lander. The selvage illustration was a photo of astronaut Charles M. Duke Jr., taken by astronaut John W. Young during the Apollo 16 mission in April 1972. Designed by Richard Sheaff, Scottsdale, Ariz. *Gravure and Hologram by Sennett Security Products. Perforated 10 1/2. 1,695,000 printed.*

CM2180 *Lunar Lander blasting off from the Moon*

CM2180		MNHVF	UseVF
$11.75	**multicolored**	22.00	10.00
	FDC *(July 8, 2000)*		25.00
	y. Sheetlet	22.00	11.00

Note: The foil hologram is affixed with water-soluble adhesive and may release from the stamp while soaking.

We regret that we cannot pass upon the authenticity of any stamp. Should you have stamps for which you desire authentication, we suggest that you contact a recognized expertizing service. Those listed here are considered competent general authorities. Expertizing committees offer opinions only, not guarantees. Opinions may vary among services, and over the years an opinion may change.

American Philatelic Expertizing Service (APEX)
P.O. Box 8000
State College, PA 16803-8000

Philatelic Foundation
501 Fifth Ave., Room 1901
New York, NY 10017

Professional Stamp Experts (PSE), Inc.
P.O. Box 43-0055
Miami, FL 33243-0055

Prior to your submitting an item for review, the expertizer should be contacted to determine fees and procedures required to accompany a submission.

2000. Escaping the Gravity of Earth Issue featured two more hologram stamps on an illustrated sheetlet issued at World Stamp Expo 2000. The Priority Mail rate stamps showed a computer-generated image of a space shuttle docking with the International Space Station (CM2181) and a model of astronauts fabricating the International Space Station (CM2182). The selvage showed astronauts David Leestma (with the red stripes on his legs) and Kathryn Sullivan in the cargo bay of the Challenger space shuttle during an October 1984 mission. Designed by Richard Sheaff, Scottsdale, Ariz. *Gravure and Hologram by Sennett Security Products. Perforated 10 1/2. 1,695,000 printed.*

CM2181 *Space shuttle;* CM2182 *Astronauts at work*

CM2181		MNHVF	UseVF
$3.20	**multicolored**	6.50	3.00
	FDC *(July 9, 2000)*		1.50

Note: The foil holograms are affixed with water-soluble adhesive and may release from the stamps while soaking.

CM2182		MNHVF	UseVF
$3.20	**multicolored**	6.50	3.00
	FDC *(July 9, 2000)*		1.50
	y. Souvenir sheet of 2	15.00	7.50
	y1. Pair, CM2181-82	15.00	6.50

2000. Probing the Vastness of Space Issue featured six International rate stamps that showed various telescopes on an illustrated six-stamp sheetlet at World Stamp Expo 2000. The selvage was a view of the Eagle Nebula, part of which was on one of the Edwin Powell Hubble stamps of 2000 (CM2119). Designed by Richard Sheaff, Scottsdale, Ariz. *Gravure by Sennett Security Products. Perforated 10 1/2. 1,695,000 printed.*

CM2183 *2.4 Meter Mirror Optical Telescopes, Hubble Space Telescope;* CM2184 *Radio Interferometer Very Large Array, National Radio Astronomy Observatory;* CM2185 *Twin 10-Meter Optical and Infrared Telescopes, Keck Observatory, Mauna Kea, Hawaii;* CM2186 *Optical Telescopes, Cerro Tololo Inter-American Observatory east of La Serena, Chile;* CM2187 *100-inch Optical Telescope, Mount Wilson Observatory near Pasadena, Calif.;* CM2188 *1,000-Foot Dish Radio Telescope, Arecibo Observatory in Puerto Rico*

		MNHVF	UseVF
CM2183			
60¢	**multicolored**	1.10	.60
CM2184			
60¢	**multicolored**	1.10	.60
CM2185			
60¢	**multicolored**	1.10	.60
CM2186			
60¢	**multicolored**	1.10	.60
CM2187			
60¢	**multicolored**	1.10	.60
CM2188			
60¢	**multicolored**	1.10	.60
	FDC *(July 10, 2000),* single		1.50
	FDC, sheetlet		15.00
	y. Pane of 6	7.00	

Each entry in this catalog has been double-checked for accuracy, but mistakes may creep into any human endeavor, and we ask your assistance in eliminating them. Please call the attention of the editors to any errors in stamp description found in this catalog. Send your comments to:

Minkus Catalog Editor
Krause Publications
700 E. State St.
Iola WI 54990

2000. Exploring the Solar System Issue featured the first pentagonal stamps issued by the United States on an illustrated five-stamp sheetlet at World Stamp Expo. The $1 stamps offered views of the Sun. The selvage depicted a montage of Saturn and several moons, imaged by *Voyager 1* in November 1980. Designed by Richard Sheaff, Scottsdale, Ariz. *Gravure by Sennett Security Products. Perforated 10 1/2. 1,695,000 printed.*

CM2189 *Solar eclipse from a satellite;* CM2190 *An illustrated cutaway view;* CM2191 *A digitally restored NASA image of sunrise from space;* CM2192 *Solar eruption taken by Skylab on Dec. 19, 1973;* CM2193 *Photo from Earth of the Sun in a partly cloudy sky*

		MNHVF	UseVF
CM2189			
$1	**multicolored**	2.00	1.00
CM2190			
$1	**multicolored**	2.00	1.00
CM2191			
$1	**multicolored**	2.00	1.00
CM2192			
$1	**multicolored**	2.00	1.00
CM2193			
$1	**multicolored**	2.00	1.00
	FDC *(July 11, 2000),* single		2.00
	FDC, pane		10.00
	y. Pane of 5	10.00	

2000. Stampin' the Future Issue featured winning designs from 120,000 contest entries by U.S. children aged 8-12. Designed by Richard Sheaff, Scottsdale, Ariz., illustrators: Zachary Canter, astronauts; Sara Lipsey, children; Morgan Hill, rocket; and Ashley Young, dog. *Self-adhesive panes of 20, offset by Ashton-Potter, USA. Die cut perforated 11. 100,000,000 printed.*

CM2194 *astronauts;* CM2195 *children;* CM2196 *rocket;* CM2197 *dog*

		MNHVF	UseVF
CM2194			
33¢	**multicolored**	.50	.20
CM2195		MNHVF	UseVF
33¢	**multicolored**	.50	.20
CM2196		MNHVF	UseVF
33¢	**multicolored**	.50	.20
CM2197		MNHVF	UseVF
33¢	**multicolored**	.50	.20
	Plate block of 4	2.00	
	FDC *(July 13, 2000)* (single)		1.50
	FDC (block)		6.00
	y. Pane of 20	10.00	

2000. California Statehood Issue in the Statehood Series featured a color photograph of cliffs at the Big Sur coastline, with the invasive plant pest iceplant blooming in the foreground. Designed by Carl Herrman, Carlsbad, Calif., from photo by Art Wolfe, Seattle Wash. *Self-adhesive panes of 20, gravure by Avery Dennison, (53,000,000 printed).*

2198 *Cliffs at the Big Sur coastline*

		MNHVF	UseVF
CM2198			
33¢	**multicolored**	.50	.20
	Plate block of 4	2.00	
	FDC *(Sept. 8, 2000)*		1.50

Please do not send us stamps to be authenticated. This type of service requires elaborate equipment and facilities not regularly available to us. We suggest that you write to the following for information:

American Philatelic Expertizing Service (APEX)
P.O. Box 8000
State College, PA 16803-8000

Philatelic Foundation
501 Fifth Ave., Room 1901
New York, NY 10017

Professional Stamp Experts (PSE), Inc.
P.O. Box 43-0055
Miami, FL 33243-0055

2000. Deep-Sea Creatures Issue for National Stamp Collecting Month showed sea life whose normal habitat is 330 feet to more than 3,300 feet below the ocean surface. Designed by Ethel Kessler, Bethesda, Md. *Gummed panes of 15, gravure by Sennett Security Products, (85,000,000 printed).*

CM2199 *Fanfin anglerfish;* CM2200 *Sea cucumber;* CM2201 *Fangtooth;* CM2202 *Amphipod;* CM2203 *Medusa*

		MNHVF	UseVF
CM2199			
33¢	**Fanfin anglerfish**	.50	.20
CM2200		MNHVF	UseVF
33¢	**Sea cucumber**	.50	.20
CM2201		MNHVF	UseVF
33¢	**Fangtooth**	.50	.20
CM2202		MNHVF	UseVF
33¢	**Amphipod**	.50	.20
CM2203		MNHVF	UseVF
33¢	**Medusa**	.50	.20
	y. Strip of 5	2.50	
	FDC *(Oct. 2, 2000)*		1.50
	y1. Pane of 15	10.00	

2000. Thomas Wolfe Issue 18th in the Literary Arts Series marked the 100th birthday of Wolfe (1900-1938), author of novels including *Look Homeward, Angel, Of Time and the River* and *You Can't Go Home Again,* based on his life in North Carolina. Wolfe died of tuberculosis. Designed by Michael J. Deas, illustrator. *Gummed panes of 20, offset by Ashton-Potter (USA) with microprinting "Author." (53,000,000 printed).*

CM2204 *Thomas Wolfe*

		MNHVF	UseVF
CM2204			
33¢	**multicolored**	.50	.20
	Plate block of 4	2.00	
	FDC *(Oct. 3, 2000)*		1.50

2000. The White House Issue marked the bicentennial of the construction of the house designed as the living quarters of the president of the United States. Designed by architect James Hoban

(CM994 and CM995) for a site chosen by President George Washington and planner Pierre L' Enfant, construction started in 1792, and it was first occupied by President John Adams and his wife, Abigail. Designed by Derry Noyes, Washington, D.C., from a photo by Patricia Fisher, Washington, D.C. *Self-adhesive panes of 20, offset by Ashton-Potter (USA), (125,000,000 printed).*

CM2205 *White House on a a winter evening*

CM2205		MNHVF	UseVF
33¢	**multicolored**	.50	.20
	Plate block of 4	2.00	
	FDC *(Feb. 25, 2000)*		1.50

2000. Edward G. Robinson Issue featured, on the sixth in the Legends of Hollywood Series, the actor known for his roles as gangsters, notably in *Little Caesar,* (1931). Born in Romania, Robinson (1893-1973) immigrated to the United States with his family as a youngster and started his professional acting career in 1913. The stamp image is based on a photo by Elmer Fryer. The selvage photo is a publicity still from the film *Five Star Final* (1931), in which Robinson played a tough newspaper editor. Designed by Howard Paine, Delaplane, Va., illustrated by Drew Struzan, Pasadena, Calif. *Gummed panes of 20, gravure by Sennett Security Products (52,000,000 printed).*

CM2206 *Edward G. Robinson*

CM2206		MNHVF	UseVF
33¢	**multicolored**	.50	.20
	Plate block of 4	2.00	
	FDC *(Oct. 24, 2000)*		1.50
	y. Pane of 20	10.00	

2001. Rose and Love Letter Issue in the Love Series. Featured a love letter written by John Adams, who would become the second U.S. president, to Abigail Smith, who would become his wife, on April 20, 1763. The excerpt is from a passage that reads: "I am at Braintree but I wish I was at Weymouth! What strange Revolutions take Place in our Breasts, and what curious Vicissitudes in every Part of human Life. This summer I shall like Weymouth better than Braintree but something prompts me to believe I shall like Braintree next Winter better than Weymouth. Writers who procure Reputation by flattering human Nature, tell us that Mankind grows wiser and wiser: whether they lie, or speak the Truth, I know I like it, better and better. _ I would feign make an original, an Exemplar, of this Letter but fear I have not an original Genius." *Designed by Lisa Catalone, Washington, D.C., from photo by Renee Comet, Washington, D.C., offset by Banknote Corporation of America (510,000,000) printed, serpentine die cut 11 3/4 on 2, 3 or 4 sides.*

CM2207 *Rose and Love Letter*

CM2207		MNHVF	UseVF
(34¢)	**multicolored**	.70	.20
	Plate block of 4	3.00	
	FDC *(Jan. 19, 2001)*		1.50

2001. Year of the Snake Issue Lunar New Year Series. Was the ninth in a series featuring the creatures of the Chinese zodiac designed in paper cut fashion and calligraphy by artist Clarence Lee. *Gummed panes of 20, offset by Sterling Sommerfor Ashton-Potter (USA) Ltd. (55,000,000) printed on phosphored paper, perforated 11 1/4.*

CM2208 *Snake*

CM2208		MNHVF	UseVF
34¢	**multicolored**	.75	.25
	Plate block of 4	3.00	
	FDC *(Jan. 20, 2001)*		1.50
	y. Pane of 20	15.00	

2001. Roy Wilkins Issue Black Heritage Series. Civil rights leader Roy Wilkins (1901-81) joined the National Association for the Advancement of Colored People (NAACP) in 1931 and was executive secretary and executive director 1955-77. The traditional black-and-white stamp image was taken from a portrait photo by Morgan and Marvin Smith in the 1940s, and designed by Richard Sheaff. *Self-adhesive panes of 20, offset by Ashton Potter (USA) Ltd. on phosphored paper, serpentine die cut 11 1/2x11 1/4.*

CM2209 *Roy Wilkins*

CM2209		MNHVF	UseVF
34¢	**multicolored**	.75	.25
	Plate block of 4	3.00	
	FDC *(Jan. 24, 2001)*		1.50

2001. American Illustrators Issue in the Classic Collection Series featured illustrations by commercial artists in the 19th and 20th centuries. Designed by Carl Herrman. *Self-adhesive panes of 20, gravure by Avery Dennison (625,000 panes) printed on phosphored paper, serpentine die cut 11 1/4.*

Users of this catalog are invited to write to us if they have information they feel will supplement or correct any material contained herein. All such communications will be answered.

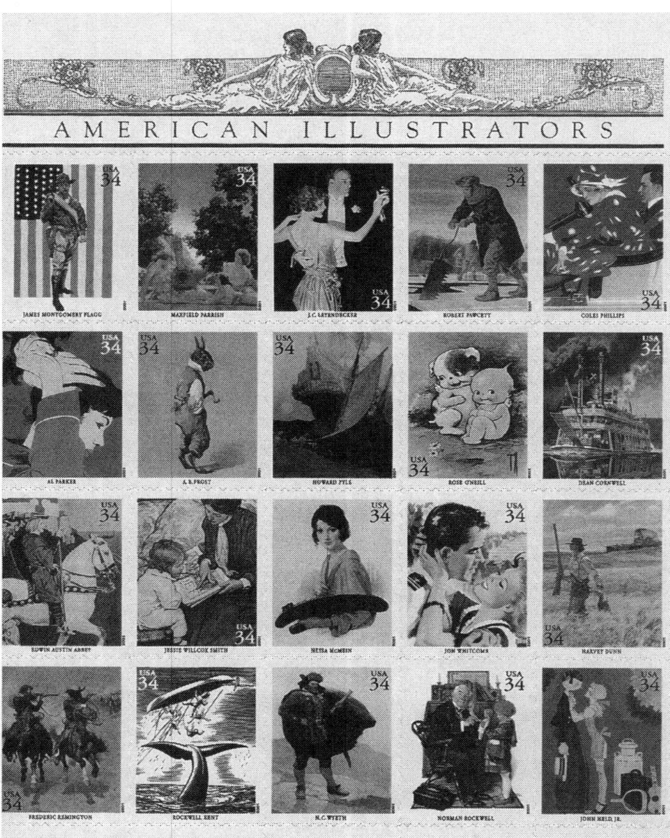

CM2210 *Marine Corps poster poster, "First in the Fight, Always Faithful," by James Montgomery Flagg;* CM2211 *"Interlude (The Lute Players)" by Maxfield Parrish;* CM2212 *Advertisement for Arrow Collars and Shirts by J.C. Leyendecker;* CM2213 *Advertisement for Carrier Corp. Refrigeration by Robert Fawcett;* CM2214 *Advertisement for Luxite Hosiery by Coles Phillips;* CM2215 *Illustration for correspondence school lesson by Al Parker;* CM2216 *"Br'er Rabbit," by A.B. Frost;* CM2217 *"An Attack on a Galleon," by Howard Pyle;* CM2218 *Kewpie and Kewpie Doodle Dog by Rose O'Neill;* CM2219 *Illustration for cover of True Magazine by Dean Cornwell;* CM2220 *"Galahad's Departure," by Edwin Austin Abbey;* CM2221 *"The First Lesson," by Jessie Willcox Smith;* CM2222 *Illustration for cover of McCall's Magazine by Neysa McMein;* CM2223 *"Back Home for Keeps," by Jon Whitcomb;* CM2224 *"Something for Supper," by Harvey Dunn;* CM2225 *"A Dash for the Timbver," by Frederic Remington;* CM2226 *Illustration for "Moby Dick" by Rockwell Kent;* CM2227 *"Captain Bill Bones," by N.C. Wyeth;* CM2228 *Illustration for cover of The Saturday Evening Post by Norman Rockwell;* CM2229 *"The Girl He Left Behind," by John Held Jr.*

		MNHVF	UseVF
CM2210			
34¢	**multicolored,** tagged (single)	.75	.25
CM2211		MNHVF	UseVF
34¢	**multicolored,** tagged (single)	.75	.25
CM2212		MNHVF	UseVF
34¢	**multicolored,** tagged (single)	.75	.25
CM2213		MNHVF	UseVF
34¢	**multicolored,** tagged (single)	.75	.25
CM2214		MNHVF	UseVF
34¢	**multicolored,** tagged (single)	.75	.25
CM2215		MNHVF	UseVF
34¢	**multicolored,** tagged (single)	.75	.25
CM2216		MNHVF	UseVF
34¢	**multicolored,** tagged (single)	.75	.25
CM2217		MNHVF	UseVF
34¢	**multicolored,** tagged (single)	.75	.25
CM2218		MNHVF	UseVF
34¢	**multicolored,** tagged (single)	.75	.25
CM2219		MNHVF	UseVF
34¢	**multicolored,** tagged (single)	.75	.25
CM2220		MNHVF	UseVF
34¢	**multicolored,** tagged (single)	.75	.25
CM2221		MNHVF	UseVF
34¢	**multicolored,** tagged (single)	.75	.25
CM2222		MNHVF	UseVF
34¢	**multicolored,** tagged (single)	.75	.25
CM2223		MNHVF	UseVF
34¢	**multicolored,** tagged, (single)	.75	.25
CM2224		MNHVF	UseVF
34¢	**multicolored,** tagged (single)	.75	.25
CM2225		MNHVF	UseVF
34¢	**multicolored,** tagged (single)	.75	.25
CM2226		MNHVF	UseVF
34¢	**multicolored,** tagged (single)	.75	.25
CM2227		MNHVF	UseVF
34¢	**multicolored,** tagged (single)	.75	.25
CM2228		MNHVF	UseVF
34¢	**multicolored,** tagged (single)	.75	.25
CM2229		MNHVF	UseVF
34¢	**multicolored,** tagged (single)	.75	.25
	FDC *(Feb. 1, 2001)*		1.50
	y. Pane of 20, tagged	15.00	

2001. Rose and Love Letter Issue in the Love Series. Featured on a 34¢ stamp a red rose against a love letter written by John Adams, who would become the second U.S. president, to Abigail Smith, who would become his wife; and, on a 55¢ stamp a pink rose against a letter from Smith to Adams. On April 20, 1763, Adams wrote, "I am at Braintree but I wish I was at Weymouth! What strange Revolutions take Place in our Breasts, and what curious Vicissitudes in every Part of human Life. This summer I shall like Weymouth better than Braintree but something prompts me to believe I shall like Braintree next Winter better than Weymouth. Writers who procure Reputation by flattering human Nature, tell us that Mankind grows wiser and wiser: whether they lie, or speak the Truth, I know I like it, better and better. _ I would feign make an original, an Exemplar, of this Letter but fear I have not an original Genius." On Aug. 11, 1763, Smith wrote, "If I was sure your absence today was occasioned, by what it generally is, either to wait upon Company, or promote some good work, I freely confess my Mind would be much more at ease than at present it is. Yet this uneasiness does not arise from any apprehension of Slight or neglect, but a fear least you are indisposed, for that you said should be your only hindrance. Humanity obliges us to be affected with the distresses and Miserys of our fellow creatures. Friendship is a band yet stronger; which causes us to feel with greater tenderness the afflictions of our Friends." *Images based on photographs by Renee Comet, Washington, D.C., designed by Lisa Catalone, Washington, D.C., offset with microprinting "USPS" by Banknote Corporation of America (4,000,000 vending booklets of CM2230 and 75,000 vending booklets of CM2231) printed on phosphored paper, self-adhesive, die cut 11 1/4 (convertible booklet and 55¢ stamp) or 10 1/2x11 1/4 (vending booklet).*

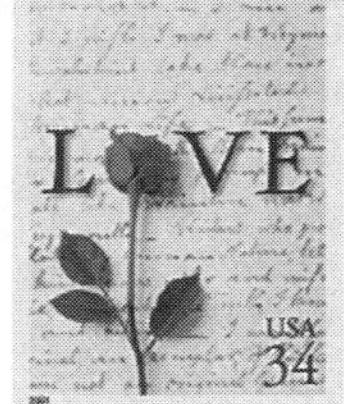

CM2230 *Rose and Love Letter*

		MNHVF	UseVF
CM2230			
34¢	**multicolored**	.70	.20
	n. Convertible booklet of 20	14.00	

CM2231 *Rose and Love Letter*

CM2231		MNHVF	UseVF
34¢	**multicolored**	.70	.20
	n. Vending booklet of 20	14.00	
	FDC		1.50

CM2232 *Rose and Love Letter*

CM2232		MNHVF	UseVF
55¢	**multicolored**	1.00	.40
	Plate block of 4	4.00	
	Pane of 20	20.00	
	FDC *(Feb. 14, 2001)*		2.00

2001. Diabetes Issue urged people to "Know More About Diabetes," which kills one American every three minutes. Self-adhesive panes of 20 illustrated by James Steinberg, Amherst, Mass., designed by Richard Sheaff, Scottsdale, Ariz., offset with "USPS" microprinting by Ashton-Potter (USA) Ltd. (100,000,000), serpentine die cut 11 1/4x11 1/2, phosphored paper.

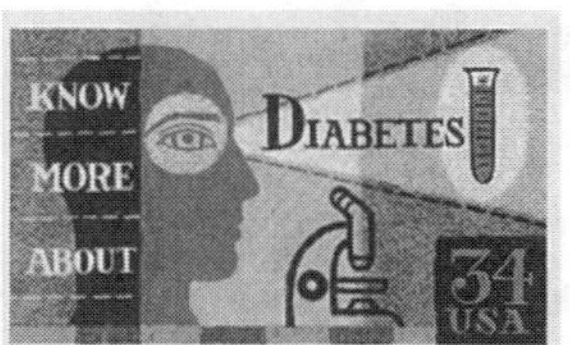

CM2233 *"Know More About Diabetes"*

CM2233		MNHVF	UseVF
34¢	**multicolored**	.70	.20
	Plate block of 4	2.80	
	FDC *(March 15, 2001)*		1.50

2001. Nobel Prize Centennial Issue honored the founding of the world's most prestigious awards for intellectual achievement. The man who endowed the prizes for physics, chemistry, physiology or medicine, literature and peace was Alfred Bernhard Nobel (1833-96), an immensely wealthy Swedish chemist and industrialist who invented dynamite and other explosives. Joint issue with Sweden, engraving by Czeslaw Slania. Designed by Olof Baldursdottir, Stockholm, Sweden, intaglio and offset by De La Rue Security Printing, Dulles, Va. (35,000,000), perforated 11, phosphored paper.

CM2234 *Alfred Bernhard Nobel (1833-96)*

CM2234		MNHVF	UseVF
34¢	**multicolored**	.65	.20
	Plate block of 4	2.60	
	FDC *(March 22, 2001)*		1.50

2001. Pan-American Exposition Centennial Issue reproduced three inverted-center stamps from the set issued for the 1901 Pan-American Exposition. The illustrated sheetlet also included 80¢ stamps based on the design of labels issued for the exposition. The background is taken from an exposition poster. *Designed by Richard Sheaff, offset and intaglio by Banknote Corporation of America (14,000,000), perforated 12 1/2x12 (1¢, 2¢, and 3¢), 12 (80¢).*

CM2235-CM2238 *Pan-American*

		MNHVF	UseVF
CM2235		**MNHVF**	**UseVF**
1¢	**green & black**	.20	.20
	FDC *(March 29, 2001)*		1.25
CM2236		**MNHVF**	**UseVF**
2¢	**carmine & black**	.20	.20
	FDC *(March 29, 2001)*		1.25
CM2237		**MNHVF**	**UseVF**
4¢	**red brown & black**	.20	.20
	FDC *(March 29, 2001)*		1.25
CM2238		**MNHVF**	**UseVF**
80¢	**red & blue**	1.60	.40
	FDC *(March 29, 2001)*		—
	y. Pane of 7	7.00	
	FDC, pane of 7		6.00

2001. Great Plains Prairie Issue third in the Nature of America Series featured the animal and plant life in one of the world's largest grasslands, stretching from the edge of the eastern woodlands and oak savannahs to the foothills of the Rocky Mountains. *Illustrated pane of 10, designed by Ethel Kessler from illustration by John D. Dawson, Hilo, Hawaii, offset by Ashton-Potter (USA) Ltd. (89,600,000), serpentine die cut 10.*

CM2239 *Animals of the Great Plains Prairie*

CM2239		MNHVF	UseVF
34¢	**multicolored,** single	.65	.20
	a. Pronghorns, Canada geese	.65	.20
	b. Burrowing owls, American bison	.65	.20
	c. American bison, black-tailed prairie dogs, wild alfalfa	.65	.20
	d. Black-tailed prairie dog, American bison	.65	.20
	e. Painted lady butterfly, American bison, prairie coneflowers, prairie wild roses	.65	.20
	f. Western meadowlark, camel cricket, prairie coneflowers, prairie wild roses	.65	.20
	g. Badger, harvester ants	.65	.20
	h. Eastern short-horned lizard, plains pocket gopher	.65	.20
	i. Plains spadefoot, dung beetle	.65	.20
	j. Two-striped grasshopper, Ord's kangaroo rat	.65	.20
	FDC *(April 19, 2001),* any single		1.25
	y. Pane of 10	7.00	
	FDC, pane of 10		7.00

2001. Peanuts Issue celebrated the cartoon dog Snoopy, in his "Red Baron" guise, created by Charles M. Schulz. At the time of the stamp issue, a year after Schulz's death, the comic strip appeared in 2,600 newspapers in 75 countries and was translated into 21 languages. *Designed by Carl Herrman from an illustration by Paige Braddock. Offset with microprinting "USPS" by Ashton-Potter (USA) Ltd. (125 million stamps), serpentine die cut 11 1/4x11 1/2.*

CM2240 "Red Baron"

CM2240		MNHVF	UseVF
34¢	**multicolored**	.65	.30
	Plate block of 4	5.00	
	FDC *(May 17, 2001)*		1.90
	y. Pane of 20	13.00	

2001. Veterans Continuing To Serve Issue paid tribute to the patriotism of the almost 25 million men and women who have served in the armed forces and are members of veterans service organizations. *Designed by Carl Herrman from a photograph of a waving American flag, 200 million stamps offset with microprinting "USA" by Ashton Potter (USA) Ltd., serpentine die cut 11 1/4x11 1/2.*

CM2241 *Veterans*

CM2241		MNHVF	UseVF
34¢	**multicolored**	.65	.20
	Plate block of 4	2.60	
	FDC *(May 23, 2001)*		1.90

2001. Frida Kahlo Issue celebrated the free-spirited Mexican artist (1907-54) who survived polio and a streetcar accident and embraced revolutionaries. Kahlo exhibited her work, predominently self-portraits with sometimes surrealistic themes, in New York, Paris and Mexico City. She is the first Mexican woman to appear on a U.S. stamp. *Designed by Richard Sheaff from* Self-portrait With Necklace *by Frida Kahlo, 55 million stamps offset, with microprinting "USPS" by Ashton-Potter (USA) Ltd.*

CM2242 *Frida Kahlo*

CM2242		MNHVF	UseVF
34¢	**multicolored**	.65	.20
	Plate block of 4	2.80	
	FDC *(June 21, 2001)*		1.50
	y. Pane of 20	14.00	

2001. Baseball's Legendary Playing Fields Issue pictured the fields where several Major League baseball teams played. Only three were still being used by the teams: Boston's Fenway Park, Chicago's Wrigley Field, and New York's Yankee Stadium. *Designed by Phil Jordan, based on vintage postcards from the collection of Ron Menchine, a former Washington Senators announcer, gravure by Avery Dennison (125 million printed).*

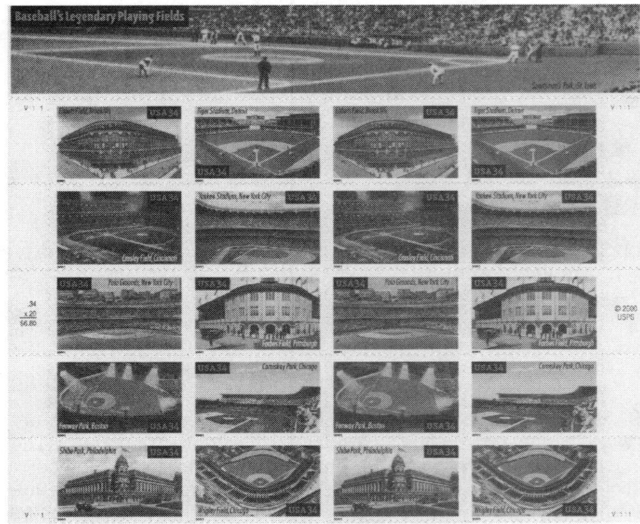

CM2243 *Ebbets Field, Brooklyn;* CM2244 *Tiger Stadium, Detroit;* CM2245 *Crosley Field, Cincinnati;* CM2246 *Yankee Stadium, New York City;* CM2247 *Polo Grounds, New York City;* CM2248 *Forbes Field, Pittsburgh;* CM2249 *Fenway Park, Boston;* CM2250 *Comiskey Park, Chicago;* CM2251 *Shibe Park, Philadelphia;* CM2252 *Wrigley Field, Chicago*

CM2243		MNHVF	UseVF
34¢	**multicolored**	.65	.20
CM2244		MNHVF	UseVF
34¢	**multicolored**	.65	.20
CM2245		MNHVF	UseVF
34¢	**multicolored**	.65	.20
CM2246		MNHVF	UseVF
34¢	**multicolored**	.65	.20
CM2247		MNHVF	UseVF
34¢	**multicolored**	.65	.20
CM2248		MNHVF	UseVF
34¢	**multicolored**	.65	.20
CM2249		MNHVF	UseVF
34¢	**multicolored**	.65	.20
CM2250		MNHVF	UseVF
34¢	**multicolored**	.65	.20
CM2251		MNHVF	UseVF
34¢	**multicolored**	.65	.20
CM2252		MNHVF	UseVF
34¢	**multicolored**	.65	.20
	FDC *(June 27, 2001), any single*		1.90
	y. Pane of 20	13.00	

Airmail

The first Airmail Series got under way in 1918, when the U.S. Post Office Department announced that an airmail service from New York to Philadelphia to Washington, D.C., would begin May 15.

Two days before the initial flight, the world's first stamp designed expressly for airmail was issued to pay the rate between any two of the three cities: 24¢ for the first ounce, including special delivery.

Later in the year, when the rate dropped to 16¢, another stamp was issued. Near the end of the year, a 6¢ stamp was issued to pay the airmail rate without special delivery.

All three stamps were of the same design, an Army Curtiss biplane used by the Air Corps, since the carrying of airmail had been entrusted to Army pilots flying Army planes. The Curtiss biplanes were called "Jennys" from their official designation, which began with the initials "JN."

All airmail issues were printed by the Bureau of Engraving and Printing unless otherwise noted. Prices for FDC are uncacheted for A1-A20.

Intaglio (flat plate press), perforated 11.

1918. Curtiss Biplane Issue

A1 *Curtiss biplane*

A1		UnFVF	UseFVF
6¢	**red orange** *(3,395,854)*	75.00	30.00
	pale orange	75.00	30.00
	Plate block of 6 w/arrow	700.00	
	Block of 4 w/arrow	2.75	1.25
	Center line block	3.00	1.15
	Double transfer	30.00	40.00
	On cover		150.00
	First flight cover *(Dec. 16, 1918)*		2,700.00
	FDC *(Dec. 10, 1918)*		26,000.00

A2 *Curtiss biplane*

A2		UnFVF	UseFVF
16¢	**green** *(3,793,887)*	90.00	40.00
	dark green	90.00	40.00
	Plate block of 6 w/arrow	1,200.00	
	Block of 4 w/arrow	425.00	150.00
	Center line block	450.00	175.00
	On cover	50.00	
	First flight cover *(July 15, 1918)*		850.00
	FDC *(July 11, 1918)*		26,500.00

A3 *Curtiss biplane*

A3v *"Inverted Jenny"*

A3		UnFVF	UseFVF
24¢	**carmine red & blue** *(2,134,888)*	90.00	45.00
	dark carmine red & blue	90.00	45.00
	Plate block of 4, blue plate number & "TOP"	450.00	
	Plate block of 4, red plate number & "TOP"	450.00	
	Plate block of 4, red plate number only	450.00	
	Plate block of 12, 2 plate numbers, arrow, & 2 "TOP" inscriptions	1,400.00	
	Plate block of 12, 2 plate numbers, arrow, & blue "TOP" only	6,000.00	
	Block of 4, w/arrow at top or left	425.00	125.00
	Block of 4, w/arrow at bottom	420.00	120.00
	Block of 4, w/arrow at right	450.00	175.00
	Center line block	450.00	150.00
	On cover		850.00
	First flight cover *(May 5, 1918)*		850.00
	FDC *(May 13, 1918)*		26,000.00
	v. Center Inverted, single	125,000.00	—
	Block of 4 center inverted	600,000.00	
	Plate block of 4 center inverted	1000,000.00	

Note: One sheet of 100 stamps with the blue vignette of the airplane upside down was purchased in a post office at Washington, D.C., by William T. Robey, who sold it to Eugene Klein of Philadelphia, who in turn sold it to Col. Edward H.R. Green. Green retained some of the errors, including the position pieces, and through Klein disposed of the rest. No. A3v is one of the most famous post office finds in U.S. stamp history.

1923. The Second Airmail Series Issue was issued for use on airmail service between New York and San Francisco. Three airmail zones were established: New York to Chicago; Chicago to Cheyenne; and Cheyenne to San Francisco. The rate of postage was 8¢ an ounce for each zone. The stamps were available through the Philatelic Agency at Washington, D.C., before they were issued to postmasters. *Intaglio, perforated 11.*

A4 *Propeller and plane radiator*

A4		UnFVF	UseFVF
8¢	**green** *(6,414,576)*	25.00	15.00
	dark green	25.00	15.00
	Plate block of 6	275.00	
	Double transfer	40.00	20.00
	On cover		22.50
	FDC *(Aug. 15, 1923)*		400.00

A5 *Airmail service insignia*

A5		UnFVF	UseFVF
16¢	**indigo** *(5,309,275)*	85.00	30.00
	Plate block of 6	1,900.00	
	Double transfer	125.00	40.00
	On cover		45.00
	FDC *(Aug. 17, 1923)*		650.00

A6 *De Havilland biplane*

A6		UnFVF	UseFVF
24¢	**carmine** *(5,285,775)*	95.00	30.00
	Plate block of 6	2,100.00	
	Double transfer	175.00	40.00
	On cover		40.00
	FDC *(Aug. 21, 1923)*		800.00

1926-27. Map Issue consisted of three denominations: 10¢, 15¢, and 20¢, reflecting new rates: 10¢ per ounce up to 1,000 miles; 15¢ to 1,500 miles; and 20¢ for distances greater than 1,500 miles or Contract Airmail routes. *Intaglio, perforated 11.*

A7-A9 *Relief map of United States and two mail planes*

		UnFVF	UseFVF
A7			
10¢	**blue** *(42,092,800)*	3.00	.45
	light blue	3.00	.45
	Plate block of 6	40.00	
	Double transfer	5.50	1.00
	FDC *(Feb. 13, 1926)*		90.00

		UnFVF	UseFVF
A8			
15¢	**olive brown** *(15,597,307)*	3.75	2.50
	light brown	3.75	2.50
	Plate block of 6	45.00	
	FDC *(Sept 18, 1926)*		100.00

		UnFVF	UseFVF
A9			
20¢	**yellow green** *(17,616,350)*	9.00	2.00
	green	9.00	2.00
	Plate block of 6	100.00	
	FDC *(Jan. 25, 1927)*		125.00

1927. Lindbergh Airmail Issue honored Charles Augustus Lindbergh (1902-1974), the 25-year-old former airmail pilot who made the first non-stop solo flight from New York to Paris, May 20-21, 1927. Stamp collectors welcomed one of the few U.S. stamps ever to honor a living person. The stamp pictures Lindbergh's Ryan monoplane, *The Spirit of St. Louis*, which is now on display in the Smithsonian Institution at Washington, D.C. *Intaglio, perforated 11.*

A10 *Lindbergh's monoplane,* Spirit of St. Louis

		UnFVF	UseFVF
A10			
10¢	**indigo** *(20,379,179)*	8.00	2.00
	Plate block of 6	145.00	
	Double transfer	11.00	3.00
	FDC *(June 18, 1927)*		150.00
	n. Booklet pane of 3	75.00	50.00
	Single, perforated 11 horizontally	12.50	
	FDC *(May 26, 1928)*		900.00

Note: First-day covers for No. A10 are from Washington, D.C., Little Falls, Minn. (where Lindbergh grew up), St. Louis, Mo., and Detroit, Mich. (his birthplace). FDCs for No. A10n are from Washington, D.C., and Cleveland, Ohio.

1928. Air Mail Beacon Issue the first airmail bicolor produced since the Curtiss Jenny stamp of 1918, reflects the 5¢-per-ounce rate that went into effect Aug. 1, 1928. Major shifts in the blue vignette are not uncommon. *Intaglio, flat plate press, perforated 11.*

A11 *Sherman Hill airmail beacon light*

		UnFVF	UseFVF
A11			
5¢	**carmine red & blue** *(106,887,675)*	4.50	.75
	Plate block of 6, 2 plate numbers & red "TOP"	45.00	
	Plate block of 6, 2 plate numbers & blue "TOP"	65.00	
	Plate block of 6, 2 plate numbers & double "TOP"	100.00	
	Plate block of 8, 2 plate numbers only	185.00	
	Block of 4 w/arrow	20.00	4.25
	Double transfer	—	
	Recut frame line at left	6.50	1.20
	FDC *(July 25, 1928)*		225.00
	v. Vertical pair, imperforate between	6,000.00	

1930. Winged Globe Issue is sometimes confused with the 5¢ rotary-press version of 1931 (A16) but is smaller — 46 3/4mm by 18 3/4mm. *Intaglio, (flat plate press), perforated 11.*

A12 *Winged globe*

		UnFVF	UseFVF
A12			
5¢	**purple** *(97,641,200)*	10.00	.50
	Plate block of 6	140.00	
	Double transfer	18.00	1.25
	FDC *(Feb. 10, 1930)*		15.00
	v. Horizontal pair, imperforate between	5,000.00	

1930. Graf Zeppelin Issue was issued for use on mail carried by the German dirigible, built and commanded by Hugo Eckener, during various stages of a single flight from Friedrichshafen, Germany, to Seville, Spain, Pernambuco, Brazil, and Lakehurst, N.J., and back to Germany during May and June. A former newspaper reporter and an early critic of Count Ferdinand von Zeppelin's experiments with dirigibles, Eckener became a pilot and in 1921 manager of the Zeppelin firm.

The three values covered postal cards or letters on various legs of the trip; a round trip letter cost $3.90. Although more than a million copies of each value were printed, sales were disappointing. After the stamps were withdrawn from circulation June 30, more than 90 percent of them were destroyed.

A13 Graf Zeppelin *in flight*

		UnFVF	UseFVF
A13			
65¢	**green** *(93,536)*	325.00	240.00
	Plate block of 6	2,750.00	
	On flight cover		325.00
	FDC *(April 19, 1930)*		1,500.00

A14 *Zeppelin spanning the Atlantic*

		UnFVF	UseFVF
A14			
$1.30	**yellow brown** *(72,428)*	650.00	450.00
	Plate block of 6	5,750.00	
	On flight cover		550.00
	FDC *(April 19, 1930)*		1,100.00

A15 *Zeppelin circling globe*

		UnFVF	UseFVF
A15			
$2.60	**blue** *(61,296)*	975.00	700.00
	Plate block of 6	8,750.00	
	On flight cover		850.00
	FDC *(April 19, 1930)*		1,200.00

1931-34. Winged Globe Issue had three values: 5¢, 6¢ and 8¢. The 5¢ stamp is sometimes confused with the 5¢ flat-plate issue of 1930 (A12), but is larger — 47 3/4mm by 19 1/4mm. *Intaglio (rotary press), perforated 10 1/2 x 11.*

A16-A18 *Winged globe*

A16		UnFVF	UseFVF
5¢	**reddish violet** *(57,340,000)*	5.50	.60
	Plate block of 4	95.00	
	FDC *(Aug. 19, 1931)*		190.00

A17		UnFVF	UseFVF
6¢	**orange** *(302,205,100)*	2.50	.35
	Plate block of 4	22.50	
	Pair, gutter between	400.00	
	FDC *(July 1, 1934)*		200.00
	FDC *(June 30, 1934)* Baltimore, Md.		225.00

A18		UnFVF	UseFVF
8¢	**yellow olive** *(76,648,803)*	2.50	.35
	Plate block of 4	40.00	
	Pair, gutter between	400.00	
	FDC *(Sept. 26, 1932)*		17.50

1933. CENTURY OF PROGRESS ZEPPELIN ISSUE was released in connection with the flight of the *Graf Zeppelin* to the Chicago World's Fair, as a goodwill gesture to publicize the event. The stamp, now known as the "Baby Zepp," remained on sale at the Philatelic Agency at Washington until 1935, but sales were disappointing, and more than 90 percent of the issue was destroyed. *Intaglio, perforated 11.*

A19 *Airship* Graf Zeppelin

A19		UnFVF	UseFVF
50¢	**green** *(324,070)*	90.00	75.00
	Plate block of 6	800.00	
	On flight cover		80.00
	FDC *(Oct. 2, 1933)*		200.00

1935-37. CHINA CLIPPER OVER PACIFIC ISSUE released primarily to pay postage on mail carried over the transpacific airmail route. *Intaglio, perforated 11.*

A20 China Clipper *over Pacific*

A20		UnFVF	UseFVF
20¢	**green** *(12,794,600)*	10.00	1.50
	dark green	10.00	1.50
	Plate block of 6	110.00	
	FDC *(Feb. 15, 1937)*		60.00

A21		UnFVF	UseFVF
25¢	**blue** *(10,205,400)*	1.50	1.00
	Plate block of 6	22.50	
	FDC *(Nov. 22, 1935)*		50.00

A22		UnFVF	UseFVF
50¢	**carmine** *(9,285,300)*	10.00	4.50
	Plate block of 6	110.00	
	FDC *(Feb. 15, 1937)*		65.00

1938. EAGLE AND SHIELD ISSUE originally designed by Franklin D. Roosevelt, was issued to coincide with the U.S. Post Office Department's promotion of National Air Mail Week. *Intaglio, perforated 11.*

A23 *Eagle and shield*

A23		UnFVF	UseFVF
6¢	**indigo & carmine** *(349,946,500)*	.50	.20
	ultramarine & carmine	.40	.20
	Block of 4, w/arrow	7.50	
	Center line block	2.50	.90
	Plate block of 10, 2 plate numbers, arrow, 2 "TOP" & 2 registration markers	15.00	
	FDC *(May 14, 1938)*		17.50
	v. Horizontal pair, imperforate vertically	10,000.00	
	v1. Vertical pair, imperforate horizontally	350.00	

1939. TRANSATLANTIC ISSUE a final Winged Globe design, celebrates the inauguration of transatlantic Airmail service. *Intaglio, perforated 11.*

A24 *Winged globe*

A24		UnFVF	UseFVF
30¢	**slate blue** *(19,768,150)*	9.00	1.50
	Plate block of 6	150.00	
	On flight cover		5.00
	FDC *(May 16, 1939)*		55.00

1941-44. TWIN MOTORED TRANSPORT PLANE ISSUE consisted of seven denominations intended to cover all airmail postage requirements. Except for the color and denomination, all of the stamps are of the same design. *Intaglio, perforated 11 x 10 1/2.*

A25 *Twin motored transport plane*

A25		MNHVF	UseVF
6¢	**rose red** *(4,746,527,700)*	.25	.20
	Plate block of 4	1.00	
	Vertical pair, gutter between	200.00	
	Horizontal pair, gutter between	—	6.00
	FDC *(June 25, 1941)*		5.00
	v. Horizontal pair, imperforate between	1,500.00	
	n. Booklet pane of 3	3.50	3.00
	FDC *(March 18, 1943)*		35.00

A26		MNHVF	UseVF
8¢	**light olive green** *(1,744,878,650)*	.30	.20
	Plate block of 4	2.00	
	Pair, gutter between	300.00	
	FDC *(March 21, 1944)*		6.00

A27		MNHVF	UseVF
10¢	**violet** *(67,117,400)*	1.40	.20
	Plate block of 4	11.00	
	FDC *(Aug. 15, 1941)*		10.00

A28		MNHVF	UseVF
15¢	**brown carmine** *(78,434,800)*	2.75	.40
	Plate block of 4	12.50	
	FDC *(Aug. 19, 1941)*		10.00

A29		MNHVF	UseVF
20¢	**emerald** *(42,359,850)*	2.75	.40
	Plate block of 4	12.50	
	FDC *(Aug. 27, 1941)*		12.50

A30		MNHVF	UseVF
30¢	**light blue** *(59,880,850)*	2.75	.50
	Plate block of 4	14.00	
	FDC *(Sept. 25, 1941)*		17.50

A31		MNHVF	UseVF
50¢	**orange** *(11,160,600)*	14.00	4.00
	Plate block of 4	90.00	
	FDC *(Oct. 29, 1941)*		32.50

1946. SKYMASTER ISSUE was released to prepay the new 5¢ airmail rate. *Intaglio, perforated 11 x 10 1/2.*

A32 *DC-4 Skymaster*

A32		MNHVF	UseVF
5¢	**carmine** *(864,753,100)*	.25	.20
	Plate block of 4	.75	
	FDC *(Sept. 25, 1946)*		2.00

1947. Small 5¢ Skymaster Issue replaced the large 5¢ stamp of 1946. *Intaglio, perforated 10 1/2 x 11.*

A33, A34 *DC-4 Skymaster*

A33		MNHVF	UseVF
5¢	**carmine** *(971,903,700)*	.25	.20
	Plate block of 4	.75	
	FDC *(March 26, 1947)*		2.00

1947. Small 5¢ Skymaster Coil Issue *Intaglio perforated 10 horizontally.*

A34		MNHVF	UseVF
5¢	**carmine** *(33,244,500)*	1.00	1.00
	Pair	1.50	1.25
	Line pair	9.00	3.00
	FDC *(Jan. 15, 1948)*		2.00

1947. Pictorial Airmail Issue consisted of three denominations intended to cover international air postage rates. *Intaglio, perforated 11 x 10 1/2.*

A35 *Pan-American Union Building, Washington, D.C.*

A35		MNHVF	UseVF
10¢	**black** *(207,976,550)*	.40	.20
	Plate block of 4	1.40	
	FDC *(Aug. 30, 1947)*		2.00
	p. Dry print	.75	.25
	Plate block of 4	2.75	

A36 *Statue of Liberty and skyline of New York City*

A36		MNHVF	UseVF
15¢	**blue green** *(756,186,350)*	.50	.20
	Plate block of 4	2.25	
	Pair, gutter between	625.00	
	FDC *(Aug. 20, 1947)*		2.50
	p. Dry print	.75	.25
	Plate block of 4	3.25	
	v. Horizontal pair, imperforate between	2,000.00	

A37 *San Francisco-Oakland Bay Bridge*

A37		MNHVF	UseVF
25¢	**blue** *(132,956,100)*	1.25	.20
	Plate block of 4	5.00	
	FDC *(July 31, 1947)*		3.00
	p. Dry print	1.50	.40
	Plate block of 4	7.00	

1948. New York City Issue commemorated the 50th anniversary of the consolidation of the five boroughs of New York City. *Intaglio, perforated 11 x 10 1/2.*

A38 *Map of the five boroughs encompassed by ring and airplanes*

A38		MNHVF	UseVF
5¢	**carmine red** *(38,449,100)*	.25	.20
	Plate block of 4	4.00	
	FDC *(July 31, 1948)*		2.50

1949. Small 6¢ Skymaster Issue reflected the raise in rates to 6¢ for domestic airmail. *Intaglio, perforated 10 1/2 x 11.*

A39-A40 *DC-4 Skymaster*

A39		MNHVF	UseVF
6¢	**carmine** *(5,070,095,200)*	.25	.20
	Plate block of 4	.75	
	FDC *(Jan. 18, 1949)*		2.00
	n. Booklet pane of 6	9.50	7.50
	FDC *(Nov. 18, 1949)*		12.50
	p. Dry print	.75	.30
	Plate block of 4	3.50	
	pn. Booklet pane of 6	15.00	

1949. Small 6¢ Skymaster Coil Issue *Intaglio, perforated 10 horizontally.*

A40		MNHVF	UseVF
6¢	**carmine**	3.50	.20
	Pair	6.00	
	Line pair	14.00	
	FDC *(Aug. 25, 1949)*		2.00

1949. Alexandria Bicentennial Issue commemorated the 200th anniversary of the founding of Alexandria, Va. *Intaglio, perforated 11 x 10 1/2.*

A41 *Carlyle House, Alexandria seal and Gadsby's Tavern*

A41		MNHVF	UseVF
6¢	**carmine** *(75,085,000)*	.20	.20
	Plate block of 4	.75	
	FDC *(May 11, 1949)*		2.25

1949. Universal Postal Union Issue commemorated the 75th anniversary of the formation of the Universal Postal Union.

A42 *Post Office Department Building, Washington*

A42		MNHVF	UseVF
10¢	**violet** *(21,061,300)*	.40	.30
	Plate block of 4	1.50	
	FDC *(Nov. 18, 1949)*		2.00

A43 *Globe surrounded by letter-carrying doves*

A43		MNHVF	UseVF
15¢	**cobalt** *(36,613,100)*	.50	.40
	Plate block of 4	2.00	
	FDC *(Oct. 7, 1949)*		3.50

A44 *Plane and globe*

A44		MNHVF	UseVF
25¢	**carmine** *(16,217,100)*	.85	.60
	Plate block of 4	6.50	
	FDC *(Nov. 30, 1949)*		4.50

1949. Wright Brothers Issue commemorated the 46th anniversary of Wilbur and Orville Wright's first flight. On Dec. 17, 1903, at Kill Devil Hill, south of Kitty Hawk, N.C., Orville took the plane aloft for 12 seconds over a distance of 120 feet. Wilbur flew 59 seconds over a distance of 825 feet in the fourth flight that day. *Intaglio, perforated 11.*

A45 *Wright brothers and their plane*

A45		MNHVF	UseVF
6¢	**carmine purple** *(80,405,000)*	.30	.20
	Plate block of 4	1.25	
	FDC *(Dec. 17, 1949)*		2.25

1952. Hawaii Airmail Issue provided a stamp to pay postage on one pound of air parcel post to the eight domestic zones (over 1,800 miles). *Intaglio, perforated 11 x 10 1/2.*

A46 *Diamond Head at Honolulu, Hawaii*

A46		MNHVF	UseVF
80¢	**bright purple** *(18,876,800)*	6.00	1.50
	Plate block of 4	32.50	
	FDC *(March 26, 1952)*		17.50

1953. Powered Flight Issue marked the 50th anniversary of the Wright brothers' first flight. *Intaglio, perforated 11 x 10 1/2.*

A47 *Old and new planes with slogan*

A47		MNHVF	UseVF
6¢	**carmine** *(78,415,000)*	.25	.20
	Plate block of 4	.80	
	FDC *(May 29, 1953)*		2.25

1954. Eagle Issue was intended primarily for use on domestic airmail postcards. *Intaglio, perforated 11 x 10 1/2.*

A48, 50 *Eagle in flight*

A48		MNHVF	UseVF
4¢	**blue** *(40,483,600)*	.25	.20
	Plate block of 4	2.00	
	FDC *(Sept. 3, 1954)*		2.00

1957. Air Force Issue marked the 50th anniversary of the U.S. Air Force. *Intaglio, perforated 11 x 10 1/2.*

A49 *U.S. military aircraft*

A49		MNHVF	UseVF
6¢	**bright Prussian blue** *(63,185,000)*	.25	.20
	Plate block of 4	1.00	
	FDC *(Aug. 1, 1957)*		2.25

1958. Eagle Issue used the flying eagle design with a 5¢ denomination because of the increase in postage rates Aug. 1. *Intaglio, perforated 11 x 10 1/2.*

A50		MNHVF	UseVF
5¢	**carmine red** *(72,480,000)*	.25	.20
	Plate block of 4	1.75	
	FDC *(July 31, 1958)*		2.00

1958. Jet Silhouette Issue met the change in domestic airmail rates Aug. 1. *Intaglio, perforated 10 1/2 x 11.*

A51-A52, A60-A61 *Jet airliner*

A51		MNHVF	UseVF
7¢	**blue** *(1,326,960,000)*	.25	.20
	Plate block of 4	1.00	
	FDC *(July 31, 1958)*		2.00
	n. Booklet pane of 6	11.00	6.75
	FDC, booklet pane		8.50

1958. Jet Silhouette Coil Issue *Coil stamp, perforated 10 horizontally.*

A52		MNHVF	UseVF
7¢	**blue** *(157,035,000)*	2.00	.20
	Pair	3.50	
	Line pair	19.00	
	FDC *(July 31, 1958)*		2.00
	Small perfs	10.00	
	Pair, imperforate	150.00	

1959. Alaska Statehood Issue commemorated the addition to the Union of the 49th state. *Intaglio, perforated 11 x 10 1/2.*

A53 *The Big Dipper and North Star superimposed on map of Alaska*

A53		MNHVF	UseVF
7¢	**deep blue** *(90,055,200)*	.30	.20
	Plate block of 4	1.00	
	FDC *(Jan. 3, 1959)*		2.00

1959. Balloon Jupiter Issue commemorated the 100th anniversary of the first U.S. transmission of airmail by balloon from Lafayette to Crawfordsville, Ind., a distance of 35 miles. *Intaglio (Giori Press), perforated 11.*

A54 *Crowd watching John Wise ascending on first flight, Aug. 17, 1859*

A54		MNHVF	UseVF
7¢	**deep blue & scarlet** *(79,290,000)*	.30	.20
	Plate block of 4	1.00	
	FDC *(Aug. 17, 1959)*		2.00

1959. Pan American Games Issue marked the opening of the Pan American Games in Chicago, Ill. *Intaglio (Giori Press), perforated 11.*

A55 *Runner holding torch*

A55		MNHVF	UseVF
10¢	**deep blue & scarlet** *(38,770,000)*	.35	.30
	Plate block of 4	1.50	
	FDC *(Aug. 27, 1959)*		2.00

1959. Hawaii Statehood Issue commemorated the admission of Hawaii to the Union as the 50th state. *Intaglio, perforated 11 x 10 1/2.*

A56 *Hawaiian warrior and map of islands*

A56		MNHVF	UseVF
7¢	**dull scarlet** *(84,815,000)*	.30	.20
	Plate block of 4	1.00	
	FDC *(Aug. 27, 1959)*		2.00

International Airmail Series was created to meet the demand for specific foreign airmail rates. The 10¢ value covered airmail to Central and South America and the West Indies exclusive of Mexico. The 15¢ denomination prepaid airmail postage to Europe and North Africa. The 25¢ stamp was for use to Asia, Africa and the Middle East. *Intaglio (Giori Press), perforated 11.*

1960. Liberty Bell Issue in the International Airmail Series.

A57 *Liberty Bell*

A57		MNHVF	UseVF
10¢	**black & green** *(39,960,000)*	1.75	.80
	Plate block of 4	7.50	
	FDC *(June 10, 1960)*		2.00

1959. Statue of Liberty Issue in the International Airmail Series.

A58 *Statue of Liberty*

A58		MNHVF	UseVF
15¢	**black & orange** *(98,160,000)*	.50	.20
	Plate block of 4	2.50	
	FDC *(Nov. 20, 1959)*		2.00

1966. Abraham Lincoln Issue in the International Airmail Series.

A59 *Abraham Lincoln*

A59		MNHVF	UseVF
25¢	**black & brown purple**	.75	.20
	Plate block of 4	3.50	
	FDC *(April 22, 1960)*		2.00
	z. Tagged	1.00	.40
	Plate block of 4	4.50	
	FDC, tagged *(Dec. 29, 1966)*		32.50

1960. Jet Silhouette Issue returned in a new color to facilitate handling of domestic airmail letters. *Intaglio, perforated 10 1/2 x 11.*

A60		MNHVF	UseVF
7¢	**bright red** *(1,289,460,000)*	.25	.20
	Plate block of 4	1.25	
	Pair, gutter between	250.00	
	FDC *(Aug. 12, 1960)*		2.00
	n. Booklet pane of 6	13.00	
	FDC *(Aug. 19, 1960)*		9.00

Decoding the Catalog

Although there is no particular difficulty in distinguishing Types I and II of the 15¢ Statue of Liberty airmail stamp, are you able to easily describe the differences based on the illustrations commonly seen in stamp catalogs?

Type I of this issue (Krause-Minkus A58) was released Nov. 20, 1959. The Bureau of Engraving and Printing produced an initial total of 98.1 million.

A double-line orange frame line surrounds the entire design, and the bottom part of Liberty's book is cropped.

On Jan. 11 and 13, 1967, respectively, two versions of the Type II 15¢ LIberty airmail were released. Type II stamps feature the same basic design as Type I, but the orange frame line has been removed from the Statue of Liberty and is replaced by a black frame. This creates the appearance of two framed images and a vertical white gutter down the center. Liberty's book is now fully seen.

The Type II version released informally on Jan. 11, 1967, in Washington, D.C. (A62z), has an all-over coating of phosphorescent tagging that glows orange-red under shortwave ultraviolet light. The version released two days later (A62) in Buffalo, N.Y., is untagged.

None of the major types of the 15¢ Statue of Liberty airmail bears any particular value premium. But it is important to learn what to search for when decoding the catalog.

1960. Jet Silhouette Coil Issue *Coil stamp, perforated 10 horizontally.*

A61		MNHVF	UseVF
7¢	**bright red** *(87,140,000)*	4.50	.40
	Pair	7.50	
	Line pair	42.50	
	FDC *(Oct. 22, 1960)*		2.00

1961. Statue of Liberty Issue in the International Airmail Series was a revision of the 1959 15¢ Statue of Liberty airmail stamp (A58), showing a revised frame line around the statue engraving. *Intaglio (Giori Press) perforated 11.*

A62 Statue of Liberty, *redesigned frame line*

A62		MNHVF	UseVF
15¢	**black & orange**	.50	.20
	Plate block of 4	2.50	
	FDC *(Jan. 13, 1961)*		2.00
	z. Tagged	1.50	.75
	Plate block of 4	16.50	
	FDC *(Jan. 11, 1967)*		32.50
	vz. Horizontal pair, imperforate vertically	11,500.00	

1961. Liberty Bell Issue in the International Airmail Series was a new denomination and color required because of new increased postal rates. *Intaglio (Giori Press), perforated 11.*

A63 *Liberty Bell*

A63		MNHVF	UseVF
13¢	**black & scarlet**	.50	.20
	Plate block of 4	2.00	
	FDC *(June 28, 1961)*		2.00
	z. Tagged	.60	.30
	Plate block of 4	2.50	
	FDC *(Feb. 15, 1967)*		32.50

1962. Airliner Over Capitol Issue was made available to meet the increase in postage rates. *Rotary press printing, perforated 10 1/2 x 11.* Although this stamp was issued Dec. 6, 1962, an experiment was started Aug. 1, 1963, in Dayton, Ohio, in which a luminescent was applied to these airmail stamps. The phosphor-tagged stamps, in conjunction with an ultraviolet sensing device, sped up airmail service.

A64, A65 *Jet over Capitol dome*

A64		MNHVF	UseVF
8¢	**carmine**	.30	.20
	Plate block of 4	1.25	
	FDC *(Dec. 5, 1962)*		2.00
	n. Booklet pane of 5, plus Mailman label	6.75	
	n1. Booklet pane of 5, plus Zone # label	47.50	
	n2. Booklet pane of 5, plus ZIP label (1964)	12.50	
	FDC *(Dec. 15, 1962)*		2.00
	p1. Printed on Hi-brite paper	—	—
	Plate block of 4	—	
	p1n. Booklet pane of 5, plus Mailman label	—	—
	z. Tagged, Type I or II	.35	.20
	Plate block of 4	1.75	
	FDC *(Dayton, Ohio, Aug. 1, 1963)*		2.00
	zn. Booklet pane of 5, plus ZIP label	1.65	1.25

Type I tagging: mat tagging, using four separate mats that did not cover entire sheet of 400 stamps (untagged areas identify the variety). Stamps from the four corners of a pane have two untagged margins.

Type II tagging: roll tagging, where continuous rolls replaced the tagging mats. Only the plate number selvage margin is partially tagged.

1962. Airliner Over Capitol Coil Issue *Type IIa tagging: wide roll tagging, where all margins are fully tagged. Coil stamp, perforated 10 horizontally.*

A65		MNHVF	UseVF
8¢	**carmine**	.60	.20
	Pair	.75	
	Line pair	6.50	
	FDC *(Dec. 5, 1962)*		2.00
	p1. On Hi-brite paper	—	—
	Pair	—	
	Line pair	—	
	z. Tagged, Type I	.40	.20
	Pair	1.00	
	Line pair	2.75	
	FDC, tagged *(Jan 14, 1965)*		32.50
	z1. Tagged, Type II	.35	.20
	Pair	1.00	
	Line pair	2.75	

1963. Montgomery Blair Issue recalled Abraham Lincoln's postmaster general and his role in the first Universal Postal Union conference in 1863. *Intaglio (Giori Press), perforated 11.*

A66 *Montgomery Blair and mail circling the globe*

A66		MNHVF	UseVF
15¢	**red, maroon & blue** *(42,245,000)*	.75	.60
	Plate block of 4	3.25	
	FDC *(May 3, 1963)*		3.00

1963. Bald Eagle Issue was prepared for use on domestic airmail postcards. *Intaglio, perforated 11 x 10.*

A67 *Bald Eagle on crag*

A67		MNHVF	UseVF
6¢	**carmine**	.25	.20
	Plate block of 4	2.00	
	FDC *(July 12, 1963)*		2.00
	z. Tagged	4.50	3.50
	Plate block of 4	95.00	
	FDC *(Feb. 15, 1967)*		55.00

1963. Amelia Earhart Issue marked the 65th birthday of America's most prominent female aviatrix, the first woman to fly across the Atlantic Ocean, and the first woman to fly across the United States non-stop. She was lost at sea while attempting to fly around the world. *Intaglio (Giori Press), perforated 11.*

A68 *Amelia Earhart*

A68		MNHVF	UseVF
8¢	**carmine red & brown purple** *(63,890,000)*	.35	.20
	Plate block of 4	1.50	
	FDC *(July 24, 1963)*		3.50

1964. Robert H. Goddard Issue marked the 50th anniversary of the first patents granted to Goddard for his multi-stage booster rockets using liquid and solid fuels. *Intaglio (Giori Press), perforated 11.*

A69 *Dr. Goddard, rocket and launching pad*

A69		MNHVF	UseVF
8¢	**multicolored** *(65,170,000)*	.45	.20
	Plate block of 4	2.25	
	FDC *(Oct. 5, 1964)*		3.00
	zo. Tagging omitted	—	

1967. Alaska Purchase Issue celebrated the 100th anniversary of the acquisition of Alaska from Russia. The date of issue, March 30, is a state holiday honoring Secretary of State William H. Seward, who arranged the sale for $7,200,000. *Intaglio (Giori Press), perforated 11.*

A70 *Totem pole*

A70		MNHVF	UseVF
8¢	**brown & light brown** *(64,710,000)*	.40	.20
	Plate block of 4	2.00	
	FDC *(March 20, 1967)*		2.00

1967. Columbia Jays Issue prepared to meet the increase in airmail rates to Europe and Mediterranean Africa. The design is similar to the 1963 5¢ Audubon commemorative (CM526) and was used again because of its aesthetic and technical excellence. *Intaglio (Giori Press), perforated 11.*

A71 *John J. Audubon's* Columbia Jays

A71		MNHVF	UseVF
20¢	**blue, brown & yellow,** tagged *(165,430,000)*	1.25	.20
	Plate block of 4	4.50	
	FDC *(April 26, 1967)*		3.00
	zo. Tagging omitted	—	

1968. Star Runway Issue met the increase in airmail rates that went into effect Jan. 7, 1968. *Intaglio, perforated 11 x 10 1/2.*

A72, A73 *Poster type art showing 50 stars*

A72		MNHVF	UseVF
10¢	**red** tagged	.40	.20
	Plate block of 4	1.35	
	FDC *(Jan. 5, 1968)*		2.00
	n. Booklet pane of 5 plus Mail Early label	3.75	3.50
	n1. Booklet pane of 5 plus ZIP slogan label	3.75	3.50
	n2. Booklet pane of 8	2.00	2.00
	n2z. Booklet pane of 8, tagging glows yellow rather than red orange	—	
	zo. Tagging omitted	—	
	nzo. Booklet pane of 5 plus Mail Early label	—	
	nzo1. Booklet pane of 5 plus ZIP slogan label	—	
	nzo2. Booklet pane of 8	—	
	v. Booklet pair, imperforate between vertically	1,750.00	

1968. Star Runway Coil Issue *Coil stamp, perforated 10 vertically.*

A73		MNHVF	UseVF
10¢	**red**	.40	.20
	Pair	.75	
	Line pair	2.00	
	FDC *(Jan. 5, 1968)*		1.75
	v. Pair, imperforate	625.00	

1968. Airmail Service Issue commemorated the 50th anniversary of the service, established May 15, 1918, when mail was carried by biplane on the Washington-New York flight. *Intaglio (Giori Press) and offset, perforated 11.*

A74 *Curtiss Jenny*

A74		MNHVF	UseVF
10¢	**black, red & blue** *(74,180,000)*	.40	.20
	Plate block of 4	2.75	
	FDC *(May 15, 1968)*		2.00
	v. red stripe on tail omitted	3,000.00	
	zo. Tagging omitted	—	

1968. USA and Jet Issue intended primarily for mail to Europe and points in North Africa. *Intaglio and offset, perforated 11.*

A75, A81 *"USA" and airplane*

A75		MNHVF	UseVF
20¢	**multicolored**	.75	.20
	Plate block of 4	3.00	
	FDC *(Nov. 22, 1968)*		2.00
	zo. Tagging omitted	—	

1969. Moon Landing Issue paid tribute to the landing of a man on the Moon July 20, 1969, when Neil A. Armstrong and Col. Edwin E. Aldrin Jr., became the first humans to land on the lunar surface. The engraved master die from which the stamps were printed was carried to the Moon by the astronauts. *Intaglio and offset, perforated 11.*

A76 *First man on the Moon*

A76		MNHVF	UseVF
10¢	**multicolored** *(152,364,800)*	.40	.20
	Plate block of 4	1.65	

		MNHVF	UseVF
	FDC *(Sept. 9, 1969)*		5.50
	v. Offset red omitted	550.00	

Note: No. A76v must have missing red from the entire design, including the dots on top of the yellow area as well as the astronaut's shoulder patch. Stamps with any red present are worth far less than the true red-omitted error.

1971. Delta Wing Silhouette Issue created to meet increased domestic and international rates. *Intaglio, perforated 10 1/2 x 11.*

A77 *Silhouette of delta wing plane*

A77		MNHVF	UseVF
9¢	**red** *(25,830,000)*	.30	.20
	Plate block of 4	1.30	
	FDC *(May 15, 1971)*		2.00

1971. Jet Silhouette Issue *Intaglio, perforated 11 x 10 1/2.*

A78-A79 *Silhouette of jet airliner*

A78		MNHVF	UseVF
11¢	**red** tagged *(317,810,000)*	.40	.20
	Plate block of 4	1.50	
	FDC *(May 7, 1971)*		2.00
	n. Booklet pane of 4 plus 2 labels	1.10	
	zo. Tagging omitted	—	
	zx. Untagged (Bureau precancel)	.60	
	FDC		80.00

1971. Jet Silhouette Coil Issue *Coil stamp, perforated 10 vertically.*

A79		MNHVF	UseVF
11¢	**red**	.40	.20
	Pair	.75	
	Line pair	.90	
	FDC *(May 7, 1971)*		2.00
	v. Pair, imperforate	275.00	

1971. Head of Liberty Issue *Intaglio (Giori Press), perforated 11.*

A80 *Head of Liberty*

A80		MNHVF	UseVF
17¢	**multicolored** tagged	.60	.20
	Plate block of 4	2.25	
	FDC *(July 13, 1971)*		2.00
	zo. Tagging omitted	—	

1971. Jet and "USA" Issue *Intaglio (Giori Press) and offset, perforated 11.*

A81		MNHVF	UseVF
21¢	**multicolored** tagged *(49,815,000)*	.75	.20
	Plate block of 4	3.00	
	FDC *(May 21, 1971)*		2.00
	zo. Tagging omitted	—	
	v. black omitted	—	

1972. National Park Issue was part of the National Parks Centennial Series (see CM674-CM680). The City of Refuge depicted is an ancient sanctuary for taboo breakers or victims of wars on a lava ledge on the southwestern part of the island of Hawaii. *Intaglio (Giori Press) and offset, perforated 11.*

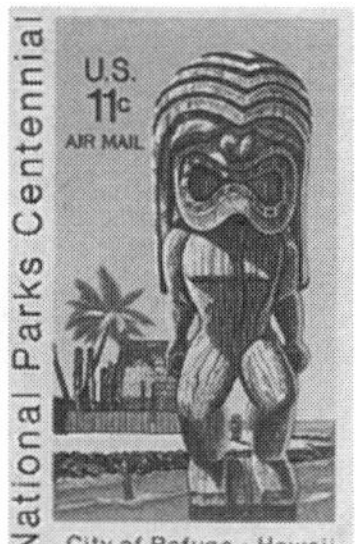

A82 *Wooden statue and palisaded temple*

A82		MNHVF	UseVF
11¢	**multicolored** *(78,210,000)*	.35	.20
	Plate block of 4	1.75	
	FDC *(May 3, 1972)*		2.00
	v. blue and green omitted	1,000.00	
	zo. Tagging omitted	—	

1972. Olympic Issue released as part of the Olympic Games Series (see CM686) for the Winter and Summer Games held in Japan and Germany. *Gravure, perforated 11 x 10 1/2.*

A83 *Skiing*

A83		MNHVF	UseVF
11¢	**multicolored** *(92,710,000)*	.40	.20
	Plate block of 10	3.75	
	FDC *(Aug. 17, 1972)*		2.00

1973. Progress in Electronics Issue was the fourth stamp and only airmail in a set commemorating advances in electronic communication. (See CM721-CM723). *Intaglio (Giori Press) and offset, perforated 11.*

A84 *Lee DeForest's audions*

A84		MNHVF	UseVF
11¢	**multicolored** tagged *(56,000,000)*	.30	.20
	Plate block of 4	1.40	
	FDC *(July 10, 1973)*		2.00
	v. Vermilion and olive omitted	1,400.00	
	zo. Tagging omitted	—	

1973. Winged Envelope Issue was created to meet the basic domestic airmail letter rate increase. *Intaglio, perforated 11 x 10 1/2.*

A85, A86 *Flying envelope*

A85		MNHVF	UseVF
13¢	**red** tagged	.40	.20
	Plate block of 4	1.60	
	FDC *(Nov. 16, 1973)*		2.00
	zx. Untagged (Bureau precancel)	.50	.20
	n. Booklet pane of 5 plus label *(Dec. 27, 1973)*	1.25	1.50

		MNHVF	UseVF
	nz. Pane of 5 plus label yellow-green, tagging (error) (rare)	—	
	zo. Tagging omitted (without precancel)	—	

1973. WINGED ENVELOPE COIL ISSUE *Rotary Press, perforated 10 vertically.*

A86		MNHVF	UseVF
13¢	**red**	.50	.20
	Pair	.75	
	Line pair	1.25	
	FDC *(Dec. 27, 1973)*		2.00
	v. Pair, imperforate	75.00	

1974. STATUE OF LIBERTY ISSUE met increases in airmail rates to foreign destinations. *Intaglio (Giori Press), perforated 11.*

A87 *Statue of Liberty*

A87		MNHVF	UseVF
18¢	**multicolored** tagged	.60	.50
	Plate block of 4	2.50	
	FDC *(Jan. 11, 1974)*		2.00
	zo. Tagging omitted	—	

1974. MOUNT RUSHMORE ISSUE

A88 *Mount Rushmore*

A88		MNHVF	UseVF
26¢	**multicolored** tagged	.75	.20
	Plate block of 4	3.50	
	Pair, gutter between	200.00	
	FDC *(Jan. 2, 1974)*		2.00
	z. yellow-green tagging (error) (rare)	—	
	zo. Tagging omitted	—	

1976. PLANE AND GLOBES ISSUE met increases in airmail rates to foreign destinations. *Intaglio (Giori Press), perforated 11.*

A89 *Stylized aircraft and globes*

A89		MNHVF	UseVF
25¢	**multicolored** tagged	.75	.20
	Plate block of 4	3.25	
	FDC *(Jan. 2, 1976)*		2.00
	zo. Tagging omitted	—	

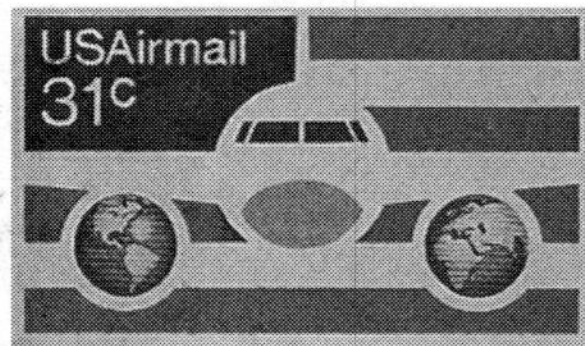

A90 *Stylized aircraft and flag, with globes*

A90		MNHVF	UseVF
31¢	**multicolored** tagged	.90	.20
	Plate block of 4	4.00	
	FDC *(Jan. 2, 1976)*		2.00
	zo. Tagging omitted	—	

Pioneers of Aviation Series

1978. ORVILLE AND WILBUR WRIGHT ISSUE the first stamps in the Pioneers of Aviation Series, marked the 75th anniversary of Orville (1871-1948) and Wilbur (1867-1912) Wright's historic first powered flight in 1903. *Intaglio (Giori Press) and offset, perforated 11.*

A91, A92 *Orville and Wilbur Wright, aviation pioneers*

A91		MNHVF	UseVF
31¢	**multicolored large portraits & biplane**	1.75	1.50
A92		**MNHVF**	**UseVF**
31¢	**multicolored, small portraits, biplane and hangar**	1.75	1.50
	Plate block of 4	4.00	
	y. Se-tenant pair A91-92	1.75	
	FDC pair *(Sept. 23, 1978)*		3.00
	vy. Pair with intaglio, black omitted	—	
	v1y. Pair with intaglio, black & ultramarine omitted	800.00	
	v2y. Pair with offset black, yellow, magenta, blue & brown omitted	2,500.00	

1978. OCTAVE CHANUTE ISSUE in the Pioneers of Aviation Series honored the biplane hang glider designed by Chanute (1832-1910), which became a standard for future glider design and aided the Wright brothers. *Intaglio (Giori Press) and offset, perforated 11.*

A93, A94 *Octave Chanute, aviation pioneer*

A93		MNHVF	UseVF
21¢	**multicolored, large portrait**	1.75	1.50
A94		**MNHVF**	**UseVF**
21¢	**multicolored, small portrait**	1.75	1.50
	Plate block of 4	4.75	
	y. Se-tenant pair A93-94		
	FDC pair *(March 29, 1978)*		3.00
	vy. Pair with intaglio, black omitted	—	
	v1y. Pair with intaglio black & ultramarine omitted	4,750.00	

1979. HIGH JUMPER ISSUE in the Olympic Games Series featured a high jumper in action. (See also CM925-28, CM932-35.) *Gravure, perforated 11.*

A95 *High jumper*

A95		MNHVF	UseVF
31¢	**multicolored** tagged	1.00	.35
	Plate block of 12	12.50	
	FDC *(Nov. 1, 1979)*		2.00

1979. Wiley Post Issue in the Pioneers of Aviation Series honored the aviator famous for record-making flights, scientific research and aircraft designs. Post (1900-1935) died with humorist Will Rogers while on a flight to Alaska. *Intaglio (Giori Press) and offset, perforated 11.*

A96, A97 *Wiley Post, aviation pioneer*

A96		MNHVF	UseVF
25¢	**multicolored, large portrait,** tagged	3.00	2.00
A97		**MNHVF**	**UseVF**
25¢	**multicolored, small portrait,** tagged	3.00	2.00
	Plate block of 4	9.00	
	y. Se-tenant pair A96-97	3.75	
	FDC pair *(Nov. 20, 1979)*		3.00

1982. Philip Mazzei Issue honored the Italian-American patriot. He collaborated with the leaders of Virginia on political ideas and promoted independence through writings published in America and in Europe. *Gravure, perforated 11.*

A98 *Philip Mazzei*

A98		MNHVF	UseVF
40¢	**multicolored** tagged	1.25	.25
	Plate block of 12	15.00	
	FDC *(Oct. 13, 1980)*		2.00
	v. Horizontal pair, imperforate vertically	—	
	v1. Pair, imperforate	3,500.00	
	v2. Perforated 10 1/2 x 11 (1982)	—	
	zo. Tagging omitted	—	

1980. Blanche Stuart Scott Issue in the Pioneers of Aviation Series commemorated the first American woman to make a solo flight in early September 1910. *Gravure, perforated 11.*

A99 *Blanche Stuart Scott*

A99		MNHVF	UseVF
28¢	**multicolored** tagged	.90	.25
	Plate block of 12	12.50	
	FDC *(Dec. 30, 1980)*		2.00

1980. Glenn Curtiss Issue in the Pioneers of Aviation Series honored an early aviator and noted aircraft designer and manufacturer (1878-1930) principally remembered for his invention and development of the aileron, and for his design and production of the first successful seaplanes and amphibious airplanes. *Gravure, perforated 11.*

A100 *Glenn Curtiss*

A100		MNHVF	UseVF
35¢	**multicolored** tagged	1.00	.25
	Plate block of 12	12.50	
	FDC *(Dec. 30, 1980)*		2.00

1983. Olympic Issues consisted of three se-tenant blocks of four commemorating the 1984 Summer Olympic Games in Los Angeles, Calif. (See CM1094-97, CM1111-14, CM1126-29, ALS19, PC96 and PC98.) *Gravure, bullseye perforated 11 1/4.*

A101 *Men's shot put*

A102 *Men's gymnastics*

A103 *Women's swimming*

A104 *Men's weight lifting*

A101		MNHVF	UseVF
40¢	**Men's shot put,** tagged	1.25	.25
	v. Line perforated 11	—	
A102		**MNHVF**	**UseVF**
40¢	**Men's gymnastics,** tagged	1.25	.25
	v. Line perforated 11	—	
A103		**MNHVF**	**UseVF**
40¢	**Women's swimming,** tagged	1.25	.25
	v. Line perforated 11	—	
A104		**MNHVF**	**UseVF**
40¢	**Men's weight lifting,** tagged	1.25	.25
	Plate block of 4	6.50	
	y. Se-tenant block of 4, A101-104	4.00	
	FDC *(April 8, 1983),* block		5.00
	v. Line perforated 11	1.35	
	Plate block of 4 line perforated 11	6.00	
	vy. Se-tenant block of 4 line perforated 11	5.00	
	v1y. Block of 4, imperforate	1,250.00	

1983. Olympics Second Issue *Gravure, perforated 11.*

A105 *Women's gymnastics*

A106 *Men's hurdles*

A107 *Women's basketball*

A108 *Soccer*

A105		MNHVF	UseVF
28¢	**Women's gymnastics,** tagged	1.25	.25

		MNHVF	UseVF
A106			
28¢	**Men's hurdles,** tagged	1.25	.25

		MNHVF	UseVF
A107			
28¢	**Women's basketball,** tagged	1.25	.25

		MNHVF	UseVF
A108			
28¢	**Soccer,** tagged	1.25	.25
	Plate block of 4	6.50	
	y. Se-tenant block of 4 A105-108	4.00	
	FDC *(June 17, 1983),* block		5.00
	v. Block of 4, imperforate vertically	—	

1983. Olympics Third Issue *Gravure, perforated 11.*

A109 *Fencing*

A110 *Cycling*

A111 *Women's volleyball*

A112 *Pole vaulting*

		MNHVF	UseVF
A109			
35¢	**Fencing,** tagged	1.25	.25

		MNHVF	UseVF
A110			
35¢	**Cycling,** tagged	1.25	.25

		MNHVF	UseVF
A111			
35¢	**Women's volleyball,** tagged	1.25	.25

		MNHVF	UseVF
A112			
35¢	**Pole vaulting,** tagged	1.25	.25
	Plate block of 4	12.50	
	y. Se-tenant block of 4 A109-112	6.50	
	FDC *(Nov. 4, 1983),* block		5.00

1985. Alfred V. Verville Issue in the Pioneers of Aviation Series honored the man (1890-1970) who designed and produced aircraft with Lawrence Sperry and Glenn Curtiss. *Gravure press, perforated 11.*

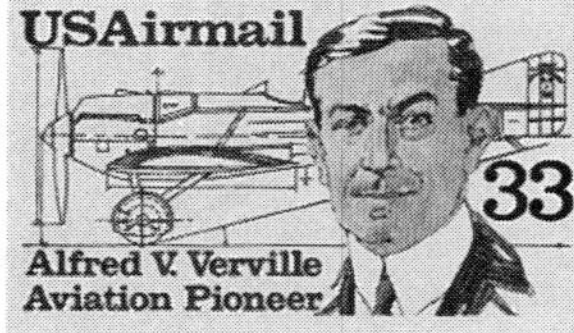

A113 *Alfred V. Verville, aviation pioneer*

		MNHVF	UseVF
A113			
33¢	**multicolored** tagged	1.00	.30
	Plate block of 4	4.50	
	FDC *(Feb. 13, 1985)*		1.75
	v. Pair, imperforate	1,100.00	

1985. Lawrence and Elmer Sperry Issue in the Pioneers of Aviation Series commemorated the father-and-son duo of Elmer Sperry (father, 1860-1930) who was awarded over 400 patents, such as the gyro-compass which revolutionized flying, and Lawrence Sperry (son, 1892-1923) who helped develop and test such aviation innovations as the automatic pilot and retractable landing gear. *Gravure press, perforated 11.*

A114 *Lawrence and Elmer Sperry, aviation pioneers*

		MNHVF	UseVF
A114			
39¢	**multicolored** tagged	1.25	.40
	Plate block of 4	5.50	
	FDC *(Feb. 13, 1985)*		2.00
	v. Pair, imperforate	1,500.00	

1986. Transpacific Airmail Issue marked the 50th anniversary of airmail service between the United States and the Far East. *Gravure, perforated 11.*

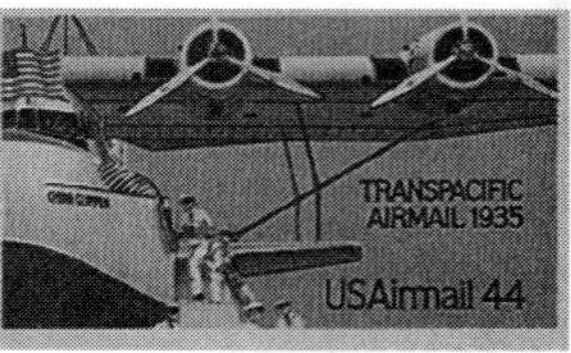

A115 *Martin M-130 China Clipper*

		MNHVF	UseVF
A115			
44¢	**multicolored** tagged	1.25	.40
	Plate block of 4	6.00	
	FDC *(Feb. 15, 1985)*		2.00
	v. Pair, imperforate	1,100.00	

1985. Junipero Serra Issue honored the Franciscan friar (1713-84) who founded the California missions. *Gravure, perforated 11.*

A116 *Junipero Serra and San Gabriel Mission*

		MNHVF	UseVF
A116			
44¢	**multicolored** tagged	1.75	.60
	Plate block of 4	11.50	
	FDC *(Aug. 22, 1985)*		2.50
	v. Pair, imperforate	18.50	

1988. Settlement of New Sweden Issue honored the 350th anniversary of the colony established by Peter Minuit. Sweden and Finland released stamps the same day (Sweden 1460, Finland 1077) with a common design to that issued by the United States. *Intaglio and offset, perforated 11.*

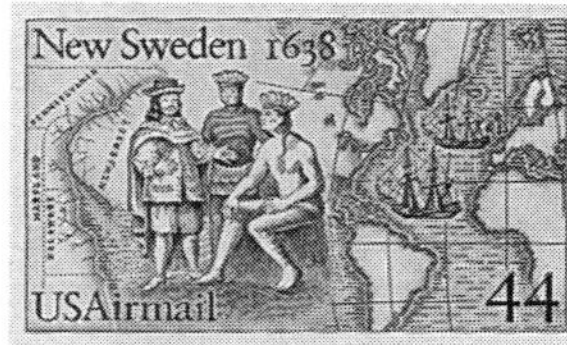

A117 *Illustration from a 1602 book on the New Sweden Colony*

		MNHVF	UseVF
A117			
44¢	**multicolored** tagged *(22,975,000)*	1.40	.50
	Plate block of 4	9.00	
	FDC *(March 29, 1988)*	2.50	

1988. Samuel P. Langley Issue in the Pioneers of Aviation Series honored the early pioneer flight engineer (1834-1906) and the 70th anniversary of airmail service. Langley's early experiments in mechanical flight laid the groundwork for the Wright brothers, Glenn Curtiss and others. *Intaglio and offset, perforated 11.*

A118 *Samuel P. Langley, unmanned Aerodrome No. 5*

		MNHVF	UseVF
A118			
45¢	**multicolored** tagged	1.40	.30
	Plate block of 4	6.00	
	FDC *(May 14, 1988)*		2.50
	v. Overall tagged	2.00	.50
	Plate block of 4	10.00	

1988. Igor Sikorsky Issue in the Pioneers of Aviation Series paid tribute to the man (1889-1972) who designed and built many early helicopters. *Intaglio and offset, perforated 11.*

36 USAirmail
Igor Sikorsky
A119 *Igor Sikorsky and VS-300*

A119		MNHVF	UseVF
36¢	**multicolored** tagged	1.25	.40
	Plate block of 4	6.00	
	FDC *(June 23, 1988)*		2.50

Note: Traces of red have been detected in all copies of a so-called "red-omitted" error of this stamp. Such stamps, on which even minute traces of red are present, are worth far less than a genuine color-omitted error would be.

1989. French Revolution Bicentennial Issue part of a joint issue with France, was released both in Washington, D.C., and in Paris. *Offset and intaglio, perforated 11 1/2 x 11.*

Equality
1789
French Revolution USAirmail 45
A120 *Liberte, Egalite and Fraternite*

A120		MNHVF	UseVF
45¢	**multicolored** tagged *(38,532,000)*	1.40	.40
	Plate block of 4	6.00	
	FDC *(July 14, 1989)*		2.50

1989. America Issue depicted a rare wooden native sculpture of the pre-Columbian era. It was one of a pair of U.S. stamps (with CM1360) that were the first stamps issued by 24 postal administrations commemorating the 500th anniversary of Christopher Columbus' arrival in America. It was part of a 1989-91 Columbian series by members of the Postal Union of the Americas and Spain (PUAS). (See A127.) *Gravure by American Book Note Co., perforated 11.*

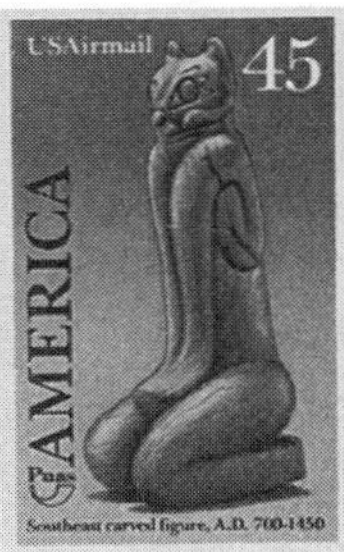
USAirmail 45
AMERICA
Puas
A121 *Key Marco Cat, Calusa culture, pre-Columbian period*

A121		MNHVF	UseVF
45¢	**multicolored** tagged *(39,325,000)*	1.50	.30
	Plate block of 4	7.50	
	FDC *(Oct. 12, 1989)*		2.00

1989. Future Mail Transportation Souvenir Sheet was part of a group of 11 postal items issued during World Stamp Expo '89 and the 20th Congress of the Universal Postal Union in Washington, D.C. *Offset and intaglio, imperforate.*

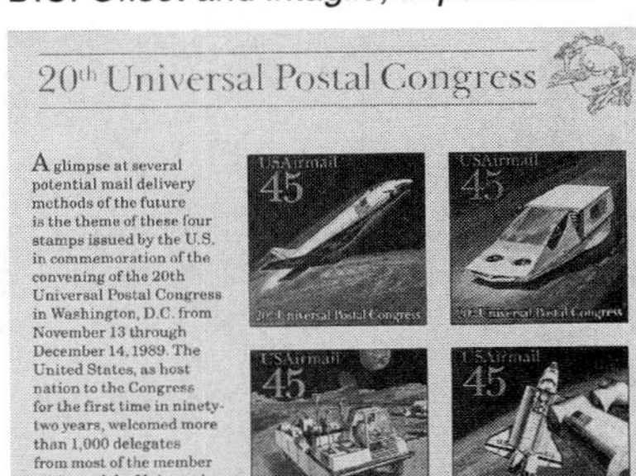
20th Universal Postal Congress
A glimpse at several potential mail delivery methods of the future is the theme of these four stamps issued by the U.S. in commemoration of the convening of the 20th Universal Postal Congress in Washington, D.C. from November 13 through December 14, 1989. The United States, as host nation to the Congress for the first time in ninety-two years, welcomed more than 1,000 delegates from most of the member nations of the Universal Postal Union to the major international event.
USAirmail 45
A122a *Hypersonic airliner*

A122b *Hovercraft*

A122c *Service rover*

A122d *Space Shuttle*

A122		MNHVF	UseVF
$1.80	**multicolored,** souvenir sheet, tagged *(1,944,000)*	7.00	5.00
	FDC *(Nov. 24, 1989)*		8.00
	a. 45¢ multicolored, tagged		
	b. 45¢ multicolored, tagged		
	c. 45¢ multicolored, tagged		
	d. 45¢ multicolored, tagged		

1989. Future Mail Transportation Issue *Offset and intaglio, perforated 11.*

USAirmail 45
20th Universal Postal Congress
A123 *Hypersonic airliner*

A124 *Hovercraft*

A125 *Service rover*

A126 *Space Shuttle*

		MNHVF	UseVF
A123			
45¢	**Hypersonic airliner,** tagged	1.25	.25
A124		MNHVF	UseVF
45¢	**Hovercraft,** tagged	1.25	.25
A125		MNHVF	UseVF
45¢	**Service rover,** tagged	1.25	.25
A126		MNHVF	UseVF
45¢	**Space Shuttle,** tagged	1.25	.25
	Plate block of 4	8.00	
	y. Se-tenant block of 4, A123-26	7.00	
	FDC *(Nov. 28, 1989)*		9.00
	vy. Plate block of 4 w/light blue omitted	1,150.00	

1990. America Issue was the second in the PUAS Columbian Series depicting scenes of the natural beauty of America prior to Columbus. *Gravure, perforated 11.*

Puas AMERICA USAirmail 45
A127 *Caribbean coast*

A127		MNHVF	UseVF
45¢	**multicolored** tagged	1.50	.50
	Plate block of 4	7.50	
	FDC *(Oct. 12, 1990)*		2.50

1991. Harriet Quimby Issue in the Pioneers of Aviation Series honored the journalist, drama critic and first licensed American woman pilot (1875-1912). *Gravure by Stamp Venturers, perforated 11.*

Harriet Quimby Pioneer Pilot
USAirmail 50
A128 *Harriet Quimby, Bleriot airplane*

A128		MNHVF	UseVF
50¢	**multicolored** tagged	1.50	.50
	Plate block of 4	7.50	
	FDC *(April 27, 1991)*		2.50
	v. Vertical pair, imperforate horizontally	2,100.00	

1991. William T. Piper Issue in the Pioneers of Aviation Series honored the "Henry Ford of Aviation," the developer of the Piper Cub aircraft. (See also A132). *Gravure by J. W. Fergusson & Sons for the American Bank Note Co., perforated 11.*

A129 *William T. Piper, Piper Cub*

A129

		MNHVF	UseVF
40¢	**multicolored** tagged	1.40	.50
	Plate block of 4	6.00	
	FDC *(May 17, 1991)*		2.50

1991. Antarctic Treaty Issue honored the 30th anniversary of the 1961 treaty dedicating the region to peaceful purposes. *Gravure by Stamp Venturers, perforated 11.*

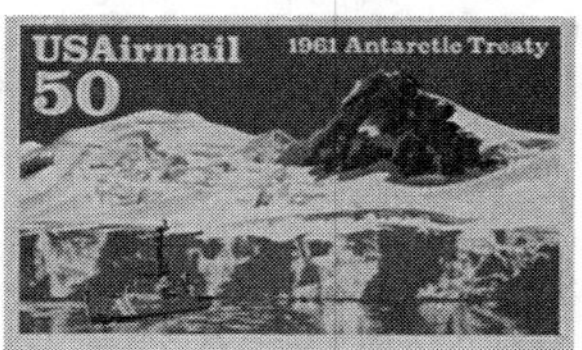

A130 *View of McMurdo Sound*

A130

		MNHVF	UseVF
50¢	**multicolored** tagged	1.50	.60
	Plate block of 4	7.00	
	FDC *(June 21, 1991)*		2.50

1991. America Issue had as its theme "Pre-Columbian Voyages of Discovery," and depicted a prehistoric Asian and the Bering land bridge by which the first native Americans are believed to have come to the Western Hemisphere thousands of years ago. *Gravure, perforated 11.*

A131 *Asian overlooking Bering land bridge*

A131

		MNHVF	UseVF
50¢	**multicolored** tagged	1.50	.50
	Plate block of 4	7.00	
	FDC *(Oct. 12, 1991)*		2.50

1993. William T. Piper Issue differs from the 1991 version (A129) in that Piper's hair touches the top edge of the design of this stamp. There was no official first day of issue for the redesigned stamp. *Printed in gravure by Stamp Venturers, perforated 11 1/4.*

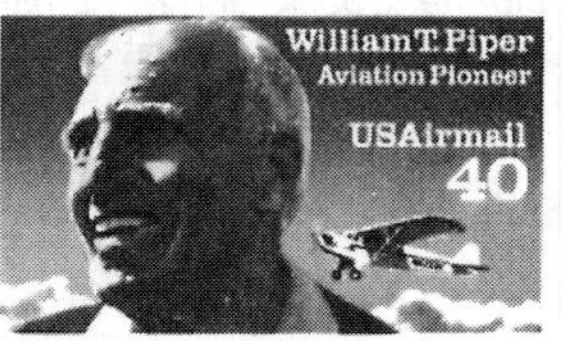

A132 *William T. Piper*

A132

		MNHVF	UseVF
40¢	**multicolored,** *(July 1993)* tagged	1.50	.50
	Plate block of 4	7.00	

Special Delivery Stamps

A special delivery stamp on any letter or article of mailable matter entitled the addressee to immediate delivery between the hours of 7 a.m. and midnight. This service began Oct. 1, 1885, and was limited to free delivery offices and post offices in towns of 4,000 population or more. At that time there were 555 such post offices. The Act of Aug. 4, 1886, extended the service to all post offices.

1885. Messenger, First Issue inscribed "At a special delivery office." *Printed by the American Bank Note Co., flat press, unwatermarked, perforated 12.*

SD1 *Messenger on foot*

SD1		UnFVF	UseFVF
10¢	**Prussian blue**	115.00	22.50
	dark blue	115.00	22.50
	Plate block of 8	6,000.00	
	Double transfer at top	250.00	
	FDC *(Oct. 1, 1885);* EKU: *Sept. 30, 1885*		10,000.00

1888. Messenger, Second Issue inscribed "At any post office." *Printed by the American Bank Note Co., flat press, unwatermarked, perforated 12.*

SD2, SD3 *Messenger on Foot*

SD2		UnFVF	UseFVF
10¢	**Prussian blue**	120.00	7.00
	dark blue	120.00	7.00
	Plate block of 8	7,500.00	
	FDD *(Sept. 6, 1888)*		
	EKU *(Dec. 18, 1888)*		

1893. Messenger, Third Issue had a change of color and was released to avoid confusion with the 1- and 4-cent Columbian commemorative stamps. SD2 went on sale again in January 1894 and remained in use until it was replaced by SD4. *Printed by the American Bank Note Co., flat press, unwatermarked, perforated 12.*

SD3		UnFVF	UseFVF
10¢	**orange yellow**	75.00	10.00
	dark orange	75.00	10.00
	Plate block of 8	5,000.00	
	FDD *(Jan. 24, 1893)*		
	EKU *(Feb. 11, 1893)*		

1894. Messenger Issue similar to SD2, with a line drawn under the words "Ten Cents." *Printed by intaglio by the Bureau of Engraving and Printing, perforated 12.*

SD4, SD5 *Messenger on foot*

SD4		UnFVF	UseFVF
10¢	**deep blue**	300.00	20.00
	bright blue	300.00	20.00
	dark blue	300.00	20.00
	Plate block of 4, w/arrow	2,000.00	
	Plate block of 6	8,000.00	
	Double transfer	750.00	
	v. Plate block of 6, imperforate & without gum	5,000.00	
	FDD *(Oct. 10, 1894)*		
	EKU *(Oct. 24, 1894)*		

1895. Messenger Issue same design as SD4. *Intaglio, perforated 12, watermarked double-line USPS (wmk187).*

SD5		UnFVF	UseFVF
10¢	**blue**	65.00	1.75
	dark blue	65.00	1.75
	deep blue	65.00	1.75
	Plate block of 6	3,000.00	
	Block of 4, w/arrow	300.00	
	Colored line through "POSTAL DELIVERY"	120.00	
	Dots in frame (curved) above messenger	150.00	
	Double transfer		10.00
	v. Printed on both sides	—	
	v1. Imperforate	—	
	FDD *(Aug. 16, 1895)*		
	EKU *(Oct. 3, 1895)*		

1902. Messenger on Bicycle Issue *Intaglio, perforated 12, watermarked double-line USPS (wmk187).*

SD6, *Messenger on bicycle*

SD6		UnFVF	UseFVF
10¢	**ultramarine**	75.00	3.00
	blue	75.00	3.00
	dark blue	75.00	3.00
	Plate block of 6	2,000.00	
	Plate block of 6, from plates 5240, 5243, 5244 or 5245, with "09" added to number	1,800.00	
	Plate block of 4, w/arrow	300.00	
	Double transfer	—	
	Transfer "damage" under "N" of "CENTS"	100.00	2.50
	FDD *(Dec. 9, 1902)*		
	EKU *(Jan. 22, 1903)*		

1908. Helmet of Mercury Issue the "Merry Widow" is the nickname for this stamp due to the resemblance to a contemporary lady's hat, of the same name. *Intaglio, perforated 12, watermarked double-line USPS (wmk 187).*

SD7 *Helmet of Mercury*

SD7		UnFVF	UseFVF
10¢	**green**	50.00	30.00
	dark green	50.00	30.00
	yellowish green	50.00	30.00
	Plate block of 6	850.00	
	Double transfer	250.00	
	on cover		200.00
	FDD *(Dec. 12, 1908)*		—
	EKU *(Dec. 14, 1908)*		

1911. Messenger on Bicycle Issue *Intaglio, watermarked single-line USPS (wmk 273), perforated 12.*

SD8-SD11 *Messenger on bicycle*

SD8		UnFVF	UseFVF
10¢	**ultramarine**	75.00	4.50
	dark ultramarine	75.00	4.50
	pale ultramarine	75.00	4.50
	violet blue	75.00	4.50
	Plate block of 6	1,800.00	
	Plate block of 6, w/imprint	2,000.00	
	v. Top frame line missing	90.00	5.00
	FDD *(Jan. 1911)*		
	EKU *(Jan. 14, 1911)*		

1914. Messenger on Bicycle Issue *Intaglio, watermarked single-line USPS (wmk 273), perforated 10.*

SD9		UnFVF	UseFVF
10¢	**ultramarine**	140.00	5.00
	blue	140.00	5.00

	pale ultramarine	140.00	5.00
	Plate block of 6	2,800.00	
	Plate block of 6, w/imprint	3,250.00	
	FDD *(Sept. 1914)*		
	EKU *(Oct. 26, 1914)*		

1916. Messenger on Bicycle Issue *Intaglio, unwatermarked, perforated 10.*

SD10		UnFVF	UseFVF
10¢	**pale ultramarine**	225.00	22.50
	blue	225.00	22.50
	ultramarine	225.00	22.50
	Plate block of 6	4,250.00	
	Plate block of 6, w/imprint	4,800.00	
	FDD *(Oct. 19, 1916)*		
	EKU *(Nov. 4, 1916)*		

1917. Messenger on Bicycle Issue *Intaglio, unwatermarked, perforated 11.*

SD11		UnFVF	UseFVF
10¢	**ultramarine**	14.50	.50
	blue	14.50	.50
	dark ultramarine	14.50	.50
	gray violet	14.50	.50
	pale ultramarine	14.50	.50
	Plate block of 6	200.00	
	Plate block of 6, w/imprint	500.00	
	v. Perforated 10 at left	—	
	FDD *(May 2, 1917)*		

1922. Messenger and Motorcycle Issue *Intaglio, unwatermarked, perforated 11.*

SD12, SD13, SD15-SD18 *Messenger and motorcycle*

SD12		UnFVF	UseFVF
10¢	**gray blue**	22.50	.25
	deep ultramarine	22.50	.25
	Plate block of 6	400.00	
	Double transfer	40.00	1.00
	FDC *(July 12, 1922)*		375.00
SD13		UnFVF	UseFVF
15¢	**red orange**	19.00	1.00
	Plate block of 6	250.00	
	Double transfer	—	
	FDC *(April 11, 1925)*		275.00

1925. Post Office Delivery Truck Issue *Intaglio, unwatermarked, perforated 11.*

SD14, SD19 *Post office delivery truck*

SD14		UnFVF	UseFVF
20¢	**black**	2.25	1.50
	Plate block of 6	40.00	
	FDC *(April 25, 1925)*		125.00

1927. Messenger and Motorcycle Issue *Rotary press printing, previous designs, perforated 11 x 10 1/2.*

SD15		UnFVF	UseFVF
10¢	**dark lilac**	1.00	.20
	gray lilac	1.00	
	red lilac	1.00	.20
	violet	1.00	.20
	Plate block of 4	7.00	
	cracked plate	75.00	
	gouged plate	100.00	
	FDC *(Nov. 29, 1927)*		100.00
	FDC, electric eye plate *(Sept. 8, 1941)*		25.00
	v. Horizontal pair, imperforate between	250.00	

1944. Messenger and Motorcycle Issue

SD16		MNHVF	UseVF
13¢	**blue**	1.00	.20
	Plate block of 4	5.00	
	FDC *(Oct. 30, 1944)*		10.00

1931. Messenger and Motorcycle Issue

SD17		MNHVF	UseVF
15¢	**yellow orange**	.75	.20
	Plate block of 4	4.00	
	FDC, Washington D.C. *(Aug. 13, 1931)*		125.00
	FDC, Easton, Pa. *(Aug. 6, 1931)*		1,500.00

1944. Messenger and Motorcycle Issue

SD18		MNHVF	UseVF
17¢	**yellow**	3.50	3.00
	Plate block of 4	27.50	
	FDC *(Oct. 30, 1944)*		10.00

1951. Post Office Delivery Truck Issue

SD19		MNHVF	UseVF
20¢	**black**	17.50	.20
	Plate block of 4	8.50	
	FDC *(Nov. 30, 1951)*		4.50

1954. Letter and Hands Issue *Rotary press printing, perforated 11 x 10 1/2.*

SD20, SD21 *Two hands and letter*

SD20		MNHVF	UseVF
20¢	**gray blue**	.75	.20
	light blue	.75	.20
	Plate block of 4	3.00	
	FDC *(Oct. 13, 1954)*		2.00

1957. Letter and Hands Issue

SD21		MNHVF	UseVF
30¢	**maroon**	.75	.20
	Plate block of 4	3.50	
	FDC *(Sept. 3, 1957)*		2.00

1969. Dual Arrows Issue for new rate. *Giori Press, perforated 11.*

SD22, SD23 *Arrows pointing in opposite directions.*

SD22		MNHVF	UseVF
45¢	**carmine & violet blue**	1.50	.50
	Plate block of 4	6.00	
	FDC *(Nov. 20, 1969)*		2.50

1971. Dual Arrows Issue new rates, same design as SD22.

SD23		MNHVF	UseVF
60¢	**violet blue & carmine**	1.50	.25
	Plate block of 4	7.50	
	FDC *(May 10, 1971)*		2.50

Airmail/Special Delivery

1934. Blue Airmail Special Delivery Stamp Issue prepaid, with one stamp, air postage and the special delivery fee. The stamp was designed by President Franklin D. Roosevelt. The first day of issue was Aug. 30 at the convention of the American Air Mail Society at Chicago. *Intaglio, unwatermarked, perforated 11.*

ASD1 *Great Seal*

ASD1		UnFVF	UseFVF
16¢	**Prussian blue** *(9,215,750)*	.90	.75
	blue	.90	.75
	FDC *(Aug. 30, 1934)*		30.00
	Plate block of 6	25.00	

Note: An imperforate, ungummed version of the blue airmail special delivery issue, CM161, is listed with other so-called Farley Series stamps among the commemorative listings.

1936. Red and Blue Airmail Special Delivery Stamp Issue used the same design as the 1934 stamp, but in two colors.

ASD2 *Great Seal*

ASD2		UnFVF	UseFVF
16¢	**carmine & blue**	.60	.30
	FDC *(Feb. 10, 1936)*		25.00
	Center line block	—	
	Plate block of 4, Type 1, thin red and blue registration line above plate nos.	12.50	
	Plate block of 4, Type II, thick red, thin blue registration line above plate nos.	225.00	
	Plate block of 4, Type III, dotted blue, thin red registration line above plate nos.	200.00	
	Plate block of 4, Type IV, thick red and blue registration line above plate nos.	15.00	
	Arrow block of 4, bottom or side arrow	—	
	v. Horizontal pair, imperforate between	—	

Offices in China

1919. Offices in China Issue Postage stamps of the 1917 United States series were overprinted and issued to the U.S. postal agency at Shanghai. The overprints are in black, except OC7 and OC16, which are in red. Sold in Shanghai at the local currency, which was one-half the value of U.S. currency at the time. These stamps were good for mail to addresses in the United States. After the closing of the China office in December 1922, the stamps were sold for a short time at the Philatelic Agency at Washington, D.C. *Intaglio, unwatermarked, perforated 11.*

OC1-OC16 *U.S. stamps 380-398 overprinted with "¢."*

	UnFVF	UseFVF
OC1		
2¢ on 1¢ green (380)	20.00	50.00
Plate block of 6	275.00	
OC2		
4¢ on 2¢ rose red (381)	20.00	50.00
Plate block of 6	275.00	
OC3		
6¢ on 3¢ violet (382)	40.00	55.00
Plate block of 6	475.00	
OC4		
8¢ on 4¢ yellow brown (383)	45.00	50.00
Plate block of 6	600.00	
OC5		
10¢ on 5¢ blue (384)	50.00	55.00
Plate block of 6	650.00	
OC6		
12¢ on 6¢ red orange (386)	65.00	80.00
Plate block of 6	750.00	
OC7		
14¢ on 7¢ black (387)	65.00	80.00
Plate block of 6	850.00	
OC8		
16¢ on 8¢ yellow olive (388)	50.00	55.00
a. olive green	40.00	45.00
Plate block of 6	600.00	
OC9		
18¢ on 9¢ salmon (389)	50.00	60.00
Plate block of 6	700.00	
OC10		
20¢ on 10¢ orange yellow (390)	45.00	50.00
Plate block of 6	650.00	
OC11		
24¢ on 12¢ brown purple (392)	50.00	60.00
a. claret brown	70.00	85.00
Plate block of 6	850.00	
OC12		
30¢ on 15¢ gray black (394)	60.00	75.00
Plate block of 6	1,000.00	
OC13		
40¢ on 20¢ pale blue (395)	90.00	120.00
Plate block of 6	1,350.00	
OC14		
60¢ on 30¢ orange red (396)	85.00	100.00
Plate block of 6	1,000.00	
OC15		
$1 on 50¢ reddish violet (397)	325.00	425.00
Plate block of 6	9,000.00	
OC16		
$2 on $1 black purple (398)	300.00	350.00
Plate block of 6	6,500.00	
Arrow block of 4	1,400.00	

1922. Offices in China Issue overprinted on No. 380. *Intaglio.*

OC17, OC18 *Overprinted "Cts."*

OC17	UnFVF	UseFVF
2¢ on 1¢ green (380)	90.00	90.00
Plate block of 6	725.00	

1922. Offices in China Issue overprinted on No. 404. *Offset.*

OC18	UnFVF	UseFVF
4¢ on 2¢ rose red (404)	75.00	75.00
Plate block of 6	725.00	
"CHINA" only	—	—
"SHANGHAI" omitted	—	—

Parcel Post Stamps

1912. Parcel Post Stamps were provided to cover the rates of postage on Fourth Class mail, set up by the Act of Congress of Aug. 24, 1912. Less than a year later, on July 1, 1913, the Postmaster General directed that ordinary postage stamps be valid for parcel post and that parcel post stamps be valid for postage purposes and be continued on sale until the supply was exhausted. The 75¢ value (PP11) outlasted all the others, and in September 1921 the remainders, consisting of 3,510,345 copies, were destroyed. The 20¢ value was the first stamp in the world to depict an airplane. *Intaglio, watermarked single-line USPS (wmk 273) and perforated 12; marginal imprints (the denomination in words) were added to the plates on Jan. 27, 1913.*

PP1 *Post Office clerk*

PP1		UnFVF	UseFVF
1¢	**carmine** *(209,691,094)*	3.00	1.25
	Double transfer	90.00	
	Plate block of 6, w/imprint	75.00	
	FDC *(Nov. 27, 1912)*		2,500.00

PP2 *City carrier*

PP2		UnFVF	UseFVF
2¢	**carmine** *(206,417,253)*	3.50	1.00
	lake	5.00	
	Double transfer	100.00	
	Plate block of 6, w/imprint	90.00	
	FDC *(Nov. 27, 1912)*		2,500.00

PP3 *Railway postal clerk*

PP3		UnFVF	UseFVF
3¢	**carmine** *(29,027,433)*	6.50	4.50
	Double transfer	17.50	
	Lower right corner retouched	17.50	
	Plate block of 6, w/imprint	150.00	
	FDC *(April 5, 1913)*		3,500.00

PP4 *Rural carrier*

PP4		UnFVF	UseFVF
4¢	**carmine** *(76,743,813)*	17.50	2.50
	Double transfer	35.00	
	Plate block of 6, w/imprint	750.00	
	FDC *(Dec. 12, 1912)*		3,500.00

PP5 *Mail train*

PP5		UnFVF	UseFVF
5¢	**carmine** *(108,153,993)*	17.50	1.75
	Double transfer	35.00	
	Plate block of 6, w/imprint	800.00	
	FDC *(Nov. 27, 1912)*		3,500.00

PP6 *Steamship and mail tender*

PP6		UnFVF	UseFVF
10¢	**carmine** *(56,896,653)*	30.00	2.50
	Double transfer	60.00	
	Plate block of 6, w/imprint	900.00	
	FDC *(Dec. 9, 1912)*		—

PP7 *Automobile*

PP7		UnFVF	UseFVF
15¢	**carmine** *(21,147,033)*	45.00	8.00
	Plate block of 6, w/imprint	2,000.00	
	FDC *(Dec. 16, 1912)*		—

PP8 *Airplane carrying mail*

PP8		UnFVF	UseFVF
20¢	**carmine** *(17,142,393)*	85.00	16.00
	Plate block of 6, w/imprint	5,000.00	
	FDC *(Dec. 16, 1912)*		—

PP9 *Manufacturing*

PP9		UnFVF	UseFVF
25¢	**carmine** *(21,940,653)*	42.50	5.00
	Plate block of 6, imprint	3,000.00	
	FDC *(Nov. 27, 1912)*		—

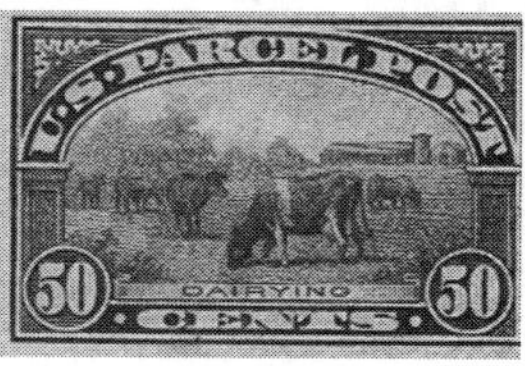

PP10 *Dairying*

PP10		UnFVF	UseFVF
50¢	**carmine** *(2,117,793)*	190.00	32.50
	Plate block of 6, imprint	17,500.00	
	FDC *(March 15, 1913)*		—

PP11 *Harvesting*

PP11		UnFVF	UseFVF
75¢	**carmine** *(2,772,615)*	55.00	25.00
	Plate block of 6, imprint	3,000.00	
	FDC *(Dec. 18, 1912)*		—

PP12 *Fruit growing*

PP12		UnFVF	UseFVF
$1	**carmine** *(1,053,273)*	250.00	20.00
	Plate block of 6, imprint	17,500.00	
	FDC *(Jan. 3, 1913)*		—

Parcel Post/Postage Due Stamps

1912. Parcel Post Postage Due Stamps were used to indicate the amount due by the addressee when parcel post was insufficiently prepaid by the sender. *Watermarked single-line USPS (wmk 273), intaglio, perforated 12.*

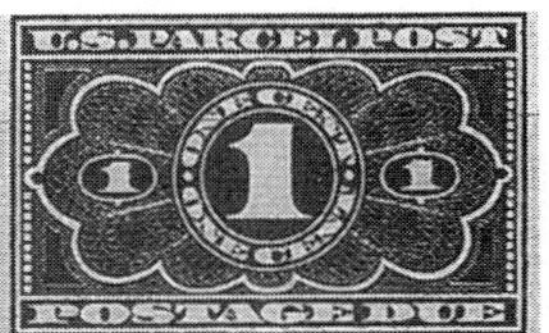

PPD1-PPD5

PPD1		UnFVF	UseFVF
1¢	**green** *(7,322,400)*	6.00	3.50
	FDD *(Nov. 27, 1912)*		
PPD2		**UnFVF**	**UseFVF**
2¢	**green** *(3,132,000)*	55.00	15.00
	FDD *(Dec. 9, 1912)*		
PPD3		**UnFVF**	**UseFVF**
5¢	**green** *(5,840,100)*	9.00	3.50
	FDD *(Nov. 27, 1912)*		
PPD4		**UnFVF**	**UseFVF**
10¢	**green** *(2,124,540)*	125.00	40.00
	FDD *(Dec. 12, 1912)*		
PPD5		**UnFVF**	**UseFVF**
25¢	**green** *(2,117,700)*	65.00	3.75
	FDD *(Dec. 16, 1912)*		

Special Handling Stamps

1925-29. Issue The Postal Service Act of 1925 provided the same service for Fourth Class matter as normally accorded First Class by payment of a 25¢ fee, for which a stamp was issued. The other denominations were issued to meet rate changes. *Intaglio, unwatermarked, perforated 11.*

The 10¢, 15¢ and 20¢ denominations were dry-printed on pregummed paper (1955). They were issued in much smaller quantities than the usual wet-printed stamps. There is a minute size difference between the wet and dry printings; the latter are on a whiter, thicker and stiffer paper.

SH1-SH5

SH1		UnFVF	UseFVF
25¢	**green**	22.50	5.50
	Plate block of 6	75.00	
	FDC *(April 11, 1925)*		225.00
SH2		**UnFVF**	**UseFVF**
10¢	**yellow green**	2.25	1.00
	FDC *(June 25, 1928)*		50.00
	p. Dry print (1955)	1.25	.90
	Plate block of 6	5.50	
SH3		**UnFVF**	**UseFVF**
15¢	**yellow green**	2.25	1.00
	FDC *(June 25, 1928)*		50.00
	p. Dry print (1955)	2.00	1.50
	Plate block of 6	25.00	
SH4		**UnFVF**	**UseFVF**
20¢	**yellow green**	3.00	1.75
	FDC *(June 25, 1928)*		50.00
	p. Dry print (1955)	2.00	1.50
	Plate block of 6	—	
SH5		**UnFVF**	**UseFVF**
25¢	**yellow green** *(1929)*	17.50	7.50
	Plate block of 6	500.00	
	"A" and "T" of "STATES" joined at top	40.00	20.00
	"A" and "T" of "STATES" and "T" and "A" of "POSTAGE" joined at top	40.00	40.00
	FDC *(April 11, 1929)*		225.00

Registration Stamp

1911. Registration Stamp Although we have had a registry since 1855, the Registry Stamp of 1911 was the only stamp issued for the specific purpose of paying registration fees. The stamp was valid for the fees only, not postage; regular postage stamps could be used to pay the fees. The Postmaster General abolished the issuance of these stamps in 1913 but allowed remaining stock to be used up. *Intaglio, single-line USPS watermark (wmk 273), perforated 12.*

REG1

REG1		UnFVF	UseFVF
10¢	**bright blue**	65.00	5.00
	Plate block of 6, w/imprint	2,000.00	
	FDC *(Dec. 1, 1911)*		10,000.00

Certified Mail Stamp

1955. Certified Mail Stamp This service provided the mailer with a receipt of mailing and required signatures of addressees or agent on delivery. *Intaglio, perforated 10 1/2 x 11.*

CER1 *U.S. mail carrier*

CER1		MNHVF	UseVF
15¢	**red**	.50	.35

Plate block of 4	12.00	
FDC *(June 6, 1955)*		3.00

Newspaper/Periodical Stamps

First issued in September 1865 to prepay postage on bulk shipments of newspapers and periodicals, they were not attached to the items mailed, but rather to the statement of mailing, which was canceled and retained by the Post Office. The stamps were discontinued July 1, 1898.

1865. First Newspaper Stamp Issue *embossed and printed in letterpress, National Bank Note Co. Thin, hard, unwatermarked paper, without gum, and perforated 12. The design size is 51 x 95mm, colored border.*

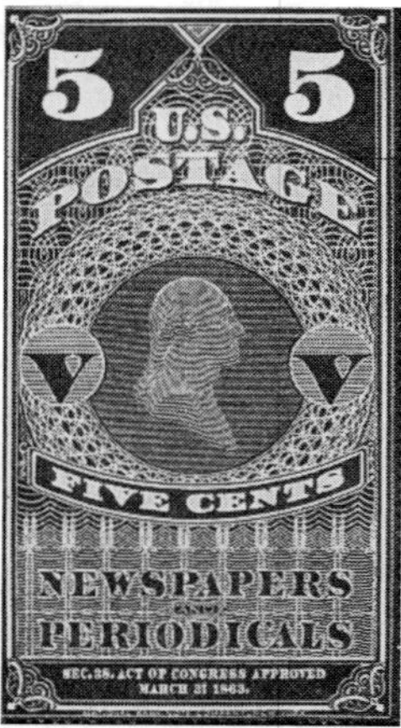

N1, N4 *George Washington*

N1		UnFVF	UseFVF
5¢	**dark blue**	250.00	—
	a. light blue	275.00	—

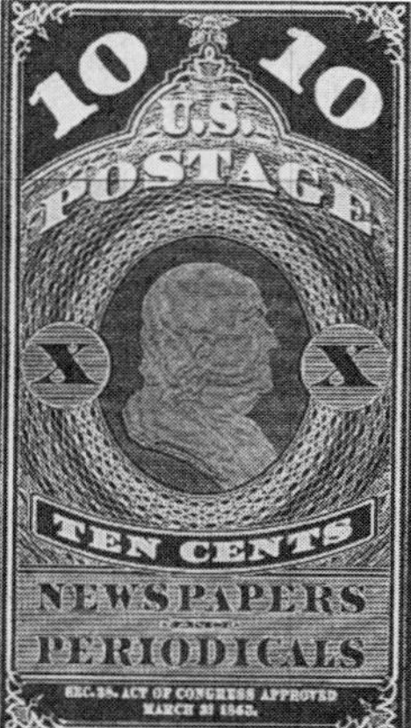

N2 *Benjamin Franklin*

N2		UnFVF	UseFVF
10¢	**green**	100.00	—
	a. blue green	100.00	—
	p. pelure paper	125.00	—

Input from stamp collectors regarding the content of this catalog and ideas to make it more useful is eagerly sought. Send your comments to:
Minkus Catalog Editor
Krause Publications
700 East State St.
Iola WI 54990

N3 *Abraham Lincoln*

N3		UnFVF	UseFVF
25¢	**orange red**	150.00	—
	a. carmine red	175.00	—
	p. pelure paper	150.00	—
N4		UnFVF	UseFVF
5¢	**blue**	75.00	—
	a. dark blue	75.00	—
	p. pelure paper	75.00	—

1875. First Special Printing of the 1865 Issue by the Continental Bank Note Co. The 5¢ with white border, the 10¢ and 25¢ with colored border. Hard, white paper, unwatermarked, issued without gum, perforated.

SPN1		UnFVF	UseFVF
5¢	**blue**	75.00	
SPN2		UnFVF	UseFVF
10¢	**bluish green**	85.00	
SPN3		UnFVF	UseFVF
25¢	**carmine**	100.00	

1881. Second Special Printing of 1865 Issue by the American Bank Note Co. White border, soft, porous paper, unwatermarked, perforated 12.

SPN4		UnFVF	UseFVF
5¢	**dark blue**	175.00	—

1875. Allegory Design Issue Intaglio, Continental Bank Note Co. Issued Jan. 1, 1875, on thin, hard paper. Design size 24 x 35mm.

N5-N11 *"Freedom" after Crawford's statue on the dome of the Capitol*

N5		UnFVF	UseFVF
2¢	**black**	25.00	12.50
	gray black	25.00	12.50
	greenish black	25.00	12.50
N6		UnFVF	UseFVF
3¢	**black**	27.50	15.00
	gray black	27.50	15.00
N7		UnFVF	UseFVF
4¢	**black**	27.50	15.00
	gray black	27.50	15.00
	greenish black	27.50	15.00
N8		UnFVF	UseFVF
6¢	**black**	30.00	20.00
	gray black	30.00	20.00
	greenish black	30.00	20.00

		UnFVF	UseFVF
N9			
8¢	**black**	45.00	24.00
	gray black	45.00	32.50
	greenish black	45.00	

		UnFVF	UseFVF
N10			
9¢	**black**	65.00	52.00
	gray black	85.00	60.00
	greenish black	65.00	52.00
	Double transfer	100.00	75.00

		UnFVF	UseFVF
N11			
10¢	**black**	45.00	32.50
	gray black	45.00	32.50
	greenish black	45.00	32.50

N12-19 *Astraea, Goddess of Justice*

		UnFVF	UseFVF
N12			
12¢	**rose**	100.00	50.00
	pale rose	100.00	50.00
N13			
24¢	**rose**	125.00	65.00
	pale rose	125.00	65.00
N14			
36¢	**rose**	150.00	75.00
	pale rose	150.00	75.00
N15			
48¢	**rose**	250.00	125.00
	pale rose	250.00	125.00
N16			
60¢	**rose**	140.00	65.00
	pale rose	140.00	65.00
N17			
72¢	**rose**	300.00	175.00
	pale rose	300.00	175.00
N18			
84¢	**rose**	450.00	200.00
	pale rose	450.00	200.00
N19			
96¢	**rose**	250.00	125.00
	pale rose	250.00	125.00

N20 *Ceres*

N21 *Victory*

N22 *Clio*

		UnFVF	UseFVF
N20			
$1.92	**brown**	350.00	225.00
	dark brown	350.00	225.00
N21			
$3	**vermilion**	475.00	175.00

		UnFVF	UseFVF
N22			
		750.00	150.00
	$6ultramarine		

N23 *Minerva*

N24 *Vesta*

N25 *Peace*

		UnFVF	UseFVF
N23			
$9	**yellow**	850.00	325.00
N24			
$12	**blue green**	1,000.00	450.00
N25			
$24	**dark gray violet**	1,000.00	450.00

N26 *"Commerce"*

N27 *Hebe*

N28 *Indian maiden*

		UnFVF	UseFVF
N26			
$36	**brown rose**	1,150.00	600.00
N27			
$48	**red brown**	1,600.00	650.00
N28			
$60	**violet**	1,600.00	650.00

1875. Special Printing of the 1875 Issue *by the Continental Bank Note Co. Hard, white paper, unwatermarked, without gum, perforated 12.*

		UnFVF	UseFVF
SPN5			
2¢	**gray black** *(19,514, quantity issued probably includes SPN 29)*	125.00	
SPN6			
3¢	**gray black** *(6,952)*	140.00	
SPN7			
4¢	**gray black** *(4,451)*	150.00	
SPN8			
6¢	**gray black** *(2,348)*	200.00	
SPN9			
8¢	**gray black** *(1,930)*	250.00	
SPN10			
9¢	**gray black** *(1,795)*	275.00	
SPN11			
10¢	**gray black** *(1,499)*	350.00	

			UnFVF	UseFVF
SPN12	12¢	**rose** *(1,313)*	425.00	
SPN13	24¢	**rose** *(411)*	600.00	
SPN14	36¢	**rose** *(330)*	700.00	
SPN15	48¢	**rose** *(268)*	800.00	
SPN16	60¢	**rose** *(222)*	850.00	
SPN17	72¢	**rose** *(174)*	1,000.00	
SPN18	84¢	**rose** *(164)*	1,250.00	
SPN19	96¢	**rose** *(141)*	1,750.00	
SPN20	$1.92	**dark brown** *(41)*	4,500.00	
SPN21	$3	**vermilion** *(20)*	8,000.00	
SPN22	$6	**ultramarine** *(14)*	10,000.00	
SPN23	$9	**yellow** *(4)*	17,500.00	
SPN24	$12	**bluish green** *(5)*	16,000.00	
SPN25	$24	**gray violet** *(2)*	—	
SPN26	$36	**brown rose** *(2)*	—	
SPN27	$48	**red brown** *(1)*	—	
SPN28	$60	**violet**	—	
SPN29	2¢	**black**	325.00	

1879. Allegory Design Issue American Bank Note Co., soft, porous paper, unwatermarked, perforated 12.

			UnFVF	UseFVF
N29	2¢	**black**	10.00	5.00
		gray black	10.00	5.00
		greenish black	19.00	5.00
		Double transfer at top	12.00	9.00
		cracked plate	—	
		v. Imperforate	—	

1879. Allegory Design Issue

			UnFVF	UseFVF
N30	3¢	**black**	12.50	5.50
		gray black		
		greenish black	12.00	5.50
		Double transfer at top	14.00	10.00
		v. Imperforate	—	
N31	4¢	**black**	12.50	5.50
		gray black	12.50	5.50
		greenish black	12.50	5.50
		intense black	12.50	5.50
		Double transfer at top	15.00	10.00
		v. Imperforate	—	
N32	6¢	**black**	22.50	12.50
		gray black	22.50	12.50
		greenish black	22.50	12.50
		intense black	22.50	12.50
N33	8¢	**black**	22.50	12.50
		gray black	22.50	12.50
		greenish black	22.50	12.50
		Double transfer at top	27.50	22.50
		v. Imperforate	—	
N34	10¢	**black**	25.00	12.50
		gray black	25.00	12.50
		greenish black	25.00	12.50
		Double transfer at top	27.50	—
		v. Imperforate	—	
N35	12¢	**red**	90.00	35.00
		v. Imperforate	—	
N36	24¢	**red**	90.00	35.00
		v. Imperforate	—	
N37	36¢	**red**	250.00	125.00
		v. Imperforate	—	
N38	48¢	**red**	225.00	75.00
		v. Imperforate	—	
N39	60¢	**red**	175.00	75.00
		v. Imperforate	—	
N40	72¢	**red**	350.00	150.00
		v. Imperforate	—	
N41	84¢	**red**	250.00	125.00
		v. Imperforate	—	
N42	96¢	**red**	175.00	75.00
		pink carmine	175.00	75.00
		v. Imperforate	—	
N43	$1.92	**pale brown**	125.00	100.00
		brown	125.00	100.00
		cracked plate	175.00	
		v. Imperforate	—	
N44	$3	**red vermilion**	125.00	75.00
		v. Imperforate	—	
N45	$6	**blue**	225.00	125.00
		ultramarine	225.00	125.00
		v. Imperforate	—	
N46	$9	**orange**	150.00	75.00
		v. Imperforate	—	
N47	$12	**yellow green**	225.00	100.00
		v. Imperforate	—	
N48	$24	**dark violet**	300.00	150.00
		v. Imperforate	—	
N49	$36	**Indian red**	350.00	150.00
		v. Imperforate	—	
N50	$48	**yellow brown**	450.00	225.00
		v. Imperforate	—	
N51	$60	**purple**	450.00	225.00
		bright purple	450.00	225.00
		v. Imperforate	—	

1885. Allegory Design Issue *Intaglio, American Bank Note Co., soft, porous paper, perforated 12.*

			UnFVF	UseFVF
N52	1¢	**black**	12.50	5.50
		gray black	12.50	5.50
		intense black	12.50	5.50
		Double transfer at top	15.00	9.00
N53	12¢	**carmine**	40.00	15.00
		deep carmine	40.00	15.00
		rose carmine	40.00	15.00
N54	24¢	**carmine**	40.00	17.50
		deep carmine	40.00	17.50
		rose carmine	40.00	17.50
N55	36¢	**carmine**	60.00	25.00
		deep carmine	60.00	25.00
		rose carmine	60.00	25.00
N56	48¢	**carmine**	85.00	40.00
		deep carmine	85.00	40.00
N57	60¢	**carmine**	125.00	50.00
		deep carmine	125.00	50.00
N58	72¢	**carmine**	150.00	60.00

			UnFVF	UseFVF
		deep carmine	150.00	60.00
		rose carmine	150.00	60.00
N59	84¢	**carmine**	300.00	140.00
		rose carmine	300.00	140.00
N60	96¢	**carmine**	225.00	100.00
		rose carmine	225.00	100.00

Imperforates of N52-B60 exist, but they were not regularly issued.

1894. Allegory Design Issue *Intaglio, Bureau of Engraving, soft, wove paper, perforated 12.*

			UnFVF	UseFVF
N61	1¢	**black**	100.00	—
		Double transfer at top	125.00	
N62	2¢	**black**	100.00	—
		Double transfer at top	125.00	
N63	4¢	**black**	125.00	—
N64	6¢	**black**	1,500.00	—
N65	10¢	**black**	225.00	—
N66	12¢	**pink**	700.00	—
N67	24¢	**pink**	700.00	—
N68	36¢	**pink**	4,500.00	—
N69	60¢	**pink**	4,500.00	—
N70	96¢	**pink**	5,500.00	—
N71	$3	**scarlet**	6,500.00	—
N72	$6	**pale blue**	8,500.00	—

1895. New Allegory Designs Issue *Intaglio, Bureau of Engraving, soft wove paper, perforated 12.*

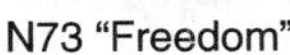

N73 "Freedom"

N76 "Freedom"

N78 "Astraea"

			UnFVF	UseFVF
N73	1¢	**black**	40.00	10.00
N74	2¢	**black**	40.00	10.00
		gray black	30.00	10.00
		Double transfer at top	45.00	
N75	5¢	**black**	50.00	15.00
		gray black	50.00	15.00
N76	10¢	**black**	100.00	45.00
N77	25¢	**carmine**	150.00	50.00
N78	50¢	**carmine**	325.00	125.00

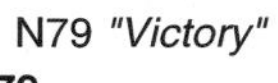

N79 *"Victory"*

N80 *"Clio"*

N81 *"Vesta"*

			UnFVF	UseFVF
N79	$2	**scarlet**	400.00	100.00
N80	$5	**ultramarine**	600.00	200.00
N81	$10	**green**	550.00	225.00

N82 *"Peace"*

N83 *"Commerce"*

N84 *Indian maiden*

			UnFVF	UseFVF
N82	$20	**slate**	825.00	400.00
N83	$50	**dull rose**	850.00	400.00
N84	$100	**purple**	1,000.00	450.00
N85	1¢	**black**	4.00	3.25
		gray black	4.00	3.25
N86	2¢	**black**	4.50	3.75
		gray black	4.50	3.75
N87	5¢	**black**	7.00	5.50
		gray black	7.00	5.50
N88	10¢	**black**	4.50	3.75
		gray black	4.50	3.75
N89	25¢	**carmine**	8.50	8.50
		lilac rose	8.50	8.50
N90	50¢	**carmine**	12.50	14.00
		rose carmine	12.50	14.00
		lilac rose	12.50	14.00
N91	$2	**scarlet**	15.00	17.50
		scarlet vermilion	15.00	17.50
N92	$5	**dark blue**	25.00	30.00
		light blue	125.00	50.00
N93	$10	**green**	25.00	30.00
N94	$20	**slate**	25.00	35.00
N95	$50	**dull rose**	30.00	40.00
N96	$100	**purple**	35.00	42.50

1899. Reprints of the 1895 Issue Special Printing In 1899 the U.S. Government sold 26,898 sets of the Newspaper Series of 1895-97 to collectors at $5 per set. Since the supply of high values was not great enough to make up the number of sets required, the values from the $5 through the $100 were reprinted. These special printings can be distinguished from the originals by the shade and whiteness of the paper and gum.

Bureau of Engraving and Printing. Designs of 1895 Issue but on double-line USPS watermark paper, with white instead of yellowish gum, perforated 12.

		UnFVF	UseFVF
SPN30		UnFVF	UseFVF
$5	**blue**	—	
SPN31		UnFVF	UseFVF
$10	**green**	—	
SPN32		UnFVF	UseFVF
$20	**slate**	—	
SPN33		UnFVF	UseFVF
$50	**rose**	—	
SPN34		UnFVF	UseFVF
$100	**purple**	—	

Official Carrier Stamps

1851. Official Carrier Stamp In the early days of the U.S. postal system the regular postage charge paid only for the delivery of mail from post office to post office. For an additional charge, the post office would act as a carrier and deliver letters to the addressee. Two stamps were issued for this purpose. Printed by Toppan, Carpenter, Casilear and Company, they were *unwatermarked and imperforate.* They were both of the 1¢ denomination although the Franklin stamp had no denomination indicated on its face.

OCS1 *Benjamin Franklin*

		UnFVF	UseFVF
OCS1		UnFVF	UseFVF
1¢	**blue on rose paper**	4,000.00	4,500.00
	Cracked plate	4,500.00	
	Double transfer	—	—
	On cover		7,750.00

OCS2 *Eagle*

		UnFVF	UseFVF
OCS2		UnFVF	UseFVF
1¢	**blue on yellowish paper**	20.00	35.00
	Double transfer	—	—
	On cover (alone)		125.00

1875. Reprint Official Carrier Stamp Special Printing reprint of the Official Carrier Stamps of 1851. The Franklin carrier was printed in a darker blue than the originals and appears on rose-colored paper as well as on a paler, thicker paper. The Eagle reprints are on hard white paper and also on a coarse paper. *Printed by the Continental Bank Note Co., by intaglio, imperforate, without gum.*

		UnFVF	UseFVF
SPOCS1		UnFVF	UseFVF
1¢	**blue on rose paper**	50.00	
	v. Perforated 12	2,500.00	
SPOCS2		UnFVF	UseFVF
1¢	**blue**	25.00	
	v. Perforated 12	175.00	

Official Stamps

The franking privilege for the various government departments was abolished July 1, 1873. On that date, official stamps were issued to be used by the departments. In addition to the name of the department, inscribed at the top, the Post Office Department stamps have large numerals as the central design, while the stamps of the other departments feature busts of the following men:

1¢ Benjamin Franklin
2¢ Andrew Jackson
3¢ George Washington
6¢ Abraham Lincoln
7¢ Edwin Stanton
10¢ Thomas Jefferson
12¢ Henry Clay
15¢ Daniel Webster
24¢ Winfield Scott
30¢ Alexander Hamilton
90¢ Oliver Perry
$2 to $20 William Seward

The first official stamps were printed in intaglio by the Continental Bank Note Co. on thin, hard paper; but in 1879 the American Bank Note Co., using the same plates, made printings on soft, porous paper. This is the principal way that they can be identified, since all the paper is unwatermarked, and all the stamps are *perforated 12.* A marginal imprint reading "Continental" does not necessarily indicate the printer. *Intaglio on thin, hard paper, unwatermarked, perforated 12.*

1873. Agriculture Dept. Issue. *Intaglio on thin, hard paper, unwatermarked, perforated 12.*

OF1

		UnFVF	UseFVF
OF1		UnFVF	UseFVF
1¢	**yellow**	95.00	75.00
	golden yellow	110.00	80.00
	olive yellow	110.00	80.00
	p. Ribbed paper	125.00	80.00
	On cover		—
OF2		UnFVF	UseFVF
2¢	**yellow**	85.00	32.50
	golden yellow	75.00	25.00
	olive yellow	75.00	27.50
	p. Ribbed paper	80.00	30.00
	On cover		—
OF3		UnFVF	UseFVF
3¢	**yellow**	65.00	6.00
	golden yellow	70.00	6.50
	olive yellow	73.00	6.50
	Double transfer	—	—
	p. Ribbed paper	73.00	7.00
	On cover		—
OF4		UnFVF	UseFVF
6¢	**yellow**	80.00	25.00
	golden yellow	80.00	27.50
	olive yellow	80.00	27.50
	On cover		—
OF5		UnFVF	UseFVF
10¢	**yellow**	150.00	100.00
	golden yellow	165.00	110.00
	olive yellow	175.00	115.00
	On cover		—
OF6		UnFVF	UseFVF
12¢	**yellow**	195.00	100.00
	golden yellow	210.00	110.00
	olive yellow	225.00	110.00
	On cover		—
OF7		UnFVF	UseFVF
15¢	**yellow**	160.00	95.00
	golden yellow	170.00	100.00
	olive yellow	175.00	100.00
	On cover		—
OF8		UnFVF	UseFVF
24¢	**yellow**	160.00	85.00

		UnFVF	UseFVF
	golden yellow	175.00	85.00
	On cover		—
OF9		UnFVF	UseFVF
30¢	**yellow**	225.00	115.00
	olive yellow	250.00	150.00
	golden yellow	235.00	140.00

1879. Agriculture Dept. Issue *American Bank Note Co., intaglio on soft, porous paper, unwatermarked, perforated 12.*

		UnFVF	UseFVF
OF10			
1¢	**yellow,** issued without gum	2,000.00	
	issued without gum	1,500.00	
	Plate pair		

Some consider No. OF10 a special printing, circa 1883.

		UnFVF	UseFVF
OF11			
3¢	**yellow**	225.00	40.00

1873. Executive Dept. Issue Intaglio on thin, hard paper, unwatermarked, perforated 12.

		UnFVF	UseFVF
OF12			
1¢	**carmine**	335.00	200.00
	dark carmine	335.00	200.00
OF13		UnFVF	UseFVF
2¢	**carmine**	210.00	100.00
	dark carmine	210.00	100.00
	Double transfer	—	—
OF14		UnFVF	UseFVF
3¢	**carmine**	260.00	100.00
	lilac red	260.00	100.00

OF15

		UnFVF	UseFVF
OF15			
6¢	**carmine**	400.00	275.00
	dark carmine	400.00	275.00
	dull carmine	400.00	275.00
OF16		UnFVF	UseFVF
10¢	**carmine**	350.00	300.00
	dark carmine	350.00	300.00
	dull carmine	350.00	300.00

1873. Interior Dept. Issue Intaglio on thin, hard paper, unwatermarked, perforated 12.

		UnFVF	UseFVF
OF17			
1¢	**orange red**	21.00	5.25
	bright orange red	21.00	5.25
	dull orange red	21.00	5.25
	p. Ribbed paper	25.00	6.00
OF18		UnFVF	UseFVF
2¢	**orange red**	16.50	3.25
	bright orange red	16.50	3.25
	dull orange red	16.50	3.25
OF19		UnFVF	UseFVF
3¢	**orange red**	28.00	3.00
	bright orange red	28.00	3.00
	dull orange red	28.00	3.00
	p. Ribbed paper	30.00	5.25
OF20		UnFVF	UseFVF
6¢	**orange red**	21.00	3.25
	bright orange red	21.00	3.25
	dull orange red	21.00	3.25
OF21		UnFVF	UseFVF
10¢	**orange red**	20.00	6.25
	bright orange red	20.00	6.25
	dull orange red	20.00	6.25
OF22		UnFVF	UseFVF
12¢	**orange red**	32.50	4.75
	bright orange red	32.50	4.75
	dull orange red	32.50	4.75

OF23

		UnFVF	UseFVF
OF23			
15¢	**orange red**	50.00	10.00
	bright orange red	50.00	10.00
	dull orange red	50.00	10.00
	Double transfer	90.00	25.00
	p. Ribbed paper	—	—
OF24		UnFVF	UseFVF
24¢	**orange red**	37.50	8.50
	bright orange red	37.50	8.50
	dull orange red	37.50	8.50
OF25		UnFVF	UseFVF
30¢	**orange red**	50.00	8.50
	bright orange red	50.00	8.50
	dull orange red	50.00	8.50
OF26		UnFVF	UseFVF
90¢	**orange red**	115.00	22.50
	bright orange red	115.00	22.50
	dull orange red	115.00	22.50
	Double transfer	160.00	—

1879. Interior Dept. Issue *Intaglio on soft, porous paper, unwatermarked, perforated 12.*

		UnFVF	UseFVF
OF27			
1¢	**orange red**	135.00	125.00
	dull orange red	135.00	125.00
OF28		UnFVF	UseFVF
2¢	**orange red**	2.50	1.25
	dull orange red	2.50	1.25
OF29		UnFVF	UseFVF
3¢	**orange red**	2.25	.75
	dull orange red	2.25	.75
OF30		UnFVF	UseFVF
6¢	**orange red**	3.50	3.75
	dull orange red	3.50	3.75
OF31		UnFVF	UseFVF
10¢	**orange red**	45.00	35.00
	dull orange red	45.00	35.00
OF32		UnFVF	UseFVF
12¢	**orange red**	90.00	60.00
	dull orange red	90.00	60.00
OF33		UnFVF	UseFVF
15¢	**orange red**	200.00	150.00
	dull orange red	200.00	150.00
	Double transfer, left side	275.00	—
OF34		UnFVF	UseFVF
24¢	**orange red**	2,500.00	—
	dull orange red	2,500.00	—

1873. Justice Dept. Issue *Intaglio on thin, hard paper, unwatermarked, perforated 12.*

		UnFVF	UseFVF
OF35			
1¢	**purple**	65.00	47.50
	dark purple	65.00	47.50
OF36		UnFVF	UseFVF
2¢	**purple**	100.00	50.00
	dark purple	100.00	50.00
OF37		UnFVF	UseFVF
3¢	**purple**	100.00	10.00
	dark purple	100.00	10.00
	Double transfer	—	—
OF38		UnFVF	UseFVF
6¢	**purple**	95.00	16.00
	bluish purple	95.00	16.00
	dull purple	95.00	16.00
OF39		UnFVF	UseFVF
10¢	**purple**	110.00	35.00
	bluish purple	110.00	35.00
	Double transfer	—	—

OF40

OF40		UnFVF	UseFVF
12¢	**purple**	85.00	22.50
	dark purple	85.00	22.50

OF41		UnFVF	UseFVF
15¢	**purple**	160.00	75.00
	Double transfer	—	—

OF42		UnFVF	UseFVF
24¢	**purple**	425.00	165.00

OF43		UnFVF	UseFVF
30¢	**purple**	375.00	95.00
	Double transfer	400.00	95.00

OF44		UnFVF	UseFVF
90¢	**purple**	700.00	240.00
	dark purple	700.00	240.00

1879. Justice Dept. Issue *Intaglio on soft, porous paper, unwatermarked, perforated 12.*

OF45		UnFVF	UseFVF
3¢	**bluish purple**	65.00	40.00
	dark bluish purple	65.00	40.00

OF46		UnFVF	UseFVF
6¢	**dark bluish purple**	150.00	100.00
	dark bluish purple		

1873. Navy Dept. Issue *Intaglio on thin, hard paper, unwatermarked, perforated 12.*

OF47		UnFVF	UseFVF
1¢	**ultramarine**	45.00	22.50
	dark ultramarine	45.00	22.50
	dull blue	45.00	22.50

OF48		UnFVF	UseFVF
2¢	**ultramarine**	35.00	10.00
	dark ultramarine	35.00	10.00
	dull blue	45.00	12.50
	gray blue	45.00	12.50
	Double transfer	—	—

OF49

OF49		UnFVF	UseFVF
3¢	**ultramarine**	35.00	5.25
	dark ultramarine	35.00	5.25
	dull blue	35.00	5.25
	pale ultramarine	35.00	5.25
	Double transfer	—	—

OF50		UnFVF	UseFVF
6¢	**ultramarine**	37.50	8.50
	bright ultrmarine	37.50	8.50
	dull blue	45.00	8.50
	Double transfer	—	—
	Vertical line through "N" of "NAVY"	65.00	14.00

OF51		UnFVF	UseFVF
7¢	**ultramarine**	210.00	85.00
	dark ultramarine	210.00	85.00
	dull blue	210.00	85.00
	Double transfer	—	—

OF52		UnFVF	UseFVF
10¢	**ultramarine**	47.50	17.50
	dark ultramarine	46.50	17.50
	dull blue	50.00	17.50
	pale ultramarine	47.50	17.50
	Cracked plate	—	125.00
	p. Ribbed paper	75.00	40.00

OF53		UnFVF	UseFVF
12¢	**ultramarine**	55.00	15.00
	dark ultramarine	55.00	15.00
	pale ultramarine	55.00	15.00
	Double transfer, left side	175.00	50.00

OF54		UnFVF	UseFVF
15¢	**ultramarine**	100.00	35.00
	dark ultramarine	100.00	35.00

OF55		UnFVF	UseFVF
24¢	**ultramarine**	100.00	35.00
	dark ultramarine	100.00	35.00
	dull blue	125.00	—

OF56		UnFVF	UseFVF
30¢	**ultramarine**	80.00	17.50
	dark ultramarine	80.00	17.50
	Double transfer	100.00	20.00

OF57		UnFVF	UseFVF
90¢	**ultramarine**	425.00	110.00
	v. Double impression	—	7,500.00

1873. Post Office Dept. Issue *Intaglio on thin, hard paper, unwatermarked, perforated 12.*

OF58		UnFVF	UseFVF
1¢	**gray black**	7.50	3.50
	black	7.50	3.50

OF59		UnFVF	UseFVF
2¢	**gray black**	8.50	3.00
	black	8.50	3.00
	v. Double Impression	325.00	—

OF60		UnFVF	UseFVF
3¢	**black**	3.00	1.00
	gray black	3.00	1.00
	Cracked plate	10.00	7.00
	Double transfer	—	—
	p. Ribbed paper	—	—
	v. Printed on both sides	—	3,500.00

OF61		UnFVF	UseFVF
6¢	**black**	9.00	2.25
	gray black	9.00	2.25
	p. Ribbed paper	—	9.00
	y. Diagonal half used as 3¢ on cover	—	4,500.00

OF62

OF62		UnFVF	UseFVF
10¢	**black**	40.00	20.00
	gray black	40.00	20.00

OF63		UnFVF	UseFVF
12¢	**black**	20.00	5.50
	gray black	20.00	5.50

OF64		UnFVF	UseFVF
15¢	**black**	27.50	9.00
	gray black	27.50	9.00
	Double transfer	—	—
	v. Pair, imperforate	—	550.00

OF65		UnFVF	UseFVF
24¢	**black**	35.00	10.00
	gray black	35.00	10.00

OF66		UnFVF	UseFVF
30¢	**black**	35.00	10.00
	gray black	35.00	10.00

OF67		UnFVF	UseFVF
90¢	**black**	50.00	10.00
	gray black	50.00	10.00
	Double transfer	—	—

1879. Post Office Dept. Issue *Intaglio on soft, porous paper, unwatermarked, perforated 12.*

OF68		UnFVF	UseFVF
3¢	**black**	9.00	3.25
	gray black	9.00	3.25
	Block of 4	200.00	—

1873. State Dept. Issue *Intaglio on thin, hard paper, unwatermarked, perforated 12.*

OF69		UnFVF	UseFVF
1¢	**green**	65.00	25.00
	dark yellow green	65.00	25.00
	pale green	65.00	25.00
OF70		UnFVF	UseFVF
2¢	**green**	130.00	40.00
	dark yellow green	130.00	40.00
	yellow green	130.00	40.00
	Double transfer	—	—
OF71		UnFVF	UseFVF
3¢	**green**	50.00	9.50
	bright green	50.00	9.50
	yellow green	50.00	9.50
OF72		UnFVF	UseFVF
6¢	**green**	50.00	11.50
	bright green	50.00	11.50
	yellow green	50.00	11.50
	Double transfer	—	—
OF73		UnFVF	UseFVF
7¢	**green**	90.00	25.00
	dark yellow green	90.00	25.00
	p. Ribbed paper	125.00	27.50

OF74

OF74		UnFVF	UseFVF
10¢	**green**	70.00	16.00
	bright green	70.00	16.00
	yellow green	70.00	16.00
	Short transfer	150.00	30.00
OF75		UnFVF	UseFVF
12¢	**green**	115.00	50.00
	Yellow green	115.00	50.00
OF76		UnFVF	UseFVF
15¢	**green**	125.00	35.00
	dark yellow green	125.00	35.00
OF77		UnFVF	UseFVF
24¢	**green**	256.00	90.00
	dark yellow green	250.00	90.00
OF78		UnFVF	UseFVF
30¢	**green**	225.00	65.00
	dark yellow green	225.00	65.00
OF79		UnFVF	UseFVF
90¢	**green**	450.00	140.00
	dark yellow green	450.00	140.00
OF80		UnFVF	UseFVF
$2	**green & black**	525.00	400.00
	yellow green & black	525.00	400.00

OF81

OF81		UnFVF	UseFVF
$5	**green & black**	4,250.00	1,800.00
	dark green & black	4,250.00	1,800.00
	yellow green & black	4,250.00	1,800.00
	Plate block of 6	42,500.00	
OF82		UnFVF	UseFVF
$10	**green & black**	2,800.00	1,400.00
	dark green & black	2,800.00	1,400.00
	yellow green & black	2,800.00	1,400.00
OF83		UnFVF	UseFVF
$20	**green & black**	1,950.00	950.00
	dark green & black	1,950.00	950.00
	yellow green & black	1,950.00	950.00

1873. Treasury Dept. Issue Intaglio on thin, hard paper, unwatermarked, perforated 12.

OF84		UnFVF	UseFVF
1¢	**brown**	25.00	3.00
	dark brown	25.00	3.00
	yellow brown	25.00	3.00
	Double transfer	35.00	5.00
OF85		UnFVF	UseFVF
2¢	**brown**	27.50	3.00
	dark brown	27.50	3.00
	yellow brown	27.50	3.00
	Cracked plate	40.00	—
	Double transfer	—	—
OF86		UnFVF	UseFVF
3¢	**brown**	17.50	1.50
	dark brown	17.50	1.50
	yellow brown	17.50	1.50
	t. Shaded circle to right of right frame line	—	—
	t1. Double impression	—	—
OF87		UnFVF	UseFVF
6¢	**brown**	23.00	2.50
	dark brown	23.00	2.50
	yellow brown	23.00	2.50
	Double transfer	—	—
	Worn plate	23.00	3.00
OF88		UnFVF	UseFVF
7¢	**brown**	55.00	15.00
	dark brown	55.00	15.00
	yellow brown	55.00	15.00
OF89		UnFVF	UseFVF
10¢	**brown**	60.00	5.50
	dark brown	60.00	5.50
	yellow brown	60.00	5.50
	Double transfer	—	—
OF90		UnFVF	UseFVF
12¢	**brown**	60.00	4.00
	dark brown	60.00	4.00
	yellow brown	60.00	4.00
OF91		UnFVF	UseFVF
15¢	**brown**	55.00	5.50
	dark brown	55.00	5.50
	yellow brown	55.00	5.50
OF92		UnFVF	UseFVF
24¢	**brown**	250.00	45.00
	dark brown	250.00	45.00
	yellow brown	250.00	45.00
	Double transfer	—	—
OF93		UnFVF	UseFVF
30¢	**brown**	85.00	6.00
	dark brown	85.00	6.00
	yellow brown	85.00	6.00
	Short transfer	—	—

OF94

OF94		UnFVF	UseFVF
90¢	**brown**	85.00	6.00
	dark brown	85.00	6.00
	yellow brown	85.00	6.00

1879. Treasury Dept. Issue *Intaglio on soft, porous paper, unwatermarked, perforated 12.*

OF95		UnFVF	UseFVF
3¢	**brown**	30.00	4.50
	yellow brown	30.00	4.50
OF96		UnFVF	UseFVF
6¢	**brown**	40.00	4.00

	yellow brown	40.00	4.00

OF97		UnFVF	UseFVF
10¢	**brown**	85.00	25.00
	dark brown	85.00	25.00
	yellow brown	85.00	25.00

OF98		UnFVF	UseFVF
30¢	**brown**	800.00	175.00
	yellow brown	800.00	175.00

OF99		UnFVF	UseFVF
90¢	**brown**	1,000.00	175.00
	dark brown	1,000.00	175.00
	yellow brown	1,000.00	175.00

1873. War Dept. Issue *Intaglio on thin, hard paper, unwatermarked, perforated 12.*

OF100		UnFVF	UseFVF
1¢	**Venetian red**	80.00	4.50
	rose red	80.00	4.50

OF101		UnFVF	UseFVF
2¢	**Venetian red**	70.00	6.50
	rose red	70.00	6.50
	p. Ribbed paper	65.00	9.00

OF102		UnFVF	UseFVF
3¢	**Venetian red**	70.00	1.75
	rose red	70.00	1.75

OF103		UnFVF	UseFVF
6¢	**Venetian red**	225.00	4.00
	dull Venetian red	225.00	4.00

OF104		UnFVF	UseFVF
7¢	**Venetian red**	70.00	40.00
	dull Venetian red	70.00	40.00
	rose red	70.00	40.00

OF105		UnFVF	UseFVF
10¢	**Venetian red**	25.00	7.50
	rose red	25.00	7.50

The crack at lower left of OF105 was on the original die and is found on all copies.

OF106		UnFVF	UseFVF
12¢	**Venetian red**	80.00	5.50
	p. Ribbed paper	110.00	7.50

OF107		UnFVF	UseFVF
15¢	**Venetian red**	19.00	6.75
	dull Venetian red	19.00	6.75
	rose red	22.50	7.50
	p. Ribbed paper	30.00	10.00

OF108

OF108		UnFVF	UseFVF
24¢	**Venetian red**	19.00	4.00
	dull Venetian red	19.00	4.00
	rose red	19.00	4.00

OF109		UnFVF	UseFVF
30¢	**Venetian red**	20.00	4.00
	rose red	20.00	4.00
	p. Ribbed paper	40.00	7.50

OF110		UnFVF	UseFVF
90¢	**Venetian red**	55.00	25.00
	rose red	55.00	25.00

1879. War Dept. Issue *Intaglio on soft, porous paper, unwatermarked, perforated 12.*

OF111		UnFVF	UseFVF
1¢	**dull rose**	3.00	2.00
	Venetian red	60.00	27.50
	rose red	60.00	27.50

OF112		UnFVF	UseFVF
2¢	**dull rose**	3.50	2.00
	dark rose	3.50	2.00
	dull vermilion	3.50	2.00

OF113		UnFVF	UseFVF
3¢	**dull rose**	3.50	1.25
	rose red	3.50	1.25
	Double transfer	6.00	4.00
	v1. Double impression	1,000.00	—
	v2. Pair, imperforate	1,500.00	—

OF114		UnFVF	UseFVF
6¢	**dull rose**	4.00	1.25
	dull vermilion	4.00	1.25
	rose red	4.00	1.25

OF115		UnFVF	UseFVF
10¢	**dull rose**	25.00	20.00
	rose red	25.00	20.00

OF116		UnFVF	UseFVF
12¢	**dull rose**	20.00	7.50
	rose red	20.00	7.50

OF117		UnFVF	UseFVF
30¢	**dull rose**	65.00	42.50
	rose red	65.00	42.50

1910-1911. Postal Savings Issue When Postal Savings Depositories were set up in 1910 under the Post Office Department, special stamps were provided for that division. Their use was discontinued in 1914, and all remainders destroyed. *Intaglio by the Bureau of Engraving and Printing, perforated 12.*

OF118 and OF119 are watermarked double-line USPS. OF120, OF121, OF122 and OF123 are watermarked single-line USPS.

OF118		UnFVF	UseFVF
2¢	**black**	17.50	1.75
	FDC *(Dec. 22, 1910)*		—
	Plate block of 6, w/imprint	250.00	
	Block of 4 (2mm apart)	45.00	6.50
	Block of 4 (3mm apart)	42.00	5.50
	Double transfer	15.00	2.50

OF119		UnFVF	UseFVF
50¢	**green**	150.00	32.50
	FDC *(Feb. 1, 1911)*		
	Plate block of 6, w/imprint	2,400.00	
	Block of 4 (2mm apart)	550.00	170.00
	Block of 4 (3mm apart)	535.00	170.00
	Margin block of 4, w/arrow	560.00	

OF120

OF120		UnFVF	UseFVF
$1	**bright blue**	150.00	10.00
	FDC *(Feb. 1, 1911)*		
	Plate block of 6 w/imprint	1,900.00	375.00
	Block of 4 (2mm apart)	400.00	45.00
	Block of 4 (3mm apart)	390.00	45.00
	Margin block of 4, w/arrow	425.00	

OF121		UnFVF	UseFVF
1¢	**dark red violet**	8.50	1.25
	FDC *(March 27, 1911)*		
	Plate block of 6, w/imprint	110.00	
	Block of 4 (2mm apart)	21.00	5.00
	Block of 4 (3mm apart)	20.00	4.75

OF122		UnFVF	UseFVF
2¢	**black**	45.00	4.25
	FDC *(March 27, 1911)*		
	Plate block of 6, w/imprint	525.00	
	Block of 4 (2mm apart)	120.00	19.00
	Block of 4 (3mm apart)	118.00	19.00
	Double transfer	32.00	4.75

OF123		UnFVF	UseFVF
10¢	**carmine**	17.50	1.25
	FDC *(Feb. 1, 1911)*		
	Plate block of 6, w/imprint	225.00	
	Block of 4 (2mm apart)	35.00	5.50
	Block of 4 (3mm apart)	33.00	5.00
	Double transfer	14.00	2.50

1983. Official Mail Issue *Intaglio perforated 11.*

OF124-OF130

OF124		MNHVF	UseVF
1¢	**blue, red & black**	.25	.25
	Plate block of 4	.60	
	FDC *(Jan. 12, 1983)*		1.75

OF125		MNHVF	UseVF
4¢	**blue, red & black**	.25	.25
	Plate block of 4	.75	
	FDC *(Jan. 12, 1983)*		1.75

OF126		MNHVF	UseVF
13¢	**blue, red & black**	.45	.75
	Plate block of 4	2.00	
	FDC *(Jan. 12, 1983)*		1.75

OF127		MNHVF	UseVF
17¢	**blue, red & black**	.50	.40
	Plate block of 4	2.50	
	FDC *(Jan. 12, 1983)*		1.75

OF128		MNHVF	UseVF
$1	**blue, red & black**	3.00	1.25
	Plate block of 4	14.00	
	FDC *(Jan. 12, 1983)*		5.00

OF129		MNHVF	UseVF
$5	**blue, red & black**	10.00	5.00
	Plate block of 4	45.00	
	FDC *(Jan. 12, 1983)*		15.00

1985. Official Mail Coil Issue *Coil, perforated 10 vertically.*

OF130		MNHVF	UseVF
20¢	**blue, red & black**	2.00	2.25
	Pair	4.50	4.50
	FDC *(Jan. 12, 1983)*		1.75
	Pair, imperforate	2,000.00	

1985. Official Mail Non-denominated Issue Postal Card "D" rate, *intaglio.*

OF131

OF131		MNHVF	UseVF
14¢	**blue, red & black**	4.50	5.50
	Plate block of 4	35.00	
	FDC *(Feb. 4, 1985)*		1.75

1985. Official Mail Coil Issue *Coil, perforated 10 vertically.*

OF132

OF132		MNHVF	UseVF
22¢	**blue, red & black,** non-denominated	4.75	3.00
	Pair	7.50	—
	FDC *(Feb. 4, 1985)*		1.00

OF133, 134

OF133		MNHVF	UseVF
14¢	**blue, red & black**	.40	.65
	FDC *(May 15, 1985)*		2.00

OF134

OF134		MNHVF	UseVF
22¢	**blue, red & black**	.75	2.25
	Pair	1.50	4.50
	FDC *(May 15, 1985)*		1.00

OF135

OF135		MNHVF	UseVF
25¢	**blue, red & black**	1.00	2.00
	FDC *(May 15, 1985)*		1.00
	Pair		

1988. Official Mail Coil Issue Design similar to OF133, coil, offset, perforated 10 vertically.

OF136

OF136		MNHVF	UseVF
20¢	**blue, red & black**	.45	.35
	Pair	1.00	.75
	FDC *(May 19, 1988)*		1.00

OF137

OF137		MNHVF	UseVF
15¢	**blue, red & black**	.45	.65
	Pair	.75	
	FDC *(June 11, 1988)*		1.00

OF138

OF138		MNHVF	UseVF
25¢	**blue, red & black**	.75	.50
	FDC *(June 11, 1988)*		1.75
	Pair	1.00	.75
	v. Pair, imperforate	2,000.00	

1989. Official Mail Issue Similar to OF133, but without the "USA" prior to the denomination, *offset, perforated 11.*

OF139

OF139		MNHVF	UseVF
1¢	**blue, red & black**	.25	.25
	FDC *(July 5, 1989)*		1.75

1991. Official Mail Coil Issue "F" rate non-denominated stamp. *Coil, offset, perforated 10 vertically.*

OF140

OF140		MNHVF	UseVF
29¢	**blue, red & black**	.75	.50
	FDC *(Jan. 22, 1991)*		1.25
	Pair	1.00	

1991. Official Mail Issue Similar to OF139, *offset, perforated 11.*

OF141

OF141		MNHVF	UseVF
4¢	**blue, red & black**	.25	.30
	FDC *(April 6, 1991)*		1.25

1991. Official Mail Issue Similar to OF139, *offset, perforated 11.*

OF142

OF142		MNHVF	UseVF
19¢	**blue, red & black**	.40	.60
	FDC *(May 24, 1991)*		1.25

OF143

OF143		MNHVF	UseVF
23¢	**blue, red & black**	.45	.60
	FDC *(May 24, 1991)*		1.75
	Pair, imperforate	475.00	

1991. Official Mail Coil Issue Similar to OF139, *coil, printed by offset, perforated 10 vertically.*

OF144

OF144		MNHVF	UseVF
29¢	**blue, red & black**	.75	.50
	Pair	1.25	1.00
	FDC *(May 24, 1991)*		1.25

1993. Official Mail Issue Similar to OF139, included a line of microprinting between the Great Seal and the denomination, *offset, perforated 11.*

OF145

OF145		MNHVF	UseVF
10¢	**blue, red & black**	.35	.55
	FDC *(Oct. 19, 1993)*		1.75

OF146

OF146		MNHVF	UseVF
$1	**blue, red & black**	2.10	1.75
	FDC *(Oct. 19, 1993)*		

1994. Official Mail Coil Issue "G" Rate non-denominated stamp. *Coil, offset, perforated 9 3/4 vertically.*

OF147

OF147		MNHVF	UseVF
32¢	**blue, red & black**	.75	.50
	FDC *(Dec. 13, 1994)*		1.00
	Pair	1.25	1.00

1995. Official Mail Issue Similar to OF139, with line of microprinting, *offset, perforated 11.*

OF148

OF148		MNHVF	UseVF
1¢	**blue, red & black**	.25	.25
	FDC *(May 9, 1995)*		1.90

OF149

OF149		MNHVF	UseVF
20¢	**blue, red & black**	.45	.55
	FDC *(May 9, 1995)*		1.25

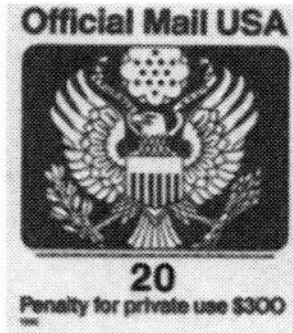

OF150

OF150		MNHVF	UseVF
23¢	**blue, red & black**	.55	.65
	FDC *(May 9, 1995)*		1.25

OF151

OF151		MNHVF	UseVF
32¢	**blue, red & black**	.75	.40
	FDC *(May 9, 1995)*		1.00

1999. Great Seal Issue showed the Great Seal of the United States in the current First Class denomination, with a line under it consisting of microprinting of the repeated phrase, "USA 1999." *Gummed coil of 100, offset by Bureau of Engraving and Printing, perforated 9 1/2.*

OF152

OF152		MNHVF	UseVF
33¢	**multicolored**	.50	.20
	Plate strip of 5	2.00	
	FDC *(Oct. 8, 1999)*		1.50
	Gummed coil of 20	7.50	

2001. Official Mail Coil Issue Official Seal *by Bureau of Engraving and Printing, offset, perforated 9 3/4 vertically, gummed.*

OF153

OF153		MNHVF	UseVF
34¢	**blue, red & black**	.65	.30
	Pair	1.30	
	FDC *(Feb. 27, 2001)*		1.50

Postage Due

1879. Postage Due Stamps Issue were authorized in 1879. They were created to denote the amount due, by the addressee, on mail that was insufficiently prepaid. The stamps were to come into use on July 1, 1879, but the four lowest denominations are known used almost two months before that date. *Engraved and printed by the American Bank Note Co., on unwatermarked paper, perforated 12.*

PD1-28

First Printing

		UnFVF	UseFVF
PD1			
1¢	**yellow brown**	40.00	8.00
PD2			
2¢	**yellow brown**	250.00	6.50
PD3			
3¢	**yellow brown**	35.00	5.00
PD4			
5¢	**yellow brown**	400.00	38.00
PD5			
10¢	**yellow brown**	450.00	30.00
PD6			
30¢	**yellow brown**	200.00	47.50
PD7			
50¢	**yellow brown**	350.00	55.00

Later Printings

		UnFVF	UseFVF
PD8			
1¢	**brown**	40.00	8.00
PD9			
2¢	**brown**	250.00	5.00
PD10			
3¢	**brown**	35.00	5.00
PD11			
5¢	**brown**	400.00	18.00
PD12			
10¢	**brown**	450.00	30.00
PD13			
30¢	**brown**	200.00	50.00
PD14			
50¢	**brown**	350.00	55.00

1887. Previous designs in changed colors.

		UnFVF	UseFVF
PD15			
1¢	**brown red**	40.00	5.00
PD16			
2¢	**brown red**	50.00	5.00
PD17			
3¢	**brown red**	700.00	150.00
PD18			
5¢	**brown red**	350.00	20.00
PD19			
10¢	**brown red**	350.00	15.00
PD20			
20¢	**brown red**	175.00	50.00
PD21			
50¢	**brown red**	1,225.00	175.00

1891. Previous designs in changed colors. *Imperforate varieties of PD22-28 exist, but they were not regularly issued.*

		UnFVF	UseFVF
PD22			
1¢	**claret**	20.00	1.00
PD23			
2¢	**claret**	25.00	1.00
PD24			
3¢	**claret**	50.00	8.00
PD25			
5¢	**claret**	60.00	8.00
PD26			
10¢	**claret**	100.00	17.50
PD27			
30¢	**claret**	350.00	150.00

PD28

PD28		UnFVF	UseFVF
50¢	**claret**	375.00	150.00

1879. Special Printings of the then current first issue of postage dues usually have mutilated perforations for they were cut apart by scissors. Known only unused.

Despite the quantities issued, the first three values are comparatively scarce. *American Bank Note Co. on soft, porous paper, unwatermarked, perforated 12.*

		UnFVF	UseFVF
SPD1			
1¢	**brown** *(4420)*	5,000.00	
SPD2			
2¢	**brown** *(1361)*	3,500.00	

		UnFVF	UseFVF
SPD3			
3¢	**brown** *(436)*	2,500.00	
SPD4			
5¢	**brown** *(249)*	1,750.00	
SPD5			
10¢	**brown** *(174)*	1,750.00	
SPD6			
30¢	**brown** *(179)*	1,750.00	
SPD7			
50¢	**brown** *(179)*	1,750.00	

1894. New Designs Issue appear in many shades. Care should be observed in soaking these stamps as the colors may run. *Printed by the Bureau of Engraving and Printing, unwatermarked, perforated 12.*

PD29-68

		UnFVF	UseFVF
PD29			
1¢	**vermilion** *(1894)*	1,300.00	300.00
PD30			
1¢	**brown carmine** *(Aug. 14, 1894)*	32.50	5.50
PD31			
2¢	**vermilion** *(1894)*	550.00	130.00
PD32			
2¢	**brown carmine** *(July 20, 1894)*	35.00	4.00
PD33			
3¢	**brown carmine** *(April 27, 1895)*	130.00	26.00
PD34			
5¢	**brown carmine** *(April 27, 1895)*	200.00	27.50
PD35			
10¢	**brown carmine** *(Sept. 24, 1894)*	200.00	25.00
PD36			
30¢	**brown carmine** *(April 27, 1895)*	350.00	90.00
PD37			
50¢	**brown carmine** *(April 27, 1895)*	900.00	250.00

1895. Same as previous designs. *Double-line USPS watermark.*

		UnFVF	UseFVF
PD38			
1¢	**brown carmine** *(Aug. 29, 1895)*	7.50	.75
PD39			
2¢	**brown carmine** *(Sept. 14, 1895)*	7.50	.70
PD40			
3¢	**brown carmine** *(Oct. 30, 1895)*	47.50	1.50
PD41			
5¢	**brown carmine** *(Oct. 15, 1895)*	50.00	1.50
PD42			
10¢	**brown carmine** *(Sept. 14, 1895)*	47.50	3.50
PD43			
30¢	**brown carmine** *(Aug. 21, 1897)*	450.00	50.00
PD44			
50¢	**brown carmine** *(March 17, 1896)*	275.00	35.00

1910. Same as previous designs. *Single-line USPS watermark.*

		UnFVF	UseFVF
PD45			
1¢	**brown carmine** *(Aug. 30, 1910)*	27.50	2.75
PD46			
2¢	**brown carmine** *(Nov. 25, 1910)*	27.50	1.25
PD47			
3¢	**brown carmine** *(Aug. 31, 1910)*	450.00	30.00
PD48			
5¢	**brown carmine** *(Aug. 31, 1910)*	75.00	6.25
PD49			
10¢	**brown carmine** *(Aug. 31, 1910)*	95.00	12.50
PD50			
50¢	**brown carmine** *(Sept. 23, 1912)*	750.00	120.00

1914. Same as previous designs. *Perforated 10.*

		UnFVF	UseFVF
PD51			
1¢	**rose red**	50.00	11.00
PD52			
2¢	**vermilion**	45.00	.30
PD53			
2¢	**rose red**	45.00	.30
PD54			
3¢	**rose red**	750.00	38.00
PD55			
5¢	**rose red**	32.00	2.50
PD56			
10¢	**rose red**	50.00	2.00
PD57			
30¢	**rose red**	200.00	16.00
PD58			
50¢	**rose red**	8,200.00	650.00

1916. Same as previous designs. *Unwatermarked.*

		UnFVF	UseFVF
PD59			
1¢	**rose red**	2,000.00	300.00
PD60			
2¢	**rose red**	125.00	20.00

1917-25. Same as previous designs. *Perforated 11.*

		UnFVF	UseFVF
PD61			
1/2¢	**carmine** *(April 13, 1925)*	1.00	.25
PD62			
1¢	**carmine**	2.25	.25
PD63			
2¢	**carmine**	2.25	.25
PD64			
3¢	**carmine**	10.00	.25
PD65			
5¢	**carmine**	10.00	.25
PD66			
10¢	**carmine**	15.00	.30
PD67			
30¢	**carmine**	80.00	.75

PD68

		UnFVF	UseFVF
PD68			
50¢	**carmine**	10.00	.30

1930. New Designs Issue *Flat press printing, perforated 11.*

PD69-76, 79-86

		UnFVF	UseFVF
PD69			
1/2¢	**carmine**	4.00	1.25
PD70			
1¢	**carmine**	2.50	.25
PD71			
2¢	**carmine**	3.50	.25
PD72			
3¢	**carmine**	20.00	1.50
PD73			
5¢	**carmine**	20.00	2.50
PD74			
10¢	**carmine**	40.00	1.00
PD75			
30¢	**carmine**	110.00	2.00

PD76

		UnFVF	UseFVF
PD76			
50¢	**carmine**	140.00	.75

PD77, 78, 87

		UnFVF	UseFVF
PD77			
$1	**carmine**	25.00	.25

PD78

		UnFVF	UseFVF
PD78			
$5	**carmine**	40.00	.25

1931. Same as previous design. *Rotary press printing, perforated 11 x 10 1/2.*

		UnFVF	UseFVF
PD79			
1/2¢	**vermilion**	1.00	.20
PD80			
1¢	**vermilion**	.20	.20
PD81			
2¢	**vermilion**	.20	.20
PD82			
3¢	**vermilion**	.25	.20
PD83			
5¢	**vermilion**	.40	.20
PD84			
10¢	**vermilion**	1.00	.20
PD85			
30¢	**vermilion**	8.00	.25
PD86			
50¢	**vermilion**	10.00	.25

1956. *Perforated 10 1/2 x 11.*

		UnFVF	UseFVF
PD87			
$1	**vermilion**	35.00	.25

1959-85. New Designs Issue for the first time in 29 years. Printed in two colors with the addition of values never before used in dues stamps. Black denomination added within intaglio frame with rubber-mat letterpress on rotary press. *Unwatermarked, perforated 11 x 10 1/2.*

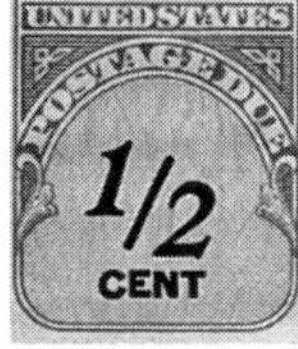
PD88

		UnFVF	UseFVF
PD88			
1/2¢	**red & black** *(June 19, 1959)*	1.25	1.00
PD89			
1¢	**red & black** *(June 19, 1959)*	.20	.20
PD90			
2¢	**red & black** *(June 19, 1959)*	.20	.20
PD91			
3¢	**red & black** *(June 19, 1959)*	.20	.20
PD92			
4¢	**red & black** *(June 19, 1959)*	.20	.20
PD93			
5¢	**red & black** *(June 19, 1959)*	.20	.20
PD94			
6¢	**red & black** *(June 19, 1959)*	.20	.20
PD95			
7¢	**red & black** *(June 19, 1959)*	.20	.20
PD96			
8¢	**red & black** *(June 19, 1959)*	.20	.20
PD97			
10¢	**red & black** *(June 19, 1959)*	.20	.20
PD98			
30¢	**red & black** *(June 19, 1959)*	.75	.20
PD99			
50¢	**red & black** *(June 19, 1959)*	1.00	.20
PD100			
$1	**red & black** *(June 19, 1959)*	1.75	.20

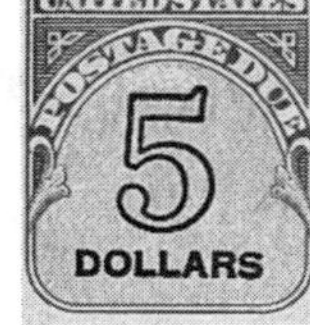
PD101

		UnFVF	UseFVF
PD101			
$5	**red & black**	9.00	.20
PD102			
11¢	**red & black** *(Jan. 2, 1978)*	.25	.20
PD103			
13¢	**red & black** *(Jan. 2, 1978)*	.25	.20
PD104			
17¢	**red & black** *(June 10, 1985)*	.40	.30

Envelopes and Wrappers

Government stamped envelopes first were authorized by the United States under an Act of Congress of Aug. 31, 1852. From the very first issue until the present they have been produced by private manufacturers under contract to the government. It is believed the first envelopes were issued some time in April 1853. The exact date is not known.

Unlike adhesive stamps, stamped envelopes are produced one at a time. Until 1965 the blanks were cut to shape by means of a cutting die (called a "knife" by collectors) much as one operates a cookie cutter. This die was placed on a pile of sheets of paper and was forced through by means of a press. Then a complex machine printed the stamp and whatever corner card might be requested, folded, gummed and sealed the flaps, applied gum to the top back flap, and counted the finished envelopes into multiples of 100 or any number desired.

Beginning in 1965 envelopes have been made from a continuous roll (web) of paper.

The embossed printing of the stamp is accomplished with a recessed printing die that strikes against a resilient undersurface, or "tympan." The tympan forces the paper into the recesses, causing the embossed effect. Later issues are printed by more contemporary processes.

Paper

While our envelopes have been made from paper of various colors, the usual color is "white." During the first issue, the customer had the choice of "white" or "buff" paper envelopes, and at various times the choice of colors available was as many as six or seven. Since 1942, envelopes have been made of white paper only.

The paper colors used throughout the issues are:

White - and various shades thereof.

Buff - in early issues from a brownish color to a yellow.

Amber - a yellowish cast that can be quite pronounced or very pale.

Cream - an intermediate shade between a yellow and a brown, was discontinued in 1886 and "buff" (sometimes known as "oriental buff") substituted.

Blue - and various shades thereof.

Orange - and various shades thereof.

Fawn - a brownish shade.

Manila - made of manila fibers.

Amber-manila - manila paper dyed yellowish.

Canary - bright yellow (used for Post Office Department envelopes only).

It will be seen that all colors vary greatly in shades. Such variation is not intentional, but merely reflects the inability to match colors exactly in various batches of paper. Even the "white" of one issue may differ by a wide margin from the "white" of another issue. Thus the colors of paper, while important to the collector, are not standardized and may be considered only within each individual issue of envelopes.

From 1853 to 1915, all envelopes were made of laid paper, and the laid lines will appear diagonal. This is the result of turning the cutting knife on the bias to the edge of the pile of paper in order to reduce waste. On the other hand, wrappers, which are rectangular in shape, presented no great waste of paper, so they were cut parallel to the edge of the paper. The laid lines on wrappers will appear horizontal or vertical, depending on how they were inserted in the press. This is the principle method of distinguishing between cut squares from wrappers and envelopes.

From 1915 to the present, envelopes have been made of wove paper, and thus show no laid lines.

Albinos and Misprints

Until the web-printing process was adopted in 1965, two envelope blanks occasionally were fed into the envelope-making machine at one time. The top sheet received an inked impression, and the bottom sheet an impression without ink. Such colorless impressions look like white "stamps" and are called "albinos." They are quite common for recent issues, including those even after web printing of envelopes began, but rather rare for early 19th century envelopes. Although they are interesting, they do not command near the premium as do envelopes with two impressions of the stamp in color (one over or partially over the other).

Collecting Envelopes and Wrappers

Envelopes and wrappers are collected as "entires" by size and watermarks and as cut squares. Cut squares are popular because, like postage stamps, they may be mounted easily into albums. Cut squares always should provide adequate margins, which in most instances would be no less than 1/4 inch of paper margin beyond the design of the stamp on all four sides.

Prices in this catalog are for cut squares with such margins. Larger squares, "full corners," or extra large corners with all back flaps attached may bring premium prices, especially for earlier issues.

Envelopes are manufactured in a variety of sizes and shapes. Thus, a single basic stamp may appear on several different-size envelopes, and some of these sizes may be more valuable than others although the stamp remains the same. Certain envelopes exist in large sizes only. In the listing that follows, an asterisk (*) designates entires available only in large size.

Catalog values are for entires of the least value. It is required by law that all envelopes be manufactured with watermarked paper. From 1853 to 1870, a single style watermark was used for all issues (wmk1), but with a new manufacturer in 1870 a new watermark was introduced, and beginning in 1874 it became the custom to change the watermark with the letting of each new contract (about every four years) through the late 1960s. It has been customary to allow remaining stocks of paper to be used up before the new watermarked paper is introduced. Most issues of envelopes, therefore, exist on at least two styles of watermarked paper and, when an issue extended over a very long period of years, there might be several watermarks involved. Indicated at the beginning of each issue are watermarks to be found on envelopes of that issue.

Watermark No. 1

Watermark No. 5 "STAR"

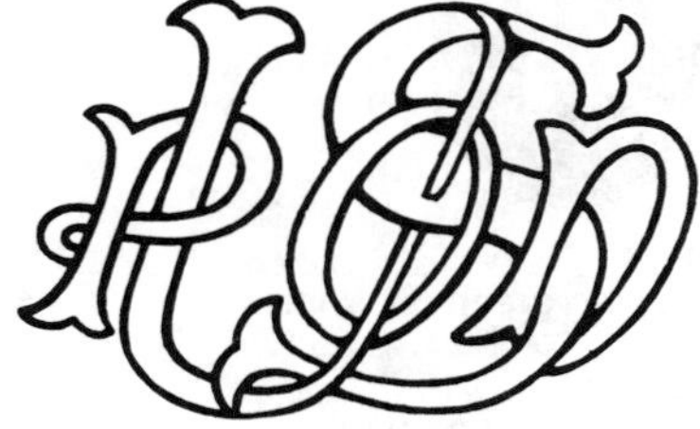

Watermark No. 6

Watermark No. 7

Watermark No. 8

Watermark No. 9

Watermark No. 10

Watermark No. 11

Watermark No. 12

Watermark No. 13

(1903-1907)

Watermark No. 15 (1907-1911)

Watermark No. 15a (1907-1911)

Watermark No. 16

USSE
1911

Watermark No. 17 (1911-1915)

US-SE
1911

Watermark No. 18 (1911-1915)

1853-55. Issue All envelopes issued from 1853 to 1870 were manufactured in New York City by the George F. Nesbitt Manufacturing Company and are known to collectors as the "Nesbitt Issues." The Nesbitt firm was established in 1795, and, at the time it was awarded the contract to produce the first U.S. government stamped envelopes in 1852, it was said to be the largest firm of manufacturing stationers in the country. Following the death of the owner in 1869, the firm lost the contract for manufacturing government envelopes, and although it entered bids on succeeding contracts for many years thereafter, it never again was successful.

Issued some time in April 1853, this issue featured the portrait of George Washington, after Houdon's bust. The complete design would appear to be adapted from the "Wyon" essay for the first stamped envelopes of Great Britain.

Watermark No. 1, also No. 1A on EN1. Wmk. 1 has the lines horizontal in the background with the letters "POD" and "US" horizontal. Background lines on wmk. 1A are diagonal.

EN1-EN2 *"THREE" within short label with curved ends. Die A, 13mm wide, 12 varieties.*

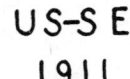

EN1		UnFVF	UseFVF
3¢	**red on white**	190.00	16.00
	entire	—	—
	entire, wmk No. 1	1,200.00	25.00
EN2		UnFVF	UseFVF
3¢	**red on buff**	70.00	10.00
	entire	750.00	20.00

EN3-EN4 *"THREE" within short label with straight ends. Die B, 16mm wide, 3 varieties.*

		UnFVF	UseFVF
EN3			
3¢	**red on white**	680.00	35.00
	entire	3,000.00	70.00
EN4		**UnFVF**	**UseFVF**
3¢	**red on buff**	195.00	15.00
	entire	1,500.00	32.00

EN5-EN6 *"THREE" within short, curved octagonal label, forming the letter "K." Die C, 2 varieties.*

		UnFVF	UseFVF
EN5			
3¢	**red on white**	3,500.00	360.00
	entire	12,500.00	500.00
EN6		**UnFVF**	**UseFVF**
3¢	**red on buff**	190.00	40.00
	entire	1,000.00	75.00

EN7-EN8 *"THREE" within wide label with straight ends. Die D, 25mm wide.*

		UnFVF	UseFVF
EN7			
3¢	**red on white**	500.00	80.00
	entire	6,200.00	130.00
EN8		**UnFVF**	**UseFVF**
3¢	**red on buff**	1,100.00	90.00
	entire	4,500.00	95.00

EN9-EN10 *"THREE" within medium wide label with curved ends. Die E. 20mm wide, 20 varieties.*

		UnFVF	UseFVF
EN9			
3¢	**red on white**	18.00	2.50
	entire	75.00	9.00
	reprint, cut square	80.00	
EN10		**UnFVF**	**UseFVF**
3¢	**red on buff**	14.00	2.25
	entire	60.00	6.00
	reprint, cut square	80.00	

EN11-EN14 *"SIX" within short label with straight ends. Die F, 4 varieties.*

		UnFVF	UseFVF
EN11			
6¢	**green on white**	175.00	100.00
	entire	300.00	150.00
	reprint, cut square	—	
EN12		**UnFVF**	**UseFVF**
6¢	**green on buff**	135.00	65.00
	entire	235.00	115.00
	reprint, cut square	80.00	
EN13		**UnFVF**	**UseFVF**
6¢	**red on white**	90.00	60.00
	entire*	210.00	105.00
	reprint, cut square	80.00	
EN14		**UnFVF**	**UseFVF**
6¢	**red on buff**	175.00	100.00
	entire*	300.00	150.00
	reprint, cut square	80.00	

EN15, EN16 *"TEN" within short label with straight ends. Die G, 16mm wide.*

		UnFVF	UseFVF
EN15			
10¢	**green on white**	175.00	100.00
	entire	325.00	150.00
EN16		**UnFVF**	**UseFVF**
10¢	**green on buff**	65.00	50.00
	entire	200.00	80.00

EN17, EN18 *"TEN" within wide label. Die H.*

		UnFVF	UseFVF
EN17			
10¢	**green on white**	200.00	100.00
	entire	350.00	150.00
	reprint, cut square	80.00	
EN18		**UnFVF**	**UseFVF**
10¢	**green on buff**	100.00	65.00
	entire	170.00	80.00
	reprint, cut square	80.00	

Reprints EN9-14, 17, 18, are on white and buff wove or vertically laid paper. Known also only as cut squares.

1860. "Star Die" Issue so-called because of the small stars at either side of the design, which do not appear on any other envelope stamp. The stars of the 1¢ denomination have five points; those of all other denominations have six points. With this series, 1¢ envelopes and newspaper wrappers were introduced for the first time. The series also introduced the 3¢ + 1¢ envelope. This was to provide for the carrier service, the fee for which was 1¢, for transporting the letter from the lamp-post letter boxes to the post office. Use of the "compound envelopes" apparently was reserved for large cities and very possibly New York City only.

A very few are known used in Baltimore, Chicago and a few other cities where carrier service was operated. Usages in any city other than New York are rare and command premium values.

The series was introduced some time during the summer of 1860 (3¢ envelopes are known used in August) and remained in use for about one year. When the Civil War broke out, steps were taken to replace the issue with a new design. However, the 1¢ and 3¢ + 1¢ envelopes continued in use and were not subjected to the general demonetization order.

Envelopes used by Southern states after their secession, as evidenced by cancellation, are scarce and command considerable premium values. Likewise, envelopes of this series overprinted (over the stamp) "CONFEDERATE STATES OF AMERICA" and other suitable indicia, used by the Confederate States postal department for official mail, are of considerable interest and value to collectors.

The buff paper for all envelopes of this series, and throughout the Nesbitt issues, exists in a multitude of shades that extend from a yellow through dark brown. None of these differences were intentional. They merely indicate various batches of paper, all of which were supposed to be "buff." Likewise, there are many shades of green of the 6¢ and 10¢ stamps, extending from "yellow green" to "dark green."

The interested collector may be advised that the extreme dark shades are less numerous than the pale or yellow shades.

Wrappers. Newspaper wrappers were introduced with this series, and were continued with succeeding series up to 1934, when they were discontinued. Wrappers may be distinguished from envelopes in that they are on paper with either vertical or horizontal laid lines. Envelopes almost invariably are on paper with diagonally laid lines.

EN19-EN23 *Franklin. Period after "POSTAGE"*

		UnFVF	UseFVF
EN19			
1¢	**blue on buff**	28.00	13.00
	entire	55.00	25.00
EN20		UnFVF	UseFVF
1¢	**blue on orange,** wove paper	—	—
	entire	1,750.00	—
EN21		UnFVF	UseFVF
1¢	**blue on buff,** wrapper	65.00	50.00
	entire	100.00	65.00
	v1. Double impression	—	—
EN22		UnFVF	UseFVF
1¢	**blue on manila,** wrapper	45.00	45.00
	entire	85.00	85.00
EN23		UnFVF	UseFVF
1¢	**blue on orange,** wrapper	1,800.00	—
	entire	2,800.00	—

EN24, EN25 *Franklin. Bust touches frame front and back*

		UnFVF	UseFVF
EN24			
1¢	**blue on orange**	410.00	360.00
	entire	480.00	425.00
EN25		UnFVF	UseFVF
1¢	**blue on white**	—	—

EN26, EN27 *No period after "POSTAGE," 2 varieties*

		UnFVF	UseFVF
EN26			
1¢	**blue on amber**	—	—
	entire	—	—
EN27		UnFVF	UseFVF
1¢	**blue on manila,** wrapper	2,600.00	2,000.00
	entire	11,000.00	3,800.00

EN28, EN29 *Washington*

		UnFVF	UseFVF
EN28			
3¢	**red on white**	27.00	13.00
	entire	37.00	23.00
	reprint, cut square	150.00	
EN29		UnFVF	UseFVF
3¢	**red on buff**	25.00	23.00
	entire	35.00	30.00
	reprint, cut square	150.00	

EN30, EN31 *Franklin. Bust does not touch frame.*

		UnFVF	UseFVF
EN30			
3¢ + 1¢	**red and blue on white**	335.00	235.00
	entire	775.00	500.00
EN31		UnFVF	UseFVF
3¢ + 1¢	**red and blue on buff**	250.00	210.00
	entire	825.00	500.00

EN32, EN33 *Franklin. Bust touches frame.*

		UnFVF	UseFVF
EN32			
3¢ + 1¢	**red and blue on white**	—	—
	entire	—	—
EN33		UnFVF	UseFVF
3¢ + 1¢	**red and blue on buff**	—	—
	entire	—	—
	reprint, cut square	100.00	

EN34, EN35

		UnFVF	UseFVF
EN34			
6¢	**red on white**	2,000.00	1,300.00
	entire*	3,700.00	
	reprint, cut square	80.00	
EN35		UnFVF	UseFVF
6¢	**red on buff**	1,700.00	950.00
	entire*	4,300.00	4,500.00
	reprint, cut square	80.00	

EN36, EN37

		UnFVF	UseFVF
EN36			
10¢	**green on white**	1,000.00	350.00
	entire	10,000.00	475.00
	reprint, cut square	80.00	
EN37		UnFVF	UseFVF
10¢	**green on buff**	1,000.00	275.00
	entire	3,800.00	475.00
	reprint, cut square	80.00	

Reprints are cut squares on vertical laid paper.

1861. Issue was introduced in the summer of 1861. The previous "Star Die" series was declared invalid for postage, due to the outbreak of the Civil War (except the 1¢ and 3¢ + 1¢ envelopes). The series presents a novelty as the higher-value envelope stamps were printed in more than one color. These also are the first bi-colored postal emissions from the United States. Still another innovation was the introduction of Letter Sheets, which, it has been stated, were issued to provide soldiers in the field with stationery and stamps in a single package. Their use did not prove popular, and they were withdrawn in April 1864.

EN38-EN41

		UnFVF	UseFVF
EN38			
3¢	**pink on white**	18.00	5.00
	entire	45.00	15.00
EN39		UnFVF	UseFVF
3¢	**pink on buff**	16.00	6.00
	entire	18.00	12.00
EN40		UnFVF	UseFVF
3¢	**pink on blue,** letter sheet	70.00	55.00
	entire	200.00	90.00

EN41		UnFVF	UseFVF
3¢	**pink on orange**	2,300.00	—
	entire	3,900.00	—

EN42, EN43

EN42		UnFVF	UseFVF
6¢	**pink on white**	90.00	85.00
	entire*	145.00	145.00
	reprint, cut square	—	—
EN43		UnFVF	UseFVF
6¢	**pink on buff**	65.00	60.00
	entire*	100.00	145.00
	reprint, cut square	—	—

Reprints, known in cut squares only, are on vertically laid paper.

EN44-EN46

EN44		UnFVF	UseFVF
10¢	**green on white**	28.00	28.00
	entire	26.00	26.00
EN45		UnFVF	UseFVF
10¢	**green on buff**	27.00	19.00
	entire	60.00	35.00

No. EN46 is not assigned.

EN47

EN47		UnFVF	UseFVF
12¢	**brown and red on amber**	175.00	150.00
	entire*	460.00	650.00

EN48

EN48		UnFVF	UseFVF
20¢	**blue and red on amber**	175.00	150.00
	entire*	460.00	775.00

EN49, EN50

EN49		UnFVF	UseFVF
24¢	**green and red on amber**	185.00	145.00
	entire*	650.00	775.00
EN50		UnFVF	UseFVF
24¢	**dark green and maroon on amber**	190.00	180.00
	entire*	650.00	1,000.00

EN51

EN51		UnFVF	UseFVF
40¢	**red and black on amber**	280.00	280.00
	entire*	850.00	1,800.00

1863-65. Issue To provide for the higher postal rates on drop letters and circular matter, it was necessary to provide 2¢ envelopes and wrappers (called "Black Jacks" because of the portrait of Andrew Jackson). At the same time, new designs were adopted for the 3¢, 6¢ and higher denominations.

EN52, EN53 *Andrew Jackson. Die A. "U.S. POSTAGE" at top. Down stroke of "2" and bottom stroke merge.*

EN52		UnFVF	UseFVF
2¢	**black on buff**	30.00	15.00
	entire	60.00	30.00
EN53		UnFVF	UseFVF
2¢	**black on manila,** wrapper	42.00	38.00
	entire	70.00	55.00

EN54, EN55 *Andrew Jackson. Die B, down stroke of figure "2" joins but does not merge with bottom stroke.*

EN54		UnFVF	UseFVF
2¢	**black on buff**	1,700.00	—
	entire	3,600.00	—
EN55		UnFVF	UseFVF
2¢	**black on orange**	1,000.00	—
	entire	2,500.00	—

EN56-EN59 *Andrew Jackson. Die C, "U.S. POST" at top. Width of design 24 to 25mm.*

EN56		UnFVF	UseFVF
2¢	**black on buff**	10.00	9.00
	entire	27.00	15.00
EN57		UnFVF	UseFVF
2¢	**black on orange**	12.00	8.00
	entire	22.00	10.00
EN58		UnFVF	UseFVF
2¢	**black on buff,** wrapper	160.00	160.00
	entire	260.00	260.00
EN59		UnFVF	UseFVF
2¢	**black on dark manila,** wrapper	35.00	22.00
	entire	120.00	60.00

EN60-EN64 *Andrew Jackson. Die D. "U.S. POST" at top. 25 1/2mm.*

EN60		UnFVF	UseFVF
2¢	**black on buff**	12.00	10.00
	entire	22.00	14.00

No. EN61 is not assigned.

EN62		UnFVF	UseFVF
2¢	**black on orange**	12.00	8.00
	entire	17.00	11.00
EN63		UnFVF	UseFVF
2¢	**black on buff,** wrapper	80.00	50.00
	entire	125.00	85.00
EN64		UnFVF	UseFVF
2¢	**black on light manila,** wrapper	12.00	11.00
	entire	25.00	20.00

EN65-EN68

EN65		UnFVF	UseFVF
3¢	**pink on white**	6.00	2.00
	entire	10.00	3.50

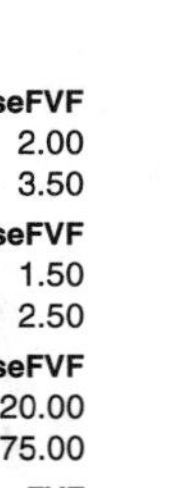

EN66		UnFVF	UseFVF
3¢	**pink on buff**	5.00	1.50
	entire	10.00	2.50

EN67		UnFVF	UseFVF
3¢	**brown on white**	38.00	20.00
	entire*	75.00	75.00

EN68		UnFVF	UseFVF
3¢	**brown on buff**	40.00	22.00
	entire*	80.00	60.00

EN69-EN73

EN69		UnFVF	UseFVF
6¢	**pink on white**	50.00	30.00
	entire*	85.00	50.00

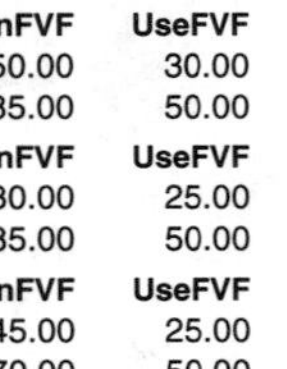

EN70		UnFVF	UseFVF
6¢	**pink on buff**	30.00	25.00
	entire*	85.00	50.00

EN71		UnFVF	UseFVF
6¢	**purple on white**	45.00	25.00
	entire	70.00	50.00

No. EN72 is not assigned.

EN73		UnFVF	UseFVF
6¢	**purple on buff**	42.00	18.00
	entire	60.00	50.00

EN74, EN75

EN74		UnFVF	UseFVF
9¢	**lemon on buff**	325.00	200.00
	entire*	500.00	500.00

EN75		UnFVF	UseFVF
9¢	**orange on buff**	95.00	75.00
	entire*	150.00	200.00

EN76, EN77

EN76		UnFVF	UseFVF
12¢	**brown on buff**	340.00	200.00
	entire*	500.00	950.00

EN77		UnFVF	UseFVF
12¢	**red brown on buff**	90.00	55.00
	entire*	130.00	185.00

EN78

EN78		UnFVF	UseFVF
18¢	**red on buff**	90.00	85.00
	entire*	180.00	800.00

EN79

EN79		UnFVF	UseFVF
24¢	**blue on buff**	95.00	80.00
	entire*	180.00	800.00

EN80

EN80		UnFVF	UseFVF
30¢	**green on buff**	60.00	50.00
	entire*	150.00	800.00

EN81

EN81		UnFVF	UseFVF
40¢	**pink on buff**	80.00	225.00
	entire*	250.00	9,300.00

1870. Issue By the end of 1869 there were various designs of stamps in use for envelopes and wrappers, none of which even closely resembled the designs of the adhesive stamps then in use. To remedy this situation and bring order to confusion, as well as to meet the public clamor against awarding the envelope contract by negotiated bid, the government advertised for bids to supply the envelopes needed for the next four years. One provision of the proposal was that the new envelopes be in denominations of the adhesive stamps then in use and that the designs of the envelope stamps be as near as possible, in color and design, to the adhesive stamps in use. After considerable controversy, the contract was awarded to George H. Reay of Brooklyn, N.Y., a former associate of Nesbitt. Reay proceeded to produce what has almost unanimously been considered the most beautiful designs and envelopes our post office ever has issued. The finely executed engravings, the beautiful inks, and careful printing on fine quality paper have earned for them the name "cameos" among collectors.

Although the contract provided that envelopes be manufactured in all denominations from 1¢ to 90¢, there was little use for envelopes in the denominations over 10¢. Hence, used examples of these high denominations are practically unknown.

EN82-EN85 *Franklin. Die A, front of the bust is narrow, back rounded. It points at letter "N" of "ONE." The neck forms a straight line between chest and chin. (Compare with EN120 and EN128.) (Watermark 2.)*

Die A

EN82		UnFVF	UseFVF
1¢	**blue on white**	28.00	23.00
	entire	50.00	28.00

		UnFVF	UseFVF
EN83			
1¢	**blue on amber**	28.00	23.00
	entire	50.00	28.00
EN84			
1¢	**blue on orange**	18.00	10.00
	entire	26.00	17.00
EN85			
1¢	**blue on manila,** wrapper	40.00	25.00
	entire	70.00	60.00

EN86-EN89 *Die B, the choker around the neck is notched top and bottom.*

Die B

		UnFVF	UseFVF
EN86			
1¢	**blue on white**	—	—
	entire	—	—
EN87			
1¢	**blue on amber**	—	—
	entire	—	—
EN88			
1¢	**blue on orange**	—	—
	entire	—	—
EN89			
1¢	**blue on manila,** wrapper	—	—
	entire	—	—

EN90-EN93 *Andrew Jackson. The figure "2" at right and left are within small circles. The top loop of "P" of "POSTAGE" is well formed. (Compare with EN142.)*

		UnFVF	UseFVF
EN90			
2¢	**brown on white**	40.00	13.00
	entire	50.00	20.00
EN91			
2¢	**brown on amber**	15.00	8.00
	entire	30.00	15.00
EN92			
2¢	**brown on orange**	10.00	7.00
	entire	13.00	10.00
EN93			
2¢	**brown on manila,** wrapper	20.00	15.00
	entire	40.00	30.00

EN94-EN96 *Small figure "3" within circles. The ponytail projects below the bust. (Compare with EN183 and EN187.)*

		UnFVF	UseFVF
EN94			
3¢	**green on white**	7.00	1.00
	entire	12.00	2.50
EN95			
3¢	**green on amber**	5.00	2.00
	entire	12.00	3.00
EN96			
3¢	**green on cream**	8.00	3.00
	entire	16.00	5.00

EN97-EN99 *Abraham Lincoln. The neck is long at the back. (Compare with EN211)*

		UnFVF	UseFVF
EN97			
6¢	**red on white**	17.00	13.00
	entire	18.00	16.00
EN98			
6¢	**red on amber**	22.00	13.00
	entire	38.00	14.00
EN99			
6¢	**red on cream**	27.00	13.00
	entire	45.00	19.00

EN97-EN99 exist in a variety of shades from dark red to vermilion.

EN100 *Edwin Stanton. The down strokes of the figure "7" do not curl up. (Compare with EN215.)*

		UnFVF	UseFVF
EN100			
7¢	**vermilion on amber**	40.00	200.00
	entire	60.00	750.00

EN101-EN104 *Thomas Jefferson. The end of the ponytail does not project. (Compare with EN219.)*

		UnFVF	UseFVF
EN101			
10¢	**olive-black on white**	375.00	375.00
	entire	475.00	850.00
EN102			
10¢	**olive-black on amber**	375.00	375.00
	entire	475.00	850.00
EN103			
10¢	**brown on white**	50.00	70.00
	entire	70.00	75.00
EN104			
10¢	**brown on amber**	70.00	50.00
	entire	85.00	70.00

EN105-EN107 *Henry Clay. The hair hides the ear. The nose is long and sharp. (Compare with EN227.)*

		UnFVF	UseFVF
EN105			
12¢	**violet-black on white**	100.00	65.00
	entire*	200.00	375.00
EN106			
12¢	**violet-black on amber**	110.00	85.00
	entire*	180.00	500.00
EN107			
12¢	**violet-black on cream**	220.00	190.00
	entire*	335.00	—

EN108-EN110 *Daniel Webster. Hair not parted, cheeks with sideburns. (Compare with EN230.)*

		UnFVF	UseFVF
EN108			
15¢	**red orange on white**	60.00	60.00
	entire*	140.00	—
EN109			
15¢	**red orange on amber**	140.00	170.00
	entire*	360.00	—
EN110			
15¢	**red orange on cream**	235.00	210.00
	entire*	325.00	—

EN111-EN113 *Winfield Scott. Ornamental lines around inner oval end in squares. (Compare with EN233.)*

		UnFVF	UseFVF
EN111			
24¢	**purple on white**	100.00	90.00
	entire	150.00	—
EN112		UnFVF	UseFVF
24¢	**purple on amber**	180.00	225.00
	entire*	335.00	—
EN113		UnFVF	UseFVF
24¢	**purple on cream**	180.00	250.00
	entire*	325.00	—

EN108-EN113 exist in various shades.

EN114-EN116 *Alexander Hamilton. The horizontal rectangles containing numerals are in alignment. Back of bust ends in narrow point. (Compare with EN236.)*

		UnFVF	UseFVF
EN114			
30¢	**black on white**	70.00	85.00
	entire*	280.00	—
EN115		UnFVF	UseFVF
30¢	**black on amber**	180.00	210.00
	entire*	500.00	—
EN116		UnFVF	UseFVF
30¢	**black on cream**	200.00	325.00
	entire*	385.00	—

EN117-EN119 *Oliver Perry. The shields containing the numerals of value do not project beyond the inner circle. (Compare with EN242.)*

		UnFVF	UseFVF
EN117			
90¢	**carmine on white**	135.00	190.00
	entire*	190.00	—
EN118		UnFVF	UseFVF
90¢	**carmine on amber**	300.00	335.00
	entire*	800.00	—
EN119		UnFVF	UseFVF
90¢	**carmine on cream**	335.00	550.00
	entire*	875.00	—

1874-76. Issue In 1874, the Post Office advertised for bids to supply envelopes. After considerable legal difficulties with George H. Reay and other bidders, the contract was awarded to the Plimpton Manufacturing Co. Reay refused to surrender his printing dies and, to futher embarrass the new contractor, is said to have engaged the services of all known die engravers. The new contractors were thus forced to employ less skilled engravers to try to duplicate the Reay designs. The resulting delay embarrassed the Post Office officials, who were forced to purchase supplies of envelopes from Reay until the new contractors could produce acceptable dies. Several unsuitable designs were accepted to take care of the situation until better dies could be made, which accounts for some of the designs of the lower denomination stamps.

Eventually the Plimpton Manufacturing Co. overcame its difficulties and, in combination with the Morgan Envelope Co., continued to be the successful bidders for the manufacture of envelopes until 1903.

The struggle George H. Reay put up to retain his contract is one of the classic stories of philately. In the end, to prevent his competitors from ever using his dies, it is stated that he finally agreed to turn them over to the authorities, only to instruct his wife to throw them overboard from a Brooklyn-Manhattan ferry. There seems to be much evidence to substantiate this story.

EN120-EN127 *Franklin. A copy of the Reay design (EN82). Die A, back of bust angles in sharp point. "O" of "POSTAGE" without network. (Compare with EN82.) Watermarks 2, 5, 6, 7, 9.*

		UnFVF	UseFVF
EN120			
1¢	**dark blue on white**	85.00	40.00
	entire	100.00	80.00
EN121		UnFVF	UseFVF
1¢	**dark blue on amber**	100.00	67.50
	entire	140.00	100.00
EN122		UnFVF	UseFVF
1¢	**dark blue on cream**	775.00	—
EN123		UnFVF	UseFVF
1¢	**dark blue on orange**	17.50	15.00
	entire	27.50	20.00
EN124		UnFVF	UseFVF
1¢	**dark blue on manila,** wrapper	50.00	32.50
	entire	67.50	60.00
EN125		UnFVF	UseFVF
1¢	**light blue on white**	100.00	70.00
	entire	130.00	100.00
EN126		UnFVF	UseFVF
1¢	**light blue on orange**	20.00	12.50
	entire	25.00	20.00
EN127		UnFVF	UseFVF
1¢	**light blue on manila,** wrapper	—	—
	entire	—	—

EN128-EN141 *A copy of Reay design (EN82). Die B, back of bust is a straight line. Front of bust broad and blunt. "O" in "POSTAGE" with network. (Compare with EN82.)*

		UnFVF	UseFVF
EN128			
1¢	**dark blue on white**	6.00	6.00
	entire	15.00	15.00
EN129		UnFVF	UseFVF
1¢	**dark blue on amber**	12.50	8.00
	entire	15.00	10.00
EN130		UnFVF	UseFVF
1¢	**dark blue on cream**	15.00	6.00
	entire	22.50	15.00
EN131		UnFVF	UseFVF
1¢	**dark blue on orange**	2.50	3.00
	entire	7.00	5.00
EN132		UnFVF	UseFVF
1¢	**dark blue on manila,** wrapper	6.00	7.50
	entire	10.00	12.50
EN133		UnFVF	UseFVF
1¢	**blue on white**	1.50	1.00
	entire	2.25	1.50
EN134		UnFVF	UseFVF
1¢	**blue on amber**	4.00	3.00
	entire	8.00	4.00
EN135		UnFVF	UseFVF
1¢	**blue on cream**	4.50	4.50
	entire	7.00	5.00
EN136		UnFVF	UseFVF
1¢	**blue on orange**	.60	.50
	entire	.75	.50
EN137		UnFVF	UseFVF
1¢	**blue on blue**	6.00	5.00
	entire	8.00	6.00
EN138		UnFVF	UseFVF
1¢	**blue on fawn**	6.00	5.00
	entire	7.00	6.00
EN139		UnFVF	UseFVF
1¢	**blue on manila**	6.00	4.00
	entire	7.00	6.00
EN140		UnFVF	UseFVF
1¢	**blue on amber-manila**	11.00	9.00
	entire	13.00	10.00

		UnFVF	UseFVF
EN141			
1¢	**blue on manila,** wrapper	1.50	1.50
	entire	3.00	2.00

The "dark blue" of EN128-EN132 is very dark, almost indigo. The "blue" of EN133-EN141 is in various shades of "blue," "pale blue," etc.

EN142-EN147 *Andrew Jackson. A copy of Reay design (EN90). Die A, thin narrow figure "2" within circles. Top loop of "P" in "POSTAGE" is very narrow. (Compare with EN90.) Watermark 2.*

		UnFVF	UseFVF
EN142			
2¢	**brown on white**	80.00	37.00
	entire	95.00	75.00
EN143		UnFVF	UseFVF
2¢	**brown and amber**	50.00	40.00
	entire	80.00	65.00
EN144		UnFVF	UseFVF
2¢	**brown on cream**	675.00	—
EN145		UnFVF	UseFVF
2¢	**brown on orange**	7,200.00	—
	entire	15,000.00	—
EN146		UnFVF	UseFVF
2¢	**brown on manila,** wrapper	80.00	40.00
	entire	85.00	60.00
EN147		UnFVF	UseFVF
2¢	**vermilion on manila,** wrapper	1,000.00	260.00
	entire	1,500.00	—

EN148-EN151 *A copy of the Reay design (EN90). Die B, Figure "2" within tall ovals. "O" in "TWO" has plain center. (Compare with EN90, EN142 and following.)*

		UnFVF	UseFVF
EN148			
2¢	**brown on white**	38.00	28.00
	entire	75.00	65.00
EN149		UnFVF	UseFVF
2¢	**brown on amber**	65.00	40.00
	entire	80.00	60.00
EN150		UnFVF	UseFVF
2¢	**brown on cream**	22,000.00	—
EN151		UnFVF	UseFVF
2¢	**brown on manila,** wrapper	15.00	14.00
	entire	20.00	18.00

EN152, EN153 *Andrew Jackson. Die B2, similar to last except tail of left figure "2" touches the oval at right.*

		UnFVF	UseFVF
EN152			
2¢	**brown on white**	55.00	25.00
	entire	75.00	65.00
EN153		UnFVF	UseFVF
2¢	**brown on amber**	160.00	55.00
	entire	175.00	85.00

EN154-EN161 *Die B3, same as EN148 but "O" in "TWO" with network in center.*

		UnFVF	UseFVF
EN154			
2¢	**brown on white**	600.00	100.00
	entire	700.00	125.00
EN155		UnFVF	UseFVF
2¢	**brown on amber**	375.00	110.00
	entire	500.00	130.00
EN156		UnFVF	UseFVF
2¢	**brown on orange**	37.50	27.50
	entire	60.00	40.00
EN157		UnFVF	UseFVF
2¢	**brown on manila,** wrapper	50.00	32.50
	entire	65.00	35.00
EN158		UnFVF	UseFVF
2¢	**vermilion on white**	17,000.00	—
EN159		UnFVF	UseFVF
2¢	**vermilion on amber**	17,000.00	—
EN160		UnFVF	UseFVF
2¢	**vermilion on orange**	17,000.00	—
EN161		UnFVF	UseFVF
2¢	**vermilion on manila,** wrapper	6,000.00	—

EN162-EN172 *Andrew Jackson. Die C, short, thick figure "2" within small size ovals. (Compare with preceding and following; also with EN90.)*

		UnFVF	UseFVF
EN162			
2¢	**brown on white**	37.50	35.00
	entire	50.00	40.00
EN163		UnFVF	UseFVF
2¢	**brown on amber**	70.00	55.00
	entire	85.00	60.00
EN164		UnFVF	UseFVF
2¢	**brown on manila,** wrapper	35.00	25.00
	entire	40.00	35.00
EN165		UnFVF	UseFVF
2¢	**brown red on orange**	—	—
	entire	—	—
EN166		UnFVF	UseFVF
2¢	**vermilion on orange**	—	—

Watermarks 2, 5 and 6.

		UnFVF	UseFVF
EN167			
2¢	**red on white**	5.50	2.50
	entire	7.00	4.50
EN168		UnFVF	UseFVF
2¢	**red on amber**	5.00	2.50
	entire	6.00	4.00
EN169		UnFVF	UseFVF
2¢	**red on cream**	11.00	5.50
	entire	13.00	8.00
EN170		UnFVF	UseFVF
2¢	**red on blue**	120.00	28.00
	entire	180.00	135.00
EN171		UnFVF	UseFVF
2¢	**red on fawn**	6.50	4.50
	entire	12.00	7.00
EN172		UnFVF	UseFVF
2¢	**red on manila,** wrapper	4.00	4.00
	entire	7.00	6.00

EN173-EN176 *Die C1, similar to last except ovals containing numerals are much heavier and there is a diagonal white line from about the letter "U" to the outer frame. (Compare with EN177.)*

		UnFVF	UseFVF
EN173			
2¢	**red on white**	50.00	30.00
	entire	55.00	35.00
EN174		UnFVF	UseFVF
2¢	**red on amber**	25.00	15.00
	entire	28.00	17.00
EN175		UnFVF	UseFVF
2¢	**red on blue**	10.00	8.00
	entire	9.00	10.00
EN176		UnFVF	UseFVF
2¢	**red on fawn**	10.00	4.00
	entire	13.00	10.00

EN177-EN179 *Andrew Jackson. Die C2, similar to last except there is no diagonal line and the middle stroke of "N" in "CENTS" is as thin as the vertical strokes. (Compare with EN173.)*

		UnFVF	UseFVF
EN177			
2¢	**red on white**	50.00	25.00
	entire	70.00	27.00
EN178		UnFVF	UseFVF
2¢	**red on amber**	250.00	75.00
	entire	335.00	100.00
EN179		UnFVF	UseFVF
2¢	**red on manila,** wrapper	16.00	9.00
	entire	40.00	12.00

EN180-EN182 *Die D, the bottom of the bust forms a complete quarter circle. (Compare with EN162.)*

		UnFVF	UseFVF
EN180			
2¢	**red on white**	525.00	100.00
	entire	625.00	300.00
EN181		UnFVF	UseFVF
2¢	**red on amber**	16,000.00	16,000.00
	entire	57,000.00	—
EN182		UnFVF	UseFVF
2¢	**red on manila,** wrapper	80.00	55.00
	entire	115.00	95.00

EN183-EN186 *Washington. Copy of Reay design (EN94). Die A, thin lettering. Long thin figures of value within tall ovals. (Compare with EN94 and EN187.) (Watermarks 2, 3, 4, 5 and 6.)*

		UnFVF	UseFVF
EN183			
3¢	**green on white**	18.00	5.50
	entire	33.00	14.00
EN184		UnFVF	UseFVF
3¢	**green on amber**	23.00	10.00
	entire	38.00	14.00
EN185		UnFVF	UseFVF
3¢	**green on cream**	33.00	10.00
	entire	40.00	15.00
EN186		UnFVF	UseFVF
3¢	**green on blue**	—	—

EN187-EN191 *Die B, thick lettering. Thick figures of value in short ovals. (Compare with EN183 and following.)*

		UnFVF	UseFVF
EN187			
3¢	**green on white**	1.25	.35
	entire	2.25	1.00
EN188		UnFVF	UseFVF
3¢	**green on amber**	1.50	.75
	entire	2.50	1.25
EN189		UnFVF	UseFVF
3¢	**green on cream**	8.00	7.00
	entire	12.00	8.50
EN190		UnFVF	UseFVF
3¢	**green on blue**	8.00	5.00
	entire	13.00	8.50
EN191		UnFVF	UseFVF
3¢	**green on fawn**	5.00	3.00
	entire	8.00	4.00

EN192-EN195 *Washington. Similar to last. Die C, the top of the head is flat at back and there is a notch above and below the knot of the ponytail. (Compare with EN187.)*

		UnFVF	UseFVF
EN192			
3¢	**green on white**	460.00	45.00
	entire	1,800.00	75.00
EN193		UnFVF	UseFVF
3¢	**green on amber**	190.00	100.00
	entire	280.00	120.00
EN194		UnFVF	UseFVF
3¢	**green on blue**	8,000.00	1,800.00
	entire	17,000.00	4,300.00
EN195		UnFVF	UseFVF
3¢	**green on fawn**	25,000.00	1,700.00
	entire	—	15,000.00

EN196-EN200 *Zachary Taylor. Die A, the numerals "5" with short thick top strokes. (Compare with EN201.) (Watermarks 2 and 5.)*

		UnFVF	UseFVF
EN196			
5¢	**blue on white**	10.00	8.00
	entire	12.00	12.00
EN197		UnFVF	UseFVF
5¢	**blue on amber**	10.00	8.00
	entire	12.00	15.00
EN198		UnFVF	UseFVF
5¢	**blue on cream**	82.00	38.00
	entire*	105.00	100.00
EN199		UnFVF	UseFVF
5¢	**blue on blue**	15.00	13.00
	entire	18.00	20.00
EN200		UnFVF	UseFVF
5¢	**blue on fawn**	100.00	50.00
	entire*	175.00	—

EN201-EN205 *Zachary Taylor. Die B, the numerals "5" with long thin top strokes. (Compare with EN196.)*

		UnFVF	UseFVF
EN201			
5¢	**blue on white**	6.00	5.50
	entire	11.00	20.00
EN202		UnFVF	UseFVF
5¢	**blue on amber**	5.50	5.50
	entire	13.00	25.00
EN203		UnFVF	UseFVF
5¢	**blue on cream**	2,500.00	—
	entire*	4,200.00	—
EN204		UnFVF	UseFVF
5¢	**blue on blue**	13.00	8.00
	entire	16.00	20.00
EN205		UnFVF	UseFVF
5¢	**blue on fawn**	88.00	43.00
	entire*	110.00	100.00

EN206-EN210 *James Garfield. (Watermarks 5, 6.)*

		UnFVF	UseFVF
EN206			
5¢	**brown on white**	3.00	2.00
	entire	5.50	15.00

EN207		UnFVF	UseFVF
5¢	**brown on amber**	4.00	2.25
	entire	7.50	18.00

EN208		UnFVF	UseFVF
5¢	**brown on buff**	90.00	60.00
	entire	120.00	—

EN209		UnFVF	UseFVF
5¢	**brown on blue**	50.00	30.00
	entire	65.00	—

EN210		UnFVF	UseFVF
5¢	**brown on fawn**	200.00	—
	entire*	250.00	—

EN211-EN214 *Abraham Lincoln. Copy of Reay design (EN97). The neck is short at the back. Lock of hair curves upward from forehead. (Compare with EN97.) (Watermarks 2, 3, 4, 5, 6.)*

EN211		UnFVF	UseFVF
6¢	**red on white**	6.00	6.00
	entire	10.00	8.00

EN212		UnFVF	UseFVF
6¢	**red on amber**	10.00	6.00
	entire	16.00	11.00

EN213		UnFVF	UseFVF
6¢	**red on cream**	16.00	10.00
	entire	20.00	16.00

EN214		UnFVF	UseFVF
6¢	**red on fawn**	17.00	9.00
	entire*	25.00	14.00

EN215, EN216 *Edwin Stanton. Copy of Reay design (EN100). The down strokes of the figure "7" curve sharply upward. (Compare with EN100.) (Watermark 2.)*

EN215		UnFVF	UseFVF
7¢	**vermilion on white**	1,500.00	—

EN216		UnFVF	UseFVF
7¢	**vermilion on amber**	90.00	55.00
	entire	120.00	—

EN217, EN218 *Thomas Jefferson. Die A, very large head, called the "booby-head." (Compare with EN101 and following.)*

EN217		UnFVF	UseFVF
10¢	**brown on white**	30.00	17.00
	entire	55.00	—

EN218		UnFVF	UseFVF
10¢	**brown on amber**	55.00	25.00
	entire	80.00	—

EN219-EN226 *Copy of Reay design (EN101). Die B, the end of the ponytail projects prominently and the head tilts downward. (Compare with EN101.)*

EN219		UnFVF	UseFVF
10¢	**brown on white**	6.00	4.00
	entire	10.00	8.00

EN220		UnFVF	UseFVF
10¢	**brown on amber**	8.00	6.00
	entire	10.00	8.00

EN221		UnFVF	UseFVF
10¢	**brown on buff**	10.00	7.00
	entire	11.00	8.00

EN222		UnFVF	UseFVF
10¢	**brown on blue**	12.00	8.00
	entire	14.00	9.00

EN219-EN222 exist in various shades.

EN223		UnFVF	UseFVF
10¢	**brown on manila**	12.00	8.00
	entire	13.00	13.00
	a. red brown on manila	12.00	9.00
	a. entire	15.00	15.00

EN224		UnFVF	UseFVF
10¢	**brown on amber-manila**	12.00	7.00
	entire*	15.00	13.00
	a. red brown on amber-manila	16.00	7.00
	a. entire	22.00	17.00

EN225		UnFVF	UseFVF
10¢	**ocher yellow on white**	1,050.00	—
	entire*	1,500.00	—

EN226		UnFVF	UseFVF
10¢	**ocher yellow on amber**	1,050.00	—
	entire*	1,500.00	—

EN227-EN229 *Henry Clay. Copy of Reay design (EN105). The head is round and small. The ear is clearly defined. (Compare with EN105.) (Watermark 2.)*

EN227		UnFVF	UseFVF
12¢	**violet black on white**	150.00	75.00
	entire*	160.00	—

EN228		UnFVF	UseFVF
12¢	**violet black on amber**	160.00	135.00
	entire*	235.00	—

EN229		UnFVF	UseFVF
12¢	**violet black on cream**	175.00	145.00
	entire*	720.00	—

EN230-EN232 *Daniel Webster. Copy of Reay design (EN108). Bust without sideburns. The hair parted. (Compare with EN108.) (Watermarks 2, 5.)*

EN230		UnFVF	UseFVF
15¢	**orange on white**	40.00	30.00
	entire*	80.00	38.00

EN231		UnFVF	UseFVF
15¢	**orange on amber**	120.00	90.00
	entire*	175.00	—

EN232		UnFVF	UseFVF
15¢	**orange on cream**	335.00	335.00
	entire*	825.00	—

EN233-EN235 *Winfield Scott. Copy of Reay design (EN111). The ornaments around the inner oval end in points. (Compare with EN111.) (Watermark 2.)*

EN233		UnFVF	UseFVF
24¢	**purple on white**	150.00	110.00
	entire*	220.00	—

EN234		UnFVF	UseFVF
24¢	**purple on amber**	150.00	110.00
	entire*	220.00	—

EN235		UnFVF	UseFVF
24¢	**purple on cream**	150.00	110.00
	entire*	700.00	—

EN236-EN241 *Alexander Hamilton. Copy of Reay design (EN114). The octagonal labels containing the figures of value are not in alignment; the one at the right tilts sharply downward. (Compare with EN114.) For brown stamps in this design, issued in 1887, see EN375-EN380. (Watermarks 2, 5, 6, 7, 9, 10.)*

		UnFVF	UseFVF
EN236			
30¢	**black on white**	55.00	30.00
	entire*	65.00	65.00
EN237		UnFVF	UseFVF
30¢	**black on amber**	70.00	55.00
	entire*	125.00	275.00
EN237A		UnFVF	UseFVF
30¢	**black on cream** (see note)	400.00	380.00
	entire*	725.00	—

The only way to distinguish EN237A and EN243A - which both appear on cream paper - from the same designs on buff paper (EN238 and EN244) is to examine the watermark. Wmk. 2 signifies cream paper.

		UnFVF	UseFVF
EN238			
30¢	**black on buff**	95.00	75.00
	entire	135.00	—
EN239		UnFVF	UseFVF
30¢	**black on blue**	100.00	75.00
	entire	110.00	—
EN240		UnFVF	UseFVF
30¢	**black on manila**	90.00	75.00
	entire	135.00	—
EN241		UnFVF	UseFVF
30¢	**black on amber-manila**	110.00	75.00
	entire	140.00	—

EN242-EN247 *Oliver Perry. Copy of Reay design (EN117). The shields containing the numerals of value project considerably within the inner circle. (Compare with EN117.) For purple stamps of same design, issued in 1887, see EN381-EN386. (Watermarks 2, 6, 7, 9.)*

		UnFVF	UseFVF
EN242			
90¢	**carmine on white**	110.00	75.00
	entire*	120.00	85.00
EN243		UnFVF	UseFVF
90¢	**carmine on amber**	150.00	195.00
	entire*	235.00	—
EN243A		UnFVF	UseFVF
90¢	**carmine on cream** (see note following EN237A)	1,100.00	—
	entire*	2,000.00	—
EN244		UnFVF	UseFVF
90¢	**carmine on buff**	200.00	230.00
	entire	235.00	
EN245		UnFVF	UseFVF
90¢	**carmine on blue**	175.00	210.00
	entire	235.00	—
EN246		UnFVF	UseFVF
90¢	**carmine on manila**	115.00	210.00
	entire*	195.00	—
EN247		UnFVF	UseFVF
90¢	**carmine on amber-manila**	110.00	175.00
	entire*	195.00	—

1876. Centennial Issue Just before the great Centennial Exposition at Philadelphia in 1876, the Plimpton Morgan Envelope Co. had developed a machine that would gum the top back flap of envelopes. Previously the machines in use would perform all operations of folding, printing and gluing together, but the gum on the top back flaps had to be applied by hand. To publicize this mechanical achievement, the company requested permission to demonstrate its new machine at the exposition. The Post Office consented and provided that a specially designed stamp should be used to commemorate the exposition, thus authorizing the world's first commemorative postage stamp. Two envelopes were authorized: The small one would have the stamp printed in green; the slightly larger one would have the stamp in red. Also, paper bearing a special watermark (wmk. 3) was ordered for these envelopes. The demand proved so great that the envelopes were manufactured at Hartford, Conn., as well as on the demonstration machine at the exposition. In all, 8,000,000 envelopes were issued, approximately 4,000,000 of each size.

EN248, EN249 *Old and new methods of carrying the post. There is a single line forming the bottom of the label containing the word "POSTAGE." (Compare with EN250.) (Watermarks 2 and 3.)*

		UnFVF	UseFVF
EN248			
3¢	**green on white**	50.00	13.00
	entire	60.00	35.00
EN249		UnFVF	UseFVF
3¢	**red on white**	55.00	25.00
	entire	70.00	45.00

EN250, EN251 *The line at the bottom of the label containing the word "POSTAGE" is made up of two thin lines which sometimes merge.*

		UnFVF	UseFVF
EN250			
3¢	**green on white**	55.00	18.00
	entire	80.00	50.00
EN251		UnFVF	UseFVF
3¢	**red on white**	19,500.00	—
	entire	28,000.00	—

1883-86. Issue With the change of the First Class rate from 3¢ to 2¢, new envelopes of the 2¢ and 4¢ denominations were called for, and new designs were adopted. The first design submitted was not considered entirely satisfactory, but so that envelopes would be available on time, it was approved. In the meantime, the new approved die was prepared and put into use in November, just one month after the new envelopes had been issued. Despite its short life, the first design (EN252-EN255) is not rare; apparently a very large supply was made. In May 1884, the color of the 2¢ envelope stamp was changed from carmine to brown to coincide with the color of the 2¢ adhesive stamp then in use. It is stated that the brown ink, because of its chemical construction, destroyed the printing dies and much recutting had to be done.

EN252-EN255 *Washington. Background of frame composed of scroll work ending in points around inner circle. (Watermarks 5, 6.)*

		UnFVF	UseFVF
EN252			
2¢	**red on white**	3.00	1.75
	entire	7.00	2.00
	a. brown on white (error), entire	2,250.00	—
EN253		UnFVF	UseFVF
2¢	**red on amber**	5.00	2.00
	entire	8.00	3.50
EN254		UnFVF	UseFVF
2¢	**red on blue**	7.00	5.00
	entire	9.00	6.00
EN255		UnFVF	UseFVF
2¢	**red on fawn**	7.00	3.50
	entire	13.00	4.00

EN256-EN265 *Four clear ornamental wavy lines within the circular frame of the design. (Compare with EN266 and EN302.) EN256-EN260 Nov. 1883. EN261-EN265 May 1884. EN266 June 1984.*

No.	Value	Description	UnFVF	UseFVF
EN256	**2¢**	**red on white**	3.00	1.50
		entire	7.00	3.00
EN257	**2¢**	**red on amber**	4.00	2.50
		entire	8.50	4.00
EN258	**2¢**	**red on blue**	7.00	5.00
		entire	11.00	6.00
EN259	**2¢**	**red on fawn**	5.00	3.00
		entire	7.00	4.00
EN260	**2¢**	**red on manila,** wrapper	8.00	4.00
		entire	13.00	8.50
EN261	**2¢**	**brown on white**	3.00	1.50
		entire	7.00	3.00
EN262	**2¢**	**brown on amber**	4.00	3.00
		entire	8.00	4.00
EN263	**2¢**	**brown on blue**	7.00	4.00
		entire	11.00	6.00
EN264	**2¢**	**brown on fawn**	5.00	3.00
		entire	7.00	4.00
EN265	**2¢**	**brown on manila,** wrapper	8.00	4.00
		entire	13.00	8.00
EN266	**2¢**	**red on white**	6.00	4.00
		entire	9.00	6.00

EN267-EN274 *Washington. Retouched dies. Similar to EN256-EN266 but the pairs of wavy lines are no longer continuous, but merge at various points.*

No.	Value	Description	UnFVF	UseFVF
EN267	**2¢**	**red on amber**	10.00	7.00
		entire	15.00	10.00
EN268	**2¢**	**red on blue**	13.00	8.00
		entire	20.00	10.00
EN269	**2¢**	**red on fawn**	10.00	7.00
		entire	13.00	8.00
EN270	**2¢**	**brown on white**	13.00	5.00
		entire	18.00	10.00
EN271	**2¢**	**brown on amber**	60.00	35.00
		entire	18.00	10.00
EN272	**2¢**	**brown on blue**	12.00	6.00
		entire	13.00	8.00
EN273	**2¢**	**brown on fawn**	10.00	9.00
		entire	14.00	13.00
EN274	**2¢**	**brown on manila,** wrapper	18.00	13.00
		entire	24.00	13.00

EN275-EN277 *There are 3 1/2 links above the left figure "2."*

No.	Value	Description	UnFVF	UseFVF
EN275	**2¢**	**red on white**	50.00	35.00
		entire	65.00	50.00
EN276	**2¢**	**red on amber**	600.00	300.00
		entire	875.00	525.00
EN277	**2¢**	**red on fawn**	—	6,500.00

EN278-EN284 *Washington. There are two links below the right figure "2." Center link below left figure "2" touches at left.*

No.	Value	Description	UnFVF	UseFVF
EN278	**2¢**	**red on white**	65.00	45.00
		entire	85.00	70.00
EN279	**2¢**	**red on amber**	120.00	65.00
		entire	135.00	85.00
EN280	**2¢**	**red on blue**	270.00	110.00
		entire	400.00	135.00
EN281	**2¢**	**red on fawn**	280.00	110.00
		entire	350.00	200.00
EN282	**2¢**	**brown on white**	80.00	35.00
		entire	180.00	90.00
EN283	**2¢**	**brown on amber**	180.00	90.00
		entire	260.00	200.00
EN284	**2¢**	**brown on fawn**	2,100.00	925.00
		entire	4,000.00	2,100.00

EN285-EN291 *A round "O" in "TWO," upright of letter "T" in "TWO" slants to right.*

No.	Value	Description	UnFVF	UseFVF
EN285	**2¢**	**red on white**	1,200.00	300.00
		entire	1,600.00	650.00
EN286	**2¢**	**red on amber**	2,100.00	775.00
		entire	3,000.00	1,000.00
EN287	**2¢**	**red on fawn**	650.00	350.00
		entire	950.00	450.00
EN288	**2¢**	**brown on white**	140.00	70.00
		entire	160.00	225.00
EN289	**2¢**	**brown on amber**	160.00	70.00
		entire	180.00	90.00
EN290	**2¢**	**brown on blue**	—	5,000.00
EN291	**2¢**	**brown on fawn**	775.00	625.00
		entire	1,100.00	750.00

EN292-EN297 *Andrew Jackson. Die A, the numeral "4" at left is narrow (2 3/4mm) and has a sharp point. (Compare with EN298.) (Watermarks 6, 7.) Oct. 1883.*

No.	Value	Description	UnFVF	UseFVF
EN292	**4¢**	**green on white**	3.00	3.00
		entire	5.00	5.00

		UnFVF	UseFVF
EN293			
4¢	**green on amber**	4.00	3.00
	entire	6.00	5.00
EN294			
4¢	**green on buff**	7.00	7.00
	entire	11.00	10.00
EN295			
4¢	**green on blue**	7.00	6.00
	entire	10.00	7.00
EN296			
4¢	**green on manila**	8.00	6.00
	entire	11.00	11.00
EN297			
4¢	**green on amber-manila**	16.00	9.00
	entire	23.00	12.00

EN298-EN301 *Die B, the numeral "4" at left is wide (3mm) and has a blunt point.*

		UnFVF	UseFVF
EN298			
4¢	**green on white**	5.00	4.00
	entire	11.00	6.00
EN299			
4¢	**green on amber**	10.00	6.00
	entire	15.00	9.00
EN300			
4¢	**green on manila**	10.00	6.00
	entire	14.00	10.00
EN301			
4¢	**green on amber-manila**	9.00	6.00
	entire	12.00	9.00

1884. JULY ISSUE The previous printing dies having proved completely unsatisfactory, new designs were introduced in July 1884. The principal change consisted of simplifying the old design by removing one pair of the wavy lines from the inner and outer circles.

At first a few impressions were made in red ink, and these are comparatively scarce. Later the stamps were printed in brown ink.

EN302-EN312 *Washington. Only two ornamental wavy lines in frame (compare with EN256), and the back of the bust forms an angle. (Compare with EN314.) (Watermarks 6, 7, 9, 10.)*

		UnFVF	UseFVF
EN302			
2¢	**red on white**	500.00	—
	entire	1,200.00	—
EN303			
2¢	**red on blue**	225.00	—
	entire	275.00	—
EN304			
2¢	**red on manila,** wrapper	100.00	—
	entire	150.00	—
EN305			
2¢	**lake on white**	25.00	20.00
	entire	30.00	24.00
EN306			
2¢	**brown on white**	.50	.25
	entire	.75	.30
EN307			
2¢	**brown on amber**	.65	.45
	entire	1.25	.55
EN308			
2¢	**brown on buff**	3.00	2.00
	entire	4.00	2.50
EN309			
2¢	**brown on blue**	2.50	.50
	entire	3.50	1.75
EN310			
2¢	**brown on fawn**	3.00	2.00
	entire	3.50	2.25
EN311			
2¢	**brown on manila**	9.00	3.50
	entire	13.00	5.00
EN312			
2¢	**brown on amber-manila**	6.00	6.00
	entire	10.00	7.00
EN313			
2¢	**brown on manila,** wrapper	5.25	5.00
	entire	7.00	6.00

EN314-EN318 *The back of the bust is rounded. (Compare with EN302.)*

		UnFVF	UseFVF
EN314			
2¢	**brown on white**	150.00	40.00
	entire	375.00	70.00
EN315			
2¢	**brown on amber**	14.00	12.00
	entire	18.00	14.00
EN316			
2¢	**brown on blue**	700.00	125.00
	entire	775.00	225.00
EN317			
2¢	**brown on fawn**	20.00	17.50
	entire	27.50	20.00
EN318			
2¢	**brown on manila,** wrapper	20.00	15.00
	entire	22.50	18.00

1886-87. ISSUE Letter sheet. Despite the failed attempt in 1861 to popularize letter sheets, Congress authorized the Postmaster General, by an Act of March 3, 1879, to make letter sheets available to the public. It stipulated, however, that no royalty should be paid for any patents on such devices. This caused the Postmaster General much difficulty, since existing letter sheets had been patented. Eventually an arrangement was made with the American Bank Note Co. to produce letter sheets under a patent owned by the United States Postal Card Co. The sheets again proved unpopular and were discontinued in 1894.

EN319 *Ulysses S. Grant. Unwatermarked or watermark "US" as above.*

		UnFVF	UseFVF
EN319			
2¢	**green on white**	—	—
	entire	22.00	11.00

Letter sheets exist with three varieties of perforations at top: 83, 41 or 33, and with guide perforations for folding at either right or left. Watermarked sheets are inscribed "Series 1" through "Series 7" and always have 41 perforations at top.

1887-99. ISSUE The new contract in 1886 again changed the designs and colors of the stamps on envelopes. The contractor, as before, was the Plimpton Morgan Envelope Co. In 1894 the contractor lost the contract to James Purcell, whose factory was at Holyoke, Mass. Purcell had great difficulty completing the terms of his contract and soon was forced to enter into negotiations with the Plimpton Morgan Co. to complete the work. Purcell's work principally is noted by the 1¢ envelopes, which he printed in a very rare dark blue ink, the 4¢ envelopes which he printed in a scarlet and sometimes orange ink, and the 5¢ envelopes for which he prepared a new printing die on which the neckline of Gen. Grant had been eliminated (EN373-374).

EN320 *Franklin. The bust leans forward and has a tremendously large lower portion. This is the so-called "Tiffany Die," which was rejected.*

EN320		UnFVF	UseFVF
1¢	**blue on white**	—	—
	entire	—	—

Watermarks 7, 8, 9, 10, 12. Wmk. 10 was intended primarily for Post Office Dept. penalty envelopes.

EN321-EN331 *The illustration at the right shows the "Spur Die," a sharp "spur" projecting downward from lower portion of the bust.*

EN321		UnFVF	UseFVF
1¢	**blue on white**	.60	.25
	entire	1.00	.35
	v. "Spur Die"	—	—
	entire	2.00	—
	v1. Double impression	—	—

EN322		UnFVF	UseFVF
1¢	**blue on amber**	3.00	1.50
	entire	6.00	4.00
	v. "Spur Die"	—	—
	entire	10.00	—

EN323		UnFVF	UseFVF
1¢	**blue on buff**	2,000.00	—
	entire	4,100.00	—
	v. "Specimen"	—	—

EN324		UnFVF	UseFVF
1¢	**blue on blue**	3,300.00	—
	entire	4,400.00	—

EN325		UnFVF	UseFVF
1¢	**blue on manila**	.65	.35
	entire	1.00	.50

EN326		UnFVF	UseFVF
1¢	**blue on amber-manila**	5.00	4.00
	entire	7.00	6.00

EN327		UnFVF	UseFVF
1¢	**blue on manila,** wrapper	.45	.30
	entire	1.00	.50

EN328		UnFVF	UseFVF
1¢	**dark blue on white**	7.00	3.00
	entire	10.00	7.00

EN329		UnFVF	UseFVF
1¢	**dark blue on amber**	45.00	25.00
	entire	60.00	30.00

EN330		UnFVF	UseFVF
1¢	**dark blue on manila**	20.00	9.00
	entire	27.50	20.00

EN331		UnFVF	UseFVF
1¢	**dark blue on manila,** wrapper	12.00	10.00
	entire	20.00	13.00

Nos. EN332-EN337 are not assigned.

EN338-EN343 *Washington. Die A, the bust points at the third colored tooth of the frame. "G" in "POSTAGE" has no cross bar. (Compare with EN344.)*

EN338		UnFVF	UseFVF
2¢	**green on white**	9.00	8.00
	entire	18.00	11.00

EN339		UnFVF	UseFVF
2¢	**green on amber**	18.00	12.00
	entire	25.00	13.00

EN340		UnFVF	UseFVF
2¢	**green on buff**	65.00	30.00
	entire	85.00	35.00

EN341		UnFVF	UseFVF
2¢	**green on blue**	2,700.00	700.00
	entire	—	4,200.00

EN342		UnFVF	UseFVF
2¢	**green on manila**	1,750.00	500.00
	entire	1,500.00	500.00

EN343		UnFVF	UseFVF
2¢	**green on amber-manila**	1,500.00	550.00
	entire	4,750.00	1,800.00

EN344-EN350 *Washington. Die B, bust points between first and second colored teeth of frame. "G" in "POSTAGE" has a cross bar. This is the common die of the series. (Compare with EN338.) The illustration at right shows the cap on "2" variety.*

EN344		UnFVF	UseFVF
2¢	**green on white**	.30	.25
	entire	.60	.25
	v. Cap on "2"	—	—
	entire	—	—
	v1. Double impression	—	—

EN345		UnFVF	UseFVF
2¢	**green on amber**	.45	.25
	entire	.60	.30
	v. Cap on "2"	—	—
	entire	—	—

EN346		UnFVF	UseFVF
2¢	**green on buff**	.60	.25
	entire	1.00	.45
	v. Cap on "2"	—	—
	entire	—	—

EN347		UnFVF	UseFVF
2¢	**green on blue**	.60	.25
	entire	1.00	.40
	v. Cap on "2"	—	—
	entire	—	—

EN348		UnFVF	UseFVF
2¢	**green on manila**	2.00	.60
	entire	2.50	1.50
	v. Cap on "2"	—	—
	entire	—	—

EN349		UnFVF	UseFVF
2¢	**green on amber-manila**	2.50	2.00
	entire	5.00	2.50
	v. Cap on "2"	—	—
	entire	—	—

EN350		UnFVF	UseFVF
2¢	**green on manila,** wrapper	3.00	2.50
	entire	7.00	6.00

EN351-EN356 *Washington. Die C, similar to last, but head larger and well rounded. The ear is formed by two lines and there are two locks of hair in front of it. (Compare with EN355.)*

EN351		UnFVF	UseFVF
2¢	**green on white**	100.00	13.00
	entire	125.00	40.00

EN352		UnFVF	UseFVF
2¢	**green on amber**	125.00	20.00
	entire	135.00	40.00

EN353		UnFVF	UseFVF
2¢	**green on buff**	150.00	40.00
	entire	160.00	60.00

EN354		UnFVF	UseFVF
2¢	**green on blue**	175.00	60.00
	entire	185.00	65.00

EN355		UnFVF	UseFVF
2¢	**green on manila**	125.00	65.00
	entire	160.00	90.00

EN356		UnFVF	UseFVF
2¢	**green on amber-manila**	325.00	80.00
	entire	375.00	120.00

EN357-EN362 *Die D, similar to EN344 but the bust has no ear.*

		UnFVF	UseFVF
EN357		UnFVF	UseFVF
2¢	**green on white**	—	—
	entire	—	—
EN358		UnFVF	UseFVF
2¢	**green on amber**	—	—
	entire	—	—
EN359		UnFVF	UseFVF
2¢	**green on buff**	—	—
	entire	—	—
EN360		UnFVF	UseFVF
2¢	**green on blue**	—	—
	entire	—	—
EN361		UnFVF	UseFVF
2¢	**green on manila**	—	—
	entire	—	—
EN362		UnFVF	UseFVF
2¢	**green on amber-manila**	—	—
	entire	—	—

EN363-EN368 *Andrew Jackson. The scarlet and orange shades of the 4¢ stamps were manufactured by James Purcell, who obtained the contract in 1894 but due to lack of adequate machinery shortly thereafter was forced to sublet his contract to the previous manufacturer.*

		UnFVF	UseFVF
EN363		UnFVF	UseFVF
4¢	**carmine on white**	1.65	1.25
	entire	3.25	1.50
	a. scarlet	2.25	1.50
	entire	5.00	4.00
	b. orange	—	—
	entire	—	—
EN364		UnFVF	UseFVF
4¢	**carmine on amber**	3.00	2.00
	entire	5.00	3.50
	a. scarlet	3.00	3.25
	entire	6.00	4.00
	b. orange	—	—
	entire	—	—
EN365		UnFVF	UseFVF
4¢	**carmine on buff**	6.00	3.00
	entire	9.00	4.00
EN366		UnFVF	UseFVF
4¢	**carmine on blue**	5.00	4.50
	entire	7.00	6.00
EN367		UnFVF	UseFVF
4¢	**carmine on manila**	7.00	6.00
	entire	9.00	7.50
EN368		UnFVF	UseFVF
4¢	**carmine on amber-manila**	5.00	3.50
	entire	3.00	4.00

EN369-EN372 *Ulysses S. Grant. There is a space between the chin and the coat. (Compare with EN373.)*

		UnFVF	UseFVF
EN369		UnFVF	UseFVF
5¢	**blue on white**	4.00	3.50
	entire	6.00	15.00
EN370		UnFVF	UseFVF
5¢	**blue on amber**	4.50	2.50
	entire	8.00	18.00
EN371		UnFVF	UseFVF
5¢	**blue on buff**	5.00	4.00
	entire	10.00	20.00
EN372		UnFVF	UseFVF
5¢	**blue on blue**	6.00	5.00
	entire	10.00	16.00

EN373, EN374 *Ulysses S. Grant. There is no space between the chin and the coat. (Compare with EN369.)*

		UnFVF	UseFVF
EN373		UnFVF	UseFVF
5¢	**blue on white**	10.00	5.00
	entire	14.00	20.00
EN374		UnFVF	UseFVF
5¢	**blue on amber**	10.00	6.00
	entire	15.00	20.00

EN375-EN380 *Alexander Hamilton. Re-issue of old design with value labels not in alignment.*

		UnFVF	UseFVF
EN375		UnFVF	UseFVF
30¢	**red brown on white**	40.00	43.00
	entire	50.00	225.00
EN376		UnFVF	UseFVF
30¢	**red brown on amber**	45.00	55.00
	entire	55.00	325.00
EN377		UnFVF	UseFVF
30¢	**red brown on buff**	40.00	45.00
	entire	50.00	360.00
EN378		UnFVF	UseFVF
30¢	**red brown on blue**	40.00	45.00
	entire	50.00	350.00
EN379		UnFVF	UseFVF
30¢	**red brown on manila**	45.00	45.00
	entire	50.00	275.00
EN380		UnFVF	UseFVF
30¢	**red brown on amber-manila**	50.00	30.00
	entire	55.00	275.00

EN381-EN386 *Oliver Perry. Re-issue of old design.*

		UnFVF	UseFVF
EN381		UnFVF	UseFVF
90¢	**purple on white**	65.00	70.00
	entire	80.00	450.00
EN382		UnFVF	UseFVF
90¢	**purple on amber**	75.00	75.00
	entire	100.00	450.00
EN383		UnFVF	UseFVF
90¢	**purple on buff**	75.00	80.00
	entire	100.00	450.00
EN384		UnFVF	UseFVF
90¢	**purple on blue**	75.00	85.00
	entire	120.00	450.00
EN385		UnFVF	UseFVF
90¢	**purple on manila**	80.00	85.00
	entire	120.00	450.00
EN386		UnFVF	UseFVF
90¢	**purple on amber-manila**	90.00	90.00
	entire	120.00	450.00

EN375-EN380 are known in various shades of brown. EN381-EN386 exist in both dark and bright purple.

1893. Columbian Exposition Issue To commemorate the Columbian Exposition, the Post Office Department ordered a special series of stamped envelopes in the 1¢, 2¢, 4¢, 5¢ and 10¢ denominations. For reasons not known, the 4¢ envelope never was issued.

The designs of all denominations are identical, except in the face value of the stamp. Four varieties are widely recognized by collectors:

- A period after "CENT"; a meridian behind head of Columbus
- A period; no meridian
- No period; a meridian
- No period; no meridian

The first three will be found on the 1¢ stamps. All four are found on the 2¢ stamps; only the first two on the 5¢ stamps. The 10¢ stamp exists only without the period, but with the meridian.

EN387-EN390 *Christopher Columbus, "Liberty," American eagle. Designs identical except for face value. (Watermark 11.)*

		UnFVF	UseFVF
EN387			
1¢	**blue on white**	2.00	1.50
	entire	3.00	1.75
EN388		UnFVF	UseFVF
2¢	**violet on white**	1.50	.75
	entire	2.50	.75
	a. slate (error)	1,900.00	—
	entire	—	—
EN389		UnFVF	UseFVF
5¢	**brown on white**	9.00	8.00
	entire*	15.00	12.00
	a. slate (error)	750.00	750.00
	entire	800.00	1,200.00
EN390		UnFVF	UseFVF
10¢	**slate on white**	40.00	30.00
	entire	60.00	45.00

1899. Issue With this issue all denominations of stamps above 5¢ values were discontinued; envelopes in higher denominations had been found to be of little use or in little demand. This was the last issue manufactured by the Plimpton Morgan Envelope Co.

EN391-EN396 *Franklin. (Watermarks 12, 13.)*

		UnFVF	UseFVF
EN391			
1¢	**green on white**	.75	.25
	entire	1.50	.75
EN392		UnFVF	UseFVF
1¢	**green on amber**	4.75	1.50
	entire	7.75	3.00
EN393		UnFVF	UseFVF
1¢	**green on buff**	10.00	4.00
	entire	13.50	4.00
EN394		UnFVF	UseFVF
1¢	**green on blue**	10.00	7.00
	entire	13.00	20.00
EN395		UnFVF	UseFVF
1¢	**green on manila**	2.00	1.00
	entire	6.50	2.50
EN396		UnFVF	UseFVF
1¢	**green on manila,** wrapper	2.00	1.00
	entire	8.75	3.00

EN397-EN400 *Washington. Die A, point of bust broad and ends over the left corner of the shield containing numeral. (Compare with EN401.)*

		UnFVF	UseFVF
EN397			
2¢	**carmine on white**	4.00	2.00
	entire	8.50	3.00
EN398		UnFVF	UseFVF
2¢	**carmine on amber**	17.50	10.00
	entire	27.50	12.00
EN399		UnFVF	UseFVF
2¢	**carmine on buff**	17.50	8.00
	entire	30.00	9.00
EN400		UnFVF	UseFVF
2¢	**carmine on blue**	60.00	30.00
	entire	75.00	35.00

EN401-EN405 *George Washington. Die B, point of bust elongated and points to the second tooth. Hair tied with ribbon at back. (Compare with EN397 and following.)*

		UnFVF	UseFVF
EN401			
2¢	**carmine and white**	.30	.25
	entire	.75	.50
EN402		UnFVF	UseFVF
2¢	**carmine and amber**	1.25	.25
	entire	3.25	.75
EN403		UnFVF	UseFVF
2¢	**carmine on buff**	1.00	.25
	entire	2.75	.75
EN404		UnFVF	UseFVF
2¢	**carmine on blue**	1.25	.50
	entire	3.50	1.75
EN405		UnFVF	UseFVF
2¢	**carmine on manila,** wrapper	6.00	3.00
	entire	12.50	6.00

EN406-EN409 *Die C, re-cut die. Similar to last but the hair is without ribbon. Many varieties of the re-cutting exist, some of which show the hair in flowing curves; some with hair pulled straight down; and others with the ribbon obliterated with short lines (Compare with EN401.)*

		UnFVF	UseFVF
EN406			
2¢	**carmine on white**	5.00	2.50
	entire	9.50	7.00
EN407		UnFVF	UseFVF
2¢	**carmine on amber**	12.00	8.00
	entire	22.50	15.00
EN408		UnFVF	UseFVF
2¢	**carmine on buff**	25.00	15.00
	entire	35.00	17.50
EN409		UnFVF	UseFVF
2¢	**carmine on blue**	10.00	7.00
	entire	22.50	15.00

There are many shades for Nos. EN406-EN409.

EN410, EN411 *Abraham Lincoln. Die A, bust pointed and undraped. Inner oval with teeth. (Compare with following.)*

		UnFVF	UseFVF
EN410			
4¢	**brown on white**	17.00	12.00
	entire	30.00	15.00
EN411		UnFVF	UseFVF
4¢	**brown on amber**	17.00	12.00
	entire	30.00	25.00

EN412 *Die B, bust is draped and point broad. Inner oval with teeth.*

		UnFVF	UseFVF
EN412			
4¢	**brown on white**	5,000.00	325.00
	entire	5,700.00	—

EN413-EN415 *Abraham Lincoln. Die C, no teeth in inner oval. Bust broad and draped. (Watermarks 12, 13, 14.)*

		UnFVF	UseFVF
EN413			
4¢	**brown on white**	10.00	7.00
	entire	25.00	11.00
EN414		UnFVF	UseFVF
4¢	**brown on amber**	37.50	15.00
	entire	50.00	20.00
EN415		UnFVF	UseFVF
4¢	**brown on manila,** wrapper	15.00	8.00
	entire	25.00	12.50

EN416, EN417 *Ulysses S. Grant. (Watermark 13.)*

		UnFVF	UseFVF
EN416			
5¢	**blue on white**	10.00	9.50
	entire	14.00	13.00
EN417		UnFVF	UseFVF
5¢	**blue on amber**	13.00	10.00
	entire	22.50	15.00

1903. ISSUE This contract is the first for the Hartford Manufacturing Co. as producers of stamped envelopes.

EN418-EN423 *Franklin. (Watermarks 13, 14.)*

		UnFVF	UseFVF
EN418			
1¢	**green on white**	.50	.25
	entire	1.25	.50
EN419		UnFVF	UseFVF
1¢	**green on amber**	12.00	3.00
	entire	18.50	4.00
EN420		UnFVF	UseFVF
1¢	**green on buff**	13.00	3.00
	entire	17.00	4.00
EN421		UnFVF	UseFVF
1¢	**green on blue**	13.00	3.00
	entire	20.00	4.00
EN422		UnFVF	UseFVF
1¢	**green on manila**	3.00	1.50
	entire	4.50	2.00
EN423		UnFVF	UseFVF
1¢	**green on manila,** wrapper	1.50	.75
	entire	2.00	1.00

EN424-EN428 *Washington. A short and two long lines of colorless shading are found in the right side of the ribbon containing the value. (Compare with EN434.)*

		UnFVF	UseFVF
EN424			
2¢	**carmine on white**	.50	.25
	entire	1.00	.50
EN425		UnFVF	UseFVF
2¢	**carmine on amber**	1.75	.50
	entire	3.75	1.50
EN426		UnFVF	UseFVF
2¢	**carmine on buff**	2.00	.50
	entire	2.50	.75
EN427		UnFVF	UseFVF
2¢	**carmine on blue**	1.50	.75
	entire	3.25	.75
EN428		UnFVF	UseFVF
2¢	**carmine on manila,** wrapper	15.00	8.00
	entire	22.50	14.00

EN429-EN431 *Ulysses S. Grant*

		UnFVF	UseFVF
EN429			
4¢	**brown on white**	20.00	12.00
	entire*	27.50	15.00
EN430		UnFVF	UseFVF
4¢	**brown on amber**	20.00	12.00
	entire*	27.50	15.00
EN431		UnFVF	UseFVF
4¢	**brown on manila,** wrapper	18.00	11.00
	entire*	40.00	30.00

EN432, EN433 *Abraham Lincoln*

		UnFVF	UseFVF
EN432			
5¢	**blue on white**	17.00	10.00
	entire	25.00	17.50
EN433		UnFVF	UseFVF
5¢	**blue on amber**	18.00	13.00
	entire	25.00	20.00

EN434-EN438 *Washington. Re-cut die. The colorless shading lines at the right of the ribbon containing the value are all short. Lettering throughout is heavier. (Compare with EN424.)*

		UnFVF	UseFVF
EN434			
2¢	**carmine on white**	.50	.25
	entire	1.00	.50
EN435		UnFVF	UseFVF
2¢	**carmine on amber**	7.00	.75
	entire	12.00	2.00
EN436		UnFVF	UseFVF
2¢	**carmine on buff**	6.00	2.00
	entire	7.50	2.00

EN437		UnFVF	UseFVF
2¢	**carmine on blue**	4.00	2.00
	entire	6.00	2.50

EN438		UnFVF	UseFVF
2¢	**carmine on manila,** wrapper	12.00	7.00
	entire	22.50	12.50

1907-16. ISSUE New contractors, The Mercantile Corp., brought a change from Hartford, Conn., where envelopes had been manufactured since 1874, to Dayton, Ohio. In 1915 the Middle West Supply Co. obtained the contract and in 1929 the International Envelope Co. was the successful bidder. These new names did not change the site of manufacture itself, and appear to reflect the merger of the corporations named. From 1929 until 1965, envelopes were manufactured by the International Envelope Co., Dayton, Ohio.

Beginning in 1915, laid paper was dropped for all envelopes in favor of wove paper, and from then on all watermarks were of the same or similar design. The watermark was changed every four years to mark each new contract. The various arrangement of the dates, at top, bottom or diagonal, is identification of the paper manufacturer. From 1929 until 1958, the diagonally placed numerals identified "Extra quality" paper. Since 1958, all envelopes are of a single quality paper.

What photo number goes here? Help me?!

Typical examples of watermarks 1915-60 (reduced size).

EN439-EN444 *Franklin. Die A, wide "D" in "UNITED." (Compare with EN445 and following.) (Watermarks 12, 14, 15, 16, 17, 18.)*

EN439		UnFVF	UseFVF
1¢	**green on white**	.30	.25
	entire	.50	.40
	v. "NITED" instead of "UNITED," entire	—	—
	v1. with added impression of 2¢ Washington (EN466)		

EN440		UnFVF	UseFVF
1¢	**green on amber**	.75	.50
	entire	1.25	.75

EN441		UnFVF	UseFVF
1¢	**green on buff**	4.00	2.00
	entire	6.00	2.50

EN442		UnFVF	UseFVF
1¢	**green on blue**	5.00	2.00
	entire	6.00	3.00

EN443		UnFVF	UseFVF
1¢	**green on manila**	3.00	2.00
	entire	4.50	2.50

EN444		UnFVF	UseFVF
1¢	**green on manila,** wrapper	.50	.25
	entire	.75	.50

EN445-EN449 *Die B, narrow "D" in "UNITED." (Compare with EN439 and following.)*

EN445		UnFVF	UseFVF
1¢	**green on white**	1.00	.50
	entire	1.25	.60

EN446		UnFVF	UseFVF
1¢	**green on amber**	1.00	.75
	entire	1.50	1.00

EN447		UnFVF	UseFVF
1¢	**green on buff**	4.00	2.00
	entire	6.00	2.50

EN448		UnFVF	UseFVF
1¢	**green on blue**	5.00	2.00
	entire	6.00	3.00

EN449		UnFVF	UseFVF
1¢	**green on manila,** wrapper	37.50	20.00
	entire	42.50	27.50

EN450-EN455 *Franklin. Die C, both "Ss" in "STATES" are broad. (Compare with other 1¢ dies.)*

EN450		UnFVF	UseFVF
1¢	**green on white**	1.00	.50
	entire	1.25	.75

EN451		UnFVF	UseFVF
1¢	**green on amber**	1.00	.80
	entire	2.00	1.00

EN452		UnFVF	UseFVF
1¢	**green on buff**	6.00	2.00
	entire	7.00	3.00

EN453		UnFVF	UseFVF
1¢	**green on blue**	5.00	4.00
	entire	5.50	4.50

EN454		UnFVF	UseFVF
1¢	**green on manila**	4.00	3.00
	entire	6.00	5.00

EN455		UnFVF	UseFVF
1¢	**green on manila,** wrapper	6.00	4.00
	entire	11.00	6.00

EN450-EN455 So-called "Dayton Dies" of which there are 13 varieties. See note after illustration of EN492.

EN456-EN460 *Die D, back of bust forms angle opposite "T" in "CENT." (Compare with other 1¢ dies.)*

EN456		UnFVF	UseFVF
1¢	**green on white**	.70	.35
	entire	.85	.50

EN457		UnFVF	UseFVF
1¢	**green on amber**	1.00	.75
	entire	1.25	1.00

EN458		UnFVF	UseFVF
1¢	**green on buff**	4.00	2.00
	entire	5.00	3.00

EN459		UnFVF	UseFVF
1¢	**green on blue**	4.00	2.00
	entire	6.00	4.00

EN460		UnFVF	UseFVF
1¢	**green on manila**	50.00	
	entire	—	

Watermarks 15 to 23 (1907-1919).

EN461-EN470 *Washington. Die A, both the "O" in "TWO" and the "C" in "CENTS" are ovals. (Compare with the following.)*

EN461		UnFVF	UseFVF
2¢	**brown red on white**	1.00	.50
	entire	1.75	.75

EN462		UnFVF	UseFVF
2¢	**brown red on amber**	6.00	3.00
	entire	8.50	7.00

EN463

		UnFVF	UseFVF
2¢	**brown red on buff**	7.00	2.00
	entire	11.00	4.50

EN464

		UnFVF	UseFVF
2¢	**brown red on blue**	5.00	2.50
	entire	7.00	4.00

EN465

		UnFVF	UseFVF
2¢	**brown red on manila,** wrapper	40.00	30.00
	entire	60.00	40.00

EN466

		UnFVF	UseFVF
2¢	**carmine on white**	.30	.25
	entire	.60	.40
	v1. with added impression of 1¢ Franklin (EN439) on reverse	325.00	400.00
	v2. with added impression of 4¢ Franklin (EN509)	300.00	

EN467

		UnFVF	UseFVF
2¢	**carmine on amber**	.30	.25
	entire	1.00	.25

EN468

		UnFVF	UseFVF
2¢	**carmine on buff**	.50	.25
	entire	.75	.25

EN469

		UnFVF	UseFVF
2¢	**carmine on blue**	.50	.25
	entire	1.00	.25

EN470

		UnFVF	UseFVF
2¢	**carmine on manila,** wrapper	5.00	3.00
	entire	9.50	5.00

EN471-EN479 *Die A2, similar to last except there is a prominent wedge-shaped lock of hair in the center of the head. (Compare with other 2¢ dies.)*

EN471

		UnFVF	UseFVF
2¢	**brown red on white**	30.00	8.00
	entire	40.00	25.00

EN472

		UnFVF	UseFVF
2¢	**brown red on amber**	110.00	50.00
	entire	130.00	75.00

EN473

		UnFVF	UseFVF
2¢	**brown red on buff**	135.00	60.00
	entire	150.00	100.00

EN474

		UnFVF	UseFVF
2¢	**brown red on blue**	135.00	110.00
	entire	170.00	140.00

EN475

		UnFVF	UseFVF
2¢	**carmine on white**	.40	.20
	entire	.75	.40

EN476

		UnFVF	UseFVF
2¢	**carmine on amber**	.40	.25
	entire	.80	.60

EN477

		UnFVF	UseFVF
2¢	**carmine on buff**	.60	.55
	entire	.90	.60

EN478

		UnFVF	UseFVF
2¢	**carmine on blue**	.45	.40
	entire	.80	.50

EN479

		UnFVF	UseFVF
2¢	**carmine on manila,** wrapper	5.00	3.00
	entire	7.00	5.00

EN480-EN487 *Washington. Die B, head is large, hair arranged in bumps. The "O" in "TWO" is circular. (Compare with EN488 and other 2¢ dies.)*

EN480

		UnFVF	UseFVF
2¢	**brown red on white**	.60	.40
	entire	.90	.50

EN481

		UnFVF	UseFVF
2¢	**brown red on amber**	3.50	2.00
	entire	5.00	2.00

EN482

		UnFVF	UseFVF
2¢	**brown red on buff**	7.00	3.25
	entire	10.00	6.00

EN483

		UnFVF	UseFVF
2¢	**brown red on blue**	5.00	2.25
	entire	7.00	4.00

EN484

		UnFVF	UseFVF
2¢	**carmine on white**	.75	.40
	entire	1.25	.60

EN485

		UnFVF	UseFVF
2¢	**carmine on amber**	1.35	.50
	entire	1.75	.80

EN486

		UnFVF	UseFVF
2¢	**carmine on buff**	7.00	4.00
	entire	11.00	6.00

EN487

		UnFVF	UseFVF
2¢	**carmine on blue**	.90	.70
	entire	1.50	.75

EN488-EN491 *Die C, prominent slits in hair resembling the gills of a shark. Lettering clear and sharp. (Compare with EN480 and other 2¢ dies.)*

EN488

		UnFVF	UseFVF
2¢	**carmine on white**	.50	.25
	entire	.75	.50

EN489

		UnFVF	UseFVF
2¢	**carmine on amber**	.40	.30
	entire	.75	.50

EN490

		UnFVF	UseFVF
2¢	**carmine on buff**	.45	.35
	entire	.70	.50

EN491

		UnFVF	UseFVF
2¢	**carmine on blue**	.50	.35
	entire	.60	.50

EN492-EN496 *Die D, the so-called "Dayton Dies" as they were made by a private die engraver on order from the factory at Dayton, Ohio. There are 13 varieties, some of which are quite valuable.*

EN492

		UnFVF	UseFVF
2¢	**carmine on white**	.60	.40
	entire	1.00	.60

EN493

		UnFVF	UseFVF
2¢	**carmine on amber**	.60	.40
	entire	1.00	.60

EN494

		UnFVF	UseFVF
2¢	**carmine on buff**	3.00	1.50
	entire	4.00	3.75

EN495

		UnFVF	UseFVF
2¢	**carmine on blue**	.75	.50
	entire	1.50	.75

EN496

		UnFVF	UseFVF
2¢	**carmine on manila,** wrapper	5.00	3.00
	entire	8.00	3.00

EN497-EN500 *Washington. Die E, front of bust tapers and the end is rounded. (Compare with EN461 and others.)*

EN497

		UnFVF	UseFVF
2¢	**carmine on white**	.40	.25
	entire	.85	.40

EN498

		UnFVF	UseFVF
2¢	**carmine on amber**	.65	.45
	entire	1.00	.60

EN499

		UnFVF	UseFVF
2¢	**carmine on buff**	.75	.50
	entire	1.25	.70

EN500		UnFVF	UseFVF
2¢	**carmine on blue**	.75	.50
	entire	1.25	.50

EN501-EN505 *Washington. Die F, upright line of the "2s" tapers. There is a very thin line where it meets the base of the numeral. The upper corner of the front end of the bust is usually, but not always, cut away in varying degrees.*

EN501		UnFVF	UseFVF
2¢	**carmine on white**	14.00	12.00
	entire	16.00	14.00
	a. vermilion	—	—
	entire	—	—
EN502		UnFVF	UseFVF
2¢	**carmine on amber**	12.00	9.00
	entire	14.00	12.00
EN503		UnFVF	UseFVF
2¢	**carmine on buff**	40.00	20.00
	entire	50.00	30.00
EN504		UnFVF	UseFVF
2¢	**carmine on blue**	15.00	9.00
	entire	20.00	16.00
EN505		UnFVF	UseFVF
2¢	**carmine on manila,** wrapper	45.00	40.00
	entire	55.00	45.00

EN506-EN508 *Die G, hair arranged as in EN471 (a wedge-shape lock in center). (Compare with EN501 and others.)*

EN506		UnFVF	UseFVF
2¢	**carmine on white**	15.00	13.00
	entire	20.00	15.00
EN507		UnFVF	UseFVF
2¢	**carmine on buff**	13.00	10.00
	entire	20.00	13.00
EN508		UnFVF	UseFVF
2¢	**carmine on blue**	15.00	10.00
	entire	18.00	16.00

EN509, EN510 *Franklin. Die A, the "F" in "FOUR" is only 1mm from the "4." (Compare with EN511.)*

EN509		UnFVF	UseFVF
4¢	**black on white**	4.00	3.00
	entire*	9.00	5.00
EN510		UnFVF	UseFVF
4¢	**black on amber**	6.00	3.00
	entire*	10.00	5.00

EN511, EN512 *Die B, the "F" in "FOUR" is 1 3/4mm from the figure "4."*

EN511		UnFVF	UseFVF
4¢	**black on white**	5.00	4.00
	entire*	10.00	6.00
EN512		UnFVF	UseFVF
4¢	**black on amber**	6.00	3.00
	entire*	12.50	7.00

EN513-EN515 *Washington. Die A, large "F" in "FIVE" (2 3/4mm high). (Compare with EN516.)*

EN513		UnFVF	UseFVF
5¢	**blue on white**	7.00	3.00
	entire	11.00	7.00
EN514		UnFVF	UseFVF
5¢	**blue on amber**	13.00	12.00
	entire	16.00	14.00
EN515		UnFVF	UseFVF
5¢	**blue on blue**	1,200.00	—
	entire	1,800.00	—

EN516-EN519 *Die B, Small "F" in "FIVE" (2 1/2mm tall). (Compare with EN513.)*

EN516		UnFVF	UseFVF
5¢	**blue on white**	7.00	3.00
	entire	12.50	6.00
EN517		UnFVF	UseFVF
5¢	**blue on amber**	13.00	12.00
	entire	22.50	15.00
EN518		UnFVF	UseFVF
5¢	**blue on buff**	1,000.00	—
	entire	—	—
EN519		UnFVF	UseFVF
5¢	**blue on blue**	1,000.00	—
	entire	—	—

1916-50. Issue The circular design used on these envelopes was introduced in 1916 and continued without change until 1950. Many dies wore out through this long tenure and many new master dies were required, which accounts for the several different dies for each denomination. The 3¢ envelopes were issued in 1917, when the rate of postage was increased from 2¢ to 3¢. The stamps were printed in a violet ink. Twenty months later the First Class rate was returned to 2¢ and the 3¢ envelopes were discontinued.

After the reduction of First Class postal rates from 3¢ (a war measure) to 2¢, the Post Office found itself with an enormous supply of 3¢ envelopes for which there was no practical use. The envelopes were revalued (1920) by running them through canceling machines with appropriate slugs to indicate the new value (2¢) inserted into them. It is estimated that some 63 million envelopes were revalued in the process.

When, in 1925, the rate for circular letters was advanced from 1¢ to 1 1/2¢, the government again found itself with an unusable supply of envelopes, this time the 1¢ denomination. Again revaluing was done by the use of canceling machines.

In July 1932, First Class rates were advanced to 3¢, which called for production of 3¢ envelopes. This new issue was printed in a bright purple ink. Wrappers were discontinued in 1934.

EN520-EN528 *Franklin. Die A, "UNITED" small and nearer inner than outer circle. (Compare with following.) Watermarks 19 to 42 (1915-1949).*

EN520		UnFVF	UseFVF
1¢	**green on white**	.25	.25
	entire	.40	.25
EN521		UnFVF	UseFVF
1¢	**green on amber**	.40	.35
	entire	.75	.50

EN522		UnFVF	UseFVF
1¢	**green on buff**	2.00	1.25
	entire	2.75	1.75

EN523		UnFVF	UseFVF
1¢	**green on blue**	.50	.40
	entire	.75	.50

EN524		UnFVF	UseFVF
1¢	**green on manila**	7.00	5.00
	entire	9.50	6.00

EN525		UnFVF	UseFVF
1¢	**green on manila,** wrapper	.25	.25
	entire	.75	.25

EN526		UnFVF	UseFVF
1¢	**green on brown** (glazed)	35.00	20.00
	entire	40.00	22.00

EN527		UnFVF	UseFVF
1¢	**green on brown,** (glazed) wrapper	65.00	—
	entire	75.00	—

EN528		UnFVF	UseFVF
1¢	**green on brown** (unglazed)	10.00	10.00
	entire	12.50	11.00

EN529, EN530 *Die B, the first "S" in "STATES" is larger than the last "S." "NT" in "CENT" are large. "U" in "UNITED" is close to circle. (Compare with EN531 and others.)*

EN529		UnFVF	UseFVF
1¢	**green on white**	85.00	65.00
	entire*	100.00	75.00

EN530		UnFVF	UseFVF
1¢	**green on amber**	325.00	200.00
	entire*	500.00	250.00

EN531-EN533 *Franklin. Die C, hair projects strongly at back, forming a "bun." (Compare with EN529 and others.)*

EN531		UnFVF	UseFVF
1¢	**green on white**	.35	.25
	entire	.40	.30

EN532		UnFVF	UseFVF
1¢	**green on amber**	1.35	.75
	entire	1.75	1.00

EN533		UnFVF	UseFVF
1¢	**green on blue**	1.00	.75
	entire	1.50	.90

EN533A		UnFVF	UseFVF
1¢	**green on manila,** wrapper	150.00	135.00
	entire	175.00	150.00

EN534-EN537 *Die D, "UNITED" large and closer to outer than inner circle. (Compare with EN520 and others.)*

EN534		UnFVF	UseFVF
1¢	**green on white**	.40	.30
	entire	.50	.35

EN535		UnFVF	UseFVF
1¢	**green on amber**	1.50	1.00
	entire	2.00	1.50

EN536		UnFVF	UseFVF
1¢	**green on buff**	4.00	1.50
	entire	.50	.35

EN537		UnFVF	UseFVF
1¢	**green on blue**	1.00	.50
	entire	1.50	.75

EN538-EN540 *"C" in "CENTS," "G" in "POSTAGE," and "U" in "UNITED" are very narrow.(Compare with all others dies.)*

EN538		UnFVF	UseFVF
1¢	**green on white**	.40	.30
	entire	.55	.50

EN539		UnFVF	UseFVF
1¢	**green on amber**	1.25	.75
	entire	1.50	1.00

EN540		UnFVF	UseFVF
1¢	**green on blue**	.75	.40
	entire	1.10	.75

EN541-EN545 *Washington. Die A, large head, well formed thick letters.*

EN541		UnFVF	UseFVF
1-1/2¢	**brown on white**	.25	.25
	entire	.60	.25
	a. purple (error)	95.00	—
	entire	120.00	—

EN542		UnFVF	UseFVF
1-1/2¢	**brown on amber**	1.00	.50
	entire	1.50	.70

EN543		UnFVF	UseFVF
1-1/2¢	**brown on blue**	1.75	1.10
	entire	2.00	1.50

EN544		UnFVF	UseFVF
1-1/2¢	**brown on manila**	7.00	4.00
	entire	12.00	7.00

EN545		UnFVF	UseFVF
1-1/2¢	**brown on manila,** wrapper	.90	.25
	entire	1.50	.60

EN546-EN548 *Die H2, slightly different head from EN541. Lettering thin and sharp; "T" with long top strokes.*

EN546		UnFVF	UseFVF
1-1/2¢	**brown on white**	.70	.35
	entire	.90	.60

EN547		UnFVF	UseFVF
1-1/2¢	**brown on amber**	1.50	.85
	entire	2.00	.90

EN548		UnFVF	UseFVF
1-1/2¢	**brown on blue**	2.00	1.50
	entire	2.25	1.50

EN549-EN555 *Washington. Die A, head large. Base line of "2s" horizontal. Lettering heavy and well formed. (Compare with following.)*

EN549		UnFVF	UseFVF
2¢	**carmine on white**	.25	.25
	entire	.50	.25
	a. green (error), entire	7,500.00	—
	p. laid paper	—	—
	entire	—	—
	v. with added impression of 1¢ green (EN520)	750.00	—
	v1. with added impression of 1¢ green (EN439)	750.00	—
	v2. with added impression of 4¢ black (EN509)	600.00	—

		UnFVF	UseFVF
EN550			
2¢	**carmine on amber**	.30	.25
	entire	.50	.25
	p. laid paper	—	—
	entire	—	—
EN551		**UnFVF**	**UseFVF**
2¢	**carmine on buff**	2.00	.75
	entire	4.50	2.00
EN552		**UnFVF**	**UseFVF**
2¢	**carmine on blue**	.25	.25
	entire	.75	.25
EN553		**UnFVF**	**UseFVF**
2¢	**carmine on manila,** wrapper	.25	.25
	entire	.50	.25
EN554		**UnFVF**	**UseFVF**
2¢	**carmine on brown** (glazed), wrapper	80.00	55.00
	entire	100.00	70.00
EN555		**UnFVF**	**UseFVF**
2¢	**carmine on brown** (unglazed), wrapper	75.00	55.00
	entire	100.00	70.00

EN556-EN559 *Washington. Die B, head very large. Base line of both "2s" slope down to right. "U" in "UNITED" far from circle. (Compare with other 2¢ dies.)*

		UnFVF	UseFVF
EN556			
2¢	**carmine on white**	10.00	7.00
	entire	16.00	10.00
EN557		**UnFVF**	**UseFVF**
2¢	**carmine on amber**	10.00	8.00
	entire	16.00	11.00
EN558		**UnFVF**	**UseFVF**
2¢	**carmine on buff**	110.00	50.00
	entire	135.00	90.00
EN559		**UnFVF**	**UseFVF**
2¢	**carmine on blue**	20.00	15.00
	entire	25.00	22.50

EN560, EN561 *Die C, as EN556 except the large inner circle and circles around the figure "2s" are very thin. (The rejected die.)*

		UnFVF	UseFVF
EN560			
2¢	**carmine on white**	35.00	30.00
	entire	50.00	40.00
EN561		**UnFVF**	**UseFVF**
2¢	**carmine on blue**	80.00	75.00
	entire	150.00	125.00

EN562-EN565 *Washington. Die D, "C" in "CENTS" very close to circle. Base line of right "2" slopes downward to right. Head slightly smaller. (Compare with EN549 and others.)*

		UnFVF	UseFVF
EN562			
2¢	**carmine on white**	10.00	8.00
	entire	13.00	11.00
EN563		**UnFVF**	**UseFVF**
2¢	**carmine on amber**	25.00	15.00
	entire	30.00	17.00
EN564		**UnFVF**	**UseFVF**
2¢	**carmine on buff**	35.00	35.00
	entire	45.00	45.00
EN565		**UnFVF**	**UseFVF**
2¢	**carmine on blue**	20.00	17.50
	entire	25.00	22.50

EN566-EN569 *Die E, smaller head than all other dies. "T" and "S" in "CENTS" close.*

		UnFVF	UseFVF
EN566			
2¢	**carmine on white**	.55	.35
	entire	.75	.50
EN567		**UnFVF**	**UseFVF**
2¢	**carmine on amber**	.60	.40
	entire	1.60	.70
EN568		**UnFVF**	**UseFVF**
2¢	**carmine on buff**	3.00	2.00
	entire	6.00	3.00
EN569		**UnFVF**	**UseFVF**
2¢	**carmine on blue**	.75	.25
	entire	1.75	.60

EN570-EN573 *Washington. Die F, base line of left "2" slopes downward to right. Heavy strands of hair resemble bumps. "T" and "S" in "CENTS" widely spaced. (Compare with other 2¢ dies.)*

		UnFVF	UseFVF
EN570			
2¢	**carmine on white**	.70	.40
	entire	1.10	.70
EN571		**UnFVF**	**UseFVF**
2¢	**carmine on amber**	1.00	.45
	entire	1.85	.85
EN572		**UnFVF**	**UseFVF**
2¢	**carmine on buff**	4.50	3.00
	entire	7.00	3.50
EN573		**UnFVF**	**UseFVF**
2¢	**carmine on blue**	.75	.30
	entire	1.25	.50

EN574-EN577 *Die H, base lines of "2s" slope downward to right. Clear sharp impressions. Thin lettering. "Ts" have short top strokes.*

		UnFVF	UseFVF
EN574			
2¢	**carmine on white**	.70	.30
	entire	1.00	.80
EN575		**UnFVF**	**UseFVF**
2¢	**carmine on amber**	.80	.40
	entire	1.60	1.00
EN576		**UnFVF**	**UseFVF**
2¢	**carmine on buff**	4.00	2.50
	entire	6.00	4.00
EN577		**UnFVF**	**UseFVF**
2¢	**carmine on blue**	.80	.40
	entire	1.50	.70
EN577A		**UnFVF**	**UseFVF**
2¢	**carmine on manila**	—	—
	entire	—	—

EN578-EN580 *Washington. Die H2, similar to EN574 except all "Ts" have long top strokes.*

		UnFVF	UseFVF
EN578			
2¢	**carmine on white**	.50	.25
	entire	.75	.55
EN579		**UnFVF**	**UseFVF**
2¢	**carmine on amber**	.70	.40
	entire	1.00	.50
EN580		**UnFVF**	**UseFVF**
2¢	**carmine on blue**	.50	.25
	entire	1.00	.50

EN581-EN585 *Die I, the letters "C," "U," and "G" are very narrow. (Compare with all other 2¢ dies.)*

		UnFVF	UseFVF
EN581			
2¢	**carmine on white**	.50	.30
	entire	.75	.50
EN582		UnFVF	UseFVF
2¢	**carmine on amber**	.60	.30
	entire	.70	.40
EN583		UnFVF	UseFVF
2¢	**carmine on blue**	.80	.25
	entire	2.25	.50

EN584-EN590 *Washington. Die A, similar to the 2¢ die (EN549). Dark violet stamps were issued from 1916-17, at which time the postage rate was reduced to 2¢. When rate again was raised to 3¢, in 1932, this denomination was reissued in a bright purple.*

		UnFVF	UseFVF
EN584			
3¢	**dark violet on white**	.60	.25
	entire	.75	.25
	a. carmine (error)	35.00	30.00
	entire	40.00	35.00
	v. with added impression of EN520, entire	650.00	—
	v1. with added impression of EN549, entire	750.00	—
EN585		UnFVF	UseFVF
3¢	**dark violet on amber**	2.50	1.50
	entire	7.00	2.75
	a. black (error)	175.00	—
	entire	210.00	—
EN586		UnFVF	UseFVF
3¢	**dark violet on buff**	25.00	2.00
	entire	32.50	3.00
EN587		UnFVF	UseFVF
3¢	**dark violet on blue**	7.00	1.75
	entire	11.00	7.50
EN588		UnFVF	UseFVF
3¢	**purple on white**	.25	.20
	entire	.50	.25
EN589		UnFVF	UseFVF
3¢	**purple on amber**	.50	.25
	entire	.75	.40
EN590		UnFVF	UseFVF
3¢	**purple on blue**	.30	.25
	entire	.75	.30

EN591-EN594 *Die E, similar to 2¢ (EN566).*

		UnFVF	UseFVF
EN591			
3¢	**dark violet on white**	1.75	1.00
	entire	3.25	1.00
	a. carmine (error)	35.00	30.00
	entire	40.00	35.00
EN592		UnFVF	UseFVF
3¢	**dark violet on amber**	5.00	3.00
	entire	9.00	4.00
	a. carmine (error)	375.00	265.00
	entire	425.00	350.00
EN593		UnFVF	UseFVF
3¢	**dark violet on buff**	30.00	1.75
	entire	27.50	1.25
EN594		UnFVF	UseFVF
3¢	**dark violet on blue**	7.00	4.50
	entire	9.00	5.00
	a. carmine (error)	300.00	300.00
	entire	425.00	775.00

EN595-EN598 *Die F, similar to 2¢ (EN570).*

		UnFVF	UseFVF
EN595			
3¢	**dark violet on white**	2.50	1.75
	entire	4.00	2.00
EN596		UnFVF	UseFVF
3¢	**dark violet on amber**	6.50	3.00
	entire	8.00	3.50
EN597		UnFVF	UseFVF
3¢	**dark violet on buff**	33.00	2.00
	entire	35.00	3.00
EN598		UnFVF	UseFVF
3¢	**dark violet on blue**	7.00	5.00
	entire	10.00	5.00

EN599-EN602 *Die H, similar to 2¢, die H (EN574).*

EN603-EN605 *Die I, similar to 2¢. (See EN581.)*

		UnFVF	UseFVF
EN599			
3¢	**dark violet on white**	1.50	1.00
	entire	3.00	2.50
EN600		UnFVF	UseFVF
3¢	**dark violet on amber**	4.00	2.00
	entire	6.00	3.00
EN601		UnFVF	UseFVF
3¢	**dark violet on buff**	32.00	4.00
	entire	37.00	8.00
EN602		UnFVF	UseFVF
3¢	**dark violet on blue**	9.00	5.00
	entire	13.00	7.00
EN603		UnFVF	UseFVF
3¢	**purple on white**	.50	.25
	entire	.50	.35
EN604		UnFVF	UseFVF
3¢	**purple on amber**	.60	.25
	entire	1.10	.40
EN605		UnFVF	UseFVF
3¢	**purple on blue**	.60	.25
	entire	1.10	.55

Nos. EN606-EN608 are not assigned.

EN609-EN611 *Franklin*

		UnFVF	UseFVF
EN609			
4¢	**black on white**	1.25	.75
	entire*	3.25	2.55
	v. with added impression of 2¢ (EN549)	—	—
	entire*	275.00	—
EN610		UnFVF	UseFVF
4¢	**black on amber**	2.75	1.00
	entire	5.50	2.00
EN611		UnFVF	UseFVF
4¢	**black on blue**	3.00	1.00
	entire	5.50	2.00

EN612-EN614 *Washington*

		UnFVF	UseFVF
EN612			
5¢	**blue on white**	3.00	2.50
	entire	6.50	3.50
EN613		UnFVF	UseFVF
5¢	**blue on amber**	4.00	1.75
	entire	7.00	3.50
EN614		UnFVF	UseFVF
5¢	**blue on blue**	4.00	3.00
	entire	9.00	4.50

EN615-EN617

		UnFVF	UseFVF
EN615			
6¢	**orange on white**	6.00	3.50
	entire*	8.00	6.00
EN616			
6¢	**orange on amber**	11.00	8.00
	entire*	15.00	10.00
EN617			
6¢	**orange on blue**	11.00	8.00
	entire*	15.00	10.00

1920. Type 1 Surcharge Revalued Envelopes When a double or triple overprint is listed it indicates that all of the overprints either are directly over the stamp or partly on the stamp. Envelopes which show overprints in various places other than on the stamp are freaks and command little or no premium value.

On 3¢ envelopes of 1916-50 issue.

Type 1 *surcharge - black overprint*

	UnFVF	UseFVF
EN618		
2¢ on 3¢ on white, Die A (EN584)	11.00	10.00
entire	16.00	12.00
EN619		
2¢ on 3¢ on white, Die E (EN591)	11.00	10.00
entire	14.00	12.00

1920. Type 2 Surcharge Revalued Envelopes

Type 2 *surcharge - rose overprint*

	UnFVF	UseFVF
EN620		
2¢ on 3¢ on white, Die A, (EN584)	7.00	6.00
entire	8.50	8.00
EN621		
2¢ on 3¢ on white, Die F (EN595)	7.00	6.00
entire	9.50	9.00
EN621A		
2¢ on 3¢ on white, Die A (EN549)	1,600.00	—
entire	—	—
EN621B		
2¢ on 3¢ on amber, Die A (EN550)	—	—
entire*	—	—
EN622		
2¢ on 3¢ on white, Die A (EN584)	2.50	2.00
entire	3.00	2.50
EN623		
2¢ on 3¢ on amber, Die A (EN585)	6.00	6.00
entire	7.00	7.00
EN624		
2¢ on 3¢ on buff, Die A (EN586)	15.00	13.00
entire	18.00	17.00
EN625		
2¢ on 3¢ on blue, Die A (EN587)	12.00	11.00
entire	13.00	11.00
EN626		
2¢ on 3¢ on white, Die E (EN591)	—	—
entire	—	—
EN627		
2¢ on 3¢ on amber, Die E (EN592)	—	—
entire	—	—
EN628		
2¢ on 3¢ on buff, Die E (EN593)	—	—
entire	—	—
EN629		
2¢ on 3¢ on blue, Die E (EN594)	—	—
entire	—	—
EN630		
2¢ on 3¢ on white, Die F (EN595)	—	—
entire	—	—
EN631		
2¢ on 3¢ on amber, Die F (EN596)	—	—
entire	—	—
EN632		
2¢ on 3¢ on buff, Die F (EN597)	—	—
entire	—	—
EN633		
2¢ on 3¢ on blue, Die F (EN598)	—	—
entire	—	—
EN634		
2¢ on 3¢ on white, Die H (EN599)	—	—
entire	—	—
EN635		
2¢ on 3¢ on amber, Die H (EN600)	—	—
entire	—	—
EN636		
2¢ on 3¢ on buff, Die H (EN601)	—	—
entire	—	—
EN637		
2¢ on 3¢ on blue, Die H (EN602)	—	—
entire	—	—

1920. Type 3 Surcharge Revalued Envelopes *On 4¢ brown envelope of 1899 issue.*

Type 3 *surcharge - black overprint*

	UnFVF	UseFVF
EN638A		
2¢ on 4¢ on white (EN413)	—	—
entire*	—	—

1920. Type 3 Surcharge Revalued Envelopes *On 4¢ brown envelope of 1903 issue.*

	UnFVF	UseFVF
EN639		
2¢ on 4¢ on white (EN429)	350.00	175.00
entire*	400.00	200.00

1920. Type 3 Surcharge Revalued Envelopes *On 4¢ brown envelope of 1899 issue.*

	UnFVF	UseFVF
EN640		
2¢ on 4¢ on amber (EN430)	350.00	125.00
entire*	400.00	175.00

1920. Type 3 Surcharge Revalued Envelopes *On envelopes of 1907-16 issue.*

	UnFVF	UseFVF
EN641		
2¢ on 1¢ on white, Die A (EN439)	21,700.00	—
entire	—	—
EN642		
2¢ on 2¢ on white, Die A (EN466)	900.00	—
entire	1,300.00	—
EN643		
2¢ on 2¢ on buff, Die A (EN468)	675.00	—
entire	775.00	—
EN644		
2¢ on 2¢ on white, Die C (EN488)	900.00	—
entire	1,300.00	—
EN645		
2¢ on 2¢ on buff, Die E (EN499)	700.00	550.00
entire	800.00	—
EN646		
2¢ on 2¢ on blue, Die E (EN500)	700.00	—
entire	800.00	—
EN647		
2¢ on 4¢ on white, Die B (EN511)	750.00	—
entire	825.00	—

1920. Type 3 Surcharge Revalued Envelopes *On 1¢ circular dies of 1916-50.*

EN648	UnFVF	UseFVF
2¢ on 1¢ on white, Die A (EN520)	900.00	—
entire	1,100.00	—

EN649	UnFVF	UseFVF
2¢ on 1¢ on white, Die C (EN531)	2,500.00	—
entire	3,250.00	—

1920. Type 3 Surcharge Revalued Envelopes *On 2¢ circular dies of 1916-1950.*

EN650	UnFVF	UseFVF
2¢ on 2¢ on white, Die A (EN549)	200.00	—
entire	250.00	—

EN651	UnFVF	UseFVF
2¢ on 2¢ on amber, Die A (EN550)	950.00	—
entire	1,300.00	—

EN652	UnFVF	UseFVF
2¢ on 2¢ on buff, Die B (EN558)	150.00	—
entire	185.00	—

EN653	UnFVF	UseFVF
2¢ on 2¢ on white, Die E (EN566)	300.00	—
entire	500.00	—

EN654	UnFVF	UseFVF
2¢ on 2¢ on buff, Die E (EN568)	275.00	—
entire	300.00	—

EN655	UnFVF	UseFVF
2¢ on 2¢ on blue, Die E (EN569)	275.00	—
entire	350.00	—

EN656	UnFVF	UseFVF
2¢ on 2¢ on white, Die F (EN570)	85.00	—
entire	160.00	—

EN657	UnFVF	UseFVF
2¢ on 2¢ on blue, Die F (EN573)	275.00	—
entire	300.00	—

EN658	UnFVF	UseFVF
2¢ on 2¢ on white, Die H (EN574)	—	—
entire	—	—

EN659	UnFVF	UseFVF
2¢ on 2¢ on buff, Die H (EN576)	275.00	—
entire	300.00	—

EN660	UnFVF	UseFVF
2¢ on 2¢ on blue, Die H (EN577)	500.00	—
entire	550.00	—

1920. Type 3 Surcharge Revalued Envelopes *On 3¢ circular dies of 1916-50.*

EN661	UnFVF	UseFVF
2¢ on 3¢ on white, Die A (EN584)	.50	.40
entire	.70	.50
v. Double overprint	15.00	8.00
entire	40.00	—
v1. Triple overprint	—	—
entire	35.00	—
v2. with added impression of 3¢ dark violet		

EN662	UnFVF	UseFVF
2¢ on 3¢ on amber, Die A (EN585)	3.00	1.50
entire	4.50	2.00
v. Double overprint	19.00	—
entire	—	—

EN663	UnFVF	UseFVF
2¢ on 3¢ on buff, Die A (EN586)	3.00	1.50
entire	3.50	1.50
v. Double overprint	13.00	—
entire	—	—
v1. Triple overprint	30.00	—
entire	—	—

EN664	UnFVF	UseFVF
2¢ on 3¢ on blue, Die A (EN587)	4.50	1.50
entire	6.00	2.00
v. Double overprint	16.00	—
entire	—	—

EN665	UnFVF	UseFVF
2¢ on 3¢ on white, Die E (EN591)	—	—
entire	—	—
v. Double overprint	—	—
entire	—	—
v1. Triple overprint	—	—
entire	—	—

EN666	UnFVF	UseFVF
2¢ on 3¢ on amber, Die E (EN592)	3.00	1.50
entire	4.50	2.00

EN667	UnFVF	UseFVF
2¢ on 3¢ on buff, Die E (EN593)	—	—
entire	—	—
v. Double overprint	—	—
entire	—	—

EN668	UnFVF	UseFVF
2¢ on 3¢ on blue, Die E (EN594)	4.25	1.00
entire	6.25	1.50
v. Double overprint	—	—
entire	12.50	—
v1. Triple overprint	—	—
entire	—	—

EN669	UnFVF	UseFVF
2¢ on 3¢ on white, Die F (EN595)	—	—
entire	—	—
v. Double overprint	—	—
entire	—	—

EN670	UnFVF	UseFVF
2¢ on 3¢ on amber, Die F (EN596)	—	—
entire	—	—
v. Double overprint	—	—
entire	—	—
v1. Triple overprint	—	—
entire	—	—

EN671	UnFVF	UseFVF
2¢ on 3¢ on buff, Die F (EN597)	—	—
entire	—	—

EN672	UnFVF	UseFVF
2¢ on 3¢ on blue, Die F (EN598)	—	—
entire	—	—

EN673	UnFVF	UseFVF
2¢ on 3¢ on white, Die H (EN599)	—	—
entire	—	—
v. Double overprint	—	—
entire	—	—
v1. Triple overprint	—	—
entire	—	—

EN674	UnFVF	UseFVF
2¢ on 3¢ on amber, Die H (EN600)	—	—
entire	—	—
v. Double overprint	—	—
entire	—	—
v1. Triple overprint	—	—
entire	—	—

EN675	UnFVF	UseFVF
2¢ on 3¢ on blue, Die H (EN602)	—	—
entire	—	—

1920. Type 3 Surcharge Revalued Envelopes *On 5¢ circular dies of 1916-50.*

EN676	UnFVF	UseFVF
2¢ on 5¢ on white (EN612)	900.00	—
entire	1,100.00	—

1920. Type 3 Surcharge Revalued Envelopes Type 3 over Type 7a - black overprint.
On 3¢ circular dies of 1916-50.

EN677	UnFVF	UseFVF
2¢ on 3¢ on white, Die F (EN595)	—	—
entire	—	—

1920. Type 4 Surcharge Revalued Envelopes *On 2¢ circular dies of 1874-76.*

Type 4 surcharge - black overprint.

EN678	UnFVF	UseFVF
2¢ on 3¢ on white (EN187)	225.00	
entire*	275.00	—

1920. Type 4 Surcharge Revalued Envelopes *On 4¢ brown envelopes of 1903 issue.*

EN679	UnFVF	UseFVF
2¢ on 4¢ on white (EN429)	12.00	9.00
entire*	25.00	15.00
v. Double overprint	40.00	—
entire*	—	—

EN680	UnFVF	UseFVF
2¢ on 4¢ on amber (EN430)	14.00	10.00
entire	22.00	13.00

1920. Type 4 Surcharge Revalued Envelopes On 2¢ carmine envelope of 1907-16 issue.

EN681	UnFVF	UseFVF
2¢ on 2¢ on white, Die E (EN497)	3,000.00	—
entire	3,700.00	—

1920. Type 4 Surcharge Revalued Envelopes *On 1¢ circular dies of 1916-21.*

EN682	UnFVF	UseFVF
2¢ on 1¢ on white, Die A (EN520)	750.00	—
entire	950.00	—

EN683	UnFVF	UseFVF
2¢ on 1¢ on white, Die C (EN531)	1,400.00	—
entire	2,250.00	

1920. Type 4 Surcharge Revalued Envelopes On 2¢ circular dies of 1874-76.

EN684	UnFVF	UseFVF
2¢ on 2¢ on white, Die A (EN549)	225.00	—
entire	275.00	—

1920. Type 4 Surcharge Revalued Envelopes On 2¢ circular dies of 1916-50.

EN685	UnFVF	UseFVF
2¢ on 2¢ on amber, Die A (EN550)	1,750.00	—
entire	2,000.00	—

EN686	UnFVF	UseFVF
2¢ on 2¢ on white, Die E (EN566)	375.00	—
entire	—	—

EN687	UnFVF	UseFVF
2¢ on 2¢ on white, Die H (EN574)	1,000.00	—
entire	1,500.00	—

1920. Type 4 Surcharge Revalued Envelopes On 3¢ circular dies of 1916-50.

EN688	UnFVF	UseFVF
2¢ on 3¢ on white, Die A (EN584)	.70	.50
entire	.90	.80
v. Double overprint	16.00	—
entire	—	—
v1. Triple overprint	25.00	—
entire	—	—

EN689	UnFVF	UseFVF
2¢ on 3¢ on amber, Die A (EN585)	3.25	2.00
entire	5.00	3.00
v. Double overprint	—	—
entire	—	—

EN690	UnFVF	UseFVF
2¢ on 3¢ on buff, Die A (EN586)	5.00	3.00
entire	7.00	5.00
v. Double overprint	20.00	—
entire	—	—

EN691	UnFVF	UseFVF
2¢ on 3¢ on blue, Die A (EN587)	3.50	1.50
entire	10.00	4.00
v. Double overprint	20.00	—
entire	—	—

1920. Type 4 Surcharge Revalued Envelopes *On Die E.*

EN692	UnFVF	UseFVF
2¢ on 3¢ on white (EN591)	—	—
entire	—	—
v. Double overprint	—	—
entire	—	—

EN693	UnFVF	UseFVF
2¢ on 3¢ on amber (EN592)	—	—
entire	—	—

EN694	UnFVF	UseFVF
2¢ on 3¢ on buff (EN593)	—	—
entire	—	—

EN695	UnFVF	UseFVF
2¢ on 3¢ on blue (EN594)	—	—
entire	—	—
v. Double overprint	—	—
entire	—	—

1920. Type 4 Surcharge Revalued Envelopes *On Die F.*

EN696	UnFVF	UseFVF
2¢ on 3¢ on white (EN595)	—	—
entire	—	—
v. Double overprint	—	—
entire	—	—

EN697	UnFVF	UseFVF
2¢ on 3¢ on amber (EN596)	—	—
entire	—	—
v. Double overprint	—	—
entire	—	—

EN698	UnFVF	UseFVF
2¢ on 3¢ on buff (EN597)	—	—
entire	—	—

EN699	UnFVF	UseFVF
2¢ on 3¢ on blue (EN598)	—	—
entire	—	—

1920. Type 4 Surcharge Revalued Envelope *On Die H.*

EN700	UnFVF	UseFVF
2¢ on 3¢ on white (EN599)	—	—
entire	—	—
v. Double overprint	—	—
entire	—	—

EN701	UnFVF	UseFVF
2¢ on 3¢ on amber (EN600)	—	—
entire	—	—

EN702	UnFVF	UseFVF
2¢ on 3¢ on buff (EN601)	—	—
entire	—	—

EN703	UnFVF	UseFVF
2¢ on 3¢ on blue (EN602)	—	—
entire	—	—

1920. Type 4 over Type 7A Surcharge Revalued Envelopes Black overprints.
On 3¢ circular dies of 1916-50.

EN704	UnFVF	UseFVF
2¢ on 3¢ on white, Die A (EN584)	—	—
entire	—	—

EN705	UnFVF	UseFVF
2¢ on 3¢ on amber, Die A (EN585)	—	—
entire	—	—

EN706	UnFVF	UseFVF
2¢ on 3¢ on white, Die E (EN591)	325.00	—
entire	450.00	—

EN707	UnFVF	UseFVF
2¢ on 3¢ on white, Die H (EN599)	750.00	—
entire	900.00	—

1920. Type 4 over Type 2 Surcharge Revalued Envelopes Black overprints.
On 3¢ circular dies of 1916-50.
On Die A.

EN708	UnFVF	UseFVF
2¢ on 3¢ on white (EN584)	75.00	—
entire	—	—

EN709	UnFVF	UseFVF
2¢ on 3¢ on amber (EN585)	60.00	—
entire	—	—

EN710	UnFVF	UseFVF
2¢ on 3¢ on buff (EN586)	60.00	—
entire	—	—

EN711	UnFVF	UseFVF
2¢ on 3¢ on blue (EN587)	180.00	—
entire	—	—

1920. Type 4 over Type 2 Surcharge Revalued Envelopes
On Die E.

EN712	UnFVF	UseFVF
2¢ on 3¢ on amber (EN592)	—	—
entire	—	—

EN713	UnFVF	UseFVF
2¢ on 3¢ on buff (EN593)	—	—
entire	—	—

EN714	UnFVF	UseFVF
2¢ on 3¢ on blue (EN594)	—	—
entire	—	—

1920. Type 4 over Type E Surcharge Revalued Envelopes
On Die F.

EN715	UnFVF	UseFVF
2¢ on 3¢ on buff (EN597)	—	—
entire	—	—

EN716	UnFVF	UseFVF
2¢ on 3¢ on blue (EN598)	—	—
entire	—	—

EN717	UnFVF	UseFVF
2¢ on 3¢ on white, Die H (EN599)	—	—
entire	—	—

1920. Type 4 over Type 3 Surcharge Revalued Envelopes
Black overprints.
On 3¢ circular dies of 1916-50.
On Die A.

EN718	UnFVF	UseFVF
2¢ on 3¢ on white (EN584)	—	—
entire	—	—

EN719	UnFVF	UseFVF
2¢ on 3¢ on amber (EN585)	—	—
entire	—	—

EN720	UnFVF	UseFVF
2¢ on 3¢ on buff (EN586)	—	—
entire	—	—

EN721	UnFVF	UseFVF
2¢ on 3¢ on blue (EN587)	—	—
entire	—	—

1920. Type 4 over Type 3 Surcharge Revalued Envelopes
On Die E.

EN722	UnFVF	UseFVF
2¢ on 3¢ on amber (EN592)	—	—
entire	—	—

EN723	UnFVF	UseFVF
2¢ on 3¢ on buff (EN593)	—	—
entire	—	—

EN724	UnFVF	UseFVF
2¢ on 3¢ on blue (EN594)	—	—
entire	—	—

EN725	UnFVF	UseFVF
2¢ on 3¢ on blue, Die F (EN598)	—	—
entire	—	—

EN726	UnFVF	UseFVF
2¢ on 3¢ on white, Die H (EN599)	—	—
entire	—	—

1920. Type 5 Surcharge Revalued Envelopes *On 3¢ circular dies of 1916-50.*

2

Type 5 *surcharge - black overprint*

EN727	UnFVF	UseFVF
2¢ on 3¢ on amber, Die A (EN585)	100.00	—
entire	130.00	—

EN728	UnFVF	UseFVF
2¢ on 3¢ on amber, Die F (EN596)	—	—
entire	—	—

1920. Type 6 Surcharge Revalued Envelopes *On 3¢ circular dies of 1916-50.*
On Die A.

2 Type 6 *surcharge - black overprint*

EN729	UnFVF	UseFVF
2¢ on 3¢ on white (EN584)	100.00	—
entire	130.00	—
x. Double overprint	—	—
entire	—	—

EN730	UnFVF	UseFVF
2¢ on 3¢ on amber (EN585)	200.00	—
entire	220.00	—

EN731	UnFVF	UseFVF
2¢ on 3¢ on white, Die E (EN591)	—	—
entire	—	—

EN732	UnFVF	UseFVF
2¢ on 3¢ on white, Die F (EN595)	—	—
entire	—	—

EN733	UnFVF	UseFVF
2¢ on 3¢ on white, Die H (EN599)	—	—
entire	—	—

1920. Type 7 Surcharge Revalued Envelopes *On 3¢ circular dies of 1916-50.*

2 Type 7 *surcharge - black overprint*

EN734	UnFVF	UseFVF
2¢ on 3¢ on white, Die A (EN584)	275.00	—
entire	325.00	—

EN735	UnFVF	UseFVF
2¢ on 3¢ on white, Die E (EN591)	—	—
entire	—	—

EN736	UnFVF	UseFVF
2¢ on 3¢ on white, Die H (EN599)	—	—
entire	—	—

1920. Type 7A Surcharge Revalued Envelopes Type 7 - violet overprint.

1 CENT

Type 7A *surcharge - violet overprint*

EN737	UnFVF	UseFVF
2¢ on 3¢ on white, Die H (EN599)	200.00	—
entire	225.00	—

1920. Type 7A Surcharge Revalued Envelopes *On 2¢ circular dies of 1916-50.*

EN738	UnFVF	UseFVF
1¢ on 2¢ on white, Die A (EN549)	—	—
entire	—	—

EN739	UnFVF	UseFVF
1¢ on 2¢ on white, Die H (EN574)	—	—
entire	—	—

1920. Type 7A Surcharge Revalued Envelopes *On 3¢ circular dies of 1916-50.*

EN740	UnFVF	UseFVF
1¢ on 3¢ on white, Die E (EN591)	200.00	—
entire	225.00	—
v1. with added 2¢ Type 4 surcharge (error)	—	—

1925. Type 8 Surcharge Revalued Envelopes *On 2¢ green envelopes of 1887 issue.*

1½

Type 8 *surcharge - black overprint*

EN741	UnFVF	UseFVF
1-1/2¢ on 2¢ on white (EN344)	600.00	—
entire	650.00	—

EN742	UnFVF	UseFVF
1-1/2¢ on 2¢ on amber (EN345)	700.00	—
entire	800.00	—

1925. Type 8 Surcharge Revalued Envelopes *On 1¢ green envelopes of 1899 issue.*

EN743	UnFVF	UseFVF
1-1/2¢ on 1¢ on white (EN391)	350.00	—
entire	650.00	—

EN744	UnFVF	UseFVF
1-1/2¢ on 1¢ on amber (EN392)	75.00	65.00
entire	120.00	100.00

1925. Type 8 Surcharge Revalued Envelopes *On 1¢ green envelopes of 1907-16. On Die A.*

	UnFVF	UseFVF
EN745		
1-1/2¢ on 1¢ on white (EN439)	5.00	4.00
entire	6.00	6.00
EN746		
1-1/2¢ on 1¢ on amber (EN440)	8.00	3.00
entire	12.00	7.00
EN747		
1-1/2¢ on 1¢ on manila (EN443)	200.00	75.00
entire	250.00	100.00

1925. Type 8 Surcharge Revalued Envelopes *On Die B.*

	UnFVF	UseFVF
EN748		
1-1/2¢ on 1¢ on white (EN445)	13.00	10.00
entire	15.00	13.00
EN749		
1-1/2¢ on 1¢ on amber (EN446)	80.00	70.00
entire	200.00	90.00
EN750		
1-1/2¢ on 1¢ on buff (EN447)	200.00	100.00
entire	225.00	110.00
EN751		
1-1/2¢ on 1¢ on blue (EN448)	75.00	55.00
entire	100.00	65.00

1925. Type 8 Surcharge Revalued Envelopes *On Die C.*

	UnFVF	UseFVF
EN751A		
1-1/2¢ on 1¢ on white (EN450)	7.00	3.00
entire	9.00	5.00
EN751B		
1-1/2¢ on 1¢ on amber (EN450)	4.50	2.50
entire*	8.00	5.00
EN751C		
1-1/2¢ on 1¢ on manila (EN454)	—	—
entire	—	—

1925. Type 8 Surcharge Revalued Envelopes *On Die D.*

	UnFVF	UseFVF
EN752		
1-1/2¢ on 1¢ on white (EN456)	—	—
entire	—	—
EN753		
1-1/2¢ on 1¢ on amber (EN457)	4.50	2.50
entire	8.00	5.00
EN754		
1-1/2¢ on 1¢ on buff (EN458)	75.00	55.00
entire	100.00	65.00
EN755		
1-1/2¢ on 1¢ on blue (EN459)	—	—
entire	—	—

1925. Type 8 Surcharge Revalued Envelopes *On 1¢ circular dies of 1916-50.*

Die A.

	UnFVF	UseFVF
EN756		
1-1/2¢ on 1¢ on white (EN520)	.35	.30
entire	.60	.50
v. Double overprint	5.00	2.50
entire	—	—
EN757		
1-1/2¢ on 1¢ on amber (EN521)	14.00	13.00
entire	21.00	16.00
EN758		
1-1/2¢ on 1¢ on buff (EN522)	4.00	2.50
entire	6.00	2.75
EN759		
1-1/2¢ on 1¢ on blue (EN523)	1.25	1.00
entire	2.50	1.50
EN760		
1-1/2¢ on 1¢ on manila (EN524)	11.00	7.00
entire	16.00	8.00
EN761		
1-1/2¢ on 1¢ on brown (glazed) (EN526)	60.00	30.00
entire	70.00	40.00
EN762		
1-1/2¢ on 1¢ on brown (unglazed) (EN528)	60.00	35.00
entire	70.00	40.00

1925. Type 8 Surcharge Revalued Envelopes *On Die B.*

	UnFVF	UseFVF
EN762A		
1-1/2¢ on 1¢ on white (EN529)	2.00	.75
entire	—	—

1925. Type 8 Surcharge Revalued Envelopes *On Die C.*

	UnFVF	UseFVF
EN763		
1-1/2¢ on 1¢ on white (EN531)	2.00	1.00
entire	—	—
x. Double overprint	—	—
entire	—	—
EN764		
1-1/2¢ on 1¢ on blue (EN533)	—	—
entire	—	—

1925. Type 8 Surcharge Revalued Envelopes *On Die D.*

	UnFVF	UseFVF
EN765		
1-1/2¢ on 1¢ on white (EN534)	—	—
entire	—	—
x. Double overprint	—	—
entire	—	—
EN766		
1-1/2¢ on 1¢ on amber (EN535)	—	—
entire	—	—
EN767		
1-1/2¢ on 1¢ on blue (EN537)	—	—
entire	—	—
x. Double overprint	—	—
entire	—	—

1925. Type 8 Surcharge Revalued Envelopes *On 1 1/2¢ circular dies of 1916-50.*

	UnFVF	UseFVF
EN768		
1-1/2¢ on 1 1/2¢ on white, Die A (EN541)	400.00	—
entire	475.00	—
EN769		
1-1/2¢ on 1 1/2¢ on blue, Die H2 (EN548)	350.00	—
entire	400.00	—

1925. Type 8 Surcharge Revalued Envelopes *On 2¢ circular dies of 1916-50.*

	UnFVF	UseFVF
EN770		
1-1/2¢ on 2¢ on white, Die A (EN549)	250.00	—
entire*	300.00	—
EN771		
1-1/2¢ on 2¢ on buff, Die E (EN568)	275.00	—
entire	300.00	—
EN772		
1-1/2¢ on 2¢ on blue, Die F (EN573)	250.00	—
entire	300.00	—

1925. Type 9 Surcharge Revalued Envelopes *On 1¢ blue envelope of 1887 issue.*

Type 9 *surcharge - black overprint*

	UnFVF	UseFVF
EN773		
1-1/2¢ on 1¢ on white (EN321)	1,000.00	—
entire	1,200.00	—

1925. Type 9 Surcharge Revalued Envelopes *On 1¢ green envelope of 1899.*

	UnFVF	UseFVF
EN774		
1-1/2¢ on 1¢ on amber (EN392)	60.00	—
entire	70.00	—

1925. Type 9 Surcharge Revalued Envelopes *On 1¢ green envelopes of 1903 issue.*

	UnFVF	UseFVF
EN775		
1-1/2¢ on 1¢ on white (EN418)	1,500.00	—
entire	2,400.00	—
EN776		
1-1/2¢ on 1¢ on amber (EN419)	14.00	12.00
entire	25.00	17.00
x. Double overprint	27.00	—
entire	33.00	—
EN777		
1-1/2¢ on 1¢ on buff (EN420)	60.00	50.00
entire	70.00	60.00

1925. Type 9 Surcharge Revalued Envelopes *On 1¢ oval dies of 1907-16.*

On Die A.

	UnFVF	UseFVF
EN778		
1-1/2¢ on 1¢ on white (EN439)	2.00	1.50
entire	3.50	2.00
x. Double overprint	8.00	—
entire	—	—
EN779		
1-1/2¢ on 1¢ on amber (EN440)	175.00	80.00
entire	200.00	100.00
EN780		
1-1/2¢ on 1¢ on buff (EN441)	7.00	5.00
entire	12.00	7.00
x. Double overprint	—	—
entire	—	—
EN781		
1-1/2¢ on 1¢ on blue (EN442)	6.00	3.00
entire	8.00	5.00
EN782		
1-1/2¢ on 1¢ on manila (EN443)	25.00	11.00
entire	35.00	25.00
EN783		
1-1/2¢ on 1¢ on white, Die B (EN445)	7.00	5.00

1925. Type 9 Surcharge Revalued Envelopes *On Die C.*

	UnFVF	UseFVF
EN784		
1-1/2¢ on 1¢ on white (EN450)	17.00	9.00
entire	25.00	13.00
EN785		
1-1/2¢ on 1¢ on manila (EN454)	55.00	40.00
entire	60.00	50.00

1925. Type 9 Surcharge Revalued Envelopes *On Die D.*

	UnFVF	UseFVF
EN786		
1-1/2¢ on 1¢ on white (EN456)	4.00	1.50
entire	7.00	3.00
EN787		
1-1/2¢ on 1¢ on buff (EN458)	18.00	15.00
entire	25.00	19.00
EN788		
1-1/2¢ on 1¢ on blue (EN459)	6.00	5.00
entire	8.00	6.00

1925. Type 9 Surcharge Revalued Envelopes *On 1¢ circular dies of 1916-50.*

On Die A.

	UnFVF	UseFVF
EN789		
1-1/2¢ on 1¢ on white (EN520)	.40	.30
entire	.70	.40
x. Double overprint	7.00	—
entire	—	—
x1. Triple overprint	13.00	—
entire	—	—
x2. Inverted overprint	11.00	—
entire	—	—
EN790		
1-1/2¢ on 1¢ on amber (EN521)	50.00	35.00
entire	60.00	45.00
EN791		
1-1/2¢ on 1¢ on buff (EN522)	5.00	2.00
entire	6.00	2.00
EN792		
1-1/2¢ on 1¢ on blue (EN523)	5.00	2.00
entire	6.00	2.00
x. Double overprint	11.00	—
entire	—	—
EN793		
1-1/2¢ on 1¢ on manila (EN524)	20.00	12.00
entire	28.00	15.00
EN794		
1-1/2¢ on 1¢ on white, Die B (EN529)	—	—
entire	—	—

1925. Type 9 Surcharge Revalued Envelopes *On Die C.*

	UnFVF	UseFVF
EN795		
1-1/2¢ on 1¢ on white (EN531)	—	—
entire	—	—
x. Double overprint	—	—
entire	—	—
EN796		
1-1/2¢ on 1¢ on blue (EN533)	—	—
entire	—	—

1925. Type 9 Surcharge Revalued Envelopes *On Die D.*

	UnFVF	UseFVF
EN797		
1-1/2¢ on 1¢ on white (EN534)	—	—
entire	—	—
x. inverted overprint	—	—
entire	—	—
EN798		
1-1/2¢ on 1¢ on amber (EN535)	—	—
entire	—	—
EN799		
1-1/2¢ on 1¢ on buff (EN536)	—	—
entire	—	—
EN800		
1-1/2¢ on 1¢ on blue (EN537)	—	—
entire	—	—

1925. Type 9 Surcharge Revalued Envelopes *On 2¢ carmine envelopes of 1916-50 issue.*

	UnFVF	UseFVF
EN801		
1-1/2¢ on 2¢ on white, Die A (EN549)	175.00	
entire	225.00	—
EN801A		
1-1/2¢ on 2¢ on white, Die E (EN566)	—	—
entire	—	—
EN801B		
1-1/2¢ on 2¢ on amber, Die E (EN567)	—	—
entire	—	—
EN802		
1-1/2¢ on 2¢ on white, Die F (EN570)	—	—
entire	—	—
EN803		
1-1/2¢ on 2¢ on white, Die H (EN574)	—	—
entire	—	—

1925. Type 9 Surcharge Revalued Envelopes Type 9 - magenta overprint *on 1¢ green envelope of 1916-50 issue.*

	UnFVF	UseFVF
EN804		
1-1/2¢ on 1¢ on white (EN531)	5.00	4.00
entire	5.00	6.00
x. Double overprint	30.00	—
entire	—	—

1925. Type 10 Surcharge Revalued Envelopes *On 1¢ circular dies of 1916-50.*

½c Paid
Santa Rosa, Cal.

Type 10 *surcharge - black overprint*

	UnFVF	UseFVF
EN805		
1¢ + 1/2¢ on white (EN520)	—	—
entire	—	—

1926. Sesquicentennial Exposition Envelope

EN806 *Liberty Bell, Center bar of "E" of "POSTAGE" shorter than top bar. Watermark 27 (1925).*

		UnFVF	UseFVF
EN806			
2¢	**carmine on white**	2.00	1.00
	entire	2.75	1.75

EN807 *The center bar of "E" in "POSTAGE" is the same length as top bar.*

		UnFVF	UseFVF
EN807			
2¢	**carmine on white**	10.00	7.00
	entire	12.50	10.00
	FDC *(July 27, 1926)*		30.00

1932. Washington Bicentennial Issue

EN808-EN813 *Mount Vernon. All of the same design; only the denomination changes. Watermark 29 (1929).*

		UnFVF	UseFVF
EN808			
1¢	**green on white** *(Jan. 1, 1932)*	2.00	1.50
	entire	2.50	1.75
EN809		UnFVF	UseFVF
1-1/2¢	**brown on white** *(Jan. 1, 1932)*	3.50	2.00
	entire	3.75	2.75
EN810		UnFVF	UseFVF
2¢	**carmine on white** *(Jan. 1, 1932)*	.50	.25
	entire	.75	.30
	a. carmine on blue (error), entire	27,000.00	—
	v. "S" of "POSTAGE" high	—	—
	entire	90.00	50.00
EN811		UnFVF	UseFVF
3¢	**purple on white** *(June 16, 1932)*	2.50	.30
	entire	4.00	.50
EN812		UnFVF	UseFVF
4¢	**black on white** *(Jan. 1, 1932)*	25.00	20.00
	entire*	30.00	25.00
EN813		UnFVF	UseFVF
5¢	**blue on white** *(Jan. 1, 1932)*	6.00	4.00
	entire	6.50	5.50

1950. Issue New Oval Design. As far back as 1941, the Post Office had submitted new designs for its envelope stamps and had ordered the necessary new printing dies to be made. The outbreak of World War II interfered with plans for the new design, and the new printing dies were not put into use. After the war, collectors brought ever-increasing pressure to bear on the Post Office Department to change the circular design, which was well into a third decade of use.

In 1950 the Post Office determined to put some of the printing dies that had been prepared in 1941 into production and ordered 1¢, 2¢ and 3¢ envelopes printed on a demonstration machine at the annual stamp exhibition sponsored by the American Stamp Dealers Association in New York. Only a very few of the old dies were found to be usable in the more modern machines then in use. However, at least one printing die in each denomination was put into use, and the envelopes were then printed and sold at the ASDA stamp show.

New printing dies immediately were developed so that the new design could replace completely the old design. These first-printed envelopes are in very short supply. *These envelopes were issued on white paper only.*

EN814 *Franklin. Die A, thick, short, "1" within heavy circle.*

		UnFVF	UseFVF
EN814			
1¢	**green,** Die A *(Nov. 16, 1950)*	6.00	2.00
	entire*	8.00	3.00

EN815 *Die B, thin, long "1" within thin circle, "E" in "ONE" has long bars and is close. (1mm) to circle.*

		UnFVF	UseFVF
EN815			
1¢	**green,** Die B	7.00	4.00
	entire	9.00	4.50

EN816 *Die C, thin long "1." "E" in "ONE" with short bars and far (1 1/2mm) from circle.*

		UnFVF	UseFVF
EN816			
1¢	**green,** Die C	7.00	4.00
	entire	9.00	4.50
	v. precanceled, entire	1.00	1.00

EN817 *Washington*

		UnFVF	UseFVF
EN817			
1-1/2¢	**brown**	5.00	4.00
	entire	6.00	5.00
	v. precanceled, entire	1.25	1.25

EN818 *Washington. Die A, figure "2" set low in heavy circle.*

		UnFVF	UseFVF
EN818			
2¢	**carmine,** Die A *(Nov. 17, 1950)*	.80	.35
	entire*	1.50	.50

EN818A *Die B, thin "2" with long hook. Center cross bar of "E" in "STATES" shorter than top or bottom bars.*

		UnFVF	UseFVF
EN818A			
2¢	**carmine,** Die B	1.50	1.00
	entire	2.00	1.10

EN819 *Die C, thin "2" set high in thin circle.*

		UnFVF	UseFVF
EN819			
2¢	**carmine,** Die C	.80	.30
	entire		

EN819A *Washington. Die D, thick cross bar in "A" of "STATES."*

		UnFVF	UseFVF
EN819A			
2¢	**carmine,** Die D	1.50	.70
	entire	1.60	.70

EN820 *Die A, tall, thick "3" within thick circle. Narrow "Es" in "THREE."*

		UnFVF	UseFVF
EN820			
3¢	**purple,** Die A *(Nov. 18, 1950)*	2.25	.85
	entire*	.30	1.50

EN821 *Die B, tall, thin, "3" in thin circle. Narrow "Es" in "THREE."*

EN821		UnFVF	UseFVF
3¢	**purple,** Die B *(Nov. 19, 1950)*	.85	.60
	entire*	1.60	.65

EN822 *Die C, short "3" in thin circle. Wide "Es" in "THREE." Line from left stand of "N" in "UNITED" to stand in "E" in "POSTAGE" well below chin.*

EN822		UnFVF	UseFVF
3¢	**purple,** Die C	.60	.35
	entire	1.00	.50

EN823 *Die D, short "3" in thin circle. Wide "Es" in "THREE." Line from left stand of "N" in "UNITED" to stand of "E" in "POSTAGE" almost touches chin. "N" in "UNITED" short; thin cross bar in "A" in "STATES."*

EN823		UnFVF	UseFVF
3¢	**purple,** Die D	.50	.25
	entire	.65	.30

EN824 *Die E, similar to EN823 except "N" in "UNITED" tall, and thick cross bar in "A" in "STATES."*

EN824		UnFVF	UseFVF
3¢	**purple,** Die E	.90	.50
	entire	1.35	.75

1958. Issue On Aug. 1, 1958, First Class postage rates were raised to 4¢. This necessitated new 4¢ stamped envelopes. In addition, to use up surplus stocks of 2¢ and 3¢ envelopes, the Post Office Department again revalued existing stocks.

EN825 *Franklin. Die A, head high in oval. Circle around "4" low (1mm from outer edge of color). Watermarks 46, 47, 48.*

EN825		UnFVF	UseFVF
4¢	**lilac,** Die A *(Aug. 1, 1958)*	.90	.25
	entire	1.00	.30

EN826 *Die B, head low in oval. Circle around "4" high (1 1/2mm from outer edge of color). To verify: right leg of "A" in "POSTAGE" shorter than left leg. Short leg on "P."*

EN826		UnFVF	UseFVF
4¢	**lilac,** Die B	1.10	.25
	entire	1.40	.35

EN827 *Die C, head centered in oval. Circle around "4" high as on Die B. To verify: legs of "A" in "POSTAGE" are about equal in length. Long leg on "P."*

EN827		UnFVF	UseFVF
4¢	**lilac,** Die C	1.25	.25
	entire	1.40	.35

1958. Type 11 Surcharge Revalued Envelopes

Type 11 *surcharge - overprint in green to left of stamp. On 3¢ purple of 1916-50 issue.*

EN828		UnFVF	UseFVF
3¢ + 1¢	**purple,** Die A (EN588)	15.00	11.00
	entire	16.00	—
EN829		**UnFVF**	**UseFVF**
3¢ + 1¢	**purple,** Die H (EN603)	12.00	10.00
	entire	15.00	—
EN830		**UnFVF**	**UseFVF**
3¢ + 1¢	**purple,** Die I (EN606)	35.00	20.00
	entire	40.00	—

1958. Type 11 Surcharge Revalued Envelopes *On 3¢ purple of 1950.*

EN831		UnFVF	UseFVF
3¢ + 1¢	**purple,** Die B (EN821)	—	—
	entire	1,100.00	—
EN832		**UnFVF**	**UseFVF**
3¢ + 1¢	**purple,** Die C (EN822)	.60	.25
	entire	.70	.35
EN833		**UnFVF**	**UseFVF**
3¢ + 1¢	**purple,** Die D (EN823)	.85	.25
	entire	1.00	.25
	quintuple surcharge		
EN834		**UnFVF**	**UseFVF**
3¢ + 1¢	**purple,** Die E (EN824)	.85	.25
	entire	1.10	.25

1958. Type 12 Surcharge Revalued Envelopes *On 2¢ circular dies of 1916-1950.*

Type 12 *surcharge - overprint in red to left of stamp.*

EN835		UnFVF	UseFVF
2¢ + 2¢	**carmine,** Die A (EN549)	4.00	2.00
	entire	4.50	—
	double surcharge		
EN836		**UnFVF**	**UseFVF**
2¢ + 2¢	**carmine,** Die H (EN574)	11.00	8.00
	entire	13.00	—
EN837		**UnFVF**	**UseFVF**
2¢ + 2¢	**carmine,** Die I (EN581)	6.00	6.00
	entire	7.50	—

1958. Type 12 Surcharge Revalued Envelopes *On 2¢ oval die of 1950.*

EN838		UnFVF	UseFVF
2¢ + 2¢	**carmine,** Die A (EN818)	.90	.40
	entire	1.10	.50
EN839		**UnFVF**	**UseFVF**
2¢ + 2¢	**carmine,** Die B (EN818A)	1.10	—
	entire	1.50	—
EN840		**UnFVF**	**UseFVF**
2¢ + 2¢	**carmine,** Die C (EN819)	.90	.35
	entire	1.10	—

EN841

		UnFVF	UseFVF
2¢ + 2¢	**carmine,** Die D (EN819A)	.90	—
	entire	1.25	—

1960. Issue Effective July 1, 1960, the Third Class postage rate for bulk mailing was raised to 2 1/2¢ for commercial users and 1 1/4¢ for non-profit organizations. These envelopes are available only precanceled and were sold only to holders of proper permits. The small size of each (No. 6 3/4), however, were made available to collectors at COMPEX in Chicago (commercial rate) and DIXIPEX in Birmingham, Ala. (non-profit rate), and were on sale at the Philatelic Agency until Dec. 31, 1960. These unprecanceled envelopes have gum on the top back flap, and the precanceled envelopes are without such gum.

EN842 *Washington*

EN842

		UnFVF	UseFVF
2-1/2¢	**blue on white** *(May 28, 1960)*	.90	.60
	entire	1.00	.70
	v. precanceled	.25	.25
	entire	.30	.30

EN843 *Die A, small "1 1/4." 2 1/4mm across bar of "4." Leaf cluster 2mm under "U."*

EN843

		UnFVF	UseFVF
1-1/4¢	**turquoise on white,** Die A *(June 25, 1960)*	.85	.60
	entire*	1.00	.65
	v. precanceled	.25	.25
	entire	.25	.25

EN843A *Die B, large "1 1/4." 2 3/4mm across bar of "4." Leaf cluster 1mm under "U."*

EN843A

		UnFVF	UseFVF
1-1/4¢	**turquoise on white**		2.00
	precanceled	3.00	3.00
	entire	3.50	3.50

EN844 *Pony Express Rider. Watermark 46.*

EN844

		UnFVF	UseFVF
4¢	**brown on white,** blue inside *(July 19, 1960)*	.65	.35
	entire	.85	.50

1963. Issue Effective Jan. 7, 1963, First Class postage rates were raised to 5¢. A new stamped envelope was prepared showing a bust of Lincoln. However, a sufficient number of working dies were unable to be delivered to service all of the machines at the factory. Hence the factory was authorized to continue printing 4¢ stamped envelopes and revalue them to 5¢. This was accomplished by using the Type 11 surcharge printed in green to the left of the stamp. The revaluing was done on unfolded envelope blanks on the regular printing machines at the factory. These blanks were then passed to another machine, which printed the 4¢ stamps and folded the envelopes. At least two different dies were used to print the added 1¢ value.

While the effective date for the new postage rates was not until Jan. 7, 1963, the Post Office made the new envelopes available as rapidly as they could be supplied. The authorized first day of issue for the 5¢ Lincoln envelope was Nov. 19, 1962. No announcement was made regarding the 4¢ revalued envelopes, but they began making their appearance at post offices in December 1962.

All of these new envelopes are known with *watermarks 47 and 48.*

Note: EN846v and EN847v are the result of using the O'Connell machines to fold blanks on which the stamps already had been printed by the Huckins (Die B) and Harris (Die C) machines, which were incapable of folding. To accomplish the folding operation, the ink fountains were removed from some of the O'Connell machines still idle for lack of working dies of the 5¢ stamp. By error, the old 4¢ die was not removed on at least one of the O'Connell machines, and this caused an albino impression of the 4¢ stamp to be printed over the 5¢ stamp. The error was not discovered until the O'Connell machine(s) had been performing the folding operation for some time.

EN845 *Abraham Lincoln. Die A, figure "5" centered in circle. Middle bar of "E" in "FIVE" equal length as top. Center bar in "E" in "POSTAGE" off center to top. Verification: small head, sharp pointed nose. Watermarks 47, 48.*

Watermark 47. Beginning in May 1961, a new watermark was introduced to mark the letting of the new contract. Two types were adopted: a star preceding the letters "USA" for paper manufactured by the International Paper Co. (wmk. 47); star following the letters "USA" (wmk. 48) for paper manufactured by the Howard Paper Co.

EN845

		UnFVF	UseFVF
5¢	**dark blue,** Die A	1.00	.35
	entire	1.00	.35

EN846 *Die B, "5" centered in circle. "FI" in "FIVE" close together. "C" in "CENTS" higher than "E." Verification: large wide head with blunt nose.*

EN846

		UnFVF	UseFVF
5¢	**dark blue,** Die B	.75	.25
	entire	1.00	.30
	v. with albino impression of 4¢, entire	75.00	—

EN847 *Die C, "5" to right in circle. Short leg on "P" in "POSTAGE."*

EN847

		UnFVF	UseFVF
5¢	**dark blue,** Die C *(Nov. 19, 1962)*	1.00	.40
	entire	1.25	.50
	v. with albino impression of 4¢, entire	75.00	—

1963. Type 11 Surcharge Revalued Envelopes Two types of the surcharge are known:

Type I: large word "CENT," dot after "U" and "S" far from letters, long angle serif on center bar of "E."

Type II: small word "CENT," dot after "U" and "S."

Type 11 *surcharge - printed in green to left of stamp on 4¢ envelope EN825.*

EN848		UnFVF	UseFVF
4¢ + 1¢	**lilac, green** Type I (EN825)	1.50	.50
	entire	1.75	.75
	v. Type II	1.50	.50
	entire	1.75	.75

1964. New York World's Fair Issue

EN849 *Globe and orbit rings*

EN849		UnFVF	UseFVF
5¢	**red on white** *(April 22, 1964)*	.70	.50
	entire	.80	.50

1965. New Issue Beginning Jan. 1, 1965, the United States Envelope Co. was awarded the contract for making envelopes. This firm established a new facility at Williamsburg, Pa., and equipped it with new machinery that would produce envelopes from a continuous web (roll) of paper. The process is very rapid, with each individual machine being capable of producing one million envelopes every 24 hours. Envelopes produced by this method are of the old low-back design.

Watermark 49

New watermarks were introduced, as illustrated. Watermarks 47 and 48 also are known on these envelopes. Watermark 49 has the star below the letter "S" of "USA" and signifies the product of the Oxford Paper Co. Watermark 50 has the star above the "S" and distinguishes the product of Crown Zellerbach.

Also, a new watermark closely resembling Watermark 47 (star before "USA") but with a star somewhat larger distinguishes the product of the Champion Paper Co.

The small size (No. 6 3/4) and large size (No. 10) of the 5¢ envelopes (EN852), both regular and window, also exist tagged, consisting of a vertical luminescent rectangle to the left of the stamp. This method of tagging also was used for the 8¢ air mail envelopes in both sizes (AEN38).

EN850 *Liberty Bell. The wavy lines at the sides indicate the stamp is precanceled.*

EN850		UnFVF	UseFVF
1-1/4¢	**brown on white** *(Jan. 6, 1965)*	.25	.25
	entire	1.00	.25

EN851 *USS Constitution "Old Ironsides" under sail*

EN851		UnFVF	UseFVF
4¢	**bright blue on white** *(Jan. 6, 1965)*	.85	.25
	entire	1.00	.25

EN852 *Eagle*

EN852		UnFVF	UseFVF
5¢	**purple on white** *(Jan. 5, 1965)*	.80	.25
	entire	.90	.30
	z. Tagged *(Aug. 15, 1967)*	1.10	.25
	entire	1.35	.35

1968. Type 12 Surcharge Envelopes Printed in red to left of stamp on 4¢ envelope (EN851).

EN853		UnFVF	UseFVF
4¢ + 2¢	**bright blue, red on white** *(Feb. 1968)*	3.50	2.00
	entire	4.50	2.50

1968. Type 11 Surcharge Envelopes *Printed in green to left of stamp on 5¢ envelope (EN852).*

EN854		UnFVF	UseFVF
5¢ + 1¢	**purple, green on white** *(Feb. 1968)*	3.50	2.00
	entire	4.25	2.50
	z. Tagged *(Feb. 5, 1968)*	3.50	2.00
	entire	4.25	2.50

1968. Type 12 Surcharge Error Envelopes Printed in red to left of stamp on 5¢ envelope (EN852).

EN854A		UnFVF	UseFVF
5¢ + 2¢	**purple, red on white**	—	—
	entire	200.00	

1968. Type 11 Surcharge Envelopes *Printed in green to left of stamp on 5¢ envelope (EN852).*

EN855 *Statue of Liberty*

EN855		UnFVF	UseFVF
6¢	**turquoise green on white,** tagged *(Jan. 4, 1968)*	.75	.25
	entire	1.00	.35

EN855 is tagged with luminescent materials mixed with the printing ink.

EN856 *Liberty Bell. The wavy lines at sides indicate the envelope is precanceled.*

EN856		UnFVF	UseFVF
1.4¢	**brown on white** *(March 26, 1968)*	.25	.25
	entire	1.25	.35
EN857		**UnFVF**	**UseFVF**
1.6¢	**orange on white** *(June 16, 1969)*	.25	.25
	entire	1.00	.25
EN858		**UnFVF**	**UseFVF**
1.7¢	**purple on white** *(May 10, 1971)*	.25	.25
	entire	.50	.25

1970. Herman Melville Issue honored the writer and the whaling industry.

EN859 *Herman Melville's* Moby Dick

EN859		UnFVF	UseFVF
6¢	**light blue on white,** tagged *(March 7, 1970)*	.50	.25
	entire	.70	.35

1971. White House Conference on Youth

EN860 *White House Conference on Youth emblem*

EN860		UnFVF	UseFVF
6¢	**light blue on white,** tagged *(Feb. 24, 1971)*	.75	.25
	entire	1.00	.50

1971. Issue Issued to meet new first class postage rate.

EN861 *Eagle*

EN861		UnFVF	UseFVF
8¢	**ultramarine on white,** tagged *(May 6, 1971)*	.50	.25
	entire	.75	.30

1971. Type 13 Surcharge Envelopes

Type 13 *surcharge - in green to left of stamp on* EN855 *or* EN860.

EN862		UnFVF	UseFVF
6¢	**turquoise green** (EN855), **+ 2¢ green on white,** tagged *(May 16, 1971)*	1.00	.50
	entire	1.25	.50

EN863		UnFVF	UseFVF
6¢	**light blue** (EN860) **+ 2¢ green on white,** tagged *(May 16, 1971)*	2.00	1.00
	entire	2.75	1.50

Sale of EN863, of which one million were produced, was limited to Washington D.C.

1971. Bowling Issue honored the seventh World Tournament of the International Bowling Federation.

EN864 *Bowling ball and pin*

EN864		UnFVF	UseFVF
8¢	**red on white,** tagged *(Aug. 21, 1971)*	.50	.25
	entire	.75	.25

Available in both #6 small and #10 large size. EN864 is the first commemorative envelope since the Washington Bicentennial of 1932 to be available in two sizes.

1971. The White House Conference on Aging Issue

EN865 *Snowflake*

EN865		UnFVF	UseFVF
8¢	**blue on white,** tagged *(Nov. 15, 1977)*	.50	.25
	entire	.75	.25

1972. First U.S. International Transportation Exposition Issue

EN866 *Transpo 72 emblem*

EN866		UnFVF	UseFVF
8¢	**red and blue on white,** tagged *(May 2, 1972)*	.75	.25
	entire	1.00	.25

1973. Issue Issued to meet new First Class postage rate.

EN867 *Liberty bell*

EN867		UnFVF	UseFVF
10¢	**turquoise green on white,** tagged *(Dec. 5, 1973)*	.50	.25
	entire	.50	.25

1973. Type 12 Surcharge Envelopes

Type 12 *surcharge - in ultramarine to left of stamp on EN861.*

EN868		UnFVF	UseFVF
8¢ + 2¢	**ultramarine, ultramarine on white,** tagged *(Dec. 1, 1973)*	.50	.25
	entire	.50	.20

1974. Tennis Centennial

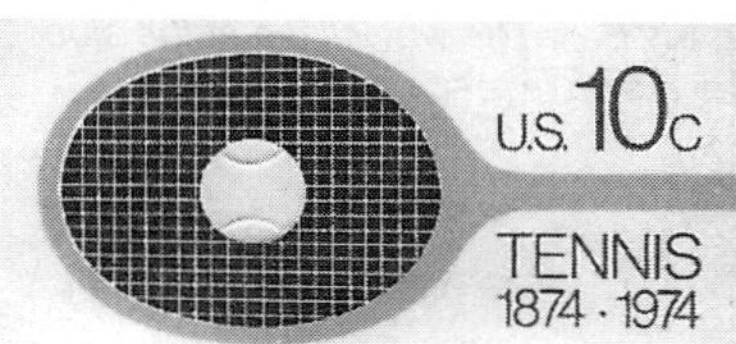

EN869 *Tennis centennial*

EN869		UnFVF	UseFVF
10¢	**yellow, green and blue on white,** tagged, *(Aug. 31, 1974)*	.85	.50
	entire	.85	.50

1974. Non-Profit Bulk Mailing

EN870 *Volunteerism*

EN870		UnFVF	UseFVF
1.8¢	**blue green on white,** tagged, *(Aug. 23, 1974)*	.35	.25
	entire	—	—

Bicentennial Era Series

1975. Seafaring Tradition Issue in the Bicentennial Era Series.

EN871 *Compass rose*

EN871		UnFVF	UseFVF
10¢	**brown and blue on light brown,** tagged, *(Oct. 13, 1975)*	.50	.25
	entire	.50	.30
	a. Brown omitted, entire	125.00	
	FDC		1.75

1975. Issue in the Bicentennial Era Series met new First Class postage rate.

EN872 *Liberty tree*

EN872		UnFVF	UseFVF
13¢	**brown on white,** tagged, *(Nov. 8, 1975)*	.50	.25
	entire	.50	.30
	FDC		1.75

1976. The American Home Maker Issue in the Bicentennial Era Series.

EN873 *Quilt pattern*

EN873		UnFVF	UseFVF
13¢	**brown and bluish green on light brown,** tagged, *(Feb. 2, 1976)*	.50	.25
	entire	.50	.30
	a. Brown omitted, entire	125.00	
	FDC		1.75

1976. American Farmer Issue in the Bicentennial Era Series.

EN874 *Sheaf of wheat*

EN874		UnFVF	UseFVF
13¢	**brown and green on light brown,** tagged, *(March 15, 1976)*	.50	.25
	entire	.50	.30
	a. Brown omitted, entire	125.00	
	FDC		1.25

1976. American Doctor Issue in the Bicentennial Era Series.

EN875 *Mortar and pestle*

EN875		UnFVF	UseFVF
13¢	**orange and brown on light brown,** tagged, *(June 30, 1976)*	.50	.25
	entire	.50	.30
	a. Brown omitted, entire	—	
	FDC		2.50

1976. American Craftsman Issue in the Bicentennial Era Series.

EN876 *Craftsman's tools*

EN876		UnFVF	UseFVF
13¢	**red and brown on light brown,** tagged, *(Aug. 6, 1976)*	.50	.25
	entire	.50	.30
	a. Brown omitted, entire	125.00	
	FDC		1.75

1976. Non-Profit Mailing Issue

EN877 *Star in pinwheel*

EN877		UnFVF	UseFVF
2¢	**red on white,** *(Sept. 10, 1976)*	.35	.25
	entire	.35	.50
	FDC		1.75

1976. Issue in the Bicentennial Era Series.

EN878 *Centennial envelope design*

EN878		UnFVF	UseFVF
13¢	**green on white,** tagged, *(Oct. 15, 1976)*	.50	.25
	entire	.50	.25
	FDC		1.75

1977. Golf Issue *Printed by gravure, in addition to embossing.*

EN879 *Golf club in motion and ball*

EN879		UnFVF	UseFVF
13¢	**blue, black and yellow green on white,** tagged, *(April 7, 1977)*	1.00	.50

	UnFVF	UseFVF
entire	1.00	.50
a. black omitted, entire*	250.00	
b. black and blue omitted, entire*	250.00	
c. blue, black and yelllow green omitted, entire*	250.00	
FDC		7.00

1977. Non-Profit Mailing Issue

EN880 *"2.1¢" in octagon*

EN880		UnFVF	UseFVF
2.1¢	**yellow green on white,** *(June 3, 1977)*	.50	.25
	entire	.50	.25
	FDC		1.75

1977. Energy Issue

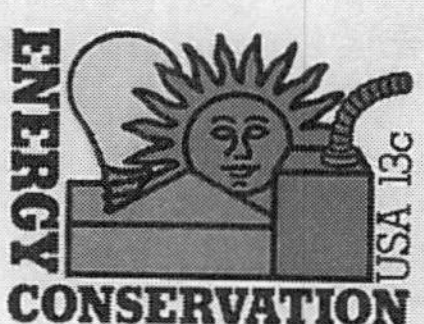

EN881 *Energy conservation*

EN881		UnFVF	UseFVF
13¢	**black, red and yellow on white,** tagged, *(Oct. 20, 1977)*	.50	.25
	entire	.50	.25
	a. black omitted, entire	—	
	b. black and red omitted, entire	475.00	
	c. red and yellow omitted, entire	—	
	d. yellow omitted, entire FDC *(Oct. 20, 1977)*	—	
	e. black, red, yellow and tagging omitted		

EN882 *Energy development*

EN882		UnFVF	UseFVF
13¢	**black, red and yellow on white**	.60	.30
	entire	.60	.30
	FDC		1.75

1978. "A" Non-Denominated Issue

to accommodate new 15¢ First Class postage rate. The envelope was printed in 1975 and 1976 and stored for contingency use.

EN883 *Stylized eagle and "A"*

EN883		UnFVF	UseFVF
15¢	**orange on white,** tagged, *(May 22, 1978)*	.60	.25
	entire	.70	.25
	FDC		2.00

1978. Uncle Sam Issue

EN884 *Stylized Uncle Sam hat and shield*

EN884		UnFVF	UseFVF
15¢	**red on white,** tagged *(June 3, 1978)*	.50	.25
	entire	.60	.25
	FDC		1.75

1978. Non-Profit Mailing Issue

EN885 *"2.7¢" over "USA"*

EN885		UnFVF	UseFVF
2.7¢	**green on white** *(July 5, 1978)*	.25	.25
	entire	.40	.25
	FDC		1.75

1978. Type 14 Surcharge Revalued Issue

Downward re-valuing.

Type 14 *surcharge - in black to left of stamp.*

EN886		UnFVF	UseFVF
15¢ on 16¢	**blue on white,** tagged *(July 28, 1978)*	.45	.25
	entire	.60	.25
	t. Surcharge omitted, entire	400.00	
	z. Tagging omitted		
	FDC		1.75

1978. Auto Racing Issue

EN887 *Indianapolis 500 racer*

EN887		UnFVF	UseFVF
15¢	**black, blue and red on white,** tagged *(Sept. 2, 1975)*	.45	.25
	entire	.50	.25
	a. black omitted, entire	175.00	—
	b. black and blue omitted, entire	—	—
	c. red omitted, entire	—	—
	d. red and blue omitted, entire	—	—
	e. black, blue and red omitted, entire	—	—
	z. Tagging omitted	—	—
	FDC		1.75

1978. Type 14 Surcharge Revalued Issue

(EN872) Liberty tree re-valued.

Type 14 *surcharge - in black to left of stamp*

EN888		UnFVF	UseFVF
15¢ on 13¢	**brown on white** (EN872), tagged *(Nov. 28, 1978)*	.40	.25

		UnFVF	UseFVF
	entire	.55	.25
	FDC		1.75

1979. Non-Profit Mailing Issue

EN889 *Authorized nonprofit organization*

EN889		UnFVF	UseFVF
3.1¢	**blue on white** *(May 18, 1979)*	.25	.25
	entire	.30	.25
	FDC		1.75

1979. Veterinary Medicine Issue

EN890 *"V" on staff of Aesculapius*

EN890		UnFVF	UseFVF
15¢	**gray and brown on white,** tagged *(July 24, 1979)*	.40	.25
	entire	.55	.25
	a. gray omitted, entire	700.00	
	b. brown omitted, entire	—	—
	c. gray, brown and tagging omitted, entire	—	—
	FDC		1.75

1979. Olympic Games Issue *Soccer*

EN891 *1980 Moscow Olympics, soccer players on envelope*

EN891		UnFVF	UseFVF
15¢	**red, green and black on white,** tagged *(Dec. 10, 1979)*	.75	.25
	entire	1.00	.25
	a. black omitted, entire	175.00	—
	b. black and green omitted, entire	175.00	—
	c. red omitted, entire	—	—
	d. red and green omitted, entire	175.00	
	e. red, green and black omitted, entire	—	—
	f. red, green black and tagging omitted, entire	—	—
	FDC		1.75

1980. Bicycling Issue

EN892 *High-wheel bicycle*

EN892		UnFVF	UseFVF
15¢	**blue and maroon on white,** tagged *(May 16, 1980)*	.50	.25
	entire	.65	.25
	a. blue omitted, entire	150.00	—
	FDC		1.75

1980. Non-Profit Mailing Issue

EN893 *Weaver violins*

EN893		UnFVF	UseFVF
3.5¢	**purple on white** *(June 23, 1980)*	.25	.25
	entire	.35	.25
	FDC		1.75

1980. America's Cup Yacht Races Issue

EN894 *Yacht*

EN894		UnFVF	UseFVF
15¢	**red & blue on white, tagged** *(Sept. 15, 1980)*	.50	.25
	entire	.65	.25
	FDC		1.75

1980. Honeybee Issue Printed by gravure, in addition to embossing.

EN895 *Orange blossom and honeybee*

EN895		UnFVF	UseFVF
15¢	**green and yellow on white,** tagged *(Oct. 10, 1980)*	.50	.25
	entire	.55	.25
	a. brown omitted, entire	200.00	—
	FDC		1.75

1981. "B" Non-Denominated Issue to accommodate new First Class postage rate.

EN896 *Stylized eagle and "B"*

EN896		UnFVF	UseFVF
18¢	**purple on white,** tagged *(March 15, 1981)*	.50	.25
	entire	.55	.25
	FDC		1.75

1981. Star Issue Denominated to meet new First Class postage rate.

EN897 *Star*

EN897		UnFVF	UseFVF
18¢	**blue on white,** tagged *(April 2, 1981)*	.50	.25
	entire	.55	.25
	FDC		1.75

1981. Blinded Veterans Association Issue

EN898 *Hand and Braille message*

EN898		UnFVF	UseFVF
18¢	**blue on white,** tagged *(Aug. 13, 1981)*	.40	.25
	entire	.60	.25
	a. red omitted, entire	250.00	
	blue omitted, entire	—	
	FDC		1.75

The hand and Braille message are embossed without color.

1981. "C" Non-Denominated Issue met the new First Class postage rate.

EN899 *Stylized eagle and "C"*

EN899		UnFVF	UseFVF
20¢	**brown on white,** tagged *(Oct. 11, 1981)*	.50	.25
	entire	.55	.25
	FDC		1.75

1981. Capitol Dome Issue

EN900 *Dome of U.S. Capitol*

EN900		UnFVF	UseFVF
20¢	**dark red on white,** tagged *(Nov. 13, 1981)*	.50	.25
	entire	5.15	.25
	z. Bar tagged	2.00	2.00
	FDC		1.75

1982. Non-Profit Bulk Mailing Issue

EN901

EN901		UnFVF	UseFVF
5.9¢	**brown on white** *(Feb. 17, 1982)*	.25	.25
	entire	.35	.25
	FDC		1.75

1982. Great Seal of the United States Bicentennial Issue

EN902 *Great Seal*

EN902		UnFVF	UseFVF
20¢	**blue, black and red on white,** tagged *(June 15, 1982)*	.50	.25
	entire	.55	.25
	a. blue omitted, entire	165.00	
	blue and red omitted		
	FDC		1.75

1982. Purple Heart Bicentennial Issue

EN903 *Purple Heart medal*

EN903		UnFVF	UseFVF
20¢	**purple and black on white,** tagged *(Aug. 6, 1982)*	.50	.25
	entire	.55	.25
	FDC		2.00

1983. Non-Profit Mailing Issue

EN904 *Olive branches*

EN904		UnFVF	UseFVF
5.2¢	**orange on white** *(March 21, 1983)*	.25	.25
	entire	.25	.25
	FDC		1.75

1983. Paralyzed Veterans Issue

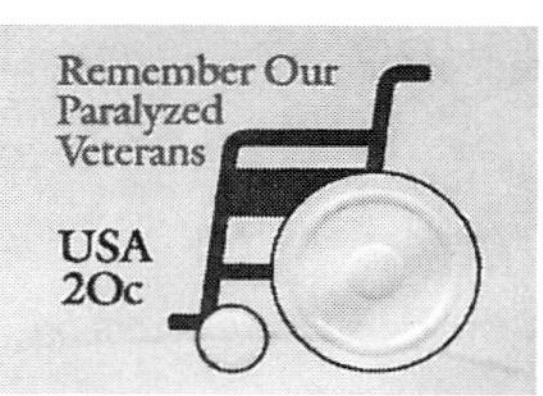

EN905 *Wheelchair*

EN905		UnFVF	UseFVF
20¢	**red, blue and black on white,** tagged *(Aug. 3, 1983)*	.50	.25
	entire	.55	.25
	a. blue omitted, entire	350.00	
	b. blue and black omitted, entire	150.00	
	c. red omitted, entire	350.00	
	d. red and black omitted, entire	150.00	
	e. black omitted, entire	325.00	
	FDC		1.75

1984. Small Business Issue

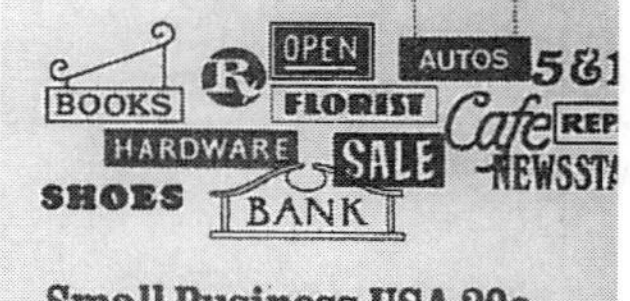

EN906 *Business signs*

EN906		UnFVF	UseFVF
20¢	**multicolored on white,** tagged *(May 7, 1984)*	.60	.25
	entire	.65	.25
	FDC		1.75

1985. "D" Non-Denominated Issue met the new First Class postage rate.

EN907 *Stylized eagle and "D"*

EN907		UnFVF	UseFVF
22¢	**green on white,** tagged *(Feb. 1, 1985)*	.50	.25
	entire	.65	.25
	FDC		1.75

1985. American Bison Issue

EN908 *Bison*

EN908		UnFVF	UseFVF
22¢	**brown on white,** tagged *(Feb. 25, 1985)*	.50	.25
	entire	.60	.25
	z. Double tagged, phosphorescent ink and separate bar tagging	—	—
	z1. Untagged (precanceled)		
	FDC		1.75

1985. Non-Profit Mailing Issue

EN909 *U.S.S. Constitution*

EN909		UnFVF	UseFVF
6¢	**aqua on white** *(May 3, 1985)*	.25	.25
	entire	.30	.25
	black omitted	—	
	FDC		1.75

1986. The *Mayflower* Issue

EN910 *Mayflower, gulls*

EN910		UnFVF	UseFVF
8.5¢	**black and gray on white,** precanceled *(Dec. 4, 1986)*	.25	.25
	entire	.35	.25
	FDC		1.75

1988. Stars Issue *Printed by letter press in addition to embossing.*

EN911 *Circle of stars*

EN911		UnFVF	UseFVF
25¢	**red and blue on white,** tagged *(March 26, 1988)*	.60	.25
	entire	.75	.35
	a. red omitted, entire	95.00	
	b. red and tagging omitted, entire	125.00	—
	z. Tagging omitted, entire	—	—
	FDC		1.75

1988. Non-Profit Mailing Issue *U.S.S. Constellation.*

EN912 *U.S.S.* Constellation

EN912		UnFVF	UseFVF
8.4¢	**black and blue on white,** precanceled *(April 12, 1988)*	.30	.25
	entire	.50	.25
	a. black omitted, entire	—	—
	z. Tagging omitted		
	FDC		1.75

1988. Holiday Greeting Snowflake Issue Printed by letterpress.

EN913 *Snowflake*

EN913		UnFVF	UseFVF
25¢	**red and green on white,** tagged *(Sept. 8, 1988)*	.60	.30
	entire	.75	.35
	FDC		1.75

1989. Philatelic Issue *Printed by letterpress.*

EN914 *Circle of stars in stamp field*

EN914		UnFVF	UseFVF
25¢	**red and blue on white,** tagged *(March 10, 1989)*	.50	.25
	entire*	.65	.30
	FDC		1.75

1989. Security Mail Issue *Printed by letterpress.*

EN915 *Circle of stars*

EN915		UnFVF	UseFVF
25¢	**red and blue on white,** tagged *(July 10, 1989)*	.50	.25
	entire	.60	.30
	FDC		1.75

Envelope is blue on inside to provide security for enclosures.

1989. Love Issue *Printed by offset and letterpress.*

EN916 *Love*

EN916		UnFVF	UseFVF
25¢	**red and blue on white,** tagged *(Sept. 22, 1989)*	.50	.25
	entire	.60	.30
	a. blue omitted, entire	—	—
	b. red and blue omitted, entire	—	—
	FDC		1.75

1989. World Stamp Expo '89 Issue *Printed by letterpress, with foil hologram used for first time by U.S.*

EN917 *Space station and shuttle*

EN917		UnFVF	UseFVF
25¢	**ultramarine,** tagged *(Dec. 3, 1989)*	.50	.30
	entire	1.00	.75
	a. ultramarine omitted, entire	575.00	
	FDC		1.75

A hologram is affixed at upper right inside, visible through a die cut window.

1990. Football Issue *Printed by letterpress, with hologram.*

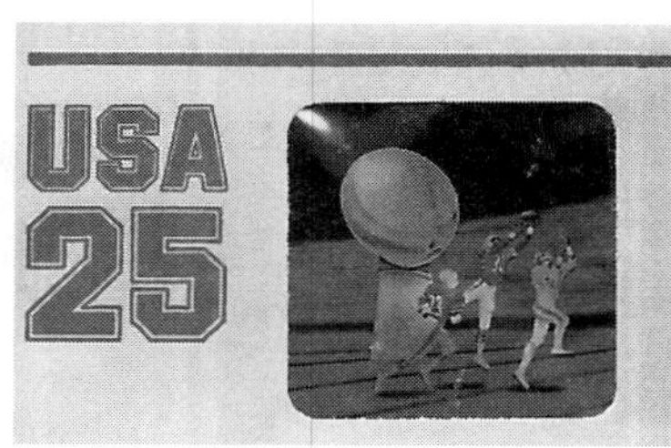

EN918 *Football players and Lombardi trophy*

EN918		UnFVF	UseFVF
25¢	**vermilion,** tagged *(Sept. 9, 1990)*	.50	.30
	entire	1.00	.75
	FDC		4.00

A hologram is affixed at upper right inside, visible through a die cut window.

1991. Star Issue met the new First Class postage rate. *Printed by letterpress, with embossing.*

EN919 *Star*

EN919		UnFVF	UseFVF
29¢	**ultramarine and rose on white,** tagged *(Jan. 24, 1991)*	.70	.35
	entire	.85	.45
	a. ultramarine omitted	750.00	
	b. rose omitted	325.00	
	FDC		1.75

1991. Non-Profit Mailing Issue *Printed by letterpress.*

EN920 *Sparrows on wires*

EN920		UnFVF	UseFVF
11.1¢	**red and blue on white,** tagged, precanceled *(May 3, 1991)*	.25	.25
	entire	.40	.30
	FDC		1.75

1991. Love Issue in the Love Series. *Printed by offset.*

EN921 *Love*

EN921		UnFVF	UseFVF
29¢	**blue, maroon and rose on white,** tagged *(May 9, 1991)*	.65	.35
	entire	.75	.40
	a. rose omitted	—	
	FDC		1.75

1991. Security Issue *Printed by letterpress.*

EN922 *Star*

EN922		UnFVF	UseFVF
29¢	**ultramarine and rose on white,** tagged *(July 20, 1991)*	.65	.35
	entire*	.75	.40
	a. ultramarine omitted, entire	575.00	
	b. rose omitted, entire	—	
	FDC		1.75

The inside of the envelope has a blue design as a security precaution for enclosures.

1991. Magazine Industry Issue *Printed by offset and letterpress, with gravure-printed vignette affixed through a die-cut window.*

EN923 *Stylized globe 250th anniversary, magazine industry*

EN923		UnFVF	UseFVF
29¢	**multicolored on white,** tagged *(Oct. 7, 1991)*	.65	.35
	entire*	.75	.40
	FDC		1.75

1991. Country Geese Issue *Printed by offset and letterpress.*

EN924 *Geese*

EN924		UnFVF	UseFVF
29¢	**bluish gray and yellow,** tagged *(Nov. 8, 1990)*	.65	.35
	entire	.75	.40
	FDC		1.75

1992. Space Station Hologram Issue *Printed by letterpress, with hologram.*

EN925 *Space station and shuttle*

EN925		UnFVF	UseFVF
29¢	**yellow green on white,** tagged *(Jan. 21, 1992)*	.65	.35
	entire*	.75	.40
	FDC		1.75

A hologram is affixed at upper right inside, visible through a die cut window.

1992. Western Americana Issue *Printed by offset and letterpress.*

EN926 *Western saddle*

EN926		UnFVF	UseFVF
29¢	**multicolored on white,** tagged *(April 10, 1992)*	.60	.35
	entire*	.75	.40
	FDC		1.75

A vignette, printed by offset, is affixed through a die cut window at upper right.

1992. Protect the Environment Issue *Printed by offset and letterpress.*

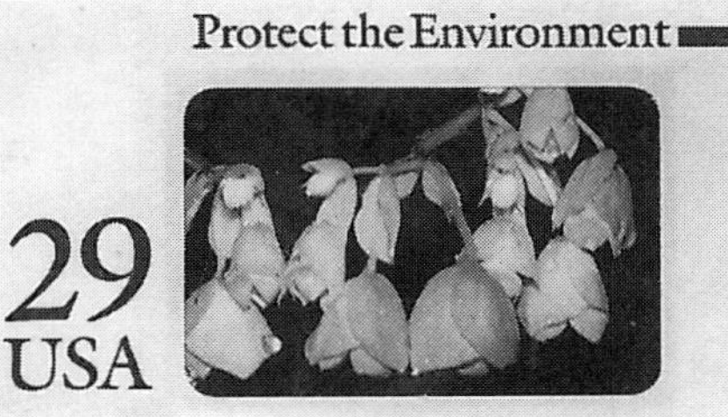

EN927 *Hillebrandia*

EN927		UnFVF	UseFVF
29¢	**multicolored on white,** tagged *(April 22, 1992)*	.60	.35
	entire*	.75	.40
	FDC		1.75

A vignette, printed by offset, is affixed at upper right inside, visible through a die cut window.

1992. Re-Issues on Recycled Paper Issue All of the envelopes in this series have the "Recycle" tri-arrow logo on the reverse. Unwatermarked envelopes and/or those available only in large (No. 10) size are marked. This series is listed only as entires, to enable inclusion both of the "Recycle" logo and to verify watermarking. *Issued May 1, 1992.*

EN928		UnFVF	UseFVF
29¢	**ultramarine on white,** unwatermarked, tagged, entire (EN919)	.80	.40

EN929		UnFVF	UseFVF
11.1¢	**red and blue on white,** unwatermarked, tagged, entire (EN920)	.40	.30

EN930		UnFVF	UseFVF
29¢	**blue, maroon and rose on white,** tagged, entire (EN921)	.80	.40

EN931		UnFVF	UseFVF
29¢	**red and blue on white,** tagged, entire* (EN922)	.80	.40

EN932		UnFVF	UseFVF
29¢	**bluish gray and yellow,** unwatermarked, tagged, entire (EN924)	.80	.40

EN933		UnFVF	UseFVF
29¢	**yellow green,** with hologram, tagged, entire* (EN925)	.80	.40

1992. Bulk Mailing Issue *Printed by offset and letterpress.*

EN934 *Star*

EN934		UnFVF	UseFVF
19.8¢	**red and blue on white,** tagged, *(May 19, 1992)*	.55	.40
	entire*	.55	.45
	FDC		1.75

1992. Disabled American Issue *Printed by letterpress.*

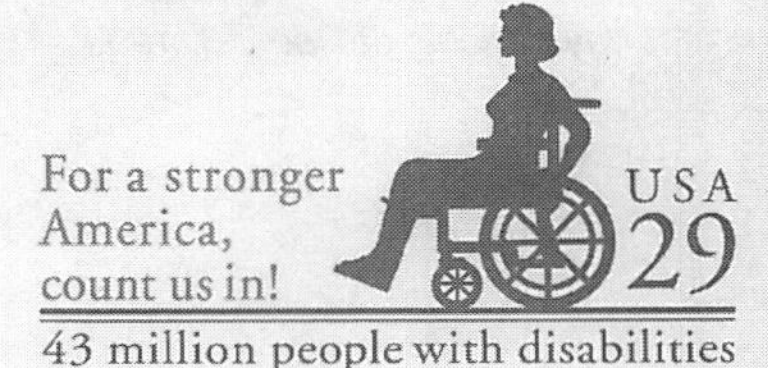

EN935 *Woman in wheelchair*

EN935		UnFVF	UseFVF
29¢	**red and blue on white,** tagged, *(July 22, 1992)*	.75	.40
	entire	.75	.40
	FDC		1.75

1993. Kitten Issue *Printed by offset and letterpress.*

EN936 *Siamese kitten*

EN936		UnFVF	UseFVF
29¢	**cyan, black and purple on white,** tagged, *(Oct. 2, 1993)*	.75	.40
	entire*	.75	.40
	FDC		1.75

A vignette, printed by offset, is affixed at upper right inside, visible through a die cut window.

1994. Football Issue *Printed by offset and letterpress.*

EN937 *Football*

EN937		UnFVF	UseFVF
29¢	**brown and black on white,** tagged, *(Sept. 17, 1994)*	.75	.40
	entire*	.75	.40
	FDC		3.00

1994. Old Glory Issue *Number 6 3/4 and 10 envelopes.*

EN938, EN939 *Flag — design continues to back of envelope*

EN938		UnFVF	UseFVF
32¢	**red and blue on white,** tagged, (No. 6 3/4)	.75	.40
	entire	.75	.40
	FDC *(Dec. 13, 1994)*		2.00

EN939		UnFVF	UseFVF
32¢	**red and blue on white,** tagged, (No. 10)	.75	.40
	entire	.75	.40
	a. red omitted, entire	.75	.40
	b. blue omitted, entire	—	
	FDC *(Dec. 13, 1994)*		2.00

Announced Jan. 12, 1995, envelopes were initially available only through mail order and received first-day cancels of Dec. 13, 1994.

1995. Liberty Bell Issue

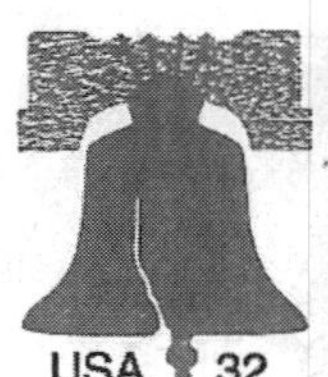

EN940, EN944 *Liberty bell*

EN940		UnFVF	UseFVF
32¢	**greenish blue and blue on white,** tagged, *(Jan. 3, 1995)*	.75	.40
	entire*	.75	.40
	a. greenish blue omitted	—	
	b. blue omitted	125.00	
	c. greenish blue and blue omitted, entire	200.00	—
	d. blue and tagging omitted	—	
	FDC		2.00

1995. Non-Profit Issue

EN941 *Sheep — design continues to back of envelope*

EN941		UnFVF	UseFVF
5¢	**green and red brown on white,** *(March 10, 1995)*	.75	.40
	entire	.75	.40
	FDC		2.00

1995. Bulk Rate Issue

EN942 *Eagle*

EN942		UnFVF	UseFVF
10¢	**dark red and blue on white,** *(March 10, 1995)*	.75	.40
	entire*	.75	.40
	FDC		2.00

1995. Heart Spiral Issue

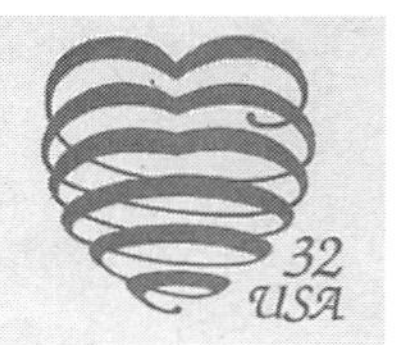

EN943 *Heart*

EN943		UnFVF	UseFVF
32¢	**red on light blue,** *(March 12, 1995)*	.75	.40
	entire	.75	.40
	FDC		2.00

1995. Liberty Bell Issue *Number 9 size security envelope.*

EN944		UnFVF	UseFVF
32¢	**greenish blue and blue on security paper,** *(May 16, 1995)*	.75	.40
	entire	.75	.40

1995. Space Hologram Issue

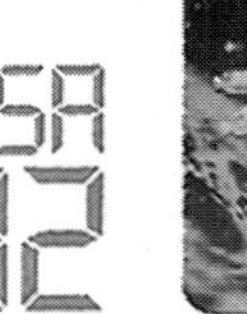

EN945 *Space station*

EN945		UnFVF	UseFVF
32¢	**red on white,** *(Sept. 22, 1995)*	.75	.40
	entire*	.75	.40
	FDC		2.00

1996. Save Our Environment Issue

EN946 *Landscape*

EN946		UnFVF	UseFVF
32¢	**multicolored on white,** *(April 20, 1996)*	.75	.40
	entire*	.75	.40
	FDC		2.00

A vignette, printed by offset, is affixed at upper right inside, visible through a die cut window.

1996. Paralympic Games Issue

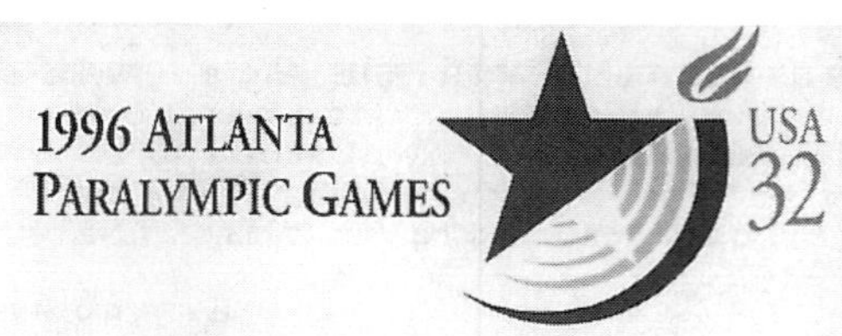

EN947 *Star, flame*

EN947		UnFVF	UseFVF
32¢	**multicolored on white,** *(May 2, 1996)*	.75	.40
	entire	.75	.40
	a. blue and gold omitted	—	

b. blue omitted —
c. black and red omitted —
FDC 2.00

1999. Flag Issue portrayed a stylized, wavy-lined American flag with a yellow staff. *Printed by Westvaco U.S. Envelope.*

EN948 *American flag with yellow staff*

EN948		UnFVF	UseFVF
33¢	**red, blue and yellow on white**	.75	.50
	entire	.75	.50
	FDC *(Jan. 11, 1999)*		1.25

1999. Flag Issue portrayed a stylized, wavy-lined American flag with a blue staff on security paper. *Printed by Westvaco U.S. Envelope.*

EN949 *American flag with blue staff*

EN949		UnFVF	UseFVF
33¢	**red and blue on white**	.75	.50
	entire	.75	.50
	FDC *(Jan. 11, 1999)*		1.25

1999. Calligraphic Love Issue in the Love Series featured "Love" and hearts in calligraphy. *Printed by Westvaco U.S. Envelope.*

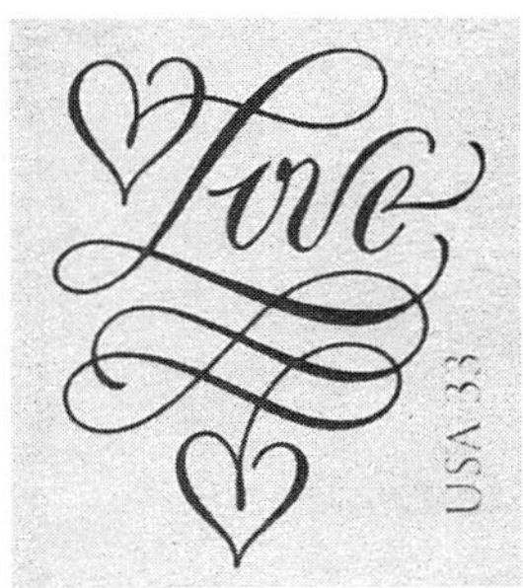

EN950 *Love*

EN950		UnFVF	UseFVF
33¢	**purple on white**	.75	.50
	entire	.75	.50
	FDC *(Jan. 28, 1999)*		1.25

1999. Lincoln Issue portrayed a bust of Abraham Lincoln, printed to appear embossed. *Offset by Westvaco U.S. Envelope.*

EN951 *Abraham Lincoln*

EN951		UnFVF	UseFVF
33¢	**blue and gray on white**	.75	.50
	entire	.75	.50
	FDC *(June 5, 1999)*		1.25

2001. Federal Eagle Issue featured a simple bald eagle design reminiscent of some postal meters but in blue-gray with a gray "34" denominatino. Designed by Michael Doret, Hollywood, Calif. Plain- and window-front envelopes were issued in each of three standard sizes: No. 10 business size, No. 9 security, and No 6 3/4 personal size. *Typographed, tagged. 75,000,000 (#10) printed, 29,000,000 (#10 window), 20,000,000 (6 3/4), 20,000,000 (6 3/4 window), 2,500,000 (#9 security), 1,800,000 (#9 security window).*

EN952 *Federal Eagle*

EN952		UnFVF	UseFVF
34¢	**blue-gray & gray**	.75	.30
	entire	.75	.30
	No. 10	.75	.30
	No. 10 window	.75	.30
	No. 9	.75	.30
	No. 6	.75	.30
	FDC *(Jan. 7, 2001)*		1.50

2001. Lovebirds Issue featured a heart-shaped line drawing of two birds as mirror images. Designed by Robert Brangwynne, Boston, Mass. Plain- and window-front envelopes were issued in each of three standard sizes: No. 10 business size, No. 9 security, and No. 6 3/4 personal size. *Tagged. 15,000,000 (6 3/4) printed, 15,000,000 (#10), 20,000,000 (6 3/4), 20,000,000 (6 3/4 window), 2,500,000 (#9 security), 1,800,000 (#9 security window).*

EN953 *Lovebirds*

EN953		UnFVF	UseFVF
34¢	**purple & red**	.75	.30
	entire	.75	
	No. 10	.75	.30
	No. 6	.75	.30
	FDC *(Feb. 14, 2001)*		1.50

2001. Community Colleges Issue

EN954 *Commuting College Student*

Airmail Envelopes

The order authorizing airmail envelopes expressly provided they be printed on white paper and have red, white and blue borders, which became known as "barber pole" borders.

Some experimenting was needed to produce these borders. On the first issues, five different types of borders are known to collectors.

Red Lozenge at Upper Right

Border 1: The lozenges (parallelograms) along the top edge and parallel to the edge measure 9 to 10mm, and with the top flap open measure along the oblique side 11 to 13mm. Small size envelopes only.

Border 2: Like Border 1 except that the lozenges measure only 7 to 8mm along the oblique side (with the top flap open). Small size envelopes only.

Border 3: Like Border 1 except the lozenges measure 11 to 12mm parallel to the edge of the envelope. Large size envelopes only.

Blue Lozenge at Upper Right - Large size envelopes only.

Border 4: Like Border 2 except with a blue lozenge at upper right corner.

Border 5: Like Border 4 except the lozenges at top point to the right (all others point to the left).

The borders are of importance to collectors, and cut squares should be preserved to include them.

After the experimentation on the first issue (AEN1-AEN2), the borders were standardized as Border 2 (red lozenge at upper right) for small size envelopes and Border 4 (blue lozenge at upper right) for large size envelopes.

1929. First Airmail Issue. The U.S. domestic airmail rate from 1929 to 1932 was 5¢, as evidenced by the 5¢ stamps (AEN1-AEN2) which were the world's first postal stationery that totally prepaid airmail postage. The airmail rate to or from Puerto Rico, however, was 10¢. Persons desiring to send airmail to or from Puerto Rico simply used a 5¢ airmail envelope to which they affixed a 5¢ adhesive stamp.

In 1932 the domestic airmail rate for the United States was advanced to 8¢, and new 8¢ airmail envelopes were issued (AEN3). In 1934 the rate was reduced to 6¢ with a resulting change in the stamps on the airmail envelopes (AEN4-AEN7).

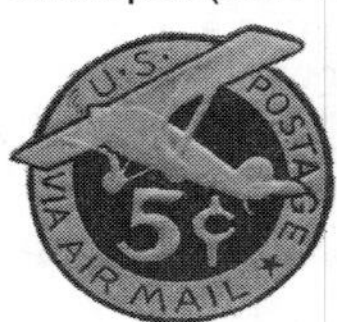

AEN1 *Vertical rudder slopes off to the left*

AEN1		UnFVF	UseFVF
5¢	**blue,** Border 1	4.00	2.50
	entire	5.50	3.00
	v. Border 2	4.00	2.50
	entire	5.50	3.00
	v1. Border 3	4.00	2.50
	entire	7.50	6.00
	v2. Border 4	4.00	2.50
	entire	9.00	6.00
	v2a. entire, 1933 watermark	750.00	—
	v2b. entire, 1937 watermark	—	—
	v3. Border 5	4.00	2.50
	entire	9.00	6.00
	v4. border omitted	700.00	—
	FDC *(Jan. 12, 1929),* size 13		40.00
	FDC *(Feb 1, 1929),* size 5		75.00
	FDC *(Feb. 1, 1929),* size 8		75.00

AEN2 *Vertical rudder is semi-circular*

AEN2		UnFVF	UseFVF
5¢	**blue,** Border 2	12.50	6.00
	entire	17.50	7.00
	entire, 1933 watermark	700.00	—
	v. Border 4	12.00	6.00
	entire	20.00	13.00
	va. entire, 1933 watermark	350.00	—
	v1. Border 5	—	—
	entire	—	—

1932. Issue

AEN3

AEN3		UnFVF	UseFVF
8¢	**olive,** Border 4	15.00	5.00
	entire	20.00	7.00
	v. Border 2	—	—
	entire	—	—
	FDC *(Sept. 26, 1932),* size 8		30.00
	FDC, size 13		11.00

1934-44. Issue With the change of the airmail rate to 6¢, the 6¢ orange design copied the old 5¢ design. The old master die of the 5¢ was used to produce blank printing dies, into each of which the figure "6" then was cut by hand. Eleven of these dies were so made; each, of course, differs materially from the other. To simplify the collecting of these, collectors divided the 11 varieties into three general classifications, as follows:

1 (AEN4): the figure "6" measures 6 1/2mm wide
2 (AEN5): the figure "6" measures 6mm wide
3 (AEN6): the figure "6" measures 5 1/2mm wide

Finally, in 1942, a new master 6¢ airmail die was made (AEN7), from which were struck as many printing dies as were necessary. All such printing dies struck from this master die were identical and may not be individually identified.

With the outbreak of World War II, there was an enormous demand by the armed forces overseas for airmail envelopes. To expedite manufacturing, the borders were ordered dropped. All borderless airmail envelopes were shipped overseas and were not available to the civilian population in this country until after the war.

AEN4-AEN6 *Vertical rudder is semi-circular*

AEN4		UnFVF	UseFVF
6¢	**orange,** Border 2	1.75	.50
	entire	2.00	.70
	v. Border 4	—	—
	entire	—	—
	v1. w/out border, entire	3.00	1.75
	FDC *(July 1, 1934),* size 13		14.00
	FDC, size 8		25.00

AEN5		UnFVF	UseFVF
6¢	**orange,** Border 2 (1942)	3.00	2.25
	entire	60.00	25.00
	v. Border 4	—	—
	entire	—	—
	v1. w/out border, entire	5.00	2.50

AEN6		UnFVF	UseFVF
6¢	**orange,** no border (1944)	1.00	.35
	entire	1.25	.50

AEN7 *Vertical rudder slopes forward*

AEN7		UnFVF	UseFVF
6¢	**orange,** Border 2 (1942)	1.75	.75
	entire	2.50	1.00
	v. Border 4	—	—
	entire	—	—
	v1. w/out border, entire	3.00	1.25
	v2. on blue paper (error) no border, entire	4,000.00	2,700.00
	v3. red lozenges of border omitted, entire	1,200.00	—

1945. Issue In March, to alleviate the enormous demand for airmail envelopes that the printer had not been able to supply, the Post Office approved the overprinting of 60 million ordinary 2¢ envelopes (AEN8-AEN14). The overprinting was done in New York, and great care was taken to keep any envelopes other than those authorized from being re-valued. All were shipped to the armed forces.

By the following September, the airmail rates had been reduced from 6¢ to 5¢, and re-valuing of the 6¢ airmail borderless envelopes was performed.

Following the war, remainders of these revalued envelopes were called in and destroyed, because they were confusing to the postal clerks. Adequate supplies, however, reached philatelic hands.

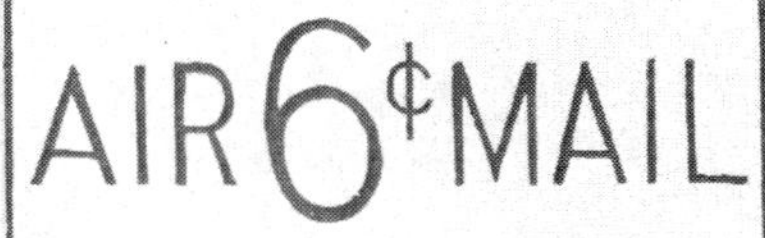

AEN8-AEN14

AEN8		UnFVF	UseFVF
6¢ on 2¢ carmine (EN549), Die A		1.50	.75
	entire	2.00	1.25

AEN9		UnFVF	UseFVF
6¢ on 2¢ carmine (EN574), Die H		—	—
	entire	—	—

AEN10		UnFVF	UseFVF
6¢ on 2¢ carmine (EN578), Die H2		—	—
	entire	—	—

AEN11		UnFVF	UseFVF
6¢ on 2¢ carmine (EN581), Die I		—	—
	entire	—	—

AEN12		UnFVF	UseFVF
6¢ on 2¢ carmine (EN810)		80.00	45.00
	entire	125.00	75.00

AEN13		UnFVF	UseFVF
6¢ on 1¢ green (EN520), Die A		1,900.00	—
	entire	2,700.00	—

On 1¢ green envelope of 1916-50 issue (error).

AEN14		UnFVF	UseFVF
6¢ on 3¢ purple (EN588), Die I		1,900.00	—
	entire	2,700.00	—

On 3¢ purple envelope of 1916-50 issue (error).

REVALUED
5¢
P.O. DEPT.

AEN15-AEN18

AEN15		UnFVF	UseFVF
5¢ on 6¢ orange (AEN4v1)		3.50	2.00
	entire	4.00	3.00
	v. Double overprint, entire	75.00	—

AEN16		UnFVF	UseFVF
5¢ on 6¢ orange (AENv1)		10.00	6.00
	entire	12.50	8.00
	v. Double overprint, entire	—	—

AEN17		UnFVF	UseFVF
5¢ on 6¢ orange (AEN6)		.75	.55
	entire	1.50	.75
	v. Double overprint, entire	65.00	—

AEN18		UnFVF	UseFVF
5¢ on 6¢ orange (AEN7v1)		1.00	.75
	entire	125.00	.75
	v. Double overprint, entire	65.00	—

Black overprint on 6¢ orange airmail envelopes, without borders, of 1934-44 issue.

1946. DC 4 Skymaster Issue

AEN19 *DC-4 Skymaster. The small projection directly below the rudder is rounded.*

AEN19		UnFVF	UseFVF
5¢	**carmine,** Border 2	.85	.25
	entire	1.25	.50
	FDC *(Sept. 25, 1946)*		

AEN20 *The small projection directly below the rudder is a sharp point.*

AEN20		UnFVF	UseFVF
5¢	**carmine,** Border 2	1.00	.35
	entire	1.25	.50
	v. w/Border 4	—	—
	entire	—	—

1947. U.S. Postage Stamp Centenary Issue complemented the Centenary International Philatelic Exhibition in New York City. The envelopes were printed on a demonstration machine at the exhibition. The envelopes also were produced at the factory in Dayton, Ohio, from both a flat and a rotary die, for distribution throughout the country. Approximately 8 million envelopes were issued, of which the rotary die printings are more common. *Flat die measures 21 3/4mm high; rotary die measures 22 1/2mm high.*

AEN21

AEN21		UnFVF	UseFVF
5¢	**carmine,** Border 2, rotary die	.50	.35
	entire	.75	.45
	v. Flat die	.60	.40
	entire	.75	.50
	FDC *(May 21, 1947)*		

1950. Issue

AEN22 *Type 1: figure "6s" lean to the right*

Type 2; figure "6s" are upright

AEN22		UnFVF	UseFVF
6¢	**carmine,** Border 2, Type 1	.50	.25
	entire	.75	.40
	v. Type 2	.90	.35
	entire	1.15	.40
	v1. Border 4, Type 1	—	—
	entire	—	—
	v2. Border 4, Type 2	—	—
	entire	—	—
	FDC *(Sept. 22, 1950)*		

1951-52. Issue The return to a 6¢ airmail rate in 1950 caused the Post Office to revalue existing supplies of 5¢ airmail envelopes in some larger post offices. The re-valuing was done on a "Ticometer," a new machine developed by Pitney-Bowes Co. This process first was done in 1951 and again in 1952. Different styles of slugs were used to make the overprint on each occasion.

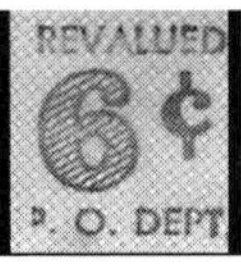

AEN23, AEN24

AEN23		UnFVF	UseFVF
6¢ on 5¢ carmine, Border 2 (AEN19)		1.00	.65
	entire	1.50	1.00
	FDC *(Sept. 29, 1951)*		

AEN24		UnFVF	UseFVF
6¢ on 5¢ carmine, Border 2 (AEN20)		.95	.65
	entire	1.40	1.10
	v. w/Border 4 (AEN20v)	—	—
	entire	—	—

Overprint in red to left of stamp on 5¢ airmail envelopes of 1946 issue.

AEN25, AEN26, AEN27

AEN25		UnFVF	UseFVF
6¢ on 5¢ (AEN19)		30.00	20.00
	entire	35.00	25.00

AEN26		UnFVF	UseFVF
6¢ on 5¢ (AEN20)		4.00	3.00
	entire	6.00	5.00
	v. w/Border 4 (AEN20v)	—	—
	entire	—	—
	FDC *(Aug. 29, 1952)*		

AEN27		UnFVF	UseFVF
6¢ on 5¢ carmine (AEN21)		—	—
	entire	1,400.00	—

Overprint in red to left of stamp on 5¢ airmail envelopes of 1946 and 1947 issues.

1956. Issue FIPEX Envelope. Issued in celebration of the Fifth International Philatelic Exhibition. The embossed stamp shows an eagle in flight.

AEN28 *Eagle in Flight*

Type I: (Left) short cloud

Type 2: (Right) long cloud

AEN28		UnFVF	UseFVF
6¢	**carmine red,** Type 1	.90	.65
	entire	1.25	1.00
	v. Type 2	—	—
	entire	—	—
	FDC *(May 2, 1956)*		1.25

1958. Issue

AEN29 *DC-4 Skymaster*

AEN29		UnFVF	UseFVF
7¢	**blue,** Border 2	.80	.70
	entire	1.25	.75
	v. Border 4	—	—
	entire	—	—
	FDC *(July 31, 1958)*		1.25

1958. Issue

AEN30, AEN36 *Jet Airliner*

AEN30		UnFVF	UseFVF
7¢	**blue,** Border 2	.70	.35
	entire	.80	.40
	v. w/Border 4	—	—
	entire	—	—
	FDC *(Nov. 21, 1958)*		1.25

1958. Issue On Aug. 1, 1958, airmail rates were advanced to 7¢, necessitating new envelopes and the re-valuing of surplus stocks of the 6¢ airmail envelopes. The same surcharging device was used as for re-valuing the 3¢ regular postage envelopes.

Type 11 *surcharge printed in green to left of stamp*

AEN31		UnFVF	UseFVF
6¢ + 1¢	**orange,** Die 1 (AEN4v1)	250.00	250.00
	entire	300.00	400.00

AEN32		UnFVF	UseFVF
6¢ + 1¢	**orange,** Die 2 (AEN5v1)	70.00	80.00
	entire	100.00	150.00

AEN33		UnFVF	UseFVF
6¢ + 1¢	**orange,** Die 3 (AEN6)	40.00	55.00
	entire	50.00	100.00

Overprinted in green to left of stamp on 6¢ orange of 1934-44 (circular die) issue, no borders.

AEN34		UnFVF	UseFVF
6¢ + 1¢	**carmine,** Border 2, Type 1 (AEN22)	1.25	.65
	entire	1.35	.80
	v. Type 2 (AEN22v)	1.25	.65
	entire	1.35	.80
	v1. Border 4, Type 1 (AEN22v2)	—	—
	entire	—	—
	v2. Border 4, Type 2 (AEN22v3)	—	—
	entire	—	—

On 6¢ carmine of 1950 (Skymaster design) issue.

AEN35		UnFVF	UseFVF
6¢ + 1¢	**carmine,** Type 1 (AEN28)	1.25	.75
	entire	1.75	1.00
	v. Type 2	—	—
	entire	—	—

On 6¢ carmine of 1956 (FIPEX) issue.

1960. Issue Type AEN30 in new color.

AEN36		UnFVF	UseFVF
7¢	**red,** Border 2	.75	.40
	entire	1.00	.45
	v. Border 4	—	—
	entire	—	—
	FDC *(Aug. 15, 1960)*		

1962. Airliner Issue

AEN37 *Airliner in flight*

AEN37		UnFVF	UseFVF
8¢	**red,** Border 2	.75	.25
	entire	1.00	.40
	v. Border 4	—	—
	entire	—	—
	FDC *(Nov. 17, 1962)*		1.25

1965. Issue

AEN38 *Jet liner with denomination*

AEN38		UnFVF	UseFVF
8¢	**red,** Border 6	.50	.25
	entire	.60	.40
	v. Border 7 (error)	—	—
	entire	25.00	—
	FDC *(Jan. 7, 1965)*		1.25
	z. Tagged (Aug. 15, 1967)	1.50	.50
	entire	2.00	1.00
	FDC *(Aug. 15, 1967)*		3.50

Border 6 has a blue lozenge above and to left of stamp. Border 7 has a red lozenge above and to left of stamp.

1968. Issue

AEN39 *Type 12 surcharge printed in red to left of stamp on 8¢ airmail envelopes AEN38*

AEN39		UnFVF	UseFVF
8¢ + 2¢	**red,** Border 6	.80	.25
	entire	1.25	.50
	FDC *(Feb. 5, 1968)*		

1968. Issue

AEN40 *Jet liner without denomination*

AEN40		UnFVF	UseFVF
10¢	**red,** Border 6, tagged	.60	.25
	entire	1.00	.25
	FDC *(Jan. 8, 1968)*		1.25

1971. Issue

AEN41 *Three circles*

AEN41		UnFVF	UseFVF
11¢	**red and blue**	.60	.25
	entire	.75	.25
	FDC *(May 6, 1971)*		1.25

1971. Issue *Revalued at left of stamp, printed on AEN40.*

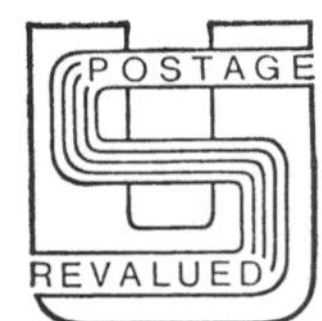

Type 13 surcharge printed in green to left of stamp

AEN42		UnFVF	UseFVF
10¢ + 1¢	**red**	1.75	.30
	entire	2.25	.65
	FDC *(June 28, 1971)*		8.00

1973. Issue

AEN43 *Stylized bird*

AEN43		UnFVF	UseFVF
13¢	**red,** luminescent ink	.40	.25
	entire	.50	.25
	FDC *(Dec. 1, 1973)*		1.25

Air Letter Sheets, Aerogrammes

Listings are for entires only.

1947. Issue *Printed by letterpress.* There are four types of inscriptions:

Type A: "AIR LETTER" on face; two-line inscription on back (when folded).

Type B: "AIR MAIL" on face; four-line inscription on back (when folded).

Type C: "AIR LETTER - AEROGRAMME" on face; four-line inscription on back (when folded).

Type D: "AIR LETTER - AEROGRAMME" on face; three-line inscription on back (when folded).

ALS1

ALS1		UnFVF	UseFVF
10¢	**carmine on bluish,** Type A	9.00	7.00
	v. blue overlay on inner side omitted	—	—
	v1. Reverse die cutting	125.00	—
	v2. Type B (Sept. 1951)	18.50	16.00
	v2a. chocolate (error of color)	450.00	—
	v2a. Reverse die cutting	300.00	—
	v3. Type C (Nov. 1953)	55.00	15.00
	v3a. Reverse die cutting	—	—
	v4. Type D (1955)	9.00	9.00
	v4a. Reverse die cutting	70.00	—
	FDC *(April 29, 1947)*		2.00

1958. Issue Paper tinted blue without overlay. *Printed by letterpress.* New inscriptions:

Type A: two-line inscription on back (when folded).

Type B: three-line inscription on back (when folded).

ALS2

ALS2		UnFVF	UseFVF
10¢	**blue and red,** Type A	7.50	6.00
	v. red omitted	—	—
	v1. blue omitted	—	—
	v2. Reverse die cutting	80.00	—
	v3. Type B	12.50	7.50
	FDC *(Sept. 12, 1958)*		1.25

1961. Issue *Printed by typography.*

ALS3

ALS3		UnFVF	UseFVF
11¢	**red and blue on bluish**	3.50	2.50
	v. red omitted	900.00	—
	v1. blue omitted	900.00	—
	v2. Reverse die cutting	40.00	—
	FDC *(June 16, 1961)*		1.25

1965. Issue "AEROGRAMME PAR AVION" on face at bottom; two-line inscription on back.

ALS4 *John F. Kennedy*

ALS4		UnFVF	UseFVF
11¢	**red and blue on bluish**	4.00	3.00
	v. Reverse die cutting	45.00	—
	FDC *(May 29, 1965)*		1.25

1967. Issue Same design as ALS4.

ALS5		UnFVF	UseFVF
13¢	**red and blue on bluish**	3.50	3.00
	v1. blue omitted	600.00	—
	v2. red omitted	600.00	—
	v3. Reverse die cutting	—	—
	FDC *(May 29, 1967)*		1.25

1968. Human Rights Issue Commemorated the 20th Anniversary of Universal Declaration of Human Rights.

ALS6

ALS6		UnFVF	UseFVF
13¢	**multicolored on bluish,** tagged GB	10.00	5.50
	v. black omitted	—	—
	v1. brown omitted	400.00	—
	v2. orange omitted	—	—
	z. Untagged (error)	—	—
	zo. Tagging omitted (error)	—	—
	FDC *(Dec. 3, 1968)*		1.25

1971. Birds Issue used the same indicium with two inscriptions — "VIA AIR MAIL • PAR AVION" for ALS7 and "AEROGRAMME • VIA AIR MAIL • PAR AVION" for ALS8.

ALS7, ALS8 *Birds in flight*

ALS7		UnFVF	UseFVF
15¢	**multicolored on bluish**	2.00	1.50
	FDC *(May 28, 1971)*		1.25

ALS8		UnFVF	UseFVF
15¢	**multicolored on bluish**	2.00	1.50
	FDC *(Dec. 13, 1971)*		1.25

1973. Hot-Air Ballooning Issue

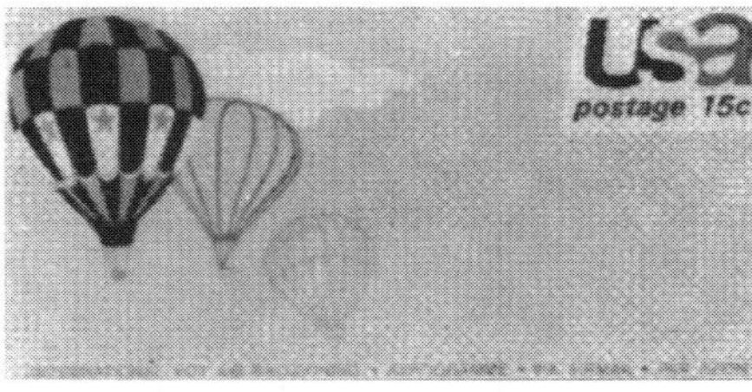

ALS9 *Hot-air balloons (same stamp indicium as previous two issues)*

ALS9		UnFVF	UseFVF
15¢	**multicolored on bluish**	1.00	1.50
	FDC *(Feb. 10, 1973)*		1.25

1974. Globe and Jet Issue

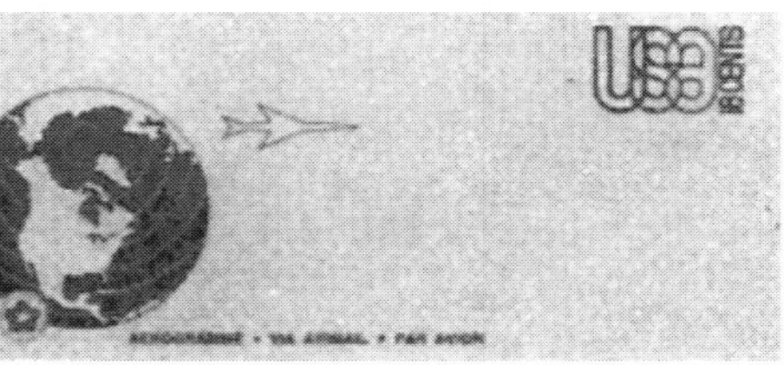

ALS10

ALS10		UnFVF	UseFVF
18¢	**red and blue on bluish,** tagged	1.25	1.50
	v. red omitted	—	—
	v1. Reverse die cutting	—	—
	FDC *(Jan. 4, 1974)*		1.25

1974. NATO Issue Commemorated the 25th anniversary of the North Atlantic Treaty Organization.

ALS11

ALS11		UnFVF	UseFVF
18¢	**red and blue on bluish,** tagged	1.25	2.00
	FDC *(April 4, 1974)*		1.25

1976. Issue

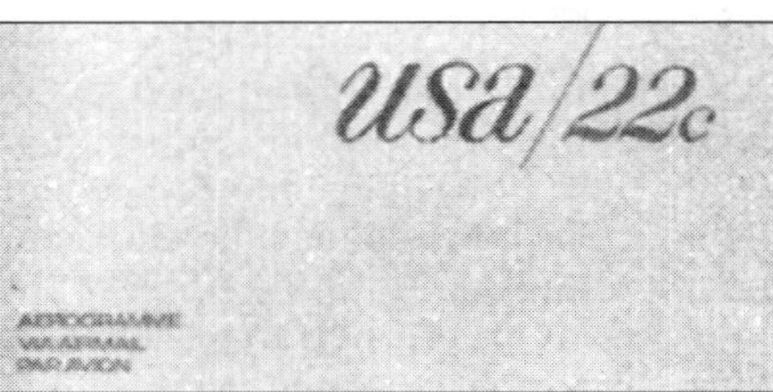

ALS12

ALS12		UnFVF	UseFVF
22¢	**red and blue on bluish,** tagged	1.25	.50
	v. Reverse die cutting	15.00	—
	FDC *(Jan. 16, 1976)*		1.25

1978. Issue

ALS13

ALS13		UnFVF	UseFVF
22¢	**blue on bluish,** tagged	1.25	.40
	v. Reverse die cutting	30.00	—
	FDC *(Nov. 3, 1978)*		1.25

1979. Olympic Issue

ALS14

ALS14		UnFVF	UseFVF
22¢	**red, green and black on bluish,** tagged	1.75	1.00
	FDC *(Dec. 5, 1979)*		1.25

1980. Tourism and Travel Issue

ALS15

ALS15		UnFVF	UseFVF
30¢	**blue, red and brown on bluish,** tagged	1.00	.40
	v. red omitted	100.00	—
	v1. Reverse die cutting	20.00	—
	FDC *(Dec. 29, 1980)*		1.25

1981. Tourism and Travel Issue

ALS16		UnFVF	UseFVF
30¢	**yellow, red, blue and black on blue,** tagged	1.00	.40
	v. Reverse die cutting	25.00	—
	FDC *(Sept. 21, 1981)*		1.25

1982. World Trade Issue

ALS17 *Made in USA*

ALS17		UnFVF	UseFVF
30¢	**multicolored on blue,** tagged	1.25	.40
	FDC *(Sept. 16, 1982)*		1.25

1983. World Communications Issue

ALS18

ALS18		UnFVF	UseFVF
30¢	**multicolored on blue,** tagged	1.25	.40
	v. Reverse die cutting	35.00	—
	FDC *(Jan. 7, 1983)*		1.25

1983. Olympics Issue

ALS19

ALS19		UnFVF	UseFVF
30¢	**multicolored,** tagged	1.25	1.00
	v. Reverse die cutting	—	—
	FDC *(Oct. 14, 1983)*		1.25

1985. LANDSAT Issue

ALS20

ALS20		UnFVF	UseFVF
36¢	**multicolored on blue,** tagged	1.25	1.00
	v. Reverse die cutting	35.00	—
	FDC *(Feb. 14, 1985)*		1.25

1985. Travel Issue

ALS21 *City skyline*

		UnFVF	UseFVF
ALS21			
36¢	**multicolored on blue,** tagged	1.25	1.00
	v. black omitted	—	—
	v1. Reverse die cutting	30.00	—
	FDC *(May 21, 1985)*		1.25

1985. Mark Twain/Halley's Comet Issue

ALS22 *Halley's Comet*

		UnFVF	UseFVF
ALS22			
36¢	**multicolored,** tagged	3.00	2.00
	v. Reverse die cutting	30.00	—
	FDC *(Dec. 4, 1985)*		1.35

1988. Issue Stylized envelope.

ALS23

		UnFVF	UseFVF
ALS23			
39¢	**multicolored,** tagged	1.25	1.00
	FDC *(May 9, 1988)*		1.50

1988. UPU Issue Abraham Lincoln and Montgomery Blair are depicted.

ALS24

		UnFVF	UseFVF
ALS24			
39¢	**multicolored,** tagged	1.25	1.00
	FDC *(Nov. 20, 1988)*		1.50

1991. Issue

ALS25, ALS26 *Eagle*

		UnFVF	UseFVF
ALS25			
45¢	**blue, gray and red on white,** tagged	1.50	.65
	FDC *(May 17, 1991)*		1.50
ALS26			
45¢	**blue, gray and red on blue,** tagged	1.50	.65

1995. Thaddeus Lowe (Balloonist) Issue

ALS27 *Thaddeus Lowe*

		UnFVF	UseFVF
ALS27			
50¢	**multicolored on blue,** tagged	1.50	.65
	FDC *(Sept. 23, 1995)*		1.50

1999. Voyageurs National Park Issue in the Scenic American Landmarks Series portrayed park scenes including the indicia, a swimming loon, a common resident of the park near International Falls, Minn. The park is named for the French traders and trappers who worked in the fur trade in the 18th and 19th centuries. *Offset by the Bureau of Engraving and Printing.*

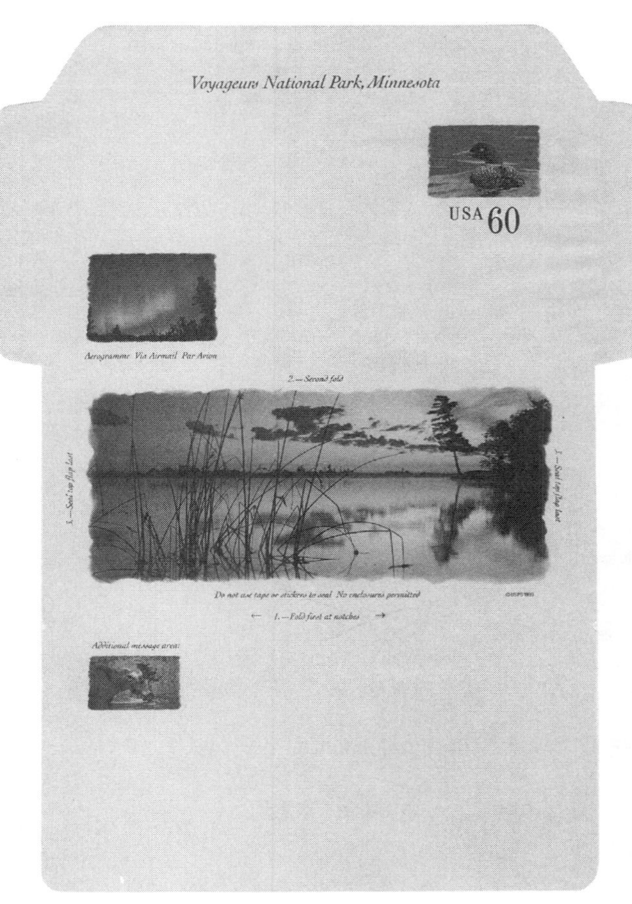

ALS28 *Voyageurs National Park*

		UnFVF	UseFVF
ALS28			
60¢	**multicolored**	1.50	1.50
	FDC *(May 15, 1999)*		1.50

Official Envelopes

When the franking privilege for government officials and departments was abolished in 1873, envelopes were issued for the Post Office and War Departments only. They were discontinued after 1879, although the War Department continued to use them for some years thereafter. Official envelope production resumed in 1983.

1873. Post Office Department Issue manufactured by George H. Reay. *Envelope Watermark 2.*

PDEN1 *Small, finely executed numeral "2"*

PDEN1		UnFVF	UseFVF
2¢	**black on canary**	11.00	7.00
	entire	15.00	11.00

PDEN2-PDEN3 *Small, finely executed numeral "3"*

PDEN2		UnFVF	UseFVF
3¢	**black on canary**	6.00	5.00
	entire	10.00	8.00
PDEN3		UnFVF	UseFVF
3¢	**black on white**	7,000.00	—
	entire	16,000.00	—

PDEN4 *Small, finely executed numeral "6"*

PDEN4		UnFVF	UseFVF
6¢	**black on canary**	13.00	11.00
	entire	19.00	16.00

1874. Post Office Department Issue manufactured by Plimpton Manufacturing Co. *Watermark 2, 4, 5.*

PDEN5, PDEN6 *Tall, heavy "2"*

PDEN5		UnFVF	UseFVF
2¢	**black on canary**	5.00	4.00
	entire	8.00	5.00
PDEN6		UnFVF	UseFVF
2¢	**black on white**	50.00	30.00
	entire	55.00	35.00

PDEN7-PDEN11 *Tall "3"*

PDEN7		UnFVF	UseFVF
3¢	**black on canary**	3.00	1.00
	entire	4.00	1.50
PDEN8		UnFVF	UseFVF
3¢	**black on white**	900.00	900.00
	entire	1,000.00	—
PDEN9		UnFVF	UseFVF
3¢	**black on amber**	40.00	29.00
	entire	50.00	45.00
PDEN10		UnFVF	UseFVF
3¢	**black on blue**	16,000.00	—
	entire	19,000.00	—
PDEN11		UnFVF	UseFVF
3¢	**blue on blue**	15,000.00	—
	entire	17,000.00	—

PDEN12, PDEN13 *Tall "6"*

PDEN12		UnFVF	UseFVF
6¢	**black on canary**	4.50	4.25
	entire	9.00	4.50
PDEN13		UnFVF	UseFVF
6¢	**black on white**	550.00	—
	entire	750.00	—

1877. Postal Service Department Issue *Unwatermarked and watermark 2, 4, 5.*

PDEN14-PDEN17

PDEN14		UnFVF	UseFVF
	black on white	4.00	3.50
	entire	6.00	5.00
PDEN15		UnFVF	UseFVF
	black on amber	30.00	21.00
	entire	90.00	40.00
PDEN16		UnFVF	UseFVF
	blue on amber	35.00	25.00
	entire	90.00	45.00
PDEN17		UnFVF	UseFVF
	blue on blue	6.00	6.00
	entire	8.00	8.00

1873. War Department Issue manufactured by George H. Reay. *Watermarks 2, 3, 4, 5, 6.*

WDEN18-WDEN20 *Benjamin Franklin, point of bust narrow and points at "N" of "ONE"*

WDEN18		UnFVF	UseFVF
1¢	**dark red on white**	500.00	300.00
	entire	750.00	350.00
WDEN19		UnFVF	UseFVF
1¢	**vermilion on white**	200.00	—
	entire	275.00	—
WDEN20		UnFVF	UseFVF
1¢	**vermilion on manila,** wrapper	11.00	8.00
	entire	20.00	15.00

WDEN21-WDEN23 *Andrew Jackson, point of bust broad and square*

WDEN21		UnFVF	UseFVF
2¢	**dark red on white**	650.00	350.00
	entire	750.00	—
WDEN22		UnFVF	UseFVF
2¢	**vermilion on white**	260.00	—
	entire	5,000.00	
WDEN23		UnFVF	UseFVF
2¢	**vermilion on manila,** wrapper	200.00	—
	entire	300.00	—

WDEN24-WDEN29 *George Washington, the ponytail projects below the bottom of the bust*

			UnFVF	UseFVF
WDEN24				
3¢	**dark red on white**		50.00	40.00
	entire		150.00	—
WDEN25			UnFVF	UseFVF
3¢	**dark red on amber**		13,000.00	—
	entire		17,000.00	—
WDEN26			UnFVF	UseFVF
3¢	**dark red on cream**		450.00	200.00
	entire		550.00	225.00
WDEN27			UnFVF	UseFVF
3¢	**vermilion on white**		75.00	40.00
	entire		150.00	—
WDEN28			UnFVF	UseFVF
3¢	**vermilion on amber**		85.00	—
	entire		250.00	—
WDEN29			UnFVF	UseFVF
3¢	**vermilion on cream**		13.00	7.00
	entire		40.00	20.00

WDEN30-WDEN33 *Abraham Lincoln, back of neck is long*

			UnFVF	UseFVF
WDEN30				
6¢	**dark red on white**		170.00	70.00
	entire		200.00	—
WDEN31			UnFVF	UseFVF
6¢	**dark red on cream**		1,400.00	350.00
	entire*		2,400.00	1,500.00
WDEN32			UnFVF	UseFVF
6¢	**vermilion on white**		—	—
	entire		—	—
WDEN33			UnFVF	UseFVF
6¢	**vermilion on cream**		350.00	—
	entire*		6,500.00	—

WDEN34, WDEN35 *Thomas Jefferson, the ponytail does not project at back*

			UnFVF	UseFVF
WDEN34				
10¢	**dark red on white**		2,700.00	280.00
	entire*		5,000.00	550.00
WDEN35			UnFVF	UseFVF
10¢	**vermilion on white**		200.00	—
	entire*		350.00	—

WDEN36, WDEN37 *Henry Clay, ear covered by hair*

			UnFVF	UseFVF
WDEN36				
12¢	**dark red on white**		100.00	40.00
	entire*		140.00	—
WDEN37			UnFVF	UseFVF
12¢	**vermilion on white**		150.00	—
	entire*		200.00	—

WDEN38, WDEN39 *Daniel Webster, face with sideburns*

			UnFVF	UseFVF
WDEN38				
15¢	**dark red on white**		100.00	45.00
	entire*		125.00	400.00
WDEN39			UnFVF	UseFVF
15¢	**vermilion on white**		250.00	—
	entire*		2,500.00	—

WDEN40, WDEN41 *Winfield Scott*

			UnFVF	UseFVF
WDEN40				
24¢	**dark red on white**		135.00	35.00
	entire*		100.00	—
WDEN41			UnFVF	UseFVF
24¢	**vermilion on white**		375.00	—
	entire*		400.00	—

WDEN42, WDEN43 *Alexander Hamilton, bust at back ends in a narrow point*

			UnFVF	UseFVF
WDEN42				
30¢	**dark red on white**		400.00	110.00
	entire*		450.00	180.00
WDEN43			UnFVF	UseFVF
30¢	**vermilion on white**		375.00	—
	entire*		475.00	—

1875. War Department Issue produced by Plimpton Manufacturing Co. *Watermarks 2, 3, 4, 5, 6.*

WDEN44-WDEN46 *Benjamin Franklin, point of bust is broad*

			UnFVF	UseFVF
WDEN44				
1¢	**red on white**		125.00	100.00
	entire		135.00	—
WDEN45			UnFVF	UseFVF
1¢	**red on amber**		750.00	—
WDEN45A			UnFVF	UseFVF
1¢	**red on orange**		18,000.00	—
WDEN46			UnFVF	UseFVF
1¢	**red on manila,** wrapper		3.00	1.75
	entire		6.00	4.00

WDEN47-WDEN50 *Andrew Jackson, forward slope of bust is rounded*

			UnFVF	UseFVF
WDEN47				
2¢	**red on white**		100.00	—
	entire		125.00	—
WDEN48			UnFVF	UseFVF
2¢	**red on amber**		25.00	15.00
	entire		35.00	25.00
WDEN49			UnFVF	UseFVF
2¢	**red on orange**		45.00	13.00
	entire		45.00	20.00
WDEN50			UnFVF	UseFVF
2¢	**red on manila,** wrapper		70.00	45.00
	entire		90.00	—

WDEN51-WDEN55 *George Washington, the ponytail does not project below bust but protrudes toward rear*

WDEN51		UnFVF	UseFVF
3¢	**red on white**	11.00	9.00
	entire	12.00	10.00
WDEN52		**UnFVF**	**UseFVF**
3¢	**red on amber**	12.00	9.00
	entire	15.00	13.00
WDEN53		**UnFVF**	**UseFVF**
3¢	**red on cream**	6.00	3.00
	entire	8.00	5.00
WDEN54		**UnFVF**	**UseFVF**
3¢	**red on blue**	4.00	3.00
	entire	5.00	4.00
WDEN55		**UnFVF**	**UseFVF**
3¢	**red on fawn**	5.00	2.00
	entire	7.00	3.00

WDEN56-WDEN58 *Abraham Lincoln, back of bust is short*

WDEN56		UnFVF	UseFVF
6¢	**red on white**	35.00	22.00
	entire	70.00	—
WDEN57		**UnFVF**	**UseFVF**
6¢	**red on amber**	70.00	30.00
	entire	75.00	—
WDEN58		**UnFVF**	**UseFVF**
6¢	**red on cream**	170.00	70.00
	entire	200.00	—

WDEN59, WDEN60 *Thomas Jefferson, the ponytail projects at back*

WDEN59		UnFVF	UseFVF
10¢	**red on white**	150.00	90.00
	entire	175.00	—
WDEN60		**UnFVF**	**UseFVF**
10¢	**red on amber**	1,100.00	—
	entire	1,400.00	—

WDEN61-WDEN63 *Henry Clay, clearly defined ear*

WDEN61		UnFVF	UseFVF
12¢	**red on white**	40.00	35.00
	entire*	100.00	—
WDEN62		**UnFVF**	**UseFVF**
12¢	**red on white**	650.00	—
	entire*	700.00	—
WDEN63		**UnFVF**	**UseFVF**
12¢	**red on cream**	600.00	—
	entire*	750.00	—

WDEN64-WDEN67 *Daniel Webster, face without sideburns*

WDEN64		UnFVF	UseFVF
15¢	**red on white**	175.00	135.00
	entire*	200.00	—
WDEN65		**UnFVF**	**UseFVF**
15¢	**red on amber**	700.00	—
	entire*	750.00	—
WDEN66		**UnFVF**	**UseFVF**
15¢	**red on cream**	650.00	—
	entire*	700.00	—

WDEN67-WDEN69*Alexander Hamilton, bust at back is broad*

WDEN67		UnFVF	UseFVF
30¢	**red on white**	150.00	125.00
	entire*	180.00	—
WDEN68		**UnFVF**	**UseFVF**
30¢	**red on amber**	1,000.00	—
	entire*	1,100.00	—
WDEN69		**UnFVF**	**UseFVF**
30¢	**red on cream**	1,000.00	—
	entire*	1,100.00	—

1910. United States Postal Savings Issue *Watermarks 15, 16, 17, 18.*

PSEN72 *Watermarks 15, 16, 17, 18*

PSEN70		UnFVF	UseFVF
1¢	**green on white**	60.00	15.00
	entire*	75.00	45.00
PSEN71		**UnFVF**	**UseFVF**
1¢	**green on buff**	185.00	60.00
	entire*	220.00	75.00
PSEN72		**UnFVF**	**UseFVF**
2¢	**carmine on white**	8.00	3.00
	entire*	13.00	9.00
PSEN73		**UnFVF**	**UseFVF**
2¢	**carmine on manila**	1,700.00	—
	entire*	2,500.00	

1983. Official Mail Issue

OEN74 *Great Seal*

OEN74		UnFVF	UseFVF
20¢	**blue on white,** entire	1.00	25.00
	FDC *(Jan. 12, 1983)*		1.25

1985. Official Mail Issue

OEN75 *Great Seal*

OEN75		UnFVF	UseFVF
22¢	**blue on white,** entire	.75	5.00
	FDC *(Feb. 26, 1985)*		1.25

1987. Official Mail Issue Used exclusively to mail U.S. Savings Bonds. *Typographed.*

OEN76 *Great Seal*

OEN76		UnFVF	UseFVF
22¢	**blue on white,** entire	.90	20.00
	FDC *(March 2, 1987)*		1.25

1988. Non-Denominated "E" Issue Used exclusively to mail U.S. Savings Bonds. *Typographed.*

OEN77 *Great Seal and "E"*

OEN77		UnFVF	UseFVF
25¢	**black and blue on white,** entire	1.00	20.00
	FDC *(March 22, 1988)*		1.25

1988. Denominated 25¢ Issue *Printed by letterpress and embossed.*

OEN78 *Great Seal*

OEN78		UnFVF	UseFVF
25¢	**black and blue on white,** entire	.75	5.00
	FDC *(April 11, 1988)*		1.25
	v. lettering as on OEN79, entire	—	—

OEN79 *Great Seal. Used exclusively to mail U.S. Savings Bonds. Typographed.*

OEN79		UnFVF	UseFVF
25¢	**black and blue on white,** entire thick lettering	.85	25.00
	FDC *(April 11, 1988)*		1.25
	v. lettering as on OEN78, entire	—	—

1990. Official Mail Issue Stars and "E Pluribus Unum" barely legible, lettering heavy: "Official" measures 13mm; "USA" measures 16mm. *Printed by letterpress.*

OEN80 *Great Seal*

OEN80		UnFVF	UseFVF
45¢	**black and blue on white,** entire	1.25	—
	FDC *(March 17, 1990)*		1.50

OEN81 *Great Seal. Used exclusively to mail U.S. passports. Typographed.*

OEN81		UnFVF	UseFVF
65¢	**black and blue on white,** entire	1.60	—
	FDC *(March 17, 1990)*		2.25

1990. Official Mail Issue Similar to above. *Printed by offset.* "Official" measures 14.5mm; "USA" measures 17mm.

OEN82 *Great Seal. Used exclusively to mail U.S. passports. Lithographed.*

OEN82		UnFVF	UseFVF
45¢	**black and blue on white,** entire	1.25	—
	FDC *(Aug. 10, 1990)*		1.50

OEN83 *Great Seal*

OEN83		UnFVF	UseFVF
65¢	**black and blue on white,** entire	1.50	—
	FDC *(Aug. 10, 1990)*		2.25

Input from stamp collectors regarding the content of this catalog and ideas to make it more useful is eagerly sought. Send your comments to:

Minkus Catalog Editor
Krause Publications
700 E. State St.
Iola WI 54990

1991. Official Non-denominated Issue Non-denominated "F" envelope. Used exclusively to mail U.S. Savings Bonds. *Typographed.*

OEN84 *Great Seal*

OEN84		UnFVF	UseFVF
29¢	**black and blue on white,** entire	1.10	20.00
	FDC *(Jan. 22, 1991)*		1.25

1991. Denominated Official Issue *Issued initially watermarked; unwatermarked evelopes are on recycled paper, and have an imprint under the flap. Lithographed and embossed.*

OEN85 *Great Seal*

OEN85		UnFVF	UseFVF
29¢	**black and blue on white,** entire	.70	2.00
	FDC *(April 6, 1991)*		1.25
	Entire, unwatermarked, *(May 1, 1992)*	.70	—

1991. Official Issue Used exclusively to mail U.S. Savings Bonds. *Typographed, unwatermarked evelopes are on recycled paper, and have an imprint under the flap.*

OEN86 *Great Seal*

OEN86		UnFVF	UseFVF
29¢	**black and blue on white,** entire	.70	20.00
	FDC *(April 17, 1991)*		1.25
	v. Entire, unwatermarked, *(May 1, 1992)*	.70	—

1992. Consular Service Bicentennial Issue Used exclusively to mail U.S. passports. *Lithographed, unwatermarked.*

OEN87 *Globe, U.S. flag*

OEN87		UnFVF	UseFVF
52¢	**blue and red on white,** entire	2.00	—
	FDC *(July 10, 1992)*		2.25

OEN88 *Globe, U.S. flag*

OEN88		UnFVF	UseFVF
75¢	**blue and red on white,** entire	4.00	—
	FDC *(July 10, 1992)*		3.25

1995. Official Mail Issue *Typographed and embossed, unwatermarked.*

OEN89 *Great Seal*

OEN89		UnFVF	UseFVF
32¢	**blue and red on white,** entire	.75	10.00
	FDC *(May 9, 1995)*		1.25

1999. Official Mail Issue featured the Great Seal of the United States. *Westvaco (2,000,000), offset and embossed, tagged.*

OEN90 *Great Seal*

OEN90		UnFVF	UseFVF
33¢	**blue and red, on white**	.75	—
	entire		
	FDC *(Feb. 22, 1999)*		1.50

2001. Great Seal Issue *typographed and embossed, unwatermarked, tagged.*

OEN91 *Great Seal*

OEN91		UnFVF	UseFVF
34¢	**blue & red**	.85	.50
	entire	.85	.50
	FDC *(Feb. 27, 2001)*		1.50

Postal Cards

Postal cards vary greatly in size. Card sizes are not indicated except in those cases where the difference is important in making proper identification. So, too, the text on the face of the cards has been changed on numerous occasions. The exact wording is not indicated except when it is the determining factor of identification.

Postal cards normally are collected intact in one of the following three conditions: mint; unused (preprinted with address or messages, but no postal marking); or used (with postal marking).

Prices for used examples of Universal Postal Union cards or other international rate cards are for overseas usages. Such cards used domestically sell for much less. Similarly, inflated values for recent used cards are based on proper use during the appropriate period.

1873. Profile of Liberty Issue *watermarked with large (90mm x 60mm) "USPOD."*

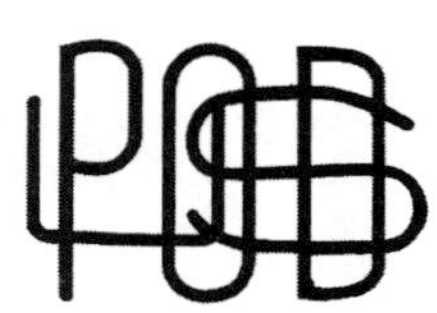

PC1, PC2, *Profile of Liberty*

PC1 *Watermark*

PC1		UnFVF	UseFVF
1¢	**reddish brown on buff**	350.00	25.00
	Preprinted	60.00	
	v. Unwatermarked	—	—
	Date of Issue *(May 12, 1873);* EKU: *May 11, 1873*		

Watermark with small (55mm x 38mm) "USPOD."

PC2		UnFVF	UseFVF
1¢	**reddish brown on buff**	75.00	3.00
	Preprinted	22.50	
	v. Unwatermarked	—	—
	Date of Issue unknown; EKU: *June 5, 1873*		

1875. Liberty Issue inscribed "WRITE THE ADDRESS ON THIS SIDE - THE MESSAGE ON THE OTHER." *Watermarked small (52mm x 36mm) "USPOD."*

PC3, PC4 *Liberty, 21 teeth below "One Cent"*

PC3		UnFVF	UseFVF
1¢	**black on buff**	2,500.00	325.00
	Preprinted	650.00	
	Date of Issue unknown; EKU: *Dec. 1, 1875*		

Unwatermarked. All subsequent U.S. Postal cards also are without watermarks.

PC4		UnFVF	UseFVF
1¢	**black on buff**	65.00	1.00
	Preprinted	6.50	
	Date of Issue *(Sept. 30, 1875)*		

1879. Universal Postal Union Card Issue frame around card. Size 5 1/8 inches x 3 inches.

PC5, PC12, PC15, *Liberty*

PC5		UnFVF	UseFVF
2¢	**blue on buff**	25.00	30.00
	Preprinted	12.50	
	a. dark blue on buff	30.00	25.00
	Preprinted	12.50	
	Date of Issue *(Dec. 1, 1879)*		

1881. Liberty Issue inscribed: "NOTHING BUT THE ADDRESS CAN BE PLACED ON THIS SIDE." There are 21 teeth or 23 teeth below "ONE CENT."

PC6 *23 teeth below "One Cent"*

PC6		UnFVF	UseFVF
1¢	**black on buff,** 21 teeth	55.00	1.00
	Preprinted	5.00	
	v. 23 teeth	950.00	50.00
	Preprinted	220.00	
	v1. Printed on both sides	1,000.00	750.00
	Date of Issue *(Oct. 17, 1881);* EKU: *(Aug. 3, 1881)*		

1885. Thomas Jefferson Issue was in production only 9 months because of difficulties in formulating a suitable ink and due to public uproar over the way Jefferson's eyes were drawn.

PC7 *Thomas Jefferson*

PC7		UnFVF	UseFVF
1¢	**brown on buff**	50.00	2.50
	Preprinted	5.00	
	a. chocolate	95.00	20.00
	Preprinted	25.00	
	b. orange brown	50.00	2.50
	Preprinted	5.00	
	c. red brown	50.00	3.00
	Preprinted	5.00	
	v. Double impression	1,100.00	
	v1. Double impression, 1 inverted	1,200.00	
	v2. Printed on both sides, same color	—	
	Date of Issue *(Aug. 24, 1885);* EKU: *Aug. 29, 1885*		

1886. Thomas Jefferson Issue

PC8 *Thomas Jefferson*

PC8		UnFVF	UseFVF
1¢	**black on buff**	20.00	1.00
	Preprinted	2.00	
	a. black on glossy dark buff	40.00	2.50
	Preprinted	5.50	
	v. Double impression	—	
	v1. Double impression, 1 inverted	—	
	v2. Missing keystone in arc above "UNITED STATES"	—	
	Date of Issue *(Dec. 1, 1886);* EKU: *May 7, 1886*		

1891. Ulysses S. Grant Issue has the same indicium on two different cards, distinguishable by their size (PC10 is known as the "Ladies Card" for short, personal notes) and by the ornate front printing (PC9 has a small, angled "of" in "United States of America;" PC10 has a small shield as part of the design).

PC9, PC10 *Ulysses S. Grant*

PC9		UnFVF	UseFVF
1¢	**black on buff,** 155mm x 95mm	35.00	1.50
	Preprinted	4.50	
	v. Double impression	1,200.00	
	Date of Issue *(Dec. 16, 1891);* EKU: *Dec. 23, 1891*		

PC10		UnFVF	UseFVF
1¢	**blue on grayish,** 117mm x 75mm	15.00	3.00
	Preprinted	7.50	
	v. Double impression, 1 inverted	1,000.00	
	v2. "Picture hanger" loop in top of portrait frame line	400.00	125.00
	Date of Issue *(Dec. 16, 1891);* EKU: *Dec. 21, 1891*		

1894. Thomas Jefferson Issue

PC11 *Thomas Jefferson with small wreath*

PC11		UnFVF	UseFVF
1¢	**black on buff**	37.00	1.00
	Preprinted	1.50	
	v. Double impression	—	
	Date of Issue *(Jan. 2, 1894);* EKU: *Jan. 4, 1894*		

1897. Universal Postal Union same design as PC5, but larger (5 1/2 inches x 3 1/2 inches).

PC12		UnFVF	UseFVF
2¢	**blue on light blue**	165.00	90.00
	Preprinted	65.00	
	Date of Issue *(Jan. 25, 1897);* EKU: *April 17, 1897*		

1897. Thomas Jefferson Issue

PC13 *Thomas Jefferson with large wreath*

PC13		UnFVF	UseFVF
1¢	**black on buff**	30.00	2.00
	Preprinted	3.00	
	v. Double impression, 1 inverted	—	
	v1. Printed on both sides	—	
	Date of Issue *(Dec. 1, 1897)*		

1898. John Adams Issue

PC14 *John Adams*

PC14		UnFVF	UseFVF
1¢	**black on buff**	45.00	27.50
	Preprinted	12.00	
	Date of Issue *(March 31, 1898)*		

1898. Universal Postal Union same design as PC5 and PC12, but without frame around card. (140mm x 82mm).

PC15		UnFVF	UseFVF
2¢	**black on buff**	12.50	10.00
	Preprinted	5.50	

1902. William McKinley (Full-Face) Issue

PC16 *U.S. seal (at left); William McKinley, full face (at right)*

PC16		UnFVF	UseFVF
1¢	**black on buff**	5,000.00	2,500.00
	Preprinted	3,250.00	
	Earliest known use: *(May 26, 1902)*		

1902. William McKinley (Profile) Issue

PC17 *U.S. seal (at left); William McKinley, profile (at right)*

PC17		UnFVF	UseFVF
1¢	**black on buff**	12.50	2.00
	Preprinted	2.00	
	v. Double impression	—	
	Earliest known use: *(July 10, 1902)*		

1907. William McKinley

PC18, PC19 *William McKinley*

PC18		UnFVF	UseFVF
1¢	**black on buff**	40.00	1.50
	Preprinted	2.00	
	Date of Issue *(June 1907)*		

1908. William McKinley same design as PC18. Message space at left side. Inscribed (vertically) at side: "THE SPACE BELOW MAY BE USED FOR CORRESPONDENCE."

PC19		UnFVF	UseFVF
1¢	**black on buff**	50.00	7.50
	Preprinted	8.00	
	Date of Issue *(Jan. 2, 1908)*		

1910. William McKinley Issue

PC20 *William McKinley, area around head shaded*

(THIS SIDE OF CARD IS FOR ADDRESS ONLY)

(THIS SIDE OF CARD IS FOR ADDRESS ONLY)

PC20		UnFVF	UseFVF
1¢	**blue on bluish**	100.00	7.50
	Preprinted	16.50	
	a. bronze blue on bluish	170.00	15.00
	Preprinted	27.50	
	b. Pointed arcs on 4 outer areas above & below "IS" in inscription to left of imprinted stamp.	2,000.00	550.00
	Preprinted	1,000.00	
	v1. Double impression	—	
	v2. Double impression, 1 inverted	—	
	v3. Triple impression	—	
	Date of Issue *(Feb. 12, 1910)*		

PC21, PC23 *William McKinley, area around head without shading*

PC21		UnFVF	UseFVF
1¢	**blue on bluish**	15.00	.50
	Preprinted	1.75	
	p. Printed on thin paper (0.008 inches thickness)	—	—
	v. Double impression, normal position	—	
	Date of Issue *(April 13, 1910)*		

1911. Abraham Lincoln Issue

PC22, PC25 *Abraham Lincoln*

PC22		UnFVF	UseFVF
1¢	**red on cream,** 127mm x 76mm	10.00	7.50
	Preprinted	3.50	
	v. Double impression	—	
	Date of Issue *(Jan. 21, 1911)*		

1911. William McKinley Issue. same design as PC21.

PC23		UnFVF	UseFVF
1¢	**carmine on cream**	12.50	7.50
	Preprinted	1.75	
	a. scarlet	—	
	v. Double impression	—	
	Date of Issue *(Aug. 10, 1911)*		

1911. Grant International Rate Issue

PC24 *Ulysses S. Grant*

PC24		UnFVF	UseFVF
2¢	**carmine on cream**	1.75	9.00
	Preprinted	1.00	
	v. Double impression	—	
	Date of Issue *(Oct. 27, 1911)*		

1913. Abraham Lincoln Issue same design as PC22; same size: 5 x 3 inches.

PC25		UnFVF	UseFVF
1¢	**green on cream**	12.50	7.50
	Preprinted		
	Date of Issue *(July 29, 1913)*		

1914. Thomas Jefferson Issue

PC26, PC27 *Thomas Jefferson*

PC26		UnFVF	UseFVF
1¢	**green on buff**	.40	.30
	Preprinted	.25	
	a. green on cream	3.75	.75
	Preprinted	1.25	
	b. green on off-white	3.75	.75
	Preprinted	1.25	
	v. Double impression	—	
	Date of Issue *(June 4, 1914)*		

1916. Thomas Jefferson Issue same design as PC26. Due to wartime shortages, an inferior rough-textured bluish gray paper was used for a short period. PC27 and PC28 were printed on this substitute paper.

PC27		UnFVF	UseFVF
1¢	**dark green on bluish gray**	2,700.00	175.00

1916. Thomas Jefferson Issue recut die consisting of heavy hair lines and distinct hair lines in queue.

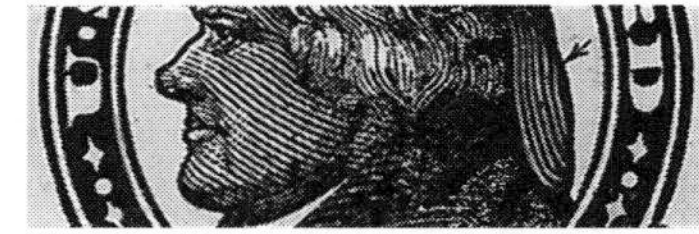

PC28 *Recut die*

PC28		UnFVF	UseFVF
1¢	**dark green on bluish gray**	3,000.00	140.00
	Date of Issue *(Dec. 22, 1916)*		

1917. Abraham Lincoln Issue Small "library" size: 5 x 3 inches.

PC29 *Abraham Lincoln*

PC29		UnFVF	UseFVF
1¢	**green on cream**	.75	.50
	Preprinted	.35	
	a. green on dark buff	1.75	.75
	Preprinted	.65	
	b green on canary	—	—
	v. Double impression	—	
	Date of Issue *(March 14, 1917)*		

1917. Thomas Jefferson Issue

PC30 *Die 1, coarse impression. Points on numerals.*

PC30		UnFVF	UseFVF
2¢	**carmine on cream**	50.00	3.00
	Preprinted	7.50	
	a. vermilion on cream	300.00	70.00
	Preprinted	75.00	
	b. lake on cream	50.00	3.00
	Preprinted	7.50	
	c. carmine on buff	40.00	3.00
	Preprinted	6.00	
	Date of Issue *(Oct. 22, 1917)*		

1918. Thomas Jefferson Issue

PC31 *Die 2, clear impression. Balls on numerals.*

PC31		UnFVF	UseFVF
2¢	**carmine on cream**	30.00	2.75
	Preprinted	4.50	
	Date of Issue *(Jan. 23, 1918)*		

1920. Jefferson Surcharge Issue

surcharged "1 CENT" in black on PC30 (die 1).

The overprints were applied by a canceling machine (below left) or a printing press (below right).

PC32, PC33

1 CENT 1 CENT

PC32	UnFVF	UseFVF
1¢ on 2¢ red on cream, *canceling machine*	55.00	12.50
Preprinted	16.00	
a. Press printing	550.00	50.00
Preprinted	110.00	
v. Double surcharge	—	
v1. Inverted surcharge	—	
Date of Issue *(April 1920)*		

1920. Jefferson Surcharge (Die 2) Issue

PC33	UnFVF	UseFVF
1¢ on 2¢ red on cream	15.00	12.50
Preprinted	2.50	
a. Press printing	225.00	35.00
Preprinted	60.00	
v. Double surcharge	90.00	
v1. Double surcharge, 1 inverted	300.00	
v2. Inverted surcharge	60.00	
v3. Triple surcharge	375.00	
Date of Issue *(April 1920)*		

1920. Jefferson Issue

PC34 *Overprinted in black on PC31 (Die 2)*

PC34	UnFVF	UseFVF
1¢ on 2¢ red on cream	4,000.00	4,500.00
Preprinted	3,000.00	
Date of Issue *(April 1920)*		

1920. Grant International Rate Surcharge Issue

2 line 1¢ surcharge on 2¢ Grant postal card (PC24). Only three or four examples known.

PC34A	UnFVF	UseFVF
1¢ on 2¢ carmine on cream	—	75,000.00
Earliest known usage: *(Dec. 16, 1920)*		—

1926. Universal Postal Union

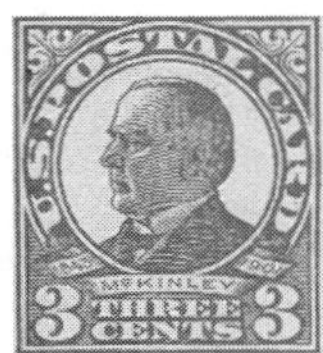

PC35 *William McKinley*

PC35		UnFVF	UseFVF
3¢	**red orange on cream**	5.00	10.00
	Preprinted	2.00	
	a. red on canary	5.50	12.50
	b. deep carmine on canary	—	—
	c. orange red on dark buff	—	—
	FDC *(Feb. 1, 1926)*		225.00

1951. Benjamin Franklin Issue

PC36 *Benjamin Franklin*

PC36		UnVF	UseVF
2¢	**carmine on buff**	.50	.30
	Preprinted	.30	
	a. lake on buff	—	—
	b. Damaged (missing) LR stamp corner	40.00	15.00
	v. Double impression	225.00	
	FDC *(Nov. 16, 1951)*		1.00

1952. 2¢ Ovpt. on Thomas Jefferson Issue

PC37 *Overprinted in green on PC26*

PC37	UnVF	UseVF
2¢ on 1¢ green on buff	.75	.40
Preprinted	.35	
v. Double surcharge	20.00	25.00
v1. Surcharge vertical at left	7.50	9.00
v2. Surcharge vertical below stamp	—	
FDC *(Jan. 1, 1952)*		12.50

Tickometer surcharge.

PC37A	UnVF	UseVF
2¢ on 1¢ green on buff	5.50	2.50

	UnVF	UseVF
Preprinted	2.00	
v. Inverted surcharge, lower left	80.00	130.00
Preprinted	60.00	
v1. Double surcharge	—	
v2. Split surcharge, top & bottom	—	
FDC *(March 22, 1952)*		

Press-printed surcharge.

1952. 2¢ OVPT. ON LINCOLN ISSUE PC29. *Surcharged, printed by Pitney Bowes Tickometer.*

PC38	UnVF	UseVF
2¢ on 1¢ green on buff	.75	.50
Preprinted	.40	
a. green on cream	.75	.50
Preprinted	.40	
b. green on canary	.75	.50
Preprinted	.40	
v. Double surcharge, normal position	—	
v1. Inverted surcharge, lower left	—	
v2. Double surcharge, 1 inverted	—	
v3. Vertical surcharge, left of stamp, reading down	7.00	5.50
FDC *(March 22, 1952)*		110.00

PC38A	UnVF	UseVF
2¢ on 1¢ green on buff	6.00	2.50
Preprinted	3.00	
v. Surcharge on back	85.00	

Press-printed surcharge.

1952. SMALL "LIBRARY" SIZE ISSUE 5 x 3 inches.

PC39 *Abraham Lincoln*

PC39		UnVF	UseVF
2¢	**carmine on buff**	.30	1.50
	Preprinted	.15	
	a. lake on buff	—	
	FDC *(July 31, 1952)*		1.00

1956. FIPEX ISSUE

PC40 *Liberty*

PC40		UnVF	UseVF
2¢	**red & dark violet blue on buff**	.30	2.00
	a. rose & dark violet blue	1.75	1.25
	v. dark violet blue omitted	475.00	250.00
	v1. Double impression of dark violet blue	18.00	11.00
	FDC *(May 4, 1956)*		1.00

1956. STATUE OF LIBERTY ISSUE International postal card.

PC41, MRC15 *Liberty*

PC41		UnVF	UseVF
4¢	**scarlet & ultramarine on buff**	1.75	75.00
	FDC *(Nov. 16, 1956)*		1.00

1958. STATUE OF LIBERTY ISSUE Domestic postal card.

PC42, MRC16 *Liberty*

PC42		UnVF	UseVF
3¢	**violet on buff**	.60	.30
	v. Double impression	—	
	v1. "I" of "IN" omitted	13.00	26.00
	x. printed precancel bars *(Sept. 15, 1961)*	4.00	3.00
	FDC *(Aug. 1, 1958)*		1.00

1958. BENJAMIN FRANKLIN ISSUE PC36 revalued in black.

ONE CENT ADDITIONAL PAID

PC43 *Overprinted in black at left of PC36*

PC43		UnVF	UseVF
2¢ & 1¢	**carmine on buff,** preprinted	175.00	500.00
	v. Surcharge inverted lower left	—	

This surcharge was authorized for use by the General Electric Co. in Owensboro, Ky., which had prepared a large number of cards for an advertising campaign prior to the 1958 rate increase. In all, some 750,000 cards were surcharged by Pitney Bowes Tickometer.

1962. ABRAHAM LINCOLN ISSUE

PC44, MRC17 *Abraham Lincoln*

PC44		UnVF	UseVF
4¢	**lilac on white,** precanceled	.30	.25
	p. Non-fluorescent paper, non-phosphorescent ink	—	—
	p1. Fluorescent paper, non-phosphorescent ink	—	—
	p2. Non-fluorescent paper, phosphorescent ink	.75	.25
	v. Double impression, normal	—	
	FDC *(Nov. 19, 1962)*		1.00

The phosphorescent ink was experimental tagging for expediting mail processing (cards placed on sale July 6, 1966).

1963. VACATIONLAND ISSUE International postal card. Designed to promote tourism to the United States.

PC45, MRC18 *Map of North America*

PC45		UnVF	UseVF
7¢	**red & blue on white**	4.50	50.00
	v. blue omitted	—	
	v1. red omitted	—	
	FDC *(Aug. 30, 1963)*		1.00

1964. U.S. Customs Service Issue honoring the 175th anniversary of the service.

PC46 *Map of United States and flags*

PC46		UnVF	UseVF
4¢	**red & blue on white**	.55	1.50
	a. blue omitted	600.00	
	v1. red omitted	—	
	FDC *(Feb. 22, 1964)*		1.00

1964. Social Security Issue in complement to the International Social Security Association conference.

PC47

PC47		UnVF	UseVF
4¢	**red & blue on white**	.50	1.50
	p. Fluorescent paper	—	—
	v. red omitted	—	
	v1. blue omitted	750.00	
	FDC *(Sept. 22, 1964)*		1.00

1965. U.S. Coast Guard Issue honoring its 175th anniversary.

PC48 *U.S. Coast Guard flag*

PC48		UnVF	UseVF
4¢	**red & blue on white**	.50	1.50
	v. blue omitted	—	
	FDC *(Aug. 4, 1965)*		1.00

1965. U.S. Census Bureau Issue honoring its 175th anniversary.

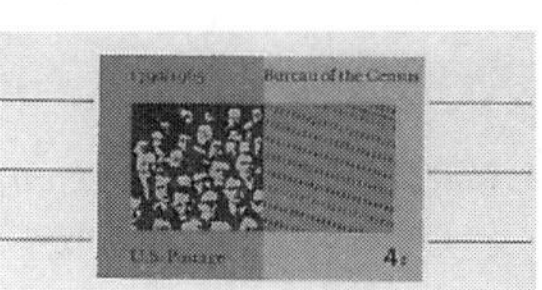

PC49 *Census anniversary*

PC49		UnVF	UseVF
4¢	**blue, light blue, & black on white**	.40	1.50
	FDC *(Oct. 21, 1965)*		1.00

1967. Vacationland Issue International postal card, design of PC45.

PC50		UnVF	UseVF
8¢	**red & blue on white**	4.25	40.00
	FDC *(Dec. 4, 1967)*		1.00

1968. Abraham Lincoln Issue

PC51, MRC20 *Abraham Lincoln*

PC51		UnVF	UseVF
5¢	**green on white**	.35	.50
	v. Double impression	—	
	FDC *(Jan. 4, 1968)*		1.00

1968. Women Marines Issue honoring their 25th anniversary.

PC52 *Women Marines*

PC52		UnVF	UseVF
5¢	**olive green and rose red on white**	.40	1.50
	v. damaged "M" in "WOMEN"	—	—
	FDC *(July 26, 1968)*		1.00

1970. Weather Services Centennial Issue

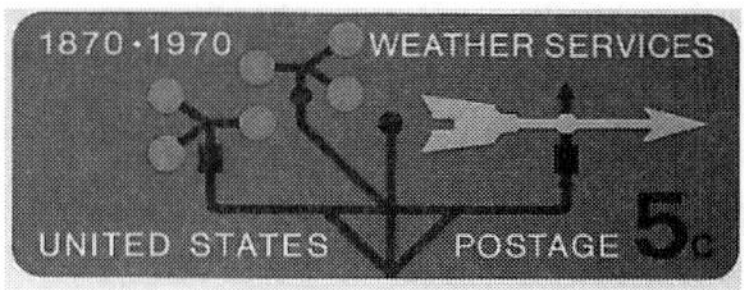

PC53 *Weather recording equipment*

PC53		UnVF	UseVF
5¢	**yellow, blue, red, and black on white,** tagged	.35	1.50
	v. black omitted	600.00	
	v1. black & yellow omitted	700.00	
	v2. blue omitted	650.00	
	FDC *(Sept. 1, 1970)*		1.00

Patriot Series

1971. Paul Revere Issue was the first in the Patriot Series.

PC54, MRC21 *Paul Revere*

PC54		UnVF	UseVF
6¢	**brown on white,** tagged	.35	2.00
	v. Double impression	325.00	—
	FDC *(May 15, 1971)*		1.00

1971. Vacationland Issue design of PC45, Vacationland.

PC55		UnVF	UseVF
10¢	**red and blue on white,** tagged	4.75	50.00
	FDC *(June 10, 1971)*		1.00

1971. New York Hospital Bicentennial Issue

PC56 *New York Hospital*

PC56		UnVF	UseVF
6¢	**multicolored on white,** tagged	.35	2.00
	v. blue & yellow omitted	700.00	
	v1. red omitted	—	
	v2. red & black omitted	—	
	v3. yellow omitted	—	
	v4. red & black impressions shifted 25mm left	—	
	za. Tagging omitted	—	
	FDC *(Sept. 16, 1971)*		1.00

1972. Tourism Year of the Americas Issue. a luminescent panel of tagging was printed at the left of the stamp. The reverse of each card is printed overall with four scenes and the words "TOURISM YEAR OF THE AMERICAS '72." (See PCA12-13.)

PC57 *Eastern Point Lighthouse, Gloucester, Mass.*

PC57		UnVF	UseVF
6¢	**black on manila,** tagged	.50	4.50
	v. Reverse blank	400.00	
	v1. Reverse inverted to front	275.00	
	zo. Tagging omitted	75.00	
	FDC *(June 29, 1972)*		1.00

PC58 *Monument Valley*

PC58		UnVF	UseVF
6¢	**black on manila,** tagged	.50	.45
	v. Reverse blank	400.00	
	v1. black missing on reverse	400.00	
	zo. Tagging omitted	75.00	
	FDC *(June 29, 1972)*		1.00

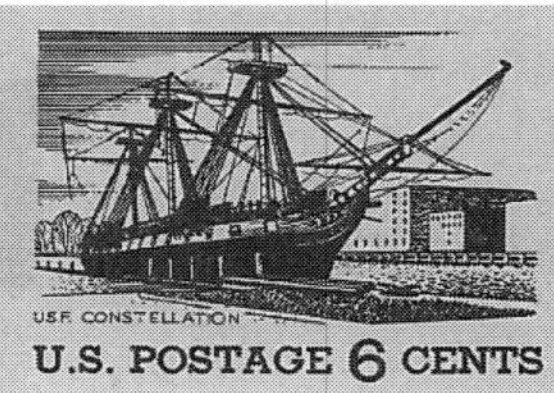

PC59 *U.S. Frigate Constellation*

PC59		UnVF	UseVF
6¢	**black on manila,** tagged	.50	.45
	v. Address side blank	400.00	
	v1. Reverse blank	400.00	
	v2. black missing on reverse	400.00	
	zo. Tagging omitted	75.00	
	FDC *(June 29, 1972)*		1.00

First-day cancels were available from any post office that had the cards in stock that day.

1972. John Hanson Issue in the Patriot Series.

PC60, MRC22 *John Hanson*

PC60		UnVF	UseVF
6¢	**blue on white,** tagged, smooth paper	.30	1.00
	FDC *(Sept. 1, 1972)*		1.00
	p. Coarse paper	1.00	1.00

1973. U.S. Postal Card Centennial Issue

PC61 *Design similar to PC1*

PC61		UnVF	UseVF
6¢	**magenta on manila**	.30	2.00
	FDC *(Sept. 14, 1973)*		1.00
	zo. Tagging omitted	75.00	
	zv. Tagging inverted to lower left	—	

1973. Samuel Adams Issue in the Patriot Series.

PC62, MRC23 *Samuel Adams*

PC62		UnVF	UseVF
8¢	**orange on white,** tagged, smooth paper	.50	1.00
	FDC *(Dec. 16, 1973)*		1.00
	v. Double impression	—	—
	p. Printed on coarse paper	.50	1.00
	v1. Double impression	250.00	

1974. Ship's Figurehead Issue International surface mail.

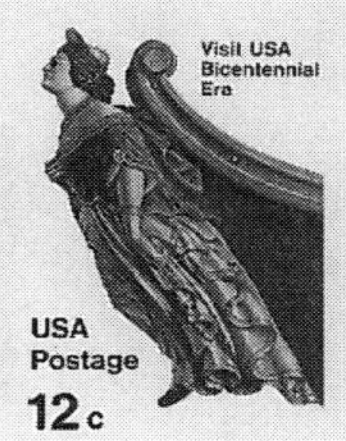

PC63 *Ship's figurehead*

PC63		UnVF	UseVF
12¢	**multicolored on white,** tagged	.40	35.00
	FDC *(Jan. 4, 1974)*		1.00
	v. yellow omitted	1,000.00	

1975. Charles Thomson Issue in the Patriot Series.

PC64, MRC24 *Charles Thomson*

PC64		UnVF	UseVF
7¢	**emerald green on white,** tagged, smooth paper	.40	7.50
	If used after Dec. 31, 1975		.35
	FDC *(Sept. 14, 1975)*		1.00
	v1. Left tip of lower precancel bar raised	—	—
	p. printed on coarse paper	.40	8.00

1975. John Witherspoon Issue in the Patriot Series.

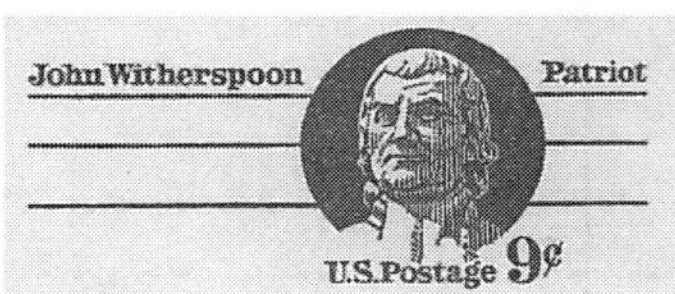

PC65, MRC25 *John Witherspoon*

PC65		UnVF	UseVF
9¢	**yellow brown on white,** tagged	.40	1.00
	FDC *(Nov. 10,1975)*		1.00

1976. Caesar Rodney Issue in the Patriot Series.

PC66, MRC26 *Caesar Rodney*

		UnVF	UseVF
PC66			
9¢	**blue on white,** tagged	.35	1.00
	v. Double impression	—	
	FDC *(July 1, 1976)*		1.00

Historic Preservation Series

1977. Federal Court House, Galveston, Texas Issue was the first in a long-running Historic Preservation Series.

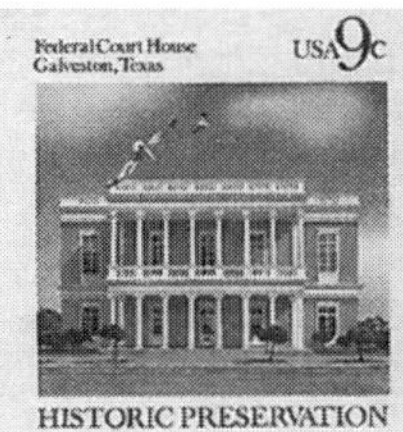

PC67 *Federal Court House, Galveston, Texas*

		UnVF	UseVF
PC67			
9¢	**multicolored on white,** tagged	.40	1.50
	FDC *(July 20, 1977)*		1.00
	v. black omitted	—	
	zo. Tagging omitted	100.00	

1977. Nathan Hale Issue in the Patriot Series.

PC68, MRC27 *Nathan Hale*

		UnVF	UseVF
PC68			
9¢	**green on white,** tagged	.35	1.00
	FDC *(Oct. 14, 1977)*		1.00
	v. Double impression	250.00	
	v1. Missing "¢"	75.00	

1978. The Music Hall, Cincinnati, Ohio Issue 2nd in the Historic Preservation Series.

PC69 *Music Hall, Cincinnati, Ohio*

		UnVF	UseVF
PC69			
10¢	**multicolored on white,** tagged	.40	1.50
	FDC *(May 12, 1978)*		1.00

1978. John Hancock (non-denominated) Issue in the Patriot Series.

PC70, MRC28 *John Hancock (for domestic use only)*

		UnVF	UseVF
PC70			
10¢	**brown orange on white,** tagged	.40	1.50
	FDC *(May 19, 1978)*		1.00

1978. John Hancock (Denominated) Issue in the Patriot Series.

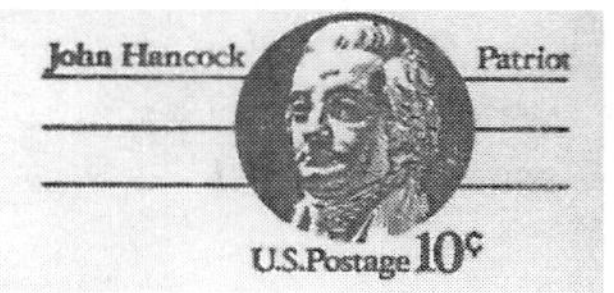

PC71, MRC29 *John Hancock (denomination as numeral)*

		UnVF	UseVF
PC71			
10¢	**orange on white,** tagged	.35	.20
	FDC *(June 20, 1978)*		1.00

1978. U.S.C.G. *Eagle* Issue International surface mail rate.

PC72 *U.S. Coast Guard Cutter* Eagle

		UnVF	UseVF
PC72			
14¢	**multicolored on white,** tagged	.45	2.00
	FDC *(Aug. 4, 1978)*		1.00

American Revolution Series

1978. Molly Pitcher Issue was the first in the American Revolution Series.

PC73 *Molly Pitcher (Mary Ludwig Hays)*

		UnVF	UseVF
PC73			
10¢	**multicolored on white,** tagged	.35	2.00
	FDC *(Sept. 8, 1978)*		1.00

1979. George Rogers Clark Issue in the American Revolution Series.

PC74 *George Rogers Clark*

		UnVF	UseVF
PC74			
10¢	**multicolored on white,** tagged	.35	2.00
	FDC *(Feb. 23, 1979)*		1.00
	v. yellow omitted	—	

1979. Summer Olympics Issue

PC75 *Sprinter*

		UnVF	UseVF
PC75			
10¢	**multicolored,** tagged	.75	2.00
	FDC *(Sept. 17, 1979)*		1.00
	zo. Tagging omitted	—	

1979. Iolani Palace, Honolulu, Hawaii Issue 3rd in the Historic Preservation Series.

PC76 *Iolani Palace, Hawaii*

		UnVF	UseVF
PC76			
10¢	**multicolored on white,** tagged	.35	2.00
	FDC *(Oct. 1, 1979)*		1.00
	zo. Tagging omitted	—	

1979. Casimir Pulaski Issue in the American Revolution Series.

PC77 *Gen. Casimir Pulaski*

		UnVF	UseVF
PC77			
10¢	**multicolored on white,** tagged	.35	2.00
	FDC *(Oct. 11, 1979)*		1.00

1980. Winter Olympics Issue International airmail rate.

PC78 *Figure skater*

		UnVF	UseVF
PC78			
14¢	**multicolored,** tagged	.75	12.50
	FDC *(Jan. 15, 1980)*		1.00

1980. Salt Lake Temple Issue 4th in the Historic Preservation Series.

PC79 *Mormon Temple, Salt Lake City, Utah*

		UnVF	UseVF
PC79			
10¢	**multicolored on white,** tagged	.35	2.00
	FDC *(April 5, 1980)*		1.00
	zo. Tagging omitted	—	

1980. Landing of Rochambeau Issue in the American Revolution Series.

PC80 *Fleet of Count Jean-Baptiste de Rochambeau*

		UnVF	UseVF
PC80			
10¢	**multicolored on white,** tagged	.35	2.00
	FDC *(July 11, 1980)*		1.00
	v. black & yellow printed on reverse, front normal	—	

1980. Battle of Kings Mountain Issue in the American Revolution Series.

PC81 *Battle of Kings Mountain, 1780*

		UnVF	UseVF
PC81			
10¢	**multicolored,** tagged	.35	2.00
	FDC *(Oct. 7, 1980)*		1.00

1980. Drake's *Golden Hinde* Issue International surface rate. Celebrated the 300th anniversary of the circumnavigation of the globe by Drake.

PC82 The Golden Hinde, *ship of Sir Francis Drake*

		UnVF	UseVF
PC82			
19¢	**multicolored on white,** tagged	.75	15.00
	FDC *(Nov. 21, 1980)*		1.00

1981. Battle of Cowpens Issue in the American Revolution Series.

PC83 *Battle of Cowpens, 1781*

		UnVF	UseVF
PC83			
10¢	**multicolored,** tagged	.35	4.00
	FDC *(Jan. 17, 1981)*		1.00

1981. Non-denominated Eagle Issue

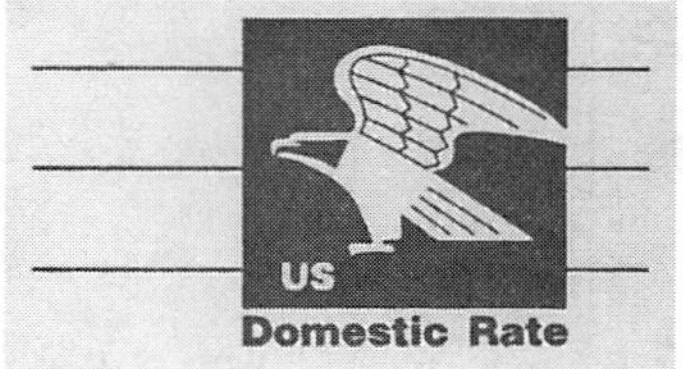

PC84, MRC30 *Stylized eagle*

		UnVF	UseVF
PC84			
12¢	**purple on white**	.40	1.00
	FDC *(March 15, 1981)*		1.00

1981. Isaiah Thomas Issue in the Patriot Series.

PC85, MRC31 *Isaiah Thomas*

		UnVF	UseVF
PC85			
12¢	**blue on white**	.35	1.00
	FDC *(May 5, 1981)*		1.00

1981. Nathanael Greene, Eutaw Springs Issue in the American Revolution Series.

PC86 *Nathanael Greene and The Battle at Eutaw Springs, 1781*

PC86		UnVF	UseVF
12¢	**multicolored on white**	.35	3.00
	FDC *(Sept. 8, 1981)*		1.00
	v. magenta & yellow omitted	—	

1981. Lewis and Clark Expedition Issue

PC87 *Lewis and Clark expedition, 1806*

PC87		UnVF	UseVF
12¢	**multicolored**	.35	4.00
	FDC *(Sept. 23, 1981)*		1.00

1981. Robert Morris (Non-Denominated) Issue in the Patriot Series.

PC88, MRC32 *Robert Morris (for Domestic use only)*

PC88		UnVF	UseVF
13¢	**brown on white**	.35	1.00
	FDC *(Oct. 11, 1981)*		1.00

1981. Robert Morris (Denominated) Issue in the Patriot Series.

PC89, MRC33 *Robert Morris (denomination as numeral)*

PC89		UnVF	UseVF
13¢	**brown on white**	.35	1.00
	FDC *(Nov. 10, 1981)*		1.00
	v. Stamp missing (copyright normal)		

1982. "Swamp Fox" Francis Marion Issue in the American Revolution Series.

PC90 *Gen. Francis Marion*

PC90		UnVF	UseVF
13¢	**multicolored on white**	.35	1.00
	FDC *(April 3, 1982)*		1.00

1982. LaSalle Claims Louisiana Issue

PC91 *LaSalle Expedition, 1682*

PC91		UnVF	UseVF
13¢	**multicolored on white**	.35	1.00
	FDC *(April 7, 1982)*		1.00

1982. Philadelphia Academy of Music Issue 5th in the Historic Preservation series.

PC92 *Philadelphia Academy of Music*

PC92		UnVF	UseVF
13¢	**brown, dark beige, red on tan**	.35	1.00
	FDC *(June 18, 1982)*		1.00
	v. brown & dark beige omitted	400.00	

1982. Old Post Office, St. Louis Issue 6th in the Historic Preservation Series.

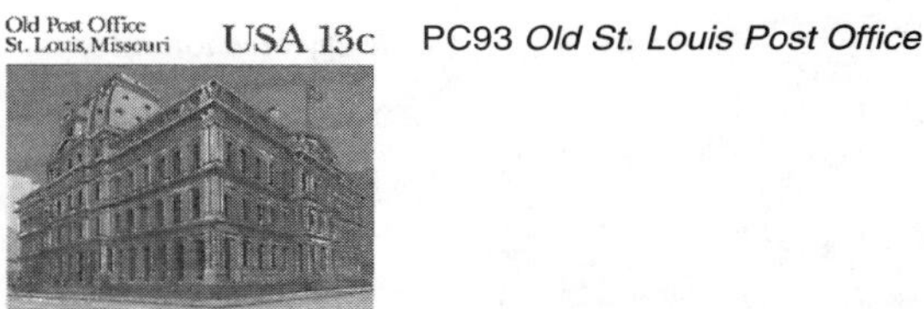

PC93 *Old St. Louis Post Office*

PC93		UnVF	UseVF
13¢	**multicolored on white**	.35	1.00
	FDC *(Oct. 14, 1982)*		1.00

1983. Landing of Gen. Oglethorpe, Georgia Issue

PC94 *Landing of James Oglethorpe in Georgia*

PC94		UnVF	UseVF
13¢	**multicolored on white**	.35	1.00
	FDC *(Feb. 12, 1983)*		1.00

1983. Old Post Office, Washington, D.C. Issue 7th in the Historic Preservation Series.

PC95 *Old Post Office, Washington, D.C.*

PC95		UnVF	UseVF
13¢	**multicolored on white**	.35	1.00
	FDC *(April 19, 1983)*		1.00

1983. Summer Olympics Issue

PC96 *Yachting*

PC96		UnVF	UseVF
13¢	**multicolored on white**	.35	1.00
	FDC *(Aug. 5, 1983)*		1.00
	v. black, magenta & yellow omitted		

1984. *Ark and Dove,* Maryland, 1634 Issue

PC97 Ark *and* Dove

PC97		UnVF	UseVF
13¢	**multicolored on white**	.35	1.00
	FDC *(March 25, 1984)*		1.00

1984. Summer Olympics Issue

PC98 *Olympic torch carrier*

PC98		UnVF	UseVF
13¢	**multicolored on white**	.35	1.00
	FDC *(April 30, 1984)*		1.00
	v. yellow & black inverted	—	
	zo. Tagging omitted	125.00	

1984. Frederic Baraga Issue

PC99 *Frederic Baraga*

PC99		UnVF	UseVF
13¢	**multicolored on white**	.35	1.00
	FDC *(June 29, 1984)*		1.00

1984. Rancho San Pedro Issue 8th in the Historic Preservation Series.

PC100 *Rancho San Pedro*

PC100		UnVF	UseVF
13¢	**multicolored**	.35	1.00
	FDC *(Sept. 16, 1984)*		1.00
	a. black & blue omitted	—	
	z. Tagging omitted	75.00	

1985. Charles Carroll (Non-Denominated) Issue in the Patriot Series.

PC101, MRC34 *Charles Carroll (for Domestic use only)*

PC101		UnVF	UseVF
14¢	**green on white,** non-denominated	.35	.50
	FDC *(Feb. 1, 1985)*		1.00

1985. Clipper *Flying Cloud* Issue International surface rate.

PC102 *Clipper* Flying Cloud, *1852*

PC102		UnVF	UseVF
25¢	**multicolored on white**	.75	7.50
	x. Cachet for CUP.PEX '87, Perth, Australia	1.25	—
	FDC *(Feb. 27, 1985)*		1.00

1985. Charles Carroll (Denominated) Issue in the Patriot Series.

PC103, MRC35 *Charles Carroll (denomination as numeral)*

PC103		UnVF	UseVF
14¢	**green on white**	.35	.25
	FDC *(March 6, 1985)*		1.00

1985. George Wythe Issue in the Patriot Series.

PC104, MRC36 *George Wythe*

PC104		UnVF	UseVF
14¢	**olive green on white**	.35	.50
	FDC *(June 20, 1985)*		1.00

1986. Settling of Connecticut Issue

PC105 *Settling of Connecticut*

PC105		UnVF	UseVF
14¢	**multicolored on white**	.30	1.00
	FDC *(April 18, 1986)*		1.00

1986. Stamp Collecting Issue

PC106

PC106		UnVF	UseVF
14¢	**multicolored on white**	.35	1.00
	x. Cachet for NAJUBRIA '86, Germany	7.50	—
	FDC *(May 23, 1986)*		1.00

1986. Francis Vigo Issue in the American Revolution Series.

PC107 *Francis Vigo, Battle of Vincennes*

PC107		UnVF	UseVF
14¢	**multicolored on white**	.35	1.00
	FDC *(May 24, 1986)*		1.00

1986. Settling of Rhode Island Issue

PC108 *Roger Williams landing at Providence, 1636*

PC108		UnVF	UseVF
14¢	**multicolored on white**	.35	1.00
	FDC *(June 26, 1986)*		1.00

1986. Wisconsin Territory Sesquicentennial Issue

PC109 *Wisconsin Territory 150th anniversary*

PC109		UnVF	UseVF
14¢	**multicolored on white**	.35	1.00
	FDC *(July 3, 1986)*		1.00

1986. National Guard Issue

PC110 *National Guard, 350th anniversary*

PC110		UnVF	UseVF
14¢	**multicolored on white**	.35	1.00
	FDC *(Dec. 12, 1986)*		1.00

1987. Self-Scouring Plow Issue

PC111 *150th anniversary, steel plow by John Deere*

PC111		UnVF	UseVF
14¢	**multicolored on white**	.35	1.00
	FDC *(May 22, 1987)*		1.00

1987. Constitutional Convention Issue in the American Revolution Series.

PC112 *Constitutional Convention, 1787*

PC112		UnVF	UseVF
14¢	**multicolored on white**	.35	1.00
	FDC *(May 25, 1987)*		1.00

1987. U.S. Flag Issue

PC113, MRC37 *Flag*

PC113		UnVF	UseVF
14¢	**black, blue, and red on white**	.35	.50
	FDC *(June 14, 1987)*		1.00
	x. Cachet for Philatelia 87 (exhibition in Koln, (Cologne) Germany	1.00	
	vz. Tagging double, 1 normal & 1 split top & bottom	—	

1987. Pride In America Issue

PC114 *Landscape*

PC114		UnVF	UseVF
14¢	**multicolored on white**	.35	1.00
	FDC *(Sept. 22, 1987)*		1.00

1987. Timberline Lodge, Mount Hood, Oregon Issue 9th in the Historic Preservation Series.

PC115 *Timberline Lodge, Mt. Hood, Ore.*

PC115		UnVF	UseVF
14¢	**multicolored on white**	.35	1.00
	FDC *(Sept. 28, 1987)*		1.00

America the Beautiful Series

1988. Prairie Scene Issue was the first of the America the Beautiful Series.

PC116, MRC38 *Bison on the prairie*

PC116		UnVF	UseVF
15¢	**multicolored on white,** non-fluorescent paper	.35	1.00
	FDC *(March 28, 1988)*		1.00
	p. Non-fluorescent paper	—	
	v. printed on both sides	650.00	
	v1. black & blue on reverse, front normal	650.00	
	v2. Double magenta and blue and triple black impressions	—	
	v3. Added printing on both sides for Myrtle Beach	2.00	1.50

1988. Blair House Issue 10th in the Historic Preservation Series.

PC117 *Blair House, Washington, D.C.*

PC117		UnVF	UseVF
15¢	**multicolored on white**	.35	1.00
	FDC *(May 4, 1988)*		1.00

1988. Square-Rigged Packet Ship *Yorkshire* Issue International surface rate.

PC118 Yorkshire

PC118		UnVF	UseVF
28¢	**multicolored**	.75	4.00
	FDC *(June 29, 1988)*		1.00

1988. Iowa Territory Sesquicentennial Issue

PC119 *Corn harvesting*

PC119		UnVF	UseVF
15¢	**multicolored on white**	.35	1.00
	FDC *(July 2, 1988)*		1.00

1988. Settling of Ohio Issue recalled the Bicentennial of the settling of Ohio, then in the Northwest Territory.

PC120 *Flatboat ferry transporting settlers*

PC120		UnVF	UseVF
15¢	**multicolored on white**	.35	1.00
	FDC *(July 15, 1988)*		1.00

1988. Hearst Castle Issue 11th in the Historic Preservation Series. Featured the estate at San Simeon, Calif., built by the newspaper magnate.

PC121 *Hearst Castle, San Simeon, Calif.*

PC121		UnVF	UseVF
15¢	**multicolored on white**	.35	1.00
	FDC *(Sept. 20, 1988)*		1.00

1988. Federalist Papers Issue

PC122 *Colonial Pressman*

PC122		UnVF	UseVF
15¢	**multicolored on white**	.35	1.00
	FDC *(Oct. 27, 1988)*		1.00

1989. Sonora Desert Issue in the America the Beautiful Series.

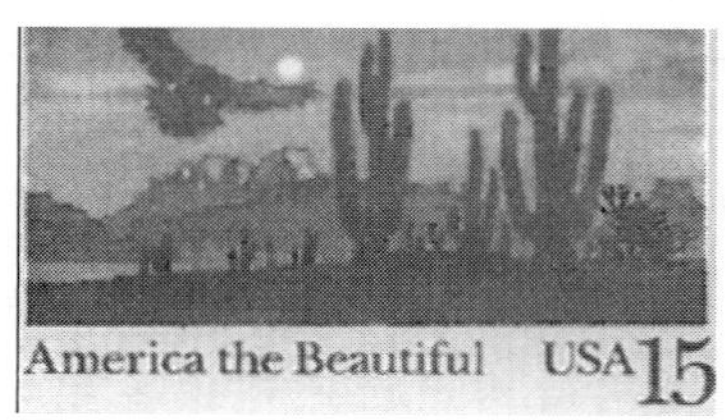

PC123 *Hawk and Sonora Desert sunset*

PC123		UnVF	UseVF
15¢	**multicolored on white**	.35	1.00
	FDC *(Jan. 13, 1989)*		1.00

College Series

1989. Georgetown University Issue was the first of the College Series, which became intertwined with the Historic Preservation Series (12th of the series).

PC124 *Healy Hall, Georgetown University*

PC124		UnVF	UseVF
15¢	**multicolored on white**	.35	1.00
	FDC *(Jan. 23, 1989)*		1.00

1989. Blue Heron and Marsh Issue in the America the Beautiful Series.

PC125 *Great Blue Heron in marsh scene*

		UnVF	UseVF
PC125			
15¢	**multicolored on white**	.35	1.00
	FDC *(March 17, 1989)*		1.00

1989. Settling of Oklahoma Issue

PC126 *Land rush scene*

		UnVF	UseVF
PC126			
15¢	**multicolored on white**	.35	.35
	FDC *(April 22, 1989)*		1.00

1989. Mountain Scene, Geese Issue in the America the Beautiful Series. Card paid surface rate to Canada.

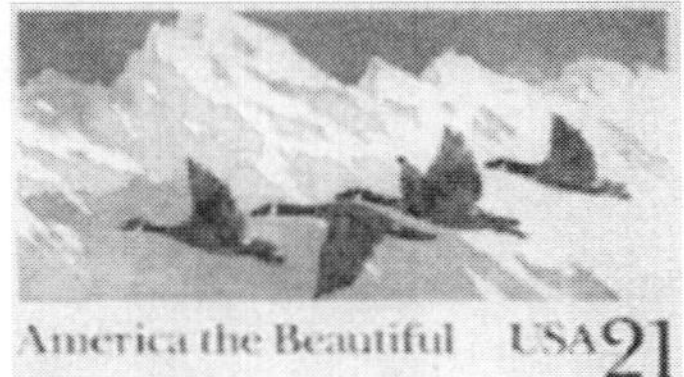

PC127 *Geese in flight*

		UnVF	UseVF
PC127			
21¢	**multicolored on white**	.65	5.00
	FDC *(May 5, 1989)*		1.00

1989. Seashore Issue in the America the Beautiful Series.

PC128 *Seashore*

		UnVF	UseVF
PC128			
15¢	**multicolored on white**	.35	1.00
	FDC *(June 17, 1989)*		1.00

1989. Forest Stream Issue in the America the Beautiful Series.

PC129 *Deer in forest*

		UnVF	UseVF
PC129			
15¢	**multicolored on white**	.35	1.00
	FDC *(Aug. 26, 1989)*		1.00

1989. Hull House Issue 13th in the Historic Preservation Series.

PC130 *Jane Addams' Hull House Community Center, Chicago*

		UnVF	UseVF
PC130			
15¢	**multicolored on white**	.35	1.00
	FDC *(Sept. 16, 1989)*		1.00

1989. Independence Hall Issue in the America the Beautiful Series.

PC131, PC136A *Independence Hall, Philadelphia*

		UnVF	UseVF
PC131			
15¢	**multicolored on white**	.35	1.00
	FDC *(Sept. 25, 1989)*		1.00

1989. Baltimore Harbor Issue in the America the Beautiful Series.

PC132, PC136 USS Constellation; *Inner Harbor, Baltimore, Md.*

		UnVF	UseVF
PC132			
15¢	**multicolored on white**	.35	1.00
	FDC *(Oct. 7, 1989)*		1.00

1989. Manhattan Skyline Issue in the America the Beautiful Series.

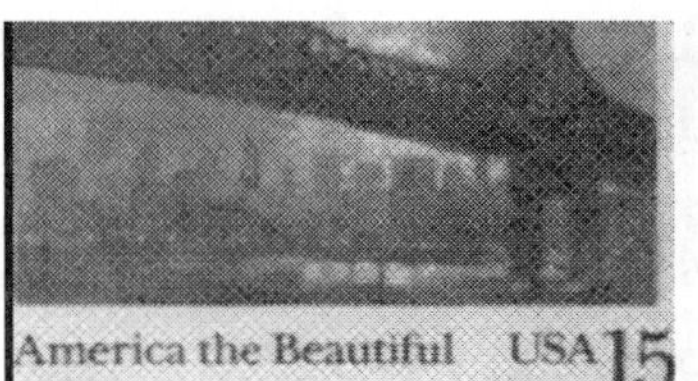

PC133, PC136C *Manhatten skyline, Queensboro Bridge*

		UnVF	UseVF
PC133			
15¢	**multicolored on white**	.35	1.00
	FDC *(Nov. 8. 1989)*		1.00

1989. U.S. Capitol Building Issue in the America the Beautiful Series.

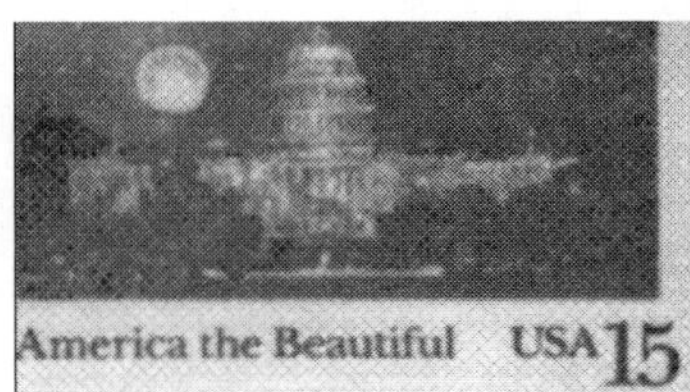

PC134, PC136B *U.S. Capitol building*

		UnVF	UseVF
PC134			
15¢	**multicolored on white**	.35	1.00
	FDC *(Nov. 26, 1989)*		1.00

1989. White House Postal Card Issue sold for 50¢ each with the illustration of the White House enlarged on the reverse.

PC135 *White House*

PC135		UnVF	UseVF
15¢	**multicolored on white**	1.25	5.00
	FDC *(Nov. 30, 1989)*		2.00

1989. America the Beautiful Se-Tenant Sheet Issue in the America the Beautiful Series. Designs of PC131-PC134 were issued in a se-tenant sheet of four cards, with rouletting between them for separation, for World Stamp Expo 89. The sheet included two labels showing the emblems of either World Stamp Expo 89 or the 20th UPU Congress. These cards do not include inscription and copyright symbols at lower left. *Rouletted 9 1/2 on two or three sides.*

PC136		UnVF	UseVF
15¢	**multicolored on white,** design of PC132	2.00	5.00
	FDC *(Dec. 1, 1989)*		1.00
PC136A		**UnVF**	**UseVF**
15¢	**multicolored on white,** design of PC131	2.00	5.00
	FDC		1.00
PC136B		**UnVF**	**UseVF**
15¢	**multicolored on white,** design of PC134	2.00	5.00
	FDC		1.00
PC136C		**UnVF**	**UseVF**
15¢	**multicolored on white,** design of PC133	2.00	5.00
	FDC		1.00
	y. Se-tenant block of 4 PC136-136C w/2 labels	12.50	

1989. Jefferson Memorial Picture Postal Card Issue sold for 50¢ each, with a different view of the Jefferson Memorial covering the reverse.

PC137 *Jefferson Memorial*

PC137		UnVF	UseVF
15¢	**multicolored on white**	1.25	4.00
	FDC *(Dec. 2, 1989)*		2.00

1990. American Papermaking Issue

PC138 *Rittenhouse Paper Mill, Germantown, Pa.*

PC138		UnVF	UseVF
15¢	**multicolored on white**	.35	1.00
	FDC *(March 13, 1990)*		1.00

Users of this catalog are invited to write to us if they have information they feel will supplement or correct any material contained herein. All such communications will be answered.

1990. World Literacy Year Issue

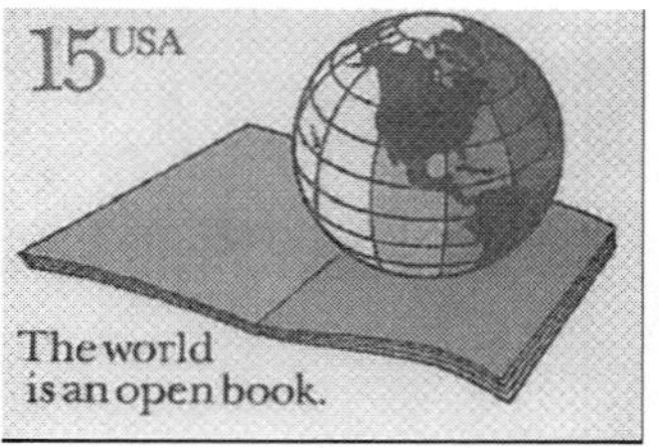

PC139 *Book and globe, World Literacy Year*

PC139		UnVF	UseVF
15¢	**multicolored on white**	.35	.50
	FDC *(March 22, 1990)*		1.00

1990. George Caleb Bingham Picture Postal Card Issue sold for 50¢, with the painting *Fur Traders Descending the Missouri* covering the reverse.

PC140 *Fur Traders on the Missouri*

PC140		UnVF	UseVF
15¢	**multicolored on white**	1.25	5.00
	FDC *(May 4, 1990)*		1.00

1990. Isaac Royall House Issue 14th in the Historic Preservation Series.

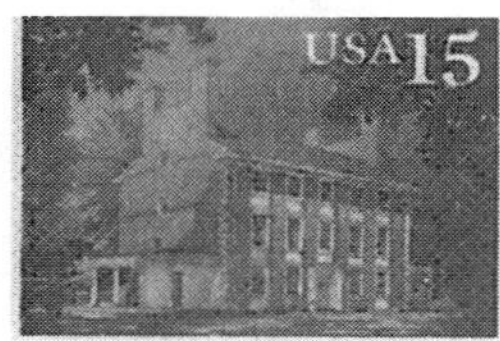

PC141 *Isaac Royall House, Medford, Mass.*

PC141		UnVF	UseVF
15¢	**multicolored on white**	.45	1.00
	FDC *(June 16, 1990)*		1.00

1990. Postal Buddy Issue computer-generated and printed USPS Eagle card, available from a vending machine under a special license agreement. The cards cost 33¢, plus state sales tax, from one of a group of test machines in Virginia. A variety of borders, messages and backs are known. The cards also were produced in sheets of four.

PC142 *Postal Buddy Card*

PC142		UnVF	UseVF
15¢	**black on white**	8.50	15.00
	FDC *(July 5, 1990)*		2.50

1990. Stanford University Issue 15th in the Historic Preservation Series and 2nd in the College Series.

PC143 *Quadrangle, Stanford University*

PC143		UnVF	UseVF
15¢	**multicolored on white**	.35	1.00
	FDC *(Sept. 11, 1990)*		1.00

1990. Constitution Hall Picture Postal Card Issue sold for 50¢ with an enlarged picture of Memorial Continental Hall, Washington, D.C., covering the reverse. Issued for the Centennial of the Daughters of the American Revolution. It is the 16th in the Historic Preservation Series.

PC144 *Constitution Hall, Washington, D.C.*

		UnVF	UseVF
PC144			
15¢	**multicolored on white**	1.25	5.00
	FDC *(Oct. 11, 1990)*		1.00

1990. Chicago Orchestra Hall Issue 17th in the Historic Preservation Series.

PC145 *Chicago Orchestra Hall*

		UnVF	UseVF
PC145			
15¢	**multicolored on white**	.45	1.00
	FDC *(Oct. 19, 1990)*		1.00

1991. Flag Issue

PC146, MRC39 *Flag*

		UnVF	UseVF
PC146			
19¢	**black, blue, and red on white**	.50	.50
	FDC *(Jan. 24, 1991)*		1.00

1991. Postal Buddy USPS Eagle Card Issue available in sheets of four from vending machines. (See PC142.)

PC147 *Postal Buddy card*

		UnVF	UseVF
PC147			
19¢	**black on white**	4.00	15.00
	FDC *(Feb. 3, 1991)*		25.00

1991. Carnegie Hall Centennial Issue 18th in the Historic Preservation Series.

PC148 *Carnegie Hall, New York City*

		UnVF	UseVF
PC148			
19¢	**multicolored on white**	.50	1.00
	FDC *(April 1, 1991)*		1.00

1991. University of Texas Medical Branch at Galveston Issue 19th in the Historic Preservation Series and 3rd in the College Series.

PC149 *Old Red, University of Texas Medical Branch, Galveston*

		UnVF	UseVF
PC149			
19¢	**multicolored on white**	.50	1.00
	FDC *(June 14, 1991)*		1.00

1991. Niagara Falls Issue in the America the Beautiful Series. International surface rate and airmail to Canada and Mexico.

PC150 *Niagara Falls*

		UnVF	UseVF
PC150			
30¢	**multicolored on white**	1.00	5.00
	FDC *(Aug. 21, 1991)*		1.00

1991. Bill of Rights Issue

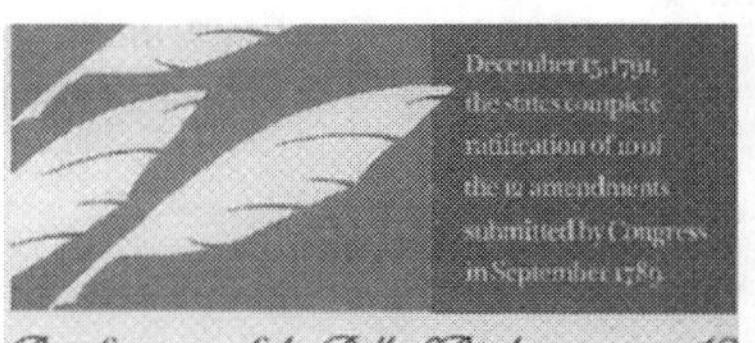

PC151 *Ratification of the Bill of Rights*

		UnVF	UseVF
PC151			
19¢	**black, blue, and red on white**	.50	.75
	FDC *(Sept. 25, 1991)*		1.00

1991. University of Notre Dame Issue 20th in the Historic Preservation Series and 4th in the College Series.

PC152 *Main Building, University of Notre Dame, South Bend, Ind.*

		UnVF	UseVF
PC152			
19¢	**multicolored on white**	.50	1.00
	FDC *(Oct. 15, 1991)*		1.00

1991. University of Vermont Issue 21st in the Historic Preservation Series and 5th in the College Series.

PC153 *The Old Mill, University of Vermont*

		UnVF	UseVF
PC153			
19¢	**multicolored on white**	.50	1.00
	FDC *(Oct. 29, 1991)*		1.00

1992. Wadsworth Atheneum Sesquicentennial Issue 22nd in the Historic Preservation Series.

PC154 *Wadsworth Atheneum, Hartford, Conn.*

PC154		UnVF	UseVF
19¢	**multicolored on white**	.50	1.00
	FDC *(Jan. 16, 1992)*		1.00

1992. University of Chicago Issue 23rd in the Historic Preservation Series and 6th in the College Series.

PC155 *Cobb Hall, University of Chicago*

PC155		UnVF	UseVF
19¢	**multicolored on white**	.50	.75
	FDC *(Jan. 23, 1992)*		1.00

1992. Willamette University Issue 24th in the Historic Preservation Series and 7th in the College Series.

PC156 *Waller Hall, Willamette University, Salem Ore.*

PC156		UnVF	UseVF
19¢	**multicolored on white**	.50	.75
	FDC *(Feb. 1, 1992)*		1.00

1992. America's Cup Picture Postal Card Issue sold for 50¢ with a picture of *The Ranger,* USA 1937, covering the reverse.

PC157 *America's Cup. The* Reliance, *USA 1903*

PC157		UnVF	UseVF
19¢	**multicolored on white**	1.25	2.00
	FDC *(May 6, 1992)*		1.00

1992. Columbia River Gorge Issue

PC158 *Columbia River Gorge*

PC158		UnVF	UseVF
19¢	**multicolored on white**	.50	.75
	FDC *(May 9, 1992)*		1.00

1992. Ellis Island Centennial Issue 25th in the Historic Preservation Series.

PC159 *Ellis Island Immigration Museum*

PC159		UnVF	UseVF
19¢	**multicolored on white**	.50	.75
	FDC *(May 11, 1992)*		1.00

1992. Postal Buddy Issue available only in sheets of four from vending machines. Price raised to 39¢ per card, plus any state sales tax (see PC142, PC147).

PC160 *Postal Buddy Post Card*

PC160		UnVF	UseVF
19¢	**multicolored on white,** tagged	15.00	35.00
	FDC *(Nov. 13, 1992)*		27.00
	p. Fluorescent paper	—	

1993. Washington National Cathedral Issue 26th in the Historic Preservation Series.

PC161 *Washington National Cathedral*

PC161		UnVF	UseVF
19¢	**multicolored on white**	.50	.75
	FDC *(Jan. 6, 1993)*		1.00

1993. College of William & Mary Issue 27th in the Historic Preservation Series and 8th in the College Series.

PC162 *Wren Building, College of William & Mary*

PC162		UnVF	UseVF
19¢	**multicolored on white**	.50	.75
	FDC *(Feb. 8, 1993)*		1.00

1993. Holocaust Memorial Picture Postal Card Issue sold for 50¢ with an aerial view of the museum covering the reverse.

PC163 *Holocaust Memorial Museum*

PC163		UnVF	UseVF
19¢	**multicolored on white**	1.25	2.00
	FDC *(March 23, 1993)*		3.00

1993. Fort Recovery Issue 28th in the Historic Preservation Series.

PC164 *Fort Recovery, Ohio*

		UnVF	UseVF
PC164			
19¢	**multicolored on white**	.50	.75
	FDC *(June 13, 1993)*		1.00

1993. University of North Carolina Issue 29th in the Historic Preservation Series and 9th in the College Series.

PC165 *Playmaker's Theatre at Chapel Hill, N.C.*

		UnVF	UseVF
PC165			
19¢	**multicolored on white**	.50	.75
	FDC *(Sept. 14, 1993)*		1.00

1993. College of the Holy Cross Issue 30th in the Historic Preservation Series and 10th in the College Series.

PC166 *O'Kane Hall, College of the Holy Cross, Worcester, Mass.*

		UnVF	UseVF
PC166			
19¢	**multicolored on white**	.50	.45
	FDC *(Sept. 17, 1993)*		1.00

1993. Illinois College Issue 31st in the Historic Preservation Series and 11th in the College Series.

PC167 *Beecher Hall, Illinois College, Jacksonville, Ill.*

		UnVF	UseVF
PC167			
19¢	**multicolored**	.50	.45
	FDC *(Oct. 9, 1993)*		1.00

1993. Bowdoin College Issue 32nd in the Historic Preservation Series and 12th in the College Series.

PC168 *Massachusetts Hall, Bowdoin College, Brunswick, Maine*

		UnVF	UseVF
PC168			
19¢	**multicolored**	.50	.75
	FDC *(Oct. 14, 1993)*		1.00

1994. Lincoln Home Issue 33rd in the Historic Preservation Series.

PC169 *Lincoln's Home, Springfield, Ill.*

		UnVF	UseVF
PC169			
19¢	**multicolored**	.50	.60
	FDC *(Feb. 12, 1994)*		1.00

1994. Wittenberg University Issue 34th in the Historic Preservation Series and 13th in the College Series.

PC170 *Meyers Hall, Wittenberg University, Springfield, Ohio*

		UnVF	UseVF
PC170			
19¢	**multicolored**	.50	.75
	FDC *(March 11, 1994)*		1.00

1994. Canyon de Chelly Issue

PC171 *Canyon de Chelly, Arizona*

		UnVF	UseVF
PC171			
19¢	**multicolored**	.50	.75
	FDC *(Aug. 11, 1994)*		1.00

1994. St. Louis Union Station Issue 35th in the Historic Preservation Series.

PC172 *St. Louis Union Station, St. Louis, Mo.*

		UnVF	UseVF
PC172			
19¢	**multicolored**	.50	.75
	FDC *(Sept. 3, 1994)*		1.00

Input from stamp collectors regarding the content of this catalog and ideas to make it more useful is eagerly sought. Send your comments to:

Minkus Catalog Editor
Krause Publications
700 E. State St.
Iola WI 54990

1994. Legends of the West Picture Postal Card Issue issued in conjunction with the 20-stamp sheetlet depicting 16 individuals and four "themes" from the Old West. Each card depicts a double-framed design from the sheetlet with the 19¢ postal card rate, while the reverse of the card is an enlarged version of the stamp design. The cards were issued Oct. 18, 1994. Sold in sets for $7.95.

PC173

PC174

PC175

		UnVF	UseVF
PC173			
19¢	Home on the Range	.60	5.00
PC174			
19¢	Buffalo Bill	.60	5.00
PC175			
19¢	Jim Bridger	.60	5.00

PC176

PC177

Chief Joseph
PC178

		UnVF	UseVF
PC176			
19¢	Annie Oakley	.60	5.00
PC177			
19¢	Native American Culture	.60	5.00
PC178			
19¢	Chief Joseph	.60	5.00

PC179

PC180

PC181

		UnVF	UseVF
PC179			
19¢	Bill Pickett	.60	5.00
PC180			
19¢	Bat Masterson	.60	5.00
PC181			
19¢	John Fremont	.60	5.00

PC182

PC183

PC184

		UnVF	UseVF
PC182			
19¢	Wyatt Earp	.60	5.00
PC183			
19¢	Nellie Cashman	.60	5.00
PC184			
19¢	Charles Goodnight	.60	5.00

PC185

PC186

PC187

		UnVF	UseVF
PC185			
19¢	Geronimo	.60	5.00
PC186			
19¢	Kit Carson	.60	5.00
PC187			
19¢	Wild Bill Hickok	.60	5.00

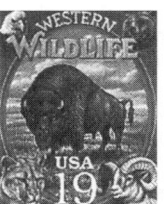

PC188

PC189

PC190

		UnVF	UseVF
PC188			
19¢	Western Wildlife	.60	5.00
PC189			
19¢	Jim Beckwourth	.60	5.00
PC190			
19¢	Bill Tilghman	.60	5.00

PC191

PC192

		UnVF	UseVF
PC191			
19¢	Sacagawea	.60	5.00
PC192			
19¢	Overland Mail	.60	5.00
	FDC (any card) *(Oct. 18, 1994)*		1.25

1994. Old Glory "G" Non-denominated Issue

PC193 *Old Glory, "G"*

		UnVF	UseVF
PC193			
20¢	**multicolored**	.40	.50
	FDC *(Dec. 13, 1994)*		1.00

1995. Red Barn Issue

PC194, MRC40 *Red Barn*

PC194 | | UnVF | UseVF
20¢ **multicolored** .40 .50
FDC *(Jan. 3, 1995)* 1.00

1995. Civil War Picture Postal Card Issue issued in conjunction with the 20 stamp sheetlet. Each card depicted a design from the sheetlet with the 20¢ post card rate, while the reverse of the card was an enlarged version of the stamp design. Issued June 29, 1995. Sold in sets for $7.95.

PC195

PC196

PC197

PC195 UnVF UseVF
20¢ *Monitor Virginia* .75 3.50
PC196 UnVF UseVF
20¢ Robert E. Lee .75 3.50
PC197 UnVF UseVF
20¢ Clara Barton .75 3.50

PC198

PC199

PC200

PC198 UnVF UseVF
20¢ Ulysses S. Grant .75 3.50
PC199 UnVF UseVF
20¢ Battle of Shiloh .75 3.50
PC200 UnVF UseVF
20¢ Jefferson Davis .75 3.50

PC201

PC202

PC203

PC201 UnVF UseVF
20¢ David Farragut .75 3.50
PC202 UnVF UseVF
20¢ Frederick Douglass .75 3.50
PC203 UnVF UseVF
20¢ Raphael Semmes .75 3.50

PC204

PC205

PC206

PC204 UnVF UseVF
20¢ Abraham Lincoln .75 3.50

PC205 UnVF UseVF
20¢ Harriet Tubman .75 3.50
PC206 UnVF UseVF
20¢ Stand Watie .75 3.50

PC207

PC208

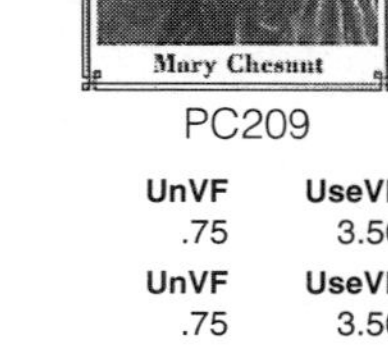

PC209

PC207 UnVF UseVF
20¢ Joseph E. Johnston .75 3.50
PC208 UnVF UseVF
20¢ Winfield Hancock .75 3.50
PC209 UnVF UseVF
20¢ Mary Chesnut .75 3.50

PC210

PC211

PC212

PC210 UnVF UseVF
20¢ Battle of Chancellorsville .75 3.50
PC211 UnVF UseVF
20¢ William T. Sherman .75 3.50
PC212 UnVF UseVF
20¢ Phoebe Pember .75 3.50

PC213

PC214

PC213 UnVF UseVF
20¢ Stonewall Jackson .75 3.50
PC214 UnVF UseVF
20¢ Battle of Gettysburg .75 3.50
FDC (any card) *(June 29, 1995)* 1.10

1995. American Clipper Ships Issue

PC215 *American Clipper Ships*

PC215 UnVF UseVF
20¢ **multicolored** .40 .50
FDC *(Sept. 3, 1995)* 1.00

1995. Comic Strip Classics Picture Postal Card Issue issued in conjunction with the sheetlet of 20 stamps commemorating the centennial of the comic strip. An enlarged version of the design appears on the reverse. Issued Oct. 1, 1995. Sold in sets for $7.95.

PC216

PC217

PC218

PC216 UnVF .60 UseVF 3.00
20¢ The Yellow Kid

PC217 UnVF .60 UseVF 3.00
20¢ Katzenjammer Kids

PC218 UnVF .60 UseVF 3.00
20¢ Little Nemo in Slumberland

PC219

PC220

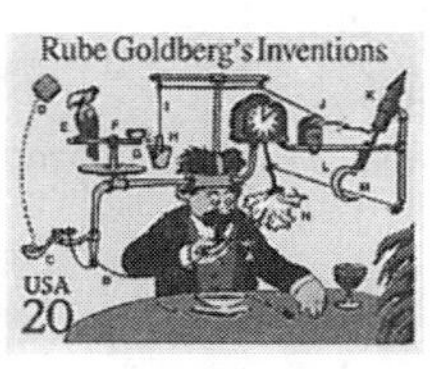

PC221

PC219 UnVF .60 UseVF 3.00
20¢ Bringing up Father

PC220 UnVF .60 UseVF 3.00
20¢ Krazy Kat

PC221 UnVF .60 UseVF 3.00
20¢ Rube Goldberg's Inventions

PC222

PC223

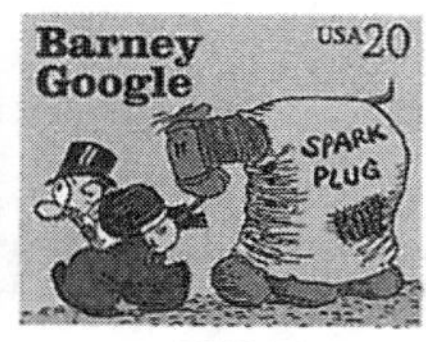

PC224

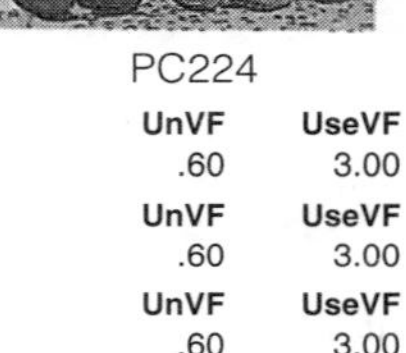

PC222 UnVF .60 UseVF 3.00
20¢ Toonerville Folks

PC223 UnVF .60 UseVF 3.00
20¢ Gasoline Alley

PC224 UnVF .60 UseVF 3.00
20¢ Barney Google

PC225

PC226

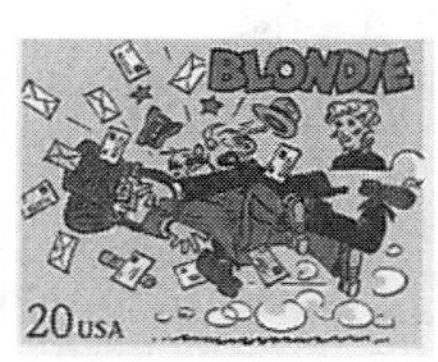

PC227

PC225 UnVF .60 UseVF 3.00
20¢ Little Orphan Annie

PC226 UnVF .60 UseVF 3.00
20¢ Popeye

PC227 UnVF .60 UseVF 3.00
20¢ Blondie

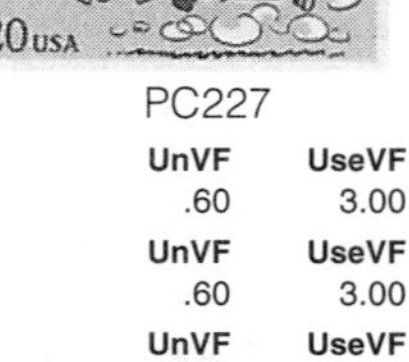
PC228

PC229

PC230

PC228 UnVF .60 UseVF 3.00
20¢ Dick Tracy

PC229 UnVF .60 UseVF 3.00
20¢ Alley Oop

PC230 UnVF .60 UseVF 3.00
20¢ Nancy

PC231 PC232 PC233

PC231 UnVF .60 UseVF 3.00
20¢ Flash Gordon

PC232 UnVF .60 UseVF 3.00
20¢ Li'l Abner

PC233 UnVF .60 UseVF 3.00
20¢ Terry and the Pirates

PC234 PC235

PC234 UnVF .60 UseVF 3.00
20¢ Prince Valiant

PC235 UnVF .60 UseVF 3.00
20¢ Brenda Starr, Reporter
FDC (any card) *(Oct. 1, 1995)* 1.00

1996. Winter Farm Scene Issue

PC236 *Winter farm scene*

PC236 UnVF .40 UseVF .50
20¢ **multicolored**
FDC *(Feb. 23, 1996)* 1.00

1996. Atlanta Olympics Picture Post Card Issue issued in conjunction with the 20 stamp sheetlet. The reverse features an enlargement of the stamp image. Issued May 2, 1996. Sold in booklets of 20 for $12.95.

PC237

PC238

PC239

PC237 UnVF .90 UseVF 5.00
20¢ Men's Cycling

PC238 UnVF .90 UseVF 5.00
20¢ Women's Diving

PC239 UnVF .90 UseVF 5.00
20¢ Women's Running

PC240

PC241

PC242

PC252

PC253

PC254

		UnVF	UseVF
PC240			
20¢	Men's Canoeing	.90	5.00
PC241			
20¢	Decathlon (Javelin)	.90	5.00
PC242			
20¢	Women's Soccer	.90	5.00

		UnVF	UseVF
PC252			
20¢	Men's Basketball	.90	5.00
PC253			
20¢	Equestrian	.90	5.00
PC254			
20¢	Men's Gymnastics	.90	5.00

PC243

PC244

PC245

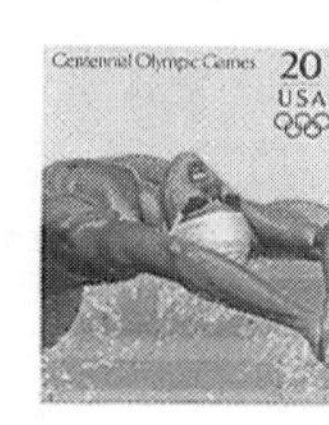

PC255

PC256

		UnVF	UseVF
PC243			
20¢	Men's Shot Put	.90	5.00
PC244			
20¢	Women's Sailboarding	.90	5.00
PC245			
20¢	Women's Gymnastics	.90	5.00

		UnVF	UseVF
PC255			
20¢	Men's Swimming	.90	5.00
PC256			
20¢	Men's Hurdles	.90	5.00
	Booklet of 20	16.00	
	FDC (any card) *(May 2, 1996)*		1.10

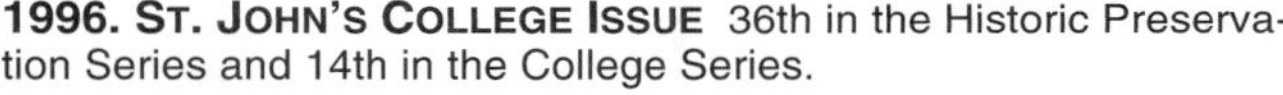

1996. St. John's College Issue 36th in the Historic Preservation Series and 14th in the College Series.

PC246

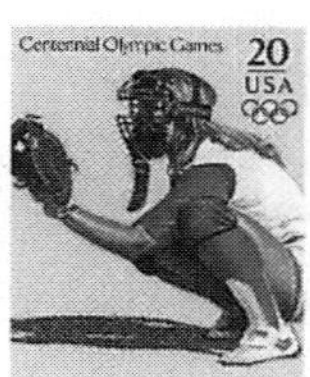

PC247

PC248

PC257 *McDowell Hall, St. John's College, Annapolis, Md.*

		UnVF	UseVF
PC246			
20¢	Freestyle Wrestling	.90	5.00
PC247			
20¢	Women's Softball	.90	5.00
PC248			
20¢	Women's Swimming	.90	5.00

		UnVF	UseVF
PC257			
20¢	**multicolored**	.50	.50
	FDC *(June 1, 1996)*		1.00

1996. Princeton University Issue 37th in the Historic Preservation Series and 15th in the College Series.

PC249

PC250

PC251

ALEXANDER HALL
USA 20
PRINCETON UNIVERSITY • 250TH ANNIVERSARY

PC258 *Alexander Hall, Princeton University*

		UnVF	UseVF
PC249			
20¢	Men's Sprints	.90	5.00
PC250			
20¢	Men's Rowing	.90	5.00
PC251			
20¢	Volleyball	.90	5.00

		UnVF	UseVF
PC258			
20¢	**multicolored**	.50	.50
	FDC *(Sept. 20, 1996)*		1.00

1996. Endangered Species Picture Postal Card Issue issued in conjunction with the 15-stamp sheetlet. Each card features an enlargement of the stamp image. Issued Oct. 2, 1996. Sold in a 5-panel booklet for $11.95. *Printed by Art Litho Co.*

PC259 PC260 PC261

		UnVF	UseVF
PC259			
20¢	Florida panther	1.10	5.00
PC260			
20¢	Black-footed ferret	1.10	5.00
PC261			
20¢	American crocodile	1.10	5.00

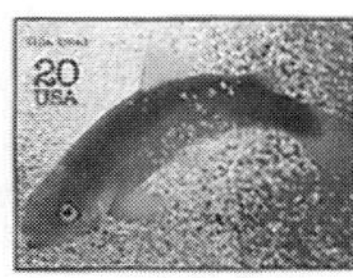
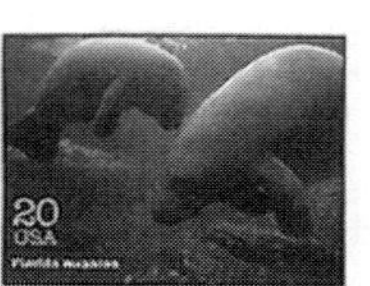
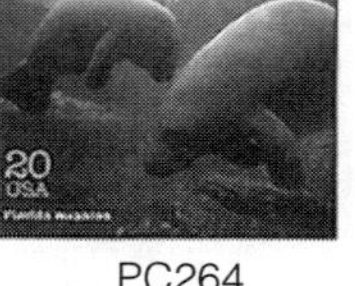

PC262 PC263 PC264

		UnVF	UseVF
PC262			
20¢	Piping plover	1.10	5.00
PC263			
20¢	Gila trout	1.10	5.00
PC264			
20¢	Florida manatee	1.10	5.00

PC265 PC266 PC267

		UnVF	UseVF
PC265			
20¢	Schaus Swallowtail butterfly	1.10	5.00
PC266			
20¢	Woodland caribou	1.10	5.00
PC267			
20¢	Thick-billed parrot	1.10	5.00

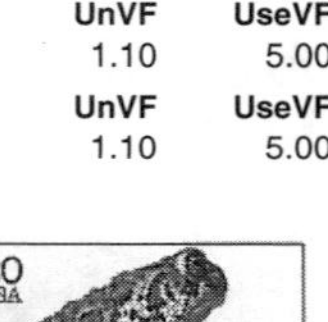

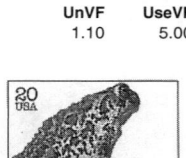

PC268 PC269 PC270

		UnVF	UseVF
PC268			
20¢	San Francisco garter snake	1.10	5.00
PC269			
20¢	Ocelot	1.10	5.00
PC270			
20¢	Wyoming toad	1.10	5.00

PC271 PC272 PC273

		UnVF	UseVF
PC271			
20¢	California condor	1.10	5.00
PC272			
20¢	Hawaiian monk seal	1.10	5.00
PC273			
20¢	Brown pelican	1.10	5.00

	UnVF	UseVF
Booklet of 15	15.00	
FDC (any card) *(Oct. 2, 1996)*		1.50

1997. Love Swans Picture Postal Card Issue current and previous Love stamp designs enlarged on back. Issued Feb. 4, 1997. Sold in sets of 12 cards (2 panels each of designs a.-d.; 1 panel of designs e.-h.) for $6.95. *Offset by Ashton-Potter (USA) Ltd.*

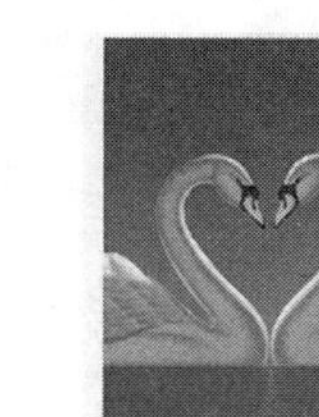

PC274 *Swans*

PC274		UnVF	UseVF
	multicolored		
	a. Bird in Rose Heart (1994)	.75	2.25
	b. 2 Birds in Rose Basket (1994)	.75	2.25
	c. Swans, vert. (1997)	.75	2.25
	d. Swans, horiz. (1997)	.75	2.25
	e. Puppy (1986)	.75	2.25
	f. Paper cut-out Heart (1987)	.75	2.25
	g. Pennsylvania-Dutch 2 birds & Heart (1990)	.75	2.25
	h. Heart Sunrise (1994)	.75	2.25
	FDC (any card) *(Feb. 4, 1997)*		1.00

1997. City College of New York Issue 38th in the Historic Preservation Series and 16th in the College Series.

PC275 *City College of New York*

PC275		UnVF	UseVF
20¢	**multicolored**	.60	1.50
	FDC *(May 7, 1997)*		1.00

1997. Golden Gate Bridge and San Francisco Harbor Issue issued in conjunction with Pacific 97 World Stamp Exhibition.

PC276 *Golden Gate Bridge, San Francisco Harbor (in daylight)*

PC276		UnVF	UseVF
20¢	**multicolored**	.60	1.00
	FDC *(June 2, 1997)*		1.00

PC277 *Golden Gate Bridge at sunset*

PC277		UnVF	UseVF
50¢	**multicolored**	.60	1.00
	FDC *(June 2, 1997)*		1.00

Warner Bros. Cartoon Characters Series

1997. Bugs Bunny Picture Postal Card Issue issued in conjunction with the self-adhesive stamp; an enlarged image appears on the back. Booklet of 10 cards sold for $5.95. *Offset by Banknote Corporation of America.*

PC278 *Bugs Bunny*

PC278		UnVF	UseVF
20¢	**multicolored**	.75	2.50
	Booklet of 10	7.50	
	FDC *(May 22, 1997)*		1.00

1997. Fort McHenry Issue 39th in the Historic Preservation Series.

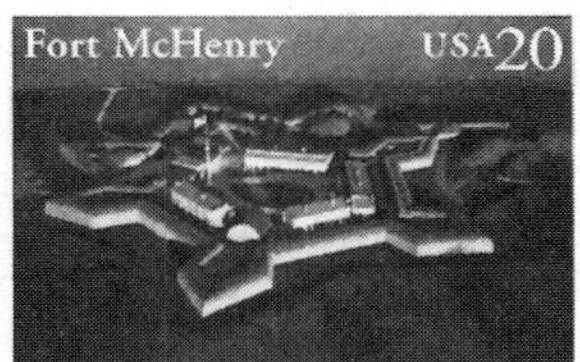

PC279 *Fort McHenry, Baltimore, Md.*

PC279		UnVF	UseVF
20¢	**multicolored**	.50	.75
	FDC *(Sept. 9, 1997)*		1.00

1997. Movie Monster Picture Postal Card Issue issued in conjuction with the 20-image sheetlet. Each postcard featured an enlargement of the stamp image. Booklet of 20 cards (four of each design) sold for $5.95. All multicolored, tagged, *offset by Ashton-Potter (USA) Ltd.*

PC280

PC281

PC282

PC280		UnVF	UseVF
20¢	Lon Chaney, Phantom of the Opera	.75	3.50
PC281		**UnVF**	**UseVF**
20¢	Bela Lugosi, Dracula	.75	3.50
PC282		**UnVF**	**UseVF**
20¢	Boris Karloff, Frankenstein	.75	3.50

PC283

PC284

PC283		UnVF	UseVF
20¢	Boris Karloff, The Mummy	.75	3.50
PC284		**UnVF**	**UseVF**
20¢	Lon Chaney, Jr., The Wolf Man	.75	3.50
	Booklet of 20	9.00	
	FDC (any card) *(Sept. 30, 1997)*		1.00

1998. University of Mississippi Issue 40th in the Historic Preservation Series and 17th in the College Series.

PC285 *The Lyceum, University of Mississippi, Oxford*

PC285		UnVF	UseVF
20¢	**multicolored**	.50	.75
	FDC *(April 20, 1998)*		1.00

1998. Sylvester & Tweety Picture Postal Card Issue in the Warner Bros. Cartoon Character Series. An enlargement of the stamp image appears on the back. Booklet of 10 cards sold for $5.95. *Offset by Ashton-Potter (USA) Ltd.*

PC286 *Sylvester & Tweety*

PC286		UnVF	UseVF
20¢	**multicolored**	.75	3.50
	Booklet of 10	7.50	
	FDC *(April 27, 1998)*		1.00

1998. Girard College Issue 41st in the Historic Preservation Series and 18th in the College Series.

PC287 *Founders Hall, Girard College, Philadelphia*

PC287		UnVF	UseVF
20¢	**multicolored**	.50	.75
	FDC *(May 1, 1998)*		1.00

1998. Tropical Birds Picture Postal Card Issue an enlargement of the stamp image appears on the back. Booklet of 20 cards (5 of each design) sold for $6.95. *Offset by Ashton-Potter (USA) Ltd., (2,000,000 printed, 100,000 sets).*

PC288

PC289

PC288		UnVF	UseVF
20¢	Antillean Euphonia of Puerto Rico	.60	3.00
PC289		**UnVF**	**UseVF**
20¢	Green-throated Carib of Puerto Rico	.60	3.00

PC290

PC291

PC290		UnVF	UseVF
20¢	Crested Honeycreeper of Hawaii	.60	3.00
PC291		UnVF	UseVF
20¢	Cardinal Honeyeater of Western Samoa	.60	3.00
	Booklet of 20	10.00	
	FDC (any card) *(July 29, 1998)*		2.50

1998. American Ballet Picture Postal Card Issue an enlargement of the stamp image appears on the back. Booklet of 10 cards sold for $5.95. *Offset by Milken Companies for Ashton-Potter (USA) Ltd.*

PC292 *Ballet dancer*

PC292		UnVF	UseVF
20¢	**multicolored,** tagged *(1,000,000)*	.75	3.00
	n. Booklet of 10	7.50	
	FDC *(Sept. 16, 1998)*		1.00

1998. Northeastern University Issue 42nd in the Historic Preservation Series and 19th in the College Series, featured a stylized window detail of Kerr Hall, a residence hall noted on the National Register of Historic Places. The institution in Boston, Mass., was founded Oct. 3, 1898. *Offset by Government Printing Office.*

PC293 *Kerr Hall, Northeastern University*

PC293		UnVF	UseVF
20¢	**multicolored,** tagged *(21,000,000)*	.50	.75
	FDC *(Oct. 3, 1998)*		1.00

1998. Brandeis University Issue 43rd in the Historic Preservation Series and 20th in the College Series, portrayed a photo of Usen Castle, which was built of colonial fieldstone between 1928 and 1940 and is an undergraduate residence hall. The nation's youngest private research university, in Waltham, Mass., was named for Louis Dembitz Brandeis, an associate justice of the U.S. Supreme Court. It was founded in 1948. *Offset by Government Printing Office.*

PC294 *Usen Castle, Brandeis University*

PC294		UnVF	UseVF
20¢	**multicolored,** tagged *(21,000,000)*	.50	.75
	FDC *(Oct. 17, 1998)*		1.00

1999. Victorian Love Picture Postal Card Issue in the Love Series designed to be used for special greetings of affection, featured a paper-lace-and-flowers motif reminiscent of the late 1800s. An enlargement of the stamp design appears on the back. Sold in packs of 20 cards (5 panels of 4 cards each) for $6.95. *Offset by Bank-note Corp. of America.*

PC295 *Victorian Valentine*

PC295		UnVF	UseVF
20¢	**multicolored,** tagged *(2,000,000)*	.50	2.50
	Pane of 4 cards	2.40	
	FDC *(Jan. 28, 1999)*		1.00

1999. University of Wisconsin-Madison Issue 44th in the Historic Preservation Series and 21st in the College Series, portrayed an old lithograph of Bascom Hill, a campus landmark. *Offset by Government Printing Office.*

PC296 *Bascom Hill, University of Wisconsin, Madison*

PC296		UnVF	UseVF
20¢	**multicolored** *(6,000,000)*	.50	.75
	FDC *(Feb. 5, 1999)*		1.00

1999. Washington and Lee University Issue 45th in the Historic Preservation Series and 22nd in the College Series, noted the 250th anniversary of the nation's sixth oldest college. It was named for George Washington, who contributed to its endowment in 1796, and Gen. Robert E. Lee, who was its president 1865-70 (see CM324). *Offset by Government Printing Office.*

PC297 *Colonnade, Washington and Lee University, Lexington, Va.*

PC297		UnVF	UseVF
20¢	**multicolored**	.50	.75
	FDC *(Feb. 11, 1999)*		1.00

1999. Redwood Library & Athenaeum Issue 46th in the Historic Preservation Series, commemorated the 250th anniversary of the nation's oldest lending library. Its original building is said to be the oldest building in the United States. The design, an old view of Newport, R.I., is based on an 1871 illustration. *Offset by Government Printing Office.*

PC298 *View of Newport, R.I., from 1871*

PC298		UnVF	UseVF
20¢	**red and black** *(6,000,000)*	.50	.75
	FDC *(March 11, 1999)*		1.00

1999. Daffy Duck Picture Postal Card Issue in the Warner Bros. Cartoon Character Series. An enlargement of the stamp image appears on the back. Booklet of 10 cards sold for $6.95. *Printed by Ashton-Potter (USA) Ltd.*

PC299 *Daffy Duck*

PC299		UnVF	UseVF
20¢	**multicolored**	.85	2.50
	Booklet of 10	8.50	
	FDC *(April 16, 1999)*		1.00

1999. Mount Vernon Issue 47th in the Historic Preservation Series, was based on a painting, *A View of Mount Vernon,* from about 1792. The estate overlooking the Potomac River was inherited by George Washington in 1751, and he lived there 1759-99. George and Martha Washington are buried there. (See EN808-13, CM172, 571.) *Offset by Government Printing Office.*

PC300 *Mount Vernon*

PC300		UnVF	UseVF
20¢	**multicolored** *(6,000,000)*	.50	.50
	FDC *(May 14, 1999)*		1.00

1999. Mount Rainier Issue in the Scenic American Landmarks Series paid a new international postal card rate to all countries other than Canada and Mexico and portrayed the snow-clad mountain that dominates the Cascade Mountain Range southeast of Tacoma, Wash. The card coincided with the 100th anniversary of Mount Rainier National Park. *Printed by Government Printing Office.*

PC301 *Mount Rainier*

PC301		UnVF	UseVF
20¢	**multicolored**	1.00	3.50
	FDC *(May 15, 1999)*		1.50

1999. Block Island Lighthouse Issue in the Scenic America Series portrayed the highest lighthouse in New England, 200 feet above the shoals and ledges that sank dozens of ships off Rhode Island. The lighthouse was established in 1875 on the island, nine miles from the mainland of Rhode Island. *Offset by Government Printing Office.*

PC302 *Block Island Lighthouse*

PC302		UnVF	UseVF
20¢	**multicolored**	.50	.75
	FDC *(July 24, 1999)*		1.00
	40-card sheets *(Nov. 10, 1999)*	20.00	

1999. All Aboard! Issue Depicted five illustrated postal cards with the same designs as the 33¢ stamps and corresponding 20¢ postcard-rate stamp indicia. Booklet of 20 cards sold for $6.95. *Printed by Ashton-Potter (USA) Ltd.*

PC303 *Daylight;* PC304 *20th Century;* PC305 *Superchief;* PC306 *Congressional;* PC307 *Hiawatha*

PC303		UnVF	UseVF
20¢	Daylight, **multicolored**	.50	2.50
PC304		UnVF	UseVF
20¢	20th Century Limited, **multicolored**	.50	2.50
PC305		UnVF	UseVF
20¢	Superchief, **multicolored**	.50	2.50
PC306		UnVF	UseVF
20¢	Congressional, **multicolored**	.50	2.50
PC307		UnVF	UseVF
20¢	Hiawatha, **multicolored**	.50	2.50
	Booklet of 20	10.00	—
	FDC (any card) *(Aug. 26, 1999)*		1.00

2000. University of Utah Issue 48th in the Historic Preservation Series and 23rd in the College Series, was released as part of the sesquicentennial celebration at the university in Salt Lake City, Utah. *Offset by the Government Printing Office.*

PC308 *University of Utah*

PC308		UnVF	UseVF
20¢	**multicolored**	.50	.75
	FDC *(Feb. 28, 2000)*		1.50

2000. Ryman Auditorium Issue 49th in the Historic Preservation Series saluted the former home of the Grand Ole Opry in Nashville, Tenn. *Offset by the Government Printing Office.*

PC309 *Ryman Auditorium*

		UnVF	UseVF
PC309			
20¢	**multicolored**	.50	.75
	FDC *(March 18, 2000)*		1.50

2000. Wile E. Coyote & Road Runner Issue Warner Bros. Cartoon Character Series. An enlargement of the stamp image appears on the back. Booklet of 10 cards sold for $6.95. Designed and illustrated by Ed Wleczyk, Los Angeles. *Offset by Banknote Corporation of America. 1,000,000 printed, (100,000 books).*

PC310 *Wile E. Coyote & Road Runner*

		UnVF	UseVF
PC310			
20¢	**multicolored**	.85	2.50
	Booklet of 10	8.50	—
	FDC *(April 26, 2000)*		1.50

2000. Adoption Issue intended to raise awareness that more than 100,000 children are available for adoption in the United States each year. Booklet of 10 cards sold for $6.95. *Offset by Banknote Corporation of America.*

PC311 *Drawing of family*

		UnVF	UseVF
PC311			
20¢	**multicolored**	.85	2.50
	Booklet of 10	9.00	—
	FDC *(May 10, 2000)*		1.50

2000. Middlebury College Issue 50th in the Historic Preservation Series and 24th in the College Series, featured the Vermont college's original three buildings, which date to 1815-61 and are known as Old Stone Row. Designed by Howard Paine, Delaplane, Va., illustrated by Arnold Holeywell, Warrenton, Va. *Offset by Government Printing Office.*

PC312 *Middlebury College, Old Stone Row*

		UnVF	UseVF
PC312			
20¢	**multicolored** *(4,000,000 printed)*	.50	.75
	FDC *(May 19, 2000)*		1.50

2000. Stars and Stripes Issue Designed by Richard Sheaff, Scottsdale, Ariz. Sold in packs of 20 cards (5 panels of 4 cards each) for $8.95. *Offset by Ashton-Potter USA. 2,000,000 cards printed, 100,000 sets of 20 cards.*

PC313
Sons of Liberty Flag

PC314
New England Flag

		UnVF	UseVF
PC313			
20¢	**multicolored**	.65	2.50
PC314			
20¢	**multicolored**	.65	2.50

PC315
Forster Flag

PC316
Continental Colors

		UnVF	UseVF
PC315			
20¢	**multicolored**	.65	2.50
PC316			
20¢	**multicolored**	.65	2.50

PC317
Francis Hopkinson Flag

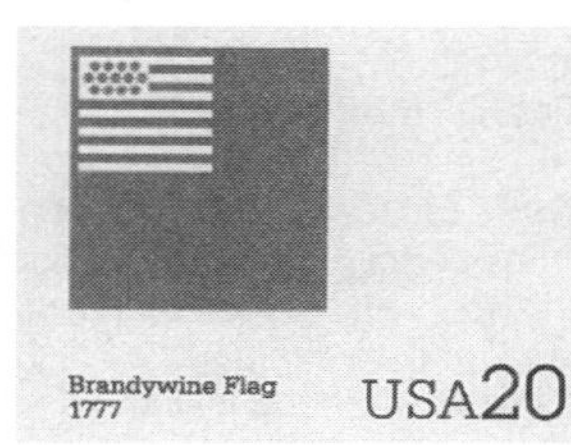

PC318
Brandywine Flag

		UnVF	UseVF
PC317			
20¢	**multicolored**	.65	2.50
PC318			
20¢	**multicolored**	.65	2.50

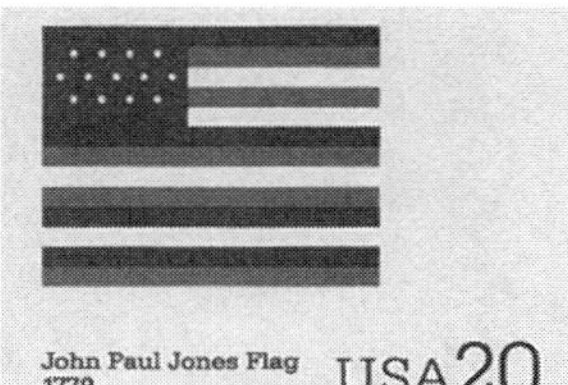

PC319
John Paul Jones Flag

PC320
Pierre L'Enfant Flag

		UnVF	UseVF
PC319			
20¢	**multicolored**	.65	2.50
PC320		UnVF	UseVF
20¢	**multicolored**	.65	2.50

PC321
Indian Peace Flag

PC322
Easton Flag

		UnVF	UseVF
PC321			
20¢	**multicolored**	.65	2.50
PC322		UnVF	UseVF
20¢	**multicolored**	.65	2.50

PC323
Star-Spangled Banner

PC324
Bennington Flag

		UnVF	UseVF
PC323			
20¢	**multicolored**	.65	2.50
PC324		UnVF	UseVF
20¢	**multicolored**	.65	2.50

PC325
Great Star Flag

PC326
29-Star Flag

		UnVF	UseVF
PC325			
20¢	**multicolored**	.65	2.50
PC326		UnVF	UseVF
20¢	**multicolored**	.65	2.50

PC327
Fort Sumter Flag

PC328
Centennial Flag

		UnVF	UseVF
PC327			
20¢	**multicolored**	.65	2.50
PC328		UnVF	UseVF
20¢	**multicolored**	.65	2.50

PC329
38-Star Flag

PC330
Peace Flag

		UnVF	UseVF
PC329			
20¢	**multicolored**	.65	2.50
PC330		UnVF	UseVF
20¢	**multicolored**	.65	2.50

PC331
48-Star Flag

PC332
50-Star Flag

		UnVF	UseVF
PC331			
20¢	**multicolored**	.65	2.50
PC332		UnVF	UseVF
20¢	**multicolored**	.65	2.50
	FDC *(June 14, 2000)* (any single)		1.50

2000. Legends of Baseball Issue Designed by Derry Noyes, Washington, D.C. Booklet of 20 cards sold for $8.95. *Gravure by Sennett Security Products.*

PC333
Jackie Robinson

PC334
Eddie Collins

PC335
Christy Mathewson

		UnVF	UseVF
PC333			
20¢	**multicolored**	.65	2.50

		UnVF	UseVF
PC334			
20¢	**multicolored**	.65	2.50
PC335			
20¢	**multicolored**	.65	2.50

PC336
Ty Cobb

PC337
George Sisler

PC338
Rogers Hornsby

		UnVF	UseVF
PC336			
20¢	**multicolored**	.65	2.50
PC337			
20¢	**multicolored**	.65	2.50
PC338			
20¢	**multicolored**	.65	2.50

PC339
Mickey Cochrane

PC340
Babe Ruth

PC341
Walter Johnson

		UnVF	UseVF
PC339			
20¢	**multicolored**	.65	2.50
PC340			
20¢	**multicolored**	.65	2.50
PC341			
20¢	**multicolored**	.65	2.50

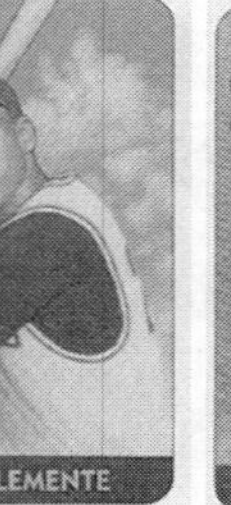

PC342
Roberto Clemente

PC343
Lefty Grove

PC344
Tris Speaker

		UnVF	UseVF
PC342			
20¢	**multicolored**	.65	2.50
PC343			
20¢	**multicolored**	.65	2.50
PC344			
20¢	**multicolored**	.65	2.50

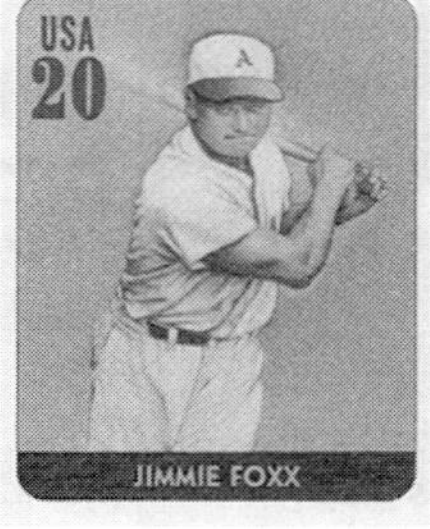

PC345
Cy Young

PC346
Jimmie Foxx

PC347
Pie Traynor

		UnVF	UseVF
PC345			
20¢	**multicolored**	.65	2.50
PC346			
20¢	**multicolored**	.65	2.50
PC347			
20¢	**multicolored**	.65	2.50

PC348
Satchel Paige

PC349
Honus Wagner

PC350
Josh Gibson

		UnVF	UseVF
PC348			
20¢	**multicolored**	.65	2.50
PC349			
20¢	**multicolored**	.65	2.50
PC350			
20¢	**multicolored**	.65	2.50

PC351
Dizzy Dean

PC352
Lou Gehrig

		UnVF	UseVF
PC351			
20¢	**multicolored**	.65	2.50
PC352			
20¢	**multicolored**	.65	2.50
	Booklet of 20	12.00	—
	FDC (any card) *(July 6, 2000)*		1.50

Read the introduction to this catalog carefully. It contains much valuable information for all stamp collectors and makes the catalog easier to use.

Holiday Contemporary Series

2000. Deer Postal Card Issue in the Holiday Contemporary Series had the same design as Christmas-season stamps issued in three formats in 1998. Designed by Tom Nikosey, Canoga Park, Calif. *Issued in packs of 5 sheets of 4 cards (blue, red, purple, green), offset by Ashton-Potter (USA), (2,000,000 printed, 100,000 sets of 5 sheets).*

PC353, PC354, PC355, PC356 *Leaping reindeer*

		UnVF	UseVF
PC353			
20¢	**red and gold**	.35	.20
PC354			
20¢	**blue and gold**	.35	.20
PC355			
20¢	**purple and gold**	.35	.20
PC356			
20¢	**green and gold**	.35	.20
	Sheet of 4	2.00	
	FDC *(Oct. 12, 2000)*		1.50

2001. Badlands National Park Issue in the Scenic American Landscapes Series, international rate, highlighted the 244,000-acre national park in southwestern South Dakota, which constitutes the largest protected mixed-grasses prairie in the United States. *Offset by the Government Printing Office.*

PC357 *Badlands scene*

		UnVF	UseVF
PC357			
70¢	**multicolored**	1.40	.50
	FDC *(Feb. 22, 2001)*		2.00

2001. Yale University Issue in the Historic Preservation Series helped to commemorate the 300th anniversary of the founding of the school in New Haven, Conn. A contemporary photo of Connecticut Hall is featured. Designed by Derry Noyes, *offset by Government Printing Office (6,000,000).*

PC358 *Yale Connecticut Hall*

		UnVF	UseVF
PC358			
20¢	**multicolored**	.40	.40
	FDC *(March 30, 2001)*		1.00

2001. University of South Carolina Issue 52nd in the Historic Preservation Series helped to commemorate the 200th anniversary of the founding of the school in Columbia, S.C. It featured a detail from a painting c 1820 of the historic Horseshoe district on the main campus. Designed by Ethel Kessler, *offset by Government Printing Office (6,000,000).*

PC359 *USC's Horseshoe District*

		UnVF	UseVF
PC359			
20¢	**multicolored**	.40	.40
	FDC *(April 26, 2001)*		1.00

2001. Northwestern University Issue in the Historic Preservation Series helped to commemorate the 150th anniversary of the founding of the school in Evanston, Ill. A drawing of the tower of University Hall, built in 1869 and the oldest building on campus, is featured. Designed by Howard Paine from the illustration by Arnold C. Holeywell, Warrenton, Va., *offset by Government Printing Office (6,000,000).*

PC360 *Northwestern's University Hall tower*

		UnVF	UseVF
PC360			
20¢	**multicolored**	.40	.40
	FDC *(April 28, 2001)*		1.00

2001. University of Portland Issue 54th in the Historic Preservation Series helped to commemorate the 100th anniversary of the founding of the school in Portland, Ore. A computer-generated illustration of Waldschmidt Hall, the oldest building on the campus, is featured. Designed by Richard Sheaff from an illustration by John Pirman, New York, N.Y., *offset by Government Printing Office (6,000,000).*

PC361 *University of Portland's Waldschmidt Hall*

		UnVF	UseVF
PC361			
20¢	**multicolored**	.40	.40
	FDC *(May 1, 2001)*		1.00

Airmail Postal Cards

1949. Inscribed. "AIR MAIL-POSTAL CARD" Issue

PCA1 *Eagle*

PCA1		UnVF	UseVF
4¢	**red orange on buff**	.75	1.00
	a. Deep red on buff	.75	1.50
	FDC *(Jan. 10, 1949)*		2.00

1958. Inscribed. "AIR MAIL-POSTAL CARD Issue

PCA2, PCA3 *Eagle in flight*

PCA2		UnVF	UseVF
5¢	**red on buff**	1.60	.80
	FDC *(July 31, 1958)*		2.00

1960. Eagle in Flight Issue with red and blue border.

PCA3		UnVF	UseVF
5¢	**red on buff**	6.50	2.25
	v. Red omitted	—	
	v1. Thinned dividing line at top	—	
	v2. Thinned dividing line at bottom	—	
	FDC *(June 18, 1960)*		2.00

1963. Bald Eagle Issue with red and blue border.

PCA4 *Bald eagle*

PCA4		UnVF	UseVF
6¢	**red on white**	.75	1.00
	p. Fluorescent paper	10.00	—
	FDC *(Feb. 15, 1963)*		5.00

1966. Visit the USA Issue with red and blue border. International rate.

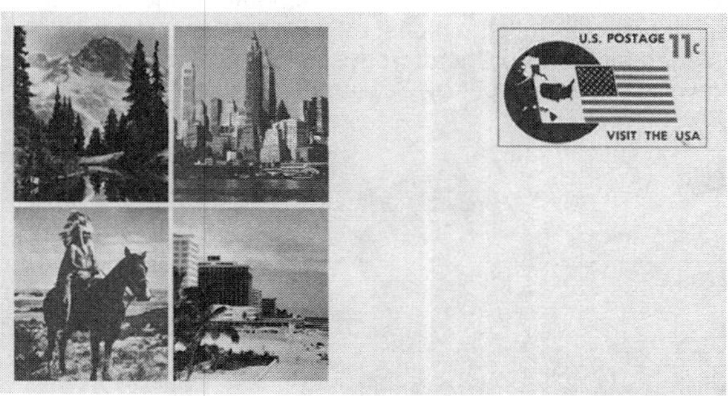

PCA5 *Map, flag and VISIT THE USA. Photos of Mt. Rainier, Washington; New York City skyline; Miami Beach, Florida; Indian on horseback.*

PCA5		UnVF	UseVF
11¢	**red and blue on white**	.75	15.00
	Fluorescent paper	—	—
	FDC *(May 27, 1966)*		1.75

1967. 50th Anniversary of Purchase of the Virgin Islands Issue with red and blue lines at bottom.

PCA6 *Virgin Islands and flag*

PCA6		UnVF	UseVF
6¢	**multicolored on white**	.50	7.50
	v. Magenta and yellow omitted	—	
	FDC *(March 31, 1967)*		1.75

1967. 12th Boy Scout World Jamboree Issue Idaho, USA.

PCA7 *Boy Scout emblem and Borah Peak.*

PCA7		UnVF	UseVF
6¢	**multicolored on white**	.50	7.50
	v. Cyan (blue) omitted	—	
	v1. Cyan (blue) & black omitted	—	
	v2. Magenta & yellow omitted	—	
	FDC *(Aug. 4, 1967)*		1.75

1967. Visit the USA Issue with design as PCA5, but without scenic pictures at left and with red and blue lines at bottom instead of border. International rate.

PCA8

PCA8		UnVF	UseVF
13¢	**red and blue on white**	1.75	10.00
	FDC *(Sept. 8, 1967)*		1.75

1968. Stylized Eagle Issue with red and blue border.

PCA9 *Stylized eagle*

PCA9		UnVF	UseVF
8¢	**red and blue on white,** non-fluorescent paper, tagged	.75	.50
	FDC *(March 1, 1968)*		1.75
	p. Slightly fluorescent paper, tagged	2.50	3.00
	p1. Tagging omitted	—	—
	FDC *(March 1, 1969)*		15.00

Flurorescent paper noted in No. PCA9 *and later issues was a function of paper manufacturers' attempt at producing whiter paper stock with the use of brighteners; such fluoresence was not a function of the tagging schemes to aid in automated canceling.*

1971. Stylized Eagle Issue with design as PCA9.

PCA10

PCA10		UnVF	UseVF
9¢	**red and blue on white,** tagged	.70	2.00
	FDC *(May 15, 1971)*		1.75

1971. VISIT THE USA ISSUE with design as PCA8. International rate.

PCA11		UnVF	UseVF
15¢	**red and blue on white,** tagged	2.25	15.00
	v. Card w/ printed cachet for sale at LUPOSTA 1971 in Berlin Germany		—
	FDC *(June 10, 1971)*		1.75

1972. TOURISM YEAR OF THE AMERICAS ISSUE

PCA12 *Grand Canyon with Statue of Liberty, Hawaii, Alaska, and San Francisco on reverse.*

PCA12		UnVF	UseVF
9¢	**black on manila,** tagged	.65	10.00
	v. Red & blue lozenges of border omitted	—	
	v1. Red lozenges omitted	—	
	zo. Tagging omitted	—	
	FDC *(June 29, 1972)*		1.75

PCA13 *Niagara Falls with Mount Vernon, Washington, D.C., Abraham Lincoln, and Liberty Bell on reverse. For international rate.*

PCA13		UnVF	UseVF
15¢	**black on manila,** tagged	.70	15.00
	v. Red & blue lozenges omitted	—	
	v1 Stamp & vertical line omitted	600.00	
	zo. Tagging omitted	—	
	FDC *(June 29, 1972)*		1.75

1974. STYLIZED EAGLE ISSUE

PCA14 *Stylized Eagle*

PCA14		UnVF	UseVF
11¢	**red, white and blue on white,** non-fluorescent paper, tagged	.75	3.00
	p. Fluorescent paper	2.00	
	zo. Tagging omitted	—	
	zv. Inverted tag bar at lower left	250.00	
	zvl. Tag bar printed double in normal position	250.00	
	FDC *(Jan. 4, 1974)*		1.75

1974. EAGLE WEATHERVANE ISSUE International rate.

PCA15 *Eagle weather vane*

PCA15		UnVF	UseVF
18¢	**multicolored on white,** non-fluorescent paper, tagged	1.00	17.50
	p. Fluorescent paper	3.00	17.50
	v. Black & yellow omitted	—	
	zo. Tagging omitted	—	
	FDC *(Jan. 4, 1974)*		1.75

1975. ANGEL WEATHERVANE ISSUE International rate.

PCA16 *Angel Gabriel weather vane*

PCA16		UnVF	UseVF
21¢	**multicolored on white,** non-fluorescent paper, tagged	.90	9.50
	v. Cyan (blue) & magenta omitted	—	
	zo. Tagging omitted	150.00	
	FDC *(Dec. 17, 1975)*		1.75

1978. AIRPLANE ISSUE International rate.

PCA17 *Curtiss "Jenny"*

PCA17		UnVF	UseVF
21¢	**multicolored on white,** non-fluorescent paper, tagged	.85	7.50
	FDC *(Sept. 16, 1978)*		1.75

1979. OLYMPIC GAMES ISSUE International rate.

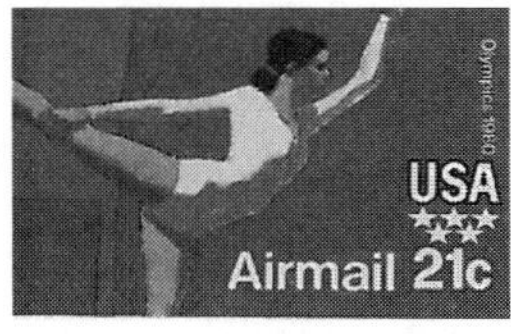

PCA18 *Gymnast*

PCA18		UnVF	UseVF
21¢	**multicolored on white,** fluorescent or non-fluorescent paper, tagged	1.25	12.50
	FDC *(Dec. 1, 1979)*		1.75

1981. 50TH ANNIVERSARY OF TRANSPACIFIC FLIGHT ISSUE International rate.

PCA19 *Clyde Pangborn, Hugh Herndon, and plane "Miss Veedol".*

PCA19		UnVF	UseVF
28¢	**multicolored on white,** fluorescent or non-fluorescent paper, tagged	1.00	7.50
	zo. Tagging omitted	—	
	FDC *(Jan. 2, 1981)*		1.75

1982. 50th Anniversary of the Founding of the Soaring Society of America Issue International rate.

PCA20 *Sailplanes*

PCA20		UnVF	UseVF
28¢	**multicolored on white,** tagged	1.00	7.50
	FDC *(March 5, 1982)*		1.75

1984. Olympics Issue International rate.

PCA21 *Speed skater*

PCA21		UnVF	UseVF
28¢	**multicolored on white**	1.00	7.50
	v. 40mm left shift of magenta and yellow	—	—
	FDC *(Dec. 29, 1983)*		1.75

1985. China Clipper Issue International rate.

PCA22 *China Clipper*

PCA22		UnVF	UseVF
33¢	**multicolored on white**	1.00	7.50
	FDC *(Feb. 15, 1985)*		1.75

1986. AMERIPEX ' 86 Issue International rate.

PCA23 *Chicago skyline*

PCA23		UnVF	UseVF
33¢	**multicolored on white**	.90	7.50
	v. Card w/ printed cachet to left, sold by U.S. Postal Service at SUDPOSTA '87, Sindelfingen, Germany	2.00	9.00
	FDC *(Feb. 1, 1986)*		1.75
	SUDPOSTA FDC *(Oct. 22, 1987)*		—

1988. DC-3 Issue International rate.

PCA24 *Douglas DC-3*

PCA24		UnVF	UseVF
36¢	**multicolored on white,** fluorescent paper, tagged	1.00	7.00
	p. Non-fluorescent paper	1.50	7.00
	v. Card w/ printed cachet to left, sold by U.S. Postal Service at a SYDPEX 88, Sydney, Australia	1.50	9.00
	FDC *(May 14, 1988)*		2.00
	SYDPEX FDC *(July 30, 1988)*		—

1991. Yankee Clipper Issue International rate.

PCA25 *Yankee Clipper*

PCA25		UnVF	UseVF
40¢	**multicolored on white**	1.00	7.50
	FDC *(June 28, 1991)*		2.00

1995. Soaring Eagle Issue International rate.

PCA26 *Soaring eagle*

PCA26		UnVF	UseVF
50¢	**multicolored on white**	1.25	8.00
	FDC *(Aug. 24, 1995)*		2.00

Official Postal Cards

1913. Postal Savings Issue produced for Postal Savings System monthly reports. In use for a very short time. 5 x 3 inches.

OPC1 *U.S. Postal Savings*

OPC1		UnVF	UseVF
1¢	**black**	325.00	150.00
	FDC *(July 1913)*		

1983. Great Seal Issue

OPC2

OPC2		UnVF	UseVF
13¢	**blue**	.60	35.00
	FDC *(Jan. 12, 1983)* at Washington, D.C.		1.00

OPC3

OPC3		UnVF	UseVF
14¢	**blue**	.60	35.00
	FDC *(Feb. 26, 1985)* at Washington, D.C.		1.00

1988. Great Seal Issue

OPC4 *Great Seal*

OPC4		UnVF	UseVF
15¢	**multicolored**	.60	35.00
	FDC *(June 10, 1988)* at New York City		1.25

1991. Great Seal Issue

OPC5 *Great Seal*

OPC5		UnVF	UseVF
19¢	**multicolored**	.55	30.00
	FDC *(May 24, 1991)* at Seattle, Wash.		1.00

1995. Great Seal Issue

OPC6 *Great Seal*

OPC6		UnVF	UseVF
20¢	**multicolored**	.40	—
	FDC *(May 9, 1995)* at Washington, D.C.		1.25

Message & Reply Cards

First issued in 1892, message and reply cards consist of two postal cards attached to each other. One card is used for sending the message, and the other card, when separated, is used to send the reply. The term "used" when referring to the unsevered card signifies a used message card and an unused reply card. Listings are for unsevered and severed (individual) cards.

1892. Issue frame around edge of card.

MRC1 *Ulysses S. Grant*

MRC1

		UnFVF	UseFVF
1¢ + 1¢	**black on buff,** unsevered	37.50	8.00
	m. Message card	7.00	1.50
	r. Reply card	7.00	1.50
	t. Message card printed on both sides, reply card blank	275.00	—
	t1. Message card blank, reply card printed on both sides	325.00	—
	FDC *(Oct. 25, 1892)*		350.00

1893. Universal Postal Union Card frame around edge of card.

MRC2, MRC10 *Liberty*

MRC2

		UnFVF	UseFVF
2¢ + 2¢	**blue on grayish white,** unsevered	18.50	25.00
	a. dark blue on grayish white	20.00	25.00
	m. Message card	6.00	7.00
	r. Reply card	6.00	7.00
	t. Message card printed on both sides, reply card blank	325.00	—
	t1. Message card blank, reply card printed on both sides	—	—
	t2. Message card normal, reply card blank	325.00	—
	FDC *(March 1, 1893)*		

1898. Issue same design as MRC1, but without frame around edge of card.

MRC3

		UnFVF	UseFVF
1¢ + 1¢	**black on buff,** unsevered	70.00	20.00
	m. Message card	15.00	3.00
	r. Reply card	15.00	3.00
	t. Message card printed on both sides, reply card blank	275.00	—
	t1. Message card blank, reply card printed on both sides	275.00	—
	t2. Message card blank, reply card normal	—	275.00
	t3. Message card normal, reply card printed on both sides	—	—
	t4. Message card without "detach annexed card/for answer"	275.00	160.00
	t5. Message card printed on both sides, reply card normal	—	—
	t6. Message card printed on both halves	—	—
	No official date of issue		

1904. Issue

MRC4m *William T. Sherman*

UNITED STATES OF AMERICA REPLY CARD
THIS SIDE IS FOR THE ADDRESS ONLY.

MRC4r *Philip H. Sheridan*

MRC4

		UnFVF	UseFVF
1¢ + 1¢	**black on buff,** unsevered	50.00	6.00
	m. Message card	10.00	2.00
	r. Reply card	10.00	2.00
	t. Message card printed on both sides, reply card blank	300.00	—
	t1. Message card blank, reply card printed on both sides	—	185.00
	t2. Message card blank, reply card normal	—	300.00
	t3. Message card normal, reply card blank	300.00	—
	FDC *(March 31, 1904)*		

1910. Issue

MRC5m *George Washington*

MRC5r *Martha Washington*

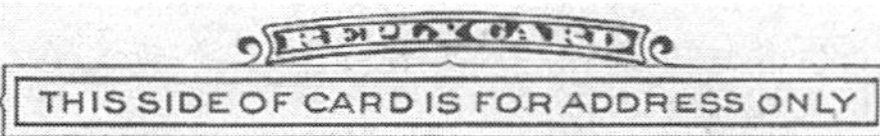

REPLY CARD
THIS SIDE OF CARD IS FOR ADDRESS ONLY

MRC5

		UnFVF	UseFVF
1¢ + 1¢	**dark blue on bluish,** unsevered	150.00	25.00
	m. Message card	11.00	4.00
	r. Reply card	11.00	4.00
	t. Message card normal, reply card blank	220.00	—
	FDC *(Sept. 14, 1910)*		

1911. Issue same design.

MRC6m *George Washington*

MRC6r *Martha Washington*

MRC6

		UnFVF	UseFVF
1¢ + 1¢	**green on cream,** unsevered	150.00	25.00
	m. Message card	25.00	6.00
	r. Reply card	40.00	45.00
	t. Message card normal, reply card blank	—	—
	FDC *(Oct. 27, 1911)*		

1915. Issue same design. Single frame around inscription.

MRC7

REPLY CARD

THIS SIDE OF CARD IS FOR ADDRESS

MRC7

		UnFVF	UseFVF
1¢ + 1¢	**green on cream,** unsevered	1.50	55.00
	dark green on buff	1.50	55.00
	m. Message card	.30	.25
	r. Reply card	.30	.25
	t. Message card normal, reply card blank	—	—
	FDC *(Sept. 18, 1915)*		

1918. Issue

MRC8m *George Washington*

MRC8r *Martha Washington*

MRC8

		UnFVF	UseFVF
2¢ + 2¢	**red on cream,** unsevered	80.00	45.00
	m. Message card	22.50	7.50
	r. Reply card	22.50	7.50
	FDC *(Aug. 2, 1918)*		

1920-21. Issue re-valued. *Surcharged in black by canceling machine.*

MRC9m *Overprinted on MRC8m*

MRC9r *Overprinted on MRC8r*

MRC9

		UnFVF	UseFVF
1¢ on 2¢ + 1¢ on 2¢	**red on cream,** unsevered	20.00	10.00
	m. Message card	6.00	4.00
	r. Reply card	6.00	4.00
	x. Message card double surcharge, reply card normal	80.00	—
	x1. Message card normal, reply card no surcharge	90.00	—
	x2. Message card normal, reply card double surcharge	80.00	—
	x3. Message card no surcharge, reply card normal	80.00	—
	x4. Message card no surcharge, reply card double surcharge	80.00	—
	x5. Message card double surcharge, reply card no surcharge	—	—
	x6. Message card no surcharge, reply card double surcharge, one inverted	—	—

MRC9A

		UnFVF	UseFVF
1¢ on 2¢ + 1¢ on 2¢	**red on cream,** unsevered	325.00	200.00
	m. Message card	95.00	45.00
	p. red on buff	—	—
	r. Reply card	95.00	45.00
	x. Message card no surcharge, reply card normal	—	—
	x1. Message card double surcharge, reply card no surcharge	—	—
	x2. Message card no surcharge, reply card double surcharge	—	—

Same surcharge press printed.

1924. Universal Postal Union Card same design and size as MRC2.

MRC10

		UnFVF	UseFVF
2¢ + 2¢	**red on buff,** unsevered	3.00	50.00
	m. Message card	.50	20.00
	r. Reply card	.50	20.00
	FDC *(March 18, 1924)*		

1926. Universal Postal Union Card same size as PC11.

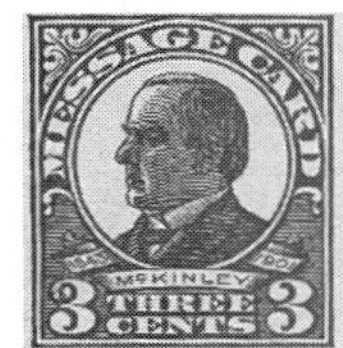

MRC11 *William McKinley*

MRC11

		UnFVF	UseFVF
3¢ + 3¢	**red on cream,** unsevered	15.00	35.00
	a. carmine on cream	—	—
	b. pale red on cream	—	—
	c. scarlet on cream	—	—
	m. Message card	3.00	16.00
	p. red on buff	—	—
	p1. red on canary	10.00	17.50
	p2. red on light buff	—	—
	p3. red on yellow buff	—	—
	r. Reply card	3.00	6.00
	FDC *(Feb. 1, 1926)*		275.00

1951. Issue same size as PC13.

MRC12 *George Washington, message card; Martha Washington, reply card.*

MRC12

		UnVF	UseVF
2¢ + 2¢	**carmine on cream,** unsevered	1.75	3.00
	m. Message card	.50	1.00
	r. Reply card	.50	1.00
	FDC *(Dec. 29, 1951)*		

1952. Issue re-valued, overprinted in green by Pitney-Bowes Tickometer.

MRC13 *Overprinted on MRC7*

MRC13

		UnVF	UseVF
2¢ on 1¢ + 2¢ on 1¢	**light green on buff,** unsevered	1.75	4.00
	m. Message card	.50	2.00
	r. Reply card	.50	2.00
	x. Both cards double surcharge	55.00	40.00
	x1. Inverted surcharge horizontal, to left of stamps	150.00	100.00
	x2. Message card double surcharge, reply card normal	45.00	30.00
	x3. Message card no surcharge, reply card normal	40.00	45.00

		UnVF	UseVF
	x4. Message card normal, reply card double surcharge	45.00	30.00
	x5. Message card normal, reply card no surcharge	40.00	45.00
	x6. Surcharge horizontal, to left of stamp	15.00	15.00
	x7. Surcharge vertical, to left of stamp	7.00	7.00
	x8. Surcharge vertical below stamp	—	—
	x9. Black surcharge vertical below stamp	—	—
	x10. Message card no surcharge, reply card double surcharge	—	—
	x11. Message card double surcharge, reply card no surcharge	—	—
	FDC *(Jan. 1952)*		

1952. Issue same as MRC13, but dark green horizontal overprint applied by printing press.

MRC14		UnVF	UseVF
2¢ on 1¢ + 2¢ on 1¢	**green on cream,** unsevered	135.00	55.00
	m. Message card	20.00	12.50
	r. Reply card	20.00	12.50
	x. Message card normal plus one on back, reply card no surcharge	—	—
	x1. Reply card normal plus one on back, with Tickometer surcharge vertical below stamp on message card	—	—

1956. Universal Postal Union Card Issue design of PC41, Liberty.

MRC15 *Statue of Liberty*

MRC15		UnVF	UseVF
4¢ + 4¢	**scarlet and ultramarine on cream,** unsevered	1.50	60.00
	m. Message card	.50	40.00
	r. Reply card	.50	35.00
	t. Message card printed on both halves	140.00	—
	t1. Reply card printed on both halves	140.00	—
	FDC *(Nov. 16, 1956)*		2.00

1958. Issue design of PC42, Liberty; the two cards are identical.

MRC16		UnVF	UseVF
3¢ + 3¢	**purple on buff,** unsevered	4.00	5.00
	t. One card blank	140.00	—
	t1. Printed by electrotype	—	—
	t2. Printed by steel plate	—	—
	FDC *(July 31, 1958)*		2.00

1962. Lincoln Precancel Issue design of PC44, Abraham Lincoln; the two cards are identical.

MRC17 *Abraham Lincoln*

MRC17		UnVF	UseVF
4¢ + 4¢	**red violet on white,** unsevered	4.50	5.00
	a. light violet	—	—
	p. Fluorescent paper, non-fluorescent ink	—	—
	t. Printed by electrotype	—	—
	t1. Printed by steel plate	—	—
	z. Non-fluorescent paper, fluorescent ink *(March 7, 1967)*	6.50	3.50
	FDC *(Nov. 19, 1962)*		1.75

1963. Universal Postal Union Card Issue design of PC45, Vacationland.

MRC18 *Map of North America*

MRC18		UnVF	UseVF
7¢ + 7¢	**red and blue on white,** unsevered	3.00	50.00
	m. Message card	.90	25.00
	r. Reply card	.90	25.00
	t. Message card blank, reply card normal	140.00	—
	t1. Message card normal, reply card blank	140.00	—
	FDC *(Aug. 30, 1963)*		2.50

1968. Universal Postal Union Cards Issue design of MRC18 (PC45), Vacationland, with 8¢ denomination.

MRC19 *Map of North America*

MRC19		UnVF	UseVF
8¢ + 8¢	**red and blue on white,** unsevered	3.50	50.00
	m. Message card	.90	25.00
	r. Reply card	.90	25.00
	FDC *(Dec. 4, 1967)*		

1968. Abraham Lincoln Issue design of PC51, Abraham Lincoln; the two cards are identical.

MRC20 *Abraham Lincoln*

MRC20		UnVF	UseVF
5¢ + 5¢	**emerald green on white,** unsevered	1.75	3.00
	t. One half blank (printed one side only)	—	—
	FDC *(Jan. 4, 1968)*		1.50

1971. Issue design of PC54, Paul Revere; the two cards are identical.

MRC21 *Paul Revere*

MRC21		UnVF	UseVF
6¢ + 6¢	**brown on white,** unsevered, tagged	1.25	2.50
	FDC *(May 15, 1971)*		1.50

1972. Issue design of PC60, John Hanson; the two cards are identical.

MRC22		UnVF	UseVF
6¢ + 6¢	**cobalt blue on white,** unsevered, tagged	1.25	2.00
	FDC *(Sept. 1, 1972)*		1.00

1973. Issue design of PC62, Samuel Adams; the two cards are identical.

MRC23		UnVF	UseVF
8¢ + 8¢	**orange on white,** unsevered, tagged	1.25	2.00
	p. Smooth paper	—	—

		UnVF	UseVF
	p1. Coarse Paper	1.35	4.00
	t. One half blank (printed one side only)	—	—
	FDC *(Dec. 16, 1973)*		1.00

1975. Issue design of PC64, Charles Thomson; the two cards are identical.

MRC24		UnVF	UseVF
7¢ + 7¢	**emerald green on white,** unsevered, tagged	1.25	5.00
	FDC *(Sept. 14, 1975)*		2.00

1975. Issue design of PC65, John Witherspoon; the two cards are identical.

MRC25		UnVF	UseVF
9¢ + 9¢	**brown on white,** unsevered, tagged	1.25	5.00
	FDC *(Nov. 10, 1975)*		1.00

1976. Issue design of PC66, Caesar Rodney; the two cards are identical.

MRC26		UnVF	UseVF
9¢ + 9¢	**blue on white,** unsevered, tagged	1.25	2.00
	FDC *(July 1, 1976)*		1.00

1977. Issue design of PC68, Nathan Hale; the two cards are identical.

MRC27		UnVF	UseVF
9¢ + 9¢	**green on white,** unsevered, tagged	1.25	2.00
	FDC *(Oct. 14, 1977)*		1.00

1978. Issue design of PC70, John Hancock (non-denominated), two cards are identical.

MRC28		UnVF	UseVF
10¢ + 10¢	**brown orange on white,** unsevered, tagged	11.00	9.00
	t. Printed with MRC28 one side, MRC29 on back side	—	—
	FDC *(May 19, 1978)*		3.50

1978. Issue design of PC71, John Hancock (with denomination); the two cards are identical.

MRC29		UnVF	UseVF
10¢ + 10¢	**brown orange on white,** unsevered, tagged	1.25	3.00
	t. One half blank (printed one side only)	—	—
	FDC *(June 20, 1978)*		1.00

1981. Issue design of PC84, stylized eagle; the two cards are identical.

MRC30		UnVF	UseVF
12¢ + 12¢	**purple on white,** unsevered, tagged	1.25	3.00
	FDC *(March 15, 1981)*		1.00

1981. Issue design of PC85, Isaiah Thomas; the two cards are identical.

MRC31		UnVF	UseVF
12¢ + 12¢	**blue on white,** unsevered, tagged	1.50	4.00
	t. Large stamp die on both sides	—	—
	t1. Large stamp die on one side, small stamp die on back	3.00	2.25
	FDC *(May 5, 1981)*		1.00

1981. Issue design of PC88, Robert Morris (non-denominated); the two cards are identical.

MRC32		UnVF	UseVF
13¢ + 13¢	**brown on white,** unsevered, tagged	2.25	4.00
	FDC *(Oct. 11, 1981)*		1.25

1981. Issue design of PC89, Robert Morris (with denomination); the two cards are identical.

MRC33		UnVF	UseVF
13¢ + 13¢	**brown on white,** unsevered, tagged	1.25	3.00
	t. One half blank (printed one side only)	—	—
	t1. Additional copyright notice, inverted on back of message card	—	—
	FDC *(Nov. 10, 1981)*		1.00

1985. Issue design of PC101, Charles Carroll (non-denomimated); the two cards are identical.

MRC34		UnVF	UseVF
14¢ + 14¢	**green on white,** unsevered, tagged	3.50	5.00
	FDC *(Feb. 1, 1985)*		1.25

1985. Issue design of PC103, Charles Carroll (with denomination); the two cards are identical.

MRC35		UnVF	UseVF
14¢ + 14¢	**green on white,** unsevered, tagged	1.25	3.00
	t. One half blank (printed one side only)	—	—
	FDC *(March 6, 1985)*		1.25

1985. Issue design of PC104, George Wythe; the two cards are identical.

MRC36		UnVF	UseVF
14¢ + 14¢	**olive green on white,** unsevered, tagged	1.20	3.00
	t. One half blank (printed one side only)	—	—
	FDC *(June 20, 1985)*		1.25

1987. Issue design of PC113, U.S. Flag; the two cards are identical.

MRC37		UnVF	UseVF
14¢ + 14¢	**black, blue and red on white,** unsevered, tagged	1.25	3.00
	FDC *(Sept. 1, 1987)*		1.50

1988. Issue design of PC116, America the Beautiful; the two cards are identical.

MRC38		UnVF	UseVF
15¢ + 15¢	**multicolored on white,** unsevered, tagged	1.25	3.00
	p. Fluorescent paper	—	—
	FDC *(July 11, 1988)*		1.25

1991. Issue design of PC146, U.S. Flag; the two cards are identical.

MRC39		UnVF	UseVF
19¢ + 19¢	**black, blue and red on white,** unsevered, tagged	1.25	3.00
	FDC *(March 27, 1991)*		1.00

1995. Issue design of PC194, Red Barn; the two cards are identical.

MRC40		UnVF	UseVF
20¢ + 20¢	**multicolored,** unsevered	1.25	3.00
	t. One half blank (printed one side only)	—	—
	FDC *(Feb. 1, 1995)*		1.25

1999. Block Island Lighthouse Issue Design of PC302 in the Scenic America Series, the two cards are identical. *Offset by Government Printing Office.*

MRC41 *Block Island Lighthouse, Rhode Island*

MRC41		UnVF	UseVF
20¢ + 20¢	**multicolored,** unsevered	1.00	.75
	FDC *(Nov. 10, 1999)*		2.00

Savings Stamps

United States Savings Stamps fall into five classifications: Postal Savings and Defense Postal Savings, both issued by the Post Office Department; and War Savings, Treasury Savings and Savings, issued by the Treasury Department.

For many years the Treasury Department objected to the listings of Savings Stamps as collectors' items, but in a letter dated July 13, 1942, these objections were withdrawn and since that date the collecting of these stamps has been encouraged.

Postal Savings Stamp Series

In 1910 the U.S. Post Office Department started a Postal Savings Department where accounts could be opened in even-dollar amounts. To enable small depositors to accumulate dollar deposits, stamps were provided with a face value of 10¢ each so that when nine were secured they could be mounted on a card with one integral stamp. The Postal Savings Department, as a banking activity, was closed April 27, 1966.

1911. FIRST ISSUE Inscribed "U.S. POSTAL SAVINGS 10 CENTS." *Intaglio, watermark double-line "USPS" (wmk. 187), perforated 12.*

PS1, PS3

PS1		UnFVF	UseFVF
10¢	**orange**	7.00	1.25
	Plate block of 6, w/imprint and open star	450.00	—
	Plate strip of 3, w/imprint and open star	45.00	—
	Block of 4, 2mm spacing between stamps	30.00	—
	Block of 4, 3mm spacing between stamps	35.00	—
	FDC *(Jan. 3, 1911)*		

1911. IMPRINTED CARD ISSUE Same design as No. PS1. Imprinted on deposit card with spaces for nine additional stamps. *Intaglio, unwatermarked, imperforate.*

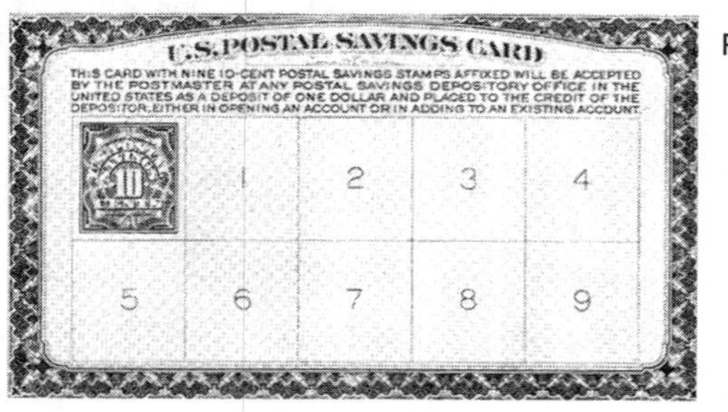

PS2

After being redeemed, these cards were canceled with a large killer device, and interesting combinations of stamps are found.

Proofs in red and blue on thin paper and a deposit card in blue, with an entirely different design showing the head of George Washington in a circle and space for nine stamps are known. It is believed that they were not issued.

PS2		UnFVF	UseFVF
10¢	**orange**	150.00	40.00
	Canceled with nine additional stamps	—	—
	FDC *(Jan. 3, 1911)*		

1911. SECOND ISSUE Aug. 14. Same design as No. PS1. *Intaglio, watermark single-line "USPS" (wmk. 237), perforated 12.*

PS3		UnFVF	UseFVF
10¢	**blue**	4.25	1.00
	Plate block of 6, w/imprint and open star	150.00	—
	Plate strip of 3, w/imprint and open star	27.50	—
	Block of 4, 2mm spacing between stamps	22.50	—
	Block of 4, 3mm spacing between stamps	25.00	—

1911. SECOND CARD ISSUE Design type of No. PS2, with change in color. Imprinted on deposit card. *Intaglio, unwatermarked, imperforate.*

PS4		UnFVF	UseFVF
10¢	**blue**	100.00	22.50
	Canceled with 9 additional stamps	—	—
	FDC *(Aug. 14, 1911)*		

In September 1920, the Post Office Department issued a new type of deposit card (Form PS333) without imprint of the first stamp. These are not listed as regular postal issues, but can be found canceled with 10 stamps of either No. PS1 or No. PS3.

1936. THIRD ISSUE Type of No. PS1. *Intaglio, unwatermarked, perforated 11.*

PS5		UnFVF	UseFVF
10¢	**blue**	4.75	1.25
	violet blue	4.75	1.25
	Plate block of 6, w/imprint and closed star	125.00	—

1940. ISSUE Inscribed "UNITED STATES" at top, "POSTAL SAVINGS" at bottom, and either "CENTS" or "DOLLAR" diagonally in center, with denomination above and below. *Intaglio, unwatermarked, perforated 11.*

PS6-PS9

PS6		MNHVF	UseVF
10¢	**blue**	12.50	6.00
	Plate block of 6	225.00	—
	FDC *(April 3, 1940)*		

PS7		MNHVF	UseVF
25¢	**red**	17.50	9.00
	Plate block of 6	325.00	—
	FDC *(April 1, 1940)*		

PS8		MNHVF	UseVF
50¢	**green**	50.00	16.00
	Plate block of 6	1,400.00	—
	FDC *(April 1, 1940)*		

PS9		MNHVF	UseVF
$1	**black**	150.00	15.00
	Plate block of 6	1,900.00	—
	FDC *(April 1, 1940)*		

Both a yellow and a manila card for 25 10¢ stamps, a salmon card for 25 25¢ stamps, a green card for 25 50¢ stamps and a manila card for 18 $1 stamps and 3 25¢ stamps were produced. Any total of $18.75 was redeemable for a $25 U.S. Savings bond.

Defense Postal Savings Stamp Series

On May 1, 1941, the Post Office Department issued Defense Postal Savings Stamps, redeemable in U.S. Treasury Defense or War Bonds. Daniel Chester French, who created the Minute Man used in the design, was one of the artists honored on the Famous Americans Series of commemorative stamps (CM229).

1941. ISSUE May 1. Inscribed "AMERICA ON GUARD/U.S. POSTAL SAVINGS/1941." *Intaglio, unwatermarked. First four values perforated 11 x 10 1/2; $5 perforated 11.*

PS10-PS14 *Minute Man*

PS10		MNHVF	UseVF
10¢	**red**	.60	—
	Plate block of 4	7.25	
	Booklet pane of 10, w/horizontal edges trimmed *(July 30, 1941)*	55.00	
	n. Booklet pane of 10, w/trimmed edges, electric eye marks at left	60.00	

		MNHVF	UseVF
	Booklet pane of 10, perforated at horizontal edges	120.00	
	Booklet pane of 10, perforated at edges, electric eye marks at left	135.00	
	FDC *(May 1, 1941)*		175.00

PS11		MNHVF	UseVF
25¢	**green**	1.85	—
	Plate block of 4	16.00	
	Booklet pane of 10 *(July 30, 1941)*	65.00	
	n. Booklet pane of 10, electric eye marks at left	70.00	

PS12		MNHVF	UseVF
50¢	**ultramarine**	4.50	—
	Plate block of 4	40.00	

PS13		MNHVF	UseVF
$1	**black**	10.00	—
	Plate block of 4	77.00	

PS14		MNHVF	UseVF
$5	**sepia**	37.00	—
	Plate block of 6	535.00	

War Savings Stamp Series

In 1917, the Treasury Department brought out the first of a series of War Savings Stamps, which were redeemable in Treasury War Certificates, War Bonds or Defense Bonds. A 25¢ Thrift Stamp was issued to enable small purchasers to accumulate them on a Deposit Card exchangeable for a $5 stamp when full.

1917. ISSUE Dec. 1. *Intaglio, unwatermarked, perforated 11.*

WS1

WS1		UnFVF	UseFVF
25¢	**green**	7.00	2.25
	Plate block of 6	750.00	
	Plate strip of 3	50.00	

1918. ISSUE In 1918, 1919, 1920 and 1921, $5 stamps were issued. They sold at $4.12 when first issued and increased in value each month until they became worth par in five years and could be cashed or applied on bonds at the face value of $5.

Nov. 17. *Intaglio, unwatermarked, perforated 11.*

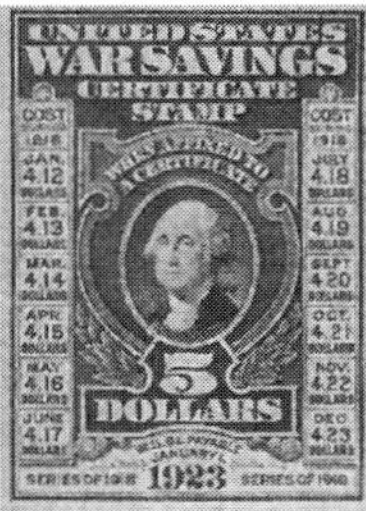

WS2 *George Washington*

WS2		UnFVF	UseFVF
$5	**green**	70.00	22.00
	Single with plate number	80.00	
	v. Vertical pair, imperforate horizontally	—	

WS2A		UnFVF	UseFVF
$5	**green**	1,100.00	—
	Single w/plate number	1,350.00	

Rouletted 7

1919. ISSUE July 3. *Intaglio, unwatermarked, perforated 11.*

WS3 *Benjamin Franklin*

WS3		UnFVF	UseFVF
$5	**blue**	275.00	—
	Single w/plate number	300.00	
	Single w/inverted plate number	325.00	

1920. ISSUE Dec. 11. *Intaglio, unwatermarked, perforated 11.*

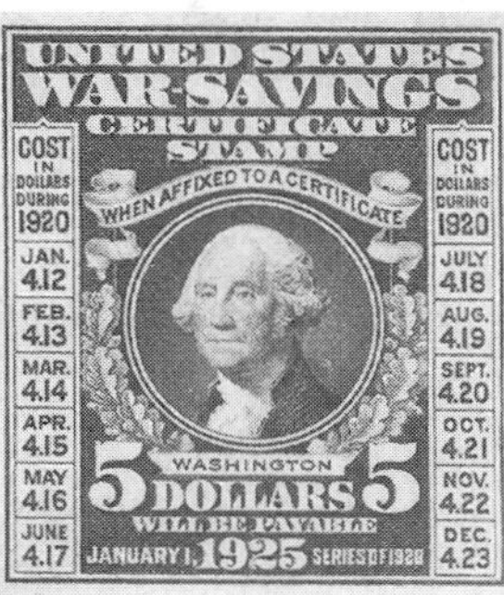

WS4 *George Washington*

WS4		UnFVF	UseFVF
$5	**carmine**	675.00	160.00
	Single w/plate number	700.00	

1921. ISSUE Dec. 21. *Intaglio, unwatermarked, perforated 11.*

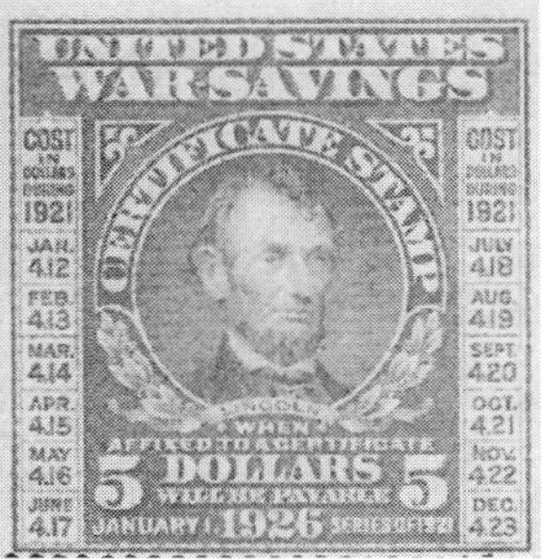

WS5 *Abraham Lincoln*

WS5		UnFVF	UseFVF
$5	**orange on green paper**	2,600.00	—
	Single w/plate number	2,750.00	

1942. ISSUE Early in 1942 the Treasury Department issued a new series of War Savings Stamps to replace the Defense Postal Savings Stamps of 1941 issued by the Post Office Department. *Intaglio, unwatermarked.*

WS6-WS10 *Minute Man*

WS6		MNHVF	UseVF
10¢	**red**	.55	—
	Plate block of 4	5.25	
	n. Booklet pane of 10 *(Oct. 27, 1942)*	40.00	
	n1. Booklet pane of 10 w/electric eye mark at left	45.00	
	a. carmine rose	.55	—
	FDC *(Oct. 29, 1942)*		

WS7		MNHVF	UseVF
25¢	**green**	1.25	—
	Plate block of 4	8.50	
	Booklet pane of 10 *(Oct. 15, 1942)*	50.00	
	Booklet pane of 10 w/electric eye mark at left	55.00	
	FDC *(Oct. 15, 1942)*		

WS8		MNHVF	UseVF
50¢	**ultramarine**	2.75	—
	Plate block of 4	27.50	
	FDC *(Nov. 12, 1942)*		

WS9		MNHVF	UseVF
$1	**black**	9.00	—
	Plate block of 4	60.00	

FDC *(Nov. 17, 1942)*

Perforated 11 x 10 1/2.

WS10		MNHVF	UseVF
$5	**violet brown**	45.00	—
	Plate block of 6	475.00	
	FDC *(1945)*		

Perforated 11.

1943. Coil Issue *Coil stamps.* Although plates for coil stamps were prepared for the 1941 issue, they were not used. Thus, this is the first Savings Stamp issued in coil form: 500 stamps to a roll.

Aug. 5. Type of No. WS6. *Intaglio, unwatermarked, perforated 10 vertically.*

WS11		MNHVF	UseVF
10¢	**red**	2.75	—
	Pair	6.00	—
	Line pair	11.00	—
WS12		MNHVF	UseVF
25¢	**green**	4.50	—
	Pair	9.50	—
	Line pair	21.00	—

Treasury Savings Stamp Series

While the $5 orange-on-green paper (No. WS5) was still current, the Treasury Department brought out a $1 stamp redeemable in War Savings Stamps or Treasury Savings Certificates. It is the scarcest of the Savings Stamps.

1921. Issue Dec. 21. *Intaglio, unwatermarked, perforated 11.*

TS1 *Alexander Hamilton*

TS1		UnFVF	UseFVF
$1	**red on green paper**	3,250.00	—
	Single with plate number	3,000.00	

Savings Stamp Series

Issued by the Treasury Department.

1954. Issue Figure of Minute Man, same as 1942 War Savings Stamps. Inscribed "UNITED STATES SAVINGS STAMP." *Intaglio, unwatermarked.*

S1 *Minute Man*

S1		MNHVF	UseVF
10¢	**red**	.60	—
	Plate block of 4	3.75	
	Booklet pane of 10 *(April 22, 1955)*	145.00	
	v. Booklet w/electric eye mark at left	155.00	
	FDC *(Nov. 30, 1954)*		

1954. Issue

S2		MNHVF	UseVF
25¢	**green**	5.75	—
	Plate block of 4	30.00	
	Booklet pane of 10 *(Aug. 15, 1955)*	145.00	
	v. Booklet pane w/electric eye mark at left	800.00	
	FDC *(Dec. 30, 1954)*		

1956. Issue

S3		MNHVF	UseVF
50¢	**ultramarine**	8.00	—
	Plate block of 4	45.00	
	FDC *(Dec. 31, 1956)*		

1957. Issue

S4		MNHVF	UseVF
$1	**black**	22.50	—
	Plate block of 4	110.00	
	FDC *(March 13, 1957)*		

1956. Issue *Perforated 11.*

S5		MNHVF	UseVF
$5	**violet brown**	70.00	—
	Plate block of 6	725.00	
	FDC *(Nov. 30, 1956)*		

1959. Issue Nov. 18. Figure of Minute Man and 48-star U.S. flag. *Intaglio (Giori Press), unwatermarked, perforated 11.*

S6 *Minute Man, flag*

S6		MNHVF	UseVF
25¢	**dark blue and carmine**	1.75	—
	Plate block of 4	8.50	
	Booklet pane of 10	65.00	
	FDC *(Nov. 18, 1959)*		

1961. Issue Figure of Minute Man and 50-star U.S. flag. *Intaglio (Giori Press), unwatermarked, perforated 11.*

S7 *Minute Man, flag*

S7		MNHVF	UseVF
25¢	**dark blue and carmine**	1.25	—
	Plate block of 4	8.00	
	Booklet pane of 10	275.00	

Revenue Stamps

Documentary Stamps

For both sides, the costs of the War Between the States were appallingly high. In human terms, the casualty rates rose to possibly 40 per cent, and almost half a million American men died for the causes of the Union and the Confederacy. In financial terms, a week before the war ended the government of the United States already had spent $3,250,000,000 — a figure larger than the total previously spent since the founding of the republic. (The final cost to both sides was more than $10,000,000,000.) During the war the Union borrowed $2,600,000,000, issued paper money to an extent that brought the value of the dollar down to 39 cents, and introduced a variety of new taxes.

In collecting some of the taxes, the government issued receipts in the form of tax stamps, which we call Revenue Stamps.

1862-64. THE FIRST DOCUMENTARY ISSUE In August 1862, the Commissioner of Internal Revenue advertised for bids for the printing of revenue stamps. The contract was awarded to Butler & Carpenter, and most of the first issue of revenues appeared near the end of 1862 and early in 1863. At first the stamps paid specific taxes on official documents, according to the designation on the stamp, but after Dec. 25, 1862, they were used indiscriminately. Different kinds of paper were used from time to time, and wide differences in shades and colors exist due to chemical reactions or fading. They are noticeable in the violets or lilacs, which often look gray, and in the reds, which are often on the brown side. Usually these stamps were canceled with pen and ink, and they are priced accordingly in this catalog. Printed cancellations are worth more; cancellations that cut into the paper are worth less.

All of the stamps came unwatermarked and perforated 12, but most of them also exist imperforate. Some stamps are perforated only horizontally and imperforate vertically, or vice versa. These are called "part perfs."

The collector should be careful of these, and make sure that they have good margins on the imperforate sides; people have been known to trim a perforated stamp in an attempt to make it look like a part perf or an imperforate stamp.

1862-64. U.S. Internal Revenue Issue. included the first U.S. bicolor stamp, R3.

No.	Denom.	Color	Perf	Part Perf	Imperf
R1	2¢	orange	.20	—	
R2	$50	green	75.00		75.00

R3

No.	Denom.	Color	Perf	Part Perf	Imperf
R3	$200	red & green	500.00		1,200.00

1862-64. Agreement Issue

No.	Denom.	Color	Perf	Part Perf	Imperf
R4	5¢	red	.20		

1862-64. Bank Check Issue

R5

No.	Denom.	Color	Perf	Part Perf	Imperf
R5	2¢	blue	.20	1.50	1.50
R6	2¢	orange	.20	.85	

1862-64. Bill of Lading Issue

No.	Denom.	Color	Perf	Part Perf	Imperf
R7	10¢	blue	.75	150.00	50.00

1862-64. Bond Issue

R8

R15

R18

No.	Denom.	Color	Perf	Part Perf	Imperf
R8	25¢	red	2.00	6.00	125.00

1862-64. Certificate Issue

No.	Denom.	Color	Perf	Part Perf	Imperf
R9	2¢	blue	25.00		10.00
R10	2¢	orange	25.00		
R11	5¢	red	.20	10.00	2.50
R12	10¢	blue	.25	165.00	190.00
R13	25¢	red	.20	5.00	7.50

1862-64. Charter Party Issue

No.	Denom.	Color	Perf	Part Perf	Imperf
R14	$3	green	4.50		900.00
R15	$5	red	6.00		225.00
R16	$10	green	20.00		450.00

1862-64. Contract Issue

No.	Denom.	Color	Perf	Part Perf	Imperf
R17	10¢	blue	.35	140.00	
		a. ultramarine	.40	160.00	

1862-64. Conveyance Issue

No.	Denom.	Color	Perf	Part Perf	Imperf
R18	50¢	blue	.20	1.25	12.50
		a. ultramarine	25.00		

R19

R20

No.	Denom.	Color	Perf	Part Perf	Imperf
R19	$1	red	3.50	375.00	10.00
R20	$2	red	2.50	1,250.00	90.00
R21	$5	red	6.00		35.00
R22	$10	green	55.00		80.00
R23	$20	orange	45.00		100.00

1862-64. Entry of Goods Issue

No.	Denom.	Color	Perf	Part Perf	Imperf
R24	25¢	red	.60	50.00	15.00
R25	50¢	blue	.25	11.50	
R26	$1	red	1.50		27.50

1862-64. Express Issue

R27

R31

No.	Denom.	Color	Perf	Part Perf	Imperf
R27	1¢	red	1.00	40.00	50.00
R28	2¢	blue	.25	16.00	10.00
R29	2¢	orange	6.00		
R30	5¢	red	.30	450.00	4.00

1862-64. Foreign Exchange Issue

No.	Denom.	Color	Perf	Part Perf	Imperf
R31	3¢	green	3.00	225.00	
R32	5¢	red	.35		
R33	10¢	blue	6.50		
		a. ultramarine	8.00		
R34	15¢	brown	12.50		
R35	20¢	red	27.50		40.00
R36	30¢	lilac	35.00	825.00	65.00
R37	50¢	blue	5.00	32.50	35.00
R38	70¢	green	6.50	75.00	275.00
R39	$1	red	.75		60.00

R40

No.	Denom.	Color	Perf	Part Perf	Imperf
R40	$1.30	orange	50.00		
R41	$1.60	green	85.00		800.00
R42	$1.90	brown violet	65.00		2,000.00

1862-64. Inland Exchange Issue

No.	Denom.	Color	Perf	Part Perf	Imperf
R43	4¢	brown	1.75		
R44	5¢	red	.20	3.50	4.25
R45	6¢	orange	15.00		
R46	10¢	blue	.25	3.50	165.00
R47	15¢	brown	1.20	10.00	25.00
R48	20¢	red	.50	15.00	14.50
R49	30¢	lilac	3.00	55.00	45.00
R50	40¢	brown	3.00	6.00	475.00
R51	60¢	orange	6.00	45.00	75.00
R52	$1	red	.50	275.00	12.50
R53	$1.50	blue	3.00		20.00
R54	$2.50	red violet	3.50		1,850.00
R55	$3.50	blue	45.00		1,500.00

1862-64. Insurance Issue

No.	Denom.	Color	Perf	Part Perf	Imperf
R56	25¢	red	.25	10.00	9.00

1862-64. Lease Issue

No.	Denom.	Color	Perf	Part Perf	Imperf
R57	50¢	blue	6.50	55.00	22.50
R58	$1	red	1.75		30.00

1862-64. Life Insurance Issue

No.	Denom.	Color	Perf	Part Perf	Imperf
R59	25¢	red	6.00	175.00	30.00
R60	50¢	blue	.75	50.00	30.00
R61	$1	red	5.00		125.00

1862-64. Manifest Issue

No.	Denom.	Color	Perf	Part Perf	Imperf
R62	$1	red	22.50		45.00
R63	$3	green	20.00		100.00
R64	$5	red	75.00		100.00

1862-64. Mortgage Issue

No.	Denom.	Color	Perf	Part Perf	Imperf
R65	50¢	blue	.35	2.25	10.00
R66	$1	red	140.00		17.50
R67	$2	red	2.25		85.00
R68	$5	red	17.50		90.00
R69	$10	green	20.00		325.00

Each entry in this catalog has been double-checked for accuracy, but mistake may creep into any human endeavor, and we ask your assistance in eliminating them. Please call the attention of hte editors to any errors in stamp description found in this catalog. Send your comments to:

Minkus Catalog Editor
Krause Publications
700 E State St
Iola, WI 54990

R70

R70		Perf	Part Perf	Imperf
$15	blue	100.00		850.00
	a. ultramarine	125.00		
R71		**Perf**	**Part Perf**	**Imperf**
$25	red	90.00		800.00

1862-64. Original Process Issue

R72		Perf	Part Perf	Imperf
50¢	blue	.40	475.00	3.00

1862-64. Passage Ticket Issue

R73		Perf	Part Perf	Imperf
50¢	blue	.70	125.00	65.00
R74		**Perf**	**Part Perf**	**Imperf**
$1	red	150.00		225.00

1862-64. Power of Attorney Issue

R75		Perf	Part Perf	Imperf
10¢	blue	.45	20.00	425.00
R76		**Perf**	**Part Perf**	**Imperf**
25¢	red	.25	25.00	5.00
R77		**Perf**	**Part Perf**	**Imperf**
$1	red	1.75		60.00

1862-64. Probate of Will Issue

R78		Perf	Part Perf	Imperf
50¢	blue	17.50	50.00	30.00
R79		**Perf**	**Part Perf**	**Imperf**
$1	red	32.50		60.00
R80		**Perf**	**Part Perf**	**Imperf**
$2	red	47.50		1,750
R81		**Perf**	**Part Perf**	**Imperf**
$5	red	17.50		400.00
R82		**Perf**	**Part Perf**	**Imperf**
$10	green	20.00		1,000
R83		**Perf**	**Part Perf**	**Imperf**
$20	orange	900.00		1,000

1862-64. Protest Issue

R84		Perf	Part Perf	Imperf
25¢	red	7.00	225.00	22.50

1862-64. Surety Bond Issue

R85		Perf	Part Perf	Imperf
50¢	blue	.25	2.50	140.00
	a. ultramarine	1.50		

1862-64. Telegraph Issue

R86		Perf	Part Perf	Imperf
$1	red	10.00		400.00
R87		**Perf**	**Part Perf**	**Imperf**
$3	green	2.50	17.50	50.00

1862-64. Warehouse Receipt Issue

R88		Perf	Part Perf	Imperf
25¢	red	20.00	200.00	40.00

*For stamps inscribed: **Playing Cards** see numbers RPC1-6 in the Playing Cards Revenues Section.*

*For stamps inscribed: **Proprietary** see numbers RP1-8 in the Proprietary Revenues Section.*

1871. The Second Documentary Issue Unscrupulous people soon found that the First Issue could be cleaned and used over again, thus avoiding the payment of taxes and cheating the government. Experiments were made and a special patented paper, violet in shade, and with tiny silk threads woven into it, was placed in use. The ink too, was special, so that any attempt to clean the stamps was disastrous. All the stamps, except for the last two values, were bi-colored, with the frames printed in blue and Washington's head in black. Each value had its individual frame. The first nine values were all small in size, and the head of Washington was enclosed in an octagon. From the 25¢ value on, they were quite tall and narrow and the Washington head was enclosed in a circle. In bi-colored printings there is a chance that a sheet after having been printed in one color, may be reversed before being put through the machine for the second color. That happened with some of these stamps, for eight of the values are known with "inverted centers," and are quite valuable. Excellent imitations of inverted centers exist; the collector interested in buying one should inspect it carefully and do business only with a firm he can trust. **Prices given are for the normal "herringbone" cancellation, a row of arrowheads, one within the other, impressed or cut into the paper.** *These stamps were printed by Joseph R. Carpenter of Philadelphia, on unwatermarked paper and perforated 12.*

R89, 120

R89		Uncut	CutCnl
1¢	blue and black	30.00	17.00
	a. Inverted center	900.00	

R90, 121, 137

R90a

R90		Uncut	CutCnl
2¢	blue and black	1.00	.20
	a. Inverted center	3,250	

R91

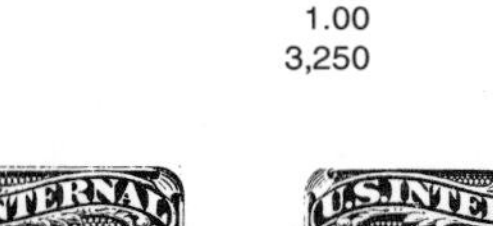
R92, 122

R93, 123

R91		Uncut	CutCnl
3¢	blue and black	12.50	8.00
R92		**Uncut**	**CutCnl**
4¢	blue and black	55.00	25.00
R93		**Uncut**	**CutCnl**
5¢	blue and black	1.40	.40
	a. Inverted center	1,400	

R94, 124

R95

R96, 125

R94		Uncut	CutCnl
6¢	blue and black	85.00	45.00

		Uncut	CutCnl
R95			
10¢	**blue and black**	.85	.20
	a. Inverted center	1,400	

		Uncut	CutCnl
R96			
15¢	**blue and black**	22.50	12.00

R97

		Uncut	CutCnl
R97			
20¢	**blue and black**	5.00	2.00
	a. Inverted center	7,000	

R104, 130

R105

R106

R98

R99, 126

R100, 127

		Uncut	CutCnl
R98			
25¢	**blue and black**	.60	.20
	a. Inverted center	7,500	

		Uncut	CutCnl
R99			
30¢	**blue and black**	60.00	30.00

		Uncut	CutCnl
R100			
40¢	**blue and black**	40.00	20.00

R101

R102, 128

R103, 129

		Uncut	CutCnl
R101			
50¢	**blue and black**	.60	.20
	a. Inverted center	750.00	
	b. Inverted center, punch cancellation		200.00
	c. Sewing machine perf.	70.00	

		Uncut	CutCnl
R102			
60¢	**blue and black**	85.00	40.00

		Uncut	CutCnl
R103			
70¢	**blue and black**	30.00	15.00
	a. Inverted center	2,500	

		Uncut	CutCnl
R104			
$1	**blue and black**	3.00	1.50
	a. Inverted center	4,000	
	b. Inverted center, punch cancellation		700.00

		Uncut	CutCnl
R105			
$1.30	**blue and black**	250.00	150.00

		Uncut	CutCnl
R106			
$1.50	**blue and black**	12.50	7.00
	a. Sewing machine perf.		450.00

R107

R108

		Uncut	CutCnl
R107			
$1.60	**blue and black**	325.00	200.00

		Uncut	CutCnl
R108			
$1.90	**blue and black**	160.00	90.00

R109

R110,132

		Uncut	CutCnl
R109			
$2	**blue and black**	12.50	7.00

		Uncut	CutCnl
R110			
$2.50	**blue and black**	25.00	15.00

R111

R112

		Uncut	CutCnl
R111			
$3	**blue and black**	30.00	17.00
R112		Uncut	CutCnl
$3.50	**blue and black**	150.00	75.00

R113,134

R114,135

		Uncut	CutCnl
R113			
$5	**blue and black**	17.50	9.00
	a. Inverted center	2,000	
	b. Inverted center, punch cancellation		600.00
R114		Uncut	CutCnl
$10	**blue and black**	90.00	50.00

R115,136

R16

		Uncut	CutCnl
R115			
$20	**blue and black**	300.00	200.00
R116		Uncut	CutCnl
$25	**blue and black**	300.00	200.00

R117

R118

		Uncut	CutCnl
R117			
$50	**blue and black**	325.00	220.00
R118		Uncut	CutCnl
$200	**blue, red and black**	4,500	2,500

R119 *("Persian rug")*

		Uncut	CutCnl
R119			
$500	**green and red, black**	10,000	

1871-72. The Third Documentary Issue The second issue was a great success in preventing the cleaning and re-use of stamps. There were, however, complaints that the stamps were difficult to distinguish because the colors were uniform in nearly all values. A third issue was therefore prepared, again by Joseph R. Carpenter of Philadelphia, using the same plates but this time with varying colors, so that identification might be much easier. *They are on violet paper with silk threads, unwatermarked and perforated 12.*

		Uncut	CutCnl
R120			
1¢	**claret and black**	25.00	15.00
R121		Uncut	CutCnl
2¢	**orange and black**	.20	.20
	a. Inverted center	275.00	
	b. claret and gray black (error of color)	500.00	
R122		Uncut	CutCnl
4¢	**brown and black**	30.00	16.00

R123			Uncut	CutCnl
5¢	**orange and black**		.20	.20
	a. Inverted center		3,000	
R124			Uncut	CutCnl
6¢	**orange and black**		30.00	15.00
R125			Uncut	CutCnl
15¢	**brown and black**		7.50	3.50
	a. Inverted center		7,500	
R126			Uncut	CutCnl
30¢	**orange and black**		12.50	6.00
	a. Inverted center		2,000	
R127			Uncut	CutCnl
40¢	**brown and black**		30.00	15.00
R128			Uncut	CutCnl
60¢	**orange and black**		55.00	28.00
R129			Uncut	CutCnl
70¢	**green and black**		35.00	28.00
R130			Uncut	CutCnl
$1	**green and black**		1.25	.50
	a. Inverted center		5,000	
R131			Uncut	CutCnl
$2	**vermilion and black**		17.50	11.00
R132			Uncut	CutCnl
$2.50	**claret and black**		30.00	18.00
	a. Inverted Center		12,500	
R133			Uncut	CutCnl
$3	**green and black**		30.00	20.00
R134			Uncut	CutCnl
$5	**vermilion and black**		17.50	10.00
R135			Uncut	CutCnl
$10	**green and black**		70.00	35.00
R136			Uncut	CutCnl
$20	**orange and black**		450.00	225.00
	a. vermilion and black		550.00	

1874. U.S. INTERNAL REVENUE ISSUE The design of the 2¢ stamp No. R121 was issued on green paper, perforated 12.

R137		Uncut	CutCnl
2¢	**orange and black on green paper**	.20	.20
	a. Inverted center	325.00	

1875-78. U.S. INTERNAL REVENUE ISSUE The Profile of Liberty was used as the central design of the new 2¢ stamps *printed on blue silk or watermarked paper. The stamps were perforated 12, imperforate or rouletted 6.*

R138-R141 *Silk paper, unwatermarked, perforated 12*

R138		UnCnl	UseFVF
2¢	**blue, on blue paper**	.75	.20
	Pair	2.50	.50
	Block of 4	8.00	1.25

1875-78. U.S. INTERNAL REVENUE ISSUE *Double-line USIR watermark, perforated 12.*

U S I R R139 *Watermark*

R139		UnCnl	UseFVF
2¢	**blue, on blue paper**	1.50	.20
	Pair	3.50	
	Block of 4	8.00	
	v. Pair, imperforate		225.00
	v1. Vertical pair, imperforate horizontally	400.00	

Note: No. R140, an imperforate version of the issue of 1875-78, has been eliminated and the stamp included as a variety of R139.

1875-78. U.S. INTERNAL REVENUE *Double-line USIR watermark, rouletted 6.*

R141		UnCnl	UseFVF
2¢	**blue, on blue paper**	30.00	30.00
	Pair	125.00	

1898. U.S. INTERNAL REVENUE ISSUE Regular Issue Nos. 189, 191, overprinted.

R142 *Overprint A*

R142		UnCnl	UseFVF
1¢	**deep green,** red overprint A	3.00	3.00

R143, R144 *Overprint B*

R143		UnCnl	UseFVF
1¢	**deep green,** red overprint B	.25	.20
	a. Inverted overprint	20.00	17.50
R144		UnCnl	UseFVF
2¢	**carmine,** blue overprint B	.30	.20
	a. Inverted overprint	2.50	1.50

The 8¢ purple brown, 10¢ dark green and 15¢ indigo of the 1895 regular postage issue exist with overprint B in magenta, but they were not officially issued. They are valued at approximately $4,000 each.

1898. NEWSPAPER STAMP ISSUE Newspaper Stamp No. N92, overprinted.

DOCUMENTARY. INT. REV. $5. — INT. REV. $5. DOCUMENTARY.

R145-158

R145		UnCnl	UseFVF
$5	**dark blue,** red overprint A, reading down	225.00	150.00
R146		UnCnl	UseFVF
$5	**dark blue,** red overprint B, reading up	100.00	75.00

1898. DOCUMENTARY ISSUE "The Battleship Issue" featured a new design, officially designated as a "Battleship, second class." The blowing-up of the battleship *Maine* in the harbor of Havana on Feb. 15, 1898, had touched off the Spanish-American War and the slogan "Remember the Maine." Many people thought the new design represented the unfortunate *Maine,* but this was officially denied. *The stamps were printed on paper with double-line watermark USIR, and rouletted 5 1/2 or hyphen-hole perforated 7.* Stamps identical with these, except that the word "Proprietary" is printed on the base instead of "Documentary" are found listed with the Proprietary stamps later on.

R147

R147		UnCnl	UseFVF
1/2¢	**orange,** rouletted	2.25	6.00
R148		UnCnl	UseFVF
1/2¢	**dark gray,** rouletted	.30	.20
R148a		UnCnl	UseFVF
1/2¢	**dark gray,** hyphen-hole	.30	.20

		UnCnl	UseFVF
R149 1¢	**pale blue,** rouletted	.35	.20
R149a 1¢	**pale blue,** hyphen-hole	.35	.20
R150 2¢	**rose,** rouletted	.25	.20
R150a 2¢	**rose,** hyphen-hole	.25	.20
R151 3¢	**indigo,** rouletted	1.25	.20
R151a 3¢	**indigo,** hyphen-hole	1.25	.20
R152 4¢	**pale rose,** rouletted	.75	.20
R152a 4¢	**pale rose,** hyphen-hole	.75	.20
R153 5¢	**lilac,** rouletted	.25	.20
R153a 5¢	**lilac,** hyphen-hole	.25	.20
R154 10¢	**gray brown,** rouletted	1.25	.20
R154a 10¢	**gray brown,** hyphen-hole	1.25	.20
R155 25¢	**lilac brown,** rouletted	1.25	.20
R155a 25¢	**lilac brown,** hyphen-hole	1.25	.20
R156 40¢	**blue lilac,** rouletted	110.00	2.00
R156a 40¢	**blue lilac,** hyphen-hole	150.00	2.00
R157 50¢	**violet gray,** rouletted	10.00	.20
R157a 50¢	**violet gray,** hyphen-hole	20.00	.20
R158 80¢	**bistre,** rouletted	55.00	.40
R158a 80¢	**bistre,** hyphen-hole	150.00	.40

1898-1900. Documentary Issue Allegorical Figure of Commerce design on the $1 through $50 values. *These stamps are rouletted 5 1/2 or hyphen-hole perforated 7, all on the Double-line USIR watermark paper. The canceled stamps usually are without gum.*

R159

		UnCnl	UseFVF	CutCnl
R159 $1	**green *(1898),*** rouletted	7.00	.20	
R159a $1	**green,** hyphen-hole	7.00	.20	
R160 $1	**carmine *(1900),*** hyphen-hole	14.00	.50	
R161 $3	**brown *(1898),*** rouletted	14.00	.75	.20
R161a $3	**brown,** hyphen-hole	14.00	.75	.20
R162 $3	**lake *(1900),*** hyphen-hole	45.00	100.00	8.00
R163 $5	**red orange *(1898),*** rouletted	17.50	1.50	.25
R164 $10	**black,** rouletted	55.00	2.50	.75
R165 $30	**red,** rouletted	175.00	85.00	40.00
R166 $50	**gray brown,** rouletted	80.00	6.00	2.00

1899. Documentary Issue Portraits in various ornate frames, each stamp inscribed: "Series of 1898." *Double-line watermark, imperforate.*

R167

		UnCnl	UseFVF	CutCnl
R167 $100	**pale brown and black** (Marshall)	90.00	30.00	17.50

R168

		UnCnl	UseFVF	CutCnl
R168 $500	**carmine lake and black** (Hamilton)	600.00	425.00	225.00
R169 $1,000	**dark green and black** (Madison)	600.00	350.00	100.00

1900. Documentary Issue Allegorical Figure of Commerce, same designs as 1898-1900, but different colors and overprinted with large outline numerals of value. *Hyphen-hole perforation 7, Double-line USIR watermark.*

R170 *Outline numeral overprint*

		UnCnl	UseFVF	CutCnl
R170 $1	**olive gray**	8.00	.25	.20
R171 $2	**olive gray**	8.00	.25	.20
R172 $3	**olive gray**	45.00	10.50	2.25
R173 $5	**olive gray**	35.00	8.50	1.25
R174 $10	**olive gray**	60.00	17.50	3.50
R175 $50	**olive gray**	600.00	350.00	75.00

1902. Documentary Issue Allegorical figure of Commerce, overprinted in black with large filigree numerals of value. A small square of water-soluble varnish was printed on the face of each stamp before it was overprinted; the part of the overprint that is on this small square of varnish will disappear when the stamp is soaked in water. *Double-line USIR watermark, hyphen-hole roulette perforated 7.*

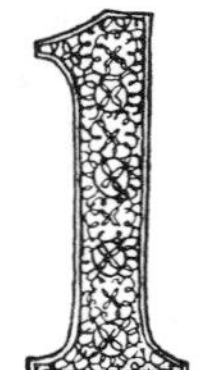

R176 *Filigree numeral overprint*

		UnCnl	UseFVF	CutCnl
R176				
$1	**green**	17.50	3.50	.25
	a. inverted surcharge		175.00	
R177		UnCnl	UseFVF	CutCnl
$2	**green**	15.00	1.50	.25
R178		UnCnl	UseFVF	CutCnl
$5	**green**	125.00	30.00	4.50
	a. Overprint omitted	55.00		

R179 *Filigree numeral overprint*

		UnCnl	UseFVF	CutCnl
R179				
$10	**green**	300.00	140.00	50.00
R180		UnCnl	UseFVF	CutCnl
$50	**green**	900.00	750.00	225.00

1914. Documentary Issue A White numeral in a circle was the new design of the small-size stamps, printed in one color. They are inscribed "Series of 1914," *offset printed on Single-line USPS watermark paper, and are perforated 10.* The unused stamps valued as with gum.

R181-R191 *Single-line USPS Watermark*

U S P S

		UnFVF	UseFVF
R181			
1/2¢	**rose**	6.50	3.50
R182		UnFVF	UseFVF
1¢	**rose**	1.50	.20
R183		UnFVF	UseFVF
2¢	**rose**	1.75	.20
R184		UnFVF	UseFVF
3¢	**rose**	45.00	27.50
R185		UnFVF	UseFVF
4¢	**rose**	11.00	2.00
R186		UnFVF	UseFVF
5¢	**rose**	4.00	.20
R187		UnFVF	UseFVF
10¢	**rose**	3.25	.20
R188		UnFVF	UseFVF
25¢	**rose**	27.50	.75
R189		UnFVF	UseFVF
40¢	**rose**	17.50	1.00
R190		UnFVF	UseFVF
50¢	**rose**	5.50	.20
R191		UnFVF	UseFVF
80¢	**rose**	80.00	10.00

1914. Documentary Issue Same design as the preceding stamps, Nos. R181-R191, but on *Double-line USIR watermark paper, perforated 10.*

		UnFVF	UseFVF
R192			
1/2¢	**red**	1.50	.60
R193		UnFVF	UseFVF
1¢	**red**	.20	.20
R194		UnFVF	UseFVF
2¢	**red**	.20	.20
R195		UnFVF	UseFVF
3¢	**red**	.60	.20
R196		UnFVF	UseFVF
4¢	**red**	3.50	.40
R197		UnFVF	UseFVF
5¢	**red**	.75	.30
R198		UnFVF	UseFVF
10¢	**red**	.50	.20
R199		UnFVF	UseFVF
25¢	**red**	5.00	1.25
R200		UnFVF	UseFVF
40¢	**red**	60.00	12.50
R201		UnFVF	UseFVF
50¢	**red**	12.50	.35
R202		UnFVF	UseFVF
80¢	**red**	90.00	17.50

1914. Documentary Issue Head of Liberty design, inscribed "Series 1914," Flat *Press printing. Double-line USIR watermark, perforated 10.*

R203

		UnFVF	UseFVF	CutCnl
R203				
$1	**yellow green**	30.00	.30	.20
R204		UnFVF	UseFVF	CutCnl
$2	**carmine**	45.00	.50	.20
R205		UnFVF	UseFVF	CutCnl
$3	**purple**	55.00	2.50	.20
R206		UnFVF	UseFVF	CutCnl
$5	**dark blue**	45.00	3.00	.50
R207		UnFVF	UseFVF	CutCnl
$10	**yellow**	100.00	5.00	1.00
R208		UnFVF	UseFVF	CutCnl
$30	**vermilion orange**	225.00	12.50	2.50
R209		UnFVF	UseFVF	CutCnl
$50	**violet**	1,200	750.00	300.00

1914-15. Documentary Issue Portraits are featured on high values *printed on Double-line USIR watermark paper, perforated 12.* These stamps always come with one or two straight edges, since they were printed in strips of four that were imperforate at the top, bottom and right side.

R210

		UnFVF	UseFVF	CutCnl
R210				
$60	**brown** (Lincoln)		115.00	45.00

R211

			UnFVF	UseFVF	CutCnl
R211	$100	**green** (Washington)		40.00	17.50
R212	$500	**blue** (Hamilton)		475.00	200.00
R213	$1,000	**yellow** (Madison)		475.00	200.00

1917. Documentary Issue White numerals in ovals were used on horizontal stamps 21mm wide and 18mm high. *Double-line USIR watermark, perforated 11.* See Nos. R237-249, for stamps of the same designs but with different perforations. *Offset printed.*

No.	Value	Color	UnCnl	UseFVF
R214	1¢	**rose**	.30	.20
R215	2¢	**rose**	.30	.20
R216	3¢	**rose**	1.50	.40
R217	4¢	**rose**	.50	.20
R218	5¢	**rose**	.30	.20
R219	8¢	**rose**	1.75	.30

R220

No.	Value	Color	UnCnl	UseFVF
R220	10¢	**rose**	.50	.20
R221	20¢	**rose**	1.25	.20
R222	25¢	**rose**	1.25	.20

R223

No.	Value	Color	UnCnl	UseFVF
R223	40¢	**rose**	1.50	.40
R224	50¢	**rose**	2.00	.20
R225	80¢	**rose**	4.50	.20

1917-33. Documentary Issue Undated Head of Liberty design (No. R203) but without dates. *Double-line USIR watermark, perforated 11.*

R226-R231 *Head of Liberty*

			UnCnl	UseFVF	CutCnl
R226	$1	**green**	6.00	.20	
R227	$2	**rose**	10.00	.20	
R228	$3	**violet**	30.00	.75	.20

R229 *Head of Liberty*

			UnCnl	UseFVF	CutCnl
R229	$4	**ochre**	22.50	1.75	.20
R230	$5	**blue**	15.00	.30	.20
R231	$10	**yellow**	27.50	1.00	.20

1917. Documentary Issue Portraits in various frames without dates. *Double-line USIR watermark, perforated 12.*

			UnCnl	UseFVF	CutCnl
R232	$30	**orange,** green numerals (Grant)	45.00	10.00	1.50
		a. blue numerals	70.00	20.00	1.50
R233	$60	**brown** (Lincoln)	50.00	7.50	1.00

R234 *George Washington*

			UnCnl	UseFVF	CutCnl
R234	$100	**pale green** (Washington)	27.50	1.50	.50
R235	$500	**blue** (Hamilton), red numerals	200.00	35.00	10.00
		a. orange numerals	—	50.00	20.00
R236	$1,000	**orange yellow** (Madison)	125.00	15.00	5.00

1928-29. Documentary Issue Similar to the 1917 issue but *perforated 10.*

			UnCnl	UseFVF	CutCnl
R237	1¢	**pale red**	2.00	1.50	
R238	2¢	**pale red**	.60	.25	
R239	4¢	**pale red**	6.00	4.00	
R240	5¢	**pale red**	1.25	.60	
R241	10¢	**pale red**	1.75	1.25	
R242	20¢	**pale red**	6.00	5.25	
R243	$1	**green**	80.00	27.50	5.00
R244	$2	**rose**	30.00	2.50	
R245	$10	**yellow**	100.00	40.00	22.50

1929-30. Documentary Issue Similar to the 1917 issue but *perforated 11 x 10.*

			UnCnl	UseFVF	CutCnl
R246	2¢	**carmine rose**	1.00	.80	
R247	5¢	**carmine rose**	.45	.40	
R248	10¢	**carmine rose**	3.50	3.50	
R249	20¢	**carmine rose**	5.50	5.25	

1940. Documentary Issue Stamps of 1917 *overprinted in black "Series 1940" and perforated 11.*

			UnCnl	UseVF	PunchCnl
R250	1¢	**pink**	2.50	2.00	.30
R251	2¢	**pink**	2.50	1.75	.40
R252	3¢	**pink**	8.00	4.00	.60
R253	4¢	**pink**	3.25	.50	.20

1940. Documentary Issue Stamps of 1917 *overprinted in black "Series 1940" and perforated 11.*

R254

			UnCnl	UseFVF	CutCnl
R254	5¢	**pink**	3.50	.75	.25
R255	8¢	**pink**	14.00	12.50	3.00
R256	10¢	**pink**	1.75	.40	.20
R257	20¢	**pink**	2.25	.50	.20
R258	25¢	**pink**	5.50	1.00	.20
R259	40¢	**pink**	5.50	.65	.20
R260	50¢	**pink**	6.00	.50	.20
R261	80¢	**pink**	10.00	.85	.20
R262	$1	**yellow green**	30.00	.50	.20
R263	$2	**rose**	30.00	1.00	.20
R264	$3	**dark violet**	45.00	25.00	3.25
R265	$4	**ochre**	75.00	30.00	5.00
R266	$5	**blue**	45.00	10.00	1.00
R267	$10	**orange yellow**	100.00	27.50	2.00

1940. Documentary Issue Stamps of 1917 handstamped in green "Series 1940." *Perforated 12, without gum.*

			UnCnl	UseFVF	CutCnl
R268	$30	**vermilion**		425.00	350.00
		a. larger, 2-line handstamp in black			
R269	$60	**brown**		625.00	450.00
		a. larger, 2-line handstamp in black			
R270	$100	**green**		900.00	800.00
R271	$500	**blue**		1,250	1,100
		a. larger, 2-line handstamp in black	2,250.00		
R272	$1,000	**orange**		600.00	375.00

No. 273 is not assigned.

1940. Documentary Issue Secretaries of the Treasury from Alexander Hamilton, the first secretary, to Salmon P. Chase, who served under Lincoln, were featured on a new series of stamps. Included were portraits of Walter Forward, the first Comptroller of the Treasury, in 1841, and Roger B. Taney, who served until his appointment was rejected by Congress. The stamps were printed in three different sizes and overprinted for use in different years. Stamps Nos. R274-R298 were overprinted in black "Series 1940." Stamps with a face value of $30 and above were issued without gum and are usually handstamped on documents. *They were issued with straight edges on 1 or 2 sides. Nos. R274-R285 size: 19 x 22mm, perforated 11.*

			MnHVF	UseVF	CutCnl	Perfin
R274	1¢	**carmine**	3.00	2.50		.75

R275 *Oliver Wolcott Jr.*

			MnHVF	UseVF	CutCnl	Perfin
R275	2¢	**carmine** (Oliver Wolcott Jr.)	4.00	2.50	1.20	1.00
R276	3¢	**carmine** (Samuel Dexter)	15.00	7.50	1.20	3.00
R277	4¢	**carmine** (Albert Gallatin)	35.00	17.50	4.50	4.00

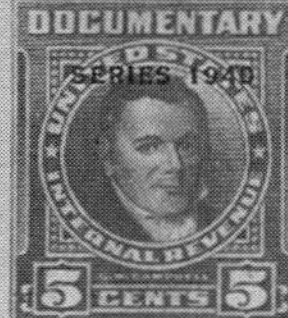

R278 *G. W. Campbell*

			MnHVF	UseVF	CutCnl	Perfin
R278	5¢	**carmine** (G.W. Campbell)	3.00	.50	.25	.20
R279	8¢	**carmine** (Alexander Dallas)	20.00	12.00	3.00	2.00

R280 *William H. Crawford*

			MnHVF	UseVF	CutCnl	Perfin
R280	10¢	**carmine** (William H. Crawford)	2.00	.35	.20	.20

R281 *Richard Rush*

			MnHVF	UseVF	CutCnl	Perfin
R281	20¢	**carmine** (Richard Rush)	3.50	2.00	1.00	.50

R282 *S. D. Ingham*

R282		MnHVF	UseVF	CutCnl	Perfin
25¢	**carmine** (S.D. Ingham)	2.50	.50	.20	.20

R283 *Louis McLane*

R283		MnHVF	UseVF	CutCnl	Perfin
40¢	**carmine** (Louis McLane)	35.00	15.00	4.00	3.00

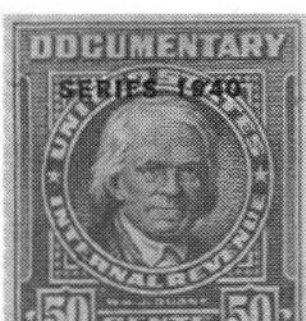

R284 *William J. Duane*

		MnHVF	UseVF	CutCnl	Perfin
R284 50¢	**carmine** (William J. Duane)	4.00	.35	.20	.20
R285 80¢	**carmine** (Roger B. Taney)	75.00	50.00	25.00	20.00

1940. Documentary Issue *Nos. R286-R292 Size: 21 1/2 x 36 1/4 mm, perforated 11.*

R286 *Levi Woodbury*

		MnHVF	UseVF	CutCnl	Perfin
R286 $1	**carmine** (Levi Woodbury)	30.00	.50	.20	.20
R287 $2	**carmine** (Thomas Ewing)	35.00	.70	.20	.20
R288 $3	**carmine** (Walter Forward)	100.00	70.00	10.00	8.50
R289 $4	**carmine** (J.C. Spencer)	60.00	30.00	6.00	2.00
R290 $5	**carmine** (G.M. Bibb)	35.00	1.25	.40	.25
R291 $10	**carmine** (R.J. Walker)	70.00	4.50	.70	.25
R292 $20	**carmine** (William M. Meredith)	1,250	500.00	300.00	300.00

1940. Documentary Issue Nos. R293-R298 *Size: 28 1/2 x 42mm, perforated 12, issued without gum.*

		MnHVF	UseVF	CutCnl	Perfin
R293 $30	**carmine** (Thomas Corwin)	100.00	35.00	11.00	10.00
R294 $50	**carmine** (James Guthrie)		1,000	900.00	500.00
R295 $60	**carmine** (Howell Cobb)	200.00	40.00	30.00	20.00
R296 $100	**carmine** (P.F. Thomas)	150.00	50.00	20.00	10.00

Users of this catalog are invited to write to us if they have information they feel will supplement or correct any material contained herein. All such communications will be answered.

R297 *J.A. Dix*

R297		MnHVF	UseVF	CutCnl	Perfin
$500	**carmine** (J.A. Dix)		800.00	450.00	250.00

R298 *S.P. Chase*

R298		MnHVF	UseVF	CutCnl	Perfin
$1,000	**carmine** (S.P. Chase)		400.00	165.00	140.00

1941. Documentary Issue Secretaries of the Treasury, designs as Nos. R274-R298, overprint reads "Series 1941." *Nos. R299-R317 perforated 11; Nos. R318-R323 perforated 12, without gum.*

		MnHVF	UseVF	CutCnl	Perfin
R299 1¢	**carmine**	2.50	1.65	.75	.60
R300 2¢	**carmine**	2.50	.75	.40	.30

R301 *Samuel Dexter*

R301		MnHVF	UseVF	CutCnl	Perfin
3¢	**carmine**	6.00	3.00	1.25	1.00

R302 *Albert Gallatin*

		MnHVF	UseVF	CutCnl	Perfin
R302 4¢	**carmine**	4.50	1.00	.30	.25
R303 5¢	**carmine**	1.00	.20	.20	.20

R304 *A.J. Dallas*

R304		MnHVF	UseVF	CutCnl	Perfin
8¢	**carmine**	12.50	6.50	3.00	2.75

No.	Denom.	Color	MnHVF	UseVF	CutCnl	Perfin
R305	10¢	carmine	1.25	.20	.20	.20
R306	20¢	carmine	2.75	.40	.20	.20
R307	25¢	carmine	1.50	.20	.20	.20
R308	40¢	carmine	8.50	2.25	1.00	.80
R309	50¢	carmine	2.25	.20	.20	.20
R310	80¢	carmine	40.00	8.50	3.00	2.50
R311	$1	carmine	8.00	.20	.20	.20

R312 *Thomas Ewing*

No.	Denom.	Color	MnHVF	UseVF	CutCnl	Perfin
R312	$2	carmine	9.00	.30	.20	.20
R313	$3	carmine	15.00	2.00	.30	.25
R314	$4	carmine	25.00	12.50	.80	.65

R315 *G.M. Bibb*

No.	Denom.	Color	MnHVF	UseVF	CutCnl	Perfin
R315	$5	carmine	30.00	.50	.20	.20

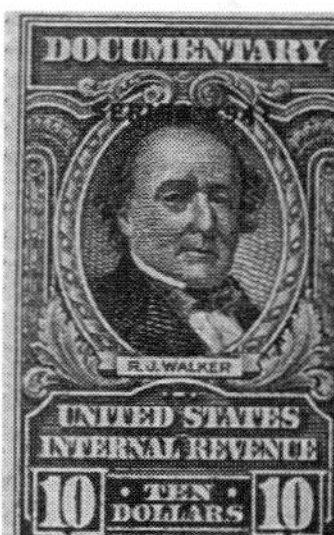

R316 *R.J. Walker*

No.	Denom.	Color	MnHVF	UseVF	CutCnl	Perfin
R316	$10	carmine	45.00	3.50	.30	.25
R317	$20	carmine	475.00	165.00	65.00	45.00
R318	$30	carmine	45.00	20.00	10.00	8.00
R319	$50	carmine	165.00	140.00	70.00	40.00
R320	$60	carmine		40.00	12.50	10.00
R321	$100	carmine	40.00	15.00	6.00	5.00
R322	$500	carmine		175.00	85.00	45.00
R323	$1,000	carmine		95.00	30.00	25.00

1942. Documentary Issue Secretaries of the Treasury, designs as Nos. R274-R298, overprint reads "Series 1942." *Nos. R324-R342 perforated 11; Nos. R343-R348 perforated 12, without gum.*

No.	Denom.	Color	MnHVF	UseVF	CutCnl	Perfin
R324	1¢	carmine	.40	.30	.20	.20
R325	2¢	carmine	.40	.30	.20	.20
R326	3¢	carmine	.60	.50	.20	.20
R327	4¢	carmine	1.25	1.00	.40	.30
R328	5¢	carmine	.40	.20	.20	.20
R329	8¢	carmine	5.00	4.00	1.00	1.00
R330	10¢	carmine	1.00	.20	.20	.20
R331	20¢	carmine	1.00	.40	.20	.20
R332	25¢	carmine	2.00	.40	.20	.20
R333	40¢	carmine	4.50	1.00	.50	.30
R334	50¢	carmine	2.50	.20	.20	.20
R335	80¢	carmine	15.00	8.00	2.50	2.00
R336	$1	carmine	7.50	.20	.20	.20
R337	$2	carmine	8.50	.20	.20	.20
R338	$3	carmine	12.50	2.00	.25	.20
R339	$4	carmine	20.00	3.50	.30	.25
R340	$5	carmine	22.50	.75	.20	.20
R341	$10	carmine	50.00	2.00	.20	.20
R342	$20	carmine	100.00	25.00	15.00	12.50
R343	$30	carmine	35.00	17.50	7.00	5.00
R344	$50	carmine	300.00	225.00	125.00	100.00
R345	$60	carmine	650.00	550.00	150.00	90.00
R346	$100	carmine	125.00	85.00	35.00	30.00
R347	$500	carmine		175.00	100.00	50.00
R348	$1,000	carmine		90.00	50.00	40.00

1943. Documentary Issue Secretaries of the Treasury, designs as Nos. R274-R298, overprint reads "Series 1943." *Nos. R349-R367 perforated 11; Nos. R368-R373 perforated 12, without gum.*

No.	Denom.	Color	MnHVF	UseVF	CutCnl	Perfin
R349	1¢	carmine	.50	.40	.20	.20
R350	2¢	carmine	.40	.30	.20	.20
R351	3¢	carmine	2.25	2.00	.50	.40
R352	4¢	carmine	.80	.80	.30	.25
R353	5¢	carmine	.40	.25	.20	.20
R354	8¢	carmine	3.50	2.75	1.50	1.25
R355	10¢	carmine	.50	.25	.20	.20

			MnHVF	UseVF	CutCnl	Perfin
R356	**20¢**	carmine	1.50	.50	.20	.20
R357	**25¢**	carmine	1.40	.20	.20	.20
R358	**40¢**	carmine	4.50	1.75	1.00	.60
R359	**50¢**	carmine	1.00	.20	.20	.20
R360	**80¢**	carmine	10.00	5.00	1.20	1.00
R361	**$1**	carmine	4.50	.30	.20	.20
R362	**$2**	carmine	8.50	.25	.20	.20
R363	**$3**	carmine	15.00	1.50	.30	.25
R364	**$4**	carmine	20.00	2.50	.40	.35
R365	**$5**	carmine	25.00	.40	.20	.20
R366	**$10**	carmine	40.00	2.50	.50	.40
R367	**$20**	carmine	90.00	17.50	5.00	4.50
R368	**$30**	carmine	30.00	17.50	4.00	3.50
R369	**$50**	carmine	60.00	20.00	7.50	5.00

R370 *Howell Cobb*

			MnHVF	UseVF	CutCnl	Perfin
R370	**$60**	carmine		65.00	12.50	9.00

R371 *P.F. Thomas*

			MnHVF	UseVF	CutCnl	Perfin
R371	**$100**	carmine		8.50	5.00	3.50
R372	**$500**	carmine		160.00	80.00	60.00
R373	**$1,000**	carmine		140.00	40.00	35.00

1944. Documentary Issue Secretaries of the Treasury, designs as Nos. R274-R298, overprint reads "Series 1944." *Nos. R374-R392 perforated 11; Nos. R393-R398 perforated 12, without gum.*

			MnHVF	UseVF	CutCnl	Perfin
R374	**1¢**	carmine	.40	.30	.20	.20
R375	**2¢**	carmine	.40	.30	.20	.20
R376	**3¢**	carmine	.40	.30	.20	.20
R377	**4¢**	carmine	.50	.40	.20	.20
R378	**5¢**	carmine	.40	.20	.20	.20
R379	**8¢**	carmine	1.50	1.00	.45	.40
R380	**10¢**	carmine	.40	.20	.20	.20
R381	**20¢**	carmine	.70	.20	.20	.20
R382	**25¢**	carmine	1.25	.20	.20	.20
R383	**40¢**	carmine	2.50	.50	.20	.20
R384	**50¢**	carmine	2.50	.20	.20	.20
R385	**80¢**	carmine	10.00	3.50	1.00	.80
R386	**$1**	carmine	5.00	.20	.20	.20
R387	**$2**	carmine	7.50	.20	.20	.20
R388	**$3**	carmine	10.00	1.25	.45	.30
R389	**$4**	carmine	15.00	9.00	1.00	.80
R390	**$5**	carmine	17.50	.25	.20	.20
R391	**$10**	carmine	35.00	1.00	.20	.20
R392	**$20**	carmine	75.00	12.50	3.00	2.75

R393 *Thomas Corwin*

			MnHVF	UseVF	CutCnl	Perfin
R393	**$30**	carmine	40.00	17.50	5.00	4.50

R394 *James Guthrie*

			MnHVF	UseVF	CutCnl	Perfin
R394	**$50**	carmine	17.50	10.00	4.50	4.00
R395	**$60**	carmine	85.00	40.00	8.50	7.50
R396	**$100**	carmine		8.00	4.00	3.00
R397	**$500**	carmine		1,000	800.00	500.00
R398	**$1,000**	carmine		155.00	50.00	40.00

1945. Documentary Issue Secretaries of the Treasury, designs as Nos. R274-R298, overprint reads "Series 1945." *Nos. R399-R417 perforated 11; Nos. R418-R423 perforated 12, issued without gum.*

No.	Denom.	Color	MnHVF	UseVF	CutCnl	Perfin
R399	1¢	carmine	.20	.20	.20	.20
R400	2¢	carmine	.20	.20	.20	.20
R401	3¢	carmine	.50	.45	.20	.20
R402	4¢	carmine	.25	.25	.20	.20
R403	5¢	carmine	.25	.20	.20	.20
R404	8¢	carmine	4.00	1.75	.50	.30
R405	10¢	carmine	.75	.20	.20	.20
R406	20¢	carmine	4.00	.75	.40	.20
R407	25¢	carmine	1.00	.25	.20	.20
R408	40¢	carmine	4.50	.80	.40	.30
R409	50¢	carmine	2.50	.20	.20	.20
R410	80¢	carmine	15.00	7.50	3.00	1.50
R411	$1	carmine	6.50	.20	.20	.20
R412	$2	carmine	6.50	.20	.20	.20
R413	$3	carmine	12.50	2.00	.80	.60
R414	$4	carmine	17.50	3.00	.50	.30
R415	$5	carmine	17.50	.30	.20	.20
R416	$10	carmine	35.00	1.25	.20	.20
R417	$20	carmine	75.00	10.00	3.00	2.50
R418	$30	carmine	55.00	18.00	6.00	5.00
R419	$50	carmine	60.00	20.00	12.50	6.00
R420	$60	carmine	100.00	35.00	12.50	10.00
R421	$100	carmine		10.00	8.00	5.00
R422	$500	carmine	185.00	150.00	65.00	50.00
R423	$1,000	carmine	100.00	80.00	20.00	15.00

1946. DOCUMENTARY ISSUE Secretaries of the Treasury, designs as Nos. R274-R298, overprint reads "Series 1946." *Nos. R424-R442 perforated 11; Nos. R443-R448 perforated 12, issued without gum.*

No.	Denom.	Color	MnHVF	UseVF	CutCnl	Perfin
R424	1¢	carmine	.25	.20	.20	.20
R425	2¢	carmine	.30	.30	.20	.20
R426	3¢	carmine	.35	.25	.20	.20
R427	4¢	carmine	.50	.40	.20	.20
R428	5¢	carmine	.25	.20	.20	.20
R429	8¢	carmine	1.00	.80	.20	.20
R430	10¢	carmine	.70	.20	.20	.20
R431	20¢	carmine	1.20	.35	.20	.20
R432	25¢	carmine	3.80	.20	.20	.20
R433	40¢	carmine	2.25	.75	.20	.20
R434	50¢	carmine	2.25	.20	.20	.20
R435	80¢	carmine	8.50	3.50	.60	.50
R436	$1	carmine	7.00	.20	.20	.20
R437	$2	carmine	8.00	.20	.20	.20
R438	$3	carmine	12.50	4.50	.90	.35
R439	$4	carmine	17.50	7.50	1.50	1.00
R440	$5	carmine	17.50	.40	.20	.20
R441	$10	carmine	35.00	1.35	.20	.20
R442	$20	carmine	75.00	7.50	2.00	1.50
R443	$30	carmine	40.00	12.50	4.00	3.00
R444	$50	carmine	17.50	8.00	4.00	3.00
R445	$60	carmine	35.00	15.00	10.00	9.00
R446	$100	carmine	40.00	10.00	3.50	3.00
R447	$500	carmine		90.00	30.00	22.00
R448	$1,000	carmine		90.00	25.00	17.00

1947. DOCUMENTARY ISSUE Secretaries of the Treasury, designs as Nos. R274-R298, overprint reads "Series 1947." *Nos. R449-R467 perforated 11; Nos. R468-R473 perforated 12, issued without gum.*

No.	Denom.	Color	MnHVF	UseVF	CutCnl	Perfin
R449	1¢	carmine	.65	.45	.20	.20
R450	2¢	carmine	.50	.40	.20	.20
R451	3¢	carmine	.50	.45	.20	.20
R452	4¢	carmine	.65	.55	.20	.20
R453	5¢	carmine	.30	.25	.20	.20
R454	8¢	carmine	1.15	.65	.20	.20
R455	10¢	carmine	1.10	.25	.20	.20
R456	20¢	carmine	1.75	.50	.20	.20
R457	25¢	carmine	2.25	.50	.20	.20
R458	40¢	carmine	3.50	.75	.20	.20
R459	50¢	carmine	3.00	.20	.20	.20
R460	80¢	carmine	7.50	6.00	.60	.20
R461	$1	carmine	5.75	.20	.20	.20
R462	$2	carmine	8.50	.40	.20	.20
R463	$3	carmine	8.50	6.50	1.00	.60
R464	$4	carmine	10.00	4.00	.40	.35
R465	$5	carmine	15.00	.40	.20	.20
R466	$10	carmine	35.00	2.00	.50	.20
R467	$20	carmine	50.00	8.50	1.00	.70
R468	$30	carmine	55.00	15.00	3.50	2.00
R469	$50	carmine	25.00	11.00	3.50	2.00
R470	$60	carmine	65.00	30.00	13.50	7.50

			MnHVF	UseVF	CutCnl	Perfin
R471	$100	carmine	25.00	8.50	3.50	2.00
R472	$500	carmine		140.00	40.00	35.00
R473	$1,000	carmine		75.00	30.00	20.00

1948. Documentary Issue Secretaries of the Treasury, designs as Nos. R274-R298, overprint reads "Series 1948." *Nos. R474-R492 perforated 11; Nos. R493-R497 perforated 12, issued without gum.*

			MnHVF	UseVF	CutCnl	Perfin
R474	1¢	carmine	.20	.20	.20	.20
R475	2¢	carmine	.30	.25	.20	.20
R476	3¢	carmine	.40	.35	.20	.20
R477	4¢	carmine	.40	.25	.20	.20
R478	5¢	carmine	.30	.20	.20	.20
R479	8¢	carmine	.75	.30	.20	.20
R480	10¢	carmine	.50	.20	.20	.20
R481	20¢	carmine	1.50	.30	.20	.20
R482	25¢	carmine	1.35	.20	.20	.20
R483	40¢	carmine	4.00	1.40	.30	.25
R484	50¢	carmine	2.25	.20	.20	.20
R485	80¢	carmine	6.50	4.00	1.00	.50
R486	$1	carmine	6.50	.20	.20	.20
R487	$2	carmine	9.00	.20	.20	.20
R488	$3	carmine	12.50	2.00	.40	.25
R489	$4	carmine	17.50	2.00	.75	.50
R490	$5	carmine	15.00	.40	.30	.20
R491	$10	carmine	35.00	1.00	.25	.20
R492	$20	carmine	75.00	8.50	3.00	1.50
R493	$30	carmine	40.00	17.50	4.00	2.50
R494	$50	carmine	40.00	15.00	4.00	2.00
R495	$60	carmine	55.00	20.00	8.00	4.50
R496	$100	carmine	45.00	8.00	3.25	2.00
R497	$500	carmine	110.00	100.00	40.00	25.00
R498	$1,000	carmine	75.00	60.00	25.00	18.00

1949. Documentary Issue Secretaries of the Treasury, designs as Nos. R274-R298, overprint reads "Series 1949." *Nos. R499-R517 perforated 11; Nos. R518-R523 perforated 12, issued without gum.*

			MnHVF	UseVF	CutCnl	Perfin
R499	1¢	carmine	.25	.20	.20	.20
R500	2¢	carmine	.50	.30	.20	.20
R501	3¢	carmine	.35	.30	.20	.20
R502	4¢	carmine	.50	.40	.20	.20
R503	5¢	carmine	.30	.20	.20	.20
R504	8¢	carmine	.65	.50	.20	.20
R505	10¢	carmine	.35	.25	.20	.20
R506	20¢	carmine	1.25	.60	.30	.20
R507	25¢	carmine	1.75	.65	.25	.20
R508	40¢	carmine	4.00	2.00	.40	.30
R509	50¢	carmine	3.50	.30	.20	.20
R510	80¢	carmine	8.00	4.50	1.25	.75
R511	$1	carmine	6.50	.40	.20	.20
R512	$2	carmine	8.50	2.00	.35	.25
R513	$3	carmine	13.50	5.75	1.50	1.00
R514	$4	carmine	17.00	6.00	2.50	1.25
R515	$5	carmine	17.00	2.50	.50	.40
R516	$10	carmine	35.00	2.50	1.00	.80
R517	$20	carmine	75.00	8.00	2.00	1.25
R518	$30	carmine	45.00	20.50	5.00	3.00
R519	$50	carmine	55.00	35.00	9.00	6.00
R520	$60	carmine		40.00	20.00	10.00
R521	$100	carmine	40.00	12.50	3.00	2.50
R522	$500	carmine		175.00	100.00	50.00
R523	$1,000	carmine		100.00	30.00	20.00

1950. Documentary Issue Secretaries of the Treasury, designs as Nos. R274-R298, overprint reads "Series 1950." *Nos. R524-R542 perforated 11; Nos. R543-R548 perforated 12, issued without gum.*

			MnHVF	UseVF	CutCnl	Perfin
R524	1¢	carmine	.20	.20	.20	.20
R525	2¢	carmine	.30	.20	.20	.20
R526	3¢	carmine	.35	.30	.20	.20
R527	4¢	carmine	.45	.35	.20	.20
R528	5¢	carmine	.30	.20	.20	.20
R529	8¢	carmine	1.20	.65	.20	.20
R530	10¢	carmine	.60	.20	.20	.20
R531	20¢	carmine	1.00	.30	.20	.20
R532	25¢	carmine	1.25	.35	.20	.25
R533	40¢	carmine	3.00	1.50	.40	.25
R534	50¢	carmine	3.50	.20	.20	.20
R535	80¢	carmine	6.50	3.50	.75	.50
R536	$1	carmine	6.50	.20	.20	.20
R537	$2	carmine	8.50	1.50	.30	.20
R538	$3	carmine	8.50	3.50	1.25	.75
R539	$4	carmine	12.50	4.50	2.00	1.00
R540	$5	carmine	17.50	.75	.30	.20
R541	$10	carmine	35.00	7.50	.75	.50

No.	Value	Color	MnHVF	UseVF	CutCnl	Perfin
R542	$20	carmine	75.00	8.00	2.00	1.50
R543	$30	carmine	60.00	40.00	10.00	8.00
R544	$50	carmine	35.00	12.50	6.50	4.50
R545	$60	carmine		50.00	15.00	8.00
R546	$100	carmine	40.00	17.50	5.00	3.00
R547	$500	carmine		100.00	45.00	30.00
R548	$1,000	carmine		70.00	20.00	18.00

1951. Documentary Issue Secretaries of the Treasury, designs as Nos. R274-R298, overprint reads "Series 1951." *Nos. R549-R567 perforated 11; Nos. R568-R573 perforated 12, issued without gum.*

No.	Value	Color	MnHVF	UseVF	CutCnl	Perfin
R549	1¢	carmine	.20	.20	.20	.20
R550	2¢	carmine	.25	.20	.20	.20
R551	3¢	carmine	.25	.20	.20	.20
R552	4¢	carmine	.30	.20	.20	.20
R553	5¢	carmine	.30	.20	.20	.20
R554	8¢	carmine	.85	.30	.25	.20
R555	10¢	carmine	.50	.20	.20	.20
R556	20¢	carmine	1.25	.40	.20	.20
R557	25¢	carmine	1.25	.40	.20	.20
R558	40¢	carmine	3.00	1.25	.20	.30
R559	50¢	carmine	2.50	.35	.20	.20
R560	80¢	carmine	5.00	2.00	1.50	.75
R561	$1	carmine	6.50	.20	.20	.20
R562	$2	carmine	8.50	.40	.20	.20
R563	$3	carmine	12.50	3.00	1.75	1.00
R564	$4	carmine	15.00	5.00	2.00	1.00
R565	$5	carmine	12.50	.50	.25	.20
R566	$10	carmine	30.00	2.50	1.00	.75
R567	$20	carmine	70.00	8.00	3.50	3.00
R568	$30	carmine	60.00	10.00	5.00	3.50
R569	$50	carmine	45.00	12.50	5.00	4.00
R570	$60	carmine		40.00	20.00	15.00
R571	$100	carmine	40.00	12.50	6.50	5.00
R572	$500	carmine	120.00	80.00	40.00	20.00
R573	$1,000	carmine		80.00	30.00	25.00

1952. Documentary Issue Secretaries of the Treasury, designs as Nos. R274-R298, and new values showing L.J. Gage (55¢, $1.10, $1.65, $2.20, $2.75 and $3.30), William Windom ($2,500), C.J. Folger ($5,000), and W.Q. Gresham ($10,000), all former secretaries of the treasury. Overprint: "Series 1952." *Nos. R574-R598 perforated 12, issued without gum.*

No.	Value	Color	MnHVF	UseVF	CutCnl	Perfin
R574	1¢	carmine	.20	.20	.20	.20
R575	2¢	carmine	.30	.20	.20	.20
R576	3¢	carmine	.25	.20	.20	.20
R577	4¢	carmine	.25	.20	.20	.20
R578	5¢	carmine	.20	.20	.20	.20
R579	8¢	carmine	.60	.40	.20	.20
R580	10¢	carmine	.40	.20	.20	.20
R581	20¢	carmine	.90	.30	.25	.20
R582	25¢	carmine	1.25	.35	.25	.20
R583	40¢	carmine	.20	.80	.50	.40
R584	50¢	carmine	2.50	.20	.20	.20
R585	55¢	carmine	17.50	10.00	1.25	1.00
R586	80¢	carmine	8.50	2.75	.75	.70
R587	$1	carmine	4.50	1.50	—	.30
R588	$1.10	carmine	30.00	20.00	10.00	6.00
R589	$1.65	carmine	120.00	40.00	25.00	20.00
R590	$2	carmine	8.00	.30	.20	.20
R591	$2.20	carmine	75.00	50.00	30.00	15.00
R592	$2.75	carmine	100.00	55.00	25.00	15.00
R593	$3	carmine	20.00	3.50	1.25	1.00
R594	$3.30	carmine	80.00	60.00	30.00	15.00
R595	$4	carmine	17.50	3.50	2.00	1.50
R596	$5	carmine	17.50	1.00	.35	.30
R597	$10	carmine	30.00	1.25	.40	.30
R598	$20	carmine	50.00	9.00	2.75	2.50
R599	$30	carmine	40.00	17.50	5.00	4.00
R600	$50	carmine	40.00	10.00	5.00	4.00
R601	$60	carmine		50.00	12.50	9.00
R602	$100	carmine	30.00	7.50	3.00	2.50
R603	$500	carmine		90.00	55.00	30.00
R604	$1,000	carmine		30.00	15.00	10.00
R605	$2,500	carmine		150.00	110.00	90.00
R606	$5,000	carmine		1,000	800.00	700.00
R607	$10,000	carmine		650.00	400.00	300.00

1953. Documentary Issue Secretaries of the Treasury, designs as Nos. R274-R298, R585, R588, R589, R591, R592, R594 and R605-R607, overprint reads "Series 1953." *Nos. R608-R632 perforated 11; Nos. R633-R640 perforated 12, issued without gum.*

No.	Value	Color	MnHVF	UseVF	CutCnl	Perfin
R608	1¢	carmine	.20	.20	.20	.20

			MnHVF	UseVF	CutCnl	Perfin
R609	**2¢**	**carmine**	.20	.20	.20	.20
R610	**3¢**	**carmine**	.25	.20	.20	.20
R611	**4¢**	**carmine**	.30	.25	.20	.20
R612	**5¢**	**carmine**	.20	.20	.20	.20
R613	**8¢**	**carmine**	.70	.70	.20	.20
R614	**10¢**	**carmine**	.35	.25	.20	.20
R615	**20¢**	**carmine**	.70	.35	.25	.20
R616	**25¢**	**carmine**	.80	.40	.25	.20
R617	**40¢**	**carmine**	1.50	1.00	.40	.35
R618	**50¢**	**carmine**	2.25	.20	.20	.20
R619	**55¢**	**carmine**	3.25	1.75	.75	.50
R620	**80¢**	**carmine**	5.50	1.75	1.40	1.25
R621	**$1**	**carmine**	3.50	.20	.20	.20
R622	**$1.10**	**carmine**	6.50	2.25	2.00	1.50
R623	**$1.65**	**carmine**	7.50	3.50	2.75	2.00
R624	**$2**	**carmine**	6.00	.55	.25	.20
R625	**$2.20**	**carmine**	9.00	6.00	2.25	2.00
R626	**$2.75**	**carmine**	12.50	6.50	3.50	2.50
R627	**$3**	**carmine**	7.50	3.00	1.50	1.25
R628	**$3.30**	**carmine**	22.50	7.50	4.50	3.25
R629	**$4**	**carmine**	15.00	7.00	2.00	1.75
R630	**$5**	**carmine**	15.00	.90	.40	.35
R631	**$10**	**carmine**	30.00	2.00	1.00	.80
R632	**$20**	**carmine**	65.00	17.50	3.00	2.00
R633	**$30**	**carmine**	40.00	12.00	5.00	4.00
R634	**$50**	**carmine**	70.00	20.00	6.50	5.00
R635	**$60**	**carmine**	275.00	125.00	80.00	50.00
R636	**$100**	**carmine**	30.00	12.50	5.00	3.00
R637	**$500**	**carmine**	225.00	100.00	30.00	20.00
R638	**$1,000**	**carmine**	125.00	55.00	20.00	15.00
R639	**$2,500**	**carmine**	450.00	450.00	250.00	225.00
R640	**$5,000**	**carmine**		1,100.00	850.00	625.00
R641	**$10,000**	**carmine**		900.00	600.00	300.00

1954. Documentary Issue Secretaries of the Treasury, designs as Nos. R274-R298, R585, R588, R589, R591, R592, R594 and R605-R607. Nos. R642-R666 are without overprint. On stamps Nos. R667-R675 overprint reads: "Series 1954." *Nos. R642-R666 perforated 11; Nos. R667-R675 perforated 12, issued without gum.*

			MnHVF	UseVF	CutCnl	Perfin
R642	**1¢**	**carmine**	.20	.20	.20	.20
R643	**2¢**	**carmine**	.20	.20	.20	.20
R644	**3¢**	**carmine**	.20	.20	.20	.20
R645	**4¢**	**carmine**	.20	.20	.20	.20
R646	**5¢**	**carmine**	.20	.20	.20	.20
R647	**8¢**	**carmine**	.25	.20	.20	.20
R648	**10¢**	**carmine**	.25	.20	.20	.20
R649	**20¢**	**carmine**	.40	.30	.20	.20
R650	**25¢**	**carmine**	.60	.30	.25	.20
R651	**40¢**	**carmine**	1.25	.60	.35	.20
R652	**50¢**	**carmine**	1.60	.20	.20	.20
R653	**55¢**	**carmine**	1.50	1.25	.50	.40
R654	**80¢**	**carmine**	2.25	1.75	1.10	1.00
R655	**$1**	**carmine**	1.50	.30	.20	.20
R656	**$1.10**	**carmine**	3.25	2.50	1.50	1.00
R657	**$1.65**	**carmine**	80.00	50.00	40.00	20.00
R658	**$2**	**carmine**	1.75	.25	.25	.20
R659	**$2.20**	**carmine**	4.50	3.50	2.50	1.50
R660	**$2.75**	**carmine**	90.00	50.00	35.00	20.00
R661	**$3**	**carmine**	3.00	2.00	1.00	.75
R662	**$3.30**	**carmine**	6.50	5.00	3.00	2.00
R663	**$4**	**carmine**	4.00	3.50	2.00	1.50
R664	**$5**	**carmine**	6.00	.45	.35	.30
R665	**$10**	**carmine**	12.50	1.25	.75	.70
R666	**$20**	**carmine**	20.00	5.25	3.00	1.75
R667	**$30**	**carmine**	30.00	12.00	4.00	3.00
R668	**$50**	**carmine**	40.00	15.00	9.00	4.50
R669	**$60**	**carmine**	65.00	20.00	12.50	9.00
R670	**$100**	**carmine**	30.00	7.00	4.50	4.00
R671	**$500**	**carmine**		75.00	22.50	18.00
R672	**$1,000**	**carmine**	150.00	50.00	17.50	14.00
R673	**$2,500**	**carmine**		175.00	80.00	45.00
R674	**$5,000**	**carmine**		700.00	500.00	350.00
R675	**$10,000**	**carmine**		450.00	175.00	135.00

1955. Documentary Issue Secretaries of the Treasury, designs as Nos. R293-R298 and R604-R607, overprint reads "Series 1955." *Perforated 12, issued without gum.*

			MnHVF	UseVF	CutCnl	Perfin
R676	**$30**	**carmine**	35.00	10.00	5.00	3.00
R677	**$50**	**carmine**	35.00	12.50	8.00	6.00
R678	**$60**	**carmine**	65.00	20.00	10.00	4.00
R679	**$100**	**carmine**	30.00	6.00	4.00	3.00

No.	Value	Color	MnHVF	UseVF	CutCnl	Perfin
R680	$500	carmine		120.00	25.00	18.00
R681	$1,000	carmine		30.00	17.50	12.50
R682	$2,500	carmine		125.00	75.00	45.00
R683	$5,000	carmine		650.00	400.00	265.00
R684	$10,000	carmine		450.00	175.00	90.00

1956. DOCUMENTARY ISSUE Secretaries of the Treasury, stamps Nos. R293-R298 and R605-R607, overprint reads "Series 1956." *Perforated 12.*

No.	Value	Color	MnHVF	UseVF	CutCnl	Perfin
R685	$30	carmine	50.00	12.50	8.00	4.00
R686	$50	carmine	50.00	17.50	4.00	4.00
R687	$60	carmine		30.00	10.00	4.50
R688	$100	carmine	50.00	12.50	5.00	4.00
R689	$500	carmine		70.00	25.00	15.00
R690	$1,000	carmine		50.00	15.00	10.00
R691	$2,500	carmine		250.00	100.00	75.00
R692	$5,000	carmine		1,100	900.00	650.00
R693	$10,000	carmine		400.00	125.00	100.00

1957. DOCUMENTARY ISSUE Secretaries of the Treasury, stamps Nos. R293-R298 and R605-R607, overprint reads "Series 1957." *Perforated 12.*

No.	Value	Color	MnHVF	UseVF	CutCnl	Perfin
R694	$30	carmine	65.00	25.00	10.00	5.00
R695	$50	carmine	40.00	22.50	10.00	4.00
R696	$60	carmine		140.00	80.00	45.00
R697	$100	carmine	40.00	10.00	8.00	4.00
R698	$500	carmine	175.00	80.00	40.00	25.00
R699	$1,000	carmine		75.00	25.00	18.00
R700	$2,500	carmine		500.00	350.00	200.00
R701	$5,000	carmine		550.00	350.00	170.00
R702	$10,000	carmine		425.00	150.00	90.00

1958. DOCUMENTARY ISSUE Secretaries of the Treasury, stamps Nos. R293-R298 and R605-R607, overprint reads "Series 1958." *Perforated 12.*

No.	Value	Color	MnHVF	UseVF	CutCnl	Perfin
R703	$30	carmine	70.00	20.00	15.00	8.00
R704	$50	carmine	60.00	20.00	12.50	6.50
R705	$60	carmine		25.00	15.00	10.00
R706	$100	carmine	50.00	10.00	5.00	2.00
R707	$500	carmine	125.00	50.00	30.00	18.00
R708	$1,000	carmine		65.00	30.00	20.00
R709	$2,500	carmine		500.00	375.00	275.00
R710	$5,000	carmine		1,200	1,000	900.00
R711	$10,000	carmine		600.00	500.00	300.00

1958. DOCUMENTARY NO-OVERPRINT ISSUE Secretaries of the Treasury, Nos. R293-R298 and R605-R607 without overprint. *Perforated 12.*

No.	Value	Color	MnHVF	UseVF	CutCnl	Perfin
R711A	$30	carmine	37.50	7.00	5.75	4.75
		v. Vertical pair, imperforate horizontally	—			
R711B	$50	carmine, cut cancel, perf. initial	42.50	7.00	3.75	3.00
		v. Vertical pair, imperforate horizontally			—	
R711C	$60	carmine, cut cancel, perf. initial	80.00	20.00	10.00	5.00
R711D	$100	carmine, cut cancel, perf. initial	19.00	4.75	3.00	2.25
R711E	$500	carmine, cut cancel, perf. initial	85.00	25.00	10.00	7.50
R711F	$1,000	carmine, cut cancel, perf. initial	55.00	20.00	10.00	7.50
		v. Vertical pair, imperforate horizontally			—	
R711G	$2,500	carmine, cut cancel, perf. initial	—	140.00	85.00	50.00
R711H	$5,000	carmine, cut cancel, perf. initial	—	150.00	85.00	60.00
R711I	$10,000	carmine, cut cancel, perf. initial	—	125.00	50.00	25.00

1962. DOCUMENTARY ISSUE For the 100th anniversary of Internal Revenue, the federal government's first commemorative documentary stamp was issued. It featured the Internal Revenue Building. This stamp was replaced at a later date with similar design but dateline removed. *Giori Press printing, perforated 11.*

R712 *Internal Revenue building*

No.	Value	Color	MnHVF	UseVF	CutCnl	Perfin
R712	10¢	blue and green	1.00	.25	.20	.20
		Plate block of 4	12.00			

1963. DOCUMENTARY ISSUE Date line removed.

R713 *Internal Revenue building*

No.	Value	Color	MnHVF	UseVF	CutCnl	Perfin
R713	10¢	blue and green	3.00	.30	.20	.20
		Plate block of 4	25.00			

Documentary stamps were no longer required after Dec. 31, 1967.

DECODING THE CATALOG

In 1962, to mark the centennial of the use of the United States revenue stamps that had been introduced to help pay the costs of the Civil War, the Internal Revenue Service introduced a curiosity among U.S. revenue stamps — a design with a commemorative inscription. This 10¢ documentary revenue stamp picturing the Internal Revenue building in Washington, D.C., has "Established 1962" below "Documentary" and above the vignette. The stamp is Minkus R712.

The following year, the same 10¢ design was used without the inscription. The stamp is Minkus R713. Mint copies catalog $3 to $3.50 — about three times the value of the 1962 commemorative version. It was the final new documentary revenue stamp. Use of the stamps was no longer required after Dec. 31, 1967.

Proprietary Stamps

1862-71. The First Proprietary Issue formed part of the first general issue of Revenue stamps. They had the same designs as the corresponding denominations and were inscribed "PROPRIETARY." Unlike other stamps in the issue, these were used only on proprietary articles, privately owned items. Prices are for used copies only. *Perforated 12.*

RP1

RP1		Perf	Part Perf	Imperf
1¢	**red** (1862)	.50	120.00	750.00

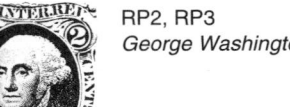

RP2, RP3
George Washington

RP2		Perf	Part Perf	Imperf
2¢	**blue** (1862)	.40	120.00	350.00
	v. ultramarine	60.00		
RP3		**Perf**	**Part Perf**	**Imperf**
2¢	**orange** (1862)	35.00		
RP4		**Perf**	**Part Perf**	**Imperf**
3¢	**green** (1862)	3.25	300.00	

RP5

RP5		Perf	Part Perf	Imperf
4¢	**purple** (1862)	6.50	210.00	
RP6		**Perf**	**Part Perf**	**Imperf**
5¢	**red** (1864)	22.50		
RP7		**Perf**	**Part Perf**	**Imperf**
6¢	**orange** (1871)	1,600.00		
RP8		**Perf**	**Part Perf**	**Imperf**
10¢	**blue** (1864)	15.00		

1871-73. Proprietary Issue Portrait of Washington in black in an oval. The stamps are of different sizes, and the frames vary in design according to the denominations. *Printed by Joseph R. Carpenter of Philadelphia on unwatermarked violet paper, perforated 12.*

RP9
George Washington

RP10, 20

RP11, 21

RP9		UnCnl	Cnl
1¢	**green and black**		4.00
	a. imperforate		80.00
	b. inverted center	2,850.00	
RP10		**UnCnl**	**Cnl**
2¢	**green and black**		4.50
RP11		**UnCnl**	**Cnl**
3¢	**green and black**		11.00
	a. inverted center	15,000.00	

RP12, 22

RP13, 23

RP14, 24

RP12		UnCnl	Cnl
4¢	**green and black**		8.00
	a. inverted center	20,000.00	
RP13		**UnCnl**	**Cnl**
5¢	**green and black**		125.00
	a. inverted center	75,000.00	
RP14		**UnCnl**	**Cnl**
6¢	**green and black**		25.00

RP15, 25

RP15		UnCnl	Cnl
10¢	**green and black**		275.00

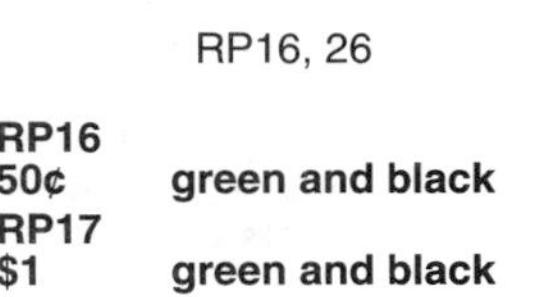

RP16, 26

RP17, 27

RP16		UnCnl	Cnl
50¢	**green and black**	550.00	
RP17		**UnCnl**	**Cnl**
$1	**green and black**	1,000.00	

Users of this catalog are invited to write to us if they have information they feel will supplement or correct any material contained herein. All such communications will be answered.

RP18, 28

		UnCnl	Cnl
RP18			
$5	**green and black**		3,000.00

1874. Proprietary Issue Green paper.

		UnCnl	Cnl
RP19			
1¢	**green and black**		6.75
RP20			
2¢	**green and black**		14.00
	a. inverted center	7,500.00	
RP21			
3¢	**green and black**		45.00
RP22			
4¢	**green and black**		15.00
RP23			
5¢	**green and black**		125.00
RP24			
6¢	**green and black**		75.00
RP25			
10¢	**green and black**	50.00	
RP26			
50¢	**green and black**		850.00
RP27			
$1	**green and black**		3,500.00
RP28			
$5	**green and black**		25,000.00

1875. Proprietary Issue Portrait of Washington in various frames engraved and printed by the National Bank Note Co. *At first the stamps were printed on green silk paper and perforated 12. Later the stamps were printed on green paper with double-line USIR watermark and perforated 12.* All prices are for used examples.

		Perf	Roul
RP29			
1¢	**green**	1.75	
RP30			
2¢	**brown**	2.50	
RP31			
3¢	**orange**	12.50	
RP32			
4¢	**red brown**	6.00	
RP33			
5¢	**black**	110.00	
RP34			
6¢	**violet blue**	25.00	

1880-81. Proprietary Issue *Green paper, watermarked USIR, perforated 12 or rouletted 6.*

		Perf	Roul
RP35			
1¢	**green**	.50	55.00
RP36			
2¢	**brown**	1.50	75.00
RP37			
3¢	**orange**	4.50	75.00
RP38			
4¢	**red brown**	5.50	
RP39			
4¢	**red**	4.50	125.00

RP40 *George Washington*

		Perf	Roul
RP40			
5¢	**black**	100.00	1,250.00
RP41			
6¢	**violet blue**	20.00	225.00
RP42			
6¢	**violet**	30.00	
RP43			
10¢	**blue**	300.00	

1898. Proprietary Issue featured a "Battleship second class," and the note over No. R147 applies here. *The stamps are watermarked double-line USIR, are rouletted 5 1/2 or hyphen-hole perforated 7.*

RP44

RP45

		Roul 5 1/2		Hyphen-Hole	
		UnFVF	UseFVF	UnFVF	UseFVF
RP44					
1/8¢	**yellow green**	.20	.20	.20	.20
RP45					
1/4¢	**chestnut**	.20	.20	.20	.20

RP46

RP48

		Roul 5 1/2		Hyphen-Hole	
		UnFVF	UseFVF	UnFVF	UseFVF
RP46					
3/8¢	**red orange**	.20	.20	.20	.20
RP47					
5/8¢	**deep blue**	.20	.20	.25	.20
RP48					
1¢	**green**	1.00	.25	25.00	15.00
RP49					
1-1/4¢	**chocolate**	.20	.20	.20	.20
RP50					
1-7/8¢	**slate blue**	7.00	1.10	20.00	6.00

RP51

RP52

		Roul 5 1/2		Hyphen-Hole	
		UnFVF	UseFVF	UnFVF	UseFVF
RP51 **2¢**	**red brown**	.80	.30	4.00	.20

		Roul 5 1/2		Hyphen-Hole	
		UnFVF	UseFVF	UnFVF	UseFVF
RP52 **2-1/2¢**	**carmine red**	2.25	.20	2.50	.20

RP53

RP54

		Roul 5 1/2		Hyphen-Hole	
		UnFVF	UseFVF	UnFVF	UseFVF
RP53 **3-3/4¢**	**greenish black**	30.00	6.00	50.00	15.00

		Roul 5 1/2		Hyphen-Hole	
		UnFVF	UseFVF	UnFVF	UseFVF
RP54 **4¢**	**dark red violet**	7.10	1.00	50.00	15.00

RP55

		Roul 5 1/2		Hyphen-Hole	
		UnFVF	UseFVF	UnFVF	UseFVF
RP55 **5¢**	**orange brown**	7.10	.90	50.00	7.50

1914. White Numeral In Circle Issue inscribed "Proprietary" across the top and "Series of 1914" under the numeral. *Nos. RP56-67 were offset printed on paper with single-line USPS watermark and Nos. RP68-88 double-line USIR watermark. Perforated 10.*

RP56, 56A

		UnFVF	UseFVF
RP56 **1/8¢**	**black**	.20	.15

RP57 RP58 RP59

		UnFVF	UseFVF
RP57 **1/4¢**	**black**	1.75	1.00
RP58 **3/8¢**	**black**	.20	.15
RP59 **5/8¢**	**black**	3.50	1.75

RP60 RP61 RP62

		UnFVF	UseFVF
RP60 **1-1/4¢**	**black**	2.50	.80
RP61 **1-7/8¢**	**black**	35.00	15.00
RP62 **2-1/2¢**	**black**	7.50	2.50
RP63 **3-1/8¢**	**black**	80.00	50.00
RP64 **3-3/4¢**	**black**	35.00	20.00
RP65 **4¢**	**black**	50.00	27.50
RP66 **4-3/8¢**	**black**	1,250.00	—
RP67 **5¢**	**black**	110.00	70.00
RP68 **1/8¢**	**black**	.20	.20
RP69 **1/4¢**	**black**	.20	.20
RP70 **3/8¢**	**black**	.60	.30
RP71 **1/2¢**	**black**	3.00	2.75
RP72 **5/8¢**	**black**	.20	.20
RP73 **1¢**	**black**	4.00	4.00
RP74 **1-1/4¢**	**black**	.30	.25
RP75 **1-1/2¢**	**black**	3.00	2.25
RP76 **1-7/8¢**	**black**	1.00	.50
RP77 **2¢**	**black**	5.00	4.00
RP78 **2-1/2¢**	**black**	1.25	1.00
RP79 **3¢**	**black**	4.00	2.75
RP80 **3-1/8¢**	**black**	5.00	3.00
RP81 **3-3/4¢**	**black**	11.00	7.50
RP82 **4¢**	**black**	.30	.20
RP83 **4-3/8¢**	**black**	14.00	8.00
RP84 **5¢**	**black**	3.00	2.50
RP85 **6¢**	**black**	50.00	40.00
RP86 **8¢**	**black**	15.00	10.00
RP87 **10¢**	**black**	10.00	6.50
RP88 **20¢**	**black**	22.00	17.00

1919. Blue Numeral In Circle Issue inscribed "Proprietary" and "U.S. Internal Revenue" across the top. *Offset printed, perforated 11, watermarked double-line USIR.*

RP89

RP89
1¢ **blue** UnFVF .20 UseFVF .20

RP90

RP91

RP92

		UnFVF	UseFVF
RP90 2¢	**blue**	.20	.20
RP91 3¢	**blue**	1.00	.50
RP92 4¢	**blue**	1.00	.50
RP93 5¢	**blue**	1.25	.50
RP94 8¢	**blue**	14.00	9.00
RP95 10¢	**blue**	5.00	2.00
RP96 20¢	**blue**	7.50	3.00
RP97 40¢	**blue**	45.00	10.00

Future Delivery Stamps

Issued to pay the tax on sales, agreements of sale or agreements to sell any products at an exchange or equivalent establishment for future delivery.

1918-34. Future Delivery Issue Documentary stamps of 1917 overprinted in black or red as illustrated. *Double-line watermark USIR, perforated 11. Nos. RFD1, 5, 12 Type 2: Words 2mm apart. Nos. RFD 2-4, 6-11 Type 1: Words about 8 1/2mm apart.*

FUTURE
DELIVERY
Type 2(RFD1,5,12)

RFD1
1¢ **rose** (2mm) Type 2 UnFVF 1.20 UseFVF .20

RFD2

FUTURE

DELIVERY

Type 1(RFD2-11,27,28)

		UnFVF	UseFVF
RFD2 2¢	**rose** Type 1	3.00	.20
RFD3 3¢	**rose** Type 1		25.00
	Cut cancellation		12.50

RFD4

RFD6

RFD7

		UnFVF	UseFVF
RFD4 4¢	**rose** Type 1	6.00	.20
RFD5 5¢	**rose** (2mm) Type 2	60.00	7.00
RFD6 10¢	**rose** Type 1	10.00	.20
	Cut cancellation	.20	
RFD7 20¢	**rose** Type 1	12.50	.20
	Cut cancellation	.20	
RFD8 25¢	**rose** Type 1	32.50	.75
	Cut cancellation		.20
RFD9 40¢	**rose** Type 1	35.00	1.00
	Cut cancellation		.20
RFD10 50¢	**rose** Type 1	7.50	.40
RFD11 80¢	**rose** Type 1	65.00	8.00
	Cut cancellation		.20
RFD12 80¢	**rose** (2mm) Type 2	50.00	3.00
	Cut cancellation		1.00

1918-34. Future Delivery Issue *Overprint words about 2mm apart, reading up.*

		UnFVF	UseFVF
RFD13 $1	**yellow green,** red overprint	25.00	.25
	Cut cancellation		.20
	a. green, black overprint		—
	Cut cancellation		125.00
	b. Overprint, reading down		275.00

RFD14 *Head of Liberty*

FUTURE
DELIVERY
RFD13-18

		UnFVF	UseFVF
RFD14 $2	**rose,** black overprint	30.00	.25
	Cut cancellation		.20
RFD15 $3	**violet,** red overprint	75.00	2.25
	Cut cancellation		.20
RFD16 $5	**blue,** red overprint	45.00	.50
	Cut cancellation		.20
RFD17 $10	**yellow**	75.00	1.00
	Cut cancellation		.20
RFD18 $20	**olive**	125.00	5.00
	Cut cancellation		.50

1918-34. Future Delivery Issue *Words 11 1/2mm apart, perforated 12.*

FUTURE
DELIVERY
RFD19-24

		UnFVF	UseFVF
RFD19 $30	**orange,** blue numerals	65.00	3.50
	Cut cancellation		1.25
RFD20 $50	**olive green**	50.00	1.00
	Cut cancellation		.35
RFD21 $60	**brown**	65.00	2.00
	Cut cancellation		.75
RFD22 $100	**pale green**	75.00	25.00
	Cut cancellation		7.00
RFD23 $500	**blue,** red numerals	65.00	12.50

			UnFVF	UseFVF
		Cut cancellation		4.00
		a. orange numerals		50.00
		Cut cancellation		11.00
RFD24			UnFVF	UseFVF
$1,000		**orange yellow**	65.00	5.25
		Cut cancellation		1.50

1918-34. Future Delivery Issue *Perforated 11.*

FUTURE RFD25-26

DELIVERY

		UnFVF	UseFVF
RFD25		UnFVF	UseFVF
$1	**green,** red overprint ('25)	25.00	1.00
	Cut cancellation		.20
RFD26		UnFVF	UseFVF
$10	**yellow,** black overprint	80.00	15.00
	Cut cancellation		9.00

1928-29. Future Delivery Issue *Offset, overprint words about 13mm apart, perforated 10.*

FUTURE RFD27-28

DELIVERY

		UnFVF	UseFVF
RFD27		UnFVF	UseFVF
10¢	**rose**		1,000.00
RFD28		UnFVF	UseFVF
20¢	**rose**		1,000.00

Stock Transfer Stamps

These stamps were used to pay the tax due on the transfer of legal title of shares or stock certificates.

1918-29. Stock Transfer Issue Documentary Stamps of 1917 overprinted in black or red. *Offset, double-line watermark USIR, perforated 11.*

STOCK RST1-10, 25-29

TRANSFER

		UnFVF	UseFVF
RST1		UnFVF	UseFVF
1¢	**rose**	.90	.20
RST2		UnFVF	UseFVF
2¢	**rose**	.30	.20
RST3		UnFVF	UseFVF
4¢	**rose**	.30	.20
RST4		UnFVF	UseFVF
5¢	**rose**	.30	.20
RST5		UnFVF	UseFVF
10¢	**rose**	.30	.20
RST6		UnFVF	UseFVF
20¢	**rose**	.60	.20
RST7		UnFVF	UseFVF
25¢	**rose**	1.25	.25
RST8		UnFVF	UseFVF
40¢	**rose**	1.25	.25
RST9		UnFVF	UseFVF
50¢	**rose**	.60	.20
RST10		UnFVF	UseFVF
80¢	**rose**	2.50	.30

STOCK TRANSFER RST11-18, 30-32

		UnFVF	UseFVF
RST11		UnFVF	UseFVF
$1	**green,** red overprint	60.00	20.00
	Cut cancellation		4.50
	a. Overprint reading down	125.00	20.00
	Cut cancellation		7.50
RST12		UnFVF	UseFVF
$1	**green,** black overprint	2.25	.25
	a. Overprint reading down		7.00
RST13		UnFVF	UseFVF
$2	**rose**	2.25	.20
	a. Overprint reading down		12.75
	Cut cancellation		2.25
RST14		UnFVF	UseFVF
$3	**violet,** red overprint	17.50	4.00
	Cut cancellation		.20
RST15		UnFVF	UseFVF
$4	**yellow brown**	7.50	.20
	Cut cancelation		.20
RST16		UnFVF	UseFVF
$5	**blue,** red overprint	5.50	.20
	a. Overprint reading down		.50
	Cut cancellation		.20
RST17		UnFVF	UseFVF
$10	**yellow**	14.00	.35
	Cut cancellation		.08
RST18		UnFVF	UseFVF
$20	**olive bistre**	70.00	20.00
	Cut cancellation		1.10

1918-29. Stock Transfer Issue *Offset, issued without gum, perforated 12.*

STOCK RST19-24

TRANSFER

		UnFVF	UseFVF
RST19		UnFVF	UseFVF
$30	**orange,** green numerals (Grant)	17.50	5.00
	Cut cancellation		2.25
	a. blue numerals		55.00
RST20		UnFVF	UseFVF
$50	**olive green** (Cleveland)	100.00	55.00
	Cut cancellation		20.00
RST21		UnFVF	UseFVF
$60	**brown** (Lincoln)	100.00	22.50
	Cut cancellation		8.50
RST22		UnFVF	UseFVF
$100	**pale green** (Washington)	22.50	5.50
	Cut cancellation		2.25
RST23		UnFVF	UseFVF
$500	**blue,** red overprint (Hamilton)	300.00	120.00
	Cut cancellation		65.00
RST24		UnFVF	UseFVF
$1,000	**orange yellow** (Madison)	160.00	75.00
	Cut cancellation		30.00

1928-32. Stock Transfer Issue Same as 1918-29 issue, *offset, perforated 10.*

		UnFVF	UseFVF
RST25		UnFVF	UseFVF
2¢	**rose**	2.25	.30
RST26		UnFVF	UseFVF
4¢	**rose**	2.25	.30
RST27		UnFVF	UseFVF
10¢	**rose**	2.00	.30
RST28		UnFVF	UseFVF
20¢	**rose**	2.75	.30
RST29		UnFVF	UseFVF
50¢	**rose**	3.50	.20
RST30		UnFVF	UseFVF
$1	**yellow green**	27.50	.20
RST31		UnFVF	UseFVF
$2	**rose**	27.50	.20
RST32		UnFVF	UseFVF
$10	**yellow**	30.00	.30

1920. Stock Transfer Issue Same as 1918-29 issue, but letters of overprint with serifs. *Offset, perforated 11.*

STOCK RST33-41

TRANSFER

No.	Denom.	Color	UnFVF	UseFVF
RST33	2¢	rose	6.50	.75
RST34	10¢	rose	1.25	.25
RST35	20¢	rose	1.25	.25
RST36	50¢	rose	2.75	.25
RST37	$1	yellow green	37.50	9.00
		Cut cancellation		.25
RST38	$2	rose	35.00	9.00
		Cut cancellation		.25

1929. Stock Transfer Issue Same as 1918 issue but letters of overprint with serifs. *Offset, perforated 10.*

No.	Denom.	Color	UnFVF	UseFVF
RST39	2¢	rose	5.00	.50
RST40	10¢	rose	1.25	.50
RST41	20¢	rose	2.00	.25

1940. Stock Transfer Issue Documentary Stamps of 1917-33 overprinted as illustrated, in black. *Offset, double-line USIR watermark, perforated 11. Nos. RST52-58 engraved.*

SERIES 1940

RST42-58 *Overprint on white numerals in ovals*

STOCK
TRANSFER

No.	Denom.	Color	MnHVF	UseVF	CutCnl
RST42	1¢	pink	2.75	.40	.20
RST43	2¢	pink	2.75	.40	.20
RST44	4¢	pink	2.75	.20	.20
RST45	5¢	pink	3.00	.20	.20
RST46	10¢	pink	3.00	.20	.20

RST47

No.	Denom.	Color	MnHVF	UseVF	CutCnl
RST47	20¢	pink	7.00	.20	.20
RST48	25¢	pink	7.00	.50	.20
RST49	40¢	pink	4.50	.50	.20
RST50	50¢	pink	5.50	.20	.20
RST51	80¢	pink	80.00	40.00	25.00
RST52	$1	green	17.50	.30	.20
RST53	$2	rose	17.50	.50	.20
RST54	$3	violet	110.00	8.00	.20
RST55	$4	yellow brown	35.00	.75	.20
RST56	$5	blue	35.00	.75	.20
RST57	$10	yellow	85.00	5.00	.40
RST58	$20	olive bistre	200.00	70.00	15.00

Stock Transfer Stamps of 1918-29 handstamped "Series 1940" in blue. Engraved, perforated 12, issued without gum.

No.	Denom.	Color	MnHVF	UseVF	CutCnl
RST59	$30	vermilion	700.00	400.00	250.00
RST60	$50	olive green	700.00	650.00	175.00
RST61	$60	brown		900.00	200.00
RST62	$100	green		500.00	125.00
RST63	$500	blue		1,750.00	1,100.00
RST64	$1,000	orange		2,100.00	1,750.00

1940. Stock Transfer Issue New designs, with same portraits as R275-298 overprinted "Series 1940" in black. *Nos. RST65-74 perforated 11, size 19 x 22mm. Nos. RST75-81 size 21 1/2 x 36 1/4mm. Nos. RST82-87 similar designs, 28 1/2 x 42mm, perforated 12.*

RST65-74

No.	Denom.	Color	MnHVF	UseVF	CutCnl
RST65	1¢	green	7.50	2.50	.40
RST66	2¢	green	5.00	1.25	.20
RST67	4¢	green	8.00	3.50	.50

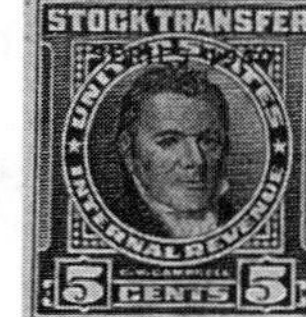

RST68 *G.W. Campbell*

No.	Denom.	Color	MnHVF	UseVF	CutCnl
RST68	5¢	green	6.00	1.25	.20
RST69	10¢	green	7.50	1.50	.20
RST70	20¢	green	25.00	7.50	.50
RST71	25¢	green	50.00	27.50	2.00
RST72	40¢	green	8.00	1.50	.25
RST73	50¢	green	65.00	45.00	20.00
RST74	80¢	green	27.50	3.50	.30

RST75-81

No.	Denom.	Color	MnHVF	UseVF	CutCnl
RST75	$1	green	30.00	8.00	.50
RST76	$2	green	50.00	10.00	.50
RST77	$3	green	50.00	10.00	.50
RST78	$4	green	225.00	175.00	60.00
RST79	$5	green	50.00	10.00	.30

No.	Value	Color	MnHVF	UseVF	CutCnl
RST80	$10	green	110.00	30.00	4.00
RST81	$20	green	400.00	70.00	8.00
RST82	$30	green		110.00	50.00
RST83	$50	green	275.00	175.00	75.00
RST84	$60	green		275.00	50.00
RST85	$100	green		160.00	60.00
RST86	$500	green		800.00	600.00
RST87	$1,000	green		700.00	500.00

1941. Stock Transfer Issue Types of 1940 overprinted "Series 1941" in black. *Nos. RST88-104 perforated 11. Nos. RST105-110 perforated 12.*

No.	Value	Color	MnHVF	UseVF	CutCnl
RST88	1¢	green	.60	.50	.20
RST89	2¢	green	.40	.20	.20
RST90	4¢	green	.35	.20	.20
RST91	5¢	green	.30	.20	.20
RST92	10¢	green	.65	.20	.20
RST93	20¢	green	1.60	.20	.20
RST94	25¢	green	1.60	.20	.20
RST95	40¢	green	2.00	.60	.20
RST96	50¢	green	3.50	.30	.20
RST97	80¢	green	17.50	7.00	.50
RST98	$1	green	10.00	.20	.20
RST99	$2	green	11.00	.20	.20
RST100	$3	green	17.50	1.25	.20
RST101	$4	green	30.00	7.00	.30
RST102	$5	green	30.00	.50	.20
RST103	$10	green	70.00	3.50	.50
RST104	$20	green	130.00	50.00	8.00
RST105	$30	green	135.00	120.00	25.00
RST106	$50	green	220.00	135.00	20.00
RST107	$60	green	400.00	160.00	140.00
RST108	$100	green		65.00	20.00
RST109	$500	green	850.00	700.00	550.00
RST110	$1,000	green		800.00	550.00

1942. Stock Transfer Issue Types of 1940 overprinted "Series 1942" in black. *Nos. RST111-127 perforated 11. Nos. RST128-133 perforated 12.*

No.	Value	Color	MnHVF	UseVF	CutCnl
RST111	1¢	green	.40	.25	.20
RST112	2¢	green	.40	.25	.20
RST113	4¢	green	2.75	.80	.45
RST114	5¢	green	.35	.20	.20
RST115	10¢	green	1.50	.20	.20
RST116	20¢	green	1.75	.25	.20
RST117	25¢	green	1.75	.25	.20
RST118	40¢	green	3.50	.25	.20
RST119	50¢	green	4.50	.20	.20
RST120	80¢	green	17.50	5.00	1.00
RST121	$1	green	11.00	.30	.20
RST122	$2	green	15.00	.30	.20
RST123	$3	green	22.50	1.00	.25
RST124	$4	green	30.00	20.00	.30
RST125	$5	green	27.50	.30	.20
RST126	$10	green	55.00	7.00	1.00
RST127	$20	green	130.00	30.00	4.00
RST128	$30	green	80.00	40.00	15.00
RST129	$50	green	125.00	80.00	15.00
RST130 100.0040.00	$60	green			
RST131	$100	green		75.00	20.00
RST132	$500	green		7,000.00	4,000.00
RST133	$1,000	green		350.00	175.00

1943. Stock Transfer Issue Types of 1940 overprinted "Series 1943" in black. *Nos. RST134-150 perforated 11. Nos. RST151-156 perforated 12.*

No.	Value	Color	MnHVF	UseVF	CutCnl
RST134	1¢	green	.40	.25	.20
RST135	2¢	green	.50	.35	.20
RST136	4¢	green	1.50	.20	.20
RST137	5¢	green	.40	.20	.20
RST138	10¢	green	.85	.20	.20
RST139	20¢	green	1.50	.20	.20
RST140	25¢	green	3.25	.20	.20
RST141	40¢	green	3.25	.20	.20
RST142	50¢	green	3.25	.20	.20
RST143	80¢	green	10.00	4.00	1.25
RST144	$1	green	10.00	.20	.20
RST145	$2	green	12.50	.20	.20
RST146	$3	green	15.00	.80	.20
RST147	$4	green	30.00	12.50	.75
RST148	$5	green	45.00	.25	.20
RST149	$10	green	60.00	4.00	.75
RST150	$20	green	120.00	30.00	12.50

No.	Denomination	Color	MnHVF	UseVF	CutCnl
RST151	**$30**	**green**	175.00	80.00	50.00
RST152	**$50**	**green**	250.00	120.00	22.50
RST153	**$60**	**green**		275.00	130.00
RST154	**$100**	**green**		50.00	17.50
RST155	**$500**	**green**		375.00	175.00
RST156	**$1,000**	**green**		250.00	150.00

1944. STOCK TRANSFER ISSUE Type of 1940 overprinted "Series 1944" in black. *Nos. RST157-173 perforated 11. Nos. RST174-182 perforated 12.*

No.	Denomination	Color	MnHVF	UseVF	CutCnl
RST157	**1¢**	**green**	.60	.60	.20
RST158	**2¢**	**green**	.40	.20	.20
RST159	**4¢**	**green**	.60	.20	.20
RST160	**5¢**	**green**	.50	.20	.20
RST161	**10¢**	**green**	.65	.20	.20
RST162	**20¢**	**green**	1.20	.20	.20
RST163	**25¢**	**green**	1.75	.30	.20
RST164	**40¢**	**green**	7.50	4.50	2.00
RST165	**50¢**	**green**	4.25	.20	.20
RST166	**80¢**	**green**	7.25	4.00	1.75
RST167	**$1**	**green**	7.25	.30	.20
RST168	**$2**	**green**	27.50	.50	.20
RST169	**$3**	**green**	22.50	1.20	.20
RST170	**$4**	**green**	27.50	4.50	.20
RST171	**$5**	**green**	25.00	.80	.20
RST172	**$10**	**green**	55.00	4.00	.40
RST173	**$20**	**green**	90.00	7.50	3.50
RST174	**$30**	**green**	110.00	55.00	12.50
RST175	**$50**	**green**	80.00	45.00	12.50
RST176	**$60**	**green**	135.00	90.00	60.00
RST177	**$100**	**green**	100.00	45.00	20.00
RST178	**$500**	**green**		375.00	250.00
RST179	**$1,000**	**green**			200.00
RST180	**$2,500**	**green** (William Windom)			
RST181	**$5,000**	**green** (C. J. Folger)			
RST182	**$10,000**	**green** (W. Q. Gresham)			1,100.00

1945. STOCK TRANSFER ISSUE Types of 1940 overprinted "Series 1945" in black. *Nos. RST183-199 perforated 11. Nos. RST200-208 perforated 12.*

No.	Denomination	Color	MnHVF	UseVF	CutCnl
RST183	**1¢**	**green**	.20	.20	.20
RST184	**2¢**	**green**	.25	.20	.20
RST185	**4¢**	**green**	.25	.20	.20
RST186	**5¢**	**green**	.25	.20	.20
RST187	**10¢**	**green**	.70	.30	.20
RST188	**20¢**	**green**	1.20	.30	.20
RST189	**25¢**	**green**	1.75	.30	.20
RST190	**40¢**	**green**	2.75	.20	.20
RST191	**50¢**	**green**	3.25	.20	.20
RST192	**80¢**	**green**	6.75	2.25	.60
RST193	**$1**	**green**	11.50	.20	.20
RST194	**$2**	**green**	15.00	.40	.20
RST195	**$3**	**green**	27.50	.50	.20
RST196	**$4**	**green**	27.50	2.25	.60
RST197	**$5**	**green**	17.50	.40	.20
RST198	**$10**	**green**	40.00	6.00	.70
RST199	**$20**	**green**	70.00	8.00	1.25
RST200	**$30**	**green**	80.00	40.00	.70
RST201	**$50**	**green**	50.00	15.00	4.00
RST202	**$60**	**green**	130.00	100.00	40.00
RST203	**$100**	**green**		20.50	12.50
RST204	**$500**	**green**		375.00	200.00
RST205	**$1,000**	**green**	1,250.00	450.00	250.00
RST206	**$2,500**	**green**			
RST207	**$5,000**	**green**			20,000.00
RST208	**$10,000**	**green**			7,000.00

1946. STOCK TRANSFER ISSUE Types of 1940 overprinted "Series 1946" in black. *Nos. RST209-225 perforated 11. No. RST226-234 perforated 12.*

No.	Denomination	Color	MnHVF	UseVF	CutCnl
RST209	**1¢**	**green**	.20	.20	.20
RST210	**2¢**	**green**	.30	.20	.20
RST211	**4¢**	**green**	.30	.20	.20
RST212	**5¢**	**green**	.30	.20	.20
RST213	**10¢**	**green**	.75	.20	.20
RST214	**20¢**	**green**	1.30	.20	.20
RST215	**25¢**	**green**	1.30	.20	.20
RST216	**40¢**	**green**	3.00	.50	.20
RST217	**50¢**	**green**	4.00	.20	.20
RST218	**80¢**	**green**	8.50	5.50	1.75
RST219	**$1**	**green**	7.50	.50	.20
RST220	**$2**	**green**	7.50	.40	.20

No.	Value	Color	MnHVF	UseVF	CutCnl
RST221	$3	green	15.00	1.20	.20
RST222	$4	green	15.00	5.00	1.75
RST223	$5	green	22.50	1.00	.20
RST224	$10	green	45.00	2.25	.50
RST225	$20	green	75.00	30.00	8.50
RST226	$30	green	65.00	25.00	16.50
RST227	$50	green	50.00	30.00	10.00
RST228	$60	green	120.00	80.00	30.00
RST229	$100	green	75.00	30.00	15.00
RST230	$500	green		150.00	90.00
RST231	$1,000	green		135.00	90.00
RST232	$2,500	green			4,500.00
RST233	$5,000	green		5,000.00	
RST234	$10,000	green			1,800.00

1947. Stock Transfer Issue Types of 1940 overprinted "Series 1947" in black. *Nos. RST235-251 perforated 11. Nos. RST252-260 perforated 12.*

No.	Value	Color	MnHVF	UseVF	CutCnl
RST235	1¢	green	.60	.50	.20
RST236	2¢	green	.50	.40	.20
RST237	4¢	green	.40	.30	.20
RST238	5¢	green	.40	.30	.20
RST239	10¢	green	.50	.40	.20
RST240	20¢	green	1.00	.40	.20
RST241	25¢	green	1.60	.40	.20
RST242	40¢	green	2.75	.60	.20
RST243	50¢	green	3.50	.25	.20
RST244	80¢	green	12.50	11.00	3.50
RST245	$1	green	7.25	.40	.20
RST246	$2	green	11.50	.60	.20
RST247	$3	green	17.50	1.25	.30
RST248	$4	green	30.00	5.00	1.00
RST249	$5	green	25.00	1.25	.25
RST250	$10	green	40.00	4.50	1.50
RST251	$20	green	80.00	25.00	5.00
RST252	$30	green	55.00	30.00	7.50
RST253	$50	green	120.00	80.00	22.50
RST254	$60	green	140.00	120.00	40.00
RST255	$100	green		25.00	12.50
RST256	$500	green		225.00	100.00
RST257	$1,000	green		80.00	40.00
RST258	$2,500	green			250.00
RST259	$5,000	green			300.00
RST260	$10,000	green			50.00

1948. Stock Transfer Issue Types of 1940 overprinted "Series 1948" in black. *Nos. RST261-277 perforated 11. Nos. RST278-286 perforated 12.*

No.	Value	Color	MnHVF	UseVF	CutCnl
RST261	1¢	green	.25	.20	.20
RST262	2¢	green	.25	.20	.20
RST263	4¢	green	.30	.25	.20
RST264	5¢	green	.20	.20	.20
RST265	10¢	green	.30	.20	.20
RST266	20¢	green	1.20	.30	.20
RST267	25¢	green	1.20	.30	.20
RST268	40¢	green	1.65	.60	.20
RST269	50¢	green	4.00	.35	.20
RST270	80¢	green	10.00	5.00	2.25
RST271	$1	green	7.50	.40	.20
RST272	$2	green	10.00	.50	.20
RST273	$3	green	12.50	3.50	1.50
RST274	$4	green	15.00	8.00	2.25
RST275	$5	green	22.50	2.25	.20
RST276	$10	green	40.00	4.00	.65
RST277	$20	green	70.00	17.50	6.00
RST278	$30	green	80.00	35.00	20.00
RST279	$50	green	50.00	35.00	10.00
RST280	$60	green	135.00	90.00	25.00
RST281	$100	green		17.50	6.00
RST282	$500	green		200.00	100.00
RST283	$1,000	green		100.00	35.00
RST284	$2,500	green	275.00	250.00	140.00
RST285	$5,000	green		225.00	150.00
RST286	$10,000	green			50.00

1949. Stock Transfer Issue Types of 1940 overprinted "Series 1949" in black. *Nos. RST287-303 perforated 11. Nos. RST304-312 perforated 12.*

No.	Value	Color	MnHVF	UseVF	CutCnl
RST287	1¢	green	.40	.35	.20
RST288	2¢	green	.40	.35	.20
RST289	4¢	green	.50	.40	.20
RST290	5¢	green	.50	.40	.20
RST291	10¢	green	1.25	.50	.20

No.	Value	Color	MnHVF	UseVF	CutCnl
RST292	**20¢**	**green**	2.00	.50	.20
RST293	**25¢**	**green**	2.50	.75	.20
RST294	**40¢**	**green**	5.00	1.25	.20
RST295	**50¢**	**green**	5.00	.20	.20
RST296	**80¢**	**green**	40.00	6.00	2.50
RST297	**$1**	**green**	9.00	.60	.20
RST298	**$2**	**green**	12.50	.75	.20
RST299	**$3**	**green**	30.00	4.00	1.00
RST300	**$4**	**green**	27.50	7.00	2.00
RST301	**$5**	**green**	35.00	2.00	.25
RST302	**$10**	**green**	40.00	4.00	1.25
RST303	**$20**	**green**	100.00	12.50	5.00
RST304	**$30**	**green**		35.00	12.50
RST305	**$50**	**green**	130.00	50.00	15.50
RST306	**$60**	**green**	150.00	130.00	40.00
RST307	**$100**	**green**		50.00	22.50
RST308	**$500**	**green**		180.00	60.00
RST309	**$1,000**	**green**		75.00	35.00
RST310	**$2,500**	**green**			300.00
RST311	**$5,000**	**green**			300.00
RST312	**$10,000**	**green**		250.00	25.00

1950. Stock Transfer Issue Types of 1940 overprinted "Series 1950" in black. *Nos. RST313-329 perforated 11. Nos. RST330-338 perforated 12.*

No.	Value	Color	MnHVF	UseVF	CutCnl
RST313	**1¢**	**green**	.35	.30	.20
RST314	**2¢**	**green**	.35	.25	.20
RST315	**4¢**	**green**	.35	.30	.20
RST316	**5¢**	**green**	.35	.20	.20
RST317	**10¢**	**green**	1.75	.25	.20
RST318	**20¢**	**green**	2.50	.40	.20
RST319	**25¢**	**green**	3.50	.50	.20
RST320	**40¢**	**green**	4.50	.80	.20
RST321	**50¢**	**green**	7.00	.30	.20
RST322	**80¢**	**green**	9.00	5.00	2.00
RST323	**$1**	**green**	9.00	.35	.20
RST324	**$2**	**green**	15.00	.60	.20
RST325	**$3**	**green**	25.00	4.00	.50
RST326	**$4**	**green**	30.00	6.50	2.50
RST327	**$5**	**green**	30.00	1.50	.20
RST328	**$10**	**green**	75.00	4.50	1.00
RST329	**$20**	**green**	100.00	22.50	4.00
RST330	**$30**	**green**	75.00	40.00	20.00
RST331	**$50**	**green**	70.00	65.00	35.00
RST332	**$60**	**green**		100.00	40.00
RST333	**$100**	**green**		32.50	20.00
RST334	**$500**	**green**		150.00	100.00
RST335	**$1,000**	**green**		65.00	25.00
RST336	**$2,500**	**green**		900.00	600.00
RST337	**$5,000**	**green**		500.00	300.00
RST338	**$10,000**	**green**			50.00

1951. Stock Transfer Issue Types of 1940 overprinted "Series 1951" in black. *Nos. RST339-355 perforated 11. Nos. RST356-364 perforated 12.*

No.	Value	Color	MnHVF	UseVF	CutCnl
RST339	**1¢**	**green**	1.00	.30	2.00
RST340	**2¢**	**green**	1.00	.30	.20
RST341	**4¢**	**green**	1.25	.40	.30
RST342	**5¢**	**green**	1.00	.30	.20
RST343	**10¢**	**green**	1.25	.30	.20
RST344	**20¢**	**green**	3.50	.75	.20
RST345	**25¢**	**green**	4.50	.80	.20
RST346	**40¢**	**green**	11.00	7.50	1.50
RST347	**50¢**	**green**	8.00	.75	.20
RST348	**80¢**	**green**	12.50	8.50	3.50
RST349	**$1**	**green**	15.00	.75	.20
RST350	**$2**	**green**	22.50	1.00	.20
RST351	**$3**	**green**	30.00	8.50	3.00
RST352	**$4**	**green**	35.00	10.00	4.00
RST353	**$5**	**green**	40.00	2.00	.20
RST354	**$10**	**green**	75.00	8.00	.20
RST355	**$20**	**green**	110.00	15.00	5.00
RST356	**$30**	**green**		40.00	20.00
RST357	**$50**	**green**		45.00	20.00
RST358	**$60**	**green**		400.00	200.00
RST359	**$100**	**green**		50.00	17.50
RST360	**$500**	**green**		125.00	75.00
RST361	**$1,000**	**green**		70.00	60.00
RST362	**$2,500**	**green**		900.00	400.00
RST363	**$5,000**	**green**		900.00	400.00
RST364	**$10,000**	**green**		100.00	50.00

1952. Stock Transfer Issue Types of 1940 overprinted "Series 1952" on black. *Perforated 11.*

No.	Denom.	Color	MnHVF	UseVF	CutCnl
RST365	1¢	green	30.00	15.00	3.00
RST366	10¢	green	30.00	15.00	3.00
RST367	20¢	green	300.00		
RST368	25¢	green	400.00		
RST369	40¢	green	70.00	20.00	8.00
RST370	$4	green	1,100.00	400.00	
RST371	$10	green	2,000.00		
RST372	$20	green	3,000.00		

Stock transfer stamps were discontinued in 1952.

Silver Purchase Stamps

The Silver Purchase Act of 1934 placed a 50% tax on net profits realized from the sale of silver bullion. The stamps were discontinued on June 4, 1963.

1934. Silver Purchase Issue Documentary Stamps of 1917 overprinted. *Under $30 perforated 11; $30 and over perforated 12 and without gum.*

RSP1

SILVER
TAX

RSP2

No.	Denom.	Color	UnFVF	UseFVF	CutCnl
RSP1	1¢	rose	1.25	1.00	
RSP2	2¢	rose	1.75	.35	
RSP3	3¢	rose	1.75	1.00	
RSP4	4¢	rose	2.25	1.75	
RSP5	5¢	rose	3.50	1.75	
RSP6	8¢	rose	4.50	3.75	
RSP7	10¢	rose	5.00	2.00	
RSP8	20¢	rose	7.00	3.50	
RSP9	25¢	rose	7.50	4.00	
RSP10	40¢	rose	7.75	5.50	
RSP11	50¢	rose	7.00	6.50	
RSP12	80¢	rose	14.00	9.50	
RSP13	$1	yellow green	22.50	11.00	
RSP14	$2	rose	22.50	15.00	
RSP15	$3	violet	55.00	25.00	
RSP16	$4	ochre	45.00	18.00	
RSP17	$5	blue	45.00	18.00	
RSP18	$10	yellow	65.00	18.00	
RSP19	$30	orange	120.00	50.00	20.00
RSP20	$60	brown	125.00	70.00	30.00
RSP21	$100	pale green	120.00	30.00	
		a. 11mm spacing on overprint	165.00	65.00	
RSP22	$500	blue	375.00	225.00	100.00
RSP23	$1,000	orange yellow		110.00	60.00
		cut cancellation		32.50	
		a. 1mm spacing on overprint		500.00	

1940. Documentary Stamps of 1917 Overprinted "Series 1940, Silver Tax." *Double-line USIR watermark, perforated 11.*

SERIES 1940 RSP24-41

SILVER
TAX

No.	Denom.	Color	MnHVF	UseVF	CutCnl
RSP24	1¢	pink	15.00		
RSP25	2¢	pink	15.00		
RSP26	3¢	pink	15.00		
RSP27	4¢	pink	17.50		
RSP28	5¢	pink	9.00		
RSP29	8¢	pink	17.50		
RSP30	10¢	pink	15.00		
RSP31	20¢	pink	17.50		
RSP32	25¢	pink	17.50		
RSP33	40¢	pink	25.00		
RSP34	50¢	pink	25.00		
RSP35	80¢	pink	25.00		
RSP36	$1	yellow green	100.00		
RSP37	$2	rose	165.00		

RSP38

No.	Denom.	Color	MnHVF	UseVF	CutCnl
RSP38	$3	violet	220.00		
RSP39	$4	ochre	400.00		
RSP40	$5	dark blue	525.00		
RSP41	$10	orange yellow	575.00		
RSP41a					

1940. Silver Tax Stamps of 1934 Handstamped Overprinted "Series of 1940" handstamped. *Perforated 12.*

No.	Denom.	Color	MnHVF	UseVF	CutCnl
RSP42	$30	orange		2,500.00	
RSP43	$60	brown		7,500.00	
RSP44	$100	pale green		3,000.00	

RSP45-46 are not assigned.

1941. Silver Tax Issue New designs similar to Stock Transfer Stamps of 1940 but inscribed "Silver Tax." Overprinted "Series 1941" as illustrated. *Double-line USIR watermark (R139). Perforated 11.*

RSP47-58 *Size: 19 x 22mm.*

No.	Value	Description	MnHVF	UseVF	CutCnl
RSP47	**1¢**	**gray** (Alexander Hamilton)	3.50		
RSP48	**2¢**	**gray** (Oliver Wolcott, Jr.)	3.50		
RSP49	**3¢**	**gray** (Samuel Dexter)	3.50		
RSP50	**4¢**	**gray** (Albert Gallatin)	5.25		
RSP51	**5¢**	**gray** (G. W. Campbell)	6.00		
RSP52	**8¢**	**gray** (A. J. Dallas)	7.00		
RSP53	**10¢**	**gray** (Wm. H. Crawford)	8.00		
RSP54	**20¢**	**gray** (Richard Rush)	12.50		
RSP55	**25¢**	**gray** (S. D. Ingham)	15.00		
RSP56	**40¢**	**gray** (Louis McLane)	25.00		
RSP57	**50¢**	**gray** (Wm. J. Duane)	30.00		
RSP58	**80¢**	**gray** (Roger B. Taney)	55.00		

RSP59-65 *Size: 21 1/2 x 36 1/2mm.*

No.	Value	Description	MnHVF	UseVF	CutCnl
RSP59	**$1**	**gray** (Levi Woodbury)	65.00	30.00	
RSP60	**$2**	**gray** (Thomas Ewing)	165.00	55.00	
RSP61	**$3**	**gray** (Walter Forward)	135.00	65.00	
RSP62	**$4**	**gray** (J. C. Spencer)	190.00	75.00	
RSP63	**$5**	**gray** (G. M. Bibb)	165.00	75.00	
RSP64	**$10**	**gray** (R. J. Walker)	260.00	95.00	
RSP65	**$20**	**gray** (Wm. M. Meredith)	450.00	300.00	

1941. Silver Tax Issue Size 28 1/2 x 42mm, perforated 12 (without gum).

No.	Value	Description	MnHVF	UseVF	CutCnl
RSP66	**$30**	**gray** (Thomas Corwin)	250.00	140.00	75.00
RSP67	**$50**	**gray** (James Guthrie)	4,500.00	4,000.00	
RSP68	**$60**	**gray** (Howell Cobb)	1,750.00	200.00	100.00
RSP69	**$100**	**gray** (P. F. Thomas)		300.00	110.00
RSP70	**$500**	**gray** (J. A. Dix)		17,500.00	
RSP71	**$1,000**	**gray** (S. P. Chase)		2,500.00	1,000.00

1942. Issue Types of 1941 overprinted "Series 1942" in black. *Perforated 11.*

No.	Value	Description	MnHVF	UseVF	CutCnl
RSP72	**1¢**	**gray**	2.50		
RSP73	**2¢**	**gray**	2.50		
RSP74	**3¢**	**gray**	2.50		
RSP75	**4¢**	**gray**	2.50		
RSP76	**5¢**	**gray**	2.50		
RSP77	**8¢**	**gray**	5.00		
RSP78	**10¢**	**gray**	5.00		
RSP79	**20¢**	**gray**	8.00		
RSP80	**25¢**	**gray**	17.50		
RSP81	**40¢**	**gray**	20.00		
RSP82	**50¢**	**gray**	20.00		
RSP83	**80¢**	**gray**	55.00		
RSP84	**$1**	**gray**	70.00		
		a. Overprint "Series 5942"	175.00		
RSP85	**$2**	**gray**	70.00		
		a. Overprint "Series 5942"	175.00		
RSP86	**$3**	**gray**	125.00		
		a. Overprint "Series 5942"	175.00		
RSP87	**$4**	**gray**	125.00		
		a. Overprint "Series 5942"	175.00		
RSP88	**$5**	**gray**	140.00		
		a. Overprint "Series 5942"	175.00		
RSP89	**$10**	**gray**	350.00		
RSP90	**$20**	**gray**	450.00		
		a. Overprint "Series 5942"	175.00		

1942. Issue *Perforated 12 (no gum).*

No.	Value	Description	MnHVF	UseVF	CutCnl
RSP91	**$30**	**gray**	800.00	75.00	
RSP92	**$50**	**gray**	650.00	600.00	
RSP93	**$60**	**gray**		950.00	550.00
RSP94	**$100**	**gray**	—	495.00	325.00
RSP95	**$500**	**gray**	—	3,000.00	2,700.00
RSP96	**$1,000**	**gray**	—	3,500.00	3,000.00

1944. Issue Types of 1941 without overprint. *Perforated 11.*

RSP97 *Alexander Hamilton*

No.	Value	Description	MnHVF	UseVF	CutCnl
RSP97	**1¢**	**gray**	1.25	.25	

RSP98 *Oliver Wolcott, Jr.*

No.	Value	Description	MnHVF	UseVF	CutCnl
RSP98	**2¢**	**gray**	1.25	—	

RSP99 *Samuel Dexter*

		MnHVF	UseVF	CutCnl
RSP99				
3¢	**gray**	1.25	—	

RSP100 *Albert Gallatin*

		MnHVF	UseVF	CutCnl
RSP100				
4¢	**gray**	1.25	—	

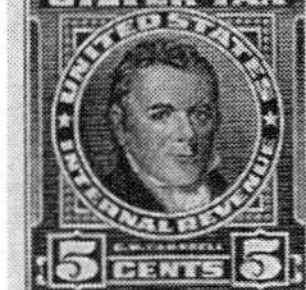
RSP101 *G.W. Campbell*

		MnHVF	UseVF	CutCnl
RSP101				
5¢	**gray**	2.25	—	

RSP102 *A.J. Dallas*

		MnHVF	UseVF	CutCnl
RSP102				
8¢	**gray**	3.50	2.50	

RSP103 *Wm. H. Crawford*

		MnHVF	UseVF	CutCnl
RSP103				
10¢	**gray**	3.50	2.50	
RSP104				
20¢	**gray**	7.00		
RSP105				
25¢	**gray**	9.00		
RSP106				
40¢	**gray**	14.00	10.00	
RSP107				
50¢	**gray**	14.00	10.00	
RSP108				
80¢	**gray**	20.00		
RSP109				
$1	**gray**	40.00	15.00	
RSP110				
$2	**gray**	60.00	35.00	
RSP111				
$3	**gray**	65.00	25.00	
RSP112				
$4	**gray**	80.00	60.00	
RSP113				
$5	**gray**	90.00	30.00	
RSP114				
$10	**gray**	125.00	50.00	15.00
RSP115				
$20	**gray**	475.00	375.00	250.00

1944. ISSUE *Perforated 12 (no gum).*

		MnHVF	UseVF	CutCnl
RSP116				
$30	**gray**	250.00	125.00	60.00
RSP117				
$50	**gray**	550.00	525.00	300.00
RSP118				
$60	**gray**		375.00	175.00
RSP119				
$100	**gray**		35.00	15.00
RSP120				
$500	**gray**		425.00	250.00
RSP121				
$1,000	**gray**		150.00	75.00

Silver Tax Stamps were discontinued on June 4, 1963.

Cigarette Tubes Stamps

1919. ISSUE Documentary Stamp of 1917 overprinted as "CIGTTE TUBES." *Double-line USIR watermark (R139), perforated 11.*

RCT1

CIGTTE

TUBES

		UnFVF	UseFVF
RCT1			
1¢	**rose**	.75	.25

1919. ISSUE Same, *perforated 10.*

		UnFVF	UseFVF
RCT2			
1¢	**rose**	30.00	10.00

1933. ISSUE Large numerals in center and inscribed "Cigarette Tubes, Series of 1933." Size: 40 x 20 1/2mm. *Double-line USIR watermark (R139), perforated 11.*

RCT3

		UnFVF	UseFVF
RCT3			
1¢	**rose**	2.50	1.00
RCT4			
2¢	**rose**	7.50	2.00

Potato Stamps

1935. ISSUE Portrait of a girl. *Unwatermarked, perforated 11.* Potato Stamps were discontinued Jan. 6, 1936, when the Agricultural Adjustment Act of Dec. 1, 1935, was discontinued.

RPS1

		UnFVF	UseFVF
RPS1			
3/4¢	**rose pink**	.30	
RPS2			
1-1/2¢	**black brown**	.75	

No.	Value	Color	UnFVF	UseFVF
RPS3	**2-1/4¢**	**yellow green**	.75	
RPS4	**3¢**	**pale violet**	.75	
RPS5	**3-3/4¢**	**olive**	.75	
RPS6	**7-1/2¢**	**orange brown**	1.50	
RPS7	**11-1/4¢**	**deep orange**	2.00	
RPS8	**18-3/4¢**	**violet brown**	4.50	
RPS9	**37-1/2¢**	**orange**	4.50	
RPS10	**75¢**	**blue**	4.50	
RPS11	**93-3/4¢**	**lake**	7.50	
RPS12	**$1.12-1/2¢**	**green**	12.50	
RPS13	**$1.50**	**brown**	12.50	

Tobacco Sale Tax Stamps

1934-35. Issue Documentary Stamps of 1917 overprinted "TOBACCO SALE TAX" in two horizontal lines except on $20 value where it is vertical, reading up. *Double line USIR watermark, perforated 11.*

No.	Value	Color	UnFVF	UseFVF
RTS1	**1¢**	**rose**	.40	.20
RTS2	**2¢**	**rose**	.40	.20
RTS3	**5¢**	**rose**	1.00	.30
RTS4	**10¢**	**rose**	1.35	.30
RTS5	**25¢**	**rose**	4.00	1.50
RTS6	**50¢**	**rose**	4.00	1.50
RTS7	**$1**	**green**	8.00	1.75
RTS8	**$2**	**rose**	15.00	2.00
RTS9	**$5**	**blue**	22.50	4.00
RTS10	**$10**	**yellow**	35.00	10.00
RTS11	**$20**	**olive**	85.00	15.00

Playing Card Stamps

These Revenue Stamps were placed on packaged decks of playing cards, first applied during the War Between the States.

1862-63. Playing Card Issue Designs of the first revenue issue, inscribed "PLAYING CARDS." *Unwatermarked, perforated 12.*

No.	Value	Color	Perf	Part Perf	Imperf
RPC1	**1¢**	**rose red**	100.00	600.00	800.00

RPC2 *George Washington*

No.	Value	Color	Perf	Part Perf	Imperf
RPC2	**2¢**	**light blue**	3.50	140.00	
RPC3	**2¢**	**orange yellow**	30.00		
RPC4	**3¢**	**dark yellow green**	100.00		

RPC5 *George Washington*

No.	Value	Color	Perf	Part Perf	Imperf
RPC5	**4¢**	**gray brown**	375.00		
RPC6	**5¢**	**rose red**	15.00		

1894-96. Playing Card Issue Inscribed "ON HAND," *unwatermarked roulletted 5 1/2.*

RPC7

No.	Value	Color	UnFVF	UseFVF
RPC7	**2¢**	**lake**	.60	.30

1894-96. Playing Card Issue Inscribed "ACT OF" instead of "ON HAND," *unwatermarked, rouletted 5 1/2.*

RPC8

No.	Value	Color	UnFVF	UseFVF
RPC8	**2¢**	**ultramarine**	12.50	2.00
		v. blue		3.00

1896-99. Playing Card Issue Same design as No. RPC8, *Double-line USIR watermark, rouletted 5 1/2 or 7.*

No.	Value	Color	UnFVF	UseFVF
RPC9	**2¢**	**pale blue**	4.50	.40
		v. ultramarine	5.00	1.20

1902. Playing Card Issue Same design as No. RPC8, *perforated 12.*

No.	Value	Color	UnFVF	UseFVF
RPC10	**2¢**	**dark blue**		35.00

This stamp was first used in 1902 although it will sometimes be found canceled 1899 from an old canceling plate.

1917. Playing Card Issue Stamp No. RPC9, handstamped in rose. *Rouletted 7.*

The overprint on No. RPC11 was applied at an Internal Revenue office; those on Nos. RPC12-RPC19 and on No. RPC21 were applied by the manufacturers and, together with the manufacturer's initials, dates, etc., formed a combination of overprint and cancellation.

ACT OF 1917
7
CENTS

RPC11 *Overprint*

No.	Value	Color	UnFVF	UseFVF
RPC11	**7¢ on 2¢**	**ultramarine**	600.00	400.00

1917. Playing Card Issue Stamp No. RPC9 with various overprints. *Rouletted 7.*

17 RPC12 *Overprinted "17" to indicate that the 7¢ tax had been paid according to the Act of 1917.*

RPC12	UnFVF	UseFVF
7¢ on 2¢ blue		35.00
a. Inverted overprint		35.00

7 RPC13 *Overprint*

RPC13	UnFVF	UseFVF
7¢ on 2¢ blue		500.00
a. Inverted overprint	375.00	375.00

7 CTS. RPC14 *Overprint reading up in red.*

RPC14	UnFVF	UseFVF
7¢ on 2¢ blue		800.00

7 CENTS RPC15 *Overprint reading up in black, violet or red.*

RPC15	UnFVF	UseFVF
7¢ on 2¢ blue		7.50
a. Overprint reading down		9.00

There are many varieties of No. RPC15 such as "double surcharge" and "7 omitted." All command premiums.

7c RPC16 *Overprinted in carmine.*

RPC16	UnFVF	UseFVF
7¢ on 2¢ blue		50.00
a. Inverted overprint		30.00

1918. Playing Card Issue New design, inscribed "Playing Cards-Class A." *Double-line USIR watermark, imperforate. Size 21 x 40mm.*

RPC17, RPC18

RPC17	UnFVF	UseFVF
7¢ pale blue	40.00	27.50

1918-19. Playing Card Issue Same as No. RPC17 but private roulette 14.

RPC18	UnFVF	UseFVF
7¢ pale blue		200.00

Both RPC17 and RPC18 served as 7¢ stamps when used before April 1, 1919, and as 8¢ stamps after that date.

7 CENTS RPC17 *Overprinted "7 CENTS" in violet, red or black, private roulette 9 1/2.*

RPC19	UnFVF	UseFVF
7¢ pale blue		35.00
a. Inverted surcharge		30.00

1919. Playing Card Issue Stamp No. RPC9 overprinted with various overprints. *Rouletted 7.*

REVENUE ACT OF 1918 8 CENTS RPC20 *Magenta or rose hand-stamp applied at an Internal Revenue office.*

RPC20	UnFVF	UseFVF
8¢ on 2¢ dark blue		75.00

8 RPC21 *Inverted carmine overprint.*

RPC21	UnFVF	UseFVF
8¢ on 2¢ blue (inverted)		500.00

8 Cts. RPC22 *Carmine overprint.*

RPC22	UnFVF	UseFVF
8¢ on 2¢ blue	100.00	.60

1922. Playing Card Issue Inscribed "Class A." *Double-line USIR watermark, rouletted 7. Size: 19 x 22mm. No denomination but valued at 8¢.*

RPC23

RPC23	UnFVF	UseFVF
8¢ pale blue	15.00	1.00

1922. Playing Card Issue Stamp No. RPC23 overprinted in carmine, blue or black.

8c RPC24 *Overprint*

RPC24	UnFVF	UseFVF
8¢ pale blue		30.00
a. Inverted overprint		30.00

1924. Playing Card Issue *Flat Plate printing, rouletted 7.*

RPC25-RPC28 *Numeral in center of design, "CENTS" in lower ribbon. Double-line USIR watermark (R139).*

RPC25	UnFVF	UseFVF
10¢ blue	10.00	.30

1926. Playing Card Issue *Rotary Press Coil Stamp, perforated 10 vertically.*

RPC26	UnFVF	UseFVF
10¢ blue		.20

1927. Playing Card Issue *Flat Plate printing, perforated 11.*

RPC27	UnFVF	UseFVF
10¢ blue	20.00	4.50

1929. Playing Card Issue *Flat Plate printing, perforated 10.*

RPC28	UnFVF	UseFVF
10¢ blue	10.00	3.50

1929. Playing Card Issue *Rotary Press Coil stamp, perforated 10 horizontally.*

RPC29 *Size 37 1/2 x 20mm.*

RPC29		UnFVF	UseFVF
10¢	light blue		.20

1929. Playing Card Issue *Flat Plate printing, perforated 10.*

RPC30		UnFVF	UseFVF
10¢	blue	10.00	1.00

1929. Playing Card Issue *Flat Plate printing, perforated 11.*

RPC31		UnFVF	UseFVF
10¢	blue	10.00	1.00

1940. Playing Card Issue Inscribed "PLAYING CARDS PACK," *size 20 x 22 1/2mm, rotary press coil stamp, perforated 10 vertically.*

RPC32

RPC32		MNHVF	UseVF
1 Pack	blue		.35

1940. Playing Card Issue *Rotary Press Coil stamp, perforated 10 horizontally.*

RPC33-RPC35 *Inscribed "PLAYING CARDS PACK," double-line USIR watermark (R139), size: 38 x 20mm.*

RPC33		MNHVF	UseVF
1 Pack	blue	2.50	.20

1940. Playing Card Issue *Flat Plate printing, perforated 11.*

RPC34		MNHVF	UseVF
1 Pack	light blue	4.50	.60

1940. Playing Card Issue *Rotary Press printing, perforated 10 x 11.*

RPC35		MNHVF	UseVF
1 Pack	light blue	160.00	75.00

The tax on playing cards was repealed effective June 22, 1965.

Wine Stamps

1914. Wine Stamp Issue These stamps were issued to pay the tax on cordials and wines. A large white numeral is in the center of the design. *Single line USPS watermark, offset printed, perforated 10. Size of design, 19 1/2 x 22 1/4mm.*

RW1-RW14

		UnFVF	UseFVF
RW1			
1/4¢	gray green	.50	.40
RW2			
1/2¢	gray green	.30	.20
RW3			
1¢	gray green	.40	.25
RW4			
1-1/2¢	gray green	2.00	1.25
RW5			
2¢	gray green	2.50	2.50
RW6			
3¢	gray green	2.50	1.00
RW7			
4¢	gray green	2.25	1.25
RW8			
5¢	gray green	.80	.40
RW9			
6¢	gray green	6.00	3.00
RW10			
8¢	gray green	3.25	1.25
RW11			
10¢	gray green	3.25	2.50
RW12			
20¢	gray green	4.00	1.50
RW13			
24¢	gray green	12.50	7.00
RW14			
40¢	gray green	2.50	.50

1914. Wine Stamp Issue Imperforate, size: 47 x 40mm.

RW15

RW15		UnFVF	UseFVF
$2	pale green	7.00	.20

1914-18. Wine Stamp Issue Same designs as 1914, *double-line USIR watermark, perforated 10.*

		UnFVF	UseFVF
RW16			
1/4¢	pale green	5.25	4.25
RW17			
1/2¢	pale green	3.50	2.50
RW18			
1¢	pale green	.25	.20
RW19			
1-1/2¢	pale green	42.50	30.00
RW20			
2¢	pale green	.25	.20
RW21			
3¢	pale green	2.25	1.50
RW22			
4¢	pale green	.75	.90
RW23			
5¢	pale green	10.00	9.00
RW24			
6¢	pale green	.40	.25
RW25			
8¢	pale green	1.75	.40
RW26			
10¢	pale green	.40	.20
RW27			
20¢	pale green	.60	.30
RW28			
24¢	pale green	12.50	.65
RW29			
40¢	pale green	27.50	10.00

1914-18 Wine Stamp Issue *Imperforate.*

RW30		UnFVF	UseFVF
$2	pale green	27.50	2.75

1914-18. Wine Stamp Issue *Perforated 11.*

RW31		UnFVF	UseFVF
2¢	pale green	70.00	80.00

1916-18. Wine Stamp Issue New design, inscribed "Series of 1916," *double-line USIR watermark.*

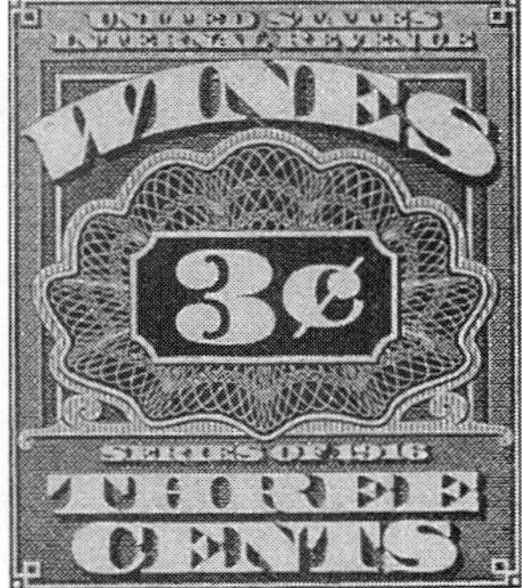

RW32-RW52 *Size 40 x 47mm, offset printing, rouletted 3-1/2.*

No.	Value	Color	UnFVF	UseFVF
RW32	1¢	green	.30	.30
RW33	3¢	green	4.25	3.75
RW34	4¢	green	.25	.25
RW35	6¢	green	1.25	.65
RW36	7-1/2¢	green	7.25	3.50
RW37	10¢	green	1.00	.35
RW38	12¢	green	2.75	3.50
RW39	15¢	green	1.50	1.50
RW40	18¢	green	22.50	20.00
RW41	20¢	green	.25	.25
RW42	24¢	green	3.75	2.75
RW43	30¢	green	3.00	2.25
RW44	36¢	green	17.50	12.50
RW45	50¢	green	.50	.40
RW46	60¢	green	3.75	1.75
RW47	72¢	green	30.00	25.00
RW48	80¢	green	.60	.50
RW49	$1.20	green	6.50	5.50
RW50	$1.44	green	8.50	2.75
RW51	$1.60	green	22.50	15.00
RW52	$2	green	1.60	1.40

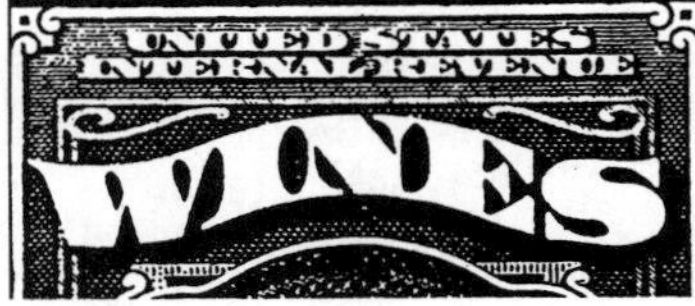

RW53-55
Flat Plate printing.

No.	Value	Color	UnFVF	UseFVF
RW53	$4	green	.80	.20
RW54	$4.80	green	3.00	2.75
RW55	$9.60	green	1.10	.25

RW56-59
Size 51 x 81mm, perforated 12 at left, Flat Plate printed.

No.	Value	Color	UnFVF	UseFVF
RW56	$20	green	80.00	35.00
RW57	$40	green	165.00	45.00
RW58	$50	green	55.00	40.00
RW59	$100	green	225.00	130.00

1933-34. Wine Stamp Issue Designs of 1916-18, slightly smaller in size. *Offset, double-line USIR watermark (R139), rouletted 7.*

No.	Value	Color	UnFVF	UseFVF
RW60	1¢	pale green	2.75	.25
RW61	3¢	pale green	7.00	2.25
RW62	4¢	pale green	1.25	.25
RW63	6¢	pale green	10.00	4.50
RW64	7-1/2¢	pale green	2.75	.40
RW65	10¢	pale green	1.75	.20
RW66	12¢	pale green	8.00	4.00
RW67	15¢	pale green	3.75	.25
RW68	20¢	pale green	4.50	.20
RW69	24¢	pale green	4.50	.20
RW70	30¢	pale green	4.50	.20
RW71	36¢	pale green	10.00	.50
RW72	50¢	pale green	4.00	.20
RW73	60¢	pale green	7.00	.20
RW74	72¢	pale green	12.00	.25
RW75	80¢	pale green	12.00	.20
RW76	$1.20	pale green	9.00	1.25
RW77	$1.44	pale green	12.00	3.50
RW78	$1.60	pale green	300.00	150.00
RW79	$2	pale green	32.50	3.50

1933-34. Wine Stamp Issue Flat Plate printing.

No.	Value	Color	UnFVF	UseFVF
RW80	$4	pale green	27.50	6.50
RW81	$4.80	pale green	27.50	12.50
RW82	$9.60	pale green	125.00	75.00

1934-40. Wine Stamp Issue New designs inscribed "Series of 1934," *double-line USIR watermark (R139). Size 28 x 25mm, offset, rouletted 7, gum.*

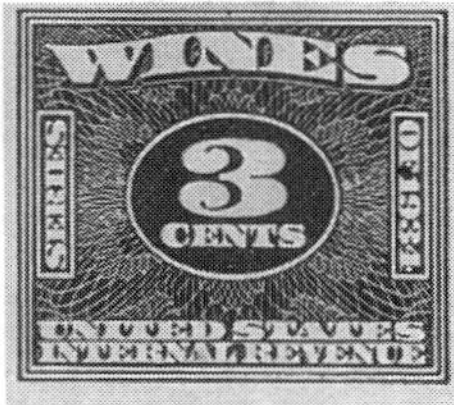

RW83-RW102

		UnFVF	UseFVF
RW83			
1/5¢	**pale green**	.70	.20
RW84			
1/2¢	**pale green**	.50	.35
RW85			
1¢	**pale green**	.60	.20
RW86			
1-1/4¢	**pale green**	.80	.70
RW87			
1-1/2¢	**pale green**	5.50	5.00
RW88			
2¢	**pale green**	1.50	.60
RW89			
2-1/2¢	**pale green**	1.50	.40
RW90			
3¢	**pale green**	4.50	3.75
RW91			
4¢	**pale green**	2.25	.20
RW92			
5¢	**pale green**	.55	.20
RW93			
6¢	**pale green**	1.65	.45
RW94			
7-1/2¢	**pale green**	2.00	.20
RW95			
10¢	**pale green**	.40	.20
RW96			
12¢	**pale green**	1.30	.20
RW97			
14-2/5¢	**pale green**	125.00	2.75
RW98			
15¢	**pale green**	.60	.20
RW99			
18¢	**pale green**	1.25	.20
RW100			
20¢	**pale green**	1.00	.20
RW101			
24¢	**pale green**	1.75	.20
RW102			
30¢	**pale green**	1.25	.20

RW103-RW109 Inscribed "Series of 1934." Size about 39 x 46mm, rouletted 7 issued without gum.

		UnFVF	UseFVF
RW103			
40¢	**pale green**	3.00	.20
RW104			
43-1/5¢	**pale green**	12.50	1.75
RW105			
48¢	**pale green**	12.50	1.00
RW106			
$1	**pale green**	15.00	10.00
RW107			
$1.50	**pale green**	27.50	12.50

1934-40. Wine Stamp Issue Intaglio, Flat Plate printing, size: 30 x 46mm. Perforated initial cancelled are worth half used price.

		UnFVF	UseFVF
RW108			
$2.50	**pale green**	30.00	15.00
RW109			
$5	**pale green**	25.00	7.00

1934. Wine Stamp Issue *Size 51 x 81mm, Flat Plate printing, perforated 12 at left.*

		UnFVF	UseFVF
RW110			
$20	**yellow green**		1,750.00
RW111			
$40	**yellow green**		3,500.00
RW112			
$50	**yellow green**		2,000.00
	a. perforated 12 1/2		1,500.00
RW113			
$100	**yellow green**	950.00	750.00
	a. perforated 12 1/2		350.00

1941-52. Wine Stamp Issue New design, inscribed "Series of 1941." The values are printed in black. *Double-line USIR watermark, size 28 x 25mm, offset printing, rouletted 7. Issued without gum.*

RW114-RW165

		MNHVF	UseVF
RW114			
1/5¢	**green**	.50	.40
RW115			
1/4¢	**green**	1.75	1.50
RW116			
1/2¢	**green**	2.25	1.75
RW117			
1¢	**green**	1.00	.65
RW117A			
1-7/10¢	**green**		10,000.00

RW118 is not assigned.

		MNHVF	UseVF
RW119			
2¢	**green**	4.50	4.50
RW120			
3¢	**green**	4.50	4.50
RW121			
3-2/5¢	**green**	50.00	45.00
RW121A			
3-1/2¢	**green**		6,500.00
RW122			
3-3/4¢	**green**	7.50	5.50
RW123			
4¢	**green**	3.25	2.75
RW124			
5¢	**green**	2.25	2.00
RW125			
6¢	**green**	2.75	2.25

RW126 is not assigned.

		MNHVF	UseVF
RW127			
7¢	**green**	5.25	4.25
RW128			
7-1/2¢	**green**	7.50	4.50
RW129			
8¢	**green**	4.50	3.50
RW130			
8-1/2¢	**green**	27.50	17.50
RW131			
9¢	**green**	8.00	7.50
RW132			
10¢	**green**	4.25	.75

RW133 is not assigned.

		MNHVF	UseVF
RW134			
11-1/4¢	**green**	4.50	4.50
RW135			
12¢	**green**	6.50	5.50
RW136			
13-2/5¢	**green**	90.00	75.00
RW137			
14¢	**green**	22.50	20.00
RW138			
15¢	**green**	4.50	3.50
RW139			
16¢	**green**	8.50	6.50
RW140			
17¢	**green**	15.00	12.50
RW141			
19-1/5¢	**green**	125.00	6.50
RW142			
20¢	**green**	5.50	1.50
RW143			
20-2/5¢	**green**	100.00	50.00
RW144			
24¢	**green**	3.75	.20
RW145			
28¢	**green**	1,750.00	1,250.00
RW146			
30¢	**green**	1.00	.20
RW147			

32¢	green	125.00	7.00
RW148		MNHVF	UseVF
33-1/2¢	green	80.00	65.00
RW149		MNHVF	UseVF
36¢	green	2.75	.20
RW150		MNHVF	UseVF
38-1/4¢	green	110.00	80.00
RW151		MNHVF	UseVF
40¢	green	2.25	.20
RW152		MNHVF	UseVF
40-4/5¢	green	3.25	.50
RW153		MNHVF	UseVF
45¢	green	5.00	.20
RW154		MNHVF	UseVF
48¢	green	12.50	5.00
RW155		MNHVF	UseVF
50¢	green	8.00	6.50
RW156		MNHVF	UseVF
51¢	green	3.75	1.00
RW157		MNHVF	UseVF
60¢	green	3.00	.20
RW158		MNHVF	UseVF
67¢	green	10.00	3.50
RW159		MNHVF	UseVF
68¢	green	3.00	.50
RW160		MNHVF	UseVF
72¢	green	9.00	.80
RW161		MNHVF	UseVF
80¢	green	250.00	9.00
RW162		MNHVF	UseVF
80-2/5¢	green	110.00	85.00
RW163		MNHVF	UseVF
84¢	green		55.00
RW164		MNHVF	UseVF
90¢	green	15.00	.20
RW165		MNHVF	UseVF
96¢	green	10.00	.20

RW167-RW209 Size 39 x 45 1/2mm. Engraved, rouletted 7.

RW166		MNHVF	UseVF
$1	green	2.00	.15
RW167		MNHVF	UseVF
$1.20	green	2.75	.15
RW168		MNHVF	UseVF
$1.44	green	1.00	.15
RW169		MNHVF	UseVF
$1.50	green	60.00	30.00
RW170		MNHVF	UseVF
$1.50-3/4	green	45.00	35.00
RW171		MNHVF	UseVF
$1.60	green	5.00	.65
RW172		MNHVF	UseVF
$1.60-4/5	**green,** (Denomination letters 1mm high, bottom "5" is oval)	4.25	.50
	Perforated, initials		7.50
	v. "Dolllar" design error	37.50	15.00
	Bottom of "5" almost circular	350.00	150.00
RW173		MNHVF	UseVF
$1.60-4/5	**green,** (Denomination letters 1 1/2mm high, bottom of "5" almost closes to a circle)	30.00	6.00
	Bottom of "5" is oval	75.00	25.00

1941-51. Wine Stamp Issue *Denomination 28 1/2mm long.*

RW174		MNHVF	UseVF
$1.68	green	85.00	45.00
	Perforated initials		32.50

> Users of this catalog are invited to write to us if they have information they feel will supplement or correct any material contained herein. All such communications will be answered.

RW175

RW175		MNHVF	UseVF
$1.80	green	2.75	.20
RW176		MNHVF	UseVF
$1.88-3/10	green	200.00	65.00
	Perforated initials		30.00
RW177		MNHVF	UseVF
$1.92	green	45.00	35.00

RW178 is not assigned.

RW179		MNHVF	UseVF
$2.01	green	3.25	.60
RW180		MNHVF	UseVF
$2.40	green	8.00	.75
RW181		MNHVF	UseVF
$2.68	green	3.25	1.10
RW182		MNHVF	UseVF
$3	green	65.00	35.00
RW183		MNHVF	UseVF
$3.36	green	70.00	25.00
RW184		MNHVF	UseVF
$3.60	green	125.00	5.50
RW185		MNHVF	UseVF
$4	green	27.50	4.50
RW186		MNHVF	UseVF
$4.08	green	60.00	30.00
RW187		MNHVF	UseVF
$4.80	green	115.00	2.50
RW188		MNHVF	UseVF
$5	green	12.50	8.50
RW189		MNHVF	UseVF
$5.76	green	210.00	100.00

RW190-RW192 are not assigned.

RW193		MNHVF	UseVF
$7.20	green	18.00	.40

RW194 is not assigned.

RW195		MNHVF	UseVF
$8.16	green	15.00	6.00
RW195A		MNHVF	UseVF
$9.60	green		3,000.00
RW196		MNHVF	UseVF
$10	green	175.00	135.00
RW197		MNHVF	UseVF
$20	green	100.00	65.00
RW198		MNHVF	UseVF
$50	green	100.00	65.00
	Perforated initials		17.50
RW199		MNHVF	UseVF
$100	green	275.00	27.50
	Perforated initials		11.50
RW200		MNHVF	UseVF
$200	green	135.00	17.50
	Perforated initials		7.50
RW200B		MNHVF	UseVF
$400	green		8,000.00
RW201		MNHVF	UseVF
$500	green		135.00
	Perforated initials		30.00
RW202		MNHVF	UseVF
$600	green		110.00
	Perforated		
RW203		MNHVF	UseVF
$900	green		4,000.00
	Perforated initials		2,500.00

		MNHVF	UseVF
RW204			
$1,000	**green**		150.00
RW205			
$2,000	**green**		1,250.00
RW206			
$3,000	**green**		180.00
RW207			
$4,000	**green**		700.00

1941-51. Wine Stamp Issue Denominations spelled out in one line.

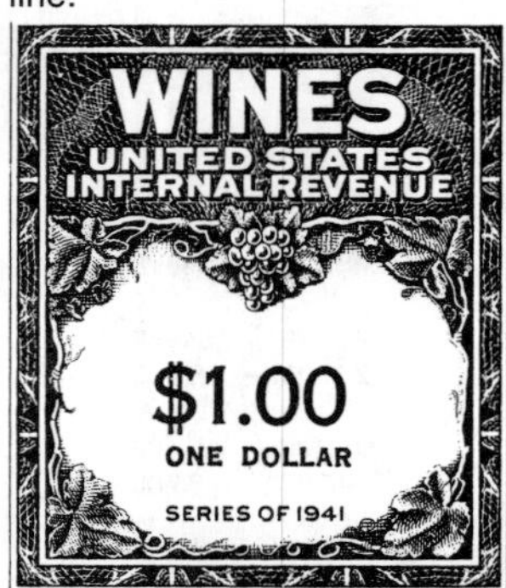

RW208

		MNHVF	UseVF
RW208			
$1	**green**	3.50	1.25
RW209			
$2	**green**	6.00	1.75
RW210			
$4	**green**	800.00	350.00
	Perforated initials		150.00
RW211			
$5	**green**		75.00
RW212			
$6	**green**		350.00
RW213			
$7	**green**	40.00	60.00
RW214			
$8	**green**	300.00	800.00
RW215			
$10	**green**	8.50	4.00
	Perforated initials		1.75
RW216			
$20	**green**	17.50	3.50
	Perforated initials		1.50
RW217			
$30	**green**	900.00	700.00

Wine stamps were discontinued Jan. 1, 1955.

Boating Stamps

1960. Federal Boating Stamps To quote from the regulation: "Effective April 1, 1960, boats of more than 10 horsepower operated on waters of the United States must be numbered under the Federal Boating Act of 1958. Boating stamps available from April 1 on are available in two denominations. The $3 denomination will cover the filing of an application and will be valid for a period of three years. A $1 stamp will cover charges for the reissuance of a lost or destroyed certificate of number."

Offset, with serial number printed by letterpress; unwatermarked, rouletted.

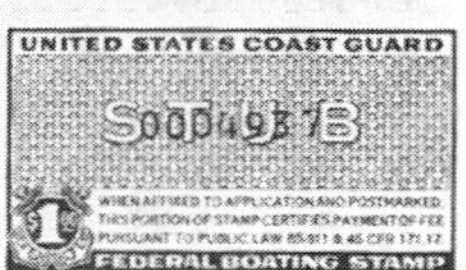

FB1 *Motor boat in action*

		MNHVF	UseVF
FB1			
$1	**carmine red, number in black**	35.00	—
	Plate block of 4	150.00	
FB2			
$3	**blue, number in red**	50.00	30.00
	Plate block of 4	210.00	

Postal Notes

Fractional currency was retired in 1876. To replace it, the Post Office Department issued the first U.S. Postal Note on Sept. 3, 1883. During the next 11 years, the Post Office Department used three different contract printers to produce seven different postal note designs. Contract periods were four years. The Homer Lee Bank Note Company contract extended from 1883-1887, the American Bank Note Company contract from 1887-1891 and the Dunlap and Clarke contract from 1891-1894. In total, 70.8 million Postal Notes were issued; at least 1,200 are known to survive.

Postal notes were issued for values up to $4.99. The postal note fee was 3¢. The last day of use was June 30, 1894.

Values are for used notes from common states in fine condition without tears, creases or stains. Territorial notes, notes from some Western and Southern states and notes with special features, such as low serial numbers or high values, command premiums.

1883. Homer Lee Bank Note Co. New York, approximately 155x85mm, date and 3¢ fee shield at left. The heavy ornate engraving often made cancels difficult to distinguish.

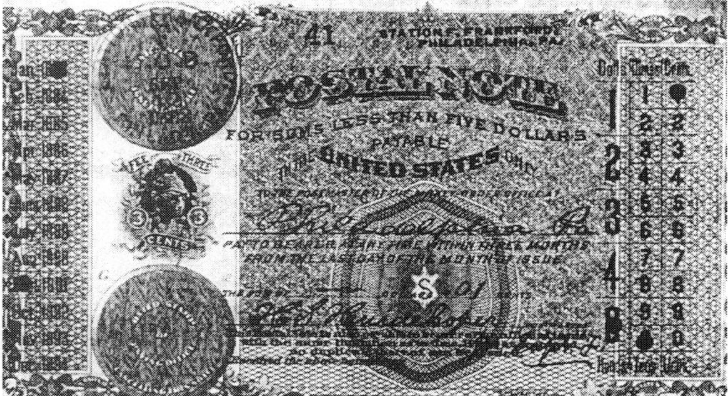

PN1 *(front)*

PN1 *(back)*

		Fine
PN1	**black on yellow;** reverse green on yellow (Sept. 3, 1883)	90.00

1884. Homer Lee Bank Note Co. imprint with red serial numbers and blue places of issue. The "pay at" city notation was written in by hand. Approximately 132x87mm, as are all succeeding notes. Dollar coupons at left were detached to indicate the dollar amount of the note; 3¢ fee shield at right.

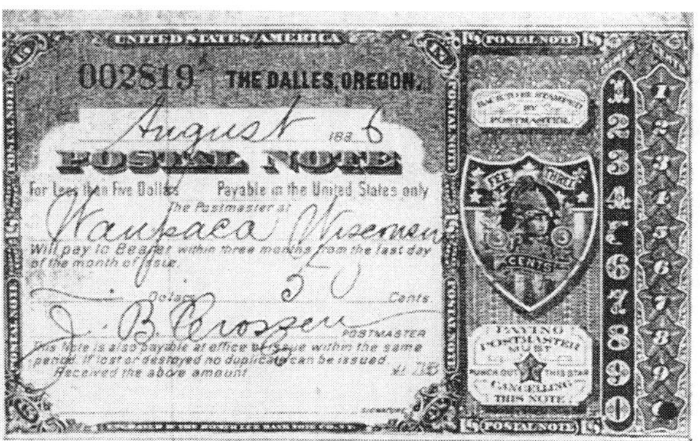

PN2 *(front)*

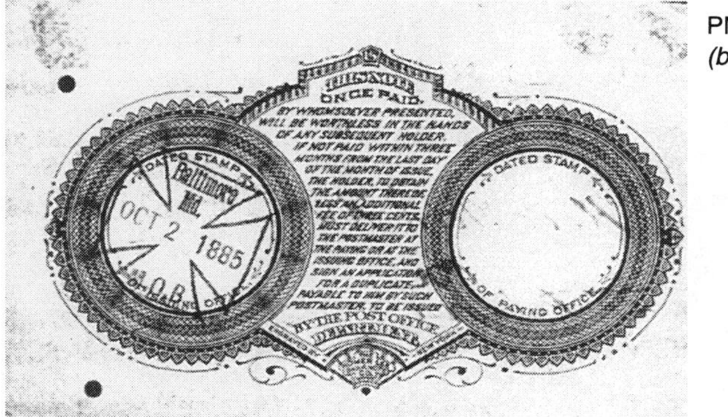

PN2 *(back)*

		Fine
PN2	**black on white;** reverse blue on white	125.00

1887. Homer Lee Bank Note Co. imprint. The pay at city notation was replaced with a handstamped "Any Money Order Office."

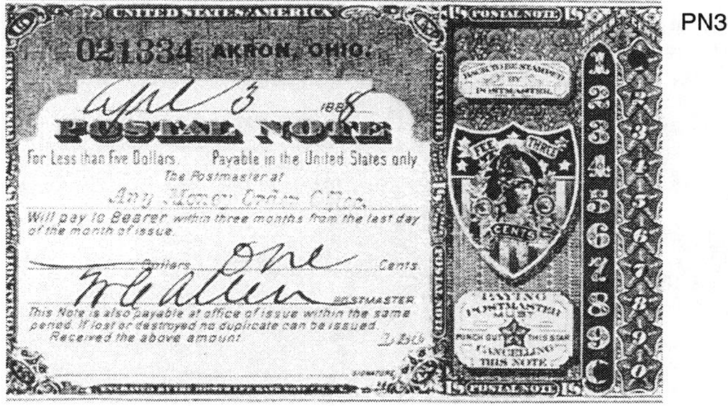

PN3

Each entry in this catalog has been double-checked for accuracy, but mistakes may creep into any human endeavor, and we ask your assistance in eliminating them. Please call the attention of the editors to any errors in stamp desciption found in this catalog. Send your comments to :
Minkus Catalog Editor
Krause Publications
700 East State ST.
Iola WI 54990

PN3	Fine
black on white; reverse blue on white	150.00

1887. Homer Lee Bank Note Co. imprint "Any Money Order Office" is printed. Redesigned text on obverse and reverse caused by changes in law, dated Jan. 3, 1887.

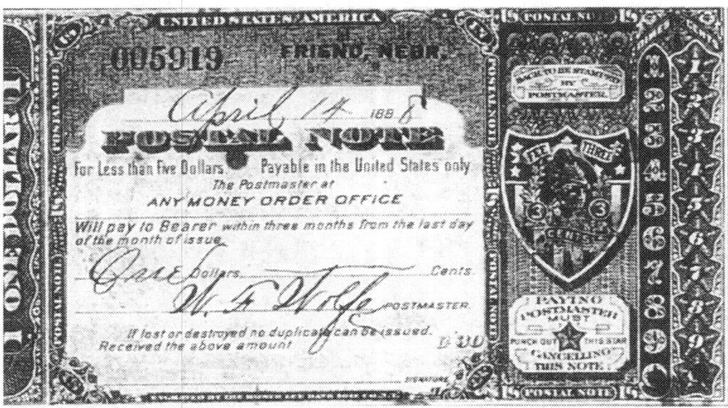

PN4 *(front)*

PN4 *(back)*

PN4	Fine
black on white; reverse blue on white	300.00

1888. American Bank Note Co. imprint. Engraved by Thomas F. Morris. Among other changes, "Any Money Order Office" line is more ornate. *"Engraved & Printed by the American Bank Note Co., N.Y." printed at bottom obverse.*

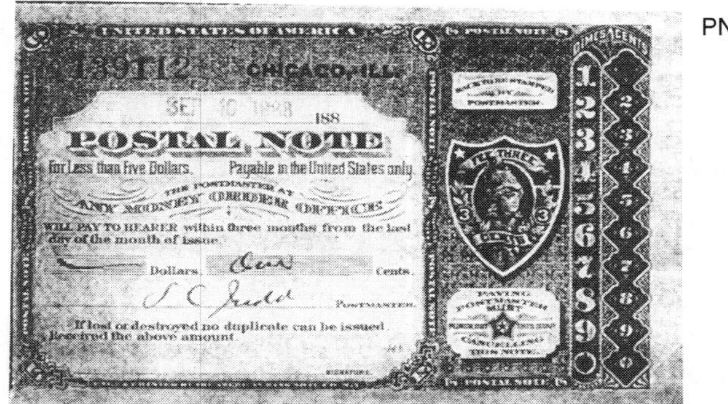

PN5

PN5	Fine
black on white; reverse blue on white *(Sept. 3, 1887)*	125.00
"1890" handwritten to replace "188_"	—

1890. American Bank Note Co. "189_" in date line.

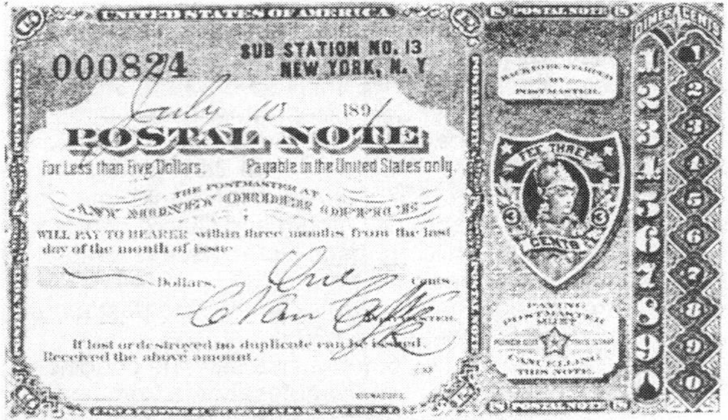

PN6 *(front)*

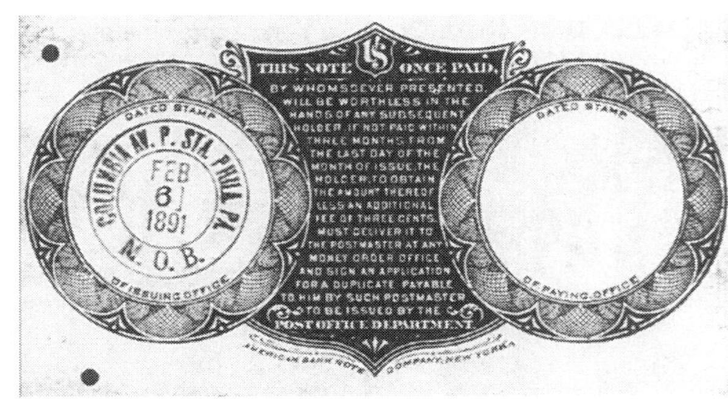

PN6 *(back)*

PN6	Fine
black on white; reverse blue on white	150.00

1892. Dunlap and Clarke imprint, identical to ABNC version except "Dunlap and Clarke, Philadelphia, Pa." replaces American Bank Note imprint at bottom obverse, and "American Bank Note Company, New York" removed from bottom reverse.

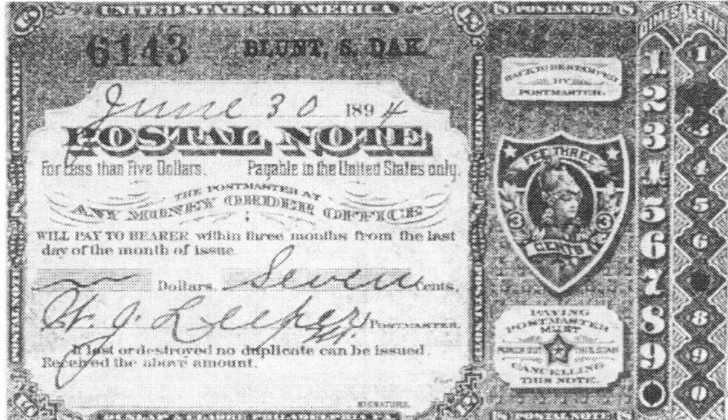

PN7 *(front)*

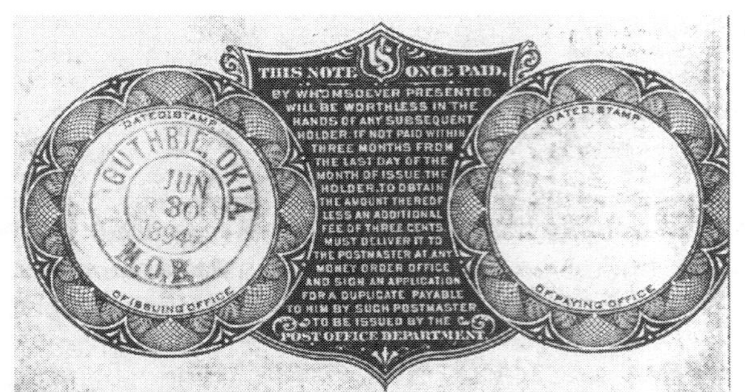

PN7 *(back)*

PN7	Fine
black on white; reverse blue on white *(Sept. 3, 1891)*	60.00

Postal Note Stamps

1945. Postal Note Issue Postal Note stamps were issued Feb. 1, 1945, to supplement the Postal Money Order service. The 18 denominations of stamps, all in the same basic design, were affixed to postal note forms and canceled to indicate the amount less than a dollar. No more than two stamps were needed to show any amount from 1¢ to 99¢. Postal Notes were discontinued effective March 31, 1951. *Intaglio, perforated 11 x 10 1/2.*

PO1-PO18

PO1		MNHVF	UseVF
1¢	**black**	.25	.20
	Plate block of 4	3.00	
	FDC *(Feb. 1, 1945)*		1.00

Postal Note Stamps were issued Feb. 1, 1945, to supplement the Postal Money Order service. The 18 denominations of stamps, all in the same basic design, were affixed to postal note forms and canceled to indicate the amount less than a dollar. No more than two stamps were needed to show any amount from 1¢ to 99¢. Postal Notes were discontinued effective March 31, 1951. Intaglio, perforated 11 x 10 1/2.

PO2		MNHVF	UseVF
2¢	**black**	.25	.20
	Plate block of 4	3.00	
	FDC *(Feb. 1, 1945)*		1.00

PO3		MNHVF	UseVF
3¢	**black**	.25	.20
	Plate block of 4	3.75	
	FDC *(Feb. 1, 1945)*		1.00

PO4		MNHVF	UseVF
4¢	**black**	.30	.20
	Plate block of 4	4.50	
	FDC *(Feb. 1, 1945)*		1.00

PO5		MNHVF	UseVF
5¢	**black**	.40	.20
	Plate block of 4	6.00	
	FDC *(Feb. 1, 1945)*		1.00

PO6		MNHVF	UseVF
6¢	**black**	.45	.20
	Plate block of 4	6.75	
	FDC *(Feb. 1, 1945)*		1.00

PO7		MNHVF	UseVF
7¢	**black**	.55	.20
	Plate block of 4	8.25	
	FDC *(Feb. 1, 1945)*		1.00

PO8		MNHVF	UseVF
8¢	**black**	.70	.20
	Plate block of 4	10.00	
	FDC *(Feb. 1, 1945)*		1.00

PO9		MNHVF	UseVF
9¢	**black**	.75	.20
	Plate block of 4	11.00	
	FDC *(Feb. 1, 1945)*		1.00

PO10		MNHVF	UseVF
10¢	**black**	1.00	.20
	Plate block of 4	14.00	
	FDC *(Feb. 1, 1945)*		1.00

PO11		MNHVF	UseVF
20¢	**black**	1.75	.20
	Plate block of 4	27.50	
	FDC *(Feb. 1, 1945)*		1.00

PO12		MNHVF	UseVF
30¢	**black**	2.50	.20
	Plate block of 4	37.50	
	FDC *(Feb. 1, 1945)*		1.00

PO13		MNHVF	UseVF
40¢	**black**	3.00	.20
	Plate block of 4	45.00	
	FDC *(Feb. 1, 1945)*		1.00

PO14		MNHVF	UseVF
50¢	**black**	3.50	.20
	Plate block of 4	52.50	
	FDC *(Feb. 1, 1945)*		1.00

PO15		MNHVF	UseVF
60¢	**black**	4.75	.20
	Plate block of 4	70.00	
	FDC *(Feb. 1, 1945)*		1.00

PO16		MNHVF	UseVF
70¢	**black**	5.25	.20
	Plate block of 4	80.00	
	FDC *(Feb. 1, 1945)*		1.00

PO17		MNHVF	UseVF
80¢	**black**	6.50	.20
	Plate block of 4	95.00	
	FDC *(Feb. 1, 1945)*		1.00

PO18		MNHVF	UseVF
90¢	**black**	7.00	.20
	Plate block of 4	110.00	
	FDC *(Feb. 1, 1945)*		1.00

Migratory Bird Hunting Permit (Duck) Stamps

An act of Congress in March 1934 authorized the issue of receipts in the form of attractive stamps to license hunters, with the proceeds going to maintain waterfowl life in the United States. When J.N. "Ding" Darling, a newspaper editorial cartoonist and artist, also Pulitzer Prize winner, designed the first "duck" stamp, the beauty and novelty of it immediately appealed to stamp collectors.

The government was adamant that the stamp was for hunters only and had to be attached to a license. The hunter had to keep it intact for a whole year; it was not for collectors, but the pressure became too great to refuse, so 15 days before the first Duck stamp issue expired, the stamps were placed on sale for stamp collectors, and ever since philatelists have happily contributed "to the maintenance of waterfowl in the United States."

Designed by some of the finest artists, stamps of great beauty have resulted, and no page in a stamp album can be more beautiful than the Duck stamp page. All the stamps are inscribed "Migratory Bird Hunting Stamp," the first five read "Department of Agriculture," and after that "Department of the Interior." From 1946 on, all the stamps are inscribed on the back, "It is unlawful to hunt waterfowl unless you sign your name in ink on the face of the stamp."

The stamps are issued on July 1 of every year, and expire on June 30 of the following year. Each stamp reads "Void after June 30th 19-," with the dashes being the year of expiration. Stamps are *unwatermarked.*

Note: Plate blocks must have selvage on two sides.

Issued in pane of 28.

1934. MALLARD ISSUE designed by J. N. Darling. *Intaglio, unwatermarked, perforated 11.*

RH1

RH1		UnFVF	UseFVF
$1	**blue**	575.00	115.00
	Plate block of 6	10,000.00	
	v. Pair, imperforate	15,000.00	
	v1. Vertical pair, imperforate horizontally	—	

1935. CANVASBACK DUCK ISSUE by Frank W. Benson. *Intaglio, unwatermarked, perforated 11.*

RH2

RH2		UnFVF	UseFVF
$1	**crimson**	525.00	135.00
	Plate block of 6	9,000.00	

1936. CANADA GEESE ISSUE by Richard E. Bishop. *Intaglio, unwatermrked, perforated 11.*

RH3

RH3		UnFVF	UseFVF
$1	**brown black**	300.00	65.00
	Plate block of 6	2,500.00	

1937. SCAUP DUCKS ISSUE by J. D. Knap. *Intaglio, unwatermarked, perforated 11.*

RH4

RH4		UnFVF	UseFVF
$1	**dull green**	250.00	45.00
	Plate block of 6	2,250.00	

1938. PINTAIL DUCK ISSUE by Roland Clark. *Intaglio, unwatermarked, perforated 11.*

RH5

RH5		UnFVF	UseFVF
$1	**violet**	250.00	45.00
	Plate block of 6	2,750.00	

1939. GREEN-WINGED TEAL ISSUE by Lynn B. Hunt. *Intaglio, unwatermarked, perforated 11.*

RH6

RH6		UnFVF	UseFVF
$1	**sepia**	140.00	40.00
	Plate block of 6	1,500.00	

1940. BLACK MALLARD ISSUE by Francis L. Jacques. *Intaglio, unwatermarked, perforated 11.*

RH7

RH7		MNHVF	UseVF
$1	**black brown**	140.00	40.00
	Plate block of 6	1,200.00	

1941. RUDDY DUCKS ISSUE by E. R. Kalmbach. *Intaglio, unwatermarked, perforated 11.*

RH8

RH8		MNHVF	UseVF
$1	**red brown**	140.00	35.00
	Plate block of 6	1,200.00	

1942. BALDPATES ISSUE by A. Lassell Ripley. *Intaglio, unwatermarked, perforated 11.*

RH9

RH9		MNHVF	UseVF
$1	**sepia**	140.00	35.00
	Plate block of 6	1,200.00	

1943. Wood Duck Issue by Walter E. Bohl. *Intaglio, unwatermarked, perforated 11.*

RH10

RH10		MNHVF	UseVF
$1	**carmine red**	60.00	35.00
	Plate block of 6	450.00	

1944. White-Fronted Geese Issue by Walter A. Weber. *Intaglio, unwatermarked, perforated 11.*

RH11

RH11		MNHVF	UseVF
$1	**red orange**	60.00	25.00
	Plate block of 6	450.00	

1945. Shoveller Ducks Issue by Owen J. Gromme. *Intaglio, unwatermarked, perforated 11.*

RH12

RH12		MNHVF	UseVF
$1	**black**	45.00	18.00
	Plate block of 6	350.00	

1946. Redhead Ducks Issue by Robert W. Hines. *Intaglio, unwatermarked, perforated 11.*

RH13

RH13		MNHVF	UseVF
$1	**chestnut brown**	35.00	13.50
	Plate block of 6	300.00	
	a. rose red	—	

1947. Snow Geese Issue by Jack Murray. *Intaglio, unwatermarked, perforated 11.*

RH14

RH14		MNHVF	UseVF
$1	**black**	35.00	13.50
	Plate block of 6	300.00	

1948. Bufflehead Ducks Issue the first by Maynard Reece, whose artwork has appeared a record five times on federal Duck stamps. *Intaglio, unwatermarked, perforated 11.*

RH15

RH15		MNHVF	UseVF
$1	**light blue**	45.00	13.50
	Plate block of 6	300.00	

1949. Goldeneye Ducks Issue by "Roge" E. Preuss. *Intaglio, unwatermarked, perforated 11.*

RH16

RH16		MNHVF	UseVF
$2	**emerald**	50.00	13.50
	Plate block of 6	350.00	

1950. Trumpeter Swans Issue by Walter A. Weber. *Intaglio, unwatermarked, perforated 11.*

RH17

RH17		MNHVF	UseVF
$2	**violet**	60.00	10.00
	Plate block of 6	400.00	

1951. Gadwall Ducks Issue Maynard Reece. *Intaglio, unwatermarked, perforated 11.*

RH18

RH18		MNHVF	UseVF
$2	**gray black**	60.00	10.00
	Plate block of 6	400.00	

1952. Harlequin Ducks Issue by John H. Dick. *Intaglio, unwatermarked, perforated 11.*

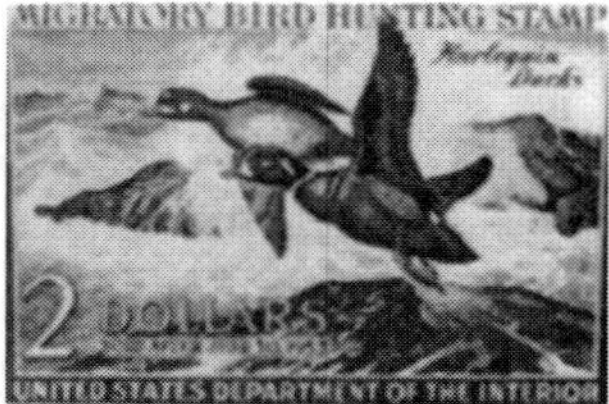

RH19

RH19		MNHVF	UseVF
$2	**deep ultramarine**	60.00	10.00
	Plate block of 6	400.00	

1953. Blue-Winged Teal Issue by Clayton Seagears. *Intaglio, unwatermarked, perforated 11.*

RH20

RH20		MNHVF	UseVF
$2	**lavender brown**	60.00	12.00
	Plate block of 6	400.00	

1954. Ring-Necked Ducks Issue by Harvey Sandstrom. *Intaglio, unwatermarked, perforated 11.*

RH21

RH21		MNHVF	UseVF
$2	**black**	60.00	8.00
	Plate block of 6	400.00	

1955. Blue Geese Issue by Stanley Searns. *Intaglio, unwatermarked, perforated 11.*

RH22

RH22		MNHVF	UseVF
$2	**deep blue**	60.00	8.00
	Plate block of 6	400.00	
	v. Writing inverted on reverse	—	

1956. American Merganser Issue by Edward J. Bierly. *Intaglio, unwatermarked, perforated 11.*

RH23

RH23		MNHVF	UseVF
$2	**black**	60.00	8.00
	Plate block of 6	400.00	

1957. American Eider Issue by Jackson M. Abbott. *Intaglio, unwatermarked, perforated 11.*

RH24

RH24		MNHVF	UseVF
$2	**yellow emerald**	60.00	8.00
	Plate block of 6	400.00	
	v. Writing inverted on reverse	3,500.00	—

1958. Canada Geese Issue by Leslie C. Kouba. *Intaglio Giori Press, unwatermarked, perforated 11.*

RH25

RH25		MNHVF	UseVF
$2	**black**	60.00	8.00
	Plate block of 6	400.00	

1959. Retriever Carrying Mallard Issue by Maynard Reece. Inscription added to the back of the stamp: "DUCK STAMP DOLLARS BUY WETLANDS TO PERPETUATE WATERFOWL." Contest rules were changed after this year to prohibit the depiction of animals besides waterfowl. From 1959 to present stamps are printed in panes of 30. *Intaglio, unwatermarked, perforated 11.*

RH26

RH26		MNHVF	UseVF
$3	**blue, orange brown & black**	85.00	8.00
	Plate block of 4	375.00	
	v. Writing inverted on reverse	—	—

1960. Redhead Ducks Issue by John A. Ruthven. *Intaglio, unwatermarked, perforated 11.*

RH27

RH27		MNHVF	UseVF
$3	**multicolored**	65.00	8.00
	Plate block of 4	350.00	

1961. Mallards Issue by Edward A. Morris. *Intaglio, unwatermarked, perforated 11.*

RH28

RH28		MNHVF	UseVF
$3	**blue, brown & yellow brown**	70.00	8.00
	Plate block of 4	375.00	

1962. Pintails Issue by Edward A. Morris. *Intaglio, unwatermarked, perforated 11.*

RH29

RH29		MNHVF	UseVF
$3	**multicolored**	70.00	8.00
	Plate block of 4	400.00	

1963. Pacific Brant Issue by Edward J. Bierly. *Intaglio, unwatermarked, perforated 11.*

RH30

RH30		MNHVF	UseVF
$3	**multicolored**	70.00	8.00
	Plate block of 4	400.00	

1964. Nene Geese Issue by Stanley Searns. *Intaglio, unwatermarked, perforated 11.*

RH31

RH31		MNHVF	UseVF
$3	**multicolored**	70.00	8.00
	Plate block of 6	2,000.00	

1965. Canvasbacks Issue by Ron Jenkins. *Intaglio, unwatermarked, perforated 11.*

RH32

RH32		MNHVF	UseVF
$3	**multicolored**	70.00	8.00
	Plate block of 4	400.00	

1966. Whistling Swans Issue by Stanley Searns. *Intaglio, unwatermarked, perforated 11.*

RH33

RH33		MNHVF	UseVF
$3	**deep green, black & blue**	70.00	8.00
	Plate block of 4	400.00	

1967. Old Squaw Ducks Issue by Leslie C. Kouba. *Intaglio, unwatermarked, perforated 11.*

RH34

RH34		MNHVF	UseVF
$3	**multicolored**	70.00	8.00
	Plate block of 4	400.00	

1968. Hooded Mergansers Issue by C. G. Pritchard. Inscription on back of the stamp changed to "BUY DUCK STAMPS SAVE WETLANDS. SEND IN ALL BIRD BANDS. SIGN YOUR DUCK STAMP." *Intaglio, unwatermarked, perforated 11.*

RH35

RH35		MNHVF	UseVF
$3	**multicolored**	55.00	8.00
	Plate block of 4	280.00	

1969. White-Winged Scoters Issue by Maynard Reece. *Intaglio, unwatermarked, perforated 11.*

RH36

RH36		MNHVF	UseVF
$3	**multicolored**	40.00	7.00
	Plate block of 4	250.00	

1970. Ross' Geese Issue by Edward J. Bierly. *Combination of intaglio and offset, unwatermarked, perforated 11.*

RH37

RH37		MNHVF	UseVF
$3	**multicolored**	40.00	7.00
	Plate block of 4	250.00	

1971. Cinnamon Teal Issue by Maynard Reece, his fifth Duck stamp. *Combination of intaglio and offset, unwatermarked, perforated 11.*

RH38

RH38		MNHVF	UseVF
$3	**multicolored**	35.00	7.00
	Plate block of 4	175.00	

1972. Emperor Geese Issue by Arthur M. Cook. *Combination of intaglio and offset, unwatermarked, perforated 11.*

RH39

RH39		MNHVF	UseVF
$5	**multicolored**	22.50	7.00
	Plate block of 4	125.00	

1973. STELLER'S EIDER ISSUE by Lee LeBlanc. *Combination of intaglio and offset, unwatermarked, perforated 11.*

RH40

RH40		MNHVF	UseVF
$5	**multicolored**	20.00	7.00
	Plate block of 4	100.00	

1974. WOOD DUCKS ISSUE by David A. Maass. *Combination of intaglio and offset, unwatermarked, perforated 11.*

RH41

RH41		MNHVF	UseVF
$5	**multicolored**	18.00	7.00
	Plate block of 4	90.00	

1975. CANVASBACKS ISSUE by James L. Fisher. *Combination of intaglio and offset, unwatermarked, perforated 11.*

RH42

RH42		MNHVF	UseVF
$5	**multicolored**	14.00	7.00
	Plate block of 4	62.50	

1976. CANADA GEESE ISSUE by Alderson Magee. *Intaglio, unwatermarked, perforated 11.*

RH43

RH43		MNHVF	UseVF
$5	**green & black**	14.00	7.00
	Plate block of 4	62.50	

1977. ROSS' GEESE ISSUE by Martin R. Murk. *Combination of intaglio and offset, unwatermarked, perforated 11.*

RH44

RH44		MNHVF	UseVF
$5	**multicolored**	14.00	7.00
	Plate block of 4	62.50	

1978. HOODED MERGANSER ISSUE by Albert Earl Gilbert. *Combination of intaglio and offset, unwatermarked, perforated 11.*

RH45

RH45		MNHVF	UseVF
$5	**multicolored**	14.00	7.00
	Plate block of 4	62.50	

1979. GREEN-WINGED TEAL ISSUE by Kenneth L. Michaelsen. *Combination of intaglio and offset, unwatermarked, perforated 11.*

RH46

RH46		MNHVF	UseVF
$7.50	**multicolored**	17.50	7.00
	Plate block of 4	55.00	

1980. MALLARDS ISSUE by Richard W. Plasschaert. *Combination of intaglio and offset, unwatermarked, perforated 11.*

RH47

RH47		MNHVF	UseVF
$7.50	**multicolored**	17.50	7.00
	Plate block of 4	55.00	

1981. RUDDY DUCKS ISSUE by John S. Wilson. *Combination of intaglio and offset, unwatermarked, perforated 11.*

RH48

RH48		MNHVF	UseVF
$7.50	**multicolored**	17.50	7.00
	Plate block of 4	75.00	

1982. CANVASBACKS ISSUE by David A. Maass. *Combination of intaglio and offset, unwatermarked, perforated 11.*

RH49

RH49		MNHVF	UseVF
$7.50	**multicolored**	17.50	7.00
	Plate block of 4	75.00	

1983. Pintails Issue by Phil Scholer. *Combination of intaglio and offset, unwatermarked, perforated 11.*

RH50

RH50		MNHVF	UseVF
$7.50	**multicolored**	17.50	7.00
	Plate block of 4	75.00	

1984. Widgeons Issue by William C. Morris. *Combination of intaglio and offset, unwatermarked, perforated 11.*

RH51

RH51		MNHVF	UseVF
$7.50	**multicolored**	17.50	7.00
	Plate block of 4	75.00	

After No. RH51's period of use had expired, 15 uncut sheets of 120 (four panes of 30 stamps per sheet, separated by gutters) were overprinted "1934-84" and "50th Anniversary" along the margins. These sheets were auctioned off by the U.S. Fish and Wildlife Service, beginning Sept. 1, 1985, with a minimum acceptable bid for each sheet of $2,000. Face value of the sheets, when valid for use, was $900. Fourteen sheets were sold, and one was donated to the Smithsonian Institution. Individual stamps of the sheet cannot be differentiated from normal copies of No. RH51. Various configurations were formed from the sheets and sold to collectors: horizontal and vertical pairs with a gutter between, cross-gutter blocks of four, and margin blocks. Sheets were submitted to The Philatelic Foundation for certification prior to being broken up, and each stamp from each of the sheets has a mark of the expertizer on the reverse. With such marks in place, individual stamps not attached to a margin were sold along with configurations noted above.

1984. Special Commemorative Issue

RH51a		MNHVF	UseVF
$7.50	**Special Commemorative Issue** (All examples must have P.F. certificates)		
	single	325.00	
	Plate block of 6	3,500.00	
	Center gutter block	6,000.00	
	Horizontal pair w/gutter between	750.00	
	Vertical pair, w/gutter between	850.00	

1985. Cinnamon Teal Issue by Gerald Mobley. *Combination of intaglio and offset, unwatermarked, perforated 11.*

RH52

RH52		MNHVF	UseVF
$7.50	**multicolored**	17.50	7.00
	Plate block of 4	75.00	

1986. Fulvous Whistling Duck Issue by Burton E. Moore Jr. *Combination of intaglio and offset, unwatermarked, perforated 11.*

RH53

RH53		MNHVF	UseVF
$7.50	**multicolored**	17.50	7.00
	Plate block of 4	75.00	
	t. Black engraved omitted	4,000.00	—

1987. Redhead Issue by Arthur G. Anderson. *Combination of intaglio and offset, unwatermarked, perforated 11 1/2 x 11.*

RH54

RH54		MNHVF	UseVF
$10	**multicolored**	20.00	10.00
	Plate block of 4	90.00	

1988. Snow Goose Issue by Daniel Smith. *Combination of intaglio and offset, unwatermarked, perforated 11 1/2 x 11.*

RH55

RH55		MNHVF	UseVF
$10	**multicolored**	20.00	7.00
	Plate block of 4	100.00	

1989. Lesser Scaup Issue by Neal R. Anderson. *Combination of intaglio and offset, unwatermarked, perforated 11 1/2 x 11.*

RH56

RH56		MNHVF	UseVF
$12.50	**multicolored**	22.50	7.00
	Plate block of 4	100.00	

1990. Black-Bellied Whistling Duck Issue by Jim Hautman. *Combination of intaglio and offset, unwatermarked, perforated 11 1/2 x 11.*

RH57

RH57		MNHVF	UseVF
$12.50	**multicolored**	22.50	7.00
	Plate block of 4	100.00	
	v. Back printing omitted	375.00	

Note: printing on back of stamp normally is on top of gum. No. RH57v can exist only unused. Beware of copies with gum removed.

1991. King Eiders Issue by Nancy Howe. *Combination of intaglio and offset, unwatermarked, perforated 11 1/2 x 11.*

RH58

RH58		MNHVF	UseVF
$15	**multicolored**	27.50	12.50
	Plate block of 4	135.00	
	t. Black engraved omitted	—	

1992. Spectacled Eider Issue by Joe Hautman, brother of Jim Hautman, whose illustration was on the 1991 stamp. *Combination of intaglio and offset, unwatermarked, perforated 11 1/2 x 11.*

RH59

RH59		MNHVF	UseVF
$15	**multicolored**	27.50	12.50
	Plate block of 4	83.00	

1993. Canvasback issue by Bruce Miller. *Combination of intaglio and offset, unwatermarked, perforated 11 1/2 x 11.*

RH60

RH60		MNHVF	UseVF
$15	**multicolored**	27.50	12.50
	Plate block of 4	135.00	
	a. Black engraved omitted	3,000.00	

1994. Red-breasted Mergansers Issue by Neal Anderson. *Combination of intaglio and offset, unwatermarked, perforated 11 1/2 x 11.*

RH61

RH61		MNHVF	UseVF
$15	**multicolored**	25.00	10.00
	Plate block of 4	135.00	

1995. Mallard Issue by Jim Hautman. *Combination of intaglio and offset, unwatermarked, perforated 11 1/2 x 11.*

RH62

RH62		MNHVF	UseVF
$15	**multicolored**	25.00	10.00
	Plate block of 4	135.00	

1996. Surf Scoter Issue by Wilhelm J. Goebel. *Combination of intaglio and offset, unwatermarked, perforated 11 1/2 x 11.*

RH63

RH63		MNHVF	UseVF
$15	**multicolored**	25.00	10.00
	Plate block of 4	135.00	

1997. Canada Goose Issue by Robert Hautman, brother of Jim and Joe Hautman, both previous winners of the U.S. duck stamp contest. *Combination of intaglio and offset, unwatemarked, perforated 11 1/2 x 11.*

RH64

RH64		MNHVF	UseVF
$15	**multicolored**	25.00	10.00
	Plate block of 4	135.00	

1998. Barrow's Goldeneye Issue By Robert Steiner. Combination of intaglio and offset, unwatermarked, perforated 11 1/2 x 11.

RH65

RH65		MNHVF	UseVF
$15	**multicolored**	25.00	10.00
	Plate block of 4	135.00	

1998. Barrow's Goldeneye Self-adhesive Issue First in a three year test of self-adhesive hunting permit stamps. Serpentine die cut.

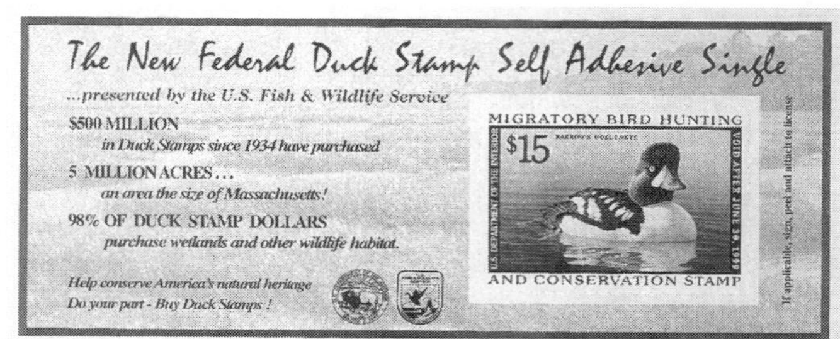

RH66		MNHVF	UseVF
$15	**multicolored**	30.00	15.00
	Plate block of 4	150.00	

1999. Greater Scaup Issue by Jim Hautman, whose illustrations were used on the 1990 and 1995 stamps. *Combination of intaglio and offset, unwatermarked, perforated 11 1/2 x 11.*

RH67

RH67		MNHVF	UseVF
$15	**multicolored**	30.00	15.00
	Plate block of 4	135.00	

1999. Greater Scaup Issue Serpentine die cut 10.

RH68		MNHVF	UseVF
$15	**multicolored**	30.00	15.00

2000. Mottled Duck Issue By Adam Grimm, age 21, the youngest artist to win the Federal Duck Stamp Art Competition. *Gravure by Bureau of Engraving and Printing.*

RH69 *Mottled Duck*

RH69		MNHVF	UseVF
$15	**multicolored**	25.00	15.00
	Plate block of 4	100.00	
	FDC *(July 1, 2000)*		25.00
	y. Pane of 20	500.00	

2000. Mottled Duck Issue *Serpentine die cut.*

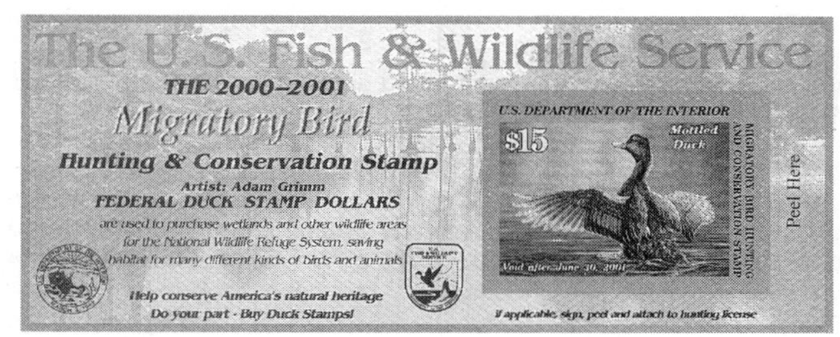

RH70 *Mottled Duck*

RH70		MNHVF	UseVF
$15	**multicolored**	25.00	15.00
	FDC *(July 1, 2000)*		25.00

2001. Northern Pintail Issue by Robert Hautman, his second win, acrylic. *Gravure by Bureau of Engraving and Printing, gummed.*
RH71 *Northern Pintail*

RH71

RH71		MNHVF	UseVF
$15	**multicolored**	25.00	15.00
	Plate block of 4	100.00	
	FDC *(June 30, 2001)*		25.00

2001. Northern Pintail Issue *Gravure by Bureau of Engraving and Printing, self-adhesive, serpentine die cut.*
RH72 *Northern Pintail*

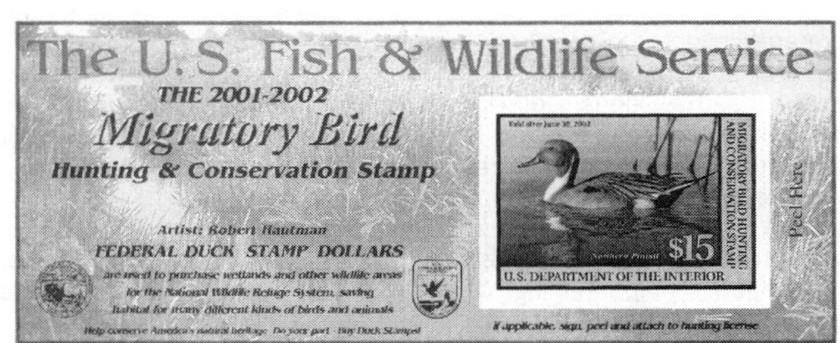

RH72		MNHVF	UseVF
$15	**multicolored**	25.00	15.00
	FDC *(June 30, 2001)*		25.00

Booklets and Panes

The first postage stamp booklets issued by the United States were made more than 100 years ago, but for many years the specialty of collecting complete booklets attracted only a few collectors who had enough knowledge to build a comprehensive collection.

In 1939, Bureau Issues Association members began work on a booklet cover numbering system to replace earlier individually prepared checklists. By pooling their collections of complete booklets and reviewing the literature available, they created a system that was first published in 1955 and updated in 1975. While many collectors find the complex BIA Booklet Cover Checklist to be confusing, it remains the definitive reference required to understand the early booklets. Copies of the 1975 Booklet Cover Checklist are available for $2 from the United States Stamp Society (formerly the BIA) through David Eeles, P.O. Box 933, Columbus, OH 43216-0933.

The BIA booklet cover numbering system showed its weaknesses with the advent of folded style booklets in 1977. While the original BIA Type Numbers worked quite well for the stapled-era booklets since the same (or similar) cover designs were often used for different booklets issued over a period of several years, the folded-style booklets all had covers with major cover differences. The old Roman numeral BIA type numbers did not work well with the frequent cover changes. So, in 1998, the BIA created a new set of cover numbers for folded-style booklets. The list, in BIA Research Paper #2, also is available for $13 from David Eeles, P.O. Box 933, Columbus, OH 43216-0933. That 100-page reference includes detailed information about all booklets issued from 1977 to date.

While collecting complete booklets was slow to catch on, interest in individual booklet panes was much greater from the start. Collectors sought out examples of panes with plate numbers in the tab or with remnants of the registration guidelines used in the manufacturing process. Early pioneers published information on them, which led to increased interest in collecting booklets as well as booklet panes.

Catalog numbers were assigned to booklet panes long before complete booklets were listed, but it wasn't until 1995 that booklets with all cover varieties were listed and priced in a major catalog. A second edition of that catalog *(The Comprehensive Catalog of United States Stamp Booklets)* was issued in 1999 by Krause Publications. And now, for the first time, a Booklet section has been added to the *Krause-Minkus Standard Catalog of U.S. Stamps.*

This booklet section is briefer than many collectors might like, but it is understandable and may be expanded as the editors receive input from collectors. It was our intent to make it as easy as possible for the average collector to use these new listings. However, with such a complex subject, it was impossible to condense all the relevant information into the listings. Collectors who want more detailed information may wish to consult the references mentioned above to increase their understanding of booklet varieties. This new section may whet your appetite.

The booklet listings are chronological in most cases. The list is a summary of all booklets and booklet panes, and, when space allows, information is included to help the reader identify the differences in the booklets and panes. Only basic information about the actual stamp (identified by Minkus number) is given since the catalog listing in the main section of this catalog goes into more detail. Throughout the booklet listings, abbreviations are used to conserve space. Most notably, "OFC" means Outside Front Cover; "IFC" means Inside Front Cover; "IBC" means Inside Back Cover; and "OBC" means Outside Back Cover. In many cases, key words or differences on a cover surface are identified in the listing, but without an actual booklet or illustration it may be hard to understand the meaning. In several cases, a number in parenthesis at the end of a booklet listing indicates the number of cover varieities that exist for that booklet. Again, the reader will need to refer to the two BIA booklet cover checklists and/or the Krause *Comprehensive Catalog of United States Stamp Booklets* to fully understand all the differences.

Values of the early booklets are very difficult to establish. Precious few complete booklets survive, and they rarely trade hands. Condition of the covers (creases, stains, tears, ink notations, etc.) has a major impact on the actual value of the early booklets. Whenever possible, individual booklet panes should be collected only with the selvage tab attached. Panes without their tabs usually are regarded as space fillers and have a greatly reduced value.

There are many levels of specialization available to booklet collectors. While a beginner might feel booklets have little to offer in the way of a challenge, many people are so fascinated by the specialty that they collect booklets and booklet panes exclusively. As with all areas of stamp collecting, there really is no limit to how each of us collects stamps, but knowledge is the key to enjoying what we do collect.

1900-03. 2¢ Washington *double line watermark, perforated 12.*

192n F-VF
red or orange-red, pane of 6, horizontal double line watermark (360 subject plates) 325.00

192n1 F-VF
red or orange-red, pane of 6, vertical double line watermark (180 subject plates) 325.00

B1 F-VF
25¢ book, black on tan, no 25¢ in corners, "Puerto Rico" on OFC 6,000.00

B2 F-VF
25¢ book, black on tan, no 25¢ in corners, "Porto Rico" on OFC 6,000.00

B3 F-VF
25¢ book, black on tan, 25¢ in corners, Special Delivery on IFC, SMITH 5,000.00

B3a F-VF
25¢ book, black on tan, 25¢ in corners, Special Delivery on IFC, PAYNE 5,000.00

25c. POST OFFICE DEPARTMENT, U. S. A. 25c.
—THIS BOOK CONTAINS 12 TWO-CENT STAMPS—
PRICE, 25 CENTS.
DOMESTIC POSTAGE RATES.
(Apply to Guam, Hawaii, Philippines, Porto Rico, Tutuila, and to Canada, Cuba, and Mexico.)
First-class. Letters and sealed matter: 2 cts. for each ounce or fraction. Postal cards, 1 ct. each.
Second-class. Newspapers and periodicals: 1 ct. for each four ounces or fraction.
Third-class. Miscellaneous printed matter: 1 ct. for each two ounces or fraction.
Fourth-class. All matter not included in first three classes: 1 ct. for each ounce or fraction
Special-delivery. A special-delivery stamp, in addition to postage, secures immediate delivery at any United States post office.

B4

B4 F-VF
25¢ book, black on tan, 25¢ in corners, Special Delivery on OFC 5,000.00

B5 F-VF
49¢ book, green on tan, no 49¢ in corners, "Puerto Rico" on OFC 7,000.00

B6 F-VF
49¢ book, black on buff, no 49¢ in corners, "Porto Rico" on OFC 7,500.00

B7 F-VF
49¢ book, black on buff, 49¢ in corners, Special Delivery on IFC, SMITH 5,500.00

B7a F-VF
49¢ book, black on buff, 49¢ in corners, Special Delivery on IFC, PAYNE 5,500.00

B8 F-VF
49¢ book, black on buff, 49¢ in corners, Special Delivery on OFC 8,500.00

B9 F-VF
97¢ book, red on tan, no 97¢ in corners, "Puerto Rico" on OFC 12,000.00

B10 F-VF
97¢ book, black on gray, no 97¢ in corners, "Porto Rico" on OFC 11,000.00

B11 F-VF
97¢ book, black on gray, 97¢ in corners, Special Delivery on IFC, SMITH 9,000.00

B11a F-VF
97¢ book, black on gray, 97¢ in corners, Special Delivery on IFC, PAYNE 9,000.00

B12 F-VF
97¢ book, black on gray, 97¢ in corners, Special Delivery on OFC 9,000.00

1907. 1¢ Franklin (Portrait) *double line watermark, perforated 12.*

211n | **blue-green,** pane of 6 | F-VF 425.00

B13 | **25¢ book, black** on green, CORTELYOU | F-VF 6,500.00

B13a | **black** on green, MEYER on OBC (5) | F-VF 6,500.00

(Number in parenthesis after a Booklet listing indicates multiple cover varieties exist.)

1903. 2¢ Washington (Flags) *double line watermark, perforated 12.*

212n | **carmine,** pane of 6 | F-VF 400.00

B14 | **25¢ book, black** on tan, PAYNE is Postmaster General on OBC | F-VF 3,500.00

B15 | **49¢ book, black** on buff, PAYNE is Postmaster General on OBC | F-VF 6,000.00

B16 | **97¢ book, black** on gray, PAYNE is Postmaster General on OBC | F-VF 12,000.00

1903. 2¢ Washington (Shield) *double line watermark, perforated 12.*

231n | **carmine,** Type I pane of 6 | F-VF 100.00

231n1 | **vermilion,** Type I pane of 6 | F-VF —

231n2 | **red,** Type I pane of 6 | F-VF —

231n3 | **carmine-rose,** Type I pane of 6 | F-VF 150.00

231n4 | **scarlet (red-orange),** Type I pane of 6 | F-VF 200.00

231n5 | **lake,** Type I pane of 6 | F-VF 2,500.00

231an | **carmine,** Type II pane of 6 | F-VF 150.00

231an1 | **lake,** Type II pane of 6 | F-VF 175.00

B17 | **25¢ book, black** on tan, 3-line Special Delivery on OFC, PAYNE | F-VF 1,000.00

B17a | **25¢ book, black** on tan, 4-line Special Delivery on OFC, WYNNE | F-VF 1,000.00

B17a1 | **25¢ book, black** on tan, No Canal Zone on OFC, CORTELYOU (3) | F-VF 1,500.00

B17b | **25¢ book, black** on tan, Canal Zone on OFC, CORTELYOU | F-VF 2,000.00

B17b1 | **25¢ book, black** on tan, 4-line Special Delivery on OFC, MEYER (5) | F-VF 1,000.00

B18 | **49¢ book, black** on buff, 3-line Special Delivery on OFC, PAYNE | F-VF 1,500.00

B18a | **49¢ book, black** on buff, 4-line Special Delivery on OFC, PAYNE | F-VF —

B18a1 | **49¢ book, black** on buff, 4-line Special Delivery on OFC, WYNNE | F-VF 1,500.00

B18a2 | **49¢ book, black** on buff, No Canal Zone on OFC, CORTELYOU (3) | F-VF 2,000.00

B18b | **49¢ book, black** on buff, Canal Zone on OFC, CORTELYOU | F-VF 2,000.00

B18b1 | **49¢ book, black** on buff, 4-line Special Delivery on OFC, MEYER (5) | F-VF 1,500.00

B19 | **49¢ book, black** on pink, 4-line Special Delivery on OFC, MEYER | F-VF 2,000.00

B20 | **97¢ book, black** on gray, 3-line Special Delivery on OFC, PAYNE | F-VF 3,500.00

B20a | **97¢ book, black** on gray, 4-line Special Delivery on OFC, WYNNE | F-VF 3,500.00

B20a1 | **97¢ book, black** on gray, No Canal Zone on OFC, CORTELYOU (3) | F-VF 4,000.00

B20b | **97¢ book. black** on gray, Canal Zone on OFC, CORTELYOU | F-VF 4,000.00

B20b1 | **97¢ book, black** on gray, 4-line Special Delivery on OFC, MEYER (5) | F-VF 3,500.00

1908. 1¢ Franklin (Profile) *double line watermark, perforated 12.*

237n | **green,** pane of 6 | F-VF 140.00

B21 | **25¢ book, black** on green, Text on OFC (3) | F-VF 2,000.00

B22 | **25¢ book, black** on green, pictorial OFC (Post Rider insignia) | F-VF 2,500.00

1908. 2¢ Washington (Profile) *double line watermark, perforated 12.*

238n | **carmine,** pane of 6, denomination shown as "TWO CENTS" | F-VF 125.00

B23 | **25¢ book, black** on tan, text on OFC (2) | F-VF 1,250.00

B24 | **25¢ book, black** on tan, pictorial OFC (Post Rider insignia) | F-VF 1,250.00

B25 | **49¢ book, black** on buff, text on OFC (2) | F-VF 2,500.00

B26 | **49¢ book, black** on pink, text on OFC | F-VF 2,500.00

B27

B27 | **49¢ book, black** on pink, pictorial OFC (Post Rider insignia) | F-VF 2,000.00

B28 | **97¢ book, black** on gray, text on OFC (3) | F-VF 3,000.00

B29 | **97¢ book, black** on gray, pictorial OFC (Post Rider insignia) | F-VF 3,000.00

1910. 1¢ Franklin *single line watermark, perforated 12.*

273n | **green,** pane of 6 | F-VF 125.00

B30 | **25¢ book, black** on green, Post Rider insignia on OFC (2) | F-VF 1,750.00

1910. 2¢ Washington *single line watermark, perforated 12.*

274n | **carmine,** pane of 6, deonimination shown as "TWO CENTS" | F-VF 100.00

B31 F-VF
25¢ book, black on tan, Post Rider insignia on OFC (2) 975.00

B32 F-VF
49¢ book, black on pink, Post Rider insignia on OFC (2) 2,000.00

B33 F-VF
97¢ book, black on gray, Post Rider insignia on OFC (2) 3,500.00

1912. 1¢ Washington *single line watermark, perforated 12.*

297n F-VF
green, pane of 6 65.00

B34 F-VF
25¢ book, black on green, Post Rider insignia on OFC (2) 1,250.00

B35 F-VF
25¢ book, green on green, Washington Post Office on OFC (3) 1,200.00

B36 F-VF
97¢ book, green on lavender, Washington Post Office on OFC 1,750.00

B43 F-VF
73¢ combination book (4-297n & 4- 298n panes), red on white 3,000.00

1912. 2¢ Washington *single line watermark, perforated 12.*

298n F-VF
carmine, pane of 6, denomination shown as "2 CENTS 2" 65.00

B37 F-VF
25¢ book, black on tan, 33mm Post Rider insignia on OFC (2) 1,000.00

B37a F-VF
25¢ book, black on tan, patented grilled wax paper interleaves 5,000.00

B38 F-VF
25¢ book, red on yellow, 27mm Post Rider insignia on OFC (3) 1,000.00

B39 F-VF
49¢ book, black on pink, 33mm Post Rider insignia on OFC (2) 1,750.00

B40 F-VF
49¢ book, red on pink, 27mm Post Rider insignia on OFC (3) 2,000.00

B41 F-VF
97¢ book, black on gray, 33mm Post Rider insignia on OFC (2) 3,000.00

B42 F-VF
97¢ book, red on blue, 27mm Post Rider insignia on OFC (3) 3,000.00

B43 F-VF
73¢ combination book (4-297n & 4-298n panes), red on white 3,000.00

(Number in parenthesis after a booklet listing indicates multiple cover varieties exist)

1914. 1¢ Washington *single line watermark, perforated 10.*

315n F-VF
green, pane of 6 4.00

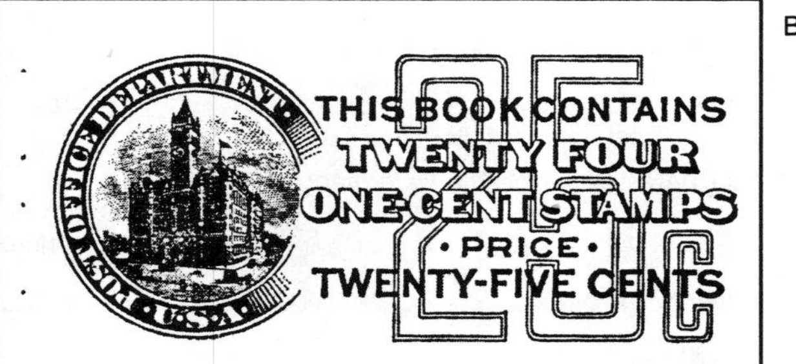

POST OFFICE DEPARTMENT
U.S.A.
THIS BOOK CONTAINS
TWENTY FOUR
ONE CENT STAMPS
• PRICE •
TWENTY-FIVE CENTS
25¢

B44

B44 F-VF
25¢ book, green on green, Washington Post Office on OFC (3) 350.00

B45 F-VF
97¢ book, green on lavender, Washington Post Office on OFC 110.00

B49 F-VF
73¢ combination book (4-315n & 4-316n panes), red on white (3) 350.00

1914. 2¢ Washington *single line watermark, perforated 10.*

316n F-VF
carmine, pane of 6 22.00

B46 F-VF
25¢ book, red on yellow, Post Rider insignia on OFC (3) 500.00

B47 F-VF
49¢ book, red on pink, Post Rider insignia on OFC (3) 1,000.00

B48 F-VF
97¢ book, red on blue, Post Rider insignia on OFC (3) 1,500.00

B49 F-VF
73¢ combination book (4-315n & 4-316n panes), red on white (3) 350.00

1916. 1¢ Washington *Unwatermarked, perforated 10.*

348n F-VF
green, pane of 6 10.00

B50 F-VF
25¢ book, green on green, Washington Post Office on OFC 750.00

B51 F-VF
97¢ book, green on lavender, Washington Post Office on OFC 500.00

B55 F-VF
73¢ combination book (4-348n & 4- 349n panes), red on white (2) 1,000.00

1916. 2¢ Washington *Unwatermarked, perforated 10.*

349n F-VF
carmine, pane of 6 85.00

B52 F-VF
25¢ book, red on buff, Post Rider insignia on OFC 750.00

B53 F-VF
49¢ book, red on pink, Post Rider insignia on OFC 1,500.00

B54 F-VF
97¢ book, red on blue, Post Rider insignia on OFC 2,500.00

B55 F-VF
73¢ combination book (4-348n & 4-349n panes), red on white (2) 1,000.00

1917. 1¢ Washington *Unwatermarked, perforated 11.*

380n F-VF
green, pane of 6 3.00

B56 F-VF
25¢ book, green on green, Washington Post Office on OFC (2) 500.00

B57

B57 F-VF
25¢ book, green on green, City Mail Carrier in 32x20mm oval, on OFC 150.00

B58 F-VF
25¢ book, green on green, City Mail Carrier in 29x18mm oval, on OFC (4) 75.00

B59 F-VF
97¢ book, green (or blue) on lavender, Washington Post Office (4) 500.00

B66 F-VF
73¢ combination book (4-380n & 4-381n panes), red on white (4) 100.00

B76 F-VF
73¢ combination book (4-380n & 4-421n panes) - red on white (3) 120.00

1917. 2¢ Washington *Unwatermarked, perforated 11.*

381n F-VF
carmine, pane of 6 5.00

B60 F-VF
25¢ book, red on buff, 27mm Post Rider insignia on OFC (2) 350.00

B61 F-VF
25¢ book, red on buff, 25mm Post Rider insignia on OFC (3) 500.00

B62 F-VF
49¢ book, red on pink, 27mm Post Rider insignia on OFC (2) 750.00

B63 F-VF
49¢ book, red on pink, 25mm Post Rider insignia on OFC (2) 500.00

B64 F-VF
97¢ book, red on blue, 27mm Post Rider insignia on OFC (2) 750.00

B64a F-VF
97¢ book, red on blue, 25mm Post Rider insignia on OFC 1,000.00

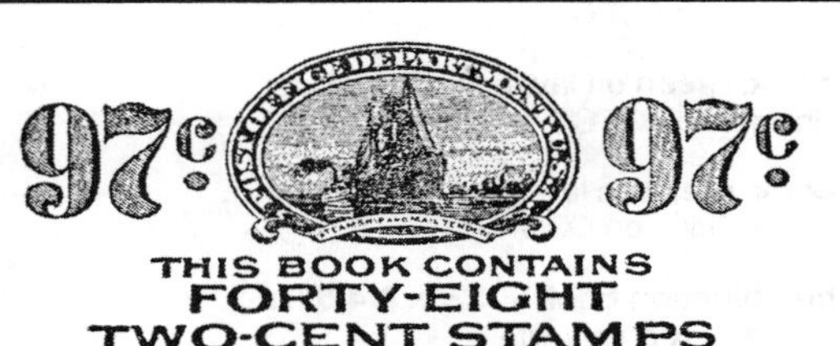

B65

B65 F-VF
97¢ book, red on blue, Steamship & Mail Tender on OFC (2) 1,500.00

B66 F-VF
73¢ combination book (4-380n & 4-381n panes), red on white (4) 100.00

1918. 1¢ Washington (AEF) *Unwatermarked, perforated 11.*

380n1 F-VF
green, pane of 30, tab at left or right, positions W1, 2, 3, or 4 1,000.00

380n1a F-VF
green, pane of 30, tab at left or right, guideline at bottom (W5 or 6) 1,250.00

380n1b F-VF
green, pane of 30, initials in tab at left or right, position W11 or 12 1,250.00

B67 F-VF
$3.00 book, black on green, "300/1 CENT POSTAGE STAMPS/$3" 15,000.00

B67x F-VF
Empty $3.00 booklet, black on green, covers and interleaving only 750.00

1918. 2¢ Washington (AEF) *Unwatermarked, perforated 11.*

381n1 F-VF
rose, pane of 30, tab at left or right, positions W1, 2, 3, or 4 25,000.00

381n1a F-VF
rose, pane of 30, tab at left or right, guideline at bottom (W5 or 6) —

381n1b F-VF
rose, pane of 30, initials in tab at left or right, position W11 or 12 —

B68 F-VF
$6.00 book, black on pink, "300/2 CENT POSTAGE STAMPS/$6" —

B68x F-VF
Empty $6.00 booklet, black on pink, covers and interleaving only 2,000.00

1917-18. 3¢ Washington *Unwatermarked, perforated 11.*

382n F-VF
violet, Type I pane of 6 60.00

382An F-VF
violet, Type II pane of 6 50.00

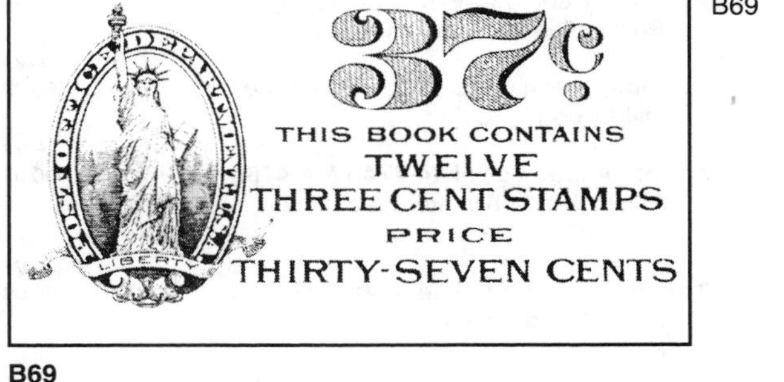

B69

B69 F-VF
37¢ book, violet on sage, Type I panes, (offset printed covers) 750.00

B70 F-VF
37¢ book, violet on sage, Type II panes, (electrotype printed covers) 175.00

1923. 1¢ Franklin *Perforated 11 (flat plate).*

419n F-VF
deep green, pane of 6 7.00

B71 F-VF
25¢ book, green on green, City Mail Carrier in 29x18mm oval (2) 75.00

B72 F-VF
97¢ book, green on lavender, Washington Post Office (3) 750.00

B77 F-VF
73¢ combination book (4-419n & 4-421n panes), red on white (3) 100.00

1923. 2¢ Washington *Perforated 11 (flat plate).*

421n F-VF
carmine, pane of 6 9.00

B73 F-VF
25¢ book, red on buff, 25mm Post Rider insignia on OFC (4) 500.00

B74 F-VF
49¢ book, red on pink, 25mm Post Rider insignia on OFC (4) 1,000.00

B75 F-VF
97¢ book, red on blue, Steamship & Mail Tender on OFC (3) 1,750.00

B76 F-VF
73¢ combination book (4-380n & 4-421n panes), red on white (3) 120.00

B77 F-VF
73¢ combination book (4-419n & 4-421n panes), red on white (3) 100.00

1926. 2¢ Washington *Perforated 10 (rotary press).*

452n F-VF
carmine, pane of 6 75.00

B78 F-VF
25¢ book, red on buff, Post Rider insignia on OFC (3) 500.00

B79 F-VF
49¢ book, red on pink, Post Rider insignia on OFC 1,000.00

B80 F-VF
97¢ book, red on blue, Steamship & Mail Tender on OFC 1,750.00

1927. 1¢ FRANKLIN *Perforated 11 x 10 1/2 (rotary press).*

		F-VF
474n	**green,** pane of 6	6.00
B81	**25¢ book, green** on green, Post Rider insignia on OFC (3)	65.00
B81a	**25¢ book, green** on green, Post Rider insignia, glassine interleaves	—
B82	**97¢ book, green** on lavender, Washington Post Office on OFC	500.00
B82a	**97¢ book, green** on lavender, Washington Post Office, glassine interleaves	—
B83	**97¢ book, green** on lavender, Post Rider insignia on OFC	500.00
B89	**73¢ combination book (4-474n & 4-476n panes), red** on white, Washington Post Office	500.00
B90	**73¢ combination book (4-474n & 4-476n panes), red** on white, 27mm Post Rider insignia	100.00
B90A	**73¢ combination book (4-474a & 4-476n panes), red** on white, 27mm Post Rider insignia, glassine interleaves	—
B91	**73¢ combination book (4-474n & 4-476n panes), red** on white, 24mm Post Rider insignia (2)	100.00

1927. 2¢ WASHINGTON *Perforated 11 x 10.5 (rotary press).*

		F-VF
476n	**carmine,** pane of 6	2.00
B84	**25¢ book, red** on buff, Post Rider insignia, wax paper interleaves (2)	7.00
B84a	**25¢ book, red** on buff, Post Rider insignia, glassine interleaves	—
B84b	**25¢ book, red** on buff, Post Rider insignia, cellophane interleaves	500.00
B85	**49¢ book, red** on pink, Post Rider insignia on OFC (2)	15.00
B86	**97¢ book, red** on blue, 25mm Post Rider insignia on OFC	175.00
B87	**97¢ book, red** on blue, 23mm Post Rider insignia on OFC (2)	30.00
B88	**97¢ book, red** on blue, Steamship & Mail Tender on OFC	750.00
B89	**73¢ combination book (4-474n & 4-476n panes), red** on white, Washington Post Office	500.00
B90	**73¢ combination book (4-474n & 4-476n panes), red** on white, 27mm Post Rider insignia	100.00
B90a	**73¢ combination book (4-474n & 4-476n panes), red** on white, 27mm Post Rider insignia, glassine interleaves	—
B91	**73¢ combination book (4-474n & 4-476n panes), red** on white, 24mm Post Rider insignia (2)	100.00

1932. 3¢ WASHINGTON *(Stuart).*

		F-VF
518n	**deep violet,** pane of 6	35.00

B92

		F-VF
B92	**37¢ book, violet** on buff, Post Rider wax seal on OFC (2)	85.00
B92a	**37¢ book, violet** on buff, Post Rider wax seal on OFC, cellophane interleaves	700.00
B93	**73¢ book, violet** on pink, Post Rider wax seal on OFC (2)	250.00

1939. 1¢ WASHINGTON *(pre-EE plates - 3mm gutter).*

		F-VF
525n	**green,** pane of 6	3.00
B94	**25¢ book, green** on green, Post Rider insignia on OFC	45.00
B95	**97¢ book, green** on lavender, Post Rider insignia on OFC	500.00
B96	**97¢ book, green** on lavender, Washington Post Office on OFC	2,000.00
B98	**73¢ combination book (4-525n & 4-527n panes), red** on white	110.00

1939. 2¢ ADAMS *(pre-EE plates - 3mm gutter).*

		F-VF
527n	**rose carmine,** pane of 6	6.00
B97	**97¢ book, red** on blue or blue-green, Post Rider insignia on OFC	30.00
B98	**73¢ combination book (4-525n & 4-527n panes), red** on white	110.00

1939. 3¢ JEFFERSON *(pre-EE plates - 3mm gutter).*

		F-VF
528n	**deep violet,** pane of 6	10.00
B99	**37¢ book, red** on blue, Post Rider insignia on OFC	65.00
B100	**73¢ book, violet** on pink, Post Rider insignia on OFC	950.00

1942. 1¢ WASHINGTON *(EE plates - 2.5mm gutter).*

		F-VF
525n1	**green,** pane of 6	2.00
B101	**25¢ book, green** on green, Post Rider wax seal on OFC	45.00
B102	**97¢ book, green** on lavender, Post Rider wax seal on OFC	500.00
B108	**73¢ combination book (4-525n1 & 4-527n1 panes), red** on white, 25mm insignia on OFC	65.00
B109	**73¢ combination book (4-525n1 & 4-527n1 panes), red** on white, 23mm insignia on OFC	65.00

B110
73¢ combination book (4-525n1 & 4-527n1 panes), red on white, 23mm wax seal on OFC — F-VF 28.00

1942. 2¢ ADAMS *(EE plates - 2.5mm gutter).*

527n1
rose carmine, pane of 6 — F-VF 6.00

B103
25¢ book, red on buff, Post Rider insignia on OFC — F-VF 15.00

B104
25¢ book, red on buff, Post Rider wax seal on OFC — F-VF 75.00

B105
49¢ book, red on pink, Post Rider insignia on OFC — F-VF 15.00

B106
49¢ book, red on pink, Post Rider wax seal on OFC — F-VF 15.00

B107
97¢ book, red on blue, Post Rider insignia on OFC — F-VF 1,000.00

B108
73¢ combination book (4-525n1 & 4-527n1 panes), red on white, 25mm insignia on OFC — F-VF 65.00

B109
73¢ combination book (4-525n1 & 4-527n1 panes), red on white, 23mm insignia on OFC — F-VF 65.00

B110
73¢ combination book (4-525n1 & 4-527n1 panes), red on white, 23mm wax seal on OFC — F-VF 28.00

1942. 3¢ JEFFERSON *(EE plates - 2.5mm gutter).*

528n1
deep violet, pane of 6 — F-VF 7.00

B111
37¢ book, violet on buff, Post Rider seal on OFC, OSWEGO on IFC — F-VF 30.00

B111a
37¢ book, violet on buff, Post Rider seal on OFC, SAINT LOUIS on IFC — F-VF 15.00

B111b
37¢ book, violet on buff, Post Rider seal on OFC, blank IFC & IBC — F-VF 1,000.00

B112
73¢ book, violet on buff, Post Rider seal on OFC, OSWEGO on IFC — F-VF 50.00

B112a
73¢ book, violet on buff, Post Rider seal on OFC, SAINT LOUIS on IFC — F-VF 35.00

B112b
73¢ book, violet on buff, Post Rider seal on OFC, blank IFC & IBC — F-VF 2,000.00

1954. 3¢ STATUE OF LIBERTY *(wet printed).*

573n
deep violet, pane of 6 — F-VF 4.00

B113
37¢ book, violet on buff, Post Rider wax seal on OFC — F-VF 12.00

B114
73¢ book, violet on pink, Post Rider wax seal on OFC — F-VF 17.00

1956. 3¢ STATUE OF LIBERTY *(dry printed).*

573pn
deep violet, pane of 6 — F-VF 5.00

B115
37¢ book, violet on buff, Post Rider wax seal on OFC — F-VF 13.00

B116
73¢ book, violet on pink, Post Rider wax seal on OFC — F-VF 20.00

1958. 4¢ LINCOLN

574n
red violet, pane of 6 — F-VF 2.00

B117
97¢ book, violet on buff, black 97¢ overprinted on 37¢ Post Rider OFC — F-VF 50.00

B118
97¢ book, violet on buff, black 97¢ overprinted on 73¢ Post Rider OFC — F-VF 25.00

B119
97¢ book, blue on yellow, Post Rider wax seal on OFC — F-VF 85.00

B120
97¢ book, blue on pink, THEIR TOWN Model Form of Address on IBC — F-VF 25.00

B120a
97¢ book, blue on pink, experimental silicone interleaving text on IFC — F-VF 80.00

B120b
97¢ book, blue on pink, HIS TOWN Model Form of Address on IBC — F-VF 10.00

(Refer to BIA Booklet Cover Checklist for detailed information on cover varieties)

1962. 5¢ WASHINGTON *(Slogan 1).*

604n1
gray blue, pane of 5 plus label ("Your Mailman"), untagged — F-VF 3.00

B121
$1.00 book (4-604n1), blue on white, Post Rider seal on OFC — F-VF 25.00

1963. 5¢ WASHINGTON *(Slogan 2).*

604n2
gray blue, pane of 5 plus label ("Use Zone Numbers"), untagged — F-VF 20.00

604n2p
Pane of 5, plus label ("Zone Numbers"), Hi-Brite paper — F-VF 30.00

604n2z
Pane of 5, plus label ("Zone Numbers"), tagged — F-VF 80.00

B122
$1.00 book (604n2), blue on white, Post Rider seal on OFC — F-VF 100.00

B122a
$1.00 book (604n2p), blue on white, Post Rider seal on OFC — F-VF 150.00

B123
$1.00 book (604n2), blue on white, Mr. Zip on OFC — F-VF 65.00

B123a
$1.00 book (604n2p), blue on white, Mr. Zip on OFC — F-VF 100.00

B125
$1.00 book (604n2z), blue on white, Mr. Zip on OFC — F-VF 300.00

1964. 5¢ WASHINGTON *(Slogan 3).*

604n3
gray blue, pane of 5 plus label ("Use Zip Code"), untagged — F-VF 4.00

604n3p
Pane of 5, plus label ("Use Zip Code"), Hi-Brite paper — F-VF 7.00

604n3z
Pane of 5, plus label ("Use Zip Code"), tagged — F-VF 2.50

B124
$1.00 book (604n3), blue on white, Domestic Rate Chart on IFC — F-VF 12.00

B124a
$1.00 book (604n3p), blue on white, Domestic Rate Chart on IFC — F-VF 250.00

B124b
$1.00 book (604n3), blue on white, Better Mail Services on IFC — F-VF 90.00

B124c F-VF
$1.00 book (604n3), blue on white, Minuteman IFC, 79373 OBC 35.00

B124d F-VF
$1.00 book (604n3), blue on white, Minuteman IFC, 00000 OBC 800.00

B126 F-VF
$1.00 book (604n3z), blue on white, Domestic Rate Chart on IFC 15.00

B126a F-VF
$1.00 book (604n3z), blue on white, Better Mail Services on IFC 30.00

B126b F-VF
$1.00 book (604n3z), blue on white, Minuteman IFC, 79373 OBC 50.00

B126c F-VF
$1.00 book (604n3z), blue on white, Minuteman IFC, 00000 OBC 8.00

1967. 6¢ Roosevelt *(pane of 8).*

622nz F-VF
black-brown, pane of 8 (320 or 400 subject plates) 1.50

B127 F-VF
$2.00 book (4-622nz & 1-616n), brown on white, 100 dots/inch OFC 7.75

B127a F-VF
$2.00 book (4-622nz & 1-616n), brown on white, 130 dots/inch OFC 7.75

1968. 1¢ Jefferson *(pane of 8).*

616n F-VF
green, pane of 8 with shiny gum (320 or 400 subject plates) 1.00

616nm F-VF
green, pane of 8 with dull-finish gum (400 subject plates) 2.00

B127 F-VF
$2.00 book (4-622nz & 1-616n), brown on white, 100 dots/inch OFC 7.75

B127a F-VF
$2.00 book (4-622nz & 1-616n), brown on white, 130 dots/inch OFC 7.75

B129 F-VF
$2.00 book (4-652n & 1-616n), blue on white, Post Rider seal OFC 8.50

B130 F-VF
$2.00 book (4-652n & 1-616n), blue on white, 27.5mm Portrait OFC 6.00

B130a F-VF
$2.00 book (4-652n & 1-616n), blue on white, 29mm Portrait OFC 750.00

B132 F-VF
$2.00 book (4-652nm & 1-616nm), blue on white, Experiment IFC 6.00

B132a F-VF
$2.00 book (4-652nm & 1-616nm), blue on white, Envelope IFC 100.00

1968. 6¢ Roosevelt *(pane of 5).*

622n1z F-VF
black-brown, pane of 5 plus Slogan 4 label ("Mail Early") 1.25

622n2z F-VF
black-brown, pane of 5 plus Slogan 5 label ("Use Zip Code") 1.25

B128 F-VF
$1.00 book (3-622n1z or 622n2z & 1-618n1 or 618n2), brown on white, Minuteman on IFC 7.00

B128a F-VF
$1.00 book (3-622n1z or 622n2z & 1-618n1 or 618n2), brown on white, Envelope on IFC 7.00

1968. 2¢ Frank Lloyd Wright *(pane of 5).*

618n1 F-VF
blue-gray, pane of 5 plus Slogan 4 label ("Mail Early"), shiny gum 1.25

618n2 F-VF
blue-gray, pane of 5 plus Slogan 5 label ("Use Zip Code"), shiny gum 1.25

B128 F-VF
$1.00 book (3-622n1z or 622n2z & 1-618n1 or 618n2), brown on white, Minuteman on IFC 7.00

B128a F-VF
$1.00 book (3-622n1z or 622n2z & 1-618n1 or 618n2), brown on white, Envelope on IFC 7.00

B131 F-VF
$1.00 book (3-652n1 or 652n2 & 1-618n1 or 618n2), blue on white 7.50

1970. 6¢ Eisenhower *(pane of 5).*

652n1 F-VF
blue, pane of 5 plus Slogan 4 label ("Mail Early") 1.25

652n2 F-VF
blue, pane of 5 plus Slogan 5 label ("Use Zip Code") 1.25

B131 F-VF
$1.00 book (3-652n1 or 652n2 & 1-618n1 or 618n2), blue on white 7.50

1970. 6¢ Eisenhower *(pane of 8).*

652n F-VF
blue, pane of 8 with shiny gum 1.25

652nm F-VF
blue, pane of 8 with experimental dull-finish gum 1.50

B129 F-VF
$2.00 book (4-652n & 1-616n), blue on white, Post Rider seal OFC 8.50

B130 F-VF
$2.00 book (4-652n & 1-616n), blue on white, 27.5mm portrait OFC 6.00

B130a F-VF
$2.00 book (4-652n & 1-616n), blue on white, 29mm portrait OFC 750.00

B132 F-VF
$2.00 book (4-652nm & 1-616nm), blue on white, experiment IFC 6.00

B132a F-VF
$2.00 book (4-652nm & 1-616nm), blue on white, envelope IFC 100.00

1971. 1¢ Jefferson *(pane of 4).*

616n1 F-VF
green, pane of 4 plus two labels (Slogans 5 and 4) .75

B134 F-VF
$1.00 book (2-663An4 & 1-616n1), claret on white, 29mm clock IBC 4.00

B134a F-VF
$1.00 book (2-663An4 & 1-616n1), claret on white, 27mm clock IBC 4.00

1971. 8¢ Eisenhower *(pane of 6).*

663An4 F-VF
reddish-brown, pane of 6, shiny gum 1.25

B134 F-VF
$1.00 book (2-663An4 & 1-616n1), claret on white, 29mm clock IBC 4.00

B134a F-VF
$1.00 book (2-663An4 & 1-616n1), claret on white, 27mm clock IBC 4.00

1971. 8¢ Eisenhower *(pane of 8).*

663An F-VF
reddish-brown, pane of 8, shiny gum 1.25

B133 F-VF
$1.92 book (3-663An), claret on white, 33mm clock on IBC 6.50

B133a F-VF
$1.92 book (3-663An), claret on white, 31mm clock on IBC 6.50

1972. 8¢ Eisenhower *(pane of 7).*

663An1 F-VF
reddish-brown, pane of 7 plus Slogan 4 label ("Mail Early"), dull-finish gum 1.75

663An2 F-VF
reddish-brown, pane of 7 plus Slogan 5 label ("Use Zip Code"), dull-finish gum 1.75

B135 F-VF
$2.00 book (1-663An3 + 2-663An2 + 1-663An1), claret on yellow 7.00

1972. 8¢ Eisenhower *(pane of 4).*

663An3 F-VF
reddish-brown, pane of 4 plus two double size message labels (Slogans 6 & 7), dull-finish gum 1.75

B135 F-VF
$2.00 book (1-663An3 + 2-663An2 + 1-663An1), claret on yellow 7.00

1973. 10¢ Jefferson Memorial *(pane of 8).*

678n2 F-VF
blue, pane of 8 1.75

B136 F-VF
$4.00 book (5-678n2), red and blue on white 8.50

1973. 10¢ Jefferson Memorial *(pane of 5).*

678n F-VF
blue, pane of 5 plus Slogan 8 label ("Paying bills?") 3.50

B137 F-VF
$1.00 book (2-678n), blue on white, (red and blue print on OBC) 3.50

1974. 10¢ Jefferson Memorial *(pane of 6).*

678n1 F-VF
blue, pane of 6 5.00

B138 F-VF
$1.25 combination book (1-A85n and 1-678n1), red and blue on white 7.25

1971-75. 2¢ Frank Lloyd Wright *(pane of 6).*

618n F-VF
blue-gray, pane of 6 with shiny gum (above pane was only used as a filler in airmail books with 11¢ stamps) 1.00

618nm F-VF
blue-gray, pane of 6 with dull-finish gum 1.00

BA24 F-VF
$1.00 book (2-A78n & 1-618n), red on white, 29mm clock IBC 5.00

BA24a F-VF
$1.00 book (2-A78n & 1-618n), red on white, 27mm clock IBC 5.00

B139 F-VF
$.90 book (1-695n & 1-618nm), red & blue on white, "$10" OBC 3.00

B139a F-VF
$.90 book (1-695n & 1-618nm), red & blue on white, "$10.00" OBC 100.00

1975. 13¢ Liberty Bell *(pane of 6).*

695n F-VF
brown, pane of 6 1.00

B139 F-VF
$.90 book (1-695n & 1-618nm), red & blue on white, "$10" OBC 3.00

B139a F-VF
$.90 book (1-695n & 1-618nm), red & blue on white, "$10.00" OBC 100.00

1975. 13¢ Liberty Bell *(pane of 7).*

695n1 F-VF
brown, pane of 7 plus Slogan 8 label ("Paying bills?") 1.75

B140 F-VF
$2.99 book (1-695n1 & 2-695n2), red & blue on white, "$10" OBC 6.00

B140a F-VF
$2.99 book, (1-695n1 & 2-695n2), red & blue on white, "$20" OBC 15.00

1975. 13¢ Liberty Bell *(pane of 8).*

695n2 F-VF
brown, pane of 8 2.00

B140 F-VF
$2.99 book (1-695n1 & 2-695n2), red & blue on white, $10 OBC 6.00

B140a F-VF
$2.99 book, (1-695n1 & 2-695n2), red & blue on white, $20 OBC 15.00

1976. 13¢ Liberty Bell *(pane of 5).*

695n3 F-VF
brown, pane of 5 plus Slogan 9 label (solid print "Collect Stamps") 1.50

695n3a F-VF
brown, pane of 5 plus Slogan 9 label (matrix print "Collect Stamps") 5.00

B141 F-VF
$1.30 book (2-695n3), red & blue on white 3.00

B141a F-VF
$1.30 book (2-695n3a), red & blue on white 10.00

1977. 9¢ Capitol Dome/ 13¢ Flag Over Capitol *Perforated 11 x 10 1/2.*

703n F-VF
Pane of 8 (1-No. 702 - green, 7-No. 703 - red & blue), perforated 11 x 10-1/2 2.75

B142 F-VF
$1.00 book, red & light blue on white, screen printed cover 3.00

B142a F-VF
$1.00 book, red & light blue on white, solid printed cover, $10 Deposit on OBC 3.00

B142b F-VF
$1.00 book, red & light blue on white, solid printed cover, $20 Deposit on OBC 5.00

B142v F-VF
$1.00 book red omitted on OFC 100.00

1977. 9¢ Capitol Dome/13¢ Flag over Capitol perforated 10.

703An F-VF
Pane of 8 (1-No. 702 - green & 7-No. 703 - red & blue), perforated 10, folded between 2nd & 3rd row 29.00

703An1 F-VF
Pane of 8 (1-No. 702A - green & 7-No. 703A - red & blue), perforated 10, folded between 1st & 2nd rows (no selvage tab on pane). 100.00

B143 F-VF
$1.00 book, red & light blue on white, screen printed cover 30.00

B144 F-VF
$1.00 book, red & light blue on white, solid printed cover, $10 DEPOSIT on OBC 30.00

B144a F-VF
$1.00 book, red & light blue on white, solid printed cover, $20.00 DEPOSIT on OBC 30.00

1978. (15¢) Non-denominated "A"

719n F-VF
orange, pane of 8 2.25

B145 F-VF
($3.60) book, orange on white 7.00

1978. 15¢ Oliver Wendell Holmes

626Bn	**maroon,** pane of 8	F-VF 2.50
626Bnv	**Pane of 8,** vertically imperforate	F-VF 1,300.00
B146	**$3.60 book, red & light blue** on white	F-VF 6.50

1978. 15¢ American Flag at Ft. McHenry

722An	**red, blue & gray,** pane of 8	F-VF 3.50
B147	**$1.20 book, red & light blue** on white	F-VF 3.75

1978. 15¢ American Roses

724n	**orange, red & green** pane of 8	F-VF 2.25
724nv	**Pane of 8,** imperforate	F-VF —
724nzo	**Pane of 8,** tagging omitted (error)	F-VF 25.00
B148	**$2.40 book, rose red & yellow green** on white	F-VF 4.00
B148v	**$2.40 book, rose red & yellow green** on white, tagging omitted on both panes	F-VF 75.00

1980. 15¢ Historic Windmills

741n	**brown** on yellow paper, pane of 10 (2 each No. 737-41)	F-VF 3.50
B149	**$3.00 book, light & dark blue** on blue	F-VF 6.00

1981. (18¢) Non-denominated "B"

749n	**purple,** pane of 8	F-VF 3.50
B150	**($4.32) booklet, dull violet,** on white	F-VF 7.00

1981. 6¢ Stars / 18¢ America the Beautiful

756n	**Pane of 8 (2 No. 755 - blue & 6 No. 756 - multicolored)**	F-VF 3.00
756nv	**Pane of 8,** vertically imperforate between, perf at outside edges	F-VF 75.00
B151	**$1.20 book, blue & red** on white, plate #1 over left stamp	F-VF 2.50
	plate #1 over right stamp	50.00
B151v	**$1.20 book, blue & red** on white, vertically imperforate between, perf at outside edges	F-VF 100.00

1981. 18¢ Wildlife

767n	**brown,** pane of 10 (No. 758-67)	F-VF 8.50
767nv	**Pane of 10,** vertically imperforate	F-VF 1,500.00
767nzo	**Pane of 10,** tagging omitted (error)	F-VF 750.00
B152	**$3.60 book, gray & olive** on white, plate #1-10 on top pane	F-VF 15.00
	plate #11-16 on top pane	35.00
B152v	**$3.60 book, gray & olive** on white, both panes untagged	F-VF —
B152v1	**$3.60 book, gray & olive** on white, bottom pane untagged, plate #11	F-VF —

1981. (20¢) Non-denominated "C"

773n	**brown,** pane of 10	F-VF 5.00
B153	**($4.00) book, brown** on blue	F-VF 8.00

1981. 20¢ Flag over Supreme Court *(pane of 6).*

781n	**black, dark red & blue,** pane of 6	F-VF 2.50
B154	**$1.20 book, blue & red** on white, Wildlife Page on OBC, unscored perfs, plate #1	F-VF 3.00
B154a	**$1.20 book, blue & red** on white, Wildlife Page on OBC, scored perfs, plate #1	F-VF 5.00
B154b	**$1.20 book, blue & red** on white, Brooklyn Bridge on OBC, scored perfs, plate #1	F-VF 5.00
B154c	**$1.20 book, blue & red** on white, Brooklyn Bridge on OBC, unscored perfs, plate #1	F-VF 5.00

1982. 20¢ Flag over Supreme Court *(pane of 10).*

781n1	**black, dark red & blue,** pane of 10	F-VF 4.50
B155	**$2.00 book, blue & red** on white, Desert Plants on IBC & OBC, unscored perfs, plate #1	F-VF 4.00
B155a	**$2.00 book, blue & red** on white, dull or Hi-brite, physical Fitness on IBC, Desert Plants on OBC, unscored perfs, plate #1	F-VF 7.50
B155b	**$2.00 book, blue & red** on white, dull or Hi-brite, Physical Fitness on IBC, Desert Plants on OBC, scored perfs, plate #1	F-VF 10.00
B155c	**$2.00 book, blue & red** on white Hi-brite, Physical Fitness on IBC, 75¢ Physical Fitness/Desert Plants on OBC, scored perfs, plate #1	F-VF 750.00
B155d	**$2.00 book, blue & red** on white Hi-brite, Physical Fitness on IBC, 75¢ Physical Fitness/Desert Plants on OBC, scored perfs, plate #4	F-VF 50.00
B155e	**$2.00 book, blue & red** on white, Physical Fitness on IBC, $1.00 Physical Fitness on OBC, unscored perfs, plate #1	F-VF 100.00
B156	**$4.00 book, blue & red** on white, unscored perfs, plate #2	F-VF 8.00
B156a	**$4.00 book, blue & red** on white, scored perfs, plate #2	F-VF 12.50
B156b	**$4.00 book, blue & red** on white Hi-brite, scored perfs, plate #2	F-VF 25.00
B156d	**$4.00 book, blue & red** on white, scored perfs, plate #3	F-VF 25.00
B156e	**$4.00 book, blue & red** on white Hi-brite, scored perfs, plate #3	F-VF 50.00
B156f	**$4.00 book, blue & red** on white Hi-brite, scored perfs, plate #4	F-VF 500.00
B156v	**$4.00 book,** blue omitted on cover, albino impression, plate #2	F-VF 750.00

1982. 20¢ Bighorn Sheep *(Type I).*

783n — F-VF
blue, pane of 10, 18-3/4mm wide, overall tagged — 5.00

783nv — F-VF
Pane of 10, vertically imperforate — —

783nzo — F-VF
Pane of 10, tagging omitted (error) — —

B157 — F-VF
$4.00 book, blue & yellow-green on white, plate number on top pane only, plate #1-6, 9-10 — 15.00
plate number on top pane, plate #16-19 — 75.00
plate number on top pane, plate #20, 22-24 — 150.00
plate number on top pane, plate #25, 26 — 250.00
plate number on top pane, plate #21, 29 — 500.00
plate number on top pane only, plate #28 — 400.00
plate number on bottom pane, plate #9, 10 — 250.00
plate number on bottom pane, plate #14, 15 — 35.00
plate number on bottom pane, plate #16-19 — 500.00
plate number on bottom pane, plate #20, 22-26 — 1,000.00

B157v — F-VF
$4.00 book, blue & yellow-green on white, both panes vertically imperforate, plate #9-10 — 225.00

B157v1 — F-VF
$4.00 book, blue & yellow-green on white, both panes with tagging omitted, plate #1-6 — 35.00

1982. 20¢ Bighorn Sheep *(Type II).*

783An — F-VF
blue, pane of 10, 18-1/2mm wide, block tagged, plate #34 — 5.00

B158 — F-VF
$4.00 book, blue & yellow-green on white, plate number on top pane, plate #34 — 20.00
plate number on bottom pane, plate #34 — 35.00

1983. $3.35 Eagle and Moon (Express Mail)

805n — F-VF
multicolored, pane of 3 — 60.00

B159 — F-VF
$28.05 book, blue & red on white, plate #1111 — 60.00

1985. (22¢) Non-denominated "D"

822n — F-VF
green, pane of 10 — 8.50

822nv — F-VF
Pane of 10, horizontally imperforate — —

B160 — F-VF
($4.40) book, green on white, plate number on top pane, plate #1, 3, 4 — 17.50
plate number on top pane, plate #2 — 875.00
plate number on bottom pane, plate #1 — 1,000.00
plate number on bottom pane, plate #3 — 250.00
plate number on bottom pane, plate #4 — 20.00

B160v — F-VF
($4.40) book, green on white, both panes horizontally imperforate — —

1985. 22¢ Flag over Capitol

830n — F-VF
black, blue & red, pane of 5 — 3.00

B161 — F-VF
$1.10 book, blue & red on white, 5-1/4 gauge cover scoring, plate #1, 3 — 5.00

B161a — F-VF
$1.10 book, blue & red on white, 4-1/4 gauge cover scoring, plate #1 — 5.00

B162 — F-VF
$2.20 book, blue & red on white, 5-1/4 gauge cover scoring, plate #1, 3 — 10.00

B162a — F-VF
$2.20 book, blue & red on white, 4-1/4 gauge cover scoring, plate #1 — 10.00

1985. 22¢ Seashells

836n — F-VF
multicolored pane of 10 (2 each No. 832-36) — 4.00

836nv — F-VF
Pane of 10, purple omitted on No. 835 — 700.00

836nv1 — F-VF
Pane of 10, vertically imperforate — 650.00

836nv2 — F-VF
Pane of 10, imperforate — —

836nzo — F-VF
Pane of 10, tagging omitted (error) — —

B163 — F-VF
$4.40 book, multicolored on white, plate #1-3 — 10.00
set of 7 sequential covers, plate #1, 3 — 65.00
set of 7 sequential covers, plate #2 — 100.00

Seven sequential B163 books are necessary to show all 25 seashells.

B164 — F-VF
$4.40 book, brown & blue on white, plate #1, 3, 5, 6, 7, 10 — 8.00
plate #8 — 10.00

B164v — F-VF
$4.40 book, brown & blue on white, purple omitted on No. 835, top pane only, plate #3 — 700.00

B164v1 — F-VF
$4.40 book, brown & blue on white, one pane vertically imperforate, plate #7 — 650.00

B164v2 — F-VF
$4.40 book, brown & blue on white, one pane imperforate — —

B164v3 — F-VF
$4.40 book, brown & blue on white, tagging omitted — —

1985. $10.75 Eagle and Moon (Express Mail) *(Type I).*

840n — F-VF
multicolored, pane of 3, Type I — 52.00

B165 — F-VF
$32.25 book, bright blue & rose red on white, plate #11111 — 55.00

B165a — F-VF
$32.25 book, navy blue & rose red on white Hi-brite, plate #11111 — 55.00

Type I shows a grainy texture in the denomination.

1989. $10.75 Eagle and Moon (International Express Mail) (Type II).

840an — F-VF
multicolored, pane of 3, Type II — 52.00

B166 — F-VF
$32.25 book, blue & red on white, plate #22222 — 55.00

Type II shows even color in the denomination.

1986. 22¢ Stamp Collecting

CM1181n — F-VF
multicolored, pane of 4 (CM1178-81) — 2.00

CM1181nv — F-VF
Pane of 4, black omitted on CM1178 & CM1181 — 45.00

CM1181nv1 — F-VF
Pane of 4, blue omitted on CM1178-80 — 2,500.00

CM1181nv2 — F-VF
Pane of 4, light brown omitted — —

B167 — F-VF
$1.76 book, purple & black on white, plate #1 — 3.00

B167v — F-VF
$1.76 book, purple & black on white, black omitted on CM1178 & CM1181, plate #1 — 100.00

B167v1 F-VF
$1.76 book, purple & black on white, blue omitted on CM1178-80, plate #1 —

B167v2 F-VF
$1.76 book, purple & black on white, light brown (lithography) omitted, plate #1 —

1986. 22¢ Fish

CM1189n F-VF
multicolored, pane of 5 (CM1185-89) 8.50

B168 F-VF
$2.20 book, blue, green & red on white, plate #11111, 22222 15.00

1986. 22¢ Special Occasions

CM1223n F-VF
multicolored, pane of 10 (2 each CM1216, CM1221 & 1 each CM1217-20, CM1222-23) 10.00

B169 F-VF
$2.20 book, blue & red on white, plate #11111, 22222 15.00

1987. 22¢ Constitution

CM1289n F-VF
multicolored, pane of 5 (CM1285-89) 4.25

CM1289nv F-VF
Pane of 5, blue omitted —

CM1289nv1 F-VF
Pane of 5, black omitted —

CM1289nv2 F-VF
Pane of 5, gray & green omitted from background 7,500.00

B170 F-VF
$4.40 book, red & blue on white, plate #1111, 1112 12.50

B170v F-VF
$4.40 book, on white, blue omitted —

B170v1 F-VF
$4.40 book, on white, black omitted —

B170v2 F-VF
$4.40 book, on white, gray & green omitted from background on one pane 7,500.00

1987. 22¢ Steam Locomotives

CM1297n F-VF
multicolored, pane of 5 (CM1293-97) 3.75

CM1297nv F-VF
Pane of 5, black omitted on one stamp —

CM1297nzo F-VF
Pane of 5, tagging omitted (error) —

B171 F-VF
$4.40 book, black & yellow on white, plate #1, 2 15.00

B171v F-VF
$4.40 book, black & yellow on white, pane with black omitted on one stamp —

B171v1 F-VF
$4.40 book, black & yellow on white, all panes untagged —

1987. 22¢ Flag with Fireworks

875n F-VF
multicolored, pane of 20 8.50

B172 F-VF
$4.40 book, multicolored on white, no plate number 9.50
plate #1111, 2222 15.00
plate #2122 20.00

B172 was made from standard sheet stamps.

1988. (25¢) Non-denominated "E"

886n F-VF
multicolored, pane of 10 6.50

B173 F-VF
($5.00) book, blue on white, scored perforations, plate #1111, 2122, 2222 10.00
unscored perforations, plate #2122 25.00

B173v F-VF
($5.00) book, blue on white, yellow plate # omitted, plate #111 —

B173v1 F-VF
($5.00) book, ultramarine on white, scored perforations, plate #2222 25.00

1988. 25¢ Pheasant

887n F-VF
multicolored, pane of 10 6.00

887nv F-VF
Pane of 10, horizontally imperforate 2,250.00

B174 F-VF
$5.00 book, multicolored on white, plate #A1111 10.00

B174v F-VF
$5.00 book, multicolored on white, one pane horizontally imperforate —

Fully imperforate panes were cut from printer's waste.

1988. 25¢ Pheasant *(red removed from background sky).*

887an F-VF
multicolored, pane of 10 75.00

B175 F-VF
$5.00 book, multicolored on white, plate #A3111 150.00
plate #A3222 125.00

1988. 25¢ Jack London *(pane of 10).*

888n F-VF
blue, pane of 10 4.50

888nzo F-VF
Pane of 10, tagging omitted (error) —

B176 F-VF
$5.00 book, multicolored on white, plate #1, 2 10.00

B176v F-VF
$5.00 book, multicolored on white, tagging omitted —

1988. 25¢ Jack London *(pane of 6).*

889n F-VF
blue, pane of 6 2.75

889nzo F-VF
Pane of 6, tagging omitted (error) 55.00

B177 F-VF
$1.50 book, blue & brown on white, plate #1 3.00

B177v F-VF
$1.50 book, blue & brown on white, tagging omitted 75.00

B178 F-VF
$3.00 book, brown & blue on white, plate #1 3.00

B178a F-VF
$3.00 book, brown & blue on white Hi-brite, plate #1 25.00

1988. 25¢ Owl and Grosbeak

893n F-VF
multicolored, pane of 10 (5 No. 892 & 5 N0. 893) 4.50

893nzo F-VF
Pane of 10, tagging omitted (error) —

B179 F-VF
$5.00 book, red & black on white, two buds on OFC, plate #1111, 1211, 2222 12.50
plate #2122 350.00

B179a F-VF
$5.00 book, red & black on white, one bud on OFC, 5-1/4 gauge cover scoring, plate #1111, 1112, 1211, 1433, 1434, 1734, 2111, 2121, 2122, 2222, 2321, 3133, 3333, 3412, 3413, 3422, 4642, 4644, 4911, 5955 12.50

plate #1133, 2221, 3233, 3512, 3521, 4941 — 20.00
plate #1414, 1634 — 75.00
plate #3822 — 25.00
plate #5453 — 250.00

B179av F-VF
$5.00 book, red & black on white, one bud on OFC, 5-1/4 gauge cover scoring, tagging omitted —

B179b F-VF
$5.00 book, red & black on white, one bud on OFC, 8-3/4 gauge cover scoring, plate #1133, 1433, 2121, 2221, 2321, 3133, 3333 — 100.00

1988. 25¢ Flag with Clouds

890An F-VF
multicolored, pane of 6 — 2.75

B180 F-VF
$3.00 book, red & blue on white, plate #1111 — 5.50

1988. 25¢ Classic Cars

CM1322n F-VF
multicolored, pane of 5 (CM1318-22) — 10.00

B181 F-VF
$5.00 book, black & red on white, plate #1 — 30.00

1988. Special Occasions

CM1332n F-VF
multicolored, pane of 6 (3 each CM1331-32 with gutter between) — 5.00
unfolded pane with First Day cancel — 20.00

CM1334n F-VF
multicolored, pane of 6 (3 each CM1333-34 with gutter between) — 5.00
mint unfolded pane — — 3,500.00
unfolded pane with First Day cancel — 20.00

CM1334nv F-VF
Pane of 6, horizontally imperforate —

B182 F-VF
$3.00 book (1-CM1332n & 1-CM1334n), multicolored on white, large print on IFC, plate #A1111 — 12.50

B182a F-VF
$3.00 book (1-CM1332n & 1-CM1334n), multicolored on white, small print on IFC, plate #A1111 — 12.50

Unfolded panes were used by USPS for first Day Programs & Souvenir pages. They were not regularily sold to the public.

1989. 25¢ Steamboats

CM1343n F-VF
multicolored, pane of 5 (CM1339-43) — 3.60
unfolded pane, plate #1 — 7.50
unfolded pane, plate #2 — 37.50

B183 F-VF
$5.00 book, blue & black on white, plate #1, 2 — 12.50

1989. 25¢ Christmas Madonna

922n F-VF
multicolored, pane of 10 — 3.00
unfolded pane, plate #1 — 10.00

922nv F-VF
Pane of 10, offset red omitted — 750.00

922nv1 F-VF
Pane of 10, imperforate —

B184 F-VF
$5.00 book, multicolored on white, plate #1 — 10.00

1989. 25¢ Sleigh

921n F-VF
multicolored, pane of 10 — 3.00
unfolded pane, plate #1111 — 12.50

921nv F-VF
Pane of 10, red omitted — 7,150.00

921nv1 F-VF
Pane of 10, horizontally imperforate —

B185 F-VF
$5.00 book, multicolored on white, plate #1111 — 10.00
plate #2111 — 25.00

1990. 25¢ Love

CM1369n F-VF
multicolored, pane of 10 — 5.00
unfolded pane, plate #1211 — 37.50

CM1369nv F-VF
Pane of 10, pink omitted — 2,000.00

B186 F-VF
$5.00 book, multicolored, on white, plate #1211, 2222 — 20.00
plate #2111, 2211 — 30.00

B186v F-VF
$5.00 book, multicolored, on white, black plate #omitted, plate 222 —

1990. 15¢ Beach Umbrella

926n F-VF
multicolored, pane of 10 — 4.25
unfolded pane, plate #111111 — 10.00

926nv F-VF
Pane of 10, blue omitted — 1,650.00

B187 F-VF
$3.00 book, multicolored on white, plate #111111 — 5.75
plate #221111 — 25.00

B187v F-VF
$5.00 book, multicolored on white, blue omitted on top pane only, plate #111111 — 1,650.00

1990. 25¢ Lighthouse

CM1382n F-VF
multicolored, pane of 5 (CM1378-82) — 4.00
unfolded pane, plate #1-3, 5 — 10.00
unfolded pane, plate #4 — 250.00

CM1382nv F-VF
Pane of 5, white omitted — 75.00

B188 F-VF
$5.00 book, blue & red on white, plate #1-5 — 15.00

B188v F-VF
$5.00 book, blue & red on white, white omitted on all panes — 300.00

1990. 25¢ Indian Headdresses

CM1393n F-VF
multicolored, pane of 10 (2 each CM1389-93) — 5.00
unfolded pane, plate #1 — 25.00
unfolded pane, plate #2 — 35.00

CM1393nv F-VF
Pane of 10, intaglio black omitted — 3,850.00

B189 F-VF
$5.00 book, multicolored on white, plate #1, 2 — 12.50

1990. 25¢ Christmas Tree

934n F-VF
multicolored, pane of 10 — 8.00
unfolded pane, plate #1211 — 10.00

B190 F-VF
$5.00 book, multicolored on white, plate #1211 — 10.00

1990. 25¢ Madonna

936n F-VF
multicolored, pane of 10 — 8.00
unfolded pane, plate #1 — 10.00

B191 F-VF
$5.00 book, multicolored on white, plate #1 — 10.00

1991. (29¢) Non-denominated "F" *(BEP).*

938n F-VF
multicolored, pane of 10 6.00

B192 F-VF
($2.90) book, yellow & multicolored on white, plate #2222 6.00

B193 F-VF
($5.80) book, green, red & black on white, plate #1111, 2222 11.00
plate #1222 50.00
plate #2111, 2121, 2212 25.00

1991. (29¢) Non-denominated "F" *(KCS).*

939n F-VF
multicolored, pane of 10 25.00
unfolded pane, plate #K1111 —
unfolded pane with first day cancel 10.00

(Unfolded panes were used by USPS on some souvenir pages; they were not sold to the public)

939nv F-VF
Pane of 10, imperforate horizontally —

B194 F-VF
($2.90) book, green, red & black on white, plate #K1111 25.00

On 939n the leaf is brighter green and the background yellow is paler than on 938n.

1991. 29¢ Tulip

948n F-VF
multicolored, pane of 10, shiny gum 8.00
unfolded pane, plate #K1111 10.00

948nv F-VF
Pane of 10, vertically imperforate 1,900.00

948nv1 F-VF
Pane of 10, imperforate horizontally 2,800.00

B195 F-VF
$5.80 book, green, red & black on white, plate #K1111, K2222 11.00

B195v F-VF
$5.80 book, green, red & black on white, top pane vertically imperforate, plate #K1111 1,900.00

1993. 29¢ Tulip *(reprint).*

948ng F-VF
multicolored, pane of 10, low-gloss gum 8.00

B195a F-VF
$5.80 book, green, red & black on white, plate #K3333 10.00

1991. 29¢ Wood Duck *(BEP - black inscription).*

950n F-VF
black & multicolored, pane of 10, overall tagging 8.00
unfolded pane, plate #1111 10.00

950nv F-VF
Pane of 10, overall tagging, imperforate horizontally 1,000.00

950nz F-VF
Pane of 10, phosphored paper 8.00

B196 F-VF
$2.90 book, black & green on white, 5-1/4 gauge cover scoring, overall tagging, plate #4444 5.75

B196a F-VF
$2.90 book, black & green on white, 8-3/4 gauge cover scoring, overall tagging, plate #4444 25.00

B196v F-VF
$2.90 book, black & green on white, 5-1/4 gauge cover scoring, phosphored paper, plate #4444 5.75

B197 F-VF
$5.80 book, black & red on white, overall tagging, plate #1111, 2222, 4444 10.00
plate #1211, 3331 150.00
plate #2122, 3222, 3333 20.00
plate #3221 75.00

B197v F-VF
$5.80 book, black & red on white, overall tagging, both panes horizontally imperforate between, perforated at top edge 1,200.00

1991. 29¢ Wood Duck *(KCS - red inscription).*

951n F-VF
red & multicolored, pane of 10 8.75
unfolded pane, plate #K11111 10.00

951nv F-VF
Pane of 10, imperforate horizontally 1,500.00

B198 F-VF
$5.80 book, black & multicolored on white, plate #K11111 11.00

1991. 29¢ Flag with Olympic Rings

952n F-VF
multicolored, pane of 10 8.00
unfolded pane, plate #K11111 10.00

952nv F-VF
Pane of 10, imperforate horizontally —

B199 F-VF
$2.90 book, black & multicolored on white, postal rate chart on OBC, plate #K11111 5.75

B200 F-VF
$2.90 book, black & multicolored on white, Free WCSE Pass on OBC, plate #K11111 5.75

B201 F-VF
$2.90 book, black & multicolored on white, Aviation Pioneers offer on OBC, plate #K11111 12.50

1991. 29¢ Love

CM1406n F-VF
multicolored, pane of 10 7.50
unfolded pane, plate #1111, 1112 10.00

B202 F-VF
$5.80 book, multicolored on white, plate #1111, 1112 11.50
plate #1113, 1123, 2223 15.00
plate #1212 25.00

1991. 19¢ Balloon

953n F-VF
multicolored, pane of 10 4.50
unfolded pane, plate #1111 5.00

B203 F-VF
$3.80 book, black & blue on white, plate #1111, 2222 7.00
plate #1222 35.00

1991. 29¢ Fishing Flies

CM1413n F-VF
multicolored, pane of 5 (CM1409-13) 5.50
unfolded pane, plate #A11111 3,000.00
unfolded pane, plate #A22122 1,000.00
unfolded pane, plate #A23124, A32225, A33233 75.00
unfolded pane, plate #A23133, A23213 10.00
unfolded pane, plate #A33213 2,000.00

CM1413v F-VF
Pane of 5, black omitted from CM1409-11 —

B204 F-VF
$5.80 book, multicolored on white, 10 gauge cover scoring, plate #A22122, A22132, A22133, A23123, A23124, A23213, A31224, A32224, A32225, A33233, A33235 25.00
plate #A11111, A23133 45.00

B204a F-VF
$5.80 book, multicolored on white, 5 gauge cover scoring, plate #A31224, A33233, A33235 25.00

B204b F-VF
$5.80 book, multicolored on white, 8 gauge cover scoring, plate #A11111, A23123, A33233, A33235 45.00

plate #A44446, A45546, A45547 25.00

Fishing Flies booklets can contain up to four different plate number combinations on the four panes. The above prices are for the listed plate number on the top pane.

1991. 29¢ Desert Storm

CM1416n F-VF
multicolored, pane of 5 4.00
unfolded pane, plate #A11121111

B205 F-VF
$5.80 book, multicolored on white, plate #A11111111 25.00
plate #A11121111 11.50

1991. 29¢ Comedians

CM1428n F-VF
multicolored, pane of 10 (2 each CM1424-28) 6.00
unfolded pane, plate #1 15.00

CM1428nv F-VF
Pane of 10, intaglio red & purple omitted 850.00

CM1428nv1 F-VF
Pane of 10, intaglio red omitted —

CM1428nv2 F-VF
Pane of 10, intaglio purple omitted —

B206 F-VF
$5.80 book, red, black & purple on white, plate #1, 2 15.00

B206v F-VF
$5.80 book, red, black & purple on white, intaglio red & purple omitted from top pane 850.00

1991. 29¢ Space Exploration

CM1441n F-VF
mulicolored, pane of 10 (CM1432-41) 8.75
unfolded pane, plate #111111 12.50

B207 F-VF
$5.80 book, blue, black & red on white, plate #111111 12.50
plate #111112 20.00

1991. (29¢) Non-denominated Santa

972An F-VF
multicolored, pane of 4 (2 each No. 972, 972A) 2.00
unfolded pane, plate #A11111 15.00

973n F-VF
multicolored, pane of 4 1.50
unfolded pane, plate #A11111 3.00

974n F-VF
multicolored, pane of 4 1.50
unfolded pane, plate #A11111 3.00

974v F-VF
Pane of 4, imperforate —

975n F-VF
multicolored, pane of 4 1.50
unfolded pane, plate #A11111 3.00

975v F-VF
multicolored, pane of 4, imperforate —

976n F-VF
multicolored, pane of 4 1.50
unfolded pane, plate #A11111 3.00

976v F-VF
Pane of 4, imperforate —

B208 F-VF
($5.80 book (1 each No. 972An-76n), multicolored on white, plate #A11111, A12111 20.00

1991. (29¢) Non-denominated Madonna

977n F-VF
multicolored, pane of 10 8.00
unfolded pane, plate #1 10.00

B209 F-VF
($5.80) book, multicolored on white, plate #1 11.50

1992. 29¢ Hummingbirds

CM1477n F-VF
multicolored, pane of 5 (CM1473-77) 4.50
unfolded pane, plate #A1111111, A2212222 15.00
unfolded pane, plate #A2212112, A2212122, A2222222 7.50

CM1477nv F-VF
Pane of 5, imperforate —

B210 F-VF
$5.80 book, multicolored on white, plate #A1111111, A2212112, A2212222, A2222222 11.50
plate #A2212122 25.00

Hummingbirds booklets exist with various plate number combinations on the four panes. The above prices are for the listed plate number on the top pane.

1992. 29¢ Pledge of Allegiance *(BEP - black inscription) - perforated 10.*

987n F-VF
black & multicolored, pane of 10 7.50
unfolded pane, plate #1111 8.50

B211 F-VF
$2.90 book, blue & red on white, plate #1111, 2222 7.50

B212 F-VF
$5.80 book, blue & red on white, plate #1111, 2222 11.00
plate #1211, 2122 250.00

1992. 29¢ Pledge of Allegiance *(BEP - black inscription) - perforated 11 x 10.*

987an F-VF
black & multicolored, pane of 10 12.00

B213 F-VF
$5.80 book, blue & red on white, plate #1111, 1211, 2122, 2222, 3333 15.00
plate #2232 15.00
plate #2333 500.00
plate #4444 25.00

1993-94. 29¢ Pledge of Allegiance *(KCS - red inscription).*

1008n F-VF
red & multicolored, pane of 10 7.50
unfolded pane, plate #K1111 8.50

B214 F-VF
$2.90 book, black, red & blue on white, 9 1/2 gauge cover scoring, plate #K1111 5.00

B214a F-VF
$2.90 book, black, red & blue on white, 6 3/4 gauge cover scoring, plate #K1111 25.00

B215 F-VF
$5.80 book, multicolored on white, plate #K1111 11.50

1992. 29¢ Wild Animals

CM1540n F-VF
multicolored, pane of 5 (CM1536-40) 2.25
unfolded pane, plate #K1111 5.00

CM1540nv F-VF
Pane of 5, imperforate 2,500.00

B216 F-VF
$5.80 book, multicolored on white, plate #K1111 11.00

1992. 29¢ Christmas Toys

1002n F-VF
multicolored, pane of 4 (No. 999-1002) 3.50
unfolded pane, plate #A111111, A222222 5.00
unfolded pane, plate #A11211 500.00

1002nv F-VF
Pane of 4, imperforate —

1002nv1 F-VF
Pane of 4, imperforate horizontally —

B217 F-VF
$5.80 book, multicolored on white, plate #111111, A112211, A222222 — 11.00

Toys booklets exist with various plate number combinations on the five panes.

1992. 29¢ Madonna

1003n F-VF
multicolored, pane of 10 — 8.00
unfolded pane, plate #1 — 9.00

B218 F-VF
$5.80 book, multicolored on white, plate #1 — 11.50

1993. 29¢ Space Fantasy

CM1547n F-VF
multicolored, pane of 5 (CM1541-45) — 3.50
unfolded pane, plate #1111, 1211 — 5.00
unfolded pane, plate #2222 — 7.00

B219 F-VF
$5.80 book, multicolored on white, plate #1111, 1211, 2222 — 11.50

1993. 29¢ Spring Garden Flowers

CM1567n F-VF
multicolored, pane of 5 (CM1563-67) — 5.50
unfolded pane, plate #1 — 10.00

CM1567nv F-VF
Pane of 5, imperforate — 2,750.00

CM1567nv1 F-VF
Pane of 5, intaglio black omitted — 350.00

B220 F-VF
$5.80 book, multicolored on white, plate #1, 2 — 11.50

B220v F-VF
$5.80 book, multicolored on white, all panes with intaglio black omitted — 2,000.00

B220v1 F-VF
$5.80 book, multicolored on white, imperforate — 5,000.00

1993. 29¢ Rock 'n' Roll

CM1583n F-VF
multicolored, pane of 8 (2 of CM1577, 1 each CM1578-83) — 4.50
unfolded pane, plate #A11111*, A13113 — 50.00
unfolded pane, plate #A22222 — 8.00

**Found only on panes of 7 (missing bottom Elvis stamp) from 1993 Commemorative mint set.*

CM1583n1 F-VF
multicolored, pane of 4 (CM1577, CM1581-83) — 2.50
unfolded pane, plate #A13113 — 75.00
unfolded pane, plate #A22222 — 5.00

Note: CM1583n1 without tab is indistinguishable from strip of the bottom 4 stamps of CM1583n.

B221 F-VF
$5.80 book (1-CM1583n & 2-CM1583n1), multicolored on white, plate #A11111, A22222 — 11.00
plate #A13113, A44444 — 15.00

Note: Rock 'n' Roll booklets exist with various plate number combinations on the three panes. The above prices are for the listed plate number on the top pane.

1993. 29¢ Broadway Musicals

CM1588n F-VF
multicolored, pane of 4 (CM1585-88) — 4.95
unfolded pane, plate #A11111, A11121, A22222 — 5.00

B222 F-VF
$5.80 book, multicolored, plate #A11111, A22222, A23233 — 11.00
plate #A11121, A23232 — 20.00

1993. 29¢ Country & Western

CM1602n F-VF
multicolored, pane of 4 (CM1599-1602) — 3.50
unfolded pane, plate #A222222 — 4.00

B223 F-VF
$5.80 book, multicolored on white, plate #A111111, A222222 — 11.50
plate #A333323 — 1,250.00
plate #A333333, A422222 — 15.00

1993. 29¢ African Violets

1018n F-VF
multicolored, pane of 10 — 5.50
unfolded pane, plate #K1111 — 6.25

B224 F-VF
$2.90 book, pink & multicolored on white, plate #K1111 — 6.00

B225 F-VF
$5.80 book, multicolored on white, plate #K1111 — 11.50

1993. 29¢ Contemporary Christmas

1026n F-VF
multicolored, pane of 10 (3 each No. 1023-24, 2 each No. 1025-26) — 6.50
unfolded pane, plate #111111 — 7.50

1026n1 F-VF
multicolored, pane of 10 (2 each No. 1023-24, 3 each No. 1025-26) — 6.50
unfolded pane, plate #111111 — 7.50

B226 F-VF
$5.80 book (1-1026n & 1-1026n1), multicolored on white, plate #111111, 222222 — 15.00

1993. 29¢ Madonna

1028n F-VF
multicolored, pane of 4 — 4.00
unfolded pane, plate #K1-11111, K1-33333, K1-44444 — 5.00
unfolded pane, plate #K2-55555 — 100.00

1028nv F-VF
Pane of 4, imperforate — —

B227 F-VF
$5.80 book, multicolored on white, plate #K1-11111, K1-33333, K1-44444, K2-55555, K2-66666 — 20.00
plate #K2-22222 — 11.50

1993. 29¢ Aids Awareness

CM1609An F-VF
multicolored, pane of 5 — 2.50
unfolded pane, plate #K111 — 3.75

B228 F-VF
$2.90 book, black & red on white, plate #K111 — 5.75

1994. 29¢ Love - Dove and Roses

CM1619n F-VF
multicolored, pane of 10 — 6.00
unfolded pane, plate #A11111 — 7.00

CM1619nv F-VF
Pane of 10, imperforate — —

B229 F-VF
$5.80 book, multicolored on white, plate #A11111, A21222 — 11.50
plate #A12111, A12112, A12211, A22122, A22222, A22322 — 20.00
plate #A11311, A12212, A21311 — 75.00

1994. 29¢ Summer Garden Flowers

CM1636n F-VF
multicolored, pane of 5 (CM1632-36) — 4.50
unfolded pane, plate #2 — 5.00

CM1636nv F-VF
Pane of 5, intaglio black omitted — 375.00

CM1636nv1 F-VF
Pane of 5, imperforate — 500.00

B230 F-VF
$5.80 book, multicolored on white, plate #1, 2 — 11.50

B230v F-VF
$5.80 book, multicolored on white, intaglio black omitted on all panes — 1,750.00

B230v1 F-VF
$5.80 book, multicolored on white, all panes imperforate 2,000.00

1994. 29¢ LOCOMOTIVES

CM1650n F-VF
multicolored, pane of 5 (CM1646-50) 4.50
unfolded pane, plate #S11111 5.00

CM1650nv F-VF
Pane of 5, imperforate —

B231 F-VF
$5.80 book, multicolored, plate #S11111 11.50

1994. 29¢ CHRISTMAS STOCKING

1047n F-VF
multicolored, pane of 20 8.50
unfolded pane, plate #P11111, P44444 15.00
unfolded pane, plate #P22222 50.00
unfolded pane, plate #P33333 3,000.00

1047nv F-VF
Pane of 20, horizontally imperforate —

B232 F-VF
$5.80 book, multicolored on white, plate #P11111, P22222, P33333, P44444 11.50

1994. 29¢ MADONNA

1049n F-VF
multicolored, pane of 10 5.50
unfolded pane, plate #1, 2 6.00

1049nv F-VF
Pane of 10, imperforate 5,000.00

B233 F-VF
$5.80 book, multicolored on white, plate #1, 2 11.50

1994. (32¢) NON-DENOMINATED "G" *(BEP - black "G") - perforated 11-1/4 x 11.*

1054n F-VF
black & multicolored, pane of 10 6.00

B234 F-VF
($3.20) book, blue & red on shiny white, plate #1111 6.00

1994. (32¢) NON-DENOMINATED "G" *(BEP - black "G") - perforated 10.*

1056n F-VF
black & multicolored, pane of 10 6.00

B235 F-VF
($3.20) book, blue & red on dull white, plate #1111, 2222 6.00

B236 F-VF
($6.40) book, blue & red on dull white, plate #1111, 2222 12.50

1994. (32¢) NON-DENOMINATED "G" *(ABNC - blue "G").*

1057n F-VF
blue & multicolored, pane of 10 6.00

1057nv F-VF
Pane of 10, perforated in the tab at the top of the stamps, otherwise imperforate —

B237 F-VF
($6.40) book, black, red & blue on white, both panes, plate #A1111, A1211, A2222, A3333, A4444 12.50
same with different plate number on bottom pane 25.00

B237v F-VF
($6.40) book, black, red & blue on white, one pane perforated in the tab at the top of the stamps, otherwise imperforate, plate #A2222 —

1994. (32¢) NON-DENOMINATED "G" *(KCS - red "G").*

1058n F-VF
red & multicolored, pane of 10 6.00

1058nv F-VF
Pane of 10, imperforate —

B238 F-VF
($6.40) book, black, red & blue on white, plate #K1111 12.50

Makeshift Vending Machine Booklets

In early 1996, the USPS contracted with Minnesota Diversified Industries (MDI) to fabricate vending machine booklets of 15 and 30 stamps in order to create $4.80 and $9.60 products. These would reduce the amount of change that would be needed to be dispensed from the vending machines. With these booklets being intended only for self-service machines, they were almost never offered from Philatelic Sales in Kansas City. These booklets all have a blue cover and window exposing up to four of the stamps. The outside back cover has a description, item number and price in varying formats.

These blue MDI books were made from stock originally intended to be made into panes of 50 and convertible booklets (self-stick sheetlets of 20). Those containing self-adhesive stamps are unique since they can not be created from the individual 20 stamp sheetlets as sold by the post office. Because of the way that they were manufactured, many different assembly varieties are found on several of the MDI booklets making it nearly impossible to collect an example of every booklet variety. It is beyond the scope of this catalog to include all of these varieties.

1996. 32¢ FLAG OVER PORCH *(MDI self-adhesive).*

1078n1 F-VF
multicolored, pane of 15 plus label 9.00

1078n2 F-VF
Pane of 16 with UL or LR stamp removed, no label 9.00

B239 F-VF
$4.80 book (1-1078n1), blue on white (4) 9.00

B240 F-VF
$4.80 book (1-1078n2), blue on white (3) 17.50

B241 F-VF
$9.60 book (2-1078n1), blue on white (3) 20.00

1078n2 can not be made from 1057n1 because the label is die cut and if removed, leaves an impression of the die cutting.

The number in parentheses indicates the number of printing variations on the OBC.

1997. 32¢ LOVE CHERUB *(MDI water activated).*

B242 F-VF
$4.80 book (15-CM1703), blue on white, plate #4222-1, 5422-1, 7633-1, 7643-1, 7644-1, 7645-1, or no plate number 9.00

1995. 32¢ LOVE CHERUB *(water activated).*

CM1704n F-VF
multicolored, pane of 10 5.50
unfolded pane, plate #1 7.50

B243 F-VF
$6.40 book, multicolored on white, plate #1 11.00

1997. 32¢ FLAG OVER PORCH *(MDI water activated).*

B244 F-VF
$4.80 book (15-No. 1080), blue on white, plate #S22222 or no plate number 9.00

1995. 32¢ FLAG OVER PORCH *(water activated).*

1081n F-VF
multicolored, pane of 10 6.25
unfolded pane, plate #11111 7.00

1081nv F-VF
Pane of 10, imperforate —

B245 F-VF
$3.20 book, multicolored on white, plate #11111, 22222, 33332 6.50
plate #23222, 44444 —

B246 F-VF
$6.40 book, multicolored on white, plate #11111, 22222, 23222, 32222, 44444 12.00

1996. 32¢ PINK ROSE *(MDI self-adhesive).*

1084n1 F-VF
multicolored, pane of 15 plus label 20.00

1084n2 F-VF
multicolored, pane of 14, no label 22.50

1084n3 F-VF
multicolored, pane of 16, no label 22.50

1084n4 F-VF
multicolored, pane of 16, stamp removed from top or bottom row, no label 22.50

B247 F-VF
$4.80 book (1-1084n1), blue on white, with cellophane wrapper (2) 20.00

B248 F-VF
$4.80 book (1-1084n1), blue on white, no cellophane wrapper (3) 15.00

B249 F-VF
$4.80 book (1-1084n4), blue on white, no cellophane wrapper 15.00

B250 F-VF
$9.60 book (1-1084n2, 1-1084n3), blue on white, with cellophane wrapper (3) 45.00

B251 F-VF
$9.60 book (2-1084n1), blue on white, no cellophane wrapper (3) 20.00

B252 F-VF
$9.60 book (2-1084n4), blue on white, no cellophane wrapper (3) 25.00

B252a F-VF
$9.60 book (1-1084n1, 1-1084n4), blue on white, no cellophane wrapper —

1084n4 can not be made from 1084n3 because the label is die cut and if removed, leaves an impression of the die cutting.

Cellophane wrapped books have the description and item number on a sticker and not on the booklet itself.

1995. 20¢ Blue Jay *(water activated).*

1087n F-VF
multicolored, pane of 10 4.25
unfolded pane, plate #S1111 5.00

B253 F-VF
$2.00 book, multicolored on white, plate #S1111 6.50

1995. 32¢ Great Lakes Lighthouses

CM1719n F-VF
multicolored, pane of 5 (CM1715-19) 3.50
unfolded pane, plate #S11111 4.00

B254 F-VF
$6.40 book, multicolored on white, plate #S11111 12.00

1995. 32¢ Peaches and Pear *(water activated).*

1090n F-VF
multicolored, pane of 10 (5 No. 1090y) 6.25
unfolded pane, plate #11111 7.00

B255 F-VF
$6.40 book, multicolored on white, plate #11111 12.00

1995. 32¢ Fall Garden Flowers

CM1762n F-VF
multicolored, pane of 5 (CM1758-62) 4.00
unfolded pane, plate #2 5.00

CM1762nv F-VF
Pane of 5, imperforate —

B256 F-VF
$6.40 book, multicolored on white, plate #2 12.00

1995. 32¢ Contemporary Christmas *(water activated).*

1101n F-VF
multicolored, pane of 5 (3 each No. 1098-99, 2 each No. 1100-01) 6.50
unfolded pane, plate #P1111 7.50

1101n1 F-VF
multicolored, pane of 5 (2 each No. 1098-99, 3 each No. 1100-01) 6.50
unfolded pane, plate #P1111 7.50

B257 F-VF
$6.40 book (1-1101n, 1-1101n1), multicolored on white, plate #P1111, P2222 or any combination 12.00

B257v F-VF
$6.40 book (2-1101n), multicolored on white, plate #P1111 —

B257v1 F-VF
$6.40 book (2-1101n1), multicolored on white, plate #P1111 —

B257v2 F-VF
$6.40 book (1-1101n & 1-1101n1), multicolored on white, bottom pane shows tab at bottom, plate #P1111 —

B257v3 F-VF
$6.40 book (1-1101n & 1-1101n1), multicolored on white, bottom pane blank, plate #P1111 —

1995. 32¢ Madonna

1113n F-VF
multicolored, pane of 10, plate number next to LL stamp 6.50
unfolded pane, plate #1 7.50

1113nv F-VF
Pane of 10, plate number next to UL stamp (miscut & misperfed) 25.00

B258 F-VF
$6.40 book (2-1113n), multicolored on white, plate #1 12.00

B258v F-VF
$6.40 book (2-1113nv), multicolored on white, plate #1 50.00

1996. 32¢ Midnight Angel *(MDI self-adhesive).*

1110n1 F-VF
multicolored, pane of 15 plus label 10.00

1110n2 F-VF
multicolored, pane of 16 with one stamp removed, no label 10.00

B259 F-VF
$4.80 book (1-1110n1), blue on white (2) 10.00

B259A F-VF
$4.80 book (1-1110n2), blue on white —

B260 F-VF
$9.60 book (2-1110n1), blue on white (3) 20.00

B261 F-VF
$9.60 book (1-1110n1, 1-1110n2), blue on white 35.00

B262 F-VF
$9.60 book (2-1110n2), blue on white (3) 20.00

1996. 32¢ Utah Centennial *(MDI water activated).*

B263 F-VF
$4.80 book (15-CM1792), blue on white, plate #P11111, P22222 or no plate number 10.00

1996. 32¢ Winter Garden Flowers

CM1797n F-VF
multicolored, pane of 5 (CM1793-97) 3.50
unfolded pane, plate #1 4.00

CM1797nv F-VF
Pane of 5 (CM1793-97), imperforate —

B264 F-VF
$6.40 book, multicolored on white, plate #1 11.00

1996. 32¢ Love Cherub *(MDI self-adhesive).*

CM1798n1 F-VF
multicolored, pane of 15 plus label 10.00

B265 F-VF
$4.80 book, blue on white (4) 10.00

B266 F-VF
$9.60 book, blue on white (3) 20.00

1996. 32¢ Fulbright Scholarships *(MDI water activated).*

B267 F-VF
$4.80 book (15-CM1806), blue on white, plate #1-1111 or no plate number 10.00

1996. 32¢ Flag over Porch *(self-adhesive).*

1125n F-VF
multicolored, pane of 10, Dated "1996" 6.50
unfolded pane, plate #21221, 22221, 22222 7.50

B268 F-VF
$6.40 book, multicolored on white, plate #11111, 13111, 21221, 22221, 22222, 44434, 55555, 55556, 66666, 77777, 88788, 88888, 99999 (4) 12.00

1996. 32¢ Georgia O'Keeffe *(MDI water activated).*

B269 F-VF
$4.80 book (15-CM1828), blue on white, plate #S1111 (2) 10.00

1996. 32¢ Tennessee Statehood *(MDI water activated).*

B270 F-VF
$4.80 book (15-CM1829), blue on white, plate #S11111 or no plate number (2) 10.00

1996. 32¢ American Indian Dances *(MDI water activated).*

B271 F-VF
$4.80 book (3-CM1835y), blue on white, plate #P1111, P2222, P3333 10.00

1996. 32¢ James Dean *(MDI water activated).*

B272 F-VF
$4.80 book (15-CM1841), blue on white, plate #S1111111 (2) 10.00

1996. 32¢ Folk Heroes *(MDI water activated).*

B273 F-VF
$4.80 book (15 from CM1842-45) blue on white (2) 10.00

The contents of B273 may vary.

1996. 32¢ Olympic Games Centennial *(MDI water activated).*

B274 F-VF
$4.80 book (15-CM1846), blue on white, plate #P1 (2) 10.00

1996. 32¢ Iowa Statehood *(MDI water activated).*

B275 F-VF
$4.80 book (15-CM1847), blue on white, plate P1111, P2222 or no plate number 10.00

1996. 20¢ Blue Jay *(self-adhesive).*

1135n1 F-VF
multicolored, pane of 4 2.00

1135n2 F-VF
multicolored, pane of 6 3.00

B276 F-VF
$2.00 book (1-1135n1 & 1-1135n2), multicolored on white, 12-1/2 gauge cover scoring, plate S1111 6.50

B276a F-VF
$2.00 book (1-1135n1 & 1-1135n2), multicolored on white, 8-1/2 gauge cover scoring, plate #S2222 6.50

Nos. 1135n1 and 1135n2 are from B276 or B276a, the peelable strip removed and the rouletting line 2mm lower than on 1135n.

1996. 32¢ Rural Free Delivery *(MDI water activated).*

B277 F-VF
$9.60 book (2 panes of 15-CM1849), blue on white, plate #1111-2, 1112-1, 1122-1, 1123-1, 2224-1, 2235-1, 3235-1 20.00

Rural free Delivery booklets exist with various plate number combinations on the two panes.

1996. 32¢ Riverboats *(MDI self-adhesive).*

B278 F-VF
$4.80 book (3 each CM1850-54), blue on white 10.00

1996. 32¢ Endangered Species *(MDI water activated).*

B279 F-VF
$4.80 book (CM1864-78), blue on white 10.00

1996. 32¢ Madonna *(MDI water activated).*

B280 F-VF
$4.80 book (15-No. 1146), blue on white, plate #1111-1, 1112-1, 2222-1, or no plate number 10.00

1996. 32¢ Hanukkah *(MDI self-adhesive).*

B281 F-VF
$4.80 book (15-CM1880), blue on white, plate #V11111, or no plate number 10.00

1996. 32¢ Yellow Rose

1149n1 F-VF
multicolored, pane of 4 3.00

1149n2 F-VF
multicolored, pane of 5 plus label, plate #S1111 on LL stamp 3.75

1149n3 F-VF
multicolored, pane of 6, plate #S1111 on LR stamp or no plate number 4.50

B282 F-VF
$4.80 book (1-1149n1 + 1-1149n2 + 1-1149n3), multicolored on white, plate #S1111 on LL stamp 10.00

B283 F-VF
$9.60 book (3-1149n3), multicolored on white, plate #S1111 on LR stamp 20.00

1997. 32¢ Flag over Porch *(self-adhesive).*

1150n F-VF
multicolored, pane of 5 plus label, dated "1997" 3.50
unfolded pane, plate #11111 4.00

1150n1 F-VF
multicolored, pane of 10, dated "1997" 6.50
unfolded pane, plate #11111 7.00

B284 F-VF
$4.80 book (1-1150n & 1-1150n1), multicolored on white, plate #11111 10.00

B285 F-VF
$9.60 book (3-1150n1), multicolored on white, plate #11111 20.00

1997. 32¢ Statue of Liberty

1154n F-VF
multicolored, pane of 4 2.50

1154n1 F-VF
multicolored, pane of 5 plus label, plate #V1111 3.25

1154n2 F-VF
multicolored, pane of 6, die cut 11 x 11, plate #V1111 on LL stamp or no plate number 4.00

1154n2v F-VF
multicolored, pane of 6, die cut 11-1/2 x 11-3/4, plate #V1111 on LL stamp or no plate number 4.00

B286 F-VF
$4.80 book (1-1154n + 1-1154n1 + 1-1154n2), multicolored on white, plate #V1111 on LL stamp 10.00

B287 F-VF
$9.60 book (3-1154n2), multicolored on white, plate #V1111 on LL stamp 20.00

B288 F-VF
$9.60 book (3-1154n2v), multicolored on white, plate #V1111 on LL stamp 30.00

1997. 32¢ Merian BotanicalPrints

1159n F-VF
multicolored, pane of 5 (1-No. 1159 sideways, 2 each No. 1157-58), plate #S11111 or no plate number 3.25

1160n F-VF
multicolored, pane of 5 (1-No. 1160 sideways, 2 each No. 1157-58) 3.50

B289 F-VF
$4.80 book (2-1159n & 1-1160n), multicolored on white, plate #S11111 10.00

1997. 32¢ CLASSIC AMERICAN DOLLS *(MDI water activated).*

B290 F-VF
$4.80 book (CM1921-35), blue on white, plate #P11111, P22222, P33333, P44444 10.00
plate #23333 300.00

1997. 32¢ HUMPHREY BOGART *(MDI water activated).*

B291 F-VF
$4.80 book (15-CM1936), blue on white, plate #S11111 10.00

1997. 32¢ STARS AND STRIPES FOREVER *(MDI water activated).*

B292 F-VF
$4.80 book (15-CM1941), blue on white, plate #1111 or no plate number 10.00

1997. 32¢ CLASSIC MOVIE MONSTERS *(MDI water activated).*

B293 F-VF
$4.80 book (3 each CM1956-60), blue on white, plate #S11111 10.00

1997. 32¢ AMERICAN HOLLY

1165n F-VF
multicolored, pane of 4 2.50

1165n1 F-VF
multicolored, pane of 5 plus label 3.25

1165n2 F-VF
multicolored, pane of 6 4.00

B294 F-VF
$4.80 book (1-1165n + 1-1165n1 + 1-1165n2), multicolored on white, plate #B1111 10.00

B295 F-VF
$9.60 book (3-1165n2), multicolored on white, plate #B1111 20.00

1998. 32¢ TROPICAL BIRDS *(MDI water activated).*

B296 F-VF
$4.80 book (15 from CM1998-2001), blue on white, plate #B1111 10.00

The contents of B296 may vary.

1998. 32¢ BALLET *(MDI water activated).*

B297 F-VF
$4.80 book (15-CM2032), blue on white, plate #P1111, P2222, P3333 10.00

1998. 32¢ SPACE DISCOVERY *(MDI water activated).*

B298 F-VF
$4.80 book (3-CM2036y), blue on white, plate #S11111 10.00

1998. 32¢ CHRISTMAS WREATHS

1190n F-VF
multicolored, pane of 4 (No. 1187-90) 2.50

1190n1 F-VF
multicolored, pane of 5 (1 each No. 1187, 1189-90, 2-No. 1188) plus label 3.25

1190n2 F-VF
multicolored, pane of 6 (2 each No. 1187, 1189, 1 each No. 1188, 1190) 4.00

B299 F-VF
$4.80 book (1-1190n + 1-1190n1 + 1-1190n2), multicolored on white, plate #B111111 10.00

1998. (33¢) NON-DENOMINATED "H" HAT

1196n F-VF
multicolored, pane of 10 7.00

B300 F-VF
($6.60) book, multicolored on white, plate #1111, 2222, 3333 14.00

1999. 33¢ FLAG AND SKYSCRAPERS *(die cut 9-3/4).*

1210n F-VF
multicolored, pane of 10 7.00

B301 F-VF
$6.60 book, multicolored on white, plate #1111, 1121 14.00

1999. 33¢ FLAG AND SKYSCRAPERS *(die cut 11).*

1211n F-VF
multicolored, pane of 4 2.50

1211n1 F-VF
multicolored, pane of 5 plus label, plate #V1111, V1112, V1121, V1122, V1212, V2212 on LL stamp 3.25

1211n2 F-VF
multicolored, pane of 6 4.00

B302 F-VF
$4.95 book (1-1211n + 1-1211n1 + 1-1211n2), multicolored on white, plate #V1111, V1112, V1121, V1122, V1212, V2212 on LL stamp 10.00

1999. 33¢ FRUIT BERRIES

1221n F-VF
multicolored, pane of 4 (No. 1218-21) 2.50

1221n1 F-VF
multicolored, pane of 5 (1 each No. 1218-19, 1221, 2-No. 1220) plus label 3.25

1221n2 F-VF
multicolored, pane of 6 (2 each No. 1218-19, 1 each No. 1220-21) 4.00

B303 F-VF
$4.95 book (1-1221n + 1-1221n1 + 1-1221n2), multicolored on white, plate #B1111, B1112, B2212, B2222 10.00
plate B2221 1,000.00

1999. 33¢ AMERICAN GLASS *(MDI water activated).*

B304 F-VF
$4.95 book (15 from CM2072-75), blue on white 10.00

The contents of B304 may vary.

1999. 33¢ CORAL PINK ROSE

1232n F-VF
multicolored, pane of 4 2.50

1232n1 F-VF
multicolored, pane of 5 plus label 3.25

1232n2 F-VF
multicolored, pane of 6, plate #S111 on reverse 4.00

B305 F-VF
$4.95 book (1-1232n + 1-1232n1 + 1-1232n2), multicolored, on white, plate #S111 on reverse 10.00

1999. 33¢ ALL ABOARD! *(MDI water activated).*

B306 F-VF
$4.95 book (3 each CM2079-83), blue on white, plate #P1111, P2222, P3333 10.00

1999. 33¢ REINDEER

1246n F-VF
multicolored, pane of 4 2.50

1246n1 F-VF
multicolored, pane of 5 plus label 3.25

1246n2 F-VF
multicolored, pane of 6 4.00

B307 F-VF
$4.95 book (1-1246n + 1-1246n1 + 1-1246n2), green & gold on white, plate #B111111, B222222 10.00

1999. 20¢ RING-NECKED PHEASANT

1248n F-VF
multicolored, pane of 5 (4-No. 1248, 1-No. 1248v sideways at top), plate #V1111 2.00

1248n1 F-VF
multicolored, pane of 5 (4-No. 1248, 1-No. 1248v sideways at bottom), plate #V1111 — 2.00

B308 F-VF
$2.00 book (1-1248n & 1-1248n1), multicolored on white, plate #V1111 in two places — 4.00

2000. 22¢/33¢/55¢/60¢/$3.20 U.S. Navy Submarines

CM2111n F-VF
multicolored, pane of 5 (CM2107-11) — 10.00

B309 F-VF
$9.80 prestige book, multicolored on white — 20.00

CM2111n was issued with two different descriptive texts. B309 contains one of each.

2000. (34¢) Non-denominated Statue of Liberty

1269n F-VF
multicolored, pane of 4, plate #V1111 on LR stamp or no plate number — 3.00

1269n1 F-VF
multicolored, pane of 6 — 4.00

B310 F-VF
($6.80) book (2-1269n & 2-1269n1), multicolored on white, plate #V1111 on LR stamp — 14.00

2000. (34¢) Non-denominated Flowers *(die cut 10-1/4 x 10-3/4).*

1277n F-VF
multicolored, pane of 4 (Nos. 1274-77), plate #S1111 on reverse or no plate number — 3.00

1277n1 F-VF
multicolored, pane of 6 (2-each No. 1274-75, 1-each No. 1276-77) — 4.00

1277n2 F-VF
multicolored, pane of 6 (1-each No. 1274-75, 2-each No. 1276-77) — 4.00

B311 F-VF
($6.80) book (2-1277n + 1-1277n1 + 1-1277n2), multicolored on white, plate #S1111 on reverse — 14.00

THIS BOOK CONTAINS
SIX
AIR TEN CENT MAIL
STAMPS
PRICE SIXTY-ONE CENTS

BA1

Airmail Booklets and Panes

1927. 10¢ Lindbergh

A10n F-VF
indigo, pane of 3 — 75.00

BA1 F-VF
61¢ book, blue on white — 175.00

1943. 6¢ Twin Motored Transport Plane

A25n F-VF
rose red, pane of 3 — 3.50

BA2 F-VF
37¢ book, red on white — 11.00

BA3 F-VF
73¢ book, red on white — 20.00

1949. 6¢ Small Skymaster *(wet printed).*

A39n F-VF
carmine, pane of 6 — 9.50

BA4 F-VF
73¢ book, red on white, wingspan 68mm on OFC, printing on IFC, large print on OBC — 25.00

BA4a F-VF
73¢ book, red on white, wingspan 68mm on OFC, blank IFC, large print on OBC — 1,000.00

BA4b F-VF
73¢ book, red on white, wingspan 68mm on OFC, blank IFC, small print on OBC — 1,000.00

BA5 F-VF
73¢ book, red on white, wingspan 60mm on OFC, blank IFC, small print on OBC — 22.50

BA5a F-VF
73¢ book, red on white, wingspan 60mm on OFC, blank IFC, large print on OBC — 1,000.00

1949. 6¢ Small Skymaster *(dry printed).*

A39pn F-VF
carmine, pane of 6 — 15.00

BA6 F-VF
73¢ book, red on white — 30.00

1958. 7¢ Jet Silhouette *(blue).*

A51n F-VF
blue, pane of 6 — 11.00

BA7 F-VF
85¢ book (overprint on 73¢ BA4 cover), red on white — 30.00

BA8 F-VF
85¢ book, blue on white — 27.50

1960. 7¢ Jet Silhouette *(red).*

A60n F-VF
red, pane of 6 — 15.00

BA9 F-VF
85¢ book, blue on white — 30.00

BA10 F-VF
85¢ book, red on white — 30.00

1962. 8¢ Airliner over Capitol *(Slogan 1).*

A64n F-VF
carmine, pane of 5 plus label ("Your Mailman"), untagged — 6.75

A64p1n F-VF
Pane of 5, plus label, Hi-brite paper — —

BA11 F-VF
80¢ book (2-A64n), black on pink, wings on OFC — 15.00

BA11a F-VF
80¢ book (2-A64p1n), black on pink, wings on OFC — —

BA12 F-VF
$2.00 book (5-A64n), red on pink, wings on OFC — 25.00

BA12a F-VF
$2.00 book (5-A64p1n), red on pink, wings on OFC — —

1963. 8¢ Airliner over Capitol *(Slogan 2).*

A64n1 F-VF
carmine, pane of 5 plus label ("Zone Numbers"), untagged — 47.50

BA13 F-VF
$2.00 book, red on pink, wings on OFC — 225.00

BA14 F-VF
$2.00 book, red on pink, Mr. Zip on OFC — 225.00

1964. 8¢ Airliner over Capitol *(Slogan 3).*

A64n2 F-VF
carmine, pane of 5 plus label ("Use Zip Code"), untagged — 12.50

A64zn F-VF
carmine, pane of 5 plus label ("Use Zip Code"), tagged 1.65

BA15 F-VF
80¢ book (2-A64n2), black on pink, wings on OFC, letter carrier on OBC 40.00

BA15a F-VF
80¢ (2-A64n2), black on pink, wings on OFC, Mr. Zip on OBC 30.00

BA16 F-VF
$2.00 book (5-A64n2), red on white, Mr. Zip on OFC 2,500.00

BA17 F-VF
$2.00 book (5-A64n2), red on pink, Mr. Zip on OFC 75.00

BA18 F-VF
80¢ book (2-A64zn), black on white, wings on OFC, "Better Mail Services" on IFC 30.00

BA18a F-VF
80¢ book (2-A64zn), black on white, wings on OFC, Minuteman on IFC 25.00

BA19 F-VF
80¢ book (2-A64zn), black on pink, wings on OFC, Mr. Zip on OBC 1,500.00

BA20 F-VF
$2.00 book (5-A64zn), red on pink, Mr. Zip on OFC 300.00

BA21 F-VF
$2.00 book (5-A64zn), red on white, Mr. Zip on OFC, Domestic Rate Chart on IFC 30.00

BA21a F-VF
$2.00 book (5-A64zn), red on white, Mr. Zip on OFC, Minuteman on IFC, 20018 on OBC 20.00

BA21b F-VF
$2.00 book (5-A64zn), red on white, Mr. Zip on OFC, Minuteman on IFC, 00000 on OBC 12.00

1968. 10¢ Star Runway *(pane of 8).*

A72n2 F-VF
red, pane of 8, red-orange tagging 2.00

A72n2z F-VF
red, pane of 8, yellow tagging —

A72n2zo F-VF
Pane of 8, tagging omitted (error) —

BA22 F-VF
$4.00 book (5-A72n2), red on white, Domestic Rate Chart on IFC 11.00

BA22a F-VF
$4.00 book (5-A72n2), red on white, envelope on IFC 15.00

1968. 10¢ Star Runway *(pane of 5).*

A72n F-VF
red, pane of 5 plus Slogan 4 label ("Mail Early") 3.75

A72nzo F-VF
Pane of 5 plus Slogan 4 label, tagging omitted (error) —

A72n1 F-VF
red, pane of 5 plus Slogan 5 label ("Use Zip Code") 3.75

A72n1zo F-VF
Pane of 5 plus Slogan 5 label, tagging omitted (error) —

BA23 F-VF
$1.00 book (1-A72n & 1-A72n1), red on white, Minuteman on IFC 11.00

BA23a F-VF
$1.00 book (1-A72n & 1-A72n1), red on white, envelope on IFC 11.00

1971. 11¢ Jet Silhouette

A78n F-VF
red, pane of 4 plus 2 labels (Slogans 5 and 4) 1.10

BA24 F-VF
$1.00 book (2-A78n & 1-618n), red on white, 29mm clock on IBC 5.00

BA24a F-VF
$1.00 book (2-A78n & 1-618n), red on white, 27mm clock on IBC 5.00

1973. 13¢ Winged Envelope

A85n F-VF
red, pane of 5 plus slogan 8 label ("Paying Bills"), red tagging 1.25

A85nz F-VF
Pane of 5, plus label, yellow-green tagging (error) —

B138 F-VF
$1.25 combination book (1-A85n & 1-678n1), red & blue on white 7.25

BA25 F-VF
$1.30 book, blue & red on white 4.00

Test Stamps

Test stamps, sometimes called familiarly "Dummy stamps," have been printed and used by the Bureau of Engraving and Printing, the U.S. Postal Service, and private companies for five purposes:

1) To develop and test stamp production equipment including printing presses and stamp and booklet manufacturing equipment by the Postal Service.

2) To develop stamp vending equipment by private companies.

3) To test and adjust stamp vending equipment at dispensing sites by the Postal Service and private companies.

4) To test stamp affixing equipment used by commercial vendors.

5) To demonstrate and promote stamp dispensing equipment.

The number of test stamps increased rapidly in the 20th century with the development and test of new stamp manufacturing equipment. Their use increased with automation of stamp manufacturing and vending, particularly with the introduction of the rotary press, coil and booklet stamps and related manufacturing equipment.

While not accountable paper, i.e. actual stamps, these stamps have generally not been made available to collectors and, in many cases, very few are known to exist. Test stamps clearly show the steps in the technological development of stamps through the years.

—*Dan Undersander and Terry Scott*

1860-80. Woman with Phrygian Hat Issue *Figure facing right (similar to 1861-66 essays of unknown origin with vignette facing left). The word* "EXPERIMENT" *appears in a straight line above vignette and* "SPECIMEN" *curved below; with 2s in lower corners. Imperforate.*

TT1-TT1D

TT1 MNHVF
green on white paper 100.00

TT1A MNHVF
black on pink paper —

TT1B MNHVF
black on yellow paper —

TT1C MNHVF
blue on yellow paper —

TT1D MNHVF
blue on pink paper —

1857. Washington Essay Issue *Lathe work background and Washington vignette engraved by Bald, Cousland, & Co. Company initials added and printed by American Bank Note Company on india paper. Imperforate.*

TT2-TT7

TT2 MNHVF
black 100.00

TT3 MNHVF
green 100.00

TT4 MNHVF
blue 100.00

TT5 MNHVF
vermilion 100.00

TT6 MNHVF
brown 100.00

TT7 MNHVF
orange 100.00

1861. Eagle and Stars Issue Eagle and stars with 8s in each corner and "SPECIMEN" above. *Imperforate.*

TT7A-TT7B

TT7A MNHVF
orange on white paper —

TT7B MNHVF
black on stiff bond paper —

1878-79. Blank Issue *Produced by Continental or American Bank Note Co. on gummed, soft paper, perforated 12.*

TT8 MNHVF
blank —

1879. African Woman Issue *Black geometric design and vignette are engraved while the blue and red coloring were likely applied by offset. The vignette has* "EXPERIMENT" *engraved above it and* "A.B.N.C." *below. Printed by American Bank Note Company, imperforate.*

TT9

TT9 MNHVF
multicolored 100.00

1910s. Rembrandt Issue Bust of Dutch artist Rembrandt with 5s in lower corners. *Printed by American Bank Note Company, perforated 12.*

TT10

TT10 MNHVF
brown on cream paper —

1890. Liberty Head Issue *Facing left with* "EXPERIMENT" *over oval of vignette. Figure 3s in squares in lower corners. Printed by American Bank Note Company on stamp paper. Perforated 12.* (Some examples exist with punch cancellations and overprinted "SAMPLE.")

TT11-TT11H

TT11 MNHVF
olive 100.00

TT11A MNHVF
purple 100.00

TT11B MNHVF
blue-green 100.00

TT11C MNHVF
blue 100.00

TT11D MNHVF
orange-red 100.00

TT11F MNHVF
light orange-red 100.00

TT11G MNHVF
yellow 100.00

TT11H MNHVF
purple-black 100.00

1890. Burt and Tobey's Issue inscribed "Burt and Tobey's" in label across top and "Stamp-Battery" bordering lower portion of oval containing image of stamp affixer. *Perforated 12.*

TT11J

TT11J MNHVF
dark green —

TT11K MNHVF
lavender —

1907. Blank Issue *Produced by Bureau of Engraving and Printing on gummed paper, watermark double-line USPS, perforated 12.*

TT12 MNHVF
blank —

1909. Mail-om-eter Coil Issue Stamp applied at the rate of 250 per minute.

TT13

TT13 MNHVF
red pair, Shermack Type III (hyphen-hole) separations —

1909. Mail-om-eter Coil Issues with "Mail-om-eter stamp applied at the rate of 250 per minute.

TT14-TT18

TT14 MNHVF
brown pair, Shermack Type III (hyphen-hole) separations —

TT15 MNHVF
brown pair, imperforate —

TT16 MNHVF
brown pair, Mail-om-eter Type I (6 large holes) separations —

TT17 MNHVF
brown pair, Mail-om-eter Type II (8 large holes) separations —

TT18 *with Mail-om-eter Type III perforations*

TT18 MNHVF
brown pair, Mail-om-eter Type III (8 small holes) separations —

1909-10. Simplex Mfg. Co. Issue "Affixed by" *on top of eagle and shield with* "Simplex Mfg. Co" in shield, "90 West St./New York" *on sides. Imperforate.*

TT19

TT19 MNHVF
red single —

1909-10. Simplex Stamp Affixer Issue "Simplex Stamp Affixer *The Drummond-Ludlow Co.*" *in oval with* "Post Haste" *in inner oval and stars and stripes inside. Imperforate.*

TT20

TT20 MNHVF
red single —

1910. Hamilton Issue with numbers 1, 2, 3, 4, in corners. Blank vignette, *offset by Bureau of Engraving and Printing, imperforate.*

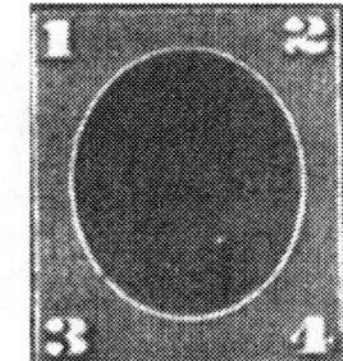

TT21

TT21 MNHVF
deep red —

1910. Hamilton Issue Vignette of Alexander Hamilton, with numbers 1, 2, 3, 4, in corners. *Offset by Bureau of Engraving and Printing, perforated 11.*

TT22-TT25

TT22 MNHVF
deep red —

1910. Hamilton Coil Issue Hamilton vignette, with numbers 1, 2, 3, 4 in corners. *Letterpress by Bureau of Engraving and Printing, perforated 12 horizontally.*

TT23 MNHVF
deep red —

1910. Hamilton Coil Issue Hamilton vignette with numbers 1, 2, 3, 4, in corners. *Letterpress by Bureau of Engraving and Printing, perforated 12 vertically.*

TT23A MNHVF
deep red —

1910. Hamilton Issue Hamilton vignette, with numbers 1, 2, 3, 4, in corners. *Intaglio by Bureau of Engraving and Printing, designs spaced 3.5mm horizontal, 2mm vertically, imperforate.*

TT24 MNHVF
deep red —

1910. HAMILTON COIL ISSUE Hamilton vignette, with numbers 1, 2, 3, 4, in corners. *Offset by Bureau of Engraving and Printing, gummed, designs spaced 2mm apart, perforated 10 horizontally.*

TT25 MNHVF
deep red —

1910. MINERVA HEAD ISSUE *Minerva looking right in shield design,* "Harris Automatic/Press Company/Series 1010/Niles,/Ohio, U.S.A." *Printed by Bureau of Engraving and Printing. Imperforate.*

TT26

TT26 MNHVF
red pair 1,500.00

1910. MINERVA HEAD ISSUE *in shield design* "Harris Automatic/Press Company/Series 1010/Niles,/Ohio, U.S.A." *with a reversed image compared to TT25. Printed by Bureau of Engraving and Printing. Imperforate.*

TT27 MNHVF
red pair 1,500.00

1910S. COLUMBIAN BANK NOTE ISSUE George Washington with "Columbian Bank Note Company" above and "SPECIMEN" below. *Imperforate.*

TT27A-TT27C

TT27A MNHVF
black on white card —
TT27B MNHVF
brown on white card —
TT27C MNHVF
light blue on white card —

1910S. STANDARD STAMP AFFIXER COIL ISSUE "Standard/Stamp /Affixer Everett, Mass." *Perforated 10.5 vertically.*

TT28

TT28 MNHVF
green pair —

1913-20S. STANDARD MAILING MACHINE CO. COIL ISSUE with "Standard" on ribbon separating "Stamp Affixer" and "Everett/Mass." *Perforated 10.5 vertically.*

TT29

TT29 MNHVF
red pair —

TT29A MNHVF
light purple, pair, perforated 10.5 vertically —

1910S. STANDARD STAMP AFFIXER COIL ISSUE "Standard Stamp Affixer/Somerville, Mass."

TT30

TT30 MNHVF
green pair, perforated 8.5 vertically 70.00
TT30A MNHVF
light green pair, perforated 8.5 vertically —
TT30B MNHVF
green pair, perforated 10.5 vertically —

1910S. STANDARD STAMP AFFIXER COIL ISSUE with shield and "Standard/Stamp/Affixer/Boston, Mass." *Perforated 10.5 vertically.*

TT31

TT31 MNHVF
red pair —

1909. AUTOMATIC VENDING CO. COIL ISSUE "United States" *above winged eagle surrounded by stars and* "Automatic Vending Co./1 Madison Ave., N.Y." *below.*

TT32

TT32 MNHVF
dark red pair, imperforate —
v. Vertical pair, horizontally imperforate —
v1. U.S. Automatic Vending Co. Type I (slit) separations —

1911-13. THE EXTENSIVE MANUFACTURING CO. COIL ISSUE "The Extensive Manufacturing Co./World Wide/Postage Stamp Affixer/90 West St New York."

TT33 MNHVF
red & blue pair, perforated 8.5 vertically —

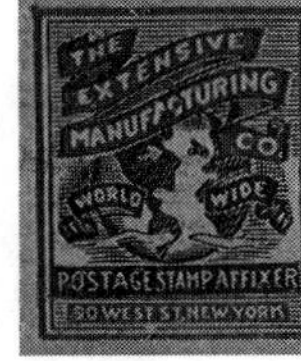
TT34

TT34 MNHVF
carmine & black pair, perforated 10 vertically —

1910-20. MULTIPOST CO. COIL ISSUE "Multipost Co./Stamp Affixers and Mailing Machines/ Rochester, N.Y."

TT35

TT35 MNHVF
red pair, perforated 9.8 vertically, full shading lines 200.00

TT36 MNHVF
carmine pair, perforated 10.2 vertically, short shading lines 200.00

1922. Mail-O-Meter Issue Inscribed "The Mail-O-Meter/ A child can run it/ seals, stamps and counts/ 250/ envelopes per minute." *Printed by Mail-O-Meter Company.*

TT36A

TT36A MNHVF
red, nine small perforation holes —

TT36B MNHVF
deep purple, 10 small perforation holes —

1910-27. Blank Coil Issue *gummed, rotary press. Imperforate.*

TT37 MNHVF
blank pair —

1927-1930s. Blank Coil Issue *Produced by Bureau of Engraving and Printing on cream paper with ribbed gum, rotary press, perforated 10 vertically.*

TT38 MNHVF
blank pair 1.25

1930-40s. Blank Coil Issue *Produced by Bureau of Engraving and Printing on white paper and smooth gum, rotary press, perforated 10 vertically.*

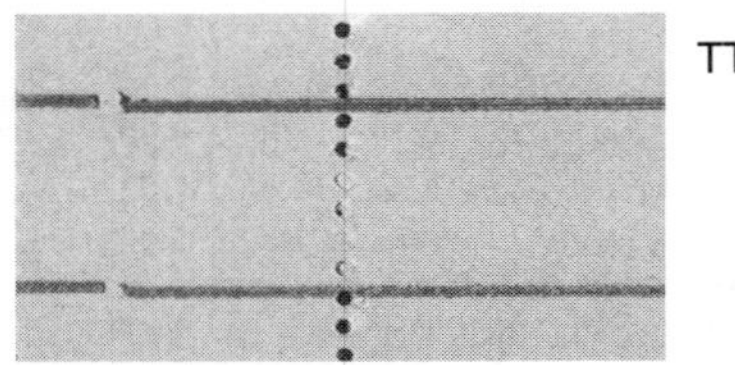
TT39

TT39 MNHVF
blank pair 1.25
2 red lines 13.5mm apart, alternating wide and narrow line gaps spaced six stamps apart, pair 3.00
either wide or narrow line gaps, pair 4.00
Strip of 10, showing both gap widths 8.00

1910-27. Blank Coil Issue *with smooth gum, rotary press.*

TT40 MNHVF
blank pair, perforated 10.5 vertically —

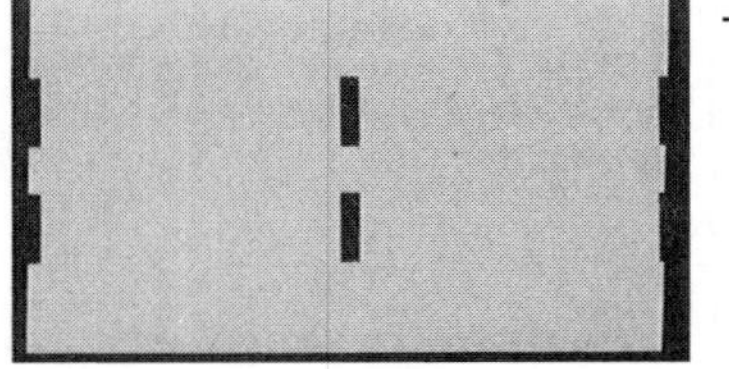
TT41

TT41 MNHVF
blank pair, Shermack Type III (hyphen-hole) separations —
paste-up pair —

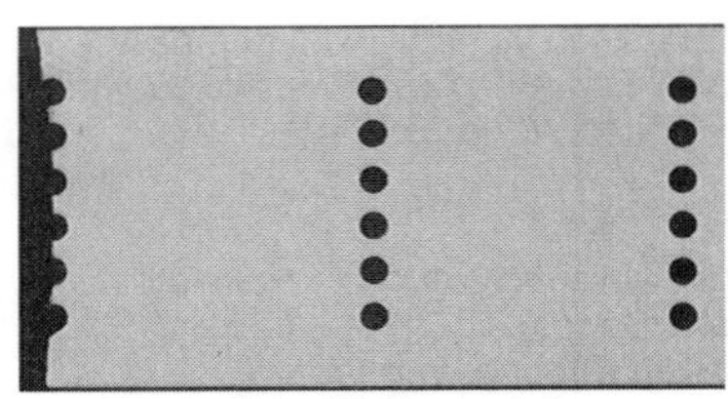
TT42

TT42 MNHVF
blank pair, Mail-om-eter Type I (6 large holes) separations —
paste-up pair —

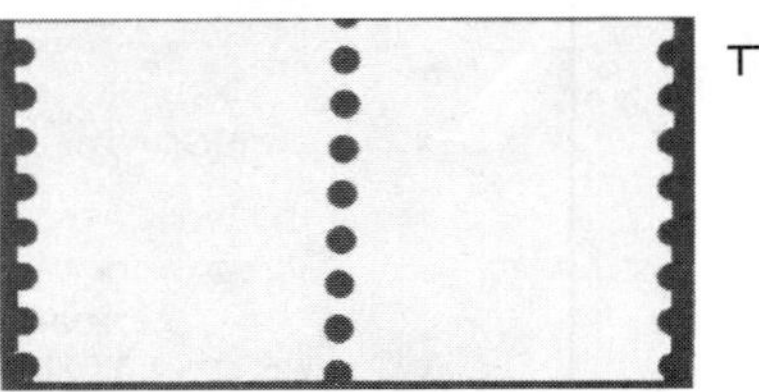
TT43

TT43 MNHVF
blank pair, Mail-om-eter Type II (8 large holes) separations —
paste-up pair —

TT44 MNHVF
blank pair, Mail-om-eter Type III (8 small holes) separations —
paste-up pair —

1897. Blank Coil Issue *Rotary press, 25.5 x 25.75mm, on tan paper, rouletted 13.25, shiny gum.*

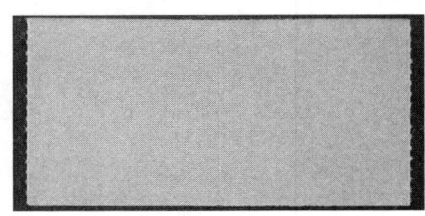

TT45

TT45 MNHVF
blank pair 50.00

1914-16. New Jersey Vending Machine Company Coil Issue *Perforated 10.5 vertically.*

TT46

TT46 MNHVF
red pair —

1912. Washington/Franklin Issue *Photogravure test design for German web-fed press, six impressions across sheet, ungummed, imperforate.*

TT47

TT47 MNHVF
brown pair 280.00

1915. NATIONAL ENVELOPE SEALING AND STAMP MFG. COIL ISSUE "National" *above eagle and shield with* "Brattleboro, Vt." *below. Perforated 8.5 horizontally.*

TT48

		MNHVF
TT48	**red & blue** pair	—
TT48A	**red** pair	—

1920s. WIZARD LABEL AFFIXER ISSUE "Made in America U.S.A./Wizard Label Affixer/Sole Manufacturers/Wizard Co./Boston, Mass." *Shermack Type III separations.*

TT49

		MNHVF
TT49	**red & blue**	—

1920s. WIZARD STAMP AFFIXER COIL ISSUE "Made in America U.S.A./Wizard Stamp Affixer/Sole Manufacturers/Wizard Co/Boston, Mass." *Perforated 10 vertically.*

TT50

		MNHVF
TT50	**red & blue** pair	—

1920s. POSTAGE STAMP MACHINE COIL ISSUE "Postage Stamp Machine Co." and "33 W. 60th St./ New York, N.Y." *in white square frame. Perforated 8.5 vertically.*

TT51

		MNHVF
TT51	**(color unknown)**	—

1920s. LICENSED SANITARY POSTAGE STATION COIL ISSUE "operated by Sanitary Postage Corp'n., New York City."

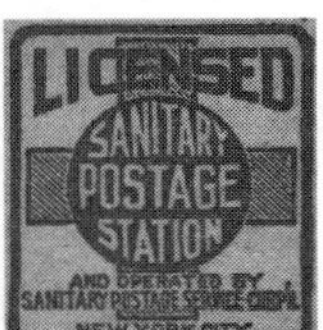

TT52-TT53

		MNHVF
TT52	**red** pair, perforated 10.5 horizontally	—
TT53	**red** pair, perforated 10.5 vertically	140.00

1920s. POSTCRAFT CO. COIL ISSUE "Postcraft Stamp Affixer" *above affixer with* "Postcraft Co./25 E. 26th St., N.Y." *Perforated 10 vertically.*

TT54

		MNHVF
TT54	**(color unknown)**	—

1920s. VIDAVER MAILING MACHINE CO. INC. COIL ISSUE Name and "Weighs/250 West 49st/New York." *Perforated 10.5 vertically.*

TT55

		MNHVF
TT55	**red** pair	120.00

1920s. AGNEW AUTO MAILING ISSUE "Agnew Auto Mailing" *over winged hourglass with* "A penny saved" *and* "Mailing Co/Boston, Mass" *below.*

TT56

		MNHVF
TT56	**red brown** pair	—

1920s. ROYALTY STAMP ISSUE Stamp affixer in oval surrounded by "Stamp Affixing Machine Patented April 23, 1925" with "Royalty Stamp" below and "No." in lower left corner.

TT56A

		MNHVF
TT56A	**red**	—

1920s-30s. STEARNS-DANIELS COMPANY COIL ISSUE "Stamp/Affixer" *with* "Ste-Dan" *in oval and* "Stearns-Daniels Co./Boston, Mass." *Perforated 10.1 vertically.*

TT57

		MNHVF
TT57	**green** pair	—

1920s-30s. EDISON DICTATING MACHINE COIL ISSUE "I pay your postage" *and* "Service Everywhere." *Perforated 10.2 vertically.*

TT58

TT58 MNHVF
red pair —

1920s-30s. Shermack Dummy Issue with "Shermack Dummy Stamps" *printed parallel to perforations, 25 x 22mm. Perforated 10.5 horizontally.*

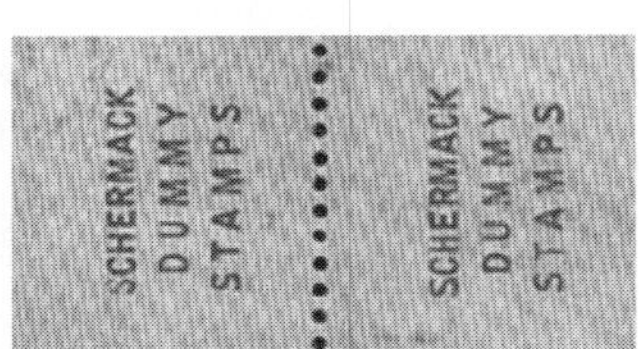

TT58A

TT58A MNHVF
red pair —

1920s-30s. National Postal Meter Company, Inc. Coil Issue *Name in circle around* "NPM" *and* "Rochester, N.Y." *at bottom. Perforated 10 vertically.*

TT59

TT59 MNHVF
red pair —

1920s-30s. Stampmasters, Inc. Coil Issue "Postmaster/Mfg. for Stampmasters Inc./Manufacturers and distributors of precision/built roll type vending machines," *with Uncle Sam and shield of stars and stripes. Perforated 10 vertically.*

TT60

TT60 MNHVF
violet pair —

1927. Mail-O-Meter Coil Issue Inscribed "The Mail-O-Meter Company/ A child can run it/ seals stamps and counts 10,000 envelopes per hour." *Perforated 10.5 vertically.*

TT61

TT61 MNHVF
bright red pair —

1930s. Central Machine & Supply Co. Issue "Central Machine & Supply Co." above oval containing "NU/E-Z/WA/STAMP/VENDOR" and "Davenport, IA" in shield at bottom.

TT61A

TT61A MNHVF
red —

1930s. Electric Vendors Inc. (Zeigle) Coil Issue *No printed design, shiny smooth gum, perforated 10.5 vertically.*

TT62 MNHVF
blue colored paper pair 35.00

TT63 MNHVF
green colored paper pair 35.00

TT64 MNHVF
yellow colored paper pair 35.00

TT65 MNHVF
white paper pair 35.00

1930s-40s. Multipost Coil Issue "GEO.A.Cleveland/Multipost Mailing Systems and Equipment/PO Box 593/St. Paul 2, Minn." *Perforated 9.5 vertically.*

TT66

TT66 MNHVF
red —

1936. Blank Issue *Produced by Bureau of Engraving and Printing, gummed with gum breakers, rotary press.*

TT67 MNHVF
blank, gum breaker ridges 5.5mm apart, perforated 11 x 10.5 25.00
v. vertical pair, horizontal gutter between —

TT68 MNHVF
blank, gum breaker ridges 11.0mm apart, perforated 10 —

1943. Overrun Countries Issue *Gummed pane of 50 horizontal commemorative-size blank stamps with manuscript marginal inscriptions. Printed by American Bank Note Co., perforated 12.*

TT68A MNHVF
blank, pane of 50 —

1944-49. Multipost Coil Issue "Multipost Stamp Affixer, Commercial Controls Corporation, U.S. Postal Meter Division," Rochester 2, N.Y. *Perforated 10 vertically.*

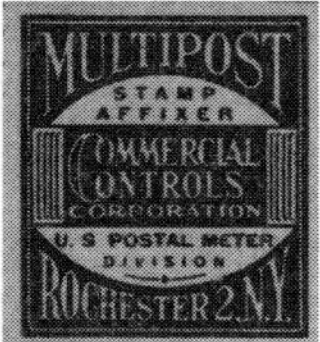

TT69, TT70, TT71

TT69 MNHVF
blue pair 50.00

TT70 MNHVF
black pair 60.00

TT71 MNHVF
blue-black pair 60.00

1944-49. Multipost Coil Issue "Commercial Controls Multipost mailMaster." *Perforated 10 vertically.*

TT72, TT73

TT72 MNHVF
purple pair 50.00

TT73 MNHVF
carmine pair 80.00

1944-49. MULTIPOST COIL ISSUE "Friden Multipost mailMaster." *Perforated 10 vertically.*

TT74

TT74		MNHVF
	carmine pair	50.00

1954. PURPLE COIL ISSUE *Vertical rectangle, framed with cross-hatch design inside. Printed by Bureau of Engraving and Printing, perforated 9.8 vertically.*

TT75-TT78

TT75		MNHVF
	purple pair, (large hole perforations)	2.00
	Line pair, (large hole perforations)	5.00
	p. Pair, (small hole perforations)	4.00
	Line pair, (small hole perforations)	20.00
	v. Coil pair, imperforate	90.00
	v1. Coil line pair, imperforate	—
	On cover and canceled "Parade of Postal Progress"	80.00

1954. CARMINE ISSUE *Vertical rectangle, framed with cross-hatch design inside. Printed by Bureau of Engraving and Printing, perforated 11 x 10.5.*

TT76		MNHVF
	carmine	240.00
	Block of 4, plate No. 141731 or 141732	—
	v. Block of 4, plate No. 141731 or 141732, imperforate	—
	Block of 4 with full vertical gutter, with EE bars between stamps	—

1954. CARMINE COIL ISSUE *Same design as TT76 but perforated 10 vertically, printed by the Bureau of Engraving and Printing.*

TT77		MNHVF
	carmine pair	275.00
	Line pair	—
	v. Pair, imperforate	200.00
	v1. Line pair, imperforate	—
	v2. Joint line block of 10 horizontally imperforate, plate Nos. 164564 or 164565	—
	v3. Joint line block of 10 imperforated, with plate Nos. 164564 or 164565	—

1958. RED VIOLET COIL ISSUE *Vertical rectangle, framed with cross-hatch design inside. Printed by Bureau of Engraving and Printing, perforated 9.8 vertically.*

TT78		MNHVF
	red violet pair, (small hole perforations)	3.00
	Line pair, (small hole perforations)	12.00
	p. Pair, (large hole perforations)	20.00
	Line pair, (large hole perforations)	125.00
	v. Pair, imperforate	300.00
	v1. Line pair, imperforate	—
	v2. Block of 8 with joint line, sheet margin and plate Nos. 165939 and 165940, imperforate horizontally	—
	cvr. On cover and canceled "Parade of Postal Progress"	85.00
	Roll of 100 in cellophane	—

1958-59. PITNEY BOWES CO. ISSUE "Postage Stamp" *above circle with* "Facsimile" *below. Imperforate.*

TT79

TT79		MNHVF
	rose carmine with overall orange tagging, Helocon paper	—
	p. Black helocon paper	—
	p1. Pink lumogen paper	—

1960-70. BLANK COIL ISSUE *with smooth gum, rotary press, perforated 10. Overall tagging, produced by Bureau of Engraving and Printing, perforated 10 vertically.*

TT80		MNHVF
	blank pair	—
	joint line pair	—

1960s. STAMP E-Z AFFIXER ISSUE Inscribed plastic postage stamp affixer and "Postage Stamp Affixer" above "STAMP-E-Z." *Imperforate.*

TT80A

TT80A		MNHVF
	light purple	—

1962-80. GRAY-BLACK FTPO COIL ISSUE Inscribed "For Testing Purposes Only," *intaglio by Bureau of Engraving and Printing, perforated 9.8 vertically.*

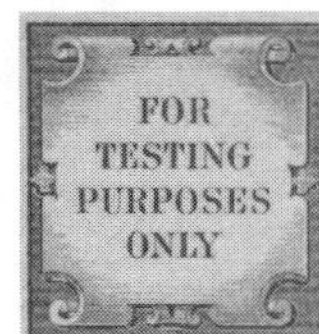

TT81-TT86, TT90-TT94, TT99, TT103-TT104

TT81		MNHVF
	gray-black pair, untagged, shiny gum	1.00
	Line pair, untagged, shiny gum	3.00
	Roll of 100 in cellophane	—

TT82		MNHVF
	gray-black pair, phosphorescent tagging, shiny gum	.75
	Line pair, phosphorescent tagging, shiny gum	3.00
	p. Pair, Hi-brite, phosphorescent tagging, shiny gum	—

TT83		MNHVF
	gray-black pair, phosphorescent tagging, pebble gum	3.00
	Line pair, phosphorescent tagging, pebble gum	12.00
	v. Pair, imperforate, phosphorescent tagging, pebble gum	50.00
	Line pair, imperforate, phosphorescent tagging, pebble gum	300.00
	Defacement lines:	—
	red, (single thin line)	—
	red, (one thick 1.5mm and two thin lines)	—
	dark red, (three thin lines and 15 to 18mm purple band)	—
	rose red, (three thin lines 10mm high and inverted "DL")	—
	blue, (single thick line 4mm wide with some streaking below)	—

blue, (single thick line at least 10mm wide)	—
blue-green, (two thin lines)	—
blue, (three thin lines)	—
green, (two thin lines)	—
orange, (one thin line)	—
orange, (two diffuse lines)	—
violet, (single irregular bar from 11 to 12mm wide, color penetrating paper and affecting gum)	—
violet, (two thick lines, bottom 3mm wide and top 3.5mm wide)	—
violet, (two thick lines, bottom 3.5mm wide and top 5.5mm wide)	—
violet, (three thin lines)	—
violet, (three thick lines 1.5mm, spaced 1.5 and 0.5mm apart)	—
violet, (four lines, spaced 7mm apart)	—
violet, (four lines, spaced 4mm between top and center and 4.5mm between center and bottom)	—
violet, (five light lines)	—
violet, (six light lines, likely from same defacer as five line)	—
yellow, (two wavy)	—
brown, (two thin lines)	—
brown (one thick line)	—
black-violet, (1 line 1.5mm wide)	—
black, (one thin line)	—
black, (one thick line)	—
black, (two lines, top thicker)	—
black, (three thin lines 0.5 to 1mm)	—
black, (three lines, bottom two thick, top thin)	—
black, (three heavy lines between, greater than 2.0mm wide)	—
black, (three heavy lines, between 1.5mm and 2.0mm wide)	—
black, (five lines, 3 about 1mm wide and 2 light)	—
black, (six lines, 3 about 1mm wide and 3 light)	—
black, (six lines)	—
grey-black, (one line)	—
grey-black, (two lines, 0.5mm to 1mm)	—
grey-black, (two heavy lines greater than 1.5mm wide)	—
grey, (three lines, spaced 1.5mm between top and center lines and 2.5mm between center and bottom lines, with very irregular print)	—
grey, (three lines, spaced 2.5mm between top and center lines and 1.5mm between center and bottom lines, with very irregular print)	—
silver, (one line)	—

TT84 MNHVF

gray-black pair, phosphorescent tagging, matte gum	4.00
Line pair, phosphorescent tagging, matte gum	20.00

TT85 MNHVF

gray-black pair, untagged, matte gum, fluorescent paper	4.00
Line pair, untagged, matte gum, fluorescent paper	12.50
p. Untagged, matte gum, non-fluorescent paper	—
p1. Untagged, matte gum, Type I paper (diagonal gum striations)	—
p2. Untagged, matte gum, Type III paper (wavy, intermittent gum striations)	—

1970. Carmine FTPO Coil Issue Inscribed "For Testing Purposes Only." *Intaglio by Bureau of Engraving and Printing, perforated 9.8 vertically, orange-red-dish tagging. Most copies soiled.*

TT86 MNHVF

carmine pair	825.00
Line pair	—

1970s. Flag Issue *Self-adhesive flag and* "United States Postal Service/Test Sample." *Produced by Avery Products Corp. Stamp imperforate mounted on backing which is rouletted 6.5.*

TT87

TT87 MNHVF

blue	200.00
paper backing imperforate	—

1970s. Proclaim Liberty Issue *Liberty Bell and Capitol with* "Proclaim Liberty" *and combined 6 and 7 followed by* "¢ Specimen-Specimen." *Perforated 12 x 11.5.*

TT88

TT88 MNHVF

blue, red & green	—

1973. Christmas Test Issue *Self-adhesive dummy for Minkus No. 684* (Dove of Peace Christmas issue), *produced by Bureau of Engraving and Printing for Avery Products Corp. to add die cutting. Stamp imperforate with rounded corners on white backing paper, which is rouletted 6.6.*

TT89

TT89 MNHVF

black	6.00
Imperforate backing	—
Block of 4, matrix intact	—
Pane of 50	—

1975. Green FTPO Coil Issue Inscribed "For Testing Purposes Only," *intaglio by Bureau of Engraving and Printing, green tagging and shiny gum, perforated 9.8 vertically.*

TT90 MNHVF

green pair	325.00
v. Pair, imperforate	—
line pair	—

1975. Green Coil Horizontally Imperforate FTPO Issue Inscribed "For Testing Purposes Only." *Intaglio by Bureau of Engraving and Printing and shipped to Germany to test coil production equipment, green tagging, shiny gum, perforated 9.8.*

TT91 MNHVF

green vertical pair, imperforate horizontally	—

1975. Green FTPO Coil Issue Inscribed "For Testing Purposes Only," *intaglio by Bureau of Engraving and Printing, untagged and matte gum, perforated 9.8 vertically.*

TT92 MNHVF

green pair	450.00
Line pair	—
v. Imperforate	375.00
Block of 12 with joint line, plate nos. 36111 and 36112	—

1980-81. Green Coil Horizontally Imperforate FTPO Issue Inscribed "For Testing Purposes Only." *Intaglio by Bureau of Engraving and Printing and shipped to Germany to test coil production equipment. Untagged and matte gum, perforated 9.8 vertically.*

TT93	MNHVF
green vertical pair, imperforate horizontally	400.00

1975. Orange FTPO Coil Issue Inscribed "For Testing Purposes Only." *Intaglio by Bureau of Engraving and Printing, on gray paper with shiny gum, tagged, perforated 9.8 vertically.*

TT94	MNHVF
orange pair	1,000.00
Line pair	—

1978. Brown FTPO Coil Issue Inscribed "For Testing Purposes Only." *Intaglio by Bureau of Engraving and Printing, matte gum, untagged, perforated 9.8 vertically.*

TT95	MNHVF
brown pair	4.00
Line pair	20.00

1980s. "Experimental" Octagon Issue "Experimental" *below 6 colored octagons. Printed by Bureau of Engraving and Printing, imperforate.*

TT96

TT96	MNHVF
multicolored pair, imperforate	—
v. Block of 4, plate No. 173404	—

1989. Flag and Eagle Flying over Trees Coil Issue *Produced by Stamp Venturers. Full rolls of each type are known.*

TT97	MNHVF
gray pair, perforated 9.9	.50
Perforated 9.9 with back number (from one roll of 3,000)	35.00

TT98

TT98	MNHVF
gray pair, rouletted	.50

1990s. Martin Marietta Issue Inscribed "For Testing Purposes Only." *Gravure by Martin Marietta Corp. with shiny gum, untagged, imperforate.*

TT99	MNHVF
gray-black pair	150.00

1990s. Blank Coil Issue *Produced by Bureau of Engraving and Printing with shiny gum on bright white paper, no tagging, perforated 9.8 vertically.*

TT99A	MNHVF
blank pair	—

1990s. Blank Coil Issue *Produced by Bureau of Engraving and Printing with dull gum on bright white paper, no tagging, perforated 9.8 vertically.*

TT99B	MNHVF
pair	—

1992. Gray-black FTPO Coil Issue *Printed on B Press by Bureau of Engraving and Printing, design 0.5mm narrower than TT81-85. Inscribed* "For Testing Purposes Only," *intaglio, matte gum, untagged, perforated 9.8 vertically.*

TT100	MNHVF
gray-black pair	1.00

1996. Coil Issue *Blue rectangle with hollow center with reversed number (every 24th stamp) etched inside square, shiny gum, perforated 9.8 vertically. Printed by Bureau of Engraving and Printing, perforated 9.8 vertically.*

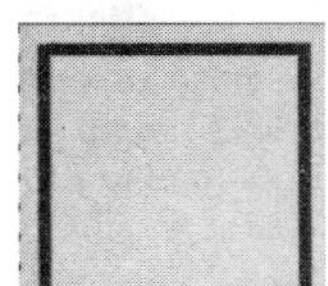
TT101

TT101	MNHVF
blue pair	350.00
Strip of 5 with reversed number "5" crudely etched	1,500.00
Strip of 5 with reversed number "12" crudely etched	—

1996. Gray-black Rectangle Coil Issue *Gray-black rectangle with hollow center, matte gum, printed by Bureau of Engraving and Printing, perforated 10 vertically, known in full rolls of 100.*

TT102	MNHVF
gray-black pair	325.00

1996. FTPO Coil Issue *Self-adhesive* "For Testing Purposes Only," *imperforate stamp on white backing paper, with 3mm gap between stamps, printed by Bureau of Engraving and Printing. Known in full rolls of 3,000 with 4-digit counting numbers on the backside of backing paper at 20 stamp intervals.*

TT103	MNHVF
black on blue	
Strip of 5 with plate number 1111	14.95
With plate number 1111 and back numbers	—

1996. FTPO Coil Issue *Self-adhesive pair* "For Testing Purposes Only," *printed by Avery Dennison. Known in rolls of 3,000 and 10,000. Stamp with simulated die cut vertical perforation, with 3mm between perforation tips. Perforated 9.8 vertically.*

TT104	MNHVF
black on white pair with simulated perforations	1.00
Strip of 5 with plate number VI	14.95

1996. Parrot Issue *Self-adhesive* Parrot with "BCA Perf Test" across bottom, *produced by Banknote Corporation of America, 31 by 22mm with die cut perforations (11.7 x 11.5).*

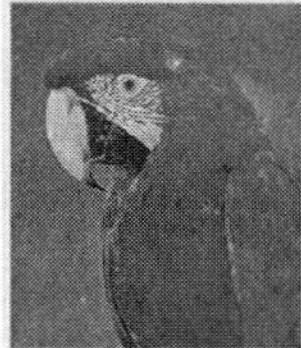

TT105

TT105	MNHVF
blue, red, green & black	—

1996. Parrot Issue Parrot with "BCA" above "00" in lower left, "c 1995 GSSC" across bottom, and "Scrambled Indicia R" vertically up right side. Stamp has hidden lettering. *Offset printed in vertical com-*

memorative format (40 x 25mm) by Banknote Corporation of America, perforated 11.5.

TT105A

TT105A MNHVF
blue, red, green and black —

1997. PACIFIC 97 ISSUE *Blank, untagged, full pane of 40, stamps 40 x 25mm gummed pane, perforated 11 by Sennett Industries at Pacific 97.*

TT106 MNHVF
blank —

1997. STYLIZED EAGLE LINERLESS TEST COIL ISSUE with 1994 stylized eagle and black "Test Specimen" overprint, *overall tagged. Produced by Bureau of Engraving and Printing in rolls of 3,000. Imperforate with simulated/printed perforations, gauge 10.0.*

TT107

TT107		MNHVF
	red, yellow, blue & black pair	130.00
	Strip of 5 with plate number 1111	975.00

1998. BLUE RECTANGLE COIL ISSUE *Self-adhesive coil, thin blue rectangle, hollow center. Produced by the Bureau of Engraving and Printing, perforated 9.8 vertically on imperforate backing paper. Known in full rolls of 3,000 with 4-digit counting numbers on the backside of the backing paper at 20 stamp intervals.*

TT108

TT108		MNHVF
	blue pair	—
	Strip of 3 with "3" printed horizontally	—

1999. FLAG OVER PORCH ISSUE Strip of 3 and each of 3 small mail boxes with test strip inside. Produced for Wal-Mart to sell in miniature post collection boxes. *Nine die cut perforation peaks on left, eight on right, light blue, low fluorescent paper.*

TT109

TT109 MNHVF
red, blue & brown 5.00

1999. FLAG OVER PORCH ISSUE Strip of 3 and each 3 small mail boxes with test strip inside. Produced for Wal-Mart to sell in miniature post collection boxes. *Eight die cut perforation peaks on left, nine on right, dark blue, medium fluorescent paper.*

TT109A MNHVF
red, blue & brown 5.00

1999. RENA ISSUE *Self-adhesive coil,* "Test" *and* "Stamp" *above and below respectively, stylized eagle with letter and* "RENA." *Imperforate stamps with rounded corners on white backing paper.*

TT110

TT110 MNHVF
blue on white paper —

2000. WORLD STAMP EXPO COIL ISSUE *Self-adhesive flying eagle with flag and "Sennett Security Products" die cut simulated perforations, gauge of 10.8.*

TT111

TT111 MNHVF
multicolored strip of 5 —

2000. WORLD STAMP EXPO ISSUE *Flying eagle with flag over trees and* "SSP." *Produced by Sennett Security Products. Perforated 11.1x11.*

TT112

TT112		MNHVF
	multicolored	—
	Plate block No. 51111	—
	Sheet of 25	—

2000. WORLD STAMP EXPO HOLOGRAM ISSUE *Image of earth, 57x57mm, adhering to glossy paper. Produced by Sennett Security Products.*

TT113

TT113 MNHVF
foil (no color) —

2000. WORLD STAMP EXPO BCA ISSUE Eagle head, with "BCA" and "00" in black on each 38x32mm self-adhesive stamp, pane of 12 stamps in different colors/combinations on white paper with "BCA" on back and "World Stamp Expo 2000" on front." *Produced by Banknote Corporation of America. Simulated perforations 11.5 x 11.*

TT114

TT114 MNHVF

	Pane, multicolored	—
a.	black, with cross hairs	—
b.	yellow	—
c.	magenta	—
d.	cyan	—
e.	black	—
f.	4-color process	—
g.	yellow & magenta	—
h.	yellow, magenta, cyan	—
i.	yellow, magneta, cyan, black	—
j.	yellow, magenta, cyan, black, varnish	—

2000. Red Mailbox Linerless Coil Issue Red mailbox in vertical coil format (25 x 22mm). *Imperforate with 1 to 2mm slit mark between stamps in the right margin.*

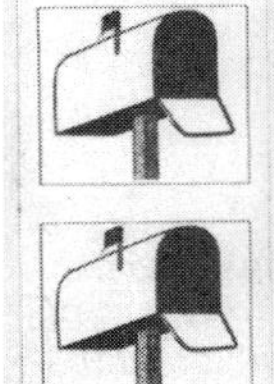
TT115

TT115 MNHVF

red pair	200.00
Strip of five with "xxx" on one stamp	—

2000. FTPO Coil Issue Self-adhesive inscribed "For Testing Purposes Only." *Printed by Bureau of Engraving and Printing, simulated vertical die cut, perforated 9.8 on white backing paper, with 2mm gap between perforation tips. Known in full rolls of 3,000 with 4-digit counting numbers on backside of backing paper at 20 stamp intervals.*

TT116 MNHVF

black pair	—
Strip of 5 with plate number 1111	—
with plate number 1111 and back numbers	—

Test Booklets

Stapled Booklets

1927-30. Post Rider Seal Issue *25¢, four blank panes with waxed glassine interleaving. Blank pane of six stamps (22x25mm) perforated 11.2 x 10.7 with tab at top and horizontal gum breakers spaced 22mm apart. Produced by Bureau of Engraving and Printing.*

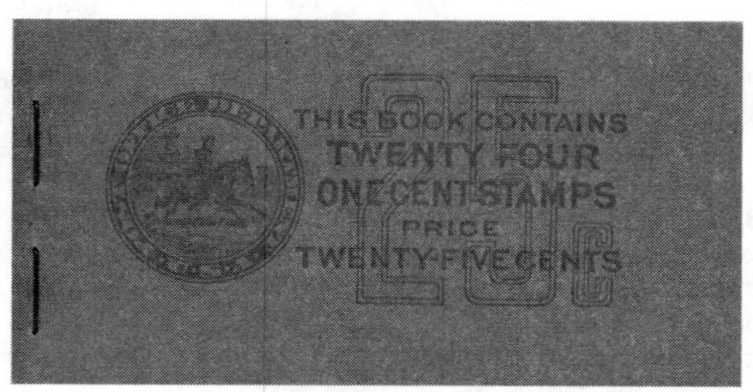

TTB1, 4, 5, 6, 7 10, 11, 12, 13, 14

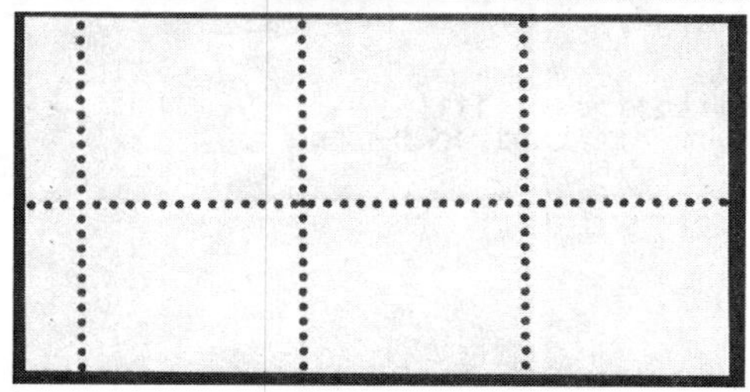

TTB1n

TTB1		MNHVF
	Cover, green on green, entire booklet	—
	n. booklet pane	—

Users of this catalog are invited to write to us if they have information they feel will supplement or correct any material contained herein. All such communications will be answered.

1930s. Post Rider Seal Issue *37¢, two horizontally uncut covers (81x86mm), two blank panes perforated 11.2 x 10.5 with tab at top and glassine interleaving. Blank pane double width of TTB1n. Produced by Bureau of Engraving and Printing.*

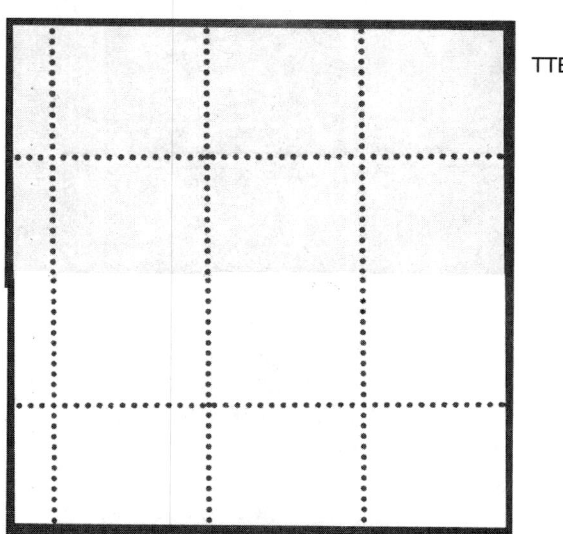

TTB2n

TTB2

TTB2		MNHVF
	Cover, violet on buff, entire booklet	—
	n. booklet pane	—

1940. Post Rider Seal Issue 37¢, two purple panes with interleaving. Purple cross-hatched rotary press printed pane, six stamps (22x25mm) perforated 11.2 x 10.5 with tab at top and horizontal gum breakers spaced 11mm apart. Intaglio by Bureau of Engraving and Printing.

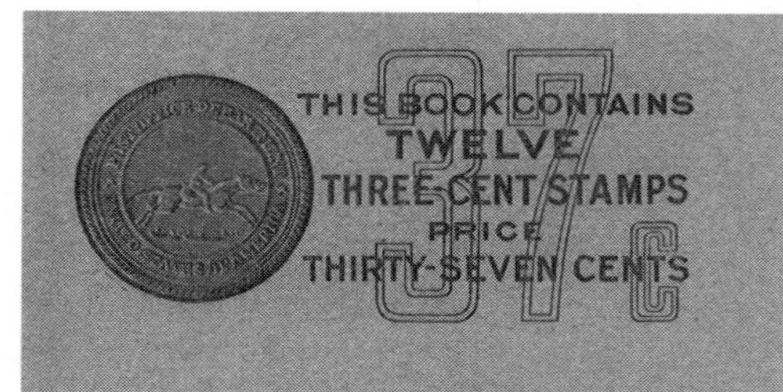

TTB3,4

TTB3, 5, 6, 8

TTB3		MNHVF
	Cover, purple on buff, entire booklet	—
	n. booklet pane	425.00

1940s. Post Rider Seal Issue 37¢, two different blank panes with waxed glassine interleaves. Blank pane (top), six stamps (22x25mm) perforated 11.2x10.5, with tab at top and horizontal gum breakers spaced 6mm apart. Blank pane (bottom), three stamps (44x25mm) perforated 11.2 x imperforate, with tab at top and horizontal gum breakers spaced 6mm apart. Produced by Bureau of Engraving and Printing.

TTB4

TTB4 MNHVF

Cover, violet on buff, entire booklet —
n1. bottom pane (three stamps) —
n. top pane (six stamps) —

1959. Post Rider Seal Issue 97¢, four blank panes with glassine interleaving. Blank pane of six stamps (22x25mm) perforated 11.2x10.5 (see TTB1n), with tab at top and horizontal gum breakers spaced 5.5mm apart and vertical gum breakers 21mm apart. Also known without gum breakers. Produced by Bureau of Engraving and Printing.

TTB5, 6, 8

TTB5 MNHVF

Cover, blue on pink, entire booklet —
n. booklet pane 150.00

1959. Post Rider Seal Issue 97¢, four blank panes with silicone interleaving. Blank pane of six stamps (22x25mm) perforated 11.2x10.5 (see TTB1n) with tab at top. Horizontal gum breakers spaced 5.5mm apart and vertical gum breakers 21mm apart. Produced by Bureau of Engraving and Printing.

TTB6 MNHVF

Cover, blue on pink, entire booklet
n. booklet pane —

1959. Wings and U.S. Airmail Issue *85¢, with two blank panes with glassine interleaving. Blank pane of six stamps (22x25mm) perforated 11.2x10.5 (see TTB1), with tab and horizontal gum breakers space 5.5mm apart. Produced by Bureau of Engraving and Printing.*

TTB7

TTB7 MNHVF

Cover, blue on white, entire booklet —
n. booklet pane 170.00

1960-62. Post Rider Seal Issue *97¢, four red violet panes and glassine interleaving. Pane red violet cross-hatched rotary press printed, six stamps (22x25mm) perforated 11.2x10.5, with tab at top and horizontal gum breakers alternating 4.5 and 6.5mm apart, vertical gum breakers spaced 22.5mm. All panes cut from coil sheet stock, and therefore are mis-cut and mis-perforated. Produced by Bureau of Engraving and Printing.*

TTB8

TTB8 MNHVF

Cover, red violet, on pink, entire booklet —
n. booklet pane —

1962-63. Small Post Rider Seal Issue $1.00, (violet DUMMY handstamp 29x4.5mm), four FTPO panes with silicone interleaving. Panes intaglio printed "For Testing Purposes Only" in gray-black vertical to stamps, six stamps (22x30mm) perforated 11.2x10.5, with perforated ends and no tab. Horizontal gum breakers spaced 5.5mm apart. Panes are cut from FTPO coil sheet stock and, therefore, are mis-cut and miss-perforated. Produced by Bureau of Engraving and Printing.

TTB9

TTB9 MNHVF

Cover, blue on white, entire booklet —
n. booklet pane —

1962-67. Blank Cover Issue With press printed hollow DUMMY black 55x7.5mm, two blank panes perforated 11.2x10.5 with tab at top and silicone interleaving. Horizontal gum breakers are spaced 11.5mm apart and vertical breakers are spaced alternating 14 and 8.5mm apart. Pane same as TTB7. Produced by Bureau of Engraving and Printing.

TTB10

TTB10 MNHVF

Cover, blank white, entire booklet 90.00

1962-67. Blank Cover Issue With press printed hollow DUMMY red 55x7.5mm, two blank panes with tab and silicone interleaving. Horizontal gum breakers are spaced 11.5mm apart and vertical breakers are spaced alternating 14 and 8.5mm apart. Pane same as TTB7n. Produced by Bureau of Engraving and Printing.

TTB11 MNHVF

Cover, blank white, entire booklet 200.00

1963-64. Mr. Zip Carrier Issue *$1 "Domestic Postage Rates" on inside front cover, violet "DUMMY" handstamp 29.5x4.5mm on cover; four blank panes with silicone interleaving. Blank pane of six stamps (22x25mm), perforated 11.2x10.5, with tab at top and gum breakers with spacing alternating 4.5 and 6.5mm horizontally and 14.0 and 8.5 vertically. Produced by Bureau of Engraving and Printing.*

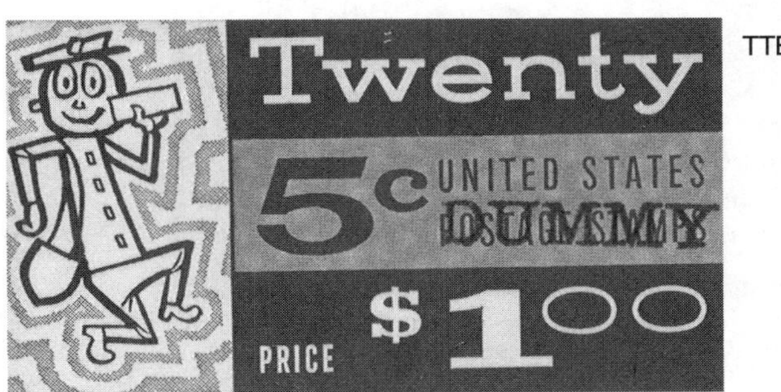

TTB12

TTB12 MNHVF

		MNHVF
Cover, blue on white, entire booklet		—
n. booklet pane		180.00

1963-64. MR. ZIP CARRIER ISSUE *$1 (red press printed hollow DUMMY (55.0x7.5mm), "Domestic Postage Rates" inside front cover, four blank panes with silicone interleaving. Blank pane of six stamps (22x25mm), perforated 11.2x10.5, with tab and horizontal gum breakers spaced 11.5mm horizontally and 14.0 and 8.5 vertically. Pane same as TTB12n. Produced by Bureau of Engraving and Printing.*

TTB13

TTB13 MNHVF

	MNHVF
Cover, blue on white, entire booklet	—
n. booklet pane	—

1963-64. MR. ZIP CARRIER ISSUE (red printed hollow DUMMY 55x7.5mm), Minute Man-Buy US Savings Bonds inside front cover, four blank panes with silicone interleaving. Blank pane of six stamps (22*25mm), perforated 11.2x10.5, with tab and horizontal gum breakers with spacing 11.5mm horizontally and 14.0 and 8.5 vertically. Pane same as TTB12n. Produced by Bureau of Engraving and Printing.

TTB14

	MNHVF
Cover, blue on white, entire booklet	50.00

1967-68. SMALL POST RIDER SEAL ISSUE *with "32 six cent and 8 one cent price $2.00" (violet handstamped DUMMY 34.5x6.5mm), five FTPO panes with silicone interleaves. Panes intaglio printed "For Testing Purposes Only" in gray-black, six stamps (22x25mm), with tab at bottom cut ends, with overall green tagging, perforated 11.2x10.5, gum breakers spaced 11mm horizontally and alternating spacing of 8.5mm and 11mm vertically. Panes were cut from FTPO coil sheet stock and, therefore, are mis-cut and mis-perforated. Produced by Bureau of Engraving and Printing.*

TTB15

TB15n

TTB15

	MNHVF
Cover, brown on white, entire booklet	50.00
n. booklet pane	70.00

1970-71. EISENHOWER PORTRAIT ISSUE *with "32 six cent & 8 one cent Price $2.00" (violet handstamped DUMMY 29.5x4.5mm), five FTPO panes with silicone interleaves.*

Panes intaglio printed "For Testing Purposes Only" in gray-black vertical with stamps, eight stamps (25x25mm) perforated 11.2x10.5, with tab and cut ends, with overall green tagging. Panes were cut from FTPO coil sheet stock and, therefore, are mis-cut and mis-perforated. One type pane with gum breakers spaced 11mm horizontally and alternating 14.0 and 8.5mm vertically. Second pane type with gum breakers spaced 11mm horizontally and 22.5mm vertically. Produced by Bureau of Engraving and Printing.

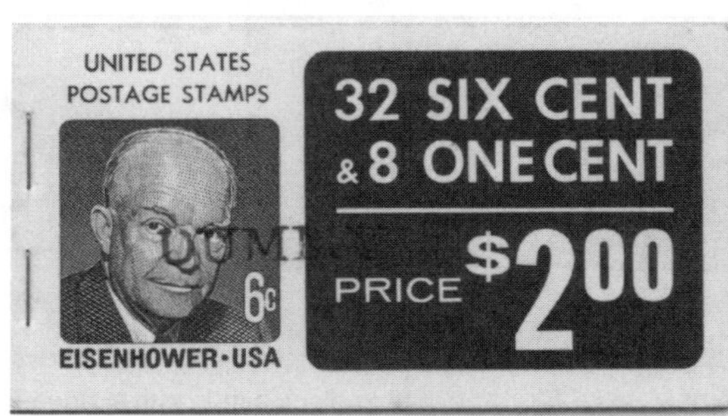

TTB16

TTB16n

TTB16

	MNHVF
Cover, blue on white, entire booklet with FTPO pane with gum breaker spacing 14.0mm and 8.5mm vertically	—
v. entire booklet with FTPO pane with gum breaker spacing 22.5mm vertically	—
n. TTB16 pane	—
n1. TTB16v. pane	—

1970-71. EISENHOWER PORTRAIT ISSUE With "32 six cent & 8 one cent price $2.00" (violet handstamped DUMMY 34.5x6.5mm), 5 FTPO panes with silicone interleaves. Occurs with TTB16. Panes were cut from FTPO coil sheet stock and, therefore, are mis-cut and mis-perforated. Produced by Bureau of Engraving and Printing.

TTB17

	MNHVF
Cover, blue on white, entire booklet with TTB16n panes	—

1970-72. STAMP SILHOUETTE ISSUE *"$1.00 with twelve 8¢ and four 1¢ stamps" (violet handstamped DUMMY 29x4.5), three FTPO panes with silicone interleaves. Panes intaglio Printed "For Testing Purposes Only" in gray-black vertical with stamps, perforated 10.5x11.2, with no tab and two cut ends, with overall green tagging, gum breakers spaced 11.0mm apart horizontally. Panes were cut from FTPO coil sheet stock and, therefore, are mis-cut and mis-perforated. Produced by Bureau of Engraving and Printing.*

TTB18

	MNHVF
Cover, claret on white, entire booklet	—
n. booklet pane	—

1970-72. STAMP SILHOUETTE ISSUE *"$1.00 with twelve 8¢ and four 1¢ stamps" (violet handstamped DUMMY 34.5x6.5), three FTPO panes with silicone interleaves. Pane same as TTB18n. Produced by Bureau of Engraving and Printing.*

TTB19 MNHVF
Cover, claret on white, entire booklet —

1970-72. Stamp Silhouette Issue *"$1.00 with twelve 8¢ and four 1¢ stamps" (violet handstamped hollow DUMMY 34.5x6.5), three FTPO panes with silicone interleaves. Pane same as TTB18n.*

TTB20 MNHVF
Cover, claret on white, entire booklet —

1971-72. Eisenhower Portrait Issue with "24 eight cent price $1.92" (violet handstamped DUMMY 29.5x4.5mm), three FTPO panes with silicone interleaves. Pane same as TTB16n. Produced by Bureau of Engraving and Printing.

TTB21

TTB21 MNHVF
Cover, claret on white, entire booklet —

1971-72. Eisenhower Portrait Issue *with "24 eight cent price $1.92" (violet handstamped DUMMY 34.5x6.5mm), three FTPO panes with silicone interleaves. Pane same as TTB16n. Produced by Bureau of Engraving and Printing.*

TTB22 MNHVF
Cover, claret on white, entire booklet —

1971-72. Stamp Silhouette Issue *with "$1.00 15 six cent & 5 two cent United States Postage Stamps" (violet handstamped DUMMY 34.5x6.5mm), four FTPO panes with silicone interleaves. Panes intaglio printed "For Testing Purposes Only" in gray-black vertical with stamps, six stamps (22x25) perforated 10.5x11.2, with no tab and one cut end, with overall green tagging and with gum breakers spaced 11.0mm apart horizontally and 22.0mm vertically. Some examples have black felt tip technician markings on either front or back covers. Produced by Bureau of Engraving and Printing.*

TTB23

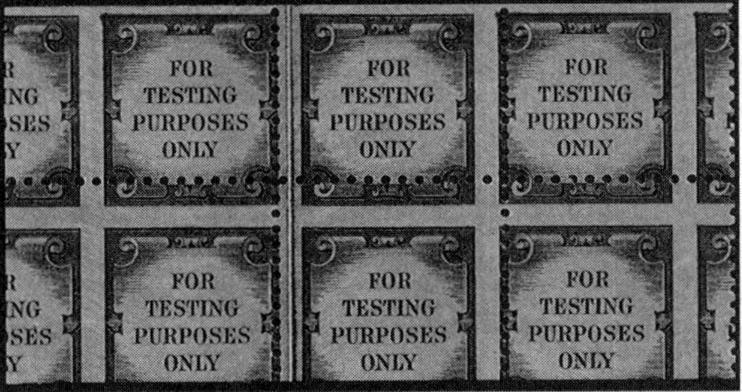

TTB23n

TTB23 MNHVF
Cover, brown on white, entire booklet 50.00
n. booklet pane 100.00

1971-72. Stamp Silhouette Issue with "$1.00 15 six cent & 5 two cent" (violet handstamped DUMMY 34.5x6.5), four FTPO panes with interleaving. Panes intaglio printed "For Testing Purposes Only" in gray-black vertical with stamps, six stamps (22x25) perforated 10.5x11.2, with no tab and one cut end, with overall green tagging and with gum breakers spaced 11.0mm apart horizontally. Panes were cut from FTPO coil sheet stock and, therefore, are mis-cut and mis-perforated. Some examples have red or black felt tip technician markings on either front or back covers. Produced by Bureau of Engraving and Printing.

TTB24n

TTB24 MNHVF
Cover, blue on white, entire booklet 45.00
n. booklet pane 90.00

1971-72. Stamp Silhouette Issue with "$1.00 ten-10¢ Airmail Stamps" (violet handstamped DUMMY 29.5x4.5mm), two FTPO panes with interleaving. Panes intaglio printed "For Testing Purposes Only" in gray-black vertical with stamps, six stamps (22x25mm), perforated 10.5x11.2, with perforated ends and no tab, with overall green tagging, with gum breakers spaced 11.0mm horizontally and alternating 14.0 and 8.5mm vertically. Produced by Bureau of Engraving and Printing.

TTB25

TTB25 MNHVF
Cover, red on white, entire booklet 50.00
n. booklet pane 150.00

Each entry in this catalog has been double-checked for accuracy, but mistakes may creep into any human endeavor, and we ask your assistance in eliminating them. Please call the attention of the editors to any errors in stamp description found in this catalog. Send your comments to:

Minkus Catalog Editor
Krause Publications
700 E. State St.
Iola WI 54990

1971-72. Stamp Silhouette Issue with "$1.00, ten-10¢ Airmail Stamps" (violet handstamped DUMMY 34.5x6.5mm), two FTPO panes with interleaving. Panes same as TTB25n. Produced by Bureau of Engraving and Printing.

TTB26 *front cover*

TTB26 *back cover*

TTB26 MNHVF

Cover, red on white, entire booklet —
n. booklet pane 100.00

Folded and Glued Booklets

Blank Cover Issue *Blank cover (48x81mm), one blank pane. Blank pane (43x112mm), eight stamps perforated 10.9x10.6, with 14mm selvage, dull gummed, untagged. Produced by Bureau of Engraving and Printing.*

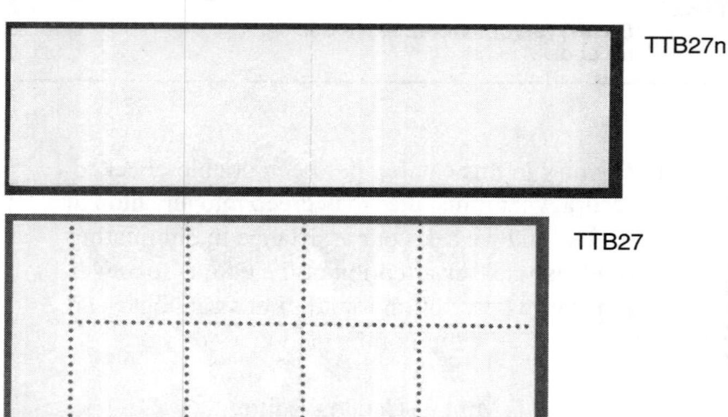

TTB27n

TTB27

TTB27 MNHVF

Cover, blank, entire booklet —
n. booklet pane —

Flag Over Supreme Court Issue *Blank cover (43x81mm), form of Flag over Supreme Court, two blank panes. Pane blank (43x137mm), 10 stamps perforated 10.0x9.8, shiny gum, untagged. Produced by Bureau of Engraving and Printing.*

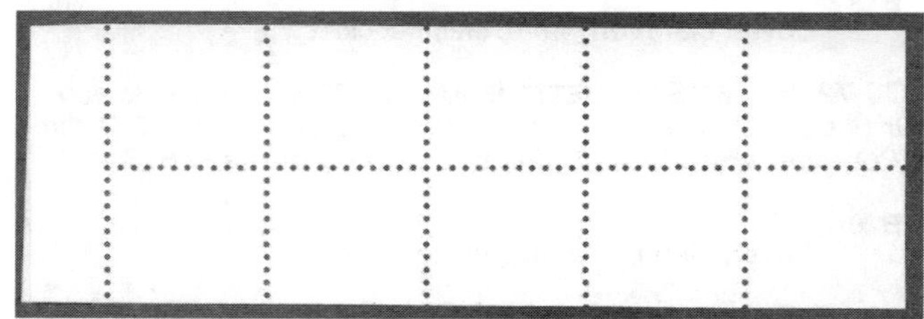

TTB28

TTB28 MNHVF

Cover, blank, entire booklet —
n. booklet pane 80.00

Blank Cover Issue *Blank fluorescent cover (48x81mm), form of 22¢ Flag over Capitol, one blank pane of five stamps. Pane blank (43x137mm), five stamps (24x44mm) perforated 10 on long side, on high gloss paper with dull gum, untagged. Tab 12mm high. Produced by Bureau of Engraving and Printing.*

TTB29n

TTB29 MNHVF

Cover, blank, entire booklet —
n. booklet pane 50.00

Blank Cover Issue *Blank cover (43x81mm), two panes of five stamps. Pane blank (43x135mm), five stamps (24x44mm) perforated 10, on high gloss paper with dull gum, untagged. Tab 12mm high. Produced by Bureau of Engraving and Printing.*

TTB30 MNHVF

Cover, blank, entire booklet —
n. booklet pane —

Blank Cover Issue *Blank cover (43x81mm), two panes of five stamps. Pane blank (43x135mm), five stamps (24x44mm) perforated 10, with shiny gum, untagged. Produced by Bureau of Engraving and Printing.*

TTB31 MNHVF

Cover, blank, entire booklet —
n. booklet pane —

Flag Over Capitol Issue *Blank cover (43x81mm), form of 22¢ Flag over Capitol, two imperforate panes. Pane blank (43x135mm), imperforate dull gum, untagged. Produced by Bureau of Engraving and Printing or, possibly, KCS Industries.*

TTB32 MNHVF

Cover, blank, entire booklet —
n. booklet pane 65.00

Blank Cover Issue *Blank cover (43x81mm), two panes with one horizontal perforation at fold. Pane blank (43x137mm), untagged, dull gum, one horizontal row of perforations (10.9) at fold. Produced by KCS Industries.*

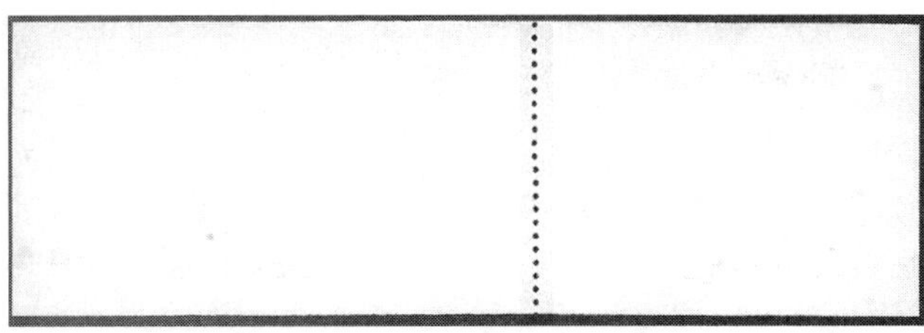

TTB33

TTB33 MNHVF

	MNHVF
Cover, blank, entire booklet	—
n. booklet pane	—

FLAG OVER CAPITOL ISSUE *Cover (43x81mm), one blank pane of five stamps. Pane blank (43x130mm), five stamps (24x44mm) perforated 10, with dull gum, untagged. Tab is about 9mm high. Produced by Bureau of Engraving and Printing.*

TTB34

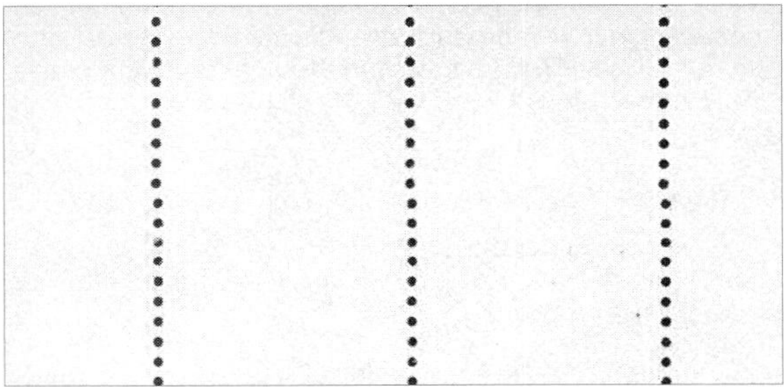

TTB34n

TTB34

	MNHVF
Cover, Flag over Capitol, entire booklet	—
n. booklet pane	40.00

1985. SEASHELLS ISSUE *$4.00, folded cover (43x81mm) with two blank panes of 10 stamps. Pane blank (43x137mm), 10 stamps perforated 10x9.8, with dull gum, untagged. Scored horizontally between stamps. Produced by Bureau of Engraving and Printing.*

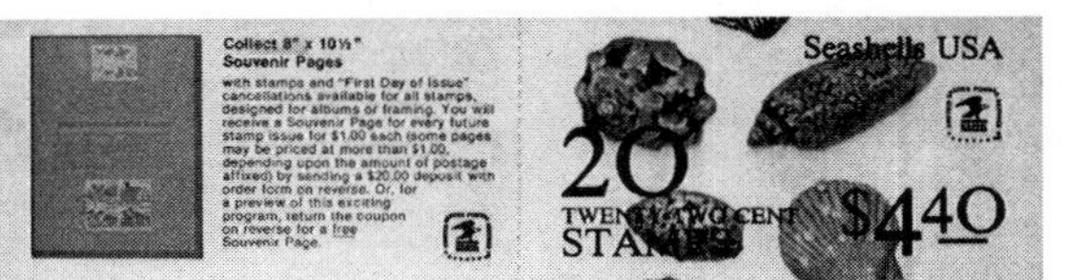

TTB35

TTB35

	MNHVF
Cover, Seashells, entire booklet	—
n. booklet pane	—

1985. SEASHELLS ISSUE *$4.00, folded cover without black printing (43x81mm), two blank panes of 10 stamps. Panes same as TTB35. Produced by Bureau of Engraving and Printing.*

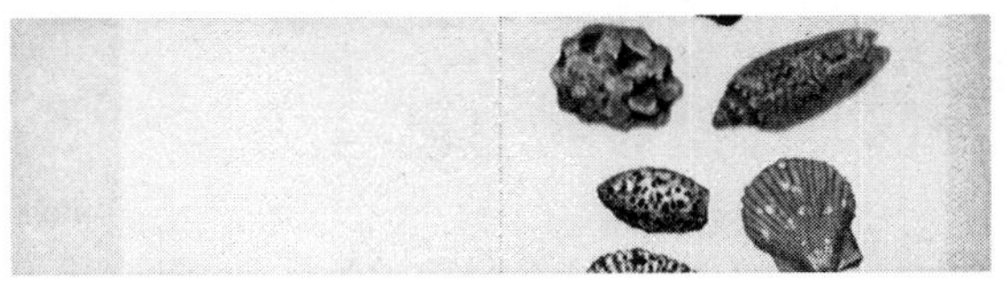

TTB36

TTB36

	MNHVF
Cover, Seashells, entire booklet	—

1985. SEASHELLS ISSUE *$4.00, folded cover without black printing (43x81mm), two blank panes of five stamps. Panes same as TTB30n. Produced by Bureau of Engraving and Printing.*

TTB37

	MNHVF
Cover, Seashells, entire booklet	—

1992. HUMMINGBIRDS ISSUE *$5.80, folded cover (41x84mm) with two blank panes of five stamps. Pane blank (41x137mm), five stamps (24x44mm) perforated 10.9, with glossy gum, untagged. Produced by American Bank Note Company.*

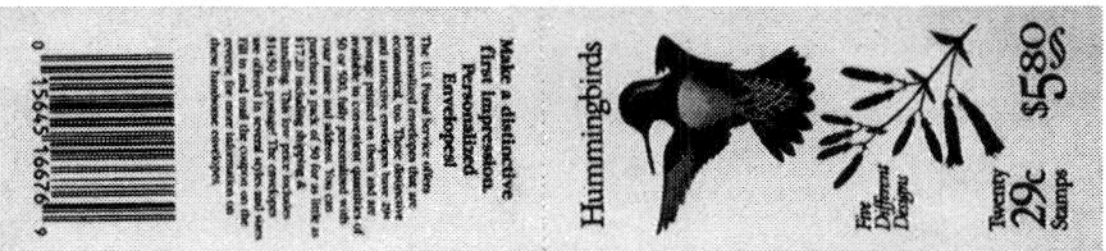

TTB38

TTB38

	MNHVF
Hummingbirds, entire booklet	
n. booklet pane	—

1994. G (FLAG) ISSUE *$6.40, folded cover (43x81mm) with two blank panes of five stamps. Possibly produced by American Bank Note Company. Panes same as TTB38n.*

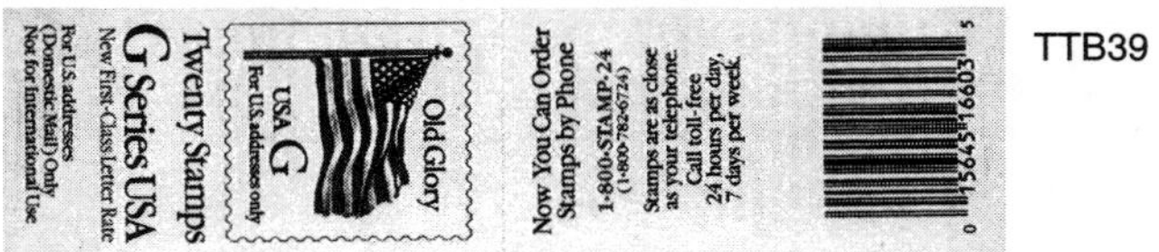

TTB39

TTB39

	MNHVF
G (Flag), entire booklet	—

1988. $5 JACK LONDON ISSUE *Folded cover (43x81mm) with $5.00 Jack London exterior and unissued "The American Garden" inside cover, with two panes. Pane of 10 stamps with blue rectangle, perforated 10.9x9.8, untagged. One stamp has a number printed within rectangle. Produced by Bureau of Engraving and Printing.*

TTB40

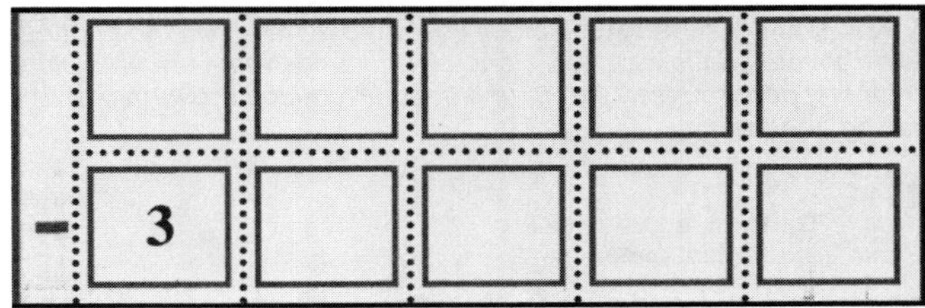

TTB40n

TTB40

	MNHVF
$5 Jack London, entire booklet	—
n. booklet pane	—

ATM Test Sheetlets

1990S. DAFFODIL ISSUE *Daffodil cover (43x81mm) with "The American Garden" inside back cover and two panes. Pane of 10 stamps* *with blue rectangle, perforated 10.9x9.8, untagged. Produced by Bureau of Engraving and Printing.*

TTB41

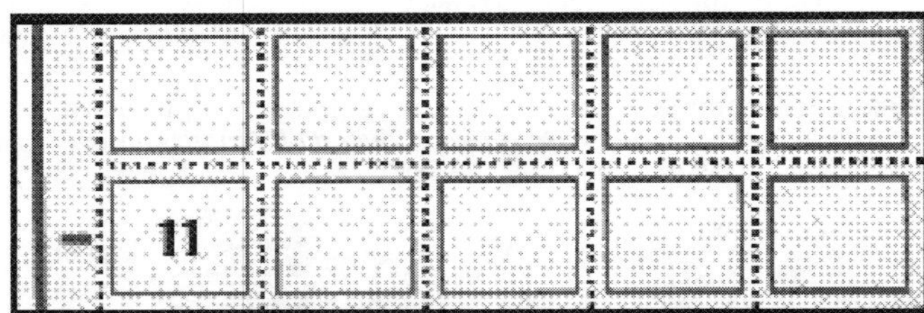

TTB41n

TTB41
Daffodil, entire booklet —
n. booklet pane —

1990s. Daffodil Issue *Daffodil cover (43x81mm) with "The American Garden" inside back cover and four panes. Pane of 10 stamps with blue rectangle, perforated 10.9x9.8, untagged. One of stamps has a number printed within rectangle. Produced by Bureau of Engraving and Printing.*

TTB42 **MNHVF**
Daffodil, entire booklet —
n. booklet pane —

1990s. Daffodil Issue *Daffodil cover (43x81mm) with "The American Garden" inside back cover and four panes. Pane of 10 stamps with very dark blue rectangle, perforated 10.9x9.8, untagged. Produced by Bureau of Engraving and Printing.*

TTB43 **MNHVF**
Daffodil, entire booklet —
n. booklet pane —

1990s. Daffodil Issue *Daffodil cover (43x81mm) with no printing inside covers and four panes. Pane of 10 stamps with very dark blue rectangle, perforated 10.9x9.8, untagged. Produced by Bureau of Engraving and Printing.*

TTB44 **MNHVF**
Daffodil, entire booklet —
n. booklet pane —

1990s. Daffodil Issue *Daffodil cover (66x87mm) with no printing inside covers and two panes. Pane of 10 stamps with black rectangle, perforated 10.9x9.8, untagged. Produced by Bureau of Engraving and Printing.*

TTB45 **MNHVF**
Daffodil, entire booklet —
n. booklet pane —

1990. Green Liberty Torch Issue *"ATM TEST/DEMONSTRATION SHEET," self-adhesive sheetlet with 18 stamp-labels with straight-line die cut separations.*

TTB50

TTB50 **MNHVF**
green, pane 45.00

1990. 25¢ Stars and Stripes Issue *25¢ Stars and Stripes self-adhesive sheetlet overprinted "SPECIMEN/FOR ATM TEST." Untagged.*

TTB50A **MNHVF**
black, blue & dark red, pane —

1992. Blank Issue *Self-adhesive ATM with 18 blank straight-line die cut labels. No printing on either front or back. Manufactured by Dittler Brothers, Inc.*

TTB50B **MNHVF**
blank, pane —

1992. Blank Issue *Self-adhesive ATM imperforate. No printing on either front or back. Liner with green "Self-Adhesive/do not wet" sloping from upper left to lower right and visible through front. Manufactured by Dittler Brothers, Inc.*

TTB50C **MNHVF**
blank, pane —

1992. 29¢ Eagle and Shield Issue *Imperforate paper sheetlet with 17 stamp-like labels overprinted dark blue "VOID" and 1 black label with text. No printing on back.*

TTB50D **MNHVF**
brown (multicolored), pane —

"NCR" and "USA" with Flag Issue *Imperforate paper sheetlet with 12 multicolored stamp-like labels, large "VOID" in background. Made by NCR.*

TTB51

TTB51 **MNHVF**
red & blue, pane 35.00

1996. "NCR & USPS" in White Strips of Flag Issue *Imperforate paper sheetlet with 12 multicolor labels. Made by NCR.*

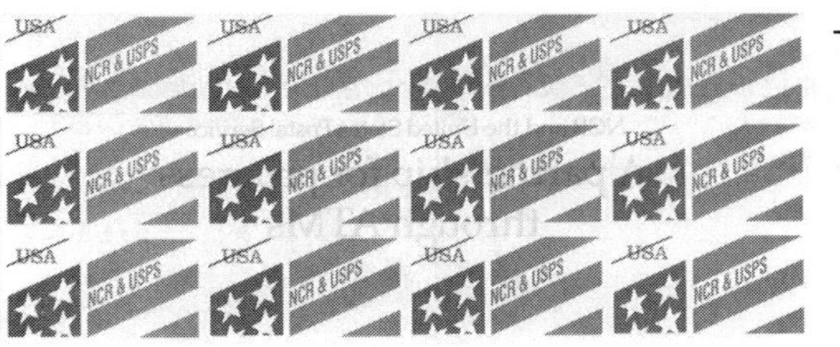

TTB52

TTB52 **MNHVF**
red & blue, pane 25.00

1997. Souvenir ATM Sheetlet from Pacific 97 Issue *Self-adhesive sheetlet with 18 multicolor stamp-like labels of San Fran-*

cisco scenes and Pacific 97 logo, with black obliterating lines and no die cut. Made by Avery Dennison.

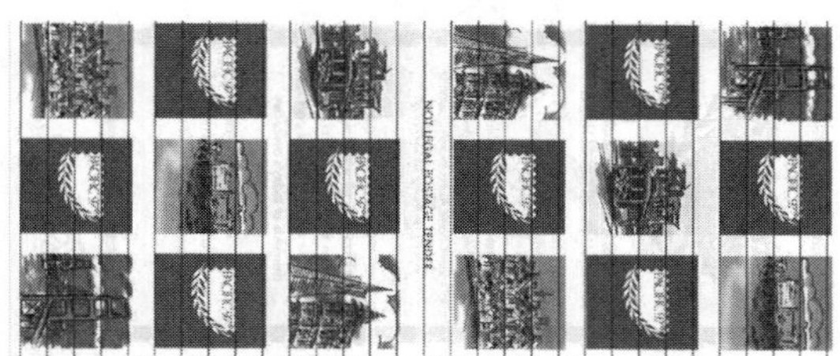
TTB53

TTB53 MNHVF
multicolored pane —

1997. Souvenir ATM Sheetlet from Pacific 97 Issue *Self-adhesive sheetlet with 18 multicolor stamp-like labels of San Francisco scenes and Pacific 97 logo, with die cuts but no black obliterating lines. Made by Avery Dennison.*

TTB54 MNHVF
multicolored pane —

Souvenir ATM Pane from Pacific 97 Issue *Self-adhesive sheetlet with 18 multicolor stamp-like labels of San Francisco Scenes and Pacific 97 logo, without obliterating lines or die cuts. Made by Avery Dennison.*

TTB55 MNHVF
multicolored pane —

"FOR ATM TESTING" and Pillars Issue *Self-adhesive sheetlet with 18 stamp-like labels of a four-column building with straight die cuts. Made by Avery Dennison for NCR.*

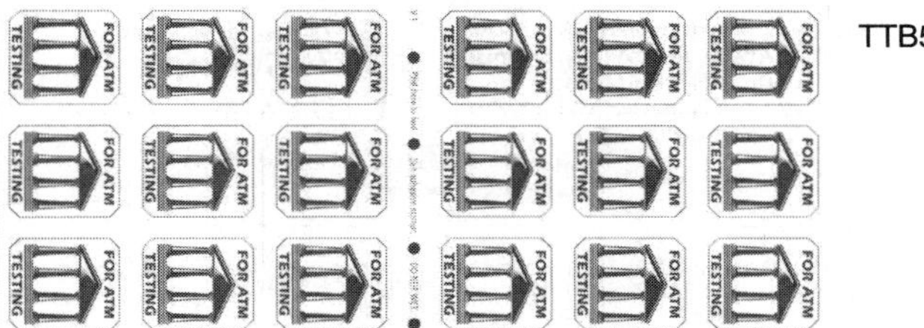

TTB56

TTB56 MNHVF
Cover, blue, pane 375.00

1997. "For Testing Purposes Only" Issue *Self-adhesive sheetlet with 18 stamp-like labels with "For Testing Purposes Only." Straight edge die cuts. Made by Avery Dennison.*

TTB57

TTB57 MNHVF
black pane 80.00

1998. FTPO Issue *Self-adhesive sheetlet with 18 stamp-like labels with "For Testing Purposes Only," serpentine die cuts gauge 7.8. Made by Avery Dennison.*

TTB58 MNHVF
black pane 40.00

2000. Souvenir ATM Issue *Self-adhesive sheetlet with two jumbo and six definitive-size stamp-like labels from World Stamp Expo 2000, straight die cuts. Made by Avery Dennison, used as "stamps" in youth area.*

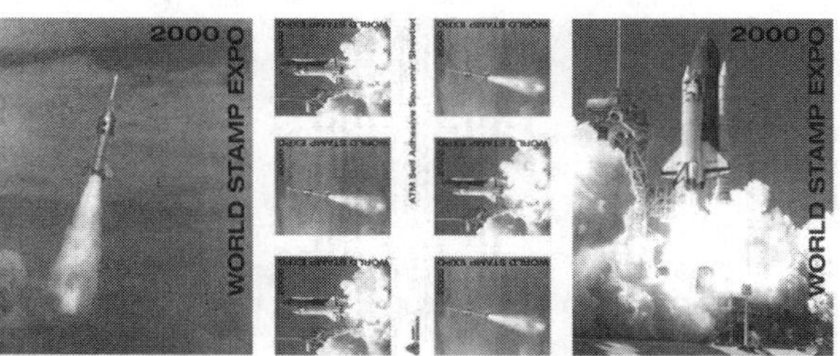

TTB59

TTB59 MNHVF
multicolored pane 5.00

2000. 29¢ Rose ATM Issue *Paper sheetlet with 18 multicolor 29¢ Rose stamp-like labels with "VOID" in faint gray and plate number 5111. Possibly made by NCR.*

TTB60 MNHVF
red & green pane —

2000. "For Testing Purposes Only Issue *Self-adhesive sheetlet with 18 stamp-like labels with "For Testing Purposes Only," serpentine die cut perforation gauge 7.8. Made by Avery Dennison.*

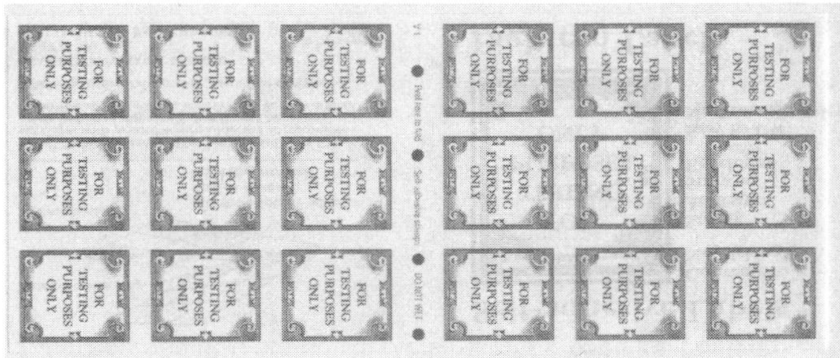

TTB61 *front*

TTB61 *back*

TTB61 MNHVF
magenta pane —

2000. NCR for ATM Testing Issue *Paper sheetlet with 18 stamp-like labels with NCR logo and "For ATM NCR TESTING." Plate number V1. Made by NCR.*

TTB62 MNHVF
black, green, blue pane —

Confederate States of America

The Confederate States of America was the government established in 1861 by the Southern states that seceded from the Union, charging that it was aggressively hostile toward their "domestic institutions."

South Carolina, the first state to secede (Dec. 20, 1860), justified its action on the grounds of continued Northern attacks on slavery, the coming to power of a sectionalist party (the Republican), and the election of a President (Abraham Lincoln) "whose opinions and purposes are hostile to slavery." It was followed, in order, by Mississippi, Florida, Alabama, Georgia, Louisiana, Texas, Virginia, Arkansas, North Carolina and Tennessee. The attack on Ft. Sumter at Charleston, S.C., on April 12, 1861, is generally considered to mark the onset of hostilities.

Upon the outbreak of the war, the Union demonetized the postal issues that had been good for postage up to June 1, 1861, so that the Confederacy could not make use of the large quantities of stamps in its possession.

The Southern states, being primarily agrarian, had little industrial capability, including printing, and the lack of postage stamps could have hampered communications.

The provisional government of six Confederate states was formed in Montgomery, Ala., on Feb. 4, 1861. By March 6, President Jefferson Davis had made his final appointment to his cabinet, Postmaster General John H. Reagan from Texas. This appointment was one of the most difficult to fill because of the importance it would have in the newly formed government.

Shortly after taking office, Reagan instructed his postmasters to "continue the performance of their duties as such, and render all accounts and pay all moneys to the order of the government of the U.S. as they had heretofore done, until the government of the Confederate states shall be prepared to assume control of its postal affairs."

On May 13, 1861, Reagan issued his proclamation assuming control and direction of postal service within the limits of the Confederate States of America as of the first day of June. Effective June 1, 1861, new rates and regulations, including a basic 5¢ letter postage rate, would go into effect. The federal government suspended operations in the Confederate states by a proclamation issued by U.S. Postmaster General Montgomery Blair on May 27, 1861, effective May 31, 1861.

3¢ 1861 Postmasters Provisionals

From the time each Southern state joined the Confederacy until June 1, 1861, the postal system operated under the rules and rates of the U.S. government, including a basic 3¢ letter postage rate. Even though the U.S. government was technically in control of the postal system, the U.S. Post Office Department was reluctant to send supplies and stamps to the seceded states.

As the southern postmasters began to run out of stamps and envelopes, they reverted back to pre-stamp times to operate in the most efficient manner they could. A few issued their own provisional postage, even though the U.S. Post Office had made the issuance of postmaster provisionals illegal many years earlier.

By June 1, 1861, five cities are known to have issued 3¢ provisionals. Nashville prepared a sixth recorded 3¢ provisional prior to Tennessee's joining the Confederacy on July 2, 1861. The unissued 3¢ Nashville provisional was produced in a state that was in the process of seceding, while the 3¢ provisionals were used in the Confederacy before the June 1 control of the Confederate postal administration.

Hillsboro, N.C., Handstamp, Adhesive

CSP66-2

CSP66-1		Mint	Used
3¢	**black,** on cover (one known)		20,000.00

Jackson, Miss., Handstamp, Envelope

CSP73-1

CSP73-1		Mint	Used
3¢	**black,** entire		—

Madison Court House, Fla., Typeset, Adhesive The earliest postmasters' provisionals issued in the Confederacy. Earliest known use: Feb 13, 1861. Printed for Postmaster Samuel J. Perry at a newspaper published by his eldest son.

CSP92-1

CSP92-1a

CSP92-1		Mint	Used
3¢	**gold,** single		17,000.00
	on Cover		65,000.00
CSP92-1a		**Mint**	**Used**
3¢	**gold,** "CNETS" error		20,000.00

Nashville, Tenn., Typeset, Adhesive

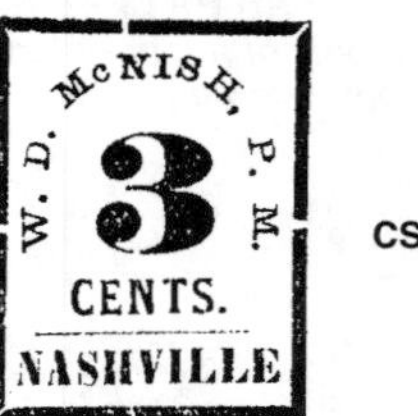

CSP102-1

CSP102-1		Mint	Used
3¢	**carmine,** single, five varieties	175.00	
	strip of 5	900.00	

Selma, Ala., Handstamp, Envelope

CSP128-1

CSP128-1		Mint	Used
3¢	**black,** entire		3,000.00

Tuscumbia, Ala., Handstamp, Envelope

CSP140-1

CSP140-1		Mint	Used
3¢	**dull red** on buff, entire		18,000.00

Confederate States Postmasters Provisionals

In the interim period from June 1, 1861, until the official issuance of Confederate stamps, as well as times that the postmasters ran out of general issue stamps, many postmasters produced other provisionals. These are:

- Adhesive postage stamps printed or handstamped on paper for separation and attachment to envelopes to signify payment of postage.
- Press-printed envelopes produced in quantity and provided by the printer to the postmaster; thus there is consistency in the paper types on which these provisionals are found.
- Handstamp provisional envelopes, which have provided a challenge to the collector. To be a provisional, the envelope must have been prepared in advance of the mailing of the envelope, in most cases sold by the postmaster and carried home for later use. Handstamp provisionals are easily confused with general handstamp covers, which were not prepared in advance. Many postmasters used the same handstamp device to produce both handstamp paid and due envelopes as well as provisional envelopes. Evidence must exist that these envelopes were prepared in advance in order to classify them as provisionals. The strongest evidence is the existence of unused examples. Handstamp provisionals come in a variety of papers as they were struck on whatever paper the postmaster might have had at the time. Many were "handbacks" to the customer in order to make necessary change as little coinage existed. For this reason, we have not attempted to differentiate the handstamp paper varieties.

The listings here represent those defined by the Confederate Stamp Alliance, an association of collectors and dealers in Confederate States material. However, it should be noted that new evidence of CSA postal material continues to surface almost 150 years after the War Between the States.

By philatelic standards, all Confederate provisionals are scarce. The most common exists in only a few hundred examples. Many exist in examples of only one or two. The prices in this section are considered retail asking prices for fine examples of entire covers and examples of off-cover stamps with little or no gum. Examples of unused stamps with major amounts of original gum would be valued at considerably more.

To date, 153 different towns have been recorded as issuing provisionals. Many more surely did. We know of many other potential provisionals; however, research has yet to prove their "prepared in advance" status. As it does, they will be added to this listing.

The illustrations provided are the best available. Please note, however, they are not to scale. Many have been reduced to fit space requirements.

Aberdeen, Miss., Handstamp, Envelope

CSP1-1

CSP1-1		Mint	Used
5¢	**black,** entire		8,000.00

CSP1-2		Mint	Used
10¢	**black,** entire, revalued 10¢ ms over 5¢		15,000.00

Abingdon, Va., Handstamp, Envelope

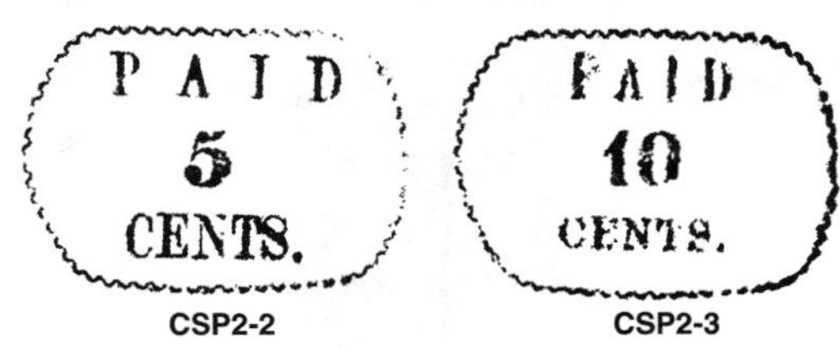

CSP2-2 CSP2-3

CSP2-1		Mint	Used
2¢	**black,** entire		15,000.00

CSP2-2		Mint	Used
5¢	**black,** entire		1,500.00
	entire, patriotic cover		3,000.00

CSP2-3		Mint	Used
10¢	**black,** entire, one mint known	5,000.00	7,500.00

Albany, Ga., Handstamp, Envelope

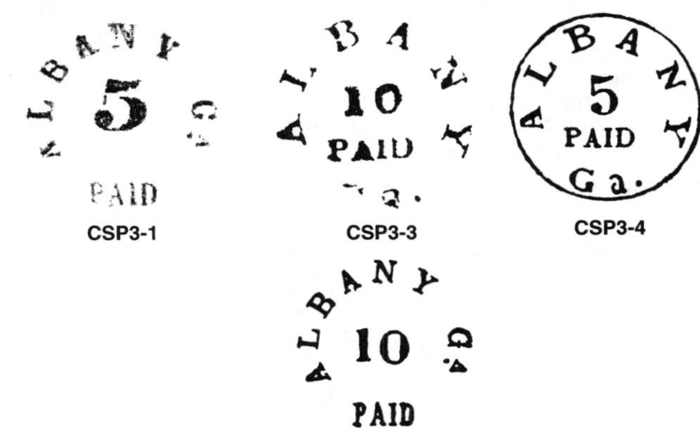

CSP3-1 CSP3-3 CSP3-4

CSP3-5

CSP3-1		Mint	Used
5¢	**greenish-blue,** entire		600.00
	on patriotic cover		—

CSP3-2		Mint	Used
10¢	**greenish-blue,** entire (similar to CSP3-1)		2,000.00

CSP3-3		Mint	Used
10¢	**greenish-blue,** entire		2,500.00

CSP3-4		Mint	Used
10¢ over 5¢	**greenish-blue,** entire (CSP3-3 over CSP3-1)		2,500.00

Anderson Court House, S.C., Handstamp, Envelope

CSP4-1 CSP4-2 CSP4-3

CSP4-1		Mint	Used
2¢	**black,** entire, no rate marking, one known		7,000.00

CSP4-2		Mint	Used
5¢	**black,** entire	500.00	2,500.00

CSP4-3		Mint	Used
10¢	**black,** entire, 10¢ in ms, one known		3,000.00

Athens, Ga., Woodcut, Adhesive Prepared for Postmaster T. Crawford from a single setting of two woodcut subjects. Each subject is similar but has distinct differences from the other, such as the size of "PAID," normally larger on the right stamp in the pair. The size of a sheet is unknown. The largest known piece is a strip of four on cover.

CSP5-1

CSP5-1		Mint	Used
5¢	**purple,** single, printed in pairs, one horizontal, one vertical	1,000.00	2,500.00
	on cover		3,500.00
	horizontal pair	2,500.00	4,200.00
	pair on cover		6,000.00
	strip of 4 on cover		10,000.00
	patriotic cover		5,000.00

CSP5-1a		Mint	Used
5¢	**purple,** vertical tete-beche pair		8,000.00
	tete-beche pair on cover		25,000.00

CSP5-2		Mint	Used
5¢	**red,** single		4,000.00
	on cover		13,500.00
	horizontal pair		10,000.00
	pair on cover, printed in pairs, one horizontal, one vertical		25,000.00

Atlanta, Ga., Handstamp, Envelope

CSP6-2 CSP6-1 CSP6-7 CSP6-6

CSP6-1		Mint	Used
2¢	**black,** entire		3,000.00
	on advertising cover		—

CSP6-2		Mint	Used
5¢	**black,** entire	150.00	500.00
	on patriotic cover		3,500.00
	on advertising cover		—

CSP6-2a		Mint	Used
10¢	**black,** entire, revalued 10¢ ms over 5¢		1,500.00

CSP6-3		Mint	Used
5¢	**red,** entire, (similar to CSP6-2)		3,000.00

CSP6-4		Mint	Used
5¢	**black,** entire (similar to CSP6-1)		1,600.00

CSP6-4a		Mint	Used
10¢	**black,** entire, revalued 10¢ ms over 5¢		2,500.00

CSP6-5		Mint	Used
5¢	**black,** entire (similar to CSP6-6 with "5" sideways)		700.00

CSP6-6		Mint	Used
10¢	**black,** entire		3,000.00

CSP6-7		Mint	Used
10¢	**black,** entire		3,000.00
	on advertising cover		—

Austin, Miss., Typeset, Envelope

CSP-8

CSP8		Mint	Used
5¢	**red** on amber, entire, canceled black PAID, one known		75,000.00

Austin, Texas, Handstamp, Adhesive

CSP9-1

CSP9-1		Mint	Used
10¢	**black,** single		—
	tied, one known on cover		—
	on cover, uncanceled, one known		1,500.00

Austin, Texas, Handstamp, Envelope

CSP9-2

CSP9-2		Mint	Used
10¢	**black,** entire		1,500.00

Autaugaville, Ala., Handstamp, Envelope Brass engraved handstamp used by Postmaster Albert William McNeel, similar to the woodcut used in Athens, Ga.

CSP10-1

CSP10-2

CSP10-1		Mint	Used
5¢	**black,** entire		12,000.00

CSP10-2		Mint	Used
5¢	**black,** entire		12,000.00

Balcony Falls, Va., Handstamp, Envelope

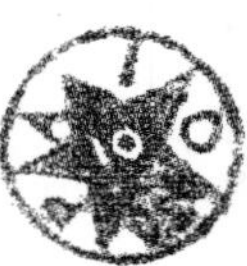
CSP-11

CSP11		Mint	Used
10¢	**black,** entire		1,800.00

Barnwell Court House, S.C., Handstamp, Envelope

CSP-12

'Control Mark'

CSP12		Mint	Used
5¢	**black,** entire		3,000.00

Baton Rouge, La., Typeset, Adhesive

CSP13-1

CSP13-2

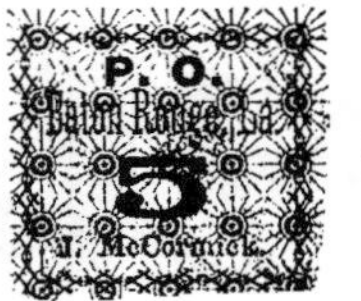

CSP13-3

CSP13-4

CSP13-1		Mint	Used
2¢	**green,** single, 10 varieties	5,000.00	6,000.00
	on cover, 10 varieties		30,000.00

CSP13-1a		Mint	Used
2¢	**green,** single, "McCcrmick," 10 varieties	12,000.00	8,000.00
	on cover, "McCcrmick," error		15,000.00

CSP13-2		Mint	Used
5¢	**green and carmine,** single, 10 varieties	1,500.00	1,500.00
	on cover, 10 varieties		7,000.00
	pair on cover		12,500.00
	strip of 3 on cover, 10 varieties		15,000.00
	strip of 5 on cover, 10 varieties		25,000.00

CSP13-2a		Mint	Used
5¢	**green and carmine,** single, "McCcrmick"	4,000.00	2,000.00
	on cover, "McCormick"		10,500.00

CSP13-3		Mint	Used
5¢	**green and carmine,** single, 10 varieties	4,000.00	1,500.00
	on cover, 10 varieties		10,000.00

CSP13-3a		Mint	Used
5¢	**green and carmine,** single, "McCcrmick," 10 varieties		3,000.00

CSP13-4		Mint	Used
10¢	**blue,** single, 10 varieties		6,000.00
	on cover, one known		75,000.00

Beaumont, Texas, Typeset, Adhesive

Earliest known use: *April 9, 1864.*

CSP14-1

CSP14-3

CSP14-1		Mint	Used
10¢	**black** on yellow, single, several varieties of each		4,500.00
	on cover, several varieties of each		75,000.00

CSP14-2		Mint	Used
10¢	**black** on pink, single, several varieties of each		15,000.00
	on cover, several varieties of each		35,000.00

CSP14-3		Mint	Used
10¢	**black** on yellow, single, one known		100,000.00

Bladon Springs, Ala., Handstamp, Envelope

CSP15-1

CSP15-2

CSP15-1		Mint	Used
ms 5¢	**black frame,** entire		2,000.00

CSP15-2		Mint	Used
10¢	**black,** entire		—

Bluffton, S.C., Handstamp, Envelope

CSP16

CSP16		Mint	Used
5¢	**black,** entire, one known		5,000.00

Bridgeville, Ala., Handstamp, Adhesive

CSP17

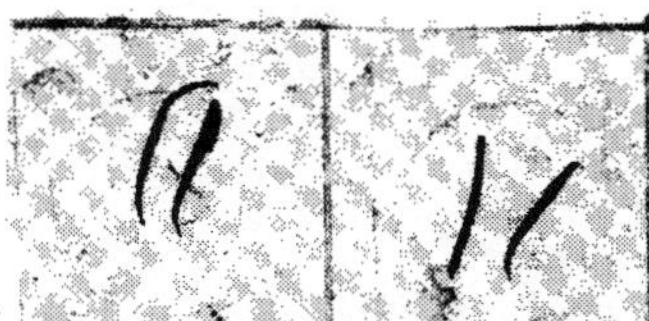

CSP17		Mint	Used
5¢	**black with red squares,** pair on cover, on pen-ruled squares		25,000.00

Camden, S.C., Handstamp, Envelope

CSP18-2

CSP18-1

CSP18-1		Mint	Used
5¢	**black,** entire		800.00

CSP18-2		Mint	Used
10¢	**black,** entire, used same as handstamp paid	500.00	

Canton, Miss., Handstamp, Envelope

CSP19-1

CSP19-1		Mint	Used
5¢	**black,** entire		2,000.00

CSP19-2		Mint	Used
10¢ over 5¢	**black,** entire, revalued 10¢ ms over 5¢		3,000.00

Carolina City, N.C., Handstamp, Envelope

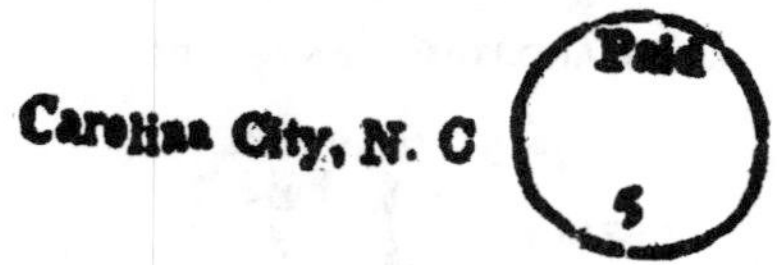

CSP20

CSP20		Mint	Used
5¢	**black,** entire (two known)		6,000.00

Cartersville, Ga., Handstamp, Envelope

CSP21

CSP21		Mint	Used
(5¢)	**red,** entire		1,500.00

Chapel Hill, N.C., Handstamp, Envelope

CSP22

CSP22		Mint	Used
5¢	**black,** entire		4,000.00
	on patriotic cover		6,500.00

Charleston, S.C., Lithograph, Adhesive Only Charleston, Lynchburg, Va., and Memphis, Tenn., produced adhesive stamps and printed envelopes at the same time.

CSP23-1

CSP23-1		Mint	Used
5¢	**blue,** single	900.00	750.00
	on cover		2,500.00
	pair	1,500.00	2,000.00
	on cover		2,000.00
	pair on cover		5,000.00
	on patriotic cover		5,000.00
	on cover with CS7, (5¢ London Print)		6,000.00
	on cover with CSP60 (forwarded)		6,000.00

Charleston, S.C., Typograph, Envelope

CSP23-2 CSP23-7

CSP23-2		Mint	Used
5¢	**blue,** entire	1,200.00	2,500.00

CSP23-3		Mint	Used
5¢	**blue** on amber, entire	1,200.00	2,500.00

CSP23-4		Mint	Used
5¢	**blue** on orange, entire	1,200.00	2,000.00

CSP23-5		Mint	Used
5¢	**blue** on buff, entire	1,200.00	2,500.00

CSP23-6		Mint	Used
5¢	**blue** on blue, entire	3,500.00	2,500.00

CSP23-7		Mint	Used
10¢	**blue** on orange, entire, one known		80,000.00

Charleston, S.C., Handstamp, Envelope

CSP23-8		Mint	Used
10¢	**black,** piece, one known		5,000.00

Charlotte, N.C., Handstamp, Envelope

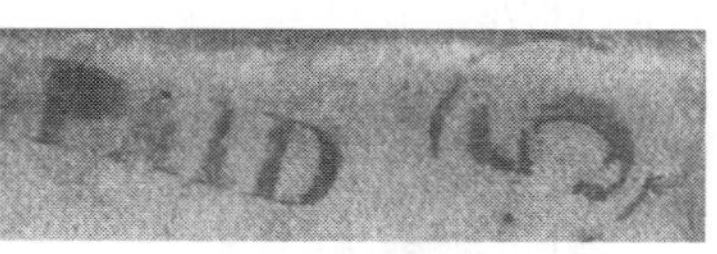

CSP23A-1

CSP23A-1		Mint	Used
5¢	**blue,** entire (two known), prepared in advance examples of handstamp paid		1,800.00

Charlottesville, Va., Handstamp, Envelope

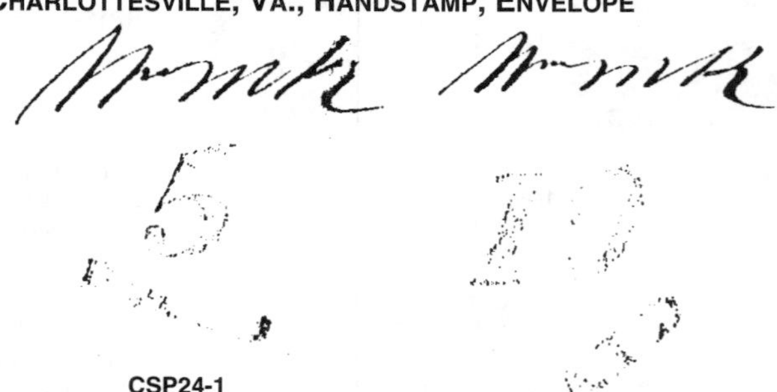

CSP24-1 CSP24-2

CSP24-1		Mint	Used
5¢	**black,** entire, with ms initials		5,000.00

CSP24-2		Mint	Used
10¢	**black,** entire, with ms initials		5,000.00

Chattanooga, Tenn., Handstamp, Envelope

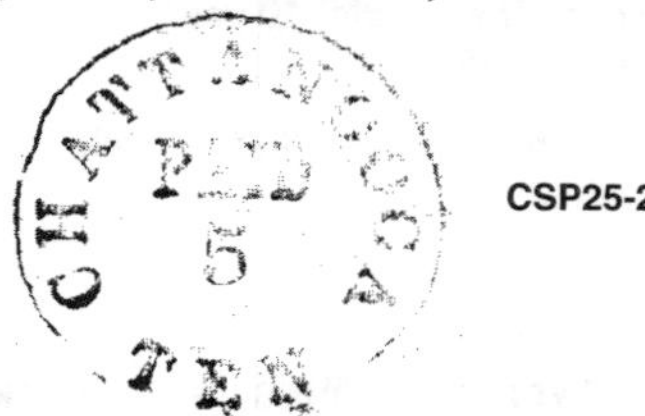

CSP25-2

CSP25-1a		Mint	Used
5¢ over 2¢	**black,** entire	3,000.00	

CSP25-2		Mint	Used
5¢	**black,** entire		1,500.00

Christiansburg, Va., Handstamp, Envelope

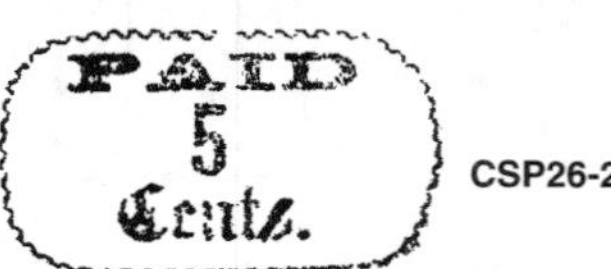

CSP26-2

CSP26-1		Mint	Used
5¢	**black** on blue, entire		2,500.00

CSP26-2		Mint	Used
5¢	**blue,** entire		1,800.00

CSP26-3		Mint	Used
5¢	**black** on orange, entire		2,200.00

CSP26-4 — Mint / Used
5¢ **green,** entire, with U.S. Minkus #EN29 — 4,000.00

CSP26-5 — Mint / Used
10¢ **blue,** entire — 3,500.00

Clarksville, Texas, Handstamp, Envelope

CSP27

CSP27 — Mint / Used
10¢ **black,** entire, same as handstamp PAID when used

Colaparchee, Ga., Handstamp, Envelope

CSP28

CSP28 — Mint / Used
5¢ **black,** entire with undated Postmark control — 3,500.00

Note: All recorded examples are used from Savannah, Ga., with a general-issue stamp on the reverse and the Colaparchee markings lined out on the front.

Columbia, S.C., Handstamp, Envelope

CSP29-1

CSP29-3

CSP29-4

CSP29-5

CSP29-6

CSP29-1 — Mint / Used
5¢ **blue,** entire — 500.00 / 700.00
blue, entire, with CS1 on cover — 3,000.00
blue, entire, used with CS8 — 7,500.00

CSP29-2 — Mint / Used
5¢ **black,** entire — 600.00 / 750.00

CSP29-3 — Mint / Used
10¢ over 5¢ blue, entire — 3,000.00

CSP29-4 — Mint / Used
5¢ **blue,** entire, seal on back, three types of "Paid" — 1,000.00
entire, seal on front, three types of "Paid" — 2,500.00

CSP29-5 — Mint / Used
10¢ **blue,** entire, seal on back, three types of "Paid" — 2,000.00

CSP29-6 — Mint / Used
5¢ **blue,** entire, 27mm seal on back, three types of "Paid" — 4,000.00

Columbia, Tenn., Handstamp, Envelope

CSP30

CSP30 — Mint / Used
5¢ **red,** entire — 3,500.00

Columbus, Ga., Handstamp Envelope

CSP31-1

CSP31-2

CSP31-1 — Mint / Used
5¢ **blue,** entire — 1,000.00
on advertising cover — —

CSP31-2 — Mint / Used
5¢ **red,** entire — 2,000.00

Courtland, Ala., Woodcut, Envelope

CSP32-1

CSP32-1 — Mint / Used
5¢ **red,** entire — 15,000.00

Cuthbert, Ga., Handstamp, Envelope

CSP33

CSP33 — Mint / Used
5¢ **black,** entire — — / —

Note: Considered a provisional only when unused, used from another town or with a general-issue stamp used over it.

Dalton, Ga., Handstamp, Envelope

CSP34-2

CSP34-1 — Mint / Used
(5¢) **black,** entire, rate omitted (similar to CSP34-2) — 750.00

CSP34-2 — Mint / Used
5¢ **black,** entire — 750.00

CSP34-2a Mint Used
10¢ over 5¢ black, entire, revalued ms 10¢ over 5¢ — 1,500.00

CSP34-3 Mint Used
10¢ **black,** entire (similar to CSP34-2) — 750.00

DANVILLE, VA., TYPESET, ADHESIVE

CSP35-1

CSP35-1 Mint Used
5¢ **red,** single, two varieties known, laid paper — 6,000.00
on cover, two varieties known, cut to shape, laid paper — 10,000.00
single, two varieties known, wove paper — 5,500.00
on cover, two varieties known, wove paper — 15,000.00
single, two varieties known, cut to shape, wove paper — 4,000.00
on cover, two varieties known, cut to shape, wove paper — 6,000.00

DANVILLE, VA., TYPOGRAPH, ENVELOPE

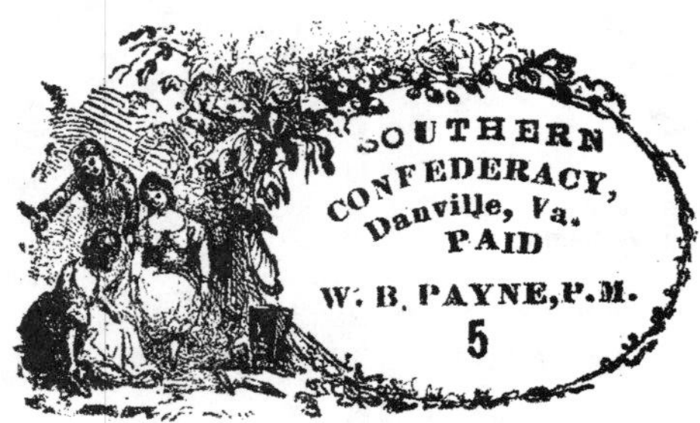

CSP35-4

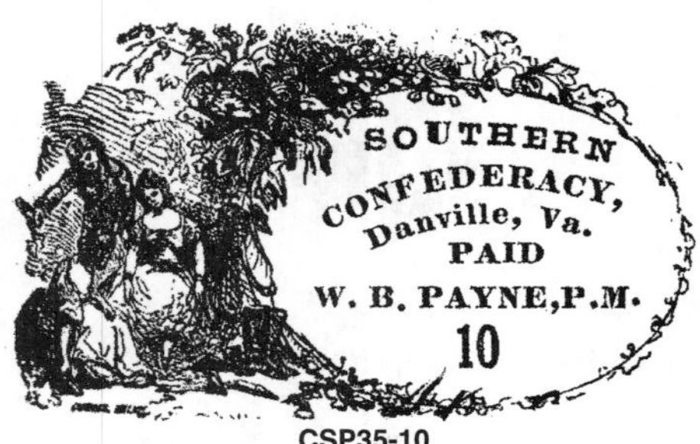

CSP35-10

CSP35-2 Mint Used
5¢ **black,** entire, "Southern" may be straight or curved — 5,000.00
used to pay postage — 7,000.00
used with other post payment evidence — 4,000.00

CSP35-3 Mint Used
5¢ **black** on amber, entire, "Southern" may be straight or curved — 5,500.00

CSP35-4 Mint Used
5¢ **black** on dark buff, entire, "Southern" may be straight or curved — 4,000.00

DANVILLE, VA., HANDSTAMP, ENVELOPE

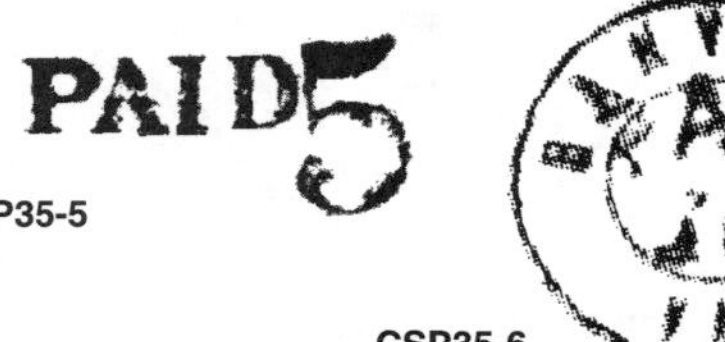

CSP35-5

CSP35-6

CSP35-5 Mint Used
5¢ **black,** entire, ms initials "WBP" — 4,000.00

CSP35-6 Mint Used
10¢ **black,** entire, (exists in red, but not sold as provisional) — 2,000.00

CSP35-7 Mint Used
10¢ **blue,** entire — 2,500.00

CSP35-8 Mint Used
10¢ **black,** entire — 2,500.00

CSP35-9 Mint Used
10¢ **black,** entire, ms initials "WBP" — 2,500.00

DANVILLE, VA., TYPOGRAPH, ENVELOPE

CSP35-10 Mint Used
10¢ **red,** entire — —

DEMOPOLIS, ALA., HANDSTAMP, ENVELOPE Postmaster J.Y. Hall.

PAID J.Y. Hall

CSP36-1

CSP36-1 Mint Used
5¢ **black,** entire, ms "J.Y. Hall" — 3,500.00

CSP36-1a Mint Used
5¢ **black,** entire, ms "Jno.Y. Hall" — 2,000.00

CSP36-2 Mint Used
ms 5¢ **black,** entire, ms "J.Y. Hall" — 3,500.00

EATONTON, GA., HANDSTAMP, ENVELOPE

CSP37-1

PAID 5 5

CSP37-2

CSP37-1 Mint Used
5¢ **black,** entire — 3,500.00

CSP37-2 Mint Used
5¢ + 5¢ **black,** entire — 3,500.00

EMORY, VA., HANDSTAMP, SELVAGE

PAID 5

CSP38-1

CSP38-1 Mint Used
5¢ **blue,** single — 3,500.00
blue, on cover, perforated 15 on 3 sides (exists with "5" above and below "Paid.") — 18,000.00

EMORY, VA., HANDSTAMP, ENVELOPE

CSP38-2

CSP38-3

CSP38-2 Mint Used
5¢ **blue,** entire — 2,000.00

CSP38-3 Mint Used
10¢ **blue,** entire — 4,500.00

Fincastle, Va., Typeset, Envelope

CSP39

CSP39		Mint	Used
10¢	**black,** entire, one known		45,000.00

Forsyth, Ga., Handstamp, Envelope

CSP40

CSP40		Mint	Used
10¢	**black,** entire		1,500.00

Franklin, N.C., Typeset, Envelope

CSP41-1

CSP41-1		Mint	Used
5¢	**blue** on buff, entire, one known		50,000.00

Franklin, N.C., Handstamp, Envelope

CSP41-2

CSP41-2		Mint	Used
5¢	**black,** entire		500.00

Frazierrsville, S.C., Handstamp, Envelope

CSP42

CSP42		Mint	Used
ms 5¢	**black,** entire, one known		2,500.00

Fredericksburg, Va., Typeset, Adhesive

CSP43-1

CSP43-3

CSP43-1		Mint	Used
5¢	**blue on bluish,** single, 10 varieties	250.00	600.00
	block of 4, 10 varieties	1,200.00	
	sheet of 20, 10 varieties	7,000.00	
	on cover, 10 varieties		4,000.00
	pair on cover, 10 varieties		15,000.00

CSP43-3		Mint	Used
10¢	**brownish-red on bluish,** single, 10 varieties	1,000.00	

CSP43-4		Mint	Used
10¢	**red** on bluish, block of 4, 10 varieties	5,000.00	

Front Royal, Va., Handstamp, Envelope

CSP44-1

CSP44-2

CSP44		Mint	Used
ms 5¢	**black,** entire, with initials		—

CSP44-2		Mint	Used
5¢	**black,** entire, with initials		—

Gainesville, Ala., Handstamp, Envelope

CSP45-1

CSP45-2

CSP45-1		Mint	Used
5¢	**black,** entire		5,000.00

CSP45-2		Mint	Used
10¢	**black,** entire, 01 instead of 10		6,000.00

Galveston, Texas, Handstamp, Envelope

CSP46-1

CSP46-2

CSP46-3

CSP46-1		Mint	Used
5¢	**black,** entire	500.00	1,500.00

CSP46-2		Mint	Used
10¢	**black,** entire		2,150.00

CSP46-3		Mint	Used
10¢	**black,** entire	600.00	2,500.00

CSP46-4		Mint	Used
20¢	**black,** entire		3,500.00

Gaston, N.C., Handstamp, Envelope

CSP47

CSP47		Mint	Used
5¢	**black,** entire, one known		6,000.00

GEORGETOWN, S.C., HANDSTAMP, ENVELOPE

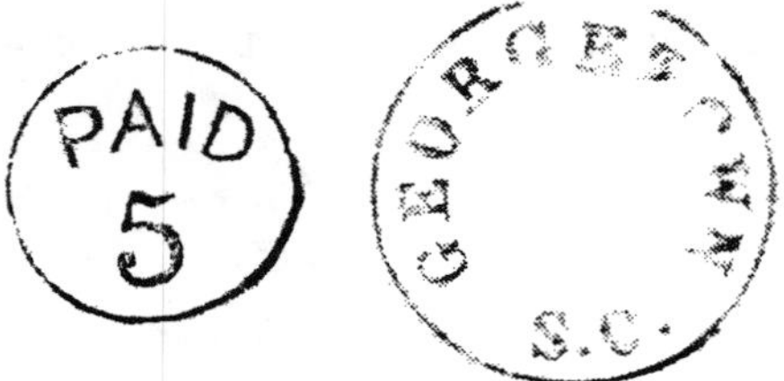

CSP48

CSP48		Mint	Used
5¢	**black,** entire		1,200.00

GOLIAD, TEXAS, TYPESET, ADHESIVE Postmaster J.A. Clarke.

CSP49-3
Type I

CSP49-6

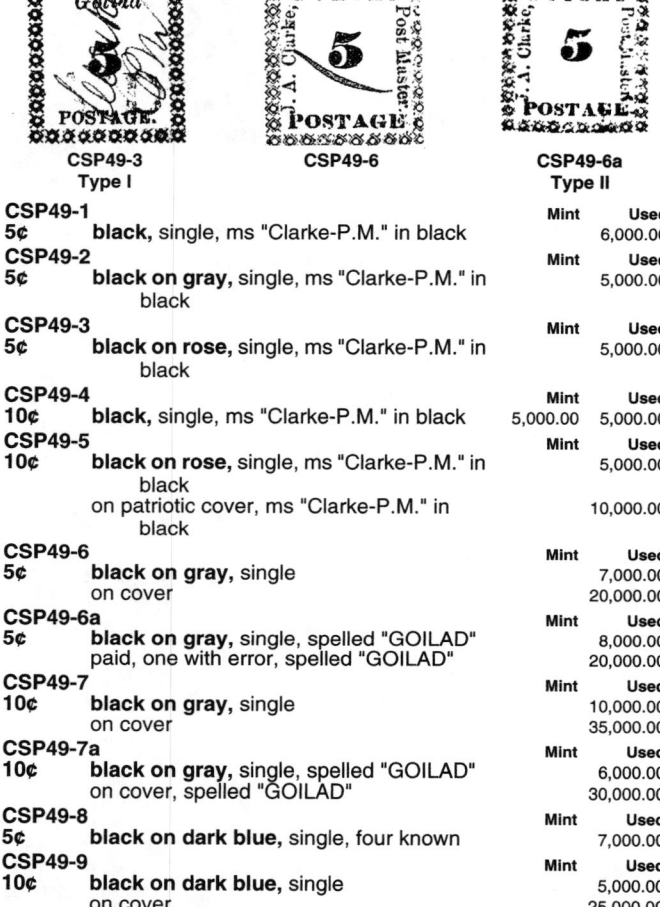

CSP49-6a
Type II

		Mint	Used
CSP49-1			
5¢	**black,** single, ms "Clarke-P.M." in black		6,000.00
CSP49-2			
5¢	**black on gray,** single, ms "Clarke-P.M." in black		5,000.00
CSP49-3			
5¢	**black on rose,** single, ms "Clarke-P.M." in black		5,000.00
CSP49-4			
10¢	**black,** single, ms "Clarke-P.M." in black	5,000.00	5,000.00
CSP49-5			
10¢	**black on rose,** single, ms "Clarke-P.M." in black		5,000.00
	on patriotic cover, ms "Clarke-P.M." in black		10,000.00
CSP49-6			
5¢	**black on gray,** single		7,000.00
	on cover		20,000.00
CSP49-6a			
5¢	**black on gray,** single, spelled "GOILAD"		8,000.00
	paid, one with error, spelled "GOILAD"		20,000.00
CSP49-7			
10¢	**black on gray,** single		10,000.00
	on cover		35,000.00
CSP49-7a			
10¢	**black on gray,** single, spelled "GOILAD"		6,000.00
	on cover, spelled "GOILAD"		30,000.00
CSP49-8			
5¢	**black on dark blue,** single, four known		7,000.00
CSP49-9			
10¢	**black on dark blue,** single		5,000.00
	on cover		25,000.00

GONZALES, TEXAS, LITHOGRAPH, ADHESIVE

CSP50-1

		Mint	Used
CSP50-1			
5¢	**gold** on dark blue, single, on glazed paper		15,000.00
	pair on cover, on glazed paper		25,000.00
CSP50-2			
10¢	**gold** on garnet, on cover, on glazed paper		15,000.00
CSP50-3			
10¢	**gold** on black, on cover, on glazed paper		15,000.00

GREENSBORO, ALA., HANDSTAMP, ENVELOPE

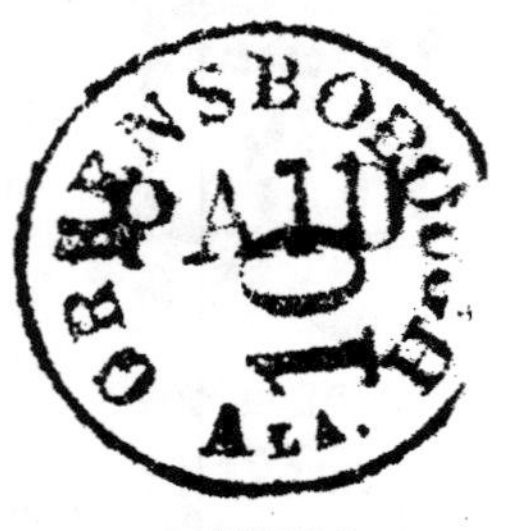

CSP51-2

		Mint	Used
CSP51-1			
5¢	**black,** entire		1,500.00
CSP51-2			
10¢	**black,** entire		3,000.00
CSP51-3			
10¢	**black,** entire		4,500.00

GREENSBORO, N.C., HANDSTAMP, ENVELOPE

CSP52-1

CSP52-2

		Mint	Used
CSP52-1			
10¢	**red,** entire		1,500.00
CSP52-1a			
10¢	**red,** entire, due 10¢ over paid 10¢, one known		2,500.00
CSP52-2			
10¢	**red,** entire, due 10¢, one known		2,500.00

GREENVILLE, ALA., TYPESET, ADHESIVE

CSP53-1

CSP53-2

		Mint	Used
CSP53-1			
5¢	**blue and red,** single, on pinkish, surface colored glazed paper	25,000.00	
	blue and red, on cover, on pinkish, surface colored glazed paper		55,000.00
CSP53-2			
10¢	**blue and red,** single, on pinkish, surface colored glazed paper	—	
	blue and red, on cover, on pinkish, surface colored glazed paper		55,000.00

GREENVILLE COURT HOUSE, S.C., HANDSTAMP, ENVELOPE

CSP55-1

CSP55-2

CSP55A

CSP55B

Control Marks

CSP55-1		Mint	Used
5¢	**black,** entire, several types of handstamp, must have control mark on reverse		3,000.00

CSP55-2		Mint	Used
10¢	**black,** entire, several types of handstamp, must have control mark on reverse		3,000.00

CSP55-3		Mint	Used
20¢	**black,** entire, ms 20¢ over 10¢ handstamp, must have control mark on reverse		4,000.00

GREENWOOD DEPOT, VA., HANDSTAMP, ADHESIVE Postmaster J. Bruce issued these primitive stamps to meet a new postal rate of 10¢, increased from 5¢, effective July 1, 1862.

CSP56

CSP56		Mint	Used
10¢	**black** on gray-blue, entire, ms signature, laid paper		20,000.00

GRIFFIN, GA., HANDSTAMP, ENVELOPE

CSP57

CSP57		Mint	Used
5¢	**black,** entire		2,000.00

GROVE HILL, ALA., WOODCUT, ADHESIVE

CSP58

CSP58		Mint	Used
5¢	**black,** single		—
	black, on cover, two known		100,000.00

HALLETTSVILLE, TEXAS, HANDSTAMP, ADHESIVE

CSP59

CSP59		Mint	Used
10¢	**black** on gray-blue, on cover, on ruled paper		25,000.00

HAMBURGH, S.C., HANDSTAMP, ENVELOPE

CSP60A

CSP60

CSP60		Mint	Used
5¢	**black,** entire		2,500.00
	black, entire, with CSP23-1 (forwarded)		6,000.00

HARRISBURGH, TEXAS, HANDSTAMP, ENVELOPE

CSP61-1

CSP61-1		Mint	Used
5¢	**black,** entire, same as handstamp paid when used	500.00	

HAYNESVILLE, ALA., TYPESET, ENVELOPE

CSP62-1

CSP62-2

CSP62-1		Mint	Used
5¢	**black,** entire, same as handstamp PAID when used	500.00	

CSP62-2		Mint	Used
10¢	**black,** entire, same as handstamp PAID when used	500.00	

HELENA, TEXAS, TYPESET, ADHESIVE

CSP63-1

CSP63-2

CSP63-1		Mint	Used
5¢	**black** on buff, single, upper case letters	7,500.00	6,000.00

CSP63-2		Mint	Used
10¢	**black** on gray, single, upper and lower case letters		6,000.00

HEMPSTEAD, TEXAS, HANDSTAMP, ENVELOPE

CSP64-1

CSP64-2

CSP64-1		Mint	Used
5¢	**blue,** entire		

CSP64-2		Mint	Used
10¢	**blue,** entire, same as handstamp PAID when used		

HIGH POINT, N.C., HANDSTAMP, ENVELOPE

CSP65

CSP65		Mint	Used
ms 5¢	**black,** entire, same as handstamp PAID when used	500.00	

Hillsboro, N.C., Handstamp, Adhesive

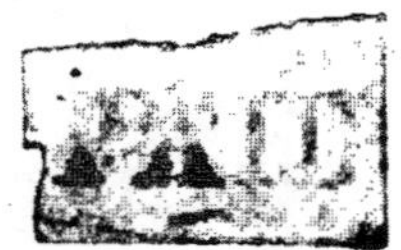

CSP66-2

CSP66-2		Mint	Used
5¢	**black,** on cover, one known		25,000.00

Note: See CSP66-1 among 3¢ 1861 Postmasters Provisionals.

Hillsboro, N.C., Handstamp, Envelope

CSP66-3

CSP66-3		Mint	Used
10¢	**black,** entire, ms "Paid 10", one known		25,000.00

Hollandale, Texas, Handstamp, Envelope

CSP67

CSP67		Mint	Used
5¢	**black,** entire		—

Houston, Texas, Handstamp, Envelope

CSP68-1

CSP68-2

CSP68-1		Mint	Used
5¢	**red,** entire, abbreviated "Txs."	—	700.00
	red, on patriotic cover, abbreviated "Txs."		4,500.00
CSP68-2		**Mint**	**Used**
10¢	**red,** entire, abbreviated "Tex."	—	1,500.00
CSP68-3		**Mint**	**Used**
10¢	**black,** entire, abbreviated "Tex."		2,300.00
CSP68-4		**Mint**	**Used**
10¢ + 5¢	**red,** entire, abbreviated "Tex."		2,500.00
CSP68-5		**Mint**	**Used**
10¢ + 10¢	**red,** entire, abbreviated "Tex."		2,500.00
CSP68-5a		**Mint**	**Used**
5¢ + ms 10¢	**red,** entire, abbreviated "Txs."		3,000.00

Huntsville, Texas, Handstamp, Envelope

CSP69-1

CSP69-1A

CSP69-2

CSP69-1		Mint	Used
5¢	**black,** entire		2,500.00
CSP69-2		**Mint**	**Used**
10¢	**black,** entire		—

Independence, Texas, Handstamp, Adhesive

CSP70-3

CSP70-1		Mint	Used
10¢	**black** on buff, on cover		28,000.00
CSP70-2		**Mint**	**Used**
10¢	**black** on dull rose, on cover		28,000.00
CSP70-3		**Mint**	**Used**
10¢	**black** on buff, on cover, small 10 and ms "Paid"		35,000.00

Isabella, Ga., Handstamp, Envelope

CSP71

CSP71		Mint	Used
ms 5¢	**black,** entire		2,000.00

Iuka, Miss., Handstamp, Envelope

CSP72		Mint	Used
5¢	**black,** entire		2,000.00
	black, on patriotic cover		4,500.00

Jackson, Miss., Handstamp, Envelope

CSP73-2

CSP73-2a

CSP73-4

Note: See CSP73-1 among 3¢ 1861 Postmasters Provisionals.

CSP73-2		Mint	Used
5¢	**black,** entire, two types of numeral		500.00
CSP73-2a		**Mint**	**Used**
5¢	**black,** on patriotic cover, two types of numeral		3,000.00
CSP73-3		**Mint**	**Used**
10¢	**black,** entire, two types of numeral		2,000.00
CSP73-3a		**Mint**	**Used**
10¢ over 5¢	**black,** entire, two types of numeral		3,000.00
CSP73-4		**Mint**	**Used**
10¢ over 5¢	**blue,** entire, two types of numeral		3,000.00

JACKSONVILLE, ALA., HANDSTAMP, ENVELOPE

CSP74

CSP74		Mint	Used
5¢	**black,** entire	—	1,500.00

JACKSONVILLE, FLA., HANDSTAMP, ENVELOPE

PAID 5

CSP75

CSP75		Mint	Used
5¢	**black,** entire, control on reverse		—

JETERSVILLE, VA., HANDSTAMP, AHESIVE

5AHA

CSP76

CSP76		Mint	Used
5¢	**black,** pair on cover, laid paper, ms initials AHA for A.H. Atwood, PM		30,000.00

JONESBORO, TENN., HANDSTAMP, ENVELOPE

CSP77-1

CSP77-1		Mint	Used
5¢	**black,** entire		3,500.00
CSP77-2		**Mint**	**Used**
5¢	**dark blue,** entire		7,000.00

KINGSTON, GA., TYPOGRAPH, ENVELOPE

CSP78-2 CSP78-1 CSP78-5 CSP78-4

CSP78-1		Mint	Used
5¢	**black,** entire, one known		2,000.00

KINGSTON, GA., HANDSTAMP, ENVELOPE

CSP78-2		Mint	Used
5¢	**black,** entire	—	3,500.00
CSP78-3		**Mint**	**Used**
5¢	**black,** entire, No "C" or "S" (similar to CSP78-2)		—
CSP78-4		**Mint**	**Used**
5¢	**black,** entire		2,500.00
CSP78-5		**Mint**	**Used**
5¢	**black,** entire		2,000.00

KNOXVILLE, TENN., WOODCUT, ADHESIVE Postmaster C.H. Charlton.

CSP79-3

CSP79-1		Mint	Used
5¢	**brick red,** single, on grayish laid paper	1,250.00	1,000.00
	single, ms cancel, on grayish laid paper		400.00
	horizontal pair, on grayish laid paper	10,000.00	2,000.00
	vertical pair, on grayish laid paper	3,000.00	
	vertical strip of 3, on grayish laid paper	6,000.00	
	on cover, on grayish laid paper		3,500.00
	on cover, ms cancel, on grayish laid paper		2,500.00
	pair on cover, on grayish laid paper		7,500.00
CSP79-2		**Mint**	**Used**
5¢	**carmine,** single, on grayish laid paper	2,000.00	1,500.00
	strip of 3, on grayish laid paper		5,000.00
	on cover, on grayish laid paper		15,000.00
	pair on cover, on grayish laid paper		40,000.00
CSP79-3		**Mint**	**Used**
10¢	**green,** on cover, on grayish laid paper		65,000.00

KNOXVILLE, TENN., TYPOGRAPH, ENVELOPE

CSP79-5

CSP79-4		Mint	Used
5¢	**blue,** entire	750.00	1,800.00
CSP79-5		**Mint**	**Used**
5¢	**blue** on orange, entire	750.00	2,000.00

KNOXVILLE, TENN., TYPOGRAPH, PIECE

CSP79-6		Mint	Used
10¢	**red,** cut to shape, one known		10,000.00
CSP79-7		**Mint**	**Used**
10¢	**red** on orange, cut to shape, one known		10,000.00

KNOXVILLE, TENN., HANDSTAMP, ENVELOPE

CSP79-8 CSP79-9

CSP79-8		Mint	Used
5¢	**black,** entire	750.00	1,500.00
	on patriotic cover		4,500.00
CSP79-9		**Mint**	**Used**
10¢ over 5¢	**black,** entire two varieties		4,000.00

La Grange, Texas, Handstamp, Envelope

CSP80-1

CSP80-2

		Mint	Used
CSP80-1			
5¢	**black,** entire	—	2,000.00
CSP80-2			
10¢	**black,** entire (two varieties)		2,500.00

Lake City, Fla., Handstamp, Envelope

		Mint	Used
CSP81			
10¢	**black,** entire		2,000.00

Laurens Court House, S.C., Handstamp, Envelope

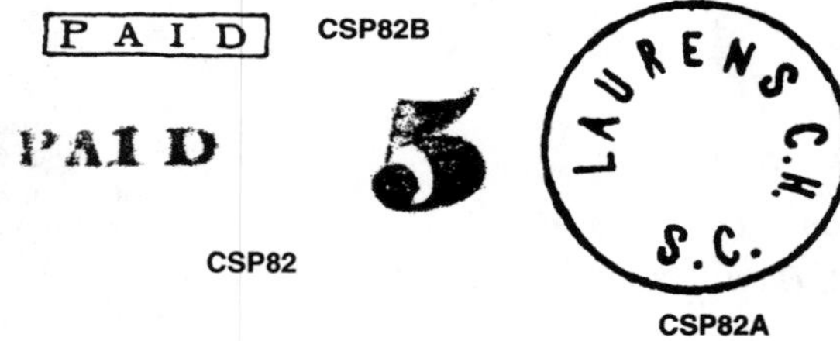

CSP82B

CSP82

CSP82A

		Mint	Used
CSP82			
5¢	**black,** entire, control mark on reverse		3,000.00

Lenoir, N.C., Woodcut, Adhesive

CSP83-1

		Mint	Used
CSP83-1			
5¢	**blue and orange,** single, white wove paper with orange ruled lines	3,500.00	3,000.00
	on cover, pen canceled, wove paper with orange ruled lines		7,000.00
	on cover, tied, white wove paper with orange ruled lines		30,000.00
	on college cover (two known)		12,000.00

Lenoir, N.C., Handstamp, Envelope

from a pear wood handstamp prepared for Postmaster James Harpan by his son in the summer of 1861.

CSP83-2

CSP83-4

		Mint	Used
CSP83-2			
5¢	**blue,** entire		4,000.00
CSP83-3			
10¢	**blue,** entire, handstamp 5¢ + 5¢, one known		25,000.00
CSP83-4			
5¢	**blue,** entire		4,500.00
CSP83-5			
5¢	**black,** entire		3,000.00

Lexington, Miss., Handstamp, Envelope

CSP84-1

		Mint	Used
CSP84-1			
5¢	**black,** entire		5,000.00
CSP84-2			
10¢	**black,** entire		5,000.00

Lexington, Va., Handstamp, Envelope

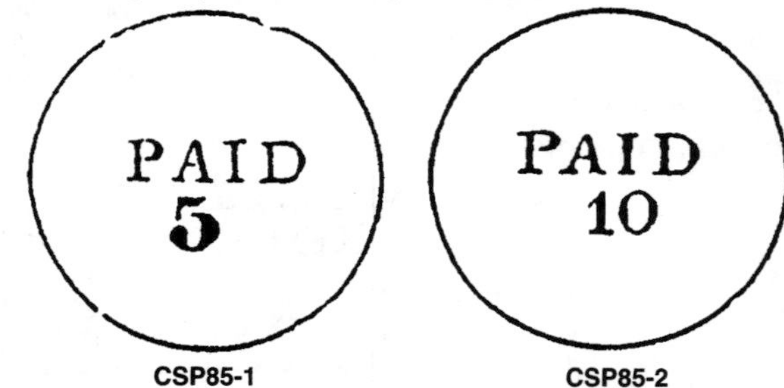

CSP85-1 CSP85-2

		Mint	Used
CSP85-1			
5¢	**black,** entire, same as handstamp paid cover when used	500.00	
	entire, with Minkus #7 for 10¢ rate, same as handstamp paid cover when used		500.00
CSP85-2			
10¢	**black,** entire, same as handstamp paid cover when used	750.00	500.00

Liberty & Salem, Va., Typeset, Adhesive

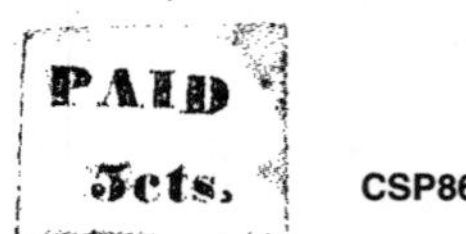

CSP86

		Mint	Used
CSP86			
5¢	**black,** on cover, either postmark		40,000.00

LIMESTONE SPRINGS, S.C., HANDSTAMP, ADHESIVE

CSP87

CSP87		Mint	Used
5¢	**black,** on cover, covers are not postmarked		10,000.00
	two on cover, covers are not postmarked		15,000.00

Note: The Postmaster applied his 5¢ handstamp to both circular and square adhesives.

LIVINGSTON, ALA., LITHOGRAPH, ADHESIVE

CSP88

CSP88		Mint	Used
5¢	**blue,** single		7,000.00
	on cover		65,000.00
	pair on cover		140,000.00

LYNCHBURG, VA., WOODCUT, ADHESIVE

Only Lynchburg, Charleston, S.C., and Memphis, Tenn., issued provisional adhesive stamps and printed envelopes at the same time.

CSP89-1

CSP89-1		Mint	Used
5¢	**blue,** single	1,500.00	1,000.00
	pair		2,500.00
	on cover		3,000.00
	pair, on cover		6,000.00

LYNCHBURG, VA., TYPOGRAPH, ENVELOPE

PAID.

CSP89-2

CSP89-2		Mint	Used
5¢	**black,** entire (this is white envelope)		2,500.00
CSP89-3		**Mint**	**Used**
5¢	**black** on amber, entire	1,500.00	2,000.00
CSP89-4		**Mint**	**Used**
5¢	**black** on buff, entire		1,500.00
	on patriotic cover		4,500.00
CSP89-5		**Mint**	**Used**
5¢	**black** on brown, entire	1,000.00	1,500.00
	on patriotic cover		10,000.00

MACON, GA., HANDSTAMP, ENVELOPE

CSP90-1

CSP90-1		Mint	Used
5¢	**black,** entire, two varieties	200.00	500.00

MACON, GA., TYPESET, ADHESIVE

CSP90-3

CSP90-4

CSP90-5

TWO CENTS

CSP90-2

CSP90-2		Mint	Used
2¢	**black** on gray-green, single		7,000.00
	on cover		65,000.00
CSP90-3		**Mint**	**Used**
5¢	**black** on light blue-green, single	850.00	600.00
	on cover		4,000.00
	on advertising cover		15,500.00
	single, (comma after "OFFICE")	1,000.00	750.00
	on cover, comma after "OFFICE"		10,000.00
	on advertising cover		15,000.00
	pair (one of each type) on cover		—
CSP90-4		**Mint**	**Used**
5¢	**black** on yellow, single	2,500.00	800.00
	on cover		5,000.00
	on advertising cover		21,000.00
	pair		2,000.00
	pair on cover		8,000.00
	pair on patriotic cover		15,000.00
CSP90-5		**Mint**	**Used**
5¢	**black** on yellow, single	2,500.00	1,250.00
	on cover		7,000.00
	on advertising cover		—
	pair		2,500.00
	pair on cover		15,000.00
	on patriotic cover		25,000.00
CSP90-5a		**Mint**	**Used**
5¢	**black** on yellow, tete beche pair, one known		—

Note: CSP90-3, CSP90-4 and CSP90-5 exist in several minor varieties and are found on laid and wove paper.

MADISON, GA., HANDSTAMP, ENVELOPE

CSP91-1

CSP91-1		Mint	Used
5¢	**red,** entire	500.00	

Note: Considered a provisional only when unused, used from another town or with a general-issue stamp used over it.

Madison Court House, Fla., Typeset, Envelope

CSP92-2		Mint	Used
5¢	**black,** on cover, one known		25,000.00

Note: See CSP92-1 among 3¢ 1861 Postmasters Provisionals.

Marietta, Ga., Handstamp, Envelope

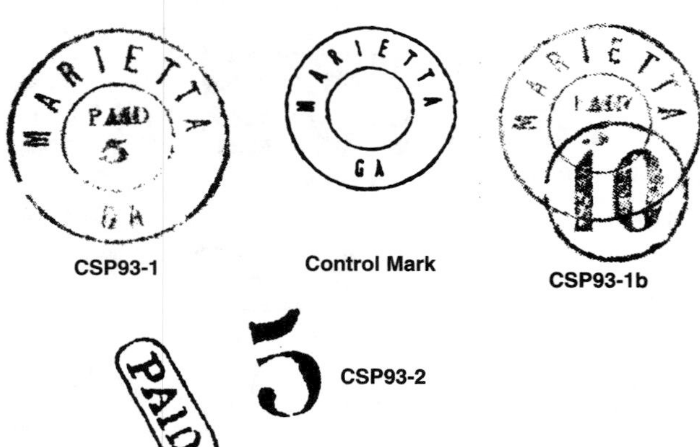

CSP93-1 Control Mark CSP93-1b

CSP93-2

		Mint	Used
CSP93-1		Mint	Used
5¢	**black,** entire		300.00
CSP93-1a		Mint	Used
10¢ over 5¢	**black,** entire, 10¢ handstamped over 5¢		2,000.00
CSP93-1b		Mint	Used
10¢ over 5¢	**black,** entire, 10¢ handstamped PAID over 5¢		—
CSP93-2		Mint	Used
5¢	**black,** entire, with undated double circle postmark control		1,800.00

Marion, Va., Typeset, Adhesive Issued by Postmaster J.H. Francis in 1861. The denomination was handstamped within the printed border.

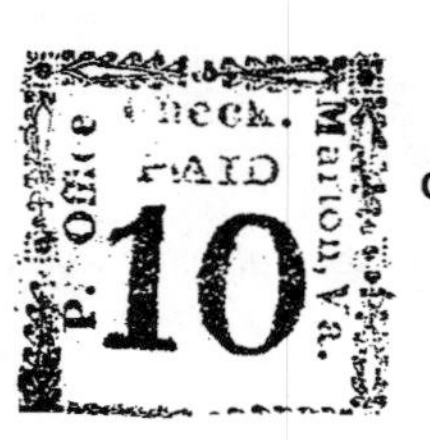

CSP94-2

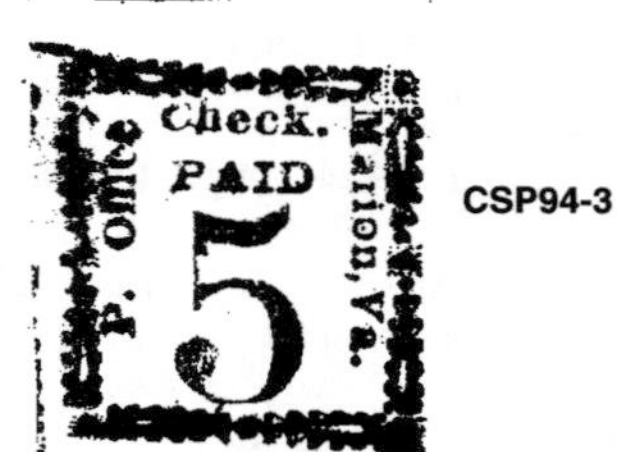

CSP94-3

		Mint	Used
CSP94-1		Mint	Used
5¢	**black,** single, handstamped numerals		12,000.00
	on cover, handstamped numerals		25,000.00
CSP94-2		Mint	Used
10¢	**black,** single, handstamped numerals	25,000.00	12,000.00
	on cover, handstamped numerals		25,000.00
CSP94-3		Mint	Used
5¢	**black** on bluish, single, handstamped numerals, laid paper	—	

Memphis, Tenn., Woodcut, Adhesive Only Memphis, Charleston, S.C., and Lynchburg, Tenn., issued provisional adhesive stamps and printed envelopes at the same time. Only Memphis entires are known with an additional 5¢ stamp to pay the 10¢ rate.

CSP95-1

CSP95-2

		Mint	Used
CSP95-1		Mint	Used
2¢	**blue,** single	100.00	1,500.00
	block of 4	600.00	
	on cover positions		10,000.00
	single, cracked plate (16,17,18)	150.00	1,500.00
CSP95-2		Mint	Used
5¢	**red,** single	150.00	175.00
	pair	350.00	500.00
	block of 4	1,100.00	
	on cover		1,750.00
	pair on cover		4,500.00
	strip of 4 on cover		7,000.00
	on patriotic cover		17,500.00
CSP95-2a		Mint	Used
5¢	**red,** tete beche pair		1,500.00
	red, tete beche pair on cover		4,000.00
CSP95-2b		Mint	Used
5¢	**red,** pair, one sideways	750.00	
CSP95-2c		Mint	Used
5¢	**red,** single, pelure paper	—	750.00

Memphis, Tenn., Typograph, Envelope

CSP95-3

		Mint	Used
CSP95-3			
5¢	**red,** entire		3,000.00
CSP95-4		Mint	Used
5¢	**red** on amber, entire		4,000.00
	entire with CS1 to make 10¢ rate		6,500.00
CSP95-5		Mint	Used
5¢	**red** on orange, entire		3,000.00
	on patriotic cover		4,000.00

Micanopy, Fla., Handstamp, Envelope

CSP96

CSP96		Mint	Used
5¢	**black,** entire		11,500.00

Milledgeville, Ga., Handstamp, Envelope

Control Mark

CSP97-3

PAID

5 10

CSP97 Examples

PAID

5

CSP97-1		Mint	Used
5¢	**black,** entire with undated postmark control		250.00

CSP97-1a	Mint	Used
10¢ over 5¢ black, entire, 10¢ handstamp over 5¢		1,000.00

CSP97-2		Mint	Used
10¢	**black,** entire (similar to CSP97-1), with undated postmark control	225.00	1,000.00

CSP97-3		Mint	Used
10¢	**black,** entire (two types)		700.00

Note: Provisionals exist with "Paid 10" inside control marks and with undated control marks with "Paid 5" and "Paid 10" handstamps.

Milton, N.C., Handstamp, Envelope

CSP98		Mint	Used
5¢ (ms)	**black,** entire, two known		2,000.00

Mobil, Ala., Lithograph,Adhesive

CSP99-1

CSP99-2

CSP99-1		Mint	Used
2¢	**black,** single	2,000.00	1,000.00
	pair	—	2,100.00
	on cover		3,500.00
	pair on cover		18,000.00
	3 singles on cover		5,500.00
	5 copies on cover		20,000.00

CSP99-2		Mint	Used
5¢	**blue,** single	275.00	300.00
	pair	675.00	700.00
	on cover		2,200.00
	pair on cover		2,000.00
	strip of 3 on cover		6,000.00
	strip of 4 on cover		7,000.00
	strip of 5 on cover		8,000.00

Montgomery, Ala., Handstamp, Envelope

CSP100-1

CSP100-3a

CSP100-7

CSP100-9

CSP100-1		Mint	Used
5¢	**red,** entire		1,000.00

CSP100-2		Mint	Used
5¢	**blue,** entire	400.00	900.00

CSP100-3		Mint	Used
10¢	**red,** entire		800.00

CSP100-3a	Mint	Used
10¢ over 5¢ red, entire		2,750.00

CSP100-4		Mint	Used
10¢	**blue,** entire		1,500.00

CSP100-5		Mint	Used
10¢	**black,** entire		800.00

CSP100-6		Mint	Used
2¢	**red,** entire		2,500.00

CSP100-7		Mint	Used
2¢	**blue,** entire		3,500.00

CSP100-8		Mint	Used
5¢	**black,** entire		2,250.00

CSP100-9		Mint	Used
10¢	**black,** entire		3,000.00

CSP100-10		Mint	Used
10¢	**red,** entire		1,500.00

Montgomery, Ala., Handstamp, Adhesive

CSP100-11	Mint	Used
Crayon 5¢ black entire, on buff, T. Welsh PM signature		13,000.00

Mt. Lebanon, La., Woodcut, Adhesive

CSP101

CSP101		Mint	Used
5¢	**red-brown,** on cover, one known		400,000.00

Nashville, Tenn., Handstamp, Envelope

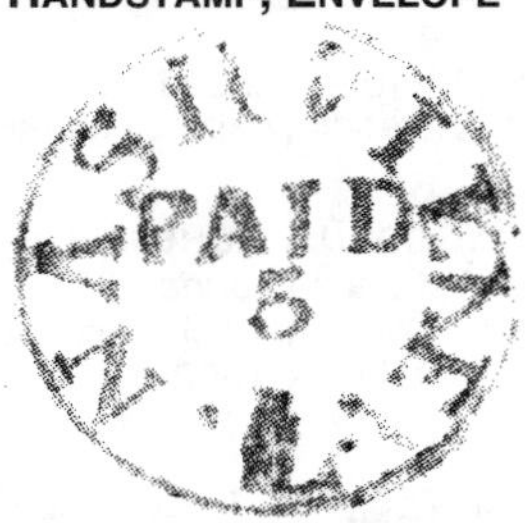

CSP102-7

CSP102-7		Mint	Used
5¢	**blue,** entire		750.00
	on patriotic envelope		1,750.00

CSP102-8	Mint	Used
10¢ over 5¢ blue, on cover with CSP102-2		2,500.00

Nashville, Tenn., Woodcut, Adhesive Postmaster W.D. McNish.

CSP102-2

CSP102-6

CSP102-5a

CSP102-2		Mint	Used
5¢	**carmine,** single, ribbed paper	850.00	900.00
	pair, ribbed paper		1,800.00
	on cover, ribbed paper		2,700.00
	on patriotic cover, ribbed paper		5,000.00
	pair on cover, ribbed paper		6,000.00
	on cover with US #27, Express Mail, ribbed paper		25,000.00

Note: See CSP102-1 among 3¢ 1861 Postmasters Provisionals.

CSP102-2a		Mint	Used
5¢	**carmine,** vertical tete beche pair, ribbed paper		3,000.00
	on cover/ tete beche pair, ribbed paper		30,500.00

CSP102-3		Mint	Used
5¢	**brick red,** single, ribbed paper	850.00	500.00
	pair, ribbed paper		1,200.00
	on cover, ribbed paper		1,000.00
	on patriotic cover, ribbed paper		6,000.00
	pair on cover, ribbed paper		6,000.00
	on US EN29 cover+US #27, Express Mail, ribbed paper		35,000.00

CSP102-4		Mint	Used
5¢	**gray,** single, ribbed paper	850.00	650.00
	on cover, ribbed paper		5,500.00
	pair on cover, ribbed paper		8,500.00
	strip of 5 on cover front, ribbed paper		15,000.00

CSP102-5		Mint	Used
5¢	**violet brown,** single, ribbed paper	750.00	450.00
	block of 4, ribbed paper	5,000.00	
	on cover, ribbed paper		5,000.00
	pair on cover, ribbed paper		6,000.00
	on patriotic cover, ribbed paper		—

CSP102-5a		Mint	Used
5¢	**violet brown,** vertical tete beche pair, ribbed paper	3,500.00	2,500.00

CSP102-6		Mint	Used
10¢	**green,** single, ribbed paper	3,000.00	3,000.00
	on cover, ribbed paper		15,000.00
	on cover with US 1857, Express, ribbed paper		95,000.00
	on cover with CSP102-2, ribbed paper		25,000.00
	on cover, with 3¢ star die, Express marking		90,000.00

New Orleans, La., Woodcut, Adhesive Postmaster J.L. Riddell prepared provisional stamps in June 1861, perhaps the red stamps first, although they were not sold until the supply of blue stamps was exhausted in January 1862.

CSP103-1

CSP103-3

CSP103-1		Mint	Used
2¢	**blue,** single	150.00	500.00
	pair	500.00	1,200.00
	block of 4	7,000.00	
	on cover		4,500.00
	pair on cover		8,000.00
	3 singles on cover		25,000.00
	strip of 5 on cover		35,000.00
	on patriotic cover		8,000.00

CSP103-1a		Mint	Used
2¢	**blue,** single, printed both sides	1,800.00	
	on cover, printed both sides		30,000.00

CSP103-2		Mint	Used
2¢	**red,** single	125.00	1,000.00
	pair	300.00	
	block of 4	1,500.00	
	on cover		35,000.00

CSP103-3		Mint	Used
5¢	**brown,** single	250.00	150.00
	pair	525.00	325.00
	on cover		400.00
	pair on cover		1,000.00
	strip of 5 on cover		6,500.00
	on cover with Minkus #31		—
	on patriotic cover		3,500.00

CSP103-3a		Mint	Used
5¢	**brown,** single, printed both sides		1,750.00
	on cover, printed both sides		7,500.00

CSP103-3b		Mint	Used
5¢	**ochre,** single	700.00	700.00
	pair		1,500.00
	on cover		2,000.00
	pair on cover		3,000.00
	on patriotic cover		5,000.00

CSP103-4		Mint	Used
5¢	**red-brown** on bluish, single	300.00	175.00
	pair	625.00	400.00
	horizontal strip of 6		3,500.00
	block of 4		2,000.00
	on cover		550.00
	pair on cover		700.00
	block of 4 on cover		5,000.00
	on cover + CS1 for 10¢ rate		7,500.00
	on patriotic cover		12,000.00

CSP103-4a		Mint	Used
5¢	**red-brown** on bluish, single, printed both sides		3,500.00

CSP103-5		Mint	Used
5¢	**yellow-brown** on off-white, single	125.00	200.00
	pair	275.00	500.00
	block of 4	650.00	
	on cover		500.00
	pair on cover		2,000.00
	strip of 5 on cover		—
	on patriotic cover		4,500.00

CSP103-6		Mint	Used
5¢	**red,** single	—	7,500.00

CSP103-7		Mint	Used
5¢	**red** on bluish, single		12,000.00

New Orleans, La., Handstamp, Envelope

J.L.RIDDELL P.M. PD 5 CTS N.O.P.O

CSP103-9

J.L.RIDDELL,P.M PD 10 CTS N.O.P.O

CSP103-10

CSP103-8		Mint	Used
2¢	**black,** entire, "J.L. Riddell" omitted		10,000.00

CSP103-9		Mint	Used
5¢	**black,** entire		4,500.00

CSP103-10		Mint	Used
10¢	**black,** entire		20,000.00

New Smyrna, Fla., Handstamp, Ahesive

CSP104

CSP104	Mint	Used
10¢ over 5¢ white/blue ruled lines, on patriotic cover, one known		50,000.00

NORFOLK, VA., HANDSTAMP, ENVELOPE

CSP105-1 CSP105-2

CSP105-1		Mint	Used
5¢	**blue,** entire, with initials		1,250.00

CSP105-2		Mint	Used
10¢	**blue,** entire, with initials		2,000.00

OAKWAY, S.C., HANDSTAMP, ADHESIVE

CSP106

CSP106		Mint	Used
5¢	**black,** on cover		75,000.00

OXFORD, N.C., HANDSTAMP, ENVELOPE

CSP107-1 CSP107-2

CSP107-1		Mint	Used
5¢	**black,** entire, same as handstamp paid when used	500.00	

CSP107-2		Mint	Used
10¢	**black,** entire, same as handstamp paid when used	500.00	

PATTERSON, N.C., HANDSTAMP, ENVELOPE

CSP108-1 CSP108-2

CSP108-1	Mint	Used
Fancy 5¢ **black,** entire, same as handstamp paid when used	500.00	

CSP108-2	Mint	Used
Fancy 10¢ **black,** entire, same as handstamp paid when used	500.00	
ms 10¢ over 5¢ black, on patriotic cover, revalued over 5¢ handstamp		15,000.00

PENSACOLA, FLA., HANDSTAMP, ENVELOPE

CSP109-1

CSP109-2

CSP109-1		Mint	Used
5¢	**black,** entire		3,500.00

CSP109-2	Mint	Used
ms 10¢ over 5¢ black, entire, revalued over 5¢ handstamp		4,500.00
on patriotic cover		15,000.00

PETERSBURG, VA., TYPESET, ADHESIVE

Printed for Postmaster W.K. Bass in horizontally arranged panes of 10.

CSP110

CSP110		Mint	Used
5¢	**red,** single	1,500.00	450.00
	pair	2,500.00	1,500.00
	block of 4	5,000.00	
	on cover		2,500.00
	pair on cover		10,000.00
	with #CS1 to make 10¢ rate		55,000.00
	on patriotic cover		6,500.00
	"C" and "G," "e" missing on cover		2,100.00

PITTSYLVANIA COURT HOUSE, VA., TYPESET, ADHESIVE

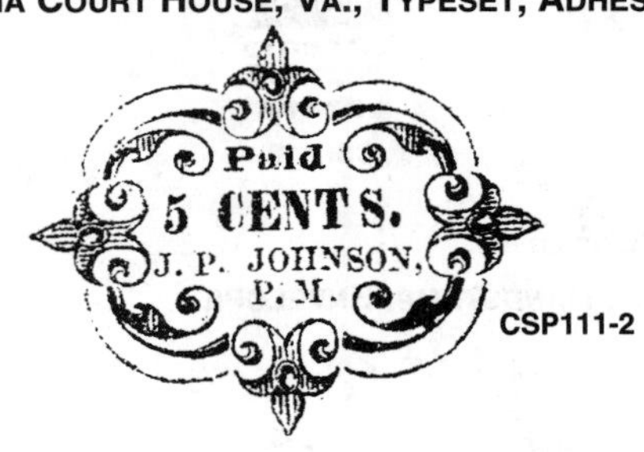

CSP111-2

CSP111-1		Mint	Used
5¢	**dull red,** single, wove paper	7,000.00	6,000.00
	single, octagonally cut, wove paper		3,000.00
	on cover, wove paper		60,000.00
	on cover, octagonally cut, wove paper		25,000.00
	on patriotic cover, octagonally cut, wove paper		30,000.00

CSP111-2		Mint	Used
5¢	**dull red,** single, laid paper		7,000.00
	single, octagonally cut, laid paper		5,500.00
	on cover, laid paper		55,000.00
	on cover, octagonally cut, laid paper		25,000.00

PLAINS OF DURA, GA., HANDSTAMP, ENVELOPE

CSP112-1 CSP112-2

CSP112-1		Mint	Used
5¢	**black,** entire, with initials used as control		500.00

CSP112-2		Mint	Used
10¢	**black,** entire, with initials used as control		500.00

Pleasant Shade, Va., Typeset, Adhesive

CSP113

CSP113		Mint	Used
5¢	**blue,** single	2,500.00	15,000.00
	pair	7,000.00	
	block of 6	25,000.00	
	on cover		30,000.00
	pair on cover		60,000.00

Plum Creek, Texas, Manuscript, Adhesive

CSP114

CSP114		Mint	Used
10¢	**black** on blue, on cover		—

Port Gibson, Miss., Handstamp, Envelope

PAID 5

CSP115

CSP115		Mint	Used
5¢	**black,** entire, with signature		—

Port Lavaca, Texas, Typeset, Adhesive

CSP116

CSP116		Mint	Used
10¢	**black,** on cover		25,000.00

Raleigh, N.C., Handstamp, Envelope

CSP118-1

CSP118-1		Mint	Used
5¢	**red,** entire		400.00
	red, on patriotic cover		2,500.00

CSP118-2		Mint	Used
5¢	**blue,** entire (four known examples)		3,000.00

Rheatown, Tenn., Typeset, Adhesive Printed for Postmaster D. Pence in the summer of 1861, using a form of three subjects, arranged horizontally, (see Tellico Plains).

CSP119

CSP119		Mint	Used
5¢	**red,** single	3,000.00	5,000.00
	single, pen cancel		3,000.00

		Mint	Used
	pair	5,000.00	
	on cover, four known		15,000.00

Richmond, Texas, Handstamp, Envelope

CSP120-2

CSP120-1		Mint	Used
5¢	**red,** entire		1,500.00

CSP120-2		Mint	Used
10¢	**red,** entire		1,000.00

CSP120-2a		Mint	Used
10¢ over 5¢ red, entire			5,000.00

CSP120-3		Mint	Used
ms 15¢	**red,** entire, revalued over 10¢ handstamp		5,000.00

Ringgold, Ga., Handstamp, Envelope

CSP121		Mint	Used
5¢	**blue-black,** entire		3,000.00

Rutherfordton, N.C., Handstamp, Adhesive

CSP122		Mint	Used
ms 5¢	**black,** on cover, cut to shape, one known		55,000.00

Salem, N.C., Handstamp, Envelope

CSP123-1

CSP123-2

CSP123-3

PAID 10

CSP123-3a

CSP123-1		Mint	Used
5¢	**black,** entire, MS Paid 5		2,000.00

CSP123-2		Mint	Used
10¢	**black,** entire, three known		6,000.00

CSP123-3		Mint	Used
5¢	**black,** entire, handstamp Paid 5		2,000.00

CSP123-3a		Mint	Used
10¢ over 5¢ black, entire, one known			3,000.00

Note: Unused reprint examples in several varieties are known. These reprints were made on wartime paper by Postmaster Keehin's son shortly after the war to sell to Northern stamp collectors. Reprints currently sell for $125.00.

SALEM, VA., (SEE LIBERTY, VA.)

SALISBURY, N.C., TYPESET, ENVELOPE

SALISBURY.
N. C.
POSTAGE

·FIVE CENTS·
M.A.SMITH•P. M.

CSP125		Mint	Used
5¢	**black** on greenish, entire, one known		6,000.00

SAN ANTONIO, TEXAS, HANDSTAMP, ENVELOPE

CSP126-1

CSP126-2

CSP126-3

CSP126-1		Mint	Used
5¢	**black,** entire		—
CSP126-2		Mint	Used
10¢	**black,** entire, paid 10 with control mark	275.00	2,000.00
CSP126-3		Mint	Used
10¢	**black,** entire		2,500.00

SANDERSVILLE, GA. HANDSTAMP, ENVELOPE

CSP126A-1

CSP126A-1		Mint	Used
10¢	**black,** entire		1,000.00

Note: Considered a provisional only when unused, used from another town or with a general issue stamp used over it.

SAVANNAH, GA., HANDSTAMP, ENVELOPE

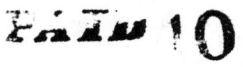

CSP127-1

CSP127-4

CSP127-1a

CSP127-2

CSP127-1		Mint	Used
5¢	**black,** entire, with rosette control		300.00
	on patriotic cover		4,500.00
CSP127-1a		Mint	Used
	10¢ over 5¢ black, entire, 10¢ handstamp over 5¢, with rosette control		1,500.00
CSP127-2		Mint	Used
5¢	**black,** entire, with rosette control		600.00
CSP127-2a		Mint	Used
	20¢ over 5¢ black, entire, 20¢ handstamp over 5¢, with rosette control		2,000.00
CSP127-3		Mint	Used
10¢	**black,** entire, with rosette control (similar to CSP127-1)		750.00
CSP127-4		Mint	Used
10¢	**black,** entire, with rosette control (similar to CSP127-2)		750.00

SELMA, ALA., HANDSTAMP, ENVELOPE

CSP128-2

CSP128-3

CSP128-2		Mint	Used
5¢	**black,** entire, signature in ms		1,500.00
CSP128-3		Mint	Used
10¢	**black,** entire, signature in ms		2,500.00
CSP128-3a		Mint	Used
	10¢ over 5¢ black, entire, signature in ms		3,000.00

Note: See CSP128-1 among 3¢ 1861 Postmasters Provisionals.

SPARTA, GA., HANDSTAMP, ENVELOPE

CSP129-1

CSP129-1		Mint	Used
5¢	**red,** entire	—	1,000.00
CSP129-2		Mint	Used
10¢	**red,** entire, (similar to CSP129-1)		2,500.00

SPARTANBURG, S.C., HANDSTAMP, ADHESIVE

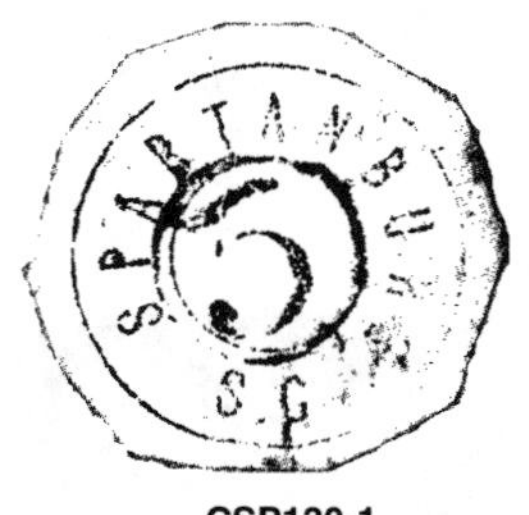

CSP130-1

CSP130-1b

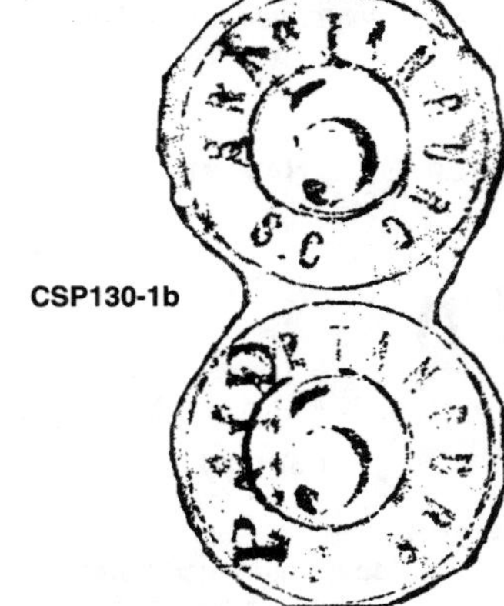

CSP130-1		Mint	Used
5¢	**black,** pair, ruled or plain wove		4,000.00
	on cover, ruled or plain wove paper		35,000.00
	pair on cover, ruled or plain wove paper		45,000.00
CSP130-1a		Mint	Used
5¢	**black,** on cover, "5" omitted, ruled or plain wove paper		35,000.00

		Mint	Used
CSP130-1b			
5¢	**black,** on patriotic cover, ruled or plain wove paper		55,000.00
CSP130-2			
5¢	**black** on brown, single, ruled or plain wove paper		5,000.00
	on cover, ruled or plain wove paper		30,000.00
CSP130-3			
5¢	**black** on bluish, single, ruled or plain wove paper		5,000.00
	on cover, ruled or plain wove paper		35,000.00

Spartanburg, S.C., Handstamp, Envelope

CSP130-4a

		Mint	Used
CSP130-4			
10¢	**black,** entire, with control mark		1,500.00
CSP130-4a			
10¢ over 5¢ black, entire, with control mark			2,000.00

Statesville, N.C., Handstamp, Envelope

CSP131-1

		Mint	Used
CSP131-1			
5¢	**black,** entire	—	1,000.00
CSP131-2			
ms 10¢ over 5¢ black, revalued in ms, way marking (one known)			6,000.00
CSP131-3			
10¢ over 5¢	**black,** entire, (two known) handstamped		6,000.00

Note: Most known mint examples are forgeries. They have strong, clear strikes and complete frames. Most genuine examples have broken boxes.

Sumter, S.C., Handstamp, Envelope

CSP132-1

CSP132-2

		Mint	Used
CSP132-1			
5¢	**black,** entire, used are same as handstamp paid	400.00	
CSP132-1a			
10¢ over 5¢ black, entire			1,500.00
CSP132-2			
10¢	**black,** entire, used are same as handstamp paid	400.00	
CSP132-2a			
ms 2¢ on 10¢ black, entire			1,500.00

Talbotton, Ga., Handstamp, Envelope

CSP133-2

CSP133-3

		Mint	Used
CSP133-1			
(5¢)	**black,** entire (no value - similar to CSP133-2)		1,500.00
CSP133-2			
5¢	**black,** entire		1,000.00
CSP133-2a			
10¢ over 5¢ black, entire, 10¢ handstamp over 5¢			2,000.00
CSP133-3			
10¢	**black,** entire		—

Talladega, Ala., Handstamp, Envelope

IE PAID 5 — CSP134-1

IE PAID 10 — CSP134-2

		Mint	Used
CSP134-1			
5¢	**black,** entire, with initials		1,000.00
CSP134-2			
10¢	**black,** entire, with initials		1,000.00

Tellico Plains, Tenn., Typeset, Adhesive Printed for Postmaster M.F. Johnson using a form of three subjects arranged horizontally, two valued at 5¢ and the right-most valued at 10¢. Probably printed by the same printer that did the Rheatown, Tenn., provisionals.

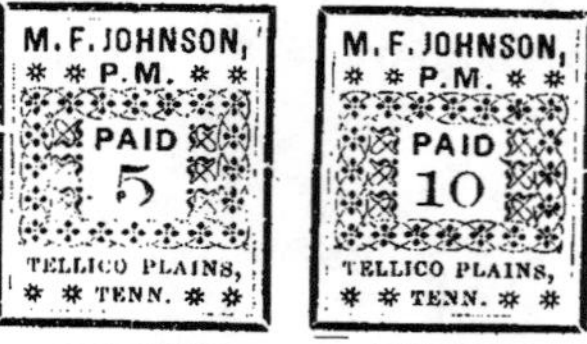

CSP135-1 CSP135-2

		Mint	Used
CSP135-1			
5¢	**red,** single, laid paper, settings of two 5¢ and one 10¢	1,300.00	—
	on cover, laid paper, one known		50,000.00
CSP135-2			
10¢	**red,** single, laid paper, settings of two 5¢ and one 10¢	2,500.00	
	se-tenant with 5¢, laid paper, settings of two 5¢ and one 10¢	4,500.00	
	strip of 3 (5¢+5¢+10¢), laid paper, settings of two 5¢ and one 10¢	8,000.00	

Thomasville, Ga., Handstamp, Envelope

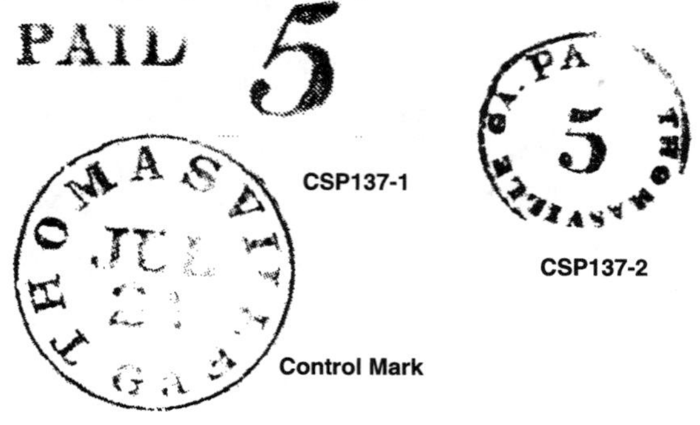

CSP137-1

CSP137-2

Control Mark

CSP137-1 Mint Used
5¢ **black,** entire, with dated postmark control on reverse — Used 500.00

CSP137-2 Mint Used
5¢ **black,** entire — Used 1,000.00
entire, patriotic cover — Used 4,500.00

TULLAHOMA, TENN., HANDSTAMP, ENVELOPE

CSP138

CSP138		Mint	Used
10¢	**black,** entire		3,000.00

TUSCALOOSA, ALA., HANDSTAMP, ENVELOPE

CSP139-1 CSP139-2

CSP139-1		Mint	Used
5¢	**black,** entire, use is same as handstamp PAID	250.00	

CSP139-2		Mint	Used
10¢	**black,** entire, use is same as handstamp PAID	250.00	

TUSCUMBIA, ALA., HANDSTAMP, ENVELOPE

CSP140-3 CSP140-4

CSP140-2		Mint	Used
5¢	**black,** entire		2,500.00
	black, entire, patriotic, See CSP140-1		4,500.00

CSP140-3		Mint	Used
5¢	**red,** entire, see CSP140-1		3,000.00

CSP140-4		Mint	Used
10¢	**black,** entire, see CSP140-1		3,500.00

Note: See CSP140-1 among 3¢ 1861 Postmasters Provisionals.

UNIONTOWN, ALA., TYPESET, ADHESIVE

CSP142-2 CSP142-5

CSP142-1		Mint	Used
2¢	**dark blue** on gray-blue, on cover, laid paper		—

CSP142-2		Mint	Used
2¢	**dark blue** sheet of 4, laid paper	55,000.00	

CSP142-3		Mint	Used
5¢	**green** on gray-blue, single, laid paper	2,500.00	2,500.00
	pair, setting of 2x2 on laid paper	—	
	on cover		6,500.00

CSP142-4		Mint	Used
5¢	**green,** single, laid paper	2,750.00	2,000.00
	on cover, laid paper		10,000.00
	pair on cover, setting of 2x2 on laid paper		20,000.00

CSP142-5		Mint	Used
10¢	**red** on gray-blue, on cover, paper		35,000.00

UNIONVILLE, S.C., HANDSTAMP, ADHESIVE

CSP143

CSP143		Mint	Used
5¢	**black** on grayish, single		—
	on cover, uncancelled		18,000.00
	on cover, tied		25,000.00
	pair on patriotic cover, one known		35,000.00

VALDOSTA, GA., HANDSTAMP, ENVELOPE

CSP144-1 Control Mark CSP144-2

CSP144-1		Mint	Used
5¢ + 5¢	**black,** entire, with undated postmark control on reverse		—

CSP144-2		Mint	Used
10¢	**black,** entire, with undated postmark control on front		2,000.00

VELASCO, TEXAS, HANDSTAMP, ENVELOPE

CSP145

CSP145		Mint	Used
10¢	**black,** entire, same as handstamp paid when used		

VICTORIA, TEXAS, TYPESET, ADHESIVE

Printed for Postmaster J.A. Moody.

TYPE I — TYPE I Typeset — TYPE II

CSP146-1 CSP146-2 CSP146-3

CSP146-1		Mint	Used
5¢	**red-brown** on green, single	20,000.00	

CSP146-2		Mint	Used
10¢	**red-brown** on green, single	7,000.00	4,500.00
	on cover		125,000.00

CSP146-3		Mint	Used
10¢	**red-brown** on green, single, bold "10", Pelure paper	7,000.00	7,000.00

Walterborough, S.C., Handstamp, Envelope

CSP147-2

CSP147-1		Mint	Used
10¢	**black** on buff, entire		4,500.00
CSP147-2		Mint	Used
10¢	**carmine**, entire		5,000.00

Warrenton, Ga., Handstamp, Envelope

CSP148-1

CSP148-1		Mint	Used
5¢	**black**, entire		1,200.00
CSP148-1a		Mint	Used
ms 10¢	**black**, entire, revalued 10¢ over 5¢		850.00

Washington, Ga., Handstamp, Envelope

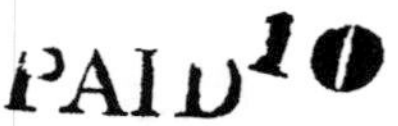

CSP149

CSP149		Mint	Used
10¢	**black**, entire, with undated postmark control on back		2,000.00

Note: Provisional covers must have the undated postmark control on the reverse. Covers with handstamped rate and paid markings and undated postmark on the front are not considered provisional uses.

Weatherford, Texas, Handstamp, Envelope

CSP150-1a

CSP150-1		Mint	Used
5¢	**black**, entire		2,000.00
CSP150-1a		Mint	Used
5¢ + 5¢	**black**, entire		15,000.00

Wilkesboro, N.C., Handstamp, Envelope

CSP151-1

CSP151-2

CSP151-1		Mint	Used
5¢	**black**, entire		6,000.00
CSP151-2		Mint	Used
10¢ over 5¢	**black**, entire, 10¢ handstamp over 5, one known		6,000.00

Winnsborough, S.C., Handstamp, Envelope

CSP152-1 CSP152-2

CSP152-1		Mint	Used
5¢	**black**, entire		1,500.00
CSP152-2		Mint	Used
10¢	**black**, entire		2,000.00

Wythville, Va., Handstamp, Envelope

CSP153

CSP153		Mint	Used
5¢	**black**, entire		900.00

Confederate States

The Confederate States of America was the government established in 1861 by the Southern states that seceded from the Union, charging that it was aggressively hostile toward their "domestic institutions."

South Carolina, the first state to secede (Dec. 20, 1860), justified its action on the grounds of continued Northern attacks on slavery, the coming to power of a sectionalist party (the Republican), and the election of a President (Abraham Lincoln) "whose opinions and purposes are hostile to slavery." It was followed, in order, by Mississippi, Florida, Alabama, Georgia, Louisiana, Texas, Virginia, Arkansas, Tennessee and North Carolina. The attack on Ft. Sumter at Charleston, S.C., on April 12, 1861.

The greatest romance to collecting Confederate States stamps is to have them on the envelopes on which they were used.

Confederate postal rates went into effect on June 1, 1861, when the Confederacy took over the operation of its own postal system. Up to that date the United States continued the postal service in the seceded states, and covers showing such after-secession usage are scarce. Confederate rates were 5¢ and 10¢ for single letters, the latter rate applying to those going over 500 miles; the rate was made 10¢ for all distances on July 1, 1862. A 2¢ rate for drop letters and unsealed printed matter remained in effect throughout.

The Confederate States Post Office Department prepared the following adhesive stamps to serve the seceded states. All of those issued were imperforate except two 10¢ blue engraved stamps on which experimental perforations, gauging 12 1/2, were officially applied to a limited number. Some private rouletting also was done. One stamp was never released.

1861. The First Issue consisted of 5¢ and 10¢ stamps, lithographed (offset) from various stones on soft, porous paper. Earliest known dates of use are given.

Hoyer and Ludwig of Richmond, Va., printed the 5¢ green stamps from three different stones. Stone A/B produced sharp, clear impressions, almost always in the olive green shade. The first printing from Stone 1 was in olive green, and others followed in various shades of green. The impressions are clear, but not as sharp as those from Stone A/B. Stone 2 impressions come in all shades of green known except olive. They are noticably poor and some were unofficially rouletted (Baton Rouge, La.).

CS1 *Jefferson Davis of Mississippi (1808-89), president of the Confederacy*

CS1		UnFVF	UseFVF
5¢	**olive green,** Stone A/B *(Oct. 16, 1861)*	275.00	175.00
	Pair	600.00	400.00
	On cover (single)		250.00
	On cover (pair)		475.00
	b1. green, Stone 1 *(Oct. 23, 1861)*	200.00	150.00
	Pair	425.00	350.00
	On cover (single)		200.00
	On cover (pair)		425.00
	b2. bright green	200.00	150.00
	b3. dark green	225.00	165.00
	b4. dull green	200.00	150.00
	b5. olive green	225.00	175.00
	c. green, Stone 2 *(Dec. 2, 1861)*	200.00	150.00
	Pair	425.00	350.00
	On cover (single)		225.00
	On cover (pair)		400.00
	c1. bright green	225.00	165.00
	c2. dark green	225.00	165.00
	c3. light green	200.00	150.00
	Earliest documented date of use: *Oct. 16, 1861*		

The 10¢ stamp lithographed (offset) by Hoyer & Ludwig from Stone 1 (CS2), are clear and distinct and in a uniform shade of dark blue. The stamps produced by J.T. Paterson & Co. of Augusta, Ga., from Stone 2 (CS3) come in a wide range of shades, and the impressions are not as clear. They show a small colored dash below the lowest point of the upper left triangle, and a line connecting the "N" in "Confederate" with the circular frame line above.

CS2, CS6 *Thomas Jefferson, who was born and died in Virginia, was an early champion of states' rights and of an agrarian economy.*

CS2		UnFVF	UseFVF
10¢	**dark blue,** *(Hoyer & Ludwig)*	400.00	225.00
	Pair	900.00	550.00
	On cover (single)		400.00
	On cover (pair)		1,250.00
	Horizontal pair, gutter between	—	
	v. Printed on both sides	—	
	Earliest documented date of use: *Nov. 8, 1861*		

CS3 *Thomas Jefferson*

CS3 *close-up*

CS3		UnFVF	UseFVF
10¢	**blue** *(Paterson)*	250.00	175.00
	dark blue	275.00	200.00
	indigo	2,200.00	1,750.00
	light blue	250.00	175.00
	Pair	550.00	400.00
	On cover (single)		250.00
	On cover (pair)		900.00
	On cover (single Stone Y)		450.00
	a. light milky blue, Stone Y	500.00	300.00
	a1. greenish blue, Stone Y	400.00	250.00
	Earliest documented date of use: *July 25, 1862*		

CS4 *Andrew Jackson, a Tennesseean and "Hero of New Orleans" in the War of 1812, was in reality a foe of the principles on which the Confederacy was founded.*

CS4		UnFVF	UseFVF
2¢	**green** (one stone)	500.00	450.00
	emerald green (very rare)	—	—
	olive yellow green	550.00	500.00
	light green	500.00	450.00
	dark green	500.00	450.00
	On cover (single)		1,500.00
	On cover (strip of 5)		10,000.00
	Earliest documented date of use: *March 21, 1862*		

Stone 2, which was used to produce CS1, was also used for the blue CS5. A second stone, Stone 3, was needed, and the printing from this newer stone was clearer. Only about 2% of the total 6.7 million 5¢ blue stamps were from Stone 3.

CS5 *Jefferson Davis*

CS5		UnFVF	UseFVF
5¢	**blue,** Stone 2 *(March 4, 1862)*	150.00	125.00
	dark blue	175.00	150.00
	milky blue	200.00	175.00
	On cover (single)		225.00
	Stone 2 on cover (pair)		425.00
	a. blue, Stone 3 *(April 10, 1862)*	200.00	125.00
	a1. dark blue	225.00	175.00
	a2. milky blue	275.00	200.00
	On cover (single)		275.00
	Stone 3 on cover (pair)		500.00
	Earliest documented date of use: *Feb. 28, 1862*		

CS6 *Thomas Jefferson*

CS6		UnFVF	UseFVF
10¢	**rose** (one stone)	700.00	400.00
	carmine	2,000.00	1,500.00
	dull rose	700.00	400.00
	dark rose	800.00	500.00
	brown rose	1,000.00	800.00
	On cover (single)		650.00
	Earliest documented date of use: *March 10, 1862*		

The carmine used on cover is a major Confederate variety. Its earliest known use is May 27, 1862. The brown rose color also is very scarce. Carmine and brown rose stamps on or off cover require certification.

1862. Second Issue of newly designed *letterpress* stamps was printed by Thomas de la Rue & Co. Ltd., London, and by Archer & Daly of Richmond, Va., from plates made by De la Rue.

The London print (CS7) is clear and distinct.

CS7 *Jefferson Davis*

CS7		UnFVF	UseFVF
5¢	**light blue**	15.00	20.00
	On cover (single London print) before July 1, 1862		125.00
	Pair	35.00	45.00
	On cover (pair)		100.00
	Earliest documented date of use: *April 16, 1862*		

The local print (CS8) from De la Rue plates show considerably less quality, both in the printing appearance and the gum.

CS8 *Jefferson Davis*

CS8		UnFVF	UseFVF
5¢	**blue,** normal paper (Richmond print)	10.00	20.00
	dark blue	9.00	22.50
	Pair	25.00	45.00
	Horizontal pair, gutter between	250.00	
	On cover (single) (overpaid drop)		200.00
	On cover (pair)		100.00
	p. blue, printed on thin glazed paper	25.00	35.00
	p1. dark blue, printed on thin glazed paper	25.00	35.00
	p2. blue, printed on thick paper	30.00	35.00
	p3. dark blue, printed on thin glazed paper	30.00	35.00
	v. pair, printed on both sides	2,000.00	800.00
	v1. "White tie"	175.00	150.00
	On cover "White tie"		400.00
	Earliest documented date of use: *Aug. 15, 1862*		

Private printings, erroneously called "Reprints," in both blue and black on modern paper were made for philatelic purposes.

After a boost in postage rates on July 1, 1862, the Confederate Post Office Department instructed the firm of Thomas de la Rue & Co. in London to alter the denominations of the two typographed (letterpress) stamps for which they had previously made plates. Thus the value line of "ONE CENT" was altered to read "TWO CENTS," and that of "FIVE CENTS" to "TEN CENTS." While these two new plates were duly shipped to the Confederacy and arrived safely, no official printing was ever made from them. The complete plate of 400 subjects of the 2¢ denomination was discovered many years ago, but only broken sections of the 10¢ plate were ever found. Various private printings have since been made from the 2¢ plate, and from the sections, and panes reconstructed from the 10¢ — the 2¢ usually in green and the 10¢ in various colors. None are officially printed government stamps, and as private emissions they have a value of only $3 to $5 each.

CS9 *John C. Calhoun of South Carolina, a leading defender of the Southern cause against the industrial North.*

CS9		UnFVF	UseFVF
1¢	**orange,** (not issued)	100.00	
	deep orange	125.00	

1863-64. Third Issue *engraved and printed by Archer & Daly in Richmond, Va., unless otherwise stated. Imperforate.*

The first printing of the later Jefferson Davis issues from Archer & Daly in 1863 show uniformly clear impressions, including sharply defined shading behind the portrait, and with an even distribution of a good quality light-colored gum. In 1864 another firm, Keatinge & Ball of Columbia, S.C., printed stamps (Nos. CS16-CS17) from the same plates. They are of poorer quality, usually with filled-in impressions; and the gum is dark and unevenly applied — even at times penetrating the paper and giving it an orange hue. Copper plate intaglio on paper that varies from thin to thick.

CS10 *Jefferson Davis.* The stamp is boxed by frame lines. Usually only parts of the frame lines are seen. Value is for stamps showing at least two lines.
Values of stamps showing more or less than two lines are adjusted accordingly.

CS10		UnFVF	UseFVF
10¢	**blue** ("Frame Line")	2,500.00	1,250.00
	milky blue	2,500.00	1,250.00
	greenish blue	2,500.00	
	dark blue	2,000.00	
	Double transfer	3,500.00	1,250.00
	On cover (single)		1,800.00
	Earliest documented date of use: *April 19, 1863*		

Certification recommended as fakes do exist.

The stamp has vertical shading lines behind the portrait. Copper plate intaglio, imperforate.

CS11 *Jefferson Davis.* The Denomination is spelled out, "TEN."

CS11		UnFVF	UseFVF
10¢	**blue** ("T-E-N")	650.00	475.00
	milky blue	650.00	475.00
	gray blue	700.00	525.00
	On cover (single)		1,250.00
	Double transfer	800.00	800.00
	Damaged plate	800.00	800.00
	Earliest documented date of use: *April 23, 1863*		

Colorless vertical gash above "N" in "CENTS," clear cross-hatching. Steel plate engraved, mainly imperforate.

CS12 *Jefferson Davis*

CS12		UnFVF	UseFVF
10¢	**blue** (Type 1)	10.00	15.00
	Pair	25.00	45.00
	milky blue	15.00	20.00
	greenish blue	15.00	20.00
	green	40.00	45.00
	Horizontal pair, gutter between	125.00	
	On cover (single)		75.00
	On cover (pair)		175.00
	v. Perforated 12 1/2	300.00	250.00
	On cover (single) perforated		450.00
	Earliest documented date of use: *April 21, 1863*		

The four corner ornaments are filled in, and a thin outline encloses the entire design. Steel plate engraved. The perforated variety requires certification.

CS13 *Jefferson Davis*

CS13		UnFVF	UseFVF
10¢	**blue** (Type 2)	10.00	15.00
	milky blue	15.00	30.00
	dark blue	10.00	15.00
	greenish blue	20.00	12.50
	green	60.00	70.00
	Pair	25.00	40.00
	On cover (single)		75.00
	On cover (pair)		175.00
	v. Perforated 12 1/2	300.00	250.00
	On cover (single) perforated		450.00
	Earliest documented date of use: *May 1, 1863*		

The perforated variety requires certification.

Because the portrait is similar to the 2¢ United States stamp of 1863, known as the "Black Jack," this stamp is sometimes called the "Red Jack." Steel plate engraved.

CS14 *Andrew Jackson*

CS14		UnFVF	UseFVF
2¢	**brown red**	50.00	275.00
	pale red *("Red Jack")*	50.00	275.00
	Double transfer	100.00	300.00
	Horizontal pair, gutter between	300.00	
	On cover (single)		1,000.00
	On cover (strip of 5)		4,000.00
	Earliest documented date of use: *April 21, 1863*		

Beware fake cancels.

CS15 *George Washington of Virginia*

CS15		UnFVF	UseFVF
20¢	**green**	35.00	350.00
	dark green	60.00	450.00
	yellow green	55.00	400.00
	On cover (single)		1,000.00
	v. Diagonal bisect, used as 10¢ on cover		2,000.00
	v1. Horizontal bisect, used as 10¢ on cover		2,500.00
	Earliest documented date of use: *June 1, 1863*		

Beware of fake cancels.

Printed by Keatinge & Ball. Cross-hatch shading behind portrait is not sharp — even undistinguishable.

CS16 *Jefferson Davis*

CS16		UnFVF	UseFVF
10¢	**deep blue** (Type I)	10.00	35.00
	On cover (single)		125.00
	Earliest documented date of use: *Sept. 4, 1864*		

Printed by Keatinge & Ball. Cross-hatch shading behind portrait is not sharp — even undistinguishable — and corner ornaments are filled in.

CS17 *Jefferson Davis*

CS17		UnFVF	UseFVF
10¢	**deep blue** (Type 2)	12.00	40.00
	On cover (single)		125.00
	Earliest documented date of use: *Sept. 4, 1864*		

Canal Zone

Former U.S. Government reservation, administered by a governor appointed by the president of the United States. Area: about 553 sq. mi. Headquarters: Balboa Heights.

100 Centavos= 1 Peso; 100 Centesimos = 1 Balboa; 100 Cents = 1 Dollar.

The Canal Zone was a strip of territory across the Isthmus of Panama, extending five miles on each side of the Panama Canal but excluding the cities of Panama and Colón. It was leased from the Republic of Panama under Varilla treaty of 1903, under Article III of which the U.S. was granted "all the rights, power and authority within the Zone which the United States would possess and exercise if it were the sovereign." The idea of a canal across Panama dated back almost to Balboa's discovery in 1513 that Panama was an isthmus. The Spanish conducted several surveys between 1534 and 1779 but, afraid of the threat to their monopoly of communication with Latin America, generally discouraged even the improvement of overland routes across the isthmus.

U.S. canal interest began with the California gold rush, when westbound settlers had to trek across the continent, sail around Cape Horn or make two sea voyages separated by a journey across Panama. A U.S. postal service using the latter route was instituted in 1848 through the Pacific Mail Steamship Company.

In 1878 the French obtained a Panamanian canal concession from the government of New Granada (Columbia) and formed a canal company headed by Ferdinand de Lesseps, who had constructed the Suez Canal. The French plan, to dig a sea-level canal following essentially the line of the Panama Railroad (completed in 1855), was later changed to include locks. Because of climate, fever-breeding mosquitoes and financial mismanagement, the French company went bankrupt in 1889 after having removed some 50,000,000 cubic meters of rock and earth and spent $287,000,000. A French receiver company was equally unsuccessful.

A U.S. commission had recommended Nicaragua as the most feasible site for an American canal project but changed its mind when the French company offered to sell its concession and works for $40,000,000. Congress authorized President Theodore Roosevelt to make the purchase, and a treaty was signed, but the Colombian Senate refused (August 1903) to ratify it. In November the Department of Panama declared itself independent of Colombia and leased the Canal Zone to the United States. The Canal was officially opened Aug. 15, 1914.

All stamps engraved and recess printed unless otherwise stated.

The Canal Zone postal service was established on June 24, 1904. Its first stamps were secured from the Republic of Panama for temporary use pending the arrival of overprinted United States stamps. They were current 2, 5 and 10 centavos provisional stamps of the Republic overprinted before deivery with the words *CANAL ZONE*. The nominal values were expressed in Colombian silver, 100 centavos of which equaled 50 cents of United States gold currency. Temporary first-class postage rates for the first issue only, in Colombian silver, were: domestic post cards, 2¢; domestic letters, 5¢ per ounce or fraction; foreign letters, 10¢ per half ounce or fraction.

A treaty signed in 1977 by U.S. President Jimmy Carter and Panamanian President Omar Torrijos mandated gradual return of the Canal Zone to Panama, a process completed on Dec. 31, 1999. The Canal Zone postal service closed on Sept. 30, 1979, and Panama assumed control over the Canal Zone post offices on Oct. 1, 1979.

100 Centavos = 1 Peso; 100 Centesimos = 1 Balboa; 100 Cents = 1 Dollar.

Regular Postal Issues

1904. Map Design Overprint Issue

1 *Map design PANAMA, 13 1/2 mm long*

		UnFVF	UseFVF
1			
2¢	**rose carmine** *(June 24, 1904)*	520.00	500.00
	v. *PANAMA* 15mm long	600.00	500.00
	v1. *PANAMA* reading up & down	650.00	500.00
	v2. *P NAMA*	600.00	500.00
	v3. *CANAL ZONE* double overprint	2,000.00	1,500.00
	v4. *CANAL ZONE* inverted overprint	850.00	600.00
	v5. *CANAL ZONE* double inverted	5,000.00	

2, 3 *Map design PANAMA, 15 mm long*

		UnFVF	UseFVF
2			
5¢	**deep blue**	250.00	180.00
	v. 2 1/4mm between bar & *A* of *PANAMA*	500.00	500.00
	v1. colon between bar & *P* of *PANAMA*	500.00	500.00
	v2. *CANAL ZONE* diagonally down to right	400.00	350.00
	v3. *CANAL ZONE* double overprint	2,250.00	1,500.00
	v4. *CANAL ZONE* inverted overprint	600.00	625.00
	v5. pair, 1 w/o overprint	5,000.00	5,000.00
3		UnFVF	UseFVF
10¢	**yellow orange**	425.00	275.00
	v. 2 1/4mm between bar & *A* of *PANAMA*	625.00	625.00
	v1. colon between bar & *P* of *PANAMA*	600.00	600.00
	v2. *CANAL ZONE* double overprint		12,500.00
	v3. *CANAL ZONE* inverted overprint	625.00	625.00
	v4. pair, 1 w/o overprint	6,000.00	5,000.00

Counterfeit CANAL ZONE handstamps and cancellations are numerous.

Nos. 1-3 were withdrawn on July 17, and overprinted. U.S. stamps were placed on sale the following day. Beginning with this issue, rates and denominations were expressed in U.S. currency or its equivalent.

1904. Canal Zone Overprint Issue

4

		UnFVF	UseFVF
4			
4¢	**deep blue green,** No. 211	30.00	25.00
5		UnFVF	UseFVF
2¢	**carmine,** No. 231	30.00	21.00
	a. scarlet	32.50	25.00
6		UnFVF	UseFVF
5¢	**deep blue,** No. 215	105.00	75.00
7		UnFVF	UseFVF
8¢	**violet black,** No. 217	160.00	110.00
8		UnFVF	UseFVF
10¢	**pale red brown,** No. 218	160.00	125.00

Dissatisfaction and concern in Panama over early United States administration led to conferences between the Panamanian authorities and William Howard Taft, U.S. Secretary of War, and a series of executive orders collectively known as the Taft Agreement.

One of the provisions required the use of Panama stamps overprinted CANAL ZONE. This automatically invalidated the current United States overprints. The new arrangements which were to cover the construction period of the Canal, required that a stable currency be established in Panama equivalent to that of the United States. Panama stamps used in the Canal Zone were to be purchased from Panama at 40 percent of their face value. Accordingly, in succeeding issues, the Canal Zone authorities were limited to whatever Panama could supply.

1904-1906. Canal Zone Overprint Issue

9, 10

CANAL

ZONE

9		UnFVF	UseFVF
1¢	**green**	2.80	2.00
	v. *CANAL* Type II	100.00	100.00
	v1. *CANA L*	125.00	125.00
	v2. *ZONE* Type II	70.00	70.00
	v3. *ZONE* (U-shaped)	275.00	275.00
	v4. inverted overprint		2,250.00
	v5. double overprint	1,250.00	1,000.00

10		UnFVF	UseFVF
2¢	**carmine red**	4.50	2.00
	v. *CANA L*	85.00	85.00
	v1. *L* sideways	2,500.00	2,000.00
	v2. *ZONE* (U-shaped)	275.00	275.00
	v3. inverted overprint	250.00	275.00

1904-06. Canal Zone Overprint Issue

11, 12, 13

11		UnFVF	UseFVF
2¢	**rose carmine,** *(Dec. 9, 1905)*	7.00	4.00
	v. *ZONE* Type II	175.00	175.00
	v1. *PANAMA* 16mm long	45.00	45.00
	v2. *PANAWA*	45.00	45.00
	v3. *PANAMA* inverted overprint	400.00	400.00

12		UnFVF	UseFVF
5¢	**deep blue**	7.50	3.00
	v. *CANAL* Type II	75.00	75.00
	v1. *CANA L*	90.00	90.00
	v2. *ZONE* Type II	75.00	75.00
	v3. *CANAL ZONE* double overprint	600.00	600.00
	v4. *PANAMA* 16mm long	40.00	40.00
	v5. *PANAWA*	40.00	40.00
	v6. *PANAM*	70.00	70.00
	v7. *ANAMA*	80.00	80.00
	v8. *PANAAM*	950.00	950.00
	v9. *PAN MA*	75.00	75.00
	v10. *PAMANA* reading up	75.00	75.00
	v11. *PAMANA* reading down	200.00	200.00
	v12. right *P* 5mm below bar	50.00	50.00
	v13. *PANAMA* inverted overprint, bar at bottom	800.00	1,000.00
	v14. *PANAMA* double overprint	1,050.00	850.00

13		UnFVF	UseFVF
10¢	**yellow orange**	20.00	10.00
	v. *CANAL* Type II	225.00	225.00
	v1. *CANA L*	200.00	200.00
	v2. *ZONE* Type II	175.00	175.00
	v3. red brown *PANAMA* overprint	29.00	29.00
	v4. *PANAMA* 16mm long	75.00	75.00
	v5. *PANAWA*	100.00	100.00
	v6. *PAMANA* reading down	200.00	200.00
	v7. right *P* 5mm below bar	150.00	150.00
	v8. left *A* touching bar	175.00	175.00
	v9. *PANAMA* double overprint	600.00	600.00

1904-06. Canal Zone Overprint Issue

14 *Large "8 cts" overprint in red - 3 varieties; "PANAMAs" (15mm) read up at left, down at right.*

8 cts

14		UnFVF	UseFVF
8¢ on 50¢ deep ochre		30.00	18.50
	v. *CANA L*	175.00	175.00
	v1. *ZONE* Type II	1,150.00	1,150.00
	v2. *CANAL ZONE* inverted overprint	425.00	400.00
	v3. right *P* 5mm below bar	175.00	175.00
	v4. red brown *PANAMA* overprint	40.00	40.00
	v5. *CANAL* Type II on v4	2,210.00	
	v6. *ZONE* Type II on v4	2,210.00	
	v7. *8¢* double overprint on v4	850.00	
	v8. omitted *8* on v4	4,250.00	

1904-06. Canal Zone Issue

15 *Large "8 cts" overprint, both "PANAMAs" (13mm) read up.*

15		UnFVF	UseFVF
8¢ on 50¢ deep ochre, overprint 14		3,000.00	4,250.00
	v. *CANA L*	4,000.00	
	v1. *PANAMA* 15mm long	3,250.00	4,750.00
	v2. *PANAMA* reading up & down	6,500.00	6,500.00
	v3. *P NAMA*	3,500.00	

1905-06. Canal Zone Issue

16 *Small "8 cts." with period, both "PANAMAs" (13mm) read up.*

8 cts.

16		UnFVF	UseFVF
8¢ on 50¢ deep ochre, (Nov. 1905)		50.00	35.00
	v. *ZONE* Type II	200.00	200.00
	v1. *PANAMA* 15mm long	80.00	70.00
	v2. *PANAMA* reading up & down	100.00	100.00
	v3. *P NAMA*	85.00	

1905-06. Canal Zone Issue

17 *Small "8 cts," both "PANAMAs" (13mm) read up.*

17		UnFVF	UseFVF
8¢ on 50¢ deep ochre, (April 23, 1906)		67.50	60.00
	v. *CANAL* Type II	200.00	200.00
	v1. *ZONE* Type II	200.00	200.00
	v2. *PANAMA* 15mm long	80.00	70.00
	v3. *PANAMA* reading up & down	100.00	100.00
	v4. *P NAMA*	85.00	
	v5. *8¢* double overprint	1,100.00	1,100.00

1904-06. Canal Zone Issue

18 *Small "8 cts." overprint in red with period; "PANAMAs" read up on left, down on right.*

18		UnFVF	UseFVF
8¢ on 50¢ deep ochre, (Sept. 1906)		70.00	60.00
	v. *CANAL* Type II	95.00	95.00
	v1. *ZONE* Type II	200.00	200.00
	v2. *PAMANA* reading up	120.00	120.00
	v3. *8¢* omitted	750.00	750.00
	v4. *8¢* double overprint	1,500.00	

Nos. 14, 15, 16, 18 without CANAL ZONE overprint were not regularly issued.

Note: The sequence for Canal Zone stamps was revised for the 2002 Minkus catalog to reflect chronological issue dates between Nos. 15 and 18.

The plate used for the CANAL ZONE overprint on Nos. 9-18 was altered five times, giving six different stages from which printings were made. A full list of the characteristic varieties and all alterations of the plate, with the approximate time they occurred and the stamps upon which the overprint is found, appears in *Bartels' Check List of Canal Zone Stamps,* second edition, 1908.

The Panama overprint was applied by a 50-subject plate to one-half of the sheet at a time and was sometimes misplaced vertically or horizon-

tally. Such misplaced overprints exist on nearly all values. When misplaced vertically the bar may appear at the bottom of the stamp instead of the top, and one row will be left without a bar. When misplaced horizontally the word PANAMA may appear once only, twice at either right or left, and three times on the same stamp. In some cases the overprint on two vertical rows of a sheet may overlap, giving the appearance of a double overprint. Although of interest to the specialist, such varieties are not worth appreciably more than the normal stamp.

Rejection by the Canal Zone authorities of a lot of 1¢ and 2¢ provisionals that Panama had prepared for its own postal needs resulted in alternate offer by Panama of some Department of Panama stock, that had not yet been overprinted. These were accepted and the bars obliterating COLOMBIA and the old values were applied by the Canal Zone authorities at the same time that *PANAMA, CANAL ZONE* and the new values were added.

1906. Canal Zone Issue

19 *first printing*

19		UnFVF	UseFVF
1¢ on 20¢ slate violet, (March 1906)		1.25	1.00

20 *second printing*

20		UnFVF	UseFVF
1¢ on 20¢ slate violet, (May 1906)		1.25	1.00

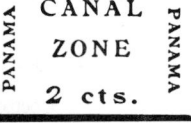

21 *third printing*

21		UnFVF	UseFVF
1¢ on 20¢ slate violet, (Sept. 1906)		1.25	1.00
	v. *C ANAL*	12.50	

22 *first printing*

22		UnFVF	UseFVF
2¢ on 1p brown lake, (March 1906)		2.00	1.75

23 *second printing*

23		UnFVF	UseFVF
2¢ on 1p brown lake, (May 1906)		2.00	1.75

24 *third printing*

24		UnFVF	UseFVF
2¢ on 1p brown lake, (Sept. 1906)		20.00	20.00

Misplaced overprints occur with bars shifted so that both bars appear at top or bottom, or occasionally only one bar altogether.

1906-07. Portrait Issue

25 *Balboa*

25		UnFVF	UseFVF
1¢	**deep blue green and black,** (Jan. 1907)	2.50	1.00
	v. *ANA* for *CANAL*	70.00	70.00
	v1. *CAN L*	80.00	80.00
	v2. *ONE* for *ZONE*	80.00	80.00
	v3. horizontal pair, imperforate		
	v4. horizontal pair, imperforate between		
	v5. vertical pair, imperforate between		
	v6. head & inverted overprint		
	v7. overprint reading up		
	v8. pair, 1 not overprint		
	v9. double overprint		
	v10. double overprint second inverted		

26		UnFVF	UseFVF
2¢	**scarlet and black,** (Oct. 1906)	30.00	27.50

27 *Córdoba*

27		UnFVF	UseFVF
2¢	**scarlet and black,** (Nov. 1906)	3.50	1.20
	a. carmine & black	3.00	1.40
	v. *CAN L*	45.00	
	v1. horizontal pair, imperforate between		
	v2. head & inverted overprint		
	v3. pair, 1 w/o overprint		
	v4. double overprint		

28 *Arosemena*

28		UnFVF	UseFVF
5¢	**blue and black,** (Dec. 1906)	7.00	2.50
	a. light blue & black	7.00	2.50
	b. cobalt & black	3.25	1.50
	c. dark blue & black	7.00	2.50
	v. *CAN L*	60.00	
	v1. *CANAL* only	35.00	
	v2. *CANAL* double overprint	500.00	350.00

29 *Hurtado*

29		UnFVF	UseFVF
8¢	**dark lilac and black,** (Dec. 1906)	20.00	9.00
	v. horizontal pair, imperforate between		

30 *Obaldia*

		UnFVF	UseFVF
30			
10¢	**dark violet and black,** (Dec. 1906)	20.00	9.00
	v. double overprint second inverted		

Earlier printings of Nos. 25-30 are on soft and thick, later printings on hard, thin paper. Nos. 25 and 30 exist imperforate between stamp and sheet margin. CA of *CANAL* spaced 1/2mm farther apart on position 50 of the sheet on later printings of Nos. 25, 27-29.

A change of printers resulted in a new series of Panama stamps and again certain denominations were obtained for Canal Zone use. These designs were in use until 1924 and appeared with several styles of overprint.

1909. Second Portrait Issue

31 *Cordoba*

		UnFVF	UseFVF
31			
2¢	**rose red and black,** (May 29, 1909)	12.50	6.50
	v. horizontal pair, 1 w/o overprint		
	v1. vertical pair, 1 w/o overprint	1,450.00	

32 *Arosemena*

		UnFVF	UseFVF
32			
5¢	**deep blue and black,** (May 28, 1909)	55.00	12.50

33 *Hurtado*

		UnFVF	UseFVF
33			
8¢	**red violet and black,** (May 25, 1909)	37.50	15.00

34 *Obaldia*

		UnFVF	UseFVF
34			
10¢	**red violet and black,** (Jan. 19, 1909)	37.50	13.50
	v. horizontal pair, 1 w/o overprint	1,450.00	
	v1. vertical pair, 1 w/o overprint		

CA of *CANAL* widely spaced on position 50 of the sheet of Nos. 31-34.

Inquiries developed that stamps could be obtained already overprinted by the manufacturer at no extra cost. The following overprint types I, II, IV and V represent stamps secured in this manner until the use of overprinted Panama stamps was discontinued in 1924. Type III was local emergency issue overprinted by The Panama Canal Press. 1¢ and 2¢ stamps were supplied in booklet form beginning late in 1911.

1909-10. Second Portrait Issue

CANAL ZONE

35-39 *CANAL ZONE reading up, spaced 10mm (1c) or 8 1/2 mm apart; "C" serifs at top and bottom.*

		UnFVF	UseFVF
35			
1¢	**deep green and black**	3.50	1.60
	v. head and inverted overprint		15,000.00
	v1. *CANAL* only	500.00	
	Booklet pane of 6	750.00	
36		UnFVF	UseFVF
2¢	**scarlet and black**	4.50	1.25
	v. pair imperforate horizontal	1,000.00	1,000.00
	v1. *CANAL* double overprint	400.00	
	Booklet pane of 6	1,000.00	
37		UnFVF	UseFVF
5¢	**deep blue and black**	19.00	3.75
	v. double overprint	180.00	180.00
38		UnFVF	UseFVF
8¢	**violet and black,** (Mar. 18, 1910)	11.00	4.75
	v. vertical pair, 1 w/o overprint	1,500.00	
39		UnFVF	UseFVF
10¢	**violet and black**	55.00	20.00

1912-16 Portrait Issue

CANAL ZONE

40-43 *"C" serif at top only, "O" tilted left.*

		UnFVF	UseFVF
40			
1¢	**deep green and black,** (July 1913)	12.00	2.60
	v. vertical pair, 1 w/o overprint	1,500.00	
	margins imperforate	750.00	
	perforate	1,150.00	
41		UnFVF	UseFVF
2¢	**scarlet and black,** (Dec. 1912)	8.00	1.40
	v. overprint reading down	175.00	
	v1. head and inverted overprint	700.00	750.00
	v2. horizontal pair, 1 w/o overprint	1,500.00	
	v3. *CANAL* only	1,100.00	
	margins imperforate	210.00	
	perforate	1,700.00	
42		UnFVF	UseFVF
5¢	**deep blue and black,** (Dec. 1912)	22.50	2.75
	t. head of 2¢		8,000.00
43		UnFVF	UseFVF
10¢	**red violet and black,** (Feb. 1916)	40.00	8.00

1915-20. Portrait Issue

CANAL ZONE

44-45 *Words spaced 9 1/2 mm apart*

		UnFVF	UseFVF
44			
1¢	**deep green and black,** (Dec. 1915)	180.00	110.00
	v. overprint reading down	315.00	
	v1. double overprint	300.00	
	v2. *ZONE* double overprint	4,250.00	
45		UnFVF	UseFVF
2¢	**scarlet and black,** (Aug. 1920)	3,000.00	150.00
46		UnFVF	UseFVF
5¢	**deep blue and black,** (Dec. 1915)	725.00	200.00

1915-20. PORTRAIT ISSUE

47-49 *"C" thick at bottom, "E" with center bar same length as top and bottom bars.*

CANAL ZONE

		UnFVF	UseFVF
47			
1¢	**deep green and black,** (Jan. 1918)	27.50	6.50
	v. overprint reading down	175.00	
	left row w/o overprint	850.00	
	right row w/double overprint	2,500.00	
48		UnFVF	UseFVF
2¢	**scarlet and black,** (Nov. 1918)	125.00	6.75
	v. overprint reading down	150.00	150.00
	v1. horizontal pair, 1 w/o overprint	2,000.00	
	left row w/o overprint	5,000.00	
49		UnFVF	UseFVF
5¢	**deep blue and black,** (April 1920)	180.00	30.00

1920-21. CANAL ZONE ISSUE

50-52 *"A" with flat top, small block type 1 3/4mm high.*

CANAL ZONE

		UnFVF	UseFVF
50			
1¢	**deep green and black,** (April 1921)	20.00	3.50
	v. overprint reading down	2.50	
	v1. horizontal pair, 1 w/o overprint	1,100.00	
	v2. *CANAL* double overprint	1,500.00	
	v3. *ZONE* only	2,750.00	1,400.00
	left row w/o overprint	3,250.00	
51		UnFVF	UseFVF
2¢	**scarlet and black,** (Sept. 1920)	10.00	2.50
	v. horizontal pair, 1 w/o overprint	1,750.00	
	v1. vertical pair, 1 w/o overprint	1,500.00	
	v2. double overprint	650.00	
	v3. double overprint second inverted	575.00	
	v4. *CANAL* double overprint	1,000.00	
	v5. *ZONE* double overprint	1,000.00	
	v6. *CANAL* only	2,250.00	
	left row w/o overprint	850.00	

52 *Perfin "P"*

		UnFVF	UseFVF
52			
5¢	**deep blue and black,** (April 1921)	300.00	45.00
	v. horizontal pair, 1 w/o overprint	825.00	

Official: Nos. 40-43, 46, 47, 50, 51 and 54 with perfin "P."

From March 1915, stamps for official mail were identified by a perforated initial (perfin) letter "P." They were replaced by overprinted stamps on March 31, 1941. The use of official stamps was discontinued Dec. 31, 1951.

A special order was placed by the Canal Zone authorities for a 13¢ stamp to handle the combined registration (8¢) and foreign letter (5¢) fees. Before the arrival of the stamps, however, the registration fee was increased to 10¢ and the stamps were overprinted accordingly. This stamp was later replaced by a 10¢ denomination in the same design. The style of the CANAL ZONE overprint is different from any other issue.

1911-14. CANAL ZONE OVERPRINT ISSUE

53-54

		UnFVF	UseFVF
53			
10¢ on 13¢	**slate,** *(Jan. 14, 1911)*	6.50	2.00
	v. *10¢* omitted	250.00	
	v1. *10¢* inverted overprint	300.00	250.00
54		UnFVF	UseFVF
10¢	**slate,** *(Jan. 6, 1914)*	45.00	9.00

Official: No. 54 with perfin P. See note after No. 52.

1914. POSTAGE DUE OVERPRINT ISSUE Prior to 1914, regular postage stamps were used to collect amounts due on unpaid matter; some stamps were specially handstamped *Postage Due.* The first set of dues comprised overprinted U.S. stamps, notwithstanding the provisions of the Taft Agreement.

CANAL ZONE

55-57 *1914, March Postage Due*

		UnFVF	UseFVF
55			
1¢	**dark carmine,** overprint on U.S. PD51	90.00	18.00
56		UnFVF	UseFVF
2¢	**dark carmine,** overprint on U.S. PD53	250.00	50.00
57		UnFVF	UseFVF
10¢	**dark carmine,** overprint on U.S. PD56	735.00	50.00

Many stamps show one or more letters of the overprint out of alignment, principally the "E" of "ZONE."

1915-19. BLUE OVERPRINT ISSUE

58, 61 *Gate to San Geronimo Castle, Portobelo, erroneously inscribed* San Lorenzo Castle, Chagres

		UnFVF	UseFVF
58			
1¢	**black brown**	10.00	5.00
	v. overprint 50 reading down	15.50	
	v1. overprint 50 reading up		5.00

59, 62, 63 *Statue of Columbus*

		UnFVF	UseFVF
59			
2¢	**black brown**	200.00	17.50

60, 65 *Pedro J. Sosa*

		UnFVF	UseFVF
60			
10¢	**black brown**	50.00	12.50

1915-19. RED OVERPRINT ISSUE

		UnFVF	UseFVF
61			
1¢ on 1¢	**black brown**	100.00	17.50

CANAL 2 ZONE

62, 63

		UnFVF	UseFVF
62			
2¢ on 2¢ black brown		35.00	12.50
63		UnFVF	UseFVF
2¢ on 2¢ black brown, overprint 44		35.00	14.00
64		UnFVF	UseFVF
4¢ on 4¢ black brown, overprint 44		40.00	18.00
	v. *ZONE* omitted	7,500.00	
	v1. *4* omitted	7,500.00	
65		UnFVF	UseFVF
10¢ on 10¢ black brown		24.00	5.00

Two spacings between 1 and *0* of *10* on No. 65.

1915. Panama National Exposition Issue Honors the 400th anniversary of the European discovery of the Pacific (1513) and the completion of the Canal (1914). *Perforated 12.*

66 *Relief map of Panama Canal*

		UnFVF	UseFVF
66			
1¢	**deep blue green and black,** *(March 1, 1915)*	7.50	6.00

67 *Balboa claims the Pacific*

		UnFVF	UseFVF
67			
2¢	**bright rose red and black**	11.00	4.50

68 *Gatun Locks*

		UnFVF	UseFVF
68			
5¢	**deep blue and black**	10.50	5.00

69 *Gaillard (Culebra) Cut*

		UnFVF	UseFVF
69			
10¢	**brown orange and black**	22.50	10.00

1917-20. Pictorials of Panama Issue

70 *SS Panama in Gaillard (Culebra) Cut*

		UnFVF	UseFVF
70			
12¢	**red violet and black,** overprinted blue	20.00	6.00

1917-20. Pictorials of Panama Issue

71 *SS Panama in Gaillard (Culebra) Cut*

		UnFVF	UseFVF
71			
15¢	**turquoise blue and black,** overprinted blue	45.00	24.00

72 *SS Cristobal in Gatun Locks*

		UnFVF	UseFVF
72			
24¢	**yellow brown and black,** overprinted blue	55.00	12.50

Official: No. 72 with perfin P. See note after No. 52.

73 *Drydock at Balboa*

		UnFVF	UseFVF
73			
50¢	**yellow orange and black** *(Sept. 4, 1920)*	300.00	140.00

74 *USS Nereus in Pedro Miquel Locks*

		UnFVF	UseFVF
74			
1b	**black purple and black** *(Sept. 4, 1920)*	160.00	60.00

1921-24. Centenary of Independence from Spain Issue
Stamps of Panama with black or red overprint.

75, 76 *José Vallarino*

		UnFVF	UseFVF
75			
1¢	**green**	3.75	1.20
	v. *CANAL* double inverted	2,750.00	
	Booklet pane of 6	1,000.00	
76		UnFVF	UseFVF
1¢	**green,** overprint 44 *(Jan. 28, 1924)*	525.00	180.00
	v. *ZONE* only, inverted overprint	19.00	
	v1. *ZONE CANAL,* inverted overprint	850.00	

77 *Land Gate, Panama City*

		UnFVF	UseFVF
77			
2¢	**carmine red**	3.00	1.25
	v. overprint reading down	225.00	
	v1. *ZONE* only	2,000.00	
	v2. pair, 1 w/o overprint	3,500.00	
	v3. double overprint	900.00	
	v4. CANAL double overprint	1,900.00	
	Booklet pane of 6	2,100.00	

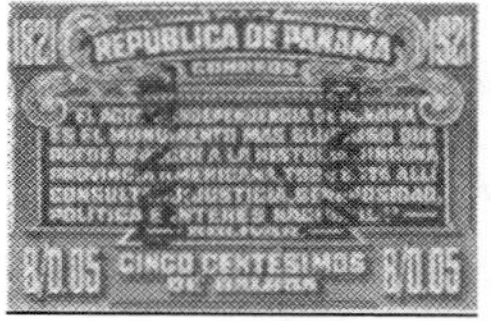

78 *Bolivar's Praise of Independence Movement*

78		UnFVF	UseFVF
5¢	**deep blue,** overprinted red	11.00	3.50
	v. overprint reading down	60.00	
	v1. red overprint 50	72.00	
	v2. black overprint 50	40.00	

79 *Municipal Building 1821 and 1921, Panama City*

79		UnFVF	UseFVF
10¢	**dark red violet**	17.50	6.00
	v. overprint reading down	100.00	

Official: Nos. 75, 77-79 with perfin P. See note after No. 52.

80 *Statue of Balboa, Panama City*

80		UnFVF	UseFVF
15¢	**light blue**	52.50	14.50

81 *T. Herrera*

81		UnFVF	UseFVF
24¢	**black brown**	57.50	20.00

82 *J. de Fábrega*

82		UnFVF	UseFVF
50¢	**black**	120.00	70.00

1924. Arms of Panama Issue

83, 84 *Arms of Panama*

		UnFVF	UseFVF
83			
1¢	**deep blue green**	12.00	4.50
84		UnFVF	UseFVF
2¢	**vermilion**	9.00	2.75
84A		UnFVF	UseFVF
5¢	**dark blue**	150.00	
84B		UnFVF	UseFVF
10¢	**violet**	150.00	
84C		UnFVF	UseFVF
12¢	**olive green**	150.00	
84D		UnFVF	UseFVF
15¢	**ultramarine**	150.00	
84E		UnFVF	UseFVF
24¢	**yellow brown**	150.00	
84F		UnFVF	UseFVF
50¢	**orange**	150.00	
84G		UnFVF	UseFVF
$1	**black**	150.00	

Nos. 84A-84G were prepared for use but not issued. 600 sets exist.

1924-33. Canal Zone Overprint Issue on U.S. Regular Issue Series. All Panama stamps overprinted *CANAL ZONE* were withdrawn from sale June 30, 1924 and were not valid for postage after Aug. 31, 1924. The formal opening of the Panama Canal was proclaimed by President Wilson July 20, 1920, signifying the end of the construction period of the Canal. The executive order comprising the Taft Agreement was subsequently abrogated by President Coolidge, effective June 1, 1924. No change was made in operations until the end of the fiscal year, June 30, 1924. As a temporary measure to replace the overprinted Panama stamps, overprinted U.S. stamps were obtained. These were used until gradually replaced by definitive designs beginning in 1928. As in the case of the Panama issues the Canal Zone authorities were obliged to accept whatever was currently available in the U.S.

85-96 *Flat top "A"*

CANAL

ZONE

85		UnFVF	UseFVF
1/2¢	**olive brown,** overprinted red *(April 15, 1925)*	1.25	.75

86, 112

86		UnFVF	UseFVF
1¢	**green**	1.40	.90
	v. *CANAL* only	1,750.00	
	v1. *ZONE* inverted overprint	450.00	450.00
	v2. *ZONE CANAL*	450.00	
	v3. *CANAL ZONE* inverted overprint	500.00	500.00
	Booklet pane of 6	44.00	

87

		UnFVF	UseFVF
87			
1 1/2¢	**yellow brown** *(April 15, 1925)*	2.00	1.40
88		UnFVF	UseFVF
2¢	**carmine**	9.00	1.80
	Booklet pane of 6	57.50	

89, 99, 116

89		UnFVF	UseFVF
5¢	**Prussian blue**	22.50	10.00

90, 100, 111, 117

		UnFVF	UseFVF
90			
10¢	**orange yellow**	45.00	22.50

91, 101

		UnFVF	UseFVF
91			
12¢	**maroon**	30.00	10.00
	v. *ZONE,* inverted overprint	37.50	30.00

92, 102, 118

		UnFVF	UseFVF
92			
14¢	**blue** *(June 27, 1925)*	24.00	18.50

93, 103

		UnFVF	UseFVF
93			
15¢	**gray black**	50.00	35.00

94, 106

		UnFVF	UseFVF
94			
30¢	**olive brown**	32.50	30.00

95, 107

		UnFVF	UseFVF
95			
50¢	**gray lilac**	80.00	45.00

96, 108

		UnFVF	UseFVF
96			
$1	**purple brown**	300.00	65.00

1925-28. Canal Zone Overprint 2nd Issue *perforated 11.*

CANAL

ZONE

97-108 *Overprint "A" with sharp-pointed top.*

CANAL

ZONE

		UnFVF	UseFVF
97			
2¢	**carmine** *(May 26, 1926)*	32.00	9.00
	v. *CANAL* only	1,500.00	1,200.00
	v1. *ZONE CANAL*	350.00	
	v2. horizontal pair, 1 w/o overprint	3,500.00	

98, 110, 114

		UnFVF	UseFVF
98			
3¢	**red violet** *(June 27, 1925)*	4.50	3.65
	v. *ZONE ZONE*	500.00	500.00
99		UnFVF	UseFVF
5¢	**Prussian blue** *(Jan. 7, 1926)*	4.50	3.65
	v. *CANAL* only	2,250.00	
	v1. *CANAL* inverted overprint	950.00	
	v2. *ZONE* only	2,000.00	
	v3. *ZONE ZONE*	1,100.00	
	v4. *ZONE CANAL*	325.00	
	v5. *CANAL ZONE* inverted overprint	500.00	
	v6. horizontal pair, 1 w/o overprint	3,250.00	
	v7. vertical pair, 1 w/o overprint, 1 w/overprint inverted	2,250.00	
100		UnFVF	UseFVF
10¢	**orange yellow** *(Aug. 1925)*	35.00	12.00
	v. *ZONE* only	3,000.00	
	v1. *ZONE ZONE*	3,000.00	
101		UnFVF	UseFVF
12¢	**maroon** *(Feb. 1926)*	22.50	15.00
	v. *ZONE ZONE*	5,000.00	
102		UnFVF	UseFVF
14¢	**blue** *(Dec. 1928)*	40.00	18.00
103		UnFVF	UseFVF
15¢	**gray black** *(Jan 1926)*	6.50	4.50
	v. ZONE only	3,200.00	
	v1. ZONE ZONE	5,500.00	
104		UnFVF	UseFVF
17¢	**black** *(April 5, 1926)*	4.50	3.25
	v. *CANAL* only	1,700.00	
	v1. *ZONE* only	800.00	
	v2. *ZONE CANAL*	200.00	
105		UnFVF	UseFVF
20¢	**carmine red** *(April 5, 1926)*	7.25	3.25
	v. *CANAL* inverted overprint	3,500.00	
	v1. *ZONE* inverted overprint	3,850.00	
	v2. *ZONE CANAL*	3,500.00	

106

		UnFVF	UseFVF
106			
30¢	**olive brown** *(Dec. 1926)*	6.75	5.00
107		UnFVF	UseFVF
50¢	**gray lilac** *(July 1928)*	250.00	200.00
108		UnFVF	UseFVF
$1	**brown** *(April 1926)*	150.00	75.00

1927. Canal Zone Overprint 3rd Issue *perforated 10.*

109 *"A" with pointed top*

		UnFVF	UseFVF
109			
5¢	**carmine** *(Jan. 1927)*	42.50	11.00
	CANAL only	2,000.00	
	v1. *ZONE* only	2,750.00	
	v2. horizontal pair, 1 w/o overprint	3,000.00	
	Booklet pane of 6	650.00	
110		UnFVF	UseFVF
3¢	**red violet** *(May 9, 1927)*	9.00	6.00
111		UnFVF	UseFVF
10¢	**orange yellow** *(May 9, 1927)*	15.00	7.25

1927-33. Canal Zone Overprint 4th Issue perforated 11 x 10 1/2.

112 *"A" with pointed top*

		UnFVF	UseFVF
112			
1¢	**green** *(June 28, 1927)*	1.75	1.40
	Vertical pair, 1 w/o overprint	3,000.00	
113		UnFVF	UseFVF
2¢	**carmine red** *(June 28, 1927)*	2.50	1.00
	Booklet pane of 6	70.00	
	CANAL double on 2 bottom stamps	875.00	
114		UnFVF	UseFVF
3¢	**red violet,** No. 477 *(Feb. 1931)*	4.00	3.00
	(handmade)	925.00	
115		UnFVF	UseFVF
3¢	**red violet,** No. 518 *(Jan. 14, 1933)*	2.80	.30
	v. *ZONE* only	1,750.00	
	v. *CANAL* only	3,500.00	
	(handmade)	72.00	
116		UnFVF	UseFVF
5¢	**blue** *(Dec. 13, 1927)*	30.00	12.00
117		UnFVF	UseFVF
10¢	**orange yellow** *(July 1930)*	17.50	12.00
118		UnFVF	UseFVF
14¢	**blue** *(Jan. 14, 1933)*	6.00	3.50
	V. *ZONE CANAL*	1,500.00	

Official: Nos. 85, 86, 88-90, 97, 99, 100, 109, 111-114, 116, 117 with perfin P. See note after No. 52.

1924-25. Overprint Postage Due 1st Issue *perforated 11.*

119 *"A" with flat top*

		UnFVF	UseFVF
119			
1¢	**deep rose**	115.00	25.00
120		UnFVF	UseFVF
2¢	**deep claret**	65.00	11.00
121		UnFVF	UseFVF
10¢	**deep claret**	250.00	55.00

1924-25. Overprint Postage Due 2nd Issue *perforated 11.*

122 *"A" with pointed top*

		UnFVF	UseFVF
122			
1¢	**deep rose**	9.00	4.50
	ZONE ZONE	1,250.00	
123		UnFVF	UseFVF
2¢	**deep rose**	18.00	5.00
	ZONE ZONE	1,500.00	
124		UnFVF	UseFVF
10¢	**deep rose**	135.00	24.00
	v. vertical pair, 1 w/o overprint	1,200.00	
	v1. double overprint	275.00	

1925. Overprint Postage Due Issue

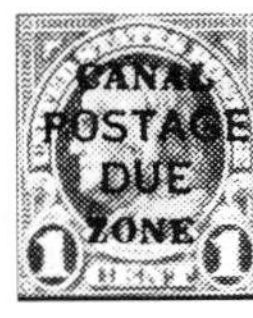
125

		UnFVF	UseFVF
125			
1¢	**green**	95.00	18.00
126		UnFVF	UseFVF
2¢	**carmine,** overprinted blue	27.50	7.50
127		UnFVF	UseFVF
10¢	**orange yellow**	55.00	12.00
	v. *POSTAGE DUE* double overprint	450.00	
	v1. *POSTAG*	450.00	
	v2. *POSTAG* double overprint	3,250.00	

1926. 150th Anniversary Declaration of Independence Issue

128 *Liberty Bell*

		UnFVF	UseFVF
128			
2¢	**carmine red**	4.75	3.50
	Plate block of 6	80.00	
	FDC *(July 6, 1926)*		45.00
	On cover		5.00

Note: Normal spacing between CANAL and ZONE of the overprint is 4.75-5mm. A few first day covers were canceled by favor on July 4, 1926, a Sunday. Price $65.00.

1928-40. First Definitive Issue

129, 257 *Maj. Gen. William C. Gorgas*

		UnFVF	UseFVF
129			
1¢	**green** dry printings	.25	.20
	v. yellow green to green, wet (early) printings	.25	.20
	v1. green, dull gum (1977)	.40	.20
	Plate block of 6	.50	
	FDC *(Oct. 3, 1928)*		11.00
	On postcard		1.75

Coil: See No. 257.

130 Maj. Gen. George Washington Goethals

		UnFVF	UseFVF
130			
2¢	**rose red**	.25	.20
	Plate block of 6	1.25	
	FDC *(Oct. 1, 1928)*		10.00
	On cover		1.00
	Booklet pane of 6	14.00	30.00

131 *Maj. Gen. George W. Goethals*

		UnFVF	UseFVF
131			
3¢	**violet** dry printings	.20	.20
	v. red violet to deep violet, wet (early) printings	.20	.20
	v1. violet, dull gum (1977)	.45	.20
	Plate block of 6	1.10	
	FDC *(Aug. 15, 1934)*		2.50
	On cover		.50
	Booklet pane of 6, handmade, perforated margins	165.00	
	Booklet pane of 6, machine made	35.00	30.00

Coil: See No. 230.

132 *Gaillard Cut. Issuance coincided with the 20th Anniversary of the openings of the Panama Canal but it is not a commemorative as it was intended to pay the domestic first class letter rate for the long term.*

132		UnFVF	UseFVF
5¢	**blue**	1.10	.40
	deep blue	1.10	.40
	Plate block of 6	8.25	
	FDC *(June 25, 1929)*		6.00
	On cover		3.50

133, 258 *Maj. Gen. Harry F. Hodges*

133		UnFVF	UseFVF
10¢	**orange** dry printings	.35	.25
	v. deep orange, wet (early) printings	.35	.25
	Plate block of 6	4.75	
	FDC *(Jan. 11, 1932)*		60.00
	On cover		3.00

Coil: See No. 258.

134 *Lt. Col. David DuBose Gaillard*

134		UnFVF	UseFVF
12¢	**brown purple** dry printings	1.00	.75
	v. purple brown, wet (early) printings	.80	.60
	Plate block of 6	10.00	
	FDC *(July 1, 1929)*		65.00
	On cover		8.00

135 *Maj. Gen. William L. Sibert*

135		UnFVF	UseFVF
14¢	**gray** dry printings	.75	.45
	dark gray, wet (early) printings	.75	.65
	Plate block of 6	7.00	
	FDC *(Jan. 11, 1932)*		50.00
	On cover		6.00

136 *Jackson Smith*

136		UnFVF	UseFVF
15¢	**gray** dry printings	.75	.45
	v. dark gray, wet (early) printings	.75	.65
	Plate block of 6	7.00	
	FDC *(Jan. 11, 1932)*		50.00
	On cover		6.00

137 Rear Adm. Harry H. Rousseau

137		UnFVF	UseFVF
20¢	**dark brown** dry printings	.95	.30
	v. olive brown to deep brown, wet (early) printings	1.00	.30
	v1. black brown, dull gum (1977)	1.75	.30
	Plate block of 6	6.00	
	FDC *(Jan. 11, 1932)*		50.00
	On cover		6.00

138 *Col. Sydney B. Williamson*

138		UnFVF	UseFVF
30¢	**black** dry printings	1.40	.65
	v. brown black, wet (early) printings	1.10	.55
	v1. black, dull gum (1977)	2.25	.65
	Plate block of 6	15.00	
	FDC *(April 15, 1940)*		9.00
	On cover		7.00

139 *Joseph C.S. Blackburn*

139		UnFVF	UseFVF
50¢	**dark lilac** dry printings	2.25	.60
	v. rose lilac, dry printings	2.25	.60
	v1. lilac, wet (early) printings	1.50	.50
	v2. rose lilac, wet (early) printings	2.00	.50
	v3. lilac, dull gum (1977)	5.00	.60
	v4 rose lilac, dull gum (1977)	3.50	.60
	Plate block of 6	17.00	
	FDC *(July 1, 1929)*		120.00
	On cover		16.00

Note: Used copies of the dull gum printings of this series cannot normally be distinguished from the dry printings of the same stamp issued prior to 1977.

Officials: Nos. 129-139 with perfin P. See note after No. 52.

1929-31. Canal Zone Overprint Airmail Issue

AIR MAIL 140, 143

10 c

140	UnFVF	UseFVF
10¢ on 50¢ red lilac *(Dec. 31, 1929)*	9.00	6.50

15 141 *Flag of 5 with serif*

141	UnFVF	UseFVF
15¢ on 1¢ green, blue overprint *(April 1, 1929)*	10.00	6.00

15 142 *Flag of 5 curved*

142	UnFVF	UseFVF
15¢ on 1¢ green, blue overprint *(March 1931)*	125.00	100.00

143	UnFVF	UseFVF
20¢ on 2¢ rose red *(Dec. 31, 1929)*	6.00	2.50
v. dropped *2* in overprint	90.00	75.00

144

144	UnFVF	UseFVF
25¢ on 2¢ rose red, blue overprint *(Jan. 11, 1929)*	5.00	3.75

Officials: Nos. 140, 143, 143v., 144 with perfin P. See note after No. 52.

1929-30. Canal Zone Postage Due Overprint Issue

145 *Postage due overprint*

145	UnFVF	UseFVF
1¢ on 5¢ blue *(March 20, 1930)*	4.50	2.75
V. W/o *POSTAGE DUE*	1,250.00	
146	UnFVF	UseFVF
2¢ on 5¢ blue *(Oct. 18, 1930)*	7.50	3.75
147	UnFVF	UseFVF
5¢ on 5¢ blue *(Dec. 1, 1930),* horizontal bars of overprint omitted	7.50	4.00
148	UnFVF	UseFVF
10¢ on 5¢ blue *(Dec. 16, 1929)*	7.50	4.00

1931-49. Canal Zone Airmail Issue

149 *Plane over canal*

		MNHVF	UseVF
149			
4¢	**rose purple**	1.15	.90
	Plate block of 6	6.00	
	FDC *(Jan. 3, 1949)*		1.75
	On postcard		2.25
150		MNHVF	UseVF
5¢	**yellow green**	.65	.35
	green	.60	.30
	Plate block of 6	6.00	
	FDC *(Nov. 18, 1931)*		9.00
	On cover		1.10
151		MNHVF	UseVF
6¢	**yellow brown**	.80	.35
	Plate block of 6	6.00	
	FDC *(Feb. 15, 1946)*		1.75
	On cover		1.00
152		MNHVF	UseVF
10¢	**orange**	1.35	.35
	red orange	1.00	.30
	Plate block of 6	12.50	
	FDC *(Nov. 18, 1931)*		8.50
	On cover		.90
153		MNHVF	UseVF
15¢	**blue**	1.25	.30
	light blue	1.25	.30
	Plate block of 6	16.00	
	FDC *(Nov. 18, 1931)*		18.00
	On cover		1.25

Note: Blue green shades have been reported but are believed to be color changelings.

154 *Plane over canal*

		MNHVF	UseVF
154			
20¢	**red violet**	2.25	.30
	deep violet	2.25	.30
	Plate block of 6	24.00	
	FDC *(Nov. 18, 1931)*		32.00
	On cover		1.75
155		MNHVF	UseVF
30¢	**rose lake**	3.50	1.15
	dull rose	3.50	1.15
	Plate block of 6	27.00	
	FDC *(July 15, 1941)*		20.00
	On cover		7.50
156		MNHVF	UseVF
40¢	**yellow**	3.25	1.25
	lemon yellow	5.00	1.75
	Plate block of 6	36.00	
	FDC *(July 15, 1941)*		100.00
	On cover		22.00
157		MNHVF	UseVF
$1	**black**	9.00	1.50
	Plate block of 6	95.00	
	FDC *(Nov. 18, 1931)*		180.00
	On cover		75.00

Officials: Nos. 150-157 with perfin P. See note after No. 52.

1932-41. Canal Zone Postage Due Issue

158-162

		UnFVF	UseFVF
158			
1¢	**claret**	.20	.20
159		UnFVF	UseFVF
2¢	**claret**	.20	.20
160		UnFVF	UseFVF
5¢	**claret**	.50	.35
161		UnFVF	UseFVF
10¢	**claret**	2.00	1.75
162		UnFVF	UseFVF
15¢	**claret** *(April 21, 1941)*	1.50	1.50

1939 25th Anniversary of Canal Issue *Perforated 11.*

163 *Balboa, June 1912, looking east from Sosa Hill; Administrative Building Site*

		UnFVF	UseFVF
163			
1¢	**light green**	.60	.30
	Plate block of 6	14.00	
	FDC *(Aug. 15, 1939)*		1.75
	On postcard		2.25

164 *Balboa, June 1936, view from Sosa, completed Administrative Building and Prado*

		UnFVF	UseFVF
164			
2¢	**carmine**	.65	.35
	Plate block of 6	15.00	
	FDC *(Aug. 15, 1939)*		2.50
	On cover		2.25

165 *Gaillard (Culebra) Cut, June 1913, deepest excavation in Canal*

		UnFVF	UseFVF
165			
3¢	**deep violet**	.40	.20
	Plate block of 6	12.00	
	FDC *(Aug. 15, 1939)*		1.25
	On cover		1.10

166 *Gaillard (Culebra) Cut, 1921, Gold and Contractor's Hills*

166		UnFVF	UseFVF
5¢	**deep blue**	2.75	.90
	Plate block of 6	18.00	
	FDC *(Aug. 15, 1939)*		2.75
	On cover		5.00

167 *Bas Obispo, Jan. 1910, view South from Panama Railroad relocation*

167		UnFVF	UseFVF
6¢	**red orange**	2.60	3.00
	Plate block of 6	48.00	
	FDC *(Aug. 15, 1939)*		5.00
	On cover		8.00

168 *Bas Obispo, July 11, 1934, USS Houston in completed cut*

168		UnFVF	UseFVF
7¢	**black**	2.50	3.00
	Plate block of 6	50.00	
	FDC *(Aug. 15, 1939)*		6.00
	On cover		10.00

169 *Gatun Lower Locks, April 15, 1911, view South from north end*

169		UnFVF	UseFVF
8¢	**green**	4.50	3.75
	Plate block of 6	60.00	
	FDC *(Aug. 15, 1939)*		7.00
	On cover		10.00

170 *Gatun Lower Locks, June 19, 1924, view of new approach*

170		UnFVF	UseFVF
10¢	**bright blue**	3.25	2.75
	Plate block of 6	60.00	
	FDC *(Aug. 15, 1939)*		5.50
	On cover		6.00

171 *Gaillard (Culebra) Cut, May 20, 1913, Pioneer Cut*

171		UnFVF	UseFVF
11¢	**blue green**	8.00	10.00
	Plate block of 6	130.00	
	FDC *(Aug. 15, 1939)*		11.00
	On cover		25.00

172 *Gaillard (Culebra) Cut, Aug. 16, 1930, SS Santa Clara*

172		UnFVF	UseFVF
12¢	**lake**	10.00	11.00
	Plate block of 6	105.00	
	FDC *(Aug. 15, 1939)*		10.00
	On cover		15.00

173 *Gamboa, July 1913, Dike, Bas Obispo Cut, Rio Chagres Bridge*

173		UnFVF	UseFVF
14¢	**dark violet**	8.50	9.50
	Plate block of 6	130.00	
	FDC *(Aug. 15, 1939)*		9.00
	On cover		20.00

174 *Gamboa, Dec. 7, 1922, ships at Rio Chagres crossing*

174		UnFVF	UseFVF
15¢	**olive green**	11.00	4.50
	Plate block of 6	135.00	
	FDC *(Aug. 15, 1939)*		10.00
	On cover		5.00

175 *Pedro Miquel Locks, June 3, 1912, construction of gates*

175		UnFVF	UseFVF
18¢	**rose carmine**	11.00	7.00
	Plate block of 6	165.00	
	FDC *(Aug. 15, 1939)*		15.00
	On cover		12.00

176 *Pedro Miquel Locks, July 16, 1927, SS Duchesa d' Aosta, president Polk*

176		UnFVF	UseFVF
20¢	**brown**	13.00	5.50
	Plate block of 6	200.00	
	FDC *(Aug. 15, 1939)*		10.00
	On cover		8.00

177 *Gatun Spillway Dam, Feb. 5, 1913, Crest Dam construction*

177		UnFVF	UseFVF
25¢	**orange**	20.00	22.00
	Plate block of 6	275.00	
	FDC *(Aug. 15, 1939)*		22.50
	On cover		45.00

178 *Gatun Spillway Dam, May 1922, Crest Dam in operation*

178		UnFVF	UseFVF
50¢	**brown purple**	24.00	5.50
	Plate block of 6	240.00	
	FDC *(Aug. 15, 1939)*		20.00
	On cover		40.00

Note: *Some of the 163-178 series, such as the 11¢, paid no specific rate and are found on cover only in combination with other stamps. Postally used copies thus sell for more than copies removed from First Day covers.*

Official: Nos. 163-166, 170, 172, 174-176 with perfin P. See note after No. 52.

1939. Airmail Issue for the 25th anniversary of the Canal opening.

179 *Douglas plane over Sosa Hill*

179		UnFVF	UseFVF
5¢	**greenish black** *(July 15, 1939)*	4.75	3.75

180 *Planes and map of Central America*

180		UnFVF	UseFVF
10¢	**red violet** *(July 15, 1939)*	4.75	3.75

181 *Sikorsky S.42 flying boat and scene near Ft. Amador*

181		UnFVF	UseFVF
15¢	**yellow brown** *(July 15, 1939)*	4.25	1.50

182 *Sikorsky S.42 flying boat at Cristobal Harbor*

182		UnFVF	UseFVF
25¢	**deep blue** *(July 15, 1939)*	15.00	10.00

183 *Sikorsky S.42 flying boat over Gaillard Cut*

183		UnFVF	UseFVF
30¢	**carmine red** *(July 15, 1939)*	12.00	9.75

184 *Sikorsky S.42 flying boat landing*

184		UnFVF	UseFVF
$1	**green** *(July 15, 1939)*	35.00	30.00

Official: Nos. 179, 180, 181, 183, 184 with perfin P. See note below No. 52.

1939. Presidential Series Overprint Issue *perforated 11 x 10 1/2.*

185

185		UnFVF	UseFVF
1/2¢	**red orange,** U.S. No. 524, *(Sept. 1, 1939)*	.25	.20
186		UnFVF	UseFVF
1 1/2¢	**yellow brown,** U.S. No. 526, *(Sept. 1, 1939)*	.30	.25

1941. Official Overprint Issue Official stamps. Definitive issues overprinted in black by Panama Canal Press with OFFICIAL PANAMA CANAL. Type I: three lines on small stamps, Nos. 129/139 (PANAMA 10mm long), two lines on large horizontal stamps (PANAMA CANAL 19 1/2mm long).

187

187		MNHVF	UseVF
1¢	**green**	3.75	.40
188		MNHVF	UseVF
3¢	**red violet**	6.00	.75
189		MNHVF	UseVF
5¢	**blue**		32.50
190		MNHVF	UseVF
10¢	**yellow orange**	10.00	2.25
191		MNHVF	UseVF
15¢	**gray black**	18.00	3.00
192		MNHVF	UseVF
20¢	**sepia**	22.50	2.75
193		MNHVF	UseVF
50¢	**red lilac**	45.00	7.50
	v. *PANAMA* 9mm, *(Sept. 22, 1941)*		800.00

1941. Official Airmail Issue overprint on No.150-175. Type II: PANAMA CANAL is 17mm long.

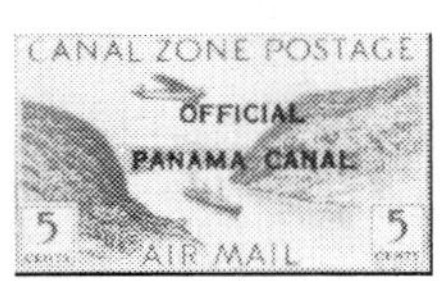
194

194		MNHVF	UseVF
5¢	**light green**	5.50	2.70
	v. Type II, *(Sept. 22, 1941)*		180.00
195		MNHVF	UseVF
6¢	**yellow brown** *(Nov. 15, 1948)*	12.50	9.00
	v. inverted overprint		2,500.00
196		MNHVF	UseVF
10¢	**orange**	8.50	3.50
	v. Type II, *(Sept. 22, 1941),*		325.00
197		MNHVF	UseVF
15¢	**light blue**	15.00	2.00
198		MNHVF	UseVF
20¢	**red violet**	18.00	4.75
	v. Type II, *(Sept. 22, 1941),*		180.00
199		MNHVF	UseVF
30¢	**carmine lake** *(May 5, 1942)*	30.00	9.00
	v. Type II, *(Sept. 22, 1941)*		55.00
200		MNHVF	UseVF
40¢	**yellow**	30.00	12.00
	v. Type II, *(Sept. 22, 1941),*		180.00
201		MNHVF	UseVF
$1	**black**	35.00	18.00

The use of official postage was restricted to departments and divisions of The Panama Canal, the Panama Railroad and certain other U.S. agencies in the Canal Zone. The stamps were used on official correspondence which did not enjoy the franking privilege, such as ordinary letters to foreign countries, certain official matter dispatched via parcel post and all airmail except official post office mail. Official stamps were also used to pay return receipt fees on registered official mail. First Class mail was almost always dispatched via airmail, and airmail official stamps are therefore not uncommon on cover. Ordinary official postage, however, was nearly always used on parcel post mail and covers are very rare.

Nos. 187-201 and 207 were sold to the public cancelled with Balboa Heights, Canal Zone between wavy lines until Dec. 31, 1951, when use of official stamps was discontinued. Mint stamps were available to the public at face for three months beginning Jan. 2, 1952. Used prices are for cancelled-to-order stamps; postally used copies are worth more. To facilitate overprinting, all sheet margins were removed and no plate numbers are known to exist.

1946-49. Issue

202 *Maj. Gen. George W. Davis, first governor*

202		MNHVF	UseVF
1/2¢	**vermilion**	.40	.25
	Plate block of 6	2.00	
	FDC *(Aug. 16, 1948)*		1.10
	On cover		1.00

203 *C. E. Magoon, second governor*

		MNHVF	UseVF
203			
1 1/2¢	**chocolate**	.45	.25
	Plate block of 6	2.25	
	FDC *(Aug. 16, 1948)*		1.25
	On cover		1.50

204 *T. Roosevelt*

		MNHVF	UseVF
204			
2¢	**light rose carmine,** dry printing	.20	.20
	v. rose carmine, wet (early) printing	.20	.20
	v1. dark rose carmine, dull gum (1977)	.40	.20
	v2. light rose carmine, dull gum	.25	.20
	Plate block of 6	.75	
	FDC *(Oct. 27, 1949)*		.80
	On cover		1.00

205, 234, 263 *John F. Stevens*

		MNHVF	UseVF
205			
5¢	**dark blue,** dry printing	.40	.20
	Prussian blue, wet (early) printing	.45	.20
	Plate block of 6	2.75	
	FDC *(April 25, 1946)*		1.00
	On cover		2.25

No.205 may have straight edges. For coil see No. 234.

206, 259 *John F. Wallace*

		MNHVF	UseVF
206			
25¢	**green,** dry printing	1.00	.50
	yellow green, wet (early) printing	2.50	.80
	Plate block of 6	7.50	
	FDC *(Aug. 16, 1948)*		3.75
	On cover		9.00

1947. Official Stamp Issue

207 *No. 205 with overprint 187, OFFICIAL/PANAMA/CANAL.*

		MNHVF	UseVF
207			
5¢	**Prussian blue**	10.00	4.00
	On cover		80.00

See note after No. 201.

1948. Canal Biological Area Issue
celebrated the 25th anniversary of the establishment of the Canal Zone Biological area.

208 *Barro Colorado Island and coatimundi. The Island, declared a biological area by Gov. Jay Johnson Morrow in 1923, was administered while under United States control by the Smithsonian Institution. The Island is in Gatun Lake, formed by the damming of the Chagres River during the building of the Canal.*

		MNHVF	UseVF
208			
10¢	**black**	1.10	1.00
	Plate block of 6	7.50	
	FDC *(April 17, 1948)*		2.75
	On cover		4.00

1949. Gold Rush Centennial Issue

209 *Forty-niners arriving at Chagres*

		MNHVF	UseVF
209			
3¢	**deep blue**	.40	.30
	Plate block of 6	4.50	
	FDC *(June 1, 1949)*		1.00
	On cover		2.00

210 *Up the Chagres River by Bungo*

		MNHVF	UseVF
210			
6¢	**deep violet**	.55	.35
	Plate block of 6	6.00	
	FDC *(June 1, 1949)*		1.00
	On cover		2.50

211 *Las Cruces Trail to Panama City*

		MNHVF	UseVF
211			
12¢	**blue green**	1.25	1.00
	Plate block of 6	16.00	
	FDC *(June 1, 1949)*		1.80
	On cover		4.00

212 *Departure for San Francisco*

		MNHVF	UseVF
212			
18¢	**deep magneta**	1.85	1.60
	Plate block of 6	20.00	
	FDC *(June 1, 1949)*		3.00
	On cover		6.00

1951. West Indian Canal Workers Issue

213 *West Indian workers in Gaillard (Culebra) Cut. During the construction period of 1904-14, 31,071 out of 45,107 workers brought to the Isthmus by the Isthmian Canal Commission were from the West Indies, and additional thousands came on their own.*

		MNHVF	UseVF
213			
10¢	**carmine**	2.00	1.60
	Plate block of 6	25.00	
	FDC *(Aug. 15, 1951)*		2.75
	On cover		5.00

1951-63. Airmail Issue *perforated 11.*

214-224 *Winged Sticker and Globe*

		MNHVF	UseVF
214			
4¢	**rose purple** *(July 16, 1951)*	1.00	.30
	v. wet print	1.25	
215			
5¢	**yellow green** *(Aug. 16, 1958)*	1.25	.60
216			
6¢	**brown** *(July 16, 1951)*	.75	.30
	v. wet print	.90	.30

		MNHVF	UseVF
217			
7¢	**olive** *(Aug. 16, 1958)*	1.40	.55
217A		MNHVF	UseVF
8¢	**carmine** *(Jan. 7, 1963)*	.70	.30
218		MNHVF	UseVF
10¢	**red orange** *(July 16, 1951)*	1.35	.45
	v. wet print	2.00	.50
219		MNHVF	UseVF
15¢	**dark purple** *(Aug. 18, 1958)*	4.75	2.00
220		MNHVF	UseVF
21¢	**blue**	10.00	4.00
	v. wet print	15.00	5.00
221		MNHVF	UseVF
25¢	**orange yellow** *(Aug. 16, 1958)*	14.00	2.75
222		MNHVF	UseVF
31¢	**deep carmine**	10.00	3.75
	v. vertical pair	350.00	
223		MNHVF	UseVF
35¢	**dark blue** *(Aug. 16, 1958)*	10.25	1.50
224		MNHVF	UseVF
80¢	**gray black** *(July 16, 1951)*	6.50	1.80
	v. wet print	12.00	1.60

Beginning June 1954, Canal Zone stamps were printed by the dry process on pre-gummed paper instead of the wet intaglio method previously employed. The same plates were used, but due to the absence of paper shrinkage and other factors, the size of the sheets is slightly larger than wet process stamps.

1955. Panama Railroad Centennial Issue

225 *Panama Railroad*

		MNHVF	UseVF
225			
3¢	**dark red violet** *(Jan. 28, 1955)*	.70	.60

1957. Gorgas Hospital Issue celebrates the 75th anniversary of the institution. *Perforated 11.*

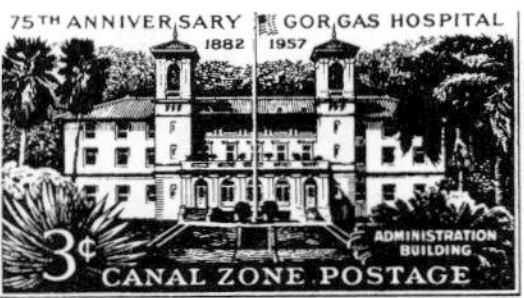

226 *Gorgas Hospital Adminstration Building with Ancon Hill in background*

		MNHVF	UseVF
226			
3¢	**black on turquoise green** *(Nov. 17, 1957)*	.40	.50

1958. SS Ancon Issue *perforated 11.*

227 *SS Ancon Panama Line*

		MNHVF	UseVF
227			
4¢	**turquoise blue** *(Aug. 30, 1958)*	.40	.35

1958. Roosevelt Centennial Issue *perforated 11.*

228 *Theodore Roosevelt medal (reverse and obverse), map of Canal*

		MNHVF	UseVF
228			
4¢	**brown** *(Nov. 15, 1958)*	.70	.40

1960. BSA 50th Anniversary Issue

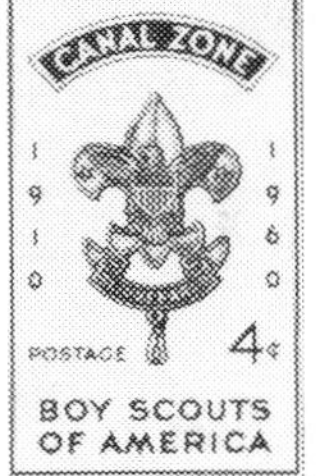

229 *First Class Boy Scout Badge and Canal Zone Community strip*

		MNHVF	UseVF
229			
4¢	**deep blue, carmel and deep ochre** *(Feb. 8, 1960)*	.55	.50

1960. Goethals Coil Issue *perforated 10 horizontal.*

		MNHVF	UseVF
230			
3¢	**violet** *(Nov. 1, 1960)*	.25	.20

1960. Administration Building Issue *perforated 11.*

231 *Administration building*

		MNHVF	UseVF
231			
4¢	**deep rose lilac** *(Nov. 1, 1960)*	.25	.20

1960. Definitive Coil Issue *perforated 10 vertically.*

		MNHVF	UseVF
232			
4¢	**dull rose lilac**	.30	.25

1960. US Army Caribbean School Issue Airmail, *perforated 11.*

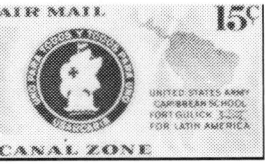

233 *Emblem*

		MNHVF	UseVF
233			
15¢	**red and deep blue** *(Nov. 21, 1961)*	1.50	.90

1961. John F. Stevens Coil Issue *perforated 10 horizontally.*

234, 263 *John F. Stevens*

		MNHVF	UseVF
234			
5¢	**Prussian blue** *(Feb. 10, 1962)*	.40	.35

1962. Girl Scouts USA 59th Anniversary Issue perforated 11.

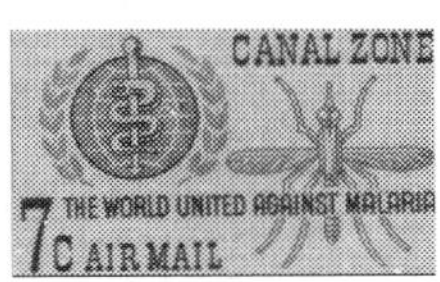

235 *Badge, tents on Gatun Lake*

		MNHVF	UseVF
235			
4¢	**turquoise blue, dark green and ochre** *(March 12, 1962)*	.40	.30

1962. Malaria Eradication Issue *perforated 11.*

236

		MNHVF	UseVF
236			
7¢	**black on lemon** *(Sept. 24, 1962)*	.70	.60

1962. Thatcher Ferry Bridge Issue *perforated 11.*

237 *Thatcher Ferry Bridge over Panama Canal and map*

		MNHVF	UseVF
237			
4¢	**black and silver** *(Oct. 12, 1962)*	.35	.30
	t. Bridge omitted	6,500.00	

No. 238 not assigned.

1962. Alliance for Progress Issue Airmail, *perforated 11.*

239 *Alliance emblem*

		MNHVF	UseVF
239			
15¢	**gray, blue and green** *(Aug. 17, 1963)*	1.50	.90

1963. Panama Canal 50th Anniversary Issue *perforated 11.*

240 *Cristobal*

		MNHVF	UseVF
240			
6¢	**green** *(Aug. 15, 1964)*	.50	.45

241 *Gatun Locks*

		MNHVF	UseVF
241			
8¢	**carmine** *(Aug. 15, 1964)*	.55	.45

242 *Madden Dam*

		MNHVF	UseVF
242			
15¢	**blue** *(Aug. 15, 1964)*	1.75	1.00

243 *Gaillard Cut*

		MNHVF	UseVF
243			
20¢	**reddish purple** *(Aug. 15, 1964)*	2.50	1.20

244 *Miraflores Locks*

		MNHVF	UseVF
244			
30¢	**chocolate** *(Aug. 15, 1964)*	3.50	3.00

245 *Balboa*

		MNHVF	UseVF
245			
80¢	**bistre** *(Aug. 15, 1964)*	5.50	4.50

1964-74. Seal and Jet Airmail Issue *perforated 11.*

246-253 *Canal Zone seal and jet plane*

		MNHVF	UseVF
246			
6¢	**green and black**	.50	.40
247			
8¢	**carmine and black**	.60	.25
248			
10¢	**salmon and black,** *(March 15, 1968)*	.45	.25
	Booklet pane of 4	5.00	
	Single *(Feb. 18, 1970)*	1.80	
248A			
11¢	**drab and black,** *(Sept. 24, 1971)*	.60	.30
	Booklet pane of 4	4.00	
248B			
13¢	**light green and black.** *(Feb. 11, 1974)*	1.25	.50
	Booklet pane of 4	6.75	
249			
15¢	**blue and black**	.75	.45
250			
20¢	**purple and black**	.90	.45
251			
25¢	**light green and black,** *(March 15, 1968)*	1.00	1.00
252			
30¢	**brown and black**	1.50	.60
253			
80¢	**bistre and black**	4.00	1.75

1965-74. Airmail Issue

255 *Goethals Memorial in in Balboa, Canal Zone*

		MNHVF	UseVF
255			
6¢	**green and blue** *(March 15, 1968)*	.45	.20

1968. Issue

256 *Ruins of Ft. San Lorenzo on bluff overlooking Chagres River at its junction with the Atlantic Ocean*

		MNHVF	UseVF
256			
8¢	**multicolored**	.45	.35
	Plate block of 4	2.75	
	FDC *(July 14, 1971)*		.90
	On cover		1.00

1975. Coil Issue *perforated 10 vertically.*

257 *Maj. Gen. William Crawford Gorgas*

		MNHVF	UseVF
257			
1¢	**green**	.20	.20
	FDC *(Feb. 14, 1975)*		.70
	On cover		1.00
	Pair	.35	.40
	Joint line pair	.90	1.35

258 *Maj. Gen. Harry Foote Hodges*

		MNHVF	UseVF
258			
10¢	**orange**	.70	.45

	FDC *(Feb. 14, 1975)*		.90
	On cover		1.25
	Pair	1.50	1.35
	Joint line pair	4.25	8.00

259 *John F. Wallace*

259		MNHVF	UseVF
25¢	**dark yellow green**	2.50	2.75
	FDC *(Feb. 14, 1975)*		2.50
	On cover		7.00
	Pair	4.00	8.00
	Joint line pair	15.00	25.00

1976. Regular Issue *perforated 11.*

260 *Cascadas,* 15 cubic yard dipper dredge built by Bucyrus Co. of New York, joined the digging fleet of Panama Canal on Oct. 31, 1915, established a world record for a day's work by an excavating machine in hard material Feb. 18, 1916 when she excavated and loaded into dump scows 23,305 cubic yards of rock and sand.

260		MNHVF	UseVF
13¢	**blue, black and green**	.45	.25
	Plate block of 4	2.25	
	FDC *(Feb. 23, 1976)*		.90
	On cover		.80
	Booklet pane of 4	3.00	2.75
	FDC booklet pane of 4 *(April 19, 1976)*		4.00

All copies of the regular issue and booklet panes of #260 have dull gum as issued. Two positions of the booklet panes exist with colored bars in the tab. Price 3x normal.

1976. Airmail Issue paid the postcard rate to overseas (not U.S.) locations. *Perforated 11.*

261

261		MNHVF	UseVF
22¢	**violet and black**	.90	2.50
	Plate block of 4	3.75	
	FDC *(May 10, 1976)*		2.65
	On postcard		9.00

All copies have dull gum as issued.

262		MNHVF	UseVF
35¢	**salmon and black**	1.25	2.50
	Plate block of 4	4.25	
	FDC *(May 10, 1976)*		2.75
	On cover		6.00

All copies have dull gum as issued.

1976. John F. Stevens Issue *perforated 11 x 10 1/2.*

263 *John F. Stevens*

263		MNHVF	UseVF
5¢	**dark blue** *(May, 1976)*	.30	.45
	v. tagged	10.00	17.00
	On cover		.75
	Plate block of 4	3.25	
	Plate block of 4, tagged	100.00	

There were 3 printings of #263. The first (1976) and third (1979) have dull gum, the second (1978) has shiny gum. Only the third printing was tagged. Exact issue dates are unknown.

1978. Regular Issue *perforated 11.*

264 *Towing locomotive ("mule") used to guide ships through the locks*

264		MNHVF	UseVF
15¢	**deep green and blue green**	.50	.30
	Plate block of 4	2.25	
	FDC *(Oct. 25, 1978)*		.90
	On cover		1.25

All copies have dull gum as issued.

Envelopes and Wrappers

1916. Stamped Envelope Issue

E1		UnFVF	UseFVF
1¢	**green and black**	15.00	11.50
	entire (350,000)	110.00	50.00
	t. head & *CANAL ZONE*	2,000.00	2,000.00
	t1. frame only	1,500.00	2,500.00

E2		UnFVF	UseFVF
2¢	**carmine and black**	12.50	5.50
	entire (incl. E2a (1,512,000)	100.00	35.00
	a. red & black	12.50	5.50
	entire	85.00	45.00
	t. head & *CANAL ZONE*	1,000.00	2,000.00
	t1. frame only, red	750.00	
	t2. frame double inverted, carmine	2,500.00	2,250.00

1918. Overprinted Panama Registration Envelope Issue

E3		UnFVF	UseFVF
10¢ on 5¢	**black and red**	125.00	85.00
	entire, size 6 (25,000)	1,500.00	2,000.00
	entire, size 8 (10,000)	1,100.00	2,000.00

1921. 100th Anniversary of Independence from Spain Issue

E4		UnFVF	UseFVF
1¢	**green**	150.00	100.00
	entire (20,681)	700.00	400.00

E5		UnFVF	UseFVF
2¢	**red**	40.00	25.00
	entire (30,000)	275.00	140.00

1923. Arms of Panama Issue

E6		UnFVF	UseFVF
2¢	**carmine**	60.00	40.00
	entire (46,041)	175.00	125.00

1924. Embossed Stamped Envelopes Issue

E7		UnFVF	UseFVF
1¢	**green**	5.00	3.00
	entire (50,000)	40.00	19.00

E8		UnFVF	UseFVF
2¢	**carmine**	5.00	2.75
	entire (100,000)	40.00	19.00

1924. Seal of Canal Zone Issue

E9		UnFVF	UseFVF
1¢	**green** *(Oct. 24, 1924)*	2.00	1.00
	entire, size 6 (205,000)	28.50	18.50

E10		UnFVF	UseFVF
2¢	**carmine** *(Oct. 24, 1924)*	.75	.30
	entire, size 6 (1,636,109)	25.00	10.50
	entire, size 8 (361,549)	25.00	10.50

1928. Stamped Envelope Overprint Issue Regular stamped envelope E10 overprinted with horizontal blue and red bars across face and box at lower left with nine lines of instructions. Additional stamps were required for airmail transmission.

E11		UnFVF	UseFVF
2¢	**red** E10, *(May 21, 1928)* entire, size 6 *(10,000)*	125.00	50.00
	entire, size 8 (5,000)	125.00	50.00

1929. Stamped Envelope Overprint Issue Regular stamped envelope E10 overprinted with horizontal blue and red bars and "VIA AIR MAIL" in blue, centered; no box of instructions.

E12		UnFVF	UseFVF
2¢	**red** E10, *(Jan. 11, 1929)* entire, size 6 *(10,000)*	150.00	85.00
	v. inscription at left, entire size 6 (45,000), *Feb. 7, 1929*	105.00	85.00
	entire, size 8 (15,200), *(Feb. 7, 1929)*	150.00	65.00

1932. Stamped Envelope Definitive Issue

E13		UnFVF	UseFVF
1¢	**green** *(April 8, 1932)*	.20	.15
	entire, size 5 (400,000)	1.50	.70
	entire, size 8 (500,000)	1.25	.70
	entire, size 13 (400,000)	1.10	.40

E14		UnFVF	UseFVF
2¢	**carmine** *(April 8, 1932)*	.30	.30
	entire, size 5 (35,000)	1.80	.70
	entire, size 7 1/2 (4,000)	6.75	6.25
	entire, size 8	1.00	.70
	entire, size 13	.85	.60

1932. Stamped Envelope Overprint Issue

E15		UnFVF	UseFVF
3¢ on 2¢	**carmine** E10, numerals 3mm high, *(July 20, 1932)*	17.50	7.50
	entire, size 8 (20,000)	225.00	125.00

E16		UnFVF	UseFVF
3¢ on 2¢	**carmine** E14, numerals 5mm high, *(July 20, 1932)*	2.40	2.00
	entire, size 5 (210,000)	6.50	6.50
	entire, size 7 1/2 (40,000)	10.50	6.75
	entire, size 8 (40,000)	8.75	6.00
	entire, size 13 (30,000)	12.00	6.00

1934. Stamped Envelope Overprint Issue

E17		UnFVF	UseFVF
3¢ on 2¢	**carmine** E10, 3 w/serifs in violet, *(Jan. 17, 1934)*	125.00	65.00
	entire, size 6 (8,000)	275.00	750.00

E18		UnFVF	UseFVF
3¢ on 2¢	**carmine** E14, 3 w/serifs in violet, *(Jan. 17, 1934)*	22.50	12.50
	entire, size 5 (5,000)	300.00	150.00
	entire, size 7 1/2 (5,500)	300.00	150.00
	entire, size 13 (12,500)	300.00	150.00

1934. Stamped Envelope Issue

E19		UnFVF	UseFVF
3¢	**purple** *(June 18, 1934)*	.20	.12
	entire, size 8	2.40	1.00
	entire, size 13	2.40	1.00

1949. Stamped Envelope Airmail Issue DC-4.

E20		MNHVF	UseVF
6¢	**blue** *(Jan. 3, 1949)*	.40	.18
	entire	5.00	2.80

1958. Stamped Envelope Issue

E21		MNHVF	UseVF
4¢	**blue** *(Nov. 1, 1958)*	.30	.15
	entire, size 6 1/4	1.50	1.00
	entire, size 8	1.50	1.00

1958. Stamped Envelope Issue

E22		MNHVF	UseVF
7¢	**red** *(Nov. 1, 1958)*	.35	.22
	entire	4.50	3.25

1963. Stamped Envelope Airmail Overprint Issue

E23		MNHVF	UseVF
3¢ + 5¢	**purple** *(June 22, 1963)*	1.80	.70
	entire	7.75	3.75

1964. Stamped Envelope Issue

E24		MNHVF	UseVF
8¢	**red** *(Jan. 6, 1964)*	.50	.18
	entire	2.25	.70

1965. Stamped Envelope Overprint Airmail Issue

E25		MNHVF	UseVF
4¢ + 4¢	**blue** *(Oct. 15, 1965)*	.50	.35
	entire	4.75	1.75

1966. Stamped Envelope Issue

E26		MNHVF	UseVF
8¢	**carmine** *(Feb. 25, 1966)*	.50	.35
	entire	5.50	1.50

1968. Stamped Envelope Overprint Issue

E27		MNHVF	UseVF
8¢ + 2¢	**carmine** *(Jan. 13, 1968)*	.50	.22
	entire	2.80	1.00

1968. Stamped Envelope Overprint Issue

E28		MNHVF	UseVF
4¢ + 4¢ + 2¢	**blue** *(Feb. 12, 1968)*	.70	.35
	entire	2.15	.85

1969. Stamped Envelope Issue

E29		MNHVF	UseVF
10¢	**ultramarine** *(April 28, 1969)*	.60	.30
	entire	3.65	3.65

1969. Stamped Envelope Overprint Issue

E30		MNHVF	UseVF
4¢ + 1¢	**blue** *(April 28, 1969)*	.18	.15
	entire	2.50	.80

E31		MNHVF	UseVF
4¢ + 2¢	**blue** *(April 28, 1969)*	.50	.30
	entire	2.50	.85

1971. Stamped Envelope Airmail Overprint Issue

E32		MNHVF	UseVF
4¢ + 5¢ + 2¢	**blue** *(May 17, 1971)*	.75	.30
	entire	3.50	1.75

1971. Stamped Envelope Overprint Issue

E33		MNHVF	UseVF
10¢ + 1¢	**ultramarine** *(May 17, 1971)*	.45	.30
	entire	4.00	2.25

1971. Stamped Envelope Issue

E34		MNHVF	UseVF
8¢	**green** *(Nov. 17, 1971)*	.35	.15
	entire	1.05	.75

1971. Stamped Envelope Airmail Issue

E35		MNHVF	UseVF
11¢	**red** *(Nov. 17, 1971)*	.40	.22
	entire	1.05	.75

1974. Stamped Envelope Overprint Issue

E36		MNHVF	UseVF
8¢ + 2¢	**green** *(March 2, 1974)*	.40	.22
	entire	1.05	.75

1974. Stamped Envelope Airmail Overprint Issue

E37		MNHVF	UseVF
11¢ + 2¢	**red** *(March 2, 1974)*	.60	.30
	entire	1.50	1.50

1975. Stamped Envelope Airmail Overprint Issue

E38		MNHVF	UseVF
8¢ + 2¢ + 3¢	**green** *(May 3, 1975)*	.60	.30
	entire	1.25	1.00

1976. Stamped Envelope Issue

E39		MNHVF	UseVF
13¢	**purple** *(Feb. 23, 1976)*	.60	.30
	entire	.95	.40

1978. Stamped Envelope Overprint Issue

E40		MNHVF	UseVF
13¢ + 2¢	**purple** *(July 5, 1978)*	.30	.20
	entire	.85	.40

Postal Cards

1907. Canal Zone Postal Card Issue

PC1 *Map of Panama; litho by American Bank Note Co., overprinted CANAL/ZONE reading up, and new value, by Isthmian Canal Commission*

PC1

	UnFVF	UseFVF
1¢ on 2¢ carmine, CANAL 15mm long *(Feb. 9, 1907) (50,000)*	40.00	25.00
v. double overprint	1,500.00	1,500.00
v1. double overprint second inverted	2,750.00	
v2. triple overprint one inverted	3,300.00	

PC2

	UnFVF	UseFVF
1¢ on 2¢ carmine, CANAL 13mm long *(10,000)* June 1907	250.00	205.00

1908-12. Canal Zone Postal Card Type 1 Issue

PC3 *Vasco Nuñez de Balboa; litho by Hamilton Bank Note Co., overprinted CANAL/ZONE reading down (6 types) or up (1 type), by Isthmian Canal Commission*

PC3

	UnFVF	UseFVF
1¢ **green and black** *(165,000)*	185.00	85.00
v. double overprint		2,000.00

1908. Canal Zone Postal Card Type 2 Issue

PC4

	UnFVF	UseFVF
1¢ **green and black** *(30,000)*	200.00	125.00
v. triple overprint	1,750.00	

1909. Canal Zone Postal Card Type 3 Issue

PC5

	UnFVF	UseFVF
1¢ **green and black** *(50,000)*	50.00	32.50
double overprint	120.00	120.00

1910. Canal Zone Postal Card Type 4 Issue

PC6

	UnFVF	UseFVF
1¢ **green and black** *(40,000)*	200.00	75.00
triple overprint		4,250.00

1908-12. Canal Zone Postal Card Type 5 Issue

PC7

	UnFVF	UseFVF
1¢ **green and black** *(40,000)*	200.00	70.00
v. double overprint		

1908-12. Canal Zone Postal Card Type 6 Issue

PC8

	UnFVF	UseFVF
1¢ **green and black** *(40,000)*	800.00	70.00

1908-12. Canal Zone Postal Card Type 7 Issue

PC9

	UnFVF	UseFVF
1¢ **green and black** *(40,000)*	200.00	70.00
v. ZONE	250.00	100.00

1913. Canal Zone V.N. Balboa Issue

PC10

	UnFVF	UseFVF
1¢ **green and black** *(634,000)*	165.00	60.00

1921. 100th Anniversary Independence from Spain Issue

PC11 *José Vallarino*

PC11

	UnFVF	UseFVF
1¢ **green** *(50,000)*	1,100.00	400.00

1924. Panama Coat of Arms Issue

PC12

PC12

	UnFVF	UseFVF
1¢ **green** *(60,000)*	700.00	800.00

U.S. Postal Card Series

1924. U.S. Postal Card Jefferson Issue

PC13

	UnFVF	UseFVF
1¢ **green on buff** *(50,000)*	90.00	35.00

1925. Seal of Canal Zone Issue

PC14

	UnFVF	UseFVF
1¢ **green on buff** *(25,000)*	95.00	35.00

1925. U.S. Postal Card Jefferson Issue

PC15

	UnFVF	UseFVF
1¢ **green on buff** *(850,000)*	9.50	5.00

1935. Canal Zone U.S. Overprint Issue

PC16

	UnFVF	UseFVF
1¢ **green on buff** *(2,900,000)*	2.00	1.65
v. double overprint	1,900.00	

1952. Canal Zone Postal Card Franklin Issue

PC17

	MNHVF	UseVF
2¢ **carmine rose on buff**	2.05	2.00

1958. Canal Zone Postal Card Ship at Lock Issue

PC18

	MNHVF	UseVF
3¢ **blue on buff**	2.00	1.75

1958. Canal Zone Airmail Postal Card Issue plane and canal over U.S. flag as border.

PC19

	MNHVF	UseVF
5¢ **red and blue**	4.00	3.75

1963. Canal Zone Overprint Issue with scene of freighter in canal.

PC20

	MNHVF	UseVF
3¢ + 1¢ **blue on buff**	4.25	4.00

PC21

	MNHVF	UseVF
5¢ + 1¢ **red and blue**	10.00	9.50

1964. Canal Zone Ship in Panama Canal Issue

PC21A

	MNHVF	UseVF
4¢ **violet blue on buff**	4.00	3.75

1965. Canal Zone Ship at Lock Issue

PC22

	MNHVF	UseVF
4¢ **green**	1.10	1.00

1965. Canal Zone Airmail Overprint Issue used PC22 with overprint value at left, "AIR MAIL" below stamp in red.

PC23		MNHVF	UseVF
4¢ + 2¢	**red and green**	4.50	4.00

1968. Canal Zone Overprint Issue

PC24		MNHVF	UseVF
4¢ + 1¢	**green,** new value in green	1.40	1.00

1968. Canal Zone Overprint Airmail Issue

PC25		MNHVF	UseVF
4¢ + 4¢	**green,** "VIA AIR MAIL" in vermilion	3.00	2.75

1969. Canal Zone Ship at Lock Issue with new value.

PC26		MNHVF	UseVF
5¢	**light ultramarine**	1.50	1.00

1971. Canal Zone Ship at Lock Overprint Issue with new value in light ultramarine.

PC27		MNHVF	UseVF
5¢ + 1¢	**light ultramarine**	.45	.80
PC28		MNHVF	UseVF
5¢ + 4¢	**light ultrmarine**	.95	.85

Additional imprint AIR MAIL.

1974. Canal Zone Ship at Lock Issue

PC29		MNHVF	UseVF
8¢	**sepia**	.95	.80

1976. Canal Zone Ship at Lock Overprint Issue

PC30		MNHVF	UseVF
8¢ + 1¢	**sepia**	.80	.60

1978. Canal Zone Ship at Lock Overprint Issue

PC31		MNHVF	UseVF
8¢ + 2¢	**sepia**	.85	.75

Cuba

After the sinking of the *USS Maine* at Havana (February 1898) the United States intervened militarily in national unrest toward Spain, destroyed the Spanish fleet at Santiago, infested the island with land forces and acquired trusteeship of Cuba in the Treaty of Paris. After three years of U.S. military administration (marked chiefly by the eradication of yellow fever), a republic was established May 20, 1902. Rebel leader Fidel Castro took control from the corrupt dictator Fulgencio Batista in 1959 and established his own Communist dictatorship.

Regular Issues

1898-1899. CUBA Puerto Principe Issue

201

201	UnFVF	UseFVF
1¢ on 1m chestnut	45.00	30.00
Inverted overprint		130.00

202	UnFVF	UseFVF
2¢ on 2m chestnut	14.50	8.50
v. inverted overprint	250.00	48.00
a. thin "2" overprint	35.00	30.00
av1. inverted overprint	275.00	100.00

203	UnFVF	UseFVF
3¢ on 2m chestnut		2,000.00
a. thin 3		3,000.00

204	UnFVF	UseFVF
3¢ on 3m chestnut	18.00	29.00
v. inverted overprint		100.00
a. thin 3	48.00	40.00
av1. inverted overprint		200.00

205	UnFVF	UseFVF
5¢ on 1m chestnut	500.00	150.00
v. inverted overprint		600.00
a. thin 5	1,200.00	425.00
av1. inverted overprint		725.00

206	UnFVF	UseFVF
5¢ on 2m chestnut	650.00	150.00
Thin 5	1,450.00	440.00

207	UnFVF	UseFVF
5¢ on 3m chestnut	1,025.00	90.00
Inverted overprint	1,450.00	290.00
a. thin 5		575.00
Inverted overprint		725.00

208	UnFVF	UseFVF
5¢ on 5m chestnut	60.00	50.00
v. inverted overprint	350.00	150.00
v1. double overprint	—	—
a. thin 5	300.00	150.00
av. inverted overprint		285.00
a2. double overprint	—	—

1898-99. Puerto Principe Red Overprint Issue

209

209	UnFVF	UseFVF
3¢ on 1¢ purple black	26.00	14.50
v. inverted overprint		190.00
a. thin 3	72.00	60.00
av1. inverted overprint		145.00

210	UnFVF	UseFVF
5¢ on 1¢ purple black	8.75	8.75
v. inverted overprint		75.00
v1. overprint sideways		2,600.00
v2. double overprint	360.00	500.00
a. thin 5	20.00	17.50
av. inverted overprint		285.00
av1. overprint sideways		1,500.00
av2. double overprint	900.00	500.00

211	UnFVF	UseFVF
10¢ on 1¢ purple black	20.00	20.00
a. broken "1"	45.00	45.00

1898-99. Puerto Principe Black Overprint Issue

212

212	UnFVF	UseFVF
1¢ on 1m chestnut	24.00	15.00
Inverted overprint		130.00
Broken 1	39.00	35.00
Double overprint		
Double overprint		225.00

213	UnFVF	UseFVF
3¢ on 1m chestnut	265.00	100.00
a2. double overprint	1,300.00	500.00
a. thin 3	1,300.00	440.00
av. double overprint	—	—

Nos. 214 and 215 are not assigned.

1898-99. Puerto Principe Black Overprint Issue

216	UnFVF	UseFVF
5¢ on 1/2m slate green	230.00	60.00
v. inverted overprint	400.00	90.00
Pair, 1 no overprint		400.00
a. thin 5 overprint	225.00	42.50
av1. double overprint, one diagonal		9,300.00
av2. inverted overprint		150.00

1898-99. Puerto Principe Black Overprint Issue

217	UnFVF	UseFVF
3¢ on 1m slate green	250.00	200.00
v. inverted overprint		225.00
a. *eents*	440.00	225.00
av. inverted overprint		725.00
a2. thin 3 overprinted	360.00	300.00
a2v. inverted overprint		440.00

1898-99. Puerto Principe Black Overprint Issue

218	UnFVF	UseFVF
3¢ on 2m slate green	650.00	130.00
v. inverted overprint		725.00
a. *eents*	725.00	225.00
av1. inverted overprint		1,300.00
a2. thin 3 overprint	1,150.00	400.00
Inverted overprint		675.00

219	UnFVF	UseFVF
3¢ on 3m slate green	800.00	130.00
Inverted overprint		300.00
a. *eents*	1,025.00	225.00
a1. inverted overprint		675.00
a2. thin 3 overprint	1,200.00	300.00
Inverted overprint		625.00

220	UnFVF	UseFVF
5¢ on 1/2m slate green	250.00	60.00
a. thin 5 overprint	360.00	

221	UnFVF	UseFVF
5¢ on 1m slate green		1,500.00
a. *eents*		2,300.00
a2. thin 5 overprint		2,300.00

Nos. 222-225 are not assigned.

1899. CUBA Regular Issue

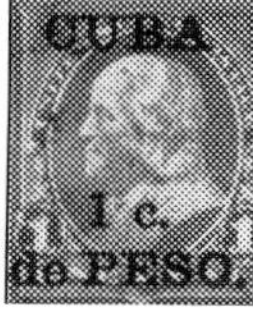

226

	UnFVF	UseFVF
226		
1¢ on 1¢ yellow green	4.50	.60
227		
2¢ on 2¢ carmine, No. 191	4.50	.70
a. orange red, No. 192a	5.00	.60
v. "CUPA"	100.00	
v1. inverted overprint	3,500.00	725.00
v2. "CUBA" at bottom	600.00	
228		
2 1/2 ¢ on 2¢ carmine, No. 191	3.25	.60
orange red, No. 192a	3.50	3.25
229		
3¢ on 3¢ dark red violet	7.50	1.50
v. CUB.A	37.50	34.25
230		
5¢ on 5¢ dark blue	8.25	1.50
v. "CUPAL"	57.50	31.00
231		
10¢ on 10¢ brown, Type I	21.00	8.00
v. on 10¢ Type III, special printing	6,000.00	

No. 228 was sold and used as 2¢. No. 229, Type I: 3 over P, Type II: 3 *to left over P.*

1899. Cuba Postage Due Issue

	UnFVF	UseFVF
232		
1¢ on 1¢ brown carmine	21.00	5.25
233		
2¢ on 2¢ brown carmine	21.00	3.60
v. inverted overprint		2,500.00
234		
5¢ on 5¢ brown carmine	18.00	2.40
v. "CUPA"	150.00	140.00
235		
10¢ on 10¢ brown carmine	17.50	2.00

236

	UnFVF	UseFVF
236		
10¢ on 10¢ indigo	180.00	87.50
v. no period after CUBA	465.00	

1899. Cuba Pictorials Issue

	UnFVF	UseFVF
237		
1¢ deep green	3.75	.25
238		
2¢ rose red	3.75	.18
Booklet pane of 6	2,000.00	
239		
3¢ slate red violet	3.75	.35
240		
5¢ deep blue	5.00	.50
241		
10¢ deep yellow brown	14.00	1.10

1899. Cuba Special Delivery Issue

	UnFVF	UseFVF
242		
10¢ yellow orange	42.00	10.00

1902. Cuba Founding of the Republic Issue

	UnFVF	UseFVF
243		
1¢ on 3¢ purple	3.75	1.25
v. overprint sideways		
v1. inverted overprint	28.00	28.00
v2. double overprint	37.50	37.50

No. 237 overprinted.

Envelopes and Wrappers

1899. Cuba Envelopes and Wrappers Issue

	UnFVF	UseFVF
E1		
1¢ on 1¢ green on buff, No. 393	2.00	3.00
entire	9.75	9.00
E2		
1¢ on 1¢ green on light blue	2.25	2.50
entire	3.75	4.25
v. double overprint		
entire	550.00	
E3		
2¢ on 2¢ green on white	1.30	1.00
entire	2.50	3.00
v. CUPA		
entire	165.00	140.00
v1. double overprint, entire	550.00	550.00
E4		
2¢ on 2¢ green on amber, No. 339	1.30	1.50
entire	3.60	3.75
v. double overprint	225.00	
entire	500.00	
E5		
2¢ on 2¢ green on buff, No. 340	7.75	5.00
entire	18.00	13.50
E6		
2¢ on 2¢ carmine on amber, No. 407	8.75	8.75
entire	18.00	19.50
E7		
2¢ on 2¢ carmine on buff, No. 408	15.50	13.50
entire	32.50	27.50
E8		
2¢ on 2¢ carmine on light blue, No. 409	1.20	1.30
entire	3.75	3.25
v. double overprint		
entire		600.00

The following envelopes exist but were not reguarly issued:

1¢ on 1¢ green on white

1¢ on 1¢ green on manila

2¢ on 2¢ carmine on white

2¢ on 2¢ carmine on oriental buff

2¢ on 2¢ carmine on light blue

4¢ on 4¢ brown on white

5¢ n 5¢ blue on white

1899. Cuba Columbus Issue

	UnFVF	UseFVF
E9		
1¢ green on white	.75	.65
E10		
1¢ green on amber	1.00	.65
E11		
1¢ green on buff	15.00	12.00
E12		
1¢ green on blue	25.00	15.00
E13		
1¢ green on laid manila, wrapper	4.00	9.00
E14		
2¢ carmine on white	1.00	.60
E15		
2¢ carmine on amber	.70	.70
E16		
2¢ carmine on buff	10.00	8.00
E17		
2¢ carmine on blue	25.00	18.00
E18		
2¢ carmine on manila, wrapper	12.00	10.00
E19		
2¢ blue on white	3.00	2.00
E20		
2¢ blue on amber	6.00	4.00

Postal Cards

1899. Cuba Postal Card Issue

	UnFVF	UseFVF
PC1		
1¢ on 1¢ black	4.50	4.25
v. no period after *Peso*	18.00	18.00
PC2		
2¢ on 2¢ black	4.50	6.00
v. no period after *Peso*	25.00	
v1. double overprint	135.00	

Danish West Indies (U.S. Virgin Islands)

A Territory of the United States, the group consists of the islands of St. Croix, St. Thomas and St. John, and about 50 smaller islands, totalling 133 square miles. The islands were discovered by Columbus in 1493, and named *Las Virgenes,* in honor of St. Ursula and her companions. Spanish forces exterminated the native Caribe population by 1596. In the period from 1650 to 1917 the islands were occupied at various times by the French, the Knights of Malta, the British and the Danes. In 1917, the Danish West Indies were purchased for 25 million dollars by the United States, following years of negotiation.

Citizenship was conferred upon the inhabitants in 1927, and in 1936 suffrage was granted to all who could read and write English. The governor and a delegate to the U.S. House of Representatives are elected.

Regular Postal Issues

1855-66. Issue *Imperforate.*

1 *Coat of arms*

		UnFVF	UseFVF
1			
3¢	**deep carmine red on yellowish**	185.00	185.00

		UnFVF	UseFVF
2			
3¢	**rose red,** *(May 1865)*	45.00	75.00
	p. thick paper	60.00	100.00
	v. privately rouletted 4 1/2	435.00	180.00

No. 1 had to be re-gummed after arrival in St. Croix. New gum was yellow or brown, same price. Original white gum rare.

1872-73. Issue *Line perforated.*

		UnFVF	UseFVF
3			
3¢	**brown red**	90.00	185.00
	p. thick paper	125.00	225.00

		UnFVF	UseFVF
4			
4¢	**dull blue,** *(Jan. 1, 1873)*	225.00	435.00
	v. pair imperforate	435.00	
	v1. pair, imperforate vertical	310.00	

Control marks. Nos. 1-3: 3 in left bottom square, C in right bottom square; engraver's mark B (A Buntzen) *over right bottom square; No. 4: engraver's mark only.*

No. 1: Many sheets destroyed when bundle with stamps fell into water while being unloaded. Remainders destroyed in 1873: No. 3 (210,000), No. 4 (200,000).

1896-1901. Issue *Perforate 14 x 13 1/2.*

5

		UnFVF	UseFVF
5			
1¢	**bright green and dull lilac,** first printing	110.00	150.00
	v. frame inverted	560.00	875.00
	a. apple green & dull lilac, second printing	175.00	125.00
	av. frame inverted	750.00	875.00
	b. blue green & deep lilac, third printing	60.00	60.00
	c. pale green & pale red lilac, thick paper, fourth printing	45.00	50.00
	d. yellowish green & claret, thick paper, fifth printing	40.00	40.00
	e. light green & red lilac, thick paper, sixth printing	28.00	35.00
	f. green & red brown, frame inverted, thick paper, seventh printing	25.00	35.00
	g. deep green & deep claret, thick paper, eighth printing	18.00	35.00
	h. yellow green & brown red, frame inverted, thick paper, ninth printing	18.00	35.00
	v2. normal frame, thick paper	37.50	30.00

		UnFVF	UseFVF
6			
3¢	**blue and rose carmine,** first printing	85.00	60.00
	v. frame inverted	500.00	500.00
	a. sky blue & carmine rose, second printing	100.00	75.00
	av. frame inverted	750.00	
	b. pale blue & dull rose, third printing	60.00	45.00
	bv. frame inverted	110.00	75.00
	c. deep blue & carmine lake, thick paper, fourth printing	50.00	28.00
	cv. frame inverted, thick paper	300.00	300.00
	cvp. pair, normal inverted frame, thick paper	500.00	435.00
	d. gray blue & dull carmine, thick paper, fifth printing	40.00	20.00
	e. bright blue & bright carmine, thick paper, sixth printing	30.00	18.00
	f. deep gray blue & lake, frame inverted, thick paper, seventh printing	27.00	18.00
	gv. normal frame, thick paper	275.00	275.00
	g. greenish blue & carmine red, thick paper, eighth printing	27.00	18.00

		UnFVF	UseFVF
7			
4¢	**deep brown and deep ultramarine,** first printing	185.00	185.00
	a. bistre brown and pale blue, second printing	12.00	15.00
	v. frame inverted	1,450.00	1,450.00

		UnFVF	UseFVF
8			
5¢	**pale green and light gray,** *(1876)* first printing	78.00	50.00
	a. grass green & gray, second printing	85.00	55.00
	b. pale green & brownish gray, thick paper, third printing	55.00	45.00
	c. bright green & deep gray, thick paper, fourth printing	30.00	18.00
	d. dark green & slate gray, thick paper, fifth printing	25.00	18.00
	e. deep green & dark brownish gray, thick paper, sixth printing	25.00	18.00

		UnFVF	UseFVF
9			
7¢	**pale lilac and orange buff,** *(1874)* first printing	100.00	95.00
	a. light violet & orange, second printing	30.00	110.00
	av. frame inverted	60.00	185.00

		UnFVF	UseFVF
10			
10¢	**pale ultramarine and yellow brown,** *(1876)* first printing	95.00	40.00
	a. pale blue & brown, second printing	75.00	45.00
	b. deep ultramarine & blackish brown, thick paper, third printing	40.00	40.00
	bv. frame inverted	435.00	435.00
	c. pale ultramarine & yellowish brown, thick paper, fourth printing	45.00	37.50
	d. bluish gray & pale yellow brown, thick paper, fifth printing	37.50	40.00
	e. light blue & black brown, thick paper, sixth printing	25.00	25.00
	f. blue & reddish brown, thick paper, seventh printing	27.00	34.00

		UnFVF	UseFVF
11			
12¢	**pale lilac and green,** *(1877)* first printing	185.00	185.00
	a. red lilac & yellow green, second printing	45.00	150.00

		UnFVF	UseFVF
12			
14¢	**lilac and green,** first printing	620.00	950.00
	v. frame inverted	2,500.00	3,750.00

		UnFVF	UseFVF
13			
50¢	**bright purple,** first printing	155.00	250.00
	a. dull gray, violet thick paper, second printing	220.00	375.00

1898. Issue *Perforate 13.*

		UnFVF	UseFVF
14			
1¢	**pale green and claret,** frame inverted *(Feb. 1898)*	12.00	18.00
	v. normal frame	225.00	370.00

1896-1901. ISSUE *Perforate 14 x 13 1/2.*

15-18

		UnFVF	UseFVF
15			
3¢	**bright blue and carmine red,** frame inverted, *(March 1898)*	9.00	12.50
	v. normal frame	185.00	310.00
16		UnFVF	UseFVF
4¢	**ochre and light gray blue,** *(March 1901)*	11.00	11.00
	v. frame inverted	250.00	310.00
17		UnFVF	UseFVF
5¢	**green and gray,** frame inverted, *(June 1896)*	45.00	50.00
	v. normal frame	750.00	1,000.00
18		UnFVF	UseFVF
10¢	**turquoise blue and brown ochre,** *(Feb. 1901)*	75.00	150.00
	v. frame inverted	925.00	1,500.00
	v1. period between *t* & *s* of *cents*	25.00	25.00

On Nos. 19-26, Type I overprint was done locally at St. Thomas; Type II was done at Copenhagen, Denmark.

I CENT 19

	UnFVF	UseFVF
19		
1¢ on 7¢ lilac and orange yellow, Type I overprint on No. 9, *(May, 12, 1987)*	75.00	185.00
v. frame inverted	110.00	310.00
v1. double overprint	200.00	310.00

20-23 *Overprint*

2
CENTS
1902

	UnFVF	UseFVF
20		
2¢ on 3¢ gray blue and rose, frame inverted, Type I overprint on No. 6 *(March 1902)*	375.00	435.00
v. normal frame	375.00	
v1. *2* w/straight tail	400.00	450.00
21	UnFVF	UseFVF
2¢ on 3¢ bright blue and carmine red, frame inverted, Type I overprint on No. 15 *(March 1902)*	6.00	25.00
v. normal frame	185.00	250.00
v1. *2* w/straight tail	11.00	25.00
v2. dated *1901*	250.00	375.00

1887-1902. ISSUE

	UnFVF	UseFVF
22		
2¢ on 3¢ bright blue and carmine red, frame inverted, dark green, Type II overprint on No. 15 *(1902)*	1,950.00	
v. normal frame	12,500.00	
23	UnFVF	UseFVF
2¢ on 3¢ bright blue and carmine red, frame inverted, Type II overprint on No. 15 *(July 1902)*	11.00	40.00
v. normal frame	250.00	375.00

8
CENTS
1902

24-25 *Overprint*

	UnFVF	UseFVF
24		
8¢ on 10¢ turquoise blue and brown ochre, Type I overprint on No. 18 *(March 1902)*	23.00	40.00
v. frame inverted	225.00	375.00
v1. period between *t* & *s* of *cents*	18.00	28.00
v2. *2* w/straight tail	28.00	46.50
25	UnFVF	UseFVF
8¢ on 10¢ turquoise blue and brown ochre, Type II overprint on No. 18 *(July 1902)*	8.00	8.00
v. frame inverted	155.00	435.00
v1. period between *t* & *s* of *cents*	9.00	15.50

26

10
CENTS
1895

	UnFVF	UseFVF
26		
10¢ on 50¢ purple, Type I overprint on No. 13 *(May 1895)*	37.50	75.00

1902-1903. ISSUE

27

		UnFVF	UseFVF
27			
1¢	**green**	3.00	3.00
28		UnFVF	UseFVF
2¢	**carmine** *(April 1903)*	7.50	25.00
29		UnFVF	UseFVF
5¢	**light blue**	17.50	25.00
30		UnFVF	UseFVF
8¢	**light brown** *(April 1903)*	28.00	50.00

1902. POSTAGE DUE ISSUE

31

		UnFVF	UseFVF
31			
1¢	**deep blue**	5.00	14.00
32		UnFVF	UseFVF
4¢	**deep blue**	9.00	18.00
33		UnFVF	UseFVF
6¢	**deep blue**	18.00	50.00
34		UnFVF	UseFVF
10¢	**deep blue**	15.50	50.00

Nos. 31-34: 5 types of each value.

1905. ISSUE

35

		UnFVF	UseFVF
35			
5b	**emerald**	4.50	3.75
36		UnFVF	UseFVF
10b	**orange**	4.50	3.75
37		UnFVF	UseFVF
20b	**light green and blue**	9.00	7.50
38		UnFVF	UseFVF
25b	**ultramarine**	9.00	9.00
39		UnFVF	UseFVF
40b	**red and brown black**	9.00	7.50
40		UnFVF	UseFVF
50b	**yellow and brown black**	11.00	11.00

1905. ISSUE

41

	UnFVF	UseFVF
41		
5b on 4¢ ochre and light gray blue	15.00	50.00
v. frame inverted overprint	37.00	75.00

No.	Denomination	Description	UnFVF	UseFVF
42	5b on 5¢ light blue		14.00	37.50
43	5b on 8¢ light brown		14.00	37.50

1905. Issue

44

No.	Denomination	Description	UnFVF	UseFVF
44	1f	**green and blue**	18.00	37.50
45	2f	**red orange and brown**	25.00	50.00
46	5f	**yellow and brown**	60.00	230.00

1905. Postage Due Issue

47

No.	Denomination	Description	UnFVF	UseFVF
47	5b	**vermilion and drab gray**	4.50	7.50
48	20b	**vermilion and drab gray**	7.50	15.00
49	30b	**vermilion and drab gray**	6.00	15.00
50	50b	**vermilion and drab gray**	5.50	30.00
		v. perforated 14 x 14 1/2, *(1913)*	30.00	150.00
		v1. perforated 11 1/2	250.00	

1907-08. Issue

51

No.	Denomination	Description	UnFVF	UseFVF
51	5b	**deep yellow green**	2.50	1.85
52	10b	**orange red,** *(Jan. 1908)*	2.50	1.85
53	15b	**red purple and chocolate,** *(Sept. 1908)*	3.75	3.75
54	20b	**yellow, emerald and blue,** *(May 1908)*	28.00	25.00
55	25b	**prussian blue**	2.50	1.85
56	30b	**claret and slate,** *(Sept. 1908)*	45.00	45.00
57	40b	**vermilion and gray** *(Sept. 1908)*	6.00	7.75
58	50b	**yellow and brown** *(Sept. 1908)*	6.00	12.00

1915-16. Issue

59

No.	Denomination	Description	UnFVF	UseFVF
59	5b	**pale green**	5.00	4.50
60	10b	**orange red** *(March 1915)*	5.00	4.50
61	15b	**red purple and red brown** *(March 1915)*	4.50	45.00
62	20b	**yellow emerald and dark blue** *(March 1915)*	4.50	45.00
63	25b	**blue and deep blue**	4.50	11.00
64	30b	**brown red and black** *(1916)*	4.50	55.00
65	40b	**orange salmon and gray black** *(1915)*	4.50	55.00
66	50b	**yellow and chocolate** *(March 1915)*	4.50	55.00

Since 1917: U.S. stamps have been used.

Envelopes and Wrappers

1877-78. Stamped Envelopes

No.	Denomination	Description	UnFVF	UseFVF
E1	2¢	**light blue** *(1878)*	5.00	15.00
		entire	20.00	75.00
		a. ultramarine	25.00	250.00
		entire	125.00	1,000.00
E2	3¢	**orange red**	5.50	15.00
		entire	20.00	75.00
		a. red orange	6.00	15.00
		entire	20.00	75.00

Postal Cards

1877. Postal Card Issue

No.	Denomination	Description	UnFVF	UseFVF
PC1	6¢	**violet**	17.50	12.00

1878-85. Postal Card Issue

No.	Denomination	Description	UnFVF	UseFVF
PC2	2¢	**light blue**	25.00	55.00
PC3	3¢	**carmine rose**	17.50	45.00

Nos. PC2 and 3 with added inscription in Danish and French.

1883. Message and Reply Card Issue

No.	Denomination	Description	UnFVF	UseFVF
PC4	2¢ + 2¢	**light blue,** unsevered	20.00	200.00
		m message card	10.00	30.00
		r. reply card	10.00	30.00
PC5	3¢ + 3¢	**carmine rose,** unsevered	20.00	100.00
		m. message card	10.00	18.00
		r. reply card	10.00	18.00

1888-98. Postal Card Issue

No.	Denomination	Description	UnFVF	UseFVF
PC6	2¢	**light blue**	10.00	22.50
PC7	3¢	**red**	10.00	22.50

Nos. PC6 and 7 with added inscription in French on message card: Carte postale avec réponse payée; on reply card: *Carte postale-réponse.*

1888-98. Message and Reply Cards

No.	Denomination	Description	UnFVF	UseFVF
PC8	2¢ + 2¢	**light blue,** unsevered		
		m. message card		
		r. reply card		
PC9	3¢ + 3¢	**red,** unsevered		
		m. message card		
		r. reply card		

1901. Message and Reply Cards

No.	Denomination	Description	UnFVF	UseFVF
PC10	1¢ on 3¢ red		50.00	200.00
PC11	1¢ on 3¢+1¢ on 3¢	**carmine rose,** unsevered	45.00	275.00
		m. message card	18.00	50.00
		r. reply card	18.00	75.00

1902. Message and Reply Cards

No.	Denomination	Description	UnFVF	UseFVF
PC12	1¢ on 2¢ light blue		30.00	150.00

1902. Message and Reply Cards

		UnFVF	UseFVF
PC13			
1¢ on 3¢ red		13.50	32.50
PC14		UnFVF	UseFVF
1¢ on 3¢+1¢ on 3¢ carmine rose, unsevered		45.00	300.00
	m. message card	25.00	60.00
	r. reply card	25.00	75.00

1903. Postal Card Issue

		UnFVF	UseFVF
PC15			
1¢	**light green**	10.00	30.00
PC16		UnFVF	UseFVF
2¢	**carmine red**	20.00	75.00

1903. Message and Reply Cards

		UnFVF	UseFVF
PC17			
1¢ + 1¢	**light green,** unsevered	20.00	75.00
	m. message card	10.00	20.00
	r. reply card	10.00	20.00
PC18		UnFVF	UseFVF
2¢ + 2¢	**carmine,** unsevered	40.00	350.00
	m. message card	20.00	50.00
	r. reply card	20.00	75.00

1905. Postal Card Issue

		UnFVF	UseFVF
PC19			
5b	**green**	10.00	24.00
PC20		UnFVF	UseFVF
10b	**red**	13.50	32.50

1905. Message and Reply Cards

		UnFVF	UseFVF
PC21			
5b + 5b	**green,** unsevered	20.00	75.00
	m. message card	10.00	20.00
	r. reply card	12.00	25.00
PC22		UnFVF	UseFVF
10b + 10b red, unsevered		25.00	90.00
	m. message card	12.50	27.50
	r. reply card	12.50	35.00

1907-08. Postal Card Issue

		UnFVF	UseFVF
PC23			
5b	**green** (1908)	10.00	24.00

1905. Message and Reply Cards

		UnFVF	UseFVF
PC24			
10b	**red**	13.50	28.50

1913. Postal Card Issue

		UnFVF	UseFVF
PC25			
5b	**green**	100.00	200.00
PC26		UnFVF	UseFVF
10b	**red**	125.00	325.00

1908. Message and Reply Cards

		UnFVF	UseFVF
PC27			
5b + 5b	**green,** unsevered	18.00	100.00
	m. message card	8.00	25.00
	r. reply card	8.00	25.00
PC28		UnFVF	UseFVF
10b + 10b red, unsevered		18.00	100.00
	m. message card	7.75	25.00
	r. reply card	7.75	35.00

1913. Message and Reply Cards

		UnFVF	UseFVF
PC29			
5b + 5b	**green,** unsevered		850.00
	m. message card		
	r. reply card		
PC30		UnFVF	UseFVF
10b + 10b red, unsevered			
	m. message card		
	r. reply card		

No. PC29: 5000 printed. No. PC30: authorized and possibly printed, but no example is known.

1915-16. Postal Card Issue

		UnFVF	UseFVF
PC31			
5b	**green**	100.00	155.00
PC32		UnFVF	UseFVF
10b	**red**	125.00	240.00

Guam

At 206 square miles, Guam is the largest of the Mariana Islands, named for Maria Ana, widow of Philip IV of Spain. Discovered in 1521 by Magellan, whose crew called the group *Islas de los Ladrones* (Thieves' Islands) because of native pilfering. Spain, which conquered the islands in the late 17th century, ceded Guam to the United States in 1898 and sold the other islands to Germany. The latter were mandated to Japan after World War I. In World War II, the small Navy forces on Guam were overcome by the Japanese on Dec. 12, 1942. Recaptured in 1944, Guam was used as a base for U.S. bomber strikes at Japan. The governor, legislature and a delegate to the U.S. House of Representatives are elected.

Regular Postal Issues

1899. Overprint Issue United States stamps overprinted "GUAM" in black or red (13 & 14), *perforated 12.*

		UnFVF	UseFVF
1			
1¢	**deep green,** U.S. No. 188	30.00	32.50
2		UnFVF	UseFVF
2¢	**carmine,** triangle III, No. 191	30.00	31.50
3		UnFVF	UseFVF
2¢	**red,** triangle III, No. 192	32.00	32.50
4		UnFVF	UseFVF
3¢	**dark red violet**	120.00	145.00
5		UnFVF	UseFVF
4¢	**chocolate**	125.00	145.00
	t. extra frame line at top (P1 793)	—	
6		UnFVF	UseFVF
5¢	**dark blue**	40.00	37.50
7		UnFVF	UseFVF
6¢	**lake**	120.00	165.00
8		UnFVF	UseFVF
8¢	**purple brown**	150.00	165.00
9		UnFVF	UseFVF
10¢	**brown,** Type I	50.00	65.00
10		UnFVF	UseFVF
10¢	**orange brown,** Type II	3,250.00	—
11		UnFVF	UseFVF
15¢	**olive green**	175.00	165.00
12		UnFVF	UseFVF
50¢	**orange,** U.S. No. 208	350.00	300.00
	a. red orange	500.00	
13		UnFVF	UseFVF
$1	**black,** Type I, overprinted red	600.00	450.00
	a. Type II red overprint, special printing	3,250.00	
14		UnFVF	UseFVF
10¢	**indigo,** U.S. No. 505 overprinted red	160.00	175.00

Hawaii

Settled by Polynesians from islands 2,000 miles to the south about 700 A.D., Hawaii was discovered in 1778 by Captain James Cook, who called the group the Sandwich Islands. He was slain there in 1779. Hawaiian chief, Kamehameha the Great, conquered and united most of the islands (1782-95), established a strong but beneficent government and encouraged foreign trade. His son Liholiho (Kamehameha II) abolished idolatry and tabu, opened Hawaii to the American missionaries, and died on a visit to England in 1824. The reign of his brother Kauikeaouli (Kamehameha III) was a period of great prosperity and enlightenment, which gave Hawaii a liberal constitutional government, full suffrage, a high rate of literacy and a patiently achieved recognition as an independent sovereign nation.

The benevolent but high-handed Kamehameha V revoked the liberal constitution of 1852. Revolution in 1887 forced King David Kalakaua to grant a constitution guaranteeing a responsible ministerial government. His sister, Queen Liliuokalani, intent upon restoring absolute monarchy, attempted to set this constitution aside early in 1893, but the resulting revolution forced her from the throne. The provisional government's attempt to have the country annexed by the United States was opposed by President Cleveland, and a republic was established July 4, 1894. In 1898, under President McKinley, a treaty of annexation was approved by a joint session of the U.S. Congress, and the Territory of Hawaii was established June 14, 1900. It became a state in 1959.

Until 1846 the Hawaiian government took no responsibility for the mails, which were carried free by ships and received or forwarded by merchants or other private persons. The 1846 Organic Act set up a postal system, but four years elapsed before this measure was carried out, when a treaty with the U.S. provided for the exchange of mails. At the same time, a post office was set up in Honolulu and postal rates established. In 1851 a revised law lowered rates and authorized issuance of the first Hawaiian stamps.

Regular Postal Issues

1851. Hawaiian Postage Issue Numerals inscribed "Hawaiian Postage." Nos. 1-3, Type I, "P" of Postage slightly to the right of "H". Type II, "P" is directly under "H".

1-3

		UnFVF	UseFVF
1			
2¢	**blue**	600,000.00	200,000.00
	pelure paper		
2		UnFVF	UseFVF
5¢	**blue**	60,000.00	35,000.00
3		UnFVF	UseFVF
13¢	**blue**	30,000.00	20,000.00

1852. H.I. & U.S. Postage Issue Numeral inscribed. *Type I 16 1/2mm Long or Type II 17 1/2 mm long.*

4

		UnFVF	UseFVF
4			
13¢	**blue**	60,000.00	37,500.00

1853-61. Kamehameha III Issue *Intaglio, imperforate.*

No. 5, 8, 9 Kamehameha III (1813-54) was 12 when he succeeded his brother as king. His statement, *The life of the land is preserved by righteousness,* is now the motto of Hawaii.

		UnFVF	UseFVF
5			
5¢	**blue**	1,650.00	6,275.00
	a. line through *HONOLULU*	3,000.00	2,500.00
	v. bright blue (Reprint)	80.00	

on 13c
6

		UnFVF	UseFVF
6			
5¢ on 13¢ dull red		8,500.00	8,000.00

7

		UnFVF	UseFVF
7			
13¢	**dull red**	725.00	800.00
	v. dull rose (Reprint)	300.00	

Thick wove paper; No. 6 with pen-written overprint.

1857-61. Kamehameha III Issue *Thin white wove paper.*

		UnFVF	UseFVF
8			
5¢	**light blue,** 1857	800.00	775.00
9		UnFVF	UseFVF
5¢	**light blue on bluish,** 1861	300.00	210.00
	a. line through *HONOLULU*	850.00	630.00
	b. Double impression		

Reprints on ordinary white wove paper.

1863. Inter-Island Issue *numerals inscribed at top; type set, imperforate. Thin paper.*

		UnFVF	UseFVF
10			
1¢	**blue on bluish**	7,000.00	5,000.00
11		UnFVF	UseFVF
2¢	**blue on bluish**	6,000.00	3,500.00

12

		UnFVF	UseFVF
12			
2¢	**deep blue on blue**	8,000.00	4,500.00

1863. Inter-Island Reprint Issue *Color changes, thin paper.*

13

		UnFVF	UseFVF
13			
1¢	**black on grayish,** 1863	600.00	1,000.00
	tete-beche pair	5,000.00	
14		UnFVF	UseFVF
2¢	**black on grayish,** 1863	900.00	750.00
	a. *2* near top of frame	3,500.00	3,000.00
	v1. *I of INTER* omitted	3,000.00	3,000.00
	v. printed on both sides	—	20,000.00
15		UnFVF	UseFVF
2¢	**black on greenish blue,** *(April 1, 1863)*	7,750.00	3,500.00
16		UnFVF	UseFVF
2¢	**black on light blue, 1864**	8,000.00	4,500.00

1864. Inter-Island Issue *White wove (17, 19) or laid (18, 20) paper.*

17

		UnFVF	UseFVF
17			
1¢	**black**	650.00	1,200.00
18		UnFVF	UseFVF
1¢	**black,** laid paper	350.00	1,200.00
	a. *HA* in left panel	2,500.00	
	b. tete-beche pair	8,000.00	
19		UnFVF	UseFVF
2¢	**black**	850.00	1,475.00
20		UnFVF	UseFVF
2¢	**black,** laid paper	350.00	1,200.00
	v. *I* of *INTER* omitted	2,250.00	
	v1. *PO TAGE*	1,000.00	

1865. Inter-Island Issue *Numerals, inscribed INTERISLAND in left panel; type-set imperforate.*

21

		UnFVF	UseFVF
21 1¢	**dark blue**	350.00	
22 2¢	**dark blue**	3,500.00	
23 5¢	**deep blue on blue**	650.00	900.00
	a. tete-beche pair	10,000.00	

1865. Inter-Island Issue *HAWAIIAN POSTAGE* in both left and right panels.

24

		UnFVF	UseFVF
24 5¢	**dark blue on blue**	900.00	630.00
	a. tete-beche pair	6,000.00	

No. 10-23; 10 different types. Gutter pair, tete-beche gutter pair exists.

1861-63. Kamehameha IV Issue *Offset.*

25 *Kamehameha IV*

		UnFVF	UseFVF
25 2¢	**pale rose red**	300.00	200.00
	a. deep rose red	2,000.00	2,000.00
	v. red (1869 Reprint)	60.00	90.00

A red reprint of No. 25 in 1869 was not issued for postal purposes. Sold at Honolulu Post Office with or without overprint CANCELLED.

		UnFVF	UseFVF
26 2¢	**pale rose red**	300.00	200.00
	a. deep rose red (1863)	275.00	300.00
	p. vertical laid paper		
	v. dull vermillion, (1886, medium, white to buff paper, Reprint)	375.00	300.00
	pv1. dull scarlet, (1889, thick, yellowish to buff paper, Reprint) horizontal laid paper	2,000.00	2,750.00

Two reprints of No. 26 were made in order to have complete sets of Hawaiian stamps for sale. In 1885 the reissue 2¢ red was sent to the American Bank Note Co., and from it a new plate was engraved and 10,000 stamps printed (5,000 of these overprinted SPECIMEN in blue). Subsequently (1887) the missing plate of the reissue was found, retouched and 37,500 stamps printed from it during 1889-90. In 1892 all remaining unsold were overprinted REPRINT.

1864-75. Portraits Issue *B.E.P., intaglio, perforated 12.*

27 *Princess Victoria*

		UnFVF	UseFVF
27 1¢	**purple,** 1871	12.00	10.00

28 *Kamehameha IV (1834-63) reigned 1854-63, vainly sought U.S. reciprocal trade agreements, made English the school language*

		UnFVF	UseFVF
28 2¢	**orange red**	20.00	12.00

29, 36, 37 *David Kalakaua (1836-91), elected king to succeed Lunalilo (No.47) in 1874. 1877 revolution forced from him a constitution guaranteeing responsible government*

		UnFVF	UseFVF
29 2¢	**deep brown,** 1875	10.00	4.00

No. 29 bisected and used with 5¢ stamp to make up 6¢ rate to U.S.

		UnFVF	UseFVF
30 5¢	**deep blue,** 1866	200.00	40.00

No. 30 traces of frame lines around design.

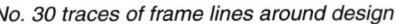

31 *Kamehameha V*

		UnFVF	UseFVF
31 6¢	**emerald green,** 1871	32.00	12.00

32, 44 *Prince William Pitt Leleiohoku, died 1877*

		UnFVF	UseFVF
32 12¢	**black,** 1875	72.50	37.00

33 *Mataio Kekuanada, father of Kamehameha*

		UnFVF	UseFVF
33 18¢	**dull carmine red,** 1871	115.00	45.00
	no gum	22.50	

1882-91. Issue *No. T29-32 and new designs; engraved, perforated 12.*

34,35 *Princess Likelike (Mrs. Archibald Cleghorn)*

		UnFVF	UseFVF
34 1¢	**Prussian blue,** 1882	8.00	12.00
35 1¢	**blue green,** 1883, T34	6.00	10.00
36 2¢	**lilac rose,** 1882 T29	80.00	35.00
37 2¢	**deep rose,** 1886, T29	5.25	1.25

1890-91. Lydia Kamehameha Issue *B.E.P., intaglio, perforated 12.*

38 *Lydia Kamehameha (Mrs. John O. Dominis, 1837-1917), sister of Kalakaua, reigned for two years as Queen Liliuokalani. Deposed in 1893, she swore allegiance to the republic after an abortive counter-revolution in 1895. She wrote the best-known Hawaiian song, "Aloha Oe"*

No.	Value	Description	UnFVF	UseFVF
38	2¢	**deep violet blue,** 1890	6.00	2.00
		v. horizontal pair, imperforate	2,500.00	
39	5¢	**bright blue,** T30	20.00	70.00
40	5¢	**deep blue,** 1891, T30	140.00	180.00

1882-83. Kalakaua Issue

No.	Value	Description	UnFVF	UseFVF
41	10¢	**black,** 1882	45.00	25.00
42	10¢	**vermilion,** 1883, T41	42.50	16.00
43	10¢	**red brown,** 1884, T41	40.00	12.00
44	12¢	**red purple,** 1883, T32	100.00	42.50

1882. Queen Kapiolani Issue

45 *Queen Kapiolani*

No.	Value	Description	UnFVF	UseFVF
45	15¢	**red brown**	85.00	35.00

1883. Kamehameha the Great Statue Issue

46 *Bronze statue, sculpted by Gould*

No.	Value	Description	UnFVF	UseFVF
46	25¢	**black violet,** 1883	165.00	75.00

1883. William C. Lunalilo Issue

47 *William C. Lunalilo (1835-74), whom the legislature unanimously elected king in 1873, was liberal, pro-American and beloved, but died within 13 months*

No.	Value	Description	UnFVF	UseFVF
47	50¢	**orange red,** 1883	200.00	110.00

1883. Queen Emma Kaleleonalani Issue

48 *Dowager Queen Emma Kaleleonalani, widow of Kamehameha IV, lost the 1874 election to Kalakaua, which caused a week's rioting in Honolulu*

No.	Value	Description	UnFVF	UseFVF
48	$1	**rose red**	300.00	180.00
		Maltese cross cancellation	65.00	

1893. Provisional Govt. Issue Overthrow of monarchy; *Nos. 27-48 overprinted. Nos. 49-60 in red, Nos. 61-69 black.*

Provisional
GOVT.
1893

49

No.	Value	Description	UnFVF	UseFVF
49	1¢	**purple**	10.00	16.50
		v. double overprint	180.00	
		v2. 189	525.00	
		v3. w/o period after *GOVT*	275.00	
50	1¢	**Prussian blue**	12.00	20.00
		v. double overprint	130.00	
		v1. w/o period after *GOVT*	180.00	180.00
		v2. pair, one w/o overprint	775.00	
51	1¢	**bright green**	2.00	4.00
		v. double overprint	850.00	600.00
		v1. pair, one w/o overprint	7,250.00	
52	2¢	**deep brown**	16.50	30.00
		v. double overprint	300.00	
		v1. w/o period after *GOVT*	350.00	
53	2¢	**slate violet**	2.00	1.65
		v. double overprint	775.00	625.00
		v1. inverted overprint	4,000.00	2,500.00
		v2. 18 3	600.00	500.00
54	5¢	**bright blue**	8.00	3.00
		v. double overprint	3,500.00	1,250.00
		v1. inverted overprint	1,250.00	
55	5¢	**indigo**	16.00	40.00
		v. double overprint	650.00	
		v1. w/o period after *GOVT*	245.00	275.00
56	6¢	**emerald green**	20.00	35.00
		v. double overprint	1,250.00	
		v1. black overprint	15,000.00	30,000.00
57	10¢	**black**	12.00	20.00
		v. double overprint	700.00	300.00
58	12¢	**black**	12.00	25.00
		v. double overprint	2,000.00	
59	12¢	**red purple**	165.00	225.00
60	25¢	**black violet**	37.00	60.00
		v double overprint	375.00	
		v1. w/o period after *GOVT*	350.00	350.00
61	2¢	**orange red**	85.00	95.00
		v. w/o period after *GOVT*	350.00	350.00
62	2¢	**deep rose**	1.65	3.00
		v. double overprint	3,000.00	
		v1. w/o period after *GOVT*	65.00	80.00
62A	6¢	**green**	20,000.00	22,500.00
63	10¢	**vermilion**	20.00	40.00
		v. double overprint	650.00	
64	10¢	**red brown**	10.00	16.50
		v. red overprint	20,000.00	23,500.00
65	12¢	**red purple**	370.00	600.00
66	15¢	**red brown**	25.00	40.00
		v. double overprint	2,000.00	
67	18¢	**dull carmine red**	35.00	45.00
		v. double overprint	400.00	
		v1. 18 3	500.00	500.00
		v2. w/o period after *GOVT*	400.00	400.00
		v3. pair, one w/o overprint	2,500.00	
68	50¢	**orange red**	80.00	120.00

		UnFVF	UseFVF
	v. double overprint	325.00	
	v1. w/o period after *GOVT*	400.00	
69		**UnFVF**	**UseFVF**
$1	**rose red**	145.00	225.00
	v. w/o period after *GOVT*	425.00	400.00

1894-99. Republic Pictorials Issue *B.E.P., intaglio, perforated 12.*

70, 82 *Arms*

		UnFVF	UseFVF
70			
1¢	**orange yellow**	2.25	1.65

71, 83 *Honolulu*

		UnFVF	UseFVF
71			
2¢	**brown drab**	3.00	.80

72 *Kamehameha I statue*

		UnFVF	UseFVF
72			
5¢	**carmine red**	5.25	2.00

73 *Hope of Statehood*

		UnFVF	UseFVF
73			
10¢	**yellow green**	8.00	6.00

74 *S.S. Arawa*

		UnFVF	UseFVF
74			
12¢	**deep blue**	16.50	22.50

75 *Sanford Ballard Dole (1858-1926), justice of Hawaiian Supreme Court, led 1893 revolution, was 1st president of Hawaii, 1894-98, 1st territorial governor, 1900-03*

		UnFVF	UseFVF
75			
25¢	**deep blue**	16.50	22.50

1896. Officials Issue *B.E.P., intaglio, perforated 12.*

76 *Lorrin Andrews Thurston (1858-1931), a leader in revolutions of 1887 and 1893. As Reform Minister of Interior, helped draft the republic constitution and led negotiations for annexation of Hawaii by the U.S.*

		UnFVF	UseFVF
76			
2¢	**yellow green**	45.00	12.00
77		**UnFVF**	**UseFVF**
5¢	**sepia**	45.00	12.00
78		**UnFVF**	**UseFVF**
6¢	**ultramarine**	45.00	12.00
79		**UnFVF**	**UseFVF**
10¢	**carmine**	45.00	12.00
80		**UnFVF**	**UseFVF**
12¢	**orange**	45.00	12.00
81		**UnFVF**	**UseFVF**
25¢	**deep violet**	45.00	12.00

1899. U.S. Government Issue T70-72 changed colors; No. 84 inscribed CENTS at bottom. *B.E.P., intaglio, perforated 12.*

82

		UnFVF	UseFVF
82			
1¢	**deep blue green**	2.00	1.60
83		**UnFVF**	**UseFVF**
2¢	**rose carmine**	1.80	1.45
	a. salmon	1.80	1.45
	v. horizontal pair, imperforate	2,250.00	
84		**UnFVF**	**UseFVF**
5¢	**deep blue**	8.50	4.00

Since 1899: U.S. Stamps have been used in Hawaii.

Envelopes and Wrappers

1884. First Issue Inside white.

EN1-5 *View of Honolulu Harbor*

		UnFVF	UseFVF
EN1			
1¢	**yellow green**	4.50	4.50
	entire	8.00	20.00
	a. green	5.00	5.00
	entire	10.00	25.00
EN2		**UnFVF**	**UseFVF**
2¢	**rose carmine**	4.50	7.00
	entire	8.00	27.50
	a. pale pink	15.00	17.50
	entire	35.00	60.00
EN3		**UnFVF**	**UseFVF**
4¢	**red**	25.00	30.00
	entire	45.00	90.00
EN4		**UnFVF**	**UseFVF**
5¢	**blue**	10.50	12.50
	entire	55.00	30.00
EN5		**UnFVF**	**UseFVF**
10¢	**black**	35.00	40.00
	entire	110.00	65.00

1884. Second Issue Inside blue.

		UnFVF	UseFVF
EN6			
2¢	**rose red**	250.00	250.00
	entire	750.00	750.00
EN7		**UnFVF**	**UseFVF**
4¢	**red**	300.00	250.00
	entire	700.00	
EN8		**UnFVF**	**UseFVF**
5¢	**deep blue**	300.00	250.00
	entire	700.00	700.00
EN9		**UnFVF**	**UseFVF**
10¢	**black**	350.00	350.00
	entire	800.00	

1885. Special Delivery Envelopes Issue *(Nos. EN5 and EN9 inscribed* Special Despatch Letter *in red in upper left corner. Prices are for entires).*

EN10		UnFVF	UseFVF
10¢	**black, inside white**	250.00	

EN11		UnFVF	UseFVF
10¢	**black, inside blue**	250.00	

1893. Provisional Government Overprint Issue *locally overprinted in black or red.*

EN12

EN12		UnFVF	UseFVF
1¢	**yellow green** red overprint	6.75	12.50
	entire	10.00	30.00
	v. double overprint	4,500.00	
	entire	1,750.00	

EN13		UnFVF	UseFVF
2¢	**rose**	4.50	7.00
	entire	6.00	18.50
	v. double overprint	500.00	
	entire	900.00	
	v1. double overprint, second inverted	140.00	
	entire	1,500.00	
	v2. triple overprint	90.00	
	entire	105.00	

EN14		UnFVF	UseFVF
5¢	**blue (shades)** red overprint	7.50	9.00
	entire	15.00	22.50
	v. double overprint	375.00	
	entire	600.00	
	v1. triple overprint		
	entire	3,000.00	

EN15		UnFVF	UseFVF
10¢	**black** red overprint, E5	18.00	20.00
	entire	32.50	120.00
	v. double overprint		
	entire	1,800.00	
	v1. triple overprint	42.50	
	entire	290.00	

EN16		UnFVF	UseFVF
10¢	**black** red overprint, E9	350.00	
	entire	1,100.00	

Postal Cards

1882-92. Hawaii Postal Card Issue

PC1, 2, 5, 6, 9 *Queen Liliuokalani*

PC1		UnFVF	UseFVF
1¢	**red on buff,** 1882	40.00	80.00

PC2		UnFVF	UseFVF
1¢	**red on flesh,** 1889	40.00	50.00

1882-92. Hawaii, Diamond Head Issue

PC3, 7, 8, 10 *Diamond Head*

PC3		UnFVF	UseFVF
2¢	**black on white**	70.00	125.00

PC3A		UnFVF	UseFVF
2¢	**black on white,** 1892	135.00	225.00

1892. Hawaii, Royal Emblem Issue

PC4 *Royal emblems*

PC4		UnFVF	UseFVF
3¢	**blue green on white**	90.00	125.00

1883-89. Hawaii, Message & Reply Cards Issue

PC5		UnFVF	UseFVF
1¢ + 1¢	**violet on buff,** entire	240.00	400.00
	m. message card	50.00	160.00
	r. reply card	50.00	160.00

PC6		UnFVF	UseFVF
1¢ + 1¢	**violet on flesh,** entire, 1889	240.00	400.00
	m. message card	50.00	160.00
	r. reply card	50.00	160.00

PC7		UnFVF	UseFVF
2¢ + 2¢	**violet blue on white,** entire	350.00	500.00
	m. message card	75.00	225.00
	r. reply card	75.00	225.00

PC8		UnFVF	UseFVF
2¢ + 2¢	**blue on white,** entire	240.00	400.00
	m. message card	50.00	150.00
	r. reply card	50.00	150.00

1893. Provisional Government Overprint Issue "Provisional Government/1893" *in black or red.*

PC9

PC9		UnFVF	UseFVF
1¢	**red on flesh**	50.00	150.00

PC10		UnFVF	UseFVF
2¢	**black on white,** red overprint	70.00	170.00

PC11		UnFVF	UseFVF
3¢	**blue green on white,** red overprint	90.00	360.00

1894. New Design Issue

PC4. Iolani palace.

PC12 *Iolani palace*

PC12		UnFVF	UseFVF
1¢	**red on flesh**	30.00	45.00

PC13 *Map of Pacific Ocean, Mercator projection*

PC13		UnFVF	UseFVF
2¢	**green on white**	60.00	100.00

Philippines

In the Spanish-American War (1898), United States forces invading the Philippines were aided by Katipunan (Revolutionary) forces. Spain ceded the islands to the U.S. (1899), and the latter decided not to relinquish control until Filipinos were ready for self-government. The Katipunans declared war on the U.S., and fighting continued until mid-1902. Despite this, U.S. civil administration began July 4, 1901. Self-rule was extended gradually until the establishment of a Commonwealth (1935). World War II brought a short period of Japanese occupation (1942-45) but following the defeat of Japan, the Philippines became a republic on July 4, 1946.

100 cents = 1 dollar. 1906: 100 centavos = 1 peso. 1962: 100 sentimos = 1 piso.

Prior to 1899: Stamps of Spanish Philippines.

Regular Postal Issues

1899. Overprint Issue

261 *1899, April 29, 1901. U.S. #182, 188-210 (triangles in upper corners) overprinted* PHILIPPINES *in black or red (#274-277); perforated 12; wmk. double-line* USPS, *#273 (U.S. #182); no wmk.*

No.		Description	UnFVF	UseFVF
261	1¢	**deep green**	4.00	.85
		x. overprint inverted	15,000.00	
262	2¢	**carmine,** (#191)	2.25	1.20
		n. Booklet pane of 6	275.00	

263

No.		Description	UnFVF	UseFVF
263	2¢	**red,** (#192)	1.65	.80
264	3¢	**dark red violet**	7.75	1.75
265	4¢	**chocolate** *(Aug. 30, 1901)*	30.00	6.00
266	5¢	**dark blue**	7.25	1.20
		x. Overprint inverted	3,725.00	3,275.00
267	6¢	**lake** *(Aug. 30, 1901)*	37.00	9.00
268	8¢	**purple** *(Aug. 30, 1901)*	37.00	10.00
269	10¢	**brown,** Type I	22.50	5.50
270	10¢	**brown,** Type II	275.00	42.50
271	15¢	**olive green** *(Aug. 30, 1899)*	40.00	10.75
		a. light olive green	42.50	12.00
272	50¢	**orange** *(Aug. 30, 1899)*	185.00	50.00

273

No.		Description	UnFVF	UseFVF
273	50¢	**orange,** no wmk., *(Aug. 30, 1899)*	525.00	350.00
274	$1	**black,** Type I, *(Aug. 30, 1901)*	575.00	570.00
275	$1	**black,** Type II, *(Aug. 30, 1901)*	3,000.00	950.00
276	$2	**dark blue** *(Aug. 30, 1901)*	1,650.00	350.00
277	$5	**dark green** *(Aug. 30, 1901)*	1,200.00	900.00

10¢: Ovals below *TEN CENTS* intact (#269), broken by ornaments (#270). $1: Circles enclosing $1 broken (#274), complete (#275).

Special printings: 1899, for the Paris Exhibition, most existing copies handstamped *Special Surcharge* on the back: 1¢, 2¢ (#262), 3¢, 5¢, 10¢ (#269), 15¢, 50¢ (#271). Few copies remain. Set $3,000 ($500 ea.).

1903, for the St. Louis Exposition, most existing copies handstamped *Special Printing* on the back: 6¢, $1 (#274), $2, $5, $800, $1,050, $1,200, $2,000.

Specimen: 1¢, 2¢ (#262), 3¢, 5¢, 10¢ (#269), 15¢, 50¢ (#272), overprinted *Specimen,* exist. $200 ea.

For O.B. and other official handstamps see note after #300.

1899-1901. Postage Due Issue U.S. #PD38-44 overprinted.

No.		Description	UnFVF	UseFVF
278	1¢	**brown carmine**	8.00	1.80
		on cover, used for regular postage: *Sept. 5-19, 1902*	290.00	110.00
279	2¢	**brown carmine**	8.00	1.80
280	3¢	**brown carmine** *(1901)*	24.00	8.00

281

No.		Description	UnFVF	UseFVF
281	5¢	**brown carmine**	20.00	3.00
282	10¢	**brown carmine**	25.00	6.30

283

No.		Description	UnFVF	UseFVF
283	30¢	**brown carmine** *(1901)*	300.00	125.00

284

No.		Description	UnFVF	UseFVF
284	50¢	**brown carmine**	290.00	120.00

Special Printings: 1889, for the Paris Exhibition, most existing copies handstamped *Special Surcharge* on the back: #278, 279, 281, 282, 284 — $1,000 ea.

1907, for the Bureau of Insular Affair on very white paper: #278-284 — $1,000 ea.

Specimen: #278, 279, 281, 282, 284, overprinted *Specimen:* exist — $40.00 ea.

1901. Special Delivery Issue Sept. 6. U.S. #SD5 overprinted in red.

285

PHILIPPINES

285		UnFVF	UseFVF
10¢	**indigo**	150.00	135.00

Special printing of 1907 for the Bureau of Insular Affairs: U.S. #SD6, 10¢ ultramarine overprinted in red, $600.

1903-04. Overprint Issue US #211-224, 231 (2¢) with black or red (R) overprint 261; perforated 12; wmk. double-line USPS.

286		UnFVF	UseFVF
1¢	**deep bluish green** *(Sept. 6, 1903)*	5.25	.50
287		UnFVF	UseFVF
2¢	**carmine** *(Sept. 6, 1903)*	10.00	1.80

288

288		UnFVF	UseFVF
2¢	**carmine,** (US #231), *(Nov. 1, 1904)*	7.25	3.00

289

289		UnFVF	UseFVF
3¢	**dark red violet** *(Nov. 1, 1904)*	90.00	16.50

290

290		UnFVF	UseFVF
5¢	**brown** *(Nov. 1, 1904)*	100.00	30.00
	a. orange brown	100.00	27.50
291		UnFVF	UseFVF
5¢	**deep blue** *(Jan. 4, 1904)*	16.50	1.15

292

292		UnFVF	UseFVF
6¢	**brown red** *(Nov. 1, 1904)*	122.50	30.00

293

293		UnFVF	UseFVF
8¢	**violet black** *(Nov. 1, 1904)*	51.00	16.50
294		UnFVF	UseFVF
10¢	**pale red brown** *(Nov. 1, 1904)*	30.00	3.25
	x. Pair, one no overprint		1,500.00

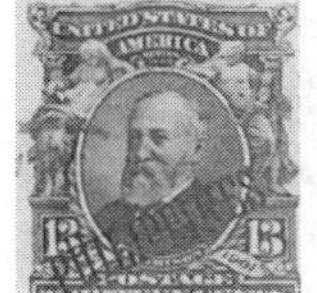
295

295		UnFVF	UseFVF
13¢	**black brown** *(Jan. 4, 1904)*	43.00	22.00

296

296		UnFVF	UseFVF
15¢	**olive green** *(Jan. 4, 1904)*	80.00	20.00

297

297		UnFVF	UseFVF
50¢	**orange** *(Sept. 6, 1903)*	182.00	45.00

298

298		UnFVF	UseFVF
$1	**black,** (R), *(Jan. 4, 1904)*	675.00	350.00
299		UnFVF	UseFVF
$2	**dark blue,** (R), *(Nov. 1, 1904)*	1,200.00	1,075.00

300

300		UnFVF	UseFVF
$5	**dark green,** (R), *(Nov. 1, 1904)*	2,425.00	1,200.00

No. 288 booklet pane (6): $1,075.

Special printings: 1903, for the St. Louis Exposition, most existing copies handstamped *Special Surcharge* on the back: 1¢, 2¢ (#288) 5¢, 13¢-$1, #286, 288, 291, 295 $1,000. ea.; #298 $2,000.

Handstamped *Special Printing* on the back: 2¢ (#287) $800.

1907, for the Bureau of Insular Affairs, on very white paper: #286, 288-297, $1,000 ea.; #298 $2,000, #299 $4,000, #300 $5,000.

On Jan. 1, 1906, all branches of the insular government began using postage stamps for official business, thus replacing the franking system in use prior to that time. Officers of these agencies were authorized, if they so desired, to overprint stamps purchased for official business with the letters *O.B.* This was done in various ways — manuscript, typewriter, and rubber stamp, with the latter in the majority. Most of these read *O.B.,* as per the directive, but other forms such as *Official Business* or

Official Mail, and variations, are known. These overprints are found on the issues of 1899 to 1906 in various colors.

1906-31. Philippine Issue

T301 *2¢ José Rizal-Mercado y Alonzo (1861-96), Philippine national hero who agitated for independence from Spain. His novel,* Noli Me Tangere *(Touch Me Not), known as the Philippine* Uncle Tom's Cabin, *forced his emigration in 1886. Given permission to revisit his homeland in 1896, he was arrested, falsely accused of instigating the Katipunan rebellion, and executed by firing squad.*

1 (1906-13): Perf. 12; wmk. 301, double-line "PIPS."

		UnFVF	UseFVF
301			
2¢	**deep green**	.35	.20
	a. yellow green *(1910)*	1.10	.20
	n. Booklet pane (6)	60.00	

T302 *4¢ President William McKinley (1843-1901) president of the United States during the Spanish-American War, was assassinated at the Pan-American Exposition in Buffalo, N.Y.*

		UnFVF	UseFVF
302			
4¢	**carmine red**	.60	.20
	a. carmine lake *(1910)*	1.50	.20
	n. Booklet pane (6)	60.00	

T303 *6¢ Ferdinand Magellan (1480-1521) was the first to circumnavigate the globe (1519-22) but was killed in the Philippines, in April 1521, while trying to force residents of a village to give him food for his crew.*

		UnFVF	UseFVF
303			
6¢	**violet**	1.50	.30

T304 *8¢ Miguel Lopez de Legazpi (1510-72), led the Spanish settlement of the islands, founded Manila in 1571.*

		UnFVF	UseFVF
304			
8¢	**brown**	3.00	1.20

T305 *10¢ Maj. Gen. Henry Ware Lawton (1843-99), fought against Katipunan leader Aguinaldo, died in action near Manila on Dec. 19, 1899.*

		UnFVF	UseFVF
305			
10¢	**blue**	2.40	.25

T306 *12¢ Abraham Lincoln (1809-1865) was assassinated while president of the United States.*

		UnFVF	UseFVF
306			
12¢	**carmine lake**	6.25	2.50
307			
12¢	**red orange** *(1910)*	12.00	4.50

T308 *16¢ Adam William T. Sampson (1840-1902), commanded the North American Squadron in the Spanish-American War.*

		UnFVF	UseFVF
308			
16¢	**black**	5.75	.60
309			
16¢	**olive green** *(1911)*	4.50	1.65

T310 *20¢ George Washington*

		UnFVF	UseFVF
310			
20¢	**pale brown**	5.50	1.25
311			
20¢	**olive yellow** *(1909)*	10.75	2.25

T312 *26¢ Francisco Carriedo*

		UnFVF	UseFVF
312			
26¢	**sepia**	8.00	3.75
313			
26¢	**deep blue green** *(1909)*	2.80	1.30

T314 *30¢ Benjamin Franklin (1706-1790), patriot, first postmaster of the United States.*

		UnFVF	UseFVF
314			
30¢	**deep olive**	6.50	2.90
315			
30¢	**ultramarine** *(1910)*	12.50	6.50

T316 *1p-10p Arms, City of Manila*

		UnFVF	UseFVF
316			
1p	**brown orange**	37.50	12.75
317			
1p	**violet** *(1909)*	40.00	6.50

318

		UnFVF	UseFVF
318			
2p	**black**	45.00	1.80

No.	Denom.	Color	UnFVF	UseFVF
319	**2p**	**dark chocolate** *(1913)*	115.00	4.00

320

No.	Denom.	Color	UnFVF	UseFVF
320	**4p**	**deep blue**	145.00	20.00

321

No.	Denom.	Color	UnFVF	UseFVF
321	**10p**	**green**	300.00	95.00

I P S

2 (1911-14) T301//321; perf. 12; wmk. 322, single-line PIPS.

No.	Denom.	Color	UnFVF	UseFVF
322	**2¢**	**green**	.80	.20
		n. Booklet pane (6)	400.00	
323	**4¢**	**carmine lake**	3.40	.25
		n. Booklet pane (6)	500.00	
324	**6¢**	**deep violet**	2.40	.20
325	**8¢**	**brown**	11.50	.60

326

No.	Denom.	Color	UnFVF	UseFVF
326	**10¢**	**blue**	4.30	.20
327	**12¢**	**orange**	3.25	.60

328

No.	Denom.	Color	UnFVF	UseFVF
328	**16¢**	**olive green**	3.75	.30

329

No.	Denom.	Color	UnFVF	UseFVF
329	**20¢**	**olive yellow**	2.40	.20
330	**26¢**	**deep blue green**	4.50	.35
331	**30¢**	**ultramarine**	4.50	.60

332

No.	Denom.	Color	UnFVF	UseFVF
332	**30¢**	**gray** *(1914)*	12.00	.65
333	**1p**	**deep lilac**	30.00	.70
334	**2p**	**dark chocolate**	37.00	1.10
335	**4p**	**deep blue**	800.00	110.00
336	**10p**	**deep green**	275.00	35.00

337 (1914-23): T301//316; perf. 10; wmk. 322, single-line PIPS.

No.	Denom.	Color	UnFVF	UseFVF
337	**2¢**	**green**	2.25	.18
		n. Booklet pane (6)	350.00	

338

No.	Denom.	Color	UnFVF	UseFVF
338	**4¢**	**carmine red**	2.25	.30
		n. Booklet pane (6)	350.00	
339	**6¢**	**violet**	57.00	11.00
		a. deep violet	50.00	8.00
340	**8¢**	**brown**	280.00	12.00
341	**10¢**	**blue**	35.00	.25

342

No.	Denom.	Color	UnFVF	UseFVF
342	**16¢**	**light yellow olive**	100.00	6.00
343	**20¢**	**orange**	25.00	1.10
344	**30¢**	**gray**	75.00	3.75

345

No.	Denom.	Color	UnFVF	UseFVF
345	**1p**	**deep lilac**	165.00	4.25

346 (1918-26): T301//316; perf. 11; wmk. 322, single-line PIPS.

No.	Denom.	Color	UnFVF	UseFVF
346	**2¢**	**green**	27.50	6.00
		n. Booklet pane (6)	500.00	

No.			UnFVF	UseFVF
347	4¢	**carmine red**	38.00	3.25
		n. Booklet pane (6)	1,250.00	
348	6¢	**violet**	52.50	2.25
349	8¢	**light brown**	280.00	40.00
350	10¢	**blue**	75.00	1.80

351

No.			UnFVF	UseFVF
351	16¢	**yellow olive**	125.00	9.50
352	20¢	**yellow**	82.50	10.50
353	30¢	**gray**	80.00	17.75

354

No.			UnFVF	UseFVF
354	1p	**deep lilac**	100.00	18.75

355 (1917-28): T301//318 and T363 (16¢), Perf. 11; #356: imperforate x perf. 11; no wmk.

No.			UnFVF	UseFVF
355	2¢	**light green**	.25	.20
		a. green	.35	.20
		v. Horizontal pair, gutter between	3,000.00	
		v1. Vertical pair, gutter between	3,500.00	
		n. Booklet pane (6)	8.75	

356

356LP

No.			UnFVF	UseFVF
356	2¢	**green,** coil *(1928)*	20.00	20.00
357	4¢	**red carmine**	.20	.20
		a. rose carmine	.40	.20
		n. Booklet pane (6)	3.60	
358	6¢	**deep violet**	.45	.20
		a. deep lilac	.70	.20
		b. purple	.70	.25
		n. Booklet pane (6)	60.00	
359	8¢	**pale yellow brown**	.30	.20
		a. deep yellow brown	.35	.20
360	10¢	**deep dull blue**	.30	.20
361	12¢	**orange**	.40	.20
362	16¢	**yellow olive,** T30	75.00	.25
		a. bistre	77.50	.25

363 Adm. George Dewey (1837-1917), hero of the Battle of Manila in the Spanish-American War.

No.			UnFVF	UseFVF
363	16¢	**olive green** *(1923)*	1.80	.25
		a. bistre	1.10	.25
364	20¢	**yellow**	.35	.20
365	26¢	**deep blue green**	.60	.60
		a. blue green	.65	.40
366	30¢	**gray black**	.70	.20
		a. black	.70	.25
367	1p	**deep lilac**	40.00	1.50
		a. red lilac	40.00	1.50
		b. rose lilac	40.00	2.25
368	2p	**dark chocolate**	37.00	1.00
369	4p	**deep blue**	35.00	.60
		a. dark blue	35.00	.60

370

No.			UnFVF	UseFVF
370	10p	**green** *(1926)*	80.00	6.50

(1931): imperforate, no watermark

No.			UnFVF	UseFVF
371	2¢	**emerald**	.30	.30
372	4¢	**red carmine**	.35	.40
373	6¢	**deep violet**	1.25	2.00
374	8¢	**yellow brown**	1.25	2.00
375	10¢	**deep dull blue**	1.50	2.50
376	12¢	**orange**	2.25	3.75
377	16¢	**bistre,** T363	1.65	2.50
378	20¢	**yellow**	1.65	2.50
379	26¢	**emerald**	1.65	2.50
380	30¢	**black**	2.00	3.25
381	1p	**violet**	6.00	10.00
382	2p	**purple brown**	16.50	21.50
383	4p	**deep blue**	46.00	80.00
384	10p	**deep green**	120.00	200.00

Note: #371-384 originally issued in 1925 in darker shades, not sold to public.

Perf. 12; wmk. 301, double-line PIPS.

1906-31. Special Delivery Issue *perforated 12; wmk. 301, double-line PIPS.*

385-389 *Special delivery; messenger, engr.*

		UnFVF	UseFVF
385			
20¢	**ultramarine**	40.00	10.00
	a. pale ultramarine	40.00	12.75

Perf. 12; wmk. 322, single-line PIPS.

		UnFVF	UseFVF
386			
20¢	**bright ultramarine** *(1911)*	24.50	2.25

Perf. 10; wmk. 322, single-line PIPS.

		UnFVF	UseFVF
387			
20¢	**deep ultramarine** *(1916)*	225.00	65.00

Perf. 11; no wmk.

		UnFVF	UseFVF
388			
20¢	**ultramarine** *(1920)*	.70	.40
	a. pale ultramarine	.70	.40
	b. black violet	1.50	.70

Imperforate; no wmk.

389

		UnFVF	UseFVF
389			
20¢	**black violet** *(1931)*	27.50	22.50
	a. dark blue violet	40.00	37.00

1926. Madrid-Manila Flight Overprint Issue

1926, May 13. Madrid-Manila Flight; #355/370, 345 (1p) overprinted in violet or red (R); perf. 11, #401: perf. 10. Capts. Ed Gallarza and J. Loriga, air navigators of the Spanish military school, left Madrid on April 4, 1926. Flying via Karachi and Macao, they made the first ocean crossing to Manila, landing there May 13.

		UnFVF	UseFVF
390			
2¢	**light green,** (R)	9.50	3.75

391x

		UnFVF	UseFVF
391			
4¢	**red carmine**	12.00	5.00
	x. Overprint variety	3,700.00	
392		UnFVF	UseFVF
6¢	**deep violet,** (R)	57.00	16.50
393		UnFVF	UseFVF
8¢	**deep yellow brown**	57.00	16.75
394		UnFVF	UseFVF
10¢	**deep dull blue,** (R)	57.00	16.75
395		UnFVF	UseFVF
12¢	**orange**	57.00	30.00
396		UnFVF	UseFVF
16¢	**yellow olive,** T308	3,000.00	2,000.00
	a. bistre, (R)	6,000.00	3,500.00
397		UnFVF	UseFVF
16¢	**olive green,** T363	65.00	30.00

398

		UnFVF	UseFVF
398			
20¢	**yellow**	65.00	30.00
399		UnFVF	UseFVF
26¢	**blue green**	65.00	30.00
	v. Perf. 12, #330	5,300.00	

400

		UnFVF	UseFVF
400			
30¢	**gray black**	65.00	30.00
401		UnFVF	UseFVF
1p	**deep lilac,** #345	240.00	140.00
402		UnFVF	UseFVF
2p	**dark chocolate,** (R)	525.00	300.00
403		UnFVF	UseFVF
4p	**dark blue,** (R)	800.00	600.00

404

		UnFVF	UseFVF
404			
10p	**green**	1,275.00	800.00

1926. Inauguration of Legislative Palace Issue *Frame lithographed; center typographed in black, perforated 12.*

405

406

		UnFVF	UseFVF
405			
2¢	**light green**	.60	.40
	v. Vertical pair, imperforate between	500.00	
	v1. Horizontal pair, imperforate between	275.00	
	FDC		3.50
406		UnFVF	UseFVF
4¢	**scarlet**	.60	.40
	v. Vertical pair, imperforate between	500.00	
	v1. Horizontal pair, imperforate between	275.00	
	FDC		3.50

407

408

		UnFVF	UseFVF
407			
16¢	**olive green**	1.30	1.00
	v. Vertical pair, imperforate between	550.00	
	v1. Horizontal pair, imperforate between	350.00	
	FDC		10.00
408		UnFVF	UseFVF
18¢	**gray brown**	1.30	1.00

		UnFVF	UseFVF
	v. Vertical pair, imperforate between	550.00	
	Double impression	550.00	
409 20¢	**yellow orange**	2.00	1.50
	a. Center in brown	500.00	
	v. Vertical pair, imperforate between	550.00	
	v1. Pair, imperforate #409	450.00	
	v2. Pair, imperforate #409a	850.00	

410

411

		UnFVF	UseFVF
410 24¢	**gray black**	1.50	1.00
	v. Vertical pair, imperforate between	550.00	
411 1p	**mauve**	60.00	45.00
	v. Vertical pair, imperforate between	625.00	

405-411 FDC (Dec. 20, 1936), $80.

1926. Official Overprint Issue Dec. 20. Officials; #405//409 overprinted in red.

412

413

Overprint **OFFICIAL**

		UnFVF	UseFVF
412 2¢	**light green and black**	2.40	1.25
413 4¢	**scarlet and black**	3.00	1.50
	v. Vertical pair, gutter between	725.00	
	x. FDC		10.00

414

415

		UnFVF	UseFVF
414 18¢	**gray brown and black**	7.25	4.00
415 20¢	**yellow orange and black**	6.75	2.50

412-415 FDC, $50.

1928 Postage Due Issue *Aug. 21, engr., perforated 11.*

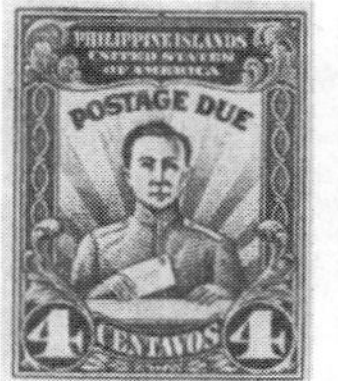
416

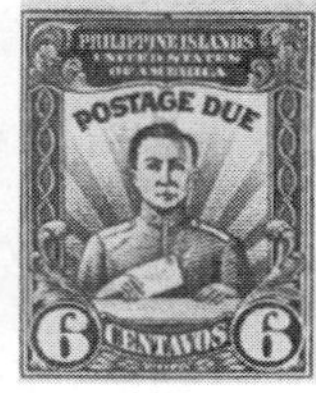
417

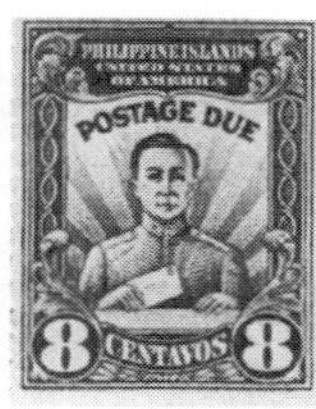
418

		UnFVF	UseFVF
416 4¢	**brown red**	.25	.25
417 6¢	**brown red**	.30	.30

		UnFVF	UseFVF
418 8¢	**brown red**	.30	.30

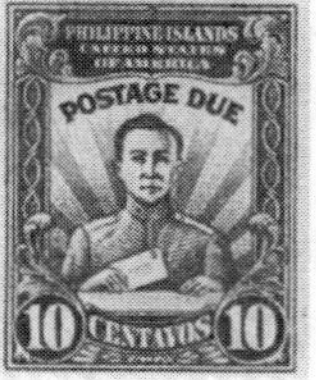
419

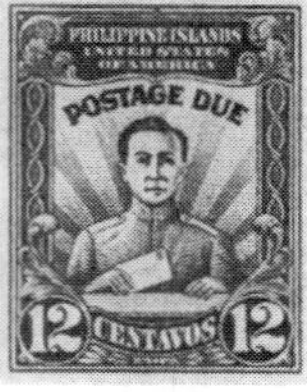
420

421

		UnFVF	UseFVF
419 10¢	**brown red**	.30	.30
420 12¢	**brown red**	.35	.35
421 16¢	**brown red**	.40	.40

422

		UnFVF	UseFVF
422 20¢	**brown red**	.30	.25

1928. London-Orient Flight Overprint Issue 1928, Nov. 9. London-Orient Flight; #355/366 and 333 (1p) overprinted in red; perf. 11, 1p: perf. 12. A flight of 4 British Southampton flying boats, commanded by Group Capt. Brown-Cave, flew from London to the Orient as a good-will gesture and an experiment toward regular airmail flights between Hong Kong and Manila.

423 *Overprint*

		UnFVF	UseFVF
423 2¢	**green**	.60	.60
424 4¢	**red carmine**	.70	.70
425 6¢	**deep violet**	2.40	2.40
426 8¢	**pale yellow brown**	2.40	2.40
427 10¢	**deep dull blue**	2.40	2.40
428 12¢	**orange**	3.75	3.75
429 16¢	**bistre**	2.40	2.40
430 20¢	**yellow**	3.75	3.75
431 26¢	**deep blue green**	11.00	8.00
432 30¢	**gray black**	11.00	8.00
433 1p	**deep lilac,** #333	60.00	32.50

1931. Official Overprint Issue May 18. Officials. #355/366 and special delivery #388 overprinted O.B.

434

434		UnFVF	UseFVF
2¢	**green**	.20	.20
	x. no period after *B*	15.00	5.00

435

435		UnFVF	UseFVF
4¢	**red carmine**	.20	.20
	x. no period after *B*	14.50	6.00

436

436		UnFVF	UseFVF
6¢	**deep violet**	.20	.20

437

437		UnFVF	UseFVF
8¢	**yellow brown**	.20	.20

438

438		UnFVF	UseFVF
10¢	**deep blue**	.40	.20

439

439		UnFVF	UseFVF
12¢	**orange**	.35	.25
	x. no period after *B*	32.50	

440

440		UnFVF	UseFVF
16¢	**olive green,** T363	.35	.20
	a. bistre	1.25	.40

441

441		UnFVF	UseFVF
20¢	**yellow**	.40	.20
	x. no period after *B*	25.00	

442

442		UnFVF	UseFVF
26¢	**deep blue green**	.50	.40
	a. blue green	1.50	.75

443

443		UnFVF	UseFVF
30¢	**gray black**	.45	.40

Special Delivery

444		UnFVF	UseFVF
20¢	**black violet**	.75	.50
	x. no period after *B*	20.00	15.00
	x1. Overprint double		

1932. Pictorial Issue *engraving, perforated 11.*

445 *Mayon Volcano (7,943 ft.), southern Luzon*

445		UnFVF	UseFVF
2¢	**light green**	.65	.40
	FDC		3.00

446 *Post Office building, Manila*

446		UnFVF	UseFVF
4¢	**carmine**	.55	.60
	FDC		4.00

447 *Pier 7, Manila Harbor*

447		UnFVF	UseFVF
12¢	**orange**	.80	1.20
	FDC		8.00

448 *Vernal Falls, Yosemite National Park, California, used in error; intended scene was Pagsanjan Falls*

		UnFVF	UseFVF
448			
18¢	**vermilion**	28.00	14.00
	FDC		20.00

449 *Rice-planting with carabao and primitive plow*

		UnFVF	UseFVF
449			
20¢	**yellow**	1.00	.85
	FDC		9.00

450 *Rice terraces*

		UnFVF	UseFVF
450			
24¢	**light purple**	1.50	1.10
	FDC		9.00

451 *Zigzag in the Kennon Road to Baguio*

		UnFVF	UseFVF
451			
32¢	**olive brown**	1.50	1.25
	FDC		9.00

1932. Von Gronau Issue Sept. 27. #445-451 overprinted in black or green (G); perf. 11. Capt. Wolfgang von Gronau, head of a commercial pilots' School at Warnemunde, Germany, and 3 companions stopped at Manila during a successful round-the-world flight in a Dornier Super-Wal flying boat. They departed for Friedrichshafen on Sept. 22.

452

		UnFVF	UseFVF
452			
2¢	**light green,** (G)	.50	.50
	FDC		2.50

453

		UnFVF	UseFVF
453			
4¢	**carmine**	.50	.50
	FDC		2.50

454

		UnFVF	UseFVF
454			
12¢	**orange,** (G)	.80	.80

455

		UnFVF	UseFVF
455			
18¢	**vermilion**	4.50	4.50

456

		UnFVF	UseFVF
456			
20¢	**yellow,** (G)	2.50	2.50

457

		UnFVF	UseFVF
457			
24¢	**light purple,** (G)	2.50	2.50

458

		UnFVF	UseFVF
458			
32¢	**olive brown,** (G)	2.50	2.50

452-458 FDC, $50.

1932. #369 overprinted in orange or red (R)

459

	UnFVF	UseFVF
459		
1p on 4p deep blue	2.40	.60
a. dark blue	3.70	1.65

460

	UnFVF	UseFVF
460		
2p on 4p dark blue, (R)	5.00	1.00
a. deep blue	5.00	1.00

Users of this catalog are invited to write to us if they have information they feel will supplement or correct any material contained herein. All such communications will be answered.

1933. Madrid-Manila Overprint Issue 1933, April 11. Madrid-Manila non-stop flight of Spanish aviator Fernando Rein y Loring; #355-366 overprinted in green.

461

F.REIN
MADRID-MANILA
FLIGHT-1933

			UnFVF	UseFVF
461	2¢	**light green**	.55	.55
		FDC		2.00

462

			UnFVF	UseFVF
462	4¢	**red carmine**	.60	.60

463

			UnFVF	UseFVF
463	6¢	**deep violet**	1.20	1.10
		FDC		4.50

464

			UnFVF	UseFVF
464	8¢	**pale yellow brown**	3.50	2.50

465

			UnFVF	UseFVF
465	10¢	**deep dull blue**	3.00	1.50

466

			UnFVF	UseFVF
466	12¢	**orange**	2.40	1.00

467

			UnFVF	UseFVF
467	16¢	**yellow olive,** T363	2.25	1.25

468

			UnFVF	UseFVF
468	20¢	**yellow**	2.25	1.65

469

			UnFVF	UseFVF
469	26¢	**deep blue green**	3.00	2.50

470

			UnFVF	UseFVF
470	30¢	**gray black**	4.00	2.50

461-470 FDC, $48.

1933. Airmail Overprint Issue May 26. #355 and #445/451 overprinted in green.

471

			UnFVF	UseFVF
471	2¢	**light green**	.85	.70
472	4¢	**carmine**	.25	.25
473	12¢	**orange**	.40	.25

474

			UnFVF	UseFVF
474	20¢	**yellow**	.40	.25

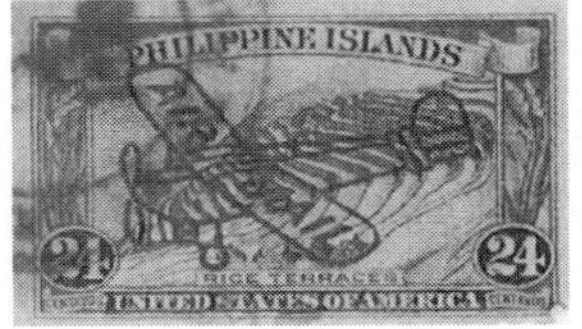

475

			UnFVF	UseFVF
475	24¢	**light purple**	.45	.35
476	32¢	**olive brown**	.65	.50

471-476 FDC, $42.50.

1934. 10TH FAR EASTERN CHAMPIONSHIP GAME ISSUE April 14. *Typo, perforated 11 1/2.*

477 *Baseball*

477		UnFVF	UseFVF
2¢	**yellow brown**	2.00	1.00
	x. *T* of *EASTERN* deformed	4.00	1.65
	FDC		2.75

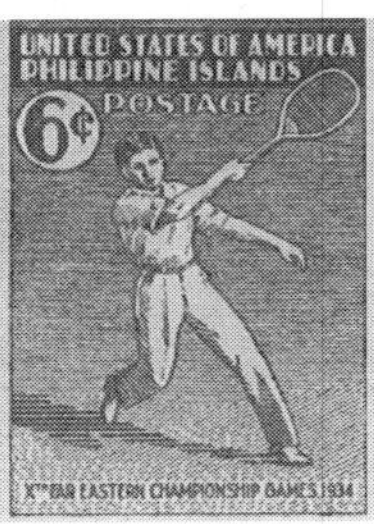

478 *Tennis*

478		UnFVF	UseFVF
6¢	**gray blue**	.35	.25
	v. Vertical pair, imperforate between	2,250.00	
	FDC		2.00

479 *Basketball*

479		UnFVF	UseFVF
16¢	**brown purple**	.65	.65
	v. Vertical pair, imperforate horizontally	1,200.00	
	FDC		2.50

1935. PICTORIAL ISSUE Feb. 15. *Engraving, perforated 11.*

480 *2¢ José Rizal:* Juan Luna painting

480		UnFVF	UseFVF
2¢	**deep rose**	.20	.20
	FDC		1.25

481 *4¢ Allegorical figure and carabao*

481		UnFVF	UseFVF
4¢	**deep yellow green**	.20	.20
	a. yellow green	.25	.20
	FDC		1.25

482 *Philippine woman*

482		UnFVF	UseFVF
6¢	**brown**	.20	.20
	FDC		1.25

483 *Pearl fishermen*

483		UnFVF	UseFVF
8¢	**red violet**	.25	.20
	FDC		2.25

484 *Santiago Fort in walled city of Manila*

484		UnFVF	UseFVF
10¢	**rose carmine**	.35	.35
	FDC		3.00

485 *Salt spring*

485		UnFVF	UseFVF
12¢	**black**	.35	.20
	FDC		3.00

486 *16¢ Magellan landing on Samar, March 16, 1521*

486		UnFVF	UseFVF
16¢	**deep blue**	.35	.20
	FDC		3.00

487 *20¢ Juan de la Cruz, national character typifying the Filipino*

487		UnFVF	UseFVF
20¢	**bistre**	.40	.20
	FDC		4.00

488 *Rice terraces*

488		UnFVF	UseFVF
26¢	**indigo**	.65	.40
	FDC		5.50

489 "The Blood Compact" *between Legazpi and Sikatuna, Chieftain of Bohol: Juan Luna painting*

		UnFVF	UseFVF
489 30¢	**deep red orange**	.55	.40
	FDC		6.00

490 *Barasoain Church*

		UnFVF	UseFVF
490 1p	**orange and black**	3.60	2.25
	FDC		15.00

491 *Battle of Manila Bay, May 1, 1898, in which the U.S. Navy's Asiatic Squadron under Commodore George Dewey destroyed the Spanish fleet*

		UnFVF	UseFVF
491 2p	**yellow brown and black**	5.50	2.50
	FDC		17.50

492 *Montalban Gorge*

		UnFVF	UseFVF
492 4p	**deep blue and black**	6.50	4.50
	FDC		25.00

493 *George Washington*

		UnFVF	UseFVF
493 5p	**deep blue green and black**	12.75	2.60
	FDC		35.00

1935. Official Overprint Issue March 14. Officials; #480-489 with overprint 494.

494

O. B.

		UnFVF	UseFVF
494 2¢	**deep rose**	.20	.20
	x. no period after *B*	15.00	5.00

495

		UnFVF	UseFVF
495 4¢	**deep yellow green**	.20	.20
	x. no period after *B*	15.00	5.00

496

		UnFVF	UseFVF
496 6¢	**brown**	.20	.20
	x. no period after *B*		

497

		UnFVF	UseFVF
497 8¢	**red violet**	.25	.20

498

		UnFVF	UseFVF
498 10¢	**rose carmine**	.25	.20

499

		UnFVF	UseFVF
499 12¢	**black**	.25	.20

500

		UnFVF	UseFVF
500 16¢	**deep blue**	.35	.20

501

		UnFVF	UseFVF
501 20¢	**bistre**	.35	.25
502 26¢	**indigo**	.60	.40
503 30¢	**deep red orange**	.65	.55

1935. Commonwealth Issue Nov. 15. Inauguration of the Commonwealth; *engr., perforated 11.*

504-508 *The Temples of Human Progress*

504		UnFVF	UseFVF
2¢	**rose red**	.25	.15
	FDC		1.25

505

505		UnFVF	UseFVF
6¢	**red violet**	.30	.25
	FDC		1.50

506

506		UnFVF	UseFVF
16¢	**dull blue**	.40	.35
	FDC		2.00

507

507		UnFVF	UseFVF
36¢	**light green**	.55	.55
	FDC		2.50

508

508		UnFVF	UseFVF
50¢	**light brown**	.85	.85
	FDC		3.00

1935. Airmail Issue Dec. 2. China Clipper flight Manila to San Francisco.

#484, 489 overprinted in gold

509		UnFVF	UseFVF
10¢	**rose carmine**	.50	.35
	FDC		3.00

510

510		UnFVF	UseFVF
30¢	**deep red orange**	.85	.60
	FDC		4.50

1936. 75th Anniversary of Rizal Issue June 19. Commemorated the birth of José Rizal (1861-1896) in Calamba, Laguna, June 19, 1861. *Typo, perforated 12.*

511 *José Rizal*

511		UnFVF	UseFVF
2¢	**orange buff**	.20	.20
	FDC		1.25

512

512		UnFVF	UseFVF
6¢	**slate blue**	.25	.25
	v. Horizontal pair, imperforate vertically	1,000.00	
	FDC		1.25

513

513		UnFVF	UseFVF
36¢	**red brown**	1.00	.85
	FDC		3.75

Read the introduction to this catalog carefully. It contains much valuable information for all stamp collectors and makes the catalog easier to use.

1936. Manila-Madrid Flight Overprint Issue Sept. 6. Manila-Madrid flight of Philippine aviators Antonio Arnaiz and Juan Calvo. *Perforated 11.*

Overprinted in blue (B) violet (V) and black

514		UnFVF	UseFVF
2¢ on 4¢ red carmine, (B)		.20	.20
	FDC		1.25

515

515		UnFVF	UseFVF
6¢ on 12¢ orange, (V)		.20	.25
	FDC		3.50

516

516		UnFVF	UseFVF
16¢ on 26¢ blue green		.35	.35
	a. green	1.50	1.00
	FDC		6.00

1936. 1st Anniversary of Commonwealth Issue Nov. 15. First President Manuel L. Quezon (1878-1944) ardently promoted independence as president of the Philippine senate (1916-35) and became president (1935-44) of the Commonwealth of the Philippines upon its inception. *Engr., perforated 11.*

517 *President Manuel L. Quezon*

517		UnFVF	UseFVF
2¢	**chestnut**	.20	.20
	FDC		1.25

518

519

518		UnFVF	UseFVF
6¢	**deep yellow green**	.20	.20
	FDC		1.25

519		UnFVF	UseFVF
12¢	**dark ultramarine**	.35	.35
	FDC		3.00

1936-38. Commonwealth Overprint Issue

COMMON-
WEALTH *#480-493 with large COMMONWEALTH overprint 520 (2¢, 6¢ and 20¢) or 521 (18 1/4 x 2 1/4mm, other values)*

520		UnFVF	UseFVF
2¢	**deep rose**	.20	.20
	n. Booklet pane (6)	3.00	1.00
	FDC		40.00

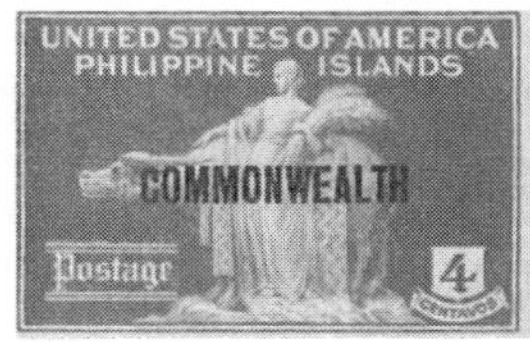

521

COMMONWEALTH

521		UnFVF	UseFVF
4¢	**deep yellow green** *(1937)*	.80	.55

522

522		UnFVF	UseFVF
6¢	**brown**	.40	.20

523

523		UnFVF	UseFVF
8¢	**red violet** *(1937)*	.35	.35

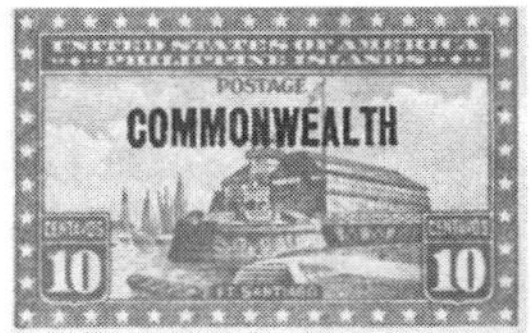

524

524		UnFVF	UseFVF
10¢	**rose carmine**	.25	.20
	x. *"commonwealt"*		
	FDC		40.00

525

525		UnFVF	UseFVF
12¢	**black** *(1937)*	.25	.20

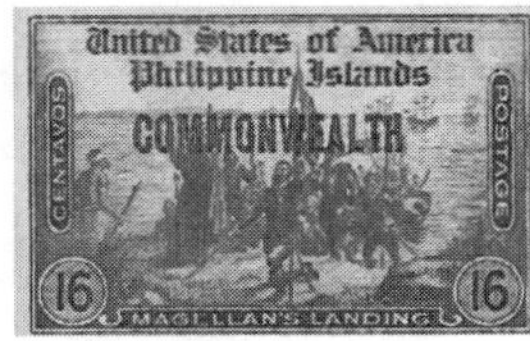

526

526		UnFVF	UseFVF
16¢	**deep blue**	.25	.20

527		UnFVF	UseFVF
20¢	**bistre** *(1937)*	1.10	.60

528

528		UnFVF	UseFVF
26¢	**indigo** *(1937)*	.65	.50

529

529		UnFVF	UseFVF
30¢	**deep red orange**	.45	.20

530

530		UnFVF	UseFVF
1p	**orange and black**	1.00	.30

531

531		UnFVF	UseFVF
2p	**yellow brown and black** *(1937)*	6.75	4.00

532

532		UnFVF	UseFVF
4p	**deep blue and black** *(1937)*	25.00	4.00

533

533		UnFVF	UseFVF
5p	**deep blue green and black** *(1937)*	2.40	2.00
	FDC		50.00

Officials. #520, 527 overprinted O.B.

534		UnFVF	UseFVF
2¢	**deep rose** *(1938)*	.20	.20
	x. no period after *B*	5.50	2.90
	FDC		50.00

535

535		UnFVF	UseFVF
20¢	**bistre** *(1938)*	1.00	.65

1937. 33RD EUCHARISTIC CONGRESS ISSUE Feb. 3. *engr., perforated 11.*

536 *33rd Eucharistic Congress*  537  538

536		UnFVF	UseFVF
2¢	**green**	.20	.20
	FDC		1.00
537		UnFVF	UseFVF
6¢	**yellow brown**	.30	.20
	FDC		1.50
538		UnFVF	UseFVF
12¢	**blue**	.30	.20
	FDC		1.75

539  540  541

539		UnFVF	UseFVF
20¢	**yellow orange**	.45	.25
	FDC		2.00
540		UnFVF	UseFVF
36¢	**red violet**	.85	.70
	FDC		2.25
541		UnFVF	UseFVF
50¢	**carmine red**	1.10	.45
	FDC		3.50

1937. City of Manila Arms Aug. 27. *Engr., perforated 11.*

542 *City of Manila Arms*

543

		UnFVF	UseFVF
542			
10p	**slate**	6.50	3.00
543		**UnFVF**	**UseFVF**
20p	**red** *b*	3.25	2.25

542-543 FDC, $75.

1937. Postage Due Issue July 29.

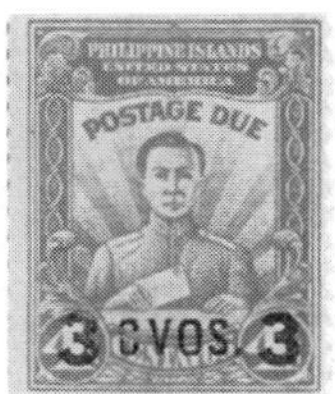

#416 over-printed

3 CVOS. 3

		UnFVF	UseFVF
544			
3¢ on 4¢	**brown red**	.25	.20
	FDC		35.00

1938-40. Commonwealth Overprint Issue #480-493 and 388 (Special delivery) with small COMMONWEALTH overprint 545 (2¢, 6¢ and 20¢) or 546 (18 1/2 x 1 1/4mm, other values).

COMMON-WEALTH

545

		UnFVF	UseFVF
545			
2¢	**deep rose** *(1939)*	.20	.20
	x. hyphen omitted		
	n. Booklet pane (6)	1.00	

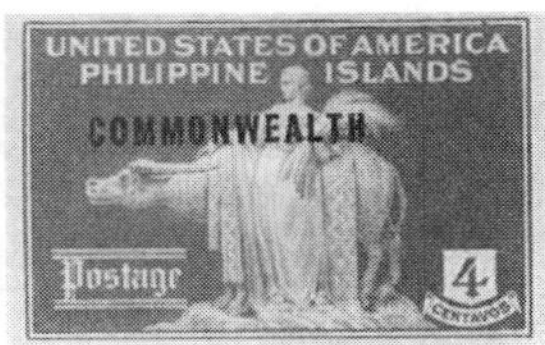

546

COMMONWEALTH

558

		UnFVF	UseFVF
546			
4¢	**deep yellow green** *(1940)*	.65	.65

547

		UnFVF	UseFVF
547			
6¢	**brown** *(1939)*	.20	.20
	a. deep brown	.20	.20
	FDC		35.00

548

		UnFVF	UseFVF
548			
8¢	**red violet** *(1939)*	.20	.20
	x. *"commonwealt"*	80.00	

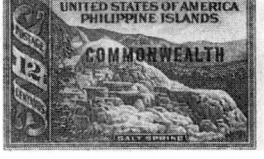

549

		UnFVF	UseFVF
549			
10¢	**rose carmine** *(1939)*	.20	.20

550

		UnFVF	UseFVF
550			
12¢	**black** *(1940)*	.20	.20

551

		UnFVF	UseFVF
551			
16¢	**deep blue** *(1938)*	.25	.20

552

		UnFVF	UseFVF
552			
20¢	**bistre** *(1939)*	.25	.20

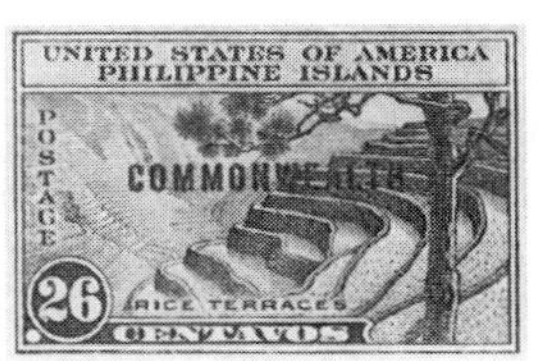

553

		UnFVF	UseFVF
553			
26¢	**indigo** *(1940)*	.35	.35

554

		UnFVF	UseFVF
554			
26¢	**deep red orange** *(1939)*	2.25	1.25

555

		UnFVF	UseFVF
555			
1p	**orange and black** *(1938)*	.65	.25
	FDC		50.00

556

		UnFVF	UseFVF
556			
2p	**yellow brown and black** *(1939)*	4.75	1.20
557		UnFVF	UseFVF
4p	**deep blue and black** *(1940)*	120.00	100.00
558		UnFVF	UseFVF
5p	**deep blue green and black** *(1940)*	6.00	4.50

Special Delivery; overprint 546

559

		UnFVF	UseFVF
559			
20¢	**violet** *(April 27, 1939)*	.50	.50

1938-40. Official Overprint Issue #545-554 with overprint 560 (2¢, 6¢ and 20¢) or 561 (other values).

O. B.

560

		UnFVF	UseFVF
560			
2¢	**deep rose**	.20	.20
	x. no period after *B*	22.00	22.00
	x1. hyphen omitted	20.00	20.00

O. B.

561

		UnFVF	UseFVF
561			
4¢	**deep yellow green**	.20	.20

562

		UnFVF	UseFVF
562			
6¢	**brown**	.20	.20

563

		UnFVF	UseFVF
563			
8¢	**red violet**	.20	.20

564

		UnFVF	UseFVF
564			
10¢	**rose carmine**	.20	.20
	x. no period after *O*	30.00	30.00

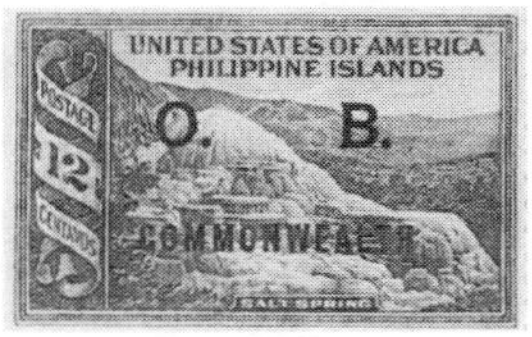

565

		UnFVF	UseFVF
565			
12¢	**black**	.20	.20

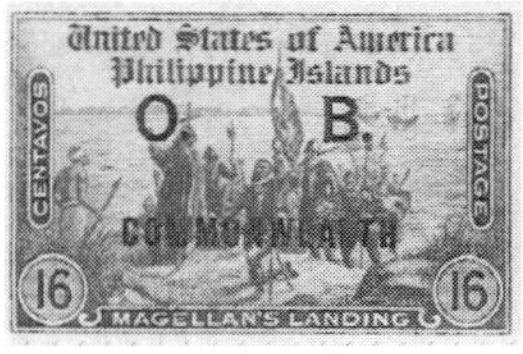

566

		UnFVF	UseFVF
566			
16¢	**deep blue**	.25	.20

567

		UnFVF	UseFVF
567			
20¢	**bistre** *(1940)*	.40	.40

568

568		UnFVF	UseFVF
26¢	**indigo**	.40	.40

569

569		UnFVF	UseFVF
30¢	**deep red orange**	.40	.40

1939. Airmail Overprint Issue Feb. 17. First Air Mail Exhibition.

#365a, 542 overprinted in black or red (R)

FIRST AIR MAIL EXHIBITION
Feb 17 to 19,1939
8 CENTAVOS 8

570	UnFVF	UseFVF
8¢ on 26¢ blue green	1.00	.60
a. green	2.25	.80
FDC		5.00

571

571	UnFVF	UseFVF
1p on 10p slate, (R)	4.00	3.00
FDC		10.00

1939. First Foreign Trade Issue July 5. First Foreign Trade Week.

#481, 365a, 543 overprinted in red (R), violet (V) or black

572	UnFVF	UseFVF
2¢ on 4¢ deep yellow green (R)	.20	.20
FDC		1.50

573

FIRST FOREIGN
TRADE WEEK

MAY 21-27, 1939
6 CENTAVOS 6

573	UnFVF	UseFVF
6¢ on 26¢ blue green (V)	.25	.25
a. green	.85	.40
FDC		2.25

574

50 CENTAVOS 50
FIRST FOREIGN
TRADE WEEK
MAY 21-27,1939

574	UnFVF	UseFVF
50¢ on 20p red brown	1.20	1.20
FDC		6.00

1939-40. 4th Anniversary of the Commonwealth 1 (Nov. 15, 1939): T575. *Engr., perforated 11.*

T575 *Triumphal Arch*

575		UnFVF	UseFVF
2¢	**yellow green**	.20	.20
	FDC		1.25

576

576		UnFVF	UseFVF
6¢	**red carmine**	.20	.20
	FDC		1.25

577

577		UnFVF	UseFVF
12¢	**deep blue**	.25	.20
	FDC		1.50

T578 *Malacañan Palace*

578		UnFVF	UseFVF
2¢	**green,** *2 (Nov. 15, 1939):* T578	.25	.20
	FDC		1.50

579

579		UnFVF	UseFVF
6¢	**yellow orange**	.30	.20
	FDC		1.50

580

		UnFVF	UseFVF
580			
12¢	**red carmine**	.40	.20
	FDC		2.00

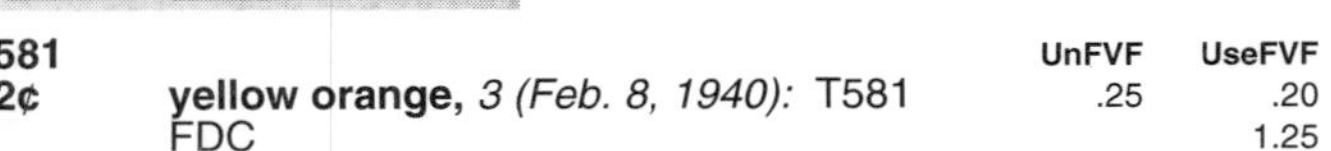

T581 *Quezon taking oath of office*

		UnFVF	UseFVF
581			
2¢	**yellow orange,** *3 (Feb. 8, 1940):* T581	.25	.20
	FDC		1.25

582

583

		UnFVF	UseFVF
582			
6¢	**green**	.30	.20
	FDC		1.25
583		UnFVF	UseFVF
12¢	**red violet**	.40	.20
	FDC		2.00

1941. José Rizal Issue April 14. *Engr.; #584: rotary press, size 19 x 22 1/2mm, perforated 11 x 10 1/2; #585: flat plate, size 14 1/4 x 22mm, perforated 11 with 1 or 2 sides imperforate.*

584 *José Rizal*

		UnFVF	UseFVF
584			
2¢	**deep apple green**	.20	.20
	FDC		1.00
585		UnFVF	UseFVF
2¢	**deep apple green,** perforated 11, *(1943)*	.25	.20
	a. light apple green	.45	.40
	Booklet pane (6)	2.00	
	Booklet pane (6), #585a	4.00	

Note: #585 issued in booklet panes only.

Official: #584, overprinted 560, O.B.

586

		UnFVF	UseFVF
586			
2¢	**deep apple green**	.20	.20

1941. Airmail Issue June 30. *Engr., perforated 11.*

587 *Boeing 314 clipper and Moro Vinta (sailing canoe)*

588

		UnFVF	UseFVF
587			
8¢	**scarlet**	1.20	.80
	FDC		2.50
588		UnFVF	UseFVF
20¢	**ultramarine**	1.10	.65
	FDC		2.50

589

590

		UnFVF	UseFVF
589			
60¢	**emerald green**	2.40	1.20
	FDC		4.50
590		UnFVF	UseFVF
1p	**sepia**	1.00	.65
	FDC		3.00

1942-44. Japanese Occupation Issue #584 2¢, 532, 547/555 overprinted with bars obliterating UNITED STATES OF AMERICA & COMMONWEALTH. *Perforated 11; #591: perforated 11 x 10 1/2.*

		UnFVF	UseFVF
591			
2¢	**deep apple green** *(March 4, 1942)*	.20	.20
592		UnFVF	UseFVF
5¢ on 6¢	**brown** *(Sept. 1, 1942)*	.20	.20
	FDC		1.50
593		UnFVF	UseFVF
12¢	**black** *(April 30, 1942)*	.30	.25
594		UnFVF	UseFVF
16¢	**deep blue** *(March 4, 1942)*	5.25	3.00
595		UnFVF	UseFVF
16¢ on 30¢	**red orange** *(Jan. 11, 1943)*	.30	.25
596		UnFVF	UseFVF
50¢ on 1p	**orange and black** *(April 30, 1943)*	.70	.70
	x. Double surcharge	300.00	
597		UnFVF	UseFVF
1p on 4p	**deep blue and black** *(April 30, 1943)*	145.00	135.00
	x. *S* inverted in *PESO*	125.00	

1943-44. Official Overprint Issue

(March 7, 1943-44): Official; #591, 592, 595 overprinted K.P. (Kagamitang Pampamahalaan = Official Business in Tagalog) and Japanese characters; #599: same overprint on #522 (large COMMONWEALTH overprint); #600: 9 1/4-10mm between bars; #601: 6mm between center bar and Japanese characters.

		UnFVF	UseFVF
598			
2¢	**deep apple green**	.20	.20
599		UnFVF	UseFVF
5¢ on 6¢	**brown** #522, *(June 26, 1944)*	35.00	35.00
600		UnFVF	UseFVF
5¢ on 6¢	**brown**	.25	.25
	x. 8-8 1/2mm between bars	.25	.25
601		UnFVF	UseFVF
16¢ on 30¢	**deep red orange**	.80	.80
	x. 1mm between bar and Japanese characters		

1942. Capture of Bataan and Corregidor Issue May. 18. Capture of Bataan and Corregidor (May 7).

#481 overprinted

		UnFVF	UseFVF
602			
2¢ on 4¢	**deep yellow green**	6.00	6.00
	x. *RATAAN*		
	FDC		4.00

1942. Postage Due Issue Oct. 13.

#544 overprinted with blue bar

		UnFVF	UseFVF
603			
3¢ on 4¢	**brown red**	35.00	35.00
	FDC		30.00

Manila post office used #544 with hand-drawn lines across *United States of America* from Sept. 1, 1942 until Oct. 13, when #603 arrived.

1942. Agriculture and Conservation Campaign Issue Nov. 12. Agriculture and conservation campaign surtax for Red Cross; *litho by Coast and Geodetic survey office; perforated 12.*

Surtax for Red Cross

		UnFVF	UseFVF
604			
2¢ + 1¢	**deep lilac**	.25	.25
605			
5¢ + 1¢	**light emerald**	.20	.20
606			
16¢ + 2¢	**orange**	25.00	25.00

604-606 FDC, $40.

1942. First Anniversary Greater East Asia War Issue Dec. 8. First anniversary of the Greater East Asia War.

#481 overprinted

		UnFVF	UseFVF
607			
5¢ on 4¢	**deep yellow green**	.80	.55
	FDC		3.00

1943. Philippine Executive Commission Issue Jan. 23. First anniversary Philippine Executive Commission.

#587, 590 overprinted

		UnFVF	UseFVF
608			
2¢ on 8¢	**scarlet**	.35	.35
609			
5¢ on 1p	**sepia**	.65	.65

608-609 FDC, $3.

1943-44. Pictorial Issue

T610, 612, 618 *Nipa palm hut*

Wmk. 610

		UnFVF	UseFVF
610			
1¢	**orange** *(June 7, 1943)*	.20	.20

T611, 614, 620 *Planting rice seedlings*

		UnFVF	UseFVF
611			
2¢	**light emerald** *(April 1, 1943)*	.20	.20
	x. Broken arm		
612			
4¢	**deep dull green** *(June 7, 1943)*	.20	.20
613			
5¢	**yellow brown** *(April 1, 1943)*	.20	.20
614			
6¢	**light scarlet** *(July 14, 1943)*	.20	.20
615			
10¢	**slate blue green** *(July 14, 1943)*	.20	.20

T616, 617, 622, 623 *Moro Vinta*

		UnFVF	UseFVF
616			
12¢	**Prussian blue** *(July 14, 1943)*	1.25	1.25
617			
16¢	**bistre brown** *(July 14, 1943)*	.20	.20
618			
20¢	**maroon** *(Aug. 16, 1943)*	1.45	1.45
619			
21¢	**blue violet** *(Aug. 16, 1943)*	.30	.30
620			
25¢	**chocolate** *(Aug. 16, 1943)*	.20	.20
621			
1p	**carmine red** *(June 7, 1943)*	.75	.75
622			
2p	**dark purple** *(Sept. 16, 1943)*	5.00	5.00
	FDC		5.50
623			
5p	**light bronze green** *(April 16, 1944)*	10.00	8.00
	FDC		7.50

1943. Capture of Bataan and Corregidor Issue May 7. First anniversary capture of Bataan and Corregidor; photo in Japan; *perforated 13.*

624, 625 *Japanese soldier and map of Manila Bay*

		UnFVF	UseFVF
624			
2¢	**deep scarlet**	.20	.20
625			
5¢	**deep emerald**	.35	.35
	x. Colorless dot after left "5"		1.50

624-625 FDC, $250.

1943. Printing Press Issue June 20. 350th anniversary printing press (Limbagan in Tagalog).

#522 overprinted

		UnFVF	UseFVF
626			
12¢ on 20¢	**bistre**		
	x. Double surcharge	—	—
	FDC		2.50

1943. Independence Issue Oct. 14. Independence; Rizal monument, Philippine woman and flag; photo; *perforated 12 or imperforate; no gum.*

Philippine woman and flag

		UnFVF	UseFVF
627			
5¢	**light blue**	.20	.20
628			
12¢	**red orange**	.25	.25
629			
17¢	**carmine rose**	.40	.40

627-629 FDC, $2.50.

Souvenir sheet (127x177) of 3: #627-629; gutter; marginal inscription Independence of the Philippines and excerpt from Rizal's Last Farewell; no gum.

		UnFVF	UseFVF
630			
5¢, 12¢, 17¢	**Sheet**	45.00	12.00
	Sheet w/FDC cancel @ Manila		3.00

1943. Flood Relief Overprint Issue Dec. 8.

#616, 618, 619 overprinted BAHA (Tagalog for flood) 1943 and add'l value

		UnFVF	UseFVF
631			
12¢ + 21¢	**Prussian blue**	.25	.25
632			
20¢ + 36¢	**maroon**	.25	.25
633			
21¢ + 40¢	**blue violet**	.25	.25

631-633 FDC, $2.

1944. Portrait Issue 5¢ Rizal. 12¢ Rev. José Burgos (1837-1872), educator and ecclesiastical reformer, who was executed, along with Fathers Mariano Gomez and Jacinto Zamora on Feb. 17, 1872 as a result of Cavite revolt; 17¢ Apolonario Mabini, the *Voice of the Revolution,* a leader, with Rizal, Marcelo del Pilar and Lopez Jaena, of *Young Filipino Party.* Also adviser to Aguinaldo. *Litho, perforated 12.*

		UnFVF	UseFVF
634			
5¢	**light Prussian blue**	.20	.20
	v. Pair, imperforate	.40	.40
635			
12¢	**light carmine red**	.20	.20
	v. Pair, imperforate	.40	.40
636			
17¢	**red orange**	.30	.30
	v. Pair, imperforate	.40	.40

Souvenir sheet (101 x 143mm) of 3; #634-636; gutter; marginal inscription; no gum.

634-636 FDC, $2. 634v-636v FDC, $3.

		UnFVF	UseFVF
637			
5¢, 12¢, 17¢	**Sheet**	5.00	3.00
	FDC		4.00

Souvenir sheet sold for 1p; surtax for care of heroes' monuments.

1944. CAPTURE OF BATAAN AND CORREGIDOR ISSUE May 7. Second anniversary of the capture of Bataan and Corregidor.

#587, 588 overprinted

No.	Description	UnFVF	UseFVF
638	**5¢ on 20¢ ultramarine**	.85	.85
639	**12¢ on 60¢ emerald green**	1.65	1.65

638-639 FDC, $3.50.

1944. OFFICIAL OVERPRINT ISSUE Aug. 10. Official; #547, 567, 590 overprinted.

640 *Overprint*

No.	Description	UnFVF	UseFVF
640	**5¢ on 6¢ brown**	.20	.20

641 *Overprint*

			UnFVF	UseFVF
641	**20¢**	**bistre**	.65	.65

642 *Overprint*

			UnFVF	UseFVF
642	**1p**	**sepia**	1.65	1.65

640-642 FDC, $4.

1945. REPUBLIC ISSUE Jan. 12. First anniversary of Republic (FDC cancelled Oct. 14, 1944); *litho; gutter; no gum.*
José P. Laurel, President of Japanese-established Philippine Republic

			UnFVF	UseFVF
643	**5s**	**light violet brown**	.20	.20
644	**7s**	**light blue green**	.20	.20
645	**20s**	**dull blue**	.25	.25

643-645 FDC, $1.50.

1944. VICTORY OVERPRINT ISSUE First Victory issue; stamps of Philippines handstamped with large VICTORY in violet, issued by Secretary of National Defense and Communications of the island of Leyte. 1 (Nov. 8-Dec. 28): Regular postage.

VICTORY

			UnFVF	UseFVF
646	**2¢**	**deep rose** *(Dec. 3, 1944),* #520	350.00	125.00
		Booklet pane of 6	2,000.00	
647	**2¢**	**deep rose** *(Dec. 14, 1944),* #545	1,600.00	
648	**2¢**	**deep apple green,** #584	3.50	3.00
649	**4¢**	**deep yellow green,** #481	32.50	30.00
650	**6¢**	**brown** *(Dec. 14, 1944),* #482	1,800.00	1,650.00
651	**6¢**	**deep yellow green** *(Dec. 3, 1944),* #518	150.00	95.00
652	**6¢**	**brown** *(Dec. 28, 1944),* #522	900.00	800.00
653	**6¢**	**red carmine** *(Dec. 14, 1944),* #576	180.00	150.00
654	**6¢**	**yellow orange** *(Dec. 14, 1944),* #579	800.00	750.00
655	**6¢**	**green,** #582	200.00	200.00
656	**8¢**	**red violet,** #548	20.00	25.00
657	**10¢**	**rose carmine,** #524	150.00	100.00
658	**10¢**	**rose carmine,** #549	180.00	150.00
659	**12¢**	**dark ultramarine** *(Dec. 3, 1944),* #519	525.00	210.00
660	**12¢**	**deep blue** *(Dec. 14, 1944),* #577	3,500.00	2,400.00
661	**12¢**	**red violet,** #583	250.00	180.00
662	**16¢**	**deep blue** *(Dec. 3, 1944),* #486	925.00	
663	**16¢**	**deep blue,** #526	600.00	430.00
664	**16¢**	**deep blue** *(Dec. 28, 1944),* #551	180.00	120.00
665	**20¢**	**bistre,** #552	37.00	37.00
666	**30¢**	**deep red orange** *(Dec. 3, 1944),* #529	300.00	210.00
667	**30¢**	**deep red orange** *(Dec. 3, 1944),* #554	425.00	350.00
668	**1p**	**orange and black** *(Dec. 3, 1944),* #555	7,500.00	5,500.00

(Dec. 3): Airmail; #472

			UnFVF	UseFVF
669	**4¢**	**carmine**	2,300.00	2,300.00

Special Delivery

			UnFVF	UseFVF
670	**20¢**	**black violet,** #388b	850.00	650.00
671	**20¢**	**violet,** #559	240.00	200.00

(Dec. 3): Postage Due; #416-422

			UnFVF	UseFVF
672	**4¢**	**brown red**	75.00	
673	**6¢**	**brown red**	110.00	
674	**8¢**	**brown red**	125.00	
675	**10¢**	**brown red**	110.00	
676	**12¢**	**brown red**	110.00	
677	**16¢**	**brown red**	115.00	
678	**20¢**	**brown red**	115.00	

Officials

			UnFVF	UseFVF
679	**2¢**	**deep rose,** #560	275.00	150.00
680	**2¢**	**deep apple green,** #586	8.75	4.50
681	**4¢**	**deep yellow green,** #495	41.00	38.00
681A	**6¢**	**dark brown,** #562	5,700.00	
682	**10¢**	**rose carmine,** #564	180.00	
683	**20¢**	**bistre,** #501	8,000.00	
684	**20¢**	**bistre,** #535	2,100.00	

1945. SECOND VICTORY OVERPRINT ISSUE Jan. 19. Stamps of the Philippines with overprint 685 (2¢, 6¢, 20¢), 695 (10p, 20p), 686 (other values). 1: Regular postage; #545/555, 542 (10p), 543 (20p).

685 *Overprint*

VICTORY

			UnFVF	UseFVF
685	**2¢**	**deep rose**	.30	.20
		FDC		3.50

686 *Overprint*

VICTORY

686		UnFVF	UseFVF
4¢	**deep yellow green**	.30	.20
	FDC		3.50

687

687		UnFVF	UseFVF
6¢	**brown**	.35	.20
	FDC		3.50

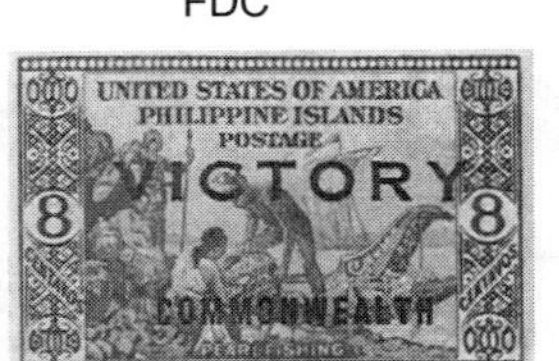
688

688		UnFVF	UseFVF
8¢	**red violet**	.35	.20
	FDC		4.50

689

689		UnFVF	UseFVF
10¢	**rose carmine**	.35	.20
	FDC		4.50

690

690		UnFVF	UseFVF
12¢	**black**	.40	.20
	FDC		5.00

691

691		UnFVF	UseFVF
16¢	**deep blue**	.50	.20
	FDC		6.00

692

692		UnFVF	UseFVF
20¢	**bistre**	.60	.25
	FDC		8.00

693

693		UnFVF	UseFVF
30¢	**deep red orange** *(May 1, 1945)*	.85	.70
	FDC		5.00

694

694		UnFVF	UseFVF
1p	**orange and black**	2.25	.50
	FDC		12.00

695 *Overprint*

VICTORY

695		UnFVF	UseFVF
10p	**slate**	80.00	17.50
	FDC		30.00
696		**UnFVF**	**UseFVF**
20p	**red brown**	70.00	22.50
	FDC		37.50

697 *2: Special delivery; #559*

697		UnFVF	UseFVF
20¢	**violet**	1.20	.80
	v. "IC" close together		3.50
	FDC		15.00

1946. José Rizal Issue May 28. *Engr., perforated 11 x 10 1/2.*

698 *José Rizal*

698		UnFVF	UseFVF
2¢	**sepia**	.30	.20

Official; #698, overprint 560, O.B.

699

			UnFVF	UseFVF
699				
2¢	**sepia** *(June 19, 1946)*		.15	.15

Since July 4, 1946: Stamps of Republic of Philippines.

Envelopes and Wrappers

1899-1906. U.S. ENVELOPES OVERPRINT ISSUE overprinted below stamp in same color, except when mentioned. 1: (1899-1900), #EN391-417 overprinted.

Prices for major numbers are for adequately margined cut squares.

EN1-8 *1¢ Philippines*

PHILIPPINES.

		UnFVF	UseFVF
EN1			
1¢	**green on white,** #391	3.50	2.00
	entire	8.00	9.00
EN2			
1¢	**green on amber,** #392	20.00	15.00
	entire	45.00	45.00
EN3			
1¢	**green on amber,** (R) #392	25.00	20.00
	entire	65.00	60.00
EN4			
1¢	**green on buff,** #393	15.00	15.00
	entire	35.00	35.00
EN5			
1¢	**green on buff,** (R) #393	35.00	35.00
	entire	75.00	75.00
EN6			
1¢	**green on blue,** #394	10.00	10.00
	entire	35.00	35.00
EN7			
1¢	**green on blue,** (R) #394	25.00	20.00
	entire	75.00	70.00
EN8			
1¢	**green on manila,** wrapper #396	1.75	1.50
	entire, wrapper	6.00	5.50

EN9-12 *2¢ Philippines*

PHILIPPINES.

		UnFVF	UseFVF
EN9			
2¢	**carmine on white,** #401	1.50	1.50
	entire	5.00	3.50
EN10			
2¢	**carmine on amber,** #402	6.00	5.50
	entire	17.50	15.00
EN11			
2¢	**carmine on buff,** #403	6.00	6.00
	entire	20.00	15.00
EN12			
2¢	**carmine on blue,** #404	6.00	7.50
	entire	15.00	12.50

EN13, 14, 15 *4¢ Philippines*

PHILIPPINES.

		UnFVF	UseFVF
EN13			
4¢	**brown on amber,** #411	45.00	45.00
	entire	90.00	90.00
	x. entire with double overprint	4,000.00	
EN14			
4¢	**brown on white,** #413	10.00	10.00
	entire	30.00	50.00
EN15			
4¢	**brown on amber,** #414	60.00	60.00
	entire	175.00	125.00

EN16, 17 *5¢ Philippines*

PHILIPPINES.

		UnFVF	UseFVF
EN16			
5¢	**blue on white,** #416	6.50	6.50
	entire	15.00	15.00
EN17			
5¢	**blue on amber,** #417	35.00	37.50
	entire	90.00	125.00

#13: bust pointed and undraped; inner oval with teeth. #14, 15: bust broad and draped; inner oval without teeth.

EN18-23 *1¢ Philippines*

PHILIPPINES.

(1905), #EN418-428, 430, 433 overprinted

		UnFVF	UseFVF
EN18			
1¢	**green on white,** #418	1.25	1.25
	entire	5.00	5.00
EN19			
1¢	**green on amber,** #419	12.00	10.00
	entire	25.00	30.00
EN20			
1¢	**green on buff,** #420	15.00	12.00
	entire	30.00	25.00
EN21			
1¢	**green on blue,** #421	12.00	10.00
	entire	30.00	30.00
EN22			
1¢	**green on manila,** #422	22.50	25.00
	entire	50.00	60.00
	x. entire, double overprint	—	—
EN23			
1¢	**green on manila,** wrapper, #423	10.00	10.00
	entire wrapper	25.00	20.00

EN24-28 *Philippines*

PHILIPPINES.

		UnFVF	UseFVF
EN24			
2¢	**carmine on white,** #423	5.00	4.00
	entire	10.00	8.00
EN25			
2¢	**carmine,** #425	20.00	17.50
	entire	40.00	45.00
EN26			
2¢	**carmine on buff,** #426	20.00	30.00
	entire	50.00	
EN27			
2¢	**carmine on blue,** #427	20.00	20.00
	entire	40.00	

		UnFVF	UseFVF
EN28			
2¢	**carmine on manila,** wrapper #428	12.00	12.00
	entire	25.00	20.00
	x. entire, double overprint	—	—
EN29		**UnFVF**	**UseFVF**
4¢	**brown on amber,** #430	60.00	80.00
	entire	150.00	200.00
	x. entire, double overprint	7,000.00	
EN30		**UnFVF**	**UseFVF**
5¢	**blue on amber,** #433	60.00	
	entire	125.00	

(1906), #EN434, 436 overprinted

		UnFVF	UseFVF
EN31			
2¢	**carmine on white,** #434	45.00	30.00
	entire	150.00	125.00
EN32		**UnFVF**	**UseFVF**
2¢	**carmine on white,** #436	70.00	125.00
	entire	250.00	300.00

1908. Rizal New Design Issue

EN33-38 *2¢ Rizal*

		UnFVF	UseFVF
EN33			
2¢	**green on white**	.60	.30
	entire	1.00	.80
EN34		**UnFVF**	**UseFVF**
2¢	**green on amber**	4.50	2.50
	entire	10.00	8.00
EN35		**UnFVF**	**UseFVF**
2¢	**green on buff**	6.00	4.00
	entire	10.00	10.00
EN36		**UnFVF**	**UseFVF**
2¢	**green on blue**	6.00	4.00
	entire	10.00	10.00
EN37		**UnFVF**	**UseFVF**
2¢	**green on manila**	10.00	
	entire	15.00	25.00
EN38		**UnFVF**	**UseFVF**
2¢	**green on manila,** wrapper	2.00	2.25
	entire	12.00	14.00

1908. McKinley New Design Issue

EN39-43 *4¢ McKinley*

		UnFVF	UseFVF
EN39			
4¢	**carmine on white**	.50	.30
	entire	1.75	1.50
EN40		**UnFVF**	**UseFVF**
4¢	**carmine on amber**	5.00	3.00
	entire	10.00	8.00
EN41		**UnFVF**	**UseFVF**
4¢	**carmine on blue**	5.00	4.00
	entire	10.00	9.00
EN42		**UnFVF**	**UseFVF**
4¢	**carmine on buff**	5.00	4.00
	entire	10.00	20.00
EN43		**UnFVF**	**UseFVF**
4¢	**carmine on manila**	10.00	12.00
	entire	25.00	30.00

1927. Rizal Issue

EN44 *Rizal*

		UnFVF	UseFVF
EN44			
2¢	**green on white**	12.50	10.00
	entire	35.00	30.00

1935. Juan de la Cruz Issue June 19.

EN45, 46 *Juan de la Cruz*

		UnFVF	UseFVF
EN45			
2¢	**carmine on white** *(1937)*	.40	.25
	entire	1.50	1.00
EN46		**UnFVF**	**UseFVF**
4¢	**olive green on white** *(1937)*	.60	.40
	entire	2.00	1.50

1944. Victory Issue #EN45, 39, 46 handstamped in violet.

		UnFVF	UseFVF
EN46A			
2¢	**green on white**	—	—
EN47		**UnFVF**	**UseFVF**
2¢	**carmine on white**	20.00	17.50
	entire	50.00	80.00
EN48		**UnFVF**	**UseFVF**
4¢	**carmine on white**		
	entire	1,000.00	1,000.00
EN49		**UnFVF**	**UseFVF**
4¢	**olive green on white**	90.00	110.00
	entire	150.00	175.00

Postal Cards, Message & Reply Cards, Official Cards

1900. U.S. #PC13, 15 Overprint Below Stamp Feb.

Prices are for entires of Postal and Official cards, for unsevered or detached Message and Reply cards.

PHILIPPINES.

		UnFVF	UseFVF
PC1			
1¢	**black on buff**	20.00	15.00
	x. no period	50.00	
PC2		**UnFVF**	**UseFVF**
2¢	**black on buff**	42.50	42.50

1900. U.S. #MRC2 Overprinted; PC1 in Blue Feb.

		UnFVF	UseFVF
PC3			
2¢ + 2¢	**blue on white,** unsevered	175.00	500.00
	m. message card	25.00	25.00
	r. reply card	25.00	25.00

1903. U.S. #PC17, 15 Overprinted Sept. 15.

PHILIPPINES

		UnFVF	UseFVF
PC4			
1¢	**black on buff**	1,500.00	1,000.00
PC5		**UnFVF**	**UseFVF**
2¢	**black on buff**	750.00	650.00

1903. U.S. #MRC1, MRC2 Overprinted in Black

PHILIPPINES.

		UnFVF	UseFVF
PC6			
1¢ + 1¢	**black on buff,** unsevered	150.00	350.00
	m. message card	25.00	25.00
	r. reply card	25.00	25.00
PC7		**UnFVF**	**UseFVF**
2¢ + 2¢	**blue on white,** unsevered	300.00	
	m. message card	50.00	
	r. reply card	50.00	

#PC7 overprinted in blue: official status doubtful.

1904. U.S. #PC17, 15 Overprinted PC6

		UnFVF	UseFVF
PC8			
1¢	**black on buff**	45.00	35.00
PC9		**UnFVF**	**UseFVF**
2¢	**black on buff**	65.00	55.00

1906. U.S. #PC17, 15 Overprinted

PHILIPPINES

		UnFVF	UseFVF
PC10			
1¢	**black on buff**	300.00	300.00

PC11-14 *Rizal*

		UnFVF	UseFVF
PC11			
2¢	**black on buff**	1,800.00	1,500.00

1907-15. Rizal 2¢ Issue

		UnFVF	UseFVF
PC12			
2¢	**black on buff**	10.00	10.00
PC13		**UnFVF**	**UseFVF**
2¢	**blue on light blue** *(1912)*	8.00	8.00
PC14		**UnFVF**	**UseFVF**
2¢	**green on buff** *(1915)*	4.00	3.50

PC15-17 *McKinley*

		UnFVF	UseFVF
PC15			
2¢	**green on amber** *(1915)*	4.00	2.00

1907-15. McKinley 4¢ Issue

		UnFVF	UseFVF
PC16			
4¢	**black on buff**	22.50	22.50
PC17		**UnFVF**	**UseFVF**
4¢	**blue on light blue** *(1912)*	25.00	25.00
PC18		**UnFVF**	**UseFVF**
4¢	**green on buff** *(1915)*	18.00	15.00

1925. Official Card #PC14 Overprinted Left of Stamp

O. B.

		UnFVF	UseFVF
PC19			
2¢	**green on buff**	40.00	40.00

1935. New Official Card Design

1935. New design

		UnFVF	UseFVF
PC20			
2¢	**red on buff**	3.00	2.00
	v. Official (O.B.) overprint		

O. B. PC21 *Official card. #PC20 overprinted*

		UnFVF	UseFVF
PC21			
2¢	**red on buff**	15.00	15.00

1938. Postal Card #PC20 Overprinted Left of Stamp

COMMONWEALTH

		UnFVF	UseFVF
PC22			
2¢	**red on buff**	2.50	1.75

COMMONWEALTH

		UnFVF	UseFVF
PC23			
2¢	**red on buff**	50.00	50.00

COMMONWEALTH

		UnFVF	UseFVF
PC24			
2¢	**red on buff**	2.50	1.65

O. B.

		UnFVF	UseFVF
PC25			
2¢	**red on buff**	15.00	15.00

1941. Official Card #PC24 Overprinted Left of Stamp

O. B. PC26 *Official card. #PC24 overprinted left of stamp*

		UnFVF	UseFVF
PC26			
2¢	**red on buff**	20.00	20.00

1941. Official Card Postal card of new design overprinted below stamp.

PC27 *Rizal*

O. B.

		UnFVF	UseFVF
PC27			
2¢	**green on buff**	175.00	180.00

#PC27: not issued without overprint.

1944. #PC14, 23, 24 Handstamped in Violet

VICTORY

		UnFVF	UseFVF
PC28			
2¢	**green on buff**	180.00	220.00
PC29		**UnFVF**	**UseFVF**
2¢	**red on buff**	650.00	
PC30		**UnFVF**	**UseFVF**
2¢	**red on buff**	300.00	500.00

1945. New Design Overprinted at Left

		UnFVF	UseFVF
PC31			
2¢	**gray brown on buff**	1.50	1.00
	FDC		3.25

Note: Not issued without overprint.

Puerto Rico

Puerto Rico, the easternmost of the Greater Antilles, was discovered by Columbus, Nov. 19, 1493. Ponce de Leon conquered it for Spain, 1509. Except for minor outbreaks, Puerto Rico remained loyal to Spain during the Spanish-American liberation movement of the early 19th century. In the Spanish-American War, however, it welcomed the American invasion of July 1898. In 1899 it was ceded to the United States by Spain.

U.S. forces landed July 25, 1898. The first military postal station opened Aug. 3 at La Playa de Ponce.

The Commonwealth of Puerto Rico is a self-governing part of the U.S. with a primary Hispanic culture. Puerto Ricans are U.S. citizens.

The commonwealth political status of Puerto Rico gives the island's citizens virtually the same control over their internal affairs as the 50 states of the United States. However, they do not vote in national elections.

Puerto Rico is represented in Congress solely by a resident commissioner who has a voice but no vote, except in committees.

Regular Postal Issues

1898. Ponce Provisional Issue

191

		UnFVF	UseFVF
191			
5¢	**violet,** handstamp on white or yellowish paper	7,500.00	

1898. Coamo Provisional Issue

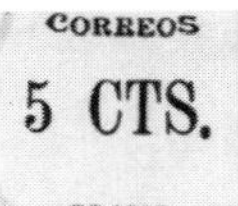

192 *Coamo provisional issue; type-set in sheet of 10; 4 varieties (Type I left); imperforate; violet control mark F. Santiago (mayor of Coamo).*

5 CTS. *Type II* 5 CTS *Type III* 5 CTS. *Type IV*

		UnFVF	UseFVF
192			
5¢	**black Type I**	600.00	975.00
	t. Type II	625.00	975.00
	t1. Type III	650.00	1,050.00
	t2. Type IV	725.00	1,125.00

1899. PORTO RICO Overprint Issue *Overprints at 36 degree angle (first listing) or 25 degree angle.*

193 *No. 193-197 overprint at 25 degree angle.*

		UnFVF	UseFVF
193			
1¢	**deep green**	4.25	1.40
	v1. pair, 36 degrees & 25 degrees	19.50	
	v2. PORTO RICU ovpt. 36 degrees	25.00	
	a. overprint 25 degrees	6.25	2.00

194 *No. 193-197 overprint at 36 degree angle.*

		UnFVF	UseFVF
194			
2¢	**carmine**	3.75	1.00
	v1. pair, 36 degree & 25 degree overprints	15.00	
	a. PORTO RICO ovpt. 25 degrees.	4.00	2.00
	av1. PORTU RICO ovpt. 25 degrees.	35.00	20.00
	av2. FORTO RICO ovpt.	—	—
	av3. PURTO RICO ovpt.		

195 *No. 193-197 overprint at 36 degree angle*

		UnFVF	UseFVF
195			
5¢	**dark blue**	6.00	2.00
196		UnFVF	UseFVF
8¢	**purple brown**	18.50	10.00
	a. ovpt. 25 degrees.	20.00	9.00
	v1. pair, 36 degree & 25 degree overprints	75.00	
	v2. FORTO RICO ovpt.	90.00	60.00
	av3. PORTO RIC ovpt.	125.00	110.00
197		UnFVF	UseFVF
10¢	**orange brown**	12.50	4.00
	v1. FORTO RICO	85.00	70.00

1899. Postage Due Issue

198 *Overprint at 36 or 25 degree angle.*

		UnFVF	UseFVF
198			
1¢	**brown carmine**	20.00	5.00
199		UnFVF	UseFVF
2¢	**brown carmine**	10.00	5.00
200		UnFVF	UseFVF
10¢	**brown carmine**	150.00	60.00

1900. PUERTO RICO Issue

201

		UnFVF	UseFVF
201			
1¢		3.25	.95
202		UnFVF	UseFVF
2¢	**carmine**	3.25	1.00
203		UnFVF	UseFVF
2¢	**red**	3.50	1.00
	v. inverted overprint	2,400.00	

Envelopes and Wrappers

1899-1900. Envelopes Overprint Issue

PORTO RICO. E1

		UnFVF	UseFVF
E1			
2¢	**green on white,** No. 344	4.25	8.00
	entire	12.50	17.50
E2		UnFVF	UseFVF
5¢	**blue on white,** No. 369	7.25	8.75
	entire	17.50	20.00

1899-1900. Wrapper Overprint In Color of Stamp Issue

PORTO RICO. E3

		UnFVF	UseFVF
E3			
1¢	**green on manila,** wrapper No. 396	1.00	1.10
	entire	2.90	42.00

1899-1900. Envelope Overprinted FOR PORTO RICO Issue

		UnFVF	UseFVF
E4			
2¢	**carmine on white**	3.00	3.00
E5		UnFVF	UseFVF
5¢	**blue on white**	8.00	9.00

1899-1900. Envelopes Overprint Issue

PORTO RICO. E6

		UnFVF	UseFVF
E6			
1¢	**green on blue,** No. 394		240.00
	entire		1,100.00
E7			
2¢	**carmine on amber,** No. 402	450.00	500.00
	entire	1,100.00	1,200.00
E8			
2¢	**carmine on buff,** No. 403		500.00
	entire		1,100.00
E9			
2¢	**carmine on buff,** No. 408		600.00
	entire		1,300.00
E10			
2¢	**carmine on blue,** No. 404		—
	entire		4,000.00
E11			
4¢	**brown on white,** No. 413	200.00	500.00
	entire	400.00	650.00

1899-1900. Envelopes Overprint PUERTO RICO Issue

PUERTO RICO. E12

		UnFVF	UseFVF
E12			
2¢	**carmine on white,** No. 401	4.00	3.00
	entire red	9.00	10.00
E13			
2¢	**carmine on buff,** No. 403	—	325.00
	entire	1,200.00	1,300.00
E14			
2¢	**carmine on buff,** No. 408		375.00
	entire		1,750.00
E15			
5¢	**blue on white,** No. 416	14.00	14.00
	entire blue	45.00	49.50

1899-1900. Envelopes Overprint Issue

PUERTO RICO. E16-E19

		UnFVF	UseFVF
E16			
1¢	**green on buff,** No. 393	20.00	40.00
	entire	70.00	75.00
E17			
1¢	**green on blue,** No. 394	20.00	40.00
	entire	90.00	100.00
E18			
1¢	**carmine on buff,** No. 403	20.00	40.00
	entire	90.00	125.00
E19			
1¢	**carmine on blue,** No. 404	20.00	40.00
	entire	70.00	125.00

Postal Cards

1899-1900. U.S. Postal Cards Issue

		UnFVF	UseFVF
PC1			
1¢	**black on buff**	150.00	160.00
	v. 20mm long imprint	1,000.00	1,300.00

No. PC1: 2 settings, one lighter than other.

		UnFVF	UseFVF
PC2			
1¢	**black on buff**	165.00	180.00
PC3			
1¢	**black on buff**	150.00	180.00

Ryukyu Islands

Government of Ryukyu (Ree-YOU-kyoo) Islands in extreme western Pacific Ocean established under U.S. Military Government after World War II.

Area: 1,003 sq. mi. (includes Okinawa, Miyako and Yaeyama groups); Population: 945,465 (1970 est.); Language: Japanese, although Ryukyans have own unwritten language; Capital: Naha, Okinawa.

B-Yen U.S. military currency: 100 sen = 1 yen (120 yen = $1.00 U.S.). 1958, Sep U.S. currency: 100 cents = 1 dollar.

Since the first Chinese invasions in 605 AD, the Ryukyus (also known as Luchu or Luchoo) have been constantly subject to such inroads by either the Japanese or the Chinese. U.S. Commodore Matthew Perry visited the islands in 1853 and in July 1854 concluded a treaty of friendship between the islands and the United States. In 1879 the Japanese dethroned the Ryukyuan regent and converted Luchu into a prefecture despite Chinese objections. With the Japanese attack on Pearl Harbor in 1941, it was apparent that any U.S. action in the area around Japan would hinge on bases in the Ryukyus, and on March 26, 1945, the U.S. 77th Infantry Division made first landings there. On July 2, 1945, the Okinawa campaign was officially termed completed — at a cost of 12,500 American dead, 36,650 wounded.

The Army Post Office (APO) was estabished when U.S. forces landed on Okinawa on April 1, 1945. About May of the same year the U.S. forces established local free mail service. Beginning in 1946 the free service was suspended and up to July 1948 all mail matter was stamped *fee paid* by the originating post office. The cancels of this period can be distinguished by the fact that the date is expressed in the international Christian form of *1946,* etc. in place of the normal Japanese imperial era date of *1921 (Showa)* etc.

During this period a provisional 7 sen stamp was created by the Kume Island postmaster with the assistance of the U.S. Navy. This was mimeographed in black and handstamped in red with the official seal of the Kume Island postmaster.

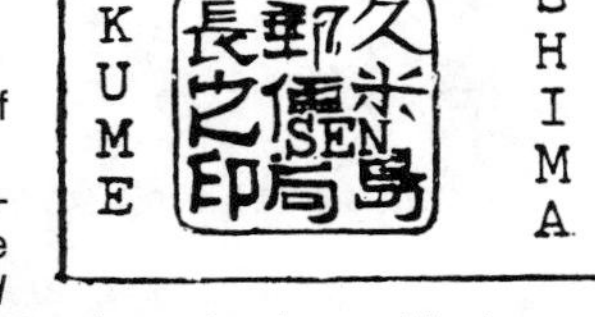

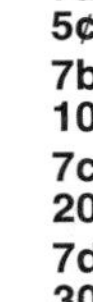

In 1947 the postal authorities secured a limited quantity of Japanese stamps. These replaced the *fee paid* hand stamps, and were of 4 types: *Ken (examined,* used in Amami Oshima area); *Hirata* (name of postmaster general of Okinawa); *Tomiyama* (postmaster general of Miyaka); and *Miyara* (postmaster general of Yaeyama).

Ken

Hirata

Tomiyama

Miyara

On May 26, 1947 use of both the hand stamped prepaid covers and the revalidated adhesives was extended to international use, and by Nov. 1, 1947 international airmail was re-established on a stampless cover basis.

Unless otherwise stated all stamps were postpaid by the Government Bureau of Japanese Ministry of Finance.

Regular Postal Issues

1948-49. First Pictorial Issue

1, 3 *Edible Cycad Bush*

No.	Value	Color	MNHVF	UseVF
1	5s	**purple magenta** *(July 1, 1948)*	2.00	4.00

2, 5 *Lily*

No.	Value	Color	MNHVF	UseVF
2	10s	**pale green**	1.50	2.25
3	20s	**pale green**	1.25	2.25

4, 6 *Trading Junk*

No.	Value	Color	MNHVF	UseVF
4	30s	**red**	2.00	3.00
5	40s	**purple magenta**	50.00	50.00
6	50s	**dull ultramarine**	1.50	4.00

7 *Farmer and dawn*

No.	Value	Color	MNHVF	UseVF
7	1y	**dull ultramarine**	400.00	225.00

1949. Second Pictorial Issue

No.	Value	Color	MNHVF	UseVF
7a	5¢	**purple magenta** *(July 18, 1949)*	2.75	2.50
7b	10¢	**pale green**	3.25	3.75
7c	20¢	**pale green**	3.25	2.75
7d	30¢	**red**	2.75	2.75
7e	40¢	**purple magenta**	2.75	2.25
7f	50¢	**dull ultramarine**	3.50	3.50
7g	1y	**dull ultramarine**	3.50	4.75

1950-58. Pictorial Issue

8 *Roof tiles*

No.	Value	Color	MNHVF	UseVF
8	50¢	**carmine rose**	.20	.15
		p. carmine rose on white paper, *(Sept. 6, 1958)*	.35	.35

9 *Girl*

9		MNHVF	UseVF
1y	**blue**	2.40	2.00

10 *Shuri Castle*

10		MNHVF	UseVF
2y	**purple**	10.00	5.00

11 *Guardian dragon*

11		MNHVF	UseVF
3y	**carmine rose**	20.00	8.00

12 *Two women*

12		MNHVF	UseVF
4y	**dark slate green**	10.00	8.00

13 *Seashells*

13		MNHVF	UseVF
5y	**emerald green**	10.00	6.00

1950. Air Mail Issue

14 *Dove and Ryukyus*

		MNHVF	UseVF
14 8y	**blue**	70.00	40.00
15 12y	**deep emerald**	40.00	17.50
16 16y	**carmine rose**	40.00	12.50

1950. Special Delivery Issue

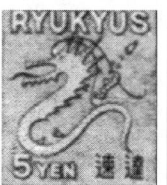

17 *Dragon*

17		MNHVF	UseVF
5y	**bright blue**	30.00	12.50

1951. Ryukyu University Issue

18 *Ryukyu University*

18		MNHVF	UseVF
3y	**chocolate** *(Feb. 12, 1951)*	50.00	20.00

1951. Arbor Week Issue

19 *Pine tree*

19		MNHVF	UseVF
3y	**emerald green** *(Feb. 19, 1951)*	25.00	15.00

1951-54. Airmail Issue

20 *Heavenly maiden*

		MNHVF	UseVF
20 13y	**Prussian blue** *(Oct.1, 1951)*	1.75	1.00
21 18y	**light green** *(Oct. 1, 1951)*	3.25	3.00
22 30y	**bright magenta** *(Oct. 1, 1951)*	4.00	1.50
23 40y	**purple** *(Aug. 16, 1954)*	6.00	4.00
24 50y	**yellow orange** *(Aug. 16, 1954)*	8.00	5.00

1952. Overprint Issue

Nos. 25, 26 overprinted in sheets of 100 (10x10).

No. 25, types 1-6: 1st printing: narrow bar spacing, top characters small (1), large (2). 2nd printing: wide bar spacing, top characters small (3), large (4) or mixed (5). 3rd printing: wide bar spacing, top characters thin, 10 yen about 7.8mm long (instead of 7mm).

No. 26, types 3-5: top characters small (3), large (4) or mixed (5).

25

25	MNHVF	UseVF
10y on 50s T1, 2 *(Jan. 1, 1952)*	10.00	8.00
v. T3, 4 *(June 5, 1952)*	30.00	20.00
v1. T5 *(June 5, 1952), T6 (Dec. 8, 1952)*	37.50	37.50

26	MNHVF	UseVF
100y on 2y purple, T4 *(June 16, 1952)*	1,200.00	900.00
v. T3		
v1. T5		

1952. Establishment of Ryukyu Island Government Issue

27 *Dove, bean sprout and Ryukyus*

27		MNHVF	UseVF
3y	**deep claret** *(April 1, 1952)*	100.00	30.00

1952-53. Historical Sites Issue

28 *Madanbashi Bridge*

28		MNHVF	UseVF
1y	**rose red**	.20	.20

29 *Main hall, Shuri Castle*

29		MNHVF	UseVF
2y	**deep emerald**	.25	.30

30 *Shuri Gate*

30		MNHVF	UseVF
3y	**turquoise**	.50	.30

31 *Stone gate, Soenji Temple*

31		MNHVF	UseVF
6y	**blue** *(Jan. 20, 1953)*	4.00	2.50

32 *Benzaiten-do Temple*

32		MNHVF	UseVF
10y	**bright rose red** *(Jan. 20, 1953)*	1.75	.70

33 *Sonohan Utaki, Shuri Castle*

33		MNHVF	UseVF
30y	**olive green** *(Jan. 20, 1953)*	8.00	5.00
	a. light olive green	25.00	

34 *Tamaudun, Shuri*

34		MNHVF	UseVF
50y	**rose purple** *(Jan. 20, 1953)*	12.00	5.00

35 Stone bridge, Hosho Pond, Enkaku Temple

35		MNHVF	UseVF
100y	**brown claret** *(Jan. 20, 1953)*	15.00	3.00

1953. Mathew Perry Issue

36 *Reception at Shuri Castle*

36		MNHVF	UseVF
3y	**purple magenta**	12.00	5.00

37 *Perry and the American fleet*

37		MNHVF	UseVF
6y	**dark cobalt**	1.50	1.50

1953. Newspaper Week Issue

38 *Chofu Ota*

38		MNHVF	UseVF
4y	**yellow brown** *(Oct. 1, 1953)*	12.00	4.00

1954-55. Industrial Arts Issue

39 *Pottery*

39		MNHVF	UseVF
4y	**brown** *(June 25, 1954)*	.75	.50

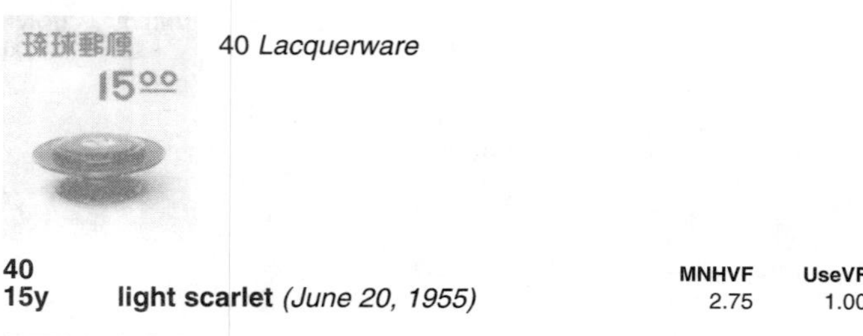

40 *Lacquerware*

		MNHVF	UseVF
40 **15y**	**light scarlet** *(June 20, 1955)*	2.75	1.00

41 *Textiles*

		MNHVF	UseVF
41 **20y**	**yellow orange** *(June 20, 1955)*	3.50	2.00

1954. Newspaper Week Issue

42 *Shigo Toma*

		MNHVF	UseVF
42 **4y**	**blue** *(Oct. 1, 1954)*	12.00	4.00

1955. Sweet Potato Issue

Celebrates the 350th anniversary of the introduction of the sweet potato to the Ryukyu Islands.

43 *Noguni Shrine*

		MNHVF	UseVF
43 **4y**	**blue** *(Nov. 26, 1955)*	10.00	6.00

1956. Arbor Week Issue

44 *Trees*

		MNHVF	UseVF
44 **4y**	**blue green** *(Feb. 18, 1956)*	10.00	4.00

1956. Ceremonial Dancers Issue

45 *Willow dance*

		MNHVF	UseVF
45 **5y**	**rose purple** *(May 1, 1956)*	1.25	.50

46 *Straw hat dance*

		MNHVF	UseVF
46 **8y**	**blue violet**	1.50	1.50

47 *Warrior costume*

		MNHVF	UseVF
47 **14y**	**dark red brown** *(June 8, 1956)*	2.75	1.75

1956. Telephone Issue

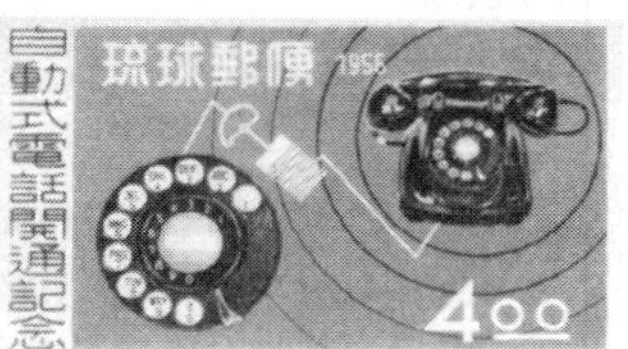

48 *Telephone*

		MNHVF	UseVF
48 **4y**	**blue violet**	15.00	6.00

1956. New Year Issue

49 *Pine, bamboo and plum*

		MNHVF	UseVF
49 **2y**	**multicolored** *(Dec. 1, 1956)*	2.50	1.00

1957. Airmail Issue

50 *Heavenly maiden with flute*

		MNHVF	UseVF
50 **15y**	**blue green** *(Aug. 1, 1957)*	5.00	2.00
51 **20y**	**deep carmine**	7.50	5.00
52 **35y**	**light green**	12.50	6.00
53 **45y**	**light red brown**	15.00	7.50
54 **60y**	**violet black**	20.00	9.00

1957. Newspaper Week Issue

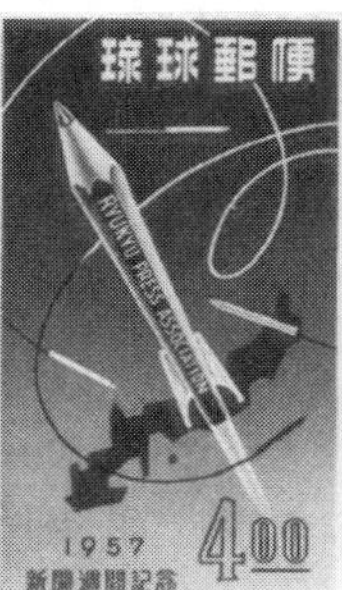

55 *Map of Okinawa*

		MNHVF	UseVF
55 4y	**deep violet blue** *(Oct. 1, 1957)*	1.00	.75

1957. New Year Issue

56 *Phoenix*

		MNHVF	UseVF
56 2y	**multicolored** *(Dec. 1, 1957)*	.40	.20

1958. Postage Stamp Issue

celebrates the 10th anniversary of Ryukyu stamps.

57 *Ryukyu stamps*

		MNHVF	UseVF
57 4y	**multicolored**	.75	.60

1958-61. Change to U.S. Currency Issue

58 *Yen symbol and potter sign*

		MNHVF	UseVF
58 1/2¢	**yellow orange**	1.00	.15
	v. pair, imperforate	750.00	.15
59 1¢	**pale green**	1.20	.15
60 2¢	**dark blue**	1.35	.15
61 3¢	**dark rose red**	1.25	.15
62 4¢	**light emerald**	1.75	.20
63 5¢	**brown salmon**	4.00	.20
64 10¢	**turquoise green**	5.00	.25
65 25¢	**blue violet**	7.00	.50
	p. gummed paper *(April 20, 1961)*	8.00	.60
66 50¢	**gray black**	15.00	.75
	p. gummed paper *(April 20, 1961)*	10.00	1.25
67 $1	**light red violet**	10.00	1.50

1958. Restoration of Shuri Mon Issue

the Gate of Courtesy is on the road to Shuri City.

68 *Gate of Courtesy*

		MNHVF	UseVF
68 3¢	**multicolored** *(Oct. 15, 1958)*	1.50	1.00

1958. New Year's Issue

69 *Lion Dance*

		MNHVF	UseVF
69 1-1/2¢	**multicolored** *(Dec. 10, 1958)*	.35	.20

1959. Arbor Week Issue

70 *Landscape*

		MNHVF	UseVF
70 3¢	**emerald green, blue and red** *(April 30, 1959)*	.80	.75
	v. red omitted		

1959. Japanese Biological Education Society Issue

71 *Yonaguni Moth*

		MNHVF	UseVF
71 3¢	**multicolored** *(July 23, 1959)*	1.50	1.00

1959. Native Flora and Fauna Issue

72 *Hibiscus*

		MNHVF	UseVF
72 1/2¢	**multicolored** *(Aug. 10, 1959)*	.30	.15

73 *Moorish Idol*

		MNHVF	UseVF
73			
3¢	**multicolored**	1.25	.25

74 *Seashell*

		MNHVF	UseVF
74			
8¢	**multicolored**	8.00	3.75

75 *Butterfly*

		MNHVF	UseVF
75			
13¢	**multicolored**	2.50	1.25

76 *Jellyfish*

		MNHVF	UseVF
76			
17¢	**deep violet blue, chestnut and yellow**	17.50	7.50

1959. New Year's Issue

		MNHVF	UseVF
77			
1-1/2¢	**multicolored on gold** *(Dec. 1, 1959)*	.60	.30

1959. Airmail Overprint Issue

78

	MNHVF	UseVF
78		
9¢ on 15y blue green *(Dec. 20, 1959)*	5.00	2.00
v. inverted overprint	700.00	
79	MNHVF	UseVF
14¢ on 20y deep carmine	8.00	4.00
80	MNHVF	UseVF
19¢ on 35y light green	9.00	5.00
81	MNHVF	UseVF
27¢ on 45y light red brown	10.00	6.00
82	MNHVF	UseVF
35¢ on 60y violet black	12.50	4.00

Several varieties of overprints exist.

1960. Ryukyu University Issue celebrates its 10th anniversary.

83 *University badge*

		MNHVF	UseVF
83			
3¢	**multicolored**	1.00	.60

1960-61. Flora and Fauna Redrawn Issue with Japanese inscription.

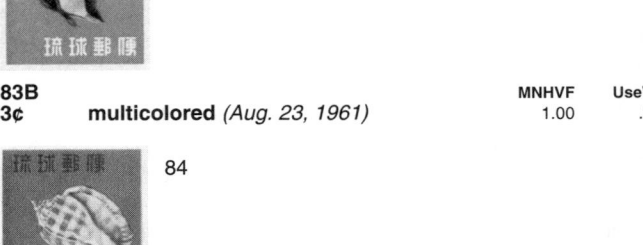

83A

		MNHVF	UseVF
83A			
1/2¢	**multicolored** *(Oct. 1961)*	.30	.30

83B

		MNHVF	UseVF
83B			
3¢	**multicolored** *(Aug. 23, 1961)*	1.00	.25

84

		MNHVF	UseVF
84			
8¢	**multicolored** *(1961)*	1.00	.75

85

		MNHVF	UseVF
85			
13¢	**multicolored** *(1961)*	1.50	.75

86

		MNHVF	UseVF
86			
17¢	**multicolored** *(1961)*	10.00	3.50

1960. Airmail Overprint on Regular Issue

87

	MNHVF	UseVF
87		
9¢ on 4y brown #39 *(Aug. 3, 1961)*	4.00	1.00
v. inverted overprint	3,500.00	

88

88	MNHVF	UseVF
14¢ on 5y rose purple, overprinted brown #45	3.00	1.25

89

89	MNHVF	UseVF
19¢ on 15y light claret, overprinted red #40	3.00	1.75

90

90	MNHVF	UseVF
27¢ on 14y dark red brown, overprinted blue #47	5.00	3.00

91

91	MNHVF	UseVF
35¢ on 20y yellow orange, overprinted green #41	6.00	3.00

1960. Dances Issue showed traditional Ryukyu dances.

92 *Munjuru*

93 *Inoha*

92		MNHVF	UseVF
1¢	**multicolored** *(Nov. 1, 1962)*	1.00	.75

93		MNHVF	UseVF
2-1/2¢	**multicolored**	2.25	1.00

94 *Batoma*

95 *Banafu*

94		MNHVF	UseVF
5¢	**multicolored**	1.00	.50

95		MNHVF	UseVF
10¢	**multicolored**	1.00	.50

1960. Athletic Issue

96 *Torch and Nago Bay*

96		MNHVF	UseVF
3¢	**light blue, deep blue green and orange red** *(Nov. 8, 1960)*	4.00	1.75

97 *Runners*

97		MNHVF	UseVF
8¢	**orange yellow and blue green**	1.00	1.00

1960. New Year's Issue

98 *Bulls fighting*

98		MNHVF	UseVF
1-1/2¢	**bistre, blue and brown red** *(Dec. 10, 1960)*	2.00	1.50

1960. Second National Census Issue

99 *Egret in flight*

99		MNHVF	UseVF
3¢	**brown**	6.00	2.00

1961. Arbor Week Issue

100 *Pine tree*

100		MNHVF	UseVF
3¢	**yellow green, red and blue green** *(May 1, 1961)*	1.75	1.25

1961. Naha City Issue

101 *City, ship and boat*

101		MNHVF	UseVF
3¢	**turquoise blue** *(May 20, 1961)*	2.00	1.00

1961-71. Dancers Issue Country name added in English.

102 *Munjuru*

102A *Inoba*

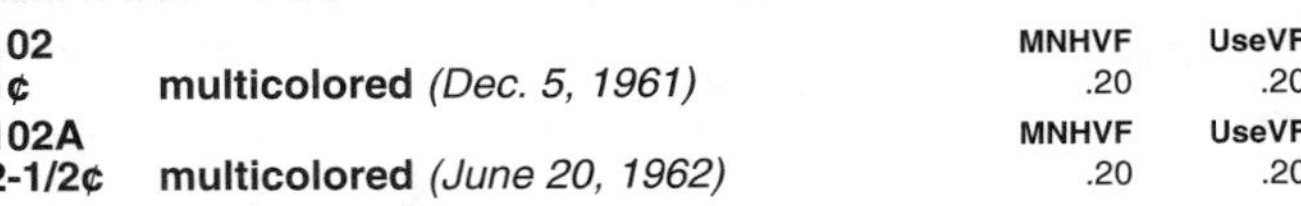

102		MNHVF	UseVF
1¢	**multicolored** *(Dec. 5, 1961)*	.20	.20

102A		MNHVF	UseVF
2-1/2¢	**multicolored** *(June 20, 1962)*	.20	.20

102B *Nuwabushi*

102C *Batoma*

102D *Banafu*

		MNHVF	UseVF
102B			
4¢	**multicolored** *(Nov. 1, 1971)*	.20	.20
102C		MNHVF	UseVF
5¢	**multicolored** *(June 20, 1961)*	.25	.20
102D		MNHVF	UseVF
10¢	**multicolored** *(June 20, 1962)*	.50	.30

103 *Shundun*

104 *Baodori*

		MNHVF	UseVF
103			
20¢	**multicolored** *(Jan. 20, 1964)*	2.25	1.25
104		MNHVF	UseVF
25¢	**multicolored** *(Feb. 1, 1962)*	1.25	1.00

105 *Nobori-kuduchi*

106 *Koteibushi*

		MNHVF	UseVF
105			
50¢	**multicolored** *(Sept. 1, 1961)*	2.50	1.00
106		MNHVF	UseVF
$1	**multicolored** *(Sept. 1, 1961)*	5.00	.50

1961. Airmail Issue

107 *Heavenly maiden*

108 *Heavenly maiden*

		MNHVF	UseVF
107			
9¢	**multicolored,** *(Sept. 21, 1961)*	.50	.20
108		MNHVF	UseVF
14¢	**multicolored**	.75	.40

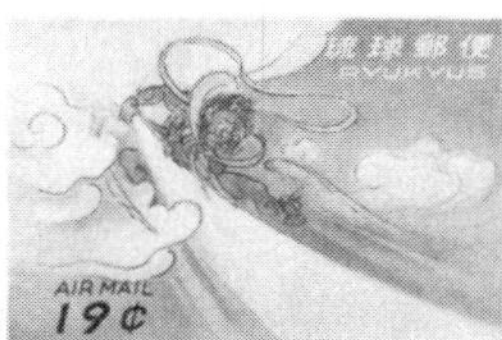

109 *Wind God*

110 *Wind God*

		MNHVF	UseVF
109			
19¢	**multicolored**	.80	.60
110		MNHVF	UseVF
27¢	**multicolored**	2.50	.75

111 *Heavenly maiden and hillside*

		MNHVF	UseVF
111			
35¢	**multicolored**	2.00	1.00

1961. Merger of Townships Issue

Takamine, Kanegushiku and Miwa merged into Itoman.

112 *White Silver Temple*

		MNHVF	UseVF
112			
3¢	**red brown** *(Oct. 1, 1961)*	2.00	1.00
	v. horizontal pair, imperforate between	300.00	
	v1. vertical pair, imperforate between	500.00	

1961. Book Week Issue

113 *Books*

		MNHVF	UseVF
113			
3¢	**multicolored** *(Nov. 12, 1961)*	1.25	1.00

1961. New Year's Issue

114 *Eagles and sun*

		MNHVF	UseVF
114			
1-1/2¢	**gold, vermilion and black** *(Dec. 10, 1961)*	2.50	1.00

Nos. 115-118 are not assigned.

1962. Ryukyu Islands Government Issue

119 *Government buildings*

No.		MNHVF	UseVF
119			
1-1/2¢	**multicolored** *(April 1, 1962)*	.70	.50
120			
3¢	**blue green, red and greenish gray**	1.00	.75

1962. Malaria Issue draws attention to the WHO drive to eradicate Malaria.

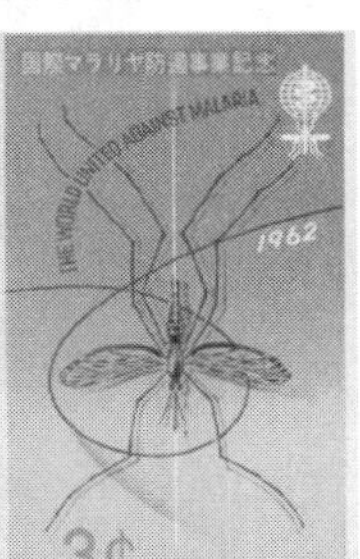

121 *Anopheles mosquito*

No.		MNHVF	UseVF
121			
3¢	**multicolored** *(April 7, 1962)*	.75	.50

122 *Malaria-eradication symbol*

No.		MNHVF	UseVF
122			
8¢	**deep blue, yellow and red**	1.00	.85

1962. Children's Day Issue

123 *Dolls and toys*

No.		MNHVF	UseVF
123			
3¢	**multicolored** *(May 5, 1962)*	1.25	.80

1962. Flower Issue

124 *Hibiscus tiliacus*

125 *Eythrila varieta orientalis*

126 *Schima superba*

No.		MNHVF	UseVF
124			
1/2¢	**multicolored** *(June 1, 1962)*	.20	.20
125			
3¢	**multicolored**	.30	.20
126			
8¢	**multicolored**	.35	.35

127 *Impatiens balsamina*

128 *Alpinia speciosa*

No.		MNHVF	UseVF
127			
13¢	**multicolored**	.50	.50
128			
17¢	**multicolored**	.75	.75

See also Nos. 142, 244, 244A.

1962. Stamp Week Issue

129 *Bowl*

No.		MNHVF	UseVF
129			
3¢	**multicolored** *(July 5, 1962)*	3.50	2.00

1962. Japan Kendo Meeting Issue

130 *Kendo practitioner*

No.		MNHVF	UseVF
130			
3¢	**multicolored**	3.75	2.00

1962. New Year's Issue

131 *Rabbit near water, textile design*

No.		MNHVF	UseVF
131			
1-1/2¢	**multicolored** *(Dec. 10, 1962)*	1.25	.75

1963. Adult Day Issue

132 *Stone relief of Man and Woman*

No.		MNHVF	UseVF
132			
3¢	**gold, black and blue** *(Jan. 15, 1963)*	1.00	.75

1963. Reforestation Issue

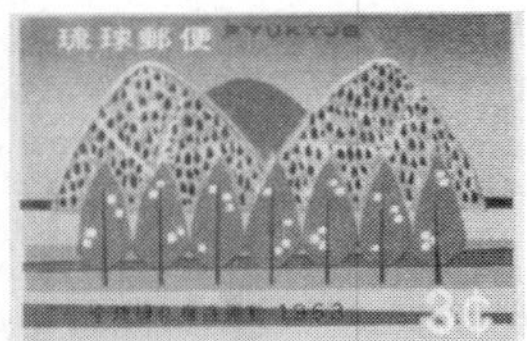

133 *Trees*

		MNHVF	UseVF
133			
3¢	**multicolored** *(March 25, 1963)*	1.00	.75

1963. Definitive Issue

134 *Gooseneck cactus*

		MNHVF	UseVF
134			
1-1/2¢	**multicolored** *(April 5, 1963)*	.20	.20

1963. Opening of Round Road Issue

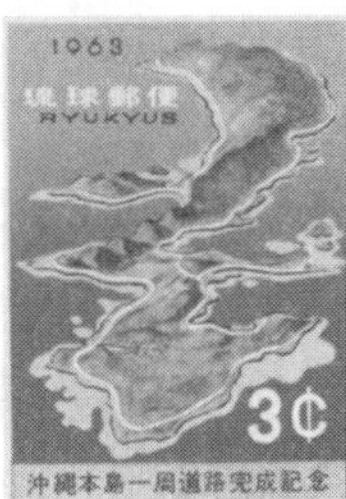

135 *Okinawa*

		MNHVF	UseVF
135			
3¢	**multicolored** *(April 30, 1963)*	1.50	.75

1963. Bird Week Issue

136 *Hawks*

		MNHVF	UseVF
136			
3¢	**multicolored** *(May 10, 1963)*	1.25	.75

1963. Shioya Bridge Issue Commemorates opening of bridge over Shioya Bay.

137 *Shioya Bridge*

		MNHVF	UseVF
137			
3¢	**multicolored** *(June 5, 1963)*	1.25	.75

1963. Stamp Week Issue

138 *Tsuikin-wan lacquerware*

		MNHVF	UseVF
138			
3¢	**multicolored** *(July 1, 1963)*	3.75	2.00

1963. Airmail Issue

139 *Plane over gate* 140 *Airliner*

		MNHVF	UseVF
139			
5-1/2¢	**multicolored** *(Aug. 28, 1963)*	.35	.20
140		**MNHVF**	**UseVF**
7¢	**multicolored**	.40	.20

1963. Junior Chamber of Commerce Issue meeting of the International organization held at Naha Okinawa.

141 *Map and JCI emblem*

		MNHVF	UseVF
141			
3¢	**multicolored** *(Sept. 16, 1963)*	.85	.60

1963. Definitive Issue

142 *Mamaomoto*

		MNHVF	UseVF
142			
15¢	*Mamaomoto (Oct. 15, 1963)*	1.00	.60

1963. National Cultural Treasures Issue

143 *Nakagusuku Castle*

		MNHVF	UseVF
143			
3¢	**multicolored** *(Nov. 1, 1963)*	.85	.50

1963. Human Rights Issue celebrates the 15th anniversary of the Universal Declaration of Human Rights.

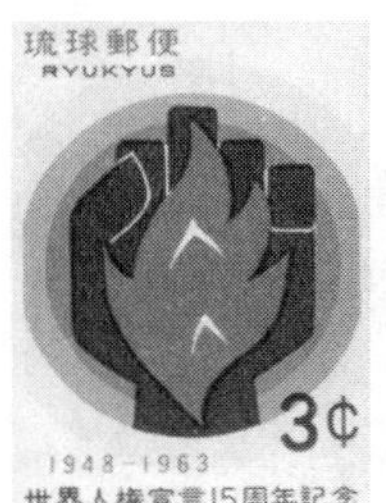

144 *Stylized flame*

		MNHVF	UseVF
144			
3¢	**multicolored** *(Dec. 10, 1963)*	.85	.50

1963. New Year's Issue

145 *Dragon*

145		MNHVF	UseVF
1-1/2¢	**multicolored** *(Dec. 10, 1963)*	.65	.20

No. 146 is not assigned.

1964. Mother's Day Issue

147 *Carnation*

147		MNHVF	UseVF
3¢	**multicolored** *(May 10, 1964)*	.50	.35

1964. Agricultural Census Issue

148 *Pineapples*

148		MNHVF	UseVF
3¢	**multicolored** *(June 1, 1964)*	.50	.35

1964. Philatelic Week Issue

149 *Minsah Obi (sash woven of kapok)*

149		MNHVF	UseVF
3¢	**multicolored, rose**	.60	.35
	a. deep carmine	.85	.50

1964. Girl Scout Issue 10th anniversary.

150 *Girl Scout*

150		MNHVF	UseVF
3¢	**multicolored** *(Aug. 31, 1964)*	.50	.35

1964. Ryukyu-Japan Microwave System Issue

151 *Shuri relay tower* 152 *Parabolic antenna*

151		MNHVF	UseVF
3¢	**green** *(Sept. 1, 1964)*	1.25	.75
	v. overprint "1" inverted overprint in date (pos 8)	25.00	20.00

152		MNHVF	UseVF
8¢	**ultramarine**	2.00	1.50

Broken type and inking varieties exits. Shifted overprints are fairly common.

1964. Olympic Torch Flight Issue The Olympic torch reached Okinawa enroute to Tokyo.

153 *Gate of Courtesy*

153		MNHVF	UseVF
3¢	**multicolored** *(Sept. 7, 1964)*	.30	.20

1964-65. Karate Issue

154 *Naihanchi stance*

155 *Makiwara*

154		MNHVF	UseVF
3¢	**multicolored** *(Oct. 5, 1964)*	.60	.25

155		MNHVF	UseVF
3¢	**multicolored** *(Feb. 5, 1965)*	.45	.25

156 *Kumite*

156		MNHVF	UseVF
3¢	**multicolored** *(June 5, 1965)*	.45	.25

1964. National Cultural Treasures Issue

157 *Miyara Dunchi, 1819*

		MNHVF	UseVF
157			
3¢	**multicolored** *(Nov. 1, 1964)*	.30	.25

1964. New Year's Issue

158 *Snake and iris*

		MNHVF	UseVF
158			
1-1/2¢	**multicolored** *(Dec. 10, 1964)*	.30	.20

1965. Boy Scout Issue

10th anniversary Ryukyuan Boy Scouts.

159 *Scouts*

		MNHVF	UseVF
159			
3¢	**multicolored** *(Feb. 6, 1965)*	.50	.25

1965. Kin Power Plant Issue

		MNHVF	UseVF
160			
3¢	**multicolored** *(July 1, 1965)*	.30	.25

1965. Onoyama Athletic Facility Issue

161 *Main stadium*

		MNHVF	UseVF
161			
3¢	**multicolored** *(July 1, 1965)*	.30	.25

1965. Philatelic Week Issue

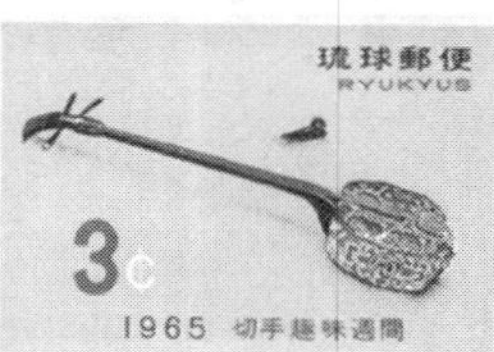

162 *Samisen*

		MNHVF	UseVF
162			
3¢	**multicolored** *(July 1, 1965)*	.50	.25

1965. International Cooperation Year Issue

		MNHVF	UseVF
163			
3¢	**multicolored** *(July 1, 1965)*	.30	.20

1965. Naha City Hall Issue

164 *Naha City Hall*

		MNHVF	UseVF
164			
3¢	**multicolored** *(Sept. 18, 1965)*	.30	.20

1965. Turtle Issue

165 *Box turtle*

166 *Hawksbill turtle*

		MNHVF	UseVF
165			
3¢	**brown** *(Oct. 20, 1965)*	.40	.25
166			
3¢	**white** *(Jan. 20, 1966)*	.40	.25

167 *Asian terrapin*

		MNHVF	UseVF
167			
3¢	**multicolored** *(April 20, 1966)*	.35	.25

1965. New Year's Issue

168 *Horse*

		MNHVF	UseVF
168			
1-1/2¢	**multicolored** *(Dec. 10, 1965)*	.20	.15
	v. gold omitted	500.00	

1966. Wild Life Conservation Issue

169 *Okinawa woodpecker*

170 *Sika deer*

171 *Dugong*

		MNHVF	UseVF
169			
3¢	**multicolored** *(Feb. 15, 1966)*	.30	.25
170			
3¢	**multicolored** *(March 15, 1966)*	.30	.25
171			
3¢	**multicolored** *(April 20, 1966)*	.30	.25

1966. Bird Week Issue

172 *Bungalow swallow*

172		MNHVF	UseVF
3¢	**multicolored** *(May 10, 1966)*	.20	.20

1966. Memorial Day Issue end of the Battle of Okinawa 1945.

173 *Lilies and ruins of city*

173		MNHVF	UseVF
3¢	**multicolored** *(June 23, 1966)*	.20	.20

1966. University of Ryukyus Issue

174 *University of Ryukyus*

174		MNHVF	UseVF
3¢	**multicolored** *(July 1, 1966)*	.20	.20

1966. Philatelic Week Issue

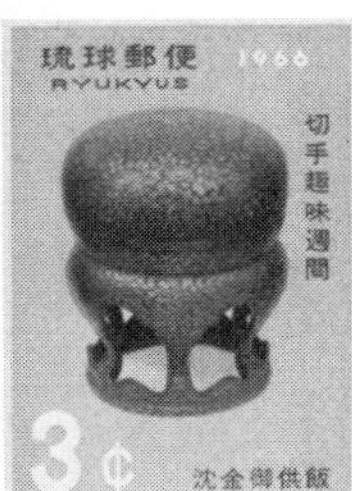

175 *18th century lacquerware*

175		MNHVF	UseVF
3¢	**multicolored** *(August 1966)*	.20	.20

1966. 20th Anniversary UNESCO Issue

176 *Tile-roofed house*

176		MNHVF	UseVF
3¢	**multicolored** *(Sept. 20, 1966)*	.20	.20

1966. Museum Issue

177 *Museum building*

177		MNHVF	UseVF
3¢	**multicolored** *(Oct. 6, 1966)*	.20	.20

1966. National Cultural Treasures Issue

178 *Tomb of Nakasone-Tuimya Genga*

178		MNHVF	UseVF
3¢	**multicolored** *(Nov. 1, 1966)*	.20	.20

1966. New Year's Issue

179 *Ram in iris wreath*

179		MNHVF	UseVF
1-1/2¢	**multicolored** *(Dec. 10, 1966)*	.20	.15

1966-67. Tropical Fish Issue

180 *Amphipron frenatus*

181 *Ostracion tuberculotus*

180		MNHVF	UseVF
3¢	**multicolored** *(Dec. 20, 1966)*	.30	.20
181		MNHVF	UseVF
3¢	**multicolored** *(Jan. 10, 1967*	.30	.20

182 *Forcipiger longirostris*

183 *Balistoides (niger) conspicilum*

182		MNHVF	UseVF
3¢	**multicolored** *(April 10, 1967)*	.30	.20
183		MNHVF	UseVF
3¢	**multicolored** *(May 25, 1967)*	.30	.20

184 *Chaetodon ephippium*

		MNHVF	UseVF
184			
3¢	**multicolored** *(June 10, 1967)*	.30	.20

No. 185 is not assigned.

1967. Philatelic Week Issue

186 *Tsuboya Urn*

		MNHVF	UseVF
186			
3¢	**multicolored** *(April 20, 1967)*	.25	.20

1967-68. Seashell Issue

187 *Mitra mitra*

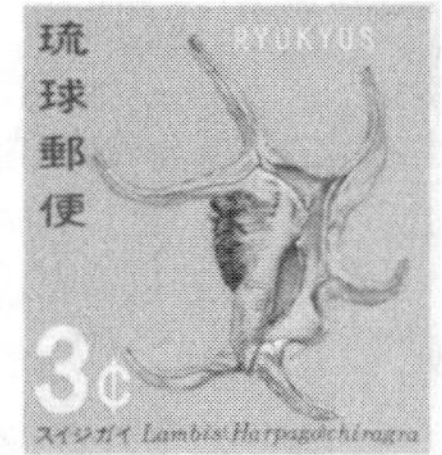

188 *Murex Aranea triremis*

189 *Lambis chiragraz*

		MNHVF	UseVF
187			
3¢	**multicolored** *(July 20, 1967)*	.25	.20
188			
3¢	**multicolored** *(Aug. 30, 1967)*	.25	.20
189			
3¢	**multicolored** *(Jan. 18, 1968)*	.30	.20

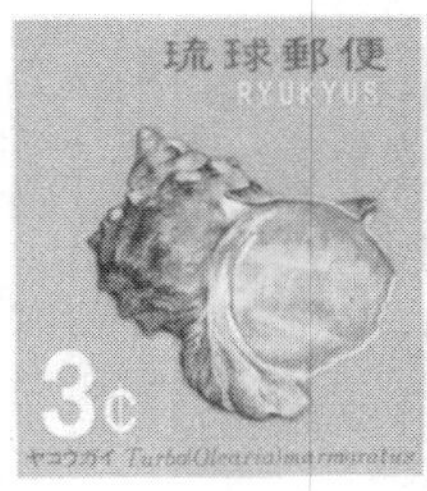

190 *Turbo mamoratus*

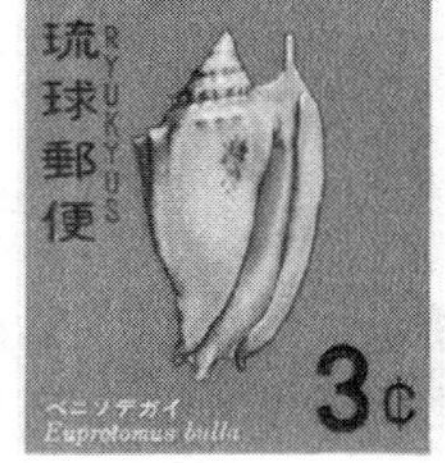

191 *Euprotomus bulla*

		MNHVF	UseVF
190			
3¢	**multicolored** *(Feb. 20, 1968)*	.30	.20
191			
3¢	**multicolored** *(June 5, 1968)*	.60	.30

1967. International Tourist Year Issue

192 *Red tiled roofs*

		MNHVF	UseVF
192			
3¢	**multicolored** *(Sept. 11, 1967)*	.25	.20

1967. Anti-Tuberculosis Issue

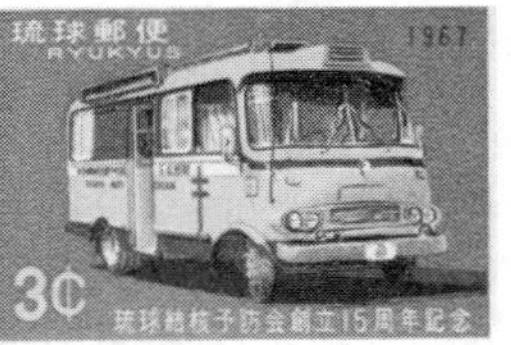

193 *Mobile TB unit*

		MNHVF	UseVF
193			
3¢	**multicolored** *(Oct. 13, 1967)*	.25	.20

1967. National Cultural Treasures Issue

194 *Hojo Bridge, Enkaku Temple*

		MNHVF	UseVF
194			
3¢	**multicolored**	.25	.20

1967. New Year's Issue

195 *Monkey*

		MNHVF	UseVF
195			
1-1/2¢	**multicolored** *(Dec. 11, 1967)*	.25	.20

1967. TV Station Issue

196 *Tower & map*

		MNHVF	UseVF
196			
3¢	**multicolored** *(Dec. 22, 1967)*	.20	.20

1968. Vaccination Issue honors 120th anniversary of first vaccinations in Ryukyu.

197 *Dr. Kijin Nakachi and assistant*

197		MNHVF	UseVF
3¢	**multicolored** *(March 15, 1968)*	.20	.20

1968. Philatelic Week Issue

198 *Pill box*

198		MNHVF	UseVF
3¢	**multicolored** *(April 18, 1968)*	.50	.40

1968. Library Week Issue

199 *Youth running toward library*

199		MNHVF	UseVF
3¢	**multicolored** *(May 13, 1968)*	.30	.20

1968. Ryukyuan Postage Issue
celebrates 20th anniversary of Ryukyuan postage stamps.

200 *Mail carriers and early stamp*

200		MNHVF	UseVF
3¢	**multicolored** *(May 13, 1968)*	.30	.20

1968. Enkaku Temple Reconstruction Issue

201 *Main gate*

201		MNHVF	UseVF
3¢	**multicolored** *(July 15, 1968)*	.30	.20

1968. Elderly People's Day Issue

202 *Old man's dance*

202		MNHVF	UseVF
3¢	**multicolored** *(Sept. 15, 1968)*	.30	.20

1968-69. Crab Issue

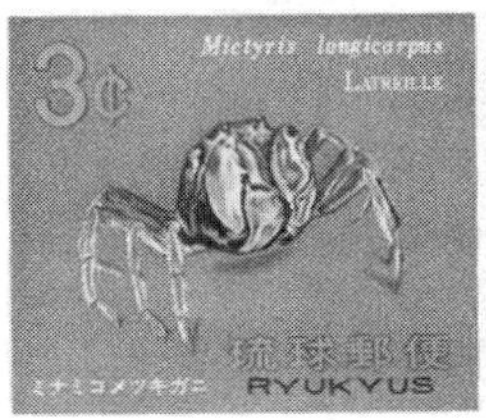

203 *Mictyris longicarpus*

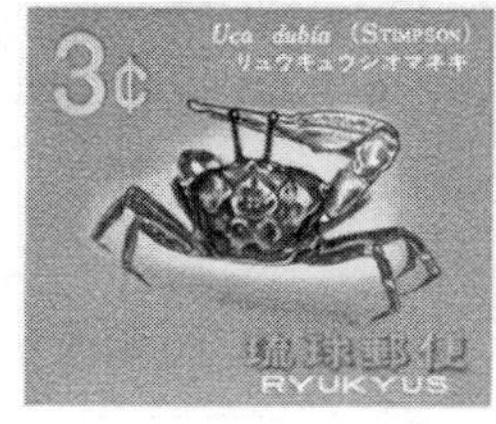

204 *Uca dubia*

203		MNHVF	UseVF
3¢	**multicolored** *(Oct. 10, 1968)*	.40	.20
204		MNHVF	UseVF
3¢	**multicolored** *(Feb. 5, 1969)*	.40	.20

205 *Baptozius vinosus*

206 *Cardisoma carnifex*

205		MNHVF	UseVF
3¢	**multicolored** *(March 5, 1969)*	.40	.25
206		MNHVF	UseVF
3¢	**multicolored** *(May 15, 1969)*	.50	.25

207 *Ocypode Ceratophthalma*

207		MNHVF	UseVF
3¢	**multicolored** *(June 2, 1969)*	.50	.25

1968. National Cultural Treasures Issue

208 *Saraswati Pavilion*

208		MNHVF	UseVF
3¢	**multicolored** *(Nov. 1, 1968)*	.30	.20

1968. All-Japan Softball Tennis Tournament Issue

209 *Tennis player*

209		MNHVF	UseVF
3¢	**multicolored** *(Nov. 3, 1968)*	.50	.20

1968. NEW YEAR'S ISSUE

210 *Cock and iris*

210		MNHVF	UseVF
1-1/2¢	**multicolored** *(Dec. 10, 1968)*	.20	.20

1969. BOXING ISSUE 20th anniversary All-Japan amateur boxing championships.

211 *Boxer*

211		MNHVF	UseVF
3¢	**multicolored** *(Jan. 3, 1969)*	.30	.20

1969. PHILATELIC WEEK ISSUE

212 *Ink slab screen*

212		MNHVF	UseVF
3¢	**multicolored** *(April 17, 1969)*	.30	.20

1969. UHF CIRCUT SYSTEM ISSUE

213 *Box antenna*

213		MNHVF	UseVF
3¢	**multicolored** *(July 1, 1969)*	.30	.20

1969. FORMATIVE EDUCATION CONFERENCE ISSUE

214 *Gate of Courtesy*

214		MNHVF	UseVF
3¢	**multicolored** *(Aug. 1, 1969)*	.30	.20

1969. FOLKLORE & FESTIVAL ISSUE

215 *Tug of war festival*

216 *Hari boat race*

215		MNHVF	UseVF
3¢	**multicolored** *(Aug. 1, 1969)*	.35	.20
216		MNHVF	UseVF
3¢	**multicolored** *(Sept. 5, 1969)*	.45	.20

217 *Izaiho ceremony*

218 *Ushideiku*

217		MNHVF	UseVF
3¢	**multicolored** *(Oct. 3, 1969)*	.45	.20
218		MNHVF	UseVF
3¢	**multicolored** *(Jan. 20, 1970)*	.55	.20

219 *Unjiyami*

219		MNHVF	UseVF
3¢	**multicolored** *(Feb. 27, 1970)*	.55	.20

1969. PROVISIONAL ISSUE overprint on No. 125.

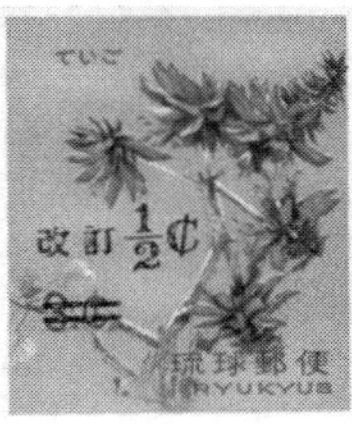

220

220	MNHVF	UseVF
1/2¢ on 3¢ multicolored	.40	.30

1969. NATIONAL CULTURAL TREASURES ISSUE

221 *Nakamura-ke farm house*

221		MNHVF	UseVF
3¢	**multicolored** *(Nov. 1, 1969)*	.20	.20

1969. New Year's Issue

222 *Dog and flowers*

222		MNHVF	UseVF
1-1/2¢	**multicolored** *(Dec. 10, 1969)*	.25	.15

1969. Emigration to Hawaii Issue

223 *Kyuzo Toyama statue*

223		MNHVF	UseVF
3¢	**multicolored** *(Dec. 5, 1969)*	.35	.20
	v. overprint *1969* omitted	2,000.00	
	v1. wide-spread bars	650.00	

1970. Philatelic Week Issue

224 *Sake flask*

224		MNHVF	UseVF
3¢	**multicolored** *(April 15, 1970)*	.30	.20

1970. Classic Opera Issue

225 *The Bell*

226 *Child and kidnapper*

225		MNHVF	UseVF
3¢	**multicolored** *(April 28, 1970)*	.50	.25
225A		MNHVF	UseVF
3¢	Sheet (4) #225	4.00	3.75
226		MNHVF	UseVF
3¢	**multicolored** *(May 29, 1970)*	.50	.25
226A		MNHVF	UseVF
3¢	Sheet (4) #226	4.00	3.75

227 *Robe of Feathers*

228 *Vengeance of Two Young Sons*

227		MNHVF	UseVF
3¢	**multicolored** *(June 30, 1970)*	.50	.25
227A		MNHVF	UseVF
3¢	Sheet (4) #227	4.00	3.75
228		MNHVF	UseVF
3¢	**multicolored** *(July 30, 1970)*	.50	.25
228A		MNHVF	UseVF
3¢	Sheet (4) #228	4.00	3.75

229 *Virgin and the Dragon*

229		MNHVF	UseVF
3¢	**multicolored** *(Aug. 25, 1970)*	.50	.25
229A		MNHVF	UseVF
3¢	Sheet (4) #229	4.00	3.75

1970. Underwater Observatory Issue

230 *Underwater observatory*

230		MNHVF	UseVF
3¢	**multicolored** *(May 22, 1970)*	.30	.20

1970-71. Great Men Issue

231 *Noboru Jahana (1865-1908)*

232 *Saion Gushichan Bunjaku (1682-1761)*

233 *Choho Giwan (1823-1876)*

231		MNHVF	UseVF
3¢	**deep carmine** *(Sept. 25, 1970)*	.60	.30
232		MNHVF	UseVF
3¢	**multicolored** *(Dec. 22, 1970)*	.90	.50
233		MNHVF	UseVF
3¢	**gray** *(Jan. 22, 1971)*	.60	.30

1970. Census Issue

234 *People*

234		MNHVF	UseVF
3¢	**multicolored** *(Oct. 1, 1970)*	.30	.20

1970. National Cultural Treasures Issue

235 *Great Cycad of Une*

235		MNHVF	UseVF
3¢	**multicolored**	.30	.20

1970. National Elections Issue

236 *Government buildings*

		MNHVF	UseVF
236			
3¢	**multicolored** *(Nov. 15, 1970)*	1.00	.25

1970. New Year's Issue

237 *Wild boar and cherry blossoms*

		MNHVF	UseVF
237			
1-1/2¢	**multicolored** *(Dec. 10, 1970)*	.20	.10

1971. Folk Craft Issue

238 *Hand loom*

239 *Filature*

		MNHVF	UseVF
238			
3¢	**multicolored** *(Feb. 16, 1971)*	.40	.20
239		MNHVF	UseVF
3¢	**multicolored** *(March 16, 1971)*	.40	.20

240 *Coat and hat*

241 *Rice huller*

		MNHVF	UseVF
240			
3¢	**multicolored** *(April 30, 1971)*	.40	.20
241		MNHVF	UseVF
3¢	**multicolored** *(May 20, 1971)*	.40	.20

242 *Fisherman*

		MNHVF	UseVF
242			
3¢	**multicolored** *(June 15, 1971)*	.40	.20

1971. Philatelic Week Issue

243 *Taku water carrier*

		MNHVF	UseVF
243			
3¢	**multicolored** *(April 15, 1971)*	.40	.20

1971. Definitive Issue

244 *Sandanka flower*

244A *Ohgocho flower*

		MNHVF	UseVF
244			
2¢	**multicolored** *(Sept. 30, 1971)*	.20	.20
244A		MNHVF	UseVF
3¢	**multicolored** *(May 10, 1971)*	.20	.20

1971. Naha City Issue 50th anniversary as a municipality.

245 *Old and new city with emblem*

		MNHVF	UseVF
245			
3¢	**multicolored** *(May 20, 1971)*	.30	.20

1971-72. Government Park Issue

246 *Mabuni Hill*

		MNHVF	UseVF
246			
3¢	**green and multicolored** *(July 30, 1971)*	.30	.20

MNHVF UseVF

247 *Mt. Arashi*

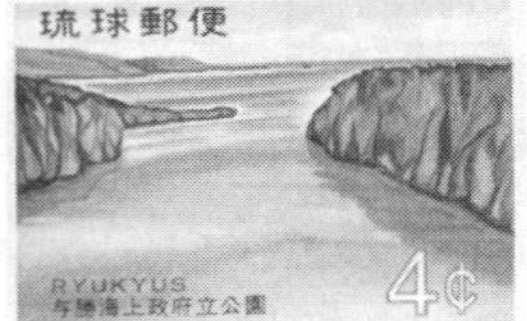

248 *Inlet*

		MNHVF	UseVF
247			
3¢	**blue and multicolored** *(Aug. 30, 1971)*	.30	.20
248		MNHVF	UseVF
4¢	**multicolored** *(Jan. 20, 1972)*	.30	.20

1971. National Cultural Issue

249 *Deva King, Torinji Temple*

249		MNHVF	UseVF
4¢	**multicolored** *(Dec. 1, 1971)*	.30	.20

1971. New Year's Issue

250 *Rat and chrysanthemums*

250		MNHVF	UseVF
2¢	**multicolored** *(Dec. 10, 1971)*	.10	.10

1971. Nurses Issue 25th anniversary of nurses' training.

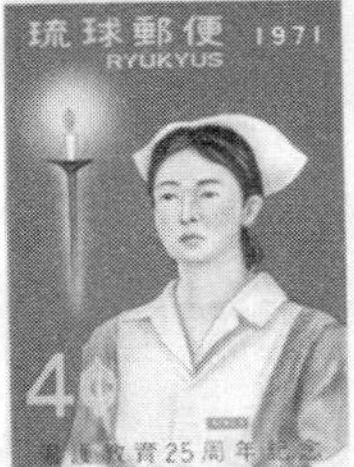

251 *Student nurse*

251		MNHVF	UseVF
4¢	**multicolored** *(Dec. 24, 1971)*	.30	.20

No. 252 not assigned.

1972. Seascapes Issue

253 *Islands*

254 *Seashore*

255 *Coral Reef*

253		MNHVF	UseVF
5¢	**multicolored** *(March 21, 1972)*	.35	.25
254		**MNHVF**	**UseVF**
5¢	**multicolored** *(March 30, 1972)*	.35	.25
255		**MNHVF**	**UseVF**
5¢	**multicolored** *(April 14, 1972)*	.35	.25

1972. Philatelic Week Issue

256 *Sake pot*

256		MNHVF	UseVF
5¢	**multicolored** *(April 20, 1972)*	.35	.25

1972. Reversion of Ryukyu Island to Japan Issue

257 *US & Japanese flags, dove*

257		MNHVF	UseVF
5¢	**multicolored** *(April 17, 1972)*	.50	.40

Ryukyu stamps were discontinued and replaced with those of Japan on May 15, 1972, as the Ryukyu Islands reverted to Japanese control.

Documentary Stamps

1952-54. First Revenue Issue *horizontally oriented numerals, offset, perforated 13 x 13 1/2.*

R1

R2

R3

R1		MNHVF	UseVF
1y	**brown** *(July 15, 1952)*	16.00	12.00
R2		**MNHVF**	**UseVF**
3y	**red** *(July 15, 1952)*	20.00	15.00
R3		**MNHVF**	**UseVF**
5y	**green** *(July 15, 1952)*	25.00	17.50

R4

R5

R6

R4		MNHVF	UseVF
10y	**blue** *(July 15, 1952)*	32.50	22.50
R5		**MNHVF**	**UseVF**
50y	**purple** *(July 15, 1952)*	40.00	27.50
R6		**MNHVF**	**UseVF**
100y	**yellow brown** *(July 15, 1952)*	62.50	35.00

			MNHVF	UseVF
R7	**500y**	**deep green** *(April 16, 1954)*	250.00	150.00
R8	**1000y**	**carmine** *(April 16, 1954)*	300.00	185.00

1958. Second Revenue Issue *vertically oriented numerals, offset, no gum, perforated 10, 10 1/2, 11 and combinations.*

R9

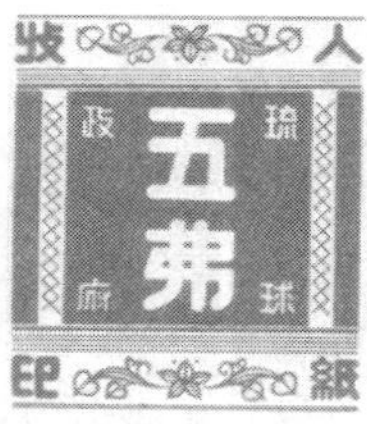
R10

R11

			MNHVF	UseVF
R9	**1¢**	**red brown** *(Sept. 16, 1958)*	32.00	32.00
R10	**3¢**	**red orange** *(Sept. 16, 1958)*	40.00	40.00
R11	**5¢**	**blue green** *(Sept. 16, 1958)*	50.00	50.00

R12

R13

R14

			MNHVF	UseVF
R12	**10¢**	**blue** *(Sept. 16, 1958)*	75.00	75.00
R13	**50¢**	**purple** *(Sept. 16, 1958)*	130.00	130.00
R14	**$1**	**yellow brown** *(Sept. 16, 1958)*	200.00	200.00

R15

R16

			MNHVF	UseVF
R15	**$5**	**deep green** *(Sept. 16, 1958)*	335.00	335.00
R16	**$10**	**carmine** *(Sept. 16, 1958)*	450.00	450.00

1959-69. Third Revenue Issue Office building. *Offset (1¢-50¢ values) and intaglio ($1-$50 values), perforated 13 x 13 1/2.*

R17

R18

R19

			MNHVF	UseVF
R17	**1¢**	**brown** *(1959)*	4.00	2.00
R18	**3¢**	**red** *(1959)*	4.00	1.50
R19	**5¢**	**purple** *(1959)*	6.00	4.00

R20

R21

			MNHVF	UseVF
R20	**10¢**	**green** *(1959)*	12.50	8.00
R21	**20¢**	**yellow brown** *(1969)*	85.00	60.00

R22 R23

			MNHVF	UseVF
R22	**30¢**	**olive** *(1969)*	92.50	75.00
R23	**50¢**	**blue** *(1959)*	40.00	17.50

R24 R25

			MNHVF	UseVF
R24	**$1**	**yellow olive** *(1959)*	55.00	17.50
R25	**$2**	**orange vermilion** *(1969)*	235.00	70.00
R26	**$3**	**purple** *(1969)*	400.00	95.00

R27 R28

			MNHVF	UseVF
R27	**$5**	**vermilion orange** *(1959)*	125.00	65.00
R28	**$10**	**dull blue green** *(1959)*	200.00	85.00
R29	**$20**	**red carmine** *(1969)*	1,100.00	245.00
R30	**$30**	**blue** *(1969)*	1,150.00	400.00

R31		MNHVF	UseVF
$50	**violet black** *(1969)*	1,750.00	800.00

Unemployment Insurance Stamps

1961. First Unemployment Issue certified, offer cancellation in an official booklet, a one-day contact for a day laborer. *Offset, unwatermarked, without gum, rouletted.*

RUI1, 3 *Dove*

RUI2 *Shield*

RUI1		MNHVF	UseVF
2¢	**violet pink** *(Jan. 10, 1961)*	800.00	800.00

RUI2		MNHVF	UseVF
4¢	**violet** *(Jan. 10, 1961)*	55.00	55.00

1966. Second Unemployment Issue *Offset, unwatermarked, perforated 13 x 13 1/2.*

RUI3		MNHVF	UseVF
2¢	**red pink** *(Feb. 1,1966)*	800.00	800.00

RUI4 *Shield, bolder denomination*

RUI4		MNHVF	UseVF
4¢	**deep violet** *(Feb. 1, 1966)*	32.50	32.50

1968. Third Unemployment Issue *Offset, unwatermarked, perforated 13 x 13 1/2.*

RUI5 *Cycad*

RUI5		MNHVF	UseVF
8¢	**brown** *(April 19, 1968)*	42.50	42.50

1967-72. Surcharged Unemployment Issue *Perforated 13 x 13 1/2.*

RUI6 *Dove overprinted 8¢*

RUI6		MNHVF	UseVF
8¢ on 2¢	**reddish pink** *(1967)*	80.00	80.00

RUI7 *Shield overprinted 8¢*

RUI7		MNHVF	UseVF
8¢ on 4¢	**deep violet** *(1972)*	42.50	42.50

RUI8 *Shield, overprinted 12¢*

RUI8		MNHVF	UseVF
12¢ on 4¢	**deep violet** *(1971)*	32.50	32.50

Allied Military Government

The rejuvenation of the postal systems of war-torn Europe was of prime importance after World War II. As part of this effort, postage stamps were produced by the United States for use in areas where American troops were involved as part of the Allied Military Government (AMG) in Italy, France, Germany and Austria.

The U.S. War Department ordered postage stamps (and currency) designed and produced for each of these areas by The Bureau of Engraving and Printing in Washington, D.C.

To augment the efforts of the BEP, additional quantities of stamps were produced locally in some of the countries by reproducing or overprinting stamps of the BEP design or by overprinting stamps available locally.

AMG - Italy

Although printed for use in all of occupied Italy by the U.S. Bureau of Engraving and Printing (BEP), only a minute quantity was ever used in Italy proper. Practically the entire printing was put on sale and used in Sicily. Therefore it acquired the name "Sicily Issue."

1943. Sicily & Southern Italy *Sept. 17, 1943. Lithographed by Bureau of Engraving and Printing, Washington, D.C. Italy and denomination in black, perforated 11, no watermark.*

IYA1

IYA2

IYA3

		FVFNH	UseFVF
IYA1 15c	**pale orange,** *(Aug. 24, 1943)*	1.00	.80
IYA2 25c	**pale yellow olive**	1.00	.80
IYA3 30c	**drab gray**	1.00	.80

IYA4

IYA5

IYA6

		FVFNH	UseFVF
IYA4 50c	**light red violet**	1.00	.80
IYA5 60c	**dull yellow,** *(Oct. 15, 1943)*	1.00	.75
IYA6 1L	**pale emerald**	1.00	.80

IYA7

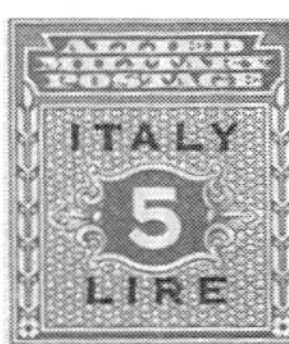

IYA8

IYA9

		FVFNH	UseFVF
IYA7 2L	**rose red,** *(Oct. 14, 1943)*	1.00	1.00
IYA8 5L	**pale turquoise blue,** *(Oct. 20, 1943)*	11.00	2.00
IYA9 10L	**pale yellow brown,** *(Oct. 20, 1943)*	1.00	3.00

1943. Italy Overprint Issue Dec. 10, 1943. Italy No. 350//354 overprinted in red (shades) or blue (B).

IYA10

		FVFNH	UseFVF
IYA10 20c	**bright rose red (B)**	1.50	3.00

IYA11

		FVFNH	UseFVF
IYA11 35c	**deep blue**	15.00	17.00

IYA11A

		FVFNH	UseFVF
IYA11A 35c	**deep blue, vermilion** overprint	15.00	17.00

IYA12

IYA12A

		FVFNH	UseFVF
IYA12 50c	**light violet**	.75	1.00
IYA12A 50c	**light violet, orange** overprint	.75	1.00

1945. Venezia Giulia Issue *Sept. 22, 1945-47. Contemporary Italian stamps with overprint size 16x12mm or 14x10mm (No. 23) or 27x14mm (No. 33, 35-43), by R. Fortuna, Trieste.*

1: Postage, on Empire issue, watermark 9 No. 348//364.

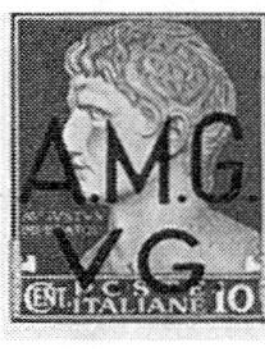

IYA13

		IFVFNH	UseFVF
IYA13 10c	**deep bistre brown** (No. 348)	.30	.35
	x. overprint inverted	3.50	3.75

IYA14

IYA17

IYA14		FVFNH	UseFVF
20c	**bright rose** (No. 350)	.40	.50

IYA15		FVFNH	UseFVF
20L	**green,** *(July 10, 1946)* (No. 364)	2.25	3.50

Note: Due to the urgent need for postage stamps, some issues were overprinted AMG-VG even though they contained the fascist symbol of the Roman ax. Values containing this symbol were the 10c brown, 20c red and the 60c green. Because a few sheets of the 20c value with the Fasces were inadvertently overprinted, a larger printing was permitted in December 1946 to prevent speculation in this issue.

No watermark, No. 733//739.

IYA16		FVFNH	UseFVF
10c	**sepia,** *(Nov. 30, 1945)* (No. 733)	.30	.20

IYA17		FVFNH	UseFVF
20c	**rose red,** *(Dec. 6, 1946)* (No. 737)	.25	.50
	x. overprint inverted	13.00	13.50

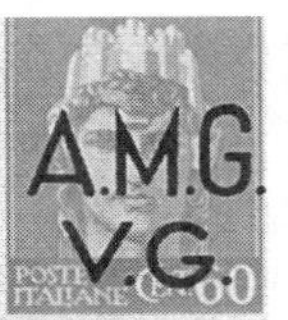

IYA18

IYA18		FVFNH	UseFVF
60c	**light orange red,** *(Nov. 30, 1945)* (No. 739)	.25	.25

Watermark 743, winged wheel, No. 743//749.

IYA19		FVFNH	UseFVF
20c	**rose red** (No. 743)	.30	.50
	x. overprint inverted	60.00	66.00
	x1. overprint doubled	120.00	120.00

IYA20

IYA20		FVFNH	UseFVF
60c	**dark blue green** (No. 744)	.45	.30
	x. overprint inverted	50.00	55.00
	x1. overprint doubled	90.00	60.00

IYA21

IYA21		FVFNH	UseFVF
1L	**dark violet** (No. 745)	.30	.30
	x. overprint inverted	45.00	46.00

IYA22

IYA22		FVFNH	UseFVF
2L	**bright rose red** (No. 747)	.35	.35
	x. overprint inverted	45.00	46.00
	x1. overprint doubled	45.00	46.00

IYA23

IYA23		FVFNH	UseFVF
5L	**rose red,** *(Oct. 16, 1945)* (No. 748)	.65	.50
	x. overprint inverted	240.00	250.00

IYA24

IYA24		FVFNH	UseFVF
10L	**deep violet** (No. 749)	.90	1.25
	x. overprint inverted	18.00	

On Peace issue, No. 798//818.

IYA25

IYA25		FVFNH	UseFVF
25c	**deep turquoise green,** *(Jan. 8, 1947)* (No. 798)	.25	.30
	x. overprint inverted		

IYA26

IYA26		FVFNH	UseFVF
2L	**dark chocolate,** *(July 17, 1947)* (No. 805)	.60	.75

YA27

IY28

IYA27		FVFNH	UseFVF
3L	**scarlet,** *(Jan. 8, 1947)* (No. 806)	.45	.30

IYA28		FVFNH	UseFVF
4L	**light orange red,** *(Jan. 2, 1947)* (No. 807)	.70	.40

IYA29

IYA29		FVFNH	UseFVF
6L	**blue violet,** *(July 17, 1947)* (No. 809)	1.75	2.25

IYA30

IYA30
20L **deep red lilac,** *(July 23, 1947)* (No. 814) FVFNH 26.00 UseFVF 1.50

YA31

IY32

IYA31
25L **dark blue green,** *(July 10, 1946)* (No. 815) FVFNH 4.25 UseFVF 6.00

IYA32
50L **deep chocolate,** *(July 10, 1946)* (No. 817) FVFNH 4.75 UseFVF 7.50

IYA33

IYA33
100L **carmine rose** *(Sept. 13, 1946)* (No. 818) FVFNH 17.50 UseFVF 25.00

Note: The 20L denomination was used extensively, resulting in one of the scarcest mint AMG-VG stamps.

2: Airmail, on No. 379, 819//826.

IYA34

IYA34
50c **dark brown** (No. 379)

	FVFNH	UseFVF
dark brown (No. 379)	.25	.50
x. overprint inverted	40.00	45.00
x1. overprint doubled	120.00	120.00

IYA35

IYA35
1L **dark slate blue,** *(July 23, 1947)* (No. 819) FVFNH .25 UseFVF .50

YA36

IY37

IYA36
2L **deep blue,** *(Jan. 16, 1947)* (No. 820) FVFNH .25 UseFVF .50

IYA37
5L **bright green,** *(Jan. 23, 1947)* (No. 822) FVFNH 1.75 UseFVF 2.50

IYA38

IYA38
10L **rose carmine,** *(Jan. 23, 1947)* (No. 823) FVFNH 1.75 UseFVF 2.50

IYA39

IYA39
25L

	FVFNH	UseFVF
deep blue, *(Sept. 13, 1946)* (No. 824)	1.75	2.50
x. overprint inverted	90.00	160.00
x1. overprint doubled	330.00	350.00

IYA40

IYA40
25L **ochre brown,** *(July 23, 1947)* (No. 825) FVFNH 15.00 UseFVF 20.00

IYA41

IYA41
50L

	FVFNH	UseFVF
dark green, *(Sept. 13, 1946)* (No. 826)	3.25	5.00
x. overprint inverted	210.00	240.00

3: On special delivery, No. 829, 832.

IYA42

IYA42
10L **deep blue,** *(Sept. 3, 1946)* FVFNH 3.50 UseFVF 4.50

IYA43

IYA43
30L

	FVFNH	UseFVF
deep violet, *(Sept. 3, 1946)*	8.50	12.25
x. overprint inverted	220.00	240.00

Note: On Oct. 1, 1947, Italian stamps overprinted AMG-VG, for use in and around the Territory of Trieste, ceased being issued. They were superseded by similar Italian stamps overprinted AMG-FTT. This was in conformity with the establishment of the Free Territory of Trieste.

AMG - France

The first issue of AMG postage stamps produced for France, titled Supplemental French Postage Stamps, because of the touchy political situation in France, was printed by the United States Bureau of Engraving and Printing (BEP) in its surface printing division. The issue was made available by the Treasury Department through the Allied Military Government authorities to the provisional French Government of Gen. Charles DeGaulle for general use throughout liberated France. Initially, these stamps replaced the existing stocks stocks of stamps used during the occupation by the German-controlled Vichy Government. The subject for the design of this series of stamps was taken from a photograph of the *Arc de Triomphe* in Paris, furnished by the Washington Public Library.

1944. France I Issue *Oct. 5, 1944. Arch of Triumph, typographed by Bureau of Engraving and Printing, Washington, perforated 11.*
1: Numerals in colors of stamps.

FLA773

FLA773 FVFNH UseFVF
5c rose purple .35 .35

FLA774

FLA774 FVFNH UseFVF
10c pearl gray .35 .35

FLA775

FLA775 FVFNH UseFVF
25c gray brown .35 .35

FLA776

FLA776 FVFNH UseFVF
50c olive bistre .50 .70

FLA777

FLA777 FVFNH UseFVF
1f light blue green .90 .90

FLA778

FLA778 FVFNH UseFVF
1.50f rose 1.90 .90

FLA779

FLA779 FVFNH UseFVF
2.50f light red violet .90 .90

FLA780

FLA780 FVFNH UseFVF
4f ultramarine 1.90 1.90

FLA781

FLA781 FVFNH UseFVF
5f gray black 1.90 1.90

FLA782 FVFNH UseFVF
10f light orange 37.50 35.00

Note: The design of the 1.50 Franc stamp was in error as the value was listed as FRANCS instead of the correct one franc fifty centimes. This was remedied on the France II issue. The FRANCE 10 Fr. value is one of the scarcest AMG stamps. Only 720,000 were printed.

1945. France II Issue The second issue, called the Committee French Postage Stamps, Series 1944, was distributed in the same manner as the first issue. No data has been found to ascertain the first date of issue of this series of stamps. The same basic design of the first issue was utilized. However, the numerals and denominational wording were not incorporated into the design but were added by overprinting the numerals and either CENTIMES, FRANC or FRANCS in black.
2: (Feb. 12, 1945): Additional values, figures in black.

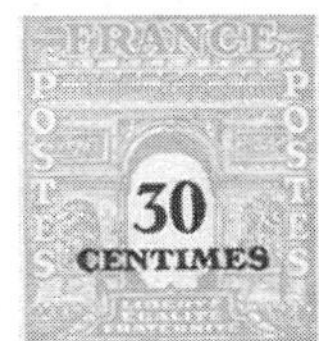
FLA783

FLA783 FVFNH UseFVF
30c orange .30 .30

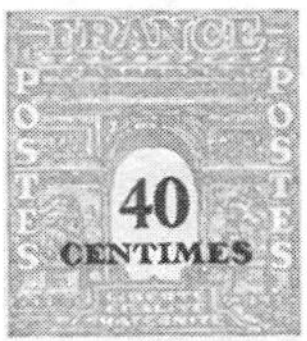
FLA784

		FVFNH	UseFVF
FLA784			
40c	**pearl gray**	.30	.30

FLA785

		FVFNH	UseFVF
FLA785			
50c	**olive bistre**	.30	.30

FLA786

		FVFNH	UseFVF
FLA786			
60c	**light violet**	.30	.30

FLA787

		FVFNH	UseFVF
FLA787			
80c	**light emerald**	.30	.30

FLA788

		FVFNH	UseFVF
FLA788			
1.20f	**gray brown**	.30	.30

FLA789

		FVFNH	UseFVF
FLA789			
1.50f	**light vermilion**	.30	.30

FLA790

		FVFNH	UseFVF
FLA790			
2f	**yellow**	.30	.30

FLA791

		FVFNH	UseFVF
FLA791			
2.40f	**carmine rose**	.30	.30

FLA792

		FVFNH	UseFVF
FLA792			
3f	**rose purple**	.30	.30

AMG - Germany

After World War II, Germany (and Berlin separately) was divided into four occupation zones with joint overall administration, except for territory east of the Oder and Neisse rivers, which was divided between USSR (Kaliningrad oblast formerly Konigsberg) and Poland (provinces of Olsztyn, Kozcalin, Szczecin, Zielona Gora, Wroclaw and Opole, formerly known as Allenstein, Koslin, Stettin, Grunberg, Breslau and Oppeln respectively). In many cases newly created districts of Germany did not follow historical boundries. The Saar, in French zone, was made autonomous. Failure of negotiations for unification of Germany led to creation of two republics: *Democratic* (East Germany — from USSR zone) and *Federal* (West Germany — British, U.S., and French zones).

100 pfennig = 1 reichsmark.

1945. U.S. and British Zones Issue *March 19-July 1945. AM POST (Allied Military), Washington printing, no white patches in spandrel, offset by Bureau of Engraving and Printing, Washington, D.C., perforated 11, thick cloudy white to tan paper; p: (early printing) (thick, smooth, clear white paper, shades.*

GDA1101

Washington printing spandrel Brunswick printing spandrel

GDA1101		FVFNH	UseFVF
3p	**bright lilac,** *(July 1, 1945)*	.20	.20
	p. early printing	.25	.25

GDA1102

GDA1102		FVFNH	UseFVF
4p	**drab gray,** *(July 1, 1945)*	.20	.20
	p. early printing	.25	.25

GDA1103

GDA1103		FVFNH	UseFVF
5p	**light yellow emerald**	.20	.20
	p. early printing	.25	.25
	pl. thin white paper	.35	.20

GDA1104

GDA1104		FVFNH	UseFVF
6p	**yellow**	.20	.20
	p. early printing	.20	.25
	pl. thin white paper	.35	.25

GDA1105

GDA1105		FVFNH	UseFVF
8p	**orange**	.20	.20
	p. early printing	.20	.25

GDA1106

GDA1106		FVFNH	UseFVF
10p	**gray brown,** *(July 1, 1945)*	.20	.20
	p. early printing	.20	.20

GDA1107

GDA1107		FVFNH	UseFVF
12p	**bright purple**	.20	.20
	p. early printing	.20	.30

GDA1108

GDA1108		FVFNH	UseFVF
15p	**carmine red,** *(July 1, 1945)*	.20	.20
	p. early printing	.20	.25

GDA1109

GDA1109		FVFNH	UseFVF
25p	**deep ulramarine,** *(July 1, 1945)*	.20	.20
	p. early printing	.25	.25

Note: The 5 pfennig value on thin paper was used mostly in the Hamburg Postal District. The 6 pfennig on thin paper was used only *in the Kiel Postal District, and it is the scarcest value of the set.*

Note: 6p, 8p and 12p sold and used in West sector of Berlin until middle September 1945.

Stamps overprinted Military/Permit/Office/Fiscal Stamp and value: revenue.

Forgeries: 3p-25p overprinted German and 8p with blue overprint 6.

Users of this catalog are invited to write to us if they have information they feel will supplement or correct any material contained herein. All such communications will be answered.

How To Differentiate Among The Three German Printings.

Entirely new plates, using the same design as that of the Washington Printing, first delivered Sept. 19, 1944, were prepared and used by Harrison & Sons, Ltd., for a British Printing, beginning in August 1945; and new plates were made by the Georg Westermann Co. of Brunswick, Germany, for a Brunswick Printing, also beginning in August 1945.

Minute variations as well as paper and gum differences permit easy identification of each of the printings.

Washington Printing

No white triangles in the corners of the arabesques

End of right leg of the "M" in the oval has a slight curve but is not concentric with the curve of the oval

Because of paper shortages during World War II, the Bureau of Engraving and Printing used whatever paper stock was available, smooth, white paper at first. The porous paper used for the subsequent printings can vary from tan to white. In addition, the gums also vary from white to tan.

British Printing

This printing is the easiest to detect. The perforations are much smaller and finer than on the other two printings. In addition, the British Printing was produced by photogravure and has a different appearance from the other two printings, which were offset lithographed.

Brunswick Printing

White triangles are found adjacent to the arabesques in the four corners but most apparent in the upper right.

End of right leg of the "M" curves concentric with the oval.

AMG - Austria

Designed, prepared and printed by the United States Bureau of Engraving and Printing (BEP), this was the final issue of the Allied Military Government produced by the BEP in Washington, D.C. All subsequent postal items needed for use in occupied or policed territory were produced in proximity to the site.

1945. American, British & French Zones Issue *June 28-Nov. 1945. Posthorn, offset by U.S. Bureau of Engraving and Printing, Washington, D.C., perforated 11, thick paper, unwatermarked.*

AXA991

AXA991 FVFNH UseFVF
1g turquoise blue, *(Nov. 20, 1945)* .20 .25

AXA992

AXA992 FVFNH UseFVF
3g orange .20 .25

AXA993

AXA993 FVFNH UseFVF
4g dull brown orange, *(July 15, 1945)* .20 .25

AXA994

AXA994 FVFNH UseFVF
5g emerald .20 .25

AXA995

AXA995 FVFNH UseFVF
6g bright purple .20 .25

AXA996

AXA996 FVFNH UseFVF
8g rose carmine .20 .25

AXA997

AXA997 FVFNH UseFVF
10g drab gray .20 .25

AXA998

AXA998 FVFNH UseFVF
12g brown drab .20 .25

AXA999

AXA999 FVFNH UseFVF
15g bright rose red, *(July 15, 1945)* .25 .25

AXA1000

AXA1000 FVFNH UseFVF
20g chestnut .25 .25

AXA1001

AXA1001 FVFNH UseFVF
25g bright blue .20 .25

AXA1002

AXA1002 FVFNH UseFVF
30g red violet .20 .25

AXA1003 AXA1004 AXA1005

AXA1003 FVFNH UseFVF
40g light blue .20 .25

AXA1004		FVFNH	UseFVF
60g	**apple green**	.25	.25

AXA1005		FVFNH	UseFVF
1s	**red lilac,** *(Aug. 13, 1945)*	.30	.40

AXA1006

AXA1007

AXA1006		FVFNH	UseFVF
2s	**yellow,** *(Aug. 13, 1945)*	.35	.55

AXA1007		FVFNH	UseFVF
5s	**deep blue violet,** *(Aug. 13, 1945)*	.55	.75

1946. Postage Due Issue All remaining stocks of the AMG Austria Issue, with the exception of the 1 and 4 groschen values, were turned over to the newly established Renner Government, operating under the sanction of the Allied authorities. As this government already had issued definitive stamps by April and May 1946, they had the AMG issue overprinted PORTO for temporary use as postage due stamps until their own definitive postage due stamps were released.

April 23-May, 1946. No. 992//1007 overprinted.

AXA1042

AXA1043

AXA1044

AXA1042		FVFNH	UseFVF
3g	**orange**	.35	.30

AXA1043		FVFNH	UseFVF
5g	**emerald**	.35	.30

AXA1044		FVFNH	UseFVF
6g	**bright purple**	.35	.30

AXA1045

AXA1046

AXA1047

AXA1045		FVFNH	UseFVF
8g	**rose carmine**	.35	.30
	x. overprint inverted	20.00	20.00

AXA1046		FVFNH	UseFVF
10g	**drab gray**	.35	.30

AXA1047		FVFNH	UseFVF
12g	**brown drab**	.40	.30

AXA1048

AXA1049

AXA1050

AXA1048		FVFNH	UseFVF
15g	**bright rose red**	.40	.30

AXA1049		FVFNH	UseFVF
20g	**chestnut**	.40	.30

AXA1050		FVFNH	UseFVF
25g	**bright blue**	.40	.30

AXA1051

AXA1051		FVFNH	UseFVF
30g	**red violet**	.40	.30

AXA1052

AXA1052		FVFNH	UseFVF
40g	**light blue**	.40	.30

AXA1053

AXA1053		FVFNH	UseFVF
60g	**apple green**	.40	.30

AXA1054

AXA1054		FVFNH	UseFVF
1s	**red lilac,** *(May 20, 1946)*	.50	.40

AXA1055

AXA1055		FVFNH	UseFVF
2s	**yellow,** *(May 20, 1946)*	.50	.40

AXA1056

AXA1056		FVFNH	UseFVF
5s	**deep blue violet,** *(May 20, 1946)*	.70	.50

Note: Inverted overprint: 3g, 8g-12g, 20g, 30g, 60g, 1s exist.

Stamps used as money

Stamps became legal tender during the American Civil War and after, 1862-1875, first by custom and then by law. These specialized uses of postage stamps are collectible today as Postage Stamp Envelopes, Encased Postage Stamps and Postage Currency.

Paper money in denominations of less than the dollar unit was required in commerce because during the Civil War the gold, silver and copper coins in circulation largely disappeared. This was due to several factors.

There was no pervading fear in the North that the armed forces of the Confederacy would prevail and shatter the Union. Rather, it would appear that a hoarding of hard money was caused by an ingrained distrust of paper money. The Yankee worker simply felt more secure when his paper wages had been converted to gold and silver. Consequently, he gave a cool reception to "greenbacks," which could not be redeemed for either gold or silver and were suspiciously regarded as "faith paper." This practically expressed preference for coins inevitably depreciated the paper money in terms of the gold standard. Gold coins commanded a premium of 3% over U.S. and state paper money in January 1862, the month following the general suspension of specie payment by banks and the Federal Treasury, and 32% by the end of 1862. At one point in 1864 it required $285 in paper to purchase $100 in gold. The distrust of the government's fiat paper was further heightened by a snowballing national debt, which reached $2.8 billion in 1865.

A monetary situation in which gold commanded a substantial premium over a like face value of paper dollars swiftly drove gold coins from commercial channels, effectively removing the United States from a gold standard. It also created a favorable condition for the exporting of silver coins, which disappeared from the marketplace, but at a less precipitous pace than gold.

Plenty of customers for gold coins existed. In 1858 Canada had adopted a decimal system of coinage with a dollar unit similar to that of the United States. In lieu of a sufficient coins of British origin, Canada unofficially adopted the coinage of the United States and used it widely in domestic trade. The West Indies and many Latin American countries also used large quantities of U.S. silver coinage.

Disappearance of gold from American trade channels and the willingness of foreign users of U.S. silver coins to pay for them with gold combined to produce a legal and highly profitable bullion trade, which speculators and bankers found irresistible: Greenbacks were exchanged for silver coins, which were then exchanged for gold in Canada, the West Indies or Latin America. The gold was then returned to the United States, where it was used to purchase more greenbacks at the metal's high premium rate. A safer round-robin route to riches can hardly be imagined.

During the last week of June and the first week of July, 1862, more than $25 million in subsidiary coins vanished from circulation in the North. Illogically, the Philadelphia Mint continued a small but steady production of silver coins during the 1860s. Bullion dealers obtained them directly from the mint and sped them abroad. In 1863, the entire production of silver coins was exported.

The withdrawal of subsidiary silver coins in the summer of 1862 all but paralyzed the institutions and practice of everyday commerce. The smallest denominations of official money available were discounted $5 Legal Tender Notes and the copper-nickel cents that had been fed into circulation in great quantities. When first forced upon the public in 1857, the copper-nickel cent, which was intrinsically worth about 60% of face value, had been considered a nuisance; it was regularly discounted 3% and more in large transactions. But with the disappearance of silver coins, the ugly duckling became the belle of the ball. It became the only alternative to walking, or going without a newspaper, or buying a pound of pomegranates and receiving change in kumquats and quince. Cents were bundled in bags of 25, 50 and 100 in a hopeless attempt to bridge the gap between the 1¢ piece and the $5 bill. By March 1863, the lowly cent commanded a premium of 20%, but few could be found.

The disappearance of nearly all official coinage from trade channels resulted in an outpouring of private emergency monies. State bank notes of $1 and $2 denominations were cut into fractional parts. Other banks issued notes in denominations of $1.25, $1.50 and $1.75. Eastern cities issued their own fractional notes. Merchants, reviving a practice prevalent during the coin shortages of 1837 and 1857, made change in their own promissory notes or "shinplasters," redeemable in merchandise at the issuer's place of business. Private issues of Civil War tokens began.

Postage Stamp Envelopes

Among the emergency monies called into use was the common postage stamp. The use of stamps as a low-denomination medium of exchange led directly to the issuing of the highly successful Postage Currency and Fractional Currency series.

By the time the Civil War began, the adhesive postage stamp had become a well-established part of the public routine. Inasmuch as they were of official origin, had a constant value throughout the country and were easily obtained, consideration of postage stamps as a medium of exchange for coin-deprived people was inevitable. In early July 1862, Horace Greeley, publisher of the politically influential *New York Tribune*, suggested that stamps pasted on a half sheet of paper, with the other half folded over the stamps to afford them protection from wear, would make an excellent coin substitute. The coin-starved public agreed.

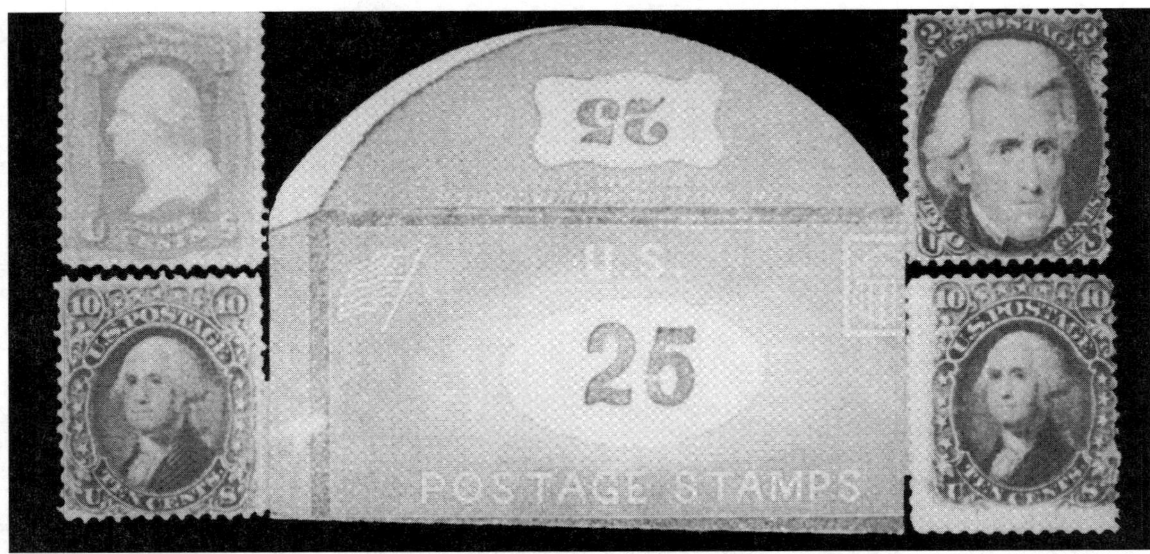

A postage stamp envelope and typical contents.

But fragile, gummed stamps could not be carried loose.

Methods of protecting the stamps were quickly devised. They were pasted on sheets of light vellum paper — with or without a protective flap — which also bore an advertising message and a large numeral indicating the total face value of the stamps. Stamps were also encased in small envelopes, approximately 70 by 35 mm in size, on the outside of which was printed the value of the contents and an advertising message.

Both methods of using stamps as emergency money had drawbacks. Pasting the stamps on sheets of paper did not provide them sufficient protection from wear. Envelopes offered better protection but provided an opportunity for petty larceny. Few recipients had the time to check the contents of each envelope to determine if it contained the proper denominational total of stamps, or if the stamps were unused, or if rectangles of colored paper had been substituted for the stamps.

Existing pieces are extremely rare. Prices given in these listings reflect the rarity of the individual envelopes and the desirability of their imprints. If any stamps are included with the envelopes there is no way of telling whether they are original.

Postage Stamp Envelopes

KL#	Name, address and notations	Value
1-25	H. Armstrong, Hosiery, Laces, etc. 140 6th Ave, (NYC)	700.
3-?	Arthur, Gregory & Co., Stationer 39 Nassau St. NYC	650.
5-25	Bergen & Tripp, Stationer 114 Nassau St, (NYC)	650.
7-25	Berlin & Jones, Stationer 134 William St, NYC	650.

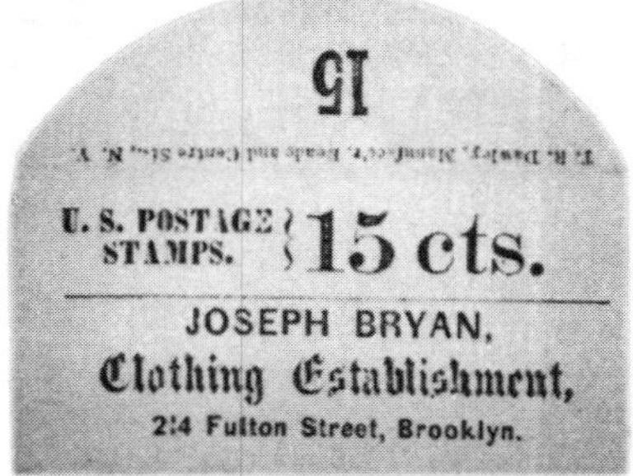

KL#	Name, address and notations	Value
9-15	Joseph Bryan, Clothing 214 Fulton St, Brooklyn	725.
9-50	Same	650.
11-25	P.D. Braisted, Jr. Billiards 14-16 4th Ave, NYC	650.
13-50	G.C. Brown, Tobacco 669 Broadway, NYC	650.
15-25	John M. Burnett, Stationer 51 William St, NYC	650.
15-25hw50		650.
15-50	Same	650.
17-25	Chas. T. Chickhaus, Tobacco 176 Broadway, NYC	725.
19-?	Clarry & Reilley, Stationer 12-14 Spruce St, NYC	725.

KL#	Name, address and notations	Value
21-50hw25	B.F. Corlies & Macy, Stationer 33 Nassau St, NYC	725.
23-30	Crook & Duff, Bar-Lunch-Dining 39-40 Park Row, (NYC)	800.
25-?	Cutter Tower & Co, Stationer 128 Nassau St, NYC	650.
27-25	Dawley, Stationer & Printer 28, 30 & 32 Center St., (NYC)	650.
28-50	T.R. Dawley, Printer Cor, Reade & Center Streets, NYC	650.
29-0hw25	Mad (Ame) A. Doubet, Importer 697 & 951 Broadway, (NYC)	725.
31-25	Francis Duffy, Oysters & Dining 239-241 8th Ave, (NYC)	725.
33-25	Embree, Stationer 130 Grand St, (NYC)	650.
34-50	Jno. C. Force Brooklyn	800.
35-25	Fox's Old Bowery Theatre (NYC)	800.
37-?	German Opera 485 Broadway, NYC	400.

KL#	Name, address and notations	Value
39-75	Gould's Dining Rooms 35 Nassau St, NYC	650.
40-50	Arthur Gregory NYC	800.
41-25	Harlem & NY Navigation Co Sylvan Shore & Sylvan Grove, (NYC) "LEGAL CURRENCY"	850.
43-5	Harpel, Printers Cincinnati	725.
45-10	Irving House, Hotel Broadway & 12th St, NYC	650.
47-25	James, Hatter 525 broadway, (NYC)	650.
49-0	Hamilton Johnston, Stationer 545 Broadway, (NYC) with Washington portrait	825.
51-25	C.O. Jones, Stationer 76 Cedar St, NYC	650.

KL#	Name, address and notations	Value
53-?	Kaiser & Waters, Stationer 104 Fulton St, NYC	650.
55-60	Kavanagh & Freeman, Billiards 10th & Broadway, NYC	725.
57-25	Lansingh's Gent's Furnishings 57-50 Albany	650.
59-10	J. Leach, Stationer 86 Nassau St, NYC Type I, Value in central diamond, most common type (vars.)	575.
59-15		650.
59-20		575.
59-25		575.
59-30		650.
59-50		575.
59-75		700.

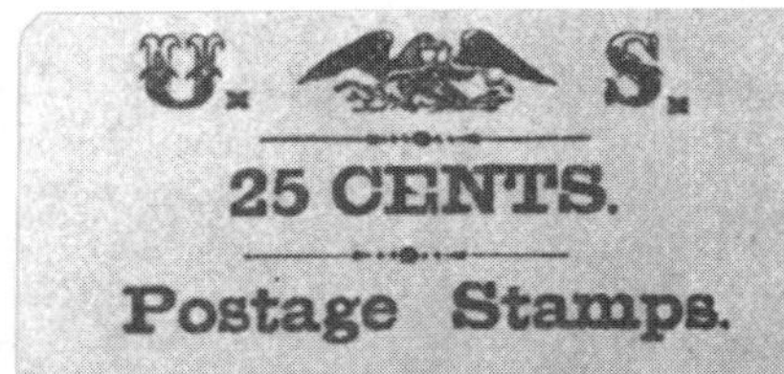

KL#	Name, address and notations	Value
60-15	As Above	700.
60-25	As Above Type II, Eagle between "U" and "S" (vars)	575.
60-50		575.
61-25	As above Type III, Large central oval with denomination (vars.)	575.
61-50	As Above Type V, Denomination in oval, flag left, shield right, similar to H. Smith design	575.

KL#	Name, address and notations	Value
62-25	As above Type IV, deonomination between flags	575.
63-50	As above	575.
71-75	D.W. Lee, Stationer 82 Nassau St, NYC	575.
72-0	R. Letson, Mercantile Dining Room, 256 Broadway, NYC	575.
73-25	J.W. Lingard New Bowery Theatre, (NYC)	650.
74-25	Macoy & Herwig, Stationers 112-114 Broadway, (NYC)	650.
75-20	Hy Maillards, Confectionery 621 Broadway, (NYC)	650.
75-25	Same	650.
75-25	Frank McElroy, Stationers 113 Nassau St, (NYC)	650.
81-10	Metropolitan Hotel NYC	650.
83-25	Miller & Grant, Importers, Laces 73 Broadway, NYC	725.

KL#	Name, address and notations	Value
85-50	W.H. Murphy (by D. Murphy's Sons) Stationers, 372 Pearl St, NYC	650.
87-?	Wm. Murphy, Stationer 438 Canal St, NYC	650.
89-25	National Express Co. 74 Broadway, NYC	800.
93-20	New York Central Railroad (N.Y.C.R.R.) NYC	725.
95-50	N.Y. Consolidated Stage Co. (NYC)	725.

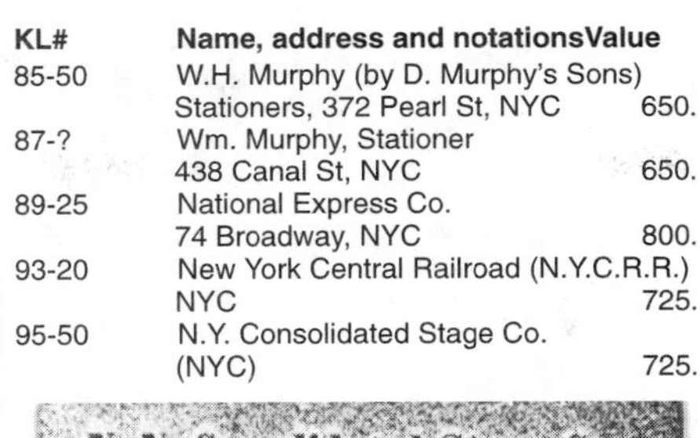

KL#	Name, address and notations	Value
97-25	Niblos Garden - Wm Wheatley (Edwin Forrest) (NYC)	725.
97-50	Same except Ravel Troupe (NYC)	725.
101-10	Nixon's Cremorne Garden, Palace of Music 14th and 6th Ave, (NYC)	975.
101-25hw10		725.

KL#	Name, address and notations	Value
101-25	Postal type hand stamp appears to read "CREMORNE (GARD)EN"	725.

KL#	Name, address and notations	Value
103-25	Chris O'Neills, Liquors Hudson Ave, Brooklyn "UNCLE SAM'S CHANGE"	800.
105-?	Oyster Bay House 553 Broadway, NYC	650.
107-25	The Oyster House 604 Broadway, NYC	650.
109-0	Pettit & Crook's Dining Rooms 136 Water St, NYC "UNCLE SAM'S CHANGE"	800.

KL#	Name, address and notations	Value
111-50	Pomroy's 699 Broadway, NYC	650.
113-50	Power, Bogardus & Co., Steamship Line Pier 34, No. River, NYC	700.
115-50	S. Raynor, Envelope Manuf'r 118 William St, NYC	650.

KL#	Name, address and notations	Value
117-25	Capt. Tom Reeves, Billiards 214 Broadway, NYC	800.

KL#	Name, address and notations	Value
119-25	Revere House 604-608 Broadway, NYC	650.
121-?	Thomas Richardson, Chop Steak & Oyster House 66 Maiden Lane, NYC	650.
122-50	E.M. Riggin, Sanford House 336 Delaware Ave., Pine St. Wharf, Philadelphia	650.
123-25	Wm Robins, Excelsion Envelope Manufactory 51 Ann St, NYC	575.
125-25	R. Scovel, Stationer 26 Nassau St, (NYC)	650.
126-25	Reuben Scovel "GOVERNMENT CURRENCY" 26 Nassau St, (NYC)	650.
126-50	Same	650.

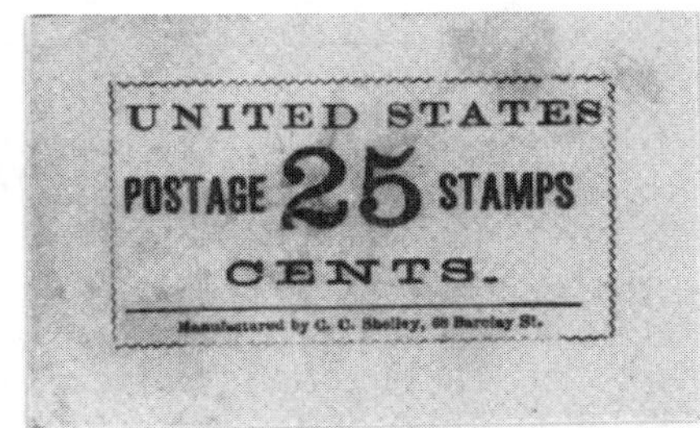

KL#	Name, address and notations	Value
127-25	C.C. Shelley, Stationer 68 Barclay St, NYC	650.
128-10	H. Smith, Stationer 137 Williams St, NYC Type I, denomination in oval, flag left, shield right (vars.)	575.
128-13	Same	575.
128-25	Same	575.
128-50	Same	575.
129-15hw50	As above Type II, fancy border, no flag, denomination below postage stamps	575.
129-50	Same	575.
130-25	Snow & Hapgood 22 Court St., Boston	650.
131-25	Sonneborn, Stationer 130 Nassau St., NYC (vars.)	650.
133-25	Taylor's Hotel Exchange Place, Jersey City (vars.)	725.
133-50	Same	725.
135-?	Dion Thomas, Stationer 142 Nassau St, NYC	725.

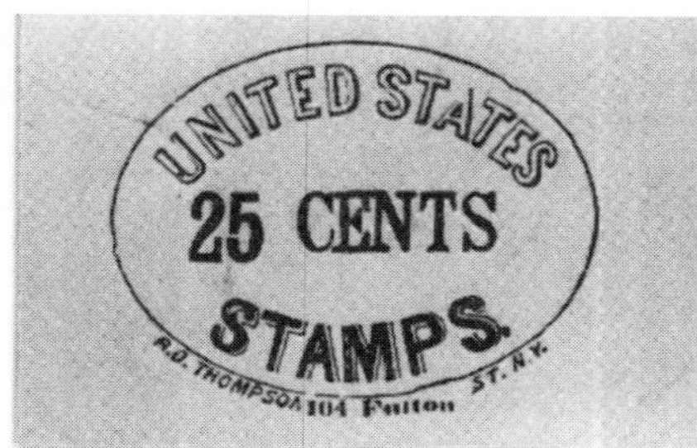

KL#	Name, address and notations	Value
137-25	R.D. Thompson, Stationer 104 Fulton St, NYC (vars.)	650.
139-25	G.W. & S. Turney 77 Chatham St, NYC	650.
140-?	S.C. Upham 403 Chestnut St., Phil.	650.
141-25	James Wiley, Wines & Liquors 307 Broadway, NYC	650.
141-50	Same	650.

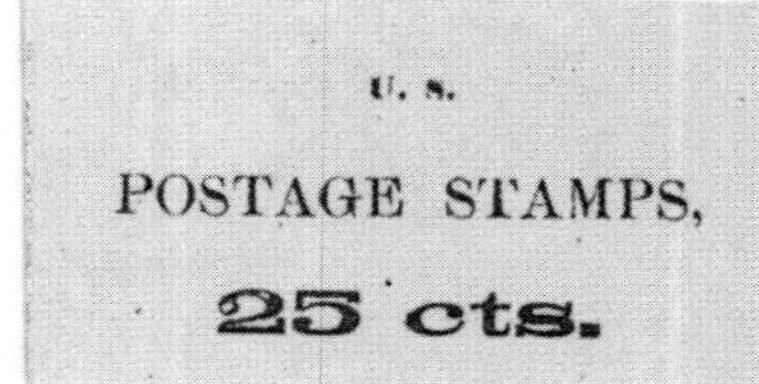

PIECES WITH NO COMPANY NAME

KL#	Name, address and notations	Value
151-25	Blank - marked by hand Envelope perhaps hand made	500.
152-10	U.S. POSTAGE STAMPS 10 CENTS	—
153-20	U.S. POSTAGE STAMPS 20 CENTS	500.

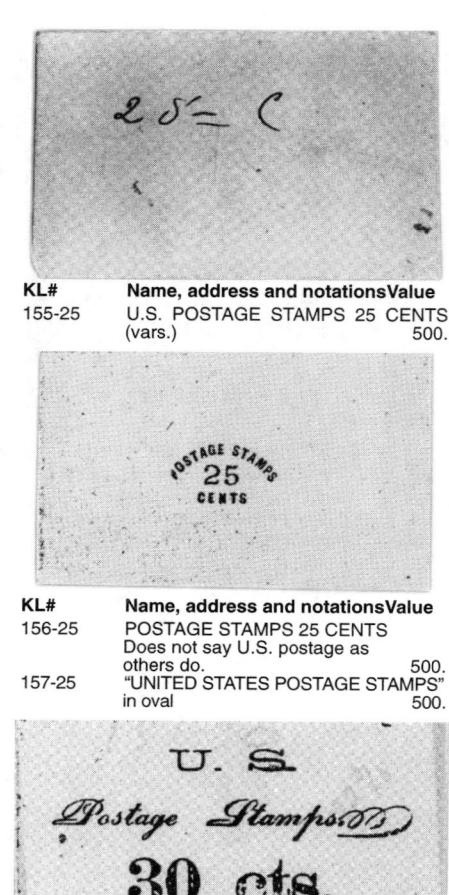

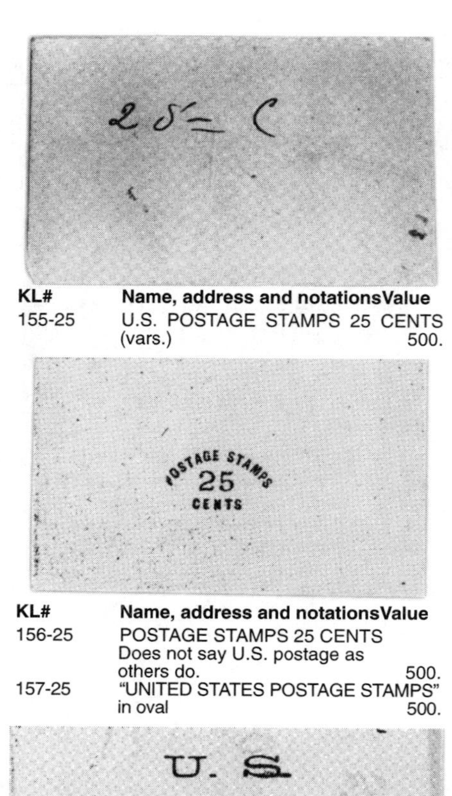

KL#	Name, address and notations	Value
155-25	U.S. POSTAGE STAMPS 25 CENTS (vars.)	500.

KL#	Name, address and notations	Value
156-25	POSTAGE STAMPS 25 CENTS Does not say U.S. postage as others do.	500.
157-25	"UNITED STATES POSTAGE STAMPS" in oval	500.

KL#	Name, address and notations	Value
157-30	U.S. POSTAGE STAMPS 30 CENTS	500.

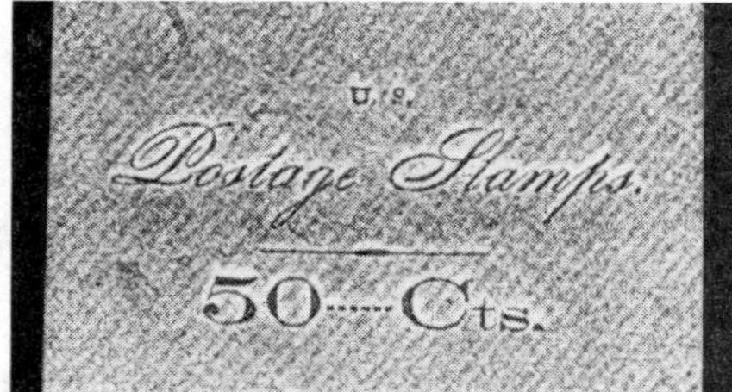

KL#	Name, address and notations	Value
159-50	U.S. POSTAGE STAMPS 50 CENTS (vars.)	500.
161-75	U.S. POSTAGE STAMPS 75 CENTS	500.

KL#	Name, address and notations	Value
163-7590	U.S. POSTAGE STAMPS 90 CENTS Hand changed from 75 cents.	650.

Envelopes come with various color ink and paper color combinations. Much of this new information became available through the sale of the Moreau hoard by Bowers & Merena. Photos on this page courtesty of Bowers & Merena.

A single hoard of these pieces consisting of a "cigar box full" is known to exist but it has not been seen or cataloged. A small group is known to have been lost in a fire some years ago. The author is indebted to Jackson Storm and to the Chase Bank Collection for some of the illustrations, and to Gene Hessler for some of the photography.

Encased Postage Stamps

The method of stamp packaging that best satisfied the dual requirements of visibility and protection was patented on Aug. 12, 1862, by a New England inventor, John Gault, who encased a single postage stamp in a round brass frame (25mm in diameter) with a clear mica frontpiece through which the stamp could be viewed.

The reverse of this case bore the advertising message of the participating merchant who purchased a quantity of Gault's "encased postage stamps" as a means of giving his customers the precise change required by their purchases.

Stamps encased by Gault were the 1¢, 3¢, 5¢, 10¢, 12¢, 24¢, 30¢, and 90¢ denominations of the Series of 1861-1869. That series also contains a 2¢ and a 15¢ stamp, but the 2¢ stamp wasn't issued until July 6, 1863, and the 15¢ value came along in 1866.

But for the eventual authorization of Postage and Fractional Currency, Gault's encased postage stamps probably would have become the chief means of "spending" postage stamps, although they, too, had their disadvantages:

The protective mica shield was easily cracked, and the encased stamps cost the distributing merchant the face value of the stamps, plus about 2¢ per holder. In view of the 20% premium existing on official coins, the additional 2¢ was of little consequence in the instance of the higher-denomination stamps, but in the case of the popular 1¢ stamp, it meant an expenditure of 3¢ for every 1¢ encased postage stamp obtained from Gault for monetary use.

The timing of the initiation of Gault's encased stamps also worked against their quantity distribution. At the time of their appearance in midsummer of 1862, the Postmaster General, Montgomery Blair, was still not reconciled to the idea of using postage stamps for money and was doing his utmost to prevent quantity sales of stamps to anyone desiring them for coinage purposes.

Three factors must be considered in concert in the grading of encased postage stamps: the stamp, the case, and the protective mica. The relative condition of each of these factors affects the overall grade.

Aerated Bread Co., New York

KL#	Denom.	Fine	VF	XF
EPS1	1¢	800.	1250.	1500.

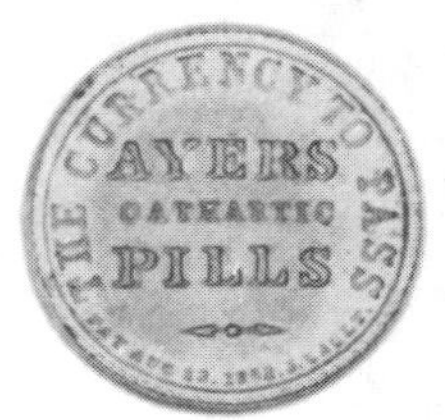

Ayer's Cathartic Pills (Long arrows variety)

KL#	Denom.	Fine	VF	XF
EPS2	3¢	100.	175.	250.
EPS3	5¢	125.	275.	350.
EPS4	10¢	250.	500.	650.

(Short arrows variety)

KL#	Denom.	Fine	VF	XF
EPS5	1¢	150.	225.	300.
EPS6	3¢	100.	175.	250.
EPS7	5¢	125.	275.	350.
EPS8	10¢	200.	350.	500.
EPS9	12¢	300.	550.	1000.
EPS10	24¢	1200.	2000.	3000.
EPS11	30¢	1500.	3000.	4000.

Take Ayer's Pills

KL#	Denom.	Fine	VF	XF
EPS12	1¢	150.	250.	325.
EPS13	3¢	100.	150.	225.
EPS14	5¢	100.	200.	300.
EPS15	10¢	175.	375.	500.
EPS16	12¢	300.	550.	1000.
EPS17	90¢Two known are both suspect as being counterfeit or altered.			

Ayer's Sarsaparilla (Small Ayer's)

KL#	Denom.	Fine	VF	XF
EPS18	1¢	300.	625.	925.
EPS19	3¢	350.	550.	750.
EPS20	10¢	300.	625.	925.
EPS21	12¢	700.	1400.	2000.

(Medium Ayer's)

KL#	Denom.	Fine	VF	XF
EPS22	1¢	150.	225.	300.
EPS23	3¢	100.	175.	225.
EPS24	5¢	150.	225.	300.
EPS25	10¢	175.	300.	450.
EPS26	12¢	300.	550.	1000.
EPS27	24¢	1200.	2000.	3000.
EPS28	30¢	1500.	3000.	4000.
EPS29	90¢	2500.	5000.	9000.

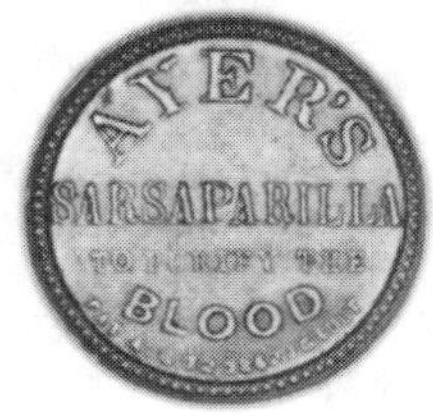

(Large Ayer's)

KL#	Denom.	Fine	VF	XF
EPS30	3¢	275.	400.	750.
EPS31	10¢	450.	700.	1000.

Bailey & Co., Philadelphia

KL#	Denom.	Fine	VF	XF
EPS32	1¢	375.	550.	1000.
EPS33	3¢	375.	550.	1000.
EPS34	5¢	400.	650.	1300.
EPS35	10¢	400.	600.	1250.
EPS36	12¢	1000.	1500.	2500.

Joseph L. Bates "Fancy Goods," Boston Fancygoods One Word

KL#	Denom.	Fine	VF	XF
EPS41	1¢	150.	225.	300.
EPS42	3¢	300.	450.	650.
EPS43	10¢	200.	375.	600.

Joseph L. Bates Fancy Goods Two Words

KL#	Denom.	Fine	VF	XF
EPS37	1¢	150.	225.	300.
EPS38	3¢	350.	675.	850.
EPS39	10¢	200.	375.	600.
EPS40	12¢	300.	550.	1000.

Brown's Bronchial Troches

KL#	Denom.	Fine	VF	XF
EPS44	1¢	225.	375.	550.
EPS45	3¢	175.	300.	400.
EPS46	5¢	175.	300.	400.
EPS47	10¢	250.	375.	500.
EPS48	12¢	600.	1000.	1400.

F. Buhl & Co., Detroit

KL#	Denom.	Fine	VF	XF
EPS49	1¢	400.	650.	1100.
EPS50	3¢	400.	700.	1250.
EPS51	5¢	400.	650.	1100.
EPS52	10¢	750.	1000.	2000.
EPS53	12¢	750.	1500.	2000.

Burnett's Cocoaine Kalliston

KL#	Denom.	Fine	VF	XF
EPS54	1¢	150.	250.	375.
EPS55	3¢	125.	175.	275.
EPS56	5¢	150.	300.	425.
EPS57	10¢	200.	550.	800.
EPS58	12¢	300.	550.	1000.
EPS59	24¢	1500.	2000.	3000.
EPS60	30¢	1750.	3000.	4000.
EPS61	90¢	2500.	5000.	9000.

Burnett's Cooking Extracts (Plain frame)

KL#	Denom.	Fine	VF	XF
EPS62	1¢	150.	250.	375.
EPS63	3¢	150.	275.	425.
EPS64	5¢	150.	250.	375.
EPS65	10¢	200.	375.	550.
EPS66	12¢	300.	550.	1000.
EPS67	24¢	1500.	2000.	3000.
EPS68	30¢	1750.	3000.	4000.
EPS69	90¢	2500.	5000.	9000.

(Ribbed frame)

KL#	Denom.	Fine	VF	XF
EPS70	10¢	350.	650.	800.

A.M. Claflin, Hopkinton, R.I.

KL#	Denom.	Fine	VF	XF
EPS71	1¢	3000.	6250.	12,750.
EPS72	3¢	3000.	4000.	6000.
EPS73	5¢	3000.	4000.	6000.
EPS74	12¢	3000.	5000.	7500.

H.A. Cook, Evansville, Ind.

KL#	Denom.	Fine	VF	XF
EPS75	5¢	350.	650.	1300.
EPS76	10¢	600.	1200.	2500.

Dougan, New York

KL#	Denom.	Fine	VF	XF
EPS77	1¢	800.	1500.	2500.
EPS78	3¢	800.	1500.	2500.
EPS79	5¢	600.	1000.	2000.
EPS80	10¢	1000.	2000.	3000.

Drake's Plantation Bitters, New York

KL#	Denom.	Fine	VF	XF
EPS81	1¢	175.	225.	300.
EPS82	3¢	125.	275.	400.
EPS83	5¢	200.	300.	400.
EPS84	10¢	225.	375.	550.
EPS85	12¢	300.	550.	1000.
EPS86	24¢	1500.	2500.	3000.
EPS87	30¢	2000.	3000.	4000.
EPS88	90¢	2750.	5500.	9000.

Ellis, McAlpin & Co., Cincinnati

KL#	Denom.	Fine	VF	XF
EPS89	1¢	600.	1250.	1850.
EPS90	3¢	600.	1250.	1750.
EPS91	5¢	800.	1650.	2300.
EPS92	10¢	600	1250.	1750.
EPS93	12¢	800.	1500.	2250.
EPS94	24¢	1200.	2000.	3000

G.G. Evans, Philadelphia

KL#	Denom.	Fine	VF	XF
EPS95	1¢	300.	600.	900.
EPS96	3¢	400.	700.	1000.
EPS97	5¢	450.	750.	1250.
EPS98	10¢	450.	750.	1250.

J. Gault (Plain frame)

KL#	Denom.	Fine	VF	XF
EPS99	1¢	150.	225.	300.
EPS100	2¢ (Three known)	—	12,000.	—
EPS101	3¢	150.	250.	350.
EPS102	5¢	150.	250.	375.
EPS103	10¢	200.	300.	500.
EPS104	12¢	300.	550.	1000.
EPS105	24¢	1250.	2000.	3000.
EPS106	30¢	1500.	3000.	4000.
EPS107	90¢	2500.	5000.	9000.

(Ribbed frame)

KL#	Denom.	Fine	VF	XF
EPS108	1¢	400.	700.	1000
EPS109	3¢	400.	700.	1000
EPS110	5¢	275.	1450.	600.
EPS111	10¢	300.	550.	700.
EPS112	12¢	500.	800.	1500.
EPS113	24¢	1500.	2750.	3500.
EPS114	30¢	1750.	3000.	4000.

L.C. Hopkins & Co., Cincinnati

KL#	Denom.	Fine	VF	XF
EPS115	1¢	700.	1250.	1750.
EPS116	3¢	600.	1150.	1500.
EPS117	5¢	800.	1500.	2250.
EPS118	10¢	700.	1250.	1750.

Irving House, N.Y. (Hunt & Nash)
(Plain frame)

KL#	Denom.	Fine	VF	XF
EPS119	1¢	150.	250.	350.
EPS120	3¢	150.	250.	350.
EPS121	5¢	400.	700.	1000.
EPS122	10¢	200.	300.	450
EPS123	12¢	300.	550.	1000.
EPS124	24¢	1250.	2000.	3000.
EPS125	30¢	1500.	3000.	4000.

(Ribbed frame)

KL#	Denom.	Fine	VF	XF
EPS126	1¢	400.	700.	1000.
EPS127	3¢	400.	700.	1000
EPS128	5¢	450.	750.	1500.
EPS129	10¢	350.	550.	750.
EPS130	12¢	500.	800.	1500.
EPS131	24¢	1500.	2750.	3500.

Kirkpatrick & Gault, New York

KL#	Denom.	Fine	VF	XF
EPS132	1¢	150.	225.	300.
EPS133	3¢	125.	200.	275.
EPS134	5¢	175.	350.	500.
EPS135	10¢	200.	300.	500.
EPS136	12¢	300.	550.	1000.
EPS137	24¢	1250.	2000.	3000.
EPS138	30¢	1500.	3000.	4000.
EPS139	90¢	2500.	5000.	9000.

Lord & Taylor, New York

KL#	Denom.	Fine	VF	XF
EPS140	1¢	400.	650.	1250.
EPS141	3¢	400.	650.	1250.
EPS142	5¢	400.	650.	1250.
EPS143	10¢	400.	700.	1500.
EPS144	12¢	800.	1500.	2000.
EPS145	24¢	1500.	2500.	3500.
EPS146	30¢	2000.	4000.	5000.
EPS147	90¢	4000.	7500.	9000.

Medum's Family Wine Emporium, New York
(Plain frame)

KL#	Denom.	Fine	VF	XF
EPS148	1¢	250.	350.	500.
EPS149	3¢	350.	500.	800.
EPS150	5¢	300.	450.	600.
EPS151	10¢	300.	450.	700.
EPS152	12¢	650.	1250.	1750.

(Ribbed frame)

KL#	Denom.	Fine	VF	XF
EPS153	10¢	400.	700.	1000.

B.F. Miles, Peoria

KL#	Denom.	Fine	VF	XF
EPS154	5¢	3500.	7000.	9000.

John W. Norris, Chicago

KL#	Denom.	Fine	VF	XF
EPS155	1¢	750.	1000.	1700.
EPS156	3¢	1000.	1750.	3000.
EPS157	5¢	1000.	1750.	3000.
EPS158	10¢	1000.	1750.	3000.

North America Life Insurance Co., New York
(Straight "Insurance")

KL#	Denom.	Fine	VF	XF
EPS159	1¢	175.	250.	350.
EPS160	3¢	175.	250.	350.
EPS161	10¢	200.	375.	600.
EPS162	12¢	450.	1000.	1500.

(Curved "Insurance")
(Trial Piece)

KL#	Denom.	Fine	VF	XF
EPS163	1¢	225.	500.	1000.
EPS164	10¢	300.	500.	750.

Pearce, Tolle & Holton, Cincinnati

KL#	Denom.	Fine	VF	XF
EPS165	1¢	1000.	1750.	3000.
EPS166	3¢	800.	1500.	2500.
EPS167	5¢	1000.	1750.	3000.
EPS168	10¢	1100.	2000.	3500.

Sands' Ale

KL#	Denom.	Fine	VF	XF
EPS169	5¢	800.	1500.	2500.
EPS170	10¢	1000.	1750.	2750.
EPS171	30¢	2000.	3500.	5000.

Schapker & Bussing, Evansville, Ind.

KL#	Denom.	Fine	VF	XF
EPS172	1¢	400.	700.	1000.
EPS173	3¢	225.	350.	600.
EPS174	5¢	450.	750.	1250.
EPS175	10¢	450.	800.	1250.
EPS176	12¢	500.	1250.	1750.

John Shillisto & Co., Cincinnati

KL#	Denom.	Fine	VF	XF
EPS177	1¢	400.	700.	1000.
EPS178	3¢	250.	350.	600.
EPS179	5¢	250.	450.	900.
EPS180	10¢	275.	425.	750.
EPS181	12¢	500.	1250.	1750.

S. Steinfeld, New York

KL#	Denom.	Fine	VF	XF
EPS182	1¢	1000.	1700.	2500.
EPS183	10¢	1000.	1600.	2500.
EPS184	12¢	1000.	1750.	2750.

N.G. Taylor & Co., Philadelphia

KL#	Denom.	Fine	VF	XF
EPS185	1¢	800.	1250.	1900.
EPS186	3¢	800.	1250.	1750.
EPS187	5¢	800.	1500.	2000.
EPS188	10¢	800.	1250.	1750.

Tremont House (Gage Brothers & Drake), Chicago

KL#	Denom.	Fine	VF	XF
EPS189	1¢	150.	225.	300.
EPS190	5¢	150.	300.	375.
EPS191	10¢	200.	325.	450.
EPS192	12¢	350.	600.	1250.

Weir & Larminie, Montreal

KL#	Denom.	Fine	VF	XF
EPS193	1¢	450.	750.	1250.
EPS194	3¢	400.	700.	1000.
EPS195	5¢	500.	800.	1500.
EPS196	10¢	600.	900.	1700.

White the Hatter, New York

KL#	Denom.	Fine	VF	XF
EPS197	1¢	750.	1000.	1900.
EPS198	3¢	800.	1500.	2500.
EPS199	5¢	900.	1750.	3000.
EPS200	10¢	800.	1500.	2500.

Read the introduction to this catalog carefully. It contains much valuable information for all stamp collectors, and also makes the catalog easier for you to use

Postage Currency

All methods of using stamps for money that had been employed prior to July 17, 1862, suffered the ultimate disadvantage of being illegal, with the consequence that the holder of the stamps could neither redeem them at the post office nor exchange them for Treasury notes.

On that date, however, President Lincoln signed into law a measure proposed in self-defense by Treasury Secretary Salmon P. Chase, providing that "postage and other stamps of the United States" were to be receivable for all dues to the U.S. and were to be redeemable at any "designated depository" in sums less than $5. The law also prohibited the issue by "any private corporation, banking association, firm, or individual" of any note or token for a sum less than $5 — a provision that was widely ignored as the private sector continued its efforts to overcome a coin shortage in the face of which the government seemed helpless.

The new law was not without its problems of practicality, either. The post office, already facing a stamp shortage before the gummed bits of paper had been declared legal tender, faced the almost impossible task of providing sufficient stamps for postal use as well as "coinage" use.

There was also the problem of which office would redeem nearly exhausted specimens of stamps that had been circulating for some time. Blair refused to take them in trade for new stamps, and Chase would not exchange them for paper money because the Treasury hadn't issued them in the first place.

Blair's obstinacy ultimately melted before the heat of public pressure, and he agreed to redeem the masses of soiled and stuck-together stamps, but he continued to insist that the actual intent of the poorly written law had been for the Treasury Department to print and distribute special stamps that would bear a general resemblance to postage stamps but would be of a different design. A compromise was finally worked out whereby the Treasury Department would sell and redeem specially marked stamps that the post office would also accept for postage. Blair agreed to print the special stamps for the Treasury.

Before the stamps could be printed, a further decision was made to issue them in a larger, more convenient size, and to print them on a heavier, ungummed paper. Credit for the final form in which Postage Currency appeared is given to Gen. F.E. Spinner, treasurer of the United States. Spinner pasted unused postage stamps on small sheets of Treasury security paper of uniform size, signed his name to some of them and passed them out to his friends as samples of currency. Congress responded to Spinner's suggestion by authorizing the printing of reproductions of postage stamps on Treasury paper in arrangements patterned after Spinner's models. In this form, the "stamps" ceased to be stamps; they became, in effect, fractional government promissory notes, a development not authorized by the initial enabling legislation of July 17, 1862. Nonetheless, the notes would be issued without legal authorization until passage of the Act of March 3, 1863, which provided for the issuing of fractional notes by the federal government.

Five issues of Postage and Fractional Currency in the total amount of $369 million were printed and released to circulation between Aug. 21, 1862, and Feb. 15, 1876. Then a flood of silver from the Comstock Lode drove down silver bullion prices, reducing the intrinsic value of silver coins to a point below face value, thereby insuring that they would remain in circulation. The silver price drop further augmented the supply of circulating silver by triggering a flow back to the United States — where they could be exchanged for their greater face value — of the hundreds of millions of silver coins that had been exported since 1862.

Congressional Acts of Jan. 14, 1875, and April 17, 1876, provided for the redemption of Postage and Fractional Currency in silver coins, and all but about $1.8 million worth was returned to the Treasury for redemption. The outstanding notes remain legal tender and can purchase their face value equivalent in goods and services today.

First Issue "Postage Currency"

August 21, 1862 - May 27, 1863

Denominations: 5¢, 10¢, 25¢, 50¢

The First Issue of U.S. government stamp money is the only one of the five issues to be identified by name as Postage Currency. The initial printing of the First Issue was released through Army paymasters on Aug. 1, 1862, and was provided for general circulation a few weeks later.

Although it is a moot point, Postage Currency probably constitutes an illegal issue of fractional notes. Rather than being strictly "postage and other stamps of the United States," and despite being "receivable for postage stamps at any U.S. post office," Postage Currency took the form of reproductions of postage stamps printed on paper that carried the promise of the United States to exchange the currency for United States Notes, which gave Postage Currency the attributes of a promissory note, a development beyond the intent of the enabling Act of July 17, 1862.

The stamps reproduced on Postage Currency are the brown or buff 5¢ stamp of the Series of 1861, bearing the portrait of Thomas Jefferson, and the green 10c stamp of the same series, with George Washington's portrait. The 25¢ and 50¢ denominations bear multiple reproductions of the appropriate stamp. Various colors of paper were used in printing the four notes of the First Issue, but the color does not influence the collector value of the individual note. Faces of the notes are printed in a color approximating the color of the genuine postage stamp, backs are all printed in black.

An interesting feature of the First Issue is the existence of notes with both perforated and straight edges. Apparently, the idea of perforated Postage Currency was a carry-over from the postage stamp printing process and was discarded when the demand for Postage Currency exceeded the capacity of the perforating machines.

Inasmuch as the Bureau of Engraving and Printing had not yet been established, contracts for printing of the First Issue were awarded to private bank note printing companies. The National Bank Note Co. printed the face, and the American Bank Note Co. printed the back. The ABNC monogram appears on the backs of some notes.

Total value of Postage Currency issued was more than $20 million.

5 CENTS

KL#	Fr#	Date	Description	VG	VF	Unc
3209	1228	17.7.1862.	Brown. One 5 cent Jefferson stamp at center. Perf. edges; ANBC's monogram on back.	14.00	16.00	155.
3210	1229		Perf. edges; back w/o ANBC's monogram.	15.00	22.00	180.
3211	1230		Straight edges; ANBC's monogram on back.	14.50	16.00	50.00
3212	1231		Straight edges; back w/o ANBC's monogram.	15.00	21.00	150.

10 CENTS

KL#	Fr#	Date	Description	VG	VF	Unc
3213	1240	17.7.1862.	Green. One 10 cent Washington stamp at center. Perf. edges; ANBC's monogram on back.	15.00	18.50	115.
3214	1241		Perf. edges; back w/o ABNC's monogram	15.50	30.00	130.
3215	1242		Straight edges; ABNC's monogram on back.	11.50	13.00	40.00
3216	1243		Straight edges; back w/o ABNC's monogram	12.50	40.00	150.

25 CENTS

KL#	Fr#	Date	Description	VG	VF	Unc
3217	1279	17.71862.	Brown. Horizontal row of five 5 cent Jefferson stamps. Perf. edges; ABNC's monogram on back.	16.00	25.00	170.
3218	1280		Perf. edges; back w/o ABNC's monogram	25.00	60.00	275.
3219	1281		Straight edges; ABNC's monogram on back.	11.50	15.00	75.00
3220	1282		Straight edged; back w/o ABNC's monogram.	13.00	60.00	300.

50 CENTS

KL#	Fr#	Date	Description	VG	VF	Unc
3221	1310	17.7.1862.	Green. Horizontal row of five 10 cent Washington stamps. #12 perf. edges; ABNC's monogram on back.	24.00	30.00	290.00
3222	1310-A		#14 perf. edges; ABNC's monogram on back	—	Rare	—
3223	1311		Perf. edges; back w/o ABNC's monogram.	30.00	70.00	300.
3224	1312		Straight edges: ABNC's monogram on back.	17.00	18.50	120.00
3225	1313		Straight edges; back w/o ABNC's monogram.	20.00	75.00	300.

Users of this Catalog are invited to write us if they have information which they feel will supplement or correct any material contained herein. All such communications will be answered

Postage and Fractional Currency Shield

The Postage and Fractional Currency Shield was one of the measures by which the Treasury Department sought to overcome and prevent the widespread counterfeiting of Fractional Currency notes.

The shields consisted of a type set of the first three issues of Postage and Fractional Currency mounted on a heavy cardboard shield surmounted by an eagle and 13 stars. Size of the framed unit was 24 by 28 inches. The shields were made available to banks and other commercial institutions in 1866-67 to provide them with a file of genuine notes to use as a reference when checking suspect notes. Those qualified to receive the shield paid face value for the notes ($4.66), plus a presumed transportation charge, for a total cost believed to be $7.50.

The 39 closely trimmed notes (20 faces and 19 backs) mounted on the shield are specimen notes printed on one side only. They include the scarce 15¢ Sherman/Grant essays and the two faces of the 3¢ note, which are distinguished by dark and light backgrounds to Washington's portrait. The shields upon which the notes were pasted are known in gray, pink and green, with gray being the most common.

Although the shields were produced in a quantity believed to be in excess of 4,500, it is presumed that fewer than 200 remain intact, with many of those folded, faded or water-stained. Apparently demand for the shields was less than the Treasury Department had anticipated, and the surplus shields were carelessly stored -- by common account in an old shed behind the Treasury Building. The number of intact shields was further reduced by early collectors who obtained them solely to secure the scarcer notes, which they removed from the shield.